THE ROUGH GUIDE TO

SOUTH INDIA
& KERALA

**ROUGH
GUIDES**

this edition updated by

Nick Edwards, Priya Ganapathy, Anurag Mallick,
Shafik Meghji, Rachel Mills and Charles Young

Contents

INTRODUCTION 4

Where to go	5	Things not to miss	14
When to go	12	Itineraries	20

BASICS 22

Getting there	23	Sports	49
Visas	24	Outdoor activities	50
Getting around	26	Yoga, meditation and ashrams	50
Accommodation	31	Culture and etiquette	53
Eating and drinking	34	Shopping	54
Health	41	Travelling with children	55
The media	46	Travel essentials	56
Festivals and holidays	47		

THE GUIDE 65

1 Mumbai	66	5 Andhra Pradesh and Telangana	272
2 Maharashtra	106	6 Kerala	296
3 Goa	154	7 Tamil Nadu	362
4 Karnataka	206	8 The Andaman Islands	440

CONTEXTS 462

History	463	Books	496
Religion	481	Language	499
Music and dance	488	Glossary	507
Wildlife	490		

SMALL PRINT & INDEX 512

Introduction to
South India
& Kerala

Though its borders are uncertain, there's no doubt that South India, the tapering half of the country's mighty peninsula, differs radically from the landlocked North. In the South, the coconut groves seem a deeper green and the rice paddies positively luminescent, the faces are a darker brown and the vermilion marks smeared over them arrestingly red. The landscape varies from tropical beaches that hug towering Ghats in the west, to the arid Deccan plateau that descends into fertile plains in the east. Under a sun whose rays feel concentrated by a giant magnifying glass, the ubiquitous colours of South India – of silk saris, shimmering classical dance costumes, lurid movie posters and frangipani flowers – radiate with a life of their own.

Despite its recent rush to modernity and pockets of over-development, South India remains one of the most relaxed parts of Asia to explore. It is also among the easiest. In all but the remotest districts, accommodation is plentiful, clean and inexpensive by Western standards. Delicious street food is available from nearly every roadside vendor. While journey times can be long, the region's extensive rail network moves vast numbers of people at all times of the day and night, and if a train isn't heading where you want to go, a bus almost certainly will be. Furthermore, South Indians are the most garrulous and inquisitive of travellers, and train rides are always enlivened by conversations that invariably begin with the refrain of "Coming from?" or "What is your native place?"

It is a credit to the region's legendary capacity for assimilating new ideas that the modern and traditional thrive side by side. Walking through central Bengaluru, you could brush shoulders with an iPhone-toting software developer one moment and a trident-wielding ascetic the next, while rickety bicycles mingle with luxury cars. There are, of course, the usual Subcontinental travel hassles: interminable queues, packed buses and constant encroachments on your personal space. Yet, just when your nerves feel stretched to breaking point, South India always offers something that makes the effort worthwhile: a glimpse of an elephant from a train window; a sumptuous vegetarian meal delicately arranged on a fresh banana leaf; or a hint of fragrant cardamom in your tea after a night dancing on a Goan beach.

Where to go

Your first impression of South India is likely to be **Mumbai**, the arrival point for most international flights. While the city gets a pretty bad press, and most people pass straight through, those who stay find themselves witness to the reality of modern-day India, from the deprivations of the city's slum-dwellings to the glitz and glamour of Bollywood movies. The surrounding state of **Maharashtra**, though not culturally or linguistically part of the South, has plenty of attractions including the extraordinary caves of Ellora and Ajanta and the thriving city of **Pune**, once a Raj-era retreat, and now a buzzing metropolis with a hip eating scene.

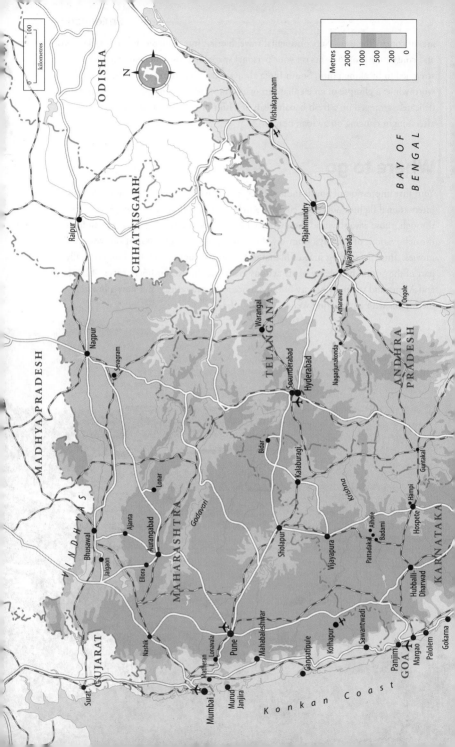

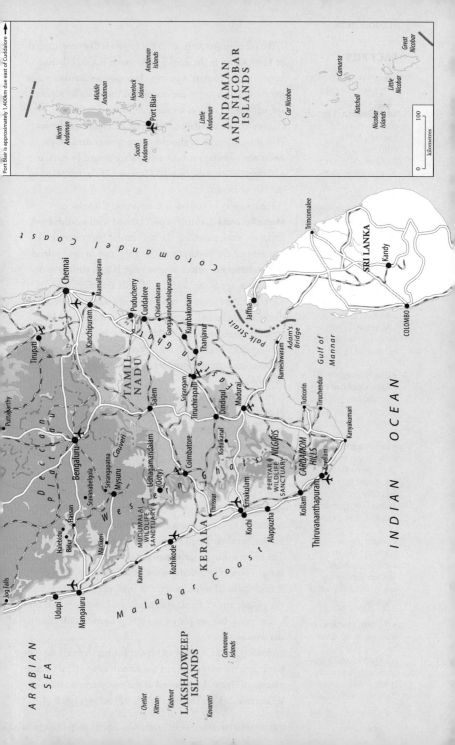

Port Blair is approximately 1,400km approximately due east of Cuddalore

ANDAMAN AND NICOBAR ISLANDS

North Andaman

Middle Andaman

Havelock Island

Port Blair

South Andaman

Little Andaman

Andaman Islands

Car Nicobar

Camorta

Katchall

Little Nicobar

Great Nicobar

Nicobar Islands

0   100   kilometres

ARABIAN SEA

Udupi

Mangaluru

Jog Falls

Deccan Plateau

Tirupati

Puttaparthy

Chennai

Mamallapuram

Kanchipuram

Bengaluru

Halebidu

Belur   Hassan

Madikeri   Sravanabelgola

Mysuru   Srirangapatna

Cauvery

Kannur

MUDUMALAI WILDLIFE SANCTUARY

Udhagamandalam (Ooty)

Kozhikode

NILGIRIS

Coimbatore

Thrissur

Ernakulam

Kochi

KERALA

Alappuzha

Malabar Coast

PERIYAR WILDLIFE SANCTUARY

CARDAMOM HILLS

Kollam

Kovalam

Thiruvananthapuram

Kanyakumari

Tinchendur

Tuticorin

Western Ghats

Eastern Ghats

Salem

Srirangam

Tiruchirapalli

Dindigul

Kodaikanal

Madurai

TAMIL NADU

Puducherry

Cuddalore

Chidambaram

Gangaikondacholapuram

Kumbakonam

Thanjavur

Coromandel Coast

Rameshwaram

Adam's Bridge

Gulf of Mannar

Palk Strait

Jaffna

Trincomalee

SRI LANKA

Kandy

COLOMBO

INDIAN OCEAN

LAKSHADWEEP ISLANDS

Chetlat

Kiltan

Kadmat

Kavaratti

Cannanore Islands

FACT FILE

• South India is referred to in some of India's oldest inscriptions as **Dravidadesa**, "Land of the Dravidians", referring to the ethnically and linguistically distinct people of the South.

• The South's Western Ghats mountain range is one of the most **biodiverse** places on earth with over 500 bird species and 139 mammals.

• Three of the the five largest **cities** in India are found in the South – Mumbai (12.4m), Bengaluru (8.4m) and Hyderabad (6.7m).

• Goans consume 40 million **coconuts** per year and the fruit finds its way into virtually every dish.

• **Languages** spoken in the South include Tamil (Tamil Nadu), Telugu (Andhra Pradesh and Telangana), Kannada (Karnataka) and Malayam (Kerala).

• India's greatest sporting hero, the cricketing master **Sachin Tendulkar** was born and raised in Mumbai.

• The **film studios** of Mumbai (Bollywood) and Chennai (Kollywood) make more movies than any other country with up to 2000 releases annually.

The other major gateway to the region is **Chennai**, capital of **Tamil Nadu**, in the deep South, which is a slightly less stressful place to start your trip. Although it's another major metropolis bursting at the seams, hidden under its surface are artful gems such as regular public performances of classical music and dance. With regular flights and ferries to Port Blair, Chennai is also the major springboard for the **Andaman Islands**, a remote archipelago ringed by coral reefs and crystal-clear seas, over 1000km east of the mainland in the Bay of Bengal.

The majority of visitors' first stop after Chennai is **Mamallapuram**, an ancient port littered with weatherworn sculpture sites, including the technicolor Shore temple. To get right off the beaten track you only have to head inland to **Kanchipuram**, whose innumerable Hindu shrines span the golden age of the illustrious Chola kingdom. Back on the coast, the former French colony of **Puducherry** retains a distinctly Gallic feel, particularly in its restaurants. Most travellers press on south to **Madurai**, the region's most atmospherically charged city, where the mighty Meenakshi-Sundareshwar temple presides over a quintessentially Tamil swirl of life.

The two other most compelling destinations in Tamil Nadu are the island of **Rameshwaram**, whose main temple features a photogenic series of pillared corridors, and **Kanyakumari**, the southernmost tip of India, where the Bay of Bengal, Indian Ocean and Arabian Sea flow together. The dark shadows visible on the horizon from here mark the start of the **Western Ghats**, lush mountains which stretch for more than 1000km in a virtually unbroken chain all the way to Mumbai, forming a sheer barrier between Tamil Nadu and neighbouring Kerala. The hill stations of **Udhagamandalam** (or Ooty, as it's still better known) and **Kodaikanal**, established by India's former colonial rulers as retreats from the summer heat of the plains, attract hordes of Indian visitors in the run-up to the rains, but see plenty of foreign tourist traffic during the winter, too.

Heading north, a string of smaller former dynastic capitals punctuate the journey across the eastern edge of the Deccan plateau to **Hyderabad**, capital of the newly created state of **Telangana** and, for the time being, still acting capital of

INDIA'S SPIRITUAL HEART

If the sacred peaks of the Himalayas are Hinduism's head, and the Ganges its main artery, then the **temple complexes** of the South are its spiritual heart and soul. Soaring high above every urban skyline, their colossal towers are emblematic of the awe with which the deities enshrined inside them have been held for centuries. Some, like the sea-washed temple at Tiruchendur in Tamil Nadu, are thought to be as old as human speech itself; others, such as the Sabarimala forest shrine in Kerala, are less ancient, but attract greater numbers of pilgrims than even Mecca. For foreign visitors, however, the most extraordinary of all have to be the colossal **Chola shrines** of Tamil Nadu (see p.383). Joining the crowds that stream through Chidambaram's Sabhanayaka Nataraja temple or Shri Ramalingeshwara in Rameshwaram will take you to the very source of the world's last surviving classical culture, some of whose hymns, prayers and rites predate the Egyptian pyramids.

Andhra Pradesh, whose principal landmarks are the Charminar and Golconda fort. Andhra's other attractions, by contrast, lie much further off the beaten track. Comparatively few Western visitors ever reach them, with the exception of **Puttaparthy**, the ashram of India's most famous living saint, Sai Baba, and Tirupati, whose temple complex on nearby Tirumala Hill receives more pilgrims than anywhere else on earth and is an essential stop for all Hindu pilgrims, especially followers of Vishnu.

West of Tamil Nadu, neighbouring **Kerala**'s appeal lies less in its religious monuments, almost all of which remain off-limits to non-Hindus, than its infectiously easy-going, tropical ambience. Covering a long thin coastal strip backed by a steep wall of hills, this is the wettest and most densely populated state in the South. It is also the most distinctive, with a culture that sets it squarely apart. Its ritualized theatre (*kathakali*), faintly Southeast Asian architecture and ubiquitous communist graffiti (Kerala was the first place in the world to gain a democratically elected communist government) are perhaps the most visual expressions of this difference. But spend a couple of days exploring the spicy backstreets of old **Kochi** (Cochin), the jungles of the **Cardamom Hills** around the Periyar Wildlife Sanctuary or the hidden aquatic world of the coastal **backwaters**, and you'll see why many travellers end up staying here a lot longer than they originally intended. If you're not pushed for time and find yourself crossing northern Kerala during the winter, set aside a few days to search for **theyyem**, a spectacular masked dance form unique to the villages around Kannur.

A short ride across the mountains takes you to **Mysuru** in **Karnataka**, whose opulent maharaja's palace, colourful markets and comfortable southern California-like climate have made it among South India's most popular tourist destinations. **Bengaluru,** India's answer to Silicon Valley, is a hectic modern capital, and most travellers press on to the state's extraordinary historic sights including the mausolea, mosques and Persian-style palaces of **Vijayapura** (Bijapur), often dubbed the "Agra of the South", and the Angkor-like faded splendour of **Hampi**, once the magnificent capital of South India's last Hindu empire.

MASALA MOVIES

Emblematic of modern India at its most highly charged and lurid are the huge, hand-painted hoardings that tower over city intersections. Featuring blood-splattered macho men, curvaceous heroines in various states of distress (and undress), chubby, bulging-eyed bad guys and explosions aplenty, they give you a pretty good taste of the kind of movies churned out by the record-beating **film industries** of Mumbai and Chennai. While many films follow the standard "hero-gets-the-girl via several song-and-dance routines" formula, the recent international success of fantasy epic *Bahubali* (notably filmed in the South Indian language of Telugu rather than Hindi), has shown that big-budget blockbusters are no longer the preserve of Hollywood. Catch the latest box-office smash at one of the big-city cinema houses, primed by our background accounts on Bollywood (p.102) and the Tamil film industry (p.370).

Only one day's journey to the west, the palm-fringed, white-sand beaches of **Goa**, formerly a Portuguese colony, offer a change of scenery from the rocky terrain of the Deccan. Succumbing to the hedonistic pleasures of warm seawater, constant sunshine and cheap drinks, many travellers find it hard to tear themselves away from the coast, but Old Goa's Portuguese churches and splendid mansions should not be missed.

When to go

The relentless tropical sun aside, the source of South India's lush scenery lies in its **high rainfall**. Unlike the north of the country, which sees only a single deluge in the summer, most of peninsular India receives **two annual monsoons** – one sucked in from the Arabian Sea in the southwest, and the other on stormy northwesterly winds off the Bay of Bengal. The heaviest rains are reserved for the Western Ghats chain of mountains, where the first summer monsoon breaks in June and lasts through to October. In a nutshell, you should, when planning a trip to South India, largely avoid the rainy seasons. The novelty of torrential downpours and the general mayhem of landslides and flooding wears off very quickly. Broadly speaking, rule out the period between April and September, when in turn firstly two months of stifling heat and then the southwest monsoon grip the whole peninsula. From late October until April, the weather is perfect in Karnataka and Goa, but less reliable in Kerala, where, by November, the "retreating", or northwest monsoon means constant grey skies and showers. Being on the eastern side of the mountains, Tamil Nadu gets even heavier rains at this time, as does coastal Andhra Pradesh. To enjoy the far south and the Andaman Islands at their best, come between January and March, before the heat starts to build up again. For more detail, read the "Best time to visit" section at the start of each chapter.

AVERAGE TEMPERATURES AND RAINFALL

	Jan	Feb	Mar	Apr	May	Jun	Jul	Aug	Sep	Oct	Nov	Dec
CHENNAI (TN)												
Max/min °C	28/20	31/21	33/23	36/26	38/27	37/27	35/26	34/26	34/25	32/24	29/22	28/21
Max/min °F	83/68	87/70	91/74	96/79	100/81	99/81	95/78	94/78	93/77	89/75	85/72	83/70
Rainfall (mm)	28	33	5	13	38	71	122	137	160	157	152	152
MUMBAI (M)												
Max/min °C	28/19	28/19	30/22	32/24	33/27	32/26	29/25	29/24	29/24	32/24	32/23	31/21
Max/min °F	82/66	82/66	86/72	90/75	91/81	90/79	84/77	84/75	84/75	90/75	90/73	88/70
Rainfall (mm)	3	3	3	0	18	485	617	340	264	64	13	3
PANJIM (GOA)												
Max/min °C	32/19	32/21	32/23	33/25	33/26	30/24	29/24	28/24	29/24	32/24	33/22	32/21
Max/min °F	90/66	90/70	90/73	91/77	91/79	86/75	84/75	82/75	84/75	90/75	91/72	90/70
Rainfall (mm)	0	0	0	0	50	580	650	400	150	90	10	0

OPPOSITE FROM TOP NILGIRI BLUE MOUNTAIN RAILWAY; AYURVEDIC MASSAGE, GOA; LALITHA MAHAL PALACE, MYSURU

Author picks

Our authors have crossed the length and breadth of South India in search of the most impressive monuments, sumptuous food and memorable journeys. Here's a list of their personal highlights.

Toy train travel Take a scenic ride on one of South India's narrow-guage "toy trains", such as the Nilgiri Blue Mountain Railway (p.436) to Ooty in Tamil Nadu or the Matheran–Neral route (p.142) in Maharashtra.

Treehouse stays Wake up to the sound of the forest in a treehouse eco-hideaway. Try the *Machan Resort* in the hills around Pune (p.145), *Kaama Kethna* near Goa (p.199) or the *Jungle Retreat* in Mudumalai Wildlife Sanctuary (p.439).

Ayurvedic massage Experience holistic Indian healthcare at its most indulgent with a traditional Ayurvedic massage at Kovalam, Varkala or a string of spa resorts in the hills (see box, p.312).

Heritage hotels There's nothing quite like treating yourself to a night or two of luxury in a stunning heritage property, such as the colonial houses in Fort Cochin (p.343), superb mansions of Chettinadu (p.423), or a former royal residence such as the *Lalitha Mahal Palace* in Mysuru (p.228) or *Taj Falaknuma Palace* in Hyderabad (p.284).

Feni firewater Distilled from cashew fruit juice or coconut sap, Goan *feni* packs a serious alcohol punch. Try it with lemonade and a twist of lime for the ultimate tropical tipple (p.165).

Marvellous markets Head to the Saturday Night Market in Arpora (p.178) for the best souvenir shopping, Goa for textiles, Kochi's Jew Town (p.346) for antiques or Devaraja Market (p.229) in Mysuru for spices.

Tiger spotting India's tigers may be under threat but you can still spot these thrilling predators in the forests of Periyar, Kerala (p.328) or Mudumalai, Tamil Nadu (p.438).

Malabari meals Sample this fragrant, Arab-influenced style of cooking in the restaurants of Kozhikode (p.354) and Kochi (p.345) in Kerala.

> Our author recommendations don't end here. We've flagged up our favourite places – a perfectly sited hotel, an atmospheric café, a special restaurant – throughout the guide, highlighted with the ★ symbol.

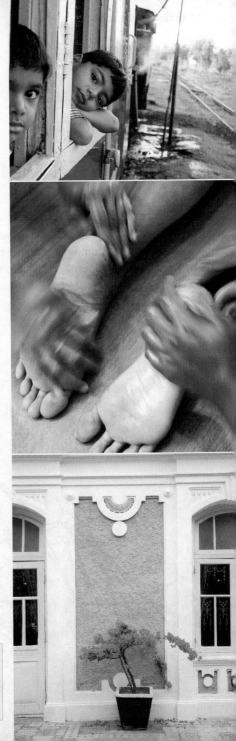

18

things not to miss

It's not possible to see everything South India has to offer in one trip, and we don't suggest you try. What follows is a selective taste of the region's highlights: outstanding temples, the best beaches, spectacular festivals and unforgettable journeys. All highlights are colour-coded by chapter and have a page reference to take you straight into the Guide, where you can find out more.

1

1 FORT COCHIN
Page 337
This atmospheric harbourside is strung with elegant Chinese fishing nets, now emblematic of Kerala.

2 HAMPI
Page 252
The capital of a great Hindu empire, sacked five centuries ago to leave a site strewn with ruins and medieval sculptures.

3 GOLCONDA FORT, HYDERABAD
Page 281
One of the most impressive forts in India – a winding series of battlements with a vividly decorated Hindu temple on top.

4 KERALAN CULTURE
Page 358
Nothing encapsulates the otherworldly feel of the deep south like the masked spirit possession *theyyem* rituals of Kerala.

5 VARKALA
Page 313
This pleasantly low-key Keralan resort boasts sheer red cliffs, amazing sea views and a legion of Ayurvedic masseurs.

6 CRICKET AT THE OVAL MAIDAN
Page 104

Join the locals at dusk as they congregate for ice cream, cricket and a chat in Mumbai's most famous maidan (park).

7 OLD GOA
Page 167

Belfries and Baroque church facades loom over trees on the banks of the Mandovi, all that remains of a once-splendid colonial city.

8 BACKWATER CRUISES, KERALA
Page 322

Explore the famous Kuttanad backwater region in a converted rice barge or punted canoe.

9 GOKARNA BEACH
Page 246

A less commercialized slice of beachside bliss, just a couple of hours or so south of Goa's crowded resorts.

10 MADURAI TEMPLE
Page 418

Madurai, perhaps the definitive South Indian city, is centred on a spectacular medieval temple.

11 BANANA-LEAF FEASTS
Page 37

Gorge yourself on delicious veggie treats served on a banana leaf.

12 YOGA RETREATS
Pages 180, 189 & 227

Discover your inner yogi at a beachside retreat in Goa or at a the world-renowned Ashtanga Institute in Mysuru.

13 MAMALLAPURAM
Page 381

A magnificent collection of eighth-century temples, set along the shore of the Bay of Bengal.

14 PUDUCHERRY
Page 394

India with a distinctly French accent, whether in its architecture or delicious food.

15 ELEPHANTS
Pages 355 & 438

Spot the most emblematic animal of South India in the reserves of Wayanad and Mudumalai.

16 TEA PLANTATIONS
Page 433

Escape the heat with a trip to the tea plantations and lush mountains of Tamil Nadu.

17 ELLORA CAVES
Page 121

A jaw-dropping complex of Buddhist, Hindu and Jain caves, carved by hand from the volcanic Deccan plateau.

18 THE ANDAMAN ISLANDS
Page 440

India's "mini Maldives" makes for a paradise tropical escape.

Itineraries

South India is simply too vast and too complex to explore in a single trip. It makes more sense to focus on one, two or perhaps three regions, depending on your time frame. The following itineraries showcase both the classic attractions and lesser known gems of three distinct regions, from the temples of Tamil Nadu to the sweltering tropical backwaters of Kerala.

MUMBAI TO GOA

Vast, bewildering Mumbai is the main arrival point for most visitors to the South and offers transport links across the region. From here you can head inland to a trio of enticing cities before heading along the tropical Konkan coast to Goa.

❶ **Mumbai** Though exhausting and often obscured by smog, Mumbai offers an impressive range of Raj-era architecture, excellent street food and the South's best nightlife and shopping. **See p.100**

❷ **Nasik** Surrounded by gorgeous vineyards, the holy city of Nasik produces the best wine in the country and makes for a relaxing stopover from Mumbai. **See p.112**

❸ **Aurangabad** A superb base from which to visit the breathtaking cave sculptures and carvings at Ellora and Ajanta. Check out, too, the city's own "false Taj", the Bibi-ka-Maqbara. **See p.116**

❹ **Matheran** Laze on shady colonial verandas, enjoy leisurely woodland walks and breathe in fresh air at this Raj-era hill station. **See p.141**

❺ **Janjira Fort** An island fortress rising sheer from the Arabian Sea makes for a diverting stop along the Konkan coast. **See p.138**

❻ **Goa** For a self-indulgent spell soaking up the rays and surf, Goa's hard to beat. Aim for one of the less-developed resorts such as Agonda or Patnem in the south of the state. **See p.203**

❼ **Gokarna** This compact pilgrimage town on the Konkan coast has plenty of traditional atmosphere, and a crop of gorgeous beaches around the headland to the south. **See p.246**

THE BEST OF KERALA

The languid, tropical state of Kerala tends to be the destination of choice for first-time visitors to South India. You'll need a good three weeks to make the most of this versatile state whether you're exploring the backwaters or taking it easy on the beach.

❶ **Fort Cochin** The heritage hotels, arty cafés and funky boutiques of Kerala's historic harbour town are the ideal starting point for a tour of the region. **See p.337**

❷ **Backwater cruises** The former colonial trading port of Alappuzha provides the entry point for trips into the surrounding backwater region of Kuttanad – a watery world like no other in Asia. **See p.322**

❸ **Varkala beach** Varkala's amazing red cliffs provide the perfect backdrop for bodysurfing and sunset yoga sessions. **See p.313**

❹ **Periyar** Scale the Western Ghat range to enter the jungles of Kerala's Cardamom Hills, where the Periyar Wildlife Sanctuary offers the

ABOVE VARKALA BEACH

chance to spot elephants from a punted raft. **See p.328**

❺ **Thrissur** Aside from being the venue for Kerala's largest temple festival, Puram, Thrissur is the best place to sample the unique artform of *kathakali* dance-drama. **See p.349**

❻ **Wayanad** Stay in a colonial-style planter's bungalow in this beautiful tea-growing region. **See p.355**

❼ **Kannur** Witness a *theyyem* ritual, one of India's most extraordinary spectacles, in the villages around Kannur. **See p.358**

TAMIL TRAILS

Even if you don't consider yourself much of a spiritual person, you will not fail to be moved by the soaring temples of Tamil Nadu. You'll also find standout cuisine, an interesting French connection and the cool, clean air of the Ghats.

❶ **Chennai** The old colonial hub of Fort St George is the standout sight of the Tamil capital, but there's also a wealth of succulent southern cuisine on offer. **See p.379**

❷ **Mamallapuram** Sculpted a dozen or more centuries ago by the Pallava kings, Mamallapuram holds a tempting combination of ancient stonework and a breezy tropical beach. **See p.381**

❸ **Puducherry** Soak up the lingering Gallic ambience of France's former colony on the Coromandel Coast, ideally from the confines of a heritage hotel. **See p.394**

❹ **Thanjavur** The mighty Brihadishwara Temple and famous collection of Chola bronzes in the town's art gallery make Thanjavur the perfect springboard for explorations of the Kaveri Delta region. **See p.407**

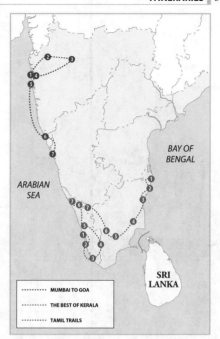

ARABIAN SEA

BAY OF BENGAL

SRI LANKA

MUMBAI TO GOA

THE BEST OF KERALA

TAMIL TRAILS

❺ **Madurai** The shrine of the Fish-Eyed Goddess is Tamil Nadu's greatest living monument, renowned for its soaring, multicoloured, deity-encrusted gateway towers. **See p.415**

❻ **The Ghats** Visit the refreshingly cool hill stations in the misty mountains of South India and sample some of the best chai in the Subcontinent. **See p.427**

❼ **Mudumalai Wildlife Sanctuary** See some of India's rarest wildlife, including sloth bears and leopards on a guided trek. **See p.438**

COMMUTERS, CHURCHGATE STATION, MUMBAI

Basics

23 Getting there

24 Visas

26 Getting around

31 Accommodation

34 Eating and drinking

41 Health

46 The media

47 Festivals and holidays

49 Sports

50 Outdoor activities

50 Yoga, meditation and ashrams

53 Culture and etiquette

54 Shopping

55 Travelling with children

56 Travel essentials

Getting there

Although many visitors reach South India overland as part of a longer tour of the Subcontinent, most people who are solely visiting the South fly into one of the gateway cities, principally Mumbai, which has numerous nonstop services from the UK, plus two from New York. From the UK, there are also nonstop scheduled flights to Chennai, Bengaluru and Hyderabad, as well as many routes into these and other southern cities via the Gulf or Southeast Asia.

Fares worldwide always depend on the season, with the highest being roughly from November to March, when the weather in India is best; fares drop during the shoulder seasons – April to May and August to early October – and you'll get the best prices during the low season, June and July. The most expensive fares of all are those coinciding with **Diwali** in October/November, when demand peaks as Indian emigrants travel home for holidays with their families, while Christmas and New Year fares are also pricey.

For Goa and Kerala, you may find it cheaper to pick up a bargain **package deal** from a tour operator (see p.24). At the time of writing a government prohibition on **flight-only charters** had been lifted, and it was even possible to buy one-way charter flights, but the law on such matters is always prone to change, so check when you are booking.

Flights from the UK and Ireland

It takes between nine and eleven hours to fly **from the UK** direct to South India. A number of carriers fly nonstop from London Heathrow to Mumbai; these currently include Air India (**W**airindia.com), Jet Airways (**W**jetairways.com), Virgin Atlantic (**W**virgin-atlantic.com) and British Airways (**W**ba .com), who also fly nonstop to Chennai, Hyderabad and Bengaluru. Numerous other European and Middle Eastern carriers offer one-stop services via their home city in Europe or the Gulf. From elsewhere in the UK and **Ireland** you'll have to take an indirect flight, changing planes at either Heathrow or somewhere else in Europe, the Middle East or Asia. Both nonstop scheduled fares and seasonal flight-only charters usually start from around £350, although indirect routes, usually via the Gulf, can be found for as little as £300 return at slack times.

Flights from the US and Canada

India is on the other side of the planet from the US and Canada. If you live on the east coast it's quicker to travel via Europe, while from the west coast it's roughly the same distance (and price) whether you travel via Europe or the Pacific. There are currently nonstop flights from **New York** to Mumbai on Air India and United (**W**united.com). Otherwise, you'll probably stop over somewhere in Europe (most often London), the Gulf, or both. Nonstop flights take around 15–16 hours, with fares from New York to Mumbai starting at around US$800, while indirect flights go from as little as US$700. You will have to change when travelling from the west coast, with fares starting at around US$900.

From Toronto to Mumbai or any other city you'll have to travel via Delhi or a connecting aiport in the US, Europe or Asia, with a minimum travel time of around 20 hours.

Flights from Australia, New Zealand and South Africa

From Melbourne and Sydney, you'll have to make at least one change of plane in Delhi or a Southeast Asian hub city (usually Hong Kong, Kuala Lumpur, Singapore or Bangkok). Flying from Melbourne or Sydney fares start from around Aus$1000, while **from Auckland** the cheapest fares start at around NZ$1400; add on approximately NZ$200 for flights from Wellington or Christchurch.

There are no nonstop flights between **South Africa** and India, with most services routing via Addis Ababa, Nairobi or the Gulf. Fares start at around ZAR5500 return.

A BETTER KIND OF TRAVEL

At Rough Guides we are passionately committed to travel. We believe it helps us understand the world we live in and the people we share it with – and of course tourism is vital to many developing economies. But the scale of modern tourism has also damaged some places irreparably, and climate change is accelerated by most forms of transport, especially flying. All Rough Guides' flights are carbon-offset, and every year we donate money to a variety of environmental charities.

Round-the-world tickets

If India is only one stop on a longer journey, you might want to consider buying a **Round-the-World (RTW) ticket**. Some travel agents can sell you an "off-the-shelf" RTW ticket that will have you touching down in about half a dozen cities (Mumbai features on many itineraries); others will have to assemble one for you, which can be tailored to your needs but is apt to be more expensive. Prices start around £1600/US\$2000 for a RTW ticket including India, valid for one year.

Packages and tours

Lots of operators run **package holidays** to South India, covering activities ranging from wildlife-watching through to general sightseeing or just lying on the beach, not to mention more specialist-interest tours focusing on anything from motorbike adventures (see p.30) to yoga and food. In addition, many companies can also arrange **tailor-made tours** where you plan your own itinerary. Specialist trips and tailor-made tours do not necessarily work out a lot more expensive than organizing everything independently, especially if you want a degree of comfort. Tour operators pay a lot less for better-class hotels and flights than you would, plus they save you time and hassle by knowing the best hotels, routes and sights to feature. On the other hand, a typical package tour can rather isolate you from the country, shutting you off in air-conditioned hotels and cars.

Agents and operators

TRAVEL AGENTS

North South Travel UK ☎ 01245 608 291, ⓦ northsouthtravel.co.uk. Friendly, competitive travel agency, offering discounted fares worldwide. Profits are used to support projects in the developing world, especially the promotion of sustainable tourism.

STA Travel UK ☎ 0333 321 0099, US ☎ 1800 781 4040, Australia ☎ 134 782, New Zealand ☎ 0800 474 400, South Africa ☎ 0861 781 781; ⓦ statravel.co.uk. Worldwide specialists in independent travel; also student IDs, travel insurance, car rental, rail passes, and more. Good discounts for students and under-26s.

Trailfinders UK ☎ 020 7368 1200, Ireland ☎ 016 777888, Australia ☎ 1300 780 212; ⓦ trailfinders.com. One of the best-informed and most efficient agents for independent travellers.

Travel CUTS Canada ☎ 1 800 667 2887; ⓦ travelcuts.com. Canadian youth and student travel firm.

USIT Ireland ☎ 01 602 1906, , Australia ☎ 1800 092 499; ⓦ usit.ie. Ireland's main student and youth travel specialists, with a branch in Australia.

TOUR OPERATORS

Audley Travel UK ☎ 01993 838 300, ⓦ audleytravel.com. Tailor-made and small-group tours that use interesting accommodation (homestays, tented camps and heritage properties).

Exodus UK ☎ 0845 287 3644, Ireland ☎ 01 804 7153, US ☎ 1 844 227 9087, Canada ☎ 1 800 267 3347, Australia ☎ 1300 131 564, New Zealand ☎ 0800 838 747; ⓦ exodus.co.uk. Experienced specialists in small-group itineraries, mixing culture with wildlife; they also conduct guided cycle tours.

Explore Worldwide UK ☎ 0845 291 4541, US ☎ 1 800 486 9096, Australia ☎ 02 8913 0700, New Zealand ☎ 0800 643 997; ⓦ explore.co.uk. Wide range of small-group adventure holidays, including Kerala backwaters.

GeoEx US ☎ 1 888 570 7108, ⓦ geoex.com. Unusual group and customized tours such as Tamil Nadu temple trips.

Insider Tours UK ☎ 07964 375 994, ⓦ insider-tours.com. Some of the most original, "hands-on" and ethical itineraries on the market, taking visitors to wonderful off-track corners of Kerala and Goa.

Kerala Connections UK ☎ 01892 722440, ⓦ kerala connections.co.uk. Itineraries for a wide range of budgets in Kerala, as well as Tamil Nadu, Karnataka, Goa, plus the Lakshadweep and Andaman islands.

Lakshmi Tours UK ☎ 01985 844183, ⓦ lakshmitoursindia.com. Special-interest tours (drawing, textiles, Ayurveda), featuring Karnataka and Kerala.

Peregrine UK ☎ 020 7408 9021, US ☎ 1 855 832 4859, Australia ☎ 1300 854 445; ⓦ peregrineadventures.com. Keenly priced small-group tours. Their Essence of South India covers a range of Tamil Nadu and Kerala highlights.

SD Enterprises ☎ 020 8903 3411, ⓦ indiarail.co.uk. Run by Indian rail experts, SD Enterprises put together itineraries for independent travellers wanting to explore South India by train, plus a range of non-choo choo choices.

Steppes Discovery UK ☎ 01285 601 645, US ☎ 1 855 203 7885; ⓦ steppesdiscovery.co.uk. Nature-tour specialist offering small groups or tailor-made trips with an accent on conservation and ecology.

Transindus UK ☎ 020 8566 3739; ⓦ transindus.co.uk. Choice of group or tailor-made tours, including the Deccan Plateau, Tamil Nadu temples and the beauty of Kerala.

Unwind Worldwide UK ☎ 0845 875 4010, ⓦ unwindworldwide.com. Wide range of group and tailor-made tours, including Taste of India, a foodies' tour of Karnataka, Tamil Nadu and Kerala.

Western & Oriental Travel UK ☎ 020 3131 5949, ⓦ wandotravel.com. Award-winning, upmarket agency with tailor-made itineraries such as southern temple tours.

Visas

Almost everyone requires a visa before travelling to India, though the process for obtaining a standard tourist visa has been streamlined a great deal in recent years, and online applications

are now accepted for shorter visits. If you're going to study or work, you'll need to apply for a special student or business visa.

e-Tourist Visas

Citizens of the UK, Ireland, the US, Canada, Australia, New Zealand, South Africa and most other countries who only plan to visit India for up to one month can apply online for an **e-Tourist Visa** (eTV) through the Indian government's official online portal (⬤indianvisaonline.gov.in). These single-entry visas are valid for **thirty days** from the date of entry and must be secured at least four days (and no more than thirty days) before travel. You have to fill in the application, upload your photo and pay the fee online, then carry a printed copy of the eTV with you to India; you'll be issued with your visa on arrival. Fees vary between zero and US$60, depending on your nationality, plus a small bank charge.

Tourist visas

If you wish to stay in India for **longer than thirty days**, or are a passport-holder from one of the few countries not covered by the eTV scheme, you will need to organize your visa in advance. Standard **tourist visas** are valid for a year (up to ten years for US citizens) from the date of issue (not of departure from your home country or entry into India), with a maximum stay during one visit of 180 days. Fees are a princely £102 for UK citizens but vary greatly for other nationalities – check on the respective websites. You're asked to specify whether you need a single-entry or a multiple-entry visa; as the same rates apply to both, it makes sense to ask for the latter to cover all eventualities. Your passport will need to have at least 180 days' validity.

Visas in the UK, US, Canada and Australia are no longer issued by Indian embassies themselves, but by various third-party companies or subcontractors (see below), for a small additional fee. The firms' websites give all the details you need to make your application. Read the small print carefully and always **make sure you've allowed plenty of time**. Processing time is usually two to five working days but it's wiser to leave at least a week. **Postal applications** take a minimum of ten working days plus time in transit, and often longer.

Elsewhere in the world, visas are still issued by the relevant local embassy or consulate, though the same caveats apply. Bear in mind too that Indian high commissions, embassies and consulates observe Indian public holidays as well as local ones, so always check opening hours in advance.

Visa agencies

In many countries it's possible to pay a **visa agency** or "visa expediter" (see above) to process the visa on your behalf, which typically costs £60–70/US$100–120, plus the price of the visa. This is worth considering if you're not able to get to your nearest Indian High Commission, embassy or consulate yourself. Prices vary from company to company, as do turnaround times. Two weeks is about standard, but you can get a visa in as little as 24 hours if you're prepared to pay premium rates. For a full rundown of services, check the company websites, from where you can usually download visa application forms.

Visa extensions

It is no longer possible to **extend a tourist visa** in India, though exceptions may be made in special circumstances such as serious illness. Many travellers who want to spend more time in South India go to a neighbouring country such as Sri Lanka for a new visa when their old one expires, but there is no guarantee a new one will be issued right away, as you are not officially allowed to spend more than six months in the country within one year.

INDIAN EMBASSIES, HIGH COMMISSIONS, CONSULATES AND VISA-PROCESSING CENTRES ABROAD

Australia c/o VFS Global (⬤ vfs-in-au.net). Offices in all states and territories except Tasmania and NT – see website for contact details.
Canada c/o BLS International (⬤ blsindia-canada.com). Nine offices countrywide – see website for contact details.
Ireland Embassy: 6 Leeson Park, Dublin 6 ☎ 01 497 0843, ⬤ indianembassy.ie.
New Zealand High Commission: 180 Molesworth St, PO Box 4045, Wellington ☎ 04 473 6390, ⬤ hicomind.org.nz.
South Africa c/o VFS Global (⬤ vfsglobal/india/southafrica). Offices in in Johannesburg, Cape Town and Durban.
Sri Lanka High Commission: 36–38 Galle Rd, Colombo 3 ☎ 011 232 7587, ⬤ hcicolombo.org; consulate: 31 Rajapihilla Mawatha, PO Box 47, Kandy ☎ 081 222 4563, ⬤ ahcikandy.org.
UK c/o VFS Global (⬤ in.vfsglobal.co.uk). Offices in twelve cities in Britain and Northern Ireland, including three in London – see website for contact details.
US c/o Travisa (⬤ indiavisa.travisaoutsourcing.com). Offices in Washington, New York, San Francisco, Chicago, Houston and Atlanta – see website for contact details.

VISA AGENCIES

CIBT Australia ☎ 1902 211 133, Canada ☎ 1 888 665 9956, UK ☎ 0844 800 4650, US ☎ 1 800 929 2428; ⓦ cibt.com.

India Visa Company UK ☎ 020 8582 1117, ⓦ indiavisacompany .com.

Travel Document Systems US ⓦ traveldocs.com. Offices in Washington DC, Atlanta, Houston, Los Angeles, New York, San Francisco and Seattle.

Visa 24 UK ☎ 0800 084 5037, ⓦ visa24.co.uk.

Visa Connection US & Canada ☎ 1 866 566 8472, ⓦ visaconnection.biz.

Visa Genie UK ☎ 020 571 0883, ⓦ visagenie.co.uk.

Getting around

Intercity transport in South India may not be the fastest or the most comfortable in the world, but it's cheap and goes more or less everywhere. You generally have the option of train or bus, sometimes plane, and occasionally even boat. Transport around town comes in even more permutations, ranging from rickety cycle rickshaws to modern metro systems.

Whether you're on road or rail, public transport or your own vehicle, India offers the chance to try out some classics: narrow-gauge railways, steam locomotives, the boneshaking Ambassador car and the Enfield Bullet motorbike – indeed some people come to India for these alone.

By train

Travelling by train is one of India's classic experiences and the rail network covers almost the whole of South India. Although the railway system might look like chaos, it does work, and generally better than you might expect. Trains are often late, of course, sometimes by hours rather than minutes, but they do run, and when the train you've been waiting for rolls into the station, the reservation you made halfway across the country several weeks ago will be on a list pasted to the side of your carriage.

It's worth bearing in mind, with journeys frequently lasting twelve hours or more, that an **overnight train** can save you a day's travelling and a night's hotel bill, assuming you sleep well on trains. When travelling overnight, always padlock your bag to your bunk; an attached chain is usually provided beneath the seat of the lower bunk.

Types of train

There are three basic types of passenger train in India. You're most likely to use long-distance **intercity trains** (called "express" or "mail") along with the odd "**super-fast**" air-conditioned train such as the *Shatabdi* expresses, daytime trains that connect major cities in the same region. Indeed you may well reach the South on a long-established *Rajdhani* express from Delhi or one of the even faster *Duronto* expresses, which also link major metropolitan areas and have fewer stops. There are also painfully slow local "**passenger**" trains, which stop everywhere, and which you'll only use if you want to get right off the beaten track. In addition to these three basic types of train, South India also boasts its own dedicated **tourist train**, the famous *Nilgiri Blue Mountain Railway* to Ooty (see box, p.436).

Classes of train travel

Indian Railways distinguishes between no fewer than eight **classes** of travel. Different types of train carry different classes of carriage, though you'll seldom have more than four to choose from any one service. The simplest and cheapest class, used by the majority of Indians, is **second class** (II or "second seating"), which are mostly unreserved. These basic carriages have hard wooden seats and often become incredibly packed during the day – bearable for shortish daytime journeys, but best avoided for longer trips and (especially) overnight travel, unless you're exceptionally hardy or unusually poor. On the plus side, fares in second-class unreserved are so cheap as to be virtually free. It also represents a way of getting on a train at the last minute if you haven't been able to secure a reserved seat.

Far more civilized, and only around fifty percent more expensive, is regular **sleeper class** (SL) consisting of carriages of three-tiered padded bunks that convert to seats during the day. All seats in these carriages must be booked in advance even for daytime journeys, meaning that they don't get horrendously overcrowded like second-class unreserved, although there's usually still plenty going on, with itinerant chai- and coffee-sellers, travelling musicians, beggars and sweepers passing through the carriages. Overnight trips in sleeper compartments are reasonably comfy. **First class** (FC) consists of non-a/c seating in comfortable if ageing compartments of two to four berths, though this class is being phased out and is now seldom found.

The other five classes are all air-conditioned (available only on inter-city and super-fast trains). **A/c chair class** (CC) cars are found almost exclusively on super-fast services and consist of comfortable reclining seats; they're really designed for daytime travel, since they don't convert to bunks, and aren't generally found on overnight services. *Shatabdi* expresses are made up entirely of chair-car carriages – ordinary a/c chair car and, for double the price, an **Executive a/c chair class** (EC) car.

There are three classes of air-conditioned sleepers. The cheapest, **a/c 3-tier** (AC3 or 3A), has open carriages with three-tier bunks – basically the same as second-class sleeper, except with a/c and bedding. Less crowded (and found on more services) is **a/c 2-tier** (AC2 or 2A), which has two-tier berths. Most comfortable of all is **a/c first-class** (AC1 or 1A), which consists of two-tier bunks in two- or four-person private compartments, complete with carpeting and relatively presentable bathrooms – although fares can work out more expensive than taking a plane.

Note that bed linen is provided free on most a/c services, while bottled water, snacks and simple meals are included in the ticket price of *Rajdhani*, *Shatabdi* and *Duronto* services.

Ladies' compartments now only exist on suburban trains in big cities, though the number of families travelling means that single women are at least unlikely to end up in a compartment with only men. You can always ask the ticket inspector to change your seat if you feel uncomfortable. Some stations also have ladies-only waiting rooms.

Timetables and fares

Fares, **timetables** and availability of berths can be checked online at Indian Railways' cumbersome website (Windianrail.gov.in), or via the more streamlined, privately run Wcleartrip.com. Indian Railways' *Trains at a Glance* (₹50; updated twice a year) contains timetables of all inter-city and super-fast trains and is available from information counters and newsstands at all main stations.

All rail fares are calculated according to the exact **distance** travelled. *Trains at a Glance* prints a chart of fares by kilometres, and also gives the distance in kilometres of stations along each route in the timetables, making it possible to calculate what the basic fare will be for any given journey. By way of comparison, the cost for each class of travel for a ticket from Chennai to Mumbai is as follows: AC1 ₹3363; AC2 ₹1949; AC3 ₹1598; CC ₹1060; SL ₹511; and II ₹296.

Reserving tickets

It's important to plan your train journeys in advance, as demand often makes it impossible to buy a long-distance ticket on the same day that you want to travel – although the Tatkal quota system (see p.28) has made life a little easier. Travellers following tight itineraries tend to buy their departure tickets from particular towns the moment they arrive to avoid having to trek out to the station again. At most large stations, it's possible to reserve tickets for journeys starting elsewhere in the country.

Online booking can be done via Indian Railways (Wirctc.co.in), which as of 2016 accepts foreign Visa cards and MasterCards, or the privately run Wcleartrip.com (with a 1.8 percent fee, plus an additional ₹20 booking charge); you will first have to register with Indian Railways in either case – check out Wseat61.com/India.htm#book-fromoutside for a clear explanation of this convoluted procedure. Bookings may be made from 120 days in advance right up to four hours before the scheduled departure time of the train. Cleartrip.com also handles Tatkal tickets (see p.28). Having booked your travel, you can then print out your own e-tickets, taking this along with some photo ID, such as a passport, when you board the train. A viable alternative to Cleartrip.com is Wmakemytrip.com, which also accepts some foreign credit cards.

When **reserving a ticket in person** at a railway station, the first thing you'll have to do is fill in a little form at the booking office stating your name, age and sex, your proposed date of travel, and the train you wish to catch (giving the train's **name and number**). Most stations have computerized booking counters and you'll be told immediately whether or not seats are available. **Reservation offices** in the main stations are generally open Monday to Saturday from 8am to 8pm, and on Sunday to 2pm. In larger cities, major stations have special tourist sections to cut queues for foreigners, with helpful English-speaking staff. Elsewhere, buying a ticket can often involve a longish wait, though women often have dedicated queues or can try simply walking to the head of the queue and forming their own "ladies' queue". A few stations also operate a number system of queueing, allowing you to repair to the chai stall until your number is called. A good alternative to queueing yourself is to get someone else to buy your ticket for you. Many **travel agents** will do this for a small fee (typically around ₹50–100); alternatively, ask at your guesthouse if they can sort it out.

Quotas and late-availability tickets

If there are no places available on the train you want, you have a number of choices. First, some seats and berths are set aside as a "**tourist quota**" – ask at the tourist counter of the reservations hall if you can get in on this, or else try the stationmaster. This quota is available in advance but usually only at major or originating stations. Failing that, other special quotas, such as one for "emergencies", only released on the day of travel, may remain unused – however, if you get a booking on the emergency quota and a pukka emergency or VIP turns up, you lose the reservation. Alternatively, you can stump up extra cash for a **Tatkal** ticket, which guarantees you access to a special ten percent quota on most trains, though certain catches and conditions apply. Bookable online and at any computerized office, these are released from 10am the day before the train departs, and there's a surcharge of ₹75–300, depending on the class of travel.

RAC – or "Reservation Against Cancellation" – tickets are another option, giving you priority if sleepers do become available. The ticket clerk should be able to tell you your chances. With an RAC ticket you are allowed onto the train and can sit until the conductor can find you a berth. The worst sort of ticket to have is a **wait-listed** one – identifiable by the letter "W" prefixing your passenger number – which will allow you onto the train (though not *Shatabdi*, *Rajdhani* or *Duronto* trains) but not in a reserved compartment; in this case go and see the ticket inspector (TTI) as soon as possible to ask him to find you a place if one is free. For short journeys or on minor routes you won't need to reserve tickets in advance.

Indrail passes

Indrail passes, sold to foreigners and Indians resident abroad, cover all fares and reservation fees for periods ranging from half a day to ninety days, but are considerably more expensive than buying tickets individually. The pass is designed for nation-wide travel, so if you only use it, say, between Mumbai, Chennai and the cities of Tamil Nadu, you won't be getting your money's worth. It does, however, save you queuing for tickets, allow you to make and cancel reservations without charge and generally smooths your way in. For example, if you need to find a seat or berth on a "full" train, pass-holders get priority for tourist quota places. Indrail passes are available, in sterling or US dollars, at main station tourist counters in India and outside the country at IR agents and sometimes at Air India offices. A seven-day pass costs US$80 in SL or II, US$135 in FC, AC2/AC3 and CC, and US$270 in AC1. There's a full list of prices and overseas IR agents at Ⓦindianrail.gov.in/international_Tourist.html.

By plane

Considering the large distances and time involved in getting around South India, **flying** is an attractive option, despite the cost – the journey from Mumbai to Chennai, for example, takes under 2 hours by plane compared to around 24 hours on the train. Delays and cancellations can whittle away the time advantage, especially over small distances, but if you're short of time and plan to cover a lot of ground, flying can be a godsend. There was a prolif-eration of private airlines in the early years of the millennium and after a few failures, most notably Kingfisher Airlines, a further crop has popped up in recent years.

Booking flights is most easily done online via the airline's website. Larger carriers also have offices in major cities, as well as at the airports they fly to; these are listed in the relevant Guide chapters. Children under twelve pay half fare and under-twos (one per adult) pay ten percent.

DOMESTIC AIRLINES

Air Asia Ⓦ airasia.com.
Air Carnival Ⓦ aircarnival.in.
Air Costa Ⓦ aircosta.in.
Air India Ⓦ airindia.com.
Air India Express Ⓦ airindiaexpress.in.
Air Pegasus Ⓦ airpegasus.in.
FLYeasy Ⓦ flyeasyindia.com.
GoAir Ⓦ goair.in.
IndiGo Airlines Ⓦ book.goindigo.in.
Jet Airways/JetKonnect Ⓦ jetairways.com.
SpiceJet Ⓦ spicejet.com.
Trujet Ⓦ trujet.com.

By bus

Although trains are generally the most atmospheric and comfortable way to travel in South India, there are some places, particularly in the Western Ghats, not covered by the rail network, or where trains are inconvenient. By contrast, **buses** go almost every-where, usually more frequently than trains (though mostly in daylight hours), and are also sometimes faster. Going by bus also usually saves you the bother of reserving a ticket in advance.

Services vary enormously in terms of price and standard. Ramshackle **government-run buses**, packed with people, livestock and luggage, cover most routes, both short- and long-distance. In addition, popular routes between larger cities, towns and resorts are usually covered by **private buses**. These tend to be more comfortable, with extra legroom, tinted windows and padded reclining seats. Note, however, that smaller private bus companies may be only semilegal and have little backup in case of breakdown.

The description of the service usually gives some clue about the level of comfort. "Ordinary" buses usually have minimally padded, bench-like seats with upright backs. "Deluxe" or "Luxury" are more or less interchangeable terms but sometimes the term deluxe signifies a luxury bus past its sell-by date; occasionally a bus will be described as a "2 by 2" which means a deluxe bus with just two seats on either side of the aisle. When applied to government services, these may hardly differ from "ordinary" buses, but with private companies, they should guarantee a softer, individual seat. It's worth asking when booking if your bus will have a video or music system (a "video bus"), as their deafening noise ruins any chances of sleep. Always try to avoid the back seats – they accentuate bumpy roads.

Luggage travels in the hatch of private buses – for which you may have to part with about ₹10–20 for the safekeeping of your bags. On state-run buses, you can usually squeeze it into an unobtrusive corner, although you may sometimes be requested to have it travel on the roof (you may be able to travel up there yourself if the bus is too crowded, though it's dangerous and illegal); check that it's well secured (ideally, lock it there) and not liable to get squashed. Baksheesh is in order for whoever puts it up there for you.

In recent years, there has been a revolution in **online booking** services, which allow you to compare schedules and fares, buy tickets online and even to select your seat. Two of the best are ⓦ makemytrip.com and ⓦ redbus.in, both of which also have downloadable apps. Buying a bus ticket at the bus station is usually less of an ordeal than buying a train ticket, although at large city bus stations there may be twenty or so counters, assigned to different routes. When you buy your ticket you'll be given the registration number of the bus and, sometimes, a seat number. As at railway stations, women can form a separate, quicker, "ladies' queue".

You can usually only pay on board on most ordinary state buses, and at bus stands outside major cities. Prior booking is usually available and preferable for express and private services, and it's a good idea to check with the agent exactly where the bus will depart from. You can usually pay on board private buses too, though doing so reduces your chances of a seat.

By boat

South India is one of the few parts of the country where you are likely to travel on water. The Andaman Islands are connected to Kolkata and Chennai by large boats – as well as to each other (see p.448) by smaller ferries. Kerala has a regular passenger service with a number of services operating out of Alappuzha and Kollam, including the popular "backwater trip" between the two (see box, p.322).

By car

It is much more usual for tourists to be driven in India than it is for them to drive themselves; **car rental** firms operate on the basis of supplying **vehicles with drivers**. You can arrange them through any tourist office or taxi firm, and local taxi drivers hanging around hotels and city ranks are also available for day hire. Cars start around ₹1800 (£22/US$27.50) per day, which should include a maximum of 200km, with additional kilometres charged at around ₹7–8 per kilometre. On longer trips, the driver sleeps in the car, for which his firm may charge an additional ₹150–200. You should generally tip the driver around ₹150 per day, too. It is important to confirm exactly what the terms and costs of the rental are before you set off.

Tourists still occasionally succumb to the romance of that quintessentially Indian automobile, the **Hindustan Ambassador** Mark IV, based on the design of the old British Morris Oxford. Sadly, however, the car's appalling suspension and back-breaking seats make it among the most uncomfortable rides in the world. All in all, you'll be much better off in a modern two- or four-door hatchback – ask your rental company for the options. Air-conditioning adds considerably to the rate, and with larger cars such as SUVs, the daily rate is higher and tends only to cover the first 80km, after which stiff additional per-kilometre charges apply.

Self-drive

A handful of big international chains offer **self-drive** car rental in India, but unless you've had plenty of experience on the country's notoriously dangerous roads, we strongly recommend you leave the driving to an expert. If you do drive yourself, expect the unexpected, and expect other drivers to take whatever liberties they can get away with. **Traffic** in the cities is particularly undisciplined; vehicles cut in and out without warning, and pedestrians, cyclists and cows wander nonchalantly down the middle of the road. In the country the roads are narrow, often in terrible repair, and hogged by overloaded Tata trucks that move aside for nobody, while something slow-moving like a bullock cart or a herd of goats can take up the whole road. It is particularly dangerous to drive at night – cyclists and cart drivers hardly ever have lights. If you are involved in an **accident**, it might be an idea to leave the scene quickly and go straight to the police to report it; mobs can assemble fast, especially if pedestrians or cows are involved.

By motorbike

Riding a **motorbike** in India is not for the faint-hearted. Besides the challenging road and traffic conditions (see above) with the resultant stress and fatigue, simply running an unfamiliar bike can become a nightmare.

Buying a motorbike in India is only for the brave. If it's an old classic you're after, the 350- or 500cc Enfield Bullet, sold cheapest in Puducherry on the Tamil Nadu coast, leads the field, with models becoming less idiosyncratic the more recent they are. If low price and practicality are your priorities, a smaller model from the likes of Bajaj, built in India but based on dependable old Japanese designs, may fit the bill if not the image. Obviously, you'll have to haggle over the price, but you can expect to pay half to two-thirds of the original price for a bike in reasonable condition. Given the right bargaining skills, you can sell it again later for a similar price – perhaps to another foreign traveller – by advertising it in hotels and restaurants. A certain amount of bureaucracy is involved in transferring vehicle ownership to a new owner but a garage should be able to put you onto a broker ("auto consultant") who, for a modest commission (around ₹1000–2000), will help you find a seller or a buyer and do the necessary paperwork.

Motorbike **rental** is available in many tourist towns and can be fun for local journeys, but the condition of the bike can be hit and miss. However, unless you know your stuff, this is a better strategy than diving in and buying a machine. Unlike with sales, it's in a rental outfit's interest to rent you a bike that works. Mechanically, the important thing to establish is the condition of the chain and sprockets, whether the machine starts and runs smoothly and, not least, whether both brakes and lights work (even so, riding at night is inadvisable). An in-depth knowledge of mechanics is not so necessary as every town has a bike mender who will be no stranger to Enfields.

Without doubt the least stressful way of enjoying India on a motorbike, especially a temperamental but characterful Enfield, is joining one of several **motorbike tours**. They focus on the best locales with minimal traffic and amazing landscapes – including Kerala – and remove much of the stress from what is still an adventure.

MOTORBIKE TOUR AGENCIES

Blazing Trails UK ☎ 05603 666788, 🖰 blazingtrailstours.com.
Classic Bike Adventure India Goa ☎ 83222 68467, 🖰 classic-bike-india.com.
Live India UK ☎ 07869 373 805, 🖰 liveindia.co.uk.

By bicycle

In many ways a **bicycle** is the ideal form of transport in India, offering total independence without loss of contact with local people. You can camp out, though there are cheap lodgings in almost every village – take the bike into your room with you – and, if you get tired of pedalling, you can put it on top of a bus as luggage, or transport it by train.

Bringing a bike from abroad requires no special paperwork but spare parts and accessories may be of different sizes and standards in India, so you may have to improvise. Bring basic spares and tools, and a pump. **Buying a bike** in India couldn't be easier, since most towns have cycle shops and even entire markets devoted to bikes. The advantages of a local bike are that spare parts are easy to get, locally produced tools and parts will fit, and your bike will not draw a crowd every time you park it. Disadvantages are that Indian bikes tend to be heavier and less state-of-the-art than ones from abroad; mountain bikes are beginning to appear in cities and bigger towns, but with insufficient gears and a low level of equipment, they're not worth buying. Selling should be quite easy: you won't get a tremendously good deal at a cycle market but you may well be able to sell privately to another traveller, or even to a rental shop.

Bicycles can be **rented** in most towns, usually for local use only, though better mountain bikes can be rented in some mountain areas: this is a good way to find out if your legs and bum can survive an Indian bike before buying one. Rates can be anything from ₹30 to ₹150 per day; you may have to leave a deposit or your passport as security. Several adventure-tour operators offer bicycle tours of the country (see p.24), with most customers bringing their own cycles.

As for **contacts**, International Bicycle Fund in the US (☎ 206 767 0848, 🖰 ibike.org) publishes information and offers advice on bicycle travel around the world and maintains a useful website. In India, the Cycling Federation of India (☎011 2375 3528, ⓦcyclingfederationofindia.org) is the main cycle-sports organization.

City transport

Transport around towns takes various forms. City **buses** can get unbelievably crowded, so beware of pickpockets, razor-carriers, pocket-slitters and "Eve-teasers" (see p.62); the same applies to **suburban trains** in Mumbai (Chennai is about the only other place where you might want to use trains for local city transport). Bengaluru, Chennai and Hyderabad all have clean, efficient and gradually expanding metro systems.

You can also take **taxis**, usually rather battered Ambassadors (painted black and yellow in the large cities) and Maruti omnivans. With luck, the driver will agree to use the meter; in theory you're within your rights to call the police if he doesn't, but the usual compromise is to agree a fare for the journey before you get in. Naturally, it helps to have an idea in advance what the fare should be, though any figures quoted in this or any other guide should be treated as being the broadest of guidelines only. From places such as main stations, you may be able to find other passengers to share a taxi to the town centre. Many stations, and certainly most airports, operate **prepaid taxi schemes** with set fares that you pay before departure; more expensive prepaid limousines are also available. **App-based taxi-booking** companies are also making their presence felt, with Uber (ⓦuber.com) now operating in 25 cities and India's own Ola (ⓦolacabs.com) becoming very popular.

That most Indian of vehicles, the **auto-rickshaw** – commonly referred to as just an "auto" – is the front half of a motor scooter with a couple of seats mounted on the back. Cheaper than taxis, better at nipping in and out of traffic, and sometimes metered in cities (you should agree a fare before setting off if that is not the case), auto-rickshaws are a little unstable and their drivers often rather reckless but that's all part of the fun. In the odd major tourist centre rickshaw-wallahs can, however, hassle you endlessly on the street, often shoving themselves right in your path to prevent you from ignoring them. In general it is better to hail a rickshaw than to take one that's been following you, and to avoid those that hang around outside posh hotels. Apps for booking auto-rickshaws are even starting to appear. Some towns also have larger versions of auto-rickshaws known as **tempos**

(or Vikrams), with six or eight seats behind, which usually ply fixed routes at flat fares.

Here and there, you'll come across horse-drawn carriages, or **tongas**. Tugged by underfed and often lame horses, these are the least popular with tourists. Slower and cheaper still is the **cycle rickshaw** – basically a glorified tricycle – but these are quite rare in South India. Foreign visitors often feel uncomfortable about travelling this way; cycle rickshaw-wallahs are invariably emaciated pavement-dwellers who earn only a pittance for their pains. In the end, though, to deny them your custom on those grounds is spurious logic; they will earn even less if you don't use them. As a foreigner you'll probably be quoted grossly inflated fares, but ask yourself if it's really worth haggling over tiny sums, which they could probably do with more than you.

If you want to see a variety of places around town, consider renting a taxi or auto-rickshaw for the day. Find a driver who speaks English reasonably well and agree a price beforehand. You will probably find it a lot cheaper than you imagine: the driver will invariably act as a guide and source of local knowledge, so tipping is usually in order.

Accommodation

There are far more Indians travelling around their own country at any one time – whether for holidays, on pilgrimages or for business – than there are foreign tourists, and a vast infrastructure of hotels and guesthouses caters for their needs. On the whole, accommodation, like so many other things in India, provides good value for money, though in the major cities, especially, there are luxury establishments that charge international prices for providing Western-style comforts and service. In recent years, there has also been a dramatic increase in the number of homestays in some parts of the country.

Budget accommodation

While accommodation prices in India are generally on the up, there's still an abundance of inexpensive **hotels** and **hostels** catering for foreign backpackers, tourists and less-well-off Indians. It's still easy to find a double room for ₹600–800, and rates outside big cities and tourist centres may fall

FIVE TOP BUDGET PLACES TO STAY

Emerald Gecko, Havelock Island
Laidback bamboo huts beside a pristine beach. See p.454
Greenlands Youth Hostel, Kodaikanal
Lovely old stone house with stunning views from the Western Ghats. See p.430
Plaza, Jalgaon Spotless, welcoming hotel, a handy stopover en route to Ajanta. See p.134
Sudha, Hampi Simple but very friendly place, right in the village. See p.259
Walton's Homestay, Fort Cochin
Beautifully converted mansion with lovely terrace and garden. See p.344

most expensive in Mumbai, Goa and resorts in Kerala, where prices are at least double those for equivalent accommodation in most other parts of the region.

The cheapest rooms usually have flimsy beds and thin, lumpy mattresses. Most places now offer en-suite bathrooms (or "**attached**" rooms, as they're known locally) and hot water, either on tap or in a bucket, though shared showers and toilets with only cold water are still fairly common at the bottom of the range – in our reviews in the Guide we have assumed that establishments have attached rooms and noted exceptions. It's always wise to check out the state of the bathrooms and toilets before taking a room. Bedbugs and mosquitoes are other things to check for – splotches of blood around the bed and on the walls where people have squashed them are telltale signs.

as low as ₹300 (roughly £3.70/US$4.60). The rock-bottom option is usually in a dormitory of a hostel or lodge, where you may even pay less than ₹100. Even cheaper still are **dharamshalas**, hostels run by religious establishments and used by pilgrims (see p.34).

Budget accommodation varies from filthy fleapits to homely guesthouses and, naturally, tends to be cheaper the further you get off the beaten track. It's

If a **taxi or rickshaw driver** tells you that the place you ask for is full, closed or has moved, it's more than likely that it's because he wants to take you to a hotel that pays him commission – added, in some cases, to your bill. Hotel touts operate in many popular tourist spots, working for commission from the hotels they take you to; this can become annoying and they should be given a wide berth unless you are desperate.

ACCOMMODATION PRICES

Accommodation prices quoted throughout this guide are for the **cheapest double room during the main tourist season**, where one exists, but not for short spikes during peak periods, such as those that occur in the hill stations from April to July or in Goa and Kerala over Christmas and New Year. Notable regional price fluctuations, including slack periods when great discounts can be had, are mentioned in the accommodation listings throughout the Guide chapters.

Where **two prices** are given, it denotes the cost of a double with shared bathroom first ("non-attached"), followed by the en-suite ("attached") option. **Dorm prices** per person are also quoted separately where applicable. If the review states that a hotel has some air-conditioned rooms, you can usually reckon on them costing 50–100 percent more than the non-a/c ones.

Not all hotels offer **single rooms**, so it can often work out more expensive to travel alone; in hotels that don't, you may be able to negotiate a slight discount. It's not unusual to find rooms with three or four beds, however – great value for families and small groups.

Like most other things in India, the price of a room may well be open to **negotiation**. If you think the price is too high, or if all the hotels in town are empty, try haggling. You may get nowhere – but nothing ventured, nothing gained.

Note that all hotels and guesthouses are required by law to have an official list of approved room prices. Some establishments, especially the cheaper ones, ignore this rule, while others do not display the rates. It is always worth asking for the "**tariff list**", if you cannot see it, as a starting point for any bargaining. In cheap hotels and hostels, you needn't expect any additions to your basic bill, but as you go up the scale, you'll find **taxes and service charges** creeping in, sometimes adding as much as a third on top of the original tariff. Service is generally ten percent, but taxes are a matter for local governments and vary from state to state. Such taxes are not included in the prices quoted in the Guide.

Mid-range hotels

Even if you value your creature comforts, you don't need to pay through the nose for them. A large clean room, freshly made bed, your own spotless bathroom and hot and cold running water can still cost as little as ₹1000 (£10/US$15) in cheaper areas. Extras that bump up the price include local taxes (see box opposite), cable TV, mosquito nets, a balcony and, above all, **air-conditioning**. Abbreviated in this book (and in India itself) as a/c, air-conditioning is not necessarily the advantage you might expect – in some hotels you can find yourself paying double for a system that is so dust-choked and noisy as to be more of a drawback than an advantage. Some offer **air-coolers** instead of a/c – these can be noisy and are less effective than full-blown a/c, but much better than just a fan. They're only found in drier climes as they don't work in areas of extreme humidity such as along the coasts. Many medium-priced hotels also have attached restaurants, and offer room service.

Most state governments run their own chain of hotels. They are usually good value but far less well run than comparable places in the private sector. We've reviewed such chain hotels throughout this guide. Bookings for state-run hotels can be made in advance through the state tourist offices throughout the country.

Upmarket hotels

Recent years have seen a proliferation in the number of luxury hotels throughout India, which charge ₹5000 and above. Roughly speaking, they fall into three categories. Pitched primarily at visiting businessmen, smart, Western-style hotels with air-conditioning and swanky interiors are to be found predominantly in towns and city centres. Because competition among them is rife, tariffs tend to represent good value for money, especially in the upper-mid-range bracket. Formal five-star chains such as Taj, India's premier hotel group, charge international rates – as most of their guests are on expense accounts or staying as part of discounted tour packages. Note that many top-end hotels offer significant **reductions to their rack rates** if you **book online**.

Holding more appeal for foreign visitors are the **heritage properties** that have mushroomed all across the country in recent years. Brimming with old-world atmosphere, they deliver a quintessentially Indian "experience", often in the most exotic locations, with turbaned bellboys and antique

FIVE TOP LUXURY PLACES TO STAY

Akkarikkulam Memoirs, Alappuzha Backwaters Converted mansion overlooking the Pamba River. See p.322

Chettinadu Mansion, Kanadukathan Delightful heritage mansion containing many original features. See p.423

Kabini River Lodge, Nagarahole National Park Beautifully refurbished former maharaja's hunting lodge. See p.239

Taj Falaknuma Palace, Hyderabad Palatial luxury in the former nizam's residence. See p.284

Taj Mahal Palace and Tower, Mumbai India's most famous hotel is the ultimate in stylish urban luxury. See p.94

automobiles adding to the colonial-era ambience. These days you can stay in fabulous Tamil mansions; colonial tea bungalows in Coorg or the Nilgiris; wooden, gabled-roofed *tharavadus* (ancestral homes) in the Keralan backwaters; and Portuguese *palacios* in Goa. Some wildlife sanctuaries also offer atmospheric, high-end accommodation in former hunting lodges, tented camps or treehouses, while down in Kerala, you can also experience the lakes and lagoons of the backwaters on a converted rice barge.

The third category, which is gaining in popularity in cities and touristic areas, is **boutique hotels**, modelled on Western lines. With much less of a corporate feel than business hotels, these tend to be smaller and place a greater emphasis on service and modern design features; some may occupy heritage properties.

Other options

Unsurprisingly, India has fully embraced the new global sharing economy and it's increasingly possible to find great places to stay via websites such as Ⓦairbnb.com and Ⓦcouchsurfing.org. **Servas** (Ⓦservas.org), established in 1949 as a peace organization, is also devoted to providing places in people's homes, representing more than six hundred hosts in India; you have to join before travelling by applying to the local Servas secretary (via the website).

Homestays, often as organized as hotels but with a far more personal touch, have been established for some time in places like Mumbai, Goa and Kerala. These have now spread far and wide,

---

CHECKOUT TIMES AND WI-FI

Checkout time is often noon, but confirm this when you arrive: some expect you out by 9am. Many others operate a 24hr system, under which you are simply obliged to leave by the same time as you arrived. Some places let you use their facilities after the official checkout time, sometimes for a small charge.

Wi-fi has proliferated in the past few years and the majority of accommodation now offer it. Reviews in the Guide only mention connectivity if it is restricted to part of the hotel, if there is a charge, or if there is no wi-fi at all.

---

encompassing other states such as Karnataka and Tamil Nadu. **Farmstays**, **rural villas** and **ecolodges** have also all mushroomed in popularity in recent years. None of these options is cheap, rarely costing less than ₹2000, but all aim to provide a more authentic experience, whether that is the chance to literally feel part of the family or to learn something about the local wildlife and environment, or even to participate in projects.

YMCAs and **YWCAs**, mostly confined to big cities, can be plusher and pricier than mid-range hotels. They are usually good value but are often full and some are exclusively single-sex. Official and non-official **youth hostels**, some run by state governments, are spread haphazardly across the country. They give HI cardholders a discount but rarely exclude non-members, nor do they usually impose daytime closing. Prices match the cheapest hotels; where there is a youth hostel, it usually has a dormitory and may well be the best budget accommodation available – which goes especially for the Salvation Army ones. A more modern, Western-style breed of **hostels** has started popping up in major cities and tourist destinations. These are aimed directly at backpackers and tend to provide better facilities than the old-style hostels, as well as pleasant communal areas ideal for socializing. One of the most widespread chains is *Zostel* (ⓦ zostel.com).

Camping is generally restricted to wildlife reserves, where the Forest Department lays on low-impact accommodation under canvas for visitors, and to beach resorts in which building is restricted by local coastal protection laws. Except on mountain treks, it's not usual simply to pitch a tent in the countryside.

Many railway stations have "**retiring rooms**": basic private rooms with a bed and bathroom (some stations have dorms, too). They can be handy if you're catching an early morning train, and are usually among the cheapest accommodation available anywhere, but can be noisy. Retiring rooms cannot be booked in advance and are allocated on a first-come-first-served basis;

as long as you have a ticket, just turn up and ask if there's a vacancy.

Finally, **religious institutions**, particularly Sikh *gurudwaras*, offer accommodation for pilgrims and visitors, which may include tourists; a donation is often expected, and certainly appreciated, but some of the bigger ones charge a fixed, nominal fee. Pilgrimage sites, especially those far from other accommodation, also have **dharamshalas** where visitors can stay – very cheap and very simple, usually with basic, communal washing facilities; some charitable institutions even have rooms with simple attached bathrooms. *Dharamshalas*, like *gurudwaras*, offer accommodation either on a donations system or charge a nominal fee, which can be as low as ₹25.

Eating and drinking

India's aromatic and delicious food has a richly deserved reputation throughout the world, and food in the South is some of the finest in the Subcontinent, with a range of cuisines that reflect the region's broad spectrum of cultures. As well as offering wonderful fresh fish, South India can be particularly special if you're a vegetarian, and even the most confirmed meat-eaters will find themselves tucking into delicious veg curries with relish.

What Westerners call a curry covers a range of dishes, each made with a different masala. The word curry probably originates from the *karhi* leaf, a type of laurel, found in much of Indian cooking, especially in the South. Commonly used **spices**, mostly grown along the lush spice belt of the Western Ghats particularly in Kerala, include pepper, cardamom, cloves, cinnamon, chilli, turmeric, garlic, ginger, coriander – both leaf and seed – cumin and saffron. Some chillis are used whole, so beware of chewing on them.

Where to eat

Broadly speaking, eating establishments divide into three main types: cheap and unpretentious local cafés (known variously as *dhabas*, *bhojanalayas* and *udupis*); Indian restaurants aimed at more affluent locals and businessmen; and tourist restaurants. The cheap cafés in the South are most commonly called **udupi** canteens (after the town in Karnataka, see p.37) or sometimes just "meals" restaurants. They offer cheap, delicious vegetarian snacks such as masala dosa, *idli*, *vada* and rice-based dishes, all freshly cooked to order and often served by uniformed waiters. Some northern-style cafés with a more meat-based menu, usually owned by Punjabis, can be found in the larger cities.

There are all sorts of **Indian restaurants**, veg and non-veg, typically catering to Indian businessmen and middle-class families. They are often attached to hotels and usually include at least some Chinese items on the menu. Prices are higher than the canteens but still remarkably good value. The more expensive Indian restaurants, such as those in five-star hotels, can be very expensive by local standards, but offer a rare chance to try top-notch classic Indian cooking, and still at significantly cheaper prices than you'd pay back home.

Tourist restaurants, found across South India wherever there are significant numbers of Western visitors, especially beach areas, cater specifically for foreign travellers with unadventurous taste buds. They dish up a stereotypical array of favourite international dishes, pancakes, omelettes, chips, muesli and fruit salad, along with a basic range of curries. The food can be very hit and miss – Indian spaghetti bolognese, enchiladas and chicken chow mein can be every bit as weird as you might expect – but the better ones may well serve excellent meat or fish. International **fast food chains** are easy to find in major cities as well as home-grown versions such as Kwality's and independently owned fast-food cafés like Pizza Corner.

Veg vs non veg

Most religious Hindus, and a large majority of people in the far south, do not eat meat, while some orthodox brahmins will not eat onions and garlic or any food cooked by anyone outside their household. Jains are even stricter and will go as far as shunning tomatoes, which remind them of blood.

Many eating places state whether they are **vegetarian** or non-vegetarian – "veg" and "non-veg". Sometimes you will come across restaurants advertising both veg and non-veg, indicating they have two separate kitchens and, often, two distinct parts to the restaurant so as not to contaminate or offend their vegetarian clientele. You'll also see "pure veg" advertised, which means that no eggs or alcohol are served.

Veganism as such is not common, however, so if you're vegan you'll need to be fairly vigilant and enquiring. Dairy products for example are prevalent in most Indian sweets, and in many restaurants and homes ghee (unclarified butter) is used for frying.

As a rule, **meat-eaters** should exercise caution in India: even when meat is available, especially in the larger towns, its quality is not assured and you won't get much in a dish anyway. Note that what is called "mutton" is in fact goat. Hindus, of course, do not eat beef, and Muslims shun pork, so you'll only find those in a few Christian enclaves such as the beach areas of Goa, in the few Tibetan communities and among the Kodavas of the Kodagu (Coorg) hill country of Karnataka, who love pork. In Kerala, due to a liberal mix of religions and cultures, attitudes to food can be more relaxed, and both beef and pork appear on the same menu.

Fish is popular throughout the region, particularly in the coastal towns and beach resorts, and fish dishes, whether as steaks or in curries, are often beautifully cooked and very good value, though (especially inland) it can be pre-frozen rather than fresh.

South Indian food

For the first-time visitor, South India's bewildering range of **regional cuisines** can challenge all preconceptions of Indian food. Occasionally, a sweeping generalization is made that the cuisine of North India is rich and spicy, while that of the South is plain. With cuisine ranging from the rich northern-style Mughlai cooking, developed within the opulent courts of Muslim Hyderabad, to the more simple vegetarian dishes of Tamil Nadu, it soon becomes clear that this is quite simply not true. The street food and snacks of Mumbai are superb, and the rest of Maharashtra is renowned for its seafood, kebabs, puris and vegetarian fare. Goan cuisine reflects strong Portuguese influences, and Karnataka draws heavily from the plain cooking of

We give more advice on **drinking water** in the Health section (see box, p.41). There's a glossary of **food terms** in the Language section (see p.504).

its southern neighbours as well as from the rich, aromatic cooking of Hyderabad. Kerala's cuisine is remarkably varied, with a range of delicious fish dishes and a lot of coconut-based recipes. And finally Tamil Nadu has the strongest vegetarian tradition in the south but nevertheless offers pockets of regional variety such as Chettinad – with its memorable chicken dishes – and the cuisine of the small, diminishing Franco-Indian population of Puducherry, which has its own unique cuisine. For more detail on many of the dishes covered here, see the Glossary on pp.504–506.

Maharashtrian cooking

Maharashtrians take their food very seriously, or in the words of a local expression "as equal to god". As the state capital, Mumbai is India's largest and most cosmopolitan city, it's no surprise to find a huge variety of flavours and food styles across the region. Maharashtrian cuisine tends to use a lot of coconut, cashews and peanuts – the oil of the latter is the main cooking medium. Another distinguishing feature is the use of a deep purple berry called *kokum*, which has a sweet and sour taste and acts as a digestif.

The most famous Mumbai dish is **Bombay duck**, a rather misleading name as it is actually a small fish which is either cooked fresh in batter or sun-dried and commonly eaten in curry (see box, p.73 for more). Another local speciality is dhansak, a lentil-based dish popular amongst Mumbai's Parsi community. Aubergines are widely used, with baby *brinjals* often stuffed with coconut. For dessert, seek out *puran poli* – *roti* stuffed with a mixture of saffron, cardamom powder, gram (chickpea) and *jaggery*.

Goan cooking

Goan cuisine is often divided into two separate traditions, based loosely on the religious or cultural differences between the Hindu and Catholic populations of the state. While Hindu Goan food has resisted Portuguese influence, the Catholic style

---

In the South – perhaps even more so than elsewhere – **eating with your fingers** is de rigueur, and cutlery may not always be available. Wherever you eat, however, remember to use only your right hand (see p.53), and wash your hands before you start. Use the tips of your fingers to avoid getting food on the palm of your hand.

FIVE TOP PLACES TO EAT: NON-VEG

Apoorva, Mumbai Top-quality Mangalorean coconut-based delights, especially seafood. See p.97

Coconut Grove, Bengaluru Gourmet cuisine from select southern regions, served on a leafy terrace. See p.220

Jina Resort, Little Andaman Exquisite fish and veg dishes in a friendly island guesthouse. See p.461

Le Club, Puducherry A stylish touch of French *je ne sais quoi* in the old Gallic colony. See p.398

Paradise Food Court, Secunderabad Huge, plush restaurant serving wonderful biriyanis and kebab dishes. See p.285

---

of cuisine has borrowed and maintained many colonial traditions. Some interesting fusions have resulted.

The hot-and-sour **vindaloo** curry, found on menus in Indian restaurants worldwide, is possibly the most famous of all Goan dishes. Vindaloo originates from the Portuguese *vinho d'alho*, literally "garlic wine", and consists of either meat or fish seasoned with vinegar, but is most traditionally made with pork. Goan food is particularly distinctive in that it uses palm vinegar, a Portuguese introduction, in many of its preparations (see box, p.165 for more).

Hyderabadi and Andhran cooking

Some connoisseurs may argue, and not without a certain justification, that the haute cuisine originating from Hyderabad in Andhra Pradesh represents the pinnacle of all **Indian Muslim cooking** (see box, p.285). Although the grandeur of a once luxurious court has faded, traditions still linger on and if you find yourself in the city, a culinary tour will leave indelible impressions. Many Hyderabadi dishes will already be familiar to visitors. Preparations such as korma (an aromatic but mild and creamy curry), pilau (aromatic fried rice; also known as *pulau*, pulao and pilaf) and biriyani (aromatic baked rice) feature prominently in India and are recognized worldwide.

As with Muslim cooking everywhere, Hyderabadi cuisine is heavily meat-orientated. However, there are also delicious **vegetarian** dishes, such as *bagheri* (or *Hyderabadi*) baingan – small aubergines cooked with peanut paste – as well as several rice preparations; like *khichari* (rice cooked with lentils and ghee), a traditional breakfast.

Outside Hyderabad, and the ubiquitous biriyani, **Andhran cuisine** is generally accepted as the hottest of South India's culinary styles, rather unsurprisingly as the state produces the legendary Guntur chilli, one of the hottest red chilli peppers in the world. There is however just about room for other flavours to seep through the firewall – a typical dish is chicken braised in red chillies, fenugreek, garlic and ginger, then pan roasted with curry leaves and dressed with lemon.

Karnatakan cooking

Sandwiched between the meat-loving Muslim enclaves of Hyderabad and the central Deccan, and the lush coastal region to the south, **Karnataka** enjoys the best of both worlds in terms of food. In Bengaluru's restaurants you can find sumptuous chicken biriyanis inspired by Andhra Pradeshi cuisine and traditional vegetarian "meals" with unlimited portions of vegetables, *sambar*, rice and *rasam* (pepper water). The state's cuisine is probably the mildest in South India, with mustard seeds used much more frequently than chillies. Palm sugar is added to many dishes to increase sweetness, while tomatoes are used in greater proportions to bring out the flavour of the local sweet tamarinds.

The most famous Karnatakan cuisine comes from the town of **Udupi**, to the north of Mangaluru, where the Udupi brahmins have gained a legendary reputation as excellent restaurateurs and hotel-keepers. Throughout the South, restaurants and hotels will often boast that they are "Udupi-run" and they are well worth seeking out, not just because of the legendary food, but also for their excellent value. An Udupi meal is typically presented on a **banana leaf** and comprises rice and a range of different vegetable curries, which vary from day to day, accompanied by pickles. Udupi restaurants are also good for *idlis*, *vada* and dosas – it's said that the ubiquitous masala dosa, wrapped around a filling of potatoes and vegetables, was invented by an Udupi brahmin.

There is further regional variety within Karnataka in the form of the meat-dominated specialities of the Kodavas (see p.238) and the North Indian-style food of the central Deccan in the north of the state, where spicy curries are accompanied by *joleata roti*, a chapati made from locally grown maize.

Keralan cooking

Kerala has a rich and varied cuisine, heavily influenced by the spice belt along the Western Ghats and its plentiful **fish** supplies along the Malabar Coast and the Kuttinad backwaters. Kerala has

always been a key centre for the **spice trade**, and has attracted traders throughout history from all over the world. These different cultures have combined to create a tolerant and liberal atmosphere that is reflected in the food.

Furthermore, the hot, steamy climate and lush mountains combine to make the state a veritable greenhouse, providing a huge range of vegetables, from beans to bitter gourds, and fruits, such as mangoes, bananas and jackfruit, all of which are used in the cuisine of this region. The main **spices** used in Keralan cuisine are cardamom, cinnamon, cloves, cumin, ginger, coriander, tumeric and peppers. Spices are recognized for their tonic properties, especially on the digestive system and are often used for specific medicinal purposes in accordance with Ayurvedic principles.

The most famous Keralan dish is its wonderful **fish curry**, or *molee*, cooked in a delicious cream of tomatoes, ground coconut and coconut milk. The coastal waters contain a huge variety of seafood including marlin and shark, and the day's catch is proudly displayed on the stands of the seaside tourist restaurants of Kovalam and Varkala. Some of the best fish comes from the backwaters, where the black *karimeen*, a flat sole-like fish that hugs the muddy bottoms, is justifiably prized.

Rice in various forms features heavily in the Keralan diet. Pilau (see Glossary, p.505) is especially popular among Muslims, and along the coast is usually served with prawns. Occasionally tapioca, known locally as *kappa*, appears an alternative staple, whether accompanying coastal fish curries or served as deep-fried chips.

FIVE TOP PLACES TO EAT: VEG

Annalakshmi, Chennai Vegetarian recipes with Ayurvedic properties are available in this beautifully decorated place. See p.379

Mango Tree, Hampi Chilled travellers' joint with a great Indian and international veg menu. See p.260

Prema Restaurant, Gokarna Sociable travellers' hangout near the town beach serving both traditional and western veg items, as well as legendary *gadbad* desserts. See p.250

Sri Krishna Bhavan, Thanjavur Great place for unlimited pure-veg Tamil "meals" and other curries. See p.412

Sri Krishna Café, Mattancherry Pure-veg Keralan meals at bargain prices. See p.345

Tamil cooking

Tamil cuisine is one of the oldest culinary heritages in India, retaining many elements of the ancient Dravidian culture that flourished in the deep south some 4000 years ago. Although meat and fish are widely available, it is also traditionally vegetarian, with a predominance of pure-veg places.

Tamil cooking uses a complex masala that includes curry leaves, coriander, cardamom, cumin, cinnamon, cloves, garlic, ginger, nutmeg, tamarind and in some dishes, rosewater. It is also one of the hottest cuisines of the South, with abundant use of chillies. Roadside cafes tend to serve unfathomably hot dishes, and you'll see free bowls of chillies provided for nibbling and delicious tongue-tingling chilli bhajis on offer. Beyond the penchant for red-hot chilli peppers, however, the deep South has an exquisite culinary tradition, most notably in the classic regional style of Chettinad (see box, p.423).

Snacks and street food

South India abounds in **snacks** and **street food**. *Idli sambhar* – lentil and vegetable sauce with rice cakes to dunk – is one ubiquitous favourite. Street finger-food includes *bhel puris* (a Mumbai speciality consisting of a mix of puffed rice, deep-fried vermicelli, potato and crunchy puri with tamarind sauce), *pani puris* (the same puris dunked in peppery and spicy water – only for the seasoned), bhajis (deep-fried cakes of vegetables in chickpea flour), samosas (vegetables or occasionally meat in a pastry triangle, fried), and pakoras (vegetables or potato dipped in chickpea flour batter and deep-fried). In the South, you'll also come across the ever-popular *vada*, a spicy deep-fried lentil cake which looks rather like a doughnut.

Kebabs rolled into griddle-fried bread, known as *kathi* or *kaati* rolls, originated in Kolkata but are now penetrating further south as well. With all street snacks, though, remember that food left lying around attracts germs – make sure it's freshly cooked. Be especially careful with snacks involving water, such as *pani puris*, and cooking oil, which is often recycled. Generally, it's a good idea to acclimatize to Indian conditions before you start eating street food.

You won't find anything called "**Bombay mix**" in India, but there's no shortage of dry, spicy snack mixes, often referred to as *channa chur*. Jackfruit chips are sometimes sold as a savoury snack – though they are rather bland – and cashew nuts are a real bargain. Peanuts, also known as "monkey nuts" or *mumfuli*, usually come roasted and unshelled.

North Indian food

Cuisine from across all of India is widely available, and those with a penchant for **North Indian food** and tandoori (clay oven) preparations will find dishes such as chicken tikka (boneless cubes of tandoori chicken, marinated with yoghurt, spices and herbs) and other favourites feature on the menus of more upmarket restaurants and five-star hotels, particularly in the evenings.

As well as the many "meals" restaurants, you'll also find more expensive thali restaurants, especially in big cities, but in South India these will serve South Indian food, with maybe one or two North Indian style dishes in them. In many thali restaurants, you can eat as much as you want ("unlimited"), with staff circulating with refills of everything, though you will also find "limited" thalis.

Sweets

Indians tend to have rather a sweet tooth and Indian **sweets**, usually made of milk, can be seriously sugar-laden. Although the emphasis on milk products is stronger in the North than in the South, sweets are popular throughout India, and sweet shops thrive in all cities and large towns. Addicts will enjoy hunting down regional specialities.

Barfi, a kind of fudge made by reducing condensed milk, varies from moist and delicious to dry and powdery. It comes in various colours and flavours from plain, creamy white, bright orange carrot to livid green *pista* (pistachio), and is sometimes sold covered with edible silver leaf. Smoother-textured, round *pedha* and thin diamonds of *kaju katri*, plus moist *sandesh* and the harder *paira*, are among many other types of sweet made from boiled-down milk. Numerous types of gelatinous **halwa** are especially popular in Hyderabad, all of them quite different in taste and texture from the Middle Eastern variety. Of the regional varieties, Mysore *pak*, made from a rich crumbly mixture of maize flour and ghee, is available all over India.

At the softer, stickier end of the spectrum, *jalebis*, those circular orange tubes dripping syrup, are made of deep-fried treacle and are just as sickly as they look. *Gulab jamuns*, deep-fried cream cheese sponge balls soaked in syrup, are just as unhealthy but utterly divine. Then there is *ladoo*, knobbly yellow balls usually made from semolina flour, which have a much drier, flakier texture.

Indian **chocolate** has improved significantly in recent years, and there is now a range of decent

Cadbury and Amul bars available everywhere. This said, some of the indigenous imitations of Swiss and Belgian chocolates present a curious take on chocolate.

Among the large **ice-cream** vendors, Kwality, Vadilal's, Gaylord and Dollops stand out; you'll see carts of ice cream being pushed around by uniformed men. The bigger companies have many, usually quite obvious, imitators; some have no scruples – stay away from water ices unless you have a seasoned constitution. Throughout southern towns and cities, ice-cream parlours selling elaborate iced concoctions, including sundaes, have really taken off. When travelling, especially around coastal Karnataka and parts of Kerala, look out for a local variation known as *gad-bad* (literally "mix-up"), where layers of ice cream come interspersed with chopped nuts and dried and glacé fruit. Be sure to try kulfi, a traditional frozen-milk preparation flavoured with pistachio, mango or cardamom. *Bhang kulfi*, not available everywhere but popular during the festival of Holi, is laced with cannabis, giving it an interesting kick, but should be approached with caution.

Fruit

What **fruit** is available varies with region and season, but there's always a fine choice. Remember that fruit should always be peeled first. Roadside vendors often sell cut and peeled fruit that is sprinkled with salt and spices but don't buy it if it looks like it's been hanging around for a while.

Mangoes are usually on offer, but not all are sweet enough to eat fresh – some are used for pickles or curries. Indians are picky about their mangoes, the ripeness of which they gauge by feel and smell before buying. Among the varieties appearing at different times in the season – from spring to summer – look out for Alphonso, which is grown in the vicinity of Mumbai, and Langra, which is grown all over South India. Oranges and tangerines are generally easy to come by, as are sweet melons and thirst-quenching watermelons, but the South is most famous for its numerous kinds of **bananas**, which are available all year round. Try the delicious red bananas of Kovalam, or the *Nanjangod* variety grown in the vicinity of Mysore, which are considered by many in the city as the best – and most extravagant.

Other **tropical fruits** available year-round include coconuts, papayas (pawpaws) and pineapples, while lychees and pomegranates are very seasonal. Among less familiar fruit, the *chiku*, which looks like a kiwi and tastes a bit like a pear, is well worth trying, as is the watermelon-sized jackfruit (*chakkai* in Malayalam), whose spiny green exterior encloses sweet, slightly rubbery yellow segments each containing a seed. The custard apple, a knobbly green case housing a scented white pulp with large black seeds, is another interesting seasonal fruit, with a sweet, creamy texture that does indeed resemble custard.

Drinks

South India is home to some of the world's premium **coffee**-growing areas and in many places coffee rivals tea in popularity. South Indian coffee is traditionally prepared with sugar and topped with large quantities of milk; in Kerala there's a whole ritual attached – the coffee is poured in flamboyant sweeping motions between tall glasses to cool it down. One of the best places to get a decent coffee is the *India Coffee House* co-operative chain, which has branches in every southern town. Good vacuum-packed filter coffee, grown in Kodagu (Coorg) in Karnataka, is available but is yet to have an impact in cafés and restaurants.

India's undisputed national drink, however, is **tea** (or **chai**) – grown in Darjeeling and Assam in the north and in the Nilgiri Hills, on the border of Kerala and Tamil Nadu, in the south. The tea gardens of the Nilgiris produce fine, full-flavoured teas and often carry a high price tag to match the altitude. Tea is sold by chai-wallahs on just about every street corner, and traditionally prepared in a different way from in the West, with lots of milk and sugar (though if you're quick off the mark you can usually get them to hold the sugar – ask for "sugar separate"). Ginger, pepper and/or cardamoms may also often added to make a *masala chai*. English tea it isn't, but many travellers find it an irresistible brew. In tourist spots and upmarket hotels, you can get a pot of European-style "tray" tea, which generally consists of a tea bag in lukewarm water – you'd do better to stick to the pukka Indian variety.

Soft drinks are widely available throughout India. Global brands like Coca Cola and Pepsi are available alongside locally produced alternatives such as Campa Cola (innocuous), Thums Up (not unpalatable), Gold Spot (fizzy orange) and Limca (lemon and lime). All contain a lot of sugar but little else. One famous advert for an Indian soft drink proudly maintained "100% artificial – contains no real fruit." None will quench your thirst for long.

Bottled water is available everywhere in 500ml, one-litre and larger bottles. In some tourist places you can refill your own bottle with treated or boiled water, a popular green initiative which helps reduce street refuse. For more on bottled water, see the box opposite.

Cartons of Frooti, Jumpin, Réal and similar brands of **fruit juice drinks**, which come in mango, guava, apple and lemon varieties are another alternative to carbonated drinks but avoid cartons which look at all mangled, as they may have been recycled. Tender coconut water from **green coconuts** is delicious, very healthy (good if you have an upset stomach) and often the cheapest drink available. Green coconuts are common in coastal areas and are sold on the roadside by vendors who will hack off the top of the coconut for you with a machete and give you a straw to suck up the coconut water (you then scoop out the flesh and eat it). Stalls selling freshly squeezed juice from just about every fruit available are also common, as is superbly refreshing sugar-cane juice, pressed through a mangle with a dash of lime.

India's greatest cold drink, **lassi** – originally from the north but now available throughout India – is made with beaten curd and drunk either salted, sweetened with sugar or mixed with fruit. It varies widely from smooth and delicious to insipid and watery, and is sold at virtually every café, restaurant and canteen in the country. Another popular soft drink, particularly enjoyed along the beaches of Mumbai, is *falooda*, which originated in Persia and was brought to India by the Parsis. It is a mixture of milk, vermicelli, basil seeds, ice cream and often flavoured with rose, saffron, mango and chocolate. Freshly made milkshakes are also commonly available at establishments with blenders, as are **fresh fruit juices**, which usually contain liquidized and strained fruit, water and sugar (or salt); street vendors selling fresh fruit juice in less than hygienic conditions are apt to add salt and *garam masala*. In the central and northern cities of South India, especially Hyderabad, Middle Eastern-inspired *sharbat* – flavoured drinks made with sugar, fruit and, often, rose essence – remain popular, especially among Muslims.

With all such drinks, however appetizing they may seem, exercise great caution in deciding where to drink them, unless you're confident your body has acclimatized; you may decide to err on the side of caution when it comes to the ice, for example, unless you establish it is from a safe source.

Alcohol

Prohibition has been making something of a comeback in Modi's India – some southern states such as Kerala, Tamil Nadu and Andhra Pradesh have partial prohibition in the form of "dry" days, high taxes, very restrictive licences and health warnings on labels.

Alcoholic enclaves in prohibition states can become major drinking centres: Puducherry and Karaikal in Tamil Nadu are the main ones. Goa is another place where the booze flows especially freely and cheaply. Interestingly, all were outside the British Raj.

Beer is widely available, if rather expensive by local standards. Price varies from state to state, but you can usually expect to pay around ₹100–240 for a 650ml bottle. A pub culture, not dissimilar to that of the West, has taken root among the wealthier classes in cities like Bengaluru and Mumbai. Kingfisher, King's Black Label and Foster's are still the leading brands but there are plenty of others, and **microbreweries** are increasingly making their presence felt in some metropolitan areas, especially Bengaluru. The mainstream lagers tend to contain chemical additives, including glycerine, but are still fairly palatable if you can get them cold. In certain places, notably unlicensed restaurants in Tamil Nadu and Kerala, beer comes in the form of "special tea" – a teapot of beer, which you pour into and drink from a teacup to disguise what it really is. A cheaper, and often delicious, alternative to beer in Goa and Kerala and other southern states is **toddy** (palm wine). Sweet and nonalcoholic when first tapped, it ferments within twelve hours.

Spirits usually take the form of "Indian Made Foreign Liquor" (IMFL), although the foreign liquor industry is expanding rapidly. Some Scotch, such as Seagram's 100 Pipers, is now being bottled in India and sold at a premium, as is Smirnoff vodka, among other known brands. Some of the brands of Indian whisky are not too bad and are affordable in comparison; gin and brandy can be pretty rough, while Indian rum is sweet and distinctive. In Goa, *feni* is a spirit distilled from coconut or cashew fruit. Steer well clear of illegally distilled *arak* (*araq*) however, which often contains methanol (wood alcohol) and other poisons. A look through the press, especially at festival times, will soon reveal numerous cases of blindness and death as a result of drinking bad hooch (or "spurious liquor" as it's called). Unfortunately, Indian **wine** – despite the efforts of a few pioneering vineyards in Maharashtra and Karnataka such as Sulu and Grover Zampa (see box, p.113) – is still generally of a poor quality, and also expensive, while foreign wine available in upmarket restaurants and luxury hotels comes with an exorbitant price-tag.

Health

There are plenty of scare stories about the health risks of travelling in India, but in fact cases of serious illness are very much the exception rather than the rule. Standards of hygiene and sanitation have increased greatly over the past couple of decades and there's no reason you can't stay healthy throughout your trip – indeed many travellers now visit the Subcontinent without even experiencing the traditional dose of "Delhi belly". Having said that, it's still important to be careful, keep your resistance high and to be aware of the dangers of untreated water, mosquito bites and undressed open cuts. It's worth knowing, if you are ill and can't get to a doctor, that almost any medicine can be bought over the counter without a prescription.

Precautions

When it comes to **food**, be wary of dishes that appear to have been reheated. Anything boiled, fried or grilled (and thus sterilized) in your presence is usually all right, though seafood and meat can pose real risks if they're not fresh; anything that has been left out for any length of time, or stored in a fridge during a power cut, is best avoided. Raw unpeeled fruit and vegetables should always be viewed with suspicion, and salads can cause problems if they have not been washed in safe water.

Be vigilant about **personal hygiene**: wash your hands often, especially before eating. Keep all cuts clean, treat them with iodine or antiseptic (a liquid or dry spray is better in the heat) and cover them to prevent infection.

Advice on avoiding **mosquitoes** is offered under "Malaria" (see p.42). If you do get bites or itches, try not to scratch them: it's difficult, but infection and tropical ulcers can result if you do. Tiger Balm and even dried soap may relieve the itching.

Finally, especially if you are going on a long trip, have a **dental check-up** before you leave home.

Vaccinations

No **inoculations** are legally required for entry into India, but tetanus, typhoid and hepatitis A jabs are recommended for travellers to many parts of the country, and it's worth ensuring that you are up to date with diphtheria, polio and other boosters. Vaccinations for hepatitis B, rabies, meningitis, Japanese encephalitis and TB are only advised if you're travelling to remote areas or working in environments with an increased exposure to infectious diseases.

Transmitted through contaminated food and water or through saliva, **hepatitis A** can lay a victim low for several months with exhaustion, fever and diarrhoea. Symptoms include yellowing of the whites of the eyes, general malaise, orange urine (though dehydration could also cause that) and light-coloured stools. If you think you have it, get a diagnosis as soon as possible, steer clear of alcohol, get lots of rest – and try to avoid passing it on. More serious is **hepatitis B**, transmitted like AIDS through blood or sexual contact.

Typhoid fever is also spread through contaminated food or water, but is increasingly rare. It produces a persistent high temperature with malaise, headaches and abdominal pains, followed by diarrhoea.

WHAT ABOUT THE WATER?

One of the chief concerns of many prospective visitors to India is whether the water is safe to drink. Tap water is best avoided, even though locals happily gulp it down, but many hotels and restaurants have modern filtration systems that remove most of the risks. **Bottled water**, available in all but the most remote places, is an even safer bet, though it has a major drawback – namely the **plastic pollution** it causes. Visualize the size of the pile of plastic you'd leave behind after getting through a couple of bottles per day, then imagine that multiplied by millions and you have something along the lines of the amount of non-biodegradable landfill waste generated each year by tourists alone.

The best solution as regards your health and the environment is to purify your own water. **Chemical sterilization** using **chlorine** is completely effective, fast and inexpensive, and you can remove the nasty taste it leaves with neutralizing tablets or lemon juice.

Alternatively, invest in some kind of **purifying filter** incorporating chemical sterilization to kill even the smallest viruses. An ever-increasing range of compact, lightweight products is available these days through outdoor shops and large pharmacies, but pregnant women or anyone with thyroid problems should check that iodine isn't used as the chemical sterilizer.

Cholera, spread the same way as hepatitis A and typhoid, causes sudden attacks of watery diarrhoea with cramps and debilitation. Again, this disease rarely occurs in India, breaking out in isolated epidemics; there is a vaccination but it offers very little protection. Most medical authorities now recommend immunization against meningococcal **meningitis (ACWY)** too. Spread by airborne bacteria (through coughs and sneezes for example), it is a very unpleasant disease that attacks the lining of the brain and can be fatal.

Rabies is widespread throughout the South, and the best advice is to give dogs and monkeys a wide berth – do not play with animals at all, no matter how cute they might look. If you're bitten or scratched and it breaks the skin, immediately wash the wound gently with soap or detergent, apply alcohol or iodine if possible, and go straight away to the nearest hospital for an anti-rabies jab.

For up-to-the-minute information, make an appointment at a travel clinic. These clinics also sell travel accessories, including mosquito nets and first-aid kits.

MEDICAL RESOURCES FOR TRAVELLERS

International Society for Travel Medicine Ⓦ istm.org. A full list of clinics worldwide specializing in travel health.

IN THE UK AND IRELAND
Hospital for Tropical Diseases Travel Clinic UK ☎ 020 3456 7891, Ⓦ www.thehtd.org.
MASTA (Medical Advisory Service for Travellers Abroad) UK ☎ 0330 100 4200, Ⓦ masta-travel-health.com. Dozens of clinics across the UK.
Tropical Medical Bureau Ireland ☎ 01 271 5200, Ⓦ tmb.ie.

IN THE US AND CANADA
Canadian Society for International Health Canada ☎ 1 613 241 5785, Ⓦ csih.org. Extensive list of travel health centres in Canada.
CDC US ☎ 1 800 232 4636, Ⓦ cdc.gov. Official US government health site, including travel.

IN AUSTRALIA, NEW ZEALAND AND SOUTH AFRICA
Netcare Travel Clinics South Africa ☎ 082 911, Ⓦ travelclinic .co.za. Travel clinics in South Africa.
Travellers' Medical & Vaccination Centre Australia Ⓦ traveldoctor.com.au. Website listing travellers' medical and vaccination centres throughout Australia and New Zealand.

Heat trouble

The sun and the heat can cause a few unexpected problems. Before they've acclimatized, many people get a bout of **prickly heat rash**, an infection of the sweat ducts caused by excessive perspiration that doesn't dry off. A cool shower, zinc oxide powder (sold in India) and loose cotton clothes should help. **Dehydration** is another possible problem, so make sure you're drinking enough liquid, and drink rehydration salts frequently, especially when hot and/or tired. The main danger sign is irregular urination (only once a day for instance); dark urine definitely means you should drink more (although it could also indicate hepatitis).

The **sun** can burn, or even cause sunstroke; a high-factor sun block is vital on exposed skin, especially when you first arrive. A light hat is also a very good idea, especially if you're doing a lot of walking around in the sun.

Finally, be aware that overheating can cause **heatstroke**, which is potentially fatal. Signs are a very high body temperature, without a feeling of fever but accompanied by headaches and disorientation. Lowering body temperature (taking a tepid shower for example) and resting in an air-conditioned room is the first step in treatment; also take in plenty of fluids and seek medical advice if the condition doesn't improve after 24 hours.

Malaria

Although much of South India is now regarded as being very low risk for **malaria**, the disease remains one of the Subcontinent's big killers. It's essential that you check with your doctor whether you'll need to take anti-malarial medication for your visit. The disease, caused by a parasite carried in the saliva of female *Anopheles* mosquitoes, can still be found in Maharashtra, Andhra Pradesh, Telangana and the Andaman Islands (there's a useful malaria map of the country at Ⓦ bit.ly/MalariaMap, showing varying levels of risk across the country). Malaria has a variable incubation period of a few days to several weeks, so you can become ill long after being bitten – which is why it's important to carry on taking the tablets even after you've returned home.

Ideas about appropriate **antimalarial medication** tend to vary from country to country and prophylaxis remains a controversial subject; it's important that you get expert medical advice on which treatment is right for you. In addition, resistance to established antimalarial drugs is growing alarmingly – none of the following provides complete protection, so avoiding being bitten in the first place remains important.

The most established regime – widely prescribed in Europe, but not in North America – is a combination of **chloroquine** (trade names Nivaquin or Avloclor) taken weekly either on its own or in conjunction with a daily dose of **proguanil** (Paludrine). You need to start this regime a week before arriving in a malarial area and continue it for four weeks after leaving. In India chloroquine is easy to come by but proguanil isn't, so stock up before you arrive. **Mefloquine** (Lariam) is a stronger treatment. As a prophylactic, you need take just one tablet weekly, starting two weeks before entering a risk area and continuing for four weeks after leaving. Mefloquine is a very powerful and effective antimalarial, though there have been widely reported concerns about its side effects, including psychological problems.

Doxycycline is often prescribed in Australasia. One tablet is taken daily, starting a day or two before entering a malarial zone and continuing for four weeks after leaving. It's not suitable for children under ten and it can cause thrush in women, while three percent of users develop a sensitivity to light, causing a rash, so it's not ideal for beach holidays. It also interferes with the effectiveness of the contraceptive pill. **Malarone** (a combination of atovaquone and proguanil) is another alternative, which you only have to start taking two days before you enter a malarial zone and continue for just a week after leaving, meaning that, although it's expensive, it can prove economical for short trips.

Malarial symptoms

The first signs of malaria are remarkably similar to a severe **flu**, and may take months to appear: if you suspect anything go to a hospital or clinic for a blood test immediately. The shivering, burning fever and headaches come in waves, usually in the early evening. Malaria is not infectious, but some strains are dangerous and occasionally even fatal when not treated promptly, in particular, the chloroquine-resistant **cerebral malaria**. This virulent and lethal strain of the disease, which affects the brain, is treatable, but has to be diagnosed early. Erratic body temperature, lack of energy and aches are the first key signs.

Preventing mosquito bites

The best way of combating malaria is, of course, to avoid getting bitten: malarial mosquitoes are active from dusk until dawn and during this time you should use mosquito **repellent** and take all necessary precautions. Sleep under a mosquito net if possible, burn mosquito coils (widely available in India, but easy to break in transit) or electrically heated repellents such as All Out. An Indian brand of repellent called Odomos is widely available and very effective, though most travellers bring their own from home, usually one containing the noxious but effective compound DEET. DEET can cause rashes and a strength of more than thirty percent is not advised for those with sensitive skin. A natural alternative is citronella or a new repellant based on eucalyptus oil called PMD, such as the UK's Mosi-guard Natural; those with sensitive skin should, however, still use DEET on clothes and nets. Mosquito "buzzers" – plug-in contraptions that smoulder tablets of DEET compounds slowly overnight – are pretty useless, but wrist and ankle bands are as effective as spray and a good alterna-

---

A TRAVELLERS' FIRST-AID KIT

Below are items you might want to take, especially if you're planning to go trekking – all are available in India itself, at a fraction of what you might pay at home:

- Antiseptic cream
- Insect repellent and cream such as Anthisan for soothing bites
- Plasters/Band-Aids
- A course of Flagyl antibiotics
- Water sterilization tablets or water purifier
- Lint and sealed bandages
- Knee supports
- Imodium (Lomotil) for emergency diarrhoea treatment
- A mild oral anesthetic such as Bonjela for soothing ulcers or mild toothache
- Paracetamol/aspirin
- Multivitamin and mineral tablets
- Rehydration sachets
- Hypodermic needles and sterilized skin wipes

tive for sensitive skin. Though active all night, female *Anopheles* mosquitoes prefer to bite in the early evening, so be especially careful at that time. Wear long sleeves, skirts and trousers, avoid dark colours, which attract mosquitoes, and put repellent on all exposed skin.

Dengue fever and Japanese encephalitis

Another illness spread by mosquito bites is **dengue fever**, whose symptoms are similar to those of malaria, plus aching bones. There is no vaccine available and the only treatment is complete rest, with drugs to assuage the fever. **Japanese encephalitis**, a mosquito-borne viral infection causing fever, muscle pains and headaches, is most prevalent in wet, rural rice-growing areas. However, it only rarely affects travellers, and the vaccine isn't usually recommended unless you plan to spend much time around paddy fields during and immediately after the monsoons.

Intestinal troubles

Diarrhoea is the most common bane of travellers. When mild and not accompanied by other major symptoms, it may just be your stomach reacting to unfamiliar food. Accompanied by cramps and vomiting, it could well be food poisoning. In either case, it will probably pass of its own accord in 24–48 hours without treatment. In the meantime, it is essential to replace the fluids and salts you're losing, so take lots of water with oral rehydration salts (commonly referred to as ORS, or called Electrolyte in India). If you can't get ORS, use half a teaspoon of salt and eight of sugar in a litre of water, and if you are too ill to keep it down, seek medical help immediately. Travel clinics and pharmacies sell double-ended moulded plastic spoons with the exact ratio of sugar to salt.

While you are suffering, it's a good idea to avoid greasy food, heavy spices, caffeine and most fruit and dairy products. Some say bananas and papaya are good, as are *kitchri* (a simple dhal and rice preparation) and rice soup and coconut water, while curd or a soup made from Marmite or Vegemite (if you happen to have some with you) are forms of protein that can be easily absorbed by your body when you have the runs. **Drugs** like Lomotil or Imodium simply plug you up – undermining the body's efforts to rid itself of infection – though they can be useful if you have to travel. If symptoms persist for more than a few days, a

course of antibiotics may be necessary; this should be seen as a last resort, following medical advice.

Sordid though it may seem, it's a good idea to look at what comes out when you go to the toilet. If your diarrhoea contains blood or mucus and if you are suffering other symptoms including rotten-egg belches and farts, the cause may be dysentery or giardia. With a fever, it could well be caused by **bacillary dysentery**, and may clear up without treatment. If you're sure you need it, a course of antibiotics such as tetracycline should sort you out, but they also destroy gut flora in your intestines (which help protect you – curd can replenish them to some extent). If you start a course, be sure to finish it, even after the symptoms have gone. Similar symptoms, without fever, indicate **amoebic dysentery**, which is much more serious, and can damage your gut if untreated. The usual cure is a course of Metronidazole (Flagyl) or Fasigyn, both antibiotics which may themselves make you feel ill, and must not be taken with alcohol. Symptoms of **giardia** are similar – including frothy stools, nausea and constant fatigue – for which the treatment is again Metronidazole. If you suspect that you have either of these, seek medical help, and only start on the Metronidazole (750mg three times daily for a week for adults) if there is definitely blood in your diarrhoea and it is impossible to see a doctor.

Finally, bear in mind that oral drugs, such as malaria pills and the Pill, are likely to be largely ineffective if taken while suffering from diarrhoea.

Bites and creepy crawlies

Worms may enter your body through skin (especially the soles of your feet) or food. An itchy anus is a common symptom, and you may even see them in your stools. They are easy to treat: if you suspect you have them, get some worming tablets such as Mebendazole (Vermox) from any pharmacy.

Biting insects and similar animals other than mosquitoes may also aggravate you. The obvious suspects are **bedbugs** – look for signs of squashed ones around beds in cheap hotels. An infested mattress can be left in the hot sun all day to get rid of them, but they often live in the frame or even in walls or floors. **Head** and **body lice** can also be a nuisance, but medicated soap and shampoo (preferably brought with you from home) usually see them off. Avoid **scratching bites**, which can lead to infection. Bites from ticks and lice can spread **typhus**, characterized by fever, muscle aches, headaches and, later, red eyes and a measles-like rash. If you think you have it, seek treatment (tetracycline is usually prescribed).

Snakes are unlikely to bite unless accidentally disturbed, and most are harmless in any case. To see one at all, you need to search stealthily – walk heavily and they usually oblige by disappearing. If you do get bitten, remember what the snake looked like (kill it if you can), try not to move the affected part, and seek medical help: antivenins are available in most hospitals. A few **spiders** have poisonous bites too. Remove **leeches**, which may attach themselves to you in jungle areas, with salt or a lit cigarette; never just pull them off.

HIV and AIDS

HIV/AIDS is as much of a risk in South India as anywhere else, and in recent years the government has heeded WHO advice by setting up its own awareness and prevention campaigns. As elsewhere in the world, high-risk groups include prostitutes and intravenous drug users. It is extremely unwise to contemplate casual sex without a condom – carry some with you (preferably brought from home as Indian ones may be less reliable) and insist upon using them.

Should you need an **injection** or a **transfusion** in India, make sure that new, sterile equipment is used; any blood you receive should be from voluntary rather than commercial donor banks. If you have a shave from a barber, make sure he uses a clean blade and don't undergo processes such as ear-piercing, acupuncture or tattooing unless you can be sure that the equipment is sterile.

Getting medical help

Pharmacies can usually advise on minor medical problems, and most doctors in India speak English. Also, many hotels keep a **doctor** on call; if you do get ill and need medical assistance, take advice as to the best facilities around. Basic medications are made to Indian Pharmacopoea (IP) standards, and most medicines are available without prescription, but always check the sell-by date.

Hospitals have variable standards: private clinics and mission hospitals are often better than state-run ones but may not have the same facilities. Hospitals in big cities, including university or medical-school hospitals, are generally pretty good, and cities such as Mumbai, Hyderabad and Bengaluru boast state-of-the-art medical facilities but at a price. Many hospitals require patients (even emergency cases) to buy necessities such as medicines, plaster casts and vaccines, and to pay for X-rays, before procedures are carried out. Remember to keep receipts for insurance reimbursements. **Government hospitals**, however,

---

AYURVEDIC MEDICINE

Ayurveda, a Sanskrit word meaning the "knowledge for prolonging life", is a five-thousand-year-old holistic medical system that is widely practised in South India. Ayurvedic doctors and clinics in large towns deal with foreigners as well as their usual patients, and some **pharmacies** specialize in Ayurvedic preparations, including toiletries such as soaps, shampoos and toothpastes.

Ayurveda assumes the fundamental sameness of self and nature. Unlike the allopathic medicines of the West, which depend on finding out what's ailing you and then killing it, Ayurveda looks at the whole patient: disease is regarded as a symptom of **imbalance**, so it's the imbalance that's treated, not the disease. Ayurvedic theory holds that the body is controlled by three forces, which reflect the forces within the self: *pitta*, the force of the sun, is hot, and rules the digestive processes and metabolism; *kapha*, likened to the moon, the creator of tides and rhythms, has a cooling effect and governs the body's organs; and *vata*, wind, relates to movement and the nervous system. The healthy body is one that has the three forces in balance. To diagnose an imbalance, the Ayurvedic **vaid** (doctor) responds not only to the physical complaint but also to family background, daily habits and emotional traits.

Imbalances are typically treated with herbal remedies designed to alter whichever of the three forces is out of whack. Made according to traditional formulae, using indigenous plants, Ayurvedic medicines are cheaper than branded or imported drugs. In addition, the doctor may prescribe various forms of yogic cleansing to rid the body of waste substances. To the uninitiated, these techniques will sound rather off-putting – for instance, swallowing a long strip of cloth, a short section at a time, and then pulling it back up again to remove mucus from the stomach. Ayurvedic **massage** with herbal oils is especially popular in Kerala where courses of treatments are available to combat a wide array of ailments.

provide all surgical and after-care services free of charge and in most other state medical institutions charges are usually so low that for minor treatment the expense may well be lower than the initial "excess" on your insurance. You will, however, need a companion to stay, or you'll have to come to an arrangement with one of the hospital cleaners, to help you out in hospital – relatives are expected to wash, feed and generally take care of the patient. Addresses of foreign consulates (who will advise in an emergency), as well as clinics and hospitals, can be found in the Directory sections in the accounts of major cities and towns in this book.

The media

With well over a billion people and a literacy rate approaching 75 percent, India produces in excess of a staggering 5000 daily papers in more than three hundred languages, plus another 40,000 journals and weeklies. There are a large number of English-language daily newspapers, both national and regional.

Newspapers and magazines

The most prominent of the **nationals** are the *Times of India* (Ⓦtimesofindia.indiatimes.com), *The Hindu* (Ⓦthehindu.com), *The Deccan Herald* (Ⓦdeccan herald.com), *The Hindustan Times* (Ⓦhindustan times.com), *The Economic Times* (Ⓦeconomictimes .indiatimes.com) and the *New Indian Express* (Ⓦnewindianexpress.com), usually the most critical of the government. All are pretty dry and sober, concentrating on Indian news, with special regional regional sections in their southern editions. The *Times of India*, *The Hindu* and *The Hindustan Times* provide the most up-to-date and detailed online news services. *The Asian Age* (Ⓦasianage.com) is a conservative tabloid that sports a motley collection of the world's more colourful stories.

India's press is the freest in Asia and attacks on the government are often quite outspoken. However, as in the West, most papers can be seen as part of the political establishment, and are unlikely to print anything that might upset the "national consensus".

There are also a number of *Time/Newsweek*-style **news magazines**, with a strong emphasis on politics. The best of these are *India Today* (Ⓦindia today.intotoday.in) and *Frontline* (Ⓦfrontline.in), published by *The Hindu*. Others include *Outlook* (Ⓦoutlookindia.com), which presents the most readable, broadly themed analysis, and *The Week* (Ⓦtheweek.in). As they give more of an overview of stories and issues than the daily papers, you will probably get a better insight into Indian politics, and most tend to have a higher proportion of inter-national news, too. Also worth checking out are Ⓦsamachar.com, one of the best news gateway sites, featuring headlines and links to leading Indian newspapers, and alternative news webzine Ⓦtehelka.com, famous for exposing corruption scandals in government.

Film **fanzines** and gossip mags are very popular – *Filmfare* (Ⓦfilmfare.com) and the online-only *Screen* (Ⓦepaper.screenindia.com) are the best, though you'd have to be reasonably *au fait* with Indian movies to follow a lot of it. Other magazines and periodicals in English cover all sorts of popular and minority interests, so it's worth having a look through what's available.

Foreign publications such as the *International Herald Tribune*, *Time* and the *Economist* are all available in the main cities, though it's easier (and cheaper) to read the day's edition for free online. For a read through the British press, try the British Council in Mumbai, Pune, Bengaluru, Hyderabad or Chennai; the USIS is the American equivalent. The UK's *Guardian* free-access website (Ⓦguardian .co.uk/world/india) is one of the best online news resources, with an extensive archive of articles.

Radio and TV

BBC World Service radio (Ⓦbbc.co.uk/worldservice radio) can be picked up at 94.3FM in most major cities, on short wave on frequencies ranging from 5790 to 15310kHz, and more sporadically on medium wave (AM) at 1413KHz (212m). It also broadcasts online. The Voice of America (Ⓦvoa.gov) can be found on 15.75MHz (19) and (75.75MHz (39.5m), among other frequencies. Radio Canada (Ⓦrcinet.ca) broadcasts in English on 6165 and 7255KHz (48.6 and 41.3m) at 6.30–7.30am and on 9635 and 11,975 KHz (31 and 25m) at 8.30–9.30pm.

The government-run **TV company**, Doordarshan, which broadcasts a sober diet of edifying programmes, has tried to compete with the onslaught of mass access to **satellite TV**. The main broadcaster in English is Rupert Murdoch's Star TV network, which incorporates the BBC World Service and Zee TV (with Z News), a progressive blend of Hindi-oriented chat, film, news and music programmes. Star Sports, ESPN and Ten Sports churn out a mind-boggling amount of cricket, extensive coverage of English Premier League football, plenty of tennis and a few other sports. Other channels include CNN, the Discovery Channel, the immensely popular Channel V, hosted by scantily clad Mumbai models and DJs, and a couple of American soap and chat stations. There are now numerous local-language channels as well, many of them showing magnificently colourful religious and devotional programmes.

Festivals and holidays

Virtually every temple in every town or village across South India has its own festival. The biggest and most spectacular include Mysuru's colourful Dasara festivities (see box, p.226) and Madurai's three annual festivals. While mostly religious in nature and usually dedicated to a particular deity, merrymaking rather than solemnity is generally the order of the day, and onlookers are invariably welcome. Indeed, if you're lucky enough to coincide with a local festival, it may well prove to be the highlight of your trip.

There isn't space to list every festival in every village here, but the most important local festivals are featured at the start of each chapter and throughout the body of the Guide. The calendar below includes details of the main regional celebrations. Hindu, Sikh, Buddhist and Jain festivals follow the Indian **lunar calendar** and their dates therefore vary from year to year – we've given the lunar month (Magha, Phalguna, Chaitra, and so on), where relevant, in the listings below. The lunar calendar adds a leap month every two or three years to keep it in line with the seasons. Muslim festivals follow the **Islamic calendar**, whose year is shorter and which thus loses about eleven days per annum against the Gregorian.

In recent years, there has been an explosion in the number of contemporary, pop, dance and fusion **music festivals**, as India develops a circuit

something like the UK and other parts of Europe. Examples include Mumbai's Mahindra Blues (ⓦmahindrablues.com), Bengaluru's Storm (ⓦstormfestivalindia.com), Sunburn at Vagator in Goa (ⓦsunburn.in) and Sula Fest at Nasik in Maharashtra (ⓦsulafest.net).

PRINCIPAL INDIAN HOLIDAYS

India has only four **national public holidays** as such: Jan 26 (Republic Day); Aug 15 (Independence Day); Oct 2 (Gandhi's birthday); and Dec 25 (Christmas Day). Each state, however, has its own calendar of public holidays; you can expect most businesses to close on the major holidays of their own religion. The Hindu lunar calendar months are given in brackets below.
Key: B=Buddhist; C=Christian; H=Hindu; J=Jain; M=Muslim; N=non-religious; P=Parsi; S=Sikh.

JAN–FEB (MAGHA)
Hampi Utsav (N). Government-sponsored music and dance festival. See box, p.211.
Pongal (H; 1 Magha). Tamil harvest festival celebrated with decorated cows, processions and *rangolis* (chalk designs on the doorsteps of houses). *Pongal* is a sweet porridge made from newly harvested rice and eaten by all, including the cows. The festival is also known as Makar Sankranti, and celebrated as such in Karnataka and Andhra Pradesh.
Vasant Panchami (H; 5 Magha). One-day spring festival in honour of Saraswati, the goddess of learning, celebrated with kite-flying, the wearing of yellow saris and the blessing of schoolchildren's books and pens by the goddess.
Republic Day (N; Jan 26). Although the live focus is the military parade in Delhi, this state celebration of India's republic-hood is marked in various places around the South too.
Teppam Floating Festival (H; 16 Magha). Meenakshi and Shiva are towed around the Vandiyur Mariamman Teppakulam tank in boats lit with fairy lights – a prelude to the Tamil marriage season in Madurai, Tamil Nadu. See p.367.
Elephanta Music and Dance Festival (N). Classical Indian dance performed with the famous rock-cut caves in Mumbai harbour as a backdrop.

FEB– MARCH (PHALGUNA)
Losar (B; 1 Phalguna). Tibetan New Year celebrations among Tibetan and Himalayan Buddhist communities, especially those at Bylakuppe in Karnataka.

INDIAN WEDDINGS
You may, while in India, be lucky enough to be invited to a **wedding**. These are jubilant affairs, always scheduled on auspicious days. A Hindu bride dresses in red for the ceremony, and marks the parting of her hair with red *sindur* and her forehead with a bindi. She wears gold or bone bangles, which she keeps on for the rest of her married life. Although the practice is officially illegal, large dowries often change hands. These are usually paid by the bride's family to the groom, and can be contentious; poor families feel obliged to save for years to get their daughters married.

Shivratri (H; 10 Phalguna). Anniversary of Shiva's *tandav* (creation) dance, and his wedding anniversary. Popular family festival but also a sadhu festival of pilgrimage and fasting, especially at important Shiva temples.

Holi (H; 15 Phalguna). Water festival held during Dol Purnima (full moon) to mark the beginning of spring, though not as vigorously celebrated in the South as in northern India. Expect to be bombarded with water, paint, coloured powder and other mixtures, so don't go out in your Sunday best.

Goa Carnival (N). Goa's own Mardi Gras features float processions and *feni*-induced mayhem in the state capital, Panjim.

MARCH–APRIL (CHAITRA)

Ramanavami (H; 9 Chaitra). Birthday of Rama, the hero of the Ramayana, celebrated with readings of the epic and discourses on Rama's life and teachings.

Easter (C; moveable feast). Celebration of the resurrection of Christ. Good Friday in particular is a day of festivity.

Pateti (P). Parsi new year, also known as Nav Roz, celebrating the creation of fire. Feasting, services and present-giving.

Khorvad Sal (P; a week after Pateti). Birthday of Zarathustra (aka Zoroaster). Celebrated in the Parsis' fire temples, and with feasting at home.

APRIL–MAY (VAISAKHA)

Baisakhi (HS; 1 Vaisakha). To the Hindus, it's the solar new year, celebrated with music and dancing; to the Sikhs, it's the anniversary of the foundation of the Khalsa (Sikh brotherhood) by Guru Gobind Singh. Processions and feasting follow readings of the Granth Sahib scriptures.

Chithirai (H). Lively procession at Madurai in Tamil Nadu. See p.367.

Mahavir Jayanti (J; 13 Vaisakha). Birthday of Mahavira, the founder of Jainism. The main Jain festival of the year, observed by visits to sacred Jain sites, such as Sravanabelagola in Karnataka.

Puram (H). Frenzied drumming and elephant parades in Thrissur, Kerala. See box, p.350.

Buddha Jayanti (B; 16 Vaisakha). Buddha's birthday. He achieved enlightenment and nirvana on the same date.

JULY–AUG (SHRAVANA)

Raksha Bandhan/Narial Purnima (H; 16 Shravana). Festival to honour the sea god Varuna. Brothers and sisters exchange gifts, the sister tying a thread known as a *rakhi* to her brother's wrist. Brahmins, after a day's fasting, change the sacred thread they wear.

Independence Day (N; Aug 15). India's biggest secular celebration, on the anniversary of Independence from the UK.

AUG–SEPT (BHADRAPARDA)

Ganesh Chaturthi (H; 4 Bhadraparda). Festival dedicated to Ganesh, especially celebrated in Maharashtra. In Mumbai, huge processions carry images of the god to immerse in the sea. See box, p.111.

Onam (H). Keralan harvest festival, celebrated with snake-boat races. The Nehru Trophy Snake Boat Race at Alappuzha (held on the 2nd Sat of Aug) is the most spectacular, with long boats crewed by 150 rowers (see box, p.301).

Janmashtami (H; 23 Bhadraparda). Krishna's birthday, an occasion for fasting and celebration, especially in Mumbai.

SEPT–OCT (ASHVINA)

Dussehra/Dasara (H; 1–10 Ashvina). Ten-day festival (usually two days' public holiday) associated with vanquishing demons, in particular Rama's victory over Ravana in the Ramayana, and Durga's over the buffalo-headed Mahishasura. Known as Dasara in South India, celebrations include performances of the Ram Lila (life of Rama). Most spectacular in Mysuru (Karnataka; see box, p.226).

Mahatma Gandhi's Birthday (N; Oct 2). Solemn commemoration of independent India's founding father.

OCT–NOV (KARTIKA)

Diwali (Deepavali) (H; 15 Kartika). Festival of lights, and India's biggest, to celebrate Rama's and Sita's homecoming in the Ramayana. Festivities include the lighting of oil lamps and firecrackers, and the giving and receiving of sweets and gifts. Diwali coincides with Kali Puja, celebrated in temples dedicated to the wrathful goddess, and often accompanied by the ritual sacrifice of goats.

Jain New Year (J; 15 Kartika). Coincides with Diwali, so Jains celebrate alongside Hindus.

Nanak Jayanti (S; 16 Kartika). Guru Nanak's birthday marked by prayer readings and processions in *gurudwaras* everywhere.

DEC–JAN (PAUSA)

Christmas (CN; Dec 25). Popular in Christian areas of Goa and Kerala, and in big cities.

Carnatic Music Festivals, Chennai (N). For around a month every year, the city hosts thirteen or so large music programmes called "conferences", each lasting several days. See p.367.

Mamallapuram Dance Festival (N). Colourful dance and music festival which runs at weekends for several weeks on a stage in front of the Arjuna's Penance bas-relief. See p.367.

Kerala Kalamandalam Festival, Cheruthuruthy (N). The annual festival of music and dance serves as a showcase for this leading arts institution, featuring the best Keralan performers and attracting musicians and dancers from all over the country. See p.353.

MOVEABLE

Kumbh Mela (H). Major festival held at four holy cities in rotation, with each location hosting once every twelve years: Nasik (Maharashtra) is on the rota but the next one is not due there until 2027.

Ramadan (M). The month during which Muslims may not eat, drink or smoke from sunrise to sunset, and should abstain from sex. Muslim areas tend to come alive in the evenings as locals break their fast after prayers (*iftar*) and shop for Id. Estimated future dates are: May 16 to June 14, 2018, and May 6 to June 4, 2019.

Id ul-Fitr (M). Feast to celebrate the end of Ramadan. The precise date of the festival depends on exactly when the new moon is sighted, and so cannot be predicted with complete accuracy. Estimated dates (though these may vary by a day or two) are: June 15, 2018, and June 5, 2019.

Sports

Cricket is by far the most popular sport in India, and a fine example of how something quintessentially British (well, English) has become something quintessentially Indian. Indian cricket now dominates the global game, responsible for as much as 80 percent of its revenue. Travellers to India will find it hard to get away from the game – it's everywhere, especially on television.

Cricketing heroes such as Virat Kohli, captain of the Indian cricket team and considered to be one of the best batsmen in the world, live under the constant scrutiny of the media and public; expectations are high and disappointments acute. India versus Pakistan matches are especially emotive, with rivalries often spilling out into bloodshed. Besides spectator cricket, you'll see games being played on open spaces all around the country.

Test matches are rare, but inter-state cricket is easy to catch – the most prestigious competition is the Ranji Trophy. Occasionally, you may even come across a match blocking a road, and will have to be patient as the players grudgingly let your vehicle continue.

Football (soccer) has undergone a revolution since the establishment of the eight-team Indian Super League (ISL) in 2013, which attracts the fourth-highest average attendances in the world as well as a massive TV audience. Teams employ high-profile coaches such as FC Goa's Brazilian legend Zico, while the players include a number of internationals, mostly from Africa. Goa has always been a stronghold of the game in general, but in 2015 Chennaiyin surprised everyone by lifting the ISL trophy, while Atlético de Kolkata won the league in both 2014 and 2016.

Horse racing can be a good day out, especially if you enjoy a flutter. Racecourses can be found in Mumbai, Pune, Hyderabad, Mysuru, Bengaluru and Ooty. Other (mainly) spectator sports include **polo**, originally from upper Kashmir, but taken up by the British to become one of the symbols of the Raj. You might come across a game but it is far more popular in the north.

After years in the doldrums, **field hockey**, which used regularly to furnish the country with Olympic medals, is making a strong comeback. The haul of medals dried up in the 1960s when international hockey moved to Astroturf – which was, and still is, a rare surface in India. However, hockey remains very popular, especially in schools and colleges. Having hosted the Hockey World Cup in 2010, India is due to stage the competition again in 2018.

Tennis in India has always been a sport for the middle and upper classes. The country has produced a number of world-class players, such as the men's duo of Mahesh Bhupati and Leander Paes, who briefly achieved a world number-one ranking in the men's doubles in 1999, but the brightest current star is undoubtedly Sania Mirza, the first Indian woman to break into the singles top 50. After injury forced her to give up the solo game she shifted her attention to doubles and was at one point number one in the WTA rankings, having partnered Martina Hingis to three successive Grand Slam titles in 2015–16, although at the time of writing she was eighth.

Volleyball is very popular throughout India, especially in the resorts of Goa. Standards aren't particularly high and joining a game is quite easy. **Golf** is widely followed, too, again among the middle classes; courses are mostly to be found in the hill stations of the Western Ghats.

INDIA'S TWENTY20 VISION

Over the last ten years, the whole global cricket scene has been massively shaken up by the brashness and glamour of the **Indian Premier League** (Ⓦ iplt20.com), the world's biggest Twenty20 cricket tournament. Held annually in April and May since 2008, the IPL features a mix of young up-and-coming locals, established Indian players and international cricketing megastars such as AB de Villiers and Chris Gayle. Each of the league's eight city team franchises supplements its home-grown playing staff by signing up star "icon players", whose services are auctioned off via a series of sealed bids – records were broken in 2015 when Delhi Daredevils picked up master-blasting batsman Yuvraj Singh for a cool US$2.4 million.

With such staggering sums of money changing hands, it's perhaps no surprise that the IPL has become as well known for its off-field controversies and financial irregularities as for the action and drama on the pitch. In 2013, three Rajasthan Royals players were arrested for spot-fixing and in 2015 both the Royals and Chennai Super Kings were booted out of the league for two years following revelations of match-fixing.

Outdoor activities

Though not the prime reason for most people to visit South India, there are a number of outdoor pursuits to be enjoyed. The most common is trekking, though snorkelling and scuba diving are well established, and a few other watersports are slowly growing in popularity.

Trekking

Although there are far more **trekking** possibilities in the mountainous north, low-level treks are available in the Western Ghats and Nilgiri Hills. Popular trekking hubs are Madikeri in the Kodagu (Coorg) region and Periyar and Munnar in Kerala's Cardamom Hills; Matheran on the outskirts of Mumbai also offers plenty of good short treks

The best time to trek is between November and March, when it's not too hot or wet, especially after New Year in the case of the Nilgiris, which can see rain from the northeast monsoon in November and December.

It isn't necessary to have any specialized gear but it is a good idea to have the following equipment: clothes to wear in layers, sturdy shoes or boots, a waterproof jacket, backpack, compass and map, pocket knife, sleeping bag, sunblock, toiletries and toilet paper, torch, water bottle, basic medical kit and some emergency provisions. It's usually best to take a guide if you are planning to get off the beaten track. They usually available at very reasonable rates; suggestions on finding guides and on specific routes are given in the relevant chapters.

Diving, snorkelling and other watersports

Because of the number of rivers draining into the sea around the Subcontinent, India's **coastal waters** are generally silt-laden and too murky for decent diving or snorkelling. However in many areas abundant hard coral and colourful fish make up for the relatively poor visibility. India also counts two beautiful tropical-island archipelagos in its territory, both surrounded by exceptionally clear seas. Served by well-equipped and reputable diving centres, the Andaman Islands and Lakshadweep offer world-class diving on a par with just about anything in Asia. Don't come here expecting rock-bottom prices though. India's dive schools cost at least as much as anywhere else, typically charging around US$70 for a two-tank outing, to US$270–300 for an open-water course.

For independent travellers, the most promising destination for both scuba diving and snorkelling is the **Andaman Islands** in the Bay of Bengal, around 1000km east of the mainland. Part of a chain of submerged mountains that stretch north from Sumatra to the coast of Myanmar (Burma), this isolated archipelago is ringed by gigantic coral reefs whose crystal-clear waters are teeming with tropical fish and other marine life. Havelock Island has by far the most dive centres, while its smaller neighbour Neil is slowly developing a scene; you can also dive on North Andaman or around Chiriya Tapu and Cinque Island, both accessed from Port Blair. If you want to do an open-water course, book ahead as places tend to be in short supply especially during the peak season, between December and February (see box, p.456).

Lakshadweep is a classic coconut-palm-covered atoll, some 400km west of Kerala in the Arabian Sea. The shallow lagoons, extensive coral reefs and exceptionally good visibility make this a perfect option for both first-timers and more experienced divers – though transport and accommodation are very pricey (see box, p.348).

PADI-approved dive schools also work out of a handful of resorts in **Goa**. Although the waters off the Goan coast have poor visibility, these schools take clients further south to an island off the shores of neighbouring Karnataka where conditions are much better.

Other niche watersports such as **kitesurfing**, which has a centre in Rameshwaram (see p.425), are also beginning to make an appearance.

Yoga, meditation and ashrams

The birthplace of yoga and the spiritual home of the world's most famous meditation traditions, India offers unrivalled opportunities for spiritual nourishment, ranging from basic yoga and pranayama classes to extended residential meditation retreats.

Yoga is taught virtually everywhere in South India and there are several internationally known centres where you can train to become a teacher. **Meditation** is similarly practised all over the region and specific courses are available in temples, meditation centres, monasteries and ashrams. **Ashrams** are communities where people work, live and study together, drawn by a common, usually spiritual, goal.

Details of yoga and meditation courses and ashrams are provided throughout the Guide. Most centres offer courses that you can enrol on at short notice, but many of the more popular ones (see p.52) need to be booked well in advance.

Yoga

Yoga (Sanskrit for "to unite" and root of the word "yoke") aims to help the practitioner unite his or her individual consciousness with the divine. This is achieved by raising awareness of one's self through spiritual, mental and physical exercises and discipline. **Hatha yoga**, the most popular form in the West, is based on physical postures called *asanas*, which stretch, relax and tone the muscular system of the body and also massage the internal organs. Each *asana* has a beneficial effect on a particular muscle group or organ, and although they vary widely in difficulty, consistent practice will lead to improved suppleness and health benefits. For serious practitioners, however, Hatha yoga is seen simply as the first step leading to more subtle stages of meditation which commence when the energies of the body have been awakened and sensitized by stretching and relaxing. Other forms of yoga include *raja* yoga, which includes moral discipline, and *bhakti* yoga, the yoga of devotion, which entails a commitment to one's guru or teacher. *Jnana* yoga (the yoga of knowledge) is centred around the deep philosophies that underlie Hindu spiritual thinking.

Many of the country's most famous teachers work from institutes in the South. **Iyengar** yoga is one of the most famous approaches studied today, named after its founder, B.K.S. Iyengar (a student of the great yoga teacher Sri Tirumalai Krishnamacharya), who died in 2014. Its main centre, the Ramamani Iyengar Memorial Yoga Institute, is in Pune, Maharashtra (Ⓦ bksiyengar.com), but there are many branches elsewhere. Iyengar's style is based upon precise physical alignment during each posture. With much practise, and the aid of props such as blocks, straps and chairs, the student can attain perfect physical balance and, the theory goes, perfect balance of mind will follow. Iyengar yoga has a strong therapeutic element and has been used successfully for treating a wide variety of structural and internal problems.

Ashtanga yoga is an approach developed by K. Pattabhi Jois of Mysuru (Ⓦ kpjayi.org; see box, p.227), who also studied under Krishnamacharya.

Unlike Iyengar yoga, which centres around a collection of separate *asanas*, Ashtanga links various postures into a series of flowing moves called *vinyasa*, with the aim of developing strength and agility. The perfect synchronization of movement with breath is a key objective throughout these sequences. Although a powerful form, it can be frustrating for beginners as each move has to be perfected before moving on to the next one.

The son of Krishnamacharya, T.K.V. Desikachar, established a third major branch in modern yoga, emphasizing a more versatile and adaptive approach to teaching, focused on the situation of the individual practitioner. This style became known as **Viniyoga**, although Desikachar has long tried to distance himself from the term. In the mid-1970s, he co-founded the Krishnamacharya Yoga Mandiram (Ⓦ kym.org), now a flagship institute in Chennai.

The other most influential Indian yoga teacher of the modern era has been Swami Vishnu Devananda, an acolyte of the famous sage Swami Sivanda, who established the International Sivananda Yoga Vedanta Center (Ⓦ sivananda .org), with more than thirty branches in India and abroad. **Sivananda**-style yoga tends to introduce elements in a different order from its counterparts – teaching practices regarded by others as advanced to relative beginners. This fast-forward approach has proved particularly popular with Westerners, who flock in their thousands to intensive introductory courses staged at centres all over India – the most renowned of them at Neyyar Dam, in the hills east of the Keralan capital, Thiruvananthapuram.

Meditation

Meditation is often practised after a session of yoga, when the energy of the body has been awakened, and is an essential part of both Hindu and Buddhist practice. In both religions, meditation is considered the most powerful tool for understanding the true nature of mind and self, an essential step on the path to **enlightenment**. In Vedanta, meditation's aim is to realize the true self as non-dual Brahman or godhead – the foundation of all consciousness and life. *Moksha* (or liberation – the nirvana of the Buddhists), achieved through disciplines of yoga and meditation, eventually helps believers release the soul from endless cycles of birth and rebirth.

Vipassana meditation (Ⓦ dhamma.org) is a technique, originally taught by the Buddha, whereby practitioners learn to become more aware of physical sensations and mental processes. Courses last for a minimum of ten days and are austere – involving 4am starts, around ten hours of meditation a day, no solid food after noon, segregation of the sexes and no talking for the duration (except with the leaders of the course). Courses are free for all first-time students, to allow everyone an opportunity to learn and benefit from the technique. Vipassana is taught in almost forty centres across the region.

Tibetan Buddhist meditation is attracting more and more followers around the world. With its four distinct schools, Tibetan Buddhism incorporates a huge variety of meditation practices, including Vipassana, known as *shiné* in Tibetan, and various visualization techniques involving the numerous deities that make up the complex and colourful Tibetan pantheon. India, with its large Tibetan diaspora, has become a major centre for people wanting to study Tibetan Buddhism and medicine. The principal location in South India is Bylakuppe, near Mysuru in Karnataka. For further details of courses available locally, see the relevant Guide chapters.

Ashrams and centres

Ashrams can range in size from just a handful of people to several thousand, and their rules, regulations and restrictions vary enormously. Some offer on-site accommodation, others will require you to stay in the nearest town or village. Some charge Western prices, others local prices and some operate on a donation basis. Many ashrams have set programmes each day, while others are less structured, teaching as and when requested. In addition to these traditional Indian place to learn yoga and meditation techniques, dozens of smaller centres open in the coastal resorts of Goa and Kerala during the winter, several of them staffed by internationally famous teachers. The more prominent of these are listed below.

COURSES AND ASHRAMS

Ashiyana Tropical Retreat Centre Mandrem, Goa Ⓦ ashiyana-yoga-goa.com. World-class yoga, massage, meditation and *satsang* tuition – from resident and visiting teachers – with treehouse accommodation and gorgeous views. See p.188.

Ashtanga Yoga Nilayam Gokulam, Mysuru, Karnataka ☎ 98801 85500, Ⓦ kpjayi.org. Run by students of Pattabhi Jois, and offering tuition in dynamic yoga, affiliated with martial arts. See box, p.227.

Brahmani Centre Anjuna, Goa ☎ 99236 99378, Ⓦ brahmaniyoga.com. Offers drop-in yoga classes – mainly Ashtanga,

with a few taster sessions in other styles, plus *pranayama* and *bhajan* devotional singing – by top-notch teachers. See box, p.180.

Harmonic Healing & Eco Retreat Centre Patnem, Goa Ⓦ harmonicingoa.com. Yoga, pilates, reiki initiations and more from internationally acclaimed teachers. See p.203.

International Society for Krishna Consciousness (ISKCON) Bengaluru ☎ 080 2357 8347; Ⓦ iskcon.org. Large and well-run international organization with a major ashram and temple in Bengaluru (see p.215) and centres in numerous other locations, both in India and abroad. Promotes *bhakti* yoga (the yoga of devotion) through good deeds, right living and chanting – a way of life rather than a short course.

Mata Amritanandamayi Math Vallikkavu, Kerala ☎ 0476 289 7578, Ⓦ amritapuri.org. The ashram of the famous "Hugging Saint", Amma, visited annually by hundreds of thousands, who pass through for *darshan* and a hug from the smiley guru, whose charitable works have earned her near-divine status in the South.

Osho Commune International Pune, Maharashtra ☎ 020 6601 9999, Ⓦ osho.com. Established by the enigmatic Osho, this "Meditation Resort" is set in 31 acres of beautifully landscaped gardens and offers a variety of courses in personal therapy, healing and meditation. See box, p.147.

Prasanthi Nilayam Puttaparthy, Andhra Pradesh ☎ 08555 87236, Ⓦ sathyasai.org. The ashram of Satya Sai Baba, one of India's most revered and popular gurus, who died in 2011. There is still a worldwide following of millions, with numerous international branches. Visitors sometimes comment on the strict security staffing and rigid rules and regulations. Cheap accommodation is available in dormitories or "flats" for four people. There is no need to book in advance, though you should phone to check availability (see p.295).

Purple Valley Centre Anjuna, Goa ☎ 0832 226 8364, Ⓦ yogagoa.com. Lovely retreat now run by Sharath Rangaswamy, grandson of the illustrious Ashtanga guru, Shri K. Pattabhi Jois. See box, p.180.

Saccidananda Ashram Thannirpalli, Kulithalai, near Tiruchirapalli, Tamil Nadu ☎ 04323 22260, Ⓦ saccidananda ashram.com. Also known as Shantivanam (meaning Peace Forest in Sanskrit), it is situated on the banks of the sacred River Kaveri. Founded by Father Bede Griffiths, a visionary Benedictine monk, it presents a curious but sympathetic fusion of Christianity and Hinduism. Visitors can join in the services and rituals or just relax here. Accommodation is in simple huts dotted around the grounds and meals are communal. Very busy during the major Christian festivals.

Sivananda Yoga Vedanta Dhanwantari Ashram Neyyar Dam, Thiruvananthapuram, Kerala ☎ 94956 30951, Ⓦ sivananda.org. An offshoot of the original Divine Life Society, this yoga-based ashram focuses on *asanas*, breathing techniques (*pranayama*) and meditation. They also run month-long yoga teacher-training programmes, but book well in advance. There are branches in Madurai, Chennai, Delhi, Uttarkashi and worldwide – see the website for details.

Vipassana International Academy Ⓦ dhamma.org. Runs a wide variety of 3- to 45-day courses in Vipassana meditation at 27 centres in Maharashtra, 12 in other parts of the South and more worldwide.

Culture and etiquette

Cultural differences extend to all sorts of little things. While allowances will usually be made for foreigners, visitors unacquainted with Indian customs may need a little preparation to avoid causing offence or making fools of themselves. The list of dos and don'ts here is hardly exhaustive: when in doubt, watch what the Indian people around you are doing.

Eating and the right-hand rule

The biggest minefield of potential faux pas has to do with **eating**. This is usually done with the fingers, and requires practice to get absolutely right. Rule one is: **eat with your right hand only**. In India, as right across Asia, the left hand is for wiping your bottom, cleaning your feet and other unsavoury functions (you also put on and take off your shoes with your left hand), while the right hand is for eating, shaking hands and so on.

Quite how rigid individuals are about this tends to vary, with brahmins (who, at the top of the hierarchical ladder, are one of the two "right-handed castes") and southerners likely to be the strictest. While you can hold a cup or utensil in your left hand, and you can get away with using it to help tear your chapatti, you should not eat, pass food or wipe your mouth with your left hand.

This rule extends beyond food. In general, do not pass anything to anyone with your left hand, or point at anyone with it either; and Indians won't be impressed if you put it in your mouth. In general, you should accept things given to you with your right hand – though using both hands is a sign of respect.

The other rule to beware of when eating or drinking is that your lips should not touch other people's food – jhutha, or sullied food, is strictly taboo. Don't, for example, take a bite out of a chapatti and pass it on. When drinking out of a cup or bottle to be shared with others, don't let it touch your lips, but rather pour it directly into your mouth. This custom also protects you from things like hepatitis. It is customary to wash your hands before and after eating.

Temples and religion

Religion is taken very seriously in India; it's important always to show due respect to religious buildings, shrines, images and people at prayer. When entering a **temple or mosque**, remove your shoes and leave them at the door (socks are acceptable and protect your feet from burning-hot stone ground). Some temples – Jain ones in particular – do not allow you to enter wearing or carrying leather articles, and forbid entry to menstruating women. In the southern state of Kerala, most Hindu temples are closed to non-Hindus, but those that aren't require men to remove their shirts before entering (women must wear long dresses or skirts).

In a mosque, non-Muslims would not normally be allowed in at prayer time and women are sometimes not let in at all. In a Hindu temple, you are often not allowed into the inner sanctum; and at a Buddhist stupa or monument, you should always walk round clockwise (ie, with the stupa on your right). Hindus are very superstitious about taking photographs of images of deities and inside temples; if in doubt, desist.

Funeral processions are private affairs, and should be left in peace. In Hindu funerals, the body is normally carried to the cremation site within hours of death by white-shrouded relatives (white is the colour of mourning). The eldest son is expected to shave his head and wear white following the death of a parent. Though not as likely as up north, you may come across cremations; such occasions should be treated with respect and photographs should not be taken.

Dress

Indian people are very conservative about dress. **Women** are expected to dress modestly, with legs and shoulders covered. Trousers are acceptable, but shorts and short skirts are offensive to many. **Men** should always wear a shirt in public, and avoid skimpy shorts away from beach areas. These rules are particularly important in temples and mosques. Cover your head with a cap or cloth when entering a dargah (Sufi shrine) or Sikh gurudwara; women in particular are also required to cover their limbs. Men are similarly expected to dress appropriately with their legs and head covered. Caps are usually available on loan, often free, for visitors, and sometimes cloth is available to cover up your arms and legs.

Never mind sky-clad Jains (see p.234) or Naga Sadhus, **nudity** is not acceptable in India. Topless bathing is not uncommon in Goa (though it is in theory prohibited), but you can be sure the locals don't like it.

In general, Indians find it hard to understand why rich Westerners should wander round in ragged clothes or imitate the lowest ranks of Indian society, who would love to have something more decent to wear. Staying well groomed and dressing "respectably" vastly improves the impression you make on local people and reduces sexual harassment for women, too.

Other possible gaffes

Kissing and **embracing** are regarded in India as part of sex: do not do them in public. In more conservative areas (ie outside Westernized parts of big cities or tourist enclaves), it is still rare for couples to hold hands, though Indian men can sometimes be seen holding hands as a sign of "brotherliness". Be aware of your **feet**. When entering a private home, you should normally remove your shoes (follow your host's example); when sitting, avoid pointing the soles of your feet at anyone. Accidental contact with one's foot is always followed by an apology.

Indian English can be very formal and even ceremonious. Indian people may well call you "sir" or "madam", even "good lady" or "kind sir". At the same time, you should be aware that your English may seem rude to them. In particular, swearing is taken rather seriously, and casual use of the f-word is likely to shock.

Meeting people

Westerners have an ambiguous status in Indian eyes. In one way, you represent the rich sahib, whose culture dominates the world, and the old colonial mentality has not completely disappeared. On the other hand, as a non-Hindu, you are an outcaste, your presence in theory polluting to an orthodox or high-caste Hindu, while to members of all religions, your morals and your standards of spiritual and physical cleanliness are suspect.

As a traveller, you will constantly come across people who want to strike up a **conversation**. English not being their first language, they may not be familiar with the conventional ways of doing this, and thus their opening line may seem abrupt if at the same time very formal. "Excuse me, gentleman, what is your native place?" is a typical one. It is also the first in a series of questions that Indian men seem sometimes to have learnt from a single book in order to ask Western tourists. Some of the questions may baffle at first ("What is your qualification?" "Are you in service?"), some may be queries about the ways of the West or the purpose of your trip, but mostly they will be about your family and your job.

You may find it odd or even intrusive that complete strangers should want to know that sort of thing, but these subjects are considered polite conversation between strangers in India, and help people place one another in terms of social position. Your family, job, even income, are not considered "personal" subjects, and it is completely normal to ask people about them. Asking the same questions back will not be taken amiss – far from it. Being curious does not have the "nosey" stigma in India that it has in the West.

Things that Indian people, especially if they are older or more traditional, are likely to find strange about you are lack of religion (you could adopt one), travelling alone, leaving your family to come to India, being an unmarried couple (letting people think you are married can make life easier) and travelling second class or staying in cheap hotels when, as a tourist, you are relatively rich. You will probably end up having to explain the same things many times to many different people; on the other hand, you can ask questions too, so you could take it as an opportunity to ask things you want to know about India. English-speaking Indians and members of the large and growing middle class in particular are usually extremely well informed and well educated.

Shopping

No country in the world produces such a tempting array of arts and crafts as India. Intensely colourful, delicately worked, exquisitely ornate and immensely varied, India's crafts have the added advantage of being amazingly inexpensive. Every part of South India has its specialities – textiles and metalwork in Karnataka, leatherware in Maharashtra and bronzes in Tamil Nadu – but everywhere you'll see beautiful souvenirs that you'll find hard to resist buying. On top of that, all sorts of things (such as made-to-measure clothes) that would be vastly expensive at home are much more reasonably priced. Even if you lose weight during your trip, your baggage might well put on quite a bit – unless of course you post some of it home.

Where to shop

Quite a few items sold in tourist areas are made elsewhere and, needless to say, it's more fun (and cheaper) to pick them up at source. Best buys are noted in the relevant sections of the Guide, along with a few specialities that can't be found outside their regions. South India is awash with **street hawkers**, often very young kids. Although they can be annoying and should be dealt with firmly if you are not interested, do not write them off completely as they sometimes have decent souvenirs at lower than shop prices and are open to hard bargaining.

Virtually all the state governments in India run handicraft **emporia**, most with branches in the major cities. Mumbai, Chennai and Bengaluru also have **Central Cottage Industries Emporiums** (Ⓦcottageemporium.in). Goods in these shops are generally of a high quality, even if their fixed prices are a little expensive, and they are worth a visit to get an idea of what crafts are available and how much they should cost.

Bargaining

Whatever you **buy** (except things like food, tickets and other daily items), you will almost always be expected to **haggle** over the price. Bargaining is very much a matter of personal style, but should always be lighthearted, never acrimonious. There are no hard and fast rules – it's really a question of how much something is worth to you. It's a good plan, therefore, to have an idea of how much you want to pay. Bid low and let the shopkeeper argue you up. If they'll settle for your price or less, you have a deal. If not, you don't, but you've had a pleasant conversation and no harm is done.

Don't worry too much about the first quoted prices. Some people suggest paying a third of the opening price, but it really depends on the shop, the goods and the shopkeeper's impression of you. You may not be able to get the seller much below the first quote; on the other hand, you may end up paying as little as a tenth of it. If you bid too low, you may be hustled out of the shop for offering an "insulting" price, but this is all part of the game, and you'll no doubt be welcomed as an old friend if you return the next day. More often, however, if you start to walk away, the price will magically come down, so that's a useful tactic. "Green" tourists are easily spotted, so try and look like you know what you are up to, even on your first day, or leave it till later; you could wait and see what the going rate is first.

Haggling is a little bit like bidding in an auction, and similar rules apply. Don't start haggling for something if you know you don't want it, and never let any figure pass your lips that you are not prepared to pay – having mentioned a price, you are obliged to pay it. If the seller asks you how much you would pay for something and you don't want it, say so.

Very occasionally rickshaw and taxi drivers stop unasked at shops where they get a small **commission** simply for bringing customers. If you're taken to a shop by a tout or driver and you buy something, you pay around fifty percent extra. Stand firm if you have no appetite for such shenanigans. If you want a bargain, shop alone, and never let anybody on the street take you to a shop – if you do, they'll be getting a commission and you'll be paying it.

Travelling with children

Travelling with kids can be both challenging and rewarding. Indians are very tolerant of children so you can take them almost anywhere without restriction, and they always help break the ice with strangers.

Most children will enjoy the vibrancy of just being in India, with festivals and temples likely to exert a special appeal. Similarly, you can't go far wrong taking them to beaches and wildlife sanctuaries, although not all Indian zoos are very happy places; the one in Mysuru (see p.226) is an honourable exception. There are, however, relatively few attractions aimed especially at kids beyond a rash of rather cheesy family theme parks that have popped up in recent years, especially in areas popular with new Indian middle-class holidaymakers, such as the coast south of Chennai. On the other hand, the more modern museums are increasingly introducing interactive displays aimed at the young that are both educational and fun.

As for the difficulties of travel, the main problem with children, especially small ones, is their extra vulnerability. Even more than their parents, they need protection from the **sun**, unsafe drinking water, heat and unfamiliar food. All that **chilli** in particular may be a problem, even with older kids, if they're not used to it. Remember too, that **diarrhoea**, perhaps just a nuisance to you, could be dangerous for a child: rehydration salts (see p.42) are vital if your child goes down with it. Make sure too, if possible, that your child is aware of the dangers of **rabies**; keep children away from animals and consider a rabies jab.

For **babies**, nappies (diapers) are available in most large towns at similar prices to the West, but it's worth taking an additional pack in case of emergencies, and bringing sachets of Calpol or similar, which aren't readily available in India. And if your baby is on powdered milk, it might be an idea to bring some of that: you can certainly get it in India, but it may not taste the same. Dried baby food could also be worth taking – any café or chaiwala should be able to supply you with boiled water.

For touring, hiking or walking, child-carrier backpacks are ideal; some even come with mosquito nets these days. As for luggage, bring as little as possible so you can manage the kids more easily. If your child is small enough, a fold-up buggy is also well worth packing, even if you no longer use a buggy at home, as kids tire so easily in the heat. If you want to cut down on long train or bus journeys by flying, remember that children under 2 travel for ten percent of the adult fare, and under-12s for half-price.

Travel essentials

Costs

For Western visitors, India is still one of the world's less expensive countries. A little foreign currency can go a long way, and you can be confident of getting good value for your money, whether you're setting out to keep your budget to a minimum or to enjoy the opportunities that spending a bit more will make possible.

What you spend obviously depends on where you go, where you stay, how you get around, what you eat and what you buy. Outside the tourist resorts of Kerala and Goa, you can still survive on a **budget** of as little as ₹1000 (£12/US$15) per day, if you eat in local *dhabas*, stay in the cheapest hotels and don't travel too much. In reality, most backpackers nowadays tend to spend around double that. On ₹2500 (£30/US$37.50) per day you'll be able to afford comfortable mid-range hotels, and meals in smarter restaurants, regular rickshaw or taxi rides and entrance fees to monuments. Spend over ₹5000 (£60/US$75) per day and you can stay in smart hotels, eat in the top restaurants, travel first class on trains and afford chauffeur-driven cars. Although it is possible to travel very comfortably in India, it's also possible to spend a great deal of money if you want to experience the very best the country has to offer, and there are plenty of hotels now charging US$500 per night, sometimes even more.

ASI ENTRANCE FEES

The Archeological Survey of India (ASI), who manage many of India's most popular monuments, currently operates a **two-tier entry system** at all its sites, whereby foreign visitors, including non-resident Indians (NRIs), pay a lot more than Indian residents. Some private attractions follow a similar policy; we've listed entrance fees for both foreigners and Indian residents (in parenthesis) throughout the Guide.

Budget **accommodation** is still very good value, however. Cheap double rooms start from around ₹400 (£4/US$6) per night, while a no-frills vegetarian **meal** in an ordinary restaurant will typically cost no more than ₹100. Long-distance **transport** can work out to be phenomenally good value if you stick to state buses and standard non-a/c classes on trains, but soon starts to add up if you opt for air-conditioned carriages on the super-fast inter-city services. The 360km trip from Bengaluru to Chennai, for example, can cost anywhere from ₹150 (£1.80/US$2.30) in second-class unreserved up to ₹1540 (£19/US$23.50) in AC first-class.

Where you are also makes a difference: Mumbai is notoriously pricey, especially for accommodation, and upscale visitor accommodation in Kerala costs almost as much as it does in Europe. Out in the sticks, on the other hand, and particularly away from your fellow tourists, you will often find things incredibly cheap, though your choice will obviously be more limited.

Don't make any rigid assumptions at the outset of a long trip that your money will last for a certain number of weeks or months. On any one day it may be possible to spend very little, but cumulatively you won't be doing yourself any favours if you don't make sure you keep yourself well rested and properly fed. As a foreigner in India, you will find yourself penalized by double-tier entry prices to museums and historic sites (see box above) as well as in upmarket hotels and airfares, both of which are levied at a higher rate and in dollars.

Some independent travellers tend to indulge in wild and highly competitive **penny-pinching**, which Indian people find rather pathetic – they have a fair idea of what you can earn at home. Bargain where appropriate, but don't begrudge a few rupees to someone who is after all far worse off than you. Even if you get a bad deal on every rickshaw journey you make, it will only add a minuscule fraction to the cost of your trip. Remember what great value you are getting in most cases and that luxury items or services at home can be affordable here. At the same time, don't pay well over the odds for something if you know what the going rate is. Thoughtless extravagance can, particularly in remote areas that see a disproportionate number of tourists, contribute to inflation, putting even basic goods and services beyond the reach of local people.

Crime and personal safety

In spite of the crushing poverty and the yawning gulf between rich and poor, India is, on the whole, a **safe** country in which to travel. As a tourist, however, you are an obvious target for the tiny number of thieves (who may include some of your fellow travellers), and stand to face serious problems if you do lose your passport and money or bank cards. Common sense, therefore, suggests a few precautions.

Beware of crowded locations, such as packed buses or trains, in which it is easy for pickpockets to operate – slashing pockets or bags with razor blades is not unheard of in certain locations, and itching powder is sometimes used to distract the unwary. Don't leave valuables unattended on the beach when you go for a swim; backpacks in dormitory accommodation are also obvious targets, as is luggage on the roof of buses. Even monkeys rate a mention here, since it's not unknown for them to steal things from hotel rooms with open windows, or even to snatch bags from unsuspecting shoulders.

Budget travellers would do well to carry a **padlock**, as these are usually used to secure the doors of cheap hotel rooms and it's reassuring to know you have the only key. You can also use them to lock your bag to seats or racks in trains, for which a length of chain also comes in handy. Don't put valuables in your luggage but keep them with you at all times. If your baggage is on the roof of a bus, make sure it is well secured. On trains and buses, the prime time for theft is just before you leave, so keep a particular eye on your gear then, beware of deliberate diversions, and don't put your belongings next to open windows. Remember that routes popular with tourists tend to be popular with thieves too. Druggings leading to theft and worse are rare but not unheard of, so if offered food or drink, make sure you are confident it's the family picnic you are sharing or have seen the food purchased from a vendor.

However, **don't get paranoid**; the best way of enjoying the country is to stay relaxed but with your wits about you. Crime levels in India are a long way below those of Western countries and violent crime against tourists is almost unheard of. Virtually none of the people who approach you on the street intend any harm: many want to sell you something (though this is not always made apparent immediately), some want to practise their English, others to chat you up, while more than a

---

DRUGS

India is a centre for the production of **cannabis** and to a lesser extent **opium**, and derivatives of these drugs are widely available. **Charas** (hashish) is produced all along the Himalayas, while **ganja** (marijuana) is the more common form in South India. The use of cannabis is frowned upon by respectable Indians – if you see anyone in a movie smoking a chillum, you can be sure it's the baddie. Sadhus, on the other hand, are allowed to smoke it legally as part of their religious devotion to Shiva, who is said to have originally discovered its narcotic properties.

Bhang (a preparation made from marijuana leaves, which it is claimed sometimes contains added hallucinogenic ingredients such as *datura*) is legal and widely available in bhang shops: it is used to make sweets and drinks such as the notoriously potent bhang lassis which have waylaid many an unwary traveller. Bhang shops also frequently sell ganja, low-quality *charas* and opium (*chandu*), mainly from Rajasthan and Madhya Pradesh. Opium derivatives morphine and heroin are widespread too, with addiction an increasing problem among the urban poor. "Brown sugar" that you may be offered on the street is number-three heroin. Use of other illegal drugs such as LSD, ecstasy and cocaine is largely confined to tourists in party locations such as Goa.

All of these drugs except bhang are strictly controlled under Indian **law**. Anyone arrested with less than five grams of cannabis, which they are able to prove is for their own use, is liable to a six-month maximum, but cases can take years to come to trial (two is normal, and eight not unheard of). Police raids and searches are particularly common in the beach areas of Goa. "Paying a fine now" may be possible on arrest (though it will probably mean all the money you have), but once you are booked in at the station, your chances are slim; a minority of the population languishing in Indian jails are foreigners on drugs charges.

few just want to add your address to their book or have a snap taken with you. Anyone offering wonderful-sounding moneymaking schemes, however, is almost certain to be a con artist.

If you do feel threatened, it's worth looking for help. **Tourism police** are found sitting in clearly marked booths in the main railway stations, especially in big tourist centres, where they will also have a booth in the main bus station. In addition, they may have a marked booth outside major tourist sites.

Be wary of **credit-card fraud**; a credit card can be used to make duplicate forms by which your account is then billed for fictitious transactions, so don't let shops or restaurants take your card away to process – insist they do it in front of you or follow them to the point of transaction. It's not a bad idea to keep US$200 or so separately from the rest of your money, along with insurance policy number and phone number for claims, and a photocopy of the pages in your passport containing personal data and your Indian visa. This will cover you in case you do lose all your valuables.

If the worst happens and you get **robbed**, the first thing to do is report the theft as soon as possible to the local police. They are very unlikely to recover your belongings but you need a report from them in order to claim on your travel insurance. Dress smartly and expect an uphill battle – city cops in particular tend to be jaded from too many insurance scams.

Losing your passport is a real hassle, but does not necessarily mean the end of your trip. First, report the loss immediately to the police, who will issue you with the all-important "complaint form" that you need to be able to travel around and check into hotels, as well as claim back any expenses incurred in replacing your passport from your insurer. The next thing to do is telephone your nearest embassy or consulate in India. Normally, passports have to be applied for and collected in person, but if you are stranded, it is usually possible to arrange to receive the necessary forms in the post. However, you still have to go to the embassy or consulate to pick up your new passport. Emergency passports are the cheapest form of replacement, but are normally only valid for the few days of your return flight. If you're not sure when you're leaving India, you'll have to obtain a more costly full passport; these can only be issued by high commissions, embassies and larger consulates, although they can be arranged through consulates in Chennai, Mumbai or Panjim (Goa), and in the case of the UK, Bengaluru and Hyderabad.

Duty-free allowance

Anyone over 17 can bring in one US quart (0.95 litre – but nobody's going to quibble about the other 5ml) of spirits, or a bottle of wine and 250ml spirits; plus 200 cigarettes, or 50 cigars, or 250g tobacco. You may be required to register anything valuable on a tourist baggage re-export form to make sure you can take it home with you, and to fill in a currency declaration form if carrying more than US$10,000 or equivalent.

Electricity

Generally 220V 50Hz AC, though direct current supplies also exist, so check before plugging in. Most sockets are triple round-pin (accepting European-size double round-pin plugs). British, Irish and Australasian plugs will need an adaptor, preferably universal; American and Canadian appliances will need a transformer too, unless multivoltage. Power cuts and voltage variations are very common; voltage stabilizers should be used to run sensitive appliances such as laptops.

Insurance

It's imperative that you take out proper **travel insurance** before setting off for India. A typical travel insurance policy usually provides cover for the loss of baggage, tickets and – up to a certain

---

ROUGH GUIDES TRAVEL INSURANCE

Rough Guides has teamed up with **WorldNomads.com** to offer great travel insurance deals. Policies are available to residents of over 150 countries, with cover for a wide range of adventure sports, 24hr emergency assistance, high levels of medical and evacuation cover and a stream of travel safety information. Roughguides.com users can take advantage of their policies online 24/7, from anywhere in the world – even if you're already travelling. And since plans often change when you're on the road, you can extend your policy and even claim online. Roughguides.com users who buy travel insurance with WorldNomads.com can also leave a positive footprint and donate to a community development project. For more information, go to Ⓦ roughguides.com/travel-insurance.

limit – cash, as well as cancellation or curtailment of your journey. Most of them exclude so-called dangerous sports unless an extra premium is paid: in South India this can mean scuba diving, kitesurfing and windsurfing, though probably not jeep safaris. Many policies can be chopped and changed to exclude coverage you don't need – for example, sickness and accident benefits can often be excluded or included at will. If you do take medical coverage, ascertain whether benefits will be paid as treatment proceeds or only after return home, and whether there is a 24hr medical emergency number. When securing baggage cover, make sure that the per-article limit – typically under £500 – will cover your most valuable possession. If you need to make a claim, you should keep receipts for medicines and medical treatment, and in the event you have anything stolen, you must obtain an official statement from the police.

Internet

Broadband has now reached more or less every-where, leading to a proliferation of **wi-fi** connec-tions. The majority of hotels and guesthouses, at least those in touristic areas, will offer wi-fi, usually free but occasionally chargeable; we have noted exceptions in our accommodation reviews. Many cafés and restaurants also have wi-fi facilities. As a result of wi-fi, the number of **internet outlets** has declined but you can usually still find somewhere with public computers in any sizeable town, charging from ₹20–40/hr in urban areas to as much as ₹300/hr in more remote places such as the Andaman Islands. Speeds can still be painfully slow and computers rather antiquated, making it difficult to load complex websites or to perform online transactions (like booking a train ticket).

Laundry

Although some hotels have washing machines and independent launderettes are starting to appear, most places still send laundry to a *dhobi*, either in-house or nearby. The *dhobi* will take your dirty washing to a *dhobi ghat*, a public clothes-washing area (the bank of a river for example), where it is shown some old-fashioned discipline: separated, soaped and given a damn good thrashing to beat the dirt out of it. Then it is hung out to dry in the sun and taken to the ironing sheds where every garment is endowed with razor-sharp creases and then matched to its rightful owner by hidden cryptic markings. Your clothes will come back

absolutely spotless, though this kind of violent treatment does take it out of them: buttons get lost and eventually the cloth starts to fray.

Left luggage

Most stations in India have "cloakrooms" (sometimes called parcel offices) for passengers to leave their baggage. These can be extremely handy if you want to go sightseeing in a town and move on the same day. In theory, you need a train ticket or Indrail pass to deposit luggage, but staff don't always ask; they may, however, refuse to take your bag if you can't lock it. If you lose your reclaim ticket expect a lot of bureaucracy before you can get your bag back. Many cloakrooms in large stations operate 24 hours but smaller ones may not. The standard charge is currently ₹15 for the first 24 hours, plus ₹20 per day afterwards.

LGBT travellers

Homosexuality is not generally open or accepted in India, and in 2013 was once again made illegal, following a decision by the conservative Modi government to reverse a 2009 declaration by the High Court that the Victorian ban on gay sex between consenting adults was unconstitutional. As of 2017, following various protests, the matter was under review by the court again. Prejudice is still ingrained, however, especially in conservative rural areas.

For **lesbians**, making contacts is difficult; even the Indian women's movement does not readily promote lesbianism as an issue that needs confronting. The only public faces of a hidden scene are the few organizations in major cities (see p.60). For **gay men**, homosexuality is no longer solely the preserve of the alternative scene of actors and artists, and is increasingly accepted by the upper classes, though Mumbai still remains much more a centre for gay life than other cities. Despite the legal uncertainties, however, gay **pride** events and clubs are becoming more common in many cities; in recent years Mumbai, Bengaluru, Chennai and some smaller cities have all hosted prides.

One **transgender** group of people you may come across are **hijras**, who were officially recog-nized as third gender by the Supreme Court in 2014. Many *hijras* are born with genitals that are neither fully male nor female, but some are male-to-female transsexual. They live in their own "families" and have a niche in Indian society, but not an easy one. At weddings, their presence is supposed to bring good luck, and they are usually given baksheesh for putting in a brief appearance. Generally, however, they have a low social status and face widespread discrimination, and many make a living by begging or prostitution.

LGBT CONTACTS AND RESOURCES

Chennai Dost Ⓦ chennai-dost.blogspot.co.uk. Useful website aimed at the LGBT community in Chennai.

Galva-108 Ⓦ galva108.org. Interesting website set up by gay and lesbian Vaishnavas and Hindus.

Gay Bombay Ⓦ gaybombay.org. Comprehensive online resource for the LGBT community in Mumbai.

Humsafar Trust Ⓦ humsafar.org. Set up to promote safe sex among gay men, with lots of links and up-to-date information.

Indian Dost Ⓦ indiandost.com. LGBT networking and info.

Outright Action International Ⓦ outrightinternational.org. Latest news on the human rights situation for LGBT people worldwide, including regular bulletins on India.

Purple Dragon ☎ +662 238 3227, Ⓦ purpledrag.com. Thai-based tour operator offering various gay-friendly tours of India and other Asian countries.

Trikone Ⓦ trikone.org. Organization campaigning for LGBT rights in South Asia.

Maps

Getting good maps of India, in India, can be difficult. The government – in an archaic suspicion of cartography, and in spite of clear coverage of the country on Google – forbids the sale of detailed maps of border areas, which includes the entire coastline.

It therefore makes sense to bring a **full country map** of India with you. Freytag & Berndt produce the best country map, while Nelles covers parts of the country with 1:1,500,000 regional maps. These are generally excellent, but cost a fortune if you buy the complete set. Ttk, a Chennai-based company, publishes basic state maps which are widely available in India, and in some specialized travel and map shops in the UK such as Stanfords; these are poorly drawn but useful for road distances. The Indian Railways map at the back of the publication *Trains at a Glance* (see p.27) is useful for planning railway journeys.

If you need larger-scale **city maps** than the ones we provide in this guide you can sometimes get them from tourist offices, though the plans published free online at Google Maps or OpenStreetMap (Ⓦ openstreetmap.org) are vastly superior (simply print them off at an internet café or before you leave home). Eicher (Ⓦ maps.eicher-world.com) has a growing series of glossy City Maps and city Road Maps. produced in India and available at all good bookshops.

As for **trekking maps**, the US Army Map Service produced maps in the 1960s which, with a scale of 1:250,000, remain sufficiently accurate on topography, but are of course outdated on the latest road developments.

Money

India's unit of currency is the **rupee**, usually abbreviated ₹ and divided into a hundred paise. Almost all money is paper, with notes of 5, 10, 20, 50, 100, 500 and 2000 rupees. Coins in circulation are 1, 2, 5 and 10 rupees, the latter two gradually replacing the paper versions, plus (rarely seen) 50 paise. Note that it's technically illegal to take rupees in or out of India (although they are widely available at overseas forexes), so you might want to wait until you arrive before changing money. If you have kept any old ₹500 or ₹1000 notes from a visit prior to November 2016, be aware that they are no longer legal tender, as they were replaced that month by new ₹500 and ₹2000 notes.

Banknotes, especially lower denominations, can get into a terrible state. Don't accept banknotes torn at the middle crease, since no one else will be prepared to take them and you'll be left saddled with the things, though you can change them at the Reserve Bank of India and large branches of other big banks. Don't pass them on to beggars; they can't use them either, so it amounts to an insult.

Large denominations can also be a problem, as change is usually in short supply. Many Indian people cannot afford to keep much lying around, and you shouldn't necessarily expect shopkeepers or rickshaw-wallahs to have it (and they may – as may you – try to hold onto it if they do). Larger notes can be changed for smaller denominations at hotels and other suitable establishments.

ATMs and banking cards

The easiest way to access your money in India is with **plastic**, though it's a good idea to also have some backup in the form of cash. You will find **ATMs** at main banks in all major towns, cities and tourist areas, though your card issuer may well add a foreign transaction fee, and the Indian bank will

> ### EXCHANGE RATES
>
> At the time of writing, the **exchange rate** was approximately ₹82 to £1, ₹71 to €1 and ₹65 to US$1. You can check current exchange rates online at Ⓦ xe.com.

also levy a small charge, generally around ₹25. Your card issuer, and sometimes the ATM itself, imposes limits on the amount you may withdraw in a day – typically ₹25,000, with no single transaction exceeding ₹10,000.

Credit cards are accepted for payment at major hotels, top restaurants, some shops and airline offices, but virtually nowhere else. American Express, MasterCard and Visa are the likeliest to be accepted. Beware of people making extra copies of the receipt, in order to fraudulently bill you later; always insist that the transaction is made before your eyes.

Visa, American Express and some other financial institutions offer **prepaid cards** that you can load up with credit before you leave home and use in ATMs like a debit card – effectively replacing the increasingly defunct travellers' cheques.

One big downside of relying on plastic as your main access to cash, of course, is that cards can easily get lost or stolen, so take along a couple of alternatives if you can, keep an emergency stash of cash just in case and make a note of your home bank's telephone number and website addresses for emergencies.

US dollars are the easiest **currency** to convert, with euros and pounds sterling not far behind. Major hard currencies can be changed easily in tourist areas and big cities, less so elsewhere. In the unlikely scenario that you enter the country with more than US$10,000 or the equivalent, you are supposed to fill in a currency declaration form.

Changing money

Changing money in regular **banks**, especially government-run banks such as the State Bank of India (SBI), can be a time-consuming business, involving lots of form-filling and queueing at different counters, so it's best to change substantial amounts at any one time. You'll have no such problems, however, with **private companies** such as Thomas Cook, American Express or forex agents. Major cities and main tourist centres usually have several **licensed currency exchange bureaux**; rates usually aren't as good as at a bank but transactions are generally a lot quicker and there's less paperwork to complete.

Outside **banking hours** (Mon–Fri 10am–2/4pm, Sat 10am–noon), large hotels may change money, probably at a lower rate, and exchange bureaux have longer opening hours. Banks in the arrivals halls at most major airports stay open 24 hours.

Wherever you change money, hold onto **exchange receipts** ("encashment certificates"); they will be required if you want to change back

any excess rupees when you leave the country and to buy air tickets and reserve train berths with rupees at special counters for foreigners. The State Bank of India now charges for tax clearance forms.

Opening hours

Standard shop opening hours in India are Monday to Saturday 9.30am to 6pm, with Sunday openings increasingly common. Most big stores, at any rate, keep those hours, while smaller shops vary from town to town, region to region and one to another, but usually keep longer hours. Government tourist offices are open Monday to Friday 9.30am to 5pm, Saturday 9.30am to 1pm, closed on the second Saturday of the month; state-run tourist offices are likely to be open Monday to Friday 10am to 5pm.

Phones

Since the mobile phone revolution, privately run phone **international direct-dialling** facilities – **STD/ISD** (Standard Trunk Dialling/International Subscriber Dialling) places – have become far less common so you can't always rely on finding one. In addition, calling from them will cost more than dialling from a mobile if you have an Indian SIM card. Most visitors bring their own phones and buy an Indian SIM to cover their trip.

SIM cards are sold through most cellphone shops and network outlets, though the process for obtaining one is rather complicated and can take up to 48 hours. You have to provide a photocopy of your passport (photo and visa pages), fill in a form

---

CALLING HOME FROM ABROAD

To make an international call from India, dial the international access code (00), then the destination's country code, before the rest of the number. Note that the initial zero is omitted from the area code when dialling the UK, Ireland, Australia and New Zealand from abroad.

Australia international access code + 61

New Zealand international access code + 64

UK international access code + 44

US and Canada international access code + 1

Ireland international access code + 353

South Africa international access code + 27

and be registered at an Indian address, though the hotel you are staying in usually suffices. There is an initial connection fee ranging from ₹50 to ₹250, depending on the dealer and network.

Coverage varies from state to state, but the largest national network providers are best – Vodafone, Airtel and Idea. Once your retailer has unlocked your phone and you have paid for the initial card, it can be topped up ("re-charged" as it's known) by amounts ranging from ₹10–1000, though only by paying specific amounts (check with the retailer) will you get the full amount in credits. Call charges to the UK and US from most Indian networks cost ₹2–3 per minute. Also, ask your card supplier to turn on the "do not disturb" option, or you'll be plagued with spam calls and spam texts from the phone company.

Indian **mobile** numbers are ten-digit, starting with a 7, 8 or (most commonly) a 9. However, if you are calling from outside the state where the mobile is based (but not from abroad), you need to add a zero in front of that.

Calling an Indian mobile or landline from a UK landline, you can save a lot of money by dialling via a company such as Planet Talk (Ⓦ planet-talk.co.uk), which requires no sign-up but uses an 0843 number, or better still by signing up cost-free with a VoIP provider such as 18185 (Ⓦ 18185.co.uk). In the US you can make cheap calls via reasonable monthly deals on Phone.com (Ⓦ phone.com).

Photography

Beware of pointing your camera at anything that might be considered "strategic", including airports and anything military. Remember too that some people prefer not to be photographed, so it's a good idea to ask before you take a snapshot of them. More likely, you'll get people, especially kids, volunteering to pose and it's quite common for Indians to ask you to be in their snaps. Almost all photo shops can now transfer digital images onto a memory stick or CD – useful in order to free up memory space.

Post

Post can take anything from six days to three weeks to get to or from India, depending on where you are and the country you are posting to; ten days is about the norm. Most **post offices** are open Monday to Friday from 10am to 5pm and Saturday from 10am to noon, but town GPOs keep longer hours (usually Mon–Sat 9.30am–1pm & 2–5.30pm). **Stamps** are not expensive, but you'll have to stick them on yourself

as they tend not to be self-adhesive (every post office keeps a pot of evil-smelling glue for this purpose). Aerogrammes and postcards cost the same to anywhere in the world. Ideally, you should also have mail franked in front of you.

Sending a parcel from India can be a performance. First take it to a tailor to have it wrapped in cheap cotton cloth, stitched up and sealed with wax. Next, take it to the post office, fill in and attach the relevant customs forms, buy your stamps, see them franked and dispatch it. Surface mail is incredibly cheap, and takes an average of six months to arrive – it may take half, or four times that, however. It's a good way to dump excess baggage and souvenirs, but don't send anything fragile this way.

Sexism and women's issues

India is not a country that provides huge obstacles to women travellers. In the days of the Raj, many upper-class women travelled through India alone, as did the female flower children of the hippie era. Plenty of women travel solo today, but few get through their trip without any hassle, so it's good to be prepared.

Indian streets are often dominated by male groups – something that may take a bit of getting used to, particularly if you find yourself subjected to incessant staring, whistling and name calling. This can usually be stopped by ignoring the gaze and quickly moving on, or by firmly telling the offender to stop looking at you. Most of your fellow travellers on trains and buses will be men, who may start up most unwelcome conversations about sex, divorce and the freedom of relationships in the West. These cannot often be avoided, but demonstrating too much enthusiasm to discuss such topics can lure men into thinking that you are easy about sex, and the situation could become threatening. At its worst in larger cities, all this can become very tiring. You can get round it to a certain extent by joining women in public places, and you'll notice an immense difference if you join up with a male travelling companion. In this case, expect Indian men to approach him (assumed, of course, to be your husband – an assumption it is sometimes advantageous to go along with) and talk to him about you quite happily as if you were not there. Beware, however, if you are (or look) of Indian origin with a non-Indian male companion: this may well cause you harassment, as you might be seen to have brought shame on your family by adopting the loose morals of the West.

In addition to staring and suggestive comments and looks, **sexual harassment**, or "Eve teasing" as it is bizarrely known, is likely to be a nuisance, but not generally a threat. It's not unlikely that you will get groped in crowds and not unusual to have men "accidentally" squeeze past you at any opportunity. It tends to be worse in cities than in small towns and villages, but being followed can be a real problem wherever you are.

In time you'll learn to gauge a situation – sometimes wandering around on your own may attract so much unwanted attention that you may prefer to stay in one place until you've recharged your batteries or your male fan club has moved on. It's always best to dress modestly – a *salwar kameez* is perfect, as is any baggy clothing – and, with the exception of one or two cosmopolitan areas of Mumbai, refrain from smoking or drinking in public.

If a loud, firm "no" fails to have the desired effect, returning an unwanted touch with a punch or slap is perfectly in order (Indian women often become aggressive when offended), and does serve to vent a little frustration. It should also attract attention and urge someone to help you, or at least deal with the offending man – a man transgressing social norms is always out of line and any passer-by will want to let him know it.

Going to watch a Bollywood movie at the cinema is a fun and essential part of your trip to India but, at cheap cinemas especially, such an occasion is rarely without hassle. If you do go to the cinema, it's best to go to an upmarket theatre, or at least to go with a group of people and sit in the balcony area, where it's a bit more expensive but the crowd is much more sedate.

Violent sexual assaults on tourists are extremely rare but the number of reported cases of rape is slowly rising – an Irish girl was gang-raped and strangled in Goa in March 2017. Consequently you should always take precautions: avoid quiet, dimly lit streets and alleys at night, as well as remote rural locations; if you find a trustworthy rickshaw/taxi driver in the day keep him for the night journey; and try to get someone to accompany you to your hotel whenever possible. While Indian women are still quite timid about reporting rape – it is considered as much a disgrace to the victim as to the perpetrator – Western victims should always report it to the police. Letting other tourists, or locals, know of any incident in the hope that pressure from the community may uncover the offender and see him brought to justice is also likely to be effective.

The **practicalities of travel** take on a new dimension for lone women travellers. In hotels watch out for "peep-holes" in your door (and in common bathrooms), and be sure to cover your window when changing and when sleeping. Often, though, you can turn your gender to your advantage. For example, on inter-city buses the driver and conductor will often take you under their wing, and there will be countless other instances of kindness wherever you travel. You'll be more welcome in some private houses than a group of Western males, and may find yourself learning the finer points of Indian cooking around the family's clay stove. Women frequently get preference at bus and railway stations where they can join a separate "ladies' queue", and use ladies' waiting rooms. On trains the enclosed ladies' compartments are peaceful havens (unless filled with noisy children); you could also try to share a berth section with a family where you are usually drawn into the security of the group and are less exposed to staring.

Lastly, bring your own supply of **tampons**, which are not widely available outside main cities.

Time

India is all in one time zone and remains the same year round: GMT+5hr 30min. This makes it 5hr 30min ahead of London, 10hr 30min ahead of New York, 13hr 30min ahead of LA, 4hr 30min behind Sydney and 6hr 30min behind New Zealand; however, daylight saving time in those places will change the difference by an hour. Indian time is referred to as IST (Indian Standard Time, which cynics refer to as "Indian stretchable time").

Tipping and baksheesh

As a well-off visitor you'll be expected to be liberal with your **tips**. Low-paid workers in **hotels and restaurants** often accept lower pay than they should in the expectation of generous tips during the tourist season. Ten percent, or a simple rounding up, should be regarded as acceptable if you've received good service – more if the staff have really gone out of their way to be helpful. **Taxi and auto-rickshaw drivers** will not expect tips unless you've made unplanned diversions or stops. What to tip your driver at the end of long tours, however, is a trickier issue, especially if you've been forking out ₹150–200 for their daily allowance, as well as paying for meals. The simple answer is to give what you think they deserve, and what you can afford. Drivers working for tour operators, even more than hotel staff and waiters, depend on tips to get through the off-season (many are paid only ₹200–300 per day because their bosses know that foreign customers tend to tip well).

Alms giving (baksheesh) is common throughout India; people with disabilities and mutilations often congregate in city centres and popular resorts, where they survive from begging. In such cases a few coins up to ₹10–20 should be sufficient. Kids demanding money, pens, sweets or the like are a different case: yielding to any request only encourages them to pester others.

Toilets

Western-style toilets are much more common in India now, especially in hotels and lodges in touristy areas, though you'll probably still come across a few traditional "squat" toilets – basically a hole in the ground. Paper, if used, often goes in a bucket next to the loo rather than down it. Instead, Indians use a jug of water and their left hand or the hose provided, a method you may also come to prefer, but if you do use paper, keep some handy, especially if staying in basic accommodation or going too far off the beaten track. Travelling is especially difficult for women as facilities are limited or nonexistent, especially when travelling by road rather than by rail. However, toilets in the a/c carriages of trains are usually kept clean, as are those in mid-range and air-conditioned restaurants. The latest development is tourist toilets at every major historical site. For ₹5 you get water, mirrors, toilet paper and a clean sit-down loo.

Tourist information

The main tourist website for India is ⓦincredibleindia.org. The Indian government also maintains a number of **tourist offices abroad**, whose staff are usually helpful and knowledgeable; addresses and contact details can be found on ⓦbit.ly/IndiaTourismoffices. Other sources of information include the websites of Indian embassies and tourist offices, travel agents (who are in business for themselves, so their advice may not always be totally unbiased), and Indian Railways representatives abroad.

Inside India, both national and local governments run tourist information offices, providing general travel advice and handing out an array of printed material, from city maps to glossy leaflets on specific destinations. The Indian government's tourist department, whose main southern office is opposite Churchgate railway station in Mumbai (see p.93), has branches in most regional capitals. These, however, operate independently of the state government information counters and their commercial bureaus are run by the state tourism development corporations, usually referred to by their initials (e.g. KTDC in Kerala, TTDC in Tamil Nadu, and so on), which offer a wide range of travel facilities, including guided tours, car rental and their own hotels. A list of state tourist office websites is given below.

Just to confuse things further, the Indian government's tourist office has a corporate wing, too. The Indian Tourism Development Corporation (ITDC) is responsible for the *Ashok* chain of hotels and operates tour and travel services, frequently competing with its state counterparts.

There's all sorts of information available about India **online** – we've listed the best websites in relevant places throughout the Guide. One particularly good general site is ⓦindiamike.com, which features lively chat rooms, bulletin boards, photo archives and banks of members' travel articles.

TRAVEL ADVICE

Australian Department of Foreign Affairs ⓦ smartraveller.gov.au.
Canadian Department of Foreign Affairs ⓦ voyage.gc.ca.
Irish Department of Foreign Affairs ⓦ dfa.ie.
New Zealand Ministry of Foreign Affairs ⓦ safetravel.govt.nz.
South African Department of Foreign Affairs ⓦ www.dirco.gov.za.
UK Foreign & Commonwealth Office ⓦ fco.gov.uk.
US State Department ⓦ travel.state.gov.

STATE TOURISM WEBSITES

Andaman and Nicobar Islands ⓦ go2andaman.com.
Andhra Pradesh ⓦ aptdc.gov.in.
Goa ⓦ goa-tourism.com.
Karnataka ⓦ karnatakatourism.org.
Kerala ⓦ keralatourism.org.
Lakshadweep ⓦ lakshadweeptourism.nic.in.
Maharashtra ⓦ maharashtratourism.gov.in.
Puducherry ⓦ tourism.puducherry.gov.in.
Tamil Nadu ⓦ tamilnadutourism.org.
Telangana ⓦ telanganatourism.gov.in.

Travellers with disabilities

Disability is common in India; many conditions that would be curable in the West, such as cataracts, are permanent disabilities here because people can't afford the treatment. Those with disabilities are unlikely to receive the best treatment available, and the choice is usually between staying at home to be looked after by your family and going out on the street to beg for alms.

For **travellers with a disability**, this has its advantages and disadvantages. Disability doesn't get the same embarrassed reaction from Indian people that it does from some able-bodied Westerners. On the other hand, you'll be lucky to see a state-of-the-art wheelchair or a disabled loo, and the streets are full of all sorts of obstacles that would be hard for a blind or wheelchair-bound tourist to negotiate independently. Kerbs are often high, pavements uneven and littered, and ramps nonexistent. There are potholes all over the place and open sewers. Some of the more expensive hotels have ramps for the movement of luggage and equipment, but if that makes them accessible to wheelchairs, it is by accident rather than design. Nonetheless, the 1995 Persons with Disabilities Act specifies access for all to public buildings, and is sometimes enforced. These days at least, most major Indian airports and metro systems have been made a lot more accessible for chair users.

If you walk with difficulty, you will find India's many street obstacles and steep stairs hard going. Another factor that can be a problem is the constant barrage of people proffering things (hard to wave aside if you are, for instance, on crutches), and all that queueing, not to mention heat, will take it out of you if you have a condition that makes you tire quickly. A light, folding camp-stool is one thing that could be invaluable if you have limited walking or standing power.

Then again, Indian people are likely to be very helpful if, for example, you need their help getting on and off buses or up stairs. Taxis and rickshaws are easily affordable and very adaptable; if you rent one for a day, the driver is certain to help you on and off, and perhaps even around the sites you visit. If you employ a guide, they may also be prepared to help you with steps and obstacles.

If complete independence is out of the question, going with an able-bodied companion might be on the cards. There are some specialist operators for tourists with limited mobility – Enable Holidays (Ⓦ enableholidays.com) offers a good "Golden Triangle" tour, for example – and some mainstream package-tour operators try to cater for travellers with disabilities, but you should always contact any operator and discuss your exact needs with them

before making a booking. You should also make sure you are covered by any insurance policy you take out.

For more information about disability issues in India, check the government website Ⓦ disability affairs.gov.in.

Volunteering

It is illegal for a foreign tourist to work in India, although some obtain a business visa to work in EFL teaching, business or high-tech. Many visitors, however, do engage in some voluntary charitable work. Several charities welcome volunteers on a medium-term commitment, say over two months, but many places also welcome much shorter-term, less formal involvement. As well as the list below, other local organizations are mentioned throughout the book.

If you want to spend your time working as a volunteer for an **NGO** (non-governmental organization), you should make arrangements well before you arrive by contacting the body in question, rather than on spec. Special visas are generally not required unless you intend to work for longer than six months. For information about which NGOs are operating across the country, log on to Ⓦ csridentity.com/india/index.asp and select options from a drop-down list, or see what's available through the worldwide VSO organization at Ⓦ vsointernational.org.

VOLUNTEERING RESOURCES

Concern India Foundation Ⓦ concernindiafoundation.org. Charitable trust supporting grassroots NGOs working with disadvantaged people, with offices in seven cities.

Goa Animal Welfare Trust (GAWT) Ⓦ gawt.org. GAWT does sterling work with stray and mistreated animals, and welcomes volunteers in centres around Goa.

Indicorps Ⓦ indicorps.org. US-based charity, contactable in Mumbai, with various projects for people of Indian origin to volunteer on.

Mango Tree Goa Ⓦ mangotreegoa.org. A British-run operation that works with disadvantaged children in Goa.

My Name Is Kumar Ⓦ mynameiskumar.org. Dutch organization providing accommodation and education to children from begging communities in Tamil Nadu. Occasional volunteers needed.

Mumbai

73 Colaba

75 Kala Ghoda and around

77 Fort

80 Central Bazaar District

81 Marine Drive

82 Malabar Hill

82 Central Mumbai: Mahalakshmi to Byculla

86 Gorai

87 Elephanta

CHHATRAPATI SHIVAJI TERMINUS (VICTORIA TERMINUS)

1

Mumbai

Ever since the opening of the Suez Canal in 1869, the principal gateway to the Indian Subcontinent has been Mumbai (Bombay), the city Aldous Huxley famously described as "the most appalling of either hemisphere". Travellers tend to regard time spent here as a rite of passage to be survived rather than savoured. But as the powerhouse of Indian business, industry and trade, and the source of its most seductive media images, the Maharashtrian capital can be a compelling place to kill time. Whether or not you find the experience enjoyable, however, will depend largely on how well you handle the heat, humidity, traffic fumes and relentless crowds of India's most dynamic, Westernized city.

First impressions of Mumbai tend to be dominated by its chronic shortage of space. Crammed onto a narrow spit of land that curls from the swamp-ridden coast into the Arabian Sea, the city is technically an island, connected to the mainland by bridges and narrow causeways. In less than five hundred years, it has metamorphosed from an aboriginal fishing settlement into a megalopolis of more than sixteen million people – India's largest city and one of the biggest urban sprawls on the planet. Being swept along broad boulevards by endless streams of commuters, or jostled by coolies and hand-cart pullers in the teeming bazaars, you'll continually feel as if Mumbai is about to burst at the seams.

The roots of the population problem and attendant poverty lie, paradoxically, in the city's enduring ability to create wealth. Mumbai alone generates one third of India's tax income, its port handles half the country's foreign trade, and its movie industry is the most prolific in the world. Symbols of prosperity are everywhere: from the phalanx of office blocks clustered on Nariman Point, Maharashtra's Manhattan, to the expensively dressed teenagers posing in Colaba's trendiest nightspots.

The flip side to the success story is the city's much-chronicled poverty. Each day, an estimated five hundred economic refugees pour into Mumbai from the Maharashtrian hinterland. Some find jobs and secure accommodation; many more end up living on the already overcrowded streets, or amid the squalor of some of Asia's largest slums, reduced to rag-picking and begging from cars at traffic lights.

However, while it would definitely be misleading to downplay its difficulties, Mumbai is far from the ordeal some travellers make it out to be. Once you've overcome the major hurdle of finding somewhere to stay, you may begin to enjoy its frenzied pace and crowded, cosmopolitan feel.

Nowhere reinforces your sense of having arrived in Mumbai quite as emphatically as the **Gateway of India**, the city's defining landmark. Only a five-minute walk north, the **Prince of Wales Museum** should be next on your list of sightseeing priorities, as much for its flamboyantly eclectic architecture as for the art treasures inside. The museum

---

BEST TIME TO VISIT

As a coastal city, the temperature in Mumbai hovers around 30°C for much of the year; the weather is most pleasant from October to March, when it's not too humid. If possible, avoid visiting the city during April and May when it's particularly hot and humid, and during the monsoon (June–Sept), which often causes flooding in the low-lying areas and disruptions to public transport.

CRICKET AT THE OVAL MAIDAN

Highlights

❶ The Gateway of India Mumbai's defining landmark, and a favourite spot for an evening stroll. **See p.73**

❷ Chhatrapati Shivaji Museum A fine collection of priceless Indian art, from ancient temple sculpture to Mughal armour. **See p.76**

❸ Maidans (parks) Where Mumbai's citizens escape the hustle and bustle to play cricket, eat lunch and hang out. **See p.77**

❹ CS (Victoria) Terminus A fantastically eccentric pile, and the greatest railway station ever built by the British. **See p.80**

❺ Haji Ali's Tomb Mingle with the crowds of Muslim worshippers who flock to the island tomb of Sufi mystic Haji Ali to listen to *qawwali* music on Thursday evenings. **See p.84**

❻ Elephanta Island Catch a boat across Mumbai harbour to see one of ancient India's most wonderful rock-cut Shiva temples. **See p.87**

❼ Bollywood blockbusters Check out the latest Hindi mega-movie in one of the city centre's gigantic Art Deco cinemas. **See p.101**

HIGHLIGHTS ARE MARKED ON THE MAP ON P.70

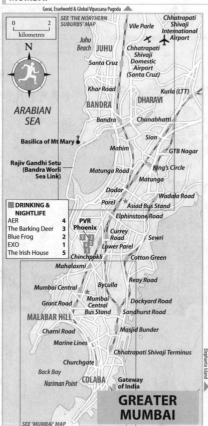

GREATER MUMBAI

SEE 'MUMBAI' MAP

Mandwa & Alibag ▼

DRINKING & NIGHTLIFE

AER	4
The Barking Deer	3
Blue Frog	2
EXO	1
The Irish House	5

provides a foretaste of what lies in store just up the road, where the cream of Bartle Frere's Bombay – the **University** and **High Court** – line up with the open maidans on one side, and the boulevards of **Fort** on the other. But for the fullest sense of why the city's founding fathers declared it Urbs Prima in Indis, you should press further north still to visit the **Chhatrapati Shivaji Terminus (CST)**, the high-water mark of India's Raj architecture.

Beyond CST lie the crowded bazaars and Muslim neighbourhoods of **central Mumbai**, at their liveliest and most colourful around **Crawford Market** and **Mohammed Ali Road**. Possibilities for an escape from the crowds include an evening stroll along **Marine Drive**, bounding the western edge of downtown, or a boat trip out to **Elephanta**, a rock-cut cave on an island in Mumbai harbour containing a wealth of ancient art.

Brief history

Mumbai originally consisted of seven **islands**, inhabited by small Koli fishing communities. In 1534, Sultan Bahadur of Ahmedabad ceded the land to the **Portuguese**, who subsequently handed it on to the English in 1661 as part of the Portuguese Infanta Catherine of Braganza's dowry during her marriage to Charles II. Bombay's safe harbour and strategic commercial position attracted the interest of the **East India Company**, based at Surat to the north, and in 1668 a deal was struck whereby they leased Bombay from Charles for a pittance.

Life for the English was not easy, however: "fluxes" (dysentery), "Chinese death" (cholera) and other diseases culled many of the first settlers, prompting the colony's chaplain to declare that "two monsoons are the age of a man". Nevertheless, the city

---

FESTIVALS IN MUMBAI

Kala Ghoda Arts Festival (Feb). The country's largest multicultural festival is held across nine days, with hundreds of events covering literature, performing and visual arts, among many other things.

Elephanta Festival (Feb/March). Two- to three-day festival that sees classical Indian dance performed against the backdrop of the eponymous caves.

Ganesh Chaturthi (Aug/Sept). Ten days celebrating the beloved elephant-headed god Ganesha: street processions, loud music and lots of dancing culminate in idols of the god being immersed in the sea on the final day.

Krishna Janmashtami (Aug). The birthday of Lord Krishna sees mass celebrations in the city, including special decorations and chanting of hymns at temples and homes, and *rangoli* (colourful floor designs).

MUMBAI OR BOMBAY?

In 1996 Bombay was renamed **Mumbai**, as part of a wider policy instigated by the right-wing Maharashtrian nationalist Shiv Sena Municipality to replace names of any places, roads and features in the city that had connotations of the Raj. The Shiv Sena asserted that the British term "Bombay" derived from the Marathi title of a local deity, Mumba Devi (see p.81). In fact, historians are unanimously agreed that the Portuguese, who dubbed the harbour "Bom Bahia" ("Good Bay") when they first came across it, were responsible for christening the site and that the later British moniker had nothing to do with the aboriginal Hindu earth goddess.

The name change was widely unpopular when it was first imposed, especially among the upper and middle classes, and non-Maharashtrian immigrant communities, who doggedly stuck to Bombay. A couple of decades on, however, "Mumbai" seems to have definitively taken root with the dotcom generation and even outgrown the narrow agenda of its nationalist originators – just as "Bombay" outlived the Raj.

established itself as the capital of the flourishing East India Company, attracting a diverse mix of settlers including Goans, Gujarati traders, Muslim weavers and the business-minded Zoroastrian Parsis. The export crisis in America following the Civil War fuelled the great Bombay **cotton boom** and established the city as a major industrial and commercial centre, while the opening of the Suez Canal in 1869 and the construction of enormous docks further improved Bombay's access to European markets, ushering in an age of mercantile self-confidence embodied by the grandiloquent colonial-Gothic buildings constructed during the governorship of **Sir Bartle Frere** (1862–67).

As the most prosperous city in the nation, Bombay was at the forefront of the **Independence** struggle; Mahatma Gandhi used a house here, now a museum, to coordinate the struggle through three decades. Fittingly, the first British colony took pleasure in waving the final goodbye to the Raj, when the last contingent of British troops passed through the Gateway of India in February 1948. Since Independence, Mumbai has prospered as India's commercial capital and the population has grown tenfold, to more than sixteen million, although the modern city has also been plagued by a deadly mixture of **communal infighting** and **terrorist attacks**.

Tensions due to the increasing numbers of immigrants from other parts of the country, and the resultant overcrowding, has fuelled the rise of the extreme right-wing Maharashtrian party, the **Shiv Sena**, founded in 1966 by Bal Thackeray, whose death and cremation in 2012 brought the state to a standstill.

Thousands of Muslim Mumbaikars were murdered by Hindu mobs following the destruction of the Babri Masjid in Ayodhya in 1992–93, while in March 1993, ten massive retaliatory **bomb blasts** killed 260 people. The involvement of Muslim godfather Dawood Ibrahim and the Pakistani secret service was suspected, and both Ibrahim and the Pakistanis have been linked with subsequent atrocities. These include the bomb blasts in August 2003, which killed 107 tourists next to the **Gateway of India**; the subsequent explosions in July 2006, when coordinated bomb blasts simultaneously blew apart seven packed commuter trains across the city; and, most dramatically, the horrific attacks of **November 26, 2008**, when a group of rampaging gunmen ran amok across the city, killing 166 people.

Despite these setbacks, Mumbai has prospered like nowhere else in India as a result of the country's ongoing **economic liberalization**. Following decades of stagnation, the textiles industry has been supplanted by rapidly growing IT, finance, healthcare and back-office support sectors. Whole suburbs have sprung up to accommodate the affluent new middle-class workforce, with shiny shopping malls and car showrooms to relieve them of their income. Even so, corruption in politics and business has drained away investment from socially deprived areas. Luxury apartments in Bandra may change hands for half a million dollars or more, but an estimated seven to eight million

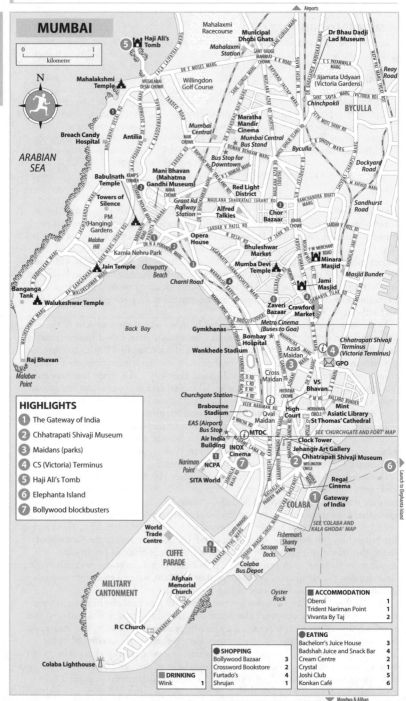

MUMBAI

0 — 1
kilometre

N

ARABIAN SEA

Mahalaxmi Racecourse

Municipal Dhobi Ghats

Dr Bhau Dadji Lad Museum

BYCULLA

Mahalaxmi Station

Chinchpokli

Jijamata Udyaan (Victoria Gardens)

Haji Ali's Tomb

Mahalakshmi Temple

Willingdon Golf Course

Breach Candy Hospital

Antilia

Mumbai Central

Maratha Mandir Cinema

Mumbai Central Bus Stand

Byculla

Dockyard Road

Sandhurst Road

Babulnath Temple

Towers of Silence

Mani Bhavan (Mahatma Gandhi Museum)

Bus Stop for Downtown

Red Light District

Alfred Talkies

Chor Bazaar

PM (Hanging) Gardens

Grant Rd Railway Station

Opera House

Bhuleshwar Market

Minara Masjid

Masjid Bunder

Malabar Hill

Kamla Nehru Park

Mumba Devi Temple

Jami Masjid

Jain Temple

Chowpatty Beach

Charni Road

Zaveri Bazaar

Crawford Market

Banganga Tank

Walukeshwar Temple

Back Bay

Gymkhanas

Metro Cinema (Buses to Goa)

Chhatrapati Shivaji Terminus (Victoria Terminus)

Bombay Hospital

Azad Maidan

GPO

Wankhede Stadium

Cross Maidan

VS Bhavan

Malabar Point

Raj Bhavan

Churchgate Station

Brabourne Stadium

Oval Maidan

High Court

Mint

Asiatic Library

St Thomas' Cathedral

SEE 'CHURCHGATE AND FORT' MAP

EAS (Airport) Bus Stop

Air India Building

MTDC

Clock Tower

Jehangir Art Gallery

INOX Cinema

Nariman Point

NCPA

Chhatrapati Shivaji Museum

Launch to Elephanta Island

SITA World

Regal Cinema

Gateway of India

COLABA

SEE 'COLABA AND KALA GHODA' MAP

World Trade Centre

CUFFE PARADE

Fisherman's Shanty Town

Sassoon Docks

Afghan Memorial Church

Colaba Bus Depot

MILITARY CANTONMENT

Oyster Rock

R C Church

Colaba Lighthouse

Mandwa & Alibag

Airports

HIGHLIGHTS

1. The Gateway of India
2. Chhatrapati Shivaji Museum
3. Maidans (parks)
4. CS (Victoria) Terminus
5. Haji Ali's Tomb
6. Elephanta Island
7. Bollywood blockbusters

ACCOMMODATION
Oberoi	1
Trident Nariman Point	1
Vivanta By Taj	2

EATING
Bachelorr's Juice House	3
Badshah Juice and Snack Bar	4
Cream Centre	2
Crystal	1
Joshi Club	5
Konkan Café	6

SHOPPING
Bollywood Bazaar	3
Crossword Bookstore	2
Furtado's	4
Shrujan	1

DRINKING
Wink	1

people (just under fifty percent of Mumbai's population) live in slums with no toilets, on just six percent of the land.

Colaba

Mumbai's main tourist enclave is the district of **Colaba**, at the far southern end of the peninsula. Even though it's a long, sweaty drive from the airport and far from representative of the city as a whole, most visitors base themselves in the neighbourhood and rarely venture beyond it. As the home of the super-swanky *Taj Mahal Palace* hotel, as well as some of the city's trendiest bars and restaurants, Colaba certainly has its glamorous side. But the dimly lit streets between its dozen or so blocks of dilapidated colonial tenements are also awash with junkies and touts, and after a day of being hissed at from doorways by sellers of "brown sugar" most people head for the bazaars and brighter lights of uptown.

The Gateway of India

Commemorating the visit of King George V and Queen Mary in 1911, India's own honey-coloured Arc de Triomphe, the **Gateway of India**, is Colaba's principal monument and the landmark most iconic of Mumbai in the Indian imagination. Featured in countless Bollywood movies, it was built in 1924 by George Wittet, whose brief was to combine the grandeur of a Roman triumphal arch with decorative motifs from Hindu and Muslim architecture. The resulting structure, every bit a symbol of "power and majesty", was originally intended to be a ceremonial disembarkation point for passengers alighting from the P&O steamers, but is, ironically, more closely associated with the moment in August 1947 when, amid much pomp and ceremony, the last remaining British soldiers on Indian soil slowly marched to their waiting troop ship as the Union Jack was lowered – to euphoric cheers from a vast crowd. The hour around sunset when thousands of visitors mill about the archway and plaza, munching *bhel puri* and having their photos taken, is the best time to visit.

The Taj Mahal Palace and Tower

Apollo Bunder

Local pride in the face of colonial oppression is the subtext of the **Taj Mahal Palace and Tower** complex, directly behind the Gateway. Its patron, the Parsi industrialist J.N. Tata, is said to have built the old *Taj* as an act of revenge after he was refused entry to what was then the best hotel in town, the "whites only" *Watson's*. The ban proved to be its undoing. *Watson's* disappeared long ago, but the *Taj* still presides imperiously over the seafront, the preserve of Mumbai's air-kissing jet set, visiting cricket teams and heads of state. Lesser mortals are allowed in to experience the tea lounge, shopping arcades and vast air-conditioned lobby (there's also a fabulously luxurious loo off the corridor to the left of the main desk).

BOMBAY DUCK

Its name suggests some kind of fowl curry, but **Bombay duck** is actually a fish – to be precise, the marine lizard fish (*Harpalon nehereus*), known in the local dialect of Marathi as *bombil*. How this long, ribbon-like sea creature acquired its English name no one is exactly sure, but the most plausible theory holds that the Raj-era culinary term derives from the Hindustani for mail train, *dak*. The nasty odour of the dried fish is said to have reminded the British of the less salubrious carriages of the Calcutta–Bombay *dak* when it pulled into VT after three days and nights on the rails, its wooden carriages covered in the stinking mould that flourished in the monsoonal humidity.

1

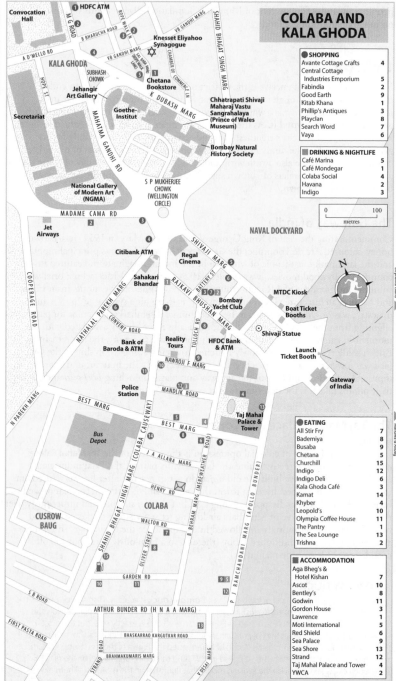

COLABA AND KALA GHODA

SHOPPING
Avante Cottage Crafts	4
Central Cottage Industries Emporium	5
Fabindia	2
Good Earth	9
Kitab Khana	1
Phillip's Antiques	3
Playclan	8
Search Word	7
Vaya	6

DRINKING & NIGHTLIFE
Café Marina	5
Café Mondegar	1
Colaba Social	4
Havana	2
Indigo	3

EATING
All Stir Fry	7
Bademiya	8
Busaba	9
Chetana	5
Churchill	15
Indigo	12
Indigo Deli	6
Kala Ghoda Café	3
Kamat	14
Khyber	4
Leopold's	10
Olympia Coffee House	11
The Pantry	1
The Sea Lounge	13
Trishna	2

ACCOMMODATION
Aga Bheg's & Hotel Kishan	7
Ascot	10
Bentley's	8
Godwin	11
Gordon House	3
Lawrence	1
Moti International	5
Red Shield	6
Sea Palace	9
Sea Shore	13
Strand	12
Taj Mahal Palace and Tower	4
YWCA	2

0   100
metres

Almost as emblematic of Mumbai as the Gateway, the building featured prominently in news coverage of the 2008 terror attacks, in which a team of Islamist jihadis occupied it for three days, killing 31 people. The subsequent refit cost US$40 million and took a year to complete, but has restored the hotel to its glittering former splendour.

Colaba Causeway

Reclaimed in the late nineteenth century from the sea, Colaba's main thoroughfare, **Shahid Bhagat Singh Marg**, better known as **Colaba Causeway**, leads south from the tourist enclave towards the quieter military cantonment area. Few tourists stray much further down it than the claustrophobic hawker zone at the top of the street, whose shops are fronted by a line of covered incense and knick-knack stalls, but it's well worth doing so, if only to see the neighbourhood's earthy **fresh produce market** a couple of blocks south of the Strand cinema.

Sassoon Docks

Mumbai's wholesale seafood market, **Sassoon Docks**, lies a ten-minute walk beyond the southern end of Colaba Causeway. The greasy quaysides are at their liveliest immediately before and after sunrise, when coolies haul the night's catch in crates of crushed ice over gangplanks, while Koli women cluster around the auctioneers. The stench, as overpowering as the noise, comes mostly from bundles of one of the city's traditional exports, **Bombay duck** (see box, p.73). Note that **photography** is strictly forbidden as the docks are adjacent to a sensitive naval area.

Afghan Memorial Church of St John the Baptist

Nanabhai Moos Marg • Buses #3, #11, #47, #103, #123 or #125 from SBS Marg (Colaba)

The **Afghan Memorial Church of St John the Baptist** was built in 1847–54 to commemorate British victims of the ill-fated First Afghan War, in which Elphinstone's expeditionary force was famously wiped out while trying to withdraw from Kabul down a tunnel of gorges to Jalalabad. Of the 16,500 troops and camp followers who set out on January 1, 1842, only forty survived the massacre, and only one British solider – William Brydon – arrived alive (a trickle of sepoys and one Greek civilian also made it back a couple of days later). The battle-scarred colours of the 44th Regiment of Foot, which provided the bulk of the British contingent, are among those displayed inside the church. Memorial plaques of coloured marble line the walls of the chancels, listing officers killed in action during the conflict.

Kala Ghoda and around

Immediately north of Colaba, **Kala Ghoda** ("Black Horse") district is named after the large equestrian statue of King Edward VII that formerly stood on the crescent-shaped intersection of MG Road and Subhash Chowk. Flanked by Mumbai's principal museum and art galleries, the neighbourhood has in recent years been rebranded as a "cultural enclave" – as much in an attempt to preserve its many historic buildings as to promote the contemporary visual arts that have thrived here since the 1950s. Fancy stainless-steel interpretive panels now punctuate the district's walkways, and on Sundays in December and January, the **Kala Ghoda Fair** sees portrait artists, potters and *mehendi* painters plying their trade in the car park fronting the Jehangir Art Gallery.

1

Chhatrapati Shivaji Museum

MG Rd • Daily 10.15am–6pm • ₹500 (₹70), phone camera ₹40, camera ₹200, video camera ₹1000 – no tripods or flash • ⓦ csmvs.in

The **Prince of Wales Museum of Western India**, or **Chhatrapati Shivaji Maharaj Vastu Sangrahalaya** as it was renamed by the Shiv Sena, ranks among the city's most distinctive Raj-era constructions. It stands rather grandly in its own gardens off MG Road, crowned by a massive white Mughal-style dome, beneath which one of India's finest collections of paintings and sculpture is arrayed on three floors. The building was designed by George Wittet, of Gateway of India fame, and stands as the epitome of the hybrid **Indo-Saracenic** style – regarded in its day as an "educated" interpretation of fifteenth- and sixteenth-century Gujarati architecture, mixing Islamic touches with typically English municipal brickwork.

The foreigners' ticket price includes an **audio tour**, which you collect at the admissions kiosk inside, though you'll probably find it does little to enhance your visit. The heat and humidity inside the building can also be a trial. To exit the museum and re-enter (which you're entitled to do) you'll have to get your ticket stamped in the admissions lobby first.

Ground floor

The **Key Gallery** in the central hall of the **ground floor** provides a snapshot of the collection's treasures, including the fifth-century-AD stucco Buddhist figures unearthed by archeologist Henry Cousens in 1909. The main **sculpture room** in the east wing displays other fourth- and fifth-century Buddhist artefacts, mostly from the former Greek colony of Gandhara. Important Hindu sculptures include a seventh-century Chalukyan bas-relief depicting Brahma seated on a lotus, and a sensuously carved torso of Mahisasuramardini, the goddess Durga, with tripod raised ready to skewer the demon buffalo.

Upper floors

The main attraction on the **first floor** has to be the museum's famous collection of **Indian painting**, which includes works from the Mughal emperors' private collections. More fine medieval miniatures are housed in the **Karl & Meherbai Khandalavala Gallery**, on the renovated east wing of this floor, along with priceless pieces of Ghandaran sculpture, Chola bronzes and some of the country's finest surviving examples of medieval Gujarati woodcarving. Indian **coins** are the subject of the **House of Laxmi Gallery**, also in the east wing, while the **second floor** showcases a vast array of Oriental ceramics and glassware. Finally, among the grisly **weapons** and pieces of armour stored in a small side gallery at the top of the building, look out for the cuirass, helmet and jade dagger which belonged to the Mughal emperor Akbar.

Jehangir Art Gallery

MG Rd • Daily 11am–7pm • Free

Technically in the same compound as the Prince of Wales Museum, though approached from further up MG Road, the **Jehangir Art Gallery** is Mumbai's longest-established venue for contemporary art, with five small halls specializing in twentieth-century arts and crafts from around the world. You never know what you're going to find – most exhibitions last only a week and exhibits are often for sale.

National Gallery of Modern Art

MG Rd, facing the museum and Mukharji Chowk • Tues–Sun 10am–5pm • ₹500 (₹20) • ⓦ ngmaindia.gov.in

Charting the development of modern Indian art from its beginnings in the 1950s to the present day, the **National Gallery of Modern Art (NGMA)** holds a mix of permanent and temporary exhibitions. The works are arrayed over five wonderfully light, semicircular galleries, interconnected by teak-and-chrome staircases. The installations, in particular, tend to be a lot more adventurous than those you'll find in the Jehangir across the road.

Around Oval Maidan

1

Northeast of Kala Ghoda stretches the yawning expanse of **Oval Maidan**, where impromptu cricket matches are held almost every day, against a backdrop of giant palms and even taller Raj-era buildings. Green during the monsoons and parched yellow for the rest of year, it is flanked on its eastern side by some of Mumbai's finest Victorian piles, dating from the high point of British power. The travel writer Robert Byron famously described them as forming an "architectural Sodom", claiming that "the nineteenth century devised nothing lower than the municipal buildings of British India. Their ugliness is positively daemonic". Today, however, they appear not so much ugly as intriguing.

High Court
Karmaveer Bhaurao Patil Marg

Dominating the east side of Oval Maidan is the **Mumbai High Court**, originally the Old Secretariat, which the Raj historian G.W. Forrest described in 1903 "a massive pile whose main features have been brought from Venice, but all the beauty has vanished in trans-shipment". With its gigantic pitched roofs and balconies shaded by enormous rattan blinds, the building has changed little since. Take a peek inside, where lawyers in black gowns, striped trousers and white tabs bustle up and down the staircases, and office desks are piled high with dusty beribboned bundles of documents – a vision of Indian bureaucracy at its most Dickensian.

Mumbai University
MG Rd

Across AS D'Mello Road from the High Court stand the two major buildings comprising **Mumbai University** (established 1857), which were designed in England by Sir Gilbert Scott, architect of the Gothic extravaganza that is London's St Pancras railway station. Funded by the Parsi philanthropist Cowasjee "Readymoney" Jehangir, whose white marble statue appears in front of it, the **Convocation Hall** greatly resembles a church. Above the entrance, a huge circular stained-glass window features a wheel with spokes of Greek pilasters separating the signs of the zodiac. With all its polished teak and brass, the interior, currently closed to visitors for security reasons, could have been transported from a Victorian public school in the home counties of England. Gilbert Scott's 79.2m-high **Rajabhai Clock Tower** is said to have been modelled on Giotto's campanile in Florence and formerly chimed tunes such as *Rule Britannia* and *Home Sweet Home*.

Fort

East of Oval Maidan stretches the spectacular **Fort** district, site of Mumbai's original British settlement and the first East India Company fort – hence the name. The sloping ramparts, moats and fortified gateways were pulled down in the mid-nineteenth century following the demise of the French threat to British supremacy in India, but this is still the commercial hub of the southern city. It's a great area for aimless wandering, with plenty of old-fashioned cafés, department stores and street stalls crammed in between the imposing Victorian buildings.

Horniman Circle

At the heart of the Fort district lies the spacious **Horniman Circle**, conceived in 1860 as the centrepiece of a newly planned Bombay by the then Municipal Commissioner, Charles Forjett, on the site of Bombay's "Green". Later, the space served as a cotton market and parade ground. The garden's wrought-iron gates and fences enclose a haven of vegetation where office workers bring their lunches and newspapers. Surrounding it

1

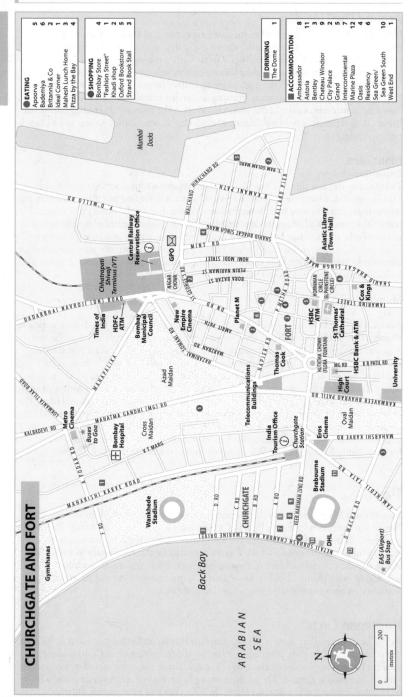

CHURCHGATE AND FORT

● EATING
Apoorva	5
Bademiya	6
Britannia & Co	2
Ideal Corner	1
Mahesh Lunch Home	3
Pizza by the Bay	4

■ SHOPPING
Bombay Store	4
"Fashion Street"	1
Khadi shop	5
Oxford Bookstore	2
Strand Book Stall	3

■ DRINKING
The Dome	1

■ ACCOMMODATION
Ambassador	8
Astoria	11
Bentley	3
Chateau Windsor	9
City Palace	2
Grand	5
Intercontinental	7
Marine Plaza	12
Oasis	4
Residency	6
Sea Green/	
Sea Green South	10
West End	1

1

are ranks of grand buildings whose paved arcades, crowned by grim-faced keystone heads, today provide accommodation for families of street sleepers.

The Asiatic Society Library

Shahid Bhagat Singh Marg • Mon–Sat 10.30am–6pm • ☎ 022 2266 0956, ⓦ asiaticsociety.org.in

The splendid Neoclassical building on the east side of Horniman Circle served as the city's former Town Hall, one of the few buildings in Mumbai that pleased Aldous Huxley: "(Among) so many architectural cads and pretentious bounders," he wrote in 1948, "it is almost the only gentleman." The Doric edifice, dating from 1833, was originally built to house the vast collection of the **Asiatic Society Library**, which is still open to the public. Save for the addition of electricity, little has changed here since the institution was founded. Reading rooms, lined with wrought-iron loggias and teak bookcases, are filled with scholars poring over mouldering tomes dating from the Raj. Among the ten thousand rare and valuable manuscripts stored here is a fourteenth-century first edition of Dante's *Divine Comedy*, said to be worth around US$3 million, which the Society famously refused to sell to Mussolini. Visitors are welcome but should sign in at the Head Librarian's desk on the ground floor.

St Thomas' Cathedral

Veer Nariman Rd • Daily 7am–6pm

Just west off Horniman Circle stands the diminutive **St Thomas' Cathedral**, reckoned to be the oldest British building in Mumbai, blending Classical and Gothic styles. After

---

DABBAWALAS

Mumbai's size and inconvenient shape create all kind of hassles for its working population. One thing the daily tidal wave of commuters does not have to worry about, however, is where to find an inexpensive and wholesome home-cooked lunch. The members of the **Nutan Mumbai Tiffin Box Suppliers Charity Trust (NMTSCT)**, known colloquially as "**dabbawalas**", see to that. Every day, around 5000 dabbawalas deliver freshly cooked meals from 200,000 suburban kitchens to offices in the downtown area. Each is prepared early in the morning by a wife or mother while her husband or son is enduring the crush on the train. She arranges the rice, dhal, *subzi*, curd and *parathas* into cylindrical aluminium trays, stacks them on top of one another and clips them together with a neat little handle.

This **tiffin box** is the linchpin of the whole operation. When the runner calls to collect it in the morning, he uses a special colour code on the lid to tell him where the lunch has to go. At the end of his round, all the boxes are carried to the nearest railway station and handed over to other dabbawalas for the trip into town. Between leaving the cook and reaching its final destination, the tiffin box will pass through at least half a dozen different pairs of hands, carried on heads, shoulder-poles, bicycle handlebars and in the brightly decorated handcarts that glide with such insouciance through the midday traffic.

WHERE TO FIND THEM

To catch them in action, head for **CST (VT)** or **Churchgate** stations around late morning, when the tiffin boxes arrive in the city centre to a chorus of "*lafka! lafka*" – "hurry! hurry!" – as the dabbawalas rush to make their lunch-hour deadlines. Nearly all come from the same small village near Pune and are related to one another. They collect around ₹2000–4000 per month in total.

One of the reasons the system survives in the face of competition from trendy fast-food outlets is that dabba lunches still work out a good deal cheaper, saving precious rupees for the middle-income workers who use the system. Competition has recently arisen from high-end takeaway joints in Mumbai, some of whom offer freshly prepared gourmet food delivered in tiffin tins. But the dabbawalas are not sitting on their heels in the face of the new competition, with a website (ⓦ mumbaidabbawala.in) to facilitate booking online and by SMS. An excellent initiative called "Share my Dabba" has also been launched to prevent wastage of uneaten food and distribute it to the needy.

1

the death of its founding father, Governor Aungier, the project was abandoned; the walls stood 5m high for forty-odd years until enthusiasm was rekindled in the second decade of the eighteenth century. It was finally opened on Christmas Day, 1718, complete with the essential "cannonball-proof roof". The whitewashed and polished brass-and-wood interior looks much the same at it did in the eighteenth century. Lining the walls are memorial tablets to British parishioners, many of whom died young, either from disease or in battle.

Chhatrapati Shivaji Terminus (Victoria Terminus)

Tours Mon–Fri 3–5pm • ₹200 • Contact Zakir Palekar ☎ 90044 11438

Inspired by St Pancras Station in London, F.W. Stevens designed **Victoria Terminus**, the barmiest of Mumbai's buildings, as a paean to "progress". Built in 1887 as the largest British edifice in India, it's an extraordinary amalgam of domes, spires, Corinthian columns and minarets that was succinctly defined by the journalist James Cameron as "Victorian-Gothic-Saracenic-Italianate-Oriental-St Pancras-Baroque". In keeping with the current re-Indianization of the city's roads and buildings, this icon of British imperial architecture has been renamed **Chhatrapati Shivaji Terminus**, in honour of the famous Maratha warlord. The new name is a bit of a mouthful, however, and locals mostly still refer to it as **VT** (pronounced "vitee").

Few of the three million or so passengers who fill almost a thousand trains every day notice the mass of decorative detail. A "British" lion and Indian tiger stand guard at the entrance, and the exterior is festooned with sculptures executed at the Bombay Art School by the Indian students of John Lockwood Kipling, Rudyard's father. Among them are grotesque mythical beasts, monkeys, plants and medallions of important personages. To minimize the sun's impact, stained glass was employed, decorated with locomotives and elephant images. Above it all, the statue of "Progress" stands atop the massive central dome.

A polished black marble memorial next to the station's main entrance commemorates the 58 passengers and staff gunned down by terrorists during the 26/11 attack (see p.71).

Central Bazaar District

Sir JJ Rd, 1km north of CST (VT) station

Lining the anarchic jumble of streets beyond Lokmanya Tilak Road is Mumbai's bustling **Central Bazaar District** – a fascinating counterpoint to the wide and Westernized streets of downtown. In keeping with traditional divisions of guild, caste and religion, most streets specialize in one or two types of merchandise. If you lose your bearings, the best way out is to ask someone to wave you in the direction of **Mohammed Ali Road**, the busy road through the heart of the district (now surmounted by a gigantic flyover), from where you can hail a cab.

Crawford Market

Crawford (aka Mahatma Phule) **Market**, ten minutes' walk north of CST, is an old British-style covered market dealing in just about every kind of fresh food and domestic animal imaginable. Before venturing inside, stop to admire the **friezes** wrapped around its exterior – a Victorian vision of sturdy-limbed peasants toiling in the fields, as designed by Rudyard Kipling's father, Lockwood, principal of the Bombay School of Art in 1865.

The **main hall** is still divided into different sections: pyramids of polished fruit and vegetables down one aisle, sacks of nuts or oil-tins full of herbs and spices down another. Around the back of the market, in the atmospheric wholesale wing, the pace of life is more hectic. Here, noisy crowds of coolies mill about with large reed-baskets held high in the air (if they are looking for work) or on their heads (if they've found some). Animal lovers should steer well clear of the market's eastern wing, where all kinds of unfortunate creatures are crammed into undersized cages; beyond the pet section, the meat hall is not for the squeamish.

Jama Masjid and Zaveri Bazaar

Sheikh Memon St

The streets immediately **north of Crawford Market** and west of **Mohammed Ali Road** form one vast bazaar area, dominated by the domes and minarets of the chintzy white **Jama Masjid**, or "Friday Mosque" (c.1800). The nucleus of the building is an ancient water tank, which now serves as an ablution pool. Pillars rise directly from the murky green pond to support the main body of the mosque, whose halls are reached by stairways. Cutting north from the Jama Masjid is **Zaveri Bazaar**, the jewellery market where Mumbaikars come to shop for dowries and wedding attire. An estimated 65 percent of all India's gold, silver and precious gems trading is carried out in the brightly lit emporia lining the market's lanes.

Mumba Devi Temple

Sheikh Memon St, Bhuleshwar

An important centre of Devi worship, the **Mumba Devi Temple** rises from one of the most densely populated square miles on the planet – a maze of twisting lanes and alleyways, lined by five- or six-storey wooden-balconied tenement buildings. The present structure, with its tapering polychrome sanctuary tower, dates only from the nineteenth century, but the black-stone deity inside it, patron goddess of the city's Koli fisherfolk, is much older. Originally she occupied a shrine further south, just outside the walls of the East India Company's fort, but that site was commandeered to make way for VT station. Colourful stalls selling floral offerings and other religious paraphernalia line the streets around it, where you'll encounter plenty of saffron-clad sadhus, their foreheads smeared with vibrant red vermilion powder.

Marine Drive

Netaji Subhash Chandra Marg, better known as **Marine Drive**, is Mumbai's seaside prom, an eight-lane highway with a wide pavement built in the 1920s on reclaimed land. The whole 3km stretch – still often referred to by Mumbaikars as the "Queen's Necklace" after the row of lights that illuminates its spectacular curve at night – is a favourite place for a stroll; the promenade next to the sea has uninterrupted views virtually the whole way along, while the peeling, mildewed Art Deco apartment blocks on the land side remain some of the most desirable addresses in the city.

Chowpatty Beach

Situated at the top of Marine Drive, **Chowpatty Beach** is a Mumbai institution. On evenings and weekends, Mumbaikars gather here in large numbers – not to swim (the sea is foul) but to wander, sit on the sand, eat kulfi and *bhel puri*, get their ears cleaned and gaze across the bay while the kids ride a pony or a rusty Ferris wheel.

At the back of the beach, a bronze bust recalls the bravery of Tukaram Omble, the policeman who lost his life capturing terrorist Ajmal Kasab during the 2008 attacks. Omble held on to the gunman's AK47 long enough for his colleagues to overpower the attacker, but was shot several times in the process and later died of his injuries.

1

Mani Bhavan

19 Laburnum Rd · Daily 9.30am–6pm · Free, with optional donation · ☎ 022 2380 5864, ⓦ gandhi-manibhavan.org · If coming by taxi, ask for the nearby Gamdevi Police Station

A ten-minute walk north from the middle of Chowpatty Beach along Pandita Ramabai Marg, **Mani Bhavan** was Gandhi's Bombay base between 1917 and 1934. Set in a leafy upper-middle-class road, the house has now been converted into a permanent memorial to the Mahatma. The lovingly maintained polished-wood interior is crammed with historic photos and artefacts – the most disarming of which is a friendly letter to Hitler suggesting world peace.

Malabar Hill

Its shirt-tails swathed in greenery and brow bristling with gigantic skyscrapers, **Malabar Hill**, the promontory enfolding Chowpatty Beach at the north end of Back Bay, has been south Mumbai's most desirable neighbourhood almost since the city was founded. The British were quick to see the potential of its salubrious breezes and sweeping sea views, constructing bungalows at the tip of what was then a separate island – the grandest of them the Government House, originally erected in the 1820s and now the seat of the serving governor of Maharashtra, **Raj Bhavan**.

Although none of Malabar's landmarks can be classed as unmissable, its Hindu shrines and surviving colonial-era residences form an interesting counterpoint to the modernity towering on all sides. Bal Gangadhar Kher Marg (formerly Ridge Road) is the district's main artery. You can follow it from Mumbai's principal **Jain Temple** (see map, p.72), with its mirror-encrusted interior dedicated to Adinath, all the way to the tip of the headland, where the famous **Walukeshwar Temple** stands as the city's oldest Hindu shrine surviving *in situ*. According to the Ramayana, Rama fashioned a lingam out of sand to worship Shiva here, which over the centuries became one of the Konkan's most important pilgrimage centres. Today's temple, erected in 1715 after the original was destroyed by the Portuguese, is of less note than the **Banganga Tank** below it – a rectangular lake lined by stone *ghats* and numerous crumbling shrines.

Central Mumbai: Mahalakshmi to Byculla

The centre of Mumbai, beyond Malabar Hill, is mostly made up of working-class neighbourhoods: a huge mosaic of dilapidated tenements, markets and industrial eyesores left over from the Victorian cotton boom. For relief from the urban cauldron, residents travel west to the seashore to worship at the **Mahalakshmi Temple** (if they're Hindus) or the island **tomb of Haji Ali** (if they're Muslims). Both make great excursions from south Mumbai, and can be combined with a foray across town to the recently

---

THE TOWERS OF SILENCE

High on Malabar Hill, screened from prying eyes by a high wall and dense curtain of vegetation (and strictly closed to visitors), stand the seven **Towers of Silence**, where the city's dwindling Zoroastrian community (better known as Parsis) dispose of their dead. Pollution of the four sacred elements (air, water, earth and, holiest of all, fire) contradicts the most fundamental precepts of the 2500-year-old Parsi faith, first imported to India when Zoroastrians fled from Sassanid Persia to escape Arab persecution in the seventh century. So instead of being buried or cremated, the bodies are laid out on top of open-topped, cylindrical towers, called *dokhmas*, for their bones to be cleaned by **vultures** and the weather. The remains are then placed in an ossuary at the centre of the tower.

1

DHARAVI: THE £700 MILLION SLUM

Sprawling over 550 acres, **Dharavi**'s maze of dilapidated shacks and narrow, stinking alleyways is home to more than a million people. An average of fifteen thousand of them share a single toilet. Infectious diseases such as dysentery, malaria and hepatitis are rife; and there aren't any hospitals.

Despite the poverty, Dharavi has been described by the UK's *Observer* newspaper as "one of the most inspiring economic models in Asia": hidden amid the warren of ramshackle huts and squalid open sewers are an estimated fifteen thousand single-room factories, employing around a quarter of a million people and turning over a staggering £700 million (US$1 billion) annually. The majority of small businesses in Dharavi are based on **waste recycling** of one kind or another. Slum residents young and old scavenge materials from across the city and haul them back in huge bundles to be reprocessed. Aluminium cans are smelted down, soap scraps salvaged from schools and hotels are reduced in huge vats, leather reworked, disused oil drums restored and discarded plastic reshaped and remoulded. An estimated ten thousand workers are employed in the plastics sector alone. Ranging from ₹3000–15,000 per month, wages are well above the national average, and though Dharavi may not have any health centres, it does hold a couple of banks, and even ATMs.

As India's most iconic slum, Dharavi has also found an unlikely niche in the history of Indian and international **cinema**. The district provided many of the settings for Danny Boyle's multiple-Oscar-winning **Slumdog Millionaire**, as well as several of its leading child actors.

Despite its burgeoning international fame, Dharavi's future remains uncertain. The entire district is living in the shadow of a proposed US$40 billion **redevelopment project** which aims to bulldoze the entire slum. In return for agreeing to eviction, residents will be entitled to apartment space in new multistorey tower blocks. Schools, roads, hospitals and other amenities have also been promised. Opposition to the scheme among Dharavites has been all but unanimous, however, with slum dwellers insisting any future development should focus not on erecting a swanky new suburb but on improving existing conditions.

You can visit Dharavi yourself by joining one of the "**Slum Tours**" run by Reality Tours and Travels out of Colaba (📞9820 822253, 🌐realitytoursandtravel.com). Tickets for these engaging guided trips start from ₹800 (including transport), with a longer and more comfortable version with an a/c car for ₹1700.

---

revamped **Dr Bhau Dadji Lad Museum** in Byculla, calling en route at the **Mahalakshmi dhobi ghats** – one of the city's more offbeat sights.

Mahalakshmi Temple

Just off Bhulabhai Desai Rd • Daily 6am–10pm • Buses #83, #124 or #132 will take you from Colaba to Haji Ali, within a stone's throw of the Mahalakshmi Temple • 📞022 2351 4732, 🌐mahalakshmi-temple.com

Mumbai's busy **Mahalakshmi Temple**, dedicated to the Hindu goddess of wealth and prosperity – the city's most sought-after attributes – stands on the shoreline off the frenetic Bhulabhai Desai intersection. The approach is via an alley lined with stalls selling spectacular floral offerings and devotional pictures. A heavy security cordon has to be crossed before entering the main shrine, where a statue of the *devi* glittering with gold jewellery and bangles, and seated astride a tiger and demon, is propitiated by a constant stream of worshippers. Donations pile so high that the temple pujaris run a money-spinning sideline reselling them. While you're here, find out what your future holds by joining the huddle of devotees pressing rupees onto the rear wall of the shrine room. If your coin sticks, you'll be rich.

Haji Ali's Tomb

Just off Lala Lajpatrai Marg • Daily 5am–10pm • Buses #83, #124 or #132 will take you from Colaba to Haji Ali • 📞022 2352 9082, 🌐hajialidargah.in

Occupying a small islet in the bay just north of the Mahalakshmi Temple is the mausoleum of the Muslim saint, Afghan mystic **Haji Ali Bukhari**. The site is a great place to head on Thursday and Friday evenings, when large crowds gather around the promontory to watch the sunset and listen to live **qawwali** music.

The tomb is connected to the mainland by a narrow concrete **causeway**, only passable at low tide. When not immersed in water, its entire length is lined with beggars supplicating passers-by and chanting verses from the Koran. Non-Muslims are welcome, but all visitors need to keep well covered (a headscarf should be worn by women).

Haji Ali Juice Centre
Daily 5am–1pm

The traditional way to round off a trip to the mausoleum is to take a glass or two of fresh fruit juice at the legendary **Haji Ali Juice Centre**, just to the right of the entrance to the causeway. Customers either cram into the tiny dining hall or else order from their cars.

Mahalakshmi dhobi ghats
Bapurao Jagtap Marg • Buses #124 (from Colaba) and #153 (from Haji Ali) go to the *dhobi ghats*; trains run from Churchgate to Mahalakshmi station. Emerging from the station, turn left and follow the road over the rail tracks – the *ghats* will be below you on your left (hawkers from the nearby slums will show you the way)

On the face of it, the idea of going out of your way to ogle Mumbai's dirty washing sounds like a very perverse pastime. If you're passing, however, the **Mahalakshmi dhobi ghats**, near Mahalakshmi suburban railway station, are a sufficiently memorable spectacle to break a trip across town to see. Washing from all over the city is brought here each morning to be soaked in concrete vats and thumped by the resident *dhobis*. A trickle of curious foreign tourists gathers on Mahalakshmi Road bridge for this uniquely Indian photo opportunity.

Dr Bhau Dadji Lad Museum
Rani Baug, Dr Ambedkar Rd, Byculla East • Daily except Wed 10am–5.30pm • ₹100 (₹10) • ☎ 022 2373 1234, ⊕ bdlmuseum.org

Way out in the postindustrial wasteland of Byculla, the **Dr Bhau Dadji Lad Museum** was originally opened in 1872 as the **Victoria and Albert Museum** – "one of the greatest boons the British have conferred on India", according to contemporary reports. The

---

ANTILIA

If Mumbai is notorious for its poverty, then the city is no less famous for the glittering wealth of its richest inhabitants, and they don't come richer than **Mukesh Ambani**, chairman of the Reliance Industries petrochemical corporation. With a net worth of US$21 billion, Ambani is officially India's richest man, and his recently built home on Altamount Rd in the Cumballa Hill district of south-central Mumbai is said to be the world's most valuable piece of real estate. The futuristic, 27-storey skyscraper – known as **Antilia** – enjoys a majestic view over the Arabian Sea on one side, and Dharavi slum area on the other. Completed in 2010, it cost an estimated US$500–600 million to build, and is valued at somewhere between US$1–2 billion. Six floors are given over to a 168-car parking area. The building boasts nine elevators, three helipads, a glittering ballroom with solid silver balustrades and ceilings festooned with crystal chandeliers, hanging gardens of hydroponic plants and an ice room where the Ambanis can beat the summer heat in flurries of man-made snow.

Reaction to this behemoth on Mumbai's skyline has been mixed, to say the least. While most of the locals and sightseers regard it with wide-eyed wonder, members of India's intelligentsia – from industrialist J.R. Tata to novelist Arundhati Roy – have been less than complimentary, deploring the Ambanis' apparent lack of social conscience.

1

elegant, Palladian-style building, set amid classically planned botanical gardens (now home to a rather depressing zoo) has been restored to its former glory, and houses a collection of fascinating lithographs, prints, documents, uniforms and models relating to the development of Bombay. In the adjacent garden, the carved stone pachyderm after which the Portuguese are said to have named Elephanta Island presides over a collection of forlorn British statues, moved here during Independence beyond the reach of angry mobs.

Gorai

Just beyond the northern limits of Mumbai, **Gorai** is a low-lying, sparsely populated peninsula separated at its tip from the mainland by tidal creek. Among the city's residents, this isolated green belt, settled by Portuguese priests and Catholic converts in the sixteenth century, is famous for two starkly contrasting attractions: if you've a day to kill in Mumbai between flights, and can't face exploring the city, either the **Esselworld** amusement park complex or adjacent **Global Vipassana Pagoda** might be worth considering – though be warned that getting to and from Gorai from downtown can take upwards of two hours at peak times.

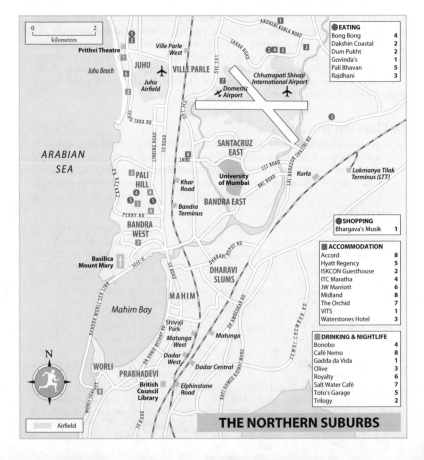

● EATING	
Bong Bong	4
Dakshin Coastal	2
Dum Pukht	2
Govinda's	1
Pali Bhavan	5
Rajdhani	3

● SHOPPING	
Bhargava's Musik	1

■ ACCOMMODATION	
Accord	8
Hyatt Regency	5
ISKCON Guesthouse	2
ITC Maratha	4
JW Marriott	6
Midland	8
The Orchid	7
VITS	1
Waterstones Hotel	3

■ DRINKING & NIGHTLIFE	
Bonobo	4
Café Nemo	8
Gadda da Vida	1
Olive	3
Royalty	6
Salt Water Café	7
Toto's Garage	5
Trilogy	2

THE NORTHERN SUBURBS

1

Esselworld

Mon–Fri 10am–7pm, Sat & Sun 10am–8pm • ₹850/₹950 regular/peak for adults; ₹500/₹600 for children; combined Esselword & Water Kingdom ₹1190 adult, ₹890 children • Ⓦ esselworld.com

Mumbai's answer to Disneyland, **Esselword** is the first-choice destination for local families who can afford the trip – an island of American-style fun and frolics on the city's green fringe. It consists of two parts: the Esselworld amusement park, with its white-knuckle roller coasters, gentler kiddies' rides, ice rink and bowling alley; and the adjacent Water Kingdom, a vast complex of aqua slides featuring the world's largest wave pool, a huge play lagoon and some brilliant family-friendly rides. Crowds in both can be oppressive on weekends and holidays, but ease off during the week when admission charges drop.

Global Vipassana Pagoda

Daily dawn–dusk • Ⓦ globalpagoda.org

Chugging across Gorai Creek on the ferry, you could be forgiven for thinking yourself on a river somewhere in Southeast Asia. From the far bank, the ethereal, gold-painted **Global Vipassana Pagoda** rises like something you'd expect to see shimmering over the waters of Burma's Ayeyarwady Delta. In fact the pagoda was built as a replica of the resplendent Shwedagon Paya in Yangon (Rangoon), Myanmar's most venerated Buddhist monument. Its gleaming golden pinnacle soars 99m – the height of a thirty-storey building – above the shoreline peaks and the adjacent amusement park, making it the world's largest freestanding dome, taller even than Vijayapura's Gol Gumbaz.

An entranceway leads to a cavernous meditation hall measuring 280m in diameter and capable of accommodating eight thousand worshippers. Genuine relics of the Buddha, donated by the government of Sri Lanka and the Mahabodhi Society of Bodh Gaya, are enshrined in the upper dome above the hall. Other structures in the landscaped complex include a 21m-tall seated Buddha carved from a single piece of marble, a massive entrance gateway and towers containing a colossal Burmese-style bell and gong.

ARRIVAL AND DEPARTURE   GORAI

By train and launch Make for Borivali or Malad station on the suburban train line. You can pick up BEST bus #294 or #247 to Gorai Creek from both stations – or better still, jump in an auto-rickshaw for the 4km trip to the river. Once at the jetty, take the Esselworld launch (₹50), not the cheaper local Gorai ferry, as the latter drops you a long way from the park.

By bus Modern Tours and Travels (Ⓣ 022 2353 0888) run a private service (2hr 30min; ₹700 plus ferry) that also runs direct to Esselworld from Colaba each day, departing from outside the Regal Cinema at 8.30am. Book in advance.

By taxi Taxis charge around ₹1000 for the 68km journey from Colaba, and can be in short supply for the return leg.

Elephanta

An hour's ride northeast across Mumbai harbour from Colaba, the island of **Elephanta** offers the best escape from the seething claustrophobia of the city – as long as you time your visit to avoid the weekend deluge of noisy day-trippers. Populated only by a small fishing community, it was originally known as **Gherapura**, the "city of Ghara priests", until the island was renamed in the sixteenth century by the Portuguese in honour of the carved elephant they found at the port – now on display outside the Dr Bhau Dadji Lad Museum in Byculla (see p.85). Its chief attraction is its unique **cave temple**, whose massive **Trimurti** (three-faced) **Shiva sculpture** is as fine an example of Hindu architecture as you'll find anywhere.

ARRIVAL AND INFORMATION   ELEPHANTA

By boat Boats set off every 30min from the Gateway of India (daily 9am–3pm; returning from Elephanta noon–5.30pm; book through the Gateway Plaza kiosks near the

Gateway of India); note that boats may be cancelled due to adverse weather conditions during the monsoon. Luxury launches (₹180 return adults; ₹125 children) include a

1

30min tour with a government guide – ask for your guide at the cave's ticket office on arrival. Ordinary Economy launches (₹145 return adults; ₹95 children) don't include the guided tour and are usually more packed. There's a tourist tax of ₹5 payable on arrival, and a further admission charge of ₹10. **Information** Cool drinks and souvenir stalls line the way up the hill, and, at the top, the MTDC *Chalukya* restaurant offers substandard food and warm beer, served on a terrace with good views out to sea. If you don't want to walk up the 120 steps to the caves there's a miniature train up from the jetty (₹10 return). Note that you cannot stay overnight on the island and that the caves are closed on Mondays.

The cave

Tues–Sun 9.30am–5pm • ₹250 (₹10)

Elephanta's impressive excavated eighth-century **cave**, covering an area of approximately 5000 square metres, is reached by climbing more than one hundred steps lined by souvenir and knick-knack stalls, to the top of the hill. Inside, the massive columns, carved from solid rock, give the deceptive impression of being structural. To the right as you enter, note the panel of **Nataraj**, Shiva as the cosmic dancer. Though spoiled by the Portuguese who, it is said, used it for target practice, the panel remains magnificent: Shiva's face is rapt, and with one of his left hands he removes the veil of ignorance. Opposite is a badly damaged panel of Lakulisha, Shiva with a club (*lakula*).

Each of the four entrances to the simple square main **shrine** – unusually, it has one on each side – is flanked by a pair of huge fanged *dvarapala* guardians (only those to the back have survived undamaged), while inside a large lingam is surrounded by coins and smouldering joss left by devotees. Facing the northern wall of the shrine, another panel shows Shiva impaling the demon Andhaka, who wandered around as though blind, symbolizing his spiritual blindness. The panel behind the shrine on the back wall portrays the marriage of Shiva and Parvati, but the cave's outstanding centrepiece is its powerful 6m bust of **Trimurti**, the three-faced Shiva, whose profile has become almost as familiar to Indians as that of the Taj Mahal.

Elephanta Hill

From Cave 1 you can follow a paved path around the north flank of the hillside past a string of other, unfinished excavations, which exemplify how the caves were originally dug out and carved. If you've the stamina, follow the dirt path that leads from the end of the paved trail beyond these to the summit of **Elephanta Hill**, a stiff hike of fifteen minutes. At the top you'll be rewarded by an encounter with a couple of rusting Portuguese cannons and a magnificent view back over Mumbai harbour to the distant city beyond.

ARRIVAL AND DEPARTURE
MUMBAI

Unless you're travelling by train to or from **Chhatrapati Shivaji Terminus** (formerly Victoria Terminus), be prepared for a long slog to or from the centre. The international and domestic **airports** are way north of the city, and ninety minutes or more by road from the main hotel areas, while from **Mumbai Central** railway or **bus station** you also face a laborious trip across town.

BY PLANE
INTERNATIONAL AIRPORT

Mumbai's busy international airport, Chhatrapati Shivaji (30km north of downtown; ☎ 022 6685 1010, ⟲ csia.in) was impressively revamped in 2015, and the iconic T2 (Terminal 2) is (surprisingly) home to India's largest public art programme. Check-in is located in the departure area (Level 4), and all airlines have offices outside the main entrance.

IN TRANSIT

If you're only passing through Mumbai between flights and need to sit out half the night, it's worth knowing that the *Leela Kempinski* and *Royal Meridien* five-stars are both a short, complimentary transfer bus ride from the international terminal at CST. Their a/c restaurants, coffee shops and bars are generally more comfortable places to kill time than the airport, though first-class and business passengers can use the luxurious lounges in T2. There's also a transit hotel on Level 1 of that terminal.

1

GETTING TO GOA

Easily the best-value way to travel the 500km from Mumbai to Goa is by **plane** – prices often compare favourably with the cost of the same journey on the Konkan Railway, which has two departures daily. If you are on a budget or unable to procure a flight or train ticket, there are several overnight **bus services** with semi-sleeper or sleeper seats.

BY PLANE

Around two dozen flights leave daily from Mumbai's domestic airport for Goa's **Dabolim airport** (code GOI). Flights are currently operated by Jet Airways, JetKonnect, IndiGo, SpiceJet, Go Air, Air India and Vistara (see p.90). One-way fares start from around ₹2700; check ⓦexpedia.co.in and ⓦcleartrip.com for the latest deals, or the websites of the airlines themselves (see p.28) for special offers and promotions.

Demand for seats can be fierce around Diwali and Christmas/New Year, when you're unlikely to get a ticket at short notice. At other times, one or other of the carriers should be able to offer a seat on the day you wish to travel – though perhaps not the lowest fares. If you didn't prebook when you purchased your international ticket, check availability as soon as you arrive.

BY TRAIN

The **Konkan Railway** line runs daily express trains from Mumbai to Goa. However, these services are not always available at short notice from the booking halls at CST and Churchgate. Don't, whatever you do, be tempted to travel "unreserved" class on any Konkan service, as the journey as far as Ratnagiri (roughly midway) is overwhelmingly crushed. There are a number of convenient overnight services (see box, p.90).

Fares range from a bargain-bucket ₹288 for basic second-class seated, to ₹423 for sleeper class, or ₹1586 for two-tier a/c. The priciest first-class tickets cost ₹2641 – roughly what you pay for a low-cost flight off peak.

BY BUS

The Mumbai–Goa bus journey is not as bad as it used to be, thanks to better road conditions, though the journey is still long. Depending on the type of bus you get and the sinuous coastal route, thirteen to fifteen hours is a realistic estimate for the journey time.

Fares start at around ₹500 for a push-back seat on a beaten-up Kadamba (Goan government) or MSRTC coach. Tickets for these services are in great demand in season with domestic tourists, so **book in advance** at Mumbai Central. Quite a few **private overnight buses** (around a dozen daily) also run to Goa, costing from around ₹600 for no-frills buses up to ₹1200 for swisher a/c Volvo coaches with berths. Tickets are best booked at least a day in advance through the bus company, or online via ⓦredbus.in. Apart from enabling you to compare services, the website also allows you to check departure and pick-up points, which vary between operators. Few leave from south Mumbai. Among those that do is the largest operator for Goa, Paulo Travels (ⓦpaulotravels.com), whose recommended sleeper services from Dhobi Talao Junction on Fashion St at 5.45pm and 7.30pm (see map, p.78), are the most comfortable buses to catch, costing ₹950 single and taking 14hr. Alternatively, Neeta Tours & Travels starts from the northern suburbs and has a pick-up point at Kalanagar bus stop in Bandra East near the Western Express highway (ⓦneetabus.in).

Taxis While many of the more upmarket hotels send out courtesy coaches or chauffeur-driven cars to pick up and drop off their guests, most people arriving in Mumbai use the prepaid taxi desk in the arrivals hall. Choose from no-frills black and yellow cabs or the a/c Cool Cabs (☎022 2216 4466, ⓦcitycoolcab.com). A prepaid taxi will cost ₹400 (or ₹500 a/c), while a Cool Cab is ₹750–950 to Colaba. Alternatively, there's a choice of fleet taxis like Tab Cab (☎022 6363 6363, ⓦtabcab.in), Meru (☎022 4422 4422, ⓦmerucabs.com) and Easy Cabs (☎022 6523 3677).

DOMESTIC AIRPORT
Internal flights land at Mumbai's domestic airport (26km to the north of downtown and 2km west of the international airport; ☎022 6685 1010, ⓦcsia.in). Terminal 1A handles Air India and Go Air, while all other carriers use terminals 1B and 1C.

Transfers If you're transferring directly from here to an international flight, take the free "fly-bus" that shuttles every 30min between the two airports; look for the transfer counter in your transit lounge.

1

RECOMMENDED TRAINS FROM MUMBAI
All the following trains run daily.

Destination	Name	No.	From	Departs	Duration
Aurangabad	*Tapovan Express*	#17617	CST	6.15am	7hr
Bengaluru (Bangalore)	*Udyan Express*	#16529	CST	8.05am	23hr 20min
Bhuj	*Kutch Express*	#19131	Bandra	5.10pm	16hr 15min
Delhi	*Rajdhani Express*	#12951	MC	5pm	15hr 35min
Goa (Margao)	*Konkan–Kanya Express*	#10111	CST	11.05pm	10hr 1min
	Jan Shatabdi	#12051	Dadar	5.25am	7hr 35min
	Mangalore Express	#12133	CST	10pm	9hr 5min
Kochi (Cochin)	*Netravati Express*	#16345	LTT (Kurla)	11.40am	25hr 25min
Kolhapur	*Sahyadri Express*	#11023	CST	5.50pm	12hr 15min
Lonavala	*Udyan Express*	#16529	CST	8.05am	2hr 30min
Nasik	*Pushpak Express*	#12534	CST	8.20pm	3hr 30min
Neral (for Matheran)	*Deccan Express*	#11007	CST	7am	1hr 25min
Pune	*Udyan Express*	#16529	CST	8.05am	3hr 35min

Information and taxis India Tourism and the MTDC both have 24hr information counters in the arrivals hall, and there's a foreign exchange counter and accommodation desk tucked away near the first-floor exit. The official "prepaid" taxi counter on the arrivals concourse charges around ₹400 to Colaba (₹500 for a/c). For a car with driver, try Cool Cab (☎ 76665 54466, ⓦ citycoolcab.in) or Meru (☎ 022 4422 4422, ⓦ merucabs.com).

Domestic airlines Air India, Air India Building, Nariman Point (☎ 1800 180 1407); Air India Express, Air India Building, Nariman Point (☎ 022 2202 3031); GoAir (☎ 092232 22111); IndiGo Airlines (☎ 099103 83838 or ☎ 1800 180 3838); Jet Airways/JetKonnect, B1, Amarchand Mansion, Ground Floor, Madam Cama Rd, Colaba (☎ 022 3989 3333); SpiceJet (☎ 096540 03333).

BY TRAIN
Three main rail networks service Mumbai: Western Railways, covering Gujarat, northern Madhya Pradesh and Rajasthan; Central Railways, covering Maharashtra and southern Madhya Pradesh; and the Konkan Railway, running south down the coast to Goa and beyond.

CHHATRAPATI SHIVAJI TERMINUS (CST)
Trains operating between Mumbai and most central, southern and eastern regions work out of Chhatrapati Shivaji Terminus or CST (formerly Victoria Terminus, or VT), the main railway station at the end of the Central Railway line. The station lies a 10- or 15min ride to/from Colaba; taxis wait at the busy rank outside the south exit, opposite the reservation hall.

MUMBAI CENTRAL
The terminus for Western Railway trains from northern India, Mumbai Central, is a 30min ride from Colaba; on arrival, take a taxi from the forecourt, or flag one down on the main road – it should cost around ₹200–250.

OTHER STATIONS
Some trains from South India run out of more obscure stations: Dadar is way up in the industrial suburbs; Kurla, arrival/departure point for a few trains to/from Bengaluru (Bangalore) and Kerala, is even further out, just south of the domestic airport. From either, it's worth asking at the station when you arrive if there is another long-distance train going to Churchgate or CST (Victoria Terminus) shortly after – far better than trying to cram into either a suburban train or bus.

RESERVATIONS
The quickest and most convenient place for foreign nationals to make reservations on any of the networks is the efficient tourist counter (#14) on the first floor of the Western Railway's booking hall, next door to the Government of India tourist office on M Karve Rd, opposite Churchgate station (Mon–Fri 8am–8pm, Sat 8am–2pm; ☎ 022 2209 7577). Mumbai's other "Tourist Ticketing Facility" is on the first floor (counter #52) of the a/c Central Railway Reservation Office at CST (VT; Mon–Sat 8am–8pm, Sun 8am–2pm; ☎ 022 2262 2859). The office is on the right of the main station entrance (as you go in), just off the concourse where taxis pull up. In theory you may be required to produce a foreign currency encashment certificate or ATM slip to buy tickets here, though it's unlikely to be asked for. Tickets for seats on the Konkan Railway can be booked at either Churchgate or CST booking halls.

BY BUS

Although taxis, working from ranks immediately outside both airports and the train stations, are by far the most convenient form of onward transport, there are a number of bus services.

GOVERNMENT SERVICES

Nearly all interstate buses work from Mumbai Central Bus Stand, a stone's throw from the railway station of the same name. Government services use the main Maharashtra State Road Transport Corporation (MSRTC) stand itself.

BOOKING COUNTERS AND RESERVATIONS

States with bus company booking counters (daily 8am–8pm) here include Maharashtra, Karnataka and Goa. Few of their services compare favourably with train travel on the same routes. Reliable timetable information can be difficult to obtain, reservations are not available on standard buses, and most long-haul journeys are gruelling overnighters. Among the exceptions are the deluxe buses run by MSRTC to Pune and Kolhapur; the small extra cost buys you more leg room, fewer stops and the option of advance booking. The only problem is that most leave from the ASIAD bus stand in Dadar, or the MSRTC stand in Thane, 30min and 60min respectively by road or rail north of Mumbai Central.

PRIVATE BUSES

Private services operate from the roadside next to Mumbai Central railway station, a 2min walk west on the opposite side of busy Dr AN Marg (Lamington Rd). They cover most of the same routes as government buses and tend to be faster, more comfortable and easier to book in advance – though

again, long-distance services invariably depart at night. Note that fares on services to popular tourist destinations such as Goa and Mahabaleshwar double during peak season.

TIMETABLES

Timetable information is most easily researched online, via websites such as ⓦ makemytrip.com, which compare fares, class of vehicles, journey durations, departure times and – crucially – departure points (services leave from different places and follow different routes out of the city).

Destinations The following refers only to MSRTC (government) services. For timetable information for private buses, check ⓦ makemytrip.com or ⓦ redbus.in.

ASIAD Dadar to: Kolhapur (4 daily; 10hr); Nasik (hourly; 4–5hr); Pune (every 15min; 4hr).

Mumbai Central to: Aurangabad (2 daily; 10hr); Bengaluru (3 daily; 24hr); Goa (2 daily; 13–16hr); Mahabaleshwar (2 daily; 7hr 30min); Udaipur (1 daily; 15–16hr); Ujjain (1 daily; 16–17hr); Vijayapura (3 daily; 12hr).

BY BOAT

Three companies – PNP, Maldar Catamarans and Ajanta – operate boat services from the Gateway of India to Mandwa jetty, on the far side of Mumbai harbour, from where buses shuttle to nearby Alibag, transport hub for the route southwards down the Konkan coast. Ranging from comfortable a/c catamarans (₹165) to bog-standard launches (₹150 upper deck; ₹125 main deck), the ferries leave roughly every hour; tickets should be purchased in advance from the PNP, Ajanta or Maldar company booths near the Gateway of India, on the north side of Shivaji Marg, next to the MTDC information counter.

GETTING AROUND

During peak hours in Mumbai **gridlock** is the norm, and you should brace yourself for long waits at junctions if you take to the roads by taxi, bus or auto. Local **trains** get there faster, but can be a real endurance test even outside rush hours.

BY TRAIN

Mumbai's local trains carry an estimated 7.5 million commuters each day between downtown and the sprawling

suburbs in the north – half the entire passenger capacity of Indian Railways (see box below). One line begins at CST (VT), running up the east side of the city; the other leaves

---

A "SUPER-DENSE" CRUSH

The suburban rail network in Mumbai is officially the busiest on the planet. No other line carries as many passengers, nor crams them into such confined spaces. At peak times, as many as 4700 people may be jammed into a nine-carriage train designed to carry 1700, resulting in what the rail company, in typically jaunty Mumbai style, refers to as "**Super-Dense Crush Load**" of fourteen to sixteen standing passengers per square metre. Not all of these actually occupy floor space, of course: ten percent will be dangling precariously out of the doors.

The busiest stretch, a 60km segment between Churchgate terminus and Virar in north Mumbai, transports nearly nine hundred million people each year, the highest of any rail network in the world. **Fatalities** are all too frequent: on average, six hundred die on the rail network annually (that's more than sixteen deaths per day), usually from falling out of the doors, crossing the tracks or because they're hit by overhead cables while riding on the roof.

1

TOURS

A number of operators around the Gateway of India offer whistle-stop one-day city "darshan" tours by bus (around ₹175–200 non-a/c, not including admission charges) – an inexpensive but usually very rushed way to cram Mumbai's tourist highlights into a single day. These trips are pitched primarily at Indian visitors, so expect slow drives past the homes of Bollywood stars and the US$200-billion skyscraper of tycoon Mukesh Ambani (see box, p.85), as well as a crossing of the Worli-Bandra Sea Link bridge. There are, however, some more foreigner-friendly alternatives.

The Bombay Heritage Walks ☎ 98218 87321, ⓦ bombayheritagewalks.com. Focusing mainly on period buildings and colonial history around Kala Ghoda and Horniman Circle, the excellent guided walks organized by architects Abha Bahl and Brinda Gaitonde last for 2hr and are offered mainly at weekends, though weekday evening outings can sometimes be arranged, depending on availability. Advance bookings essential. ₹3750 minimum for a group of up to five people.

MTDC Maharashtra Tourism's 1hr after-dark tours of downtown Mumbai's illuminated landmarks are on an open-top bus. Tickets bookable at the MTDC kiosk near the Gateway of India, which is also where they leave from. Weekends 7pm & 8.15pm; upper deck ₹150,

lower deck ₹50.

Mumbai Magic ⓦ mumbaimagic.com. A range of interesting walking and driving tours delving into various aspects of the city, from colonial architecture to Jewish heritage. Two-hour walking tour ₹3000/person.

Reality Tours and Travels ⓦ realitytoursandtravel .com. Memorable trips out to the huge Dharavi shantytown (see box, p.84).

World of Bollywood Tours and Travels ☎ 99305 66780, ⓦ worldofbollywoodtoursandtravels.com. Several excursions and tours in and around Mumbai including a Dharavi Slum Tour (US$70/person), a Bollywood Tour (US$115/150 for half/full day) and City tour.

Churchgate, travelling via Mumbai Central and Dadar to Santa Cruz and beyond. Services depart every few minutes from 5am until midnight, stopping at dozens of small stations. Carriages are packed for most of the day, with passengers dangling precariously out of open doors to escape the crush, so start to make your way to the exit at least three stops before your destination. Peak hours (approximately 8.30–10am & 4–10pm) are the worst of all. Women are marginally better off in the "ladies carriages"; look for the crowd of colourful saris and *salwar kameez* grouped at the end of the platform. Travel during non-peak hours (11am–3.30pm) can be comparatively easier.

METRO

The Mumbai Metro (☎ 022 3031 0900, ⓦ reliancemumbai metro.com) connects Versova in the west to Ghatkopar in the east, a 12km elevated network that stops at twelve stations en route, most importantly Andheri, Western Express Highway and Airport Road, close to the inter-national airport and the clutch of hotels around it. At the moment, the metro doesn't stretch to central Mumbai but this looks likely to change in the future.

BUSES

BEST (☎ 022 2285 6262, ⓦ bestundertaking.com) operates a bus network of labyrinthine complexity, covering every part of the city. You can check routes and bus numbers on their website; recognizing bus numbers in the street, however, can be more problematic, as numerals are written in Marathi

(although in English on the sides). Avoid rush hours at all costs and aim, wherever possible, for the "Limited" ("Ltd") services, which stop less frequently. Tickets are bought from the conductor on the bus.

TAXIS AND CAR RENTAL

With rickshaws banished to the suburbs, Mumbai's ubiquitous black-and-yellow taxis are the quickest and most convenient way to nip around the city centre. In theory, all should have meters; in practice, particularly at night or early in the morning, many drivers refuse to use them. If this happens, either flag down another or haggle out a fare. As a rule of thumb, expect to be charged ₹22 for the first 1.5km and ₹14.84/km thereafter, plus a small sum for heavy luggage (₹10/article). A fifty percent supplement is levied for journeys between midnight and 5am. For more comfort, try a Cool Cab (☎ 022 2216 4466, ⓦ citycoolcab .in), blue taxis with a/c and tinted windows; rates are around forty percent higher than in a normal cab.

CARS WITH DRIVERS

Cars can be rented per 8hr day (₹1500–1700 for non-a/c, or from 1800 for a/c, depending on the car), plus ₹300/day driver allowance if the trip involves an overnight stay (the driver sleeps in the car). A minimum kilometre rate applies (usually 250km), after which there is a charge for every additional kilometre covered. A recommended travel agent who can arrange cars and drivers in Mumbai is Garha Tours & Travels (☎ 79264 63818, ⓦ garhatours.in).

Their office is near the airport at 104 Atlantic Apartments, Swami Samarth Nagar, Lokhandwala Complex, Andheri (W).

For car hire, try CarJee (☎ 022 2830 1941 or ☎ 99673 91103, ⓦ carjee.com).

INFORMATION

Tourist information The best source of information in Mumbai is the excellent India Tourism (Mon–Fri 9am–6pm, Sat 9am–2pm; ☎ 022 2207 4333 or ☎ 022 2207 4334, ⓔ indiatourism-mum@mic.in) at 123 M Karve Rd, opposite Churchgate station's east exit, with exceptionally helpful staff and lots of free maps and brochures. The Maharashtra State Tourism Development Corporation (MTDC) office is on Madame Cama Rd opposite the LIC Building at Nariman Point (Mon–Sat 9.30am–5.30pm; ☎ 022 2284 5678, ⓦ maharashtratourism.gov.in); staff here can reserve rooms in MTDC resorts, and also sell tickets for city sightseeing tours (see box opposite).

Listings For detailed listings, the most complete source is Mumbai's *Time Out* (ⓦ timeout.com/mumbai). Alternatively, check out the "Metro" page in the *Indian Express* or the "Bombay Times" section of the *Times of India*. All are available from street vendors around Colaba and downtown.

ACCOMMODATION

Finding **accommodation** at the right price when you arrive in Mumbai can be a real problem. Budget travellers, in particular, can expect a hard time finding decent but affordable accommodation. The best low-cost places tend to fill up days or weeks in advance, so you should book well ahead to avoid a stressful, sweaty room hunt. Tariffs in mid-range and upmarket places are also especially high for India. State-imposed **luxury tax** (currently ten percent), and **service charges** levied by the hotel itself further bump up bills; both these add-ons are included in the prices quoted in the following reviews. A short ride from the railway stations, **Colaba** makes a handy base and is where the majority of foreign visitors head first. The streets around the Gateway of India are chock-full of accommodation, and the area also offers more in the way of food and entertainment than neighbouring districts. At the western edge of the downtown area, swanky **Marine Drive** (officially Netaji Subhash Chandra Marg) is lined with four- and five-star hotels taking advantage of the panoramic views over Back Bay and the easy access to the city's commercial heart.

COLABA AND KALA GHODA

Aga Beg's & Hotel Kishan Ground, 2nd & 3rd floor, Shirin Manzil, Walton Rd ☎ 022 2284 2227; map p.74. Muslim-run pair of budget guesthouses on different floors of the same building. Their differently priced rooms (up to ₹3000) are nice and clean, some jazzily decorated. A/c costs ₹350 extra. **₹1800**

Ascot 38 Garden Rd ☎ 022 6638 5566, ⓦ ascothotel .com; map p.74. One of the oldest and most comfortable small hotels in Mumbai, updated with contemporary glass-and-marble designer interiors and spacious modern rooms. Their Deluxe rooms (₹8310) are twice the size of the Superiors. **₹7120**

Bentley's 17 Oliver Rd ☎ 022 2284 1474, ⓦ bentleyshotel .com; map p.74. Dependable old Parsi-owned favourite in five different colonial tenements, all on leafy backstreets. Rooms are quiet, secure and spacious, if a little worn, though the overall shabbiness isn't compensated for by the rates, which are higher than you'd expect for the level of comfort. Singles ₹2425. **₹3375**

Godwin Jasmine Building, 41 Garden Rd ☎ 022 2287 2050, ⓦ hotelgodwin.in; map p.74. Smart three-star with large, international-standard rooms and great views from the rooftop garden restaurant and upper floors (ask for #804, #805 or #806). Not quite in the same league as the nearby (and comparably priced) *Ascot* but a sound choice nonetheless. **₹7720**

Gordon House 5 Battery St ☎ 022 2289 4400, ⓦ ghhotel

.com; map p.74. Chic designer boutique place behind the Regal cinema. Each floor has a different theme: Scandinavian, Mediterranean and Country, plus there's a Versailles Suite. **₹12,000**

Lawrence 3rd floor, 33 Sri Sai Baba Marg (Rope Walk Lane), off K Dubash Marg, behind TGI's ☎ 022 2284 3618 or ☎ 6633 6107; map p.74. Close to the Jehangir Art Gallery, this is arguably south Mumbai's best rock-bottom choice, with five well-scrubbed doubles (plus two singles and two triples for ₹900 and ₹1800 respectively) with fans, and not-so-clean shared shower-toilets. Be warned though, it's a long slog up three floors of filthy wooden steps if the (decrepit) lift isn't working. No wi-fi. Advance booking essential. **₹1000**

Moti International 10 Best Marg ☎ 022 2202 1654, ⓔ hotelmotiinternational@yahoo.co.in; map p.74. Quiet and friendly hotel in a characterful old colonial building. Rooms are cosy and clean; most (but not all) have windows. All come with a/c, fridge, TV and complimentary soap and towels. Good value. **₹3200**

Red Shield Red Shield House, 30 Boram Behram (Mereweather) Rd, near the Taj hotel ☎ 022 2284 1824, ⓔ red_shield@vsnl.net; map p.74. Ultrabasic bunk beds in cramped, stuffy dorms (lockers available), or larger doubles. Rates include a basic breakfast, served in a sociable canteen. Maximum one-week stay. Gates close midnight; check on 9am. No wi-fi. Dorms **₹350**, doubles **₹1300**

1

Sea Palace Kerawalla Chambers, 26 PJ Ramchandani Marg (Apollo Bunder) ☎022 2284 1828, ⓦseapalace hotel.net; map p.74. Best of the three mid-range hotels at the quiet end of the harbour front, although the rooms come as a bit of a disappointment for the price, with old-fashioned decor and worn furnishings. All are a/c but sea views cost extra. Breakfast and light meals are served in the rooftop café. ₹6500

Sea Shore 4th floor, 1-49 Kamal Mansion, Arthur Bunder Rd ☎022 2287 4237; map p.74. Among the best budget deals in Colaba, with singles for ₹700. The sea-facing rooms with windows are much nicer and cost only ₹100 more than the airless cells on the other side. Friendly management and free, safe baggage store. Non-attached bath only. *India Guest House* (☎022 2283 3769), one floor below, has very ordinary box rooms with thin partition walls and a hostel-like appeal from ₹500. ₹1200

Strand PJ Kerawalla Chambers, Ramchandani Marg (Apollo Bunder) ☎022 2288 2222, ⓦhotelstrand.com; map p.74. Popular mid-scale option on the seafront, with good harbour views from the pricier deluxe rooms. It's nicely situated and efficiently run, but very dowdy, with smudged walls, tired colour schemes, worn carpets and cheap mattresses. ₹5000

Taj Mahal Palace and Tower PJ Ramchandani Marg ☎022 6665 3366, ⓦtajhotels.com; map p.74. Perhaps India's most famous hotel and the haunt of Mumbai's *beau monde*, with 560 luxury rooms, shopping arcades, a huge outdoor pool and a good spread of bars and restaurants. The hotel was at the centre of the terrorist attacks of November 2008 (see p.71), but reopened within a month, and has now been restored to its former glory after a US$40-million refit. Prices are considerably more in the *Palace* than the *Tower*. ₹17,200

Vivanta By Taj 90 Cuffe Parade ☎022 6665 0808, ⓦtajhotels.com; map p.72. Modern, business-oriented five-star occupying a seventeen-floor skyscraper just south of Colaba. A much more competitively priced option than its sister concern, the *Taj Mahal Palace and Tower*, though lacking old-world style and atmosphere. There is a large outdoor pool, three restaurants, a spa and gym and steam room. ₹12,760

★**YWCA** 18 Madam Cama Rd ☎022 2202 5053, ⓦywcaic.info; map p.74. Relaxing, secure and quiet hostel (open to men as well as women) with spotless attached rooms. Singles for ₹2436. Rates include breakfast and a generous buffet dinner – a bargain for south Mumbai. Advance booking online is obligatory with minimum payment of one night's stay. Temporary membership for ₹50. ₹3690

MARINE DRIVE

Ambassador VN Rd ☎022 2204 1131, ⓦambassador india.com; map p.78. Landmark four-star hotel established in 1930 with smart modern rooms and a choice location close to the sea and cafés. The revolving restaurant on the top floor is unfortunately still closed for renovation but there's also a bar, restaurant and bakery on site. ₹10,090

Astoria Jamshedji Tata Rd ☎022 6654 1234, ⓦastoria mumbai.com; map p.78. Smart business hotel in a refurbished 1930s Art Deco building near the Eros cinema. The rooms are nowhere near as ritzy as the lobby but offer good value this close to the centre. ₹7100

Bentley 3rd floor, Krishna Mahal, Marine Drive ☎022 2281 5244, ⓦbentleyhotel.in; map p.78. Not to be confused with *Bentley's* in Colaba (see p.93), this small, friendly guesthouse is near the cricket stadium. The nineteen marble-lined a/c rooms are clean and comfortable, though five share shower-toilets. Rates include Continental breakfast. ₹2730/₹3500

★**Chateau Windsor** 5th floor, 86 Veer Nariman Rd ☎022 6622 4455, ⓦchateauwindsor.com; map p.78. Impeccably neat and central, with unfailingly polite staff and a selection of attractively renovated rooms – many of them quaintly old-fashioned. Their "penthouse" on the fifth floor is particularly nice, comprising an individual bungalow surrounded by pot plants. Very popular, so reserve well in advance. Singles for ₹4750. ₹5250

Intercontinental 135 Marine Drive ☎022 3987 9999, ⓦmumbai.intercontinental.com; map p.78. Ultra-chic boutique hotel whose rooms have huge sea-facing windows and state-of-the-art gadgets. There's a rooftop pool, outdoor dining with sheesha, and the *Long & Short* restaurant serves great breakfast buffets (₹650) and brunches, plus the *Dome* (see p.99). Wi-fi around ₹1000/day. ₹14,250

Marine Plaza 29 Marine Drive ☎022 2285 1212, ⓦhotelmarineplaza.com; map p.78. Ritzy but small luxury hotel on the seafront, with the usual five-star facilities and a (pseudo) Art Deco atrium lobby topped by a glass-bottomed rooftop pool. Sea-view rooms cost ₹2000 extra. ₹11,870

Oberoi Nariman Point ☎022 6632 5757, ⓦoberoi hotels.com; map p.72. Enjoying a prime spot overlooking Back Bay, this hotel is traditionally the first choice of business travellers to the city – lacking the heritage character of the *Taj Mahal Palace and Tower*, but with fine views from its soaring tower and an atmosphere of glittering opulence throughout. It was severely damaged during the 2008 terror attacks, in which 32 staff and guests lost their lives, but has been fully renovated since. ₹34,000

Sea Green/Sea Green South 145 Marine Drive ☎022 6633 6525, ⓦseagreenhotel.com & 145-A Marine Drive ☎022 6633 6535, ⓦseagreensouth.com; map p.78. Jointly owned and enduringly popular pair of seafront hotels. Decor is old-fashioned going on shabby, and rates are quite high, although the sweeping bay views from front-facing rooms partly compensate. ₹5720

Trident Nariman Point (formerly the Hilton Towers) Nariman Point ☎022 6632 4343, ⓦtridenthotels.com;

map p.72. Sitting next to the *Oberoi* (see opposite) on Nariman Point, the *Trident* suffered slight damage during the 2008 attacks but reopened shortly afterwards. Currently the city's premier business hotel, with full five-star facilities and trimmings, including sea views from its pool. ₹14,000.

West End 45 New Marine Lines ☎022 4083 9121, ⓦwestendhotelmumbai.com; map p.78. A large economy hotel established in 1948 in the heart of South Mumbai with a/c rooms and suites, great Continental, Tandoori and Mughlai food in the *Gourmet* restaurant, plus a lounge bar. ₹6300

AROUND CHHATRAPATI SHIVAJI (VICTORIA) TERMINUS

City Palace 121 City Terrace ☎022 2261 5515, ⓦhotel citypalace.net; map p.78. Large and popular hotel bang opposite the station. The twenty economy rooms are tiny and windowless (almost like in a capsule hotel), but have a/c and are perfectly clean. Deluxe rooms higher up the building are larger and have bird's-eye views. Singles ₹3200. ₹4200

Grand 17 Shri SR Marg, Ballard Estate ☎022 6658 0506, ⓦgrandhotelbombay.com; map p.78. Characterful British-era three-star near the old docks, almost a century old though nicely refurbished, with well-equipped rooms at competitive rates and a decent restaurant. ₹6560

Oasis 276 Shahid Bhagat Singh Marg, near the GPO ☎022 3022 7886, ⓦhoteloasisindia.in; map p.78. Very well placed for CST station, and the best-value budget option in this area: rooms have good beds, clean linen and TVs. It's worth splashing out on a top-floor "deluxe" room as they offer better views. ₹3000

★**Residency** 26 Rustom Sidhwa Marg, off DN Rd ☎022 2262 5525, ⓦresidencyhotel.com; map p.78. Great little mid-range hotel, close to the best shopping areas. Its variously priced rooms (all with safe and complimentary breakfast) offer unbeatable value, especially the no-frills "standard" options. Some rooms are cramped and lack external windows, but they're well furnished and clean, and staff are courteous. Book a fortnight in advance. ₹4870

JUHU AND AROUND THE AIRPORTS

★**Accord** 32 Jawaharlal Nehru Rd, Near Canara Bank, Santa Cruz (East) ☎022 2611 0560, ⓦhotelaccordindia .com; map p.86. If all you want is a simple, inexpensive, clean, secure, attached room for the night within easy reach of the airport, you won't do better than this place. Don't expect a palace: the decor is faded and the location, amid a tangle of busy roads and overpasses, is dreadful; but they get the basics right. The windows are well sound-proofed; staff are courteous; breakfast is included; and there's a 24hr complimentary transfer car to or from the airport, just 15min away. ₹3500

Hyatt Regency Airport Rd, Andheri (East) ☎022 6696 1234, ⓦmumbai.regency.hyatt.com; map p.86. Ancient Hindu precepts on architecture and design were incorporated into this ultra-luxurious five-star, right next to the airport. The results are impressive, with floor-to-ceiling windows and rain showers, plus a spa and fitness centre. ₹12,250

ISKCON Guesthouse Juhu Church Rd, Juhu ☎022 2620 6860, ⓦiskconmumbai.com (follow the "Guest House" link under "Temple" on the drop-down menu); map p.86. Idiosyncratic hotel run by the International Society for Krishna Consciousness. Rooms (some with a/c, ₹1500 extra) are very large and impeccably clean and comfortable for the price, though certain restrictions apply (no alcohol, meat or caffeine may be consumed on the premises). Wi-fi costs ₹600/day. Forty days' advance booking is recommended. ₹4000

ITC Maratha Sahar Rd, Andheri (East) ☎022 2830 3030, ⓦitchotels.in; map p.86. This palatial luxury hotel close to the airport has made an attempt to infuse some Maharashtra character into its decor, and holds a particularly pleasant pool in its central courtyard. Check for early bird offers. ₹15,000

JW Marriott Juhu Tara Rd, Juhu ☎022 6693 3000, ⓦmarriott.com; map p.86. Palatial five-star complex with five opulent restaurants, three pools (one of them filled with treated salt water), a top-notch spa and blocks of luxury rooms looking through landscaped grounds to the beach. ₹16,000

Midland Jawaharlal Nehru Rd, Santa Cruz (East) ☎022 2611 0414, ⓦhotelmidland.com; map p.86. Dependable two-star with well-furnished twin-bedded rooms, just a short ride from the airport. It's right in front of the *Accord* (see above) but not as good value. Courtesy bus and breakfast included in the price. ₹5200

The Orchid 70-C Nehru Rd, Vile Parle (East) ☎022 2616 4040, ⓦorchidhotel.com; map p.86. Award-winning "Eco-Five-Star", built with organic and recycled materials and using low-toxin paints. Every effort is made to minimize waste of natural resources, with a water-recycling plant and "zero garbage" policy. Breakfast included. ₹11,800

VITS Andheri Kurla Rd, International Airport Zone, Andheri (East) ☎022 6151 7555, ⓦvitshotels.com; map p.86. An "Eco-Four-Star at Three-Star prices" is how this environment-friendly hotel describes itself, designed using energy-saving materials and with "green" trimmings such as jute slippers and recycling bins in the rooms. A very comfortable option for the price. ₹6720

Waterstones Hotel Sahar, Andheri (East) ☎022 4090 6633, ⓦwaterstoneshotel.com; map p.86. India's trendiest boutique hotel just five minutes away from the International Airport. Rooms are swanky, and there's a terrific bar and grill, a "movie lounge", Olympic-sized pool and a spa. Breakfast included. ₹10,000

1

EATING

Mumbai is crammed with interesting **places to eat**, from glamorous rooftop lounge bars to hole-in-the-wall kebab shops. The cafés, bars and restaurants of **Colaba** encompass just about the full gamut of possibilities, while a short walk or taxi ride north, **Kala Ghoda** and **Fort** are home to some of the best cafés and restaurants in the city, including its last traditional Parsi diners, whose menus (and sometimes decor as well) have changed little in generations. Watch out for the service charges levied on your bill by some of the more expensive places.

COLABA

All Stir Fry Gordon House Hotel; map p.74. Cool modern restaurant specializing in build-your-own meals using a selection of fresh veg, meat, fish, noodles and sauces, flash-cooked in a wok in front of you. The wok buffet is ₹730/948 (veg/non-veg) for unlimited servings, and there's an extensive *dim sum* menu (₹275–550). Daily 7–10am, 12–3.30pm & 7pm–1am.

Bademiya Behind the Taj Mahal Palace & Tower on Tulloch Rd ❶022 2284 8038, ⓦbademiya.com; map p.74 & map 78. Legendary Colaba kebab-wallah serving delicious flame-grilled chicken, mutton and fish steaks (all at ₹120–150), as well as veg alternatives (₹90), wrapped in paper-thin, piping hot *rotis*, from benches on the sidewalk. Families from uptown drive here on weekends, eating in their car bonnets, but there are also little tables and chairs if you don't fancy a takeaway. For a sit-down meal, try their restaurant on nearby Navroji F Rd (❶022 2202 1447; map p.78) or their fine-dining branch near the State Central Library at Horniman Circle (❶022 2265 5657). Daily 6.30pm–late.

Busaba 4 Mandlik Marg ❶022 2204 3769, ⓦbusaba .net; map p.74. Sophisticated bar-restaurant specializing in Far Eastern cuisine (₹450–600). Thai, Korean, Vietnamese and Tibetan staples run alongside exotic salads. The big signature dish here, however, is Burmese *kaukswe*: a mound of noodles in a smooth, rich, coconut broth, topped with tender meat, fresh ginger, lime, fried onions and crispy wonton noodles. One of *the* places the city's high rollers like to pose (if they can't get a table at *Indigo* next door). Daily noon–3pm & 6.30pm–midnight.

Churchill 103 Colaba Causeway; map p.74. Tiny a/c Parsi diner, with a vast choice of filling, Continental comfort food, from pizza to pasta and burgers – ideal if you've had your fill of spicy food. For dessert or an afternoon treat, check the famous

Churchill fridge for freshly baked treats such as gooey chocolate cake or blueberry cheesecake (₹105). No alcohol, no washrooms. Most mains ₹390–445. Daily 11am–midnight.

Indigo 4 Mandlik Marg ❶022 6636 8980, ⓦfood indigo.com; map p.74. One of the city's most fashionable restaurants, specializing in superb international and modern European cooking with a gourmet Indian twist (Cochin crab tortellini, for example). Mains ₹600–885 or ₹2400/head for three courses; wine prices are astronomical. Reservations essential. Daily noon–3pm & 7pm–1am.

Indigo Deli Ground Floor, Pheroze Building, Chattrapati Shivaji Maharishi Marg ❶022 6655 1010; map p.74. This much-loved gastro café-restaurant is a stalwart of the south Mumbai scene thanks to its menu of Continental comfort foods and NY deli-style staples – from burgers (₹565–725) and hot dogs to thin-crust pizzas and perfect steak frites – served in sleek designer comfort. Pick of the all-day breakfast selection is the chef's special Eggs Benedict (or "Eggs Benny" as it's known here). For dessert, try the organic lime pie (₹395), or croissant bread pudding with brandy sauce. They serve single origin coffees and teas. Most mains ₹565–800. Daily 8.30am–12.30am.

Kamat SB Singh Rd, Colaba Causeway ❶022 2287 4734; map p.74. Friendly little restaurant serving the best South Indian breakfasts in the area, as well as the usual range of southern snacks (*idli*, *vada*, *sambhar*), delicious dosas and (limited) thalis for ₹110–250, besides Punjabi and Chinese. Daily 8.30am–10.30pm.

★**Konkan Café** Vivanta By Taj Hotel, Cuffe Parade ❶022 6665 0808; map p.72. Sophisticated five-star hotel restaurant, done up in earthy terracotta red and banana-leaf green hues in homage to a Mangalorean home. They serve fine regional cuisine from coastal Maharashtra, Goa, Karnataka and Kerala. Choose from their thali platters (₹1950) or go à la carte: butter-pepper-garlic crab is to die

STREET FOOD

Mumbai is renowned for distinctive street foods – especially **bhel puri**, a quintessentially Mumbai masala mixture of puffed rice, deep-fried vermicelli, potato, crunchy puri pieces, chilli paste, tamarind water, chopped onions and coriander. More hygienic, but no less ubiquitous, is **pao bhaji**, a round Portuguese-style bread roll served on a tin plate with griddle-fried, spicy vegetable stew, and **kanji vada**, savoury doughnuts soaked in fermented mustard and chilli sauce. And if all that doesn't appeal, a pit-stop at one of the city's hundreds of **juice bars** probably will. There's no better way to beat the sticky heat than with a glass of cool milk shaken with fresh pineapple, mango, banana, *chikoo* (small brown fruit that tastes like a sweet pear) or custard apple. Just make sure they hold on the ice – which may be made with untreated water.

1

for. Quite simply some of the most mouthwatering South Indian food you'll ever eat. Daily noon–2.45pm & 7–11.45pm.

Leopold's Colaba Causeway; map p.74. A Mumbai institution that played a starring role in Gregory David Roberts' *Shantaram*, *Leopold's* is the number-one hangout for India-weary Western travellers, who continue to cram onto its small tables for overpriced Indian, Continental and Chinese food. The café was one of the leading targets of the 2008 terror attacks, though its bullet-ridden walls have now been discreetly hidden with pictures. Mains ₹310–570; beer ₹210–510. Daily 7.30am–midnight.

Olympia Coffee House Rahim Mansion, Colaba Causeway ☎022 2202 1043; map p.74. *Fin-de-siècle* Irani café with marble tabletops, wooden wall panels, fancy mirrors and a mezzanine floor for women. Waiters in Peshwari caps and *salwar kameez* serve melt-in-the-mouth kebabs and delicious curd-based dips. It gets crowded at breakfast for cholesterol-packed *masala kheema* (fried mutton mince), which regulars wash down with bright orange chai. A quint-essential (and inexpensive) Bombay experience. Mains ₹70–160. Mon–Thurs, Sat & Sun 7am–11.45pm, Fri 7–11.45am & 1.30–11.45pm.

The Sea Lounge Taj Mahal Palace and Tower; map p.74. Atmospheric 1930s-style lounge café on the first floor of the *Taj*, with fine Gateway and harbour views – good for high tea (from around ₹750) or a decadent breakfast (₹1160–1225). Daily 7am–midnight.

KALA GHODA

Chetana 34K Dubhash Marg ☎022 2284 4968, ⦿chetana.com; map p.74. Sumptuous pure-veg thalis (Maharashtrian, Rajasthani or Gujarati, with a healthy low-calorie option at lunchtime; ₹420–450) served in a mellow, Indian-style interior (a/c) with booths and traditional art on the walls. You won't find better *desi* cooking at this price anywhere else in south Mumbai. Daily 12.30–3.30pm & 7.30–11.30pm.

Kala Ghoda Café 10 Rope Walk Lane ☎022 2263 3866, ⦿kgcafe.in; map p.74. This tiny café makes a hip little pit-stop if you're visiting the nearby museums. High, whitewashed walls, long skylights and wood benches give a feeling of space even though it's pint-sized. The coffee and teas are first rate, and they do freshly baked light bites, sandwiches (₹145–240), salads (₹260–395), soups, waffles and fruit sundaes (₹160–250), as well as more filling main meals like pasta (₹390–420) after 7.30pm. Free wi-fi (except between 12.30 and 3.30pm). Daily 8.30am–11.45pm.

★**Khyber** 145 MG Rd, opposite Jehangir Art Gallery ☎022 4039 6666, ⦿khyberrestaurant.com; map p.74. You enter this romantic Mughlai restaurant through a finely carved, cusp-arched sandstone facade, and the interior is no less enchanting. The cuisine is "Northwest Frontier" style:

rich, creamy curries made with sublime blends of spices, and choice cuts of seafood, chicken or mutton kebabs flame-grilled or braised in traditional *tava* pans. Mains ₹495–700. Daily 12.30–4pm & 7.30–midnight.

The Pantry Yeshwant Chambers, Ground Floor, Military Square Lane ☎022 2267 8901; map p.74. A great option for a heat-beating light bite or gourmet brunch: with its cement floors, recycled Burmese hardwood table tops, white walls and dabs of pastel colour, the café has a fresh, airy feel and a menu featuring Continental crowd pleasers such as quiche (₹250), gorgonzola and apple sandwiches (₹345) and waffles (₹295–395), alongside freshly baked pastries. Mains ₹275–525. Daily 8.30am–11.30pm.

Trishna 7 Sai Baba Marg (Ropewalk Lane), Kala Ghoda ☎022 2270 3213, ⦿trishna.co.in; map p.74. Visiting dignitaries and local celebs, from the President of Greece to Bollywood stars, have eaten in this dimly lit Mangalorean restaurant. There are wonderful fish dishes in every sauce going, including the signature butter-pepper-garlic crab (₹1200) and superb pomfret stuffed with green masala (₹1400), plus cheaper North Indian standards. Very small, so book in advance. Mon–Sat noon–3.30pm & 6.30pm–midnight, Sun noon–3.30pm and 7.30pm–midnight.

CHURCHGATE AND FORT

★**Apoorva** SA Brelvi Rd ☎022 2287 0335; map p.78. Popular Mangalorean restaurant, hidden up a side street off Horniman Circle (look for the tree trunk wrapped with fairy lights). The cooking is authentic and the seafood – simmered in spicy coconut-based gravies – comes fresh off the boat each day. Try their definitive Bombay duck, *surmai* (kingfish) in coconut gravy or delicious prawn *gassi*, served with perfect *sannas* and *appams*. Mains ₹290–900. Daily 11:30am–4pm & 6.30pm–midnight.

★**Britannia & Co** Shri SR Marg, Ballard Estate ☎022 2261 5264; map p.78. Quirky little Parsi restaurant set up in 1923, famous for its quaint period atmosphere and wholesome Irani food, like the mouthwatering berry pulao (chicken, mutton or vegetable), made with deliciously tart dried berries imported from Tehran (₹350/650 veg/non-veg, but portions are gigantic). For afters, there's the house caramel custard. One of the city's unmissable eating experiences. Mon–Sat noon–4pm.

Ideal Corner 12 F/G Hornby View, Gunbow St ☎022 2262 1930; map p.78. Another Parsi café with a cult following, dishing up delicious home-made specialities like *salli boti* (meat curry with potato stick toppings), *patra ni machi* (fish steamed in banana leaf), lamb or veg dhansak, and exceptional *lagan nu* custard – a Zoroastrian take on the classic British pud, flavoured with rose water and cardamom. Most mains ₹100–190. Tues–Sun noon–3.30pm & 5.30–10.45pm.

★**Mahesh Lunch Home** 8-B Cawasji Patel St ☎022 2287 0938, ⦿maheshlunchhome.com; map p.78. Much

1

like *Trishna* (see p.97) only a good bit cheaper and less touristy, this Mangalorean diner in the depths of Fort is famous across the city for its flavoursome seafood specialities, especially the Koliwada prawns (₹450), pomfret *gassi* (₹590) and fish curry (₹380), and the jumbo butter-garlic crab, sold by weight. Reservations recommended on weekends. Mon–Sat 11.30am–4pm & 6pm–midnight, Sun 7pm–midnight.

Pizza By the Bay Soona Mahal, 143 Marine Drive ☏ 022 2284 3646, ⊚ pizzabythebay.in; map p.78. This bustling, high-end Italian on the corner of VN Rd and Marine Drive does a brisk trade in authentic pasta (₹610), pizza (₹580–800) and freshly baked treats, as well as European-style breakfasts (7–11am). Reserve ahead for a table next to the window for breezy bay views. Long waits on weekends are the norm, even if you book. Count on spending upwards of ₹1500 for three courses. Happy hour Mon–Fri noon–7pm. Daily 7am–1am.

CHOWPATTY

Bachelorr's Juice House Chowpatty Sea Face, opposite Birla Krida Kendra, near Charni Rd station ☏ 022 2368 1408; map p.72. There's no better antidote to the brouhaha of the nearby beach than a "Strawberry Cream" at *Bachelorr's* – a tall milkshake crammed with whipped cream and pieces of fresh strawberry, which they do in any number of chocolate-based variations. No points for ambience. Daily 10am–1am.

Cream Centre Fulchand Niwas 25/B, Chowpatty Sea Face ☏ 022 2367 9222; map p.72. This immaculately clean, pure-veg fast-food joint facing Chowpatty Beach serves a huge range of Indian snacks, but the best, by far, is their famous *channa batura* (₹150) – a frisbee-sized pillow of deep-fried puri, which you poke with your finger to deflate and use to mop up a bowl of creamy masala chickpeas, diced potatoes and onions. Daily noon–11.30pm.

Crystal 19 Chowpatty Sea Face, near Wilson College ☏ 022 2369 1482; map p.72. Lovers of North Indian home-cooking travel here from across the city to eat *dhaba*-style dhal *makhani*, *alu matar* and other spicy vegetarian dishes, served from a soot-blackened kitchen. For dessert, there's divine *kheer* (cardamom-flavoured rice pudding) and *amras* (mango pulp). A great little budget option if you're not fazed by the grime, with most mains under ₹100. Daily noon–3.30pm & 7–10.30pm.

CRAWFORD MARKET AND THE CENTRAL BAZAARS

Badshah Juice and Snack Bar Opposite Crawford Market, Lokmanya Tilak Rd ☏ 022 2342 1943; map p.72. Delicious kulfi, and dozens of freshly squeezed fruit juices, though most locals come for the *faloodas* (₹95–135) – an incomparable, quintessentially Mumbai mix of vermicelli, basil seeds and tapioca pearls steeped in milk,

ice cream and rose syrup. The ideal place to round off a trip to the market. Daily 7am–12.30am.

★**Joshi Club** 381-A Narottamwadi, Kalbadevi Rd ☏ 022 2205 8089; map p.72. Also known as *The Friends Union Joshi Club*, this eccentric thali canteen serves what many aficionados regard as the most genuine and tasty Gujarati-Marwari meals in the city, on unpromising Formica tables against a backdrop of grubby walls. ₹200 buys you unlimited portions of four vegetable dishes, dhal and up to four different kinds of bread, with all the trimmings (and banana custard). Daily 11am–3pm & 7–10pm.

THE NORTHERN SUBURBS

Bong Bong 5 Silver Croft CHS, corner of 16th Rd and 33rd Rd, Bandra West ☏ 022 6555 5567; map p.86. The best of a select band of authentic Bengali restaurants in the suburbs, catering mainly for homesick movie-makers. Decorated with memorabilia, rickshaw murals and old photographs of Kolkata, it has a cosy and sociable vibe and serves food packed with astounding flavours. Mains from ₹260–400. Daily noon–3.30pm & 7pm–12.30am.

★**Dakshin Coastal** ITC Maratha, Sahar Rd, near the airport ☏ 022 2830 3030; map p.86. A far cry from your regular Udupi vegetarian joint, *Dakshin Coastal* showcases the sublime and varied cuisine of the South Indian shoreline. From the sun-dried chillis soaked in buttermilk appetizer to main-course delights such as Keralan-style prawns delicately cooked with raw mango and fresh coconut, everything is packed with intense flavours and exquisitely presented. Count on ₹2000–2500/head for the works. Mon–Sat 7–11.45pm, Sun 12.30–2.45pm.

★**Dum Pukht** ITC Maratha, Sahar Rd, near the airport ITC Maratha, Sahar Rd ☏ 022 2830 3030; map p.86. One of the few kitchens in India that faithfully re-creates the cuisine of the Muslim nawabs of Hyderabad and Awadh, where chefs developed a technique of slow cooking known as *dum*. If you've a monster appetite, go for the *raan-e-dum pukht* – a leg of marinated lamb stuffed with spices, baked in dough and finished with a shell of dried fruit, coconut and oven juices. The decor's as regal as the cooking. Count on ₹2000–2500/head for three courses. Daily 7–11.45pm.

Govinda's ISKCON Hare Krishna Mandir, Juhu Tara Rd, Juhu ☏ 022 2620 0337; map p.86. Sumptuous vegetarian thalis of sattvic cooking (no garlic or onions). Everything's been ritually offered to Krishna before being served, guaranteeing what the management describe as a "transcendental dining experience". At ₹450/head, it's certainly great value for Mumbai and there's often live *bhajan* singing. Daily 7am–3pm & 7.30–10.30pm.

Pali Bhavan 10 Adarsh Nagar, Pali Naka, near Costa Coffee, Bandra (West) ☏ 022 2651 9400; map p.86. An aura of Old India hangs over this quirkily styled restaurant up in Bandra, which delights as much for its decor of sepia

1

photos and antique woodwork as its classy pan-Indian cuisine. The huge menu features dishes from across the country, given classy gourmet twists (₹1000–1500/head). Daily noon– 2.45pm & 7pm–12.30am.

Rajdhani Level 2 Phoenix Market City, LBS Marg, Kurla (West); map p.86. Outstanding, eat-till-you-burst vegetarian thali joint serving home-style Gujarati and Marwari fare. The friendly waiters have unique hand signals to transmit messages to servers dishing out an endless procession of over a dozen treats. At ₹460 for an unlimited thali, it's great value for money. Daily noon–3.30pm & 7–11pm.

DRINKING

Mumbaikars have an unusually easy-going attitude to alcohol; popping into a **bar** for a beer is very much accepted (for men at least), even at lunchtime. **Colaba Causeway** is the focus of the travellers' and local students' social scene but to sample the cutting edge of the city's nightlife, you'll have to venture to the **suburbs**, where the trendiest places have turned the city's draconian licensing laws to their advantage by serving gourmet food to complement the range of imported beers, wines and cocktails.

★**AER** Four Seasons Hotel, 114 Dr E Moses Rd, Worli ☎022 2481 8000, ⓦ fourseasons.com; map p.70. With its all-white, *Miami Vice*-style jigsaw furniture and astounding panoramic views over the city, this alfresco bar on the 34th floor of a luxury skyscraper hotel has become the poster boy of Mumbai's lounge bars, even out-blinging the *Dome* on Marine Drive (see below). Cocktails and champagne are half-price between 5.30 and 8.30pm. Otherwise, it's Moët & Chandon at ₹1400/glass (or Kingfishers for a more reasonable ₹450). Cover charges after 10pm, ₹2500/head admission on Fri & Sat. Daily 5.30pm–1.30am.

The Barking Deer Mathuradas Mill Compound, Senapati Bapat Marg, Lower Parel ☎022 3015 1377; map p.70. Mumbai's first brewpub, serving fresh craft beer like Bombay Blonde, Flying Pig Belgian Wit or Honey Bee Braggot (₹300 glass, ₹1150 pitcher), alongside great finger food. The Deer Belly Lunch (Mon–Thurs noon–3pm; ₹650) offers a four-course multicuisine set meal with a goblet of beer or choice of mocktail. Happy hours 5–8pm. Daily 11.30pm–12.30am.

Bonobo 1 Kennilworth Phase II, 2nd Floor, off Linking Rd, Bandra ☎022 2605 5050; map p.86. *Bonobo* is the current high court of cool, hosting live gigs and DJ sets on Fridays and Saturdays in a (tiny) a/c performance space – from drum 'n' bass to dubstep. A balmy rooftop bar soaks up the overspill, and doubles as a gastro diner with delicious dishes like picante prawns and calamari (₹424). Drinks ₹250–450. Daily 5.30pm–1.30am.

★**Café Marina** Sea Palace Hotel, Kerawalla Chambers, Apollo Bunder, Colaba; map p.74. If lounge-resto isn't your thing, and all you want is a reasonably priced cold beer, and something tasty to munch while savouring an expansive view, this place ticks all the boxes. Overlooking the harbour from a great rooftop vantage point, it offers local and imported bottled beers from ₹290–525. Daily 8.30am–11.30pm.

Café Mondegar Colaba Causeway; map p.74. Draught and bottled beer (₹220–440) and deliciously fruity cocktails are served in this small café-bar. The atmosphere is very relaxed, the music on the famous jukebox tends towards cheesy rock classics and the clientele is a mix of Westerners and local students; murals by famous Goan cartoonist Mario Miranda give the place a cheerful ambience. Breakfast menu till 11.30am. Daily 8.30am–1.30pm.

Café Nemo 329/A Thadani House, off Worli Sea Face and New Prabhadevi Rd, near the Indian Coast Guard office ☎022 2430 1127, ⓦ cafenemo.com; map p.86. Located in an antique bungalow in a backstreet across the water from Bandra, this used to be a hub for Mumbai's underground music scene but was recently renovated into a yuppie café with a slick yellow-and-grey colour scheme. Besides cocktails (₹450-550), a range of international food, including Korean fried chicken, is on offer (from ₹250), and one of the rooms is still used for live music events. Daily noon–1.30am.

Colaba Social 24 Glen Rose Building, BK Boman Behram Marg, Apollo Bunder ☎022 2282 8484, ⓦ socialoffline .in; map p.74. Colaba's latest hangout with industrial interiors, exposed brick and piping, metal chairs and a ceiling studded with funky egg trays. Expect a decent range of craft beer (₹225–325), wine (₹250–575) and cocktails (₹295–625), alongside all-day breakfast (till 7.30pm) and sharing plates (from ₹290). Daily 8.30am–1.30pm.

The Dome Hotel InterContinental, 135 Marine Drive; map p.78. After *AER* in Worli, this cool rooftop bar is easily south Mumbai's most alluring spot for a sundowner. Plush white sofas and candlelit tables surround the domed rotunda and a very sexy raised pool, while the views over Back Bay make even the sky-high drink prices (₹800 plus for a cocktail) feel worth it. ₹2000/head. Daily 5.30pm–1.30am.

Gadda da Vida Novotel Mumbai, Balraj Sahani Marg, Juhu Beach ☎022 6693 4444, ⓦ novotel.com; map p.86. Beach-front bars are like hens' teeth in Mumbai, but at *Gadda da Vida* (named after a hit from 1970s prog-rock band Iron Butterfly) you can sip your Caipiroska by the poolside as the sun sets over Juhu's churning waves. House DJs spin electro jazz early on, followed by dance anthems as the place fills up. ₹430 for a beer and ₹800 for cocktails.

1

Cover charge ₹1200/per person. Happy hours 3–7pm. Daily 5.30pm–1.30am.

Havana Gordon House Hotel, Battery St, Colaba; map p.74. The retro *Polly Esther's* has been revamped into a warm-toned Cuban-style café and bar with wooden railway sleepers and hand-painted signs of Che and Castro, plus a separate cigar room. Cover charge ₹1000–2000. Tues–Thurs & Sun 12.30–3pm & 5pm–1.30am, Fri & Sat 12.30–3pm & 5pm–3am.

Indigo 4 Mandlik Rd, Colaba ☎ 022 6636 8981, ⊛ food indigo.com; map p.74. Attached to the fashionable *Indigo* restaurant (see p.96), this is the coolest hangout in Colaba, with edgy, stripped-bare decor and frequented by young media types and would-be wine buffs. Beer from ₹250, cocktails from ₹560. Daily 6.30pm–1.30am.

The Irish House Phoenix Mills Compound, Senapati Bapat Marg, Lower Parel ☎ 022 4347 1111, ⊛ theirish house.in; map p.70. Rustic wooden decor and booths create the chatty ambience of a typical Irish pub. Fresh draught beer (₹220) is served out of wooden kegs, and there's an extensive range of bottled beers. Their popular pub grub includes fish 'n' chips (₹395) and BBQ sandwiches (from ₹275). Happy hours 5–8pm. Daily noon–1.30am.

Olive 4 Union Park Rd, Pali Hill (between Juhu and Bandra) ☎ 022 4340 8228, ⊛ olivebarandkitchen.com; map p.86. If you want to rub shoulders with Mumbai's party crowd, the theme bar night on Thursday evening (aka TGIT or Thank God It's Thursday) is your best bet, though dress to kill – and come armed with a full wallet. Cocktails are around ₹1000. Mon–Sat 7.30pm–1am, Sat & Sun noon–3.30pm & 7.30pm–1.30am.

Salt Water Café Rose Minar Annexe, 87 Chapel Rd, next to Mount Carmel Church, Bandra (West) ☎ 022 2643 4441, ⊛ saltwatercafe.in; map p.86. This smart all-day diner in swanky Bandra is renowned for its relaxed atmosphere, warm-toned designer decor, gastro food and drink-till-you-drop happy hours. During the day you can down unlimited quantities of sangria for ₹600, and on Wed–Sat between 11pm and 1am, ₹750 buys you unlimited vodka cocktails and Budweiser. Sunday brunch ₹1500/head without alcohol. Happy hours 4–7pm. Daily 9am–1am.

Toto's Garage 30 Lourdes Heaven, Pali Junction, Bandra (West) ☎ 022 2600 5494; map p.86. Neon-lit, garage-themed bar with a VW hanging from its ceiling, belting mostly 80s rock. It's tiny and packed to the gills most of the time with the lads piling in for pitchers of draught beer after work (from ₹200/pint). Daily 6pm–1am.

Wink Vivanta by Taj, G.D. Somani Rd, 90 Cuffe Parade ☎ 022 6665 0808; map p.72. This stylish lounge bar a short hop from Colaba is split into two areas, separated by a Japanese gauze screen: a sleek island bar, famous for its Winktini cocktails (₹700–1000); and a chillout area with brick walls and comfy couches where you can chat and munch on wasabi peas until the DJ cranks up the volume around 11pm. It gets very busy on weekends. Theme nights during the week, such as ladies' night on Wed and Bollywood on Fri. Sun–Thurs 6pm–1am, Fri & Sat 6pm–3.30am.

NIGHTLIFE

Despite a 1.30am curfew (only clubs within hotels are allowed to carry on later), Mumbai's **clubbing** scene remains the most full-on in India. Tiny, skin-tight outfits that show off razor-sharp abs and pumped-up pecs are very much the order of the day for boys, and spray-on mini-dresses and kitten heels are *de rigueur* for the girls. Dancefloors get as rammed as a suburban commuter train and the cover charges can be astronomical on weekends. Door policies and dress codes tend to be strict ("no ballcaps, no shorts, no sandals"), and, in theory, most clubs have a "couples-only" policy. In practice, if you're in a mixed group and don't appear sleazy you shouldn't have any problems.

★ **Blue Frog** D/2 Mathuradas Mills Compound, NM Joshi Marg, Lower Parel ☎ 022 6158 6158, ⊛ bluefrog .co.in; map p.70. Housed in an old warehouse in Mumbai's former mill district, *Blue Frog* is the city's hippest and most happening live music venue, showcasing leading Indian and international music acts and DJs – anything from rock to hip-hop and Indo-jazz fusion. Admission is free before 9pm (except on Sun), otherwise ₹350 Tues–Thurs & Sun, or ₹600 on Fri & Sat. Tues–Sat 6.30pm–1.30am, Sun 11.30am–5pm & 6.30pm–1.30am.

EXO St Regis Hotel, Senapati Bapat Marg, Lower Parel ☎ 022 6162 8422, ⊛ stregismumbai.com; map p.70. Mumbai's hottest nightclub, spread over two floors (Level 37–38 of the swish *St Regis*, with floor-to-ceiling windows, Osler chandeliers, leather upholstery and foot-tapping house music. Around ₹5000 cover charge for two people. Wed, Thurs & Sun 7pm–1am, Fri & Sat 7pm–3am.

Royalty G1/B, Krystal Building, Waterfield Road, Bandra West ☎ 022 4229 6000 ⊛ royaltyindia.com; map p.86. European Renaissance meets Indian royalty, with plush interiors and extensive gold-leafing; the main club area spreads over ten thousand square feet with an elevated VIP Members area and a separate Baroque-style Red Room. Resident DJs spin popular EDM and hip-hop, and there are frequent gigs by guest DJs. Wed–Sat 10pm–1.30am.

★ **Trilogy** Hotel Sea Princess, Juhu Tara Rd, Santacruz (W) ☎ 022 2646 9500, ⊛ trilogy.in; map p.86. This place has it all: rude doormen, bartenders in fedoras, a glittering staircase, VVIP lounges, a huge dancefloor (a rarity in Mumbai) and sparkly LED chandeliers that festoon the ceiling and change colours in sync with the music. The DJs play mostly hip-hop for a mixture of teenyboppers, Bollywood wannabes and thirty-somethings. Drink prices are top whack (₹400 for beers, double for shots and cocktails). Entry ₹2000/couple. Daily 10pm–3am.

CINEMA

Not surprisingly for a city obsessed with the movies, Mumbai has hundreds of **cinema houses**, among them a handful of glorious Art Deco halls dating from the twilight of the Raj. However, only a handful regularly screen **English-language** films. The rest feature the latest Bollywood blockbusters, which of course aren't shown with subtitles. For the latest **reviews and listings**, get hold of a copy of *Time Out Mumbai* magazine (₹50). Alternatively, look for the biggest, brightest hoarding, and join the queue. **Seats** in a comfortable a/c cinema cost ₹170–300, or less if you sit in the stalls (not advisable for women).

Eros Cambata Building, 42 M. Karve Rd, opposite Churchgate station ☎022 2282 2335, ⊛eroscinema .co.in. Another Art Deco behemoth, the Eros can accommodate over a thousand people. Screens mainly Hindi and Marathi movies, with occasional English-language offerings.

Inox CR2 Mall, 2nd Floor, Barrister Rajni Patel Marg, Nariman Point ☎022 6152 2888, ⊛inoxmovies.com. Another big multiscreen venue, in the retro Mumbai-Art Deco style.

Metro Big MG Rd, Dhobi Talao Junction, Marine Lines ☎022 3984 4060 or ☎93241 41119, ⊛bigcinemas .com. Opened by Metro-Goldwyn-Mayer in 1938, this is the granddaddy of the city's movie houses, transformed into a six-screen multiplex in 2006. Facilities are top-notch. Screens mainly Hindi movies, but does show the odd Hollywood hit.

Regal Shahid Bhagat Singh Rd, Colaba ☎022 2202 1017. One of Mumbai's oldest and best-loved cinema halls, the Regal showed Laurel and Hardy's *The Devil's Brother* on its opening night in 1933. There's still only one screen, and the auditorium is filled with velvet seats. Shows both Hollywood and Bollywood, mainly to affluent middle-class professionals and students, so the vibe is generally civilized. The handiest cinema if you're based in south Mumbai.

SHOPPING

Mumbai is a great place to shop and prices compare well with other Indian cities. Locally produced **textiles** and export-surplus clothing are among the best buys, as are **handicrafts** from far-flung corners of the country. In the larger shops, rates are fixed and **credit cards** are often accepted; elsewhere, particularly when dealing with street vendors, it pays to haggle. Uptown, the **central bazaars** are better for spectating than serious shopping.

ANTIQUES

Bollywood Bazaar Mutton St ☎022 2347 2427; map p.72. The Chor Bazaar area, and Mutton Street in particular, is the centre of Mumbai's antiques trade. And one shop that's worth the trip alone for Indian film fans is the wonderful Bollywood Bazaar, which sells old posters and memorabilia. The priciest pieces are hand-painted specimens dating from the 1950s, but they also stock plenty of repro versions that make great souvenirs. Sat–Thurs 10am–8pm.

Phillip's Antiques Madame Cama Rd, opposite Regal Cinema ⊛phillipsantiques.com, Colaba; map p.74. Although much more expensive than Chor Bazaar, this famous antique shop is well worth a browse – even if you're not buying. Brass, bronze and wood Hindu sculpture, silver jewellery, old prints and aquatints form the mainstay of its collection. Mon–Sat 10am–7pm.

CLOTHES AND TEXTILES

Mumbai produces the bulk of India's clothes, mostly the lightweight, light-coloured "shirtings and suitings" favoured by droves of uniformly attired office-wallahs. Better-quality cotton clothes (often stylish designer-label rip-offs) are available in shops along Colaba Causeway and Mandlik Marg (behind the *Taj Mahal Palace and Tower*).

PERFORMING ARTS IN MUMBAI

Mumbai is a major centre for traditional **performing arts**, attracting the finest **Indian classical musicians** and **dancers** from all over the country. Frequent concerts and recitals are staged at venues such as Bharatiya Vidya Bhavan, KM Munshi Marg (☎022 2363 0224), the headquarters of the international cultural (Hindu) organization, and the National Centre for the Performing Arts, Nariman Point (NCPA; ⊛ncpamumbai.com).

For **drama**, head out to the Prithvi Theatre (☎022 2614 9546, ⊛prithvitheatre.org) on Juhu Church Road, a small but lively venue focusing mainly on Hindi-language theatre, along with some English productions.

1

BOLLYWOOD REVOLUTION

Film is massive in India. The country produces around 1200 movies annually, half of them in the studios of north Mumbai. Known as "**Bollywood**", the home of the All-India cinema industry has experienced a sea change over the past decade, as its output has started to reach mass audiences of expat Indians in Europe and North America. The resulting global revenues have financed much higher production standards and a completely new approach to plot, acting styles and scripts – rendering redundant the old cinematic stereotypes of the so-called "masala format", which dominated Indian film for decades.

Big song-and-dance numbers still very much have their place in the modern Bollywood blockbuster, as does melodrama. But the overall tone these days tends to be much more sophisticated, with glamorous foreign locations, more plausible story lines, cutting-edge camera work and even state-of-the-art CGI deployed to wow cinemagoers at home and abroad. Much of it is now developed in-house, helmed by VFX studios like Red Chillies.

Whereas in the past, hit movies tended to incorporate a bit of everything – romance, laughs, fight scenes, chases, lurid baddies, a set of instantly recognizable stock characters and convoluted plots that emphasized traditional values – now the industry is making big bucks from more nuanced genre flicks. The highest grossing movies of the past decade were a cross-border comedy drama (*Bajrangi Bhaijaan*; 2015); a sci-fi comedy satirizing religious dogma (*PK*; 2014); a caper (*Dhoom 3*; 2013); an action flick (*Ek Tha Tiger*; 2012); and a love story (*Bodyguard*; 2011) – radical departures from the Bollywood mainstream. Though "commercial" film-makers like Karan Johar and Rohit Shetty continue to churn out tried-and-tested formulaic films, a crop of directors like Vishal Bhardwaj, Dibakar Banerjee and Anurag Kashyap are unafraid to experiment with themes.

Some elements, however, remain consistent. Not even the most serious Indian movie can do without at least two or three "item numbers" – the set-piece song-and-dance sequences that give all hit films their essential anthems. And the cult of the Bollywood star shows no sign of abating. A-listers in the industry enjoy almost god-like status (only the country's top cricketers come close to matching their exalted mass appeal). Images of the current heartthrobs appear everywhere, from newspapers to cheesy TV ads.

At the top of the heap stands the veteran, white-bearded éminence grise of Bollywood, **Amitabh Bachchan**, whose record-breaking career as a screen hero saw a startling revival in the 2000s after he came out of de facto retirement to host India's version of *Who Wants To Be A Millionaire*, called *KBC* (*Kaun Banega Crorepati*). Only a notch behind him comes **Shah Rukh Khan**, the smouldering lead of countless romantic blockbusters and the man the *Los Angeles Times* dubbed "the world's biggest movie star" in 2011. SRK has great overseas appeal, and the Khan trilogy is completed by Bollywood bad boy **Salman Khan** and **Aamir Khan**, the actor-director-producer behind hits such as *Lagaan*, *Ghajini*, *3 Idiots* and *PK*. Other leading men of the moment include action stars Akshay Kumar and Ajay Devgan, dancing sensation **Hrithik Roshan**, newcomer **Ranveer Singh** and talented **Ranbir Kapoor** who represents the fourth generation of the illustrious Kapoor clan, India's first family of cinema.

Not surprisingly in such an image-obsessed industry, **female leads** tend to have a shorter shelf life than their male counterparts, although contemporary starlets such as **Priyanka Chopra**, **Deepika Padukone**, **Katrina Kaif**, **Anushka Sharma** and **Kangna Ranaut** are tackling increasingly demanding roles in an attempt to prove themselves as serious actresses.

Even so, their off-screen antics and romantic dalliances continue to capture more attention than their acting skills, as do any public appearance of India's biggest celebrity couple, star actor **Abhishek Bachchan** (son of Amitabh) and his wife **Aishwarya Rai**. A former Miss World whose extreme beauty and svelte figure are often credited as spearheading the crossover of Bollywood into Western cinemas, Aishwarya has maintained her great popularity despite having had her first child in 2011. The career trajectory of Bollywood actresses has tended to be downwards after marriage (the assumption being that Indian audiences aren't prepared to accept a married woman, or even worse, a mother, as a romantic heroine). But with several other Bollywood queens – **Madhuri Dixit Nene, Karisma Kapoor, Rani Mukherjee** and **Vidya Balan** – making comebacks after starting a family, the times may well be changing.

Fabindia Jeroo Bldg, 137 MG Road, Kala Ghoda ☎022 2262 6539, ⊛fabindia.com; map p.74. It's worth checking out the local branch of the nationwide Fabindia chain, which has an excellent and very affordable selection of stylish modern Indian-style shirts, *kurtas*, *salwar kameez*, as well as beautifully made items for the home. Daily 10am–8pm.

"Fashion Street" MG Rd; map p.78. For cheap Western clothing, you can't beat this long row of stalls strung out along MG Rd between Cross and Azad maidans west of CST, specializing in reject and export-surplus goods ditched by big manufacturers: mainly T-shirts, jeans, summer dresses and sweatshirts. Daily 10am–9pm.

Khadi shop (signed "Mumbai Khadi Gramodyog Sangh") 286 Dr D.N. Marg, near the Thomas Cook office; map p.78. For traditional Indian clothes, look no further than here. As Whiteaway & Laidlaw, this rambling Victorian department store used to kit out all the newly arrived burrasahibs with pith helmets, khaki shorts and quinine tablets. These days, its old wooden counters and shirt and sock drawers stock dozens of different hand-spun cottons and silks, sold by the metre or made up as vests, *kurtas* or block-printed *salwar kameez*. Mon–Sat 10.30am–6.30pm.

Shrujan Saagar Villa, 38 Bhulabahi Desai Rd, opposite Navroz Apartment ☎022 2352 1693, ⊛shrujan.org; map p.72. A dazzling array of bags, belts, cushion covers, trousers, quilts, saris, shawls, skirts, tops and wall hangings, embroidered by tribal women from the Kutch region of Gujarat. All profits go to community development schemes. Mon–Sat 10.30am–6.30pm.

Vaya Tanna House Annexe, Nathalal Parekh Marg ☎022 2202 9115; map p.74. Charming collective of hand-woven and heritage textiles from across India with artisan shawls, saris and fabrics sourced directly from weavers. Mon–Sat 11am–7pm.

LIFESTYLE

Bombay Store Western India House, Sir PM Rd, Fort ☎022 2288 5048; map p.78. This department store in the Fort district is a great place to shop for souvenirs, with vibrant displays of traditional handicrafts, textiles, woodwork, silverware, repro vintage photos and funky fashion accessories and designer artefacts from the Elephant Company. Mon–Sat 10.30am–8pm, Sun 11am–6.30pm.

Good Earth 2 Reay House, next to Taj Mahal Palace and Tower Hotel ☎022 2202 1030; map p.74. Fine tableware, luxury bed linen, lanterns and exquisite clothes made from traditional Indian fabrics. Prices reflect its proximity to the *Taj*, but their stock is all original and beautifully displayed. Daily 11am–8pm.

Playclan 1st Floor, Vaswani House, 7 BEST Marg, near Taj Mahal Palace and Tower Hotel, Colaba ☎022 2283 3577, ⊛theplayclan; map p.74. Colourful range of stationery, prints and mugs decorated with Indian icons such as

Ambassador cars, *kathakali* dancers, Bombay taxis and auto-rickshaws – perfect souvenirs. Daily 11am–9.30pm.

HANDICRAFTS

Regionally produced handicrafts are marketed in assorted state-run emporia at the World Trade Centre, down on Cuffe Parade, and along Sir PM Rd, Fort. The quality is consistently high – as are the prices, if you miss out on the periodic holiday discounts. Mereweather Rd (now officially B Behram Marg), behind the *Taj Mahal Palace and Tower*, is awash with Kashmiri handicraft stores stocking overpriced papier-mâché pots and bowls, silver jewellery, woollen shawls and rugs. Avoid them if you find it hard to shrug off aggressive sales pitches. Down at the south end of Colaba Causeway, around Arthur Bunder Rd, shops with mirrored walls and shelves are stacked with cut-glass carafes full of syrupy, fragrant essential oils. Incense is hawked in sticks, cones and slabs of sticky *dhoop* on the pavement nearby (check that the boxes haven't already been opened and their contents sold off piecemeal).

Avante Cottage Crafts 12 Oriental Mansion, Wodehouse Rd, Colaba ☎022 2202 0873, ⊛avantecrafts.com; map p.74. One of the pioneering handicraft retailers in town selling a wide range of metal, wood and stone artefacts, folk paintings and textiles. Daily 11.30am–8.30pm.

Central Cottage Industries Emporium 34 Shivaji Marg, near the Gateway of India in Colaba ☎022 2202 7537; map p.74. The size, central location and big range of inlaid furniture, wood- and metalwork, miniature paintings, jewellery, toys, clothing and textiles make this the single best all-round place to hunt for souvenirs. Also purveyors of a fine range of teas. Mon–Sat 10.30am–6.30pm.

BOOKSHOPS

Crossword Bookstore Mohammed Bhai Mansion, NS Patkar Marg, Kemp's Corner, a 10min walk north of Chowpatty Beach ☎022 6627 2104; map p.72. Mumbai's largest retailer, in a/c premises, complete with its own coffee bar. Mon–Fri 11am–8.30pm, Sat & Sun 11am–9pm.

Kitab Khana Somaiya Bhavan, MG Rd ☎022 6170 2276; map p.74. Eclectic bookshop in a restored heritage building with high ceilings, polished woodwork and a café. Daily 10.30am–7.30pm.

Oxford Bookstore Apeejay House, 3 Dinsha Vacha Rd, Churchgate ☎022 6636 4477; map p.78. Not quite as large as Crossword, but almost, and much more easily accessible if you're staying downtown or in Colaba. It also has a very cool a/c café. Daily 10am–9pm.

Search Word Metro House, Shahid Bhagat Singh Marg (Colaba Causeway) ☎022 2285 2521; map p.74. The best bookshop in Colaba, with shelves full of guides and a great range of Indian fiction – at discounts only rivalled by the Strand Book Stall in Fort. Daily 11am–8.30pm.

1

Strand Book Stall Next door to Canara Bank, off PM Rd, Fort ☎022 2266 1994; map p.78. The best-value bookshop in the city centre, with a big selection of discounted Penguins and Indian literature. Daily 10.30am–9pm.

MUSIC AND MUSICAL INSTRUMENTS

Bhargava's Musik 4/5 Imperial Plaza, 30th Rd, Bandra ☎022 2641 1842, ⓦbhargavasmusik.com; map p.86. The city's foremost music shop, up in the northern suburb of Bandra, stocks every conceivable kind of Indian instrument, from sitars and sarods to bamboo flutes and *shruti* boxes, as well as Western guitars, strings and drums. Mon–Sat 10.30am–8pm.

Furtado's Jer Mahal, Dhobitalao ☎022 6622 5454, ⓦfurtadosonline.com; map p.72. Mostly Western-style woodwind, brass, keyboard and percussion, with a basic stock of Indian instruments. It's more easily accessible than Bhargava's if you're based in south Mumbai. Mon–Sat 10am–8pm.

SPORTS

In common with most Indians, Mumbaikars are crazy about **cricket**. Few other spectator sports get much of a look-in, although the **horseracing** at Mahalakshmi draws large crowds on Derby days. Previews of all forthcoming events are posted on the back pages of the *Times of India*, and in *Time Out Mumbai*.

CRICKET

Cricket provides almost as much of a distraction as movies in the Maharashtrian capital, and you'll see games in progress everywhere, from impromptu sunset knockabouts on Chowpatty Beach to more formal club matches in full whites at the gymkhanas lined up along Marine Drive. The Indian season runs from October through February. Tickets for cup and test matches are almost as hard to come by as seats on commuter trains, but foreign visitors can sometimes gain preferential access to quotas through the Mumbai Cricket Association's offices on the first floor of Wankhede (see below; ☎022 2279 5500, ⓦmumbaicricket.com).

Brabourne Stadium Off Marine Drive. The world's most prolific batsman in both test and one-day cricket, Sachin Tendulkar, still lives in the city and plays regularly for its league-winning club side at the Brabourne Stadium.

Oval Maidan South Mumbai. This is the place to watch local talent in action, set against a wonderful backdrop of imperial-era buildings. Something of a pecking order applies here: the further from the path cutting across the centre of the park you go, the better the wickets and the classier the games become. Pitches like these are where Sachin Tendulkar (see above), cut his cricketing teeth.

Wankhede Stadium Off Marine Drive. This 45,000-capacity stadium is where major test matches are hosted, amid an atmosphere as intense, raucous and intimidating for visiting teams as any in India.

HORSERACING AND HORSERIDING

Mahalakshmi Racecourse Near the Mahalakshmi Temple, just north of Malabar Hill ⓦarcmumbai.com. This is the home of the Royal Western India Turf Club – a throwback to British times that still serves as a prime stomping ground for the city's upper classes. Race meets are held twice weekly, on Wednesdays and Saturdays between November and March, and big days such as the 2000 Guineas and Derby attract crowds of 25,000. Entrance to the public ground is by ticket on the day. Seats for the colonial-era stand, with its posh lawns and exclusive *Gallops Restaurant* are, alas, allocated to members only.

LAUGHTER YOGA

On the principle that laughter is the best medicine, Mumbai doctor Madan Kataria and his wife Madhuri – aka "the Giggling Gurus" – have created a new kind of therapy: *hasya* (laughter) yoga. There are now more than three hundred **Laughter Clubs** in India and many more worldwide; around fifty thousand people join the Laughter Day celebrations in Mumbai on the first Sunday of May each year, with tens of thousands more participating in seventy countries worldwide.

Fifteen-minute sessions start with adherents doing yogic breathing while chanting "Ho ho ha ha", which develops into spontaneous "hearty laughter" (raising both hands in the air with the head tilting backwards), "milkshake laughter" (everyone laughs while making a gesture as if they are drinking milkshake), and "swinging laughter" (standing in a circle saying "aaee-oo-eee-uuu") before the rather fearsome "lion laughter" (extruding the tongue fully with eyes wide open and hands stretched out like claws, and laughing from the tummy). The session then winds up with holding hands and the chanting of slogans ("We are the laughter club member [sic]…Y…E…S!").

Laughter Clubs take place between 6am and 7am at various venues around the city, including Colaba Woods in Cuffe Parade and Juhu Beach. For the full story, go to ⓦlaughteryoga.org.

Race cards are posted in the sports section of the *Times of India* and at ⓦrwitclive.com. On non-race days, the Mahalakshmi ground doubles as a riding track. Temporary membership of the Amateur Riding Club of Mumbai, another bastion of elite Mumbai, entitles you to use the club's thoroughbreds for classes. Full details on how to do this, along with previews of forthcoming club polo matches, are posted on the website.

DIRECTORY

Ambulance ⓣ101 for general emergencies; but you're nearly always better off taking a taxi.

Banks and exchange There are dozens of ATMs dotted around the city. All the major state banks downtown change foreign currency (Mon–Fri 10.30am–2.30pm, Sat 10.30am–12.30pm); some (eg the Bank of Baroda) also handle credit cards and cash advances. Thomas Cook's big Dr D.N. Marg branch (Mon–Sat 9.30am–6.30pm; ⓣ022 6160 3333), between the Khadi shop and Hutatma Chowk, can also arrange money transfers from overseas.

Consulates and high commissions Note that most of India's neighbours, including Bangladesh, Bhutan, Burma, Nepal and Pakistan, only have embassies in New Delhi and/or Kolkata (Calcutta). All of the following are open Mon–Fri only: Australia, Level 10, A Wing, Crescenzo Building, G Block, Plot C 38-39, Bandra Kurla (ⓣ022 6757 4900, ⓦmumbai .consulate.gov.au); Canada, Indiabulls Finance Centre, 21st Floor, Tower 2, Senapati Bapat Marg, Elphinstone Rd West (ⓣ022 6749 4444, ⓦcanadainternational.gc.ca); Republic of Ireland, Kamanwalla Chambers, 2nd Floor, Sir PM Rd, Fort (ⓣ022 6635 5635); South Africa, Gandhi Mansion, 20 Altamount Rd (ⓣ022 2351 3725, ⓦdha.gov.za); United Kingdom, Naman Chambers, C/32 G Block, Bandra Kurla Complex, Bandra East (ⓣ022 6650 2222, ⓦgov.uk); US, C-49, G-Block, Bandra Kurla Complex, Bandra East (ⓣ022 2672 4000, ⓦmumbai.usconsulate.gov).

Hospitals The best hospital in the centre is the private Bombay Hospital, New Marine Lines (ⓣ022 2206 7676, ⓦbombayhospital.com), just north of the government tourist office on M Karve Rd. Breach Candy Hospital (ⓣ022 2367 1888, ⓦbreachcandyhospital.org) on Bhulabhai Desai Rd, near the swimming pool, is also recommended by foreign embassies.

Internet A couple of cramped 24hr places (₹40/hr) can be found in Colaba on Nawroji F Marg. If you have your own computer, wi-fi access is available at most of the city's mid- and high-end hotels, as well as at local branches of the *Barista* coffee shop chain (there's a branch next to the Regal cinema in Colaba).

Libraries Asiatic Society (see p.79), Shahid Bhagat Singh Marg, Horniman Circle, Ballard Estate (Mon–Sat 10.30am–7pm); British Council (for British newspapers and magazines), A Wing, 1st floor, Mittal Tower, Nariman Point (Tues–Sat 10am–6pm); Bombay Natural History Society, Hornbill House, next to the Chhatrapati Shivaji Museum (ⓦbnhs.org; Mon–Fri 9.30am–5.30pm), has an international reputation for the study of wildlife in India. Visitors may obtain temporary membership, which allows them access to the library, natural history collection, occasional talks and the opportunity to join organized walks and field trips.

Pharmacies Saharkari Bandar Chemist at the top of SBS Marg, Colaba, is open until 8.30pm.

Police The main police station in Colaba (ⓣ022 2204 3702) is on the west side of Colaba Causeway, near the crossroads with Best Marg.

Postal services The GPO (Mon–Sat 9am–8pm, Sun 9am–4pm) is around the corner from CST (VT) station, off Nagar Chowk. The parcel office (10am–4.30pm) is behind the main building on the first floor. Packing-wallahs hang around on the pavement outside. DHL (ⓣ1800 111 345) has seventeen offices in Mumbai, the most convenient being the 24hr one under the *Sea Green Hotel* at the bottom of Marine Drive.

Travel agents The following travel agents are recommended for booking domestic and international flights, and cars with drivers: Cox and Kings India, 16 Bank St, Fort (ⓣ1800 221235, ⓦcoxandkings.co.in); Sita World, 11th Floor, Bajaj Bhavan, Nariman Point; Thomas Cook, 324 Dr DN Rd, Fort (ⓣ022 6160 3333, ⓦthomascook.in); Garha Tours & Travels, 104 Atlantic Apartments, Swami Samarth Nagar, Lokhandwala Complex, Andheri (W) (ⓣ022 2635 0035 or 98670 28232, ⓦgarhatours.in).

Maharashtra

112 Nasik and around

116 Aurangabad and around

121 Ellora

128 Ajanta

133 Lonar

134 Jalgaon

135 Nagpur

135 Around Nagpur

138 The Konkan coast

141 Matheran

143 Lonavala and around

145 Pune

151 Mahabaleshwar and around

152 Kolhapur

KAILASH TEMPLE, ELLORA

Maharashtra

Vast and rugged, the modern state of Maharashtra is the third largest in India, and one of the most visited by foreign tourists, though most people venture no further than its seething port capital, Mumbai. As soon as you leave the seemingly endless concrete housing projects, industrial works and swamplands of Mumbai, you enter a different world with a different history. Undoubtedly, Maharashtra's greatest treasures are its extraordinary cave temples and monasteries; the finest of all are found near Aurangabad, renamed after the Mughal emperor Aurangzeb and home to the Bibi-ka-Maqbara, dedicated to his wife. The busy commercial city is the obvious base for visits to the Buddhist caves at Ajanta, with their fabulous and still-vibrant murals, and the monolithic temples of Ellora, where the astonishing Hindu Kailash temple was carved in its entirety from one single rock.

Despite Maharashtra's early importance as a centre of Buddhism, Hinduism is very much at the core of the life in the state. Balancing modern industry alongside ancient associations with the Ramayana, the main pilgrimage centre has always been **Nasik**, a handy place to break journeys en route to Aurangabad. One of the four locations of the Kumbh Mela, the city is always a hive of devotional activity, and lies close to one of India's most sacred Shiva shrines, reached from the village of **Trimbak**. In the state's far northeastern corner, the city of **Nagpur** lies close to **Sevagram**, where Mahatma Gandhi set up his headquarters during the struggle for Independence.

Away from the cities, one of the most characteristic features of the landscape is a plenitude of **forts**. Rising abruptly a short distance inland from the sea, the Sahyadri Hills – part of the **Western Ghats** – form a series of huge steps that march up from the narrow coastal strip to the edge of the **Deccan plateau**. These flat-topped hills could easily be converted into forts where small forces could withstand protracted sieges by large armies. Today, visitors can scale such windswept fortified heights at **Pratapgadh** and **Daulatabad**.

During the nineteenth century, the mountains found another use. When the summer proved too much for the British in Bombay, they sought refuge in nearby **hill stations**, the most popular of which, **Mahabaleshwar**, now caters for droves of domestic tourists. **Matheran**, 800m higher, has a special attraction: a rickety miniature train. South of Matheran, a further series of magnificent rock-cut caves clustered around another town, **Lonavala**, provides the main incentive to break the journey to the modern, cosmopolitan city of **Pune**, famous for its **Osho** resort founded by the New Age guru Bhagwan Rajneesh, but most appealing for its atmospheric old town and burgeoning restaurant and bar scene.

To the west, Maharashtra occupies 500km of the **Konkan coast** on the Arabian Sea, from Gujarat to Goa. The little-explored palm-fringed coast winds back and forth with countless inlets, ridges and valleys; highlights include **Murud-Janjira**, whose extraordinary

---

BEST TIME TO VISIT

The best time to visit Maharashtra is the October–February period, when it is typically hot and dry (though the eastern side of the state may get a few showers). Temperatures ramp up from March to May, when it can get uncomfortable, and thunderstorms are not uncommon. The monsoon generally hits in June and lasts till September, with July the wettest month; most hotels in the hill station of Matheran (see p.141) close during this period. It is also well worth trying to coincide your visit with one of the state's many festivals (see box, p.111).

FIFTH-CENTURY CAVE MURAL, AJANTA

Highlights

1 Nasik Pilgrimage centre and capital of India's nascent wine industry, this city is a fascinating combination of ancient and modern. **See p.112**

2 Ellora caves A World Heritage Site with breathtaking Hindu, Buddhist and Jain caves carved from solid volcanic rock, as well as the stunning Kailash temple. **See p.121**

3 Ajanta caves Hidden in a remote horseshoe-shaped ravine, Ajanta's caves contain the finest surviving gallery of art from any of the world's ancient civilizations. **See p.128**

4 Gandhi ashram, Sevagram Learn about the great man's life and beliefs at the last ashram he lived in. **See p.136**

5 The Konkan coast This stretch of coastline remains relatively unspoilt with several appealing places to stay, including the small port of Murud-Janjira. **See p.138**

6 Miniature train to Matheran Fantastic views across the Western Ghats are revealed during the switchback train journey up to this former British hill station. **See p.142**

7 Pune Known as the "Oxford of the East", this sophisticated city is home to an absorbing old town, a riveting museum and some excellent places to eat and drink, plus the Osho ashram. **See p.145**

HIGHLIGHTS ARE MARKED ON THE MAP ON P.110

fortress was the only one never conquered by the Mughals, and **Ganpatipule**, the region's chief pilgrimage centre, with kilometres of virtually deserted, palm-fringed beaches. By the time you reach **Kolhapur**, the main town in the far south of the state, famous for its temple and palace, Mumbai feels a world away.

Brief history

Maharashtra enters recorded history in the second century BC, with the construction of its first Buddhist caves. These lay in peaceful places of great natural beauty, and were created with the wealth generated by the nearby caravan trade routes between north and South India.

The region's first Hindu rulers – based in Badami, Karnataka – appeared during the sixth century, and Buddhism was almost entirely supplanted by the twelfth century. Hinduism, in the form of the simple faith of Ramdas, the "Servant of Rama", provided the philosophical underpinning behind the campaigns of the Maharashtra's greatest warrior, **Shivaji** (1627–80), who remains a potent symbol for Maharashtrans. The fiercely independent Maratha chieftain united local forces to place insurmountable obstacles in the way of any prospective invader; so effective were their guerrilla tactics that he could even take on the mighty Mughals, who by 1633 had got as far as capturing Daulatabad. By the time he died, in 1680, he had managed to unite the Marathas into a stable and secure state, funded by the plunder gleaned through guerrilla raids as far afield as Andhra

HIGHLIGHTS

1. Nasik
2. Ellora caves
3. Ajanta caves
4. Gandhi ashram, Sevagram
5. The Konkan coast
6. Miniature train to Matheran
7. Pune

MAHARASHTRA

FESTIVALS IN MAHARASHTRA

Makar Sankranti (Jan). Marks the end of Dakshinayana (the southward movement of the sun) and the start of Uttarayan (the northward movement of the sun; kite-flying, bathing in sacred rivers and/or with sesame oil, lighting oil lamps to honour ancestors, and exchanging sesame sweets all feature in the festivities.

Ratha Saptami (Jan). This festival heralds the start of spring and the harvest, when offerings are made to the sun god, Surya.

Gudhi Padwa (usually March). Hindu celebration marking the start of the new year, the day Brahma created the universe. People raise a bright green or yellow flag outside households and kick off festivities by eating a paste made from neem leaves and jaggery.

2

Narali Purnima/Raksha Bandhan (Aug). The "coconut festival" marks the end of the monsoon, and heralds the start of the fishing season – it is celebrated enthusiastically by communities on the Konkan coast (see p.138).

Ganesh Chaturthi (Aug/Sept). Dedicated to one of Hinduism's most popular deities, this ten-day festival finishes with a procession and the immersion of large Ganesh effigies into rivers, water tanks or the sea.

Marabats and Badgyas (Aug/Sept). Celebrated with particular fervour in Nagpur (see p.135), where effigies personifying evils such as corruption and bribery are taken on a procession and then burned.

Navarata (Sept/Oct). The "Nine nights" festival dedicated to the worship of Shakti, the mother goddess, and by extension the importance of women generally. A Maharashtran characteristic of the festival is *bondhla*, folk dances performed by girls each evening.

Tripuri Purnima (Nov). The most important Shiva festival after Shivrati, Tripuri Purnima marks the god's victory over the demon Tripurasura. Celebrations include ritual bathing, and in places such as Nasik (see p.112) lit candles are floated on the Godavari River.

Pradesh. In response, Mughal Emperor **Aurangzeb** moved his court and capital south to the Deccan, first to Bijapur (now Vijayapura) in 1686 and then Golconda in 1687, but still failed to subdue Shivaji's dynasty. Yet by the end of the eighteenth century the power of both had weakened and the British were able to take full control.

Maharashtra claims a crucial role in the development of a nationalist consciousness. The Indian National Union, originally convened in Pune, held a conference in Bombay in 1885; thereafter it was known as the **Indian National Congress**. This loose congregation of key local figures from around the country changed the face of Indian politics. At first, its aim was limited to establishing a national platform to raise the status of Indians, and it remained loyal to the British. In the long term, of course, it was instrumental in the achievement of Independence 62 years later, with many of the Congress's factional leaders over the years hailing from Maharashtra.

With Independence, the Bombay Presidency, to which most of Maharashtra belonged, became known as Bombay State. Maharashtra as such was created in 1960 from the state's Marathi-speaking regions. Its manufacturing industries, centred on Mumbai and to a lesser extent cities such as Nagpur, Nasik, Aurangabad, Sholapur and Kolhapur, now account for around fifteen percent of the nation's output. Textiles have long been important – the Deccan soils supplied the world with cotton in the nineteenth century after its main source was interrupted by the American Civil War – but this is now also one of the premier high-tech industry regions, especially along the Mumbai–Pune corridor. Still, the majority of Maharashtra's population of more than 114 million are still engaged in agriculture.

MTDC HOTELS

The Maharashtra Tourism Development Corporation (**MTDC**) runs a number of hotels across the state, often occupying superb locations – though standards are variable – and it can also organize homestays and B&Bs. The most useful of its resorts are listed in this chapter and can be booked either at MTDC offices or at ⓦ maharashtratourism.gov.in.

Nasik and around

Lying at the head of the main pass through the Western Ghats, the city of **NASIK** (or Nashik) makes an interesting stopover en route to or from Mumbai, 187km southwest. It is one of the four sites of the world's largest religious gathering, the **Kumbh Mela**, most recently hosting it in 2015 (it won't return until 2027). Even outside festival times, the *ghat*-lined banks of the **River Godavari** are always animated.

According to the Ramayana, Nasik was where Rama (Vishnu in human form), his brother Lakshmana and wife Sita lived during their exile from Ayodhya, and the arch-demon Ravana carried off Sita from here in an aerial chariot to his kingdom, Lanka, in the far south. The scene of such episodes forms the core of the busy

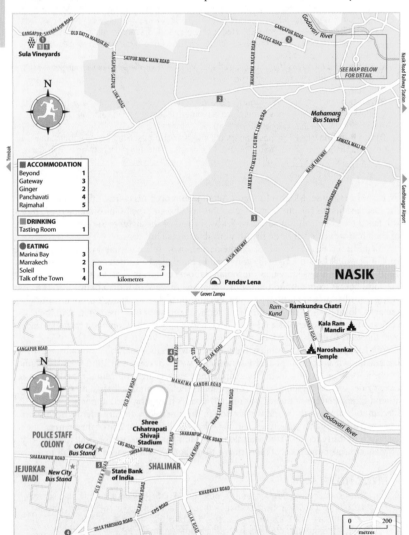

INDIA'S WINE CAPITAL

With its temperate winters, rich soil and gently undulating landscape, Nasik's arid and dusty hinterland has over the past two decades proved itself to be – incongruously enough – ideal for growing wine grapes, and the city has firmly established itself at the centre of India's fast-expanding wine industry. Note that Maharashtra has eleven "dry days" when it is illegal to sell alcohol; check the Sula website for dates.

TOURS AND TASTINGS

Grover Zampa 32km southwest of Nasik ☎0255 320 4379, ⓦgroverzampa.in. Based in the Sanjegaon Valley, Grover Zampa is India's second-biggest wine producer (after Sula), and offers tours and tastings lasting 1hr 30min–2hr (daily 9.30am–5pm; ₹400 for the tour, ₹500 for the tour and five tastings, ₹650 for the tour and seven tastings). Book in advance.

Sula Vineyards 14km west of Nasik ☎0253 302 7777, ⓦsulawines.com. The best-established producer,

enthusiastically supported by Mumbai's urban sophisticates, Sula Vineyards is a slick operation that wouldn't feel out of place in the Napa Valley. It runs 30min tours of its winery (hourly: Mon–Fri 11.30am–6.30pm, Sat & Sun 11.30am–7.30pm; ₹250 for four wine tastings, ₹350 for six – the latter is only available at the weekend), concluding with a tasting session. There's also the *Tasting Room* wine bar and the *Soleil* restaurant (see p.115).

---

pilgrimage circuit – a lively enclave packed with religious specialists, beggars, sadhus and street vendors touting puja paraphernalia.

However, Nasik has a surprising dearth of historical buildings, and its only real monuments are the rock-cut caves at nearby **Pandav Lena**. Excavated at the peak of Buddhist achievement on the Deccan, these 2000-year-old cells hark back to the days when, as capital of the powerful **Satavahana** dynasty, Nasik dominated the all-important trade routes linking the Ganges plains with the ports to the west.

From Nasik, you can make an interesting day-trip to the highly auspicious village of **Trimbak**, from which a steep climb takes you to **Brahmagiri**, the source of the Godavari. Somewhat in contrast to its religious importance, Nasik is also the centre of Maharashtra's burgeoning **wine region** (see box above).

Ram Kund

Around 1.7km northeast of the Old City Bus Stand

Always buzzing with a carnival atmosphere, the **Ram Kund** is the reason most people come to Nasik, although this sacred bathing tank can look more like an overcrowded municipal swimming pool than one of India's most ancient holy places. Among the Ram Kund's more arcane attributes is its capacity to dissolve bones – whence the epithet of **Astivilaya Tirth** or "Bone Immersion Tank".

Kala Ram Mandir

At the end of the narrow, uphill street opposite Ram Kund • No fixed opening times • Free

The square around the **Kala Ram Mandir**, or "Black Rama Temple", is the city's second most important sacred area. Among the well-known episodes from the Ramayana to occur here was the event that led to Sita's abduction, when Lakshmana sliced off the nose of Ravana's sister after she had tried to seduce Rama by taking the form of a voluptuous princess. Sita's cave, or **Gumpha**, a tiny grotto known in the Ramayana as Parnakuti ("Smallest Hut"), is just off the square.

The Kala Ram temple itself, at the bottom of the square, houses unusual jet-black deities of Rama, Sita and Lakshmana; these are very popular with visiting pilgrims, as access is free from all caste restrictions. The best time to visit is around sunset, after evening puja, when a crowd, mostly of women, gathers in the courtyard to listen to a traditional storyteller recount tales from the Ramayana and other epics.

Pandav Lena

8km southwest of Nasik • Daily sunrise–sunset • ₹100 (₹5) • An auto-rickshaw costs ₹350–400 return, including waiting time

A steep fifteen-minute climb up one of the precipitous conical hills that overlook the Mumbai–Agra road is **Pandav Lena**, a small group of 24 rock-cut caves famous for their well-preserved Pali inscriptions and fine ancient stone sculpture. Cave 18, the only *chaitya* hall, is one of the earliest, dating from the first century BC, and is notable for its striking facade, while Cave 3, the largest *vihara*, boasts some superb exterior stonework.

2

Trimbak

Buses leave regularly from Nasik's Old City Bus Stand (every 30min; 45min). To return, you can catch a bus (which run until around 8pm) or one of the shared taxis that wait outside Trimbak Bus Stand

Crouched in the shadow of the Western Ghats, 28km west of Nasik, the village of **TRIMBAK** – literally "Three-Eyed", another name for Lord Shiva, in Marathi – marks the spot where one of the four infamous drops of immortality-giving *amrita* nectar fell to earth from the *kumbh* vessel during the struggle between Vishnu's vehicle Garuda and the Demons – the mythological origin of the Kumbh Mela.

Trimbakeshwar Mandir

Among India's most sacred Shiva centres (it houses one of the twelve holiest Shiva temples, known as *jyotirlingas*), the **Trimbakeshwar Mandir**, in the centre of the village, is closed to non-Hindus. Its impressive eighteenth-century *shikhara*, however, can be glimpsed from the backstreets nearby.

The source of the Godavari

Trimbak is also close to the source of one of India's longest and most venerated rivers, the **Godavari**; the spring can be reached via an ancient trail that cuts through a cleft in an awesome, guano-splashed cliff face. The round trip to **Brahmagiri**, the source of the Godavari, takes between two and three hours. It's a strenuous walk, particularly in the heat, so take enough water.

From the trailhead at the edge of the village, the way is paved and stepped as far as the first level outcrop, where there are some welcome chai stalls and a small hamlet. Beyond that, either turn left after the last group of huts and follow the dirt trail through the woods to the foot of the **rock-cut steps** (20min), or continue straight on to the three **shrines** clinging to the base of the cliff above. The first is dedicated to the goddess Ganga, the second – a cave containing 108 lingams – to Shankar (Shiva), and the third to the sage Gautama Rishi, whose hermitage this once was.

The steps climb 550m above Trimbak to the remains of **Anjeri Fort** – a site that was, over the years, attacked by the armies of both Shah Jahan and Aurangzeb before it fell into the hands of Shaha-ji Raj, father of the legendary rebel-leader Shivaji. The **source** itself is another twenty minutes further on, across **Brahmagiri Hill**, in the otherwise unremarkable Gaumukh ("Mouth of the Cow") temple. From its rather unimpressive origins, this paltry trickle flows for nearly 1000km east across the entire Deccan to the Bay of Bengal.

ARRIVAL AND DEPARTURE   NASIK AND AROUND

By plane Gandhinagar airport is around 5km southeast of the city and has irregular flights to/from Mumbai; a taxi to/from the city centre costs around ₹300.

By bus Buses from Mumbai pull in at the Mahamarga Bus Stand, 10min by rickshaw from the city centre, while Aurangabad and Pune buses terminate at the central New City Bus Stand. The Old City Bus Stand is around 500m north along the Old Agra Rd (also known as Swami Vivekanand Rd), and is primarily useful for buses to Trimbak; it's an easy walk from either stand to several inexpensive hotels and restaurants.

Destinations Aurangabad (every 1–2hr; 4hr–4hr 30min); Mumbai (hourly; 4hr); Pune (every 30min; 4–5hr); Trimbak (every 30min; 45min).

By train Nasik Road is the nearest railway station, 8km southeast of the centre; local buses regularly ply the route into town, and there is no shortage of shared taxis and auto-rickshaws (₹150–250). There's a ticket booking office (Mon–Sat 8am–8pm, Sun 8am–2pm), near HDFC House, around 1km west of the city bus stands, though it is easier to book online or via a travel agent.

Destinations Agra (4 daily; 17–21hr); Aurangabad (4 daily; 3hr–3hr 40min); Delhi (4 daily; 20hr–26hr); Jalgaon (23 daily; 2hr 30min–3hr); Mumbai (45 daily; 3hr 30min–5hr 30min); Nagpur (11 daily; 9hr–20hr); Pune (1 daily; 7hr).

INFORMATION

Tourist information The helpful MTDC tourist office (Mon–Sat 10am–5.30pm; ☎ 0253 257 0059) is at T1, Golf Club, Old Agra Rd, most easily reached by cutting across the park opposite the New City Bus Stand.

Services The State Bank of India, between the two city bus stands on Old Agra Rd, changes money. Internet access is available at the Shree Sadguru Cyber Café, next to the *Panchavati* hotel complex.

ACCOMMODATION

Most of Nasik's hotels, stretching along the Mumbai–Agra road en route to Pandav Lena, are pitched at business travellers, though there are a few more budget-friendly exceptions around the Old City Bus Stand chowk.

Beyond Sula Vineyards, 14km west of Nasik ☎ 0253 223 0141, ⓦ sulawines.com. Each of the super-stylish rooms is named after a grape variety at this tranquil hotel in the grounds of Sula Vineyards. There's also an infinity pool, spa and gym, and you can go hiking or cycling. The rate listed here is for weekends; prices drop during the week. ₹7000

Gateway 7km southwest on the Mumbai–Agra road ☎ 0253 660 4499, ⓦ thegatewayhotels.com. Set amid beautifully landscaped grounds, with a gleaming marble lobby designed in mock-Maratha style, the *Gateway* is one of the most luxurious places to stay in the area, though rooms are somewhat overpriced. Facilities include a pool, gym, restaurant and bar. ₹7500

Ginger Satpur MIDC ☎ 0253 661 6333, ⓦ gingerhotels .com. Nasik outpost of this reliable mid-range chain offering efficient service, comfortable if bland rooms, a small gym and a branch of *Café Coffee Day*. The downside is the location, on a busy road 4km northwest of the Mahamarga Bus Stand. It's much cheaper to book online in advance. ₹2400

Panchavati 430 Chandak Vadi ☎ 0253 257 2291, ⓦ panchavatihotels.com. Set mercifully off noisy MG Rd a 15min walk from the New City Bus Stand, this complex has rooms to suit most pockets, all of them clean, attached and good value for money, though overall it's a little worn and institutional. At the bottom of the range is the budget *Panchavati Guest House*, followed by the mid-range *Panchavati Yatri*, the slightly swisher *Hotel Panchavati* and, at the top of the range, the *Panchavati Millionaire*. ₹900

Rajmahal Sharanpur Rd ☎ 0253 258 0501, ⓦ hotel rajmahalnashik.com. Solid, centrally located, though not the friendliest hotel, the *Rajmahal* has simple, but clean and fairly modern rooms (ask for one of the quieter ones away from the very noisy main road). Good value. ₹1550

EATING

Nasik's best-value meals are to be had in its traditional thali restaurants, where for less than the price of a beer you can enjoy carefully prepared and tasty vegetable, pulse and lentil dishes, often including such regional specialities as *bajra* (wholemeal *rotis*) and *bakri* (hot oatmeal biscuits).

Marina Bay Panchavati hotel complex, 430 Chandak Vadi ☎ 0253 257 7871, ⓦ facebook.com/marinabay. Appealing restaurant with dishes from across India's coastal regions, including Goa, Kerala and Bengal – the crab masala is a standout. Plenty of meat and veg dishes too, including some tasty Mughal- and Afghan-style kebabs. Mains ₹180–650. There's another, flashier branch in the City Centre Mall, off Ambedkar Marg. Daily 11.30am–3.30pm & 7–11.30pm.

Marrakech Patil Lane 3, just off College Rd ☎ 73044 99888, ⓦ marrakech-restaurant.com. For something a little different, head to this small chain for some quality Moroccan and Lebanese cuisine (plus numerous standard Indian options). Try the falafel wrap, lamb kofta, or *mouttabal* (mains ₹90–230). Daily 11am–11pm.

Soleil Sula Vineyards, 14km west of Nasik ☎ 0253 223 0575, ⓦ sulawines.com. The classiest place to eat in and around Nasik, *Soleil* makes full use of the Sula's organic farm to produce top-quality French, modern Mediterranean and Indian cuisine (mains ₹350–700). Wi-fi available. Tues–Sun 12.30–3.30pm & 7–10.30pm.

Talk of the Town Suyojit Chambers, Trimbak Rd, near the New City Bus Stand ☎ 0253 257 1961. One of central Nasik's smarter restaurant-bars with a choice of dining halls, from the family-friendly to the smoky and masculine. The North Indian veg and non-veg dishes (mains ₹195– 435) are generally pretty tasty, and there's a long list of alcoholic drinks. Daily 11am–11pm.

> ### GOING DOOLALLY
>
> In the days of the Raj, soldiers who cracked under the stresses and strains of military life in British India were packed off to recuperate at a psychiatric hospital in the small Maharashtran cantonment town of **Deolali**, near Nasik. Its name became synonymous with madness and nervous breakdown; hence the English phrase "to go doolally".

2

DRINKING

Ironically, given that the surrounding region is the country's prime wine region, Nasik's religious associations tend to mean that meat and alcohol are less easily available than elsewhere in Maharashtra, but most of the larger hotels have bars (known as "permit rooms") and several of the more expensive restaurants serve beers and spirits too.

★**Tasting Room** Sula Vineyards, 14km west of Nasik ☏0253 223 0575, ⊛sulawines.com. This breezy bar looks out over acres of neat rows of vines towards the scenic Gangapur tank. The wine list focuses on Sula's range of whites, reds and rosés (the Merlot-Malbec and the Shiraz are well worth sampling), as well as a small selection from other (mainly New World) producers. A glass of wine costs ₹150–250, while snacks will set you back ₹165–400; there's a ₹300 cover charge at weekends. Wi-fi available. Daily 11am–11pm.

Aurangabad and around

Many travellers regard **AURANGABAD** as little more than a convenient, though largely uninteresting, place in which to kill time on the way to **Ellora** and **Ajanta**, yet given a little effort, this city can compensate for its architectural shortcomings. Scattered around its ragged fringes, the remains of fortifications, gateways, domes and minarets – including those of the most ambitious Mughal tomb garden in western India, the **Bibi-ka-Maqbara** – bear witness to an illustrious imperial past; the small but fascinating crop of **rock-cut Buddhist caves**, huddled along the flanks of the flat-topped, sandy yellow hills to the north, are remnants of even more ancient occupation.

Modern Aurangabad is one of India's fastest growing commercial and industrial centres, specializing in car, soft drink and beer production. It's an upbeat place, boasting plenty of restaurants, bars and interesting shops in the old city. Easy day-trips include the dramatic fort of **Daulatabad**, and, just a little further along the Ellora road, the tomb of Emperor Aurangzeb at the Muslim village of **Khuldabad**.

Brief history

The city was founded in the early seventeenth century by **Malik Ambar**, an ex-Abyssinian slave and prime minister of the independent Muslim kingdom of the Nizam Shahis; many of the **mosques** and palaces he erected still endure, albeit in ruins. Aurangabad really rose to prominence, however, towards the end of the seventeenth century, when **Aurangzeb** decamped here from Delhi. At his behest, the impressive city walls and gates were raised in 1682 to withstand the persistent Maratha attacks that bedevilled his later years. Following his death in 1707, the city was renamed in his honour as it changed hands once again. The new rulers, the **Nizams of Hyderabad**, staved off the Marathas for the greater part of 250 years, until the city finally merged with Maharashtra in 1956.

The old city

The **old city**, laid out on a grid by Malik Amber in the early seventeenth century, still forms the core of Aurangabad's large **bazaar** area. It's best approached via **Gulmandi Square** to the south, along any of several streets lined with colourful shops and stalls. Sections of Aurangzeb's city wall survive, though more impressive is the network of city **gates**, some of which have been restored to something approaching their former glory.

The Panchakki

Panchakki Rd, about 600m northwest of the Central Bus Stand • Daily 6.15am–9.15pm • ₹100 (₹5)

On the left bank of the Kham River is an unusual watermill known as the **Panchakki**. Water pumped underground from a reservoir in the hills 6km away drives a small grindstone, once used to mill flour, and collects in an attractive fish-filled tank, shaded by a large banyan tree. The Panchakki forms part of the **Dargah** of Baba Shah Muzaffar, a religious compound built by Aurangzeb as a memorial to his spiritual mentor, a Chishti mystic. The complex makes a lively place to wander around in the early evening with lots of chai shops, *mehendi* (henna hand-painting) artists and souvenir shops.

Bibi-ka-Maqbara

Around 2.5km north of the city centre • Daily sunrise–10pm • ₹100 (₹5) • The easiest way to get here is by auto-rickshaw; a round trip encompassing the Bibi-ka-Maqbara and the Aurangabad caves (see p.118) costs ₹300–350

Although it's the most impressive Islamic monument in Maharashtra, Aurangabad's Mughal tomb-garden, the **Bibi-ka-Maqbara**, has always suffered from comparison with the Taj Mahal, built forty years earlier, of which it's an obvious imitation. Completed in 1678, the mausoleum was dedicated by **Prince Azam Shah** to the memory of his mother **Begum Rabi'a Daurani**, Aurangzeb's wife. Lack of resources dogged the 25-year project, and the end result fell far short of expectations. Looking at the mausoleum from beyond the ornamental gardens and redundant fountains in front of it, the truncated minarets and ungainly entrance arch make the Bibi-ka-Maqbara appear ill-proportioned compared with the elegant height and symmetry of the Taj, an impression not enhanced by the abrupt discontinuation of marble after the first 2m – allegedly a cost-saving measure.

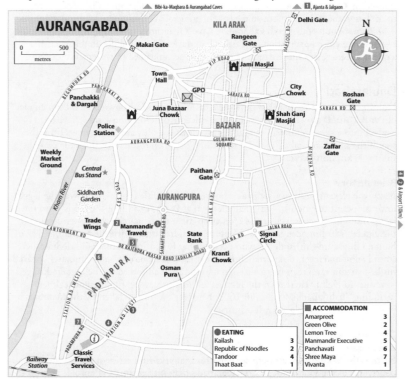

An enormous brass-inlaid **door** – decorated with Persian calligraphy naming the maker, the year of its installation and chief architect – gives access to the archetypal *charbagh* garden complex. Of the two entrances to the mausoleum itself, one leads to the inner balcony while the second drops through another beautiful door to the **vault** (visitors may no longer climb the minarets). Inside, an exquisite octagonal **lattice-screen** of white marble surrounds the raised plinth supporting Rabi'a Daurani's grave. Like her husband's in nearby Khuldabad, it is "open" as a sign of humility. The unmarked grave beside it is said to be that of the empress's nurse.

2

Aurangabad caves

Around 3.5km north of the city centre • Daily sunrise–sunset • ₹100 (₹5) • The most practical way of getting to the caves is by auto-rickshaw; a round trip encompassing the Bibi-ka-Maqbara and caves costs around ₹300

Carved out of a steep-sided spur of the Sahyadri Range overlooking the Bibi-ka-Maqbara, Aurangabad's own **caves** bear no comparison to those in nearby Ellora and Ajanta, but their fine **sculpture** makes a worthwhile introduction to rock-cut architecture. In addition, the infrequently visited site is peaceful and pleasant in itself, with commanding views over the city and surrounding countryside.

The caves, all Buddhist, consist of two groups, eastern and western (a third group is inaccessible), around 500m apart. The majority were excavated between the fourth and eighth centuries, under the patronage of two successive dynasties: the **Vakatkas**, who ruled the western Deccan from Nasik, and the **Chalukyas**, a powerful Mysore (now Mysuru) family who emerged during the sixth century. All except the much earlier Cave 4, which is a *chaitya* hall, are of the *vihara* (monastery) type, belonging to the Mahayana school of Buddhism. **Cave 3** is the most impressive of the western group, with vivid friezes adorning the pillars in the main chamber. In the eastern group, Cave 6 has some finely carved *bodhisattvas*, but it's the superb sculpture in **Cave 7** that provides the real highlight, including a couple of *zaftig* representations of Tara and, to the left of the Buddha in the sanctuary, a celebrated frieze showing a dancer in classic pose accompanied by six female musicians.

Daulatabad

Dominating the horizon 13km northwest of Aurangabad, the awesome hilltop citadel of **DAULATABAD** crowns a massive conical volcanic outcrop whose sides have been shaped into a sheer 60m wall of granite. Not least for the panoramic **views** from the top of the hill, Daulatabad makes a rewarding pause en route to or from the caves at Ellora, 17km northwest.

Brief history

It was the eleventh-century **Yadavas** who were responsible for scraping away the jagged lower slopes of the mount – originally known as **Deogiri**, "Hill of the Gods" – to form its vertical-cliff base, as well as the 15m-deep moat that encircles the upper portion of the citadel. Muslim occupation of Deogiri began in earnest with the arrival in 1327 of Sultan Ghiyas-ud-din **Tughluq**, who decreed that his entire court should decamp here from Delhi, an epic 1100km march that cost thousands of lives, and ultimately proved futile – within seventeen years, drought and famine had forced the beleaguered ruler to return to Delhi. Thereafter, the fortress fell to a succession of different regimes, including Shah Jahan's **Mughals** in 1633, before it was finally taken by the **Marathas** midway through the eighteenth century.

The fortress

Daily 6am–6pm • ₹100 (₹10)

Beyond the formidable sets of outer defences that enclose a series of high-walled courtyards at the foot of the hill, Daulatabad's labyrinthine **fortress** unfolds around the enormous **Chand Minar**, or "Victory Tower", erected in 1435. The Persian blue-and-turquoise tiles that once plastered it in complex geometric patterns have disappeared, but it remains an impressive spectacle, rising from the ruins of the city that once sprawled from its base. The **Jama Masjid**, back along the main path, is Daulatabad's oldest Islamic monument. Built in 1318, the well-preserved mosque comprises 106 pillars plundered from the Hindu and Jain temples that previously stood on the site. It now functions as a Bharatmata temple, much to the chagrin of local Muslims. Adjoining the mosque, the large stone-lined "Elephant" **tank** was once a central component in the fort's extensive water-supply system. Two giant terracotta pipes channelled water from the hills into Deogiri's legendary fruit and vegetable gardens.

From the Chand Minar, the main walkway continues through another set of bastions and fortified walls before emerging close to the **Chini Mahal**, or "Chinese Palace". The impressive **Mendha Tope** ("Ram-headed Cannon"), inscribed in Persian, rests on a squat stone tower just above. From here onwards, a sequence of macabre traps lay in wait for the unwary intruder. First, a moat infested with man-eating crocodiles (now spanned by an iron bridge) had to be crossed to reach the main citadel. Next the attackers would have had to clamber through a maze of claustrophobic, zigzagging passageways, the last of which was closed with an iron cover that could be heated to generate toxic gases.

From the final tunnel, it's a fairly steep ten-minute climb up a broad flight of steps to the **Baradari**, an attractive octagonal pavilion used by Shah Jahan during his visits to Daulatabad. The **views** from the flat roof of the building are superb, but an even more impressive panorama is to be had from the **look-out post** perched on the summit of the hill, marked with another grand cannon.

ARRIVAL AND INFORMATION   DAULATABAD

By bus/taxi Although Daulatabad features on the guided tours of Ellora from Aurangabad (see p.120), you'll have more time to enjoy it by travelling here on one of the buses (every 30min; 30min) that shuttle between Aurangabad and the caves. From Daulatabad, it is easy to catch another bus or shared taxi on to Khuldabad and Ellora; the stop is opposite the main entrance to the fort.

Visiting independently If you're not on a tour, try to arrive early as the place is often overrun, and bring a torch as some of the passages in the fort are pitch-black and hopelessly confusing – one reason why you might also consider hiring a guide (around ₹700).

Khuldabad

22km north of Aurangabad • Tombs sunrise–10pm • Free, but small tips and donations are expected • Buses run every 30min between Aurangabad and Ellora, stopping en route at Khuldabad's small bus stand (30min from Aurangabad, 10min from Ellora), a 10min walk from the tombs

Nestled on a saddle of high ground, **KHULDABAD**, also known as **Rauza**, is an old walled town famous for a wonderful crop of onion-domed **tombs**. Among the Muslim notables deemed worthy of a patch of earth in this most hallowed of burial grounds ("Khuldabad" means "Heavenly Abode") were the Emperor Aurangzeb himself, who raised the town's granite battlements and seven fortified gateways, a couple of nizams, and a fair few of the town's Chishti founding fathers.

Aurangzeb's tomb lies inside a whitewashed **dargah**, midway between the North and South gates. The grave itself is a humble affair decorated only by the fresh flower petals scattered by visitors, open to the elements instead of sealed in stone. The devout emperor insisted that it be paid for not out of the royal coffers, but with the money he raised in the last years of life by selling his own hand-quilted white skullcaps. Aurangzeb chose this as his final resting place primarily because of the presence, next door, of **Sayeed Zain-ud-din**'s tomb, which occupies a quadrangle separating Aurangzeb's grave from those of his wife and second son, Azam Shah. Locked away behind a small door in the mausoleum is Khuldabad's most jealously guarded relic, the **Robe of the Prophet**, revealed to the public once a year on the twelfth day of the Islamic month of Rabi-ul-Awwal, when the tomb attracts worshippers from all over India. Directly opposite Zain-ud-din's tomb is the **Dargah of Sayeed Burhan-ud-din**, a Chishti missionary buried here in 1334. The shrine is

2

said to contain hairs from the Prophet's beard, which magically increase in number when they are counted each year.

ARRIVAL AND DEPARTURE

BY PLANE
Chikal Thana airport Aurangabad's airport is 10km east of the city; a taxi to/from the city centre costs around ₹400. Most of the smarter hotels offer a pick-up service. Jet Airways and Air India have daily flights to Mumbai (50min) and Delhi (1hr 50min).

BY TRAIN
Aurangabad railway station The railway station is on the southwest edge of the city centre, at the southern end of Station Rd West. As Aurangabad is not on the main line, trains to and from the city are fairly limited (Jalgaon, 166km north, has the nearest mainline station, with services to a far greater range of destinations; see p.134). The quickest train to Mumbai is the #12072 *Jan Shatabdi Express* (daily 6am; 6hr 30min); if you prefer to travel overnight, try the #17058 *Devagiri Express* (daily 11.25pm; 7hr 45min).
Destinations Delhi (1 daily; 22hr 30min); Hyderabad/Secunderabad (4 daily; 10hr–12hr 30min); Jalgaon (1 daily;

AURANGABAD AND AROUND

4hr 15min); Mumbai (4 daily; 6hr 30min–8hr); Nasik (4 daily; 3hr–3hr 40min).

BY BUS
State buses The hectic Central Bus Stand is 2.5km north of the railway station, off Dr Ambedkhar Rd. All the state transport corporation (MSRTC) buses arrive and depart from here.
Destinations Ellora (every 30min; 40min) via Daulatabad and Khuldabad; Jalgaon (every 30min; 3hr 30min–4hr) via Fardapur for Ajanta (2hr 30min–3hr); Mumbai (5–7 daily, including a nightly "luxury" bus; 8–10hr); Nagpur (around 5–6 daily; 12hr); Nasik (every 30min–1hr; 4hr 30min); Pune (every 30min–1hr; 5hr).
Private buses For a little more comfort, numerous private companies run a/c buses to most of the larger destinations; you can save yourself a lot of hassle by heading straight to the calm and efficient Manmandir Travels on Adalat Rd (☎0240 236 5748, ⓦmanmandir.co.in), which operates services to a wide range of destinations from its own private terminus – a far cry from the usual bedlam.

GETTING AROUND

By auto-rickshaw Aurangabad's sights lie too far apart to take in on foot. The city is, however, buzzing with auto-rickshaws; longer sightseeing trips work out much cheaper if you settle on a fare in advance (₹600–700/day).
By taxi Taxis can be hailed in the street or found at the

railway station and cars with drivers can be hired through travel agents such as the efficient Classic Travel Services (☎0240 233 7788, ⓦclassictravelservicesaurangabad.tripod.com), on the ground floor of the Tourist Reception Centre. Expect to pay around ₹1400/day.

INFORMATION AND TOURS

Tourist information A counter at the airport (opens to meet incoming flights) provides basic information, while more detailed enquiries are fielded at the Tourist Reception Centre on Station Rd East, where helpful offices of both India Tourism (Mon–Fri 8.30am–6pm, Sat 8.30am–1.30pm; ☎0240 233 1217, ⓦincredibleindia.org) and MTDC (Mon–Fri plus 1st & 3rd Sat of month 10am–1pm & 1.30–5.45pm; ☎0240 234 3169, ⓦmaharashtratourism.gov.in) are on the first floor.
Tour operators Several companies run guided tours

of Aurangabad and the surrounding area, all operating similar itineraries and departure times, and all generally rushed. Ellora and City tours usually include the Bibi-ka-Maqbara, Panchakki, Daulatabad Fort, Aurangzeb's tomb at Khuldabad, and the Ellora caves (though not the Aurangabad ones). Ajanta tours go to the caves only, but it's a long round-trip to make in a day – if you want to spend more time at the site, stay at Fardapur (see p.133) or travel on to Jalgaon (see p.134). Classic Travel Services (see above) runs the best of the tours (₹350–500, excluding entry fees).

ACCOMMODATION

Aurangabad's proximity to some of India's most important monuments, together with its "boom-city" status, ensures a profusion of **hotels**, though standards are variable. For local guesthouses, contact the MTDC.

Amarpreet Jalna Rd ☎0240 621 1133, ⓦamarpreet hotel.com. This whitewashed, vaguely Art Deco upper- to mid-range hotel, on a main road just south of the old city, is a reliable choice. Rooms are large and well furnished (if a bit dated), and there's a quality non-veg restaurant and a bar. Good value, especially if you book online. ₹4300

★**Green Olive** CBS Rd ☎0240 232 9490, ⓦhotel greenolive.com. A swish newcomer that has set a benchmark for its competitors: staff are friendly and efficient; the rooms are clean, modern and well equipped (nice toiletries, kettle and so on); there's a great restaurant (try the ₹450 buffet dinner); and rates – particularly if you book online

– are very reasonable. ₹3700

Lemon Tree 7/2 Chikalthana ☎ 0240 660 3030, ⓦ lemon treehotels.com. Set around a large pool, this is the brightest and cheeriest of the high-end hotels lining the airport road. It has a couple of good restaurants (see below) and the appealing *Slounge* bar. The rate given here is for booking online in advance; rack rates are significantly higher. ₹6000

Manmandir Executive Adalat Rd ☎ 0240 236 5777, ⓦ manmandirmotels.com. Well-maintained, low-cost business hotel above a private bus terminus (see opposite), with a range of sizeable, blandly comfortable rooms (the non-a/c options are particularly good value), plus a reasonable a/c dorm for those on a really tight budget. Dorms ₹300, doubles ₹1500

Panchavati Off Station Rd West ☎ 0240 232 8755, ⓦ hotelpanchavati.com. Decent, if unspectacular, hotel

on the western edge of the city centre with economical rooms (some with a/c), welcoming staff and a restaurant (whose menu even features a few Korean options). ₹1125

Shree Maya Bharuka Complex, Padampura Rd, off Station Rd West ☎ 0240 233 3093. Friendly and popular place with large, cleanish rooms (some a/c); standards vary, so ask to look at a few. There's also a sociable restaurant with good food. ₹1000

Vivanta Ajanta Rd, 4km north of the centre ☎ 0240 661 3737, ⓦ vivantabytaj.com. Part of the Taj group, Aurangabad's most luxurious option is a domed, gleaming-white, wedding-cake confection. Rooms are tastefully finished in dark wood, and all come with bathtubs and a balcony. Facilities include a spa, large pool and croquet on the palm-fringed lawn. ₹7000

EATING

Aurangabad is full of places to eat, with most restaurants serving either strictly vegetarian **Gujarati** food or meat-oriented North Indian dishes. As elsewhere in the state, non-veg places tend to be synonymous with dim lights, drawn curtains and a male clientele – with a few exceptions – while the veg restaurants attract families. **Drinking** is an exclusively male preserve in Aurangabad, usually carried out in the many specially segregated bars (aka "permit rooms"), as well as the larger, more tourist-oriented restaurants and hotels.

Kailash Station Rd East ☎ 0240 233 8916. This pure-veg restaurant serves inexpensive South Indian (including tasty dosas; ₹40–110) and Punjabi food (mains ₹90–120) – plus some so-so Chinese dishes – and is a popular local spot. Daily 9am–11pm.

Republic of Noodles Lemon Tree hotel ☎ 0240 660 3030. If you fancy something a little different, head to this award-winning Southeast Asian restaurant, which has an alfresco dining area by the pool. As well as some classic Thai and Vietnamese dishes, there are a few more unusual Burmese, Indonesian and Singaporean options. Expect to pay around ₹650-plus for dinner. Wi-fi available. Daily 7am–11pm.

Tandoor Shyam Chambers, Station Rd East ☎ 0240 232

8481. Dominated by an imposing bust of Egyptian pharaoh Tutankhamun, this travellers' favourite is one of the city's best-established non-veg restaurants. Tandoori chicken and mutton kebabs (₹170–285) are the house specialities, while for monster appetites there's the full-on "sizzling tandoori platter" (big enough for two; ₹605). Daily 10.30am–4pm & 6.30–11pm.

Thaat Baat Beneath Embassy Hotel, near Vivekanand College, Samarth Nagar Rd ☎ 0240 233 4666. There's a festive air at this fun, family-friendly thali place, where armies of waiters breezily ladle out dollops of tasty pure veg against a backdrop of Rajasthani puppets, paintings and handicrafts. A hearty meal (and soft drink) costs around ₹170. Daily 11am–3.30pm & 7–11pm.

DIRECTORY

Banks and exchange An efficient foreign exchange service is provided at this branch of national chain Trade Wings on CBS Rd (daily 9am–7pm; ☎ 0240 235 7480, ⓦ tradewings.in).

Textiles Aurangabad is famous for its Himroo and Paithani textiles, which are on sale (alongside an array of cheaper imitations) throughout the city; Classic Travel Services runs a tour (see opposite) to the Paithani Weaving Centre.

Ellora

Palaces will decay, bridges will fall, and the noblest structures must give way to the corroding tooth of time; whilst the caverned temples of Ellora shall rear their indestructible and hoary heads in stern loneliness, the glory of past ages, and the admiration of ages yet to come. Captain Seely, *The Wonders of Ellora*

Maharashtra's most visited ancient monument, the **ELLORA** caves, 29km northwest of Aurangabad, may not enjoy as grand a setting as their older cousins at Ajanta, but their amazing wealth of **sculpture** more than compensates – this is an unmissable stop if you're

2

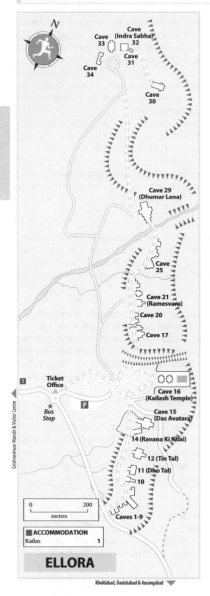

heading to or from Mumbai, 400km southwest. In all, 34 Buddhist, Hindu and Jain caves – some excavated simultaneously, in competition – line the foot of the 2km-long Chamadiri escarpment as it tumbles down to meet the open plains. The site's principal attraction, the colossal **Kailash temple**, rears from a huge, sheer-edged cavity cut from the hillside – a vast lump of solid basalt fashioned into a spectacular complex of colonnaded halls, galleries and shrines.

Brief history

The original reason why this apparently remote spot became the focus of so much religious and artistic activity was the busy **caravan route** that passed through here on its way between the prosperous cities to the north and the ports of the west coast. Profits fuelled a 500-year spate of excavation, beginning midway through the sixth century AD at around the same time that Ajanta, 100km northeast, was abandoned. This was the twilight of the **Buddhist** era in central India; by the end of the seventh century, **Hinduism** had begun to reassert itself. The Brahmanical resurgence gathered momentum over the next three hundred years under the patronage of the Chalukya and Rashtrakuta kings – the two powerful dynasties responsible for the bulk of the work carried out at Ellora, including the eighth-century Kailash temple. A third and final flourish of activity on the site took place towards the end of the first millennium AD, after the local rulers had switched allegiance from Shaivism to the **Jain** faith. A small cluster of more subdued caves to the north of the main group stand as reminders of this age.

Unlike the isolated site of Ajanta, Ellora did not escape the iconoclasm that accompanied the arrival of the **Muslims** in the thirteenth century. The worst excesses were committed during the reign of Aurangzeb who ordered the demolition of the site's "heathen idols". Although Ellora still bears the scars from this time, most of its best pieces of sculpture have remained remarkably well preserved, sheltered from centuries of monsoon downpours by the hard basalt hillside.

The caves

Daily except Tues dawn–dusk · ₹250 (₹10) · If you've come in an auto-rickshaw or a taxi you will also need to buy a ₹10 parking ticket

The **caves** are numbered, following a roughly chronological plan. Numbers 1 to 12, at the southern end of the site, are the oldest, from the Vajrayana Buddhist era

(500–750 AD). The Hindu caves, 13 to 29, overlap with the later Buddhist ones and date from between 600 and 870 AD. Further north, the Jain caves – 30 to 34 – were excavated from 800 AD until the late eleventh century. Because of the sloping hillside, most of the cave entrances are set back from the level ground behind open courtyards and large colonnaded verandas or porches.

To see the oldest caves first, turn right opposite Cave 16, the vast Kailash temple, and follow the main pathway down to Cave 1. From here, work your way gradually northwards again, avoiding the temptation to look around Cave 16, which is best saved until late afternoon when the bus parties have all left and the long shadows cast by the setting sun bring its extraordinary stonework to life.

2

The Buddhist group

The **Buddhist caves** line the sides of a gentle recess in the Chamadiri escarpment. All except Cave 10 are *viharas*, or monastery halls, which the monks would originally have used for study, solitary meditation and communal worship, as well as the mundane business of eating and sleeping. As you progress through them, the chambers grow steadily more impressive in scale and tone. Scholars attribute this to the rise of Hinduism and the need to compete for patronage with the more overtly awe-inspiring Shaivite cave-temples being excavated so close at hand.

Caves 1 to 9

Cave 2 is the first cave of interest, a large central chamber supported by twelve massive, square-based pillars while the aisles are lined with seated Buddhas. The doorway into the shrine room is flanked by two giant, bejewelled *dvarapalas*, or guardian figures: an unusually muscular Padmapani, the *bodhisattva* of compassion, on the left, and an opulent Maitreya, the "Buddha-to-come", on the right. Both are accompanied by their consorts. Inside the sanctum itself, a stately Buddha is seated on a lion throne, looking stronger and more determined than his serene forerunners in Ajanta.

Caves 3 and 4 lack the artifice of Cave 2, though the latter retains some fine capital work. **Cave 5** is the largest single-storey *vihara* in Ellora. Its enormous 36m-long rectangular assembly hall is thought to have been used by the monks as a refectory, and has two rows of benches carved from the stone floor.

Caves 6–9 were excavated at roughly the same time in the seventh century, and are reached via a single door and stairwell cut into the rock. On the walls of the antechamber at the far end of the central hall in **Cave 6** are two of Ellora's most famous and finely executed figures: Tara, the buxom female consort of the *bodhisattva* Avalokitesvara, stands to the left; on the opposite side, the Buddhist goddess of learning, Mahamayuri, is depicted with her emblem, the peacock, while a diligent student sets a good example at his desk below. From Cave 6, a short flight of steps leads up to diminutive **Cave 9**, with a fine frieze decorating the facade.

Caves 10, 11 and 12

Excavated in the early eighth century, **Cave 10** is one of the last and most magnificent of the Deccan's rock-cut *chaitya* halls. Steps lead from the left of its large veranda to an upper balcony, where a trefoil doorway flanked by flying threesomes, heavenly nymphs and a frieze of playful dwarfs leads to an interior balcony. Inside the long apsidal hall (which you may need to ask to be unlocked), the rib-vaulting effect on the ceiling imitates the beams that would have appeared in earlier freestanding wooden structures. A slender Buddha sits enthroned in front of a votive *stupa*, the hall's devotional centrepiece.

In spite of the rediscovery in 1876 of its hitherto hidden basement, **Cave 11** continues to be known as the **Dho Tal**, or "Two Floors" cave. Its top storey is a long, columned assembly hall housing a Buddha shrine and, on its rear wall, images of Durga and Ganesh, the elephant-headed son of Shiva – evidence that the cave was converted into a Hindu temple after being abandoned by the Buddhists. **Cave 12** next door – the **Tin Tal**, or "three floors" – is another triple-storey *vihara*, approached via a large open courtyard. Again, the main highlights are on the uppermost level. The shrine room at the end of the hall, whose walls are lined with five large *bodhisattvas*, is flanked on both sides by seven Buddhas – one for each of the Master's previous incarnations.

The Hindu group

Ellora's seventeen **Hindu caves** are grouped around the middle of the escarpment, to either side of the majestic Kailash temple. Excavated at the start of the Brahmanical revival in the Deccan during a time of relative stability, the cave-temples throb with a vitality absent from their restrained Buddhist predecessors. In place of benign-faced Buddhas, huge **bas-reliefs** line the walls, writhing with dynamic scenes from the Hindu scriptures. Most are connected with **Shiva**, the god of destruction and regeneration (and the presiding deity in all of the Hindu caves on the site), although you'll also come across numerous images of Vishnu (the Preserver) and his various incarnations.

The same tableaux crop up time and again, a repetition that gave Ellora's craftsmen ample opportunity to refine their technique over the years leading up to their greatest achievement, the Kailash temple (Cave 16). Covered separately (see p.126), the temple is the highlight of any visit to Ellora, but you'll appreciate its beautiful sculpture all the more if you visit the earlier Hindu caves first. Numbers 14 and 15, immediately south, are the ones to go for if you're pushed for time.

Cave 14

Dating from the start of the seventh century AD, and among the last of the early excavations, **Cave 14** was a Buddhist *vihara* converted into a temple by the Hindus. The entrance to the bare sanctum is guarded by two impressive river goddesses, Ganga and Yamuna, while lining the ambulatory wall behind and to the right, seven heavy-breasted fertility goddesses, the **Sapta Matrikas**, dandle chubby babies on their laps. Shiva's son, Ganesh, sits to their right beside two cadaverous apparitions, Kala and Kali, the goddesses of death. Superb **friezes** adorn the cave's long side walls.

Cave 15

Like its neighbour, the two-storey **Cave 15**, reached via a long flight of steps, began life as a Buddhist *vihara* but was hijacked by the Hindus and became a Shiva shrine. Behind the Natya Mandapa ("Hall of Dance") in the centre of the courtyard, make for the upper level of the main structure to find some of Ellora's most magnificent sculpture. The cave's name, **Das Avatara**, is derived from the sequence of panels along the right wall, which show five of **Vishnu**'s ten incarnations (avatars).

A carved panel in a recess to the right of the antechamber shows Shiva emerging from a lingam. Brahma and Vishnu stand before the apparition in humility and supplication – symbolizing the supremacy of Shaivism in the region at the time the conversion work was carried out. Finally, halfway down the left wall of the chamber as you're facing the shrine, the cave's most elegant piece of sculpture shows Shiva as Nataraja, poised in a classical dance pose.

Caves 17 to 29

Only three of the Hindu caves strung along the hillside north of the Kailash temple are really worth exploring in depth. **Cave 21** – the **Ramesvara** – was excavated late in the sixth century. Thought to be Ellora's oldest Hindu cave, it harbours some well-executed sculpture, including a fine pair of river goddesses on either side of the veranda, two wonderful door guardians and some sensuous loving couples, or *mithunas*, dotted around the walls of the balcony. **Cave 25**, further along, contains a striking image on the exterior ceiling of the main shrine of the sun god **Surya** speeding in his chariot towards the dawn.

FROM TOP SAILING BOAT, JANJIRA FORT (P.138); NASIK VINEYARD (P.113) >

2

From here, the path picks its way past two more excavations, then drops steeply across the face of a sheer cliff to the bottom of a small river gorge. Once under the seasonal **waterfall**, the trail climbs the other side of the gully to emerge beside **Cave 29**, the huge **Dhumar Lena**. Dating from the late sixth century, the cave boasts an unusual cross-shaped floor plan similar to the Elephanta cave in Mumbai harbour. Pairs of rampant lions guard its three staircases while, inside, the walls are covered with huge **friezes**. On the right-hand side of the (southern) entrance, a dice-playing scene shows Shiva teasing Parvati by holding her arm back as she prepares to throw. Left of the exit, Shiva skewers the Andhaka demon, while in the opposite wall panel he foils the many-armed Ravana's attempts to shake him and Parvati off the top of Mount Kailash; look for the cheeky dwarf baring his bum to taunt the evil demon.

The Kailash temple (Cave 16)

Cave 16, the colossal **Kailash temple**, is Ellora's masterpiece. Here, the term "cave" is not only a gross understatement but a complete misnomer. For although the temple was, like the other excavations, hewn from solid rock, it bears a striking resemblance to earlier freestanding structures in South India. The monolith is believed to have been the brainchild of the Rashtrakuta ruler **Krishna I** (756–773). One hundred years and four generations of kings, architects and craftsmen elapsed, however, before the project was completed. Climb up the track leading along the lip of the compound's north-facing cliff to the ledge overlooking the squat main tower, and you'll see why.

The sheer scale is staggering. Work began by digging three deep trenches into the top of the hill using pickaxes and lengths of wood which, soaked with water and stuffed into narrow cracks, expanded to crumble the basalt. Once a huge chunk of raw rock had been exposed in this way, the royal sculptors set to work. In all, around a quarter of a million tonnes of chippings and debris were cut from the hillside, with no room for improvisation or error. The temple was conceived as a giant replica of Shiva and Parvati's Himalayan abode, the pyramidal **Mount Kailash**. Today, all but a few fragments of the thick coat of white-lime plaster that gave the temple the appearance of a snowy mountain have flaked off, to expose elaborately carved surfaces of grey-brown stone beneath. Around the rear of the tower, these have been bleached and blurred by centuries of erosion, as if the giant sculpture is slowly melting in the fierce Deccan heat.

The temple

The main **entrance** to the temple is through a tall stone screen, intended to mark the transition from the profane to the sacred realms. After passing between two guardian river goddesses, Ganga and Yamuna, you enter a narrow passage that opens onto the main forecourt, opposite a panel showing **Lakshmi**, the goddess of wealth, being lustrated by a pair of elephants. Custom requires pilgrims to circumambulate clockwise around Mount Kailash, so descend the steps to your left and head across the front of the courtyard towards the near corner.

From the top of the concrete steps in the corner, all three principal sections of the complex are visible: first, the shrine above the entrance housing Shiva's vehicle, **Nandi**, the bull; next, the intricate recessed walls of the main assembly hall, or **mandapa**, which still bear traces of the coloured plaster that originally coated the whole edifice; and finally, the sanctuary itself, surmounted by the stumpy, 29m pyramidal tower, or **shikhara** (best viewed from above). These three components rest on an appropriately huge raised platform, borne by dozens of lotus-gathering elephants. As well as symbolizing Shiva's sacred mountain, the temple also represented a giant **chariot**. The transepts protruding from the side of the main hall are its wheels, the Nandi shrine its yoke, and the two life-sized, trunkless elephants in the front of the courtyard (disfigured by Muslim raiders) are the beasts of burden.

Most of the main highlights of the temple itself are confined to its side walls, which are plastered with vibrant **sculpture**. Lining the staircase that leads up to the north side of the *mandapa*, a long, lively narrative panel depicts scenes from the Mahabharata, and below this the life of **Krishna**. Continuing clockwise, the majority of the panels around the lower sections around the temple are devoted to **Shiva**. On the south side of the *mandapa*, in an alcove carved out of the most prominent projection, you'll find the finest piece of sculpture in the compound. It shows Shiva and Parvati being disturbed by the multiheaded **Ravana**, who has been incarcerated inside the sacred mountain and is now shaking the walls of his prison with his many arms. Shiva is about to assert his supremacy by calming the earthquake with a prod of his toe. Parvati, meanwhile, nonchalantly reclines on her elbow as one of her handmaidens flees in panic.

From here, head up the steps at the southwest corner of the courtyard to the **Hall of Sacrifices**, with its striking frieze of the seven mother goddesses, the Sapta Matrikas, and their ghoulish companions Kala and Kali (shown astride a heap of corpses). The sixteen-columned assembly hall is shrouded in a gloomy half-light designed to focus worshippers on the presence of the deity within. Using a portable arc light, the chowkidar will illuminate fragments of painting on the ceiling, where Shiva, as **Nataraja**, performs the dance of death.

The Jain group

Ellora's small cluster of four **Jain caves** is north of the main group, just a five-minute walk north along the path from Cave 29 or, alternatively, reachable from the Kailash temple via a curving asphalt road.

Excavated in the late ninth and tenth centuries, after the Hindu phase had petered out, the Jain caves are Ellora's swansong, featuring some fine decorative carving and a few exquisite paintings. Of principal interest is **Cave 32**, the **Indra Sabha** ("Indra's Assembly Hall"), a miniature version of the Kailash temple. The lower of its two levels is plain and incomplete, but the upper storey, guarded by huge *yaksha* and *yakshi* figures facing each other across the veranda, is crammed with elaborate stonework, notably the ornate pillars and the two *tirthankaras* guarding the entrance to the central shrine. The naked figure of Gomatesvara, on the right, is fulfilling a vow of silence in the forest. He is so deeply immersed in meditation that creepers have grown up his legs, and animals, snakes and scorpions crawl around his feet.

The Grishneshwar Mandir

Rising above the small village west of the caves, the cream-coloured *shikhara* of the eighteenth-century **Grishneshwar Mandir** pinpoints the location of one of India's oldest and most sacred deities. The lingam enshrined inside the temple's cavernous inner sanctum is one of the twelve "self-born" **jyotirlingas** ("linga of light"), thought to date back to the second century BC. Non-Hindus are allowed to join the queue for *darshan*, but men have to remove their shirts before entering the shrine itself.

ARRIVAL AND INFORMATION   **ELLORA**

Most visitors use Aurangabad as a base for day-trips to the caves; if you prefer to take in the caves at a more leisurely pace and climb Daulatabad Hill, either spend the night at Ellora or leave Aurangabad early in the morning.

By bus There are regular MSRTC buses (every 30min; 40min) from Aurangabad to Ellora.

By tour Travel agencies in Aurangabad offer tours (see p.120), though these tend to be rather rushed.

By auto-rickshaw/taxi An auto-rickshaw for the round trip from Aurangabad costs ₹700–800, including waiting time; a taxi costs ₹1200–1500.

Guides Official multilingual guides are on hand to take you on a tour of the most interesting caves (groups of up to five people around ₹750).

Tourist information There's a new visitor centre (same opening times as the caves) with a selection of exhibits on the caves, plus temporary exhibitions.

ACCOMMODATION

Apart from the mediocre MTDC canteen inside the complex and the roadside *dhabas* opposite the bus stand, the only place to eat is at the restaurant inside the *Kailas* hotel.

Kailas Opposite the entrance to the caves ☎02437 244543, ⓦhotelkailas.com. This small, peaceful hotel has a mix of simple rooms (a/c costs ₹1000 extra) close to the road and smarter cottages (₹3500) facing the caves themselves. There's a decent restaurant, and a range of activities on offer, including trips to local markets, hikes, massages and even paragliding. ₹2000

Ajanta

Hewn from the near-vertical sides of a horseshoe-shaped ravine, the caves at **AJANTA** occupy a site worthy of the spectacular ancient art they contain. Less than two centuries ago, this remote spot was known only to local tribespeople; the shadowy entrances to its abandoned stone chambers lay buried deep under a thick blanket of creepers and jungle.

The chance arrival in 1819 of a small detachment of East India Company troops, however, brought the caves' obscurity to an abrupt end. Led to the top of the precipitous bluff that overlooks the gorge by a young "half-wild" scout, the tiger-hunters spied what has now been identified as the facade of Cave 10 protruding through the foliage.

The British soldiers had made one of the most sensational archeological finds of all time. Further exploration revealed a total of 28 colonnaded caves chiselled out of the chocolate-brown and grey basalt cliffs lining the River Waghora. More remarkable still were the immaculately preserved **paintings** writhing over their interior surfaces. For, in addition to the rows of stone Buddhas and other **sculpture** enshrined within them, Ajanta's excavations are adorned with a swirling profusion of murals, depicting everything from battlefields to sailing ships, city streets and teeming animal-filled forests to snow-capped mountains. Even if you aren't wholly familiar with the narratives they portray, it's easy to see why these paintings are regarded as the finest surviving gallery of art from any of the world's ancient civilizations.

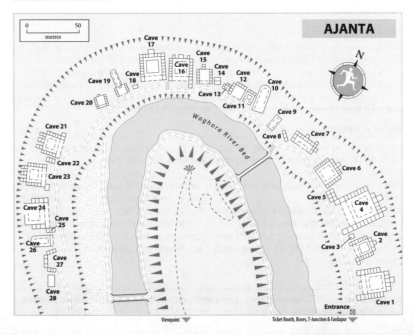

ROCK-CUT CAVES OF THE NORTHWESTERN DECCAN

The **rock-cut caves** scattered across the volcanic hills of the northwestern Deccan rank among the most extraordinary religious monuments in Asia. Ranging from tiny monastic cells to elaborately carved temples, they are remarkable for having been hewn by hand from solid rock. Their third-century-BC origins seem to have been as temporary shelters for Buddhist monks when heavy monsoon rains brought their travels to a halt. Modelled on earlier wooden structures, most were sponsored by **merchants**, for whom the casteless new faith offered an attractive alternative to the old, discriminatory social order. Gradually, encouraged by the example of the Mauryan emperor Ashoka, the local ruling dynasties also began to embrace Buddhism. Under their patronage, during the second century BC, the first large-scale monastery caves were created at **Karla**, **Bhaja** and **Ajanta**.

THE HINAYANA SCHOOL

Around this time, the austere **Hinayana** ("Lesser Vehicle") school of Buddhism predominated in India. Caves cut in this era were mostly simple worship halls, or **chaityas** – long, rectangular apsed chambers with barrel-vaulted roofs and two narrow colonnaded aisles curving gently around the back of a monolithic **stupa**. Symbols of the Buddha's enlightenment, these hemispherical burial mounds provided the principal focus for worship and meditation, circumambulated by the monks during their communal rituals.

THE MAHAYANA SCHOOL

By the fourth century AD, the Hinayana school was losing ground to the more exuberant **Mahayana** ("Greater Vehicle") school. Its emphasis on an ever-enlarging pantheon of **bodhisattvas** (merciful saints who postponed their accession to nirvana to help mankind towards enlightenment) was accompanied by a transformation in architectural styles. *Chaityas* were superseded by lavish monastery halls, or **viharas**, in which the monks both lived and worshipped, and the once-prohibited image of the Buddha became far more prominent. Occupying the circumambulatory recess at the end of the hall, where the *stupa* formerly stood, the colossal **icon** acquired the 32 characteristics, or **lakshanas** (including long dangling ear-lobes, cranial protuberance, short curls, robe and halo) by which the Buddha was distinguished from lesser divinities. The peak of Mahayana art came towards the end of the Buddhist age. Drawing on the rich catalogue of themes and images contained in ancient scriptures such as the **Jatakas** (legends relating to the Buddha's previous incarnations), Ajanta's exquisite wall **painting** may, in part, have been designed to rekindle enthusiasm for the faith, which was, by this point, already starting to wane in the region.

THE VAJRAYANA SECT

Attempts to compete with the resurgence of **Hinduism**, from the sixth century onwards, eventually led to the evolution of another, more esoteric religious movement. The **Vajrayana**, or "Thunderbolt" sect stressed the female creative principle, **shakti**, with arcane rituals combining spells and magic formulas.

BRAHMANISM

Ultimately, however, such modifications were to prove powerless against the growing allure of Brahmanism. The ensuing shift in royal and popular patronage is best exemplified by **Ellora** where, during the eighth century, many old *viharas* were converted into temples, their shrines housing polished *shivalinga* instead of *stupas* and Buddhas. Hindu cave architecture, with its dramatic mythological **sculpture**, culminated in the tenth century with the magnificent **Kailash temple**, a giant replica of the freestanding structures that had already begun to replace rock-cut caves. It was Hinduism that bore the brunt of the iconoclastic medieval descent of Islam on the Deccan, Buddhism having long since fled to the comparative safety of the Himalayas, where it still flourishes.

Brief history

Located close enough to the major trans-Deccan trade routes to ensure a steady supply of alms, yet far enough from civilization to preserve the peace and tranquillity necessary for meditation and prayer, Ajanta was an ideal location for the region's itinerant Buddhist

2

VISITING AJANTA

In spite of its comparative remoteness, **Ajanta** receives an extraordinary number of visitors. If you want to enjoy the site in anything close to its original serenity, avoid coming on a weekend or public holiday – it takes a fertile imagination indeed to picture Buddhist monks filing softly around the rough stone steps when hundreds of riotous schoolchildren and throngs of tourists are clambering over them. Among measures to minimize the impact of the hundreds of visitors who daily trudge through is a ban on flash photography – though the introduction of low-impact lighting has aided close viewing – and strict limits on the numbers allowed into the most interesting caves at any given time. Another significant move to reduce the ecological impact on the area has been the creation of the **Ajanta T-junction** (see p.133).

The best seasons to visit are either during the monsoon, when the river is swollen and the gorge reverberates with the sound of the waterfalls, or during the cooler winter months between October and March. At other times, the relentless Deccan sun beating down on the south-facing rock can make a trip around Ajanta a real endurance test. Whenever you go, take a hat, some sunglasses, a good torch and plenty of drinking water.

monks to found their first permanent monasteries. Donative inscriptions indicate that its earliest cave excavations took place in the second century BC.

In its heyday, Ajanta sheltered more than two hundred monks, as well as a sizeable community of painters, sculptors and labourers employed in excavating and decorating the cells and sanctuaries. Sometime in the seventh century, however, the site was abandoned – whether because of the growing popularity of nearby Ellora, or the threat posed by the resurgence of Hinduism, no one knows. By the eighth century, the complex lay deserted and forgotten, overlooked even by the Muslim iconoclasts who wrought such damage to the area's other sacred sites during the medieval era.

The caves

Tues–Sun 9am–5pm • ₹250 (₹10), "amenities fee" ₹10 • Entry tickets are sold at the booth at the main entrance, a 4km bus ride (a/c bus ₹20, non-a/c bus ₹10 one way) from the Ajanta T-junction

An obvious path leads up from the ticket booth to the grand **Mahayana** *viharas*; if you'd prefer to see the caves in chronological order, however, start with the smaller **Hinayana** group of *chaitya* halls at the bottom of the river bend (caves 12, 10 and 9), then work your way back up, via Cave 17. For help getting up the steps, sedan-chair bearers (around ₹500), or dhooli-wallahs, stand in front of the stalls below, while porters (around ₹150) are on hand to carry bags. Official **guides** make two-hour tours (around ₹750) which can be arranged through the ticket office; most deliver an interesting spiel but you may well feel like taking in the sights again afterwards at a more leisurely pace.

Cave 1

There's always a queue for **Cave 1**, which contains some of the finest and stylistically most evolved paintings on the site. By the time work on it began, late in the fifth century, *viharas* served not only to shelter and feed the monks, but also as places of worship in their own right. In common with most Mahayana *viharas*, the extraordinary murals lining the walls and ceilings depict episodes from the Jatakas, tales of the birth and former lives of the Buddha.

Left of the doorway into the main shrine stands another masterpiece. **Padmapani**, the lotus-holding form of Avalokitesvara, is surrounded by an entourage of smaller attendants, divine musicians, lovers, monkeys and a peacock. His heavy almond eyes and languid hip-shot *tribhanga* (or "three-bend") pose exudes a distant and sublime calm. Opposite, flanking the right side of the doorway, is his counterpart, **Vajrapani**, the thunderbolt holder. Between them, these two *bodhisattvas* represent the dual aspects of Mahayana Buddhism: compassion and knowledge.

The real focal point of Cave 1, however, is the large sculpted Buddha seated in the shrine room – the finest such figure in Ajanta. Using portable electric spotlights, guides demonstrate how the expression on the Buddha's exquisitely carved face changes according to where the light is held.

On the way out, you should be able to spot this cave's other famous *trompe l'oeil*, crowning one of the pillars (on the fourth pillar on the left as you face the exit): the figures of four apparently separate stags that, on closer inspection, all share the same head.

Cave 2

Cave 2 is another impressive Mahayana *vihara*, dating from the sixth century. Here, the ceiling is decorated with complex floral patterns, including lotus and medallion motifs. Sculpted friezes in the small subsidiary shrine to the right of the main chapel centre on a well-endowed fertility goddess, **Hariti**, the infamous child-eating ogress, and Kubera, the god of wealth. The side walls teem with lively **paintings** of the Jatakas and other mythological episodes. A mural on the left veranda shows the birth of the Buddha, emerging from under his mother's arm, and his conception when a white elephant appeared to her in a dream (bottom left).

Caves 3 to 9

Cave 3 is inaccessible but unfinished **Cave 4**, the largest *vihara* in the complex, is worth a quick look for its 28 pillars and huge Buddha. It's also worth popping into **Cave 6**, a two-storey *vihara* with a finely carved doorjamb and lintel around the entrance to its shrine room. Cave 8 is always closed; it contains the generator for the lights.

Cave 9, which dates from the first century BC, is the first *chaitya* you come to along the walkway. Resting in the half-light shed by a characteristic *peepal*-leaf-shaped window in the sculpted facade, the hemispherical **stupa**, with its inverted pyramidal reliquary, forms the devotional centrepiece of the 14m-long hall. The fragments of painting that remain, including the procession scene on the left wall, are mostly superimpositions over the top of earlier snake deities – *nagarajas*.

Cave 10

Although, like Cave 9, marred by the unsightly wire meshing used to keep out bats, the facade of **Cave 10**, a second-century-BC *chaitya* hall – the oldest of its kind in the ravine – is still a grand sight. The cave's main highlights, however, are far smaller and more subdued. Along the left wall, you may be able to pick out the fading traces of painting (now encased in glass) that depict a scene in which a raja and his retinue approach a group of dancers and musicians surrounding a garlanded *bodhi* tree – a symbol of the Buddha (the Hinayanas preferred not to depict him figuratively); it's believed to be the earliest surviving Buddhist mural in India. Elsewhere on the walls is graffiti scrawled by the British soldiers who rediscovered the caves in 1819.

The apsidal-ended hall itself, divided by three rows of painted octagonal pillars, is dominated by a huge monolithic **stupa** at its far end. If there's no one else around, test out the *chaitya*'s amazing acoustics.

Caves 16 and 17

The next cave of interest, **Cave 16**, is another spectacular fifth-century *vihara*, with the famous painting known as the **Dying Princess** near the front of its left wall. The "princess" was actually a queen named **Sundari**, and she isn't dying, but fainting after hearing the news that her husband, King Nanda (Buddha's cousin), is about to renounce his throne to take up monastic orders. The opposite walls show events from Buddha's early life as **Siddhartha**.

Cave 17, dating from between the mid-fifth and early sixth centuries, boasts the best-preserved and most varied paintings in Ajanta. While you wait to enter, have a look at the frescoes on the **veranda**. Above the door, eight seated Buddhas, including Maitreya, the Buddha-to-come, look down. To the left, an amorous princely couple share a last

2

CAVE PAINTING TECHNIQUES

The basic **painting techniques** used by the artists of Ajanta to create the caves' lustrous kaleidoscopes of colour changed little over the eight centuries the site was in use, from 200 BC to 650 AD. First, the rough stone surfaces were primed with a thick coating of paste made from clay, cow-dung, animal hair and vegetable fibre. Next, a finer layer of smooth white lime was applied. Before this was dry, the artists quickly sketched the outlines of their pictures using red cinnabar, which they then filled in with an undercoat of *terre-verte*. The **pigments**, all derived from natural water-soluble substances (kaolin chalk for white, lamp soot for black, glauconite for green, ochre for yellow and imported lapis lazuli for blue), were thickened with glue and added only after the undercoat was completely dry. Thus the Ajanta paintings are not, strictly speaking, frescoes (always executed on damp surfaces), but **tempera**. Finally, once dry, the murals were painstakingly polished with a smooth stone to bring out their natural sheen. The artists' only sources of **light** were oil-lamps and sunshine reflected into the caves by metal mirrors and pools of water (the external courtyards were flooded expressly for this purpose), a constraint that makes their extraordinary mastery of line, perspective and shading – which endow Ajanta's paintings with their characteristic otherworldly light – all the more remarkable.

---

glass of wine before giving their worldly wealth away to the poor. The wall that forms the far left side of the veranda features fragments of an elaborate "Wheel of Life". Inside the cave, the murals are, once more, dominated by the illustrations of the Jatakas, particularly those in which the Buddha takes the form of an animal to illustrate certain virtues. This is also where you'll find the exquisite and much-celebrated portrait of a sultry, dark-skinned princess admiring herself in a mirror while her handmaidens and a female dwarf look on. The chowkidars will demonstrate how, when illuminated from the side, her iridescent eyes and jewellery glow like pearls against the brooding, dark background.

Cave 19

Excavated during the mid-fifth century, when the age of Mahayana Buddhism was in full swing, **Cave 19** is indisputably Ajanta's most magnificent *chaitya* hall, its **facade** teeming with elaborate sculpture. Inside, the faded frescoes are of less note than the sculpture around the tops of the pillars. The standing Buddha at the far end, another Mahayana innovation, is even more remarkable. Notice the development from the stumpier *stupas* enshrined within the early *chaityas* (caves 9 and 10) to this more elongated version. Its umbrellas, supported by angels and a vase of divine nectar, reach right up to the vaulted roof.

Caves 21 to 26

Caves 21 to 26 date from the seventh century, a couple of hundred years after the others, and form a separate group at the far end of the cliff. Apart from the unfinished **Cave 24**, whose roughly hacked trenches and pillars give an idea of how the original excavation was carried out here, the only one worth a close look is **Cave 26**. Envisaged on a similarly grand scale to Cave 19, this impressive **chaitya** hall was never completed. Nevertheless, the sculpture is among the most vivid and sensuous at Ajanta. On the left wall as you enter the cave, the colossal image of **Parinirvarna** (Siddhartha reclining on his deathbed) is the essence of tranquillity. Note the weeping mourners below, and the flying angels and musicians above, preparing to greet the sage as he drifts into nirvana. Two panels down, and in dramatic contrast, the **Temptation of Mara** frieze depicts Buddha ensconced under a *peepal* tree as seven tantalizing sisters try to seduce him. Their father, the satanic Mara, watches from astride an elephant in the top left corner. The ruse to lead the Buddha astray fails, of course, eventually (bottom right) forcing the evil adversary and his daughters to retreat.

The viewpoint

The climb to the **viewpoint** from where the British hunting party first spotted the Ajanta caves is well worth the effort – the panorama over the Waghora gorge and its surrounding walls of bare, flat-topped mountains is spectacular. From the far side of the iron footbridge beneath Cave 8, steps lead up the opposite side of the ravine to a small tin-roofed shelter, where the full majesty of the sheer-sided gorge becomes clear. From here it's a stiff twenty-minute climb straight ahead to the clearly visible viewpoint at the ridge of the hill.

ARRIVAL AND DEPARTURE
AJANTA

By bus All MSRTC buses (every 30min; the last one returns around 5pm) between Aurangabad (2hr 30min–3hr), 108km southwest, and the nearest railhead at Jalgaon (1hr), 58km north, stop on request at the Ajanta T-junction, which is 4km from the caves on the main road. Provided that you catch an early enough service up here, it's possible to see the caves, grab a bite to eat, and then head off

again in either direction (there are facilities for storing your luggage here).

By taxi A taxi for the round trip from Aurangabad, with waiting time, costs ₹2800–3000; from Jalgaon you can expect to pay ₹1500–1700.

By tour Travel agencies in Aurangabad offer rather rushed tours (see p.120) of Ajanta.

GETTING AROUND AND INFORMATION

The Ajanta T-junction All vehicles (including taxis and tour buses) must terminate at the Ajanta T-junction, where you'll find a tourist complex with snack joints, toilets and hawker stalls. There is also a new visitor centre (Tues–Sun 9am–5pm) that houses a museum with replicas of four

of the caves, plus three restaurants. After paying a ₹10 "amenities fee" to enter the complex, you catch one of the supposedly ecofriendly green buses that regularly ply the route to and from the caves (non-a/c ₹15, a/c ₹20 one way).

ACCOMMODATION

As the first bus from the T-junction to the caves doesn't leave until 9am, there's little advantage in staying locally, though there are some reasonable accommodation options. For food, apart from the uninspiring MTDC dining halls just outside the entrance to the caves and at the *MTDC Ajanta Tourist Resort*, you have a choice of *Padmapani Park*'s pure-veg restaurant and the nearby string of *dhabas* that line the main highway.

MTDC Ajanta Tourist Resort Fardapur ⊕ 02438 244230, ⊛ maharashtratourism.gov.in. Located around 1.5km from the T-junction in the village of Fardapur, this hotel is pretty basic, with spartan rooms with fans or a/c, as well as an unremarkable restaurant. ₹1600

MTDC T-Junction Guest House Close to the tourist complex ⊕ 02438 244230, ⊛ maharashtratourism.gov .in. Set in attractive gardens a short wander from the tourist complex and the bus stop, this faded guesthouse has five

spacious, split-level rooms, all a/c, with small verandas. The main drawback is that, apart from the nearby snack stalls, there's nowhere to eat. ₹1800

Padmapani Park Fardapur ⊕ 02438 244280, ⊛ hotel padmapaniparkajanta.com. At the edge of Fardapur, a 1km walk from the *MTDC Ajanta Tourist Resort*, is this just-about-adequate, low-cost alternative to the MTDC hotels: rather shabby rooms, but a good restaurant. ₹1000

Lonar

Few visitors reach the crater at **LONAR** but those who do find this **meteorite-formed lake** an amazing and tranquil place. Referred to as "Taratirth" in a Hindu legend that correctly claimed it was created by a shooting star, the gigantic hole in the ground was formed about 50,000 years ago when a lump of space rock survived its fiery descent through the atmosphere to bury itself here. As the only such crater formed in basalt rock in the world, the site is not just a geological curiosity but also highly valuable to scientists – NASA has made extensive studies due to its apparent similarity to some lunar and Martian landscapes; though many of the lake's mysteries, such as the extreme alkalinity of its thick, sulphurous water, continue to baffle.

Numerous steep paths lead down to the lake from the rim, the principal one starting around 500m from the *MTDC Holiday Resort* and emerging in the basin near a twelfth-century temple dedicated to Shiva. A complete circuit of the lake, surrounded

2

by forest and home to a rich array of birdlife, takes around three hours. En route you will discover numerous other seemingly lost Shaivite shrines. While huddling along a ravine etched into the crater's northeastern slope – an alternative path back up – is a fascinating cluster of temples, fed by a spring, or *dhar*, supposedly originating from the Ganges. Before leaving, it's well worth searching out the tenth-century Chalukyan **Daitya Sudana** temple in Lonar village, its walls inside and out crawling with a profusion of exquisite carvings of mythological scenes.

ARRIVAL AND INFORMATION LONAR

By taxi The easiest way to get to Lonar is by taxi from Aurangabad, which costs ₹2500–3500 for a day-trip.
By bus There are two morning buses direct from Aurangabad (4hr), with the last bus back around 4pm; services stop in the

centre of Lonar village, around 2km from the lake.
Guides For more on the crater, it's worth hiring a local guide; Gajanan Kharat (☎ 07260 221428) is recommended.

ACCOMMODATION

MTDC Holiday Resort Opposite the crater ☎ 07260 22160, ⓦ maharashtratourism.gov.in. The only accommodation in Lonar is this rather ghostly hotel built for a tourist

rush that never came. The attached rooms are comfortable, though uninspiring, but the restaurant has a superbly sited terrace from which to view the lake. **₹1500**

Jalgaon

Straddling an important junction on the Central and Western Railway networks, as well as the main trans-Deccan trunk road, NH-6, **JALGAON** is a prosperous market town for the region's cotton and banana growers, and a key jumping-off point for travellers heading to or from the Ajanta caves, 58km south. Even though the town holds nothing of interest, you may find yourself obliged to hole up here to be well placed for a morning departure.

ARRIVAL AND DEPARTURE JALGAON

By train The railway station, on Station Rd, appropriately enough, is well served by mainline trains between Delhi, Kolkata and Mumbai, and convenient for most cities to the north on the Central Railway. Express services also pass through en route to join the Southeastern Railway.
Destinations Agra (7 daily; 14–18hr); Aurangabad (1 daily; 4hr 15min); Bengaluru (1 daily; 24hr 20min); Bhopal (10 daily; 6hr 45min–8hr 40min); Chennai (1 daily; 23hr); Delhi (7 daily; 18–23hr); Gwalior (7 daily; 12hr 15min–16hr); Mumbai (23 daily; 7hr 20min–19hr); Nagpur (14 daily; 5hr 45min–9hr); Nasik (23 daily; 2hr 30min–3hr); Pune (6 daily; 8hr 30min–11hr 15min); Wardha Junction (for Sevagram; 15 daily; 5hr 30min–6hr 30min);

Varanasi (9 daily; 19–29hr).
By bus The busy MSRTC Bus Stand is 1.5km across town from the railway station (₹30–40 in an auto-rickshaw). There are frequent buses to Aurangabad (every 30min; 3hr 30min–4hr), 160km away, all of which stop at the Ajanta T-junction (1hr). MSRTC also runs buses to Mumbai (1–2 daily; 9–11hr), Nagpur (1–2 daily; 9–10hr) and Pune (4–5 daily; 9–10hr), but preferable are the (generally overnight) buses run by the private companies such as Shree Durga Travels (☎ 0257 222 8124, ⓦ redbus.in) and Uncle Travels (☎ 0257 224 1294); tickets can be booked at the travel agents on Station Rd.

ACCOMMODATION AND EATING

★**Plaza** Station Rd, 2min walk from the railway station ☎ 0257 222 7354, ⓔ hotelplaza_jal@yahoo .com. By far the best place to stay in Jalgaon – in fact one of the best budget hotels in Maharashtra – is this welcoming and very spruce hotel. Immaculately clean rooms feature a cool, white minimalist design; the huge a/c "deluxe" room (₹1650) is particularly good. The owner is very friendly and well informed, and staff will provide tea in your room if you're leaving early in the morning. **₹900**

Royal Palace Mahabal Rd, 10–15min auto-rickshaw ride from the railway station ☎ 0257 223 3888, ⓦ hotel royalpalace.in. The grand marble lobby, decorated with a glitzy chandelier, a reproduction of the *Mona Lisa* and fountain filled with fish, raise expectations that the mid-range rooms fail to match; still, they are comfortable enough, and there's a good restaurant. Book online for a ten- to twenty-percent discount. **₹1975**

Nagpur

Capital of the "land of oranges", **NAGPUR** is the focus of government attempts to develop industry in the remote northeastern corner of Maharashtra – most foreign visitors come for business rather than pleasure. In the city itself, the most prominent landmark is the Sitabuldi Fort, standing on a saddle between two low hills above the railway station, though it's closed to the public. North and west of the fort, the pleasantly green Civil Lines district holds some grand Raj-era buildings, dating from the time when this was the capital of the vast Central Provinces region.

2

ARRIVAL AND DEPARTURE   NAGPUR

Geographically at the virtual centre of India, Nagpur is handily placed for connections all across the country – though a long way from anywhere.

By plane The airport is around 8km southwest of the centre (around ₹250 by auto-rickshaw, more by taxi).
Destinations Delhi (3 daily; 1hr 30min); Kolkata (1 daily; 1hr 30min); Mumbai (7 daily; 1hr 20min); Pune (3 daily; 1hr 15min); Raipur (1 daily; 40min).

By train Nagpur's busy central mainline railway station is a short auto-rickshaw (around ₹30–40) ride from the main hotel district along Central Ave. The quickest train to Mumbai is the #12290 *Nagpur CSTM Duront* (daily 8.40pm; 11hr 15min).
Destinations Bhopal (20 daily; 5hr 15min–8hr 30min); Chennai (9 daily; 14hr 40min–23hr 30min); Delhi (17 daily;

14–22hr); Hyderabad (11 daily; 8hr 30min–11hr); Jabalpur (6 daily; 8hr 40min–19hr 40min); Jalgaon (14 daily; 5hr 45min–9hr); Kolkata (10 daily; 17hr 30min–21hr 30min); Mumbai (11 daily; 11hr 15min–23hr 30min); Nasik (11 daily; 9–20hr); Pune (3 daily; 15–17hr 45min); Wardha Junction (for Sevagram; 15 daily; 1hr).
By bus MSRTC buses pull in at the State Bus Stand, 2km southeast of the railway station.
Destinations Aurangabad (6 daily; 12hr); Jabalpur (2–3 daily; 7–8hr); Jalgaon (2–3 daily; 9hr); Pune (4–5 daily; 16hr); Ramtek (every 30min; 1hr 30min); Wardha (every 30min; 2–3hr).

INFORMATION

Tourist information The MTDC tourist office (Mon–Sat 10am–6pm; ☎0712 253 3325) is 2.5km west of the centre on West High Court Rd in Civil Lines, but is only useful for booking accommodation. If you're heading to Madhya Pradesh, you can get information from the helpful MP

Tourism office on the fourth floor of the Lokmat Building, Wardha Rd (Mon–Sat 10am–5pm except 2nd & 3rd Sat of month; ☎0712 244 2378).
Services The State Bank of India on Kingsway, near the railway station, changes foreign currency.

ACCOMMODATION AND EATING

Grand Just off Central Ave, around 1km east of the bus stand ☎0712 661 7850. The *Grand* is one of the better budget hotels on Central Ave, though as standards are generally low, this isn't a ringing endorsement. The cleanish rooms here are a bit shabby, but OK for a night. ₹800
Naivedhyam 198 Rani Jhansi Chowk, Sitabuldi ☎0712 256 3070. This swish, first-floor restaurant, right in the centre of town, is a Nagpur institution, serving up delicious veg Indian/Chinese food and sizzlers (mains ₹200–300). There are various good-value meal combos, especially at lunchtime (₹220–360). Daily 11am–11pm.
Pride Wardha Rd, opposite the airport ☎0712 229 1102, ☜pridehotel.com. One of Nagpur's best top-end

hotels, the *Pride* often plays host to visiting cricket teams. The rooms are spacious and well equipped, though some have rather kitsch 1970s-era decor. Facilities include a pool and gym, a clutch of fine cafés/restaurants and an appealing bar. Good online discounts available. ₹5000
Tuli International 1km northwest of the railway station ☎0712 665 3555, ☜tuligroup.com. Of Nagpur's numerous business-traveller-oriented hotels, this hotel in the quiet Sadar district probably has the most charm; its chandeliered lobby, carpeted corridors and chintzy decor give it an endearingly old-fashioned feel. Rooms are comfortable and there's a good restaurant, coffee shop and "pub". If you want a bit more luxury, try sister hotel *Tuli Imperial*. ₹4250

Around Nagpur

The trickle of visitors who pass through Nagpur tend to visit en route to Madhya Pradesh, or the Gandhian ashrams at **Sevagram** and **Paunar**, a two-hour journey southwest. The other worthwhile excursion is the ninety-minute bus ride northeast to the hilltop temple complex at **Ramtek**.

Ramtek

The picturesque cluster of whitewashed hilltop temples and shrines at **RAMTEK**, 40km northeast of Nagpur on the main Jabalpur road (NH-7), is one of those alluring apparitions you spy from afar on long journeys through central India. According to the Ramayana, this craggy, scrub-strewn outcrop was the spot where Rama, Sita and Lakshmana paused on their way back from Lanka. Although few traces of these ancient times have survived, the site's old **paved** pilgrim trails, sacred lake, tumbledown shrines and fine views across the endless plains more than live up to its distant promise.

Ram Mandir and the Kalidas Smarak
Around 4.5km from the bus stand • Kalidas Smarak daily 8.30am–8pm • ₹10

On the fringes of the town a flight of stone steps climbs steeply up the side of Ramtek hill to the **Ram Mandir**. Built in 1740, the temple stands on the site of a fifth-century structure, of which only three small sandstone shrines remain. Just beneath the temple complex stands the circular **Kalidas Smarak**, a modern memorial to the great Sanskrit poet, Kalidasa. The pavilion's interior walls are decorated with painted panels depicting scenes from his life and works.

Ambala Lake
Just off the road that runs between the bus stand and the Ram Mandir

Another of Ramtek's sacred sites is Ambala Lake, a holy bathing tank that lies 1.5km along a pilgrims' trail at the bottom of the gully, enfolded by a spur of parched brown hills. Its main attractions are the temples and *ghats* clinging to its muddy banks. More energetic visitors can combine a look with a *parikrama*, or circular tour of the tank, taking in the semi-derelict cenotaphs and weed-choked shrines scattered along the more tranquil north and western shore.

ARRIVAL AND DEPARTURE   RAMTEK

By bus Frequent buses shuttle between Nagpur and Ramtek (every 30min; 1hr 30min). From the bus stand, an auto-rickshaw will take you the 4.5km to the Ram Mandir via Ambala Lake for around ₹150.

Sevagram
9km east of Wardha • **Main ashram compound** Daily 6am–6pm • Free • **Visitors' centre** Daily except Tues 10am–6pm • Free • ☎ 71522 84753, ⓦ gandhiashramsevagram.org

SEVAGRAM, Gandhi's model "Village of Service", is deep in the serene Maharashtran countryside. The Mahatma moved here from his former ashram in Gujarat during the 1936 monsoon, on the invitation of his friend Seth Jamnalal Bajaj. At the centre of the Subcontinent, within easy reach of the Central Railway, it made an ideal headquarters for the national, nonviolent Satyagraha movement, combining seclusion with the easy access to other parts of the country Gandhi needed in order to carry out his political activities.

These days, the small settlement is a cross between a museum and living centre for the promulgation of Gandhian philosophies. Interested visitors are welcome to spend a couple of days here, helping in the fields, attending discussions and prayer meetings, and learning the dying art of hand-spinning. The older ashramites, or *saadhaks*, are veritable founts of wisdom when it comes to the words of their guru, Gandhiji.

Once past the absorbing visitors' centre, which documents Gandhi's life, the real focal point of the ashram is the sublimely peaceful main compound entered a few hundred metres along the road. These modest huts – among them the Mahatma's main residence – have been preserved exactly the way they were when the great man and his disciples lived here in the last years of the Independence struggle. A small shop sells handloomed cloth and other products made on site.

ARRIVAL AND DEPARTURE
SEVAGRAM

By train Wardha Junction railway station, 77km south-west of Nagpur and 9km west of Sevagram, has regular services to/from Nagpur (15 daily; 1hr) and Jalgaon (15 daily; 5hr 30min–6hr 30min).

By bus Local buses (every 30min; around 20min) run between Wardha and the crossroads outside the Kasturba

Gandhi Hospital, from where it's a 1km walk to the ashram. Buses also connect Nagpur and Wardha (every 30min; 2–3hr).

By auto-rickshaw An auto-rickshaw from the bus stand to Sevagram and Paunar (see below) costs around ₹300.

ACCOMMODATION

Rustam Bhavan Guest House In the main ashram compound ☎ 07152 284753, ⓦ ghandiashramsevagram .org. If you want to spend some time at the ashram, you can stay in the basic but spotless *Rustam Bhavan Guest House*,

though you will be expected to do a couple of hours' communal work a day. Simple, super-healthy veg meals are on offer. **₹500**

Paunar

Vinoba Bhave's ashram at **PAUNAR**, 3km from Sevagram has a more dynamic feel than its more famous cousin at Sevagram. Bhave (1895–1982), a close friend and disciple of Gandhi, best remembered for his successful Bhoodan, or **land gift**, campaign to persuade wealthy landowners to hand over farmland to the poor, founded the ashram in 1938 to develop the concept of **swarajya**, or "self-sufficiency". Consequently, organic gardening, milk production, spinning and weaving have an even higher profile here than the regular meditation, prayer and yoga sessions. Another difference between this institution and the one up the road is that the *saadhaks* here are almost all female.

In the living quarters, Bhave's old **room** is kept as a shrine. Stone steps lead down from the upper level to a small terrace looking out over the **ghats**, where two small memorials mark the spots where a handful of Gandhi's, and later Bhave's, ashes were scattered onto the river. Every year, on January 30, the *ghats* are inundated with half a million people who come here to mark the anniversary of Gandhi's death.

ARRIVAL AND DEPARTURE
PAUNAR

By bus Paunar can be reached by bus from Wardha (every 30min; 2–3hr); hop off at the old stone bridge, which is close to the ashram.

On foot Alternatively, you can walk the 3km from Sevagram

(see opposite). The path, a cart track that runs over the hill opposite the hospital crossroads, comes out in the roadside village 1km west of the Paunar ashram.

ACCOMMODATION AND EATING

Paunar Ashram 3km from Sevagram ☎ 07152 288388. As with Sevagram, it is possible to stay in one of the visitors' rooms at the ashram, though you should call in advance

to check there's space. Meals, made from organic, home-grown produce, are available on request. **₹500**

Tadoba Andhari Tiger Reserve

Daily except Tues: March & April 5.30–10am & 3–6.30pm; May & June 5–9.30am & 3.30–7pm; Oct & Nov 6–10am & 2.30–6.30pm; Dec–Feb 6.30–11am & 2–6pm; closed rest of year

Visitor numbers are slowly increasing at the **Tadoba Andhari Tiger Reserve**, 140km south of Nagpur, but it remains a great place to spot a big cat (there are an estimated 64 tigers here) without the crowds you get at some of India's other parks. The forests and lakes of the reserve, which spans over 625 square kilometres, are also home to mugger crocodiles, leopards, hyenas, and honey badgers, plus 195 species of bird.

ARRIVAL AND INFORMATION

By car The park is a 2hr drive from Nagpur; a taxi/rental car and driver costs ₹3500–4500.

By bus There are buses (3–4 daily; 3hr 30min–4hr) from Nagpur to the city of Chandrapur, around 5km from the reserve.

Safaris The following prices are all per safari: ₹750 (₹1000 at

TADOBA ANDHARI TIGER RESERVE

weekends) per jeep/car, ₹1500 (₹2000 at weekends) per minibus, ₹300 per guide per safari. Vehicle numbers are restricted, so book ahead. Many lodges will do this for you; if not visit ⓦ mahaecotourism.gov.in. A range of other activities are available, including hikes in the "buffer zone" around the park, and canoe and boat trips. Book via your lodge.

ACCOMMODATION AND EATING

MTDC Tadoba Moharli gate ⓣ02168 260318, ⓦ maharashtratourism.gov.in. The best budget option near the park, beside a lake, this lodge has simple, clean but rather austere rooms with either fan or a/c. There's a restaurant and staff can help organize safaris. ₹**1850**

Svasara Jungle Kolara gate ⓣ 93700 08008, ⓦ svasara

resorts.com. Just 300m from one of the park gates, this top-end resort has twelve luxury suites (each with a private veranda), pool and spa amid expansive grounds. Rates include full board, and the well-informed staff can organize safaris and transfers for you. ₹**14,500**

The Konkan coast

Despite the recent appearance of a string of resorts aimed at wealthy urbanites, the coast stretching south from Mumbai, known as the **Konkan**, remains relatively unspoilt. Empty beaches, backed by casuarina and areca trees and coconut plantations, regularly slip in and out of view, framed by the distant Western Ghats, while little fortified towns preserve a distinct coastal culture, with its own dialect of Marathi and fiery cuisine. The number of rivers and estuaries slicing the coast meant that for years this little-explored area was difficult to navigate, but the Konkan railway, which winds inland between Mumbai and Kerala via Goa, now renders it more easily accessible; proposals for a seaplane service from Mumbai have rumbled on for years – check the latest with the MTDC.

There are numerous appealing **homestays** along the Konkan coast; ZaraHutke (ⓣ98670 00918, ⓦzarahutke.in) has a good selection.

Murud-Janjira

The first interesting place to break the journey south is the small port of **MURUD-JANJIRA**, 165km south of Mumbai. A traditional trade centre that once belonged to a dynasty of former Abyssinian slaves known as the Siddis, it still has plenty of attractive wooden houses, some brightly painted and fronted by pillared verandas. The gently shelving beach is wide and generally safe for swimming, though the sea is more inviting further south or north. Currents throughout the region, however, can be strong, and people have drowned here in recent years.

In Murud, the 1661 Kasa Fort sits in the open sea 2km off the beach but cannot be visited, nor can the impressive nineteenth-century palace of the last nawab, which dominates the northern end of the bay. Fine views of the coast and surrounding country-side can be had, however, from the hilltop **Dattatreya Temple**, sporting an Islamic-style tower but dedicated to the triple-headed deity comprising Brahma, Vishnu and Shiva.

Janjira Fort

5km south of Murud • Daily 7am–dusk • Free • Local *hodka* boats (20min) sail to the fort from the Rajpuri jetty, a short auto-rickshaw ride away, though, since they seat twenty and only leave when full, at quiet times you may have to charter the boat yourself (₹500–600)

Just offshore some 5km south of Murud-Janjira stands the imposing sixteenth-century **Janjira Fort**, one of the few the Marathas failed to penetrate, and now a picture of majestic dereliction. The boat trip to the fort is a serene one, and once there you're given an hour so to explore the formidable battlements, though the interior lies mostly in ruins.

2

By bus and catamaran or ferry The nearest railhead is Roha, a 2hr bus ride away, which is why most travellers still reach the town via one of the hydrofoil catamarans or regular ferries (roughly hourly; 1hr) from the Gateway of India in Mumbai to Mandawa, on the southern side of Mumbai harbour (see p.91). Buses meet the boats and shuttle passengers to Alibag (45min), from where you can catch a bus to Murud (every 1–2hr; 2hr). Most direct bus services (every 1–2hr) from Mumbai Central take 6hr; there are also two faster buses (4hr 30min) which must be booked in advance. Buses stop along Murud's main street, Durbar Rd, parallel to the coast.

Services Bring enough cash to cover your stay – at the time of writing there was no ATM or currency exchange facilities.

Golden Swan Resort On the edge of town, 1km north of the chowk ☏ 02144 274078, ⊚ goldenswan.com. This resort is the most comfortable option, with a/c cottages (₹6550) sleeping up to six people and smart a/c rooms (some with views of the sea and the fort); weekend rates (given here) include full board; prices drop by about a third during the week, but only breakfast is included. Bike rental is available. ₹5500

Sea Shell Resort Darbar Rd, next to the police station ☏ 02144 274306, ⊚ seashellmurud.com. This centrally located, resort-style hotel has decent if rather plain rooms (with fans or a/c) overlooking the sea and a small pool shaded by palm trees, and a restaurant. Staff can arrange dolphin-spotting boat trips. ₹2500

Raigad Fort

Around 100km southeast of Murud-Janjira are the impressive remains of the sixteenth-century **Raigad Fort**. Once the capital of Maratha king Shivaji, the fort was sacked by the British in 1818. Described by some as the "Gibraltar of the East", the fort is perched on top of an 820m rocky hill. It is accessed via some 1450 steps (a 3hr–3hr 30min climb) or a "ropeway" (see below).

By taxi Raigad Fort is a challenge to get to without your own wheels; the easiest option is to hire a taxi in Murud-Janjira (₹2200–2500 return, with waiting time).

Ropeway If you don't fancy climbing the 1450 odd steps, a ropeway (cable car) runs to the peak (daily 9.30am–5.30pm; ₹200 return; ☏ 02145 202122, ⊚ raigadropeway.com).

Ganpatipule

Some 215km south of Murud-Janjira lies **GANPATIPULE**, a tiny village centred on a modern **Ganapati temple**. Approached via a long covered walkway, the temple is built around a Ganapati *omnar*, a naturally formed – though hardly accurate – image of the elephant god, which attracts thousands of Indian pilgrims each year. Much more impressive is Ganpatipule's spectacular white-sand **beach**, which extends for several kilometres either side of the village. The sea is generally safe for swimming, though you should exercise caution between June and October, when currents can be particularly strong.

By train/bus To get to Ganpatipule, either make your way to Ratnagiri (on the Konkan railway and well connected by buses to other cities in the state) and take a local bus (every 30min–1hr; 1hr 30min) the last 32km, or catch one of the direct MSRTC services from Mumbai (1–2 daily; 10hr) or Kolhapur (every 2–3hr; 4hr). Buses usually stop outside the *MTDC Resort*, though at festival times you may be dropped along the main road at the edge of the village, a 1.5km walk or rickshaw ride from the beach.

★**Atithi Parinay** 12km south of Ganpatipule ☏ 90499 81309, ⊚ atithiparinay.com. Owned by an interior designer and her mother, this delightful homestay is a great place to unwind. Choose to stay in a comfortable "Swiss" tent (with attached bathroom), cottage, bungalow, or very atmospheric treehouse. Home-cooked veg meals are on offer, as are yoga, hiking, beach and river visits, and trips to local palaces, temples and a traditional boat-making centre. ₹6000

MTDC Resort In the centre of Ganpatipule ☏ 02357 235248, ⊚ maharashtratourism.gov.in. Set around neat lawns right at the heart of the village, this state-run resort has reasonable rooms, some with breezy balconies, occupying a row of attractive two-storey villas a stone's throw from the sea; the "Konkani Huts", in a shaded beachside compound a 10min walk north, are poorly maintained and disappointing, however. There's a good restaurant-bar. ₹2250

Malvan and Tarkali Beach

In the far south of the Konkan coast, 195km south of Ganpatipule, the scenic town of **MALVAN** is a relaxing place to spend a few days. Just offshore lies the eye-catching Sindhudurg Fort, and 6km to the south is the palm-fringed **Tarkali Beach**, where the Karli River meets the sea. Boat trips along the river and dive trips to the nearby coral reefs are both popular activities; staff at the *MTDC Tarkali Beach Resort* (see below) can advise on reputable companies (there are several unscrupulous and inexperienced dive shops in and around Malvan).

ARRIVAL AND DEPARTURE   MALVAN AND TARKALI BEACH

By train/bus The nearest railway station is 40km away in Kudal, from where there are regular buses (every 1–2hr during the day; 1hr). There are also buses to Kolhapur (5–6 daily; 4hr 30min–6hr).

ACCOMMODATION AND EATING

MTDC Tarkali Beach Resort Tarkali Beach ☎ 02365 252390, ⓦ maharashtratourism.gov.in. One of the more comfortable options in the area, right on the beach, has attached cabins – large and clean but decorated in the typically unimaginative MTDC style – as well as a decent restaurant serving Indian and Chinese standards. ₹2400

Matheran

The Raj-era hill station of **MATHERAN**, 108km east of Mumbai, is set on a narrow north–south ridge at an altitude of 800m in the Sahyadri Range. From evocatively named viewpoints, at the edge of sheer cliffs that plunge into deep ravines, you can see way across the hazy plains – on a good day, so they say, as far as Mumbai. The town itself, shrouded in thick mist for much of the year, has, for the moment, one unique attribute: cars, buses, motorbikes and auto-rickshaws are banned. That, added to the journey up, on a **miniature train** that chugs its way through spectacular scenery to the crest of the hill, gives the town an agreeably quaint, time-warped feel.

Matheran ("mother forest") has been a popular retreat from the heat of Mumbai since the nineteenth century. These days, few foreign visitors venture up here, and those who do only hang around for a couple of days, to kill time before a flight or to sample the charms of Matheran's colonial-era hotels. The tourist season lasts from mid-September to mid-June (at other times it's raining or misty), and is at its most hectic around Diwali and Christmas, in April and May, and over virtually any weekend. There's really nothing to do but relax, explore the woods on foot or horseback and enjoy the views.

As the crow flies, Matheran is only 6.5km from Neral on the plain below, but the train climbs up on 21km of track with no fewer than 281 curves, said to be among the sharpest on any railway in the world. Sadly, the steam engines that once handled the demanding haul puffed their last in 1980, to be replaced by cast-off diesels from Darjeeling, Shimla and Ooty. The train ride is a treat, especially if you get a window seat, but be prepared for a squash unless you travel first class.

2 The points and forest walks

Matheran occupies a long, narrow, semicircular plateau, bounded for most of its extent by sheer cliffs. These taper at regular intervals into outcrops, or **points**, revealing through the tree canopy wonderful panoramas of distant hills and plains.

For a quick taster, head south from the main bazaar past *Lords Central* hotel on Matheran's eastern flank to Alexander Point, pressing on beyond it to Chowk Point – the most southerly of the mountain's spurs. This shouldn't take more than a couple of hours return. Another enjoyable route on an old cart track winds around the western rim, past a series of gorgeous British-era bungalows to Louisa, Coronation and Sunset (or Porcupine) points, the last regarded as the choicest place to see the sun go down.

Accurate topographical maps of the mountain and its many paths are all but impossible to come by, although there's a wonderful old British one proudly on display in the dining room of *Lords Central* hotel, which walkers are welcome to consult.

All the viewpoints are walkable, and horses and rickshaws are available (see below).

ARRIVAL AND INFORMATION   MATHERAN

By train To reach Matheran by rail you must first get to Neral Junction, served by trains from Mumbai (2–3 daily; around 1hr 30min); other trains travel between Mumbai and Karjat, from where you can backtrack to Neral on suburban services. One or two daily fast trains (2hr 40min) travel between Neral and Pune; there are more frequent services between Pune and Karjat. From mid-Oct to mid-June, narrow-gauge trains chug up from Neral to Matheran (2–5 daily; 2hr). During the monsoon services are weather dependent and unreliable. All trains are timed to tie in with incoming mainline expresses, so don't worry about missing a connection if the one you're on is delayed – the toy train should wait. Nevertheless it's worth booking a day in

advance at weekends. Matheran railway station is in the town centre on MG Rd, which runs roughly north–south.

By minibus or taxi A taxi from Mumbai (2hr 30min–3hr) to Matheran costs from around ₹2000, one to Pune costs from around ₹2200 (2hr 30min–3hr). Shared taxis and minibuses (both 30min) shuttle regularly between Matheran and Neral. All motorized transport parks at the taxi stand next to the *MTDC Resort* at Dasturi Naka, 2km from central Matheran.

Services Neither of Matheran's banks offers foreign exchange, though the ATM at the Union Bank, just south of the station, accepts foreign cards; nevertheless, it is worth bringing some cash with you just in case.

GETTING AROUND

By porter, horse and rickshaw From the taxi stand – after paying the entry toll (₹50 adults, ₹25 children) – you can walk with a porter (₹150–250), be led by a rather fragile-looking horse (₹150–300) or take a hand-pulled rickshaw (₹350–450) to your hotel; you are expected to

haggle. If you're happy to carry your own bags, follow the rail tracks, which cut straight to the middle of Matheran, rather than the more convoluted dirt road. Trips to the town's various viewpoints cost from ₹300 by horse and ₹450 by rickshaw.

ACCOMMODATION

Matheran has plenty of **hotels**, though all are pricey – particularly at weekends, when rates almost double (book ahead), and during peak periods when they become astronomical. Most are near the railway station on MG Rd. Note that 10–11am checkouts are standard, and many places close down during the rainy off-season. The town's hoteliers almost universally refuse beds to "stags" (single male travellers). Most places only have hot water in the morning. Many provide **full** or **half-board** at reasonable rates; there are also numerous thali joints near the station.

Bombay View Southwest of Paymaster Park, 1.5km from the station ☎02148 230453, ⌨bombayview

hotelmatheran.com. Housed in a huge converted colonial-era mansion and annexe, this establishment is a notch pricier than the more basic places down by the station, but just about worth the extra. The rooms are dated, but most have plenty of space, as well as forest or garden views. Gujarati and Jain food is on offer. ₹3500

Hope Hall MG Rd, opposite Lords Central ☎ 99691 25299, ⓦ hopehallmatheran.com. Situated at the quiet end of town and open since 1875, *Hope Hall* has decent-sized, clean, attached "small" and "large" rooms (sleeping up to four and five people respectively; the better ones come with high ceilings and a shared veranda) scattered across a secluded yard. Badminton and table-tennis facilities available. ₹2500

Lords Central MG Rd ☎ 02148 230228, ⓦ matheran hotels.com. Though worn at the edges – its wonky verandas, poinsettias, hard beds and tasty (and copious) set meals give

it the feel of a 1930s boarding house – eccentric, Raj-era *Lords* is one of Matheran's best-loved institutions, thanks in no small part to its irreverent, anecdote-loving Parsi owners. It also boasts spectacular views from its poolside terrace garden. Rates include full board. ₹5500

★**The Verandah in the Forest** 2km southwest of station ☎ 02148 230810, ⓦ the-verandah-in-the-forest. neemranahotels.com. Hidden away in the woods, just above Charlotte Lake, this sumptuously restored nineteenth-century bungalow is reason enough to visit Matheran. As well as period decor and furnishings, its greatest asset is a huge west-facing veranda smothered in foliage – one of the most perfect spots in India for lunch (₹600; pre-book) or afternoon tea and biscuits (though beware the pilfering monkeys). ₹5000

Lonavala and around

Forty years ago, **LONAVALA** (also spelt Lonavla), 110km southeast of Mumbai and 62km northwest of Pune, was a quiet town in the Sahyadri Hills. Since then, the place has mushroomed to cope with hordes of weekenders and second-home owners from the state capital, and is now only of interest as a base for the magnificent **Buddhist caves** of **Karla** and **Bhaja**, some of the finest rock-cut architecture in the northwest of the Deccan region. Though not as impressive as Ajanta and Ellora, they have some beautifully preserved ancient sculpture.

Bhaja

9km east of Lonavala • Daily 9am–5.30pm • ₹100 (₹5) • Local trains run roughly hourly from Lonavala (20–30min) to Malavli railway station, 2km from the caves; from here follow the road south of the station until it peters out (1.5km), from where it's a steep 10min climb up to the caves

The excavations at **caves** at **BHAJA** are among India's oldest, dating from the late second to early first century BC, during the earliest, Hinayana, phase of Buddhism. You enter

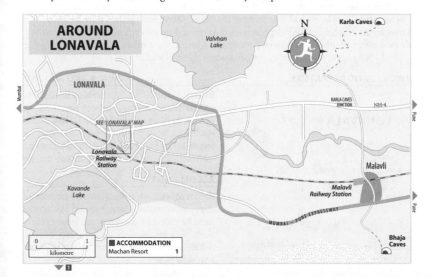

VISITING BHAJA AND KARLA

The two sites lie some 6km apart, to the east of Lonavala, and can be covered by bus and/or train in a day, if you are prepared for a good walk (bring plenty of water), though it is easier to hire an **auto-rickshaw** (₹500–600) or taxi (₹1000–1500) for the tour, both of which can usually be found at Lonavala railway station. Avoid weekends if you want to enjoy the caves in peace; Karla, in particular, gets swamped with noisy day-trippers to its Hindu shrine.

---

the complex opposite Bhaja's apsidal **chaitya** hall, which contains a *stupa* but no figures. Its 27 plain bevelled pillars lean inwards, mimicking the style of wooden buildings, and sockets in the stone of the exterior arch reveal that it once contained a wooden gate or facade. Most of the other caves consist of simple halls – *viharas* – with adjoining cells that contain plain shelf-like beds; many are fronted by rough verandas. Further south, beyond a mysterious dense cluster of fourteen **stupas**, the veranda of the **last cave**, a *vihara*, is decorated with superb carvings, which scholars have identified as the figures of the Hindu gods, Surya and Indra.

Karla

3km north of the Karla Caves junction on the Mumbai–Pune road and 11km from Lonavala • Daily 9am–5pm • ₹100 (₹5) • Three morning buses (generally 9am, 10am & 11.30am; 30min) head for the caves directly from Lonavala, with the last bus returning from Karla at 5pm

The rock-cut Buddhist *chaitya* hall at **KARLA** (also Karli), reached by steep steps that climb 110m, is the largest and best preserved in India, dating from the first century AD. Though partially obstructed by a modern Hindu temple housing a shrine to Ekviri, the enormous 14m-high facade of the hall, topped by a horseshoe-shaped window, is still an impressive sight. To the left of the entrance stands a *simhas stambha*, a tall column capped with four lions, while in the porch of the cave, dividing its three doorways, are panels of figures in six couples, presumed to have been the wealthy patrons of the hall. With their expressive faces and sensuous bodies, it's hard to believe these figures were carved around two thousand years ago.

Two rows of octagonal columns with pot-shaped bases divide the interior into three, forming a wide central aisle and, on the outside, a hall that allowed devotees to circumambulate the monolithic *stupa* at the back. Above each pillar's fluted capital kneel a pair of finely carved elephants, each mounted by two riders, one with arms draped over the other's shoulders. Amazingly, some of the timber rafters supporting the arched roof appear to date from the time when the hall was in use.

ARRIVAL AND DEPARTURE

LONAVALA AND AROUND

By bus The Central Bus Stand is just off the old Mumbai–Pune road, but the train is an infinitely preferable way to travel.
By train The railway station is in the south of town, a 10min walk from the bus stand. Lonavala is on the main railway line between Mumbai (every hour or so; 2hr–2hr 30min) and Pune (every hour or so; around 1hr), and most express trains stop here.

ACCOMMODATION

With the odd exception, Lonavala's limited accommodation offers poor value, mainly because demand well outstrips supply for much of the year. **Rates** drop between Oct and March. Numerous shops sell the local sweet speciality, **chikki** – a moreish amalgam of nuts, seeds or coconut set in rock-solid jaggery.

Citrus D Shahani Rd, a 5min auto-rickshaw ride from the bus or railway station ☎ 02114 279531, ⓦ citrushotels.com; map p.144. Slick, business-traveller-focused hotel, somewhat incongruously tucked into a sleepy backstreet. The minimalist rooms are arranged within lemon-fragranced blocks. There's a spa and a chic Astroturf-covered courtyard, and the excellent Italian/Mediterranean restaurant is the best of the hotel selection. ₹**5000**

Machan Resort Jambulne, 17km south of Lonavala ☎ 95940 53113, ⓦ themachan.com; map p.143. Easily the best place to stay in the area (for those with deep pockets), the *Machan* is an "off-grid" (all the electricity is generated by solar and wind power) ecofriendly resort in a rural location surrounding by 25 acres of grounds. Accommodation is provided in luxurious treehouses high above the canopy, making them a haven for birders, as well as in a charming cabin (₹8000). Massages are available and rates include half-board. ₹**12,000**

Pune

At an altitude of 598m, the sophisticated city of **PUNE** (sometimes anglicized as Poona), Maharashtra's second largest, lies close to the Western Ghat mountains (known here as the Sahyadri Hills), on the edge of the Deccan plains as they stretch away to the east. Capital of the Marathas' sovereign state in the sixteenth century, its rulers were deposed by the Brahmin Peshwa family. Pune was – thanks to its cool, dry climate – chosen by the British

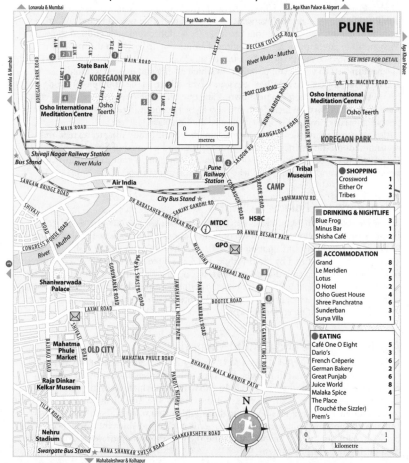

in 1820 as an alternative headquarters for the Bombay Presidency. Since colonial days, Pune has continued to develop as a major industrial city and is one of India's fastest growing business and tech centres. Signs of prosperity abound, from multistorey apartment blocks and gated estates, to coffee shops, air-conditioned malls and hip boutiques. Pune also has a couple of spiritual claims to fame: Koregaon Park is home to the famous Osho ashram (see opposite), while on the city's outskirts is *yogacharya* BKS Iyengar's illustrious yoga centre.

Pune's centre is bordered to the north by the **River Mula** and to the west by the **River Mutha** – the two join in the northwest to form the Mutha-Mula, at Sangam Bridge. The principal shopping area, and the greatest concentration of restaurants and hotels, is in the streets south of the railway station, particularly Connaught and, further south, **MG Road**. The old Peshwa part of town, by far the most interesting to explore, is towards the west between the fortified **Shaniwarwada Palace** and fascinating **Raja Dinkar Kelkar Museum**; old wooden *wadas* – palatial city homes – survive on these narrow, busy streets, and the Victorian, circular **Mahatma Phule Market** is always a hive of activity.

Raja Dinkar Kelkar Museum

1378 Shukrawar Peth • Daily 10am–5.30pm • ₹200 (₹50) • ☎ 020 2446 1556, ⑩ rajakelkarmuseum.com

Dinkar Gangadhar Kelkar (1896–1990), aside from being a celebrated Marathi poet published under the name Adnyatwasi, spent much of his life travelling and collecting arts and crafts from all over the country. In 1975, he donated his collection to the Maharashtran government for the creation of a museum dedicated to the memory of his son, Raja, who died at the age of 12. Housed in a huge old-town mansion, the **Raja Dinkar Kelkar Museum** is a wonderful potpourri in which beauty and interest is found in artistic and everyday objects, though the sheer scale of the collection – 21,000 pieces strong – means that only a fraction can be shown at any one time. Paraphernalia associated with *paan*, the Indian passion, includes containers in every conceivable design: some mimic people, animals or fish, others are egg-shaped and in delicate filigree.

Also on show are musical instruments, superb Marathi and Gujarati textiles and costumes, domestic shrines, puppets, ivory games and a model of Shaniwarwada Palace; while curiosities include a suit of fish-scale armour, a collection of intricate noodle-makers and an entire cabinet full of "erotic nut cutters".

Shaniwarwada Palace

1km north of the Kelkar Museum • **Palace** Daily 8am–6pm • ₹100 (₹5) • **Sound-and-light show** Daily except Tues 8pm • ₹25

In the centre of the oldest part of town only the imposing high walls of the **Shaniwarwada Palace** survived a huge conflagration in 1828. The chief residence of the Peshwas from 1732 until it was captured by the British in 1817, the building has little to excite interest today, though there's a **sound-and-light show** in English. The entrance is through the Delhi gate on the north side, one of five set into the perimeter wall, whose huge teak doors come complete with nasty elephant-proof spikes. The interior of the palace is now grassed over, the seven-storey building entirely absent.

Aga Khan Palace and Gandhi Memorial

5km northeast of the city centre • Daily 9am–5.30pm • ₹100 (₹5) • An auto-rickshaw costs around ₹100 from the city centre

In 1942, Mahatma Gandhi, his wife Kasturba and other key figures of the freedom movement were interned at the grand **Aga Khan Palace**, which is set in quiet leafy gardens across the river, 5km northeast of the centre. The Aga Khan donated the palace to the state in 1969, and it is now a small **Gandhi museum**, typical of many all over India, with captioned photos and simple rooms unchanged since they were occupied by the freedom fighters. A **memorial** behind the house commemorates Kasturba, who died during their imprisonment.

Tribal Museum

Koregaon Rd, 1.5km east of the railway station • Daily 10.30am–5.30pm • ₹200 (₹10)

The Tribal Research and Training Institute, which runs the **Tribal Museum**, is dedicated to the protection and documentation of Maharashtra's forty-plus tribal groups, who number around ten million. The museum's photos, artefacts and outdoor dioramas serve as an excellent introduction to this little-known world, but the highlights are the wonderful collections of dance masks and Worli paintings.

2

Osho International Meditation Resort

17 Koregaon Park Rd, 2km northeast of the railway station • ☎ 020 2401 9999, ⓦ osho.com • **Welcome Center** Daily 9am–1pm & 2–4pm • Registration for first-time visitors ₹1560, one-day pass ₹1790 (₹870), spa/pool entry ₹290/day • **Osho Teerth** Daily 6–9am & 3–6pm • Free with day-pass

Pune is the headquarters of the infamous **Osho International Meditation Resort**. Set amid 28 acres of landscaped gardens and woodland, the ashram of the now-deceased

---

OSHO

It is almost half a century since followers began to congregate around **Bhagwan Rajneesh** (1931–90), the self-proclaimed New Age guru better known to his tens of thousands of acolytes worldwide as **Osho**. Underpinned by a philosophical mishmash of Buddhism, Sufism, sexual liberation, Tantric practices, Zen, yoga, hypnosis, Tibetan pulsing, disco and unabashed materialism, the first Rajneesh ashram was founded in Pune in 1974. It rapidly attracted droves of Westerners, and some Indians, who adopted new Sanskrit names and a uniform of orange or maroon cottons and a bead necklace (*mala*) with an attached photo of the enlightened guru, in classic style, sporting long greying hair and beard.

FULFILMENT, UTOPIANISM AND TAX EVASION

Few early adherents denied that much of the attraction lay in Rajneesh's novel approach to fulfilment. His dismissal of Christianity ("Crosstianity") as a miserably oppressive obsession with guilt struck a chord with many, as did the espousal of liberation through sex. Rajneesh assured his devotees that material comfort was not to be shunned. Within a few years, satellite ashrams were popping up throughout Western Europe, and by 1980 an estimated 200,000 devotees had liberated themselves in 600 meditation centres across 80 countries.

To protect itself from pollution, nuclear war and HIV/AIDS, the organization poured money into a utopian project, **Rajneeshpuram**, on 64,000 acres in Oregon, US. It was at this point that the media really got interested in Rajneesh, now a multimillionaire. Infiltrators leaked stories of strange goings-on at Rajneeshpuram and before long its high-powered female executives became subject to police interest. Charges of tax evasion, drugs, fraud, arson and a conspiracy to poison several people in a neighbouring town to sway a local election vote provoked further sensation. Although he claimed to know nothing of this, Rajneesh pleaded guilty to breaches of US immigration laws and was deported in 1985. Following protracted attempts to resettle in 21 different countries, Rajneesh returned home to Pune, where he died in 1990, aged 59.

POST-RAJNEESH

The ashram went through internal squabbles and financial trouble in the 1990s. At his death, Rajneesh appointed an inner circle to manage the group, though several departed and the Osho "brand" – which sells millions of books each year, supplemented by CDs, DVDs, paintings and photos – is now controlled from Zurich and New York. The Pune ashram wasn't seeing enough of this to meet its costs and consequently has had to relaunch and restyle itself and the pattern of life inside its walls; in its heyday an average stay was three to six months, today people typically stay no more than two weeks.

It was partly due to Osho's enduring popularity with foreigners that the nearby *German Bakery*, Koregaon Park's erstwhile hippie hangout, was targeted for a Mumbai-style terrorist attack in February 2010, which left seventeen dead and around sixty injured – a huge shock for this normally peaceful little enclave. Resolutely, the café itself reopened in 2013 (see p.150).

2

New Age guru, Shri Bagwan Rajneesh, aka "Osho" (see box, p.147), comprises a dreamy playground of cafés, marble walkways, Olympic-size swimming pool, spas, tennis courts and clinics, with a shop selling Osho paraphernalia. Courses at its multiversity are offered in a variety of therapies and meditation techniques, alongside more offbeat workshops.

This ecofriendly bubble follows a strict door policy, with security beefed up following the revelation of visits to Osho by Mumbai 26/11 conspirator **David Headley**, and in the wake of Pune's own attack in 2010. If you're interested in taking a course, you must take your passport to the Welcome Center, where you'll have to take an on-the-spot HIV test in order to register. You'll need **two robes** (maroon for daywear, white for evenings), on sale at the ashram's "mini-mall". It is also possible to stay inside the resort at the pricey *Osho Guest House* (see opposite).

The beautiful gardens laid out to the east of the main Osho complex, the **Osho Teerth**, are open to day-pass holders. They make a serene place for a stroll, with babbling streams, stands of giant bamboo, mature trees and Zen sculpture artfully placed amid the greenery.

ARRIVAL AND DEPARTURE   PUNE

Pune is very well connected, but demand for seats on planes, trains and buses far exceeds supply; book onward transport as soon as you can.

BY PLANE

Lohagaon airport Pune's airport, 10km northeast of the city centre, is a major hub, with regular direct flights to cities throughout India. It's a 15–30min journey to/from the city centre, depending on traffic; a taxi costs ₹300–500. Plans for a new international airport have been mooted.

BY TRAIN

Pune railway station The railway station is in the centre of the city, south of the river; an auto-rickshaw to/from Koregaon Park costs ₹60–80. It is one of the last stops for numerous long-distance trains to and from Mumbai, so rail services are excellent – despite many of them departing in the early morning; some terminate at Dadar or (worse still) Kurla, so always check first. Some services are much more convenient than others (see box below). Reservations for all trains should be made as far in advance as possible online, via a travel agency or at the reservation centre next to the station itself (Mon–Sat 8am–8pm, Sun 8am–2pm). Destinations Bengaluru (8 daily; 18hr 30min–24hr 30min); Chennai (4 daily; 19hr 30min–25hr 30min); Delhi (5 daily; 24hr 20min–28hr 30min); Ernakulam (for Kochi; 1 daily; 33hr 20min); Hyderabad/Secunderabad (11 daily; 8hr 30min–13hr 20min); Jalgaon (6 daily; 8hr 30min–11hr 15min); Kolhapur (6 daily; 7hr–8hr 50min); Lonavala (roughly hourly; 1–2hr); Madgaon (for Goa; 1 daily; 13hr); Mumbai (1–2 hourly; 2hr 30min–5hr); Nagpur (3 daily; 15hr–17hr 45min); Nasik (1 daily; 7hr).

BY SHARED TAXI

For Mumbai, 24hr shared taxis leave from agencies at the taxi stand in front of Pune railway station – they're quicker than the buses, but only take you as far as Dadar.

TRAINS TO AND FROM PUNE

Of the myriad rail services feeding in and out of Pune, the following are recommended as the fastest and/or most convenient:

Destination	Name	No.	Frequency	Departs	Arrives
Bengaluru	*Nagarcoil Express*	#16339	Daily	3.50pm	10.28am+
Chennai	*Mas Garibrath*	#06027	Daily	2.15pm	11.35am+
Delhi	*Jhelum Express*	#11077	Daily	5.20pm	8.45pm +
Goa	*Goa Express*	#12780	Daily	4.35pm	5.40am+
Hyderabad/ Secunderabad	*Shatabdi Express*	#12025	Daily	5.50am	2.20pm
Kolhapur	*Sahyadri Express*	#11023	Daily	9.18pm	6.05am
Mumbai	*Deccan Queen*	#12124	Daily	7.15am	10.25am

+ next day

BY BUS

Pune has three main bus stands. If you're unsure which station you require for your destination, ask at the enquiries hatch of the City Bus Stand or at the MTDC counter at the railway station. More comfortable private buses depart from offices throughout Pune; tickets can be bought from travel agencies in Koregaon Park.

City Bus Stand Next to the railway station, City Bus Stand is split into two sections, one serving Pune itself (with signs and timetables only in Marathi), the other for destinations south and west. Regular buses to Mumbai (via Lonavala)

also leave from here.

Destinations Goa (3–4 daily; 11hr); Kolhapur (hourly; 5–6hr); Mahabaleshwar (hourly; 3hr 30min–4hr); Mumbai (every 15min; 3hr 15min).

Swargate and Shivaji Nagar stands The Swargate Bus Stand, about 5km south, close to Nehru Stadium, services Karnataka and some of the same destinations as City, while the stand next to Shivaji Nagar railway station, 3km west of the centre, runs buses every 30min to points north, such as Aurangabad (5hr) and Nasik (4–5hr).

INFORMATION

Tourist information The spectacularly unhelpful MTDC Tourist Office (Mon–Fri plus 1st & 3rd Sat of month 10am–5.45pm; ☎ 020 2612 6867, ⓦ maharashtratourism.gov.in) is inside "I" block of Central Building (enter between Ambedkar Chowk and Sadhu Vaswani Circle). It also has an information counter (officially the same times) opposite the railway station's first-class booking office and at the airport (opens to meet incoming flights).

ACCOMMODATION

Top-end hotels are springing up all over Pune, but there's a chronic shortage of budget and mid-range places, which explains why prices are high and vacancies like gold dust: book as far in advance as possible.

Grand MG Rd, near the Dr Ambedkar statue ☎ 020 2636 0728, ⓦ grandhotelpune.co.in. Set behind a dimly lit beer garden, the colonial-era *Grand* doesn't live up to its name, but is an acceptable budget choice: the high-ceilinged doubles in the rear annexe are pretty clean, though scruffy; the bathroom-less, wood-partitioned singles (₹400), however, are best avoided. ₹990

Le Meridien RBM Rd, just northwest of the railway station ☎ 020 6641 1111, ⓦ starwoodhotels.com. Once the biggest hotel in Pune, this vast cathedral of marble still feels like its most opulent and luxurious. Spacious rooms come with thick honey-coloured carpets and huge beds; the rooftop bar (complete with two-tiered pool) is one of the city centre's most heavenly spaces for an evening drink and is open to non-guests. Rates vary wildly online, and there are often good deals to be had. ₹7500

Lotus Plot No. 356, Lane No.5, Koregaon Park ☎ 020 2613 9701, ⓦ hotelsuryavilla.com. In an unassuming salmon-pink block in tranquil, leafy surroundings, this is Koregaon's Park's best-value hideaway. Bright, clean rooms with big windows, comfy beds and balconies; a/c cost extra. A basic breakfast (included) is served to the rooms, and the location is handy for the city's best restaurants/bars. ₹1900

★**O Hotel** North Main Rd ☎ 020 4001 1000, ⓦ ohotels india.com. Goa chic in Pune: outside, a forbidding sandstone-coloured tower block; inside, a designer playground of bold textures, shades and shapes. Rooms are suitably Zen-like, blending simple lines and stylish details with warm, muted tones and natural materials, and facilities include a gorgeous spa and spectacular rooftop infinity pool and bar, plus Indian and Japanese restaurants. ₹5500

Osho Guest House Osho International Meditation Resort, 17 Koregaon Park Rd ☎ 020 6601 9900, ⓦ osho .com. Part of the Osho ashram, and open only to attendees, this luxury hotel offers stylish minimalist rooms – though be warned that the hotel is situated above the main auditorium, which, as the ashram likes to put it, can make the 6am meditation session "very hard to resist". ₹7285

Shree Panchratna 7 Tadiwala Rd ☎ 020 2605 9999, ⓦ hotelshreepanchratna.in. Aimed at business travellers and located on a quiet side-street close to the railway station, *Shree Panchratna* is well maintained and efficiently run, if unexciting. The plain rooms all have a/c, kettles, mini-fridges, and a fresh feel; some also have balconies (though no views). ₹3200

Sunderban 19 Koregaon Park ☎ 020 2612 4949, ⓦ hotelsunderban.chobs.in Attractive Art Deco mansion, set behind an immaculate expanse of lawn, and sited beside the Osho ashram. The older rooms in the main house, furnished in swathes of leather and acres of teak and mahogany, are better value than those in the flashier modern garden block, though there are big discounts April–Sept. There's a great Italian restaurant (see p.150) and a spa. ₹4000

Surya Villa 294/1 Koregaon Park ☎ 020 2612 4501, ⓦ hotelsuryavilla.com. Under the same management as *Lotus* (see above) and slightly cheaper, *Surya Villa* has sizeable if somewhat spartan rooms (with fans or a/c) spread over four floors in a suburban block close to Osho. It's very popular, mainly with long-staying foreign ashramites, and has a good restaurant filled with traveller favourites. ₹1500

2

EATING

Pune's affluent young things have money to burn these days, and new, innovative places to eat and drink open up every month to relieve them of their tech salaries, the largest concentration of them up at the eastern end of Koregaon Park. Booking is advisable at the smarter places at weekends. In addition to those listed below, several of the hotels have good restaurants, including *Surya Villa* and *O Hotel* (see p.149); *Shisha Café* (see opposite) also has excellent food.

★**Café One O Eight** Precious Gem, Lane 6, Koregaon Park ☎90118 04770. Hip Aussie-style café and yoga studio that's an easy place to while away a few hours. As well as excellent coffee – including a proper flat white – and fresh juices (₹150–320), there are top-notch all-day-breakfast options, toasted sandwiches (including one with Vegemite; ₹150–280), inventive bruschettas and pasta dishes. The food's mostly organic and there are plenty of veggie, vegan and gluten-free options. Wi-fi available. Mon–Fri 7am–9pm, Sat & Sun 8am–9pm.

Dario's Sunderban ☎020 2605 3597, ⓦdarios.in. A tranquil, Italian veg restaurant with a lovely patio filled with plants and birdsong. The food – sandwiches, a huge range of salads, risottos, pastas and pizzas, plus crêpes, waffles and pastries for breakfast – is pretty authentic, and it is a great place for a glass of wine or a proper espresso or cappuccino. Mains ₹480–620. Wi-fi available. Daily 8am–11.30pm.

French Crêperie 5 Jewel Tower, Lane 5, Koregaon Park ☎90110 16829, ⓦfrenchcreperie.com. With a giant Moulin Rouge mural on the wall and a cool split-level dining area, *French Crêperie* is gaining a following among Pune's hip young things. As well as savoury and sweet crêpes (₹120–400), the menu features sandwiches, waffles, soups and pasta dishes. Wi-fi available. Daily 10am–1pm.

German Bakery 291 Koregaon Park ☎020 3939 5551. Open again after the 2010 terrorist attack (see p.147), *German Bakery* is a good spot throughout the day with breakfast options, main meals ranging from thin-crust pizzas to bangers and mash, and – of course – plenty of cakes (₹80–130), including *Sachertorte* and lamingtons. On the downside, it's right on the main road, and the music choices can be questionable. Wi-fi available. Daily 7.30am–11.45pm.

Great Punjab 5 Jewel Tower, Lane 5, Koregaon Park ☎020 2614 5060. One of Koregaon Park's most popular north Indians, offering generous kebabs, grills and tandoori dishes – and a long list of cocktails and spirits – in smart if subdued surroundings. Dedicated carnivores should sample the *karela* kebab, a mountain of succulent tandoori chicken stuffed with a robust mix of minced meat and herbs. Mains ₹280–900. Daily 11am–11pm.

Juice World 2436/B East Street Camp ☎020 2611 4318. Freshly squeezed fruit juices, milkshakes and *faloodas* (₹65–230) are the mainstay of this buzzing haunt just east of the top of MG Rd; lychee, *chikoo* and musk melon are some of the more unusual flavours on offer. It also serves piping-hot snacks and meals (₹75–220) such as stuffed *paratha*, tangy Bombay-style *pao bhaji*, and biryani. Daily 8am–10pm.

Malaka Spice Lane 5, Koregaon Park ☎020 2615 6293, ⓦmalakaspice.com. This Southeast Asian specialist serves up pretty authentic stir-fries, curries and noodle dishes (mains ₹285–650) in arty surroundings. It's relaxed at lunchtime and intimate in the evening when the candlelit covered veranda and garden terrace twinkle with fairy lights. It's also a good spot for a drink. There are a couple of other branches, but this is the most convenient. Wi-fi available. Daily 11am–11pm.

The Place (Touché the Sizzler) 7 Moledina Rd ☎020 2613 4632. Huge, succulent sizzlers (veg, fish, pork, mutton or beef; ₹350–480), steaks, fish and chips, and veal escalope are among the house specialities of this Parsi-run old-timer in the city centre (somewhat bizarrely, the founder of the restaurant later opened a sizzler restaurant on the Isle of Man in the UK). Daily 11.30am–3.30pm & 7–10.45pm.

Prem's Main Rd, Koregaon Park ☎020 6601 2413. Tucked away from the main road, this cool, modern restaurant-bar is a hit for both its spot-on Indian and Chinese dishes (there are also a few decent Continental options) and its range of beers (including draught Hoegaarden) and spirits – plus "detox" drinks (₹40–120) if you've overindulged. Mains ₹240–500. Daily 8am–11pm.

DRINKING AND NIGHTLIFE

Blue Frog Ishanya Mall, just off Airport Rd ☎020 4005 4001, ⓦbluefrog.co.in. Pune outpost of the famous Mumbai club, and one of the best live music venues in town with international and Indian acts, often performing acoustic sets, plus DJs at the weekends (check the website to see who's playing). There's a lively bar and a good restaurant serving "modern European with Asian influences". Wi-fi available. Tues–Sun 6pm–12.30am.

★**Minus Bar** O Hotel ☎020 4001 1000, ⓦohotelsindia .com. High over the cityscape, the *O*'s lantern-lit rooftop bar is Pune's most elegant spot for a sundowner. Sink into a low-slung white-cushioned sofa, settle onto a beanbag or dip your toes in the infinity pool as you choose from an enterprising list of cocktails (around ₹650–850; beers are cheaper) and soak up the views. Wi-fi available. Daily noon–11.30pm.

★**Shisha Café** ABC Farms, Koregaon Park ☎020 6520 0390, ⓦshishajazzcafe.in. One of Pune's most congenial watering holes: a cavernous restaurant-bar filled with plants and capped with a huge thatched roof hung with Persian carpets. Indo-Iranian food, notably kebabs (mains ₹330–450) dominate the menu, and they serve a good range of beers (from ₹190), wines and spirits, plus hookahs and Turkish coffee. The walls are lined with posters of jazz greats, and live jazz and blues bands often play in the evenings. Daily 10am–11.30pm.

SHOPPING

The Koregaon Park area has several quality – if pricey – clothes and craft shops, especially in the area between Lane 7 and Lane 5. For less expensive options – and a considerably more bustling environment – head to the streets south of the railway station, especially Connaught, which have a wide range of shops and stalls.

Crossword Koregaon Park Plaza mall, Main Rd ☎020 6704 0225, ⓦcrossword.in. This national chain has numerous stores around town: this one, on the second floor of the mall, is one of the most convenient. It has an extensive range of English-language fiction and nonfiction. Daily 11am–9pm.

Either Or 24 Sohrab Hall, Sassoon Rd ☎020 2605 7225, ⓦeitheror.in. This classy shop is an excellent place for souvenir shopping, with an extensive range of textiles,

jewellery, household furnishings, crafts and music. Daily 10.30am–8pm.

Tribes Kamdhenu Building, Senepati Bapat Marg ☎97679 96355, ⓦtribesindia.com. This government-backed shop stocks a wide range of crafts and artworks – including paintings, pottery, textiles, home furnishings and food items – that have been produced by the country's tribal groups. Daily 10am–7pm.

DIRECTORY

Banks and exchange For changing currency, Thomas Cook is at 13 Thacker House, just off General Thimmaya Rd (☎020 2634 6171, ⓦthomascook.in).

Post office The efficient GPO is on Sadhu Vasavani (Connaught) Rd.

Mahabaleshwar and around

The former capital of the Bombay Presidency, the hill station of **MAHABALESHWAR**, 250km southeast of Mumbai, is easily reached from Pune, 120km northeast. The highest point in the Western Ghats (1372m), it is subject to extreme **weather** conditions. Early June brings heavy mists and a dramatic drop in temperature, followed by a deluge of biblical proportions. Tourists tend only to visit between October and early June; during April and May, at the height of summer, the place is packed.

For most foreign visitors, Mahabaleshwar's main appeal is its location midway between Mumbai and Goa, but it has some good **hiking trails**, and a boating lake, and is close to the Pratapgadh fort (see below). Otherwise, the main activity is to amble up and down the pedestrianized **main bazaar** (Dr Sabne Road) and graze on the locally grown **strawberries** for which the town is famous.

Pratapgadh

Around 24km west of Mahabaleshwar • Daily dawn–dusk • ₹100 (₹20) • Taxis charge around ₹700 for the return trip to Pratapgadh, with waiting time; state buses (1hr) also do the journey each day, leaving the bus stand around 9am and returning around 11am

The seventeenth-century fort of **PRATAPGADH** stretches the full length of a high ridge affording superb views over the surrounding mountains. Reached by a flight of five hundred steps, it is famously associated with the Maratha chieftain, **Shivaji**, who lured the Mughal general Afzal Khan here from Bijapur (now Vijayapura) to discuss a possible truce. Neither, it would seem, intended to keep to the condition that they should come unarmed. Khan attempted to knife Shivaji, who responded by killing him with the gruesome *wagnakh*, a set of metal claws worn on the hand. Today visitors can see Afzal Khan's tomb, a memorial to Shivaji, and views of the surrounding hills.

2

ARRIVAL AND INFORMATION

By bus The State Bus Stand is at the northwest end of the bazaar. There are regular MSRTC buses to/from Mumbai (5–7 daily; around 7hr), Pune (every 30min–1hr; 3hr 30min) and Kolhapur (4–5 daily; 5hr 30min), and one to Panaji in Goa

(12hr); for the latter, numerous agents in the bazaar sell tickets for more comfortable private buses.

Entry fees There is a ₹20 entry fee for visitors, collected at toll booths at each end of town.

MAHABALESHWAR AND AROUND

GETTING AROUND

By taxi Auto-rickshaws are banned in Mahabaleshwar but taxis line up at the west end of the bazaar, charging ₹50–80 for short hops in and around town.

By bike Bikes can be rented from a stall at the *Dreamland* hotel (see below).

ACCOMMODATION

Despite an abundance of hotels, at peak times prices in Mahabaleshwar are well above average. Room rates are a moveable feast, particularly at the lower end of the scale, but fall roughly into three categories: peak months are April and especially May, when as at Diwali, Christmas and New Year, rates at the cheaper places double or even treble and the place is well worth avoiding. Prices quoted are for off-season, which broadly covers most of the rest of the year, bar long weekends ("mid-season"). The cheapest places to stay are on the Main Bazaar and the road parallel to it, Murray Peth. Two points to note: hoteliers in Mahabaleshwar refuse to take in single male travellers ("stags"), and many places close during the monsoon.

Dreamland Below the State Bus Stand ☎ 02168 260228, ⌨ hoteldreamland.com. Large, well-established hotel surrounded by extensive gardens. Rooms range from simple "cottages" to spacious a/c rooms (₹5500) with stupendous views. There's a pool, jacuzzi and sauna, café and pure-veg restaurant. Prices rise at weekends. ₹3500

MTDC Holiday Resort 2km southwest of the centre

☎ 02168 260318, ⌨ maharashtra.gov.in. A sprawling campus with a wide choice of accommodation, ranging from austere economy rooms through high-ceilinged standard rooms to spruce modern cottages accommodating four (₹3650), in a peaceful location; a 10min walk from Mumbai Point. ₹1450

EATING AND DRINKING

Grapevine Western end of Masjid Rd, which is parallel with the main bazaar ☎ 02168 261100. For something a bit different, make for the idiosyncratic *Grapevine*, where a decent list of wines, beers and spirits complements a

delightfully eclectic (if expensive) menu ranging from Parsi home-cooking to lamb burgers and fish and chips (mains from ₹180). Daily noon–3pm & 7–10.30pm.

Kolhapur

KOLHAPUR, on the banks of the River Panchaganga 225km south of Pune, is thought to have been an important centre of the Tantric cult associated with Shakti worship since ancient times. The city probably grew around the sacred site of the present-day **Mahalakshmi temple**, still central to the life of the city, although there are said to be up to 250 other shrines in the area. Today it is a major industrial centre, but has retained enough Maharashtran character to make it worthy of a stopover.

Mahalakshmi temple

In the centre of the old town, overlooking the town square • Daily dawn–10.30pm • Free

The **Mahalakshmi temple**, whose cream-painted sanctuary towers embellish the centre of Kolhapur's old town, is thought to have been founded in the seventh century, though what you see today dates from the early eighteenth century. The devout queue around the block from the complex's east gate for *darshan* at the image of the goddess Mahalakshmi, beneath the largest of five domed towers; tourists are welcome to join them.

Rajwada (Old Palace)

Near the Mahalakshmi temple • No fixed opening times • Free

The **Rajwada**, or Old Palace, is still occupied by members of the former ruling Chhatrapati family, though its entrance hall is usually busy with worshippers to its Bhawani temple – you can access it by passing under the pillared porch that extends out into the town square.

Wrestling pit (motibaug)

Close to the Rajwada • **Wrestler training** June–Sept daily except Sat 6–9am & 4–6pm • Free

Kolhapur is famous as a centre for traditional wrestling, or *kushti*. On leaving the Old Palace gates, turn right and head through the low doorway in front of you, from where a path picks its way past a couple of derelict buildings to the *motibaug*, or **wrestling pit**. You can watch wrestlers training; matches take place at the nearby **Khasbag Maidan** stadium.

New Palace

Shahaji Chhatrapati, 2km north of the town centre • Tues–Sun 9.30am–1pm & 2.30-6pm • ₹75 (₹20)

The maharaja's **New Palace** was built in 1884, following a fire at the Rajwada. Designed by Major Mant, founding father of the Indo-Saracenic school of so much British colonial architecture, it fuses Jain and Hindu influences with local touches from the Rajwada while remaining indomitably Victorian, with a prominent clock tower. The present maharaja lives on the first floor, while the ground floor houses the **Shahaji Chhatrapati Museum**, a dozen or so rooms crammed with fascinating memorabilia that demonstrates above all else the Chhatrapati family's extraordinary history of bloodlust: among the maharaja's collection of portraits, costumes, embroidery, riding paraphernalia and old Raj-era photos is an astonishing array of swords (including one that belonged to Mughal emperor Aurangzeb), rifles and torture equipment, a gruesome display cabinet of a huntsman's homeware – fans fashioned from tails, an elephant's-foot table – and, in the final room, a scandalous Who's Who of stuffed endangered species. Rather less macabre is the spectacular church-like Durbar Hall, with its superb carvings and mosaic floor.

ARRIVAL AND INFORMATION — KOLHAPUR

By train The railway station is 400m west from the bus stand on Station Rd, near the centre of town. There are services to Pune (6 daily; 7hr–8hr 50min) and Mumbai (3 daily; 11–13hr).

Tourist information The MTDC tourist office (Mon–Fri plus 1st & 3rd Sat of month 10am–5pm; Ⓣ 0231 269 2935, Ⓦ maharashtratourism.gov.in) is on Assembly Rd, a 15min walk north of the railway station (ask locally for the Collector's Office).

ACCOMMODATION AND EATING

There's no shortage of decent, good-value **accommodation** in Kolhapur, which is famous for its fiery **cuisine**. In addition to the hotel restaurants – notably *Woodland* and *Padma* – there are good, inexpensive places to eat around Station Square.

Padma Guest House Near Padma Talkies, Laxmipuri Ⓣ 0231 264 1387, Ⓦ padmakolhapur.com. A reliable budget hotel with decent rooms (all with private bathrooms and TVs) and an excellent restaurant specializing in Kolhapuri cuisine – the tongue-tingling mutton curries are not to be missed. **₹600**

Tourist Station Rd Ⓣ 0231 265 0421, Ⓦ hoteltourist.co.in. The pick of a row of welcoming mid-range hotels a few minutes' walk east of the bus stand. Rooms (all are attached; a/c costs about ₹600 extra) are unfussy but large and well maintained; ask for one away from the road. It has veg and non-veg restaurants, and a "permit room" (bar). 24hr checkout. **₹1200**

★ **Woodland** 204 "E" Ward, Tarabai Park Ⓣ 0231 265 0941, Ⓦ hotelwoodland.net. Good-value and welcoming mid-range hotel, in a peaceful suburb 2km north of the railway and bus stations. It has spacious and bright a/c rooms, plus a terrific non-veg garden/veranda restaurant, *Sunderban*, and a bar. 24hr checkout. **₹3100**

Goa

162 Central Goa

172 North Goa

191 South Goa

PALOLEM BEACH

Goa

The former Portuguese enclave of Goa, midway down India's southwest coast, has been a holiday destination since colonial times, when British troops and officials used to travel here from across the country for a spot of "R&R". Back then, the three Bs – bars, brothels and booze – were the big attractions. Now it's the golden, palm-fringed beaches spread along the state's 105km coastline that pull in the tourists – around two million of them each winter. Cheap air travel has made it a major package tour destination for Europeans, and there has been a dramatic rise in the number of newly affluent domestic visitors in recent years. Luckily, in spite of the increasing chaos of Goa's main resorts, it's still possible to find the odd quiet corner if you're prepared to explore and can avoid the busy Christmas/New Year period. If you know where to go, Goa can still be a wonderful place.

Serving as the linchpin for a vast trade network for more than 450 years, Goa was Portugal's first toehold in Asia. However, when the Portuguese empire began to flounder in the seventeenth century, so too did the fortunes of its capital. Cut off from the rest of India by a wall of mountains and hundreds of kilometres of unnavigable alluvial plain, it remained aloof from the wider Subcontinent until 1961, when the exasperated prime minister, Jawaharlal Nehru, finally gave up trying to negotiate with the Portuguese dictator Salazar and sent in the army.

It was shortly after the "Liberation" (or "Occupation" as some Goans still regard it), that the first **hippie travellers** came to the region on the old overland trail. They found a way of life little changed in centuries: back then Portuguese was still very much the lingua franca of the well-educated elite, and the coastal settlements were mere fishing and coconut cultivation villages. Relieved to have found somewhere culturally undemanding to party, the "freaks" got stoned, watched the mesmeric sunsets over the Arabian Sea and danced like lunatics on full-moon nights.

Since then, the state has been at pains to shake off its reputation as a druggy drop-out zone, and its beaches have grown in popularity year on year. Around two dozen stretches of soft white sand indent the region's coast, from spectacular 25km sweeps to secluded palm-backed coves. The level of development behind them varies a great deal; while some are lined by swanky Western-style resorts, the most sophisticated structures on others are palm-leaf shacks.

Which beach you opt for largely depends on what sort of holiday you have in mind. Developed resorts such as **Calangute** and **Candolim** in the north, and **Colva** and **Benaulim** in the south, offer more accommodation than elsewhere. **Anjuna**, **Vagator** and **Chapora**, where places to stay are generally harder to come by, are the places to aim for if you've come to Goa to party. However, the bulk of budget

BEST TIME TO VISIT

The best time to come to Goa is during the dry, relatively cool **winter months** between late November and mid-March. At other times, either the sun is too hot for comfort, or the humidity, clouds and rain make life miserable. During peak season, from mid-December to the end of January, the weather is perfect, with temperatures rarely nudging above 32°C. Finding a room or a house to rent at that time, however – particularly over Christmas and New Year when tariffs double, or triple – can be a real hassle.

SATURDAY NIGHT MARKET, ARPORA

Highlights

❶ **Beach shacks seafood** Tuck into a fresh kingfish, lobster or tandoori pomfret, washed down with an ice-cold beer. **See p.165**

❷ **Old Goa** The belfries and Baroque church facades looming over the trees on the banks of the Mandovi are all that remains of this once splendid colonial city. **See p.167**

❸ **Saturday Night Market, Arpora** Cooler and less frenetic than the flea market, with appealing goods on sale and a fun atmosphere. **See p.178**

❹ **Flea market, Anjuna** Goa's famous tourist bazaar is the place to pick up the latest party gear, shop for souvenirs and watch the crowds go by. **See p.179**

❺ **Aswem** The hippest spot on the north Goan coast to swim, fine dine and dance under the stars with the stars. **See p.186**

❻ **Palacio do Deão** An extravagant, painstakingly restored colonial-era mansion in south Goa, where you can eat lunch on a leafy garden terrace. **See p.194**

❼ **Sunset stroll, Palolem** Tropical sunsets don't come much more romantic than at this idyllic palm-fringed cove in the hilly deep south. **See p.200**

HIGHLIGHTS ARE MARKED ON THE MAP ON P.158

travellers taking time out from tours of India end up around **Palolem**, in the far south beyond the reach of the charter transfer buses – though be warned that it too has become a major resort over the past decade, attracting literally thousands of long-stay visitors in peak season. For a quieter scene, you could head for **Patnem**, just over the headland from Palolem, or **Agonda**, further up the coast, where development is limited to a string of more upmarket hut camps and family guesthouses. The only place where the **hippie scene** endures to any significant extent

HIGHLIGHTS

1. Beach shacks seafood
2. Old Goa
3. Saturday Night Market, Arpora
4. Flea market, Anjuna
5. Aswem
6. Palacio do Deão
7. Sunset stroll, Palolem

FESTIVALS IN GOA

With its diverse cultural mix, Goa's festivals range from Christian and Hindu celebrations to hedonistic parties and arty events. The **Christmas and New Year** period attracts many thousands to techno and dance parties – of which the Sunburn Festival is the largest. Outside this period, however, less touristy, more authentic draws – Carnival or Narkasur Parades, for example – go to show that Goa is not all beaches and parties.

Goa Carnival (Pre-Lent). Four-day party held throughout the state with parades of colourful floats surrounded by masked revellers (especially in Panjim) as well as live music and street stalls.

Shigmotsav/Gulalotsav (March). Goa's answer to Holi; the state's biggest spring festival. Huge dance troupes perform folk dances in the streets through the night.

Narkasur Parades (Oct; eve of Diwali). A festival unique to Goa, when giant demon effigies (narkasurs) dance through the streets before being burned to mark the festival of lights. The main parades are in Panjim (see p.162), Margao (see p.192), Mapusa (see p.172), Vasco and Ponda.

International Film Festival of India (IFFI) (Late Nov; ⊛ iffi.nic.in). A lively, glittering, contemporary event held in Panjim.

St Francis Xavier's Feast (Dec 3). Ceremonies to commemorate the saint's death attract thousands of pilgrims to Old Goa (see p.167).

Mary Immaculate Conception Church Feast (Early Dec). One of the major festivals in Panjim (see p.164), this three-day event sees street stalls set up around the church, and firework displays.

Christmas/New Year (Dec 25/Jan 1). Celebrated in Goa more than anywhere else in the country. The state heaves with foreign and domestic tourists set to party – and accommodation prices can double or triple.

Sunburn Festival (Dec 27–30; ⊛ sunburn.in). The biggest techno/house party of the year in Goa (if not Asia) at five arenas in Vagator. See p.182.

is **Arambol**, in the far north of the state, where you can dip in to any number of yoga sessions and holistic therapies between spells on the beach.

Some 10km from the state capital, **Panjim**, the ruins of the former Portuguese capital at **Old Goa** are foremost among the attractions away from the coast – a sprawl of Catholic cathedrals, convents and churches that draw crowds of Christian pilgrims from all over India. Another popular day-excursion is to Anjuna's Wednesday **flea market**, a sociable place to shop for souvenirs and dance gear. In the south, the district of Salcete, and its main market town, **Margao**, is also littered with distinctively hybrid buildings in the form of Portuguese-era mansions, churches and seminaries. Finally, wildlife enthusiasts may be tempted into the interior to visit the nature reserves at **Cotigao** and **Netravali** in the far south.

Brief history

Goa's sheer inaccessibility by land has always kept it out of the mainstream of Indian history; on the other hand, its control of the seas and the lucrative spice trade made it a much-coveted prize for rival colonial powers. Until a century before the arrival of the Portuguese, Goa had belonged for more than a thousand years to the kingdom of the **Kadamba** dynasty. They, in turn, were overthrown by the Karnatakan Vijayanagars, the Muslim Bahmanis and Yusuf Adil Shah of Bijapur, but the capture of the fort at Panjim by **Afonso de Albuquerque** in 1510 signalled the start of a Portuguese occupation that was to last 451 years.

Goa Dourada ("Golden Goa")

As the colony expanded, its splendid capital (dubbed as "Goa Dourada", or "Golden Goa", due to its incredible prosperity) came to hold a larger population than Paris or London. Though Ismail Adil Shah laid siege for ten months in 1570, and the Marathas came very close to seizing the region, the greatest threat was from other European maritime nations, principally Holland and France. Meanwhile, conversions to

Christianity, started by the Franciscans, gathered pace when St Francis Xavier founded the **Jesuit** mission in 1542. With the advent of the **Inquisition** soon afterwards, laws were introduced censoring literature and banning any faith other than Catholicism. Hindu temples were destroyed, and converted Hindus adopted Portuguese names, such as Da Silva, Correa and De Sousa, which remain common in the region. Thereafter, the colony, whose trade monopoly had been broken by its European rivals, went into gradual decline, hastened by the unhealthy, disease-ridden environment of its capital.

"Liberation"

Despite certain liberalization, such as the restoration of Hindus' right to worship and the final banishment of the dreaded Inquisition in 1820, the nineteenth century saw widespread civil unrest. During the British Raj many Goans moved to Bombay, and elsewhere in British India, to find work.

The success of the post-Independence Goan struggle for freedom owed as much to the efforts of the Indian government, which cut off diplomatic ties with Portugal, as to the work of freedom fighters such as **Menezes Braganza** and **Dr Cunha**. After a "liberation march" in 1955 resulted in a number of deaths, the state was blockaded. Trade with Bombay ceased, and the railway was cut off, so Goa set out to forge international links, particularly with Pakistan and Sri Lanka: that led to the building of Dabolim airport, and a determination to improve local agricultural output. In 1961, prime minister Jawaharlal Nehru finally sent in the armed forces. Mounted in defiance of a United Nations resolution, "**Operation Vijay**" met only token resistance, and the Indian army overran Goa in two days. Thereafter, Goa (along with Portugal's other two enclaves, Daman and Diu) became part of India as a self-governing **Union Territory**, with minimum interference from Delhi.

Goa today

After Independence Goa continued to prosper, bolstered by iron-ore exports and a booming tourist industry. However, dominated by issues of statehood, the status of Konkani and the ever-rising levels of immigration, its political life has been dogged for decades by chronic **instability**, with frequent changes of government and chief ministers, interrupted by occasional periods of **President's Rule** when the state had to be governed directly from New Delhi.

At the start of the 21st century, renewed fears over the pace of change on the coastal strip started to dominate the news. A sudden influx and just as sudden disappearance of **Russian charter tourists** has now been replaced by high-rolling **property developers** from Delhi and Mumbai who have provoked a backlash from successive ruling coalitions, with a state-sponsored land grab of expatriate property. Hundreds of resident Europeans had their assets confiscated, and fled. A series of high-profile attacks on, and unexplained deaths of foreigners has done little to improve the state's image abroad. Meanwhile, as ever-improving infrastructural links with the rest of India render Goa's borders more porous, the survival of the region as a culturally distinct entity continues to hang in the balance.

ARRIVAL AND DEPARTURE   GOA

TO AND FROM MUMBAI

By plane A couple of dozen flights shuttle between Mumbai and Goa's Dabolim airport daily, with fares from as low as ₹2000 if you book well in advance with one of the no-frills airlines – or as much as ₹40,000 on New Year's Eve. Try SpiceJet, IndiGo, Go Air or JetKonnect (see p.28). Flying with Air India or Jet Airways will set you back around ₹4000–8000 each way. The cheaper flights are usually at inconvenient times.

By train Seven or so more trains run daily on the Konkan Railway from Mumbai, the most convenient being the overnight *Mangalore Junction Express* (#12133), which departs from CST at 10pm and arrives in Goa at 7.05am the following morning. Travelling to Mumbai, the service to go for is the overnight *Konkan Kanya Express* (#10112), which departs from Margao/Madgaon (see p.193) at 6pm (or Karmali, near Old Goa, 11km west of Panjim, at 6.32pm), arriving at Mumbai CST at 5.50am the following day. The other fast train from Goa to CST, the *Mandovi Express* (#10104), departs Margao/Madgaon at 9.15am (or Karmali at 9.50am) and arrives at 9.40pm the same evening. Note that all Konkan trains book up within days of the seats being released.

By bus A fleet of night buses covers the 500km between Goa and Mumbai – a terrible 16hr journey, best avoided. If you have to go this way, choose Paulo Travels, which offers a range of services from no-frills buses for ₹600 to swisher a/c Volvo coaches with berths (₹1425). For tickets, contact their office just north outside the Kadamba bus stand, Panjim (☎0832 2277036, ⓦpaulotravels.com). In south Goa, the firm's main outlet is just north of the bus station in Margao (☎0834 273 3355). Information on all departures and fares is available online.

TO AND FROM HAMPI

By train The most stress-free and economical way to travel between Goa and Hosapete, the jumping-off place for Hampi, is the *Vasco–Howrah Express* (#18048), which departs Vasco da Gama every Tues, Thurs, Fri and Sun at 7.10am (Margao/Madgaon 7.50pm), arriving 7hr 38min later. Fares range from ₹235 for a seat in a second-class sleeper compartment to ₹890 for second-class a/c – the comfiest option. Tickets can be bought on the day, but

arrive at Margao/Madgaon by at least 6.30am, as the "queues" are invariably more like rugby scrums. There are also trains from Hosapete to Goa via Hubballi (see p.250).

By bus The bus journey covering the same route is no cheaper than the train (sleeper class) and is far more gruelling. Two or three clapped-out government services leave Panjim's Kadamba stand (platform #9) each morning for Hosapete, the last one at 10.30am. Brace yourself for a long, hard slog; all being well, it should take 9 or 10hr, but delays and breakdowns are frustratingly frequent.

TO AND FROM GOKARNA

By train The fastest and most convenient way to travel along the coast between Goa and Gokarna is on the Konkan Railway. The *Madgaon–Mangaluru Passenger* (#56641) leaves Margao/Madgaon at 1pm, passing through the market town of Canacona/Chaudi at 1.52pm en route to Gokarna Rd, the town's railhead, where it arrives at 3.35pm. The return train (#56640) leaves Gokarna Rd at 10.11am, stopping at Canacona/Chaudi at 11.38pm, and arriving at Margao/Madgaon at 12.40pm. As this is classed as a passenger service, you don't have to buy tickets in advance; just turn up at the station 30min before departure and pay at the regular ticket counter.

GETTING AROUND

By local bus Although often crowded, local buses can get you most places in Goa, and for shorter journeys cost only ₹10–15. Most services run from around 6am until around 7pm, though often later for inter-urban routes.

By taxi Most foreign visitors travel around Goa in white or yellow-and-black Maruti van taxis or the slightly cheaper

auto-rickshaw. Fares are often posted at ranks and the official per-kilometre rates for all taxis and rickshaws can be found at ⓦgoatourism.gov.in/inside-goa – you should always clearly settle the fare before you start your journey.

By motorcycle taxi If you're not weighed down with luggage, motorcycle taxis – known throughout Goa as

EASY RIDING

Zipping round Goa on a **rented motorbike** is very much part of the Goa experience for most people, but before you take to the road there are a few things to consider. Officially, you need an international **driver's licence** to rent and ride anything, but in practice a standard licence will probably suffice if you're stopped and asked to produce your papers by the local police. All rented motorcycles should carry special yellow-and-black **licence plates**; make sure yours does, to avoid harassment by Goa's notoriously corrupt traffic cops. Although recent changes mean that police checks on foreigners have reduced considerably, if you are caught without a licence the bike owner will be fined ₹10,000 so they are very unlikely to rent to you without seeing one. Make sure the lights and brakes are in good shape, wear a helmet, and be especially vigilant at night. Rates for motorbikes vary according to season, duration of rental and vehicle; most owners also insist on a **deposit** and/or passport as security. The cheapest bike, a scooter-style **Honda Activa** 100cc, which has automatic gears, costs ₹250–350 per day. Other options include the perennially stylish **Enfield Bullet** 350cc, although these are heavy, unwieldy and – at upwards of ₹700–1000 per day – the most expensive bike to rent. It's worth bearing in mind that road traffic accidents are the biggest cause of death of foreigners in India, with those riding Enfields being the lion's share of these cases, so if you're not an experienced motorcyclist they are best avoided. **Fuel** is sold at service stations around the state (known locally as "petrol pumps"). In smaller settlements, including the resorts, it's sold in mineral-water bottles at general stores or through backstreet suppliers – but you should avoid these as some bulk out their petrol with low-grade kerosene or industrial solvent, which makes engines misfire and smoke badly.

"pilots" – offer a faster alternative and generally cost less than half the taxi rate. Just remember that with motorcycle taxis there are old pilots and there are bold pilots, but no old, bold pilots – it's always best to choose a more mature driver (as well as haggle hard on the rate).

By bike A cheaper alternative is to rent a bicycle (gearless, Indian-made cycles) which are on offer in all the resorts for around ₹150–200/day.

By motorbike Many people travel around Goa by motorbike, but there are a number of issues to bear in mind (see box, p.161).

Central Goa

Known as the *Velhas Conquistas* ("Old Conquests"), the land wedged between the Mandovi and Zuari rivers in Central Goa was the first territory to be colonized by the Portuguese in the early sixteenth century, and still retains a more Christian feel than outlying districts. Gabled, whitewashed churches dominate most village squares, and you'll see plenty of old-style Portuguese dresses worn by Catholic women.

The Lusitanian atmosphere is most discernible of all in the older districts of the state capital, **Panjim**, and although the town attracts far fewer visitors than the coastal resorts, it certainly deserves a day or two's break from the beach, if only to visit the remains of **Old Goa**, a short bus ride away upriver. Further inland, the forested lower slopes of the Western Ghats, cut through by the main Panjim–Bengaluru (Bangalore) highway, shelter the impressive **Dudhsagar falls**, reachable only by 4WD jeep, and a small, but beautifully situated, medieval Hindu temple at **Tambdi Surla**.

Panjim

Stacked around the sides of a lush terraced hillside at the mouth of the River Mandovi, **PANJIM** (also known by its Marathi name, **Panaji** – "land that does not flood") was for centuries little more than a minor landing stage and customs house, protected by a hilltop fort and surrounded by stagnant swampland. It only became state capital in 1843, after the port at Old Goa had silted up, and its rulers and impoverished inhabitants had fled the plague.

Today, the town ranks among the least congested and hectic of any Indian capital. Conventional sights are thin on the ground, but the backstreets of the old quarter, **Fontainhas**, have retained a faded Portuguese atmosphere, with their colour-washed houses, *azulejo*-tiled street names and Catholic churches.

Panjim's annual hour in the spotlight comes at the end of November each year when it hosts the **International Film Festival of India**, or **IFFI** (🖰iffi.nic.in), for which a galaxy of Bollywood glitterati, and the odd foreign director, turn up to strut their stuff.

Fontainhas

The town's oldest and most interesting district, **Fontainhas**, comprises a dozen or so blocks of Neoclassical houses nestled at the foot of leafy Altinho Hill on the eastern edge of Panjim, across the creek from the bus stand. Many have retained their traditional coat of ochre, pale yellow, green or blue – a legacy of the Portuguese insistence that every Goan building (except churches, which had to be white) should be colour-washed after the monsoons. While some have been restored, the majority remain in a state of charismatic decay.

One of the district's oldest structures is the **Chapel of St Sebastian**, which stands at the centre of Fontainhas, at the head of a small square. The eerie crucifix inside, brought here in 1812, formerly hung in the Palace of the Inquisition in Old Goa. Unusually, Christ's eyes are open – allegedly to inspire fear in those being interrogated by the Inquisitors.

Just off the bottom of the square is a small workshop where you can watch traditional Goan *azulejos* being made. The main sales room, **Velha Goa Galeria** (Mon–Sat 10am–9pm; 🕿0832 2426 628, 🖰velhagoa.net), is a couple of blocks away at 191 Rua de Ourem.

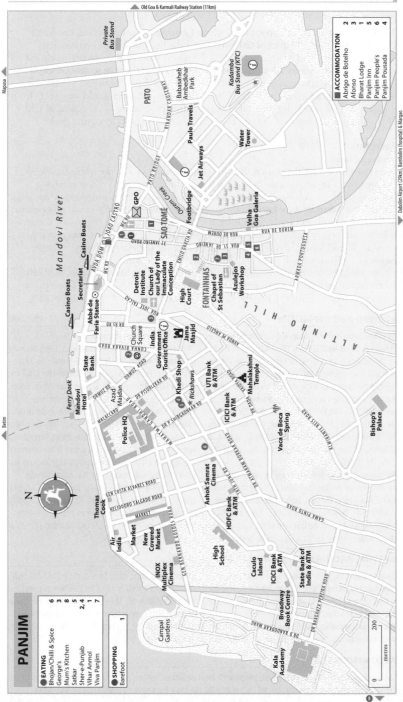

Old Goa & Karmali Railway Station (11km)

Dabolim Airport (29km); Bambolim (hospital) & Margao

PANJIM

● EATING
Bhojan/Chilli & Spice	6
George's	3
Mum's Kitchen	8
Satkar	5
Sher-e-Punjab	2, 4
Vihar Anmol	1
Viva Panjim	7

● SHOPPING
Barefoot	1

■ ACCOMMODATION
Abrigo de Botelho	2
Afonso	3
Bharat Lodge	1
Panjim Inn	5
Panjim People's	6
Panjim Pousada	4

Mandovi River

PATO

Private Bus Stand

Ribandar Causeway

Babasaheb Ambedkhar Park

Kadamba Bus Stand (KTC)

Water Tower

Paulo Travels

Pato Bridge

Jet Airways

Quirem Creek

Footbridge

Velha Goa Galeria

GPO

SÃO TOMÉ

RUA DE OUREM

RUA 31 DE JANEIRO

Casino Boats

Secretariat

Casino Boats

AVDA DOM JOÃO CASTRO

Detroit Institute

Church of our Lady of the Immaculate Conception

High Court

FONTAINHAS

Chapel of St Sebastian

Azulejos Workshop

ARMADA PORTUGUESA

ALTINHO HILL

Ferry Dock

Abbé de Faria Statue

Mandovi Hotel

State Bank

Church Square

India

Government Tourist Office

Jama Masjid

Khadi Shop

Rickshaws

UTI Bank & ATM

Mahalakshmi Temple

ICICI Bank & ATM

Vaca de Boca Spring

Bishop's Palace

Azad Maidan

Police HQ

Ashok Samrat Cinema

Thomas Cook

GEN COSTA ALVARES ROAD

HELIODORO SALGADO ROAD

Air India

Market

New Covered Market

High School

Caculo Island

HDFC Bank & ATM

ICICI Bank & ATM

Broadway Book Centre

State Bank of India & ATM

INOX Multiplex Cinema

Campal Gardens

Kala Academy

GAMA PINTO ROAD

DR D BANDODKAR MARG

DR BRAGANZA PEREIRA ROAD

N

0   200

metres

3

8

Church Square

The leafy rectangular park opposite the India Government tourist office, known as **Church Square** or the **Municipal Gardens**, forms the heart of Panjim's commercial district. Presiding over its southeast side is the town's most distinctive landmark, the whitewashed Baroque facade of the **Church of Our Lady of the Immaculate Conception**. At the head of a crisscrossing laterite walkway, the church was built in 1541 for the benefit of sailors arriving here from Lisbon. The weary mariners would stagger up from the quay to give thanks for their safe passage before proceeding to the capital at Old Goa – the original home of the enormous bell that hangs from its central gable.

Secretariat

Avda Dom João Castro

Running north from the church, Rua José Falcão brings you to the riverside, where Panjim's main street, Avenida Dom João Castro, holds the town's oldest surviving building. With its sloping tiled roofs, carved-stone coats of arms and wooden verandas, the stalwart **Secretariat** looks typically colonial. Yet it was originally the summer palace of Goa's sixteenth-century Muslim ruler, the Adil Shah. Later, the Portuguese converted it into a temporary resthouse for the territory's governors (who used to overnight here en route to and from Lisbon) and then a residence for the viceroy. Today, it houses municipal offices, though plans are afoot to transform it into a museum.

A hundred metres east, a peculiar statue of a man holding his hands over the body of an entranced reclining woman represents **Abbé de Faria** (1755–1819), a Goan priest who emigrated to France to become one of the world's first professional hypnotists.

ARRIVAL AND DEPARTURE   PANJIM

By plane European charter planes and domestic flights arrive at Dabolim airport (☎ 0832 254 0788), 29km south of Panjim on the outskirts of Vasco da Gama, Goa's second city. Prepaid taxis into town (45min; ₹790), booked at the office directly opposite the main exit, can be shared by up to four people, though if you turn right as you exit and go down the hill, you can get one for ₹500–600. Motorcycle taxis are about ₹300–350.

Destinations Bengaluru (8 daily; 1hr); Chennai (1 daily; 1hr 35min); Delhi (13 daily; 2hr 30min); Hyderabad (2 daily; 1hr 30min); Kolkata (1 daily; 3hr); Mumbai (16–18 daily; 1hr 15min).

By train There's no railway station in town itself; the nearest one, on the Konkan Railway, is at Karmali (11km east of Panjim near Old Goa). State buses to central Panjim await arrivals. Bookings can be made in town at the KRC Reservations Office, on the first floor of the Kadamba bus stand, Panjim (Mon–Fri 8am–6pm; ₹10 booking fee).

Book as far in advance as possible.

Destinations Gokarna Rd (3–4 daily; around 2hr); Hosapete for Hampi (4 weekly; 7hr); Mumbai (6–8 daily; 8hr 35min–11hr 40min); Pune (1–3 daily; 12hr 30min–14hr 40min).

By bus Long-distance and local buses work out of Panjim's busy Kadamba bus stand, 1km east of the centre in the district of Pato. Tickets can be bought in advance at the booking counters here (daily 9–11am & 2–5pm). Trips for private services are sold by the many travel agents immediately outside the station. Buses tend to depart in the afternoon/evening, and arrivals are in the morning. Within Goa, note that KTC shuttle buses are always faster than normal services.

Destinations Arambol (3–4 daily; 1hr 45min); Calangute (every 30min; 45min); Gokarna (2 daily; 5hr 30min); Hampi (1 nightly; 10hr); Mapusa (every 15min; 25–40min); Margao (every 15min; 45–55min); Mumbai (12 daily/nightly; 16hr); Pune (7–8 daily; 12hr).

GETTING AROUND AND INFORMATION

By auto-rickshaw Auto-rickshaws are the most convenient way of getting around Panjim; flag one down at the roadside or head for one of the ranks around town. The trip from the bus stand to Fontainhas costs around ₹50.

Tourist information The Government of Goa tourist information counter, inside the concourse at the main

Kadamba bus stand (daily 9am–5pm; ☎ 0832 222 5620, ⓦ goatourism.gov.in) is useful for checking train and bus timings, but little else. The more reliable India Government tourist office is across town on Church Square (Mon–Fri 9.30am–6pm, Sat 9.30am–1pm; ☎ 0832 222 3412, ⓦ incredibleindia.org).

ACCOMMODATION

The heritage properties in the atmospheric and peaceful **Fontainhas** are the best places to stay, while more modern and expensive hotels cluster in the area around 18th of June Rd. Finding a room can be a problem during **Dussehra** (Sept &

Oct), Diwali (mid-Nov), the **IFFI film festival** (see p.159) in late Nov, and over Christmas and New Year. Note that **checkout times** vary.

Abrigo de Botelho Rua de Natal, Fontainhas ☎98221 00867, ⓦhadbgoa.com. The newest of the district's heritage boutique hotels, set on a quiet corner in one of the prettiest backstreets. Its rooms, which come in three categories (₹3000–5000), are all a/c, large and tastefully decorated, with beautiful wood and tiled floors. Complimentary breakfast is served in a secluded rear garden. ₹3000

★**Afonso** St Sebastian Chapel Square, Fontainhas ☎0832 222 2359 or ☎97643 00165, ⓔafonso guesthouse@gmail.com. This refurbished colonial-era house in a picturesque square is a safe bet if you can't quite afford the *Panjim Inn* down the road. Spotless attached rooms, friendly owners and leafy rooftop terrace with views and cool ceramic mosaic floors – though someone's gone overboard with the textured wall paint. ₹2500

Bharat Lodge Sao Tome Rd, near the GPO ☎0832 222 4862, ⓔthebharatlodge@gmail.com. Good-value budget guesthouse, located at the heart of the old quarter in a terracotta-washed, 150-year-old building that has retained many of its original features despite extensive

modernization. The rooms are large for the price, have quiet fans and good-sized bathrooms: ask for no. 106 or 102 if they're vacant. A/c ₹500 extra. ₹1000

★**Panjim Inn/Panjim Pousada** E–212, Rua 31 de Janeiro, Fontainhas ☎0832 222 6523, ⓦpanjiminn .com. Grand three-hundred-year-old townhouse, managed as a homely heritage hotel, with period furniture, antique photos, balconies and a veranda where meals and drinks are served. Their adjacent three-storey wing overlooking the river is in the same style, but with better views, while the *Pousada* annexe over the road has two lovely rearside rooms sharing a wooden balcony that overlooks a secret courtyard. Buffet breakfast available. ₹6400

Panjim People's Rua 31 de Janeiro, Fontainhas ☎0832 222 6523, ⓦpanjiminn.com. Sister concern of the *Panjim Inn*, in a former high school opposite the original house (see above). It's more upmarket than their other two buildings, with rooms fitted with antique rosewood furniture, gilded pelmets, lace curtains and bathtubs. Rates include buffet breakfast. ₹16,000

EATING

Catering for the droves of tourists who come here from other Indian states, as well as fussy, more price-conscious locals, Panjim is packed with good **places to eat**. Most are connected to a hotel, but there are also plenty of other independently run establishments offering quality food for far less than you pay in the coastal resorts. If you're unsure about which

---

GOAN FOOD AND DRINK

Not unnaturally, after 451 years of colonization, Goan **cooking** absorbed a strong Portuguese influence – palm vinegar (unknown elsewhere in India), copious amounts of coconut, tangy *kokum* and fierce local chillies also play their part. Goa is the home of the famous **vindaloo** (from the Portuguese *vinho d'alho*, literally "garlic wine"), originally an extra-hot and sour pork curry, but now made with a variety of meat and fish. Other **pork** specialities include spicy *chouriço* sausages; *sorpotel*, a hot curry made from pickled pig's liver and heart; *leitão*, suckling pig; and *balchao*, pork in a rich brown sauce. Another traditional Goan Catholic dish is mutton *xacuti*, made with a sauce of lemon juice, peanuts, coconut, chillies and spices. The choice of **seafood**, often cooked in fragrant masalas (such as the sour and spicy *ambotik*), is excellent – clams, mussels, crab, lobster, giant prawns – while **fish**, depending on the type, is either cooked in wet curries, grilled, or baked in a *tandoor*. Chicken dishes include *cafrea*, a spicy stew with origins in Africa. *Sanna*, like the South Indian *idli*, is a steamed cake of fermented rice flour, but here sweetened with palm toddy. Sugar fiends will adore *bebinca*, a rich, delicious, solid egg custard with coconut, and the toffee-like *dodol*.

As for **drinks**, locally produced wine, spirits and beer are cheaper than anywhere in the country, thanks to lower rates of tax. The most famous and widespread **beer** is Kingfisher, which tastes less of glycerine preservative than it does elsewhere in India, but you'll also come across pricier Fosters, brewed in Mumbai and nothing like the original. Goan **port**, a sweeter, inferior version of its Portuguese namesake, is ubiquitous, served chilled in large wine glasses with a slice of lemon. Local **spirits** – whiskies, brandies, rums, gins and vodkas – come in a variety of brand names for less than ₹50–150 a shot, but, at half the price, local speciality **feni**, made from distilled cashew or from the sap of coconut palms, offers strong competition. Cashew *feni* is usually drunk after the first distillation, but you can also find it double-distilled and flavoured with ginger or cumin, producing a smooth liqueur.

3

regional cooking style to go for, head for **The Fidalgo Food Enclave**, in the *Hotel Fidalgo* on 18th June Rd, which hosts six different outlets, from Goan to Gujarati.

Bhojan/Chilli & Spice Hotel Fidalgo, 18th June Rd ☎ 0832 222 6291. Authentic, pure-veg Gujarati thali joint, in the a/c restaurant complex of a popular upscale hotel. You won't eat finer Indian vegetarian cuisine anywhere in Goa. ₹350 for the works. For equally superb non-veg, North Indian food (kebabs, curries, tandoori and the like) head next door to *Chilli & Spice*. Daily noon–3pm & 7.30–11pm.

George's Emilio Gracia Rd ☎ 0832 242 6821. This great little Goan-Catholic café serves proper local food (though at slightly more than local prices, thanks to the guidebooks), on cramped tables near the Immaculate Conception church. Grab a seat under a fan and tuck into calamari chilli fry, prawn-curry-rice, or the superb and spicy beef tongue roast – mains ₹150–300. They also do good-value fish curry rice meals (₹180). Mon–Sat 10am–10pm.

★ **Mum's Kitchen** Dr D Bandodkar (DB) Marg (Panjim–Miramar Rd) ☎ 90110 95559, ⓦ mumskitchengoa.com. The owners of this great Goan restaurant in the suburb of Miramar, 10min by auto from the centre of Panjim, collected old family recipes from mothers, grandmas and aunties across the state in an attempt to revive disappearing culinary traditions. The results, such as *kombdechem sukhem* (spicy boneless chicken), are as authentic and flavour-packed as any you'll encounter in Goa. Around ₹500–600 / head. Daily 11am–11pm.

Satkar 18th June Rd ☎ 0832 222 1922. Popular vegetarian South Indian snack and juice joint. There's a huge range of dishes, including Chinese and North Indian,

but most people go for their fantastic masala dosas (₹50) and piping hot, crunchy Goan samosas (₹50) – the best in town. Daily 7am–10.30pm.

Sher-e-Punjab Above Hindu Pharmacy, Cunha Rivara Rd, Church Square ☎ 0832 242 5657. This North Indian restaurant, an old Panjim favourite, occupies a funky, glass-sided dining hall overlooking the square. Steer clear of the Goan and Chinese menu – Mughlai is the thing here: chicken, mutton and *paneer* (₹210–400) prepared in the *tandoor* or steeped in rich, spicy and creamy sauces, which you scoop up with flaky naan breads. There's another branch near *Satkar*. Daily noon–3.30pm & 7–11pm.

Vihar Anmol Near the petrol station on MG Rd. Very clean, and one of the best places in town for South Indian snacks (₹25–80); they serve hearty thalis (₹80) and good North Indian food, too. It's more conveniently situated than its competitors if you're staying in Fontainhas, though it does suffer from traffic noise; best avoided during rush hours. Daily 7am–10pm.

★ **Viva Panjim** 178 Rua 31 de Janeiro, behind Mary Immaculate High School, Fontainhas ☎ 98504 71263. Award-winning traditional Goan home-cooking – *xacutis*, vindaloo, prawn *balchao*, *cafrea*, *ambotik* and delicious freshly grilled fish – served by a charming local woman, Linda de Souza, in a pretty colonial-era backstreet. This place should be your first choice for dinner if you're staying in Fontainhas. Most mains ₹175–300. Mon–Sat 11.30am–3pm & 7–10.30pm, Sun 7–10.30pm.

SHOPPING

The main shopping area in the city is on and around **18th June Rd**, though there are a few more interesting shops in Fontainhas.

Barefoot 1/26 Rua 31 de Janeiro, Fontainhas (near the petrol station) ☎ 0832 243 6815, ⓦ barefootgoa.com. A step above the normal tourist tat, this place sells a range of

quality (and of course pricey) clothes, jewellery and assorted knick-knacks, ideal for last-minute shopping before you go home. Mon–Sat 10am–11pm.

DIRECTORY

Banks Nearly all the banks in town have ATMs, where you can make withdrawals using Visa or MasterCard. The most efficient place to change currency is Thomas Cook, near the Air India/Indian Airlines office at 8 Alcon Chambers, Dr D Bandodkar (DB) Marg (April–Sept Mon–Sat 9am–6pm; Oct–March also Sun 10am–5pm; ☎ 0832 663 9257).

British Consular Assistant The British High Commission of Mumbai has a one-woman Consular Section in Panjim – a useful contact for British nationals who've lost passports, got into trouble with the law or need help dealing with a death. It's on the far western end of town, opposite the five-star *Marriott Hotel* at 303–304 Casa del Sol, Miramar (Mon–Thurs 9.30am–3pm, Fri 9.30am–12.30pm; ☎ 83224 61110 or ☎ 83224 61113, ✉ assistance@goaukconsular.org;

emergency out-of-hours number ☎ 11 241 9 2100).

Cinema Panjim's swanky multiplex, the 1272-seater INOX, is in the northwest of town on DB Marg (☎ 0832 242 0999, ⓦ inoxmovies.com). It screens all the latest Hindi block-busters and some Hollywood movies.

Hospital The state's main medical facility is the new Goa Medical College, aka GMC (☎ 0832 245 8700, ⓦ gmc.goa .gov.in), 7km south on NH-17 at Bambolim, where there's also a 24hr pharmacy. Ambulances (☎ 102) are likely to get you there a lot less quickly than a standard taxi. Conditions are grim by Western standards. Less serious cases can receive attention at the Vintage Hospital, next to the fire brigade headquarters in Panjim's St Inez district (☎ 0832 564 4401 to 4405). Better medical facilities are available

in Margao, less than an hour away by road (see p.192).
Pharmacies Hindu Pharma, near the tourist office on Church Square (Mon–Sat 9am–8pm; ☎0832 222 3176),

stocks a phenomenal range of Ayurvedic, homeopathic and allopathic medicines.

Old Goa

Just 10km from Panjim, and at one time a byword for oriental splendour, Portugal's former capital in India, **OLD GOA**, was virtually abandoned following malaria and cholera epidemics from the seventeenth century onwards. Today, despite its UNESCO World Heritage Site status, you need considerable imagination to picture the once-great city at its zenith, when it boasted a population of several hundred thousand. The maze of twisting streets, piazzas and ochre-washed villas has vanished, and all that remains is a score of cream-painted churches and convents. Foremost among the surviving monuments is the tomb of **St Francis Xavier**, the legendary sixteenth-century missionary, whose desiccated remains are enshrined in the **Basilica of Bom Jesus** – the object of veneration for Catholics from across Asia and beyond.

3

Viceroy's Archway

Old Goa's grandest mansions formerly lined the riverfront, and the best direction from which to approach the site is still from the north. Begin your tour at the **Viceroy's Archway** (1597), which would have been the first structure to greet new arrivals in the seventeenth century. Constructed to commemorate Vasco da Gama's first landfall in India, it features a Bible-toting figure resting his foot on the cringing figure of a "native" on one side, and a statue of Da Gama himself on the other.

Church of St Cajetan

A short way up the lane from the Archway, the spectacular domed **Church of St Cajetan** (1651) was modelled on St Peter's in Rome by monks from the Theatine Order. While it boasts a Corinthian exterior, non-European elements are also evident in the decoration, such as the cashew-nut designs in the carving of the pulpit.

The Sé (St Catherine's Cathedral)

The Portuguese viceroy Redondo (1561–64) commissioned the **Sé**, or **St Catherine's Cathedral**, southwest of St Cajetan's, to be "a grandiose church worthy of the wealth, power and fame of the Portuguese who dominated the seas from the

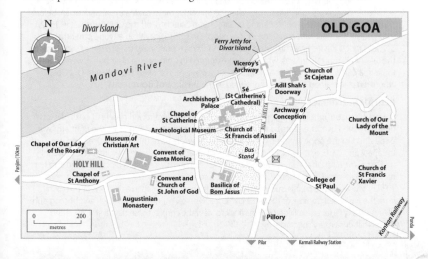

Atlantic to the Pacific". Today it stands larger than any church in Portugal, although it was beset by problems, not least a lack of funds and the motherland's temporary loss of independence to Spain. It took eighty years to build and was not consecrated until 1640.

On the Tuscan-style exterior, the one surviving tower houses the **Golden Bell**, cast in Cuncolim (south Goa) in the seventeenth century. During the Inquisition its tolling announced the start of the gruesome autos-da-fé that were held in the square outside, when suspected heretics were subjected to public torture and burned at the stake. The scale and opulence of the Corinthian-style interior is overwhelming; no fewer than fifteen altars are arranged around the walls, among them one featuring a **Miraculous Cross**, said to heal the sick. The staggeringly ornate, gilded main **altar** is surrounded by panels depicting episodes from the life of St Catherine of Alexandria (died 307 AD).

Convent of St Francis of Assisi

Archeological Museum Daily except Fri 10am–6pm • ₹10

3

On the north side of Old Goa's central square stands the **Convent of St Francis of Assisi**, built by Franciscan monks in 1517. Today, the core of the **Archeological Museum** inside consists of a gallery of **portraits** of Portuguese viceroys, painted by local artists under Italian supervision. Other exhibits include coins, domestic Christian wooden sculpture, and downstairs in the cloister, pre-Portuguese Hindu sculpture. Next door, the **Church of St Francis of Assisi** (1521) features fine decorative frescoes, *hidalgos'* tombstones in the floor paving and paintings on wood showing the life of St Francis.

Basilica of Bom Jesus

Site of the world-famous mausoleum of St Francis Xavier, the **Basilica of Bom Jesus**, on the south side of the main square, is India's most revered and architecturally

---

ST FRANCIS XAVIER

Francis Xavier, the "Apostle of the Indies", was born in 1506 in the old kingdom of Navarre, now part of Spain. When the Portuguese king, Dom Joao III (1521–57), received reports of corruption and dissolute behaviour among the Portuguese in Goa, it was Xavier whom the Jesuit Order selected to restore the moral climate of the colony.

Arriving after a year-long journey, the young priest embarked on a programme of missionary work throughout southern India, converting an estimated thirty thousand people – primarily by performing such miracles as raising the dead and curing the sick with a touch of his beads. Subsequent missions took him further afield to Sri Lanka, Malacca (Malaysia) and Japan, before his death from dysentery on the island of San Chuan (Sancian), off the Chinese coast in 1552.

Although credited with converting more people to Christianity than anyone other than St Paul, Francis Xavier owes his subsequent canonization principally to the legend surrounding the fate of his mortal remains, which, when exhumed in China a year after burial, were found to be in a perfect state of preservation. His body was later removed and taken to Old Goa, where it has remained ever since, enshrined in the **Basilica of Bom Jesus**.

PLUNDERED RELICS

St Francis's incorruptible corpse, however, has never rested entirely in peace. Chunks of it have been removed over the years by **relic hunters** and curious clerics: in 1614, the right arm was dispatched to the pope in Rome (where it allegedly wrote its name on paper), a hand was sent to Japan, and parts of the intestines to Southeast Asia. One Portuguese woman, Dona Isabel de Caron, even bit off the little toe of the cadaver; apparently, so much blood spurted into her mouth, it left a trail to her house and she was discovered.

Every ten years (the next is due in 2024), the saint's body is carried in a three-hour ceremony from the Basilica of Bom Jesus to the Sé cathedral, where visitors file past, touch and photograph it. Around a quarter of a million pilgrims flock to view the corpse, these days a shrivelled and somewhat unsavoury spectacle.

accomplished church. Work on the building was started in 1589 and took sixteen years to complete. In 1964, it became the first church in South Asia to be promoted to a Minor Basilica, by order of Pope Pius XII, and today forms the main focus for Christian worship in the old colonial capital.

Is it believed that the design of the basilica is derived from the Gesù, the Jesuits' headquarters in Rome, and, with its idiosyncratic blend of Neoclassical restraint and Baroque extravagance, is typical of the late Renaissance. The sumptuous **facade**, the most ornate in Goa, is dominated by the IHS motif, standing for Iesus Hominum Salvator ("Jesus Saviour of Men") – a feature of all Jesuit churches.

The interior

The **interior** is positively plain by comparison to the exterior, but no less impressive, dominated by a massive gilt altarpiece and a huge central statue of St Ignatius Loyola, founder of the Jesuit Order, accompanied by the Infant Jesus. Swathed in lush gold leaf, the gigantic **reredos** filling the far end of the nave remains the basilica's most arresting feature. Its undisputed treasure, however, is to be found in the south transept: the **mausoleum of St Francis** was installed in 1698, a century and a half after his death, gifted to the Jesuits by the last of the Medicis, Cosimo III (1670–1723), Grand Duke of Tuscany, in exchange for the pillow on which the saint's head was laid to rest. It took Florentine sculptor Giovanni Batista Saggini a decade to design and was made from precious marble and coloured jaspers shipped from Italy.

Holy Hill

If the heat hasn't got the better of you, head west up the lane leading from the bus stand to take in the cluster of monuments on **Holy Hill**, some of which date from the earliest phase of Christian building in Goa.

Convent of Santa Monica

The lane winds uphill, passing the weed-choked **Convent of Santa Monica** on the right. This was the only Goan convent at the time of its construction in 1627, and the largest one in Asia in its era. It housed around a hundred nuns and offered accommodation to women whose husbands were called away to other parts of the empire. As they had to remain away from the public gaze, the nuns attended Mass in the choir loft of the adjacent **chapel**, where a Miraculous Cross rises above the figure of St Monica at the altar.

Museum of Christian Art

Daily 9.30am–5pm • ☎ 0832 228 5299 • ₹20

Next door to the Convent of Santa Monica stands Goa's foremost **Museum of Christian Art**. Exhibits include processional crosses, ivory ornaments, damask silk clerical robes and some finely sculpted wooden icons dating from the sixteenth and seventeenth centuries, among them an unusual statue of John the Baptist wearing a tiger-skin wrap (in the style of the Hindu god Shiva).

Chapel of Our Lady of the Rosary

Crowning the very top of the Holy Hill, the **Chapel of Our Lady of the Rosary**, constructed in 1526 in the Manueline style (after the Portuguese king Manuel I, 1495–1521), features Ionic plasterwork with a double-storey portico, cylindrical turrets and a tower that commands fine views across the river from the terrace where Albuquerque surveyed the decisive battle of 1510. Its cruciform interior is unremarkable, except for the marble tomb of **Catarina a Piró**, believed to have been the first European woman to set foot in the colony. A commoner, she eloped here to escape the scandal surrounding her romance with Portuguese nobleman Garcia de Sá, who later rose to be governor of Goa. Under pressure from no less than Francis Xavier, Garcia eventually married her, but only in *articulo mortis* as she lay on her deathbed. Her finely carved tomb, set in the wall beside the high altar, incorporates a band of intricate Gujarati-style ornamentation, probably imported from the Portuguese trading post of Diu.

ARRIVAL AND DEPARTURE	OLD GOA

Given how short the trip is, and the high each-way charges levied by local **taxis** (₹400) and **auto-rickshaws** (₹250), this is one excursion that's eminently doable by public transport. Just 15–20min by road from the state capital, Old Goa is served by **buses** every 10min from Panjim's Kadamba bus stand (₹10).

Tambdi Surla

Six or seven hundred years ago, the Goan coast and its hinterland were littered with scores of richly carved stone temples. Only one, though, made it unscathed through the Muslim onslaught and the religious bigotry of the Portuguese era. Erected in the twelfth or thirteenth century, the tiny **Mahadeva temple** at **TAMBDI SURLA**, 65km from Panjim and deep in the interior of Goa, owes its survival to its remote location in a tranquil clearing deep in the forest at the foot of the Western Ghats, which enfold the site in a wall of impenetrable vegetation.

The temple, dedicated to Shiva, was built from the finest weather-resistant grey-black basalt, carried across the mountains from the Deccan Plateau and richly carved in situ by the region's most accomplished craftsmen.

Despite its remoteness, Tambdi Surla sees large numbers of visitors, especially on weekends, when it becomes the target for numerous school trips – so if you want to enjoy the site's essential tranquillity come during the week.

ARRIVAL AND DEPARTURE	TAMBDI SURLA

By bus A single daily bus leaves Panjim's Kadamba bus stand at 10.50am and arrives at the temple at 1.10pm. The return bus leaves late afternoon.

By taxi To get to Tambdi Surla you have to follow the course of NH-4 east from the central Goan town of Ponda, which, used by streams of iron-ore trucks, is a nightmare on a scooter or motorbike. Go by taxi if you can afford it: drivers charge around ₹3000 for a return trip from the coast.

Dudhsagar waterfalls

Measuring a mighty 600m from head to foot, the famous **Dudhsagar waterfalls**, on the Goa–Karnataka border, are some of the highest in India, and a spectacular enough sight to entice a steady stream of visitors from the coast into the rugged Western Ghats. The Konkani name for the falls, which literally translated means "sea of milk", derives from clouds of foam kicked up at the bottom when the water levels are at their highest. Overlooking a steep, crescent-shaped head of a valley carpeted with pristine tropical forest, Dudhsagar is set amid impressive **scenery** that is only accessible on foot or by jeep.

The **best time to visit** is immediately after the monsoons, from October until mid-December, when water levels are highest, although the falls flow well into April.

ARRIVAL AND INFORMATION	DUDHSAGAR WATERFALLS

By jeep The only practical way to get to Dudhsagar and back is by 4WD jeep from Colem/Kulem (get to Colem by train from Vasco, Margao and Chandor, or by taxi from the north coast resorts for around ₹3000). Look for the "Controller of Jeeps" in Colem, near the station. The cost of the onward 30- to 40min trip from Colem to the falls, across rough forest tracks and three river fords, is ₹2100/six-person jeep (you may have to wait for the vehicle to fill up); the drive ends with an enjoyable 10min hike.

Entrance fee The park entrance fee is ₹20, with an extra ₹300 for a camera.

North Goa

Development in North Goa is concentrated mainly behind the 7km strip of white sand that stretches from the foot of **Fort Aguada**, crowning the peninsula east of Panjim, to Baga creek in the north. Encompassing the resorts of **Candolim**, **Calangute** and **Baga**, this is Goa's prime charter belt and an area most independent travellers steer well clear of.

Since the advent of mass tourism in the 1980s, the alternative "scene" has drifted progressively north away from the sunbed strip to **Anjuna** and **Vagator** – site of some of the region's loveliest beaches – and scruffier **Chapora**, which still has the feel of a fishing village (although overfishing means few boats actually go out these days). Further north still, **Arambol** has thus far escaped any large-scale development, despite the completion of the new road bridge across the Chapora River. **Aswem** and **Mandrem**, just south of Arambol, are this stretch of coast's hot tips: still reasonably off-track, though rapidly filling up.

3

ARRIVAL AND DEPARTURE   NORTH GOA

North Goa's market town, **Mapusa**, is the area's main jumping-off place if you're arriving overland from out of state. Travelling here by train via the **Konkan Railway**, get off at **Tivim** (Thivim), 12km east of Mapusa, from where you'll have to jump in a bus or taxi for the remaining leg.

Mapusa

MAPUSA (pronounced "Mapsa") is the district headquarters of Bardez *taluka*. A dusty collection of dilapidated, mostly modern buildings ranged around a busy central square, the town is of little more than passing interest, although it does host a lively daily fresh produce **market**. Anjuna's market may be a better place to shop for souvenirs, but Mapusa's is much more authentic. Local specialities include strings of spicy Goan sausages (*chouriço*), bottles of toddy (fermented palm sap) and large green plantains from nearby Moira.

Whatever you're looking for in the Mapusa market, it's a good idea to arrive as early in the morning as possible to beat the heat. After 11am temperatures can be stifling.

ARRIVAL AND DEPARTURE   MAPUSA

By train Tivim (Thivim), the nearest railway station to Mapusa, is 12km east in the neighbouring Bicholim district. Buses should be on hand to transport passengers into town. The Konkan Railway's *Konkan Kanya Express* #10111 arrives in Tivim from Mumbai's CST at around 9am, leaving plenty of time to find accommodation in the coastal resorts west of Mapusa.

Destinations Cancona (for Palolem; 3 daily; 1hr 30min–2hr); Gokarna Rd (Fri; 2hr 30min); Mumbai (5–7 daily; 8hr 20min–11hr 30min).

By bus You can pick up local services to Calangute, Baga, Anjuna, Vagator, Chapora and Arambol. These leave

from the Kadamba bus stand, a 5min walk west of the main square, where all state-run services from Panjim also pull in.

Destinations Anjuna (hourly; 30min); Arambol (every 30min; 1hr); Calangute (every 30min; 30min); Chapora (every 30min; 30–40min); Mumbai (24 daily; 16hr); Panjim (every 10–15min; 25min); Pernem (6 daily; 1hr 45min); Vagator (every 30min; 25–35min).

By taxi Motorcycle taxis hang around the square to whisk lightly laden shoppers and travellers to the coast for around ₹150. Taxis charge considerably more (around ₹300), but you can split the fare with up to five people.

SWIMMING IN GOA: A WARNING

Be very careful where you swim in Goa. Many places are subject to vicious **currents** (even in relatively shallow water) and during the season at least one tourist a week drowns here – often after they have consumed drugs or alcohol. It's safest to stick to the beaches with lifeguards and flags indicating the safe areas to swim. Swimming anywhere during the **monsoon** would be suicidal.

EATING

FR Xavier Municipal Market. For quick, authentic Goan food, you won't do better than the recently renovated *FR Xavier*, which has been here since the Portuguese era. It serves scrumptious veg patties and beef "chops" (rissoles), as well as spicy meals of fish, prawn and chicken curry, and other local standards such as *cafrea* and *xacuti*. Most mains cost less than ₹150. Mon–Sat 9am–9pm.

Ruchira Fifth floor, Hotel Satyaheera, by the roundabout past the taxi stand ☏ 0832 226 3869. The best and most comfortable of the eating options around the main intersection, serving decent but expensive local and Indian dishes such as Goan chicken chilli fry and prawn biryani. Daily 11am–11pm.

SHOPPING

Other India Bookstore Above the Mapusa Clinic ☏ 0832 226 3305, ⓦ otherindiabookstore.com. Hidden away above the Mapusa Clinic, this bookstore is a treasure trove with a vast range of titles relating to ecology, the environment and Goa in general; a full stock list is available online. Mon–Fri 9am–5pm, Sat 9am–1pm.

Candolim and around

CANDOLIM is prime package-tourist country, and not a resort that sees many backpackers, but, with a few pleasant places to stay in the village by the fort, it can make a good first stop if you've just arrived in Goa – and its predominantly more mature clientele make it much less rowdy than Calangute/Baga. The busy strip running through the middle of town holds a string of banks and handy shops where you can stock up with essentials before moving further afield, and there are some great places to eat and drink, frequented mostly by boozy, middle-aged Brits and, increasingly, domestic tourists.

Fort Aguada

The one sight worth seeking out in the area is **Fort Aguada**, crowning the rocky flattened headland to the south, at the end of the beach. Built in 1612 to protect the northern shores of the Mandovi estuary from Dutch and Maratha raiders, the bastion encloses several natural springs, the first source of drinking water available to ships arriving in Goa after the long sea voyage from Lisbon. The ruins of the fort can be reached by following the main drag south from Candolim as it bears left, past the turning for the *Vivanta Resort*; keep going for 1km until

CANDOLIM & FORT AGUADA

you see a right turn, which runs uphill to a small car park. Panoramic views extend from the top of the hill where a four-storey Portuguese **lighthouse**, erected in 1864 and the oldest of its kind in Asia, looks down over the vast expanse of sea, sand and palm trees.

Sinquerim Beach

From the base of the walled *Vivanta Resort* on the northern flank of the headland, a rampart of red-brown laterite juts into the bay at the bottom of what's left of **Sinquerim Beach**, which was virtually wiped out by a series of particularly heavy monsoon storms in 2009. This was among the first places in Goa to be singled out for upmarket tourism. The Taj group's *Vivanta* resort, among the most expensive hotels in India, lords it over the sands from the slopes below the battlements.

ARRIVAL AND DEPARTURE

By bus Buses from and to Panjim and Calangute stop every 10–15min or so at the stand by the crossroads in the middle of Candolim and a few head south here to the Sinquerim terminus by the fort; you can also flag them down from anywhere along the main road to Calangute.

CANDOLIM AND AROUND

Destinations Calangute (every 15min; 15min); Panjim (every 15min; 25min).

GETTING AROUND AND INFORMATION

By motorbike During the season there is often a dearth of motorcycles for rent, in which case search for one in Calangute. The nearest petrol pump lies 5km east on the main Panjim road, just beyond Nerul.

Services There are lots of ATMs dotted along the main drag and you can change money at any number of private exchange places in Candolim, although their rates are unlikely to be as competitive as those in Calangute. Dive Goa, at the SinQ Beach Club, offers diving trips (☎93250 30110, ⊛divegoa.com).

ACCOMMODATION

Candolim is charter-holiday land, so **accommodation** tends to be expensive for most of the season. That said, if bookings are down you can find some great bargains here, and **Sinquerim**, east of the fort, is a genuinely nice place to stay.

★**Dona Florina** Monteiro's Rd, Escrivao Waddo ☎99230 49076, ⊛donaflorina.co.in. Large guesthouse in a superb location, overlooking the beach in a secluded corner of the village. Its friendly owner has added a breezy rooftop terrace with ceramic mosaic floors where guests can practise yoga. Well worth paying ₹500 extra for if you want idyllic sea views. No car access. ₹2000

Marbella Sinquerim ☎0832 247 9551, ⊛marbellagoa .com. Individually styled suites and spacious rooms in a beautiful house built to resemble a traditional Goan mansion. Everything is gorgeous, especially in the top-floor "Penthouse" (₹6000), and the whole place is screened by a giant mango tree. Unashamedly romantic. ₹3000

Pretty Petal Camotim Waddo ☎96375 56149, ⊛pretty petalsgoa.com. Very large modern rooms, all with fridges, quality mattresses, balconies and relaxing, marble-floored communal areas overlooking lawns. Their top-floor apartment, with windows on four sides and a huge balcony, is the best choice, though more expensive. Use of nearby swimming pool included. ₹1700

Shanu Holiday Home Escrivao Waddo ☎0832 248 9899, ⊛shanu.in. Eighteen good-sized, well-furnished rooms with narrow balconies right on the dunes, some of them with uninterrupted views of the sea. The a/c rooms cost double. Ask the hospitable owners for no. 120 (or failing that 118, 111, 110 or 107). Breakfast (₹200–300) is served in your room. ₹700

EATING

Candolim's numerous beach **cafés** are a cut above your average seafood shacks, with pot plants, high-tech sound systems and prices to match. The further from the *Vivanta* complex you venture, the lower the prices become. Fancier places serving more ambitious cuisine line busy Fort Aguada Rd, alongside a string of enduringly popular local joints.

★**Bomra's** 247 Fort Aguada Rd, Souza ☎97675 91056. Understated, relaxed place, on a dimly lit gravel terrace by the roadside. From the outside you'd never know this was one of Goa's gastronomic highlights, but the food – contemporary Burmese and Kachin cuisine – is superb. The menu's reassuringly short; try their aromatic-flavoured pickle tea-leaf salad for a starter, and the beef in peanut curry or snapper with lemongrass and galangal for a main. They also do fantastic mojitos and, for dessert, delicious ginger crème brûlée. Count on ₹1200–1400 for three courses. Daily noon–2.30pm &7–11pm.

Café Chocolatti 409 Fort Aguada Rd, Dando Waddo

📞 93261 12006. Nazneen, the British-raised owner of this delightful café in south Candolim, has conjured up a chocoholic heaven. Order a perfect cup of freshly ground coffee or a milkshake to drink in the garden, and indulge in gourmet Belgian-style truffles, tinged with chilli, mocha and orange, a succulent marmalade brownie, or crunchy almond-flavoured Italian biscuits. ₹200–250 for coffee and a treat. Their decent full English is ₹430. Daily 10am–9pm.

Pete's Shack Sequeira Beach. One beach shack that deserves singling out, because it's always professional and serves great healthy salads (₹200–250) with real olive oil, mozzarella and balsamic vinegar. All the veg is carefully washed in chlorinated water first, so the food is safe and fresh. The same applies to their seafood sizzler and tandoori main courses. For dessert, try the wonderful home-made *matka kulfi* (served in an earthenware pot) or a cooling mint lassi. Daily 8am–10pm.

Viva Goa! Fort Aguada Rd, Ana Waddo 📞 0832 248 9677. Tasty, no-nonsense Goan food fresh from the market – mussel-fry, barramundi (*chonok*), lemonfish (*modso*) and sharkfish steaks fried *rechado* style in chilli paste or in millet (*rawa*) – served on a roadside terrace. It used to be a locals' place, but the customers are mostly tourists these days, and although not as authentic as it used to be, it's good value with most seafood mains around ₹200–300. Daily 11am–3.30pm & 6.30–11.30pm.

Calangute and Baga

3

A 45-minute bus ride up the coast from Panjim, **CALANGUTE** was, in Portuguese times, where well-to-do Goans would come for their annual *mudança*, or change of air, in May and June, when the pre-monsoon heat made life in the towns insufferable. It remains the state's busiest resort, but has changed beyond recognition since the days when straw-hatted musicians in the beachfront bandstand would regale smartly dressed strollers with Lisbon *fados* and Konkani *dulpods*. Mass package tourism, combined with a huge increase in the number of Indian visitors (for whom this is Goa's number-one beach resort), has placed an impossible burden on the town's rudimentary infrastructure. Hemmed in by four-storey buildings and swarming with traffic, the market area, in particular, has taken on the aspect of a typical makeshift Indian town of precisely the kind that most travellers used to come to Goa to get away from. That said, the south end of the beach around **Maddo Waddo** is quite mellow and there are marginally fewer domestic lager louts than in Baga to the north.

Baga

BAGA is pretty much an extension of Calangute, though the scenery in the far north is somewhat more varied and picturesque. Overlooked by a rocky headland draped in vegetation, a small tidal **river** flows into the sea at the top of the village, past a spur of soft white sand where ranks of brightly coloured fishing boats are moored.

Since the package boom, Baga has developed more rapidly than anywhere else in the state and today looks less like the Goan fishing village it was in the early 1990s and more like a small-scale resort on the Spanish *costas*, with a predominantly young, male, Indian clientele. These "stags", lured to Goa by advertising hinting at cheap booze, hard partying and erotic encounters with exotic foreign women, can be annoying. Beyond the rowdy bars where they hang out, however, you'll find a crop of excellent **restaurants** and some lively **nightlife**.

ARRIVAL AND INFORMATION   CALANGUTE AND BAGA

By bus Buses from Mapusa (every 30min; 30min) and Panjim (every 15min; 45min) pull in at the small bus-stand-cum-market-square in the centre of Calangute. Some continue to Baga, stopping at the crossroads behind the beach en route.

By taxi From Mapusa a taxi should cost around ₹400 and from Panjim around ₹500, with motorcycle taxis costing around half that and rickshaws somewhere in between.

Services There are more than 27 ATMs along the main streets, all of which will give cash with Visa or MasterCard. Private currency changers on the same street (many of which also do money wiring) include Wall Street Finances (Mon–Sat 9.30am–6pm), opposite the *Plantain Leaf* and in the shopping complex on the beachfront, who exchange cash at bank rates.

ACCOMMODATION

In spite of the encroaching mayhem, plenty of travellers get hooked on **Calangute**'s mix of market town and beach resort, returning year after year to stay in little family guesthouses in the fishing *waddo*. Nowhere is far from the shore, but sea

3

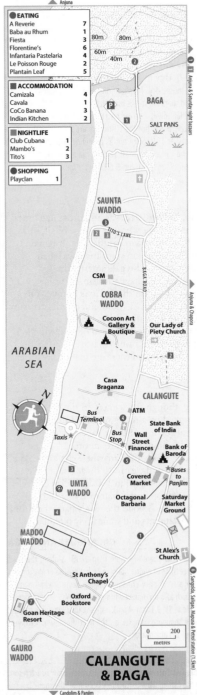

● EATING	
A Reverie	7
Baba au Rhum	1
Fiesta	3
Florentine's	6
Infantaria Pastelaria	4
Le Poisson Rouge	2
Plantain Leaf	5

■ ACCOMMODATION	
Camizala	4
Cavala	1
CoCo Banana	3
Indian Kitchen	2

■ NIGHTLIFE	
Club Cubana	1
Mambo's	2
Tito's	3

● SHOPPING	
Playclan	1

CALANGUTE & BAGA

views are a rarity. Accommodation is harder to find in **Baga**, as even rooms in smaller guesthouses tend to be booked up well before the season gets under way. The majority of family-run places lie around the north end of the beach, where nights have been a lot more peaceful since Goa's premier club, *Tito's*, acquired soundproofing.

Camizala 5–33B Maddo Waddo ☎96891 56449. A lovely, breezy haven amid the brouhaha of Calangute, with four rooms, common verandas and sea views. About as close to the beach as you can get, and the *waddo* is quiet. Cheap, considering the location, and a popular long-stay option. ₹800

Cavala Baga Rd ☎0832 227 7587, ⓦcavala.com. Modern hotel in tastefully traditional laterite, with a pool in a plot across the road surrounded by banana groves. Some rooms have separate balconies front and back; the rear-side ones look across open fields. Rooms range from simple non-a/c doubles (₹3900) to luxurious suites (₹7250). ₹3900

★**CoCo Banana** 1195 Umta Waddo ☎0832 227 6478 or ☎0832 227 9068, ⓦcocobananagoa.com. Very comfort-able, spacious chalets, all with bathrooms, fridges, fans, mosquito nets, kettles and extra-long mattresses. Down the lane beyond *Electric Cats* restaurant, it is run by a welcoming Goan-Swiss couple, Walter and Marina Lobo, who have been here for more than 35 years – a chat with the former about the cultural history of Goa is reason enough to stay here. They also have a few much quieter a/c rooms closer to the beach for ₹1400. ₹950

Indian Kitchen Behind Our Lady of Piety Church ☎98221 49615, ⓦindian-kitchen-goa.com. Highly decorated guesthouse with crazy mosaic tiling, brightly patterned walls and lanterns. The rooms, all attached, have fridges and TV – and, amazingly for a budget hotel, there's a little pool to the rear. They also have more expensive a/c rooms (₹2000) and quieter chalets round the back (₹1500). ₹880

EATING

This has long been a destination where people come as much to **eat** as for a stroll on the beach, and even if you stay in resorts elsewhere you'll doubtless be tempted down here for a meal.

A Reverie Near Goan Heritage Resort, Gauro Waddo ☎98231 74927 or ☎98235 05550. Over-the-top gourmet place on the south side of Calangute, centred on a grand, multilevel, terracotta-tiled canopy. Both the gastronomic menu and ambience are about as extravagant as Goa gets, but the prices aren't top whack (around ₹1500–2000/head, plus drinks). Signature dishes include the little BBQ (beef or lamb steak cooked at the table), and lobster cooked in a risotto, poached or with Goan spices. Reservations recommended. Daily 7–11.30pm.

Baba au Rhum Arpora ☎ 96572 10468. This cool French patisserie-cum-pizzeria hidden deep in the expat enclave of Arpora is a bit off the beaten track, but worth hunting out for its crumbly croissants, baguettes, *pains au raisin*, fruit salads, juices and perfect *café au lait*, served on heavy wood tables, with infectious World grooves playing in the background. To find it, turn left off the main Calangute–Anjuna road when you see their signboard. Around ₹300–500/head for meals, with desserts and pastries at around ₹100–200. Wed–Mon 9am–11pm.

Fiesta Tito's Lane ☎ 0832 227 9894, ⓦ fiestagoa.com. Baga's most sumptuously decorated restaurant enjoys a perfect spot at the top of a long dune, with sea views from the veranda of a 1930s house. Conch-shell lanterns and an old fishing boat filled with scatter cushions set the tone. The contemporary Mediterranean food is as delectable as the decor. Try their carpaccio of beef for starters, followed by cannelloni, spag bol or the succulent wood-fired pizzas (₹350–750). Most starters and mains ₹350–650. Reservations recommended. Daily 7pm–midnight.

Florentine's 4km east of St Alex's Church at Saligao, next door to the Ayurvedic Natural Health Centre ☎ 0832 227 8122. It's well worth venturing inland to taste Florence D'Costa's legendary chicken *cafreal* (₹300) made to a jealously guarded family recipe that pulls in crowds of locals and tourists from across north Goa. The restaurant

is a down-to-earth place, with prices to match, serving only chicken, some seafood and vegetarian snacks. Daily 11.30am–3pm & 6.30–10.30pm.

Infantaria Pastelaria Next to St John's Chapel, Baga Rd ☎ 0832 329 1290. Roadside terrace café that gets packed out for its stodgy croissants, freshly baked apple pie and traditional Goan sweets (such as *dodol* and home-made *bebinca*). Top of the savouries list, though, are the prawn and veg patties (₹120), which locals buy by the boxload. Also has a mid-priced multicuisine menu. Daily 7.30am–midnight.

★**Le Poisson Rouge** Baga Creek ☎ 98238 50276, ⓦ gregorybazire.com. An established star on north Goa's gastronomic map, this Gallic-run restaurant is situated in an elegantly styled palm garden lit by pretty tea lights. An ever-changing menu mixes classic French technique with local flavour, with dishes such as king fish dosa bhaji and bisque – check the website for the latest offerings. Around ₹1500/head for three courses, plus extra for wine. Reservations recommended. Daily 7–10.30pm.

Plantain Leaf Market area ☎ 72649 20949. The best Udupi-style restaurant outside Panjim, if not all Goa, where waiters in matching shirts serve the usual range of delicious dosas and other spicy snacks in a clean, cool marble-lined canteen. Try their definitive *idli-vada* breakfasts, delicious masala dosas (₹70) or the cheap and filling set thalis (₹120). Daily 8am–midnight.

NIGHTLIFE

Nightlife is centred around Baga and the various bars and clubs along **Tito's Lane**, named after *Tito's Club*, the most famous club in Goa, if not India. This is where the Indian "stags" come to fulfil their Goa fantasies, so single women may feel uncomfortable with the level of attention – although on the upside single women will rarely have to pay for entry or drinks. Otherwise, take your pick from the string of shacks lined up along the beach or bars on **Baga Rd**, which stay open until the last punter staggers home.

Club Cubana Arpora ☎ 91582 57000, ⓦ clubcubanagoa .com. *Cubana*, which occupies a hilltop just inland from the strip, is the most civilized nightspot in the area, especially for women. Only couples are admitted (₹2000 for two, includes drink); and there's even a ladies-only dancefloor. The music's so-so, but the vibe is much more chilled than male-dominated *Tito's*. Jeeps shuttle punters up the hill, and you can wallow in a curviform pool. On Wed women get in for free (₹800 admission for guys). Daily 9.30pm–late.

Tito's/Mambo's Tito's Lane, Saunta Waddo ⓦ titosgoa .com. Baga's legendary nightlife is largely attributable to *Tito's* and its various offspring, including the latest, more

techno-orientated, *Mambo's*. Every night hundreds of revellers, many of them single men from other states, are lured in by TV images of women in skimpy dancewear and a thumping sound-and-light system. For Western women in particular, this can make for an uncomfortably loaded atmosphere. Biggest nights are Fri and Sat; music policy is loungey till 11pm, then hip-hop, house, techno and, at *Tito's*, Bollywood hits. At both, entry and drinks are usually free for women, otherwise you might pay anything from ₹1000 to ₹3000 including drinks (₹1500 for couples), depending on how busy they are. At Christmas, prices can soar above ₹3000. Nov & Dec daily 10pm–3am; off-season closes earlier.

SEXUAL HARASSMENT IN GOA

While the vast majority of **harassment** of female tourists in Goa is relatively harmless (though unacceptable) – the surreptitious use of cellphones to take photos of scantily clad women on beaches, for example (report them to the beach police and they'll be forced to delete the pictures), or unwanted attempts at conversation by large groups of men – there have been more serious cases of sexual crimes. Women should avoid walking alone in remote places (or on the beach), especially after dark, and never accept drinks from strangers.

SATURDAY NIGHT BAZAARS

One of the few genuinely positive improvements to the north Goa resort strip over the last fifteen years has been the **Saturday Night Market** (W snmgoa.com), held on a plot inland at **Arpora**, midway between Baga and Anjuna. Originally the brainchild of an expat German called Ingo, it's run with great efficiency and a sense of fun that's palpably lacking these days from the Anjuna flea market (see opposite). The balmy evening temperatures and pretty lights are also a lot more conducive to relaxed browsing than the broiling heat of mid-afternoon on Anjuna beach. Although far more commercial than its predecessor in Anjuna, many old Goa hands regard this as far truer to the original spirit of the flea market. A significant proportion of the stalls are taken up by foreigners selling their own stuff, from reproduction Indian pop art to antique photos, the latest trance party gear, stunning antique and coconut-shell jewellery and techno DJ demos. There's also a mouthwatering array of ethnic food and a stage featuring live music from around 7pm until 3am, when the market winds up, as well as a couple of trendy bars with live music or DJs. Admission is free.

The night market from which Ingo's splintered – Mackie's (W mackiesnitebazaar.com) – lies nearby, close to the riverside In Baga. Spurned by the expatriate designers and stallholders, it is not quite as lively as its rival, though in recent years has made an effort to close the gap, with better live acts and more foreign stallholders.

SHOPPING

Playclan Shop no. S–3, Ida Maria Resort, next to HDFC Bank ☎ 93722 80862, W playclan.com. Delhi-based design collective Playclan have a great shop in Calangute offering quirky souvenirs and gifts. They create an alternative universe of instantly recognizable Indian symbols – gods, *kathakali* dancers, rickshaws and "horn-ok-please" lorries – with which they decorate T-shirts, mugs, lighters and underwear. Daily 11am–8pm.

Anjuna

ANJUNA, the next sizeable village up the coast from Baga, was, until a few years back, the last bastion of alternative chic in Goa – where the state's legendary full-moon parties were staged each season, and where the Beautiful Set would rent pretty red-tiled houses for six months at a time, make trance mixes and groovy dance clothes, paint the palm trees fluoro colours and spend months lazing on the beach. A small contingent of fashionably attired, middle-aged hippies still turn up, but thanks to a combination of the Y2K music ban (see box, p.181) and overwhelming growth in popularity of the flea market, Anjuna has seriously fallen out of fashion for the party crowd.

As a consequence, the scattered settlement of old Portuguese houses and whitewashed churches, nestled behind a long golden sandy beach, nowadays more closely resembles the place it was before the party scene snowballed than it has for a decade or more. There is, however, a downside to staying here: levels of substance abuse, both among visitors and locals, remain exceptionally high, and the village suffers more than its fair share of dodgy characters.

The beach

The north end of **Anjuna beach**, just below where the buses pull in, is no great shakes by Goan standards, with a dodgy undertow and lots of even dodgier Kashmiris selling hash, as well as parties of whisky-filled day-trippers in constant attendance. The vibe is much nicer at the far, southern end, where a pretty and more sheltered cove accommodates a mostly twenty-something tourist crowd. A trance soundtrack thumps from the shacks behind it, cranking up to become proper parties after dark, when *Curlie's* and neighbouring *Shiva Valley* take turns to max their sound systems, hosting international DJs through the season. Chai ladies and food stallholders sit in wait on the sands, just like in the raves of old, and on Thursdays, when they seem to have come to an arrangement with authorities, the party continues till daylight. Every other night things grind to a halt at 10pm sharp.

Flea market

The biggest crowds gather on Wednesdays after Anjuna's **flea market**, held in the coconut plantation behind the southern end of the beach, just north of *Curlie's*. Along with the Saturday Night Market at Arpora (see box opposite), this is the place to indulge in a spot of **souvenir shopping**. Two decades or so ago the weekly event was the exclusive preserve of backpackers and the area's seasonal residents, who gathered here to smoke chillums and to buy and sell party clothes and jewellery. These days, however, it's all more mainstream. Pitches are rented out by the metre, drugs are banned and the approach roads to the village are choked all day with air-conditioned buses and Maruti taxis ferrying in tourists from resorts further down the coast. Even the beggars have to pay **baksheesh** to be here. The mayhem is, however, fun to experience at least once.

What you end up paying for the exotic merchandise on offer – from Rajasthani handicrafts to South Indian stone carving and everything in between – largely depends on your ability to **haggle**. Prices are sky-high by Indian standards. Be persistent, though, and cautious, and you can usually pick things up for a reasonable rate (except from the Western designers, who are not so fond of haggling).

Even if you're not spending, the flea market is a good place just to sit and watch the world go by. Mingling with the suntanned masses are bands of strolling musicians, mendicant sadhus and fortune-telling bulls. And if you happen to miss the show, rest assured that the whole cast reassembles every Saturday at Baga/Arpora's night markets (see box opposite).

ANJUNA map including: DE MELLO WADDO, Oxford Arcade, STARCO'S CROSSROADS, Bus Stop, Connexions, SORONTO WADDO, Supermarket, Police Post, Bank of Baroda, Paddy Fields, Speedy Travel, Motorcycle Repairs, MONTEIRO WADDO, Orchard Stores, Flea Market Ground, PEQQEM, PEDDEM

SHOPPING
Artjuna House 1

EATING
Artjuna 3
German Bakery 5
Laguna Anjuna 1
Martha's Breakfast Home 4
Villa Blanche 2
Xavier's 6

NIGHTLIFE
Curlie's/Shiva Valley 1

ACCOMMODATION			
Anjuna Beach Resort	1	Manali	4
Anjuna Palms	2	Martha's	8
Banyan Soul	9	Renées	7
Blue Nest	3	Yoga Magic	6
Granpa's Inn	5		

ARRIVAL AND DEPARTURE   ANJUNA

By bus Buses from Mapusa (hourly; 30–40min) drop passengers at various points along the tarmac road across the top of the village, which turns north towards Chapora at the main Starco's crossroads. If you're looking for a room on spec, get off here as it's close to many of the guesthouses.

ACCOMMODATION

Anjuna Beach Resort De Mello Waddo ☎0832 227 4499 or ☎98221 76753 (Joseph), ⊚anjunabeachresort .com. This place offers 32 spacious, comfortable rooms with balconies, fridges, attached bathrooms and solar-heated water in two concrete blocks ranged around a pool. Those on the upper floors are best. There's also a block of apartments for long-stayers; both are very good value, though the complex is showing signs of age. A/c ₹500 extra. ₹2000

Anjuna Palms De Mello Waddo ☎0832 227 3268 or ☎98226 86817 (Felix), ⊚anjunapalms.com. Cosy budget guesthouse just a 10min walk from the beach, tucked away behind an old Portuguese-era house next door to the Oxford Arcade, with more character than most. It offers three types of rooms: larger, a/c ones with high ceilings (₹900), more ramshackle attached and non-attached options, and dorm beds. All of them open on to a garden courtyard. Dorms ₹225, doubles ₹550/₹700

Banyan Soul Peqqem Peddem, off Flea Market Rd ☎98207 07283, ⊚thebanyansoul.com. Leafy, designer-chic hotel on the quiet, southeastern fringes of the village, near the *German Bakery*. Shaded by an old banyan tree, the rooms are attractively decorated – though small for the price – and each has a private outdoor sitout that's well screened from the neighbours. Some readers find this place a bit overpriced and boxed in; others love its tucked-away feel. ₹3000

3

YOGA IN ANJUNA

Thanks to the presence on its fringes of two world-class centres, Anjuna is a great place to develop your **yoga** skills.

Brahmani Centre Tito's White House, Anjuna ☎ 99236 99378, ⊛ brahmaniyoga.com. Brahmani offers drop-in Ashtanga yoga classes by expert teachers at a studio on the outskirts of the village just off the main Siolim Rd; all levels of ability are catered for.

Purple Valley Arpora ⊛ yogagoa.com. If you're looking for a fully fledged retreat or course, you won't do better than Purple Valley, which has accommodation for up to forty guests and what must be one of the loveliest yoga *shalas* (practice areas) in India. Their teachers were all

students of the late Ashtanga guru Shri K. Pattabhi Jois.

Satsanga Retreat Verla Canca, 4km inland from Anjuna ☎ 0832 247 2823, ⊛ satsangaretreat.com. Offering retreats, yoga holidays and teacher training, Satsanga describes itself as a "home away from home" but with palm trees, tropical gardens and a swimming pool in a small village between Anjuna and Mapusa. The yoga space is beautiful and there are plenty of chill-out areas and hammock spots. Ayurvedic food and massage are on offer too.

Blue Nest Soronto Waddo ☎ 97630 63379. Joseph and Cecilia's little row of five old-fashioned rooms, with pitched-tiled roofs and wood rafters, is close to the main road through the village, but you wouldn't know it. Neatly painted, they're large for the price and have good thick mattresses, as well as nice little tiled verandas looking out over woodland. No wi-fi. ₹300

Granpa's Inn Gaun Waddo ☎ 0832 227 3270, ⊛ granpas inn.com. *Granpa's* occupies a lovely 200-year-old house set in half an acre of lush gardens, with a kidney-shaped pool and shady breakfast terrace. They offer three categories of rooms: non-a/c standards (₹4000), a/c suites in the main house (₹4500) and poolside suites (₹5500). Very popular despite the high tariffs, so book well ahead. ₹4000

Manali South of Starco's crossroads ☎ 0832 227 4421. Anjuna's most popular all-round budget guesthouse offers recently renovated, simple, clean attached rooms with fans, opening onto a yard. Services include a safe deposit, money exchange, library and a sociable terrace-restaurant. No wi-fi, but there is an adjoining bookshop/cybercafé. Booking recommended. ₹700

Martha's 907 Monteiro Waddo ☎ 0832 227 3365, ✉ mpd8650@hotmail.com. Spotless attached rooms

(₹900 for non-a/c, ₹1500 for a/c) run by a friendly family. Amenities include kitchen space, and running, solar-heated water. Two pleasant houses and a villa also available – ideal for families (around ₹1500/night). And their breakfasts are famous (see opposite). ₹900

Renées Monteiro Waddo ☎ 0832 227 3405 or ☎ 98504 62217. This is a little gem of a guesthouse. Swathed in greenery, welcoming and family run, it holds just half a dozen rooms, most of them surprisingly spacious, with garden-facing balconies. A few have simple kitchenettes and fridges. It's a tad pricier than the competition, but worth it. A/c ₹200 extra. ₹500

★**Yoga Magic** ☎ 0832 652 3796 or ☎ 93705 65717, ⊛ yogamagic.net. Innovative "Canvas Ecotel", offering low-impact luxury on the edge of Anjuna in Rajasthani hunting tents. The structures, ranging from standard lodges (₹9000/night) to swankier suites (₹12000) are all decorated with block-printed cotton and furnished with cushions, silk drapes and solar halogen lights. Loos are of the biodegradable, non-smelly compost kind. All prices include breakfast, and they also do seven-day yoga packages. And there's a pool. ₹12500

EATING

Responding to the tastes of its visitors, Anjuna boasts a good crop of quality cafés and restaurants, many of which serve healthy vegetarian dishes and juices. If you're hankering for a taste of home, call in at Orchard Stores on the southeastern side of the village, or the rival Oxford Arcade, on the opposite, north side, which both serve the expatriate and tourist community with a vast range of pricey imported delights and organic produce from around India.

Artjuna 972 Monteiro Waddo, on the flea market road ☎ 0832 227 4794, ⊛ artjuna.com. Pretty little garden café serving delicious salads, pesto omelettes, sandwiches of all varieties, a few sweet treats (₹130–320) and great coffee. There's a play area for kids, yoga, Zumba for all ages and a beautiful shop. Sun–Fri 7am–10.30pm, Sat 7am–7pm.

★**German Bakery** South Anjuna, on the road to Nirvana Hermitage ☎ 90960 58775, ⊛ german-bakery

.in. The original and inimitable outlet of this much-copied wholefood café-restaurant, hidden away in a tree-shaded garden on the south side of the village, is Goa's ultimate travellers' hangout. Sitting beneath old trees strung with Tibetan prayer flags and Pipli lanterns, you can consume buckwheat porridge (₹120), *kombucha* tea, wheatgrass and lovely crunchy salads (₹200–300). There is a full menu of Italian, Indian and Tibetan dishes and seafood, and, of course, the bakery's famous cakes and coffee. Daily 8am–11pm.

Laguna Anjuna De Mello Waddo, close to the flea market ☎ 0832 227 4131, ⓦ lagunaanjuna.com. Pretty poolside restaurant in a chic little boutique hotel, offering large Goan fish thalis (₹350) and a full range of Indian delights such as chicken dhansak (₹350) with the other mains at ₹250–500. Daily 8am–11pm.

Martha's Breakfast Home Martha's guesthouse, 907 Monteiro Waddo ☎ 0832 227 3365. Secluded, very friendly breakfast garden serving fresh Indian coffee, crêpes, healthy juices, apple and cinnamon porridge, fruit salads with curd and – the house speciality – melt-in-the-mouth waffles with proper maple syrup (₹300–400). They also have less expensive omelettes, sandwiches and salads. Daily 8–11am.

Villa Blanche Assagao ☎ 98221 55099, ⓦ villablanche -goa.com. A short drive from Anjuna on the road to Mapusa, this great bistro-cum-bakery serves terrific light bites, including smoked salmon bagels with capers (₹350), heavier mains such as German-style beef meatballs (₹400), and everything from healthy sprout salads to home-made ice cream. On Sun it hosts a popular brunch (10am–3pm) which just keeps on giving for ₹700; booking is essential. Mon–Sat 9am–11pm, Sun 10am–4pm.

Xavier's South Anjuna. Nestled in the palm forest just inland from the flea market ground, *Xavier's* has formed the hub of the south Anjuna alternative scene for decades, and is still going strong. Most people come for the seafood, kebabs, tikkas and tandoori dishes (₹200–300), but they also serve tasty Chinese grub. Look for the sign on the left off the market lane. Daily 11am–3pm & 6.30–11pm.

NIGHTLIFE

Anjuna is far from being the rave spot it once was, but at least one big **party** is still held in the area around the Christmas/New Year full-moon period. The rest of the time, serious tranceheads make the trek up to Vagator (see p.182) or Aswem (see p.186).

Curlie's/Shiva Valley South beach, Anjuna. A pair of adjacent shacks that together form the focus of a rather heavy, druggy scene, with large, mixed crowds of both Indian and Western tourists gathering from sunset until 10pm. A small dance area between the two hosts trance parties every Thurs from sunset till very late. Drinks at regular shack prices; admission free. Daily sunset–10pm.

THE DARK SIDE OF THE MOON

Lots of visitors come to Goa expecting to be able to party on the beach every night, and are dismayed when most places to dance turn out to be mainstream clubs they probably wouldn't look twice at back home. The truth is that the full-on, elbows-in-the-air **beach party** of old, when tens of thousands of people would space out to huge techno sound systems under neon-painted palm trees, is – for now – pretty much a thing of the past in Goa.

Goa's coastal villages saw their first big parties back in the 1960s with the influx of hippies to Calangute and Baga. Much to the amazement of the locals, the preferred pastime of these wannabe sadhus was to cavort naked on the sands together on full-moon nights, amid a haze of chillum smoke and loud rock music. At first the villagers took little notice of these bizarre gatherings, but with each season the scene became better established, and by the late 1970s the Christmas and New Year parties, in particular, had become huge events, attracting travellers from all over the country.

In the late 1980s, the local party scene received a dramatic shot in the arm with the coming of Acid House and techno. LSD and ecstasy became the preferred dance drugs as the rock and dub scene gave way to rave culture, with ever-greater numbers of young clubbers pouring in for the season on charter flights. Goa soon spawned its own distinctive brand of psychedelic music, known as **Goa Trance**, cultivated by artists such as Goa Gill, Juno Reactor and Hallucinogen.

The golden era for Goa's party scene, and Goa Trance, was in the early 1990s, when big raves were held two or three times a week in beautiful locations around Anjuna and Vagator. For a few years the authorities turned a blind eye. Then, quite suddenly, the plug was pulled: during the run-up to the Y2K celebrations a ban on amplified music was imposed between 10pm and 7am. Nearly twenty years later, the **curfew** is still officially in place but routinely flaunted: some places pay backhanders to stay open until the early hours, while during an election year it's early to bed for everyone again. Today's **rave scene** is limited to a few established, above-board clubs – notably the *Nine Bar* and *Hilltop* in Vagator (see p.184), and *Marbela Beach* at Aswem (see p.187). The recent drop in foreign tourist numbers, however, has led to talk of the legislation being changed.

SHOPPING

Artjuna House 972 Monteiro Vaddo ☎0832 227 4794, ⓦartjuna.com. Chock full of everything from cute kids' clothes to antique furniture, *Artjuna's* delightful boutique offers an eclectic mix of jewellery by expat designers Moshe and Simona Bassi, as well as tribal adornments from Nagaland. They also do a fantastic collection of women's clothes and create unique leatherwork – all displayed in a lovely Portuguese villa. There's a nice little café too. Daily 8am–10.30pm.

DIRECTORY

Banks and exchange ATMs are clustered along the Mapusa Rd near the Bank of Baroda, which itself will make encashments against Visa cards, but doesn't offer foreign exchange.

Post office The village post office is on the Mapusa Rd near the bank.

Vagator

Barely a couple of kilometres of clifftops and parched grassland separate Anjuna from the southern fringes of **VAGATOR**. Spread around a tangle of winding back lanes, this is a more chilled, undeveloped resort that appeals, in the main, to southern European beach bums who come back year after year.

With the red ramparts of **Chapora fort** looming above it, Vagator's broad sandy beach – known as "Big Vagator" – is undeniably beautiful. However, a peaceful swim or lie on the sand is out of the question here as it's a prime stop for bus parties of domestic tourists. A much better option, though one that still sees more than its fair share of day-trippers, is the next beach south. Backed by a steep wall of crumbling palm-fringed laterite, **Little** (or "Ozran") **Vagator beach** is actually a string of three contiguous coves. To reach them you have to walk from where the buses park above Big Vagator, or drive to the end of the lane running off the main Chapora–Anjuna road (towards the *Nine Bar*), from where footpaths drop sharply down to a wide stretch of level white sand (look for the mopeds and bikes parked at the top of the cliff). Long dominated by Italian tourists, the southernmost – dubbed "Spaghetti Beach" – is the prettiest, with a string of well-established shacks, at the end of which a **face carved out of the rocks**, staring serenely skywards, is the most prominent landmark. Relentless racquetball, trance sound systems and a particularly sizeable herd of stray cows are the other defining features.

ARRIVAL AND INFORMATION

VAGATOR

By bus Buses from Panjim and Mapusa, 9km east, pull in every 15min or so at the crossroads on the far northeastern edge of Vagator, near where the main road peels away towards Chapora. From here, it's a 1km walk over the hill and down the other side to the beach.

Services *Bethany Inn*, on the north side of the village, has a foreign exchange licence (for cash and travellers' cheques), and an efficient travel agency in the office on the ground floor. The nearest ATM is in Anjuna (see p.182).

ACCOMMODATION

Bethany Inn Just south of the main road ☎0832 227 3731 or ☎83222 73731. Eleven immaculate, self-contained rooms with minibar fridges, balconies and attached bathrooms; plus four additional a/c options in a new block, with big TVs, larger balconies and more spacious tiled bathrooms (₹2600). ₹850

★**Boon's Ark** Near Bethany Inn ☎0832 2274045 or ☎98221 75620, ⓦboonsark.com. Honest, clean, family-run place offering modern rooms with excellent beds, stone shelves, fridges and pleasant little verandas opening on a well-tended courtyard garden. Owners Peter and Jessie Hungu also offer room service, money exchange and bikes to rent. A/c ₹500 extra. ₹1800

Dolrina Vagator Beach Rd ☎0832 227 4896. Nestled under a lush canopy of trees near the beach, Vagator's largest budget guesthouse, although showing its age, has attached and non-attached rooms, a couple of larger family options, individual safe deposits and roof space. Single rates are available, and breakfast can be served in your room. ₹450/₹800

★**Jackie's Daynite** Beach Rd ☎0832 227 4320 or ☎98221 33789. The best all-round budget place in the village, perfectly placed within easy reach of both the *Nine Bar* and *Hilltop*. Jackie De Souza has been running a café and shop here for almost forty years, and added rooms behind. They're clean and great value, though often booked up, so reserve in advance. A/c ₹700 extra. ₹800

Vista Mare Little Vagator clifftop ☎98221 20980, ⓦvistamarevagator.com. Lovely big rooms behind a (quiet-ish) restaurant on the clifftop, boasting a/c, king-size beds, spacious attached bathrooms, marble-topped tables and huge verandas. A top location and good value, they also have a six-person room for ₹4000. ₹2500

Yellow House Big Vagator ☎98221 25869. Henriquita Moniz and son Jubert renovated this guesthouse behind Big Vagator beach, which now looks better than ever after more than twenty years in business. It's peaceful and secluded, despite the proximity of the surf, and the rooms are neat and pleasantly furnished. A/c ₹500 extra. ₹1000

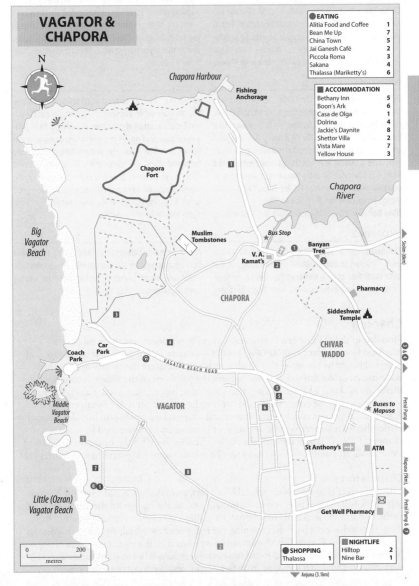

VAGATOR & CHAPORA

N

Chapora Harbour

Fishing Anchorage

EATING
Alitia Food and Coffee	1
Bean Me Up	7
China Town	5
Jai Ganesh Café	2
Piccola Roma	3
Sakana	4
Thalassa (Mariketty's)	6

ACCOMMODATION
Bethany Inn	5
Boon's Ark	6
Casa de Olga	1
Dolrina	4
Jackie's Daynite	8
Shettor Villa	2
Vista Mare	7
Yellow House	3

Chapora Fort

Chapora River

Big Vagator Beach

Muslim Tombstones

Bus Stop

Banyan Tree

V. A. Kamat's

CHAPORA

Pharmacy

Siddeshwar Temple

CHIVAR WADDO

Coach Park

Car Park

VAGATOR BEACH ROAD

VAGATOR

Buses to Mapusa

Middle Vagator Beach

St Anthony's   ATM

Little (Ozran) Vagator Beach

Get Well Pharmacy

0   200
metres

Salim (6km)

Petrol Pump

Mapusa (9km)   Petrol Pump & ⓐ

SHOPPING
Thalassa	1

NIGHTLIFE
Hilltop	2
Nine Bar	1

Anjuna (3.1km)

3

EATING

Bean Me Up Near the petrol pump ☎ 0832 227 3479, ⓦ beanmeup.in. North Goa's only raw and vegan joint – the last word in Goan gourmet healthy eating. Design-your-own salads and fresh juices, various tofu, tempeh and seitan combos steeped in creamy sauces, and pizzas from a real wood-fired oven. Mains (₹180–300) come with steamed spinach, fresh brown bread and hygienically washed greens. Daily 8am–11pm.

China Town Chapora crossroads, next to Bethany Inn ☎ 98221 42230. This small roadside restaurant, tucked away just south of the main drag, is perennially popular for its budget eats. The menu includes tasty Goan seafood dishes (₹200–250) in addition to a large Chinese selection and all the usual Goa-style travellers' grub. Daily 9am–11pm.

★ Thalassa (Mariketty's) Ozran clifftop ☎ 98500 33537, ⓦ thalassagoa.com. Stylish and hospitable, *Thalassa* serves high-end, flavoursome and scrupulously authentic Greek cooking with excellent service, against a backdrop of swaying palms and rippling ocean. Try and get there in time for the stunning sunset from the large (and popular) terrace. Especially recommended are the kebabs – you can often see them spit-roasting a whole lamb as you enter. Count on ₹1000 for three courses plus drinks; double that if you have seafood. Booking essential. Daily 9am–11.30pm.

NIGHTLIFE

Hilltop Vagator ☎ 96047 72788, ⓦ facebook.com /hilltopgoa. *Hilltop*'s big night is Sun, when bumper crowds take to its pretty, circular dancefloor, set in a coconut grove just back from the clifftop. The PA is heavy duty, the palm trunks painted regulation neon, chai mamas ring the arena with their flickering kerosene lamps and freshly baked nibbles, and overseas DJs do the honours on stage. They also host their own night market on Fri. Admission ₹1000–1500, though occasionally free. Fri & Sun 4–10pm.

Nine Bar Above Small Vagator beach ☎ 96231 02102, ⓦ club9bar.com. The spiritual home of Goa trance, where you can space out on a large open-air dancefloor as the sun sets behind a curtain of palm trees and DJs spin beats from a chest-thumping rig. It's got a very welcoming vibe and admission is free – but note that photography is strictly prohibited. They play trance every Mon, with different dance genres on one or two other nights a week during the season. During the day it serves food, including a very good Greek breakfast (₹300). Daily 9am–sunset for food; 5pm–sunrise on party nights.

SHOPPING

Thalassa Ozran clifftop ☎ 98500 33537, ⓦ thalassagoa .com. Attached to the popular Greek restaurant of the same name (see above), this boutique offers a range of stylish beach and evening wear, from beautiful floaty dresses to hand-made textiles. There is also a selection from resident designer Martino Caramia, who favours light cotton and bright colours – perfect attire for sipping sangria sundowners. Daily 11am–11pm.

Chapora

Huddled in the shadow of a Portuguese fort on the opposite, northern side of the headland from Vagator is **CHAPORA**, north Goa's main fishing port. The anchorage and boatyard below its brown-walled citadel – where you can see the mostly now disused boats drawn up on the shore – used to form the backbone of the village's economy, but there's always been a hard-drinking, heavy-smoking hippie tourist scene alongside it, revolving around the coffee shops and bars on the main street. For a brief period a few years back, Russian mafia types took over and squeezed the freaks out, but like migrating turtles they've returned to their old hangout in numbers undiminished by Goa's recent changes. Today Chapora remains the commuter dormitory for the freaks on the party scene in Vagator and Anjuna – many rent houses or rooms long-term here year after year.

Chapora fort

Chapora's chief landmark is its venerable old **fort**, most easily reached from the Vagator side of the hill. At low tide, you can also walk around the bottom of the headland, via the anchorage and the secluded coves beyond it to Big Vagator, then head up the hill from there. The red-laterite bastion, crowning the rocky bluff, was built by the Portuguese in 1617 on the site of an earlier Muslim structure (thus the village's name – from Shahpura, "town of the Shah"). Deserted in the nineteenth century, it lies in ruins today, although the views up and down the coast from the weed-infested ramparts are still superb.

ARRIVAL AND DEPARTURE

CHAPORA

By bus Buses run between Chapora and Panjim (3 daily), and from Mapusa (every 15min), with departures until 7.30pm. Most drop passengers at the old banyan tree at the far end of the main street, where the motorcycle pilots all hang out.

ACCOMMODATION

Chapora specializes in **long-term rentals** of rooms and houses (by the week or month) to repeat visitors; these economical options can be found by asking around the village.

Casa de Olga 📞0832 227 4355 or 📞98221 57145, ✉eadsouza@yahoo.co.in. By far the most comfortable guesthouse in Chapora, this immaculate, red-and-white-painted little place, near the fishing anchorage, is run with great efficiency and enthusiasm by hosts Edmund and Elisa. Their nicest rooms are in a new block to the rear, which are all attached and have good-sized balconies; the cheaper, non-attached alternatives are at the front. No wi-fi. ₹500/₹900

Shettor Villa Off the west side of the main street 📞0832 227 3766 or 📞98221 58154, ✉brianlive@hotmail.com. More basic than *Casa de Olga*, with five attached rooms with fans, ranged around a sheltered backyard; there's also a (sometimes noisy) rooftop restaurant where you can use the wi-fi. ₹500

EATING

Alitia Food and Coffee On the main street 📞90499 97468. Chapora's main street is a bit of a low-key bar-hopping zone most nights for locals and foreign residents; this tiny shack is a good place to refuel on tasty crêpes, waffles and toasties (₹130–200), made with fresh or imported ingredients like mozzarella, chorizo and smoked ham. Outstanding coffee, too. Daily dusk–dawn.

Jai Ganesh Café Just up from the banyan tree. The focal point of the tourist scene, where Chapora's resident Westerners watch the world go by over fresh fruit juices and milkshakes (₹50–80) and perhaps a cheese or chocolate croissant (₹60). Daily 8am–sunset.

Piccola Roma 1km southwest of Chapora on the Mapusa Rd 📞75078 06821. One of the few restaurants in the area that stays open year-round, this Indian-run joint serves very good Italian food, with particularly good wood-oven pizzas (₹180–500) and steak with porcini sauce (₹400). They also deliver within 5km (₹50). Daily noon–11pm.

Sakana 1km southwest of Chapora on the Mapusa Rd, opposite Piccola Roma 📞98901 35502. Generally considered one of the best Japanese places in Goa, this smart and stylish joint decorated with paper lanterns and red tablecloths serves fresh sashimi (from ₹400), veg and non-veg sushi (₹200–370) and a set menu of tuna teriyaki (₹480). Daily noon–midnight.

Morjim

Relatively isolated, the village of **MORJIM** was where Goa's first Russian tourists headed in the early noughties. Once dubbed "Morjimograd" by other foreign visitors, it's now returned (thanks to the crash of the ruble) to a more mixed resort, attracting more middle-aged Brits and Indians than Russians. That said, the atmosphere in the guesthouses and restaurants along and behind the beach can feel less than friendly (probably as few Russians speak any English), and most Western travellers find the experience of staying here disconcerting – not to mention eye-wateringly expensive. Many prefer to continue north to the more culturally mixed resorts of Aswem and Mandrem.

Morjim beach itself is dramatic and well worth at least a walk, especially in the early morning, when you may see teams of fishermen hauling giant handnets from the surf. The spit at its southern end, opposite Chapora fort, is also a great birding hot spot.

ARRIVAL AND DEPARTURE

MORJIM

By bus Half a dozen buses a day skirt Morjim en route to Panjim, the first at 7am; heading the other way, you can pick up a direct bus from Panjim at 5pm, and there are hourly services from Mapusa via Siolim after 11am. They'll drop you on the main road, a 5min walk from the beachfront area at Vithaldas Waddo.

ACCOMMODATION

Because of the unwelcoming vibe, the hotels and guesthouses immediately behind the beach, in the dunes and along the beachfront road, are best avoided. One really nice option, however, stands on the riverfront south of the village.

★Jardin d'Ulysse Facing the riverbank on the village's south side ☎98225 81928, ✉ulyssemorjim@gmail.com. Delightful Goan/French-run place comprising five a/c "cottages" with tiled roofs, ochre-washed floors and kitchenettes. Down in the front garden, a small restaurant whips up an eclectic menu of steaks, scrumptious lasagne, Tibetan *momos* and salads for mostly French and British travellers – at least ₹400–500/head for a meal without drinks. Owners Fleur and Gilbert are charming hosts, always on hand to help arrange excursions, boat trips and scooters. ₹3000

EATING

★Sublime Morjim beach ☎98224 84051, ⓦfacebook.com/SublimeMorjim. Run by celebrity chef Chris Saleem Agha Bee, this funky little gastro beach shack in the heart of Morjim rustles up stylish, innovative cuisine deploying novel combos of fresh local ingredients: try the fish carpaccio (₹290) or ginger batter calamari (₹290) for starters, and Asiatic beef with wasabi mashed potatoes (₹550) or nut-crusted white fish with nori sesame stuffing (₹440) for mains. Ample veggie options include the popular mega organic salad (₹350). Booking essential. Daily noon–3pm & 6–11pm.

Aswem

Pretty **ASWEM**, the next settlement north of Morjim, could hardly be described as a proper resort. Officially inside the Coastal Protection Zone, its beachfront holds few permanent buildings and most of the accommodation is in temporary structures. And yet, over the past few seasons, the strip of soft white sand nestled beneath its *mand* of slender palms has become the place to see and be seen by India's seriously cool set – Mumbai millionaires, Bollywood A-listers and international celebs are regularly spotted in the swanky resorts and clubs in the dunes. A more down-to-earth scene holds sway around the headland to the south, which is family friendly, with lots of children playing on the beach. How long this stretch can hold out against the rising tide of bling, however, is anyone's guess.

ARRIVAL AND DEPARTURE   ASWEM

By bus Buses from Panjim (3 daily; 1hr 30min) cover the quiet stretch of road running parallel to the beach inland, from where a 5min walk across paddy fields brings you to the shacks and hut camps attached to them. More frequent buses can be caught from the stop 2km away in Morjim.

ACCOMMODATION

With accommodation either ultrabasic or staggeringly expensive, most visitors ride up to Aswem for the day on scooters and decamp after sunset. A handful of places, however, offer reasonable **value**.

Anahata ☎98225 90123, ⓦanahataretreat.com. This spot, in the coconut plantation under the Ajoba temple just north of *La Plage* restaurant, is arguably the finest nook on the coast hereabouts. The place holds eleven octagonal huts made from dark mango wood. The cheapest are in the garden, with some on the beach (₹9000) and others with sea views (₹11000). They're large, well spaced, have wraparound verandas, and are naturally cross-ventilated, with quality beds and simple, relaxing decor. There is also a yoga space and a great restaurant and lounge area on the beach. ₹7500

Leela Cottages Near La Plage ☎0840 792 4040, ⓦleelacottage.com. Beautiful designer huts (all a/c) of various sizes and prices (up to ₹1300), grouped in a gated property under the palms. The interiors are furnished with antiques collected from all over India. It's just a stone's throw from the beach, but far enough away from the restaurants to remain peaceful and quiet (and free from cooking smells). ₹7000

Nifa Aswem Morjim Rd, opposite the Madji Organic Café ☎0832 224 4400 or ☎98221 33370, ⓦhotelnifa.com. A cheaper alternative set back on the roadside inland, *Nifa* has clean, comfortable, fan and a/c (₹200 more) rooms as well as sea-facing options (₹400 extra) a short walk from the beach. There is a small pool on site. ₹1200

Otter Creek ☎98200 37387, ⓦaseascape.com. You have to cross a rickety footbridge to reach these luxury tents, nestled on the riverbank just behind the dunes, in the thick of a coconut plantation. Each is fitted with a bamboo four-poster, bathroom, veranda and jetty on the river. €103

★Yab Yum ☎0832 651 0392, ⓦyabyumresorts.com. A campus of beautiful domed structures made from palm thatch, mango wood and laterite, with curvy moulded concrete floors and walls painted pale purple. Large and attractively furnished inside, the rooms have beds on platforms and comfy mattresses, glitter balls, paper lanterns and muslin drapes – though such alt-chic comes at a price (up to ₹8100 for suites). ₹5000

EATING

Gopal Just south of La Plage ☎ 98221 47416. Once the only shack on Aswem beach, now almost hidden by its more famous neighbour *La Plage*, *Gopal* still commands a loyal following of customers who want simple Indian food. It offers a typical Goan menu – fish/prawn curry rice and a bit of everything from all over the world – with meals costing around ₹300–400. Daily 8am–10pm.

★ **La Plage** Aswem beach ☎ 98221 21712. Nestled in a shady coconut grove and with very comfy seats, *La Plage* does a brisk trade in cool Gallic-Mediterranean snacks and drinks, served up by Nepali waiters in black *lunghis*. The menu changes a little each season but expect marinated kingfish gravlax (₹320), their signature hamburger (₹450), seared rare tuna (₹490) and, last but not least, a tempting chocolate thali offering five choco-rich desserts (₹670; it's not obligatory to share). Booking essential for dinner and Sun lunch. Daily 8.30am–11pm.

Maa Raw and Vegan Café Leela Cottages, near La Plage ☎ 0840 792 4040, ⓦ leelacottage.com. If you've never tried raw or vegan food, this is the place to start. Sandwiches, salads, burritos, lasagne and pizzas are beautifully presented and delicious; especially good is the Tesero zucchini pasta with creamy cashew sauce. About ₹500/head with a coffee. Daily 11am–3pm & 6–10pm.

Pink Orange Just south of La Plage ☎ 91688 26747. A great place to chill out, with low seating and comfy cushions. They serve up tasty breakfasts featuring pesto omelettes and a range of locally made cheeses (₹240), as well as a great choice of salads (₹250–450), thalis (₹200–250) and delicious home-made pesto gnocchi (₹220). Hosts Alex and Jai also run *Café Esperanto* on the roadside, which stays open during monsoon. As Jai doubles as a DJ, you can expect chilled beats and the odd daytime party here. Daily 9am–10pm.

Roma Aswem beach road, before Anahata ☎ 0832 227 5126. Pretty, Italian-run garden restaurant with delicious wood-fired pizzas (₹260–350), and an interesting (and similarly priced) selection of home-made pastas, including very good ravioli with mushroom sauce. A cut above the usual Italian dishes, and they have a children's play area too. Daily 11am–11pm.

NIGHTLIFE

Aswem has emerged as a new face of Goan nightlife, with a few chic beachfront **clubs** where you can jump off the dancefloor straight on to the sand. In addition to *Marbela Beach* there are a couple of other choices – such as *Club Fresh* – but whether they are good or not depends very much on which crew are on the decks in any one year.

Marbela Beach Aswem ⓦ marbelabeach.com. Probably the chicest club in Goa, this white-themed resort on the beachfront features a lounge bar, champagne bar and three open-air dancefloors blasting dance mixes into the night air from outsized PAs. Admission is usually free (unless they have a big-name international DJ), with drinks at ₹250–300 for beers or ₹350–500 for shots and cocktails. Daily 9pm–3am or later.

SHOPPING

Jade Jagger Aswem beach, south of La Plage. Aswem is renowned for its designer boutiques. This place features beautifully chic and eye-wateringly expensive beach creations from the renowned designer, with floaty dresses and jewellery set with precious stones. Thurs–Tues noon–6.30pm.

Mandrem

From the far side of the creek bounding the edge of Aswem, a magnificent and largely empty beach stretches north towards Arambol – the last unspoiled stretch of the north Goan coast. Whether or not **MANDREM** can continue to hold out against the developers remains to be seen, but for the time being, nature still has the upper hand here. Olive ridley marine **turtles** nest on the quietest patches, and you're more than likely to catch a glimpse of one of the white-bellied **fish eagles** that live in the casuarina trees – their last stronghold in the north of Goa.

ARRIVAL AND INFORMATION   MANDREM

By bus Connected by regular buses from Mapsua (9 daily; 1hr 30min), the market area at Madlamaz is easy to reach by public transport, but getting to the beach area is trickier as auto-rickshaws are few and far between. Ask your guesthouse or hut camp for help.

Services A couple of small grocery stores, internet cafés, ATMs and travel agents are on hand.

ACCOMMODATION

Most of the village's accommodation is tucked away inland at **Junasa Waddo**, where a growing number of small guesthouses, hotels and **yoga retreats** cater to a mixed, peace-and-quiet-loving crowd – costs are generally higher than at Arambol (see below), however.

Ashiyana Junasa Waddo ⓦ ashiyana-yoga-goa.com. If you like your yoga retreats to be drop-dead gorgeous, look no further than here. Perched on the banks of the Mandrem River facing the sea from the middle of an old coconut *mand*, the centre offers world-class yoga, massage, meditation and satsang tuition with accommodation in Indonesian-style boutique treehouses and ecolodges. Some of them boast glorious sea views, and there's a wholefood-Ayurvedic-veg restaurant on site (guests only). Rates include workshops and full board. Per person/day €70

Mandala Just upriver from Ashiyana ⓣ 96578 98021, ⓦ themandalagoa.com. Beautifully painted murals adorn the buildings at *Mandala*, a "back-to-nature boutique resort".

You can stay in the main house with all mod cons and a/c (₹4500), in beautiful two-tier bamboo chalets based on the design of Keralan houseboats (₹5500) or in more basic fan-cooled beach huts. It's close to the beach, but there's no direct road access. Yoga classes available. ₹2200

Villa River Cat ⓣ 0822 224 7928 or ⓣ 98236 10001, ⓦ villarivercat.com. Quirky riverside hotel, screened from the beach by the dunes, with distinctive hippie-influenced decor and furniture. The sixteen rooms (up to ₹5000) are all individually designed: mosaics, shells, devotional sculpture and hammocks set the tone. Host Rinoo Seghal is an animal-lover, so brace yourself for the menagerie of cats and dogs. ₹4000

EATING

★**Café Nu** Junnaswada, small track before D'Souzas Residency ⓣ 98506 58568. Lovely open-sided restaurant in a pretty garden, serving sublime, light gourmet bites. There are plenty of fish dishes (₹400–500), the famous house hamburger (₹380; lunchtime only) and, for the health-conscious, a copious organic salad (₹260). The bon bon dessert (₹220) is legendary around these parts. Booking essential for dinner. Daily 11.30–2.30pm & 6–10.30pm.

O'Saiba Mandrem beach. Great views from this beach shack, which serves up high-quality versions of the usual Indian and tandoori food. Expect delicious seafood including *hariyali* fish tikka with fresh mint sauce (₹250), a flavoursome *palak paneer* (₹200) and a fair number of Western favourites. Daily 7am–11pm.

Arambol

ARAMBOL, 32km northwest of Mapusa, is easily the most populous village in the far north, and the area's main tourist hub. Traditionally a refuge for a hard-core hippie fringe, it nowadays attracts a lively and eclectic mix of travellers, the majority of whom stick around for the season, living in rented rooms, hut camps and small houses scattered behind the magnificent white sand beach. As in most of north Goa, there's also a showing of young, often quite alternative, Russians here, joining the spiritually inclined types from northern Europe who have long formed Arambol's mainstay. The overall vibe is inclusive and positive, with plenty of **live music**, lots of relaxed places to eat and drink, and more opportunities to learn new **yoga** poses and reshuffle your chakras than you could get through in several lifetimes. Beach life is generally laidback too – except on weekends, when day-tripping drinkers descend en masse in SUVs from nearby Maharashtra.

The village and beaches

Arambol's main drag is a winding road lined cheek-by-jowl with clothes and bedspread stalls, travel agents, internet cafés and souvenir shops. The lane bends downhill to the **main beach** – one of the most picturesque in South India, dotted with wooden outriggers. The best view of it is from the crucifix and small **Parasurama shrine** on the hilltop to the north, which is an especially serene spot at sunset. **After dark**, when the Hula-Hoopers, fire jugglers and *bhajan* singers have turned homewards, the candles and fairy lights of the shacks illuminate the beachfront to magical effect.

Swimming is possible here during the daytime, but less inspiring than around the headland at Paliem or "Lakeside" beach, reached by following the track through a series of rocky-bottomed coves. The path emerges at a broad strip of soft white sand hemmed in by cliffs. Behind here a small freshwater lake extends along the bottom of the valley into the jungle, lined with sulphurous mud, which, when smeared over the body, dries to form a surreal, butter-coloured shell.

Keep following the path around the back of the lake and you'll soon come to Paliem's famous **banyan tree**, a monster specimen with giant runners extending more than 60m – a popular chillum-smoking spot. Keen walkers can continue over the cliffs immediately north – Arambol's prime parascending venue – to reach the generally quiet **Kerim beach**.

ARRIVAL AND DEPARTURE ARAMBOL

By bus Buses run between Panjim and Arambol, via Mapusa's main town stand, every 30min until noon, and every 90min till 8pm, terminating at the small bus stop on the main road in Arambol. A faster private minibus service from Panjim bus stand arrives daily opposite the chai stalls at the beach end of the village. If you're heading for the Chapora/Vagator/Anjuna area, taking the same bus to Siolim and taking a taxi (₹300) or rickshaw (₹200) from there will save you changing at Mapusa.

By taxi Taxis charge ₹1500–1650 for the run from Dabolim airport to Arambol, and ₹700–800 for the 30min trip from the nearest railhead at Tivim (Thivim).

ACCOMMODATION		EATING	
Arun Huts	3	Cheeky Monkey	6
Atman	5	Double Dutch	7
Famafa	2	Dylan's (Toasted and Roasted)	9
Go-Ym	6	Eyes of Buddha	1
Ivon's	4	Fellini's	4
Om Ganesh		Lamuella	5
Cottages	1	Relax Inn	3
Surf Club	7	Rice Bowl	2
		Sai Deep	8

SHOPPING	
Lamuella	1

NIGHTLIFE	
Ash	1
Surf Club	2

ACTIVITIES

Posters pinned to palm trees and café noticeboards around Arambol advertise an amazing array of activities, from **kitesurfing** to **reiki**. Good places to get a fix on what's happening are the noticeboard at *Lamuella* (see p.191) and *Double Dutch*'s "Bullshit Info" corner (see p.190), which displays details for just about everyone who does anything – including their own popular *dokra* bronze-casting workshops, held annually each January.

YOGA IN ARAMBOL

Yogis and **yoga classes** are ubiquitous in Arambol, and of varying quality. Here are two of our favourites.

Sharat Yoga Modlo Waddo ⓦ hiyogacentre.com. Iyengar yoga teacher Sharat holds five-day classes (Nov–March, courses start on Mon; ₹5000) in his studio. Prospective students should sign up at the centre from 1–3pm. To find it, head for the *Priya Guest House* and follow the "HIYC" signs from there.

Viriam Kaur's Kundalini Yoga Kundalini Rooftop Garden, Girkar Waddo ⓦ organickarma.co.uk. These classes, held in the leafy rooftop garden, have a strong following – not least because it's among the few places in India where you can learn Kundalini yoga. Also trained in Western and Ayurvedic massage, Viriam and her partner Adam Divine offer individual sessions and training, plus workshops and courses on chakra healing and other therapeutic techniques.

Dance Temple of Dance, Girkar Waddo, signposted off the road close to the Kundalini Rooftop Garden, offers tribal fusion to contemporary, salsa, Bollywood and belly dance styles, and hosts a festival (Feb 9–11) with workshops and performances.

Paragliding Tandem rides from the clifftops above Lakeside beach, run by an ever-changing combination of Indian and international fliers. Costs include all equipment and full instruction. For more information, go to the Western India Paragliding Association shack, just in front of the lake.

ACCOMMODATION

The **cost** of accommodation in Arambol has risen sharply over the past few seasons, reflecting the village's popularity with more affluent hippies, but it's still nearly all pitched at budget travellers: no-frills, Goan-run guesthouses and expat-inspired hippie-chic predominate here.

Arun Huts Near Narayan Temple ☎ 98500 96468. Quirky little hut camp, run by local beautician, Mrs Mala Singh, in the thick of Arambol village. Just 60m from the sea, it comprises two rows of neatly painted wood huts, fitted with decent mattresses, attached shower toilets and fans. The whole earth-floored compound is smothered in banana trees, palms and flowers, and very atmospheric, especially in the evening. Good value but no wi-fi. ₹1000

Atman Girkar Waddo ☎ 86988 80135, ⊕ atmangoa .com. Lovely bamboo-and-wood tree huts on the south side of the beach, prettily thatched and decorated with coco mats, colourful sari drapes, original fractal-fluoro wall hangings and bolsters on their spacious sitout areas. Smiling Italian-Indian owners, Michaela and Sunil, also run a yoga space and courses and small boutique, as well as a restaurant. ₹2000

Famafa Khalcha Waddo ☎ 75078 59842, ⊕ famafa arambolgoa.com. Large, anodyne concrete place just off the main drag; very close to the beach and great value. One of the few places with hot showers. They don't take bookings and operate a 10am checkout, so get here early for a room. ₹1600

Go-Ym Bag Waddo, close to Atman ☎ 89751 54961, ⊕ go-ym.com. Large mid-range resort with twelve tiled, vibrantly coloured cottages close to the beach. The taste-fully decorated rooms have comfortable beds. ₹2500

Ivon's Girkar Waddo ☎ 0832 224 2672 or ☎ 98221 27398. The pick of the budget bunch: immaculately clean, tiled rooms, all with attached bathroom (with hot water) some fronted by good-sized tiled balconies opening onto the dunes or a well-groomed family compound. Wi-fi in their restaurant next door. ₹800

Om Ganesh Cottages In the cove between the village and Lakeside beach ☎ 94212 57688, or book at the Om Ganesh stores on the main drag ☎ 0832 229 7614. The most desirable of the cottages stacked up the cliffside just south of Lakeside beach, with superb sea views from the verandas. Rates vary wildly according to demand, and advance booking (with a deposit) is all but essential by mid-season. ₹600

Surf Club South end of the beach ☎ 98505 54006, ⊕ surfclubgoa.com. Simple, clean, very good value rooms at the quietest end of the beach, with excellent bedding and hot water. The rooms upstairs (₹1600) are much larger and lighter than those downstairs; they also have an annexe with even better eco-cottages (₹3000). ₹1200

EATING

Thanks to its annually replenished pool of expat **gastronomic talent**, Arambol harbours a handful of unexpectedly good restaurants – not that you'd guess from their generally lacklustre exteriors. The village's alternative, Western European contingent cares more about flavours than fancy decor, and prices in the village reflect this. The more affluent short-term visitors, meanwhile, tend to gravitate towards the fancier seafood joints along the beachfront, where the day's catch is displayed on cold trays for selection, then grilled alfresco in front of you. Prices can be eye-popping, so get a quote before you order.

Cheeky Monkey Arambol beach ☎ 98508 23926. A cut above your average beach shack, offering a great variety of salads, home-made pastas and stir-fried noodle dishes. Try the warm beetroot salad (₹180), mushroom ravioli (₹210) and the only dessert on the menu, a knockout chocolate pudding with cinnamon ice cream (₹250). Daily 9am–11pm.

★ **Double Dutch** Main St, halfway down on the right (look for the yellow signboard) ☎ 70838 89420. Spread under a palm canopy in the heart of the village, this laidback café is the hub of alternative Arambol. Renowned for its melt-in-the-mouth apple pie (₹210), it also offers a tempting range of home-baked buttery biscuits, cakes, healthy salads (₹110–230) and sumptuous main meals (from ₹210), including fresh

buffalo steaks (₹290–440), Indonesian noodles (₹250) and perennially popular "mixed stuff" (stuffed mushrooms and capsicums with sesame pesto; ₹320). Daily 7am–11pm.

Dylan's (Toasted and Roasted) Behind Kinara restaurant and Golden Hands jewellers ☎ 96047 80316. Owner Raj insists that it's not *just* about the coffee and the cookies, but both are exceptional – he also sells ground coffee and beans. In the evening, as well as serving a decent veg thali (₹150), he hosts regular concerts and art shows (see opposite). Mon–Sat 9am–11pm.

Eyes of Buddha North end of beach ☎ 80073 83755. Enduringly popular travellers' hangout in a perfect spot overlooking the main beach. It's renowned above all for its mountainous fruit salad and curd breakfasts, and they serve up great North Indian food, tandoori fish (₹250) and a few local Goan dishes, too: try the succulent *paneer* (₹180) and chicken kebabs (₹250) with hot naan bread. Daily 8am–11pm.

Fellini's Main St. Italian-run place serving delicious wood-fired pizzas (₹230–350), and authentic pasta or gnocchi with a choice of more than twenty sauces. It gets horrendously busy in season, so get here early if you want snappy service. Daily 11am–11pm.

★**Lamuella** Main St ☎98224 86314. Hiding behind the boutique of the same name, *Lamuella* serves healthy breakfasts, toasties, hummus plates and filling salads during the day, as well as energizing juice combos and herb teas. After sunset you can order from an eclectic menu with amazing home-made mushroom ravioli and grilled fish (₹420), with chocolate fondant ice cream for dessert (₹150). Daily 8.30am–11pm.

Relax Inn North end of beach. Top-quality seafood straight off the boats, and authentic pasta (you get even more expat Italians in here than at *Fellini's*) – try the *vongole* (clam) sauce. Inexpensive (most mains around ₹200–300), but expect a wait as they cook to order. Daily 8–10.30pm.

Rice Bowl North end of beach ☎0832 651 0856. This cliffside place serves the best Chinese food in Arambol, with a perfect view of the beach to match, and a pool table (₹120/hr). Any of their tasty noodle dishes are safe bets, as are the Japanese and Tibetan specialities (₹150–350). Daily 8am–11pm.

Sai Deep At the bottom end of the village ☎90490 51266. This little *dhaba* is noted among those in this stretch and has a devoted following. They serve copious fruit salads as well as a good travellers' breakfast menu of pancakes, eggs and curd all at rock-bottom prices – the veg thali is a mere ₹70. Daily 8.30am–8.30pm.

NIGHTLIFE

Many of the shacks on the beach have occasional live music, though **Dylan's** (see opposite) has the most going on, with some kind of (usually) low-key performance most nights.

Ash Girkar Waddo ☎98225 83584. With amazing art work, this Russian-run open-air venue hosts two or three events a week during the season, with everything from Russian shamanic singers to gypsy folk musicians and Sufi bands – the musicianship is of a consistently high standard. Event nights only 6.30–11pm.

Surf Club South end of the beach ☎98505 54006, ⓦ surfclubgoa.com. Secret little hippie drinking establishment decorated with some trippy tiles, this place has a great vibe and hosts some very good psychedelic rock acts every week or so on its small stage. Daily 8am–10pm.

SHOPPING

Lamuella Opposite Shiv Krupa Store, Main St. In the heart of Arambol, *Lamuella* holds a great collection of clothes for women and children – with a few options for men – mostly from expat local designers. They also stock beautiful jewellery for every budget and homeware from fair-trade collectives in India. There's a café in the back garden (see above). Daily 10am–10pm.

DIRECTORY

Banks and exchange There is an ATM close to the bus stand, and several places along the main village lane change money and do cash advances on debit and credit cards: try SS Travels opposite Om Ganesh General Store.

Post office On the east side of the village, 1km out on the Querim–Arambol–Agarwada Rd, just before the petrol pump.

South Goa

Backed by a lush band of coconut plantations and green hills, Goa's south coast is fringed by some of the region's finest **beaches**. An ideal first base if you've just arrived in the region is **Benaulim**, 6km west of the state's second city, **Margao**. The most traveller-friendly resort in the area, Benaulim stands slap in the middle of a spectacular 25km stretch of pure white sand. Although increasingly carved up by Mumbai time-share companies, low-cost accommodation here remains plentiful and of a consistently high standard. Nearby **Colva**, by contrast, has degenerated over the past decade into an insalubrious sink resort. Frequented by huge numbers of day-trippers, and boasting few discernible charms, it's best avoided.

With the gradual spread of package tourism down the coast, **Palolem**, a ninety-minute drive south of Margao along the main highway, is Goa's most happening beach, attracting droves of sun seekers from November through March. Set against a backdrop of forest-cloaked hills, its bay is spectacular, though the crowds can feel overwhelming in high season. For a quieter scene, try **Agonda**, just up the coast, or **Patnem**, immediately south of Palolem. Among the possible day-trips inland, a crop of Portuguese-era mansions at **Chandor** and **Quepem** are your best options; and in the far south, the **Cotigao Wildlife Sanctuary** affords a rare glimpse of unspoiled forest and its fauna.

Margao

The capital of prosperous Salcete *taluka*, **MARGAO** – referred to in railway timetables and on some maps by its official government title, **Madgaon** – is Goa's second city, and if you're arriving in the state on the Konkan Railway, you'll almost certainly have to pause here to pick up onward transport by road. Surrounded by fertile rice paddy and plantain groves, the town has always been an important agricultural market, and was once a major religious centre, with dozens of wealthy temples and *dharamshalas* – however, most of these were destroyed when the Portuguese absorbed the area into their **Novas Conquistas** ("New Conquests") during the seventeenth century. Today, Catholic churches still outnumber Hindu shrines, but Margao has retained a cosmopolitan feel due to a huge influx of migrant labour from neighbouring Karnataka and Maharashtra.

Largo de Igreja and around

It's a short auto-rickshaw ride from the centre to **Largo de Igreja** (Church Square), at the north end of town, where **Church of the Holy Spirit** is the main landmark of Margao's dishevelled colonial enclave. Built by the Portuguese in 1675, the church ranks among the finest examples of late Baroque architecture in Asia, with an interior dominated by a huge gilt reredos dedicated to the Virgin.

Just northeast, overlooking the main Ponda road, stands one of the state's grandest eighteenth-century *palacios*, **Sat Burzam Ghor** ("Seven Gables house"). Just three of its original seven high-pitched roof gables remain, but the mansion is still an impressive sight, its facade decorated with fancy scrollwork and huge oyster-shell windows.

Market area

Colonial-era vestiges aside, the main reason to come to Margao is to shop at the town's **market**, the hub of which is a labyrinthine covered area and shopping centre, and the open-air **Gandhi Market** just south. Just up the road, on the southeast side of the town's hectic main square, **Praça Jorge Barreto**, stands the little government-run **Khadi Gramodyog** shop, which sells the usual range of hand-spun cottons and raw silk by the metre, as well as ready-made traditional Indian garments.

MARGAO

O & Kadamba Bus Stand

Pilar, Sat Burzam Ghor, Largo de Igreja, Lutolim & Ponda

DA COSTA ROAD
M MENEZES ROAD
MIGUEL LOYOLA FURTADO ROAD
Mumbai, Colva & Benaulim

Praça Jorge Barreto

Khadi Gramodyog
Bank of Baroda & ATM

Lorenzo Mall (HDFC Bank & ATM)

Municipal Building

Buses for Panolem & Benaulim

LUIS MIRANDA ROAD

(i)

State Bank of India

Hindu Pharmacy

New Market

IGNACIO DE LOYOLA RD

Bobcards & Bank of Baroda

Gandhi Market

Railway Station (Madgaon) & Karnataka

Vasco da Gama

0   100
metres

BHARATKA HEGDE DESAI ROAD

Karwar

ACCOMMODATION

| Nanutel | 1 |

EATING

Café Coffee Day	2
Longuinho's	4
Tato	1, 3

ARRIVAL AND DEPARTURE

By train Margao's huge railway station, Madgaon Junction, lies 3km south of the centre, its reservation office (Mon–Sat 8am–4.30pm, Sun 8am–2pm; ☎0832 271 2940) divided between the ground and first floors. Tickets for trains to Mumbai are in short supply, so make your reservation as far in advance as possible. If you're catching the train to Hosapete (for Hampi) get here early to avoid long queues. Several principal trains stop in Margao at unsociable times of night, but there's a 24hr information counter (☎0832 271 2790) and a round-the-clock prepaid auto-rickshaw and taxi stand outside the exit.

Destinations Canacona/Chaudi (6–7 daily; 30–45min); Gokarna (2 daily; 1hr 30min–2hr 30min); Hosapete (4 weekly; 7hr); Mangaluru (4–5 daily; 5–6hr); Mumbai (3 daily; 9hr 30min–11hr 50min).

By bus All interstate and state buses arrive at and depart from the Kadamba bus stand, 3km north of the centre, with auto-rickshaws charging around ₹100 to get into town. Buses to destinations on the south coast also stop in front of the *Kamat Hotel*, on the east side of Praça Jorge Barreto. Paulo Travel's deluxe coach to and from Hampi works from a lot 300m or so north of the Kadamba bus stand, on the left just before the large yellow government building.

Destinations Agonda (4 daily; 2hr); Benaulim (every 30min; 15min); Chandor (hourly; 45min); Canacona/Chaudi (every 30min; 1hr 40min); Gokarna (2 daily; 4hr 30min); Hampi (1 nightly; 10hr); Mangalaru (5 daily; 7hr); Mapusa (10 daily; 2hr 30min); Mumbai (2 daily; 16–18hr); Panjim (every 30min; 50min); Panolem (every 30min; 2hr); Pune (1 daily; 12hr).

ACCOMMODATION

Nanutel Rua Padre Miranda ☎0832 270 0900, ⊕nanu hotels.in. With Colva and Benaulim so close, it's hard to think of a reason why you'd want to stay in Margao, but if you're stuck then this three-star multistorey block, north of Praça Jorge Barreto, is a possibility. Pitched at visiting businesspeople, it has 55 comfortable central a/c rooms and a small pool, with friendly staff. Breakfast included. **₹4500**

EATING

After a browse around the market, most visitors make a beeline for *Longuinho's*, once the hangout of Margao's English-speaking middle classes (now it's mostly tourists), before heading home. If you are on a tight budget, try one of the South Indian-style pure-veg cafés along Station Rd.

Café Coffee Day Shop 18/19 Vasanth Arcade, Da Costa Rd near Popular High School ☎93722 80847. India's answer to *Starbucks* has a super-cool a/c branch tucked away off Praça Jorge Barreto, popular with local college kids. Aside from a good latte (₹97), it serves spicy savouries (such as mini-pizzas and sandwiches; ₹110–140) and, most memorably, a sinful "sizzle dazzle" brownie (₹185). Daily 8.30am–10.30pm.

Longuinho's Luis Miranda Rd. Old-fashioned café serving meat, fish and veg mains (₹120–200), with cheaper freshly baked savoury snacks, cakes and drinks. The food isn't up to much these days – though they do a decent Bombay duck (₹120) – and the 1950s Goan atmosphere has dwindled

with the tourist trade, but it's a pleasant enough place to catch your breath over a beer. Daily 8.30am–10.30pm.

Tato Tucked up an alley off the east side of Praça Jorge Barreto, and opposite the yellow government building north of the Kadamba bus stand. The town's brightest and best South Indian café chain serves the usual range of hot snacks (including especially good samosas at breakfast, and masala dosas from noon). For a proper meal, climb the stairs to their cool a/c floors, where you can order wonderful thalis (veg ₹75, fish ₹150) and North Indian dishes, as well Udupi nibbles (₹20–170). Tues–Sun 8am–9.30pm.

DIRECTORY

Cinema Margao boasts south Goa's principal cinema, the Osia Multiplex (☎0832 270 1616), out in the north of town near the Kadamba bus stand. It screens Hollywood as well as Bollywood releases; tickets cost ₹120–200.

Hospitals Hospicio (☎0832 270 5664 or ☎0832 270 5754), Rua Do Miranda, and the Apollo Victor Hospital, in the suburb of Malbhat (☎0832 272 8888 or ☎0832 272 6272, ⊕apollovictorhospital.com).

Post office The GPO is at the top of Praça Jorge Barreto.

Around Margao

For a good dose of quirky colonial architecture, head **inland from Margao**, where villages such as **Loutolim** and **Chandor** are littered with decaying old Portuguese houses, most of them empty – the region's traditional inheritance laws ensure that old family homes tend to be owned by literally dozens of descendants, few of whom are willing or can afford to maintain them.

Braganza-Perreira/Menezes-Braganza house

Chandor • Daily except holidays, no set hours – just turn up between 10am and noon or 3 and 6pm, go through the main entrance, up the stairs and knock at either of the doors • Recommended donation ₹200/person • ☎ 0832 278 4227 or ☎ 98221 60009

Thirteen kilometres east of Margao across Salcete district's fertile rice fields lies sleepy **Chandor** village, a scattering of tumbledown villas and farmhouses ranged along shady tree-lined lanes. The main reason to venture out here is to see the splendid **Braganza-Perreira/Menezes-Braganza house**, regarded as the grandest of Goa's colonial mansions. Dominating the dusty village square, the house, built in the 1500s by the wealthy Braganza family for their two sons, has a huge double-storey facade, with 28 windows flanking its entrance. Braganza de Perreira, the great-grandfather of the present owner, was the last knight of the king of Portugal; more recently, Menezes Braganza (1879–1938), a journalist and freedom fighter, was one of the few Goan aristocrats actively to oppose Portuguese rule. Forced to flee Chandor in 1950, the family returned in 1962 to find their house, amazingly, untouched. The airy tiled interiors of both wings contain a veritable feast of **antiques**.

Exploring the house

The house is divided into two separate wings, owned by different (and contrasting) branches of the old family. Furniture enthusiasts and lovers of rare Chinese porcelain, in particular, will find plenty to drool over in the **Menezes-Braganza** wing (to the right as you face the building). Next door, in the **Braganza-Perreira** portion, an ornate oratory enshrines St Francis Xavier's diamond-encrusted toenail, retrieved from a local bank vault. The house's most famous feature, however, is its ostentatiously grand ballroom, or **Great Salon**, where a pair of matching high-backed chairs, presented to the Braganza-Perreiras by King Dom Luís of Portugal, occupy pride of place.

Fernandes House

Chandor • Mon–Sat 10am–5pm; telephone in advance • A donation of around ₹200/person is expected • ☎ 0832 278 4245

An air of charismatic dilapidation hangs over the **Fernandes House**, on the south side of Chandor village. One of the oldest surviving *palacios* in Goa, its core is of pre-conquest Hindu origin, overlaid by later accretions. Sara Fernandes, the present owner, receives visitors in the wonderful **salon** that extends the length of the building's first floor, abutting a bedchamber containing its original, ornately carved four-poster. Hidden in the bowels of the building below, a narrow passage fitted with disguised gun holes was where the family used to shelter when attacked by Hindu rebels and bandits such as the Ranes.

Palacio do Deão

Quepem • Guided tours daily except Fri 10am–6pm • Free • ☎ 0832 266 4029, ⓦ palaciododeao.com

A superb colonial-era *palacio* stands at **Quepem**, a thirty-minute drive southeast of Margao on the fringes of the state's iron-ore belt. In 1787, a high-ranking member of the Portuguese clergy, **Father José Paulo de Almeida**, built a country house in the town. Known as the **Palacio do Deão**, it grew to become one of the grandest in the colony, and later served as a retreat for its viceroys. The *palacio* was recently restored to its former glory, and what you see today is a faithful approximation of how the house would have looked in José Paulo's day. The engaging guided **tour** lasts around half an hour, winding up on the lovely rear terrace overlooking the river where you can enjoy a delicious Goan lunch, dinner or afternoon tea by prior arrangement (at least a day in advance; around ₹500).

FROM TOP ASWEM BEACH (P.186); PALACIO DO DEÃO >

Colva

A hot-season retreat for Margao's moneyed middle classes since long before Independence, **COLVA** is the oldest and largest – and least appealing – of south Goa's resorts. Its outlying *waddos* are pleasant enough, dotted with colonial-style villas and ramshackle fishing huts, but the beachfront is dismal: a lacklustre collection of concrete hotels, souvenir stalls and flyblown snack bars strewn around a bleak central roundabout. The atmosphere is not improved by the heaps of rubbish dumped in a rank-smelling ditch that runs behind the beach, nor by the stench of drying fish wafting from the nearby village. Benaulim, just a five-minute drive further south, has a far better choice of accommodation and range of facilities, and is altogether more salubrious.

Benaulim

The predominantly Catholic fishing village of **BENAULIM** lies in the dead centre of Colva beach, scattered around coconut groves and paddy fields 7km west of Margao. Two decades ago, the settlement had barely made it onto the backpackers' map. Nowadays,

3

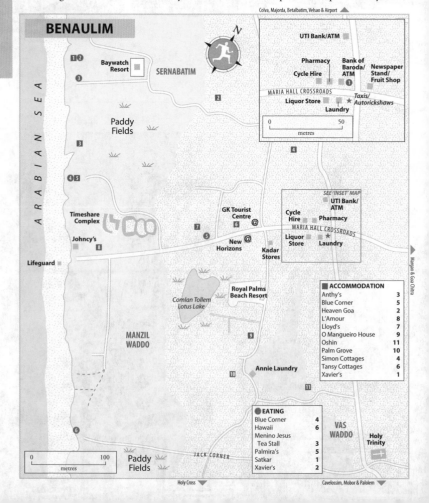

though, affluent holiday-makers from metropolitan India come here in droves, staying in the huge resort and time-share complexes mushrooming on the outskirts, while long-staying, heavy-drinking Brit pensioners and thirty-something European couples taking time out of trips around the Subcontinent make up the bulk of the foreign contingent.

Benaulim's rising popularity has certainly dented the village's old-world charm, but time your visit well (avoiding Diwali and the Christmas peak season), and it is still hard to beat as a place to unwind. The seafood is superb, accommodation and motorbikes cheaper than anywhere else in the state, and the **beach** is breathtaking, particularly around sunset, when the brilliant white sand and churning surf reflect the changing colours to magical effect. Shelving away almost to Cabo da Rama on the horizon, it is also lined with Goa's largest, and most colourfully decorated, fleet of **wooden outriggers**, which provide welcome shade during the heat of the day.

Goa Chitra

Tues–Sun 9.15am–6pm, last tour 5.15pm • ₹300 • ☎ 0832 657 0877, ⊛ goachitra.com • To get to Goa Chitra by bike or motorcycle, head east from Maria Hall crossroads towards Margao, and take the first turning on your left at a fork after 1.5km; when you reach the T-junction ahead, turn sharply right – the museum lies another 500m on your right

Conventional sights are thin on the ground along this stretch of coast, though one exception stands out on the eastern fringes of Benaulim: a splendid new ethnographic museum, **Goa Chitra**. Set against a backdrop of a working organic farm, the exhibition comprises a vast array of antique agricultural tools and artefacts, ranging from giant cooking pots and ecclesiastical robes to tubas and sugar-cane presses. The idea is to promote appreciation of the region's traditional agrarian lifestyle – a world of knowledge and skills fast disappearing.

ARRIVAL AND DEPARTURE   BENAULIM

By bus Buses from Margao run every 20min or so from the Kadamba bus stand to the Maria Hall crossroads in Benaulim. There is a taxi and auto-rickshaw rank at the crossroads, from where you can pick up transport to the beach, 1.5km west.

By motorbike or bicycle Signs offering motorbikes for rent are dotted along the lanes off Maria Hall crossroads:

rates are standard, descending in proportion to the length of time you keep the vehicle (₹250–350/day is about average for a Honda Activa). Worth bearing in mind if you're planning to continue further south is that motorbikes are much cheaper to rent (and generally in better condition) here than in Palolem. Bicycle rental costs around ₹100/day.

ACCOMMODATION

Aside from the unsightly time-share complexes and five-stars that loom in the fields around the village, most of Benaulim's accommodation consists of small budget **guesthouses**, scattered around the lanes 1km or so back from the beach.

Anthy's Sernabatim ☎ 0832 277 1680 or ☎ 99228 54566, ⊜ anthysguesthouse@rediffmail.com. Nicely furnished rooms right on the sea, with high ceilings, tiny bathrooms and breezy verandas. It also boasts a restaurant and offers free sunbeds for guests on the beach. A/c ₹400 extra. **₹1600**

Blue Corner Sernabatim ☎ 98504 55770, ⊛ blue-corner-goa.com. Popular hut camp on the beach, run by an enthusiastic young crew. Large palm-leaf structures with fans, mosquito nets, attached shower-toilets and plywood sitouts. Quiet and secure, and the bar-restaurant is one of the most happening places on the beach in the evenings. **₹1200**

★**Heaven Goa** 1 Ambeaxir, Sernabatim ☎ 0832 275 8442 or ☎ 75076 60997, ⊛ heavengoa.in. Welcoming Swiss-run guesthouse in a block of a dozen or so rooms occuping a plum spot, 10min back from the sea beside a

lily pond alive with frogs, egrets and water buffalo. The rooms are spacious and well set up (with wooden shelves, mosquito nets, shiny tiled floors and balconies overlooking the water). Seven rooms offer a/c for ₹400 more. Unbelievable value in this bracket. **₹1200**

L'Amour Beach Rd ☎ 0832 277 0404, ⊛ lamourbeach resortgoa.com. Benaulim's oldest hotel comprises a comfortable 21-room complex; the rooms are fan-only but chalets (₹3000) are spacious, a/c and cool, with ceramic tiled floors and little verandas opening onto a central garden. Reasonable rates, and hot water. **₹1500**

Lloyd's 1554/A Vas Waddo ☎ 0832 277 1492, ⊛ lloyd touristrooms@gmail.com. With its garish yellow exterior, this place on the beach side of the village stands out in more ways than one. The rooms are really big for the price, with high ceilings, quality beds and fans, plus neat mozzie screens over the windows. Also various-sized a/c apartments (from ₹2500) upstairs for longer stays. ₹**600**

O Mangueiro House 1685/A, Vas Waddo (next to Carina Beach Resort) ☎0832 277 0408 or ☎99225 42217, ⓦmangogrovegoa.com. One of the oldest budget guesthouses in Benaulim, run by the affable Mr Caetano. Just 400m from the beach, the rooms are on the small side, but neat and clean, freshly painted each season, and with quality mattresses. Some have tiny balconies opening onto a sandy courtyard; others face the road. There's an equally good-value studio for longer stays (₹800) and a two-bedroom apartment (₹1400). ₹**550**

Oshin Mazil Waddo ☎0832 277 0069, ⓦoshins-guesthouse.com. Large complex of old-style budget rooms set well back from the road. Opening onto leafy terraces, they're spacious and clean with attached bathrooms, balconies, fresh towels and complimentary soap; those on the top floor afford views over the treetops. A notch above most places in this area, and good value, but quite a walk from the beach. ₹**600**

Palm Grove Tamdi-Mati, 149 Vas Waddo ☎0832 277 0059, ⓦpalmgrovegoa.com. Secluded hotel surrounded by beautiful gardens, offering three classes of a/c rooms, ranging from ropy to luxurious. A 10- to 15min walk (or bike ride) back from the beachfront, but very pleasant, and the management is welcoming. ₹**2000**

Simon Cottages Ambeaxir, Sernabatim ☎0832 277 0581, ⓔsimoncottages@yahoo.com. Perennially among the best budget deals in Benaulim, in a quiet spot 1km from the beach at the unspoiled north side of the village. Huge rooms on three storeys, all with shower-toilets and verandas, opening onto a sandy courtyard. Some have a/c (₹550 extra). ₹**450**

Tansy Cottages Beach Rd ☎0832 277 0574, ⓔtansycottages@yahoo.in. Not the best of locations, and the shocking green-and-purple paintwork is hard to live with, but the rooms are some of the nicest budget options in Benaulim: a generous size, with tiled floors and new attached bathrooms. A/c ₹400 extra. ₹**600**

★**Xavier's** Sernabatim ☎0832 277 1489, ⓔjovek @vsnl.in. Well-maintained, large rooms ranged around a lovely garden, virtually on the beach but within walking distance of the village centre. All rooms have private terraces, extra-thick king-sized mattresses, and low-slung cane chairs to lounge on, and the local owners, who have been here for decades, are genuinely hospitable. A peaceful, perfectly situated option – and great value. A few rooms have a/c for ₹1800. ₹**1200**

EATING

Benaulim's proximity to Margao market, along with the presence of a large Christian fishing community, means its **restaurants** serve some of the tastiest, most competitively priced seafood in Goa. The largest and busiest shacks flank the beachfront area, where *Johncy's* catches most of the passing custom. However, you'll find better food at lower prices at places further along the beach, which seem to change chefs annually; wander by and see who has the most customers.

Blue Corner Sernabatim ☎98504 55770. Great little beachside joint specializing in seafood and authentic Chinese dishes. House favourites include "fish tomato eggdrop soup" (₹140), scrumptious "dragon potatoes" (₹150) and, best of all, their "Dave's steak" (₹395). Also featured on the eclectic menu are tasty Italian dishes, sizzlers and, for homesick veggies, a pretty good cauliflower cheese (₹220). Daily 7.30am–late.

Hawaii South end of beach ☎09373 167016. Nadia and Vinod from Himachal Pradesh have run this welcoming little shack for more than a decade, and can claim one of the most loyal clienteles in the village, most of whom come for the Italian dishes, prepared with home-made pasta, fresh herbs, olive oil and proper cheese. The prawn lasagne (₹350) and moussaka (₹250) also get the thumbs up, and they do a zingy, fresh-mint mojito (₹150). During the day, a kids' play area is an additional attraction. Daily 8am–late.

Menino Jesus Tea Stall Sernabatim. If you've ever wondered what beach shacks were like thirty years ago, check this place out. It's where the local rickshaw drivers refuel on spicy fish-curry-rice plates (₹180), piping-hot slices of millet-fried mackerel and *pao bhaji* for just ₹50. Rough and ready, but the food's delicious, and the sea view is perfect. Daily 6am–7.30pm.

Palmira's Beach Rd ☎0832 277 1309. Benaulim's best breakfasts: wonderfully creamy and fresh set curd, copious fruit salads with coconut (₹80), real espresso (₹50), warm local bread (*bagri*) and the morning paper. For a light lunch, try their delicious prawn toast (₹90) or tomato or ginger-carrot soups (₹80). Daily 7am–10pm.

Satkar Maria Hall Crossroads. No-frills locals' Udupi canteen that's the only place in the village where you can order regular Indian snacks – samosas (₹10), masala dosas (₹50), hot pakoras and spicy chickpea stew (*channa*) – and full thalis (₹90)– at regular Indian prices. The *bhaji pau* breakfast (₹33) is a must. Daily 8am–9.30pm.

★**Xavier's** Sernabatim ☎93261 29443. Host Jovek's mum prepares and cooks most of the masala at this breezy beachside restaurant, so the Goan dishes – prawn vindaloo, coconut-rich fish *caldin* (both ₹300) and a knockout *chouriço* chilli-fry (₹190) are highly recommended. Less spicy alternatives include a tasty lemon rice (₹120); and, of course, they do the usual range of market-fresh seafood. Facing one of the most tranquil stretches of the beach, the terrace is most atmospheric at night, with the waves crashing in just a few metres away. Daily 8am–late.

DIRECTORY

Banks and exchange The Bank of Baroda (Mon–Fri 9am–2pm, Sat 9–11.30am) on Maria Hall crossroads has an ATM, as does the UTI Bank. Currency may be changed at the two travel agents GK Tourist Centre, at the crossroads in the village centre, and New Horizons, diagonally opposite. It's worth comparing rates at the two.

General stores You'll find a couple of well-stocked general stores near the Maria Hall crossroads.

Internet GK Tourist Centre and New Horizons each have broadband connections (₹50/hr).

Laundry Annie's, opposite *Palm Grove* hotel, offers an inexpensive same-day laundry service. The Frank Bela laundry on the Maria Hall crossroads charges slightly more.

Pharmacy There is a pharmacy at the Maria Hall crossroads.

Agonda

AGONDA, 10km northwest of the market town of **Chaudi** (known to outsiders as **Canacona**), comes as a pleasant surprise after the chaos elsewhere in Goa. Accommodation in this predominantly Catholic fishing village is in small-scale, family-run guesthouses and upper-end hut camps, the restaurant scene is relatively unsophisticated, and the clientele easy-going and health-conscious. Granted, you don't get a dreamy brake of palm trees as a backdrop, but the surrounding hills and forest are exquisite, and the sand is as clean as any in the state.

The smart money says Agonda could all too soon go the way of Palolem, but for the time being the village deserves to be high on the list for anyone seeking somewhere quiet and wholesome, with enough amenities for a relaxing holiday and plenty of local atmosphere.

3

ARRIVAL AND DEPARTURE   AGONDA

By bus Agonda is served by four daily buses from the nearest market town, Canacona/Chaudi (20–30min); two run to Margao (2hr). Most services stop at the junction on the main Palolem road, 1km east (you can usually find a rickshaw for the trip into the village), but a couple go as far as the church in the centre of Agonda.

ACCOMMODATION

Agonda gets packed in **peak season**, and over Christmas and New Year you'll be lucky to find a bed anywhere on spec. Tariffs rocket by fifty percent or more at this time, but after Jan 15 settle back down again and remain on a par with those in Patnem and Palolem. Except for the upscale camps (which require payment in advance online) few places accept advance bookings so you'll probably have to plod around to find somewhere that suits, or else phone ahead from the comfort of a café table (though note that mobile coverage tends to be patchy hereabouts).

★**Agonda White Sand Beach Huts** 900m north of St Anne's Church ☎ 98221 57541, ⊛ agondavillas.com. This campus of stylish huts has raised the bar in Agonda. Made of local wood, thatch and bamboo, with stone-tiled floors, the cottages are furnished like chic hotel rooms – though ranged around a busy bar-restaurant – and there's a minimum stay of three nights. For greater seclusion, and unparalleled luxury on the beach, treat yourself to a stay in one of their gorgeous villas (three nights ₹9000) – huge, five-star boutique chalets in Balinese and Keralan styles, with decadent open-to-sky bathrooms and uninterrupted sea views from private terraces. Three nights ₹4500

Chris-Joana Just south of St Anne's church ☎ 0832 264 7306 or ☎ 94211 55814, ✉ chrisjoana92@yahoo.com. Smart modern house on the roadside. Its bargain rooms are clean, light and airy, with decent beds – two have a/c for ₹1500. Go for one on the rear side, overlooking the rooftops and creek toward coconut plantations; the front ones get warm in the afternoons. ₹900

Jardim A Mar Doval Kazan ☎ 94208 20470, ⊛ jardim -a-mar.com. Professionally run "palm-tree-garden resort", offering budget rooms and pricier beachside huts (₹2000), nicely decorated with Rajasthani quilts and blockprint throws. Partly German-owned, it has a slicker feel than most of the competition. ₹800

★**Kaama Kethna** Gurawal, 2km southeast of Agonda off the Palolem road ⊛ kaamakethna.net. This German-run ecotourism and permaculture project just outside the village – a 15min cycle from the beach – offers simply furnished treehouses (₹1500–2500), built high in the cashew canopy from palm leaf panels and wood, plus a few bamboo huts with spacious terraces at ground level. The site is wonderfully quiet and leafy, with colourful birds and monkeys flitting through the branches. Food grown on the farm is served in their little restaurant; they also offer yoga and meditation courses and natural therapies. ₹1000

Monsoon 1km north of St Anne's Church ☎ 99235 49360, ⊛ monsoon-goa.com. Low-slung thatched huts

(₹1500–4000 depending on size and season) and rooms in a secluded, peaceful setting behind the north end of the beach. Efficiently run by the resident German owner, it offers a pleasant parachute-shaded chillout terrace and dining area (see below) with a tiled roof. Family-friendly (no bar). Prices are especially high over Christmas. ₹1200

EATING

Agonda's restaurants are as much **hangouts** as places to eat. Most are furnished with relaxing cane chairs, pretty Himalayan lanterns and lounge areas with bolsters, and are on or near the beach.

Agonda White Sand 900m north of St Anne's church. One of the more sophisticated menus in Agonda, including eggs rösti for breakfast (₹250), steaks with pepper or blue cheese sauce (₹480), seafood, tandoori chicken and cashew brown rice with beetroot *raita* (₹180) for lunch and dinner, as well as a good range of cocktails (₹300–400). Daily 8am–late.

Fatima Corner and Thali Opposite the bank at the main junction. The place for tourists to get a local-food fix, this shady little restaurant has a pleasant vibe and serves the usual mix of Indian and Continental dishes as well as excellent thalis (₹120/₹150). Also popular for its set breakfasts (₹150–200). Daily 8am–9pm.

Jardim A Mar Doval Kazan ☎ 94208 20470, ⓦ jardim -a-mar.com. A café-restaurant that ticks all the boxes: it's slap on the sand, well shaded (under palms and a Ladakhi parachute), with comfy cane chairs and silk cushions scattered on lounge mats. And it's a great breakfast spot, churning out fresh fruit juices, proper coffee, grilled baguettes and, the house speciality, rice pudding, as well as a popular all-day menu. Around ₹200–500 for a main meal. Daily 7am–11pm.

Madhu's North side of beach. For years the best tandoori outfit on the beach: great for fresh local fish and Indian dishes alike (₹140–300). It's inexpensive and always busy, so get here early. The chicken tikka *malai* kebab (₹250) is especially good. Daily 8am–11pm.

Monsoon 1km north of St Anne's Church ☎ 99235 49360, ⓦ monsoon-goa.com. One for the healthy eaters: great house muesli and copious fresh salads for breakfast (₹150–280); pasta (₹150–250), Tibetan *momos* (₹180), seared fish steaks (₹400–600) and a focused selection of curries the rest of the day. Served on a small sandy terrace on the beach. Daily 8am–10.30pm.

DIRECTORY

Banks and exchange You will find ATMs at the junction opposite St Anne's church.

Internet A string of places along the tarmac lane leading north of the church offer internet access.

Palolem

Nowhere else in peninsular India conforms so obediently to the archetypal image of a paradise beach as **PALOLEM**, 35km south of Margao. Lined with a swaying curtain of coconut palms, the bay forms a perfect curve of golden sand, arcing north from a giant

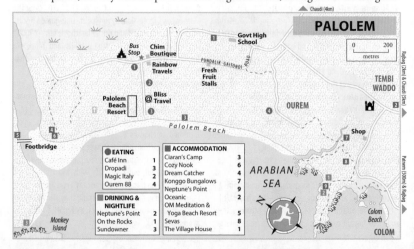

pile of boulders to a spur of the Sahyadri Hills, which tapers into the sea draped in thick forest. Palolem, however, has become something of a paradise lost over the past decade. It's now the most popular resort in Goa among independent foreign travellers, and is deluged from late November. Visitor numbers become positively overwhelming in peak season, when thousands of people spill across a beach backed by an unbroken line of shacks and Thai-style hut camps.

Basically, Palolem in full swing is the kind of place you'll either love at first sight or want to flee from as quickly as possible. If you're in the latter category, try smaller, less frequented **Patnem** beach, a short walk south around the headland, where the shack scene is more subdued and the sands marginally emptier.

ARRIVAL AND DEPARTURE   PALOLEM

By bus Regular buses run between Margao and Palolem, stopping at the end of the lane leading from the main street to the beachfront. Frequent services also run between Margao and Karwar (in Karnataka) via the nearby market town of Canacona/Chaudi (every 30min; 2hr), 2km southeast across the rice fields.

By train Canacona/Chaudi is also the nearest railhead to Palolem; the station lies a short way north of the main bazaar. Rickshaws charge ₹80–100, taxis ₹200–250, for the ride to the beach.

GETTING AROUND AND ACTIVITIES

Bike rental A stall halfway along the main street charges around ₹50–100/day.

Surf canoes Available for rent at various places along the beach for ₹200/hr – great for paddles to Monkey Island at the top of the bay, or, weather permitting, around the headland to "Butterfly Beach".

Trekking Goa Jungle Adventure (☎ 98504 85641, ⓦ goajungle.com or ⓦ facebook.com/goajungleadventure) runs guided treks to natural swimming sites and features a mix of trekking, canyoning, swimming and abseiling in the mountain area inland from Palolem. You will need to be reasonably fit. Full-day trips ₹1990–3690, including transport and equipment.

ACCOMMODATION

The local municipality's strict enforcement of a rule banning new concrete construction in Palolem (it went so far as to bulldoze without warning the entire resort a few years back) has ensured that most of the village's accommodation consists of simple palm-leaf huts.

Ciaran's Camp Centre of Palolem Beach ☎ 0832 264 3477, ⓦ ciarans.com. "Camp" understates the sophistication of this compact resort whose coir, coconut wood and terracotta-tiled chalets are ranged around a neatly manicured central lawn. You've a choice of sea-facing or super-plush a/c rooms (₹5000). The whole place is exceptionally well run, with a popular double-decker bar-restaurant on site, safe lockers and a pair of friendly large hounds. **₹4500**

Cozy Nook North end of the beach, near the island ☎ 0832 264 3550, ⓦ cozynookgoa.com. One of the most attractive set-ups in Goa, comprising bamboo huts in three styles. The nicest are the Robinson Crusoe-esque deluxe options (₹3500), which have two storeys, with a chillout floor on top and bedroom below. The sea-facing ones (₹4500) are ramshackle and jazzy, decked out in Rajasthani furniture; the semi-deluxe only have upper-floor rooms. Opening onto the lagoon on one side and the beach on the other, the site occupies a prime spot at the scenic north end of the bay. **₹2500**

Dream Catcher North end of the beach behind Cozy Nook ☎ 0832 264 4873 or ☎ 77700 89572, ⓦ dream catcher.in. Individually styled, very glam Keralan-style huts in a neatly swept sandy compound, with more space, better mattresses, nicer textiles, bigger windows and sturdier foundations than most, in a plum position by the riverside. There's also a shaded yoga *shala* for classes (₹400), and a "chillout-ambient bar". Prices are on the high side, to say the least (up to ₹7700 depending on the category of hut), but so are the standards. **₹2750**

Konggo Bungalows Ourem ☎ 94220 59217, ⓦ konggo .in. The most interesting huts currently on offer in Palolem, ingeniously constructed around cliffs and rocks in a beautiful tropical garden alive with birds and butterflies, just behind the far south end of the beach. The larger ones (₹3000–4000) are huge, with long, deep decks, and plenty of room to do yoga and even cook your own meals – and the bathrooms have proper plumbing. Good value given the great location. **₹1500**

Neptune's Point South Palolem ☎ 91584 32629, ⓦ neptunepoint.com. *Neptune's* occupies the sweet spot atop the boulder headland dividing Palolem and Patnem, and its huts, stacked up on the hillside under giant coconut palms, make the most of the stupendous views. They're

3

basic by today's standards, but comfortable enough, and having the sea on three sides is a unique selling point. The only downside is the Sat party night and Wed movie evenings (see below), held on the premises, which bring in big crowds. ₹1500

Oceanic Tembi Waddo ☎0832 264 3059, ⊛hotel-oceanic.com. A 10min walk inland from the beach (and also reachable via the backroad to Canacona/Chaudi), *Oceanic* is owned and managed by a resident British couple. Its marble-floored rooms are stylishly designed, fresh, cool and relaxing, with large mosquito nets, block-printed bedspreads and bedside lamps. There's also a pool on a forested patio behind, and a quality restaurant. ₹3250

★ **OM Meditation & Yoga Beach Resort** Far northern end of Palolem beach, on the far side of the creek (look for the rickety footbridge to the right as you head for the island) ☎0832 264 3550. Run by the guys at *Cozy Nook* (where you can access wi-fi), this isolated tent camp is a silent space with music and noise prohibited – there's also a small yoga area. The tents are quite well equipped, with comfortable

beds, and the attached bathrooms are open to the sky. ₹1000

Sevas Far southern end of the beach, on the hill dividing Palolem from Colom ☎0832 264 3977 or ☎94220 65437, ⊛sevaspalolemgoa.com. Beautiful "ethnic" cabanas sporting traditional rice-straw roofs, mud-and-dung floors, hygienic squat-style loos and bucket baths. The huts come in two sizes: cottage and cabana (₹1800–2400; sleeps four). They also offer massages and yoga classes, and there's a pleasant restaurant serving very good thalis for ₹200. ₹1000

The Village House #196, near Government High School ☎99604 87627, ⊛villageguesthousegoa.com. This British-run boutique guesthouse, on the fringes of Palolem a 10min walk from the beach, is the most comfortable and stylish place to stay in the area. Furnished with four-posters and vibrant silk bed covers, the a/c rooms are either "cosy" or large (for ₹1400 more) – and the designer bathrooms palatial. A shady rear garden serves as a common breakfast area, and you can take your drinks out onto the veranda in the evenings. ₹4500

EATING

Palolem's **restaurants** reflect the cosmopolitan make-up of its visitors. Each year, a fresh batch of innovative, ever more stylish places opens, many of them managed by expats.

Café Inn Pundalik Gaitondi Rd ☎98503 49021. The best coffee in Palolem, made with a proper Italian coffee machine by an Israeli duo. They get packed out for an international range of set breakfasts (₹160–300), and have a small but eclectic menu, including tasty *shakshuka*, smoked chicken pastrami sandwiches (₹250), tortilla wraps (₹280), cakes and pastries. The best reason to come here, though, is for the Belgian waffles (₹160–250). Daily 10am–11pm.

Dropadi Beachfront ☎0832 264 4555. This place enjoys both a top location and Palolem's best Indian chef, who specializes in rich, creamy Mughlai dishes and tandoori fish. Go for the superb *murg makhini* (₹350), crab masala with spinach (₹700) or tandoori jumbo prawns in basil sauce (₹350 each). Daily noon–11pm.

Magic Italy Beach Rd ☎88057 67705. Italian-run and on the busy approach to the seafront, this is in the running

to be south Goa's number-one Italian restaurant, serving authentic home-made ravioli and tagliatelle (₹280–450) and scrumptious, large wood-fired pizzas (from ₹320). Reservation recommended. Daily 5–11pm.

★ **Ourem 88** On a lane running behind south side of beach (behind Rococo Pelton Bar) ☎86988 27679. Tiny garden restaurant run by Brit expats Jodie and Brett, serving cleverly-thought-out Euro gastro dishes made from fresh local ingredients. Try their superb steak with béarnaise sauce, melt-in-the-mouth chicken Kiev or oven-baked barramundi filet in a herb and parmesan crust, leaving room for the divine chocolate fondata. Absolutely the finest dining in Palolem, though prices are reasonable given the quality of the cuisine (around ₹2000 for three courses, not including drinks). Tues–Sun 6.30–11pm, by reservation only (several days beforehand in season).

DRINKING AND NIGHTLIFE

Goa's 10pm amplified **music ban** (see p.181) is officially observed in Palolem, although *On the Rocks* has found a way of circumventing the rule and *Neptune's Point* has seemingly come to an arrangement with the authorities.

Neptune's Point South side of beach. A dreamy location for a sundowner. On Wed at 7.30pm they screen free movies, which you can watch while enjoying a mojito (₹250) from the bar, and on Sat they host techno dance parties (9pm–4am; ₹800). Drinks won't break the bank either. Daily 11am–late.

On the Rocks Southern end of the beach ☎86051 06600, ⊛silentnoise.in. On the rocky promontory at the far south

end of the bay, the Silent Noise collective stages weekly headphone parties here on Sat nights (₹600), where the music is broadcast digitally to individual headsets instead of through PAs. You've a choice of house, electro and big beats on three separate channels, synced with live AV screens, lights and lasers. Can be a bit weird when you don't have headphones on, but many people seem to enjoy it. They also run a Wed afternoon market and other events. Sat 9pm–4am.

Sundowner Opposite Monkey Island, across the estuary at the north of the beach ☎ 98602 13524. As indicated by the name, this open-air bar is the top spot for a sunset tipple with its sweeping view across the bay, although – you may have to wade across the estuary to get there – there is a rickety bridge slightly inland and you can clamber around the rocks if you can't find the crossing point. They have a range of cocktails (₹200–350), and if you book ahead they can cook a seafood barbecue (₹800/person) – otherwise it's snacks only. Daily 10am–midnight.

DIRECTORY

Banks and exchange Several agents in Palolem are licensed to change money; LKP forex in the *Palolem Beach Resort* offers competitive rates. Sai Baba, Sun Moon Travel and Rainbow Travels on the main street all do cash advances against Visa and MasterCard. The nearest ATMs are 2km away towards the market town of Canacona/Chaudi on the main road.

Doctor Dr Sandheep, at the private Dhavalikar Hospital (☎ 0832 264 3147), 2km out of Palolem at Devabag on the road to Agonda.

Internet Among a few cybercafés along the main road, Bliss Travel, on the left near the main entrance to the beach, charges ₹50/hr for the village's fastest broadband.

Pharmacy Palolem's main pharmacy is 1km out of the village on the Chaudi Rd, to your right just after the Agonda turning. It's closed on Sun, but out of hours you can call at the pharmacist's house immediately behind the shop.

3

South of Palolem

If the bright lights of Palolem start to lose their allure, wander around the headland to the south, where the Hindu fishing hamlet of **Colom** offers a more sedate scene. The shacks and bar strip resurfaces in earnest once around the next promontory at **Patnem**, but even in peak season the beach here rarely gets packed. Finally, to the south of Patnem, **Rajbag** is a worthwhile destination for a fitness walk, but little more, thanks to the massive luxury resort behind it.

Colom

Once across the creek and boulder-covered spur bounding the south end of Palolem beach, you arrive at **COLOM**, a largely Hindu fishing village scattered around a series of rocky coves. Dozens of long-stay rooms, leaf huts and houses are tucked away under the palm groves and on the picturesque headland running seawards. This is the best place in the village to start an accommodation hunt – the lads at the *Boom Shankar* bar (see p.204) will know of any vacant places – but be warned that most of the rooms here can be basic.

Patnem

A string of hut camps and shacks lining the beach south of Colom, **PATNEM** is one of the mellower spots in these parts. The beach, curving for roughly 1km to a steep bluff, is broad, with little shade, and shelves quite steeply at certain phases of the tide, though the undertow rarely gets dangerously strong. On the headland dividing Patnem from Colom, the **Harmonic Healing & Eco Retreat Centre** (☎ 98225 12814, ⌨ harmonicingoa .com) hosts daily yoga, reiki, pilates and Thai massage classes, as well as lessons in Bollywood dance and classical Indian singing, in a greenery-swathed site with panoramic views of the beach.

Rajbag and beyond

At low tide, you can walk around the bottom of the steep-sided headland dividing Patnem from neighbouring **RAJBAG**, another kilometre-long sweep of white sand. Sadly, its remote feel has been entirely submerged by the massive five-star recently erected on the land behind it – much to the annoyance of the locals, who campaigned for four years to stop the project.

It's possible to press on even further **south from Rajbag** by crossing the Talpona River via a hand-paddled ferry, which usually has to be summoned from the far bank (fix a return price in advance). Once across, a short walk brings you to **Talpona beach**, backed by low dunes and a line of straggly palms. From here, you can cross the headland at the end of the beach to reach **Galjibag**, a remote white-sand bay that's a protected nesting site for olive ridley marine **turtles**. A strong undertow means swimming isn't safe here.

ARRIVAL AND DEPARTURE   SOUTH OF PALOLEM

By train The nearest railway station is Canacona/Chaudi.
By auto-rickshaw or taxi Most beaches can be reached by auto-rickshaw from Canacona/Chaudi for around ₹75. Auto-rickshaws and taxis for the return trip hang around along the beachfront lane.

By bus Patnem's bus stop is 1km or so closer to Canacona/ Chaudi than Palolem's, with buses starting at the Kadamba bus stand at the north end of Chaudi's bazaar and dropping passengers at the end of the short lane leading to Patnem beach.

ACCOMMODATION

April 20 Patnem ☎ 99609 16989, ⓦ goyam.net. Luxury, two-storey wooden bungalows painted pretty pastel colours, with tariffs ranging up to ₹5000, depending on size and time of year. Partly screened by casuarina trees, each is smartly furnished and fitted with bathrooms, mosquito nets and swings on sea-facing balconies; those at the front are the village's number-one des reses. **₹2500**

Boom Shankar Colom ☎ 97651 87294. Simply furnished, clean, attached rooms on the southern edge of the village, with lots of lounging space and fine views across the cove. They can also help you root out longer-term rentals in houses nearby. **₹1500**

Home Patnem ☎ 0832 264 3916, ⓦ homeispatnem .com. A chic little local-run guesthouse within sight of the beach, comprising an annexe of attached rooms under Mangalorean tiles, pleasantly decked out with textiles, coconut mats, lampshades and other touches to justify their tariffs. No wi-fi. **₹1500**

★**Laguna Vista** Just east of Colom beach ☎ 85549 498110, ⓔ agunavistapatnem@gmail.com. Basic but beautifully located thatched huts on their own quiet cove, with fans, loos, comfy mattresses, mozzie nets, fresh towels, safe lockers and perfect sunset views. There's a lovely yoga *shala* on site and a relaxing lounge-resto (see below). Run by a dynamic young Delhiite, this is a very nicely put-together camp and perfect for seclusion, with a sociable hangout on the doorstep. **₹1500**

Namaste Patnem ☎ 98504 77189. A standout choice among the string of budget traveller camps in Patnem, this dependable, lively budget option is run by the amiable Satay. Fan rooms cost up to ₹3000 depending on size and comfort of the hut, time of year and how far back you are from the sand, and there are also a/c options (₹4000); all have individual shower-toilets. **₹1500**

Papaya's Patnem ☎ 99230 79447, ⓦ papayasgoa.com. A delightfully green oasis, where water is recycled to keep the plants in their prime and power comes from solar panels. The eco-huts have four-posters, thick mattresses, breezy little sitouts and shaggy palm-frond fringes made from locally sourced materials. **₹2500**

EATING AND DRINKING

It's a safe bet you'll spend a few hours each day in one or other of the cafés in **Colom** or behind **Patnem beach**, and a couple of commendable places are tucked away just inland.

April 20 North end of Patnem beach ☎ 99609 16989. This swanky beachside restaurant, an offshoot of the popular *Dropadi* in Palolem (see p.202), does superb seafood prepared in rich North Indian tandoori style: crab *makhini*, avocado prawns and tandoori sea bass (₹500–600) are their signature dishes. Daily 8am–11pm.

Boom Shankar Colom. *Boom Shankar* does a great range of food – including its perennially popular fresh mozzarella and tomato salads (₹210) and inexpensive seafood dishes (₹190–380) – and, with a rear terrace overlooking the bay and gorgeous views, is the perfect place for a sundowner. Daily 11am–late.

Capital Patnem beach, opposite Patnem Chai Shop ☎ 99235 33015. It's worth ambling up the lane from the beach for a meal at *Capital*. The roadside location isn't up to much, but they do fantastic salads (₹170–300) and a knockout spinach-mushroom cheeseburger (₹260), to name but two of the healthy, freshly prepared dishes on an extensive multicuisine menu. Daily 8.30am–11pm.

Casa Fiesta Patnem beach. Popular place near the centre of the beach, offering an appetizing menu of world cuisine: hummus, Greek salad, Mexican specialities and fish *pollichathu*. Mains (mostly under ₹400) come with delicious roast potatoes. They also have one of the most impressive selections of fresh fish on the beach, though for considerably more. Daily 7.30am–11.30pm.

★**Home** Middle of Patnem beach. Patnem's nicest beach café, serving meze, freshly baked bread, Swiss rösti (₹210), fresh salads (₹190–290), proper Lavazza espresso and wonderful desserts (banoffee pie, warm apple tart with fresh cream and legendary brownies are all ₹150). It's a particularly pleasant option for breakfast, with Chopin on the sound system and sparrows chirping in the palms. Daily 8.30am–9.30pm.

Laguna Vista Colom ☎ 99230 94676. Full-flavoured, healthy, organic meals made from local ingredients and served on a dreamy, wave-lapped terrace by a young crew. The menu is eclectic and international – bruschette, crunchy salads, chapatti wraps, falafels and Indian dishes – and prices restrained (count on ₹550 for two courses). They also do a range of thalis for ₹190–250. Daily 7.30am–11pm.

Papaya Middle of Patnem beach. Succulent grilled seafood steaks and potato wedges (₹250) are the big hit at *Papaya*, but they also do a roaring trade in zingy Thai curries (₹300) and prawns with more-ish rösti potatoes and mushrooms (₹350). Daily 8am–11pm.

Patnem Chai Shop At the end of the lane leading from Patnem beach, on the corner. The village chai shop is famous hereabouts for its crunchy samosas (₹8), *bhaji pao* (₹15) and delicious tea, attracting as many discerning expats as locals to its tiny interior. Daily 6.30am–6.30pm.

Cotigao Wildlife Sanctuary

The **Cotigao Wildlife Sanctuary**, 10km southeast of Canacona/Chaudi, was established in 1969 to protect a remote and vulnerable area of forest lining the Goa–Karnataka border. Best visited between October and March, Cotigao is a peaceful and scenic park that makes a pleasant day-trip from Palolem, 12km northwest. Encompassing 86 square kilometres of mixed deciduous woodland, the reserve is certain to inspire tree lovers, but less likely to yield many wildlife sightings: its tigers and leopards were hunted out long ago, while the gazelles, sloth bears, porcupines and hyenas that allegedly lurk in the woods rarely appear. You do, however, stand a good chance of spotting at least two species of monkey, a couple of wild boar and the odd gaur (the primeval-looking Indian bison), as well as plenty of birdlife.

A network of trails winds from the trailhead 3km beyond the centre to various named sites in the forest, but aren't waymarked and are very hard to follow. It is worth noting that some visitors complain about walking for hours without seeing anything of interest.

ARRIVAL AND INFORMATION

COTIGAO WILDLIFE SANCTUARY

By bus Any of the buses running south on the NH-17 to Karwar via Canacona/Chaudi will drop you within 2km of the gates. However, to explore the inner reaches of the sanctuary, you really need your own transport.

Interpretative Centre You have to pay your entry fees

(₹20, plus ₹100 for a car, ₹30 for a motorbike; ₹30 for a camera permit) at the reserve's small interpretative centre. The wardens here will show you how to get to a 25m-high treetop watchtower, overlooking a waterhole that attracts a handful of animals around dawn and dusk.

ACCOMMODATION AND EATING

Cottages Book through the Deputy Conservator of Forests in Margao ☎ 0832 273 5361. You can stay in the sanctuary at one of four cottages, in the compound behind the main reserve gates. ₹800

Eating Food and drink may be available by prior arrangement (at least 4hr), and there's a shop at the nearest village, 2km inside the park.

Karnataka

212 Bengaluru (Bangalore) and around

222 Mysuru (Mysore)

229 Around Mysuru

231 Hassan and around

236 Kodagu (Coorg)

240 Mangaluru (Mangalore)

244 North of Mangaluru: coastal Karnataka

250 Hubballi (Hubli)-Dharwad

251 Hosapete (Hospet)

252 Hampi (Vijayanagar)

260 Badami, Aihole and Pattadakal: Monuments of the Chalukyas

264 Vijayapura (Bijapur) and the north

MYSORE PALACE, MYSURU

Karnataka

Created in 1956 from the princely state of Mysore, Karnataka – a derivation of the word *karu nadu* meaning "black soil" in the local language, Kannada – marks a transition zone between central India and the Dravidian deep south. Along its borders with Maharashtra, Andhra Pradesh and Telangana, a string of medieval walled towns studded with domed mausoleums and minarets recall the era when this part of the Deccan was a Muslim stronghold. The coastal and hill districts that dovetail with Kerala are, in contrast, quintessential Hindu South India, lush with tropical vegetation and soaring temple *gopuram*. In between are scattered several extraordinary sites, notably the ruined Vijayanagar city at Hampi, whose lost temples and derelict palaces stand amid an arid, rocky landscape of surreal beauty.

Fed by the southwest monsoon (see box below) and draped in dense deciduous forests, the **Western Ghats**, recognized among the world's top eight biodiversity hotspots (see p.239), run in an unbroken line along the state's palm-fringed coast, impeding the path of the rain clouds east. As a result, the landscape of the interior – comprising the southern apex of the triangular Deccan trap, known as the **Mysore Plateau** – is considerably drier. Three of South India's most sacred rivers, the Kaveri (also spelt Cauvery), Tungabhadra and Krishna, flow across this sun-baked terrain, draining east to the Bay of Bengal.

Karnataka's principal attractions are concentrated at opposite ends of the state, with a handful of less-visited places dotted along the coast between Goa and Kerala. Road and rail routes dictate that most itineraries take in the brash state capital, **Bengaluru (Bangalore)**, a go-ahead, modern city that epitomizes the aspirations of the country's new middle class, with glittering malls, fast-food outlets and a nightlife unrivalled outside Mumbai. The state's second city, **Mysuru (Mysore)**, appeals more for its Raj-era ambience, nineteenth-century palaces and vibrant produce and incense markets. It also lies within easy reach of several important historical monuments.

A clutch of unmissable sights lie further northwest, dotted around the dull railway town of **Hassan**. Around nine centuries ago, the Hoysala kings sited their grand dynastic capitals here, at the now middle-of-nowhere villages of **Belur** and **Halebidu (Halebid)**, where several superbly crafted temples survive intact. More impressive still, and one of India's most extraordinary sacred sites, is Gomateshwara, the 18m Jain colossus at **Sravanabelagola**, which stares serenely over idyllic Deccan countryside.

West of Mysuru, the Ghats rise in a wall of thick jungle cut by deep ravines and isolated valleys. Within, the coffee-growing district of **Kodagu (Coorg)** offers an entrancing, unique culture and lush, misty vistas. Most Coorg agricultural produce is

---

BEST TIME TO VISIT

Coastal Karnataka is one of the wettest regions in India, its climate dominated by the seasonal monsoon, which sweeps in from the southwest in June, dumping an average of 4m of rain on the coast before it peters out in late September. October to April is therefore the best time to visit. **Bengaluru and Mysuru**, to the south of the Deccan Plateau, have a temperate climate with mild weather most of the year. The **northern tracts** and the coast get really hot in summer (April–June), with monsoon bringing some respite between July and October.

KUDLE BEACH, GOKARNA

Highlights

❶ Bengaluru Booming silicon city offers the best shopping, nightlife and dining this side of Mumbai, not to mention a few great parks, plus the odd palace and temple. **See p.212**

❷ Mysuru (Mysore) The sandalwood city oozes relaxed, old-world charm and has lots to see, including the opulent palace and a photogenic market. **See p.222**

❸ Halebidu and Belur Two wonderfully ornate and architecturally unique Hoysala temples set deep in the slow-paced Karnataka countryside. **See p.232 & p.233**

❹ Gokarna This vibrant Hindu holy town is blessed with atmospheric temples and exquisite crescent beaches and is ideal for serious unwinding. **See p.246**

❺ Hampi The crumbling remains of the Vijayanagar kingdom, scattered among a stunning boulder-strewn landscape bisected by the Tungabhadra River. **See p.252**

❻ Vijayapura (Bijapur) Known as the "Agra of the South" for its splendid Islamic architecture, most famously the vast dome of the Gol Gumbaz. **See p.264**

❼ Bidar Rarely visited Muslim outpost in the remote northeast of the state, famed for *bidri* metalwork and magnificent medieval monuments. **See p.269**

HIGHLIGHTS ARE MARKED ON THE MAP ON P.210

FESTIVALS IN KARNATAKA

Hampi Utsav (early to mid-Jan). Celebrated since Vijayanagar times and revived by the Government of Karnataka, this three-day festival is a cultural showcase of music, dance, costume dramas, puppet shows, fireworks, processions and *kushti* (wrestling) that once received royal patronage.

Makar Sankranti (mid-Jan). The transition of the sun into the zodiacal sign of Makara (Capricorn) is when the harvest festival (*suggi habba*) is celebrated. Temple festivities, cultural programmes and kite-flying, especially in northern Karnataka, mark the occasion.

Bangalore Karaga (April). Bengaluru's oldest festival is celebrated over eleven days around the Dharmaraya Swamy Temple in the old city. The festival honours Draupadi, considered a form of Shakti, and is named after the *karaga* or large floral pyramid borne by the appointed carrier during a night-time procession to the accompaniment of music and acrobatics.

Mysore Dasara (Sept/Oct). The biggest of them all, Karnataka's *naada habba* (state festival) culminates in a grand procession on its tenth and final day (see box, p.226).

Kadalekai Parishe (Dec/Jan). Bengaluru's unique groundnut fair, held near the Bull Temple in Basavanagudi (see p.215) with rural produce on sale.

shipped out of **Mangaluru (Mangalore)**, a useful stopover on the journey along Karnataka's beautiful **Karavali coast**. Interrupted by countless mangrove-lined estuaries, the state's 320km-long coastline contains plenty of fine beaches. Attractions of the coastal belt include the famous Krishna temple at **Udupi**, an important Vaishnavite centre, **Jog Falls** – India's second highest cataract – set amid some of the region's most spectacular scenery, though for many the region's biggest draw is the atmospheric Hindu pilgrimage town of **Gokarna**, further north up the coast, a well-established hideaway for Western budget travellers owing to its string of exquisite beaches.

However, the state's undisputed highlight lies in the hinterland of **northern Karnataka**: the UNESCO-listed ghost city of Vijayanagar, better known as **Hampi**. Scattered around boulder hills on the south banks of the Tungabhadra River, the ruins of this once splendid capital provide a magical setting, often prompting travellers to overstay. The main access point to Hampi is **Hosapete (Hospet)**, from where buses leave for the journey north across the rolling Deccan plains to **Badami, Aihole** and **Pattadakal**, the last another UNESCO World Heritage Site. Now lost in countryside, these tiny villages – once capitals of the **Chalukya** dynasty – are still littered with ancient rock-cut caves and finely carved stone temples.

Further north, in one of Karnataka's most remote and poorest districts, craggy hilltop citadels and crumbling wayside tombs herald the formerly troubled buffer zone between the Muslim-dominated northern Deccan and the Dravidian-Hindu south. **Bijapur**, capital of the Bahmanis – now formally **Vijayapura** – harbours South India's finest collection of Islamic architecture, including the world's second largest freestanding dome, the Gol Gumbaz. The first Bahmani capital, **Gulbarga** (now **Kalaburagi**) site of a famous Muslim shrine and theological college, has retained little of its former splendour but the more isolated **Bidar**, where the Bahmanis moved in the sixteenth century, deserves a detour en route to or from Hyderabad. Perched on a rocky escarpment, its crumbling red ramparts include Persian-style mosaic-fronted mosques, mausoleums and a sprawling fort complex evocative of Samarkand on the Silk Route.

Brief history

Like much of southern India, Karnataka has been ruled by successive Buddhist, Hindu and Muslim dynasties. The influence of Jainism has also been marked; India's very first emperor, **Chandragupta Maurya**, is believed to have converted to Jainism in the fourth century BC, renounced his throne and fasted to death at Sravanabelagola, now one of the most visited Jain pilgrimage centres in the country.

During the first millennium AD, this whole region was dominated by power struggles between the various kingdoms controlling the western Deccan. The period between the third and fifth centuries saw the rise of dynasties like the **Satavahanas**, the **Kadambas** and the **Gangas** of Talakad. From the sixth to the eighth centuries, the **Chalukya** kingdom of Vatapi (Badami) included Maharashtra, the Konkan coast on the west and the whole of Karnataka. The **Rashtrakutas** and the **Hoysalas** dominated until the thirteenth century, when the Deccan kingdoms were overwhelmed by General Malik Kafur, a convert to Islam.

By the medieval era Muslim incursions from the north laid the foundation of the **Bahmani** kingdom and forced the hitherto warring and fractured Hindu states of the South into close alliance, with the mighty **Vijayanagar** kings emerging as overlords. Their lavish capital, Vijayanagar, ruled an empire stretching from the Bay of Bengal to the Arabian Sea and south to Cape Comorin. The Bahmani empire split into five independent kingdoms in 1490 but joined forces as a confederacy, the Deccan Sultanate, in 1565 at the Battle of Talikota, and laid siege to Vijayanagar, plundering its opulent palaces and temples.

Thereafter, a succession of Muslim sultans held sway over the North, while in the south of the state, the independent **Wadiyar rajas** of Mysore, whose territory was comparatively small, successfully fought off the Marathas. In 1761, the brilliant Muslim campaigner Haider Ali, with French support, seized the throne. His son, Tipu Sultan, turned Mysore into a major force in the South before he was killed by the British at the **battle of Srirangapatnam** in 1799. After Tipu's defeat, the British restored the Wadiyar family to the throne. Apart from a further half-century of colonial rule in the mid-nineteenth century, they kept it until Karnataka was created by the merging of the states of Mysore and the Madras Presidencies in 1956.

Bengaluru (Bangalore) and around

The political hub of the region, **BENGALURU** is a world apart from the rest of the state and in many ways India's most Westernized urban centre. Once a sleepy cantonment, the charming, verdant "Garden City" of just over 600,0000 people at Independence has been completely transformed by the technology boom into both a trendy, racy business hub and a bustling, smog-choked megalopolis of around 8.5 million, perhaps the fastest growing city in India. These days, signs of the West are thick on the ground: big-brand fashion stores and branches of *CCD* or *Barista* on nearly every corner; a swanky international airport and ultramodern metro (still far from completion); and legions of hard-working, free-spending twenty- and thirty-somethings in designer T-shirts and miniskirts.

Despite its lush environs and cosmopolitan air, Bengaluru's few attractions are no match for those elsewhere in the state. That said, it's an efficient transport hub, well served by plane and bus, and paired with first-rate shopping, dining and nightlife, and a calendar packed with big-ticket events in music, dance, art, literature, theatre or folk arts, this vibrant city can still deliver a few days' respite from South India's more taxing inconveniences.

The centre of modern Bengaluru lies about 4km east of Kempe Gowda Circle (and the bus and railway stations), near **MG Road**, where you'll find most of the mid-range accommodation, restaurants, shops, tourist information and banks. Leafy **Cubbon Park**, and its less than exciting museums, lie on its eastern edge, while the oldest, most "Indian" part of the city extends south from the railway station, a warren of winding streets at their most dynamic in the hubbub of the **City** and **Gandhi markets**. Bengaluru's tourist attractions are spread out: monuments such as **Tipu's Summer Palace** and the **Bull Temple** are some way south of the centre. Most, if not all, can be seen on a half-day tour, but if you explore on foot, be warned that Bengaluru has some of the worst pavements in India.

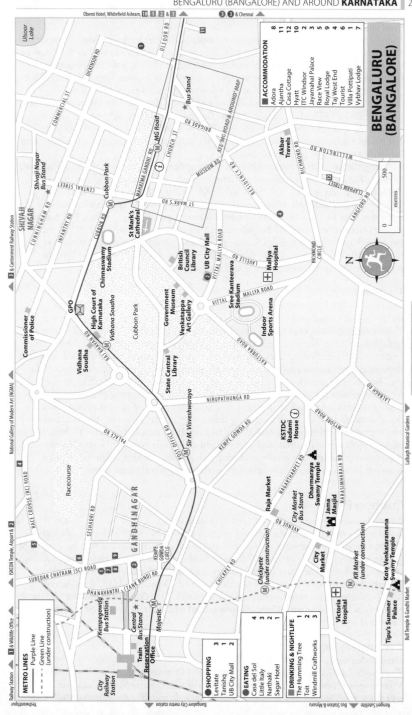

BENGALURU (BANGALORE)

METRO LINES
— Purple Line
‑ ‑ ‑ Green Line
(under construction)

ACCOMMODATION
Adora	8
Ajantha	11
Casa Cottage	12
Hyatt	10
ITC Windsor	2
Jayamahal Palace	3
Race View	5
Royal Lodge	9
Taj West End	4
Tourist	6
Villa Pottipati	1
Vybhav Lodge	7

SHOPPING
Levitate	3
Tanishq	1
UB City Mall	2

EATING
Casa del Sol	4
Little Italy	3
Narthaki	2
Sagar Hotel	1

DRINKING & NIGHTLIFE
The Humming Tree	2
Toit	1
Windmill Craftworks	3

0 — 500 metres

4

Brief history

A stone inscription near a tenth-century temple in the eastern part of the city describes a battle fought on this ground in 890, in a place called "Bengaval-uru," or the "City of Guards". This marks the earliest historical reference to the city that was **renamed** Bengaluru in 2006. (Another legend ascribes the city's origins to "benda-kal-ooru", or "village of boiled beans", after a Hoysala ruler was offered a humble meal of boiled beans on a hunting expedition and founded a town at the site.) The city was established more firmly in 1537 when Magadi **Kempe Gowda**, a feudatory chief of the Vijayanagar empire, set up a *pete* (town) here. His son Kempe Gowda II built a mud fort and erected four watchtowers outside the *pete*, predicting that it would one day extend that far (the city now stretches far beyond).

During the first half of the seventeenth century, Bangalore fell to the Muslim sultanate of Bijapur and changed hands several times before being returned to Hindu rule under the Mysore Wadiyar rajas. In 1758, Chikka Krishnaraja Wadiyar II was deposed by the military genius **Haider Ali**, who set up arsenals here to produce muskets, rockets and other weapons for his formidable anti-British campaigns. He and his son, **Tipu Sultan**, greatly extended and fortified Bangalore until Tipu was overthrown in 1799 by the British, who established a military cantonment and passed the administration over to the maharaja of Mysore in 1881. With the creation of Karnataka state in 1956, the erstwhile maharaja became governor and Bangalore the capital.

The modern city

Even before 1947, the city had already begun to transform into a scientific and technological capital with the establishment of numerous colleges and universities. Until well after Independence, political leaders, film stars and VIPs flocked to buy or build homes here. The so-called "Garden City" offered many parks and leisurely green spaces, not to mention theatres, cinemas and a lack of restrictions on alcohol. In recent decades Bengaluru has experienced a **seismic societal shift**, predominantly due to the endless job opportunities presented by computer software and back-office services. The 1990s high-tech boom saw skyscrapers, swish stores and shopping malls springing up, while the city's infrastructure buckled. The stumbles prodded several multinationals to decamp to Hyderabad, itself a growing technology centre, upsetting the local economy and temporarily threatening Bengaluru's treasured status as India's main IT hub. Led by rapid growth in the international telecom and call-centre sectors, the city has bounced back in recent years, though sky-rocketing living costs, choking pollution, regular power failures and crippling seasonal water shortages remain a problem.

Cubbon Park

ⓂVidhana Soudha or buses #296B, #114B and #114C from Kempegowda Bus Station

A welcome green space in the heart of the city, shaded by massive clumps of bamboo, **Cubbon Park** is entered from the western end of MG Road, presided over by a statue of Queen Victoria. Several prominent historic landmarks are located within its sprawling expanse, including the **State Central Library**, one of the oldest and largest in the country, housed in the impressive red Sheshadri Iyer Memorial Hall (daily except Mon 8.30am–6pm), and the colonnaded, red-brick **High Court of Karnataka** (Attara Kacheri), while the famous **Chinnaswamy cricket stadium** and domed **St Mark's Cathedral** sit nearby.

Government Museum

Kasturba Rd • Tues–Sun 10am–5pm • ₹10

The poorly labelled and maintained **Government Museum** features prehistoric artefacts, Vijayanagar, Hoysala and Chalukya sculpture, musical instruments, Thanjavur paintings and Deccani and Rajasthani miniatures. It includes the adjacent **Venkatappa**

Art Gallery, which exhibits twentieth-century landscapes, portraits, abstract art, wood sculpture and occasional temporary art shows.

Vidhana Soudha
On the northwest edge of Cubbon Park • No public entry

Built in 1956, Bengaluru's vast State Secretariat, **Vidhana Soudha**, is the largest civic structure of its kind in the country. Kengal Hanumanthaiah, chief minister at the time, wanted a "people's palace" that, following the transfer of power from the royal Wadiyar dynasty to a legislature, would "reflect the power and dignity of the people". In theory its design is entirely Indian, but its overall effect is not unlike the bombastic colonial architecture built in the so-called Indo-Saracenic style.

Lalbagh Botanical Gardens
Daily 6am–7pm • ₹10 • Buses #25, #25A & #25B and #25E from Kempegowda Bus Station • ⓥ bit.ly/LalbaghBangalore

Inspired by the splendid gardens of the Mughals and the French botanical gardens at Puducherry in Tamil Nadu (see p.396), Sultan Haider Ali set to work in 1760 laying out the **Lalbagh Botanical Gardens**, 4km south of the centre. Originally covering forty acres, just beyond his fort – where one of Kempe Gowda's original watchtowers can still be seen – the gardens were expanded under Ali's son Tipu, who introduced numerous exotic species of plants, and today they house an extensive horticultural seedling centre. The British brought in gardeners from Kew in 1856 and built a military bandstand and a glasshouse, based on London's Crystal Palace, which hosts wonderful flower shows. Now spreading over 240 acres, the gardens are pleasant to visit during the day, but tend to attract unsavoury characters after around 6pm. Great sunsets and city views can be had from the central hill, which is topped by a small shrine.

Tipu's Summer Palace and around
KR Market • Daily 10am–6pm • ₹100 (₹5) • Buses #15E, #31 & #31E and #210A from Kempegowda Bus Station

Just southwest of the crowded City Market (aka KR Market), near the fairytale-like **Jama Masjid** – whitewashed and rambling and still in regular use – lies **Tipu's Summer Palace**, a two-storey, mostly wooden structure built in 1791. Similar in style to the Daria Daulat Bagh at Srirangapatna (see p.230), the palace is in a far worse state, with most of its painted decoration destroyed. Next door, the **Kote Venkataramana Swamy Temple**, dating from the early eighteenth century, was built by the Wadiyar rajas.

Bull Temple
Basavanagudi • Daily 7.30am–1.30pm & 2.30–8.30pm • Buses #15E, #31, #210A and #210E from Kempegowda Bus Station

Lying 6km south of the Kempegowda Bus Station, in the Basavanagudi area, Kempe Gowda's sixteenth-century **Bull Temple** houses a massive monolithic Nandi bull, its grey granite made black by the application of charcoal and oil. The temple is approached along a path lined with mendicants and snake charmers; inside, for a small donation, the priest will offer you a string of fragrant jasmine flowers.

Don't miss the **Dodda Ganesha Temple** (daily 6.30am–12.30pm & 5.30–8.30pm), featuring a mammoth monolith of Ganesha, 5.5m tall and 5m wide, below the Bull Temple.

Sri Radha Krishna Mandir (ISKCON temple)
Hare Krishna Hill, Chord Rd • Daily 7.15am–1pm & 4.15–8.30pm • Buses #78A, #78E, #19E, 258CC from Kempegowda Bus Station

Some 8km north of the centre lies ISKCON's (International Society of Krishna Consciousness) gleaming temple, a hybrid of ultramodern glass and vernacular South

Indian architecture. Also known as **Sri Radha Krishna Mandir**, it's a huge, lavish showpiece crowned by a gold-plated dome. Barriers guide visitors on a one-way journey through the well-organized complex to the inner sanctum, an octagonal hall resplendent with colourfully painted ceilings and golden images of the god Krishna and his consort Radha. Collection points throughout and inescapable merchandizing on the way out are evidence of the organization's highly successful commercialization.

National Gallery of Modern Art (NGMA)

Manikyavelu Mansion, Palace Rd • Tues–Sun 10am–5pm; 1hr guided tours Wed 11am & Sat 3pm • ₹500 (₹20); camera ₹1000/image • ☎ 080 2846 6313, ⓦ ngmaindia.gov.in

Opened in February 2009 and set in a former Wadiyar mansion, the **National Gallery of Modern Art** (one of three in India – the others are in Delhi and Mumbai) is a fabulous repository of 17,000 paintings, sculptures and graphic prints capturing Indian art from the early eighteenth century to present times.

Around Bengaluru

While most visitors push straight on to Mysuru, there are several places of interest within easy reach of Bengaluru, especially for those with interest in folk culture, wildlife or spiritual renewal.

Nrityagram Dance Village

Hesaraghatta • Tues–Sat 10am–2pm • Village entrance fee ₹50; guided tours with lunch and performance (book in advance) ₹1500/person (minimum ten) • ☎ 080 2846 6313, ⓦ nrityagram.org

Anyone wishing to see or study classical dance in a rural environment should check out **Nrityagram Dance Village**, a delightful, purpose-built model village 30km northwest of Bengaluru, designed by the award-winning architect Gerard de Cunha and founded by the late Protima Gauri. Gauri had a colourful career in media and film, and eventually came to be renowned as an exponent of Odissi dance. Attracting pupils from all over the world, the school hosts regular performances and lectures on Indian mythology and art, and also offers courses in different forms of Indian dance.

Nandi Hills

Daily 6am–10pm • ₹10 • ☎ 080 2659 9231, ⓦ horticulture.kar.nic.in/nandi.htm • You can stay at *Nehru Nilaya* (bookings via ⓔ nandihillsreservations.in) or KSTDC's *Mayura Pine Top* (☎ 0815 6250906, ⓦ karnatakaholidays.net) • Regular government buses from Kempegowda Bus Station (2hr)

Some 60km north of Bengaluru in Chikkaballapur district, **Nandi Hills** is named after the hilltop shrine of Yoga Nandishwara, dedicated to Shiva. The erstwhile summer retreat of Tipu Sultan and the British, the hills rise to almost 1500m and offer panoramic views and invariably pleasant weather. You can hike to **Tipu's Drop**, a dreaded 600m clifftop from which convicts were hurled to their death by Tipu Sultan, while other draws include the spring-fed Amrita Sarovar tank and *Nehru Nilaya*, the guesthouse where ex-PM Jawaharlal Nehru stayed.

Bannerghatta National Park

Daily 9.30am–5pm • Zoo ₹80; Butterfly Park ₹30; bus safari adults ₹400 (₹260), children ₹300 (₹130); boating ₹60; camera ₹20, video camera ₹200 • ⓦ bannerghattabiologicalpark.org • Bus BIG-10 AC4 from MG Rd, #365/#V365 from Kempegowda Bus Station or #366 from City Market; buses stop at Nagammana Doddi, 400m from the park

The key attraction of the 104-square-kilometre **Bannerghatta National Park**, 22km south of Bengaluru, is a compact "biological park", which houses a zoo, butterfly enclosure, crocodile farm, reptile park and aviary. Safaris are organized to see lions, tigers, herbivores and sloth bear in a wilderness habitat.

ART OF LIVING INTERNATIONAL CENTRE

Ved Vignam Maha Vidya Peeth (daily 9am-6.30pm; ☎ 080 6726 2626, ⊛ artofliving.org), the main centre of the **Art of Living** organization founded in 1982 by **Sri Sri Ravi Shankar** (not to be confused with the great sitar maestro), occupies 24 acres of lush, green, hilly land 21km south of Bengaluru on Kanakapura Road in Udayapura. Its centrepiece is the splendid, lotus-like **Vishalakshmi Mantap** temple, which is surrounded by more shrines, an amphitheatre and an ashram boasting lodgings, restaurants and a host of other facilities including a wellness centre, bookshop, Ayurvedic spa and even a wedding hall. The organization – now with centres worldwide and NGO status – was founded by the guru after he discovered **Sudarshan Kriya**, a powerful stress-reducing breathing technique that is the focal point of his teachings. Those interested in courses or volunteering can register through the website, or simply drop in to attend regular events like music, meditation and *darshan* led by the guru (most Wed & Sat 4.30pm). Get here by taking bus #211A, #211B, #211C or #211F from Kempegowda Bus Station or #213 or #214D from City Market.

Janapada Loka Folk Arts Museum

On the Mysuru road • Daily except Tues 9am–5.30pm • Museum ₹100 (₹20); video show ₹5; boating ₹10 • ☎ 96866 01166, ⊛ jaanapadaloka.org • Any Bengaluru–Mysuru bus, except nonstop express services, can drop you here

The **Janapada Loka Folk Arts Museum**, 53km southwest of Bengaluru, gives a fascinating insight into the region's culture. The collection is impressive: there's an amazing array of hunting implements, weapons, ingenious household gadgets, masks, dolls and shadow puppets, plus carved wooden *bhuta* (spirit) sculptures and larger-than-life temple procession figures, manuscripts, musical instruments and *yakshagana* theatre costumes. A small **restaurant** serves simple food, and the adjacent *Kamat Lokaruchi* restaurant is a popular stopover for Bengaluru–Mysuru travellers.

4

ARRIVAL AND DEPARTURE   BENGALURU (BANGALORE) AND AROUND

BY PLANE

Airport Bengaluru International Airport (⊛ bengaluru airport.com) is 35km northeast of the city in Devanahalli. It's the busiest in South India and the most spacious in the country, with top-notch facilities. Until the much-discussed high-speed rail link is up and running, you can get into the city by Meru Airport Taxi (₹700–800; ☎ 080 4422 4422, ⊛ merucabs.com) or efficient a/c Vayu Vajra bus; the most useful routes to visitors are the round-the-clock #9 to/from Central Bus Stand (every 20–50min; 45min–1hr 15min; ₹180) and #7A to/from MG Rd (11 daily; 50min–1hr 20min; ₹180). KSRTC (see p.218) also runs direct FlyBus services from the airport to Mysuru (8 daily), and an overnight service (departing 9pm) to Kundapur on the coast, via Mangaluru and Udupi.

Airlines Air India (☎ 080 6678 5161); Go Air (☎ 080 4740 6091); Indigo (☎ 080 6678 5450); Jet Airways (☎ 080 3989 3333); SpiceJet (☎ 1 800 180 3333).

Destinations Chennai (24 daily; 50min); Delhi (37–43 daily; 2hr 30min–3hr 30min); Goa (6 daily; 1hr); Hyderabad (20 daily; 1hr–1hr 30min); Kochi (10 daily; 1hr–1hr 20min); Mumbai (33 daily; 1hr 30min–1hr 45min); Thiruvananthapuram (6 daily; 1hr 10min).

BY TRAIN

Stations Bengaluru is well connected by train to all parts of India. Bangalore City railway station is west of the centre, near Kempe Gowda Circle, opposite the main bus stands; for the north of the city, it's better to board or disembark at Bangalore Cantonment station north of the centre. Bangalore City has prepaid auto-rickshaw and taxi booths in the forecourt, and is connected (via Majestic station) to MG Road and points east in the city by Namma Metro's newly completed Purple Line. Trains to Goa and a handful of trains to other destinations leave from Yeshwanthpur railway station (☎ 080 2337 7161) in the north of the city; Namma Metro's Green Line from Nagasandra has stops at Yeshwanthpur and currently runs south as far as Sampige Road station, a 20min walk from Kempegowda Bus Station.

Bookings The computerized reservation office at Bangalore City (Mon–Sat 8am–2pm & 2.15–8pm, Sun 8am–2pm; ☎ 132) is in a separate building, to the left as you approach the station; counter 14 is for foreigners.

Destinations The most useful services from Bangalore City include: *Shatabdi Express* #12028 (daily except Wed 4.25pm; 5hr) to Chennai; *Karnataka Express* #12627 (daily 7.20pm; 38hr 35min) to Delhi; *Hampi Express* #16592 (daily 10pm; 9hr 10min) to Hosapete; *Udyan Express* #11302 (daily 8.45pm; 21hr 45min) to Mumbai; *Shatabdi Express* #12007 (daily except Wed 11am; 2hr), *Tippu Express* #12614 (daily 3pm; 2hr 30min) or *Chamundi Express* #16216 (daily 6.15pm; 2hr 55min) to Mysuru; *Kacheguda Express* #12786 (daily 6.20pm; 11hr 20min) to Hyderabad (Kacheguda station) and *Kanya-kumari Express* #16526 (daily 8pm) to Thiruvananthapuram (16hr) via Ernakulam (for Kochi; 12hr 20min).

BY BUS

Government buses Long-distance government buses, including those from other states like Goa and Maharashtra, arrive at the busy Central Bus Stand, opposite the railway station (T 77609 90562, W ksrtc.in). There is a comprehensive timetable in English in the centre of the Central Bus Stand concourse. Most services can be booked in advance at the computerized counters near Bay 13 (daily 7.30am–7.30pm).

Private buses Tickets for the numerous private bus companies can be bought from the agencies on Tank Bund Rd, on the opposite side of the bus stand from the train station; operators include Sharma (T 080 2670 2447, W sharmatransports.com), Vijayanand Travels or VRL (T 080 2297 1245, W vrlbus.in), Paulo (T 080 2238 4040, W paulo travels.com), SRS (T 080 2680 1616, W srsbooking.com) and National (T 080 2660 3112, W nationaltravels.in), which advertise a multitude of destinations, including sleeper coaches to Goa and Mumbai.

Destinations Chennai (hourly; 6–7hr); Hassan (every 15–30min; 4hr); Hosapete (2 daily; 10hr); Hyderabad (6 daily; 15–16hr); Madikeri (hourly; 6hr); Mangaluru (every 30min–1hr; 9–10hr); Mumbai (2–4 daily; 23–24hr); Mysuru (every 10–15min; 3hr); Ootacamund (6 daily; 7hr 30min–8hr); Puttaparthy (every 30min–1hr; 4hr); Tirupati (hourly; 7hr).

GETTING AROUND

By bus Bengaluru's extensive bus system radiates from the Kempegowda Bus Station (T 080 222 2542), near City railway station. Most buses from platform 17 travel past MG Rd. Along with regular buses, BMTC (T 1800 425 1663, W mybmtc.com) also operates a deluxe express service, Pushpak, on a number of set routes (#P109 terminates at Whitefield, by the famous Sai Baba ashram) as well as a handful of night buses. Other important city bus stands include the City Market Bus Stand at Kalasipalayam (T 080 2295 2333), near the railway station, and Shivaji Nagar (T 080 2295 2324) to the northeast of Cubbon Park.

4

By metro Opening in stages since 2012, Bengaluru's Namma Metro (W bmrc.co.in) has struggled to take off, though the opening of the full length of the east–west Purple Line in mid-2016 will increase its usefulness to travellers markedly, linking the main train and bus stations (via Majestic/Kempegowda station) with points east including Cubbon Park, MG Road and Indiranagar. The north–south Green Line is slated to open in full in December 2016, when it will intersect with the Purple Line at Majestic before continuing south via Chikpete, KR Market and Lalbagh. Trains run every 10–15min from 6am to 10pm, and tickets cost ₹10–40.

By auto-rickshaw The easiest way of getting around is by metered auto-rickshaw, which can now even be summoned by app (W mgaadi.com). Fares start at ₹25 for the first kilometre and ₹8/km thereafter; one-and-a-half or double-meter rates usually apply 9pm–6am, and there's an extra surcharge of ₹20 to suburban areas. Most meters do work and drivers are usually willing to use them, although you will occasionally be asked for a flat fare, especially during rush hour. Expect to pay ₹80–100 from the Kempegowda Bus Station to MG Rd.

By taxi You can book chauffeur-driven cars and taxis through several agencies including EasyCabs (T 080 4343 4343, W easycabs.com), EZI Drive (T 080 4240 0000, W ezidrive.in) or Carzonrent (T 88822 22222, W carzonrent .com), or use Ola or Uber.

Car rental Avis has outlets at the airport and the *Oberoi* hotel, 37–39 MG Rd (T 080 2558 5858, W avis.com). Hertz (T 080 4330 2201, W hertz.com) has counters at the airport and on Swami Vivekananda Rd, east of MG Rd. Zoom (W zoomcar.com) is a decent Indian self-drive option. For long-distance car rental and tailor-made itineraries, try one of the travel agents listed in the Directory (see p.222) or any KSTDC office (see below).

INFORMATION AND TOURS

India Tourism For information on Bengaluru, Karnataka and neighbouring states, go to the excellent India Tourism Office (Mon–Fri 9.30am–6pm, Sat 9am–1pm; T 080 2558 5417), in Triumph Tower, 48 Church St, where you can pick up free maps for both city and state.

KSTDC Apart from booths at the City railway station (daily 7am–8pm; T 080 2287 0068) and at the airport, Karnataka State Tourist Development Corporation (W karnatakatourism .org) also has an office at Badami House, NR Square (daily 6am–10pm; T 080 4334 4334), where you can book tours (W karnatakaholidays.net).

Listings For information about what's on, pick up the twice-monthly listings magazine *Travel & Shop* (W travelandshop .in), available at most hotels and tourist offices, or the online guide *Time Out Bangalore* (W timeout.com/bangalore).

National parks information For information on any of Karnataka's national parks, call at the Wildlife Office, Forest Department, Aranya Bhavan, Malleswaram (T 080 2334 1993), or try Jungle Lodges & Resorts, Floor 2, Shrungar Shopping Centre, off MG Rd (T 080 2559 7021, W jungle lodges.com). The latter, a quasi-government body, promotes ecotourism through a number of upmarket forest lodges, including the much-lauded *Kabini River Lodge* (see p.239) near Nagarahole.

Walking tours Bangalore Walks (W bangalorewalks.com) organizes engaging theme-based walks (₹500, plus optional breakfast ₹200) regularly around the city. Bengaluru by Foot (T 080 4120 3095, W bengalurubyfoot.com) lead a range of fascinating cultural and food tours in and around Bengaluru (from ₹600), as well as in Mysuru.

ACCOMMODATION

Due to the great number of business visitors it receives, Bengaluru offers a wealth of upmarket lodgings, as well as serviced apartments. Decent **budget accommodation** is also available, mostly concentrated around the Central Bus Stand and railway station.

MG ROAD AND AROUND

★**Ajantha** 22-A MG Rd ☎080 2558 4321, ⓦhotel ajantha.in; map p.213. Best value in this area, with 61 basic yet large rooms and four spacious cottages (₹2650), located at the end of a quiet lane but close to all the action. Complimentary breakfast at the veg restaurant. ₹1650

★**Casa Cottage** 2 Clapham St ☎080 2227 0754, ⓦcasa cottage.com; map p.213. Tranquillity awaits at these cottages, set in well-maintained grounds just over 1km south of MG Rd. The cottages and apartments are enormous, comfortable and well appointed, and the free breakfasts are excellent. ₹3900

Empire International 36 Church St ☎080 4041 4041, ⓦhotelempire.in; map p.219. Smart, newish hotel with a popular restaurant and very comfortable rooms boasting modern decor and good facilities. The slightly cheaper sister concern *Hotel Empire*, a few blocks north of MG Rd on Central St, is similar but lacks the finer touches, and charges ₹1572 for a double. ₹2475

Hyatt 1/1 Swami Vivekananda Rd ☎080 2555 8888, ⓦbangalore.hyatthotels.hyatt.com; map p.213. Formerly the *Ista*, this ultra-luxurious hotel is a secluded sanctuary, with an infinity pool, jacuzzi and gym, plus breezy, safari-themed *Liquid Lounge* bar. Some of the spacious rooms have marble baths and views of Ulsoor Lake; suites have large garden balconies. Online deals available. ₹7000

The Park Residency Pinto Towers, 36 Residency Rd ☎080 2558 2151, ⓦparkresidency.net; map p.219. This concrete behemoth offers good value, considering the central location, with clean, sizeable rooms, all with fridge, TV and some a/c. Hearty Indian or Continental breakfast included. ₹2200

Shangrila 182 Brigade Rd ☎080 4112 1622, ⓔshangrila _htl@yahoo.co.in; map p.219. A welcoming Tibetan-run lodge that's right in the thick of things; the comfy standard rooms are decent value and the a/c ones are a great deal. Good Tibetan/Chinese restaurant, too. No wi-fi. ₹1000

AROUND THE RAILWAY STATION AND CENTRAL BUS STAND

Adora 47 SC Rd ☎080 2220 0025; map p.213. Above a quality South Indian veg restaurant, this large hotel is a top budget place and popular backpacker choice. Though bland, the rooms are clean and sizeable, and some have a/c. Wi-fi only in lobby. ₹884

Royal Lodge 252 SC Rd ☎080 2226 6951, ⓦroyallodge .in; map p.213. A large, functional budget hotel, which has been recently upgraded without much of a price hike. All rooms are attached, with TV, except a few poky singles. No wi-fi. ₹700

Tourist Ananda Rao Circle, Race Course Rd ☎080 2226 2381; map p.213. One of Bengaluru's best all-round budget lodges, with four floors wrapped round a courtyard and a veg restaurant. Small rooms, long verandas, friendly family management and no reservations, so it fills up fast. No wi-fi. ₹400

Vybhav Lodge 42 SC Rd ☎080 2287 3997; map p.213. A tad grubby and frayed at the edges but not a bad fall-back.

4

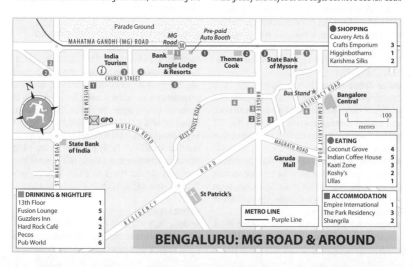

BENGALURU: MG ROAD & AROUND

All the rooms are extremely compact and the cell-like attached singles with TV are very inexpensive. No wi-fi. ₹600

NORTH OF THE CENTRE

ITC Windsor 25 Golf Course Rd ☎080 2226 9898, ⓦitchotels.in/hotels/itcwindsor.aspx; map p.213. Ersatz palace, now a luxurious five-star, mainly for overseas businesspeople with rates to match. Facilities include a gym, pool, jacuzzi, fine restaurant and popular Irish pub, *Dublin*. ₹8500

Jayamahal Palace 1 Jayamahal Rd ☎080 4058 0444, ⓦjayamahalpalace.com; map p.213. A charming heritage hotel tucked in a leafy precinct near Cantonment railway station. The large rooms have parquet flooring and balconies overlooking lawns. ₹4500

Race View 25 Race Course Rd ☎080 4069 6111; map p.213. Large business hotel with sizeable wood-panelled

rooms. Those at the front do overlook the racecourse but also the busy road. The a/c rooms cost just a little more. No wi-fi. ₹1150

Taj West End Race Course Rd ☎080 2225 5055, ⓦtaj hotels.com; map p.213. Begun as a British-run boarding house in 1887, these lodgings were later upgraded with fabulous gardens and long colonnaded walkways. The old wing is bursting with character, with broad verandas overlooking acres of grounds. Good online deals. ₹12,500

Villa Pottipati 142 4th Main, 8th Cross, Malleswaram ☎080 2336 0777, ⓦvilla-pottipati.neemranahotels .com; map p.213. A heritage hotel in the northwestern suburbs, wrapped in a garden of jacaranda trees and flowering shrubs. Its rooms ooze old-world style, with pillared verandas, deep bathtubs and direct access to an outdoor swimming pool. Gourmet Indian and Continental meals are also served. ₹4500

EATING

Bengaluru's profusion of cafés and restaurants makes up for its deficit of tourist sights with a gastronomic variety unparalleled in South India. Around **MG Rd**, and in **Indiranagar** (east of the centre) and the southeastern suburb of Koramangala, pizzerias, burger chains, ritzy ice-cream parlours and gourmet restaurants stand cheek by jowl with regional cuisine from Andhra Pradesh, Tamil Nadu, Kerala, Bengal and Punjab, besides Mumbai *chaat* cafés and snack bars. Stand-up local eateries called **darshinis** are popular for a quick bite. In addition to the places below, many of the establishments listed under "Drinking and nightlife" (see opposite) also serve good food.

MG ROAD AND AROUND

★**Casa del Sol** 3rd floor, Devatha Plaza, 131 Residency Rd, 3km south of MG Rd ☎080 4151 0101; map p.213. The ₹250 lunch buffet is worth every paise and the Sunday brunches are festive, all-you-can-drink affairs. An evening cocktail on the cool, comfortable terrace is a real treat. Daily 11am–11pm.

Coconut Grove 86 Church St ☎080 2559 6262; map p.219. Mouthwatering gourmet cuisine from Kerala, Chettinad and Coorg. Veg, fish and meat preparations are served in traditional copper thalis on a leafy terrace, and there's a wide range of seafood dishes. Main dishes ₹480–650. Its *Coco Grove* cocktail bar is a good spot for a drink. Daily 12.30–3.30pm & 7–11.30pm.

Indian Coffee House Church St ☎080 2558 7088, ⓦindiancoffeehouse.com; map p.219. Now occupying incongruous modern premises but still old-fashioned at heart, with turbaned waiters serving tasty finger foods (₹32–65) and fine filter coffee. The perfectly fluffy scrambled eggs are superb. Daily 8am–8.30pm.

Kaati Zone Church St ☎080 6566 0000, ⓦkaatizone .com; map p.219. Fast, clean and wallet-friendly, the popular chain serves delicious *kaati* rolls (₹120), biryani, curry meals and "Rolls-Rice". It has a busy outlet at the airport with dine-in and delivery stores across town. Daily 11am–11pm.

★**Koshy's** St Mark's Rd ☎080 2221 3793; map p.219. A popular hangout for theatre folk, artists and old-timers, this atmospheric colonial-style café with pewter teapots

and cotton-clad waiters serves tasty Indian specialities and international favourites. The fish biryani, beef fry and chilli pork are legendary. Its adjacent sister concern, *Jewel Box*, is more upmarket with a/c. Daily 9am–11pm.

Ullas 1st floor, Public Utility Building, MG Rd ☎080 2558 7486; map p.219. Superb pure-veg restaurant, with a terrace and indoor section. Excellent lunchtime thalis (₹50–100) and a good choice of curries, plus Bombay *chaat*. Daily 9am–10pm.

AROUND THE RAILWAY STATION AND CENTRAL BUS STAND

Narthaki Just off SC Rd ☎94485 53274; map p.213. The best restaurant in the railway station and bus stand area. Veg meals are served on the first floor, while the restaurant-cum-bar on the second offers a full range of Indian and Chinese dishes. The chicken chilli is a belter. Mains ₹200–250. Daily 11.30am–11.30pm.

Sagar Hotel 48 SC Rd ☎080 2291 4197; map p.213. First-floor Andhra-style family restaurant serving filling biryanis for little more than ₹100, as well as dishes from other parts of India. There's an a/c bar upstairs. Daily 11.30am–4pm & 6.30–11pm.

INDIRANAGAR

★**Little Italy** 1135 100 Feet Rd, Indiranagar, 6km east of MG Rd ☎080 2520 7171, ⓦlittleitaly.in; map p.213. Fantastic vegetarian Italian food – try the risottos or tomato-based pasta dishes (₹400–500) – served on the bamboo-bordered terrace or in the elegant dining room.

There's also an extensive wine list. Daily noon–3.30pm & 6.30–11pm.

DRINKING AND NIGHTLIFE

Bengaluru's progressive outlook has fostered a thriving nightlife for urban youth and tourists alike. A night on the town generally kicks off with a bar crawl along the old colonial quarter of **Brigade Rd**, **Residency Rd** and **Church St**, which are lined with scores of swish **pubs**. Drinking alcohol does not have the seedy connotations it does elsewhere in India; you'll even see young Indian women enjoying a beer with their mates. While some prefer an elegant tipple in five-star hotels, it's the latest crop of microbreweries serving craft beer that are now all the rage. Most **clubs** operate a couples-only policy.

★**13th Floor** 13th Floor, Ivory Tower, 84 MG Rd ☎080 4178 3355; map p.219. Sip your poison and take in the sunset view (or glittering city lights) from a fine vantage point: classy and cosmopolitan, with cool postmodern decor, *13th Floor* is an absolute must. Come early because it fills up fast (happy hour till 7pm). Daily 5–11pm.

Fusion Lounge 185 Deena Complex, Brigade Rd ☎080 4114 2912; map p.219. Dazzling high-tech lounge-cum-nightclub with different spaces for pricey but excellent food, DJ nights, karaoke and live performances. Daily 11.30am–11.30pm (till 1am Fri & Sat).

Guzzlers Inn 48 Rest House Rd, off Brigade Rd ☎080 4112 2513; map p.219. Long-established watering hole serving up classic rock, live sports, draught beer and good affordable Indian food. Half-price afternoon happy hour extends till 8pm on weekdays. Daily 11am–11.30pm.

★**Hard Rock Café** 40 St Mark's Rd, at Church ☎080 4124 2222, ⓦhardrock.com/cafes/bengaluru; map p.219. This gorgeous, multiroom space inside an old stone library is well established as the buzzing nexus of Bengaluru nightlife, not to mention the finest bar and grill in town. With high vaulted ceilings, grey stone walls and subtle accents, it feels both lived in and new. Daily noon–11pm.

★**The Humming Tree** 12th Main Rd, Indiranagar ☎98866 18386, ⓦbit.ly/HummingTreeBangalore; map p.213. A popular venue for music gigs with a lounge bar serving wicked drinks and good food in a friendly

atmosphere. Daily noon–11.30pm (till 1am Fri & Sat).

Pecos 34 Rest House Rd, off Brigade Rd ☎080 2558 6047, ⓦpecospub.com; map p.219. Three dank levels of rock posters and ageing wood make up the definitive Bengaluru dive. The tunes are hard-driving, the beer's cheap and the Indian grub ain't half bad. Daily 10.30am–11pm.

Pub World 65 Laxmi Plaza, Residency Rd ☎080 2558 5206; map p.219. The city's second oldest pub, this stylish place has lots of TVs and semi-private booths with crimson couches, popular with trendy young professionals. Daily 11am–11pm.

★**Toit** 100 Ft Rd, Indiranagar II Stage ☎90197 13388, ⓦtoit.in; map p.213. A lively, loud brewpub across multiple levels with warm brick and wood interiors and eclectic decor. Terrific finger food is on offer and a drinks menu encompassing branded Belgian and German beer to cocktail pitchers. It's always crowded, so reserve a table or grab a stool near the bar. ₹750 entry on Wed, Fri & Sat. Daily noon–11pm.

★**Windmills Craftworks** 331 Rd 5B, EPIP Zone, Whitefield, 16.5km from MG Rd ☎88802 33322, ⓦwindmillscraftworks.com; map p.213. Exclusive space that blends gourmet food, music and books to browse with the best craft beer in town. Their *Terrace Buffet* (Mon–Fri noon–3pm & 7–11pm) features North Indian fare (lunch ₹700, dinner ₹900) and global flavours for Sunday brunch (11.30am–3.30pm). Mon–Thurs & Sun 11.30am–11.30pm, Fri & Sat till 1am.

SHOPPING

The bustling area around **MG Rd** is the hub of Bengaluru shopping, with lots of stores along its main section selling designer goods a little cheaper than in the West, as well as quality Indian clothing and accessories, and handy including UB City (see p.222), Bangalore Central and Garuda Mall. **Dickenson Rd** and **Commercial St** nearby are particularly strong on good jewellery and clothing. The free *Travel & Shop* magazine carries a huge list of establishments. At occasional **flea markets** like Kitsch Mandi (ⓦkitschmandi.com) and Soul Santhe (ⓦsundaysoulsante.com) you can find the traveller's garb and trinkets so evident in places like Hampi or Gokarna, and Raja Market and the crowded lanes of **Chickpet** are atmospheric for shopping for ethnic items.

Cauvery Arts & Crafts Emporium 49 MG Rd ☎080 2558 1118, ⓦcauveryhandicrafts.net; map p.219. This state government-run outlet sells all manner of wooden toys and gadgets, sandalwood sculptures, inlaid rosewood coffee tables, metalwork, carpets, rugs and hundreds of other gift items. Daily 10am–9pm.

Higginbothams 74 MG Rd ☎080 2558 6574; map p.219. The main Bengaluru branch of the venerable

national chain has a diverse collection of fiction, plus academic and reference books. Daily 9.30am–8.30pm.

Karishma Silks 45 MG Rd ☎080 2558 1606; map p.219. Vast, colourful range of pure silks, embroidered saris, cottons and *salwar kameez*, to suit most budgets. Daily 10.15am–8.45pm.

Levitate Above 100 Ft Boutique Restaurant, 100 Ft Rd, Indiranagar ☎98453 17776; map p.213. A quirky lifestyle boutique selling handwoven cotton scarves, handcrafted leather footwear, funky bags and trinkets, besides kitsch and retro Bollywood posters. Daily 11am–10pm.

Tanishq 121 Dickenson Rd ☎ 080 2555 0907, ⍵ tanishq .co.in; map p.213. If you have money to splash out on some really special jewellery, head for this treasure-trove of diamonds, gold and silver. Daily 10am–8pm.

UB City Mall Vittal Mallya Rd ⍵ ubcitybangalore.in; map p.213. Upmarket global luxury brands from Louis Vuitton to Jimmy Choo, fancy pubs, fine dining, an art gallery and Angsana spa announce where and how the rich come to roost and splurge.

DIRECTORY

Banks and exchange Thomas Cook, 70 MG Rd (☎ 1800 209 9100); TT Forex, 180 Cunningham Rd (☎ 080 2225 1201); Weizmann Forex Ltd, 56 Residency Rd (☎ 080 6628 4463) are all open Mon–Sat 10am–6.30pm. Banks have better rates; the State Bank of Mysore on MG Rd is the most convenient. There are ATMs all over, especially in the MG Rd area.

Hospitals Victoria Hospital, near City Market (☎ 080 2670 1150); Mallya (☎ 080 2227 7979), close to MG Rd.

Internet Internet cafés are widely available across the city, and generally charge ₹20–30/hr. They're usually open until 9pm or later.

Libraries The British Council (English-language) library, 23 Kasturba Rd Cross (Mon–Sat 10.30am–6.30pm; ☎ 080 2248 9220), has newspapers and magazines that visitors are welcome to peruse in a/c comfort.

Pharmacies Most pharmacies attached to hospitals are open 24/7; try Al-Siddique Pharma Centre, opposite Jama Masjid near City Market, and Janata Bazaar, in the Victoria Hospital.

Police ☎ 100.

Post office On the corner of Raj Bhavan Rd and Cubbon Rd, at the northern tip of Cubbon Park (Mon–Sat 10am–7pm, Sun 10.30am–1.30pm).

Travel agents For flight bookings and train, bus or hotel reservations, try Akbar Travels at 131 Brigade Rd, Shoolay Circle (☎ 080 2222 7645, ⍵ akbartravels.com). For cultural tours and adventure trails contact Gulliver Adventures & Travels (☎ 94813 78912, ⍵ gulliveradventures.in).

4

Mysuru (Mysore)

A centre of sandalwood-carving, silk and incense production, and dotted with palaces and gardens, **Mysore**, officially renamed **MYSURU** in 2014, is one of South India's more appealing cities. Nearly 160km southwest of Bengaluru, the city is Karnataka's cultural capital and the most popular tourist destination, attracting about 2.5 million visitors each year. Nevertheless, it remains a charming, old-fashioned place, changed by neither an IT boom nor its now well-established status as a top international yoga destination. That said, the erstwhile capital of the Wadiyar rajas can be underwhelming at first blush: upon stumbling off a bus or train you're not so much embraced by the scent of jasmine blossoms or gentle wafts of sandalwood as smacked by a cacophony of tooting, careening buses, bullock carts, bikes and tongas. Still, give it a few days and Mysuru will cast a spell on you.

In addition to its established tourist attractions, chief among them the **Mysore Palace**, Mysuru is a great city simply to stroll around. The evocative, if dilapidated, pre-Independence buildings lining market areas such as **Ashoka Road** and **Sayaji Rao Road** lend an air of faded grandeur to a busy centre that teems with vibrant street life.

Brief history

In the tenth century Mysuru was known as Mahishur – "the town where Mahishasura, the demon buffalo was slain" (by the goddess Durga; see box, p.226). Presiding over a district of many villages, the city was ruled from about 1400 until Independence by the Hindu **Wadiyars**. Their rule was only broken from 1761, when the Muslim Haider Ali and his son Tipu Sultan took over. Two years later, the new rulers demolished the labyrinthine old city to replace it with the elegant grid of sweeping, leafy streets and public gardens that survive today. However, following Tipu Sultan's defeat in 1799 by the British colonel Arthur Wellesley (later the Duke of Wellington), Wadiyar power was restored. As the capital of Mysore state, the city thereafter dominated a major part of southern India. In 1956, when Bangalore became capital of newly formed Karnataka, its maharaja was appointed governor. Following the demise in 2013 of

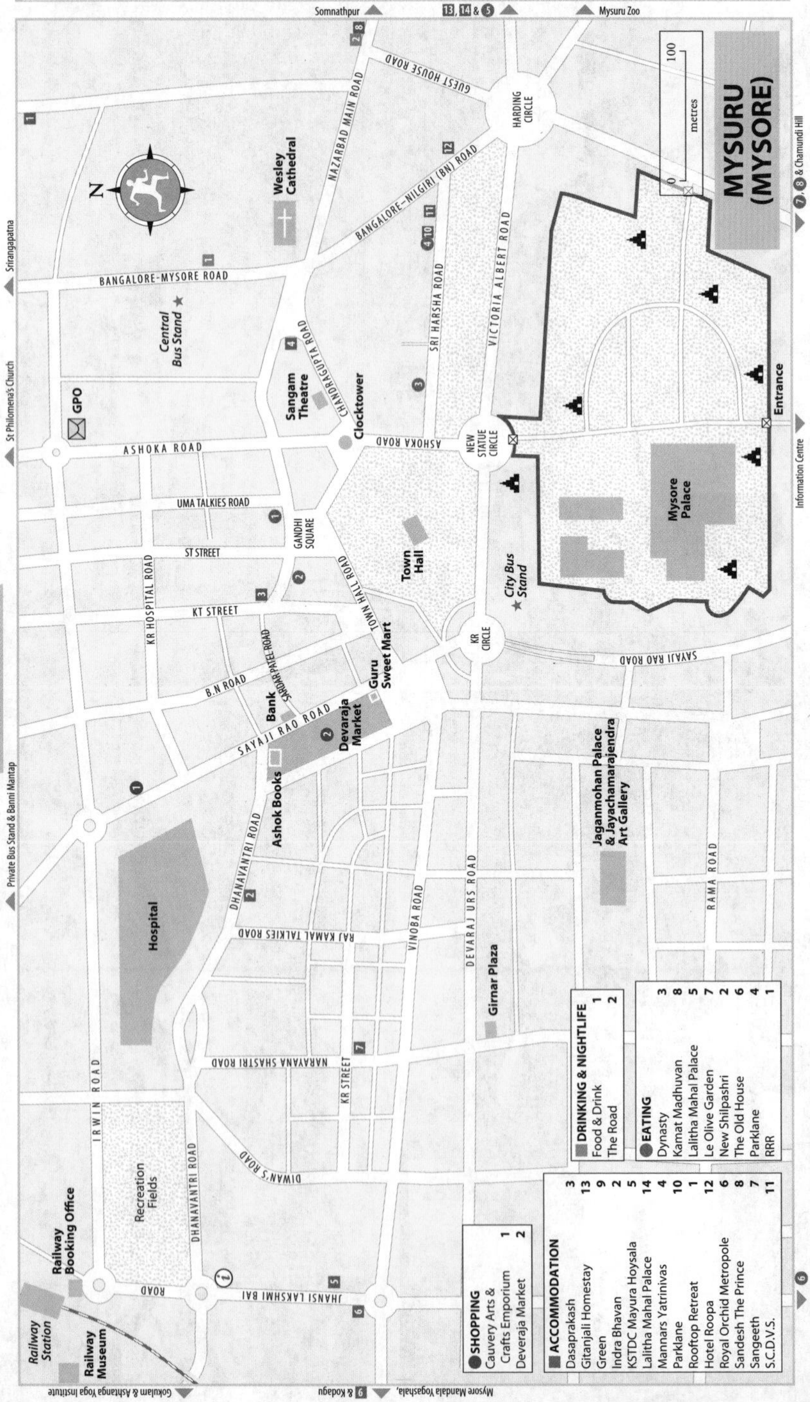

MYSURU (MYSORE)

Somnathpur
13, 14 & 5
Mysuru Zoo

HARDING CIRCLE

NAZARBAD MAIN ROAD
GUEST HOUSE ROAD
BANGALORE–NILGIRI (BN) ROAD
VICTORIA ALBERT ROAD
SRI HARSHA ROAD
CHANDRAGUPTA ROAD
BANGALORE–MYSORE ROAD
ASHOKA ROAD
ASHOKA ROAD
UMA TALKIES ROAD
ST STREET
KT STREET
KR HOSPITAL ROAD
B. N ROAD
SARDAR PATEL ROAD
SAYAJI RAO ROAD
TOWN HALL ROAD
DHANVANTRI ROAD
RAJ KAMAL TALKIES ROAD
VINOBA ROAD
DEVARAJ URS ROAD
RAMA ROAD
NARAYANA SHASTRI ROAD
KR STREET
DIWAN'S ROAD
IRWIN ROAD
DHANVANTRI ROAD
JHANSI LAKSHMI BAI ROAD
SAYAJI RAO ROAD

Wesley Cathedral
Central Bus Stand
GPO
Sangam Theatre
Clocktower
Gandhi Square
Town Hall
City Bus Stand
New Statue Circle
KR Circle
Guru Sweet Mart
Devaraja Market
Bank
Ashok Books
Hospital
Girnar Plaza
Mysore Palace
Entrance
Information Centre
Jaganmohan Palace & Jayachamarajendra Art Gallery
Recreation Fields
Railway Booking Office
Railway Station
Railway Museum

Srirangapatna
St Philomena's Church
Private Bus Stand & Banni Mantap
Gokulam & Ashtanga Yoga Institute
Mysore Mandala Yogashala
Kodagu
7, 8 & Chamundi Hill
7, 8 & Chamundi Hill

0 metres 100

N

● **SHOPPING**
| Cauvery Arts & Crafts Emporium | 1 |
| Devaraja Market | 2 |

■ **ACCOMMODATION**
Dasaprakash	3
Gitanjali Homestay	13
Green	9
Indra Bhavan	2
KSTDC Mayura Hoysala	14
Lalitha Mahal Palace	4
Mannars Yatrinivas	10
Parklane	1
Rooftop Retreat	12
Hotel Roopa	6
Royal Orchid Metropole	8
Sandesh The Prince	7
Sangeeth	11
S.C.D.V.S.	5

■ **DRINKING & NIGHTLIFE**
| Food & Drink | 1 |
| The Road | 2 |

● **EATING**
Dynasty	3
Kamat Madhuvan	8
Lalitha Mahal Palace	5
Le Olive Garden	7
New Shilpashri	2
The Old House	6
Parklane	4
RRR	1

Srikantadatta Narasimharaja Wadiyar, who had held the now titular role since 1974, his 23-year-old nephew Yaduveer Krishnadatta Chamaraja Wadiyar was ceremonially crowned as Mysuru's new king on May 28, 2015.

Mysore Palace

There are six gates in the perimeter wall but entrance is only via the Varaha Gate on the south side • Daily 10am–5.30pm • ₹200 (₹40); shoes and cameras must be left in the cloakroom • ☎ 0821 2421051, ⓦ mysorepalace.gov.in

Mysuru's centre is dominated by the walled maharaja's palace, popularly known as **Mysore Palace**, a fairytale spectacle topped with a shining brass-plated dome. It's especially magnificent on Sunday nights and during festivals, when it is illuminated by nearly 100,000 lightbulbs. The palace was completed in 1912 for the 24th Wadiyar raja, on the site of the old wooden palace that had been destroyed by fire in 1897. In 1998, after a lengthy judicial tussle, the courts decided in favour of formally placing the main palace in the hands of the Karnataka state government but the royal family, who still hold a claim, have lodged an appeal, which is ongoing. Twelve temples surround the palace, some of them of much earlier origin.

Entrance area and outer buildings

An extraordinary amalgam of styles from India and around the world crowds the lavish interior. Entry is through the Gombe Thotti or **Dolls' Pavilion**, once a showcase for the figures featured in the city's lively Dasara celebrations and now a gallery of European and Indian sculpture and ceremonial objects. Halfway along, the brass **Elephant Gate** forms the main entrance to the centre of the palace, through which the maharaja would drive to his car park. Decorated with floriated designs, it bears the Mysore royal symbol of Ganda-Berunda, a mythical double-headed eagle, now the state emblem. To the north, past the gate, stands a ceremonial elephant *howdah*. Elaborately decorated with 84kg of 24-carat gold, it appears to be inlaid with red and green gems – in fact the twinkling lights are battery-powered signals that would have let the *mahout* know when the maharaja wished to stop or go.

The main halls

Walls leading into the octagonal **Kalyana Mandapa**, the royal wedding hall, are lined with a meticulously detailed frieze of oil paintings, executed over a period of fifteen years by four Indian artists, illustrating the great Mysore Dasara festival (see box, p.226) of 1930. The hall itself is magnificent, a cavernous space featuring cast-iron pillars from Glasgow, Bohemian chandeliers and a domed ceiling featuring multicoloured Belgian stained glass arranged in peacock designs.

Climbing a staircase with Italian marble balustrades, past an unnervingly realistic figure of Krishnaraja Wadiyar IV, lounging comfortably with his bejewelled feet on a stool, you come into the **Public Durbar Hall**, an orientalist fantasy like something from *One Thousand and One Nights*. A vision of brightly painted and gilded colonnades, open on one side, the massive hall affords views out across the parade ground and gardens to Chamundi Hill. The maharaja gave audience from here, seated on a throne made from 280kg of solid gold, though these days the hall is only used during the Dasara festival, when it hosts classical concerts. The smaller Ambavilas, or **Private Durbar Hall**, features especially beautiful stained glass and gold-leaf painting. Before leaving you pass two embossed silver doors – all that remains of the old palace.

Residential Museum

Behind the Private Durbar Hall • Daily 10am–5.30pm • ₹60

Privately owned by the present scion of the royal family, and housed within the residential part of the palace, the **Residential Museum** displays royal treasures, paintings, musical instruments, children's toys, furniture, trousseaux and armoury.

Jayachamarajendra Art Gallery

300m west of Mysore Palace • Daily 8.30am–5.30pm • ₹120 (₹30); no cameras • ☎ 0821 2423693

Built in 1861, the three-storey **Jaganmohan Palace** was used as a royal residence until 1915, when it was turned into a picture gallery and museum, the **Jayachamarajendra Art Gallery**, by Maharaja Krishnaraja Wadiyar IV. Most of the "contemporary" art on show dates from the 1930s, when a revival of Indian painting was spearheaded by E.B. Havell and the Tagore brothers, Rabindranath and Gaganendranath, in Bengal.

The ground-floor gallery, centring on a large wooden Ganesh seated on a tortoise, is lined with paintings, including Krishnaraja Wadiyar sporting with the "inmates" of his zenana during Holi. Games including circular *ganjifa* playing cards illustrated with portraits of royalty or deities, and board games delicately inlaid with ivory are also displayed on the ground floor. Nineteenth- and twentieth-century **paintings** dominate the first floor; among them the work of pioneering oil painter Raja Ravi Varma who has been credited for introducing modern techniques to Indian art. The second floor displays a cluster of musical instruments, among them a brass *jaltarang* set and a glass xylophone. Besides folk exhibits, leather puppets, temple chariots and wooden statues, also on display is a sandal soap used by Mahatma Gandhi during his visit to Karnataka.

Mysuru Zoo

Zoo Main Rd, 1km east of Mysore Palace • Daily except Tues 8.30am–5.30pm • ₹50 (₹60 Sat, Sun & hols), camera ₹20, video camera ₹150 • ☎ 0821 2520302, ⓦ mysorezoo.info

Officially named Sri Chamarajendra Zoological Gardens, **Mysuru Zoo** is one of the oldest and best in India. Established as far back as 1882, it was opened to the public in 1902 and has grown to encompass 245 beautifully landscaped acres, with admirably spacious compounds for most of the animals that live here. The zoo boasts all the usual big **mammals**, including some fine leopards and tigers, and there are also many species of bird and reptile to be admired, though some of their cages do not make viewing the animals easy. The zoo even has a very cheap canteen and an admirable policy of charging a deposit on water bottles, which can be claimed back at the exit. As always, it pays to visit early morning or late afternoon when the animals are most active.

Chamundi Hill

Temple Daily 7am–2pm, 3.30–6pm & 7–9pm • Free but special entrance ₹10 • Bus #201 from the City stand

Chamundi Hill, 12km southeast of the city, is topped with a temple to the chosen deity of the Mysore rajas – the goddess Chamundi, or Durga, who slew the demon buffalo Mahishasura. It's a pleasant, easy bus trip to the top; the walk down takes about thirty minutes. Take drinking water, especially in the middle of the day – the walk isn't very demanding, but by the end of it, after more than a thousand steps, your legs are likely to be a bit wobbly.

MYSURU DASARA FESTIVAL

Following the tradition set by the Vijayanagar kings, the ten-day festival of **Dasara** (Sept/Oct), to commemorate the goddess Durga's slaying of the demon buffalo, Mahishasura, is celebrated in grand style at Mysuru. Scores of cultural events include concerts of South Indian classical (Carnatic) music and dance performances in the great Durbar Hall of the **Mysore Palace**. On Vijayadashami, the tenth and last day of the festival, a magnificent procession of mounted guardsmen on horseback and caparisoned elephants – one carrying the palace deity, Chamundeshwari, on a gold *howdah* – marches 5km from the palace to Banni Mantap, site of a sacred banyan tree. There's also a floating festival in the temple tank at the foot of **Chamundi Hill**, and a procession of chariots around the temple at the top. A torchlit parade (Jamboo Savari) takes place in the evening, followed by a massive firework display and much jubilation on the streets.

YOGA IN MYSURU

Despite the passing in 2009 of its founder, Sri Pattabhi Jois, the world-renowned **Ashtanga Yoga Institute** (☎98801 85500, ⓦkpjayi.org), 3.5km northwest of town in Gokulam, is still a revered pilgrimage destination for devotees. The surrounding neighbourhood has in recent years turned into a bustling expat haven, filled with cafés, guesthouses, restaurants and internet cafés. The institute doesn't offer drop-in classes; students must register for a minimum of one month (around ₹30,000), and book at least two months in advance.

There are several other centres clustered around Gokulam, including Bharath Shetty's popular **IndeaYoga** (☎0821 241 6779, ⓦyoga-india.net) at 144E 7th Main Rd, which offers early morning courses of between two and eight weeks' duration, and **Yoga Bharata**, 810 Contour Rd (☎0821 424 2342, ⓦyogabharata.com), who welcome drop-ins (₹300 per class) and offer courses of one to four weeks (from ₹2000).

Some 3km south of town, **Mysore Mandala Yogashala**, at 897/1 Narayan Sastry Rd, Lakshmipuram (☎0821 425 6277, ⓦmandala.ashtanga.org; closed Mon & Sat), is a self-contained retreat, offering excellent instruction, an organic café, well-tended garden, cultural events and drop-in classes. Two-hour Ashtanga classes (₹500) run at 6am, 8.30am and 4.30pm, with the slightly less strenuous ninety-minute Hatha classes (₹400) at 7am and 4.30pm.

Inside the twelfth-century **temple**, which is open to non-Hindus, is a solid gold Chamundi figure. Outside, in the courtyard, stands a fearsome, if gaily coloured, statue of Mahishasura. Overlooking the path down the hill, the magnificent 5m **Nandi**, carved from a single piece of black granite in 1659, is an object of worship himself, adorned with bells and garlands. Minor shrines, dedicated to Chamundi and the monkey god Hanuman, among others, line the side of the path; at the bottom, a little shrine to Ganesh lies near a chai shop. From here you can pick up an auto-rickshaw or bus back into the city, but at weekends the latter are often full. If you walk on towards the city, passing a temple on the left with a big water tank (the site of the floating festival during Dasara), you'll reach the main road between the *Lalitha Mahal Palace* (see p.228) and the centre; there's a bus stop, and often auto-rickshaws, at the junction.

ARRIVAL AND DEPARTURE

MYSURU (MYSORE)

By train The railway station is 1.5km northwest of the centre. For long hauls, the best way to travel is by train, usually with a change at Bengaluru (6–7 daily; 2–3hr); the fastest service is the a/c *Shatabdi Express* #2008 (daily except Wed 2.15pm; 2hr), which continues to Chennai (7hr 10min). There are ten services daily to Hassan, of which the *Talguppa Intercity Express* #16206 (5.50am; 1hr 50min) is the fastest.

By bus Mysuru has three bus stands: major long-distance KSRTC and other state services pull in to Central, near the heart of the city, where there are advance booking counters. The Private stand is about 1km northwest of here and a host of agents there can make bookings for private buses to many destinations. Local buses, including services for Chamundi Hill and Srirangapatna, stop at the City stand, next to the northwestern corner of Mysore Palace.

Destinations from Central Bus Stand Channarayapatna (for Sravanabelagola; hourly; 2hr 30min); Hassan (every 15–30min; 3hr); Hubballi (4–6 daily; 9hr); Kochi (6 daily; 11–12hr); Madikeri (every 30min–1hr; 3hr); Mangaluru (every 30min–1hr; 7hr); Ootacamund (via Bandipur National Park; 8 daily; 5hr).

Destinations from Private Bus Stand Overnight services to Goa leave at 4pm and 5pm, getting to Panjim at 9am and 10am respectively.

INFORMATION AND TOURS

Karnataka Tourism The helpful Karnataka Tourism office (Mon–Sat 9.30am–5.30pm; ☎0821 242 2096) is located at the Department of Tourism, *Hotel Mayura Hoysala*, 2 Jhansi Lakshmi Bai Rd, Metropole Circle. They run marathon city bus tours (8.30am–8.30pm; ₹210) for a minimum of twelve passengers, and rushed tours of Belur, Halebidu and Sravanabelagola.

Bike tours MYcycle Tours (☎98867 05179, ⓦbit.ly /MYcycle) organizes rickshaw rides and cycling trips covering Mysuru and Srirangapatna (3hr; ₹1450).

ACCOMMODATION

Finding a room is only a problem during Dasara (see box, p.226) and the Christmas/New Year period, when the popular places are booked up weeks in advance and prices predictably soar. Checkout is generally noon.

Dasaprakash Gandhi Square ☎0821 244 2444, ⓦmysoredasaprakashgroup.com. Large, crumbling yet charming hotel complex arranged around a spacious paved courtyard. It's busy, clean and efficient, with some rather overpriced a/c rooms, reasonable singles and an excellent veg restaurant. ₹675

★**Gitanjali Homestay** Siddharthanagar, 6km east of the centre ☎0821 247 4646, ⓦgitanjalihomestay.com. Run by a Coorg family, this peaceful homestay located at the base of the Chamundi hills has four rooms in a cottage-style unit with a large common veranda opening out to a garden. Excellent home-cooked Kodava cuisine. ₹4500

★**Green** Chittaranjan Palace, 2270 Vinoba Rd, Jayalakshmipuram ☎0821 251 2536, ⓦgreenhotelindia .com. This former royal palace among landscaped gardens on the western outskirts has been refurbished as an elegant, eco-conscious two-star hotel. The 31 rooms are a decent size, and facilities include lounges, verandas, a croquet lawn and well-stocked library. All profits go to charities and environmental projects. Book in advance to arrange a pickup. ₹3750

Indra Bhavan Dhanavantri Rd ☎0821 242 3933, ⓔhotel indrabhavan@rediffmail.com. A dilapidated old lodge full of character, with attached singles and doubles, that is currently undergoing renovation. The "ordinary" rooms are a little grubby, but the good-value "deluxe" ones (₹500) have clean tiled floors, TVs and open onto a wide common veranda. Two good veg restaurants. No wi-fi. ₹300

KSTDC Mayura Hoysala 2 Jhansi Lakshmi Bai Rd ☎0821 242 6160, ⓦkarnatakaholidays.net. Reasonably priced rooms and suites in a colonial-era mansion (a/c rooms ₹2750). There's a terrace restaurant and beer garden, which is good value, but the food is uninspiring. The budget *Yatri Niwas* (☎0821 2423492) in the same compound offers rooms for ₹900. Rate includes tax. No wi-fi. ₹1500

Lalitha Mahal Palace T. Narasipur Rd, 5km east of the city ☎0821 252 6100, ⓦlalithamahalpalace.in. On a slope overlooking the city in the distance, this white Neoclassical palace was built in 1931 to accommodate the maharaja's foreign guests. Now it's a Raj-style fantasy, decked with stunning period furniture and popular with tour groups. Rooms range from the cute turret rooms to the "Viceroy Suite" (₹50,000). The tea lounge, restaurant (see opposite) and pool are open to non-residents (₹350). ₹8600

Mannars Yatrinivas Chandragupta Rd ☎0821 2521148, ⓦmannarsyatrinivas.com. Budget hotel near the Central Bus Stand and Gandhi Square. Spruced up of late but overall still very plain; of its 24 rooms only the "deluxe" have TV (₹1400). Deservedly popular with backpackers but no advance booking. ₹850

★**Parklane** 2720 Sri Harsha Rd ☎0821 243 0400, ⓦparklanemysore.com. A complete overhaul has transformed the *Parklane* into a swish yet affordable boutique hotel. Appealingly misshapen rooms, all with a/c, contemporary furnishings and most with balconies, encircle a skylit atrium. ₹2100

★**Rooftop Retreat** 165 3rd Main Rd, Gayathripuram ☎0821 245 0483. This delightful apartment homestay in a tranquil neighbourhood 2.5km from Central Bus Stand comes with a warm welcome, superb food and rooftop patio. Bright blues and cosy creams dominate the mostly wood furnishings. Reserve in advance. ₹2500

Hotel Roopa 2724-C Bangalore–Nilgiri Rd ☎0821 244 0044, ⓦhotelroopa.com. Bright modern hotel block with compact but comfy rooms at surprisingly reasonable prices and a good complimentary buffet breakfast. Centrally located near the station, and ideal for the palace. ₹1295

Royal Orchid Metropole 5 Jhansi Lakshmi Bai Rd ☎0821 425 5566, ⓦroyalorchidhotels.com. Luxurious heritage hotel set in pleasant gardens built in 1920 by the maharaja of Mysore. Its thirty rooms have high ceilings and a sense of grandeur. There's also a small outdoor pool and gym. The fine *Tiger Trail* multicuisine restaurant serves buffet breakfast (included) and lunch in the central courtyard; the *Shikari* restaurant hosts barbecue dinners. ₹7000

Sandesh The Prince 3 Nazarbad Main Rd ☎0821 243 6777, ⓦsandeshtheprince.com. Smart, stylish four-star with comfortable, well-furnished rooms and an impressive, skylit foyer. Facilities include travel desk, foreign exchange, outdoor pool (₹300/day to non-residents) with barbecue, and an excellent Ayurvedic centre and beauty parlour. ₹5000

Sangeeth 1966 Narayana Shastri Rd, near the Udipi Krishna temple ☎0821 242 4693. One of Mysuru's best all-round budget deals: bland and a bit boxed in, but friendly and very good value, with a rooftop restaurant. ₹500

S.C.D.V.S. Sri Harsha Rd ☎0821 242 1379, ⓦhotel scvds.com. Friendly modern lodge with some a/c rooms and cable TV in most. Some of the upper-storey rooms have balconies overlooking the palace. ₹1250

EATING

Mysuru has scores of **places to eat**, from numerous South Indian "meals" joints dotted around the market to the opulent *Lalitha Mahal Palace*. To sample the renowned **Mysore pak**, a sweet, rich crumbly mixture made of ghee and maize flour, queue at Guru Sweet Mart, a small stall at KR Circle that's considered to be the best sweetshop in town. Another speciality is the soft, fragrant *mallige idli*, named after the delicate jasmine flower for which the city is known.

Dynasty Palace Plaza hotel, Sri Harsha Rd ☎0821 241 7592. Dynasty offers a wide range of Indian, Chinese and Continental fare (mains ₹150–200), served either in the ground-floor dining hall or breezy covered rooftop terrace, great in the evening. Full bar. Daily 7.30am–11pm.

Kamat Madhuvan Near Gun House, Nanjangud Rd ☎99800 04507. A traditional veg hotel 1km south of the palace, serving and north Karnataka cuisine such as *jolada roti* (flatbread), plus thalis (veg ₹150, special ₹215), to a soundtrack of light classical music in the evening. Daily 7am–10.30pm.

Lalitha Mahal Palace T. Narasipur Rd ☎0821 252 6100, ⒲lalithamahalpalace.in. Sample the charms of this palatial five-star hotel with a hot drink in the atmospheric tea lounge, or an à la carte lunch in the grand dining hall, accompanied by live sitar music. Buffet dinners for around ₹1000 on special occasions. The old-style bar also boasts a full-size billiards table. Daily 12.30–3pm & 8–11pm.

★**Le Olive Garden** The Windflower Spa, Maharanapratap Rd, 3km southeast of town ☎0821 252 2500. Excellent, reasonably priced Indian, Chinese and Western dishes served to the sound of falling water and croaking frogs at this quasi-jungle hideaway. Daily noon–11pm.

★**New Shilpashri** Gandhi Square ☎0821 244 8558. Encircled by leafy potted plants, this rooftop terrace is one of the best spots in the city to enjoy a sun-dipped egg and toast breakfast or a cool evening cocktail. Quality North Indian food like tasty tandoori and foreign dishes such as chicken stroganoff go for ₹100–150. Plenty of good veg options too. Daily 8am–10.30pm.

The Old House Jhansi Lakshmi Bai Rd, RTO Circle, 2km west of the palace ☎0821 233 3255. Overlooking a leafy garden, this lovely café and patisserie serves wood-fired pizzas, pastas, salads and juices, besides a variety of fresh breads from the in-house bakery. Drop by at the adjoining Maya boutique, housed in a charming colonial building, for knick-knacks. Daily 7.30am–10pm.

Parklane Sri Harsha Rd ☎0821 243 0400, ⒲parklane mysore.com. Congenial courtyard restaurant-cum-beer balcony, with moderately priced veg and non-veg (meat sizzlers are a speciality), fake trees and live Indian classical music every evening. The hotel rooftop space is a real stunner, with full bar, pool and fantastic views. Popular with travellers and locals alike. Daily 8am–11pm.

RRR Gandhi Square ☎0821 244 1979. Superb Andhra canteen with a small but plush a/c room at the back. Gets packed at lunchtimes and at weekends, but it's well worth the wait for its excellent chicken biryani, fried fish and set menus served on banana leaf. Daily 11.30am–4.30pm & 7–11pm.

DRINKING AND NIGHTLIFE

Food & Drink Maharaja Shopping Complex, Bangalore–Mysore Rd ☎92415 57015. Advertising itself as a music bar, this joint is still more of a drinking den, with a wide selection of drinks and a jarring mixture of Western and Indian sounds. Daily noon–11pm.

The Road Sandesh The Prince, 3 Nazarbad Main Rd ☎0821 243 6777. Lined with plush booths – several of which are inside faux classic cars – this upmarket, American road trip-themed restaurant/club serves a good lunch menu before the tables are cleared at 7pm and patrons take to the circular wooden dancefloor, usually to guest DJs (₹300–400 cover at weekends). Daily noon–11.30pm.

SHOPPING

Cauvery Arts and Crafts Emporium Sayaji Rao Rd ☎0821 252 1258, ⒲cauverycrafts.com. Souvenir stores spill over with the famous sandalwood in Mysuru but the best place to get a sense of what's on offer is this government-run store, which stocks a wide range of local crafts that can be shipped overseas. Daily 10.30am–8pm.

Devaraja Market Sayaji Rao Rd. One of South India's most atmospheric produce markets: a giant complex of covered stalls groaning with bananas (the delicious Nanjangud variety), luscious mangoes, blocks of sticky jaggery and conical heaps of lurid *kumkum* powder. Daily 5.30am–8.30pm.

Around Mysuru

Mysuru is a jumping-off point for some of Karnataka's most popular destinations. At **Srirangapatna**, the fort, palace and mausoleum date from the era of Tipu Sultan, the "Tiger of Mysore", while the superb Hoysala temple of **Somnathpur** is an architectural masterpiece. Nagarahole National Park (see p.239) is also accessible within three hours of the city.

Srirangapatna

The island of **Srirangapatna**, in the River Kaveri, 20km northeast of Mysuru, measures 5km by 1km. Long a site of Hindu pilgrimage, it is named after its tenth-century

Sriranganathaswamy Vishnu temple. The Vijayanagar kings built a fort here in 1454, and in 1616 it became the capital of the Mysore Wadiyar rajas. However, Srirangapatna is more famously associated with **Haider Ali**, who deposed the Wadiyars in 1761, and his son **Tipu Sultan**. During his seventeen-year reign – which ended with his death in 1799, when the future Duke of Wellington took the fort at the bloody battle of "Seringapatnam" – Tipu posed a greater threat than any other Indian ruler to British plans to dominate India. Born in 1750, of a Hindu mother, he inherited his father Haider Ali's considerable military skills, but was also an educated, cultured man, whose lifelong desire to rid India of the hated British invaders naturally brought him an ally in the French. He obsessively embraced his popular name of the **Tiger of Mysore**, surrounding himself with symbols and images of tigers; much of his memorabilia is decorated with the animal or its stripes, and, like the Romans, he is said to have kept tigers for the punishment of criminals.

Sri Ranganathaswamy temple

300m east of station • Daily 7.30am–1pm & 4–8pm

At the heart of the fortress, the great temple of **Sri Ranganathaswamy** still stands proud and virtually untouched by the turbulent history that has flowed around it, and remains, for many devotees, the island's prime draw. Developed by succeeding dynasties, it consists of three distinct sanctuaries and is entered via an impressive five-storeyed gateway and a hall built by Haider Ali. The innermost sanctum, the oldest part of the temple, contains an image of a reclining Vishnu.

Daria Daulat Bagh

2km east of the station • Daily 9am–5pm Fri • ₹100 (₹5)

The former summer palace, the **Daria Daulat Bagh**, literally "wealth of the sea", was built in 1784 to entertain Tipu's guests. At first sight, this low, wooden colonnaded building set in an attractive formal garden fails to impress. But the superbly preserved interior is remarkable, with its ornamental arches, tiger-striped columns and floral decoration on every centimetre of the teak walls and ceiling. A much-repainted mural on the west wall relishes every detail of Haider Ali's victory over the British at Pollilore in 1780.

Gumbaz mausoleum

3km east of Daria Daulat Bagh • Daily except Fri 9am–5pm • Free

An avenue of cypresses leads from an intricately carved gateway to the **Gumbaz mausoleum**. Built by Tipu Sultan in 1784 to commemorate Haider Ali, and later also to serve as his own resting place, the lower half of the grey-granite edifice is crowned by a dome of whitewashed brick and plaster, spectacular against the blue sky. Ivory-inlaid rosewood doors lead to the tombs of Haider Ali and Tipu, each covered by a pall (tiger stripes for Tipu), and an Urdu tablet records Tipu's martyrdom.

ARRIVAL AND GETTING AROUND   SRIRANGAPATNA

Srirangapatna is a small island, but places of interest are quite spread out; tongas, auto-rickshaws (around ₹300 for a 2hr tour) and bicycles are available on the main road near the bus stand.

By train All the Mysuru–Bengaluru trains pull in to the station near the temple and fort, taking only 15min from Mysuru.

By bus Frequent buses (including #307, #313 and #316) leave from Mysore City Bus Stand (30min); #316 drops you near the Gumbaz.

ACCOMMODATION AND EATING

Mayura River View 3km south of the railway station ☎08236 252114, ⊚ karnatakaholidays.net. The KSTDC hotel-cum-restaurant occupies a pleasant spot beside the River Kaveri. Its rooms and cottages (all a/c) are overpriced, however. **₹2500**

New Amblee Holiday Resort 2km east of the railway station ☎08236 252357, ⊚ambleeresort.in. Located along the banks of the picturesque Kaveri River, this hotel offers luxury and deluxe rooms with or without a/c. **₹1500**

Somnathpur: Keshava Vishnu temple

Daily 9am–5.30pm • ₹100 (₹5)

Built in 1268, the exquisite **Keshava Vishnu temple**, in the sleepy hamlet of **SOMNATHPUR**, was the last important temple to be constructed by the Hoysalas; it is also the most complete and the finest example of this singular style (see box, p.232). Somnathpur itself, just ninety minutes from Mysuru by road, is little more than a few neat tracks and some attractive simple houses with pillared verandas.

Built on a star-shaped plan, like other Hoysala shrines, the Keshava temple is a *trikutachala*, "three-peaked hills" type, with a tower on each shrine. Its high plinth (*jagati*) provides an upper ambulatory, which allows visitors to marvel at the profusely decorated walls. Among the many superb images here is a life-size statue of Krishna playing the flute, and as at Halebidu, a lively frieze details countless episodes from the Ramayana, Bhagavata Purana and Mahabharata. Unusually, the temple is autographed, bearing the signatures of its sculptors. Outside the temple stands a flagstaff (*dhvajastambha*), which may originally have been surmounted by a figure of Vishnu's bird vehicle Garuda.

It's best to visit as early as possible, as the black stone gets hot in the day, making it tough to walk barefoot.

ARRIVAL AND DEPARTURE   SOMNATHPUR

By bus There are no direct buses from Mysuru to Somnathpur. Private buses run from Mysuru to Tirumakudal Narasipur (1hr), from where there are regular buses to Somnathpur (20min).

ACCOMMODATION AND EATING

There is nowhere to stay near the temple and the only food available is biscuits or maybe a samosa or fruit from a street-seller.

Talakadu Jaladhama 30km southeast of Somnathpur ☏ 080 4123 9306, ⊛ jaladhama.net. Tucked in the backwaters of a dammed section of the Kaveri River, this large resort offers secluded cottages, some with rooftop hot tubs and herb gardens. A popular weekend getaway, it arranges boating and sports activities as well as bonfires and a tacky rain dance set to Bollywood tunes. ₹**4500**

Hassan and around

The nondescript town of **HASSAN**, 118km northwest of Mysuru, is visited in large numbers because of its proximity to the Hoysala temples at **Belur** and **Halebidu**, both northwest of the town, and the Jain pilgrimage site of **Sravanabelagola** to the southeast. Some travellers end up staying a couple of nights but with a little forward planning you shouldn't have to linger for long, as Belur, Halebidu and Sravanabelagola, deep in the serene Karnataka countryside, offer more appealing surroundings.

ARRIVAL AND INFORMATION   HASSAN

By train The railway station, served by regular trains from Mysuru (10 daily; 2–3hr), is 2km east of the town centre on BM Rd. There are also several daily trains to Mangaluru (5–6hr), one of them overnight.

By bus Hassan's KSRTC Bus Stand is in the centre of town, at the northern end of Bus Stand Rd, and served by frequent buses from Mysuru (every 15–30min; 3hr). In order to see the surrounding sights by bus, you'll need at least two days. Belur and Halebidu can be comfortably covered in one day; it's best to take one of the earliest hourly buses to Halebidu (1hr) and move on to Belur (30min), from where services back to Hassan are more frequent (6.30am–6.15pm; 1hr 10min). Sravanabelagola, however, is in the opposite direction, and not served by direct buses; you have to head to Channarayapatna (every 30min from 6.30am; 1hr), aka "CR Patna", on the main Bengaluru highway and pick up one of the regular buses (30min) or any number of minibuses from there.

By car Apart from taking a tour, the only way to see Sravanabelagola, Belur and Halebidu in one day is by car, which some visitors share; most of the hotels can fix this up for around ₹2500/day.

Tourist information AVK College Rd (Mon–Sat 10am–5.30pm; ☏ 08172 268862).

4

ACCOMMODATION AND EATING

DR Karigowda Residency BM Rd, under 1km west from railway station ☎ 96868 41686. Immaculate budget hotel: friendly, comfortable and amazing value. Single occupancy possible; a/c ₹200 extra. No wi-fi. **₹700**

Harsha Mahal Below Harsha Mahal Lodge, Harsha Mahal Rd ☎ 08172 268533. Excellent veg canteen that serves freshly cooked *idli*, dosas and other South Indian fare. Meals ₹50. Daily 6.30am–9.30pm.

Hoysala Village Resort Belur Rd, 6km northwest of the centre ☎ 08172 256065, ⓦ hoysalavillageresorts .com. Ethnic luxury cottages and suites in a quiet rural

setting, with a multicuisine restaurant and a pool. **₹8800**

Southern Star BM Rd, 500m from the train station ☎ 08172 251816, ⓦ hotelsouthernstar.com. Newish hotel with a variety of rooms and all mod cons. It's better value than most and the *Hoysala* multicuisine restaurant is excellent. **₹3300**

Suvarna Gate Suvarna Regency, PB 97, BM Rd ☎ 08172 264006. This plush non-veg restaurant and bar with a few tables overlooking the garden is one of Hassan's finest. The varied menu is not cheap, with most curries going for at least ₹200. Daily 7am–11pm.

Halebidu (Halebid)

Now little more than a scruffy village of brick houses and chai stalls, **HALEBIDU** (formerly **Halebid**), 32km northwest of Hassan, was the second capital of the powerful Hoysala dynasty, which held sway over south Karnataka from the eleventh until the early fourteenth centuries and its peak stretched from coast to coast. Once known as **Dora Samudra** (Gateway to the Sea), the capital city became *Hale-bidu*, or "Old City", after successive raids by the Delhi sultanate between 1311 and 1326 reduced it to rubble. Despite the sacking, several large Hoysala temples (see box below) survive, two of which, the **Hoysaleshvara** and **Kedareshvara**, are superb, covered in exquisite carvings. Note that Belur (see opposite) has superior facilities to those found in Halebidu, making it a far better base for exploration of the Hoysala region.

Hoysaleshvara temple

Temple Daily 6am–6pm • Free **Archeological museum** Daily except Fri 10am–5pm • ₹5

The **Hoysaleshvara** temple, in the centre of the village, was started in 1121 and still unfinished even after a century of work; this possibly accounts for the absence here of the type of towers that feature at Somnathpur. Two large, ornately carved idols of Nandi, the bull, face its double shrine, with a Ganesha figure to the south. Each shrine contains a lingam.

HOYSALA TEMPLES

The **Hoysala** dynasty, who ruled southwestern Karnataka between the eleventh and thirteenth centuries, built a series of distinctive temples centred primarily at three sites: **Belur** and **Halebidu**, close to modern Hassan, and **Somnathpur**, near Mysuru. At first sight, and from a distance, the buildings, all based on a star-shaped plan, appear to be modest structures, compact and even squat. Yet on closer inspection, their profusion of fabulously detailed and sensuous sculpture, covering every centimetre of the exterior, is astonishing. Detractors often class Hoysala art as decadent and overly fussy, but anyone with an eye for craftsmanship will be sure to marvel.

The intricacy of the carvings was made possible by the material used in construction: a soft **soapstone** that on oxidization hardens to a glassy, highly polished surface. The level of detail, similar to that seen in sandalwood and ivory-work, became increasingly free and more fluid as the style developed, and reached its highest point at Somnathpur. Beautiful bracket figures, often delicate portrayals of voluptuous female subjects, were placed under the eaves, fixed by pegs top and bottom. A later addition (except possibly in the Somnathpur temple), these serve no structural function.

Another technique more usually associated with wood is the unusual treatment of the massive stone **pillars**: lathe-turned, they resemble those of the wooden temples of Kerala. They were probably turned on a horizontal plane, pinned at each end, and rotated with the use of a rope. It may be no coincidence that, to this day, wood-turning is still a local speciality.

Hoysaleshvara also features many Vaishnavite images. The **sculptures**, which have a fluid quality lacking in the earlier work at Belur, include Brahma aboard his swan, Krishna holding up Mount Govardhana and Vishnu (Trivikrama) spanning the world in three steps. One of the most remarkable images is of the demon king **Ravana** shaking Shiva's mountain abode, Mount Kailash, populated by numerous animals and figures with Shiva and Parvati seated atop. You'll also come across the odd erotic tableau featuring voluptuous, heavily bejewelled maidens. A narrative frieze, on the sixth register from the bottom, follows the length of the Nandi *mandapas* and illustrates scenes from the Hindu epics.

A small **archeological museum** next to the temple houses a collection of Hoysala art and other finds from the area.

The Jain basadis

600m south of the Hoysaleshvara temple

Halebidu's Jain *basadis* (temples) stand virtually unadorned; their only sculptural decoration consists of ceiling friezes inside the *mandapas* and elephants at the entrance steps, where there's an impressive donation plaque. The thirteenth-century temple of **Adi Parshwanatha** is dedicated to the 23rd *tirthankara*, Parshvanath, while the sixteenth-century **Vijayanatha** is dedicated to the sixteenth *tirthankara*, Shantinath. The chowkidar will demonstrate various tricks made possible by the carved pillars' highly polished surfaces; some are so finely turned they sound metallic when struck.

Kedareshvara temple

400m east of the *basadis* • Daily 6.30am–6pm • Free

With its magnificently carved outer walls, tower, doorway and ceiling, the Shaivite **Kedareshvara temple**, built in 1219, has been described by architectural historian James Fergusson as "a gem of Indian architecture". The multitude of sculpted friezes at the base of the exterior depict elephants, horses, lions, mythical animals, swans and scrolls illustrating stories from Hindu epics, while the upper sections bear 180 finely carved images of gods and goddesses standing under elegantly designed floral arches. Inside, the ceilings are of most interest, replete with dancing images and other carvings.

ARRIVAL AND DEPARTURE   HALEBIDU (HALEBID)

Buses run until 7pm to Hassan (every 30min–1hr; 1hr) and to Belur (hourly; 30min).

ACCOMMODATION

Mayura Shantala Halebeedu Opposite Hoysaleshvara temple ☎ 08177 273224. KSTDC hotel set in a small garden offering three comfortable, if overpriced, doubles with verandas, plus a four-bed room – all should be booked in advance. This is also the only place to eat, apart from a handful of daytime chai stalls. No wi-fi. ₹1500

Belur

BELUR, 37km northwest of Hassan, on the banks of the Yagachi River, was the Hoysala capital prior to Halebidu, during the eleventh and twelfth centuries. Still in active worship, the **Chennakeshava temple** is a fine and early example of the singular Hoysala style, built by King Vishnuvardhana in 1117 to celebrate his conversion from Jainism, victory over Chola forces at Talakad and his independence from the Chalukyas. Today, its grey-stone *gopura*, or gateway tower, soars above a small, bustling market town – a popular pilgrimage site from October to December, when busloads of Ayappan devotees stream through en route to Sabarimala (see box, p.331). The **car festival** held around March or April takes place over twelve days and has a pastoral feel, attracting farmers from the surrounding countryside who conduct a bullock cart procession through the streets to the temple.

Chennakeshava temple

West of the bus stand • Daily 7.30am–7.30pm; main shrine opens for worship 8–10am, 11am–1pm, 2.30–5pm & 6.30–7.30pm

Chennakeshava temple stands in a huge walled courtyard, surrounded by smaller shrines and columned *mandapa* hallways. Both the sanctuary and *mandapa* are raised on the usual plinth (*jagati*), creating the jagged star shape. The quantity of **sculptural decoration**, if less mature than in later Hoysala temples, is staggering. The bracket figures depict celestial nymphs with intricately carved make-up, ornaments and hair, such detail being exclusive to Belur. Notable are the stunning sculpture of Darpanasundari ("lady with a mirror"), the pillars in the Navaranga hall and the 2m-high statue of Sri Keshava depicted with four hands.

Within the same enclosure, the **Kappe Channigaraya temple** has some finely carved niche images and a depiction of Narasimha (Vishnu as man-lion) killing the demon Hiranyakashipu. A few metres west, fine sculptures in the smaller **Viranarayana** shrine include a scene from the Mahabharata of Bhima killing the demon Bhaga.

ARRIVAL AND INFORMATION   BELUR

By bus Buses from Hassan and Halebidu arrive at the small bus stand in the middle of town, a 10min walk west along the main street from the temple.

Bike rental There are auto-rickshaws available, but a good way to explore the area, including Halebidu, is to rent a bicycle (₹5/hr) from one of the stalls around the bus stand.

Tourist information The tourist office (Mon–Sat 10am–5pm) is located within the KSTDC *Mayuri Velapuri* compound on Temple Rd.

ACCOMMODATION AND EATING

Kalpavriksha Just off Temple Rd ☎ 98276 30455. Just about the only place to eat meat in Belur, this small bar and restaurant offers a standard range of Indian and Chinese main courses for around ₹100–150, as well as South Indian snacks. Daily 7am–10pm.

Mayuri Velapuri Temple Rd ☎ 08177 222209. This KSTDC hotel is a clean and comfortable place to stay, with five non-a/c and eight a/c rooms. The two dorms are rarely occupied, except in the March–May pilgrim season. Dorms ₹150, doubles ₹1000

Sumukha Residency Temple Rd ☎ 08177 222181. Close to the temple and bus stand, this fairly modern and comfortable place has singles for ₹350 and a/c rooms for ₹850. No wi-fi. ₹500

Vishnu Lodge Main Rd, near the bus stand ☎ 08177 222263. Above a great veg restaurant and sweet shop, this is the best-value place, with sizeable rooms (some with TV) but tiny attached bathrooms where hot water is only available in the mornings. No wi-fi. ₹500

Sravanabelagola

The sacred Jain site of **SRAVANABELAGOLA**, 49km southeast of Hassan and 93km north of Mysuru, consists of two hills and a large tank. On one of the hills, Indragiri (also known as Vindhyagiri), stands an extraordinary 18m-high monolithic statue of a naked male figure, **Gomateshvara**. Said to be the largest freestanding sculpture in India, this tenth-century colossus, visible from kilometres away, makes Sravanabelagola a key pilgrimage centre. At the **Mahamastakabhisheka** or "great head anointing ceremony", held every twelve years, devotees congregate to pour libations over the statue. The next will be held in February 2018. Spend a night or two in the village, and you can climb Indragiri Hill before dawn to enjoy the serene spectacle of the sun rising over the sugar cane fields and outcrops of lumpy granite that litter the surrounding plains – an unforgettable sight.

Sravanabelagola is linked in tradition with the Mauryan emperor Chandragupta, who starved himself to death on the second hill around 300 BC, in accordance with a Jain practice. The hill was renamed Chandragiri, marking the arrival of Jainism in southern India. At the same time, a controversy regarding the doctrines of Mahavira, the last of the 24 Jain **tirthankaras** (literally "ford-makers", who assist the aspirant to cross the "ocean of rebirth"), split Jainism into two separate branches – *svetambara*, "white-clad" Jains, more common in North India, and *digambara*, "sky-clad", who usually go naked and are associated with the South.

The monuments at Sravanabelagola probably date from no earlier than the tenth century, when a General Chavundaraya is said to have visited Chandragiri in search of a Mauryan statue of Gomateshvara. As a result of a vision in the rock face, having failed to find it, he decided to have one made. From the top of Chandragiri he fired an arrow across to Indragiri Hill; where the arrow landed, he had a new Gomateshvara sculpted from a single rock.

Indragiri Hill

Gomateshvara is approached from the tank between the two hills south of the main road by 612 steps, cut into the granite of **Indragiri Hill**, which pass numerous rock inscriptions on the way up to a walled enclosure. Shoes must be deposited at the stall to the left of the steps, and you can leave bags at the site office nearby. Take plenty of water if it's hot, as there is none available on the hill. Entered through a small wagon-vaulted *gopura*, the **temple** is entirely dominated by the towering figure of Gomateshvara. With elongated arms and exaggeratedly wide shoulders, his proportions may seem unnatural but depict the idealized physical features possessed by great thinkers and sages. The sensuously smooth surface of the white granite is finely carved: particularly the hands, hair and serene face. As in legend, ant hills and snakes sit at his feet and creepers appear to grow on his limbs.

Chandragiri Hill

Leaving your shoes with the keeper at the bottom, take the rock-cut steps to the top of the smaller **Chandragiri Hill**, north of the main road. Fine views stretch south to Indragiri and, from the north on the far side, across to a river, paddy and sugar cane fields, palms and the village of Jinanathapura, where there's another ornate Hoysala temple, the Shantishvara *basadi*.

Rather than a single large shrine, as at Indragiri, Chandragiri holds a group of *basadis* in late Chalukya Dravida style, within a walled enclosure. Caretakers will take you around and open up the closed shrines. Save for pilasters and elaborate parapets, all the temples have plain exteriors. Named after its patron, the tenth-century **Chavundaraya** temple is the largest of the group, dedicated to Parshvanath. Inside the twelfth-century **Chandragupta**, superb carved panels in a small shrine tell the story of Chandragupta and his teacher Bhadrabahu. Traces of painted geometric designs survive and the pillars feature detailed carving. Elsewhere in the enclosure stands a 24m-high *manastambha*, "pillar of fame", decorated with images of spirits, *yakshis* and a *yaksha*. No fewer than 576 inscriptions dating from the sixth to the nineteenth centuries are dotted around the site, on pillars and on the rock itself.

Bhandari Basadi and monastery (math)

The road east from the foot of the steps at Chandragiri leads to two interesting Jain buildings in town. To the right as you face the hill, the **Bhandari Basadi** (1159), housing a shrine with images of the 24 *tirthankaras*, was built by Hullamaya, treasurer of the Hoysala raja Narasimha. Two *mandapa* hallways, where naked *digambara* Jains may sometimes be seen discoursing with devotees clad in white, lead to the shrine at the back.

At the end of the street, the *math* (monastery) was the residence of Sravanabelagola's senior *acharya*, or guru. Thirty male and female monks are attached to the *math*; normally a member of staff will be happy to show visitors around. Among the rare palm-leaf manuscripts in the library, some more than a millennium old, are works on mathematics and geography, and the Mahapurana, hagiographies of the *tirthankaras*. Next door, a covered walled courtyard edged by a high platform on three sides has a chair placed for the *acharya*. A collection of tenth-century bronze *tirthankara* images is housed here, and vibrant murals detail the various lives of Parshvanath. The hills where the *tirthankaras* stood to gain *moksha* are represented in a model, somewhat resembling a jelly mould, with tacked-on footprints.

ARRIVAL AND INFORMATION

By bus You can reach Sravanabelagola from Hassan with one change of bus (see p.231), although many people choose the easier option of a tour from Mysuru or Bengaluru.
Bike rental Crisscrossed by winding back roads, the idyllic countryside around Sravanabelagola is mostly flat and thus perfect cycling terrain. Bicycles are available for rent at Saleem Cycle Mart, on Masjid Rd, opposite the northeast corner of the tank.

ACCOMMODATION AND EATING

There are plenty of *dharamshalas* to choose from if you want to stay. Managed by the temple authorities, they offer simple, scrupulously clean rooms, many with their own bathrooms and sitouts, set around gardens and courtyards, and costing under ₹300 per night. The 24hr office of the Shravanabelagola Digambara Jain Managing Committee (☎ 08176 257258), located inside the *SP Guest House*, next to the bus stand clock tower, allocates rooms.

Hotel Raghu Opposite the main tank ☎ 08176 257238. Very simple attached rooms but clean enough and the only private option around (a/c rooms ₹900). It also has the best of the many small local restaurants – try the excellent thali. ₹600

Kodagu (Coorg)

The hill region of **Kodagu**, formerly known as **Coorg**, lies 100km west of Mysuru in the Western Ghats, its eastern fringes merging with the Mysore plateau. India's leading coffee-producing region, Kodagu is also the birthplace of the River Kaveri and home to the martial Kodavas, whose customs, language and appearance set them apart from their neighbours (see box, p.238). Its rugged mountain terrain is interspersed with cardamom valleys and fields of lush paddy, as well as coffee plantations, making it one of South India's most beautiful areas. Yet much has changed since Dervla Murphy spent a few months here with her daughter in the 1970s (the subject of her classic travelogue, *On a Shoestring to Coorg*) and was entranced by the landscape. **Homestays** have given tourism in Kodagu a big boost, and larger hotel chains and resorts have moved in to cater to weekend visitors, making the main towns feel much more crowded.

Nonetheless, the countryside is still idyllic and the climate refreshingly cool even in summer. Many visitors **trek** through the unspoilt forest tracts and ridges that fringe the district. On the eastern borders of Kodagu around Kushalnagar, large **Tibetan settlements** have transformed the once barren countryside of Bylakuppe into fertile farmland dotted with monasteries, some of which house thousands of monks. To its south, and three hours southwest of Mysuru, **Nagarahole National Park** can be rewarding if visited at the right time of year.

If you plan to cross the Ghats between Mysuru and the coast, the route through Kodagu is definitely worth considering. A good time to visit is during the festival season in early December, or during the **Blossom Showers** around March and April when the coffee plants bloom with white flowers that scent the air.

Brief history

The first records of a kingdom here date from the eighth century, when it prospered from the salt trade passing between the coast and the cities on the Deccan. Under the Hindu **Haleri rajas**, the state repulsed invasions by its more powerful neighbours, including Haider Ali and his son Tipu Sultan (see p.214). A combination of hilly terrain, absence of roads (a deliberate policy on the part of defence-conscious Kodagu kings) and the tenacity of its highly trained warriors ensured Kodagu was never conquered.

In 1834, after ministers appealed to the British to help depose their despotic king, Chikkaviraraja, Kodagu became a princely state with nominal independence, which it retained until the creation of Karnataka in 1956. **Coffee** was introduced during the Raj and, despite plummeting prices on the international market, this continues to be the linchpin of the local economy, along with pepper and cardamom. Although Kodagu is

Karnataka's wealthiest region, despite being its smallest, and provides the highest tax revenue, it does not reap the rewards – some villages are still without electricity – and this, coupled with the distinct identity and fiercely independent nature of the Kodavas (see box, p.238), has given rise to movements for autonomy, such as the **Codava National Council**.

Madikeri (Mercara) and around

Nestling beside a curved stretch of craggy hills, **MADIKERI**, capital of Kodagu, undulates around 1300m up in the Western Ghats, roughly midway between Mysuru and the coastal city of Mangaluru. The gradually increasing number of foreigners who travel up here find it a pleasant enough town, with red-tiled buildings and undulating roads that converge on a bustling bazaar, but most move on to home and plantation stays in the verdant Coorg countryside within a couple of days.

Omkareshwara temple
1km northwest of bus stand

The red-roofed **Omkareshwara temple**, built in 1820 and dedicated to Shiva, features an unusual combination of Hindu features, Islamic-influenced domes and even Gothic elements. The annual Teppothsava or boat festival takes place in November or December.

Madikeri Fort
1km northwest of bus stand • Tues–Sun 10am–5.30pm • **Museum** Tues–Sun 9am–5pm, except 2nd Sat • Free

Housed within the old **Madikeri Fort**, the original mud **palace** of Haleri king Muddu Raja was rebuilt in stone by Tipu Sultan in 1781 and further modified by the British in the nineteenth century; it now serves as government offices. The fort also houses the old prison and an ancient Kote Ganapati temple, as well as St Mark's Chapel, which has been converted into a small **museum** containing British memorabilia, Jain and Hindu deity figures and weapons.

Around 2km north of the fort and temple, at Gaddige, the huge square **tombs of the rajas**, with Islamic-style gilded domes and minarets, are also worth a look.

Raja's Seat and around
The Kodagu kings chose an ideal vantage point from which to watch the sunset: **Raja's Seat** (daily 6am–8pm; ₹5), a grassy park and garden on the western edge of town, fills up just before dusk for a water-and-light show at 7pm. Nearby, **Gandhi Mantap** marks the site where Mahatma Gandhi addressed the townsfolk in 1934.

Abbi Falls
8km southeast of the town • Auto-rickshaws charge ₹300 for the return journey including waiting time

The pleasant road to **Abbi Falls**, Madikeri's famous 21m cascade, winds through the hill country and makes for a good day's outing. A gate near the car park leads through a private coffee and cardamom plantation to the base of the cascade (fenced off to dissuade swimming). Viewed from a hanging bridge, the falls are at their best during and after the monsoons.

ARRIVAL AND INFORMATION | MADIKERI AND AROUND

By bus Madikeri has regular bus connections with Bengaluru (hourly; 6hr), Hassan (6 daily; 4hr), Mangaluru (every 30min–1hr; 4hr) and Mysuru (every 30min–1hr; 3hr). The KSTRC state bus stand is at the lowest part of town, towards its eastern side, below the main bazaar; private buses from villages around the region pull into a car park 100m west.

Tourist information Travel Coorg (daily 5am–11.30pm; ☎08272 228080, ⊛www.travelcoorg.in), located at the bus stand, offers useful information on the area, including treks and homestays. Coorg Travels (☎08272 225817) also arranges treks, tours and homestays. For information on Kodagu's forests and booking forest bungalows contact the Deputy Conservator of Forests (☎08272 228305) at the fort. To arrange coffee plantation visits, contact the Codagu Planters Association on Mysore Rd (☎08272 226273, ⊛cpa.org.in).

THE KODAVAS

Theories abound as to the origins of the **Kodavas**, or **Coorgs**, who today comprise less than one sixth of the hill region's population. Fair-skinned and with their own language and customs, they are thought to have migrated to southern India from Kurdistan, Kashmir or even Greece, though no one knows exactly why or when. One popular belief holds that this staunchly martial people, who since Independence have produced some of India's leading military brains, are a branch of Indo-Scythians; some even claim connections with Alexander the Great's invading army. Whatever their origins, the Kodavas have managed to retain a distinct identity apart from the freed plantation slaves, Moplah Muslim traders and other immigrants who have settled here. Their language is Dravidian, yet their religious practices, based on ancestor veneration and worship of nature spirits, sacred groves (*devarakadu*) and the river, differ markedly from those of mainstream Hinduism. Land tenure in Kodagu is also quite distinctive: women have a right to inheritance and ownership, and, are also allowed to remarry.

Spiritual and social life for traditional Kodavas revolves around the **ain mane**, or ancestral homestead. Built on raised platforms to overlook the family land, these large, detached houses, with their beautiful carved wood doors and beaten-earth floors, generally have four wings and courtyards to accommodate various branches of the extended family, as well as shrine rooms, or **Karona Kalas**, dedicated to the clan's most important forebears. Key religious rituals and rites of passage are always conducted in the *ain mane*, rather than the local temple. However, you could easily travel through Kodagu without ever seeing one, as they are invariably away from roads, deep in the plantations.

ACCOMMODATION

Kodagu has a huge range of stay options from rustic cottages to ritzy resorts, though its charm lies in the profusion of traditional homestays, many in plantation bungalows, which offer the legendary hospitality of the Kodavas. For more see ⓦ coorghomestays.com.

IN AND AROUND TOWN

★**Caveri** School Rd ☎08272 225492, ⓦ hotelcaveri .com. Below the private bus stand, this large hotel has been upgraded but remains good value, with spacious and nicely furnished double rooms. There's a ground-floor restaurant, serving the spicy local delicacy *pandi* (pork) curry, and adjacent bar. ₹850

Chitra School Rd ☎08272 225372, ⓦ hotelchitra.co.in. Good-value hotel near the private bus station. Neat, well-kept rooms have cable TV, and there's also an excellent veg restaurant-cum-bar downstairs. No wi-fi. ₹750

Coorg International Convent Rd ☎08272 228071, ⓦ coorginternational.com. A 10min rickshaw ride west of the centre, this large hotel has comfortable Western-style rooms, a multicuisine restaurant, exchange facilities, and shops. Wi-fi only in the lobby. ₹7500

Daisy Bank Heritage Inn General Thimaya Rd (aka Mysore Rd) ☎08272 321172. Housed in a converted mansion, the original *East End Hotel* has nine double rooms with high ceilings and subtle decor. All rooms, named after flowers, have spotless bathrooms and flatscreen TVs; prices vary according to size. No wi-fi. ₹1250

★**Gowri Nivas** New Extension ☎94481 93822, ⓦ gowri nivas.com. Bops and Muthu's charming homestay in the heart of town has two rooms in a separate cottage and one in the main house, decorated with lovely artefacts. Delicious Kodava cuisine is on offer. ₹4000

Mayura Valley View Raja Rd ☎08272 228387, ⓦ karnatakaholidays.net. A stiff walk up past Raja's Seat, this KSTDC hotel offers large old-fashioned rooms, many with excellent views. The restaurant serves booze and has an open terrace with epic views. ₹3000

OUTSIDE TOWN

★**Palace Estate** Near Nalaknad Palace, Kakkabe, 35km southwest of Madikeri ☎98804 47702, ⓦ palace estate.co.in. Set at the base of Thadiyendamol, Coorg's loftiest mountain, this pioneering homestay is a 1hr 15min drive from Madikeri. A backpacker favourite, it has panoramic views, home-style food, warm hosts and a private waterfall, making it the perfect spot to linger. There's even a single room for ₹1400. ₹2000

★**Rainforest Retreat** 13km north of Madikeri, near Galibeedu village ☎08272 265636, ⓦ rainforestours .com. Informed hosts and botanists Sujata and Anurag Goel run a 20-acre organic farm, with warmly furnished eco cottages and two tents set amid lush rainforest. Produce such as pepper, cardamom and coffee are sold under their "Don't Panic, It's Organic" brand, with profits going to their NGO, WAPRED, which fosters environmental awareness and sustainable agriculture in the region. Tariff includes breakfast and a plantation walk. Their new self-catering *Faraway Cottage* is ideal for long-stayers (₹5000/week). ₹2000

EATING

Athithi Opposite the Town Hall ☎ 99010 40200. Tucked just off the main road, this place has an outdoor terrace, as well as indoor seating, where you can enjoy South Indian and tandoori pure-veg cuisine for ₹60–150. Daily 7am–10pm.

★Choice Junior College Rd ☎ 08272 225585. This popular three-storey restaurant has had a facelift, with the addition of a spacious roof "garden" upstairs. Tuck into huge portions of Indian and Chinese food; the American chop suey is a winner at ₹170. Daily 8am–10pm.

★East End General Thimaya Rd ☎ 08272 229996. Though the landmark hotel has shifted to a new building behind East End petrol pump, the restaurant has retained the same flavours and menu as before. Try the *keema ball*

curry (₹200) or biryanis for lunch, snacks like *keema dosa* (₹160), and mutton cutlet (served only the 4.30–7pm) for dinner. Daily 8am–10pm.

Karavali Fish Land Down the lane opposite the Fort ☎ 98457 89989. Sparkling-clean family restaurant that specializes in fish, including a great-value ₹60 thali, although there are plenty of veg and meat options too. Daily 8am–10.30pm.

West End Near KSRTC bus stand, Kohinoor Rd. A grubby hole-in-the-wall bar and restaurant popular among locals for spicy *pandi* curry, served with *akki otti* (rice rotis) roasted on a wood fire. Daily 9.30am–10.30pm.

Nagarahole National Park

90km south from Madikeri • ₹1000 (₹200), camera ₹20 payable at check post

Nagarahole ("Snake River") **National Park**, together with Bandipur and Tamil Nadu's Mudumalai national parks, forms the **Nilgiri Biosphere Reserve**, one of India's most extensive tracts of protected forest. Straddling Kodagu and Mysore districts, the park extends 640 square kilometres north from the River Kabini, which has been dammed to form a picturesque artificial lake. During the dry season (Feb–June), this perennial water source attracts large numbers of animals to its muddy riverbanks and grassy swamps, or *hadlus*, making it a potentially prime spot for sighting gaur (Indian bison), elephant, *dhole* (wild dog), deer, boar, and even the odd tiger or leopard. The forest here is of the moist deciduous type – thick jungle with a 30m-high canopy – and more impressive than Bandipur's drier scrub. The park is best avoided altogether during the monsoon season.

4

ARRIVAL AND INFORMATION   NAGARAHOLE NATIONAL PARK

By bus Buses from Mysuru's Central stand go to Hunsur (2 daily; 3hr), 10km from the park's north gate, where you can find transport, mostly in the form of jeeps, to the Forest Department's two guesthouses. From Madikeri, there are regular buses to the southern entrance at Kutta (hourly; 2hr); buses headed for Kozhikode stop there too.

Auto-rickshaws and jeeps from the Kutta stand drop you at the park entrance and reservation office.

Tours Jeep safaris cost ₹3000–5000 depending on group size. Bus tours (6–9am & 4–6.30pm; ₹100) can be arranged at the visitor centre.

ACCOMMODATION

Forest Department guesthouses Inside the park; bookings through the Project Tiger office in Mysuru ☎ 0821 248 0901 or Forest Department in Hunsur ☎ 0822 252 041. These simple rustic cabins are scantily furnished and you must arrive (either by jeep or rented vehicle) at the park gates well before dusk – the road through the reserve to the lodges closes at 6pm, and is prone to "elephant blocks". ₹500

The Jade Manchalli, Kutta ☎ 08228 244396, ⊚ thejade coorg.com. Kabir and Megha's heritage homestay is just 10km from the park's southern entrance and a great base for trekking in the Brahmagiri range to Irpu Falls. The classy rooms overlook the garden and hills. Excellent Kodava cuisine; breakfast and dinner included. ₹3700

Jungle Inn Veerana Hosahalli, Hunsur ☎ 08222 246022, ⊚ jungleinn.in. Close to the park's northern entrance, this highway lodge has a mix of rooms of different sizes plus huge Swiss tented cottages. Staff can arrange pick-up from Hunsur. ₹3500

Kabini River Lodge Approached via the village of Karapura, east of the park ☎ 08228 264403, ⊚ jungle lodges.com. Set in its own leafy compound overlooking the Kabini reservoir, this former maharaja's hunting lodge offers all-in deals that include meals, forest entry charges and safaris around the park with expert guides. It's impossible to reach by public transport, so you'll need to rent a car to get here. Choose from cottages, rooms and tented cottages. All-inclusive from ₹33,092

Mangaluru (Mangalore)

Most visitors dismiss **Mangalore**, now officially renamed **MANGALURU**, as a stopover between Goa and Kerala, or as a strategic hub from which to access Coorg and Hassan. However, this bustling multicultural town is packed with history and some visit just to relish its famed coastal cuisine.

Named after the ancient temple of Mangaladevi at Bolar, 3km from the city centre, Mangalore was one of the most famous ports of South India and frequented by Arab traders. It was already well known overseas in the sixth century as a major source of pepper; the fourteenth-century Muslim writer Ibn Battuta noted its trade in pepper and ginger and the presence of merchants from Persia and Yemen. In the mid-1400s, the Persian ambassador Abdu'r-Razzaq saw Mangalore as a lucrative "frontier town" of the Vijayanagar empire (see p.254), which was why it was captured by the Portuguese

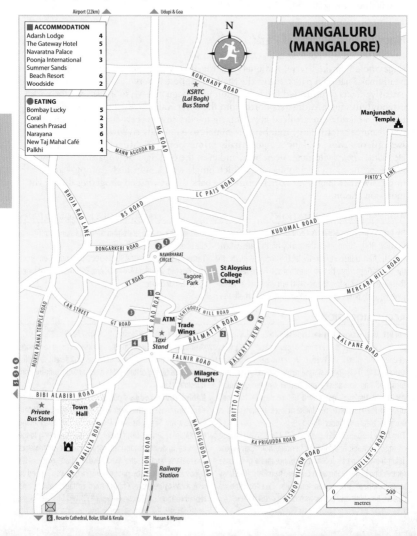

MANGALURU (MANGALORE)

Airport (22km)   Udupi & Goa

ACCOMMODATION
Adarsh Lodge	4
The Gateway Hotel	5
Navaratna Palace	1
Poonja International	3
Summer Sands Beach Resort	6
Woodside	2

EATING
Bombay Lucky	5
Coral	2
Ganesh Prasad	3
Narayana	6
New Taj Mahal Café	1
Palkhi	4

KONCHADY ROAD
KSRTC (Lal Bagh) Bus Stand
Manjunatha Temple
MG ROAD
MANN AGUDDA RD
PINTO'S LANE
BHOJA RAO LANE
BS ROAD
LC PAIS ROAD
KUDUMAL ROAD
DONGARKERI ROAD
NAVABHARAT CIRCLE
St Aloysius College Chapel
Tagore Park
VT ROAD
MERCARA HILL ROAD
CAR STREET
GT ROAD
ATM
KS RAO ROAD
LIGHTHOUSE HILL ROAD
Trade Wings
BALMATTA ROAD
BALMATTA NEW RD
KALPANE ROAD
MUKYA PRANA TEMPLE ROAD
Taxi Stand
FALNIR ROAD
Milagres Church
BRITTO LANE
BIBI ALABIBI ROAD
Private Bus Stand
Town Hall
NANDIGUDDA ROAD
KA PRIGUDDA ROAD
DR UP MALIYA ROAD
STATION ROAD
Railway Station
BISHOP VICTOR ROAD
MULLER'S ROAD

0   500
metres

, Rosario Cathedral, Bolar, Ullal & Kerala   Hassan & Mysuru

in 1529, and later Tipu Sultan and the British. Nowadays, the modern port, 10km north of the city proper, is principally known for the processing and export of coffee and cocoa (mostly from Kodagu), and cashew nuts (from Kerala). It is also a centre for the production of *beedis* (local cigarettes).

Mangaluru's strong Christian influence can be traced back to the arrival of St Thomas further south. Some 1400 years later, in 1526, the Portuguese founded one of the earliest churches on the coast, although today's **Rosario Cathedral**, with a dome based on St Peter's in Rome, dates only from 1910. Closer to the centre, on Lighthouse Hill Road, fine restored fresco, tempera and oil murals by the Italian Antonio Moscheni adorn the Romanesque-style **St Aloysius College Chapel**, built in 1882.

Manjunatha temple

Atop the Kadri Hill, 3km north of the centre

Mangaluru's tenth-century **Manjunatha temple** is believed to be the oldest Shiva temple in the city and an important centre of the tantric **Nathapanthi cult**, a divergent form of Hinduism and similar to cults in Nepal. Enshrined in the sanctuary are a number of superb **bronzes**, including a 1.5m-high seated Matsyendranatha, made in 958 AD. To see it up close, visit at *darshan* times (6am–1pm & 4–8pm), although the bronzes can be glimpsed through the wooden slats on the side of the sanctuary. If possible, time your visit to coincide with *mahapuja* (8am, noon & 8pm) when the priests give a fire blessing to the accompaniment of raucous music. Opposite the east entrance, steps lead via a reddish-coloured path to a curious group of minor shrines. Beyond this complex stands the **Shri Yogishwar Math**, a hermitage set round two courtyards.

Ullal

10km south of Mangaluru • Local bus #44A runs to Ullal from the junction at the south end of KS Rao Rd (centre of town)

To escape the city for a few hours, head to the suburb of **ULLAL**, where a long sandy **beach** stretches for kilometres, backed by wispy casuarina trees. It's a popular place for a stroll, particularly in the evening when Mangaloreans come out to watch the sunset, but a strong undertow makes swimming difficult, and at times unsafe. You might be better off using the pool at the *Summer Sands Beach Resort* (see p.242), immediately behind the beach. Towards the centre of Ullal, and around 700m from the main bus stand, is the *dargah* of **Seyyid Mohammad Shareeful Madani**, a sixteenth-century saint who is said to have come from Medina in Arabia, floating across the sea on a handkerchief. The extraordinary nineteenth-century building with garish onion domes houses the saint's tomb, which is one of the most important Sufi shrines in southern India. Visitors are advised to follow custom and cover their heads and limbs and wash their feet before entering.

ARRIVAL AND DEPARTURE

MANGALURU (MANGALORE)

By plane Bajpe airport, 22km north of the city (bus #22 or #47A or taxis for ₹400–500), has regular flights to Bengaluru (9 daily; 50min–1hr 10min) and Mumbai (6 daily; 1hr 30min) besides services to Goa, Hyderabad and Kochi. There are also daily connections with the Gulf states.

By train The railway station, to the south of the city centre on Station Rd, sees daily services from cities all over India. Though rail services to Goa and Mumbai operate from Mangaluru, note that Konkan Railway through trains do not stop at the city terminus. A better choice of train connections north and south is at Kankanadi, around 10km north, or Kasaragod, an easy bus ride across the Kerala border.

Destinations From Mangaluru itself, the best northbound trains are: the fast *Madgaon Express* #22636 (departs 8.15am) to Margao (5hr 45min) via Udupi (1hr 40min) and the *Matsyaganda Express* #12620 (departs 2.35pm) to Gokarna (4hr), Margao (5hr 55min) and Mumbai's Lokmanya Tilak station (14hr 35min). Services south through all major points in Kerala to Thiruvananthapuram include the *Ernad Express* #16605 (departs 7.20am; 13hr 40min) and the *Malabar Express* #16630 (departs 6.15pm; 14hr 10min).

By bus Mangaluru's busy KSRTC Bus Stand (known locally as the "Lal Bagh" Bus Stand) is nearly 3km north of the town centre, in Hampankatta, from where you can catch city buses to most local destinations. Private buses use the much more central stand near the Town Hall. Agents for luxury and overnight services to Bengaluru and beyond include Anand Travels (☎0824 244 6737, ⓦanandbus .com) and Ideal Travels (☎0824 242 4899, ⓦidealtravels .co), both opposite Milagres Church on Falnir Rd, and Vijayanand Travels (☎0824 249 3536, ⓦvrlbus.in).

Destinations Bengaluru (every 30min–1hr; 9–10hr);

Hassan (hourly; 5–6hr); Kannur (hourly; 3hr); Kasaragod (every 30min; 1hr); Kozhikode (every 1–2hr; 5hr); Madikeri (every 30min–1hr; 4hr); Mysuru (hourly; 7hr); Udupi (every 10–15min; 1hr). The only direct bus to Gokarna leaves Mangaluru at 1.30pm; otherwise, change at Kumta. There are plenty of state buses heading north to Udupi and south along the coast into northern Kerala, though it is easier to pick up the more numerous private services to those places.

INFORMATION

Services You can change money at Trade Wings on Lighthouse Hill Rd (Mon–Sat 9.30am–5.30pm; ☎0824

242 6225). There are many ATMs, especially on KS Rao Rd.

ACCOMMODATION

The main area for hotels, **KS Rao Rd**, runs south from the bus stand and has an ample choice to suit most pockets. You can also stay out of town by the beach in **Ullal**, 10km south of the city.

Adarsh Lodge Market Rd ☎0824 244 0878. No-frills, compact but clean rooms – good value, especially the singles for ₹330. No wi-fi. **₹490**

The Gateway Hotel Old Port Rd, 1.5km from the railway station ☎0824 666 0420, ⓦthegatewayhotels .com. Modern Taj group business hotel; all rooms are a/c and some offer fine views of the Netravathi River joining the sea. Travel desk, exchange, pool, bar, two classy restaurants (*Gad* and *Cardamom*) and 24hr coffee shop. **₹4500**

Navaratna Palace KS Rao Rd ☎0824 244 1104, ⓦnavaratnapalace.com. Rooms are musty but its proximity to the railway station and bus stand makes it a convenient choice for travellers. **₹1499**

Poonja International KS Rao Rd ☎0824 244 0171,

ⓦhotelpoonjainternational.com. Smart, mostly a/c, high-rise hotel with well-appointed rooms (some a/c) and good views from the upper floors. South Indian buffet breakfast included. **₹1699**

Summer Sands Beach Resort Chota Mangalore, Ullal ☎0824 246 7690, ⓦsummersands.in. Near the beach, with a pool and a bar-restaurant serving local specialities, Indian and Chinese food. Unfortunately the spacious rooms and villa-style cottages are rather run-down. Price inclusive of breakfast, dinner and tax, though wi-fi is chargeable. **₹7000**

Woodside Balmatta Rd ☎0824 244 0296, ⓦhotel woodsidemangalore.com. Pegged as a business hotel, this place offers unfussy spacious rooms (some a/c) and a good veg restaurant, *Xanadu*. Singles ₹990. **₹1370**

EATING

Bombay Lucky Near North Police Station, Mohammed Ali Rd, Bunder, 4km from the bus stand ☎0824 242 3710. Dating back to 1917, this late-opening restaurant, legendary for its Muslim cuisine, has been renovated but the quality remains high. Try the ghee rice, chicken korma, chicken or mutton biryani (₹140) or *bheja* (brain-fry) chicken or mutton fry, washed down with Suleimani (lemon) tea. Reasonably priced and lightning-quick service. Daily 9.30am–midnight.

Coral Ocean Pearl hotel, Navabharat Circle ☎0824 241 3800, ⓦtheoceanpearl.in. As the name suggests, there's an excellent seafood selection here and at reasonable prices despite the luxury hotel setting, including delicious fish thalis (lunchtime only; ₹331) and *koliwada* (crunchy, fried) prawns (₹632). Daily noon–3pm & 7–11pm.

Ganesh Prasad Down a lane running off KS Rao Rd ☎0824 425 5932. Classic pure-veg canteen, churning out all the South Indian favourites, from crispy dosas to gut-

busting lunchtime "meals" (₹60). Daily 7am–9.30pm.

Narayana Near Indian Overseas Bank, Azizuddin Rd, Bunder ☎0824 244 0891. A humble yet popular place near the harbour dishing out the best fish curry in town, served with boiled rice, and a choice of fried fish. Always packed like a tin of sardines. Daily 12.30–3.30pm & 7–9.30pm.

New Taj Mahal Café Kodialbail, KS Rao Rd ☎0824 426 9335. Open early doors, this Mangalore institution (since the 1920s) is a great choice for breakfast. Try local savouries like *ambade* (lentil fritters), *kadle upkari* (spiced chickpeas), *thuppa* dosa (slathered with clarified butter; ₹35), *godi* (wheat) halwa and banana halwa. Daily 6am–9.30pm.

Palkhi Balmatta Rd ☎0824 244 4929. This airy family rooftop restaurant offers a wide menu of North Indian, Chinese and Continental cuisine, with main courses around ₹230. Daily noon–3.15pm & 7–11.15pm.

North of Mangaluru: coastal Karnataka

Whether you travel the **Karnataka (Karavali) coast** on the Konkan Railway or along the busy NH-17, southern India's smoothest highway, the route between Goa and Mangaluru ranks among the most scenic anywhere in the country. Crossing countless palm- and mangrove-fringed estuaries, the railway line stays fairly flat, while the recently upgraded road, dubbed by the local tourist board as "The Sapphire Route", scales several spurs of the Western Ghats, which here creep to within a stone's throw of the sea, with spellbinding views over long, empty beaches and deep blue bays. Highlights are the pilgrim town of **Udupi**, site of a famous Krishna temple, and **Gokarna**, another important Hindu centre that provides access to exquisite unexploited beaches. A decent inland road winds through the mountains to **Jog Falls**, India's biggest waterfall, which can also be approached from the east.

Udupi

UDUPI (also spelt Udipi), on the west coast, 60km north of Mangaluru, is one of South India's holiest Vaishnavite centres. The Hindu saint **Madhva** (1238–1317) was born here, and the **Krishna temple** and *mathas* (monasteries) he founded are visited by hundreds of thousands of pilgrims each year. The largest numbers congregate during the late winter, when the town hosts a series of spectacular **car festivals** and gigantic, bulbous-domed chariots are hauled through the streets around the temple. Even if your visit doesn't coincide with a festival, Udupi is a good place to break the journey along the Karavali coast. Thronging with pujaris and pilgrims, its small sacred enclave is wonderfully atmospheric.

The Krishna temple and mathas

Udupi's **Krishna temple** lies five minutes' walk east of the main street, surrounded by the eight **mathas** founded by Madhva in the thirteenth century. Legend has it that the idol enshrined within was discovered by the saint himself after he prevented a shipwreck. The grateful captain of the vessel offered Madhva his precious cargo as a reward, but the holy man asked instead for a block of mud, which he broke open to

---

KAMBLA

If you're anywhere between Mangaluru and Bhatkal from October to April and come across a crowd gathering around a waterlogged paddy field, chances are they're there to watch the spectacular rural sport of **Kambla**, or **buffalo racing**. It's a centuries old tradition unique to Dakshina Kannada, the southernmost district of coastal Karnataka.

Two contestants, usually local rice farmers, take part in the race, riding on a wooden plough-board tethered to a pair of buffaloes. The object is to reach the opposite end of the field first, but points are also awarded for style, and riders gain extra marks – and roars of approval from the crowd – if the muddy spray kicked up from the plough-board splashes the special white banners, or *thorana*, strung across the course at a height of 6–8m. In simpler formats of the competition contestants may be tugged by a single buffalo, connected by a rope or even hold the animal's tail.

Generally, race days are organized by wealthy landowners on fields specially set aside for the purpose. Villagers flock in from all over the region, as much for the fair (*shendi*), as the races themselves: men huddle in groups to watch cockfights (*korikatta*), women haggle with bangle sellers and kids roam around sucking sticky *kathambdi goolay*, the local bonbons. It is considered highly prestigious to be able to throw such a party, especially if your buffaloes win any events or, better still, come away as champions. Pampered by their doting owners, racing buffaloes are massaged, oiled and blessed by priests before big events, during which large sums of money are often won and lost. In recent years, however, the sport has come under the scanner of animal activists leading to a request for a ban on the practice by the Animal Welfare Board of India, though time will tell whether a law will be enforced.

expose a perfectly formed image of Krishna. Believed to contain the essence (*sannidhya*) of the god, this deity draws a steady stream of pilgrims, and is the focus of almost constant ritual activity. It is looked after by *acharyas*, or pontiffs, from one of the *mathas* on a two-year rotation system. They perform pujas (5.30am–8.45pm) that are open to non-Hindus; men are only allowed into the main shrine bare-chested.

ARRIVAL AND INFORMATION   UDUPI

By train Udupi's railway station is at Indrali on Manipal Rd, 3km west from the centre, and there are at least five trains in each direction daily.

By bus Udupi's three bus stands are dotted around the amorphous square in the centre of town: the KSRTC and private stands form a practically indistinguishable gathering spot for the numerous services to Mangaluru and more long-distance buses to Mysuru and Bengaluru and between northern Kerala and Goa. There are hardly any direct buses to Gokarna or Jog Falls, so you usually have to change at Kumta or Honnavar for both. The City stand is down some steps to the north and handles private services to local villages.

Tourist information There's a tourist information centre near the temple in the Krishna Building, on Car St (☏ 0820 429 3222), and a tourist office at Rajasadri, Manipal End Point (Mon–Sat 10am–5.30pm; ☏ 0820 257 4868).

ACCOMMODATION

As a busy pilgrimage town, Udupi offers ample inexpensive **accommodation**, which is only likely to approach capacity during a major festival.

Durga International Just west of City Bus Stand ☏ 0820 253 6971, ⌨ hoteldurgainternational.com. Airy and efficient lodge with a variety of attached rooms, all with TV and some with a/c, on the upper storeys of a modern block. Also has a good multicuisine restaurant. No wi-fi. ₹**900**

Janardana Next to KSRTC Bus Stand ☏ 0820 252 3880, ⌨ www.janardanahotel.in. Clean but fairly mundane hotel with simple attached rooms of different sizes, most with cable TV and some a/c. No wi-fi. ₹**900**

Sriram Residency Opposite the GPO ☏ 0820 253 0761, ⌨ hotelsriramresidency.in. Plushest place in the centre, though costing no more than most, with a smart lobby and comfortable a/c rooms. One of the two restaurants serves fine non-veg, and there's a bar too. No wi-fi. ₹**1035**

Sri Vidyasamudra Choultry Opposite Krishna temple ☏ 0820 252 0820. Foreigners are welcome in this ultra-basic lodge for pilgrims. The front rooms overlooking the temple are incredibly atmospheric. No wi-fi. ₹**150**

Vyavahar Lodge Kankads Rd ☏ 0820 252 2568. Basic but friendly and clean lodge between the bus stands and temple. Singles are just ₹300. No wi-fi. ₹**500**

EATING

As you might expect of the **masala dosa**'s birthplace, there are many fine, simple South Indian restaurants in Udupi, where you can sample these and other veg favourites. The vast majority of places are pure veg: for non-veg food or alcohol, you'll have to try a posh hotel restaurant such as the *Sriram Residency* (see above).

Diana Jodukatte, Ajjarkad, 1.5km southwest of the Krishna temple ☏ 0820 252 0505, ⌨ hoteldianaudupi .com. This long-established restaurant on the first floor of the *Diana* hotel is the birthplace of the *gadbad* ice cream (₹85), a famous dish invented hurriedly (*gadibidi* is Kannada for confusion) when several layers of different ice creams were mixed with chopped nuts and chewy dried fruit. Local snacks like dosas, *poori kurma* (veg curry with fried bread) and veg cutlets are also available, besides tandoori and Chinese. Daily 8am–9pm.

Mitra Samaj Car St ☏ 98801 99678. Established in 1949, this cramped place shares wall space with the Chandra-mouleshwara shrine close to the Krishna temple. Try the bullet *idlis* (₹30; available only after 2pm), *goli bajji* (a spongy, fried snack, ₹30; after 4pm) or dosa served with typical Udupi *sambhar* (₹50). Daily 5.30am–9pm.

Pooja Below Janardana hotel ☏ 7204 022221. Formerly called *Adarsha*, this pure-veg eatery rustles up tasty South Indian tiffin, filling masala dosa (₹85), *upma* (thick semolina or rice-flour porridge; ₹15) and wholesome thalis (₹50). Daily 6am–9pm (Sun till 4pm).

Jog Falls

Vehicle entry fee ₹10 per person • Musical fountain and laser show Mon–Sat 7.15–8.15pm, Sun 7.15–9.15pm

Hidden in a remote, thickly forested corner of the Western Ghats 240km northeast of Mangaluru, **Jog Falls** are the highest waterfalls in India. Today, however, they are rarely as spectacular as they were before the construction of a large dam upriver, which impedes the flow of the River Sharavati over the sheer red-brown sandstone cliffs. Still, the surrounding scenery is gorgeous, with dense scrub and jungle carpeting sparsely populated, mountainous terrain. The views of the falls from the opposite side of the gorge is also impressive, though during the monsoons mist and rain clouds tend to envelop the cascades. Another reason not to come during the wet season is that the extra water, and abundance of leeches at this time, make the excellent **hike** to the floor valley a trial; if you can, head up here between October and January. The trail starts just below the bus park and winds steeply down to the water, where you can enjoy a refreshing dip. The whole patch opposite the falls has been landscaped for appealing viewing, with its own entrance gate and reception centre.

ARRIVAL AND INFORMATION   JOG FALLS

By bus Jog Falls is connected by the well-paved NH-206 that crosses the Ghats from the coast south of Kumta (6 buses daily to the falls from Kumta; 3hr), which is connected by frequent buses to Gokarna. Coming from the south, it is slightly quicker to connect at Honnavar (4–6 daily; 2hr 30min). On the inland side, there are hourly services to Shivamogga (Shimoga), from where you can change onto buses for Hosapete and Hampi. Change at Sagar (40km) instead for buses to Udupi, Mysuru, Hassan and Bengaluru.

Tourist information The tourist office (Mon–Sat 10am–1.30pm & 2.30–5.30pm), upstairs at the new reception centre, opens rather erratically but can supply information on transport and vehicle rental.

ACCOMMODATION AND EATING

Apart from the standard government canteen at the *Mayura Gerusoppa Jogfalls* hotel, the only other food options are at the enclave of small chai stalls and shops that cluster around the reception centre.

JMJ Homestay More than 1km southeast of the reception centre, beyond the canal ☎ 94822 08755. Friendly homestay with four comfortable, rustic rooms. Food served on request. No wi-fi. ₹500

Matthuga Homestay Talavata, BH Rd, 8km from Jog Falls ☎ 98807 99975, ⊚ matthuga.in. Popular homestay, close to nature, set in a plantation bungalow with lovely attached rooms and cottages (₹2900). Fixed pure-veg menu (breakfast ₹80; lunch/dinner ₹130). No TV, no wi-fi. ₹1700

Mayura Gerusoppa Jogfalls 200m west of reception centre ☎ 08186 244732, ⊚ karnatakaholidays.net.

Predictable concrete KSTDC hotel whose vast, old-fashioned a/c and non-a/c rooms are comfortable enough but grossly overpriced, especially at weekends. It has two blocks: the more basic *Tunga*; and *Sharavati*, with better views of the falls. No wi-fi. *Tunga* ₹800, *Sharavati* ₹2000

PWD Inspection Bungalow 400m west of the reception centre ☎ 08186 244333. Nicely situated on a hillock above the main road, with four spacious a/c attached rooms and five decent non-a/c rooms. No wi-fi but food is made on request (veg ₹75, non-veg ₹400). ₹500

Gokarna

Among India's most scenically situated sacred sites, **GOKARNA** lies between a broad white-sand beach and the verdant foothills of the Western Ghats, 230km north of Mangaluru. Yet this compact little coastal town – a Shaivite centre for more than two millennia – remained largely "undiscovered" by Western tourists until the early 1990s, when it began to attract dreadlocked and didgeridoo-toting neo-hippies fleeing the commercialization of Goa, just over 60km north. Now it's firmly on the tourist map, although the town retains a charming local character, as the Hindu pilgrims pouring through still far outnumber the foreigners who flock here in winter.

A hotchpotch of wood-fronted houses and red terracotta roofs, Gokarna is clustered around a long L-shaped bazaar. Its broad main road – known as **Car Street** – runs west to the town beach, which is a sacred site in its own right. Hindu mythology identifies it as the place where Shiva was reborn from the underworld after a period of penance through the ear of a cow, or *go-karna*, thus giving the town its name.

Gokarna is also the home of one of India's most powerful *shivalingas* – the **atmalinga**, which took root here having being carried off by Ravana, the evil king of Lanka, from

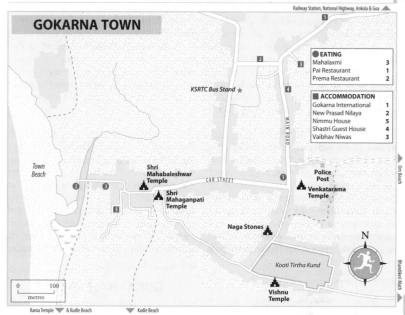

GOKARNA TOWN

EATING
Mahalaxmi	3
Pai Restaurant	1
Prema Restaurant	2

ACCOMMODATION
Gokarna International	1
New Prasad Nilaya	2
Nimmu House	5
Shastri Guest House	4
Vaibhav Niwas	3

Shiva's home on Mount Kailash. It is said Ravana's brute force distorted the *shivalingam* to resemble the shape of a cow's ear – another theory behind the town's name.

The temples

The *atmalinga* (or *pranalinga*) is enshrined in the medieval **Shri Mahabaleshwar temple**, at the far west end of the bazaar. It is regarded as so auspicious that a mere glimpse of it will absolve a hundred sins, even the murder of a brahmin. Pilgrims shave their heads, fast and take a ritual dip in the sea before *darshan*. For this reason, the tour of Gokarna traditionally begins at the beach, followed by a puja at the **Shri Mahaganpati temple**, a stone's throw east of the Mahabaleshwar shrine, to propitiate the elephant-headed god Ganesh. Foreign tourists are not allowed into the inner sancta of the main two temples but the parts you can visit are still extremely atmospheric. One interesting holy place you can get right into is **Bhandikeri Math**, a short way east of the bathing tank. This three-hundred-year-old temple and learning centre has shrines to the deities Bhavani Shankar, Uma Maheshwari and Maruthi.

The beaches

While Gokarna's numerous temples, shrines and tanks are the big draw for Indian pilgrims, most Western tourists head for the beautiful **beaches** to the south of the more crowded town beach. Beyond the lumpy, reddish-coloured headland that overlooks the town, lie a series of sandy strips connected by short seaside walks and motley shacks offering varied cuisine.

To pick up the trail, take a left off Car Street beside the Shri Mahaganpati temple and follow the cemented path for twenty minutes uphill and across a rocky plateau to **Kudle Beach**. This wonderful 1km-long sweep of golden-white sand sheltered by a pair of steep-sided promontories is now punctuated by dozens of restaurant-cum-hut ventures. This is the longest and broadest of Gokarna's beaches, with decent surf too, though the water can be dangerous.

It takes around twenty minutes more to hike over the headland from Kudle to exquisite **Om Beach**, so named because its distinctive twin crescent-shaped bays resemble the auspicious Om symbol. Apart from the luxury resort set well back from the beach, largely flimsy huts and the odd hammock still populate the palm groves, usually belonging to restaurants. Large groups of male travellers tend to descend on the beach at weekends – female sunbathers may prefer to press on further south.

Gokarna's two most remote beaches lie another thirty-minute walk over the rocky hills. **Half Moon** and **Paradise** beaches are mainly for intrepid sun-lovers happy to pack in their own supplies. If you're looking for near-total isolation – a sense of Goa perhaps thirty years ago – these are your best bet.

ARRIVAL AND DEPARTURE   GOKARNA

By train Gokarna Road railway station is 9km inland but buses, taxis and auto-rickshaws (₹200) are available to take you into town. Gokarna Road has two daily trains in each direction: the southbound services are the *Matsyagandha Express* #12619 (departs 3.08am) and the *Bangalore Express* #16524 (departs 3.12pm), both to Udupi and Mangaluru; the trains north are the *Matsyagandha Express* #12620 (departs 6.40pm) to Margao and Mumbai and the *Madgaon Passenger* #56640 (departs 10.11am) to Margao. A couple of

other weekly expresses also call here, such as the *Maru–Sagar Express* #12978 (dep. Fri 2.48pm) to Ernakulam and *Poorna Express* #11098 (dep. Mon 11.22am) to Pune, but more regular express connections can be found in either Kumta or Ankola.

By bus The KSRTC Bus Stand, 300m north of Car St, is within easy walking distance of Gokarna's limited accommodation. The town is well connected by direct daily bus to Goa (5hr) and several towns in Karnataka, including Bengaluru

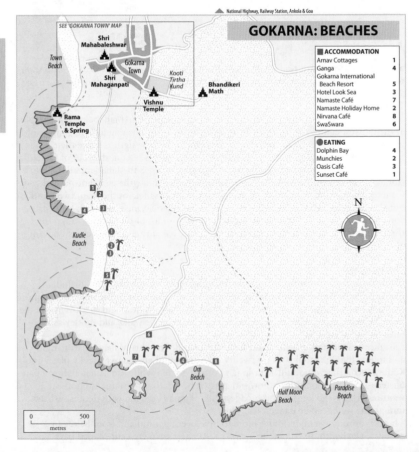

▲ National Highway, Railway Station, Ankola & Goa

GOKARNA: BEACHES

SEE 'GOKARNA TOWN' MAP

Shri Mahabaleshwar
Town Beach
Gokarna Town
Shri Mahaganpati
Kooti Tirtha Kund
Bhandikeri Math
Vishnu Temple
Rama Temple & Spring
Kudle Beach
Om Beach
Half Moon Beach
Paradise Beach

N

0   500
metres

ACCOMMODATION

Arnav Cottages	1
Ganga	4
Gokarna International Beach Resort	5
Hotel Look Sea	3
Namaste Café	7
Namaste Holiday Home	2
Nirvana Café	8
SwaSwara	6

EATING

Dolphin Bay	4
Munchies	2
Oasis Café	3
Sunset Café	1

(13–14hr), Hosapete/Hampi (10hr) and Mysuru (13hr), via Mangaluru (6hr) and Udupi (5hr). You can change at Ankola on the main highway for more services north into Goa. For more buses to Hosapete and Hampi and the best connections to Jog Falls, change at Kumta.

GETTING AROUND

By bike Bicycles are available for rent from a stall next to *Pai Restaurant* for ₹50/day.

By auto-rickshaw and taxi Auto-rickshaws and taxis cost ₹150–200 to Om Beach. There's no motorable road to Kudle Beach but auto-rickshaws charge just ₹80 along the paved path that goes three-quarters of the way.

ACCOMMODATION

There is a better range of **guesthouses** than of bona fide **hotels** in Gokarna. As a last resort, you can nearly always find a bed in one of the spartan **dharamshalas** dotted around town. There's an increasing number of options at the **beaches**, from basic huts to resorts. Prices can double over the Christmas/New Year period.

GOKARNA TOWN

Gokarna International On the main road into town ⓣ08386 256622, ⓔhotelgokarn@yahoo.com; map p.247. Popular mid-scale place in a four-storey block on the edge of town, offering good value, from no-frills singles to deluxe, carpeted a/c doubles. The better ones (₹1400) have balconies overlooking the palm tops. Restaurant and bar on the premises. **₹866**

New Prasad Nilaya On the lane near the bus stand ⓣ08386 257135; map p.247. Very clean budget place with helpful management. The pricier rooms have cable TV and balconies. **₹700**

Nimmu House Southwest of Car St, towards Kudle Beach ⓣ08386 256730, ⓦnimmuhouse.in; map p.247. This foreigners' favourite is in a great leafy location but prices spike in peak season. Double rooms in the attractive modern block are spacious, attractive and have decent mattresses, while those in the old wing are much plainer. Many upper rooms have balconies with fine beach views. **₹800**

Shastri Guest House 100m east of the bus stand ⓣ08386 256220, ⓔnarasimha.shastri@gmail.com; map p.247. Tucked behind the Shastri Clinic on the main road, this quiet place offers attached plus a handful of non-attached rooms with rock-bottom single rates (₹175), as well as four roomier cottages (₹700) up the hill. Only slightly more in high season. No phone or online bookings done. **₹400**

Vaibhav Niwas Off the main road, a few minutes from the bus stand ⓣ08386 256714, ⓔvaibhavnivas97@gmail.com; map p.247. Friendly, cheap and justifiably popular guesthouse pitched at foreigners, with a rooftop café-restaurant; rock-bottom rooms with shared facilities and some attached with TV. **₹500**

GOKARNA BEACHES

Arnav Cottages Kudle hill ⓣ90360 44212; map p.248. Barely a 5min walk from the beach, with simple but very clean cottages, bikes for hire plus a yoga hall, good in-house restaurant and German bakery. Its biggest assets? Amazing views of Kudle Beach and attentive host and staff. **₹2000**

Ganga North end of Kudle Beach ⓣ08386 257195; map p.248. One of the more established beach joints, with simple huts (all with common bathrooms), an excellent terrace restaurant and high-speed internet. Beach-view huts cost more. **₹400**

★**Gokarna International Beach Resort** Kudle Beach ⓣ08386 257843, ⓦgokarnabeachresort.com; map p.248. Set back from the beach in a small garden dotted with coconut trees, this compact hotel offers simple comforts in neat laterite cottages and rooms fitted with small kitchenettes and verandas, some of them sea-facing. Rates drop as low as ₹800 off season. **₹2400**

Hotel Look Sea Kudle Beach ⓣ93411 56506; map p.248. All but four of these basic huts and rooms have shared facilities but many enjoy excellent beach views. Fine muesli in the morning; football matches on the telly and beer in the evening. **₹150/₹400**

Namaste Café Northwest end of Om Beach ⓣ08386 257141, ⓦnamastegokarna.com; map p.248. One of the more popular beach options. Each room has a different theme: in one, everything is round (including the bed); another resembles a rustic log cabin. Ther's also a pleasant, shaded restaurant. The same folk also run *Namaste Sanjeevini*, a pricier option on Kudle Beach with a/c and non-a/c (₹4000) and more budget-conscious *Namaste Samudra*. **₹1080**

Namaste Holiday Home Kudle Beach ⓣ08386 257454, ⓦspiritualland.com; map p.248. Sea-view cottages, rooms and tree houses amid lush greenery, with an organic vegetable patch. Dressed with good linen, rugs and cheery curtains, plus well-equipped bathrooms, the clean, airy spaces guarantee secluded relaxation. Besides complimentary yoga, river kayak tours and Thai massages are available. **₹2400**

Nirvana Café Southeast end of Om Beach ⓣ08386 257429, ⓔsuresh.nirvana@gmail.com; map p.248. A dozen bamboo huts with solid attached brick bathrooms (not all attached), neatly arranged behind a congenial restaurant with raised concrete loungers. **₹450/₹800**

SwaSwara Above Om Beach ☎08386 257133, ⓦswaswara.com; map p.248. The first luxury resort in Gokarna, this CGH Earth property offers beautifully designed wood villas spread over terraces on a hillside overlooking the bay. There's a pool, yoga dome and an Ayurvedic treatment centre, all set in extensive gardens. Minimum five-night stay; all-inclusive packages per villa **€2295**

EATING

Gokarna town offers a good choice of **places to eat**, with a string of busy "meals" joints along Car St and the main road. The beaches now have a plethora of places offering travellers' favourites. Look out for the local sweet speciality *gadbad* (see p.245).

GOKARNA TOWN

Mahalaxmi At the beach end of Car St ☎99450 59215; map p.247. Service can be rather slow, but you won't feel much need to hurry, waiting on this sea-view rooftop perch. The menu includes tasty veg curries or veg with a creamy cheese sauce (all under ₹100). Daily 8am–10pm.

Pai Restaurant Main Rd ☎08386 256755; map p.247. An excellent spot for fresh and tasty veg thalis (₹70), masala dosas and crisp *vadas*, plus teas and coffees any time of day. Daily 7am–9.30pm.

★**Prema Restaurant** Car St, 150m west of the Mahabaleshwar temple ☎94810 52117; map p.247. Welcoming and hugely popular veg canteen with a varied menu encompassing delicious dosas, superb toasted English muffin sandwiches, lots of other veg dishes and the best *gadbad* in town. Daily 8am–8.30pm.

GOKARNA BEACHES

Dolphin Bay Southeastern Om Beach ☎98452 65608; map p.248. Typically laidback place at the back of the beach, offering Western and Indian food, plus a fine range of lassis. Fish costs ₹180–200. Daily 8am–10pm.

Munchies South-central Kudle Beach ☎96482 37456; map p.248. One of the newer and most relaxing spots on Kudle, with pleasant shady seating and known for its pancakes, banoffee pie and garlic cheese naan. Also offers tasty grilled seafood and curries in the ₹150–200 range. Daily 8am–11pm.

Oasis Café South-central Kudle Beach; map p.248. You can dig your feet in the soft sand at this friendly hangout, nicely decorated with colourful lanterns and wall hangings. A range of offerings from lamb to *momos*, plus Thai dishes at only around ₹150. Daily 8am–11pm.

Sunset Café Central Kudle Beach ☎98868 97597; map p.248. This very popular restaurant offers a range of veg, chicken and seafood dishes such as calamari sizzler for ₹230, and guarantees prime sunset views accompanied by Arabian Sea breezes. Daily 8am–10.30pm.

Hubballi (Hubli)-Dharwad

Karnataka's second most industrialized city, **Hubli**, now officially known as **HUBBALLI**, just east of the Ghats and 418km northwest of Bengaluru, has little of interest except for its transport connections to Mumbai, Goa, the coast of Uttar Kannada (North Canara), Hampi and other points in the interior. Its twin city, the cultural hub of **DHARWAD**, 20km northwest, has a little more to offer fans of Indian classical music.

Gangothri

Dharwad Yellapur Rd, Shukravarpet • Regular KSRTC buses and taxis ply between Hubballi and Dharwad

The birthplace of several renowned Indian classical singers, Dharwad's biggest attraction is **Gangothri**, the childhood home of Dr Gangubai Hangal (1913–2009), a doyenne of Hindustani classical music who broke boundaries of tradition, gender and stereotype with her deep powerful voice. Her greatness lay in her simplicity, and her humble home has been converted into a museum showcasing her life, musical achievements and memorabilia.

ARRIVAL AND DEPARTURE   HUBBALLI (HUBLI)-DHARWAD

By train Hubballi's railway station is right in the town centre and is well connected.

Destinations Bengaluru (10–15 daily; 7hr 25min–9hr); Hassan (*Dharwar Mysore Express* #17302 dep. 9.15pm; 6hr 50min); Hosapete (9–10 daily; 2hr 20min–2hr 50min); Mumbai (2–5 daily; 14hr 30min–18hr); Pune (4–5 daily;

9hr 30min–12hr).

By bus Hubballi's efficient KSRTC Bus Stand is 2km south of the centre, and can be reached by bus from the railway station or the chaotic City Bus Stand, about 1km west of the

station. There are connections to most towns in Karnataka, most usefully to Ankola (every 30min–1hr; 3hr 30min–4hr) for Gokarna; handy if you do not happen to coincide with one of the four daily direct buses.

ACCOMMODATION

Ajanta JC Nagar Rd ☎0836 236 2216. This no-frills lodge near the station has a range of rooms, including very cheap singles with shared bathroom, and various doubles. ₹400

Kailash Lamington Rd ☎0836 235 2235. Conveniently located between the railway station and the bus stand, this

efficient business hotel offers good-value a/c rooms and a decent restaurant. ₹600

Shri Renuka Lodge Opposite the City Bus Stand ☎0836 225 3615. This large and well-organized lodge offers a range of reasonable rooms, some with a/c, and has its own veg restaurant. ₹500

EATING

Don't leave Dharwad without picking up a box of Dharwad *pedha*, a caramel-brown, milk-based sweet dusted with caster sugar, which can be bought at Babusingh's Thakur Pedha in Line Bazar or numerous outlets of Mishra Pedha.

Basappa Khanavali Opposite Civil Court, PB Rd ☎93426 79111. This 1930 pure-veg eatery serves excellent North Karnataka thalis for ₹70, served with *bhakri* (*jowar roti*). Gets rather busy at lunchtime. 10.30am–3.30pm & 7.30–10.30pm.

Kamat Hotel ☎0836 236 2845, ⊛kamatyatri.in. The two branches of the famous South Indian food chain dish

out excellent vegetarian meals and snacks. One is by the traffic island at the bus stand end of Lamington Rd, the other opposite the railway station. Both daily 7am–10pm.

Megh Darshini Subhash Rd ☎0836 243 5147. A popular restaurant serving excellent South Indian fare, with budget meals and generously large puris. Daily 7am–10pm.

4

Hosapete (Hospet)

Charmless **Hospet**, now reverted to its traditional name of **HOSAPETE** ("New City"), about ten hours from both Bengaluru and Goa, is of little interest except as the jumping-off place for the extraordinary ruined city of **Hampi** (Vijayanagar), 13km northeast. If you arrive really late, or want a more upmarket hotel, it makes sense to stay here and catch a bus or auto-rickshaw out to the ruins the following morning.

ARRIVAL AND DEPARTURE

HOSAPETE (HOSPET)

By train Hosapete's railway station is 1.5km north of the centre. Note that the Hosapete-based auto-rickshaws that gather on the forecourt charge at least ₹200 to Hampi but if you walk a short way along the road, you can usually bargain a returning Hampi auto down to under ₹100. Hosapete has one direct train daily to Bengaluru, the overnight *Hampi Express* #16591 (dep. 9.05pm; 9hr 5min); change at Guntakal Junction (3hr) for numerous southbound and northbound expresses. For connections to the coast and Goa, take the *Amaravathi Express* #18047 (dep. Mon, Tues, Thurs & Sat 6.20am; 7hr 35min) or head west to Hubballi (4 daily; 3–4hr). For connections to Badami and Vijayapura, change at Gadag (4 daily; 1hr 20min–2hr).

By bus The bus stand is in the centre, just off MG (Station) Rd, which runs south from the railway station. Bookings for long-distance routes can be made at the ticket office on the bus stand concourse (daily 8am–noon & 3–6pm), where there's also a left-luggage facility. Regular buses run the 30min route to Hampi, some via

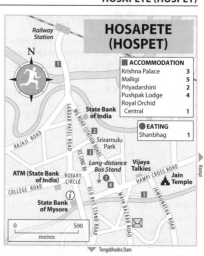

HOSAPETE (HOSPET)
■ **ACCOMMODATION**	
Krishna Palace	3
Malligi	5
Priyadarshini	2
Pushpak Lodge	4
Royal Orchid Central	1
● **EATING**	
Shanbhag	1

Kamalapura, until around 7.30pm. There are KSRTC buses to destinations throughout the state, but journeys are slow so the only ones worth taking are to Gadag (every 30min; 2hr), Hubballi (every 30min; 3hr) or Guntakal (hourly; 2hr 30min–3hr), for the better rail and road connections in those towns. Many tourists opt for the apparently easy option of a private sleeper coach to Goa or Gokarna which depart between 7 and 8pm (9–10hr; ₹800), operated by Paulo Travels (☎08394 225867, ⓦpaulotravels.com) from beside the hotel *Priyadarshini*. Unfortunately, these are usually overbooked, overcrowded and, if you are travelling to Gokarna, you will be offloaded for a transfer at Ankola in the wee hours.

INFORMATION

Tourist information The tourist office at the Rotary Circle (Mon–Sat: April & May 8am–1.30pm; June–March 10am–5.30pm; ☎08394 228537) offers limited information and sells tickets for KSTDC tours of Hampi.

Services Full exchange facilities are available at the *Malligi* hotel. Enfield motorbikes are available for rent (or sale) from Bharat Motors (☎08394 224704) near Vijaya Talkies cinema.

ACCOMMODATION

Krishna Palace MG Rd ☎08394 294300, ⓦkrishna palacehotel.com. Offering a bit of luxury surprising for Hosapete, this central and snazzy a/c hotel has smartly furnished rooms and an ostentatious lobby, plus spa massages. Sadly, the restaurant food disappoints. ₹4000
Malligi 10/90 JN Rd, a 2min walk southeast of the bus stand ☎08394 228101, ⓦmalligihotels.com. A 40-year-old institution that's been renovated from a tourist home to swanky hotel with several blocks of luxurious a/c rooms and suites separated by manicured lawns. There is also a large outdoor swimming pool (₹100/hr for non-residents), two smart restaurants, a gym and spa, in addition to a small bookshop and an efficient travel service. ₹2500

Priyadarshini MG Rd ☎08394 228838. Large and bland, but spotless and decent value, especially the a/c rooms (some with balconies). Two good restaurants: the veg *Naivedyam* and, in the garden, the excellent non-veg *Manasa*, which has a bar. ₹1200
Pushpak Lodge MG Rd ☎08394 421380. With basic but clean attached rooms, this is the best low-priced lodge in town and is conveniently, if noisily, located right by the bus stand. ₹400
Royal Orchid Central MG Rd ☎08394 300100, ⓦroyal orchidhotels.com. New luxury hotel with swish rooms, poolside bar, rooftop dining, travel desk and helpful staff. ₹4000

EATING

Shanbhag Next to the bus station. The excellent Udupi restaurant at this old hotel is a perfect pit stop before heading to Hampi, particularly since it opens early for breakfast. Daily 6.30am–9.30pm.

Hampi (Vijayanagar)

Among a surreal landscape of golden-brown boulders and leafy banana fields, the ruined "City of Victory," **Vijayanagar**, better known as **HAMPI** (the name of the main local village), spills from the south bank of the River Tungabhadra. This once dazzling Hindu capital was devastated by a six-month Muslim siege in the second half of the sixteenth century. Only stone, brick and stucco structures survived the ensuing sack – monolithic deities, crumbling houses and abandoned temples dominated by towering *gopuras* – as well as the irrigation system that channelled water to huge tanks and temples, some of which are still in use today.

Thus, Hampi's monuments appear a lot older than their four or five hundred years. With its wooden superstructure burnt and past buried in ruins, excavations by the Archaeological Survey of India (ASI) can only piece together the fragmented history of this sophisticated city. Grappling with years of encroachment and the constant tussle between preservation and modernization, the Hampi World Heritage Area Management Authority (HWHAMA) has controversially pressed ahead with plans to revamp **Hampi Bazaar** and the adjoining "heritage zone" (see box, p.256). Yet, at least for the time being, the serene riverside setting and air of magic that still lingers over the site, sacred for centuries before a city was founded

HAMPI / VIJAYANAGAR

ANEGUNDI

Tungabhadra River

Hanuman Temple &

VIRUPAPURAGADDA

SEE 'HAMPI BAZAAR & VIRUPAKSHA TEMPLE' MAP

Coracle Jetty

Vitthala Temple

King's Balance

Agni Temple & Kotilinga Complex

Narasimha Temple

Sacred Ghats

Virupaksha Temple

Bus Stand

Rama Temple

Achyutha Bazaar

Nandi Temple

HAMPI BAZAAR

Achyutharaya Temple

Hemakuta Hill

Matanga Hill

Krishna Temple

Veerabhadra Temple

Ugra Narasimha Statue

Palace

Guards' Quarters

Gateway

Elephant Stables

Lotus Mahal

Hazara Rama Temple

Madhava Temple

"Underground" Temple

Yellamma Temple

Palace

King's Audience Hall

Mahanavami-Dibba

Queen's Bath

Jain Temple

Bhima's Gate

Archeological Museum

KAMALAPURA

Kamalapura Bus Stand

N

Not to Scale

Hosapete

EATING

Laughing Buddha	1
Shiv Moon	2

ACCOMMODATION

The Goan Corner	3
Hampi's Boulders	1
Mowgli	7
Sai Plaza	5
Sunny Guest House	4
Umashankar Lodge	6
Uramma Heritage Homes	2

4

here, make it one of India's most extraordinary locations. Many find it difficult to leave and spend weeks chilling out in cafés, wandering to whitewashed hilltop temples and gazing at the spectacular sunsets.

Although spread over 26 square kilometres, the **ruins** of Vijayanagar are mostly concentrated in two distinct groups: the designated **Sacred Centre** around Hampi Bazaar and the nearby riverside area, encompassing an enclave of temples and *ghats*; and the **Royal Enclosure** – 3km south of the river, just northwest of **Kamalapura** village – which holds the remains of palaces, pavilions, elephant stables, guardhouses and temples. Between the two stretches is a long boulder-choked hill and scores of banana plantations, fed by ancient irrigation canals.

Brief history

According to the Ramayana, the region was once the mythical Kishkinda, ruled by the monkey king Bali, with his brother Sugriva and their ambassador, Hanuman. The unpredictably placed rocks – some balanced in perilous arches, others heaped in colossal, hill-sized piles – are said to have been flung down by their armies in a show of strength. It was here that Lord Rama raised his monkey army to rescue Sita from demon king Ravana's clutches.

While Hampi's mythic status was grand, its chronological evolution into the capital of a vast empire was no less extraordinary. The rise of the **Vijayanagar empire** seems to have been a direct response, in the first half of the fourteenth century, to the expansionist aims of Muslims from the North, most notably Malik Kafur and Mohammed-bin-Tughluq. Two Hindu brothers from Andhra Pradesh, Harihara and Bukka, who had been employed as treasury officers in Kampili, 19km east of Hampi, were captured by the Tughluqs and taken to Delhi, where they supposedly converted to Islam. Assuming them to be suitably tamed, the Delhi sultan despatched them to quell civil disorder in Kampili, which they duly did, only to abandon both Islam and allegiance to Delhi shortly afterwards, preferring to establish their own independent Hindu kingdom. Within a few years they controlled vast tracts of land from coast to coast. In 1343, guided by their spiritual guru Vidyaranya Swami, they founded their new capital, Vijayanagar, on the southern banks of the River Tungabhadra, a location long considered to be sacred by Hindus.

The city's most glorious period was under the reign of **Krishna Deva Raya** (1509–29), when it enjoyed a near monopoly of the lucrative trade in Arabian horses and Indian spices passing through the coastal ports and was the most powerful Hindu capital in the Deccan. Travellers such as the Portuguese chronicler Domingo Paez, who stayed for two years after 1520, were astonished by its size and wealth, telling tales of markets full of silk and precious gems, bejewelled courtesans, ornate palaces and fantastic festivities. Records reveal how it was once larger than Rome, with palaces grander than those of Lisbon.

Thanks to its natural features and massive fortifications, Vijayanagar was virtually impregnable. Yet in 1565, following his interference in the affairs of local Muslim sultanates, the regent Rama Raya was drawn into a battle with a confederacy of Muslim forces to the north and ultimately defeated. Rama Raya was captured and suffered a grisly death at the hands of the **sultan of Ahmadnagar**. Vijayanagar then fell victim to a series of destructive raids, and its days of splendour were brought to an abrupt end.

Hampi Bazaar and around

Hampi's long, straight main street, **Hampi Bazaar**, runs east from the entrance to the Virupaksha temple, and is lined by the remains of Vijayanagar's ruined, columned bazaar. While the Bazaar has been cleared of all shops under a restoration initiative (see box, p.256), the area north of the temple towards the river still houses a maze of restaurants, hotels and other businesses.

The Virupaksha temple

Daily 6.30am–12.30pm & 2–8.30pm • ₹2 but free during *aarti* (daily 6.30–8am & 6.30–8.30pm)

Dedicated to a form of Shiva known as Virupaksha ("the terrible-eyed one"), the **Virupaksha temple** dominates the village, drawing a steady flow of pilgrims, with its 50m-high nine-storey tower, the tallest *gopura* in Karnataka, acting like a beacon. The temple is at its liveliest during *aarti* (worship). The small three-headed Nandi outside the main entrance supposedly represents the past, present and future of Hampi. In the 1565 siege, Nandi's third head, representing the future, was defaced; Hampi never regained its glory.

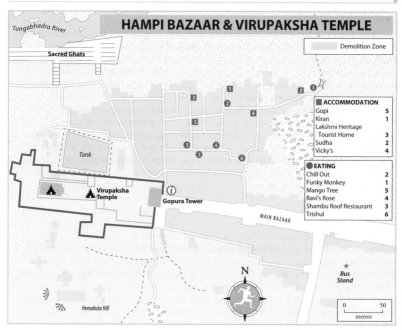

The complex consists of two courts, each entered through a towered *gopura*. From the smaller *gopura* near the ticket counter you enter the inner court, surrounded by a colonnade which is usually filled with pilgrims dozing or singing religious songs. If the temple elephant, Lakshmi, is around when you enter, you can get her to bless you by placing ₹10 in her trunk. In the middle, the principal temple is approached through a *mandapa* hallway whose carved columns feature rearing animals. Rare Vijayanagar-era paintings on the *mandapa* ceiling include aspects of Shiva, a procession with the sage Vidyaranya, the ten incarnations of Vishnu and scenes from the Mahabharata. In a side passage of the main shrine, guides show the inverted image of the *gopura*, illustrating an early example of a pin-hole camera.

The riverside

The sacred **ford** in the river is reached from the Virupaksha's north *gopura*; you can also get there by following the lane around the impressive temple **tank**. A *mandapa* overlooks the steps that originally led to the river, now some distance away. A small **motorboat** (₹15 [₹10]) runs from this part of the bank, ferrying villagers to the fields and tourists to the increasingly popular enclave of **Virupapuragadda**. The road left from the sacred ford through the village eventually loops back towards the hilltop Hanuman temple, about 5km east, and on to Anegundi – a recommended circular walk.

Matanga Hill

The place to head for sunrise is the boulder hill immediately east of Hampi Bazaar. From the end of the main street, an ancient paved pathway winds up a rise, topped by the magnificent Achyutharaya temple (see p.256) on the eastern ridge of **Matanga Hill**. The views improve as you progress up towards the small Veerabhadra temple at its summit, which provides an extraordinary vantage point. Muggings have been reported along this path early in the morning, so be vigilant if there are only one or two of you.

The riverside path

Walking east from the Virupaksha temple along the length of Hampi Bazaar, turn left before the huge monolithic **Nandi** statue to get to Vitthala temple (see below). This riverside path, peppered by conch-blowing sadhus and ragged mendicants, winds past cafés and numerous shrines, including a Rama temple – home to hordes of fearless monkeys. Beyond at least four Vishnu shrines, a paved and colonnaded **bazaar** leads due south to the **Achyutharaya temple** (aka Tiruvengalanatha), whose beautiful stone carvings – among them some of Hampi's famed erotica – are being restored by the ASI. Back on the main path again, make a short detour across the rocks leading to the river to see the little-visited waterside **Agni temple**; next to it, the Kotilinga complex consists of 1008 tiny lingas, carved on a flat rock. As you approach the Vitthala temple, to the south is an archway known as the **King's Balance**, where the rajas were weighed against gold, silver and jewels to be distributed to Brahmins and the needy on festive occasions.

Vitthala temple

Daily 6am–6pm • ₹250 (₹10); ticket also valid for the Lotus Mahal (see p.258) on the same day

Although the area of the **Vitthala temple** does not show the same evidence of early cult worship as Virupaksha, the ruined bridge to the west probably dates from before Vijayanagar times. The bathing *ghat* may be from the Chalukya or Ganga period, but as the temple has fallen into disuse it seems that the river crossing (*tirtha*) here lacks the sacred significance of the Virupaksha site. Now part of the UNESCO World Heritage Site, the Vitthala temple was built for Vishnu, who according to legend was too embarrassed by its ostentation to live here.

The **Saptasvara Mandapa** (Open Dancing Hall) features slender monolithic granite musical **pillars** which were constructed so as to sound the notes of the scale when struck. Today, due to vandalism and erosion from being repeatedly beaten, heavy security makes sure that no one is allowed to touch them. Guides, however, will happily demonstrate the musical resonance of other pillars on an adjacent structure. Outer columns sport characteristic Vijayanagar rearing horses, while friezes of lions, elephants and horses on the moulded basement display sculptural trickery – you can transform one beast into another simply by masking one portion of the image.

In front of the temple, to the east, a stone representation of a wooden processional **rath**, or chariot, houses an image of Garuda, Vishnu's bird vehicle. Now cemented, at one time the chariot's wheels revolved.

SACRILEGE IN A SACRED SETTING?

Until 2011, the local people of Hampi Bazaar had lived a peaceful and largely idyllic existence amid the Vijayanagar ruins. Indeed, in recent decades many had been making a decent living from tourists who came to hang out in the cafés and guesthouses while marvelling at the sights. All that changed abruptly when a long-pending **government scheme** to fence off the whole 26-square-kilometre area in order to protect its UNESCO World Heritage status finally got out of legal gridlock and began to be implemented, and residents were forced to move out of the bazaar to a rehabilitation area 4km away. Amid protests, the **bulldozers** cleared a 30–40m swathe of modern buildings flanking the bazaar and the main lane from the temple to the river. Ironically, even the tourist office was flattened.

While the heritage conservation project may take years to complete, locals who run guesthouses near the river and on the opposite bank feel they are living on borrowed time, fearing the next round of demolition. With authorities having to comply to strict conservation norms and locals facing displacement with paltry **compensation packages**, Hampi is in a Catch-22 situation. For travellers who have been enchanted by Hampi over the years it is heartbreaking that the magic of staying amid the ruins seems certain to disappear.

Anegundi and beyond

With more time, and a sense of adventure, you can head across the River Tungabhadra to **ANEGUNDI** (also spelt **Anegondi**), a fortress town predating Vijayanagar, and its fourteenth-century headquarters. The most pleasant way to get here is to take a coracle from the ford 1.5km east of the Vitthala temple; these circular baskets, which are today reinforced with plastic sheets, also carry bicycles, which are a good way to visit Hampi's many monuments. A contentious bridge was constructed at this point but collapsed some years ago. A new one is being built outside the core heritage zone, at Bukkasagar, further downstream.

Forgotten temples and fortifications litter Anegundi village and its quiet surroundings. The ruined **Huchchappa-matha** temple, near the river gateway, is worth a look for its lathe-turned black stone pillars and fine panels of dancers. **Aramane**, a ruined palace in the centre, stands opposite the home of the descendants of the royal family; also in the centre, the **Ranganatha temple** is still active. A huge wooden temple chariot stands in the village square. Limited **accommodation** is available here in village houses and you can get basic snacks at the local stalls.

Pampa Sarovar

To complete a five-kilometre loop back to Hampi from Anegundi (the simplest route if you have wheels), head left (west) through the old gateway just north of the village, which winds through sugar cane fields and eventually comes out near Virupapuragadda. En route you can visit the Vali Kila fort, a Durga temple and the sacred **Pampa Sarovar**, signposted down a dirt lane to the left. The small temple above this square bathing tank is dedicated to the goddess Lakshmi and holds a cave containing a footprint of Vishnu. If you're staying around Anegundi, this quiet spot is best visited early in the evening during *aarti*.

Hanuman temple

A worthwhile detour off the road north of the river leading west from Anegundi is the hike up to the tiny whitewashed **Hanuman temple**, perched on the rocky hilltop of Anjanadri. Believed to be the birthplace of Hanuman (also called Anjaneya, the son of Anjana), the spot holds a strange attraction for monkeys. The steep climb takes around thirty minutes and affords superb views over Hampi, especially at sunrise and sunset. Further west of Anjanadri, you reach an impressive old **stone bridge** dating from Vijayanagar times. The bridge no longer spans the river but just beyond it to the west, back at Virupapuragadda, the motorboat (₹15 [₹10]) returns you to the Virupaksha temple.

Hemakuta Hill and around

Directly above Hampi Bazaar, **Hemakuta Hill** is dotted with pre-Vijayanagar temples that date from the ninth to eleventh centuries. Aside from the architecture, the main reason to clamber up is to admire the **views** of the ruins and surrounding countryside. With views across the boulder-covered terrain and banana plantations, the sheer western edge of the hill is Hampi's top sunset spot, attracting crowds of tourists most evenings, along with entrepreneurial chaiwalas and little boys posing for photos in Hanuman costumes.

A couple of interesting monuments lie on the road leading south towards the southern group of ruins. The first of these, a walled **Krishna temple complex** to the west of the road, dates from 1513. Although dilapidated in parts, it features some fine carving and shrines.

Hampi's most-photographed monument stands just south of the Krishna temple in its own enclosure. Depicting Vishnu in his incarnation as the Man-Lion, the monolithic **Ugra Narasimha** statue, with its bulging eyes and crossed legs strapped into yogic pose, is one of Vijayanagar's greatest treasures.

The southern and royal monuments

The most impressive remains of Vijayanagar, the city's **royal monuments**, lie some 3km south of Hampi Bazaar, spread over a large expanse of open ground. Before tackling the ruins proper, it's a good idea to get your bearings with a visit to the small **Archeological Museum** (daily except Fri 10am–5pm; free) at Kamalapura, which can be reached by bus from Hosapete or Hampi. Among the sculptures, weapons, palm-leaf manuscripts and paintings from Vijayanagar and Anegundi, the highlight is a superb scale model of the city, giving an excellent bird's-eye view of the entire site.

Bhima's Gate

The route to the monuments is well signposted. After 200m or so you reach the partly ruined massive **inner city wall**, made from granite slabs, which runs 32km around the city, in places as high as 10m. Just beyond the wall, the **citadel area** was once enclosed by another wall and gates, of which only traces remain. To the east, the small *ganigitti* ("oil-woman's") fourteenth-century **Jain temple** features a simple stepped pyramidal tower of undecorated horizontal slabs. Beyond it is **Bhima's Gate**, once one of the principal entrances to the city, named after the Titan-like Pandava prince and hero of the Mahabharata. Like many of the gates, it is "bent" with two 90° turns, a form of defence against any frontal assault. Bas-reliefs depict such episodes as Bhima avenging the honour of his wife, Draupadi, by killing the general Dushasana. Draupadi vowed she would not dress her hair until Dushasana was dead; one panel shows her tying up her locks, the vow fulfilled.

Queen's Bath

To the west of the Jain temple, the plain facade of the 15m-square **Queen's Bath** belies its glorious interior, open to the sky and surrounded by corridors with 24 different domes. Eight projecting balconies overlook the now dry tank; traces of Islamic-influenced stucco decoration survive. Women from the royal household would bathe here and umbrellas were placed in shafts in the tank floor to protect them from the sun. The water supply channel can be seen outside.

Mahanavami-Dibba

Northwest of the Queen's Bath is **Mahanavami-Dibba** or "House of Victory", built to commemorate a successful campaign in what is now Odisha. A 12m pyramidal structure with a square base, it is said to have been where the king gave and received honours and gifts. From here he watched the magnificent parades, music and dance performances, martial arts displays, elephant fights and animal sacrifices that made celebration of the ten-day Dasara festival famed throughout the land. Carved reliefs decorate the sides of the platform.

King's Audience Hall

To the west of the Mahanavami-Dibba, another platform – the largest at Vijayanagar – is thought to be the basement of the **King's Audience Hall**. Stone bases of a hundred pillars remain, in an arrangement that has caused speculation as to how the building could have been used; there are no passageways or open areas.

Lotus Mahal

Daily 6am–6pm • ₹250 (₹10); ticket also valid for the Vitthala temple on the same day

The two-storey **Lotus Mahal**, in the north of the compound and part of the **zenana enclosure**, or women's quarters, was designed for the pleasure of Krishna Deva Raya's queen: a place where she could relax, particularly in summer. Displaying a strong Indo-Islamic influence, the pavilion is open on the ground floor, whereas the inaccessible upper level contains windows and balcony seats. A moat surrounding the building is thought to have provided water-cooled air via tubes.

Elephant Stables

Just northeast of the Lotus Mahal, the **Elephant Stables**, a series of high-ceilinged, domed chambers entered through arches, are the most substantial surviving secular buildings at Vijayanagar – a reflection of the high status accorded to elephants, both ceremonial and in battle.

Hazara Rama temple

To the west of the compound, on Hemakuta Hill, is the small **Hazara Rama** ("One thousand Ramas") temple. Thought to have been a private palace shrine, the rectangular enclosure features a series of medallion figures and bands of detailed friezes showing scenes from the Ramayana.

ARRIVAL AND INFORMATION	HAMPI (VIJAYNAGAR)

By bus Buses from Hosapete terminate close to where the road joins the main street in Hampi Bazaar, halfway along its dusty length.

Tourist information A tourist information counter (☎ 08394 241339) is situated in the main Hampi Bazaar area. The numerous private agencies can also help with most travel-related enquiries.

Services Stalls such as Raju, just up the lane from *Vicky's* guesthouse, has motorbikes and scooters for rent (around ₹150–200/day). Most guesthouses rent bicycles (₹80/day) but the bumpy terrain does make cycling hard work. There are no ATMs or banks but agents can offer exchange; rates are rather poor, so it's better to stock up on cash in Hosapete.

ACCOMMODATION

Hampi Bazaar remains the best place to stay for access to the sites, choice of restaurants and other facilities. There are no fancy hotels but a number of guesthouses of varying size and calibre. Some travellers prefer to stay across the river in **Virupapuragadda**, which is now well developed and has caught up in price. Prices are pretty low most of the year apart from the Christmas to mid-January peak, when they at least double.

HAMPI BAZAAR

Gopi Centre of the village ☎ 08394 241695, ⊛ gopi -guesthouse.com; map p.255. One of the more established places with small, simple rooms in the old building and smart but more expensive a/c options (₹1500) in another block round the corner. ₹1000

Kiran Beside the river ☎ 08394 204159, ⊜ gowda kiran96@yahoo.co.in; map p.255. The basic rooms here are compact but clean enough and among the cheapest left in the area. The rooftop restaurant has fine views of the river and the temple. ₹800

★ **Lakshmi Heritage Tourist Home** Down the lane towards the river ☎ 08394 241456; map p.255. There's nothing heritage about this modern guesthouse, whose smart a/c rooms have big mirrors around the headboards. Those downstairs are better. A tad noisy, but has hot running water all the time. Good discounts at slack times. ₹1000

★ **Sudha** Northeast end of the village ☎ 94810 42336; map p.255. One of the nicest, friendliest places to stay. The rooms vary in size but are generally larger and decorated more nicely on the slightly pricier upper storey. Rooftop Korean restaurant. ₹400

Vicky's Just east of the village centre ☎ 94805 61010, ⊜ vickyhampi@yahoo.co.in; map p.255. Small, clean rooms in one of the village's oldest lodges. Friendly and deservedly popular for its rooftop restaurant. ₹800

ACROSS THE RIVER

The Goan Corner 500m inland and east of boat crossing, Virupapuragadda ☎ 08762 626999, ⊛ thegoancorner .wordpress.com; map p.253. Large complex between lush paddy fields and attractive boulders with 36 rooms in thatched huts plus a 24-bed "million star" rooftop dorm. The lively restaurant has a good view of the boulders. Dorm ₹250; ₹600/₹800

Hampi's Boulders Narayanpet, Bandi Harlapur ☎ 94480 34202, ⊛ hampisboulders.com; map p.253. Overlooking a bend in the River Tungabhadra, this small, quirky resort hotel is the best upscale option, a 30min drive from Hampi Bazaar. There are four grades of cottages, from non-a/c to executive suites (₹12,800), moulded around giant boulder outcrops, with palms and mango trees for shade. Meals are so-so South Indian buffets but they have a natural rock-cut swimming pool. ₹5600

★ **Mowgli** Far west end of main road, Virupapuragadda ☎ 08533 287033, ⊛ mowglihampi.com; map p.253. The smartest option right across the river, offering thirty rooms and cottages, including two with a/c, with comfy sitouts and private balconies, some with garden and river views, as well as a welcoming restaurant, set against a gorgeous paddy and river backdrop. ₹1200

Sai Plaza Main road, Virupapuragadda ☎ 08533 287017, ⊛ saiplazahampi.com; map p.253. These fifteen bunga- lows enclosing an attractive courtyard garden are relaxed and

4

welcoming. The restaurant has delicious lassis and sandwiches and excellent views across the river. ₹400

★ **Sunny Guest House** 500m inland of boat crossing, Virupapuragadda ☎ 08533 287005, ⓦ sunnyguest house.com; map p.253. Nicely landscaped gardens with brightly painted bungalows and two sets of compact rooms, some with piped hot water. Their *Sheesh Besh* restaurant is a popular hangout. ₹400

Umashankar Lodge Main road, Virupapuragadda ☎ 94495 32394; map p.253. Cosy, popular spot with small but clean attached rooms (the upstairs ones rather overpriced) set round a leafy courtyard. Has a shaded

garden restaurant. ₹600

Uramma Heritage Homes Anegundi ☎ 08533 267792, ⓦ urammaheritagehomes.com; map p.253. A series of rustic homestays in renovated heritage homes that have retained the vernacular architecture. Choose from the seven *Uramma Cottages*, set within a farm, each with thatched roof and traditional food on offer, or individual rural villas such as beautiful two-room *Uramma House*. Nearby *Peshegar House*, originally a home of the book-keepers of Vijayanagar, has five doubles with shared baths and common dining in the garden courtyard. Rooms half-price in the off-season summer months. *Peshegar House* ₹850, *Uramma Cottage* ₹3500

EATING

Hampi has a plethora of traveller-oriented **restaurants**, with many of the most popular attached to guesthouses in the bazaar, or among the growing row of joints in Virupapuragadda. As a holy site, the main village is strictly alcohol-free and almost entirely vegetarian. There are no such restrictions on the other side of the river.

Chill Out Centre of village ☎ 94820 48655; map p.255. One of the cooler hangouts, with cushioned seating and bright decoration. Veg sizzlers go for ₹160. Daily 8am–10.30pm.

Funky Monkey Netra Guest House, Hampi Bazaar ☎ 08394 241775; map p.255. New rooftop restaurant with a relaxed vibe, great river views, decent Continental food and beverages like herbal teas and passion fruit lemonade. Daily 8am–10.30pm.

Laughing Buddha Main road, Virupapuragadda ☎ 94827 67374; map p.253. Good for set breakfasts and meat dishes such as *schnitzel* (₹150), with a relaxed atmosphere and film screenings every evening. Daily 8am–late.

★ **Mango Tree** Centre of village ☎ 94487 65213; map p.255. Relocated from its riverside spot, this famous place is renowned for its veg food, especially banana pancakes and pasta dishes (around ₹100). Daily 7.30am–9.30pm.

Ravi's Rose East end of village; map p.255. This small rooftop joint is one of the best places for authentic Indian

food (₹80–160); there are even some genuinely spicy dishes on request, and great lassis too. Good sound system, playing mostly Western music. Daily 7am–10pm.

Shambu Roof Restaurant Centre of village ☎ 94487 95096; map p.255. Set breakfasts, snacks, a variety of dosas and a special thali for ₹100 are among the items available. The rooftop setting guarantees fine views of the temple, particularly at dawn and sunset. Daily 8am–10.30pm.

Shiv Moon Riverside path, 500m east of the village ☎ 94807 26462; map p.253. A good place to break the journey to or from the Vitthala temple, serving pastas and standard curries, all in the ₹100–150 range. Daily 6am–10pm.

★ **Trishul** Southeast side of village ☎ 94484 81332; map p.255. Featuring chicken, tuna, lasagne, pizza and apple crumble, plus Mexican and Israeli cuisine, this is one of Hampi's widest menus, promising the rare treat of non-veg dishes. Daily 7am–11pm.

Badami, Aihole and Pattadakal: Monuments of the Chalukyas

Now quiet villages, **Badami**, **Aihole** and **Pattadakal**, the last a UNESCO World Heritage Site, were once the capital cities of the **Chalukyas**, who ruled much of the Deccan between the fourth and eighth centuries. The astonishing profusion of **temples** in the area beggars belief. Badami's and Aihole's cave temples, stylistically related to those at Ellora (see p.121), are some of the most important of their type. Among the many freestanding temples are some of the earliest in India, and at Pattadakal, uniquely, it is possible to see both northern (*nagara*) and southern (Dravida) architectural styles side by side, besides the *vesara*, a fusion of the two.

Badami

Surrounded by a yawning expanse of flat farmland, **BADAMI**, capital of the Chalukyas from 543 to 757 AD, extends east into a gorge between two red sandstone hills, topped by an ancient fortified complex. The southern hill is riddled with cave temples, while the northern one is studded with early structural temples and fort remains. Beyond the village, to the east, is an artificial lake, **Agastya Teertha**, said to date from the fifth century. Badami's selection of hotels and restaurants makes it an ideal base from which to explore the Chalukyan remains at Aihole and Pattadakal, as they do not possess such facilities. Be aware that the whole Badami area is home to numerous troupes of monkeys, especially around the monuments, and they will crawl all over you if you carry food.

Southern Fort cave temples

Daily sunrise–sunset • ₹100 (₹5)

Badami's earliest monuments are a group of sixth-century **caves** cut into the hill's red sandstone, each connected by steep steps leading up the hillside.

About 15m up the rock face and reachable after forty steps is **Cave 1**, dedicated to Shiva. The entrance is through a triple opening into a long porch raised on a plinth guarded by images of Shiva's dwarf attendants, the *ganas*. On the right is a striking 1.5m-high image of an eighteen-armed Nataraja illustrating 81 dance postures. Guides dramatically point out certain arm positions to highlight various *mudras*.

A little higher, **Cave 2** is a Vishnu shrine that holds some impressive sculpture and painting. Climbing again, steps and slopes lead upwards past a natural cave containing a smashed image of the Buddhist *bodhisattva*, Padmapani (he who holds the lotus), before steps on the right lead up to the fort.

Cave 3 (578 AD), another Vishnu shrine, stands beneath a 30m-high perpendicular bluff, and holds an image of Vishnu seated on a coiled snake. The oldest and largest of the group, with a facade measuring 21m from north to south, it is also considered to be the finest for the quality of its sculptural decoration. Treatment of the pillars is

4

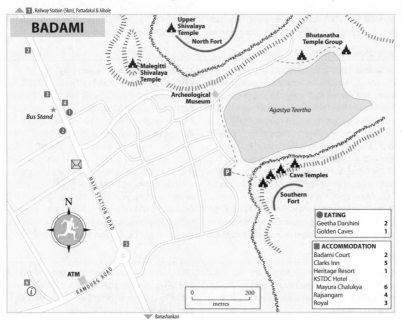

BADAMI

1, Railway Station (5km), Pattadakal & Aihole

Upper Shivalaya Temple
North Fort
Bhutanatha Temple Group
Malegitti Shivalaya Temple
Archeological Museum
Agastya Teertha
Bus Stand
P
Cave Temples
Southern Fort
MAIN STATION ROAD
N
ATM
RAMDURG ROAD
Banashankari

EATING	
Geetha Darshini	2
Golden Caves	1

ACCOMMODATION	
Badami Court	2
Clarks Inn	5
Heritage Resort	1
KSTDC Hotel Mayura Chalukya	6
Rajsangam	4
Royal	3

0   200
metres

extremely elaborate, featuring male and female bracket figures, lotus motifs and medallions portraying amorous couples.

To the east of the others, **Cave 4** is a Jain temple that overlooks Agastya Teertha and the town. It's a simpler shrine, dating from the sixth century. Lining the walls are figures of the 24 *tirthankaras*, both seated and standing and mostly without their identifying emblems. Here, the rock is striped.

After seeing the caves it is possible to climb up to the fort and walk east where, hidden in the rocks, a carved panel shows Vishnu reclining on the serpent Adisesha, attended by a profusion of gods and sages. Continuing, you can skirt the gorge and descend on the east to the Bhutanatha temples at the lakeside.

North Fort

North of Agastya Teertha, a number of structural temples can be reached by steps. The small **Archeological Museum** (daily except Fri 10am–5pm; ₹2) contains sculpture from the region. Although now dilapidated, the **Upper Shivalaya temple** is one of the earliest Chalukyan buildings. Scenes from the life of Krishna decorate the base and various images of him can be seen between pilasters on the walls. Only the sanctuary and tower of the **Lower Shivalaya** survive. Perched on a rock, the **Malegitti Shivalaya** (late seventh century) is the finest southern-style, early Chalukyan temple in existence. Its shrine is adjoined by a pillared hallway with small pierced stones and a single image on each side: Vishnu on the north and Shiva on the south.

ARRIVAL AND INFORMATION   BADAMI

By bus Badami bus stand, in the centre of the village on Main Station Rd, sees frequent daily services to Gadag (2hr), Hubballi (3hr) and Vijayapura (4hr), as well as local buses to Aihole and Pattadakal. The direct Hosapete buses all leave by 8.30am (5hr); at other times you should change in Gadag.

By train The railway station is 5km north; large auto-rickshaws-cum-*tempos* connect it with the town centre for ₹10/person; drivers are reluctant to cram in travellers with big bags, but you should be able to secure a whole vehicle for ₹80–100. The line from Vijayapura to Gadag via Badami carries five daily trains in each direction; some services continue to Hubballi.

Tourist information The friendly tourist office (Mon–Sat 10am–5.30pm; ☎ 08357 220414) is located inside the *KSTDC Hotel Mayura Chalukya* (see below).

ACCOMMODATION

★**Badami Court** Main Station Rd ☎ 08357 220207, ⓦ hotelbadamicourt.com. A prime location, superior a/c rooms and efficient staff make this a top choice for travellers. Additional perks include a pool to beat the heat and good-quality cooking at the restaurant. ₹**2500**

★**Clarks Inn** Veerpulakeshi Circle, Main Station Rd ☎ 08357 220150, ⓦ clarksinn.in. Part of a large chain, this new hotel is a short hop from the bus station (2km from railway station). Swanky, elegantly decorated rooms present superb views of the caves. Has a 24hr coffee shop on the ground floor. Super online deals, too. ₹**4000**

★**Heritage Resort** Station Rd ☎ 08357 220250, ⓦ theheritage.co.in. Spacious and attractively furnished detached a/c cottages arranged around verdant lawns. Also an excellent multicuisine restaurant. ₹**2500**

KSTDC Hotel Mayura Chalukya Ramdurg Rd ☎ 08357 220046, ⓦ karnatakaholidays.net. This renovated government hotel has 26 sizeable rooms, the majority of which are a/c, plus pleasant gardens and a bar-restaurant. ₹**1000**

Rajsangam Opposite the bus stand ☎ 08357 221991, ⓦ hotelrajsangaminternational.com. Spacious singles, deluxe doubles, suites with balconies and two good restaurants: the *Banashree* serves pure-veg food and the *Shubashree* is non-veg and has a bar. ₹**1400**

Royal 50m north of the bus stand ☎ 08357 220114. Good-value newish lodge, built of brightly painted concrete and marble, with simply furnished but clean attached rooms, all with flatscreen TVs, and a veg restaurant. ₹**1000**

EATING

Geetha Darshini 100m south of the bus stand ☎ 90363 56378. This is a small but top-notch South Indian joint whose *idlis*, *vadas* and dosas are out of this world. Daily 6am–9pm.

Golden Caves Just opposite the bus stand ☎ 94487 29812. Good, inexpensive non-veg Indian and Chinese food, served indoors or in the airy courtyard, though service is slow. Try the tandoori chicken (full: ₹450), thali (₹90) or good-value fish. Daily 8am–11.30pm.

Aihole

No fewer than 125 temples, dating from the Chalukyan and the later Rashtrakuta periods (sixth to twelfth centuries), are found in the tiny village of **AIHOLE** (Aivalli), near the banks of the River Malaprabha. Lying in clusters within the village, in surrounding fields and on rocky outcrops, many of the temples are remarkably well preserved. Reflecting both its geographical position and spirit of architectural experimentation, Aihole boasts northern (*nagara*) and southern (Dravida) temples, as well as variants that failed to survive subsequent stylistic developments.

Two of the temples are **rock-cut caves** dating from the sixth century. The Hindu **Ravalaphadi cave**, northeast of the centre, a Shiva shrine with a triple entrance, contains fine sculptures of Mahishasuramardini, a ten-armed Nateshan (the precursor of Nataraja) dancing with Parvati, Ganesh and the Sapta Matrikas ("seven mothers"). A two-storey cave, plain save for decoration at the entrances and a panel image of Buddha in its upper veranda, can be found partway up the hill to the southeast, overlooking the village. At the top of that hill, the Jain **Meguti** temple, which may never have been completed, bears an inscription on an outer wall dating it to 634 AD. You can climb up to the first floor for fine views of Aihole and the surrounding country.

Durga temple

In the Archaeological Survey compound near the centre of the village • Daily 6am–6pm • ₹100 (₹5)

The late seventh- to early eighth-century **Durga temple**, one of the most unusual, elaborate and large in Aihole, stands close to others on open ground. The horseshoe-shaped shrine derives its name not from the goddess Durga but from the Kannada *durgadagudi*, meaning "temple near the fort". A series of pillars – many featuring amorous couples – form an open ambulatory path around the whole building. Other sculptural highlights include the decoration on the entrance to the *mandapa* hallway and niche images on the outer walls.

Archeological Museum

Just outside the entrance to the Durga temple • Daily except Fri 10am–5pm • Free

The small **Archeological Museum** displays a modest collection of early Chalukyan sculpture and sells the booklet *Glorious Aihole*, which includes a site map and accounts of the monuments.

Ladh Khan temple

A short way south of the Durga temple, beyond several other shrines

The **Ladh Khan** temple, perhaps the best known of all at Aihole, was one of the early temple prototypes. Originally a royal assembly and marriage hall dating back to the fifth century, it was named after the Muslim soldier who later made it his home. Inside are a Nandi bull and a small sanctuary containing a *shivalingam* next to the back wall. Both may have been later additions, with the original inner sanctum located at the centre.

ARRIVAL AND DEPARTURE   **AIHOLE**

Six daily **buses** run to Aihole from Badami (1hr 30min) via Pattadakal (45min) from 5.30am to 9pm; the last bus returns around 6pm.

Pattadakal

On a bend in the River Malaprabha 22km northeast of Badami, the village of **PATTADAKAL** served as the ceremonial site of Chalukyan coronations between the seventh and eighth centuries; in fact, it may have been used solely for such ceremonies (*pattada kallu* means "coronation stone" in Kannada). Like Badami and Aihole, the area boasts fine Chalukyan architecture, with particularly large mature examples; as at Aihole, both northern and southern styles can be seen. Pattadakal is connected by regular state buses and hourly private buses to Badami (45min) and Aihole (45min).

Temple compound

Daily 6am–6pm • ₹250 (₹10)

Pattadakal's main group of monuments stand together in a well-maintained **temple compound**, next to the village, and have been designated a UNESCO World Heritage Site. The site is used for a major annual **dance festival** at the end of January or early February.

Earliest among the temples, the **Sangameshwara**, also known as **Shri Vijayeshwara** (a reference to its builder, Vijayaditya Satyashraya; 696–733), shows typical southern features. To the south, both the **Mallikarjuna** and the enormous **Virupaksha**, side by side, are in the southern style, built by two sisters who were successively the queens of Vikramaditya II (733–46). Along with the Kanchipuram temple in Tamil Nadu, the Virupaksha was probably one of the largest and most elaborate in India at the time. Interior pillars are carved with scenes from the Ramayana and Mahabharata, while in the Mallikarjuna the stories are from the life of Krishna.

The largest northern-style temple, the **Papanatha**, further south, was probably built after the Virupaksha in the eighth century. Outside walls feature reliefs from the Ramayana (some of which bear the sculptors' autographs), including Hanuman's monkey army on the south wall.

Vijayapura (Bijapur) and the north

The dry and dusty far northern region of Karnataka is as distinct culturally as it is in landscape. Predominantly Muslim, at least in the larger settlements, it boasts some wonderful Islamic architecture and shrines in the venerable city of **Bijapur**, or **Vijayapura**, bustling **Kalaburagi (Gulbarga)** and rather forlorn **Bidar**.

Vijayapura (Bijapur)

Boasting some of the Deccan's finest Muslim monuments, **Bijapur** – now officially **VIJAYAPURA** – is often billed as "the Agra of the South". The comparison is partly justified: for more than three hundred years, this was the capital of a succession of powerful rulers, whose domed mausoleums, mosques, colossal civic buildings and

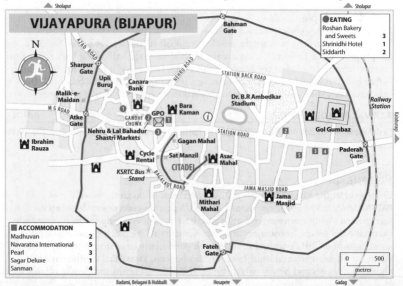

fortifications recall a lost golden age of unrivalled prosperity and artistic refinement. Yet there the similarities between the two cities end. A provincial market town of around 300,000 inhabitants, modern Vijayapura is a world away from the urban frenzy of Agra. With the exception of the mighty **Gol Gumbaz**, which attracts busloads of day-trippers, its historic sites see only a slow trickle of tourists, while the ramshackle town centre is surprisingly laidback, dotted with peaceful green spaces and colonnaded mosque courtyards. In the first week of February the town hosts an annual **music festival**, which attracts several renowned musicians from both the Carnatic (South Indian) and the Hindustani (North Indian) classical music traditions.

Unlike most medieval Muslim strongholds, Bijapur lacked natural rock defences and had to be strengthened by the Adil Shahis with huge **fortified walls**. Extending some 10km around the town, these ramparts, studded with cannon emplacements (*burjs*) and watchtowers, are breached in five points by *darwazas*, or strong gateways, and several smaller postern gates (*didis*). In the middle of the town, a further hoop of crenellated battlements encircled Bijapur's **citadel**, site of the sultans' apartments and durbar hall, of which only fragments remain. The Adil Shahis' **tombs** are scattered around the outskirts, while most of the important **mosques** lie southeast of the citadel.

Brief history

Still generally known as Bijapur, a name that stuck until the city's rechristening in 2014, Vijayapura (the Chalukyas' "City of Victory") was established around the tenth century. Taken by the Vijayanagar empire, it passed into Muslim hands for the first time in the thirteenth century with the arrival of the sultans of Delhi. The Bahmanis administered the area for a time, but it was only after the local rulers, the **Adil Shahis**, won independence from Bidar by expelling the Bahmani garrison and declaring this their capital that Bijapur's rise to prominence began.

Burying their differences for a brief period in the late sixteenth century, the five Muslim dynasties that issued from the breakdown of Bahmani rule – based at Golconda, Ahmadnagar, Bidar and Gulbarga – formed a military alliance to defeat Vijayanagar. The spoils of this campaign, which saw the total destruction of Vijayanagar (Hampi), funded a two-hundred-year building boom in Bijapur during which the city's most impressive monuments were built. However, old enmities between rival Muslim sultanates on the Deccan soon resurfaced, and the Adil Shahis' royal coffers were gradually squandered on fruitless and protracted wars. By the time the British arrived on the scene in the eighteenth century, the Adil Shahis were a spent force, locked into a decline from which they and their capital never recovered.

Gol Gumbaz

Daily 6am–6pm • ₹100 (₹5)

The vast **Gol Gumbaz** mausoleum, Vijayapura's most famous building, soars above the town's east walls, visible for kilometres in every direction. Inspired by a seven-storey structure in Arabia and built for muezzins to offer *azaan* (call for prayer) from its summit, the original name Bol Gumbaz was corrupted over the years to Gol Gumbaz.

The cubic tomb, enclosing a 170-square-metre hall, is crowned with a single hemispherical **dome**, only 5m smaller than St Peter's in Rome, once the largest in the world. Spiral staircases wind up the four seven-storey octagonal towers that buttress the building to the famous **Whispering Gallery**, a 3m-wide passage encircling the interior base of the dome from where, looking carefully down, you can get a real feel of the sheer size of the building. Arrive here just after opening time to avoid the bus tours and to experience the extraordinary acoustics. The **view** from the mausoleum's ramparts, which overlook the town and its monuments to the dark-soiled Deccan countryside beyond, is superb.

Set on a plinth in the centre of the hall below are the gravestones of the ruler who built the Gol Gumbaz, **Mohammed Adil Shah**, along with those of his wife, daughter, grandson and favourite courtesan, Rambha. At one corner of the grounds stands the simple gleaming white shrine to a Sufi saint of the Adil Shahi period, **Hashim Pir**, which attracts *qawwals* (singers of devotional *qawwali* music) each February to the annual three-day *urs*.

Jama Masjid

A little under 1km southwest of the Gol Gumbaz • Modest clothing is advised – no shorts or skirts

The **Jama Masjid** was commissioned by Ali Adil Shah, the ruler credited with constructing the city walls and complex water supply system, as a monument to his victory over the Vijayanagar empire at the battle of Talikota in 1565. Still an active place of worship, it is widely regarded as one of the finest mosques in India.

Simplicity and restraint are the essence of the colonnaded prayer hall below, divided by gently curving arches and rows of thick plaster-covered pillars. Aside from the odd geometric design and trace of yellow, blue and green tile-work, the only ornamentation is found in the mihrab, or west- (Mecca-) facing prayer niche, which is smothered in gold leaf and elaborate calligraphy. The marble floor of the hall features a grid of 2500 rectangles, known as *musallahs* (after the *musallah* prayer mats brought to mosques by worshippers). These were added by the Mughal emperor Aurangzeb, allegedly as recompense for making off with the velvet carpets, long golden chain and other valuables that originally filled the prayer hall.

Mithari Mahal

800m west of the Jama Masjid

Although of modest size, the delicately carved three-storey gatehouse known as the **Mithari Mahal** (or Mehtar Mahal) is one of Vijayapura's most beautiful buildings, with ornate projecting windows and minarets crowning its corners. Once again, it was erected by Ali Adil Shah, along with the mosque behind, using gifts presented to him during a state visit to Vijayanagar.

Asar Mahal

Just beyond the eastern battlement of the citadel

The dilapidated **Asar Mahal**, a large open hall fronted by a stagnant step-well, was built in 1646 by Mohammed Adil Shah as a seat of justice. It was later chosen to house hair strands from the Prophet's beard, thereby earning the title **Asar-i-Sharif**, or "place of illustrious relics". Women are not permitted inside to view the upper storey, where fifteen niches are decorated with Persian-style pot-and-foliage murals.

The citadel

Vijayapura's **citadel** stands in the middle of town, hemmed in on all but its north side by battlements. Most of the buildings inside have collapsed, or have been converted into government offices, but enough remain to give a sense of how imposing this royal enclave must once have been.

The best-preserved monuments lie along, or near, the citadel's main north–south artery, Anand Mahal Road, reached by skirting the southeast wall from the Asar Mahal. The latter route brings you first to the **Gagan Mahal**. Originally Ali Adil Shah's "Heavenly Palace", this now-ruined hulk later served as a durbar hall for the sultans, who would sit in state on the platform at the open-fronted north side, watched by crowds gathered in the grounds opposite. West off Anand Mahal Road, the five-storey **Sat Manzil** was the pleasure palace of the courtesan Rambha. In front stands an ornately carved water pavilion, the **Jal Mandir**, now left high and dry in an empty tank.

Malik-e-Maidan and Upli Buruj

Guarding the principal western entrance to the city is the Burj-i-Sherza ("Lion Gate"), one of several bastions that punctuate Vijayapura's battlements. This one sports a colossal cannon, known as the **Malik-e-Maidan**, literally "Lord of the Plains". It was brought here as war booty in the sixteenth century, and needed four hundred bullocks, ten elephants and an entire battalion to haul it up the steps to the emplacement. Inscriptions record that the cannon, whose muzzle features a relief of a monster swallowing an elephant, was cast in Ahmadnagar in 1551.

A few more discarded cannons lie atop the watchtower, a short walk northeast of the Malik-e-Maidan. Steps wind around the outside of the oval-shaped **Upli Buruj**, or "Upper Bastion", to a gun emplacement that affords unimpeded views over the city and plains.

Ibrahim Rauza

Under 1km west of the ramparts • Daily 6am–6pm • ₹100 (₹5)

Set in its own walled compound, the **Ibrahim Rauza** represents the apogee of Bijapuri architecture. Whereas the Gol Gumbaz impresses primarily by its scale, the appeal of this tomb complex lies in its grace and simplicity. It's also a haven of peace, with cool, colonnaded verandas and flocks of iridescent parakeets careening between the mildewed domes, minarets and gleaming golden finials.

Opinions differ over whether the tomb was commissioned by Ibrahim Adil Shah (1580–1626), or his favourite wife, Taj Sultana, but the former was the first to be interred here, in a gloomy chamber whose only light enters via a series of exquisite pierced-stone windows. Made up of elaborate Koranic inscriptions, these are the finest examples of their kind in India. More amazing stonework decorates the exterior of the mausoleum, and the equally beautiful **mosque** opposite, the cornice of whose facade features a stone chain carved from a single block. The two buildings, bristling with minarets and cupolas, face each other from opposite sides of a rectangular raised plinth, divided by a small reservoir and fountains. Viewed from on top of the walls that enclose the complex, you can see why its architect, Malik Sandal, added a self-congratulatory inscription in his native Persian over the tomb's south doorway, describing his masterpiece as "A beauty of which Paradise stood amazed".

4

ARRIVAL AND INFORMATION

VIJAYAPURA (BIJAPUR)

By train The railway station is just east of the Gol Gumbaz, outside the old city walls, and 3km northeast of the bus stand. Departing at 5pm, the daily *Golgumbaz Express* #16536 links Vijayapura with Badami, Gadag and Hubballi, while the *Basava Express* #17308 (dep. 4.35pm) runs daily via Kalaburagi (5hr 20min) to Bengaluru (arr. 10.45am). Destinations Badami (4–6 daily; 2hr 20min–2hr 55min); Gadag (2–5 daily; 4hr 10min–4hr 50min); Hubballi (4–7 daily, 5hr 45min–6hr 30min).

By bus State and interstate buses from as far afield as Mumbai and Aurangabad pull into the KSRTC Bus Stand on the southwest edge of the town centre. KSRTC run deluxe buses to Bengaluru, Hubballi, Mumbai and Hyderabad.

Heading to Badami, it is often quicker to take the first bus to Bagalkot and change there. VRL runs private services to Bengaluru (3 buses from 7pm) and operates other overnight buses to Mangaluru (via Udupi) and Mumbai. These can be booked through Vijayanand Travels, terrace floor, Shastri Market, Gandhi Chowk (☏ 08352 251000, ⍈ vrlbus .in) or its other branch just south of the bus stand. Destinations Aurangabad (12hr); Badami (4hr); Bagalkot (2hr); Bengaluru (13hr); Hubballi (6hr); Hyderabad (10hr); Kalaburagi (4hr); Mangaluru (15hr); Mumbai (12hr). **Tourist information** The tourist office (Mon–Sat 10am– 5.30pm; ☏ 08352 250359) behind the *Hotel Adil Shahi* annexe on Station Rd, can help with arranging itineraries and guides.

GETTING AROUND

By bus Frequent local buses, largely uncrowded, connect the bus stand with the Gol Gumbaz and the train station. **By auto-rickshaw** Auto-rickshaws don't have meters and charge a minimum of ₹25; although most of Vijayapura is covered by a fare of ₹60, they are a much more expensive way of getting around the monuments, when they charge at least ₹300 for a 4hr tour.

By tonga or tempo Tongas are available from near the bus stand, while *tempos* ply the main road between the bus stand, the Gol Gumbaz and the train station. **By bike** Vijayapura is flat, relatively uncongested, and generally easy to negotiate by bicycle; rickety Heros are available for rent from stalls outside the bus stand for ₹10/hr.

ACCOMMODATION

Madhuvan Station Rd ☏ 08352 255571. With a bright yellow exterior and a variety of rooms, from overpriced ordinary doubles to more comfortable a/c options, this is a safe bet. The veg restaurant serves good-value thalis at lunchtime. Currency exchange available for guests. ₹1040

Navaratna International Just off Station Rd ☏ 08352 222771. The huge, shiny-tiled rooms at this quiet hotel are great value for this price. Good service, veg and non-veg restaurants and a popular palm-shaded dining (and drinking) area. ₹800

★ **Pearl** Station Rd ☏ 08352 256002. Bright modern hotel with clean, sizeable rooms. The front ones have balconies and

those at the top afford views of the Gol Gumbaz. The smart attached annexe at the back has quality a/c rooms. ₹1200

Sagar Deluxe Near Bara Kaman ☏ 08352 259234. A budget option close to the action yet tucked away on a quiet side street. Simple but adequate rooms, including cheap singles and great-value a/c. ₹600

Sanman Station Rd ☏ 08352 251866. Best value among the budget places, if a tad grubby, and right opposite the Gol Gumbaz. The more expensive rooms have TV and the rooftop restaurant/bar offers excellent evening views of the mausoleum. ₹500

EATING

Roshan Bakery and Sweets MG Rd. Among other goodies, this popular place whips up the perfect budget takeaway brunch: flaky croissants filled with boiled egg or veg. Most items cost less than ₹20. Daily 7am–9pm.

Shrinidhi Hotel Ashram Rd ☏ 98441 45240. Probably the best choice for good South Indian veg food, from *vada*,

dosa and snacks to full-on thalis for just ₹100. Daily 7am–8pm.

★ **Siddarth** Gandhi Chowk ☏ 93416 11635. Above the main market, this sprawling rooftop bar-restaurant offers tasty non-veg Indian cuisine such as tandoori chicken for ₹300, plus a good selection of booze. Daily 10am–10pm.

4

Kalaburagi (Gulbarga)

Gulbarga, officially renamed **KALABURAGI**, 165km northeast of Vijayapura, was the founding capital of the Bahmani dynasty and the region's principal city before the court moved to Bidar in 1424. Later captured by the Adil Shahis and Mughals, it has remained a staunchly Muslim town, and bulbous onion domes and mosque minarets still soar prominently above its ramshackle concrete-box skyline. The town is also famous as the birthplace of the Sufi saint, Hazrat Gesu Daraz (1320–1422), whose tomb, situated next to one of India's foremost Islamic theological colleges, is a major shrine.

In spite of Kalaburagi's religious and historical significance, its **monuments** pale in comparison with those at Vijayapura, or even Bidar. Unless you're particularly interested in medieval Muslim architecture, few are worth breaking a journey to see.

The Dargah

The one monument that warrants a look is the **Dargah**, a tomb complex on the edge of town around 2km northeast of the train station. Approached via a broad bazaar, this marble-lined enclosure centres on the tomb of **Hazrat Gesu Daraz Banda Nawaz**, or "the long-haired one who brings comfort to others". The saint was spiritual mentor to the Bahmani rulers, and it was they who erected his beautiful double-storeyed mausoleum, now visited by thousands of Muslim pilgrims each year. Women are not allowed inside, and men must wear long trousers. The same applies to the neighbouring tomb, whose interior has retained its exquisite Persian paintings. The Dargah's other important building, open to both sexes, is the **madrasa**, founded by Banda Nawaz and enlarged during the two centuries after his death.

ARRIVAL AND DEPARTURE   KALABURAGI (GULBARGA)

By train Kalaburagi's mainline railway station lies 1.5km east of the bus stand, along Mill Rd. Station Rd, the town's other main artery, runs due north of here past the lake to the busy Chowk crossroads, at the heart of the bazaar. Destinations Bengaluru (5–9 daily; 10hr 5min–14hr 40min); Chennai (3–4 daily, 13hr 35min–16hr 45min);

Hyderabad (6–12 daily; 3hr 40min–5hr 35min); Mumbai (9–13 daily; 9hr 40min–12hr); Pune (13–17 daily; 5hr 15min–8hr).

By bus Daily KSRTC buses from Vijayapura, Bidar and beyond pull in to the State Bus Stand on the southwest edge of town. Frequent local buses such as #206 run from the bus stand via the crossroads near the station to the Dargah.

Destinations Hourly to Vijayapura (4hr) and Bidar (3hr); less frequently further afield.

ACCOMMODATION

Central Park Station Rd, 1km north of the railway station ☎ 08472 273231. Clean, modern business hotel whose simple but smart rooms have TV; some have a/c (₹1200). Good veg restaurant. ₹**990**

Golden Regency Opposite GESCOM, Station Rd, 1km north of the railway station ☎ 08472 266688, ⊛ golden

regency.in. Centrally located modern hotel with large, neat rooms and complimentary breakfast. Singles for ₹800. ₹**1100**

Heritage Inn SB Temple Rd ☎ 08472 224093. Modern hotel next to Gulbarga's deserted fort with deluxe rooms and suites, separate veg and non-veg restaurants, a bar and complimentary breakfast and pick-up/drop. ₹**1675**

EATING

Kamat The venerable chain restaurant has several branches in Kalaburagi including a pleasant one at Station Chowk, specializing in veg "meals"; try *jolada roti*, an unleavened local bread made from sorghum cooked either hard and crisp or soft like a chapatti. Daily 7am–10pm.

Rajdhani Mill Rd ☎ 97417 37143. Most of the mains such as chicken and mutton cost well under ₹200 at this simple basement restaurant on the way towards the station from the bus stand. Daily 11am–11pm.

Bidar

Lost in the far northeast of Karnataka, **BIDAR**, 284km northeast of Vijayapura, is a provincial backwater, known for its fighter-pilot training base, gently decaying monuments and the most important Sikh shrine in Karnataka. The town, half of whose 210,000-strong population is Muslim, has a gritty charm, with narrow red-dirt streets ending at arched gates and open vistas across the plains. Littered with tile-fronted tombs, rambling fortifications and old mosques, it merits a visit if you're travelling between Hyderabad (150km east) and Vijayapura, although you should expect little in the way of Western comforts, and lots of curious approaches from locals.

In 1424, following the break-up of the Bahmani dynasty into five rival factions, **Ahmad Shah I** shifted his court from Gulbarga to a less constricted site at Bidar. Revamping the town with a new fort, splendid palaces, mosques and ornamental gardens, the Bahmanis ruled from here until 1487, when the Barid Shahis took control. They were succeeded by the Adil Shahis from Vijayapura, and later the Mughals under Aurangzeb, who annexed the region in 1656, before the nizam of Hyderabad acquired the territory in the early eighteenth century.

The heart of Bidar is its medieval **old town**, encircled by crenellated ramparts and eight imposing gateways (*darwazas*). This predominantly Muslim quarter holds many Bahmani-era mosques, havelis and *khanqahs* – "monasteries" set up by the local rulers for Muslim cleric-mystics and their disciples.

Mahmud Gawan's madrasa

The highlight of the old town is the impressive ruins of **Mahmud Gawan's madrasa**, whose single minaret soars high above the city centre. The distinctively Persian-style building, originally surmounted by large bulbous domes, once housed a world-famous library. However, this burnt down after being struck by lightning in 1696, and several of the walls and domes were blown away when gunpowder stored here by Aurangzeb's occupying army caught fire and exploded. Today, the madrasa is little more than a shell, although its elegant arched facade has retained large patches of the vibrant Persian glazed tile-work that once covered most of the exterior surfaces.

The Fort

At the far north end of the street running past the madrasa

A rambling, crumbling Monument Valley to the fifteenth-century Bahmani Empire, the Bidar **Fort** retains a serene, austere beauty. Though locals have incorporated the vast rolling

BIDRI

Bidar is renowned as the home of a unique damascene metalwork technique known as **bidri**, developed by the Persian silversmiths who came to the area with the Bahmani court in the fifteenth century. These highly skilled artisans engraved and inlaid their traditional Iranian designs onto a metal alloy composed of lead, copper, zinc and tin, which they blackened and polished. The resulting effect – swirling silver floral motifs framed by geometric patterns and set against black backgrounds – has since become the hallmark of Muslim metalwork in India.

Bidri objets d'art are displayed in museums and galleries all over the country. But if you want to see pukka *bidri*-wallahs at work, take a walk down Bidar's **Siddiq Talim Road** (or Chaubara Road), which cuts across the south side of the old town, where skull-capped artisans tap and burnish vases, goblets, plates, spice boxes, betel-nut tins and ornamental hookah pipes, as well as less traditional objects – coasters, ashtrays and bangles – that crop up (at vastly inflated prices) in silver emporiums as far away as Delhi and Kolkata.

spaces into their lives – young boys play cricket in the grassy turf, terraces are planted with rice, and scooters and small trucks ply its roads – its appeal remains undiminished.

The fort was founded by the Hindu Chalukyas and strengthened by the Bahmanis in the early fifteenth century. Despite repeated sieges, it remains largely intact, encircled by 10km of ramparts that drop away in the north and west to 300m cliffs. The main southern entrance is protected by equally imposing man-made defences: gigantic fortified gates and a triple moat formerly crossed by a series of drawbridges. You can complete the round of **the ramparts** in ninety minutes, taking time out to enjoy the views over the red cliffs and across the plains.

Rangeen Mahal

The first building of note inside the fort is the exquisite **Rangeen Mahal**, on the left after the third and final entrance gateway. Mahmud Shah built this "Coloured Palace" after an unsuccessful uprising of Abyssinian slaves in 1487 forced him to relocate to a safer site inside the citadel. The palace's relatively modest proportions reflect the Bahmanis' declining fortunes, but its interior comprises some of the finest surviving Islamic art in the Deccan, with superb woodcarving above the door arches and Persian-style mother-of-pearl inlay on polished black granite surfaces. If the doors to the palace are locked, ask for the keys at the nearby **ASI Museum** (daily 8am–1pm & 2–5pm; free).

Solah Khamb Masjid
Opposite the ASI Museum

An expanse of gravel is all that remains of the royal gardens, overlooked by the austere **Solah Khamb** mosque (1327), Bidar's oldest Muslim monument, whose most outstanding feature is the intricate pierced-stone calligraphy around its central dome. From here, continue west through the ruins of the former royal enclosure – a rambling complex of half-collapsed palaces, baths, zenanas and assembly halls – to the fort's west walls.

Ashtur: the Bahmani tombs

As you look from the fort's east walls, a cluster of eight bulbous white domes floats alluringly above the trees in the distance. Nearly 5km east of Bidar (leave the old town via Dulhan Darwaza gate) and dating from the fifteenth century, the mausoleums at **Ashtur** are the final resting-places of the Bahmani sultans and their families, including the son of the ruler who first decamped from Gulbarga, Ala-ud-din Shah I. His tomb is by far the most impressive, with patches of coloured glazed tiles on its arched facade, and a large dome whose interior surfaces bear sumptuous Persian paintings. Reflecting sunlight onto the ceiling with a small pocket mirror, the chowkidar picks out the highlights, among them a diamond, barely visible among the bat droppings.

The tomb of Ala-ud-din's father, the ninth and most illustrious Bahmani sultan, Ahmad Shah I, stands beside that of his son, decorated with Persian inscriptions. Beyond this are two more minor mausoleums, followed by the partially collapsed tomb of Humayun the Cruel (ruled 1458–61), cracked open by a bolt of lightning. Continuing along the line, you can chart the gradual decline of the Bahmanis as the mausoleums diminish in size, ending with a sad handful erected in the early sixteenth century, when the sultans were no more than puppet rulers of the Barid Shahis.

Gurudwara Nanak Jhira Sahib

1km north of bus stand • Headscarves are mandatory, and provided just outside the shrine

Guru Nanak, the founder of Sikhism, came to Bidar during his second Udasi (sacred journey) in 1512, when the region was in the grips of a famine. Since Bidar had brackish water, forcing its denizens to travel far away for potable water, the Guru uttered a mantra ("Sat kartar"), shifted a stone with his wooden sandal, and a spring (*jhira*) miraculously emerged from a laterite trap in the hill, which now fills the water tank known as **Amrit Kund** (Pool of Nectar). Built in 1948 beside the spring and recently expanded, the **Gurudwara Nanak Jhira Sahib** is the largest in Karnataka and open to people of all faiths. Drop by at the **Sikh Museum**, to the left of the *gurudwara* entrance, where pictures and paintings depict key events in Sikh history, and don't leave without having a meal at the *langar* (free community kitchen), run by volunteers for pilgrims round the clock.

ARRIVAL AND DEPARTURE   BIDAR

By train Bidar lies on a branch line of the main Mumbai–Secunderabad–Chennai rail route and can only be reached by slow passenger train.

By bus Most visitors arrive by bus at the KSRTC Bus Stand on the far northwestern edge of town, around 2km from the centre. The best connections are with Kalaburagi (every 15min; 3hr) and Hyderabad (every 30min; 4hr).

ACCOMMODATION AND EATING

Extremely grubby lodges predominate in Bidar but the good news is that none of the handful of better **hotels** listed below cost very much. These are generally the best **places to eat** too, along with the odd basic veg restaurant.

Ashoka Near Deepak Theatre, Basaveshwara Circle, 2km southeast of bus stand ☎ 08482 227621. Standard business hotel with reasonably comfortable, good-value deluxe rooms, some of them a/c. The restaurant serves both veg and non-veg. No wi-fi. ₹600

Mayura Opposite the bus stand ☎ 08482 228142. Ugly concrete block but with large rooms; deluxe a/c rooms are ₹1000. The restaurant food is tasty but it doubles as a slightly unsavoury bar. No wi-fi. ₹600

Rohit Inside gurudwara arch, near town police station ☎ 08482 223425. Great Punjabi fare close to Gurudwara Nanak Jhira Sahib, including excellent *dal makhani* (₹100) and *paneer* dishes. Daily 12.30–10pm.

Sapna International Udgir Rd, 300m north of the bus stand ☎ 08482 222081, ⊚ hotelsapnacontinental.com. Bidar's nicest lodgings, with big, clean rooms and a good non-veg restaurant. ₹1200

Udupi Krishna On Dr Ambedkar Circle ☎ 92065 77811. A very humble place but undoubtedly one of the best independent restaurants in town, serving up unlimited pure-veg thalis for lunch and South Indian breakfasts. Daily 6.30am–9.30pm.

Andhra Pradesh and Telangana

277 Hyderabad/Secunderabad

286 Telangana

288 Eastern and northern Andhra Pradesh

292 Southern Andhra Pradesh

CHARMINAR, HYDERABAD

5

Andhra Pradesh and Telangana

Although Andhra Pradesh and the newly created state of Telangana together occupy a great swathe of eastern India, stretching more than 1200km along the coast from Odisha to Tamil Nadu and reaching far inland from the fertile deltas of the Godavari and Krishna rivers to the semi-arid Deccan Plateau, most foreign travellers simply pass through en route to their better-known neighbours. This is understandable, as places of interest are few and far between, but the sights the two states do offer are absorbing enough to warrant at least a brief stop-off.

A major high-tech hub and, for the time being, the joint capital of both states, **Hyderabad** is an atmospheric, predominantly Muslim city with lively bazaars, the eclectic Salar Jung Museum, impressive Chowmahalla Palace and the mighty **Golconda Fort**. **Warangal**, 150km northeast, has Muslim and Hindu remains from the twelfth and thirteenth centuries, while the region's Buddhist legacy is preserved in museums at sites such as **Nagarjunakonda** and **Amaravati**. In the east, the city of **Vijayawada** has little to recommend it, though it is a convenient access point for Amaravati. Similarly, in the northeast, the fast-growing city of **Visakhapatnam** is little more than a handy place to break up a long trip, but between the two the delightful region around the **Godavari Delta** is well worth a detour. By contrast, the temple town of **Tirupati** in the far southeast is a fascinating, impossibly crowded pilgrimage site. In the southwest, **Puttaparthy** attracts a more international pilgrim crowd, who still flock to the ashram of the late spiritual leader Sai Baba.

Although modern industries have grown up around the capital, and shipbuilding, iron and steel are important on the coast, most people in Andhra Pradesh and Telangana remain poor. Away from the Godavari and Krishna deltas, where the soil is rich enough to grow rice and sugar cane, the land is in places impossible to cultivate, which has contributed to the desperate plight of many farmers (see p.276).

Brief history

The earliest accounts of the region, from the third century BC, refer to a people known as the Andhras. The **Satavahana dynasty** (second century BC to second century AD), also known as the Andhras, came to control much of central and southern India from their second capital at Amaravati on the Krishna. They enjoyed extensive international trade and were great patrons of Buddhism. Subsequently, the Pallavas, the Chalukyas and the Cholas all held sway. By the thirteenth century, the Kakatiyas of Warangal were under constant threat from Muslim incursions; while later on, after the fall of their city at Hampi, the Hindu Vijayanagars transferred operations to Chandragiri near Tirupati.

The next significant development was in the mid-sixteenth century, with the rise of the Muslim **Qutb Shahi dynasty**. In 1687, the son of the Mughal emperor Aurangzeb seized Golconda. Five years after Aurangzeb died in 1707, Hyderabad's viceroy declared independence and established the Asaf Jahi dynasty of **nizams**. In return for allying

BEST TIME TO VISIT

As with the rest of the South, the ideal time to come to Andhra Pradesh and Telangana is during the winter months from December to mid-March. April to June is blazing hot, particularly inland towards the Deccan Plateau. The southern part of Andhra Pradesh misses most of the main summer monsoon but is hit by the northeast monsoon between September and November, when cyclones can create havoc, especially in the coast areas.

PILGRIMS AT TIRUMALA HILL

Highlights

❶ Hyderabad A predominantly Islamic city, as well as a focal point of twenty-first-century high-tech India, with a compelling combination of monuments, museums and bazaars. **See p.277**

❷ Golconda Fort Set in a lush landscape just west of Hyderabad, the Qutb Shahi dynasty's capital boasts a dramatic and well-preserved fort with amazing acoustics. **See p.281**

❸ Warangal This sleepy town features two important Hindu monuments: a rambling medieval fort and an exquisitely carved thousand-pillared Shiva temple. **See p.286**

❹ Nagarjunakonda Now surrounded by a vast artificial lake, this peaceful place boasts various Buddhist monuments, including a huge statue, and a fine museum. **See p.287**

❺ The Godavari Delta With a mixture of verdant hills, mangrove swamps and the lush Konaseema area, this is a fine region to explore. **See p.289**

❻ Tirumala Hill The world's most visited pilgrimage centre, crowned by the crowded, vibrant and colourful Venkateshvara Vishnu temple. **See p.292**

HIGHLIGHTS ARE MARKED ON THE MAP ON P.276

5

with the British against Tipu Sultan of Mysore, the nizam dynasty was allowed to retain a certain degree of autonomy even after the British had come to dominate India.

During the Independence struggle, harmony between Hindus and Muslims in Andhra Pradesh disintegrated. **Partition** brought matters to a climax, as the nizam wanted to join other Muslims in the soon-to-be-created state of **Pakistan**. In 1949 the capital erupted in riots, the army was brought in and Hyderabad state was admitted to the Indian Union. Andhra Pradesh state was created in 1956 from Telugu-speaking regions (although Urdu is widely spoken in Hyderabad) that had previously formed part of the Madras Presidency on the east coast and the princely state of Hyderabad to the west. Today almost ninety percent of the population is Hindu, with Muslims largely concentrated in the capital.

In 1999, the pro-business Telugu Desam party eventually wrested the power long held by Congress, and over the following five years there was huge development around Hyderabad, most famously, **HITEC City**. However, rural areas – where drought and economic crisis led to thousands of farmer suicides – were neglected. In 2004 Congress regained control of the state government, although they were also criticized for not doing enough to help farmers, and suicides have continued with alarming frequency, though numbers have fallen in recent years.

In December 2009, following a high-profile hunger strike, the Indian government surprisingly bowed to pressure from the Telangana Rashtra Samithi (TRS) party and announced plans to carve a new state, **Telangana**, out of northwestern Andhra Pradesh.

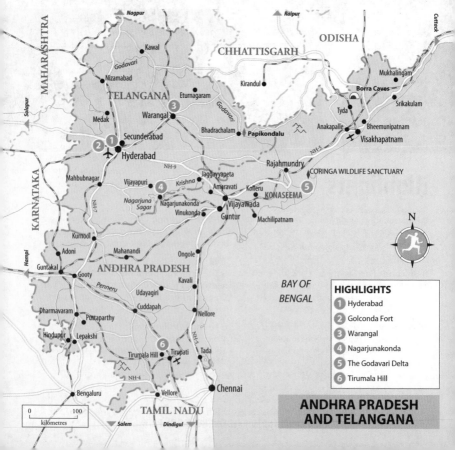

HIGHLIGHTS
1 Hyderabad
2 Golconda Fort
3 Warangal
4 Nagarjunakonda
5 The Godavari Delta
6 Tirumala Hill

ANDHRA PRADESH AND TELANGANA

FESTIVALS IN ANDHRA PRADESH AND TELANGANA   **5**

Sankranti (Jan). Celebrated all over both states with lively music and dance, especially in the Konaseema region (see p.290).

Antarvedi Chariot Festival (Jan/Feb). Impressive temple chariot festival celebrating the marriage of Lord Narasimha and the goddess Lakshmi in the East Godavari district (see p.290).

Muharram (Oct/Nov). The sacred month of the Muslim New Year is celebrated with verve by the large Shia population in Hyderabad (see p.279).

Vaikunta Ekadashi (Dec/Jan). One of the most important festivals at Tirumala (see p.292), when Vishnu's victory over the demon Muran is commemorated.

Despite widespread protests, strikes and political resignations a commission was set up to examine the practicalities of the issue, and in July 2013 a resolution was unanimously passed in Congress agreeing to the bifurcation. Almost a year later, on June 2, 2014, Telangana officially ceded from Andhra Pradesh to become India's twenty-ninth state, with Hyderabad serving – in a rather complicated arrangement – as capital of both states until the new Andhran capital at Amaravati is complete.

Hyderabad/Secunderabad

A melting pot of Muslim and Hindu cultures, the joint capital of Andhra Pradesh and Telangana comprises the twin cities of **HYDERABAD** and **SECUNDERABAD**, with a combined population of around eight million. Secunderabad, of little interest, is the modern administrative city founded by the British, whereas Hyderabad, the old city, has teeming **bazaars**, **Muslim monuments**, the absorbing **Salar Jung Museum** and magnificent **Chowmahalla Palace**. Hyderabad declined after Independence, with tensions often close to the surface due to lack of funding. Nowadays, although the overcrowded old city still suffers from substandard amenities, the conurbation as a whole is booming. In recent years Hyderabad has overtaken Bengaluru to become India's foremost computer and **IT centre**.

The Hyderabad metropolitan area has three distinct sectors: **Hyderabad**, divided between the old city and newer areas towards HITEC City; **Secunderabad**, the modern city; and **Golconda**, the old fort. The two cities are basically one big sprawl, separated by an artificial lake, **Hussain Sagar**. The most interesting area, the **old city** south of the River Musi, holds the bazaars and **Charminar**, the city's principal landmark, as well as the Salar Jung Museum and Chowmahalla Palace. North of the river, the traditional shopping areas are found around **Abids Circle** and **Sultan Bazaar**. Four kilometres west of Hyderabad railway station lies the posh **Banjara Hills** district, full of gleaming malls and fancy restaurants. Beyond here is the exclusive residential area of **Jubilee Hills**, while a further 6km brings you to **HITEC City**.

Brief history

Hyderabad was founded in 1591 by **Mohammed Quli Shah** (1562–1612), 8km east of Golconda, the fortress capital of the Golconda empire. Unusually, the new city was laid out on a grid system, with huge arches and stone buildings that included Hyderabad's most famous monument, **Charminar**. At first it was a city without walls; these were only added in 1740 as defence against the Marathas. Legend has it that a secret tunnel linked the city with the spectacular **Golconda Fort**, 11km away.

For the three hundred years of Muslim reign, there was harmony between the predominantly Hindu population and the minority Muslims. Hyderabad was the most important focus of Muslim power in South India at this time; the princes' fabulous wealth derived primarily from the fine gems, particularly diamonds, mined in the Kistna Valley at Golconda. The famous **Koh-i-Noor** diamond was found here – the only time it was ever captured was by Mughal emperor Aurangzeb, when his son seized the Golconda Fort in 1687. It ended up, cut, in the British royal crown.

5

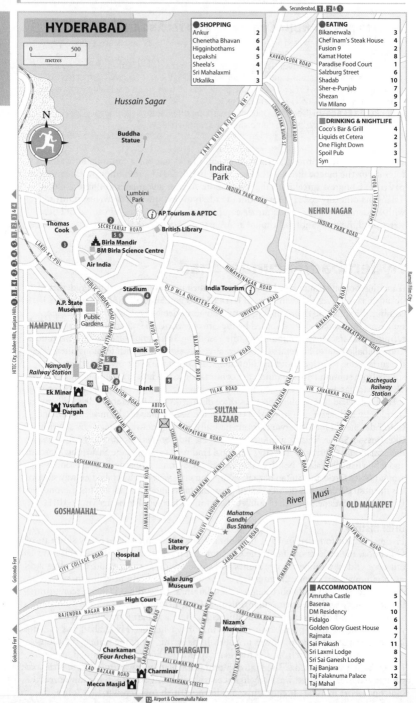

HYDERABAD

Secunderabad, **1**, **2** & **1**

0 500 metres

● SHOPPING
Ankur	2
Chenetha Bhavan	6
Higginbothams	4
Lepakshi	5
Sheela's	4
Sri Mahalaxmi	1
Utkalika	3

● EATING
Bikanerwala	3
Chef Inam's Steak House	4
Fusion 9	2
Kamat Hotel	8
Paradise Food Court	1
Salzburg Street	6
Shadab	10
Sher-e-Punjab	7
Shezan	9
Via Milano	5

■ DRINKING & NIGHTLIFE
Coco's Bar & Grill	4
Liquids et Cetera	2
One Flight Down	5
Spoil Pub	3
Syn	1

■ ACCOMMODATION
Amrutha Castle	5
Baseraa	1
DM Residency	10
Fidalgo	6
Golden Glory Guest House	4
Rajmata	7
Sai Prakash	11
Sri Laxmi Lodge	8
Sri Sai Ganesh Lodge	2
Taj Banjara	3
Taj Falaknuma Palace	12
Taj Mahal	9

Hussain Sagar

Buddha Statue

Indira Park

Lumbini Park

AP Tourism & APTDC

NEHRU NAGAR

Thomas Cook

SECRETARIAT ROAD

British Library

Birla Mandir
BM Birla Science Centre

Air India

INDIRA PARK ROAD

HIMAYATNAGAR ROAD

Stadium

India Tourism

A.P. State Museum

Public Gardens

NAMPALLY

OLD MLA QUARTERS ROAD

UNIVERSITY ROAD

Bank

RAJA REDDY ROAD

KING KOTHI ROAD

Nampally Railway Station

Bank

Ek Minar

STATION ROAD

TILAK ROAD

VIR SAVARKAR ROAD

Kacheguda Railway Station

Yusufian Dargah

MUKARRAMJAHI ROAD

ABIDS CIRCLE

MAHIPATRAM ROAD

SULTAN BAZAAR

BHAGYA REDDI ROAD

GOSHAMAHAL ROAD

JAMBAGH ROAD

GOSHAMAHAL

River Musi

OLD MALAKPET

Mahatma Gandhi Bus Stand

State Library

Hospital

CITY COLLEGE ROAD

Salar Jung Museum

High Court

RAJENDRA NAGAR ROAD

CHATTA BAZAR RD

Nizam's Museum

PATTHARGATTI

Charkaman (Four Arches)

LAD BAZAAR ROAD

Charminar

Mecca Masjid

RATHKHANA STREET

12, Airport & Chowmahalla Palace

5

Since the creation of **Telangana** in 2014, Hyderabad has been leading a double life as joint capital of the new state as well as Andhra Pradesh. Officially it belongs to Telangana, as evidenced by the fact that government offices bear the new state's name, but it will continue to act as the administrative centre of Andhra Pradesh until the latter's new capital is created at Amaravati (see p.289). This transition is supposed to be complete inside ten years but that may be optimistic.

The old city

By far the most atmospheric part of Hyderabad is the **old city**, immediately south of the River Musi. This is easily the most Islamic enclave in South India, where the majority of women wear full black burqa and many men sport fine beards. This is where you will find the city's liveliest and most interesting bazaars, as well as many of its most important sights, from the eclectic **Salar Jung Museum**, through the majestic minarets of **Charminar** to the extensive complex of **Chowmahalla Palace**.

Salar Jung Museum

Daily except Fri 10am–5pm • ₹500 (₹20), camera ₹50 • ⓦ salarjungmuseum.in

The unmissable **Salar Jung Museum**, on the south bank of the River Musi opposite the ornate bulbous domes of the Osmania General Hospital, houses part of the huge collection of Salar Jung, one of the nizam's prime ministers, and his ancestors. A well-travelled man of wealth, he bought whatever took his fancy from both East and West, from the sublime to, in some cases, the ridiculous. His extraordinary hoard includes Indian jade, miniatures, furniture, lacquerwork, Mughal opaque glassware, fabrics, bronzes, Buddhist and Hindu sculpture, manuscripts and weapons. At the time of writing, it was planned to reorganize the somewhat haphazard collection into geographical themes with the use of two new buildings that have been constructed either side of the old one. The museum gets very crowded at weekends, especially on Sunday.

Charminar

Daily 9am–5.30pm • ₹100 (₹10)

A maze of bazaars teeming with people, the old city has at its heart **Charminar** or Four Towers, a triumphal arch built at the centre of Mohammed Quli Shah's city in 1591 to commemorate an epidemic of the plague. It features four graceful 56m-high minarets, housing spiral staircases to the upper storeys. The (now defunct) mosque on the roof is the oldest in Hyderabad. The yellowish colour of the building is due to a special stucco made of marble powder, gram and egg yolk. In the evening (7–9pm), the edifice is attractively lit up. The **Charkaman**, or Four Arches, north of Charminar, were built in 1594; the western arch, **Daulat-Khan-e-Ali**, was at one time adorned with rich gold tapestries.

Lad Bazaar

Charminar marks the beginning of the fascinating **Lad Bazaar**, which leads to Mahboob Chowk, a market square featuring a mosque and Victorian clock tower. Lad Bazaar specializes in everything you could possibly need for a Hyderabadi marriage, including bangles, rosewater, herbs, spices and cloth. You'll also find silver filigree jewellery, antiques, *bidri*-ware, hookah paraphernalia and, in the markets near Charminar, **pearls** – so beloved of the nizams that they ground them into powder to eat. Hyderabad is still the centre of India's pearl trade.

Nizam's Museum

Daily except Fri 10am–5pm • ₹80 (₹10)

Just over 1km northeast of Charminar, the faded and peeling white-painted facade of the **Nizam's Museum** does not hold much promise but behind its solid wooden doors there is quite a treasure-trove of royal family memorabilia. The first two of the four rooms display

5

a motley collection of silver boxes, model planes and boats, Koranic inscriptions, cylindrical caskets, china and glass objects, photos and paintings, plus larger pieces such as thrones. The third room proclaims itself to be the **City Museum** and showcases some quite detailed and very informative historical displays from the Megalithic era to the present day, while the last room has numerous costumes in long dark-wood cabinets.

Mecca Masjid
Daily 8am–noon & 3–8pm

Southwest, behind Charminar, the **Mecca Masjid** was constructed in 1598 and can hold three thousand devotees, with room for up to ten thousand more in the courtyard. On the left of the courtyard are the tombs of the nizams, while the ornamental walls and lattice archways delight throughout the building. In May 2007, the mosque was rocked by a powerful bomb; the incident killed fourteen people. The perpetrators were never caught and since this and subsequent bombings, security has been very tight throughout the city.

Chowmahalla Palace
Khilwat 20-4-236, Motigalli · Daily except Fri 10am–5pm · ₹200 (₹50), camera ₹50 · ⓦ chowmahalla.co.in

The 150-year-old **Chowmahalla Palace**, southwest of the Mecca Masjid, was built between 1857 and 1869 by the nizams to entertain royal visitors and official guests. Inspired by the Shah's palace in Tehran, it is actually a complex of four palaces, other imposing edifices, elegant courtyards and fountain-filled gardens.

The grand **Kilwat Mubarak** (Durbar Hall) is the most impressive building, containing a hall dominated by opulent chandeliers and other rooms full of furniture, ornaments, costumes, china crockery and displays on the history of the nizams. The oldest part is the southern courtyard, where you can visit the two-storeyed **Aftab Mahal**, which houses more costumes and some intricate wall hangings, as well as the smaller Afzal Mahal, Mahtab Mahal and Tahniyat Mahal. At the rear of the complex there is a collection of carriages and vintage motorcars.

North of the river

The area around Hyderabad Deccan railway station, known locally as Nampally, and north towards Hussain Sagar contains some interesting places. Just south of the station itself, tucked in the lanes behind the striking bulbous yellow dome of the **Ek Minar mosque**, the atmospheric **Yusufian Dargah** is the shrine of a seventeenth-century Sufi saint of the venerable Chishti order. About 1km north of the station, set in tranquil public gardens, the **Telangana State Museum** (daily except Fri & 2nd Sat of month 10.30am–5pm; ₹10) displays a modest collection of bronzes, prehistoric tools and weapons.

Kala Pahad Hill

The **Birla Venkateshvara Mandir** (daily 7am–noon & 3–9pm; no photography) on **Kala Pahad ("black mountain") Hill**, north of the public gardens, is open to all. Constructed in 1976, the temple itself is not of great interest, but affords fine views and is a notable landmark, tapering towards the sky in elegant fashion. Nearby is the mildly diverting **BM Birla Science Centre** (daily 10.30am–8pm, closes 3pm on Fri; ₹35; ⓦbirlasciencecentre.org), which has a lot of satellite hardware and photos, sensory perception machines and a small dinosaur display, plus a **planetarium** (English shows at 11.30am, 4pm & 6pm; ₹40). In a very unscientific manner, the centre also incorporates the **Nirmala Birla Gallery of Modern Art**, featuring the works of Indian painters such as Krishnan Kanna and Amitava Dhar.

Hussain Sagar

Hussain Sagar, the large expanse of water separating Hyderabad from Secunderabad, lends a welcome air of tranquillity to the busy conurbation, and the pedestrianized sections of its banks are popular areas for a stroll, especially at sunset. In the centre of the artificial lake stands a large stone statue of the **Buddha Purnima** ("Full Moon Buddha"), erected in 1992. Regular **boats** (₹60 return) chug out to the statue from Lumbini Park (daily 9am–9pm; ₹10), just off Secretariat Road, which offers some shady spots and also has a toy railway. The park was the site of one of two bombs that exploded in August 2007, claiming 44 lives, so security is predictably tight.

Golconda Fort

Daily 9am–5pm • ₹100 (₹5) • Sound-and-light show: English: March–Oct 7pm, Nov–Feb 6.30pm; 1hr; ₹80–110 • Bus #66G from Charminar via Nampally

Golconda, 122m above the plain and 11km west of old Hyderabad, was the capital of the seven Qutb Shahi kings from 1518 until the end of the sixteenth century, when the court moved to Hyderabad itself. Well preserved and set in thick green scrubland, it is one of India's most impressive forts, boasting 87 semicircular bastions and eight mighty gates, complete with gruesome elephant-proof spikes. Set aside a day to explore the fort, which covers an area of around four square kilometres.

Entering the **fort** by the Balahisar Gate, you come into the Grand Portico, where guards clap their hands to show off the fort's acoustics. To the right is the **mortuary bath**, where the bodies of deceased nobles were ritually bathed prior to burial. If you follow the arrowed anticlockwise route, you pass the two-storey residence of ministers Akkana and Madanna before starting the stairway ascent to the Durbar Hall. Halfway along the steps, you arrive at a small, dark cell named after the court cashier **Ramdas**, who while incarcerated here produced the clumsy carvings and paintings that litter the gloomy room.

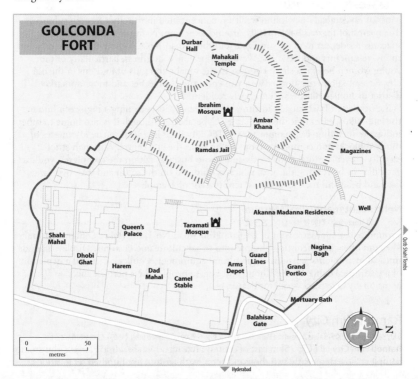

5

Nearing the top, you come across the small, pretty mosque of Ibrahim Qutb Shah; beyond here is an even tinier temple to Durga. The steps are crowned by the three-storey **Durbar Hall** of the Qutb Shahis, on platforms outside which the monarchs would sit and survey their domains.

The ruins of the **queen's palace**, once elaborately decorated with multiple domes, stand in a courtyard centred on an original copper fountain that used to be filled with rosewater. You can still see traces of a "necklace" design on one of the arches, at the top of which a lotus bud sits below an opening flower with a cavity at its centre that once contained a diamond. At the entrance to the **palace** itself, four chambers provided protection from intruders. Passing through two rooms, the second of which is overgrown, you come to the **Shahi Mahal**, the royal bedroom. Originally it had a domed roof and niches on the walls that once sheltered candles or oil lamps. Golconda has a nightly **sound-and-light show**.

Tombs of the Qutb Shahi kings
Daily except Fri 9.30am–4.30pm • ₹20 • Bus #123 or #142S from Charminar

There are no less than seventy monuments, including the famous **tombs of the Qutb Shahi kings** about 1km north of Golconda Fort's outer wall. Set in peaceful and beautifully landscaped gardens, the forty mausoleums commemorate commanders, relatives of the kings, dancers, singers and royal doctors, as well as all but two of the Qutb Shahi kings. Now whitewashed, they were once brightly coloured in turquoise and green. Other buildings include more than twenty mosques, five step-wells, some pavilions and a hamam. The whole complex is in the process of undergoing a ten-year conservation programme at the expense of the Aga Khan Foundation.

The western suburbs

Most of Hyderabad's newfound wealth is concentrated in the city's western suburbs. The nearest of these is **Banjara Hills**, around 4km from Nampally, which comprises spacious residences in quiet streets surrounding Road No.1, a glitzy strip of trendy shops, restaurants and bars. The Western appearance and dress, particularly of the young women here, is a sharp contrast to the niqabs and saris ubiquitous in the old city. Several kilometres further west you enter the even leafier and more upmarket district of **Jubilee Hills**, which is largely residential.

The upturn in Hyderabad's fortunes was driven by its becoming a high-tech hub in the late 1990s, earning it the nickname "Cyberabad", although it is also home to other industries including car manufacture. **HITEC City** itself is several square kilometres of modern blocks and complexes about 10km from the city centre. Although strict security prevents casual visits by those with no business within the complexes, you can get a flavour by touring the area, which is bordered on the south and west by a large lake and beautiful rock formations, reminiscent of Hampi.

Nehru Centenary Tribal Museum
Mon–Sat 10.30am–5pm • ₹100 (₹10) • ☎ 040 2339 1270

Around half a kilometre west of Banjara Hills Road No.1, the **Nehru Centenary Tribal Museum** offers an interesting glimpse into tribal culture and customs. Displays include musical instruments, costumes, agricultural equipment, a bullock cart and a depiction of a traditional dance by the Khond and Bagata peoples. Live performances occasionally take place – call for details.

Ramoji Film City
Daily 9am–8pm • ₹1000 • **Sahas Adventure Park** Daily 9am–5.30pm • ₹900 • Combined ticket ₹1500 • ⓦ ramojifilmcity.com

Ramoji Film City (RFC), 25km east of central Hyderabad, is the world's largest film studio complex. Covering nearly two thousand acres, with around five hundred set locations,

5

it can produce up to sixty movies simultaneously. Although you cannot see films actually being made, you can tour the facades, enjoy rides such as the Ramoji Tower simulated earthquake and watch a dance and stunt show. The adjacent **Sahas Adventure Park** is packed with activities such as zip-lining, zorbing, quad biking and other adrenaline-filled fun. The easiest way to get here is on a tour from Hyderabad (see below).

ARRIVAL AND DEPARTURE

By plane Modern and efficient Rajiv Gandhi International Airport (ⓦ hyderabad.aero) is around 20km south of central Hyderabad. Until the metro connection is complete, the airport is only linked to the city by taxis (about ₹1000) and Pushpak Airport Liner buses (every 10–15min; ₹100–250); heading to the airport, you can catch these from the Secretariat.

Destinations There are frequent international flights and excellent domestic connections to Bengaluru (12–15 daily; 1hr–1hr 30min); Chennai (13–15 daily; 1hr–1hr 30min); Delhi (14–16 daily; 2–4hr); Goa (2–3 daily; 1hr 45min); Kochi (2–4 daily; 1hr 45min); Kolkata (4–5 daily; 2–3hr); Mumbai (15–18 daily; 1hr 15min–3hr 30min) and many other cities.

By train Many long-distance trains terminate at Secunderabad; your ticket is valid for any connecting train to Hyderabad (Nampally) railway station. The two stations are also linked to each other – and other points in the city, such as Banjara Hills and HITEC City – by the overground Hyderabad Metro (or MMTS). The railways reservations office at Hyderabad (daily 8am–8pm) is to the left as you enter the station: counter 211 is for tourists. The Secunderabad reservation complex is more than 400m to the right as you exit the station: counter 34 is for foreigners.

HYDERABAD/SECUNDERABAD

Destinations Daily train services from Hyderabad (Nampally) station include: the *Charminar Express* #12760 to Chennai (6.30pm; 13hr 45min); the *Sabari Express* #17230 to Trivandrum via Ernakulam (noon; 30hr 55min); the *Mumbai Express* #17032 to Mumbai (8.40pm; 16hr 25min); the *East Coast Express* #18646 to Kolkata (9.50am; 30hr 25min) via Vijayawada, Visakhapatnam and Bhubaneswar; and the *Rayasaleema Express* #17429 to Tirupati (4.15pm; 14hr 25min). Most northeast-bound services call at Warangal and Vijayawada. From Secunderabad, the *Konark Express* #11020 travels to Mumbai (11.45am; 16hr 10min). The *Bangalore Express* #12785 (7.05pm; 11hr 20min) departs from Kacheguda station, around 3km east of Nampally.

By bus The long-distance Mahatma Gandhi Bus Stand occupies an island in the River Musi, 3km southeast of Nampally railway station.

Destinations From the long-distance bus stand, regular bus services run to destinations throughout the state and beyond, including Bidar (hourly; 4hr), Tirupati (10 daily; 12hr), Vijayapuri for Nagarjunakonda (6 daily; 4hr), Vijayawada (every 15min; 6hr) and Warangal (every 15min; 3hr). Various "deluxe" private buses depart for Bengaluru, Chennai, Mumbai and other major cities from outside Hyderabad (Nampally) railway station.

INFORMATION AND TOURS

Tourist information The AP Tourism (daily 9am–6pm; ☏ 040 2340 5656, ⓦ aptourism.gov.in) and Telangana Tourism (daily 7am–9pm; ☏ 1800 4254 6464, ⓦ telangana tourism.gov.in) offices are next to each other on Secretariat Rd, near the huge flyover. The APTDC office also in the same complex (daily 7am–8pm; ☏ 040 2345 3036, ⓦ aptdc.gov.in) and the other APTDC office, on Sardar Patel Rd, Secunderabad (☏ 040 2789 3100), exist principally to book their tours. The Incredible India office is in the new tourist plaza at Begumpet (Mon–Fri 9am–5pm; ☏ 040 2326 1360), along with the offices of many other states. A good source of information is the online magazine, *Channel 6* (ⓦ channel6.in).

Guided tours Telangana Tourism operates a number of

good-value guided tours. The times quoted below are when tours set off from the Secunderabad office; the pick-up time in Hyderabad is 15–20min later. There's a Heritage-cum-Museum city tour (daily 7.30am–7.30pm; non-a/c ₹250, a/c ₹350); a Ramoji Film City tour (daily 7.30am–6.30pm; non-a/c ₹1300, a/c ₹1400 including entry); and several fascinating heritage walks, mostly departing from Charminar (on demand 7.30–9am; ₹50, including breakfast; ☏ 040 2345 0444). The Nagarjuna Sagar tour (Sat & Sun 7.30am–10pm; ₹550 excluding entry) is a rushed but convenient way to reach this fascinating area (see p.287).

Car and driver All travel agents can arrange a car and driver (see p.286).

ACCOMMODATION

The area to the east of **Hyderabad (Nampally) railway station** has the cheapest accommodation, but you're unlikely to find anything acceptable for less than ₹500: avoid the grim little collection of five lodges with "Royal" in their name. A little over 1km north of Secunderabad railway station, several decent places can be found on **Sarojini Devi Rd**.

HYDERABAD
Amrutha Castle 5-9-16 Saifabad, opposite the

Secretariat ☏ 040 4443 3888, ⓦ amruthacastle.com. This extraordinarily kitsch hotel, which looks like a fairy castle,

5

won't be to everyone's taste, but is undoubtedly a fun place to stay. The turreted attached rooms have faux wooden beams, fortified doors and paintings of famous royals. Although there's no moat, you can take a dip in the rooftop pool. ₹4800

★ **DM Residency** 5-8-196/B Nampally ☎ 040 6644 7734, ✉ hoteldmresidency@gmail.com. Set back from the Nampally hubbub, this new hotel is kept scrupulously clean by the overtly helpful staff. The rooms are comfortable, with flatscreen TVs and there's wi-fi in the lobby. Good single and a/c rates. ₹1300

Fidalgo Nampally High Rd ☎ 040 3061 6161, ⓦ hotel fidalgo-goa.com. A business traveller-oriented hotel with central a/c and comfy attached rooms set around a looming atrium. While the standard rooms are fine, the "classic" ones are pretty slick, particularly their plate glass desks. ₹4300

Golden Glory Guest House Road No.3, Banjara Hills ☎ 040 2355 4765, ⓦ goldengloryguesthouse.com. Billing itself as a business and family guesthouse, this modest place with neat modern rooms, some with balconies, is one of the more affordable places in the area. A/c rooms are not much more than non-a/c. ₹1300

Rajmata Nampally High Rd, opposite railway station ☎ 040 6666 5555, ✉ royalrajmata@gmail.com. Set back from the popular *Rajmata* has a slightly over-priced collection of cleanish attached rooms: all have TVs and some also boast a/c. Wi-fi in the lobby. ₹900

Sai Prakash Station Rd ☎ 040 2461 1726, ⓦ hotel saiprakash.in. The vast marble lobby gives way to keenly priced all a/c rooms with flatscreen TVs and contemporary blue-and-brown flower motifs on the walls: the bathrooms, however, are decidedly cramped. It also has two decent restaurants. ₹1800

Sri Laxmi Lodge Gadwal Compound, Station Rd ☎ 040 6663 4200. Down a small lane opposite the *Sai Prakash*, *Sri Laxmi* is one of the city's better shoestring options. The rooms – if not always the sheets – are clean and have attached showers and squat toilets. A TV costs ₹50 extra. No wi-fi. ₹450

Taj Banjara Road No.1, Banjara Hills ☎ 040 6666 9999, ⓦ tajhotels.com. In a pleasant lakeside location, with all the usual top-notch facilities including a pool, three classy restaurants and a 24hr coffee shop. Online specials with particularly good weekend rates. ₹4725

★ **Taj Falaknuma Palace** Road No.1, Banjara Hills ☎ 040 6666 9999, ⓦ tajhotels.com. The opulent and beautiful former residence of the nizams is now a top-notch Taj group hotel, with superb grounds, rooms, restaurants and exceptional service. A real treat if you can afford it. ₹33,000

Taj Mahal 4-1-999 Abids Rd ☎ 040 6651 1122, ⓦ hotel tajmahalindia.com. This classy white-and-pale-green 1920s heritage building has a patio garden, spiral staircase and plenty of character. The rooms themselves are plainer, but feature high ceilings, a/c, flatscreen TVs and fridges; the pricier upper-storey rooms are better. ₹1750

SECUNDERABAD

Baseraa Sarojini Devi Rd ☎ 040 2770 3200, ⓦ baseraa .com. The smartest hotel within walking distance (around 15min) of the station, *Baseraa* boasts modern attached rooms with a/c, cable TV and minibars. ₹2900

Sri Sai Ganesh Lodge St John's Rd ☎ 040 2780 6633. With some a/c rooms, this modern concrete-and-glass hotel with largish attached rooms is one of the best options in the immediate station area. No wi-fi. ₹1200

EATING

HYDERABAD

Bikanerwala 6-3-190/Z Road No.1, Banjara Hills ☎ 040 6666 1111. At this bustling fast-food joint the focus is firmly on North Indian cuisine, with authentic *bhel puri*, *chana bhatura* and *aloo tikki* (₹50–150) all on offer, as well as sweets. Daily 8.30am–11.30pm.

Chef Inam's Steak House Road No.12, Banjara Hills ☎ 040 6999 4858. American-roadhouse-style joint serving a dozen different char-grilled steaks for ₹550–850, plus a variety of burgers, kebabs, chicken and seafood dishes, as well as Boston Creameries ice cream. Daily 11am–midnight.

★ **Fusion 9** 6-3-249/A Road No.1, Banjara Hills ☎ 040 6557 7722, ⓦ fusion9.in. Expensive (mains ₹400–750) but quality cuisine from regions as diverse as Mexico, Europe, the Middle East and Southeast Asia, served in a smart modern lounge. There's a smart deli below and the same owners have several other outlets – check the website. Mon–Sat 12.30–3.30pm & 7–11.30pm, Sun 1–4pm & 7–11.30pm.

Kamat Hotel Station Rd, opposite Sai Prakash hotel ☎ 040 2320 3351. At this conveniently located branch of the hygienic veggie chain, waiters in white shirts with red lapels serve up inexpensive veg dosas, *idlis*, *vadas*, thalis and mains (₹50–170). Daily 7am–10pm.

Salzburg Street Amrutha Castle hotel, 5-9-16 Saifabad ☎ 040 4443 3880. Overlooking the lobby's water feature, this restaurant has unusual, but well-executed, options such as wok-tossed garlic prawns for ₹450 and the Korean-Indian fusion *kimchi paneer* as well as some more traditional Indian and Chinese dishes. Most mains ₹200–300. Daily 7.30–10.30am, 12.30–3pm & 7.30–11pm.

Shadab High Court Rd, Old City ☎ 040 2456 1648. While there are some fine meat and fish tandoori items on the menu, the main reason to visit the *Shadab* hotel is for its excellent mutton and chicken biryanis (₹150–200), some of the best in the city. You may have to queue for a table, but it's worth the wait. Daily 5am–11pm.

Sher-e-Punjab Corner of Nampally High Rd and station slip road ☎ 040 2320 4448. In a convenient, if not particularly appealing location, this popular basement restaurant offers tasty North Indian veg and non-veg

HYDERABADI AND ANDHRA CUISINE

5

Hyderabadi cooking is derived from Mughlai court cuisine, featuring sumptuous meat dishes with northern ingredients such as cinnamon, cardamom, cloves and garlic. The city is also the home of the world-famous biryani, where mutton, chicken or veg is mixed with rice and spices including nutmeg and cloves. **Andhra cuisine** encompasses traditional southern vegetarian dishes with an array of flavourings such as cassia buds, peanuts, coconut, tamarind leaves, mustard seeds and red chillies. Fish and prawns are commonly eaten in coastal areas.

food from ₹150, while a full tandoori chicken goes for ₹300. Daily 10am–10.30pm.

Shezan MJ Rd, Nampally ☎ 040 2461 7867. People flock to this hotel restaurant for the excellent and gut-busting biryanis, a snip at ₹180. Some Western and Chinese dishes are also served in the tiered open-air dining hall. Daily noon–11pm.

Via Milano 1259 Road No.36, Jubilee Hills ☎ 040 6455 5544. Swish Italian bar-restaurant that does a range of pasta, risotto, pizza and main courses for ₹400–500. On the third floor above equally trendy *Eat*

India and *Urban Asia*. Daily noon–11pm.

SECUNDERABAD

★**Paradise Food Court** Sarojini Devi Rd ☎ 040 6631 3721, ⓦ paradisefoodcourt.com. This very popular modern multi-restaurant complex, with several other branches all over the city, bashes out fine Hyderabadi cuisine, as well as Chinese. The biryanis are recommended, but don't miss out on the succulent mutton kebabs. Mains ₹260–350. Daily 8am–11pm.

DRINKING AND NIGHTLIFE

There are plenty of **bars**, particularly along Road No.1 in Banjara Hills and the burgeoning Jubilee Hills area further west, although a lot of young professionals in Hyderabad prefer to party in each others' homes in comparison with Bengaluru.

★**Coco's Bar & Grill** 217 Road No.2, Banjara Hills ☎ 040 2354 0600, ⓦ cocosbarngrill.com. Airy rooftop terrace with comfortable, cushioned bamboo armchairs, where you can enjoy a beer or cocktail to the nightly live music. Daily noon–midnight.

Liquids et Cetera Road No.1, Banjara Hills ☎ 040 6625 9907, ⓦ liquidsetc.com. Very trendy nightclub that hosts theme nights such as Foreplay Thursdays and Bollywood Bling on Sundays. Attracts celebrities from the Mumbai entertainment scene. Daily 8pm–2am.

One Flight Down Nampally High Rd ☎ 97044 98713. Just about the only bar in the station area, this basement

bar underneath *Hotel Fidalgo* has comfy leather seats, jazzy lighting and dubious taste in disco music. Daily 8pm–2am.

Spoil Pub Road No.1, Jubilee Hills ☎ 040 6451 3333. Popular pub that offers a range of entertainment from Ladies Nite to House of Noise. Cheap snacks and happy hour drinks until 8.30pm. Daily 5–11pm.

Syn Taj Deccan hotel, Road No.1, Banjara Hills ☎ 040 6666 3939. Although some of the food is overpriced for the quality, futuristic *Syn* features a *teppanyaki* counter and a slick bar that, alongside the usual range of alcoholic drinks, also serves "detox cocktails". Daily noon–11pm.

SHOPPING

All the shops listed below operate core hours of Mon–Sat 10am–8pm, sometimes later. Lad Bazaar (see p.279) in the old city remains the most absorbing place to browse for anything from saris to spices.

Ankur 6-1-84 Secretariat Rd ☎ 040 2323 4901. A huge range of beautiful silks and saris of varying quality and extent can be found at this well-stocked shop.

Chenetha Bhavan A little south of the railway station, Nampally ☎ 040 2460 2845. This modern shopping complex is stuffed with handloom shops, specializing in both clothes and carpets.

Higginbothams 9 Lal Bahadur Stadium ☎ 040 2323 7918. The main Hyderabad branch of the venerable national chain has a diverse collection of novels, reference and academic books.

Lepakshi Gunfoundry, MG Rd ☎ 040 2323 5028. The flagship branch of the AP government emporium stocks a

wide range of handicrafts from all over the state.

Sheela's 17 Lal Bahadur Stadium Complex ☎ 040 2323 6944. Keenly priced souvenir shop selling lots of jewellery, leather bags and various handicrafts.

Sri Mahalaxmi 1264 Road No.36, Jubilee Hills ☎ 96768 04991. Upmarket jewellers displaying a dazzling range of pearls and large pieces in brightly lit cases.

Utkalika Opposite DGP Office, Saifabad ☎ 040 2324 0510. This government of Odisha handicrafts emporium has a modest selection of silver filigree jewellery, handloom cloth, *ikat* tie-dye, Jagannath papier-mâché figures and buffalo bone carvings.

5

DIRECTORY

Banks and exchange State Bank of Hyderabad, MG Rd, and Federal Bank, first floor, Orient Estate, MG Rd, exchange foreign currency; both open Mon–Fri 10.30am–2.30pm, the latter also Sat 10.30am–12.30pm. Alternatively try Thomas Cook (☎ 040 2329 6521) at Nasir Arcade, Secretariat Rd, or LKP forex (☎ 040 2321 0094) on Public Gardens Rd, a 10min walk north of Nampally station; both open Mon–Sat 9.30am–6pm. ATMs are ubiquitous.

Hospitals The government-run Gandhi Hospital is in Secunderabad (☎ 040 2770 2222); the private CDR Hospital is in Himayatnagar (☎ 040 2322 1221); and there's a Tropical Diseases Hospital in Nallakunta (☎ 040 2766 7843).

Library You must be a member or a British citizen to use the British Library, Secretariat Rd (Tues–Sat 11am–7pm; ☎ 040 2323 0774).

Pharmacies Apollo Pharmacy (☎ 040 6060 2424) has branches throughout the city, some open 24hr.

Police ☎ 040 2323 0191. In an emergency call ☎ 100.

Travel agents Sagar Tours & Travels, with branches in Afzal Gunj and Lakdi-Ka-Pul (☎ 98480 82716, ☜ sagartravels hyderabad.com); Classic Travels in Secunderabad (☎ 040 2775 5645); Sri Sai International Travels in Ameerpet (☎ 040 2374 2604, ☜ srisaitravels.com).

Telangana

The principal places of interest in the rest of Telangana lie about the same distance in opposite directions from the capital. As you head north from Hyderabad, the landscape becomes greener and hillier, sporadically punctuated by photogenic black-granite rock formations. There is little to detain visitors here except **Warangal**, which has a medieval fort and a Shiva temple, and nearby **Palampet**, with its Kakatiya temple. South of the capital, swathes of flat farmland stretch into the centre of the state, where the **Nagarjuna Sagar** dam has created a major lake with the important Buddhist site of **Nagarjunakonda**, now an island, in its waters.

Warangal and around

WARANGAL – "one stone" – 150km northeast of Hyderabad and just about possible to visit as a day-trip, was the Hindu capital of the Kakatiyan empire in the twelfth and thirteenth centuries. Like other Deccan cities, it changed hands many times between the Hindus and the Muslims – something reflected in the remains you see today.

Warangal's **fort** (daily 9am–5pm; ₹100 [₹5]), 4km south of the city, is famous for its two circles of fortifications: the outer made of earth with a moat, and the inner of stone. Four roads into the centre meet at the ruined Shiva temple of **Swayambhu** (1162). At its southern gateway, another Shiva temple, from the fourteenth century, is in much better shape; inside, the remains of an enormous lingam came originally from the Swayambhu shrine. Also inside the citadel is the **Shirab Khan**, or **Audience Hall**, an early eleventh-century building very similar to Mandu's Hindola Mahal.

Some 6km north of town just off the main road beside the slopes of Hanamkonda Hill, the largely basalt Chalukyan-style "**thousand-pillared**" **Shiva temple** (daily 6am–6pm) was constructed in 1163. A low-roofed building on several stepped stages, it features superb carvings and shrines to Vishnu, Shiva and Surya, the sun god. They lead off the *mandapa*, whose numerous finely carved columns give the temple its name. In front, a polished Nandi bull was carved out of a single stone. A Bhadrakali temple stands at the top of the hill.

Palampet

PALAMPET, around 70km northeast of Warangal, is a remote village that is worth the effort to get to for its splendid thirteenth-century **Ramappa temple**. Created by the same Kakatiyan artisans who built the Hanamkonda temple near Warangal, the temple is built on a 1.8m-high cruciform plinth and crowned by a central *shikhara*, delicately carved with scenes from the Puranas, while the inner sanctum boasts a 2.7m-tall lingam. There is also an impressive Nandi statue and bathing tank.

ARRIVAL AND INFORMATION

By train There are at least twenty services daily between Hyderabad and Warangal, taking 2–3hr.

By bus There are buses every 15–30min between Warangal and Hyderabad, taking around 3hr. There is no direct bus from Warangal to Palampet, so change in Mulugu.

Getting around The easiest way to cover the sites near

WARANGAL AND AROUND

Warangal is to rent a bike from one of the stalls on Station Rd (₹50/day). An auto-rickshaw to either the fort or the temple costs around ₹120, if you negotiate hard.

Tourist information There's a Telangana Tourism office (☏0870 257 1339; Mon–Sat 10am–5pm) at Nakalgutta in Hanamkonda.

ACCOMMODATION AND EATING

Ashoka Main Rd, Hanamkonda ☏0870 257 8491, ☜hotelashoka.in. Near the thousand-pillared temple, this place has carpeted a/c rooms with TV and fridge but dodgy service. The restaurant provides Indian and Chinese standards; there's also an attached bar. ₹1200

Bharati Mess Station Rd, Warangal. The best of the simple vegetarian restaurants in the station area, offering huge and wholesome unlimited refill meals for around ₹80, all made with fresh ingredients. Daily 7am–10pm.

Harita Kakatiya Main Rd, Hanamkonda ☏0870 256 2236, ☜telanganatourism.gov.in. Not far from the thousand-pillared temple, this government hotel is the best in the area, with large spacious a/c rooms and a good restaurant. ₹1850

Surya Station Rd, Warangal ☏0870 244 1834. A decent budget option very close to the station, with clean attached rooms and a good restaurant serving a range of inexpensive food. ₹750

Vijaya Lodge Station Rd, Warangal ☏0870 225 1222. The pick of the basic lodges near the station, quite large and modern with fairly hygienic rooms, many of them with shared bathrooms. Simple but OK restaurant. ₹300/₹500

Nagarjunakonda

NAGARJUNAKONDA, or "Nagarjuna's Hill", 166km south of Hyderabad and 175km west of Vijayawada, is all that remains of the vast area, rich in archeological sites, that was submerged when the huge Nagarjuna Sagar dam was built across the River Krishna in 1960. Ancient settlements in the valley had first been discovered in 1926, and extensive excavations carried out between 1954 and 1960 uncovered more than one hundred sites dating from the early Stone Age to late medieval times. Nagarjunakonda was once the summit of a hill, where a fort towered 200m above the valley floor; now it is just a small oblong island near the middle of Nagarjuna Sagar lake. The new border between Telangana and Andhra Pradesh runs right through the lake and both states claim it as their own in tourist literature. It certainly falls more within the compass of Hyderabad, eventually to be solely the capital of Telangana, which manages the local resort (see p.288).

Several Buddhist monuments have been reconstructed, in an operation reminiscent of that at Abu Simbel in Egypt, and a **museum** exhibits the more remarkable ruins of the valley. **VIJAYAPURI**, the village on the shore of the lake, overlooks the colossal dam itself, which produces electricity for the whole region, and is the jumping-off point for visiting **Nagarjunakonda island** (daily 9am–5pm). Boats arrive on the northeastern edge of the island, at what remains of one of the gates of the fort, built in the fourteenth century and renovated by the Vijayanagar kings in the mid-sixteenth century. Low, damaged, stone walls skirting the island mark the fort's edge, and you can see ground-level remains of the Hindu temples that served its inhabitants. Well-kept gardens lie between the jetty and the museum, beyond which nine Buddhist monuments from various sites in the valley have been rebuilt. West of the jetty, there's a reconstructed third-century-AD bathing *ghat*.

The stupas

The **maha-chaitya**, or *stupa*, constructed at the command of King Chamtula's sister in the third century AD, is the area's earliest Buddhist structure. It was raised over relics of the Buddha – said to include a tooth – and has been reassembled in the southwest of the island. Nearby, a towering **Buddha statue** stands beside a ground plan of a monastery that enshrines a smaller *stupa*. Close by are other **stupas**; the brick walls of the *svastika chaitya* have been arranged in the shape of swastikas, common emblems in early Buddhist iconography.

5

The museum

Daily except Fri 10.30am–5pm • ₹100 (₹5)

The **museum** houses stone friezes decorated with scenes from the Buddha's life, and statues of the Buddha in various postures. Earlier artefacts include metal axe-heads and knives (dating from the first millennium BC). Later exhibits include inscribed pillars from Ikshvaku times. Medieval sculptures include a thirteenth-century *tirthankara* (Jain saint) and a seventeenth-century Ganesh.

ARRIVAL AND INFORMATION   NAGARJUNAKONDA

By bus Nagarjunakonda can easily be reached from Hyderabad (4hr; all the regular Macherla services stop at Vijayapuri) or Vijayawada (6hr; a direct service runs daily at 11am and frequent services leave from Guntur).

By boat Tickets for boats to the island (daily 9.30am, 11.30am & 1.30pm; 45min; ₹90) go on sale 25min before

departure. Each boat leaves the island 90min after it arrives, so if you want to see the ruins and museum in detail, take a morning boat and return in the afternoon.

Tourist information The AP Tourism office (Mon–Sat 10am–5pm; ☎ 08680 277364) is near the bus stand.

ACCOMMODATION

Accommodation at Vijayapuri is limited and there are two distinct settlements 6km apart on either side of the dam. For easy access to the sites it's better to stay near the jetty on the right bank of the dam; ask the bus driver to leave you at the launch station.

Haritha Vijay Vihar On the near side of the dam as you approach the lake from Hyderabad ☎ 08680 277362, ⓦ harithahotel.com. APTDC runs the comfortable all-a/c *Vijay Vihar*, complete with swimming pool. Rooms are over fifty percent more expensive at weekends. **₹1600**

Nagarjuna Motel Complex 500m beyond the boat jetty ☎ 08642 278188. This functional but drab-looking concrete complex has adequate rooms, some with a/c, and a basic restaurant. **₹600**

Eastern and northern Andhra Pradesh

One of India's least visited areas, **eastern Andhra Pradesh** is sandwiched between the Bay of Bengal in the east and the red soil and high peaks of the Eastern Ghats in the north. Its one architectural attraction is the ancient Buddhist site of **Amaravati**, designated to be the new capital of Andhra Pradesh (see p.279), near the business hub of **Vijayawada**, whose sprinkling of historic temples is far overshadowed by impersonal, modern buildings. For anyone with a strong desire to explore, however, pockets of natural beauty along the coast and in the hills of eastern Andhra Pradesh can offer rich rewards, especially the **Godavari Delta** around Rajahmundry. At the northern tip of the state, the nondescript industrial port city of **Visakhapatnam** is a useful place to break up a journey to northern India.

Vijayawada

Almost 450km north of Chennai, a third of the way to Kolkata, **VIJAYAWADA** is a bustling commercial centre on the banks of the Krishna Delta, 90km from the coast. This mundane city, alleviated by a mountain backdrop of bare granite outcrops and some urban greenery, is seldom visited by tourists, but is an obvious stop-off point for a visit to nearby **Amaravati**. The **Kanaka Durga** (also known as Vijaya) **temple** on Indrakila Hill in the east, dedicated to the city's patron goddess of riches, power and benevolence, is the most interesting of Vijayawada's handful of temples. Across the river, roughly 6km southwest of town, is an ancient, unmodified cave temple complex at **Undavalli** (daily 9am–5pm; ₹100 [₹5]) a tiny rural village on the local #301 bus service to Amaravati. There are shrines to all three of the *trimurti*, with the reclining Vishnu statue on the upper level being the most impressive feature.

ARRIVAL AND INFORMATION   VIJAYWADA

By train Vijayawada's railway station, on the main Chennai–Kolkata line, is in the centre of town: the daily *East Coast Express* #18645 (11.35am; 6hr 55min) is a convenient service to Hyderabad (Secunderabad).

By bus The Pandit Nehru bus stand is 1.5km west of the station, on the other side of the Ryes Canal. The efficient #301 bus to Amaravati via Undavalli (every 20–30min;

1hr 30min) leaves from platform 47. There are also regular services to Hyderabad (every 15min; 6hr) and Visakha-patnam (hourly; 6–9hr).

Tourist information There's a tourist office (Mon–Sat 10am–5pm; ☎ 0866 252 3966) at the railway station, and APTDC has an office in the town centre at the *Hotel Ilapuram* complex, Gandhi Nagar (same times; ☎ 0866 257 0255).

ACCOMMODATION AND EATING

Monika Lodge Just off Elluru Rd about 300m northeast of the bus stand ☎ 0866 257 1334. Cheap, no-frills lodge, with small attached rooms, some a/c, perfectly salubrious enough for a night. No wi-fi. ₹575

Narayana Swamy Atchutaramaiah St ☎ 0866 257 1221. Good-value lodge, with spotless rooms, some with a/c and TV. If full, try the similar *Sitara* nearby on the other side of the road. ₹925

Raj Towers Elluru Rd ☎ 0866 257 1311, ⊕ hotelrajtowers .com. Mid-range hotel in a tall modern block, which offers

pleasantly furnished a/c rooms with cable TV and has a decent restaurant. The owner has the budget *Hotel Comforts* opposite. ₹2000

Swarna Palace Corner of Atchutaramaiah St and Elluru Rd ☎ 0866 257 7222, ✉ swarnapalace@rediffmail.com. Reliable place, with spacious and comfortable singles that can sleep two, though the a/c rooms cost over twice as much. Its fourth-floor *Palace Heights* restaurant serves hearty portions of Indian, Chinese and Continental food, and there's a bar. ₹900

Amaravati

Daily except Fri 10am–5pm • ₹100 (₹5); museum ₹2

For centuries **AMARAVATI**, 33km from Vijayawada, has been little more than a village on the banks of the Krishna. All that is due to change in the coming decade, however, as this is the location that has been chosen to be the brand-new **capital** of Andhra Pradesh, following the secession of Telangana (see p.279). If the hoardings are to be believed and enough investment is forthcoming, an ultramodern city of gleaming skyscrapers will rise from the quiet fields, although the ground had barely been broken at the time of writing.

Pending this building frenzy, Amaravati remains famous as the site of a Buddhist settlement formerly known as Chintapalli, where a *stupa* larger than those at Sanchi in Madhya Pradesh was erected over relics of the Buddha in the third century BC, during the reign of Ashoka. The *stupa* no longer stands, but its size is evident from the mound that formed its base. There was a gateway at each of the cardinal points, one of which has been reconstructed, and the meticulously carved details show themes from the Buddha's life. A Kalachakra initiation programme was conducted by the Dalai Lama here in January 2006 to commemorate 2550 years since the Buddha's birth.

Exhibits at the small but fascinating **museum** date from the third century BC to the twelfth century AD and include Buddha statues with lotus symbols on the feet, tightly curled hair and long ear lobes – all traditional indications of an enlightened teacher.

ARRIVAL AND DEPARTURE   AMARAVATI

By bus Bus #301 runs every 20–30min from Vijayawada to Amaravati (1hr 30min). The excavated site and museum

are less than 1km from the bus stand but it's better to jump off when the bus turns onto the main street.

ACCOMMODATION AND EATING

RKS Rest House Temple St ☎ 08645 255516. Typical of the handful of basic lodges dotted around the temple,

this place offers no creature comforts but is OK for a night. ₹400

The Godavari Delta

A previously uncharted region that is just beginning to open up to tourism, though still mostly aimed at domestic visitors, is the enchanting **Godavari Delta**, where the mighty

5

river ends its journey of almost 1500 miles across India from its source in the Western Ghats. The best base for exploration of the area is **Rajahmundry**, roughly halfway between Vijayawada and Visakhapatnam. From there, you can take a trip upriver to the verdant **Papikondalu Hills**, delve into the lush **Konaseema** region to the south or visit the **Coringa Wildlife Sanctuary** to the southeast.

Rajahmundry

Busy but not unpleasant **RAJAHMUNDRY** sprawls along the east bank of the Godavari, still 80km from the sea, yet the river is so wide at this point that it takes over five minutes to cross it by rail or road. Although the main reason to come here is to explore the rural areas that surround it, the lively riverfront merits a stroll. Being the last major town on India's second holiest river, the banks are a riot of temples, shrines and bathing *ghats*, always bustling with pilgrims and locals alike.

Papikondalu Hills

As the best spots in the green riverside **Papikondalu Hills** to the north of Rajahmundry are only accessible by boat, it is best to take a tour (see below) to reach them. You are first taken 35km by road to the muddy jetty at **Polavaram** and then transferred onto a double-decker boat that sedately cruises upstream to **Bhadrachalam**, visiting some temples en route and giving you the option to stay overnight in rustic bamboo huts at **Kolluru**, beside a tributary where you can bathe in the clear rushing waters.

Konaseema

Billing itself as Andhra's answer to the renowned Keralan backwaters (see p.322), **Konaseema** is a palm-rich region of fertile islands and grassy marshes created by the seven mouths of the Godavari. This sleepy area, home to water buffalo, farmers and fishermen, is just waking up to tourism, especially around the nearby villages of **Razole** and **Dindi**, around 50km south of Rajahmundry, which offer waterfront resorts and houseboats for groups.

Coringa Wildlife Sanctuary

Daily 7am–6pm • ₹200 (₹10)

Roughly 45km southeast of Rajahmundry, the **Coringa Wildlife Sanctuary** contains the largest area of **mangrove swamps** in India apart from the Sundarbans in West Bengal. There's a boardwalk through the muddy groves and a small jetty for boat trips when the tide is high enough, plus an ugly concrete viewing platform that does allow great views all around. Among the birdlife to be spotted here is the ubiquitous egret, the open-billed stork, kingfishers and even the Brahminy kite, while the elusive otter is the most notable resident mammal. The surrounding bay is also a major breeding ground for the olive ridley turtle.

ARRIVAL AND INFORMATION   **THE GODAVARI DELTA**

By train Rajahmundry's railway station, on the main east-coast line, is on the south side of the city centre: all of the 15–20 daily trains between Vijayawada (2hr 30min–3hr) and Visakhapatnam (3hr–3hr 30min) stop here.

By bus The bus stand is 3km northeast of the station. There are regular services to Dindi (hourly; 2hr), Hyderabad (every 30min–1hr; 9–10hr), Razole (hourly; 2hr), Vijayawada (every 15–30min; 3–4hr) and Visakhapatnam (every 30min–1hr;

3hr 30min–4hr 30min). For Coringa Wildlife Sanctuary, you can take a bus to Kakinada (every 15–30min; 1hr 30min and get an auto-rickshaw or Yanam-bound bus from there.

Tourist information and tours The best source of information and place to book tours of the region is the efficient Konaseema Tourism office (daily 8am–8pm; ☏ 80087 57111, ⓦ konaseematourism.com), 200m north of Rajahmundry railway station.

ACCOMMODATION AND EATING

Foodway 200m north of Rajahmundry railway station ☏ 99599 84550. Better than the fast-food-joint appearance suggests, this modern place serves a range of special thalis

and biryanis plus other Indian and Chinese dishes, all under ₹200. Daily 11am–10pm.

Haritha Coconut Country Resort Dindi ☏ 98487

80524, @aptdc.gov.in. Unusually attractive government resort with large rustic rooms, a multicuisine restaurant, swimming pool and a couple of luxury two-room houseboats for rent. ₹2300

★**Podarillu Resort** Razole ☎80087 27333, @kona seematourism.com. Spacious a/c rooms with uninterrupted views across the tranquil waters. The huge ground-floor bathrooms have shrubs growing in the sandy soil. Food by arrangement. ₹2900

Sri Ishwarya Residency Opposite Rajahmundry railway station ☎0883 243 7315. Standard station-area lodge with decent-sized rooms that are clean enough but rather haphazard service. No wi-fi. ₹750

Transit Bay 200m north of Rajahmundry railway station ☎0883 244 1000. Modern hotel with central a/c and smart business-oriented rooms painted in bright colours. Overlooks the tracks so suffers from train noise. ₹1350

Visakhapatnam and around

Andhra Pradesh's second largest city, 650km east of Hyderabad and 350km north of Vijayawada, **VISAKHAPATNAM** (commonly known as Vizag) is a busy port and home to major shipbuilding, oil refining and steel industries. Apart from having a decent beach, some interesting temples and a couple of museums, for most travellers it only serves to break up a long journey along the east coast. Those who do linger in the area, however, can enjoy the seaside area of **Waltair** and will be rewarded by visiting outlying places such as **Bheemunipatnam**, **Mukhalingam** and the **Borra caves**.

Kursura Submarine Museum

Beach Rd • Tues–Sat 2–8.30pm, Sun also 10am–12.30pm & 2–8.30pm • ₹40

Housed in a decommissioned submarine named INS *Kursura*, which is now landed like a beached whale in a dry dock on the seafront, the **Kursura Submarine Museum** is mainly of interest to nautical fanatics. It gives you the chance to see the inner workings of the vessel and get an idea of what life must have been like on board.

Vishaka Museum

Beach Rd • Mon–Fri 11am–7pm, Sat & Sun noon–8pm • ₹5

The surprisingly well-laid-out and well-labelled **Vishaka Museum** covers seafaring from ancient times to post-Independence, with plenty of paintings and naval equipment, though with perhaps a little too much emphasis on and glorification of military prowess.

Kailashagiri Hill and beach

The best beach for swimming is below **Kailashagiri Hill**, several kilometres north of the port. The popular hilltop park boasts fantastic coastal and city vistas, and a hilarious viewing deck in the shape of the *Titanic*'s bow, as well as the usual modest funfair paraphernalia and stalls. The park is also linked to the coast road and fine sandy beach by a **cable car** (₹30 one way).

Around Visakhapatnam

Various traces of older civilizations lie within a day's journey of the city. At **Bheemunipatnam**, 30km north, you can see the remains of a Dutch fort and a peculiar cemetery with slate-grey pyramidal tombs. You'll need a car to get to **Mukhalingam**, 100km north of Bheemunipatnam, where three Shaivite temples, built between the sixth and twelfth centuries, rest in low hills. Their elaborate carvings and well-preserved towering *shikharas* display slight local variations from the otherwise standard Odishan style.

Ninety kilometres inland on a minor road that winds through the Eastern Ghats and the Araku forest, **Borra** boasts a set of dark and eerie limestone **caves**, pierced with age-old stalactites and stalagmites (daily 10am–1pm & 2–5pm; ₹40).

ARRIVAL AND INFORMATION   **VISAKHAPATNAM AND AROUND**

By train Visakhapatnam's railway station, on the main Chennai–Kolkata line, is close to the port. The best service

in both directions is the superfast *Coromandel Express* #12842 (10.10pm) to Bhubaneswar (6hr 25min) and

5

Kolkata (13hr 40min); #12841 (4.40am) to Chennai (12hr 50min) and Vijayawada (5hr 40min).

By bus Regular buses for Vijayawada (every 30min; 6–8hr), Rajahmundry (every 30min–1hr; 3hr 30min–4hr

30min) and Hyderabad (hourly; 11–13hr) leave from the bus stand, south of the city centre.

Tourist information The APTDC office is in the RTC Complex in the city centre (Mon–Sat 9am–5pm; ☎ 0891 278 8820).

ACCOMMODATION

VISAKHAPATNAM

Gateway Beach Rd ☎ 0891 662 3670, ⊛ thegateway hotels.com. The top-end Taj Hotels-run *Gateway* has recently renovated sea-facing attached rooms and an excellent Chinese restaurant. Good online deals. ₹5500

Haritha Hotel Beach Rd ☎ 0891 256 2333, ⊛ aptdc .gov.in. This mid-range APTDC hotel offers comfortable, if slightly institutional, standard and a/c rooms. Breakfast included. ₹1600

★ **Karanths Hotel** 33-1-55 Patel Marg, Visakhapatnam ☎ 0891 256 0347. By far the best place if you're just overnighting between trains and want to stay by the station. Very clean attached rooms with cable TV and polite service. No wi-fi. ₹550

The Park Beach Rd, Visakhapatnam ☎ 0891 304 5678,

⊛ theparkhotels.com. This branch of the nationwide chain is Vizag's classiest hotel, with elegantly furnished rooms and all mod cons, including fine dining, lush gardens and a pool. Breakfast included. ₹10,250

YMCA Beach Rd, Visakhapatnam ☎ 0891 275 5826, ⊛ ymcavizag.org. The reliable and predictably popular *YMCA*, which boasts a splendid seaside location, has a few economical attached rooms and a dorm. No wi-fi. Dorms ₹150, doubles ₹800

AROUND VISAKHAPATNAM

Jungle Bells Tyda ⊛ aptdc.gov.in. This mid-range APTDC hotel has fair-sized rustic rooms and is the nearest place to Borra caves. Buffet breakfast included. ₹1200

EATING

Flying Spaghetti Monster Waltair Rd, Visakhapatnam ☎ 0891 276 6652. An unexpected find for such a city, serving pizzas, pasta and some Mexican dishes for ₹300–500. Daily noon–10.30pm.

Sandy Lane Beach Rd, Visakhapatnam ☎ 0891 273 6997. Housed in an attractive Raj-era mansion and with seating at the back of the beach, this bar-restaurant offers chilled beer and fresh seafood for ₹150–300. Daily 11am–11pm.

Southern Andhra Pradesh

The further south you travel from the fertile lands watered by the great Krishna and Godavari rivers, the less hospitable the terrain becomes, especially in the rocky southwest of the state. For Hindus, the main attraction in southern Andhra Pradesh is the **Venkateshvara temple**, outside **Tirupati**, India's most popular Vishnu shrine, where several thousand pilgrims come each day to receive *darshan*. **Puttaparthy**, the community founded by the deceased spiritual leader Sai Baba, and the **Oneness University** (see box opposite) are the only other places in the region to attract significant numbers of visitors. All three places are closer to Chennai in Tamil Nadu and Bengaluru in Karnataka than to other points in Andhra Pradesh.

Tirumala Hill and Tirupati

Set in a stunning position, surrounded by wooded hills capped by a ring of vertical red rocks, the **Sri Venkateshvara temple** at **Tirumala**, 170km northwest of Chennai, is said to be one of the richest places of pilgrimage in the world, and is certainly the most popular, drawing more devotees than Rome or Mecca. With its many shrines and *dharamshalas*, the whole area around Tirumala Hill, an enervating drive 700m up in the Venkata Hills, provides a fascinating insight into contemporary Hinduism practised on a large scale.

The road trip up Tirumala Hill is a lot less terrifying now that there's a separate route down; the most devout, of course, climb the hill by foot. The steep **trail** starts at Alipuri, 4km from the centre of Tirupati; all the pilgrim buses pass through – look out for a large Garuda statue and the soaring *gopura* of the first temple. There are drinks stalls all along the route, which is covered for most of the way. The walk takes at least four hours, and an early start is recommended. When you get to the top, you will see barbers giving pilgrims tonsures as part of their devotions.

At the bottom of the hill, the **Sri Kapileswaraswami** temple at Kapilateertham is the only Tirumala temple devoted to Shiva.

The Venkateshvara temple

General entry free; *sudarshan* ₹50; special entry and *e-darshan* ₹300 • Ⓦ tirumala.org

The **Venkateshvara temple** (aka Sri Vari) dedicated to **Vishnu** and started in the tenth century, has been renovated to provide facilities for the thousands of pilgrims who visit daily; weekends, public holidays and festivals are even busier. Unless your visit is intended to be particularly rigorous, you should buy one of the **special darshan** tickets, as this can reduce the time it takes to get inside by quite a few hours, perhaps even more than a day. All types of tickets can be purchased from booths near the temple entrance and even in advance online. Before entering the temple non-Hindus have to sign a declaration of faith in Lord Venkateshvara and provide photocopies of the picture and visa pages from their passports, along with the originals. Note that **no electronic devices** are allowed inside the temple.

At the entrance is a colonnade, lined with life-sized copper or stone statues of royal patrons. The *gopura* gateway leading to the inner courtyard is decorated with sheets of embossed silver; a gold *stambha* (flagstaff) stands outside the inner shrine next to a gold upturned lotus on a plinth. Outside, opposite the temple, is a small museum, the **Hall of Antiquities** (daily 8am–8pm). Your *darshan* tickets entitle you to enter the museum via shorter queues opposite the exit.

Tirupati

The hill is 11km as the crow flies from its service town of **TIRUPATI**, but double that by road. The town is almost entirely modern and pretty unappealing, as well as being predictably crowded with the constant flow of pilgrims. A five-minute walk from the railway station, the one temple in Tirupati itself that's definitely worth a look is **Govindarajaswamy**, whose modern grey *gopura* is clearly visible from many points in town.

THE ONENESS UNIVERSITY AND TEMPLE

A few kilometres from the small town of Tada, around 70km east of Tirupati, lies the startling complex of the **Golden City**, home to the **Oneness University**. The focal point of this community is the stunning and gigantic three-storey **Oneness Temple**, built in brilliant white marble and visible for miles around. The largest pillarless hall in Asia, it is capable of housing up to five thousand people. The huge edifice has an impressive meditation hall on the upper storey and beneath it areas for communal worship and events, most notably *darshan* with the founders of the Oneness Movement, **Sri Bhagavan** (born March 15, 1949 in Natham, Tamil Nadu) and his partner **Amma** (born August 15, 1954 in Sangam, Andhra Pradesh). Often referred to as Kalki Bhagavan, as many followers have declared him to be the tenth incarnation of Vishnu, the guru has always disavowed this title, concentrating instead on promoting his core message of seeking union with the divine.

After the couple married in 1976, they founded the Jeevashram school in 1984, originally located at Satyaloka, a remote location in the Eastern Ghats near the Andhra and Karnataka borders. Here they developed the philosophy of Oneness, wherein every individual feels connected to all that is and gradually awakens to a state of higher consciousness. This is achieved by the process of **deeksha blessing**, whereby divine energy is transferred directly to the recipient by a gentle touching of the head around the crown chakra. In the early 1990s, the school relocated to **Nemam**, in Tamil Nadu north of Chennai, before finding its new home at the Golden City at the turn of the millennium.

The temple is not open to casual visitors but those genuinely interested can arrange a visit in advance and be given a tour. You can find out more about the movement and get details on the four-week-long **deepening process** at the university by logging onto Ⓦ onenessuniversity.org. If you do arrange to go independently, it is better to hire a taxi from Tirupati or Chennai as the complex is very difficult to reach by public transport.

5

The inner sanctum is open to non-Hindus and contains a splendid, large, black reclining Vishnu. In its own compound by the side entrance stands the fine little Venkateshvara Museum of Temple Arts (daily 8am–8pm; ₹5). The temple's impressive bathing tank lies 200m to the east.

Tiruchanur Padmavati temple

Between Tirupati and Tirumala Hill, the **Tiruchanur Padmavati temple** is another popular pilgrimage halt. A gold *vimana* tower with lions at each corner surmounts the sanctuary, which contains a black stone image of goddess Lakshmi with one silver eye. A ₹50 ticket allows you to jump the queue to enter the sanctuary.

Chandragiri Fort

Daily except Fri 10am–5pm · ₹100 (₹5) · **Sound-and-light show (in English)** Nov–Feb 7.30pm, March–Oct 8pm; 45min; ₹40

In the sixteenth century, **Chandragiri**, 11km southwest of Tirupati, became the third capital of the Vijayanagars. It was here that the British negotiated the acquisition of the land to establish Fort St George, the earliest settlement at what is now Chennai. The original fort, thought to date from around 1000 AD, was taken over by Haider Ali in 1782, followed by the British in 1792. A small **museum** is housed in the main building, the Indo-Saracenic Raja Mahal. Another building, the **Rani Mahal**, stands close by, while behind that is a hill with two freestanding boulders that was used as a place of public execution during Vijayanagar times. There's a nightly **sound-and-light show**.

ARRIVAL AND DEPARTURE — TIRUMALA HILL AND TIRUPATI

By plane There are flights to Hyderabad (6 daily; 1hr) and Visakhapatnam (1 daily; 1hr 15min) from the airport, 14km outside Tirupati.

By train Trains from Chennai (6–8 daily; 2hr 30min–4hr) pull in at Tirupati's central railway station. There are several connections to Hyderabad (4–6 daily; 12–15hrs).

By bus The bus stand is 500m east of the train station. From Hyderabad it's a long haul (8–10 daily; 12–15hrs). Frequent express bus services run to Chennai (every 15–30min; 3hr 30min–4hr). There are hourly buses to both Kanchipuram (5hr), two of which continue to Mamallapuram (7hr), and Bengaluru (7hr).

GETTING AROUND AND INFORMATION

By bus A special section at the back of Tirupati bus stand has services every few minutes to Tirumala Hill; you can also access the hill via a local bus stop outside the railway station.

Tourist information The AP Tourism office (daily 7am–9pm; ☎ 0877 225 5385) is on the second floor of the Sri Devi Complex, Tilak Rd.

ACCOMMODATION AND EATING

Unless you're a pilgrim seeking accommodation in the *dharamshalas* near the temple, all the decent places to stay are in Tirupati. Eating is almost exclusively vegetarian, and there are many cheap "meals" places in town and on Tirumala Hill.

Annapurna 349 G Car St, opposite the railway station ☎ 0877 225 0666, ⊕ hotelannapurna.in. On a busy corner, this modern hotel has spacious, sparsely furnished attached rooms with tiled floors, TVs and either fans or a/c. The a/c restaurant serves South Indian snacks, thalis, Chinese and North Indian dishes. ₹1100

Bhimas Deluxe 34–38 G Car St, near the railway station ☎ 0877 222 5521, ⊕ bhimasdeluxehotel.com. Despite an unappealing grey colour scheme, the attached a/c rooms with TV here are a decent choice; 12hr "transit rooms" are available for two thirds of the regular rate. ₹1750

Mayura 209 TP Area ☎ 0877 222 5925, ⊕ mayura hotels@yahoo.co.in. The best of the mid-range hotels opposite the bus station, offering average rooms with clean bathrooms and TV. No wi-fi. ₹1500

★ **The Orchid** Fortune Kences hotel, opposite the bus stand ☎ 0877 225 5855. The excellent ₹799 evening buffet is one of the few places to enjoy non-veg food, with superb chicken and lamb dishes, followed by a great range of desserts. À la carte available too. Daily 7–11pm.

Sindhuri Park Opposite the bathing tank ☎ 0877 225 6430, ⊕ hotelsindhuri.com. One of the smartest places in the town centre, this all-a/c hotel has comfortable – if unremarkable – attached rooms with good views of the tank and temple. The restaurant offers a good range of Indian *paneer* and veg dishes, as well as banana splits for dessert. ₹2340

Sri Vignesh Residency 191 Railway Station Rd ☎ 0877 645 2547. The bright yellow exterior rather masks the dingy interior. Still, the cell-like attached rooms are among the best budget deals in town. No wi-fi. ₹450

Puttaparthy

5

Deep in the southwest of the state, amid the arid rocky hills bordering Karnataka, a thriving community has grown up around the once insignificant village of **PUTTAPARTHY**, birthplace of spiritual leader **Sai Baba**. Centring on **Prasanthi Nilayam** (Abode of Peace), the ashram where Sai Baba used to reside most of the year, the town has schools, a university, hospital and sports centre that offer up-to-date and free services to all. The ashram itself is a huge complex, with canteens, shops, a museum and library, and a vast assembly hall. The museum (daily 10am–noon) contains detailed displays on the world's major faiths and presents a positive unitarian message.

ARRIVAL AND DEPARTURE

PUTTAPARTHY

By train The railway station, named Sri Satya Sai Prasanti Nilayam, is 8km from town on the main north–south route but it is only served by infrequent passenger trains. For express services go to Dharmavaram, 42km away, connected to Puttaparthy by regular buses.

By bus Buses from Bengaluru (every 30min–1hr; 4hr), Hyderabad (4–6 daily; 12–13hr), Tirupati (hourly; 6–7hr) and Chennai (8–10 daily; 8–9hr) stop at the stand outside the ashram entrance.

ACCOMMODATION AND EATING

Many visitors stay in the ashram accommodation, which is strictly segregated by sex, except for families. Costs are minimal, and although you can't book in advance, you can enquire about availability at the secretary's office (☏ 08555 287583). Outside the ashram, many of the hotels are overpriced. The ashram also has a canteen open to non-residents.

Bamboo Nest Chitravathi Rd ☏ 99064 34576. Delicious Tibetan *momos* (dumplings) and *thukpas* (thick noodle soups) are available at this popular and sociable haunt. Most items under ₹100. Daily 9.30am–2pm & 4.30–9pm.

Sai Ganesh Guest House Gopuram Rd ☏ 08555 287460. This small and cosy lodge near the police station is one of the best budget options. No wi-fi. ₹**500**

Sai Towers Near the ashram entrance ☏ 0855 287270,

ⓦ saitowers.com/hotel. Charges a lot for its smallish fan and a/c rooms, except for some much cheaper singles, but has a good veg restaurant downstairs. ₹**2300**

Sri Sai Sadan Gopuram Rd ☏ 08555 287507, ✉ srisai sadan@yahoo.com. Decent-value hotel, whose rooms all have a fridge, TV, phone and balcony with views of the countryside or the ashram, plus there's a meditation room and rooftop restaurant. No wi-fi. ₹**1000**

SHRI SATYA SAI BABA

Born on November 23, 1926, in Puttaparthy, **Satyanarayana Raju** allegedly displayed prodigious talents from an early age. His apparently supernatural abilities initially caused some concern to his family, who took him to Vedic doctors and eventually to be exorcised. Having been declared possessed by the divine rather than the diabolical, at the age of 14 he calmly announced he was the new incarnation of **Sai Baba**, a saint from Shirdi in Maharashtra who died eight years before Satya was born.

Gradually his fame spread and a large following developed. In 1950 the **ashram** was inaugurated and a decade later Sai Baba was attracting international attention; he still has millions of devotees worldwide, more than five years after his death on April 27, 2011. Just 5ft tall, with a startling Hendrix-style Afro, his smiling, saffron-clad figure can be seen on posters, photos and murals all over South India. Though his **miraculous powers** reportedly included the ability to materialize *vibhuti*, sacred ash, with curative properties, Sai Baba always claimed this to be unimportant, emphasizing instead his message of **universal love**. During his last years a number of ex-followers made serious accusations about coercion and even sexual abuse on the part of the guru himself, which have been vehemently denied.

Predictably, following the passing of the guru, there have been further rumours of corruption by the trustees of his organization, casting its future into some doubt. Whatever your feelings about the divinity of Sai Baba, the atmosphere around the ashram remains undeniably peaceful. You can find out more about the Sai organization at ⓦ saibaba.ws.

Kerala

302 Thiruvananthapuram

309 Kovalam

312 South of Kovalam

313 Varkala and around

317 Kollam (Quilon)

319 Alappuzha (Alleppey)

324 Mararikulam

325 Kottayam and around

328 Periyar and around

332 Munnar and around

335 Kochi (Cochin)

347 Around Kochi

349 Thrissur (Trichur)

352 Around Thrissur

353 Kozhikode (Calicut)

355 Wayanad

357 The far north

PAPANASAM BEACH, VARKALA

Kerala

The state of Kerala stretches for 550km along India's southwest coast, divided between the densely forested mountains of the Western Ghats inland and a lush, humid coastal plain of rice paddy, lagoons, rivers and canals. Its intensely tropical landscape, fed by the highest rainfall in peninsular India, has intoxicated visitors since the ancient Sumerians and Greeks sailed in search of spices to the shore known as the Malabar coast. Equally, Kerala's arcane rituals and spectacular festivals – many of them little changed since the earliest era of Brahmanical Hinduism – have dazzled outsiders for thousands of years.

Travellers weary of India's daunting metropolises will find Kerala's cities smaller and more relaxed. The most popular is undoubtedly the great port of **Kochi** (Cochin), where the state's long history of peaceful foreign contact is evocatively evident in the atmospheric old quarters of Mattancherry and Fort Cochin. In Kerala's far south, the capital, **Thiruvananthapuram** (Trivandrum), is gateway to the nearby palm-fringed beaches of **Kovalam** and **Varkala**, and provides visitors with varied opportunities to sample Kerala's rich cultural and artistic life.

One of the best aspects of exploring Kerala, though, is the actual travelling – especially by **boat**, in the spellbinding Kuttanad region, around historic **Kollam** (Quilon) and **Alappuzha** (Alleppey); travellers are increasingly setting out from **Kumarakom** too. Cruisers and beautiful wooden barges known as *kettu vallam* ("tied boats") ply the **backwaters**, offering tourists a window on village life in India's most densely populated state. Furthermore, it's easy to escape the heat of the lowlands by heading for the **hills**, which rise to 2695m. Roads pass through landscapes dotted with churches and temples, tea, coffee, spice and rubber plantations, and natural forests, en route to wildlife reserves such as **Periyar**, where herds of mud-caked elephants roam freely in vast tracts of jungle.

Kerala is short on the historic monuments prevalent elsewhere in India, and most of its ancient **temples** are closed to non-Hindus. Following an unwritten law, few buildings in the region, whether houses or temples, are higher than the surrounding trees, which in urban areas often creates the illusion that you're surrounded by forest. Typical features of both domestic and temple architecture include long, sloping tiled and gabled roofs that minimize the excesses of rain and sunshine, and pillared verandas; the definitive examples are Thiruvananthapuram's **Puttan Malika Palace**, and **Padmanabhapuram Palace**, in neighbouring Tamil Nadu but easily reached from the capital.

BEST TIME TO VISIT

The period from **December to February** is generally considered to be the best time to visit Kerala, especially if you're planning some beach time – the skies are blue and the humidity isn't too fierce. From March the heat builds up until the skies open in June for the state's first **monsoon**, which lasts until August and is more intense than October's "retreating" monsoon. A word of warning, however, for budget travellers. Kerala's **accommodation** is pricey (though it tends to be of a high standard) and in high season cheap places to stay are thin on the ground everywhere, but especially in the hill stations and backwater areas, where it's not uncommon to pay upwards of ₹2000 for a room in a modest guesthouse. March, April and May are good months to negotiate discounts and the best time to hike in the cooler climes of the Western Ghats.

Summer is noted for its festivals (see box, p.301), including the traditional snake boat races held during monsoon.

KETTU VALLAM, THE BACKWATERS

Highlights

❶ Varkala Chill out in a clifftop café, sunbathe on the beach or soak up the atmosphere around the town's busy temple tank. **See p.313**

❷ The backwaters Explore the beautiful waterways of Kerala's densely populated coastal strip on a rice barge or punted canoe, following the narrow, overgrown canals right into the heart of the villages. **See box, p.322**

❸ Hiking around Munnar The tea plantations, grassy mountains and dazzling viewpoints around Munnar are the perfect antidote to the heat and humidity of the coast. **See p.333**

❹ Fort Cochin Dutch, Portuguese, British and traditional Keralan townhouses line the backstreets of Malabar's old peninsular port.

Stay in a heritage hotel, see the fisherman hauling their catch at sunrise and take in a performance of *kathakali* – elaborately costumed ritual theatre. **See p.337**

❺ Temple festivals Parades of extravagantly decorated elephants, backed by drummers and firework displays, form the focal point of Kerala's Hindu festivals, among them Thrissur's famed Puram; you can also see intimate *theyyem* spirit-possession rituals in the north of the state. **See boxes, p.350 & p.358**

❻ Wayanad Engage a local guide to take you on foot to explore the dense forests and grasslands that cover this isolated mountain region. **See p.355**

HIGHLIGHTS ARE MARKED ON THE MAP ON P.300

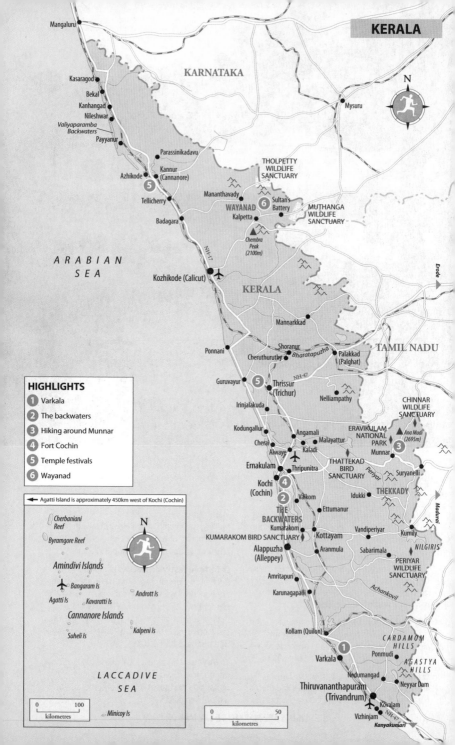

FESTIVALS IN KERALA

Huge amounts of money are lavished upon many, varied, and often all-night **festivals** associated with Kerala's temples. Fireworks rend the air, while processions of caparisoned elephants are accompanied by some of the loudest (and deftest) drum orchestras in the world. Thrissur's famous **Puram** festival (see box, p.350) is the most astonishing, but smaller events take place throughout the state, with everyone welcome to attend. Between December and March it's possible to spend weeks hopping between village **theyyems** in northern Kerala, experiencing rituals little altered in centuries (see box, p.358). The **snake boat races** in June, August and September are an incredible sight, while **Christmas** sees paper lanterns and fairy lights decorating homes and churches. Kerala's Hindu festivals are fixed according to the Malayalam Calendar, so dates change from year to year – see ⓦ keralatourism.org.

Swathi Sangeetotsavam (Jan). Held in honour of composer Sri Swathi Thirunal (maharaja of Travancore 1813–46), free evening performances of Karnatic and Hindustani music take place on the raised porch of Thiruvananthapuram's Puttan Malika Palace (see p.304), with spectators seated on the lawn.

Maha Shivrati (Usually early March; the moonless night). The night of the worship of Shiva is an all-night vigil at temples across the state. A *shivalingam* rises out of the banks of the River Periyar near Kochi, attracting thousands of devotees.

Vishu (Mid-April). A festival of lights and fireworks on Hindu New Year's Day. On this day it's believed that the first object seen is auspicious, so items including rice, fruit, flowers and gold are set out in homes.

Nehru Trophy Snake Boat Race (Second Sat in Aug). The most spectacular of the boat races attracts huge crowds to Punnamda Lake near Alappuzha (see p.319). Following a grand procession, the magnificently decorated longboats – each carrying more than one hundred oarsmen rowing to the rhythmic *vanchipattu* ("song of the boatman") – compete in knockout rounds. Similar races can be seen at Aranmula (Aug–Sept) and Champakulam (June–July).

Onam (Ten days in Aug or Sept). Kerala's harvest festival is marked by singing, *kathakali*, *pookalam* (floral "carpets"), traditional food and in Thrissur, *pulikali* (the dance of the tigers). Four of the days are state holidays.

6

As well as **festivals** (see box above), **theatre** and **dance** also abound; not only the region's own female classical dance form, **mohiniyattam** ("dance of the enchantress"), but also the martial-art-influenced **kathakali** dance drama, which has for four centuries brought gods and demons from the Mahabharata and Ramayana to Keralan villages. Its two-thousand-year-old predecessor, the Sanskrit drama **kudiyattam**, is still performed by a handful of artists, while localized rituals known as **theyyem** (see box, p.358), where dancers wearing decorative masks and hats become "possessed" by temple deities, remain a potent ingredient of village life in the north of the state.

Brief history

Ancient Kerala is mentioned as the land of the **Cheras** in a third-century-BC Ashokan edict, and in several even older Sanskrit texts, including the Mahabharata. Pliny and Ptolemy also testify to thriving trade between the ancient port of Muziris (now known as Kodungallur) and the Roman Empire. Kodungallur is also tipped to be where one of the twelve disciples, St Thomas, first set foot in 52 AD; today Christians account for some 21 percent of Kerala's population. Little is known about the region's early rulers, whose dominion covered a large area, but whose capital, Vanji, has not so far been identified. At the start of the ninth century, King Kulashekhara Alvar – a poet-saint of the Vaishnavite *bhakti* movement known as the *alvars* – established his own dynasty. His son and successor, Rajashekharavarman, is thought to have been a saint of the parallel Shaivite movement, the *nayannars*. The great Keralan philosopher **Shankaracharya**, whose *advaitya* ("non-dualist") philosophy influenced the whole of Hindu India, was alive at this time.

Eventually, the prosperity acquired by the Cheras through trade with China and the Arab world proved too much of an attraction for the neighbouring **Chola** empire, which embarked upon a hundred years of sporadic warfare with the Cheras at the end of the tenth century. Around 1100, the Cheras lost their capital at Mahodayapuram in the north, and shifted south to establish a new capital at Kollam (Quilon).

Direct trade with Europe commenced in 1498 with the arrival in the capital, Calicut, of a small Portuguese fleet under **Vasco da Gama** – the first expedition to reach the coast of India via the Cape of Good Hope and Arabian Sea. After an initial show of cordiality, relations between him and the local ruler, or Zamorin, quickly degenerated, and da Gama's second voyage four years later was characterized by appalling massacres, kidnapping, mutilation and barefaced piracy. Nevertheless, a fortified trading post was soon established at Cochin from which the Portuguese, exploiting old enmities between the region's rulers, were able to dominate trade with the Middle East. This was gradually eroded away over the ensuing century by rival powers France and Holland. An independent territory was subsequently carved out of the Malabar Coast by Tipu Sultan of Mysore, but his defeat in 1792 left the British in control right up until Independence.

Kerala can claim some of the most startling **radical** credentials in India. In 1957 it was the first state in the world to democratically elect a communist government, and still regularly returns communist parties in elections. Due to reforms made during the 1960s and 1970s, Kerala currently has the most equitable land distribution of any Indian state. Poverty appears far less acute than in other parts of the country, with life expectancy and per capita income well above the national averages. Kerala is also justly proud of its reputation for healthcare and education, with **literacy** rates that stand, officially at least, at 96 percent for men and 92 percent for women. Industrial development is negligible, however: potential investors from outside tend to fight shy of dealing with such a politicized workforce.

Thiruvananthapuram

Kerala's capital, **THIRUVANANTHAPURAM** (still widely known as **Trivandrum**), is set on seven low hills just a couple of kilometres inland from the Arabian Sea. Despite its administrative importance – demonstrated by wide roads, multistorey office blocks and gleaming white colonial buildings – it's an easy-going state capital by Indian standards, with enclaves of traditional red-tiled gabled houses breaking up the bustle of its modern concrete core, and a swathe of parkland spreading north of the centre. Although its principal sight, the **Sri Padmanabhaswamy temple**, is closed to non-Hindus, the city holds enough of interest to fill a day. Foremost among its attractions is the splendid **Puttan Malika Palace**, one of the state's best museums, and a typically Keralan market, **Chalai Bazaar**.

Both the palace and bazaar are in the oldest and most interesting part of the city, the **Fort** area in the south. At the opposite, northern side of the centre, the **Sri Chitra Art Gallery** and **Napier Museum** showcase painting, crafts and sculpture in a leafy park. In addition, schools specializing in the martial art *kalarippayat* and the dance/theatre forms of **kathakali** and **kudiyattam** offer an insight into the Keralan obsession with physical training and skill.

Sri Padmanabhaswamy temple

Padmanabha, the god Vishnu reclined on a coiled serpent with a lotus flower sprouting from his belly button, is the presiding deity of the **Sri Padmanabhaswamy temple**, a vast complex of interlocking walled courtyards, shrines and ceremonial walkways in the south of the city. The iconic image of the temple's seven-tiered, Tamil-style *gopura* gateway, reflected in the waters of the adjacent bathing tank, graced the front pages of many newspapers across the world in June 2011 when it was discovered that a vast horde of **treasure** had been discovered in vaults below its inner sanctum. Sealed inside the secret chambers were sacks of diamonds, a thousand kilograms of gold, thousands

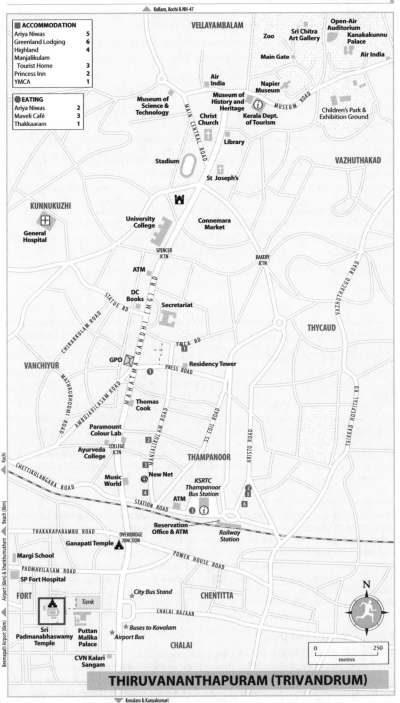

THIRUVANANTHAPURAM (TRIVANDRUM)

6

KERALAN RITUAL THEATRE

Among the most magical experiences a visitor to Kerala can have is to witness one of the innumerable ancient drama rituals that play such an important role in the cultural life of the region. **Kathakali** is the best known; other less publicized forms, which clearly influenced its development, include the classical Sanskrit **kudiyattam**.

Many Keralan forms share broad characteristics. A prime aim of each performer is to transform the mundane into the world of gods and demons; his preparation is highly ritualized, involving otherworldly costume and mask-like make-up. In *kathakali* and *kudiyattam*, this preparation is a rigorously codified part of the classical tradition.

One-off **performances** of various ritual types take place throughout the state, building up to fever pitch during April and May before pausing for the monsoon (June–Aug). Finding out about such events requires a little perseverance, but it's well worth the effort; enquire at tourist offices, or buy a Malayalam daily paper such as the *Malayalam Manorama* and ask someone to check the listings for temple festivals – most of the action invariably takes place within the temples. Tourist *kathakali* is staged daily in **Kochi** (see p.339) but to find authentic performances, contact **performing arts schools** such as Thiruvananthapuram's Margi (see p.306) and Cheruthuruthy's Kerala Kalamandalam (see p.353); *kudiyattam* artists work at both, as well as at Natana Kairali at Irinjalakuda, which is accessible from Thrissur (see p.352).

KATHAKALI

Here is the tradition of the trance dancers, here is the absolute demand of the subjugation of body to spirit, here is the realization of the cosmic transformation of human into divine.

Mrinalini Sarabhai, classical dancer

The image of a *kathakali* actor in a magnificent costume with extraordinary make-up and a huge gold crown has become Kerala's trademark. Traditional performances, of which there are still many, usually take place on open ground outside a temple, beginning at 10pm and lasting until dawn, illuminated by the flickers of a large brass oil lamp centre-stage. Virtually nothing about *kathakali* is naturalistic, because it depicts the world of gods and demons; men play both the male and female roles.

Standing at the back of the stage, two musicians play driving rhythms, one on a bronze gong, the other on heavy bell-metal cymbals; they also sing the dialogue. Actors appear and disappear from behind a hand-held curtain and never utter a sound, save the odd strange cry. Learning the elaborate hand gestures, facial expressions and choreographed movements, as articulate and precise as any sign language, requires rigorous training which can begin at the age of 8 and last ten years. At least two more **drummers** stand left of the stage; one plays the upright *chenda* with slender curved sticks, the other plays the *maddalam*, a horizontal barrel-shaped hand drum. When a female character is "speaking", the *chenda* is replaced by the hourglass-shaped *ettaka*, a "talking drum" on which melodies can be played. The drummers

---

of pieces of gem-encrusted jewellery and, the pièce de résistance, an exquisite 1m-tall gold **image of Vishnu** shimmering with precious stones. Experts are still debating the value of the items, with estimates ranging from US$40–200 billion. Either way, the find makes this by far the richest place of worship in the world.

Non-Hindus are unfortunately not permitted inside, but the main approach road to Sri Padmanabhaswamy, with its stalls full of religious souvenirs and offerings, makes an atmospheric place for a stroll, particularly in the early morning when worshippers take ritual baths in the tank.

Puttan Malika Palace

Tues–Sun 8.30am–12.45pm & 3–4.45pm • ₹50, camera ₹30; guided tour only

The **Puttan Malika Palace**, immediately southeast of the Sri Padmanabhaswamy temple, became the seat of the Travancore rajas after they left Padmanabhapuram at the end of the nineteenth century. The cool chambers, with highly polished plaster floors and

keep their eyes on the actors, whose every gesture is reinforced by their sound, from the gentlest embrace to the gory disembowelling of an enemy.

Although it bears the unmistakeable influences of *kudiyattam* and indigenous folk rituals, *kathakali*, literally "story-play", is thought to have crystallized into a distinct theatre form during the seventeenth century. The plays are based on three major sources: the **Hindu epics** the Mahabharata, Ramayana and the Bhagavata Purana. While the stories are ostensibly about god-heroes such as Rama and Krishna, the most popular characters are those that give the most scope to the actors – the villainous, fanged, red-and-black-faced *katti* ("knife") antiheroes; these types, such as the kings Ravana and Duryodhana, are dominated by lust, greed, envy and violence. David Bolland's *Guide to Kathakali*, widely available in Kerala, gives invaluable scene-by-scene summaries of the most popular plays and explains in simple language a lot more besides.

When **attending a performance**, arrive early to get your bearings before it gets dark, even though the first play will not begin much before 10pm. (Quiet) members of the audience are welcome to visit the dressing room before and during the performance. The colour and design of the mask-like make-up, which specialist artists take several hours to apply, reveal the character's personality. The word *pacha* means both "green" and "pure"; a green-faced *pacha* character is thus a noble human or god. Red signifies *rajas*, passion and aggression; black denotes *tamas*, darkness and negativity; and white is *sattvik*, light and intellect. Once the make-up is completed, elaborate wide skirts are tied to the waist, and ornaments of silver and gold are added. Silver talons are fitted to the left hand. The transformation is complete with a final prayer and the donning of waist-length wig and crown. Visitors new to *kathakali* will almost undoubtedly get bored during such long programmes, parts of which are very slow indeed. If you're at a village performance, you may not always find accommodation, so you can't leave during the night. Be prepared to sit on the ground for hours, and bring some warm clothes. Half the fun is staying up all night to witness, just as the dawn light appears, the gruesome disembowelling of a villain or a demon *asura*.

KUDIYATTAM

Three families of the Chakyar caste and a few outsiders perform the Sanskrit drama **kudiyattam**, the oldest continually performed theatre form in the world. Until recently it was only performed inside temples and then only in front of the uppermost castes. Visually it is very similar to its offspring, *kathakali*, but its atmosphere is infinitely more archaic. The actors, eloquent in sign language and symbolic movement, speak in the compelling intonation of the local brahmins' Vedic chant, unchanged since 1500 BC.

A single act of a *kudiyattam* play can require ten full nights; the entire play takes forty. A great actor, in full command of the subtleties of gestural expression, can take half an hour to do such a simple thing as murder a demon, berate the audience or simply describe a leaf fall to the ground. Unlike *kathakali*, *kudiyattam* includes comic characters and plays. The ubiquitous Vidushaka, narrator and clown, is something of a court jester, and traditionally has held the right to criticize openly the highest in the land without fear of retribution.

delicately carved wooden screens, house a crop of dusty royal heirlooms, including a solid crystal throne gifted by the Dutch. The real highlight, however, is the elegant Keralan architecture itself. Beneath sloping red-tiled roofs, hundreds of wooden pillars, carved into the forms of rampant horses (*puttan malika* translates as "horse palace"), prop up the eaves, and airy verandas project onto the surrounding lawns.

The royal family have always been keen patrons of the arts, and the **Swathi Sangeetotsavam festival**, held in the grounds in January, continues this tradition (see box, p.301).

CVN Kalari Sangam

S St, East Fort • Fighting exercises Mon–Sat 6.30–8am • ☎ 0471 247 4182, ⓦ cvnkalari.in

Around 500m southeast of the temple in East Fort, the redbrick **CVN Kalari Sangam** ranks among Kerala's top **kalarippayat** gymnasiums. It was founded in 1956 by C.V. Narayanan Nair, one of the legendary figures credited for the martial art's revival, and attracts students from across the world. Every morning except Sunday you can watch fighting exercises in the sunken *kalari* pit that forms the heart of the complex. Foreigners may join courses, arranged through the head teacher, or *gurukkal*, although prior experience of martial arts and/or dance is a prerequisite.

Chalai Bazaar

Thiruvananthapuram's main source of fresh produce and everyday items is the kilometre-long **Chalai Bazaar**, which runs east from MG Road in East Fort, from opposite the main approach to the temple. Lined with little shops selling flowers, incense, spices, bell-metal lamps and fireworks, it's a great area for aimless browsing (most shops open daily 10am–8pm). On your left (north side) as you enter the street, look out for **United Umbrella Mart**, which sells brightly coloured temple parasols used in elephant processions. Further down on the opposite side of the road, the delightfully old-fashioned **Ambal Coffee Works** is another source of authentic Keralan souvenirs.

Margi School

West Fort · ☎ 0471 247 8806, ⓦ margitheatre.org

Thiruvananthapuram has for centuries been a crucible for Keralan classical arts, and the **Margi School**, at the western corner of the Fort area, is one of the foremost colleges for **kathakali** dance drama and the more rarely performed **kudiyattam** theatre form (see box, p.304). Most visitors venture out here to watch one of the authentic *kathakali* or *kudiyattam* performances staged once each month in its small **theatre**, details of which are posted on the school's website.

To reach Margi, head to the SP Fort Hospital on the western edge of Fort and then continue 200m north; the school is set back from the west side of the main road in a large red-tiled and tin-roofed building, behind the High School (the sign is in Malayalam).

Napier Museum

LMS Vallayambalam Rd · Tues–Sun 10am–5pm · ₹10

A minute's walk east from the north end of MG Road, opposite Kerala Tourism's information office, brings you to the entrance to Thiruvananthapuram's **public gardens**. As well as serving as a welcome refuge from the noise of the city, the park holds the city's best museums. Give the dusty and uninformative Natural History Museum a miss and head instead for the more engaging **Napier Museum**. Built at the end of the nineteenth century, it was an early experiment in what became known as the "Indo-Saracenic" style, with tiled, gabled roofs, garish red-, black- and salmon-patterned brickwork, and a spectacular interior of stained-glass windows and loud turquoise, pink, red and yellow stripes. Highlights of the collection include fifteenth-century Keralan woodcarvings, terrifying Ceylonese (Sri Lankan) masks, a carved temple chariot (*rath*) and Chola and Vijayanagar bronzes.

Sri Chitra Art Gallery

Next to Zoological Gardens · Tues–Sun 10am–5pm · ₹20

You pass through the main ticket booth for the city's depressing, faded zoo to reach the **Sri Chitra Art Gallery**, which shows paintings from the Rajput, Mughal and Tanjore schools, along with pieces from China, Tibet and Japan. The meat of the collection, though, is made up of works by the celebrated artist **Raja Ravi Varma** (1848–1906), a local aristocrat who achieved fame and fortune as a producer of Hindu mythological prints – forerunners of India's quirky calendar art. Varma's style was much criticized by later generations for its sentimentality and strong Western influence, but in his time he was regarded as the nation's greatest living artist.

Also on view at the Sri Chitra, in rooms to the rear of the main building, are a couple of minor **Tagores**, and some striking, strongly coloured Himalayan landscapes by the Russian artist-philosopher and mystic, **Nicholas Roerich**, who resided in the Himalayan Kullu Valley for two decades until his death in 1947.

ARRIVAL AND DEPARTURE   THIRUVANANTHAPURAM   **6**

BY PLANE
Beemapalli airport Connected to most major Indian cities, as well as Sri Lanka, the Maldives and the Middle East, Beemapalli airport lies 6km southwest of town. You'll find a Kerala Tourism information booth (in theory 24hr), ATM, Vodafone stand (where you can buy an Indian SIM) and a Thomas Cook foreign exchange facility just before the exit of the arrivals concourse.

GETTING INTO TOWN
By shuttle The best way to get to and from the airport is on the a/c airport bus (₹30), which runs between the arrivals concourse and the City bus stand in East Fort. See ⓦ aanavandi.com for the schedule.
By auto-rickshaw and taxi Auto-rickshaws can get you into the centre for around ₹150 and there's also a handy prepaid taxi service (pay before departure; ₹350 for Thiruvananthapuram railway station, ₹500 for Kovalam's Lighthouse Beach).

BY BUS
Interstate buses The long-distance KSRTC Thampanoor bus station is opposite the railway station in the southeast of the city, within walking distance of most of the city's budget accommodation. This is the place to catch services to Varkala as well as long-distance buses heading north up the coast (to Kollam, Alappuzha, Ernakulam or Thrissur). For the latter aim for the 6am or 5.30pm "super-deluxe a/c" specials – you can buy tickets for all long-distance routes at the reservations hatch, main bus stand concourse (daily 6am–10pm). The Tamil Nadu bus company, TNSRTC,

has its own counter on the same concourse. Numerous private bus companies also run interstate services; many of the agents are on Aristo Rd near the *Greenland Lodging*.
Local services Local buses (including those for Kovalam) depart from City bus stand, in East Fort, a 10min walk south from the KSRTC Thampanoor and railway stations. Services to Kovalam leave from the stand on the roadside – be prepared for a crush if you attempt this journey in the late-afternoon rush hour.
Destinations Alappuzha/Alleppey (every 15–20min; 3hr 30min); Ernakulam/Kochi (every 30min; 5hr); Kanyakumari (5 daily; 2hr 15min); Kollam/Quilon (every 15–20min; 1hr 40min); Kovalam (from East Fort; every 20–30min); Kumily/Periyar (3 daily; 7hr 45min); Madurai (8 daily; 7hr); Neyyar Dam (hourly; 1hr 30min); Varkala (8 daily; 90min).

BY TRAIN
Kerala's capital is well connected by train with other towns and cities. Although you can buy a ticket just before departure, getting seats at short notice on long-haul journeys can be a problem, so make reservations as far in advance as possible from the efficient computerized booking office at the station (24hr). There's a handy prepaid auto-rickshaw counter on the arrivals concourse.
Destinations Alappuzha/Alleppey (10 daily; 2hr 15min–3hr); Chennai/Madras (6 daily; 16hr–17hr 30min); Ernakulam/Kochi (25 daily; 3hr 25min–5hr 15min); Kanyakumari (2 daily; 2hr 40min–3hr); Kollam/Quilon (31 daily; 55min–1hr 20min); Madurai (3 daily; 6hr 50min–10hr 50min); Varkala (20 daily; 35min).

RECOMMENDED TRAINS FROM THIRUVANANTHAPURAM
The following trains are recommended as the fastest and/or most convenient from Thiruvananthapuram.

Destination	Name	No.	Departs	Arrives
Alappuzha	*Netravati Express**	#16346	daily 9.50am	12.45pm
Chennai	*Chennai Mail**	#12624	daily 2.40pm	7.20am+
Ernakulam/Kochi	*Jan Shatabdi*	#12082	daily 2.30pm	6.20pm
Kanyakumari	*Kanyakumari Express*	#16381	daily 9.55am	12.30pm
Kollam	*Kerala Express*	#12625	daily 11.15am	12.10pm
Madurai	*Anantapuri Express*	#16724	daily 4.10pm	11pm

*via Kollam, Varkala, Kottayam and Ernakulam, + = next day

6

INFORMATION AND TOURS

Tourist information In addition to at the airport (see p.307), Kerala Tourism has an information counter at the KSRTC Thampanoor bus station (Mon–Sat 10am–5pm; ☎ 0471 232 7224), while in Vellayambalam on Museum Rd, next to the unremarkable Museum of History and Heritage, KTDC hosts a visitor reception centre where you can book accommodation in their hotel chain and tickets for various guided tours (daily 7am–9pm; ☎ 0471 232 1132).

Tours Most of the KTDC tours, including the city tours (daily 1.30–6.45pm; ₹400), are too rushed, but if you're really pushed for time and want to reach the tip of India, try the Kanyakumari tour (daily 7.30am–9pm; ₹700), which takes in Padmanabhapuram Palace (except Mon), Suchindram Temple and Kanyakumari in Tamil Nadu.

ACCOMMODATION

Accommodation is a lot easier on the pocket in Thiruvananthapuram than at nearby Kovalam Beach. That said, this is one city where budget travellers, in particular, should consider spending a couple of hundred rupees more than they might usually.

Ariya Niwas Manorama Rd, Thampanoor ☎ 0471 233 0789, ✉ ariyanivas.tvm@gmail.com. Large, spotless and airy rooms with comfy beds and great city views from its upper floors. Good value, 24hr checkout and just 2min walk from the railway station, with an excellent "meals" restaurant on the ground floor (see below). A/c ₹1100 extra. ₹1070

Greenland Lodging Aristo Rd, Thampanoor ☎ 0471 232 8114. An efficient lodge with immaculate rooms (some a/c). The best low-cost option near the bus stand and railway station – though you'll have to book ahead. ₹680

Highland Manjalikulam Rd, Thampanoor ☎ 0471 233 3200, ⊕ highland-hotels.com. The rooms in this lower-to mid-range option fail to live up to the promise of the six-storey concrete-and-tinted-glass facade, but it's well managed, a short walk from the stations, and easy to find. A/c ₹700 extra. ₹1100

Manjalikulam Tourist Home Manjalikulam Rd, Thampanoor ☎ 0471 233 0776, ⊕ manjalikulam.com.

Don't be fooled by the shining glass-and-marble ground floor – above lurks a basic budget place offering variously priced rooms, all of them clean and with good, comfy mattresses. No single occupancy. A/c ₹500 extra. ₹700

Princess Inn Manjalikulam Rd, Thampanoor ☎ 0471 233 9150, ✉ princess_inn@yahoo.com. Well-scrubbed, respectable cheapie close to the stations. One of the more welcoming and better-value small hotels in this busy enclave, though it's a bit more of a plod up the lane from Station Rd than some. A/c ₹400 extra. ₹900

★ **YMCA** YMCA Rd, near the Secretariat ☎ 0471 233 0059, ⊕ ymcatvm.org. Neat, smartly furnished rooms at good rates for the levels of comfort. The "luxury" options (₹1200) are enormous and have high ceilings, quiet fans (some with a/c), TVs and spacious bathrooms. Not the bargain it once was, but you'll still need to book at least two weeks in advance. No wi-fi. ₹800

EATING

Freshly cooked dosas, *idli-vada-sambhar*, biryanis and other traditional snacks are available at streetside cafés across town, including the perennially popular **Indian Coffee House** chain, which runs several branches in the city centre – most famously the circular *Maveli Café* next to the KSRTC bus stand in Thampanoor.

★ **Ariya Niwas** Ariya Niwas hotel, Manorama Rd, Thampanoor. Top-class South Indian vegetarian thalis (₹100) dished up on banana leaves in a scrupulously clean non-a/c dining room on the hotel's ground floor, or in the pricier a/c dining hall on the first storey. Hugely popular with everyone, and deservedly so: there's nowhere better to eat in the city. Daily 7.30am–9.30pm.

Maveli Café Next to the bus station on Station Rd, Thampanoor ☎ 0471 321 4505. Part of the *Indian Coffee House* chain, this bizarre redbrick, spiral-shaped café (designed by the renowned expatriate British architect, Laurie Baker) is a Thiruvananthapuram institution. Inside, waiters in the trademark *ICH pugris* serve dosas (₹40),

vadas, greasy omelettes, mountainous biryanis (meat ₹105, ₹veg 55) and china cups of the usual (weak and sugary) filter coffee. An obligatory pit stop, though a grubby one. Daily 7am–10pm.

Thakkaaram Pulimood Junction, Press Rd ☎ 97454 64444 or ☎ 97454 74444. On the ground floor of Naaz Tower, this cool and clean non-veg a/c restaurant serves mouthwatering Malabari food in booths that look like train carriages. The menu is tricky to navigate, but you can't go wrong with the *kozhi chuttathu* (chargrilled chicken; ₹230 for half) and roti fresh from the *tandoor* (₹20). Great lunchtime biryani specials too (₹229 with tea and dessert). Daily noon–11pm.

DIRECTORY

Banks and exchange A string of big banks along MG Rd have ATMs and change currency; there are additional ATMs next to the information counter across the road from the railway station, and immediately outside the station exit, next to the reservations hall. Thomas Cook has a foreign exchange counter at the airport and at its travel agency on the ground floor of the Soundarya Building (near the big Raymond's tailoring store), MG Rd (Mon–Sat 9.30am–6pm). **Hospitals** SP Fort Hospital (☎ 0471 245 0540), just down the road from the Margi School in West Fort, has a 24hr casualty and specialist orthopaedic unit; the private Cosmopolitan Hospital in Pattom (☎ 0471 244 8182) is also recommended. **Internet** New Net on Manjalikulam Rd charges ₹30/hr and is convenient if you're staying in Thampanoor.

Kovalam

6

You have to envy the travellers who discovered **KOVALAM** back in the 1970s. Before the appearance of the crowds and sunbeds that nowadays spill over the resort's quartet of beaches, not to mention the warren of hotels, shops and restaurants crammed into the palm groves behind them, this must have been a heavenly location. Four decades of unplanned development, however, have wrought havoc on the famous headland and its golden sand bays. Virtually every conceivable patch of dry ground behind the most spectacular of them, **Lighthouse Beach**, has been buried under concrete, but it's still a popular base for Ayurveda and yoga. The proximity of Kovalam to the city means domestic tourism is booming; closest to the bus and taxi stand, **Howah Beach** in particular attracts a lot of day-trippers, who leave behind a trail of rubbish.

Kovalam beaches

Kovalam consists of **four coves**, each with markedly different characters. It takes around 45 minutes to an hour to walk from one end of them to the other, but there's no shortage of potential pit stops along the way to restore your energies.

Lighthouse Beach

The largest and most developed cove at Kovalam, known for obvious reasons as **Lighthouse Beach**, is where most foreign tourists congregate. Lined by a paved esplanade, its seafront of shops and hotels extends along the full length of the bay, overlooked by the eponymous **lighthouse** at the southern end (daily 3–5pm; ₹25 [₹10], camera ₹20). You can scale the 142 spiral steps and twelve ladder rungs to the observation platform for a fine view.

Hawah Beach

A small rocky headland divides Lighthouse Beach from **Hawah Beach** (or **Eve's Beach**) – almost a mirror image of its busier neighbour, although backed for most of its length by empty palm groves. In the morning, before the sun-worshippers arrive, it functions as a base for local fishermen, who hand-haul their massive nets through the shallows, singing and chanting as they coil the endless piles of rope.

Kovalam Beach

Kovalam Beach, the third of the coves, is dominated from on high by the angular chalets of the five-star *Leela* resort. Coachloads of excited Keralan day-trippers descend here on weekends, but at other times it offers a peaceful alternative to the beaches further south. To get there, follow the road downhill past the bus terminus.

WARNING: SWIMMING SAFETY IN KOVALAM

Due to unpredictable rip currents and a strong undertow, especially during the monsoons, **swimming** from Kovalam's beaches is not always safe. The introduction of blue-shirted lifeguards has reduced the annual death toll, but at least a couple of tourists still drown here each year, and many more get into difficulties. Follow the warnings of the safety flags at all times and keep a close eye on children. There's a first-aid post midway along Lighthouse Beach.

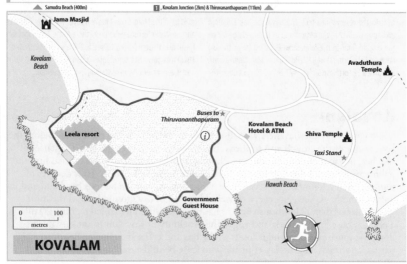

KOVALAM

Samudra Beach

The most northerly of Kovalam's quartet, **Samudra Beach** was until recently a European package-tourist stronghold. Nowadays the large hotels clustered just beyond it, on the far side of a low, rocky headland, host mainly metropolitan Indian and Russian holiday-makers.

ARRIVAL AND INFORMATION   KOVALAM

By bus Buses from Thiruvananthapuram loop through the top of the village before coming to a halt outside the gates of the *Leela* resort, on the promontory dividing Hawah and Kovalam beaches. If you don't intend to stay at this northern end of the resort, get down just after *Hotel Blue Sea* where the road bends – a lane branching to the left drops steeply downhill towards the top of Hawah Beach. The bus journey generally takes 30 to 45 minutes. Heading in the other direction (into the city) pick up the bus from outside the gates of the *Leela*. Long-distance services heading down the coast towards Kanyakumari stop at

Kovalam Junction on the main highway.
By auto-rickshaw or taxi You can cover the 14km from Thiruvananthapuram more quickly by auto-rickshaw (₹150–200) or taxi (₹500–600).
Tourist information The friendly tourist office (daily 10am–5pm, closed Sun in low season; ☏0471 248 0085, ⊛keralatourism.org), just inside the *Leela* resort gates, close to where the buses pull in, stocks the usual range of glossy leaflets and can offer up-to-date advice about cultural events in the area.

ACCOMMODATION

Kovalam is chock-full of **accommodation** in all categories. Little of it could be considered great value by Keralan standards, but you may be able to pick up last-minute discounts outside the Dec/Jan high season. Expect to be plagued by commission touts as you arrive; to avoid them, approach via the back paths.

★**Amruthamgamaya (Amrutam)** Panagodu, near Venganoor, 6km northeast ☏0880 6020629 or ☏09967 222152, ⊛amruthamgamaya.com. A great option if you want to base yourself away from the busy coastal strip, but within striking distance of the beaches. It's essentially an Ayurveda centre, but with comfortable accommodation in beautiful, large rooms overlooking a terraced garden. Veg meals are served on a high rooftop overlooking a sea of palm trees, and there's a gorgeous pool. Great value, but

tricky to find: phone ahead for directions. Rates are for double occupancy and include superb Keralan food. Half board ₹8000, full board ₹8500
Beach Hotel II Above Fusion restaurant, Lighthouse Beach ☏0471 248 6575, ⊛thebeachhotel-kovalam .com. Stylish, German-run hotel at the quiet end of Lighthouse Beach. Its twelve rooms (some a/c) all have big, sea-facing balconies, and are light, spacious and airy, with terracotta-tiled floors and block-printed cotton bedspreads.

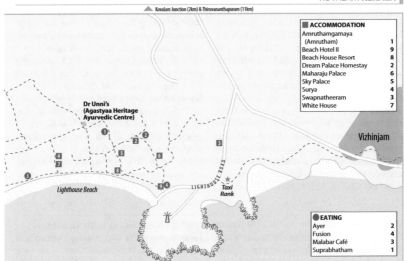

Kovalam Junction (2km) & Thiruvananthapuram (11km)

ACCOMMODATION

Amruthamgamaya (Amrutham)	1
Beach Hotel II	9
Beach House Resort	8
Dream Palace Homestay	2
Maharaju Palace	6
Sky Palace	5
Surya	4
Swapnatheeram	3
White House	7

Dr Unni's (Agastyaa Heritage Ayurvedic Centre)

Vizhinjam

Lighthouse Beach

Taxi Rank

EATING

Ayer	2
Fusion	4
Malabar Café	3
Suprabhatham	1

Not to be confused with its sister concern, *Beach Hotel I*, below *Waves* restaurant, which isn't nearly as nice. A/c ₹1000 extra. **₹4000**

Beach House Resort Lighthouse Beach ☏81294 13850 (Naza). Tiny, garish yellow place on the seafront offering unusually large rooms with kitchenettes that have a fridge. Sadly the wood-panelled penthouse has had a permanent resident these last couple of years, but the two rooms below each have a breezy balcony and sea view. A/c 800 extra. **₹2000**

Dream Palace Homestay Lighthouse Beach ☏94472 91922 (John), ✉dreampalacekovalam@gmail.com. Half a dozen pleasant rooms in a modern block set a 3min walk back from the beachfront, with marble floors, dark varnished furniture, sprung mattresses, kitchenettes, fancy headboards and tiny balconies. Excellent value. **₹1000**

Maharaju Palace 30m behind Lighthouse Beach ☏0471 248 5320 or ☏99468 54270, ⌨maharajupalace .com. This Dutch-owned guesthouse, a block in from the beach, offers boutique style at affordable rates. Occupying a modern house in a well-kept tropical garden, its marble-lined rooms are impeccably clean and decorated with Indian handicrafts and comfy cane chairs on the verandas. Breakfast included. **₹3000**

Sky Palace Lighthouse Beach ☏97458 41222. Basic but comfortable option two blocks back from the waterfront, just a thirty-second walk from the beach. The very clean rooms, opening onto a sociable common veranda, are a good size, with gleaming floors and crisp white sheets. **₹800**

Surya Lighthouse Beach ☏0471 248 1012, ✉kovsurya @yahoo.co.in. Professionally run, budget travellers' guest-house down a narrow lane from the seafront. It's secure and quiet, with pleasant rooms for the price. A/c ₹500 extra. If it's full, try the *White House* next door (see below). **₹1000**

Swapnatheeram (formerly Sri Krishna Palace) Lighthouse Beach ☏0471 248 4685, ⌨swapnatheeram .com. Great-value mid-range place run by an exceptionally friendly local family, nestled on the left side of the road a 1min walk from the beach. Their thirteen rooms are spacious and immaculately clean, with quality mattresses and complimentary towels and soap – some, which cost a little more, have sea views. Breakfast included. A/c ₹600 extra. **₹1500**

White House Lighthouse Beach ☏0808 9791292, ✉whitehousekovalamag@gmail.com. Basic guesthouse fronting a leafy plot. Quiet, clean and set back from the beach. Rooms 203 and 204 are the pick of the crop. A/c ₹600 extra. **₹1000**

EATING

Lighthouse Beach is lined with identikit cafés and restaurants specializing in **seafood**: pick from displays of fresh fish, lobster, tiger prawns, crab and mussels that are then weighed, grilled over a charcoal fire or cooked in a *tandoor* (traditional clay oven), and served with rice, salad or chips. Meals are **pricey** by Indian standards and service is often painfully slow, but the food is generally very good and the ambience convivial. **Nightlife** in Kovalam is sedate, revolving around the beachfront cafés. Beer and spirits are served in most places, albeit in discreet china teapots from under the table due to tight liquor restrictions.

Ayer Lighthouse Beach. The open kitchen at this popular Ayurvedic restaurant behind *Hotel California* churns out delicious veggie burgers and curries and has Ayurvedic rice, rye and wholemeal wheat options. The mozzies are particularly ferocious back here, next to their large pond, but friendly staff provide coils to burn under your table. Set dinner ₹430. Daily 7.30am–10pm.

★ **Fusion** Lighthouse Beach. Along with *Waves* further along the main beach, this is the liveliest place in Kovalam, with three innovative menus (Eastern, Western and fusion), served on a first-floor terrace overlooking the bay. Try the fish fillet sautéed in coconut jus, one of the Keralan seafood specialities, or home-made tagliatelle and chilli pesto. Most mains ₹200–550. Daily 7.30am–10pm.

Malabar Café Lighthouse Beach. Deservedly one of the most popular spots on the beachfront, serving a jack-of-all-trades menu of pizzas, burgers, superb tandoori seafood and choose-your-own lobsters, as well as Keralan staples such as fish *pollichathu* (₹350) and fish curry with tapioca (₹350). Most other mains ₹120–350. Daily 7.30am–late.

Suprabhatham Behind Lighthouse beach, next to a small Shiva temple. Simple, popular vegetarian café-restaurant in a well-shaded courtyard, where you can order Indian breakfasts (*idli* ₹80), as well as an extensive multicuisine menu: the "Bengali aubergine" is popular. Staff tend to start on stiff whisky slammers around 10.30pm, after which the service and cooking degenerate rapidly. Daily 8am–11pm.

DIRECTORY

Banks and exchange There's an ATM in the *Kovalam Beach Hotel*, on the road leading up from the southern end of Hawah Beach; otherwise, the nearest are up at Kovalam Junction, 2km inland on the national highway (roughly ₹100 return in an auto-rickshaw), where both ICICI and Canara Bank have sub-branches. Pheroze Framroze, near the entrance to the *Leela* resort and bus stand, offers competitive rates for currency and travellers' cheques.

Tailors Dozens of little tailor shops are crammed in to the alleyways behind Lighthouse Beach; Suku's (near *Keerthi* restaurant) is recommended. You can have light cotton clothes made to measure, or ask them to copy your favourite garment from home, using a wide choice of coloured calico.

South of Kovalam

A tightly packed cluster of tiled fishermens' huts, **VIZHINJAM** (pronounced "Virinyam"), on the opposite (south) side of the headland from Lighthouse Beach, was once the capital of the Ay kings, the earliest dynasty in south Kerala. A number of simple small shrines survive from those times, and can be made the focus of a pleasant afternoon's stroll through coconut groves, best approached from the centre of the village rather than

AYURVEDA IN KERALA

"Health tourism" is very much a buzz phrase in Kerala, and resorts such as Kovalam and Varkala are packed with places to de-stress and detox – the majority of them based on principles of **Ayurveda medicine**. The Keralan approach to India's ancient holistic system of medicine has two distinct elements: first, the body is cleansed of toxins generated by imbalances in lifestyle and diet; secondly, its equilibrium is restored using herbal medicines, mainly in the form of plant oils applied using a range of different **massage** techniques. A practitioner's first prescription will often be a course of **panchakarma** treatment – a five-phase therapy during which harmful impurities are purged through induced vomiting, enemas and the application of medicinal oils poured through the nasal cavity. Other less onerous components, tailored for the individual patient, may include: *dhara*, where the oils are blended with ghee or milk and poured on to the forehead; *pizhichi*, in which four masseurs apply different oils simultaneously; and, the weirdest looking of all, *sirovashti*, where the oils are poured into a tall, topless leather cap placed on the head. Alongside these, patients are prescribed special balancing foods, and given vigorous full-body massages each day.

Standards of both treatment and hygiene vary greatly between establishments, as do the prices. Female travellers also sometimes complain of sexual harassment at the hands of opportunistic male masseurs; cross-gender massage is forbidden in Ayurveda. The application of dodgy oils that can cause skin problems is another risk you might be exposed to at a backstreet clinic. Your best bet is to follow tips from fellow travellers and, if you're unsure, check the state of any treatment rooms in advance.

the coast road – brace yourself for the sharp contrast between hedonistic tourist resort and workaday fishing village. Note too another stark divide: between the Christian quarter to the south, with its towering Catholic church, and Muslim quarter to the north, spreading below a gigantic mosque.

Golden-sand beaches fringe the shore stretching **southwards from Vizhinjam**, interrupted only by the occasional rock outcrop and tidal estuary. This dramatic coastline, with its backdrop of thick coconut plantations, can appear peaceful compared with Kovalam, but it's actually one of the most densely populated corners of the state. Over the past decade, virtually every metre of land backing the prettiest stretches of coast has been bought up and built on. Even so, it's worth renting a scooter to explore the back lanes and more secluded beaches, where poor Christian fishing villages stand in surreal juxtaposition with luxury beach resorts and Ayurveda spas.

6

Padmanabhapuram Palace

50km southeast of Kovalam • Tues–Sun 9am–4.30pm • ₹300 (₹35), camera ₹20 • Frequent buses along the main highway from Thiruvananthapuram and Kovalam; hop on any service heading to Nagercoil or Kanyakumari and get off at Thakkaly (sometimes written Thuckalai)

Although now officially in Tamil Nadu, **PADMANABHAPURAM**, 63km southeast of Thiruvananthapuram, was the capital of Travancore between 1550 and 1750, and maintains its historic links with Kerala, from where it is still administered. With its exquisite wooden interiors, coconut-shell floors and antique furniture and murals, the **palace** represents the apogee of regional building, and fully merits a visit. Just **avoid weekends**, when the complex gets overrun with bus parties.

ACCOMMODATION   **SOUTH OF KOVALAM**

Should you decide to prolong exploring the Vizhinjam coastline and its surrounds, you can choose from a few lovely resorts and **heritage properties**.

Bethsaida Hermitage Pulinkudi ☎ 0471 226 7554, ⓦ bethsaidahermitage.com. An "ecofriendly Ayurveda beach resort" with a difference. The huge, well-furnished rooms in brick cottages or imposing modern blocks, two large pools, à la carte restaurant and prime location next to a beautiful cove are standard for the area – here, however, the profits support a church-run orphanage, a great initiative that's been doing a fine job for more than a decade. ₹8000

Thapovan Nellinkunnu ☎ 0471 248 0453, ⓦ thapovan .com. This German-run heritage resort comprises two parts: one in a grove by the seashore, and another higher up the cliffside. The latter's elevated position and views across the palm canopy to Vizhinjam give it the edge. The traditional teak chalets and gardens are lovely. ₹5985

Travancore Heritage Chowara ☎ 0471 226 7828, ⓦ thetravancoreheritage.com. The centrepiece of this extravagant complex is a splendid 150-year-old mansion, fronted by a kidney-shaped pool and sun terrace. Below it are sixty relocated antique bungalows (₹8000–12,000), some boasting alfresco garden bathrooms and their own plunge pools. ₹7200

Varkala and around

Devout Hindus have for hundreds, and possibly thousands, of years travelled to **VARKALA**, 54km north up the coast from Thiruvananthapuram, to scatter ashes of recently deceased relatives on **Papanasam beach**. The beach, 4km from Varkala town itself, is dramatically set against a backdrop of superb, burnt-clay-coloured cliffs, which, coupled with comparatively low-key development, makes this a more appealing place to spend a beach holiday than Kovalam. Tightly crammed along the rim of crumbling North Cliff, its row of restaurants and small hotels stare out across a vast sweep of ocean – a view that can seem almost transcendental after sunset, when a myriad tiny fishing boats light up their lanterns.

Papanasam beach

Known in Malayalam as Papa Nashini ("sin destroyer"), Varkala's beautiful white-sand **Papanasam beach** (also known just as **Varkala beach**) has long been associated with ancestor worship. Devotees come here after praying at the ancient Janardhana Swamy Temple on the hill to the south, then perform mortuary rituals on the beach, directed by specialist pujaris (priests). The best time to watch the rites is in the **early morning**, just after sunrise – though out of respect, it's best to keep your camera in your bag.

Western sun-worshippers keep to the northern end of the bay, where whistle-happy lifeguards ensure the safety of **swimmers** by enforcing the no-swim zones beyond the flags: the undercurrent is often strong, claiming lives every year. **Dolphins** are often seen swimming quite close to the coast, and, if you're lucky, you may be able to swim with them by arranging a ride with a fishing boat. Sea otters can also occasionally be spotted playing on the cliffs by the sea.

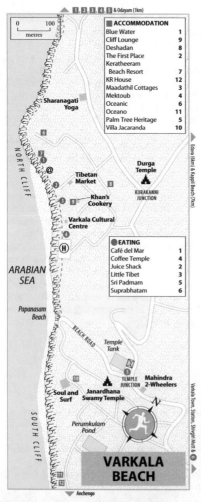

North Cliff

Few of Varkala's Hindu pilgrims make it as far as the **North Cliff** area, the focus of a well-established tourist scene where bamboo and palm-thatch cafés, restaurants and souvenir shops jostle for space close to the edge of the mighty escarpment that plunges vertically to the beach below. Several steep flights of steps cut into the rock provide shortcuts from the sand, or you can also get here via the gentler path that starts from the beachfront.

South Cliff

Dotted with mid-range hotels and guesthouses, the clifftop area running south of the main beachfront – known locally as **South Cliff** – is a much quieter neighbourhood of leafy lanes and large residential houses – a legacy of the lingering presence of numerous clean-living brahmin families. The beach below the cliff, reached via rock-cut steps from several of the hotels, largely disappears at low tide, but offers a blissfully secluded spot to swim when the water recedes, though you should watch out for the sharp laterite boulders lurking in the surf.

Janardhana Swamy Temple

Varkala's ancient **Janardhana Swamy Temple** is reached by heading up the lane that climbs steeply south from the beachfront area. **Non-Hindus** are not permitted to enter the inner sanctum of the shrine, but you can peep over the perimeter walls from the encircling path – a pleasant stroll in the morning, when the temple elephant is led around the lanes on her exercise walk.

Enshrining a form of Vishnu, the temple is adorned with brightly painted images of Hanuman, Rama's monkey general. Among its treasures is a bell salvaged from a Dutch ship that was wrecked on the beach in the eighteenth century – the ship's captain donated it in a gesture of thanksgiving after his entire crew escaped with their lives.

North of Varkala

Just **north of Varkala** the shoreline grows a lot less densely populated, though the large, gaudily painted houses dotted around its hinterland of leafy lanes bear witness to the considerable affluence flooding in with remittance cheques from the Gulf states. You can comfortably walk the kilometre or so from the north end of Varkala cliff as it descends to **ODAYAM**, a mixed Hindu and Muslim village where a cluster of resorts and modest guesthouses has sprung up around the small black-sand beach. Room rates are on the high side, but it can be well worth paying for the extra seclusion when Varaka's clifftop area is firing on all cylinders.

Around 7km north is **Kappil Beach**, a scenic spot where the sea meets the backwaters. A narrow road separates the pretty stretch of sand from Edava-Nadayara Lake, where **Priyadarshini Boat Club** has rowing boats and pedaloes to rent (☎0470 266 2323).

ARRIVAL AND DEPARTURE

VARKALA

By train The town's railway station – Varkala-Sivagiri – is 500m north of the central junction, served by express and passenger trains from Thiruvananthapuram, Kollam and most other Keralan towns on the mainline.
Destinations Alappuzha/Alleppey (3 daily; 2hr); Ernakulam/ Kochi (hourly; 3hr 30min–4hr 30min); Kollam/Quilon (every 30min; 25min); Thiruvananthapuram (every 30min; 1hr).

By bus While some buses from Thiruvananthapuram's Thampanoor stand, and from Kollam to the north, continue on to within walking distance of the beach and clifftop area, most terminate in Varkala town.
Destinations from Varkala Junction Alappuzha/Alleppey (1 daily; 3hr 30min); Kollam/Quilon (3 daily; 1hr); Thiruvananthapuram (every 30min; 1hr 30min–2hr).

GETTING AROUND

By bus and auto-rickshaw Auto-rickshaws between the town and beach shouldn't cost more than ₹80, and frequent local buses also cover the route (₹5).
By motorcycle Scooters may be rented from Mahindra2-Wheelers (Mon–Sat 9.30am–5pm; ☎98467 01975), near Temple Junction, and Wheels of South India, a business of

no fixed abode that works up in North Cliff (☎98470 80412 or ☎93879 74698). The nearest petrol pump is in Varkala town – 300m north of the main circle, on the left side of Station Rd as you head towards the railway station.
By taxi Unni (☎98466 90300) is recommended for airport drops and local sightseeing day-trips.

ACTIVITIES

Yoga and meditation Many guesthouses offer morning yoga for around ₹300–400; just ask around to find a good class. For a real retreat, Sharanagati Yoga (☎90486 94762, ⓦsharanagati-yogahaus.com), on the Thiruvambadi road behind North Cliff, offers expert tuition in both yoga and meditation. Most students sign up for an all-inclusive package (₹3500/day, plus ₹500 for anyone sharing the same room), covering two daily yoga and two daily meditation sessions, all

(vegetarian) meals and comfortable accommodation.
Surfing Although Varkala has a reputation for surf that dumps you right on the sand, it's an undeveloped scene and you won't be fighting to get on a wave. Husband-and-wife team Ed and Sofie set up Soul and Surf (☎98955 80106, ⓦsoulandsurf.com) in 2010 and offer lessons (₹2300/1hr 30min), board rental (₹1500/day) and surf packages with accommodation on South Cliff.

ACCOMMODATION

Varkala offers a wide choice of **accommodation**. The hotels up on **North Cliff** are most people's first choice, with more inspiring views than those lining the road to the beach, but there are some even better options on quieter **South Cliff** if you don't mind being away from the thick of things. For greater seclusion and a vivid taste of the area's lush palm forest and paddy fields, try **Odayam**, 1km north along the coastal path. All areas are accessible by road. You're likely to be able to negotiate a discount if you contact the hotel direct – and don't forget that rates plummet outside high season.

6

NORTH CLIFF

Cliff Lounge ☎ 94465 92002 or ☎ 99463 90217, ⓦ cliff lounge.com. This mid-range place is set back behind the strip but with uninterrupted sea views from its spacious double rooms, which are clean and simple, and with balconies. It's recently changed hands and now has a focus on Ayurvedic medicine, with a clinic on site (ⓦ mother ayurvedics.com). ₹1000 extra for a/c. ₹1600

Deshadan ☎ 98460 31005, ⓦ deshadan.com. The smartest and most efficiently run of Varkala's small-scale resort complexes, a 10min walk from the clifftop. Centred on a great little swimming pool, its fourteen individually themed rooms are tastefully styled, with hand-painted furniture and ethnic colour schemes. A pair of two-bedroomed cottages (₹8000) in the garden suit families well. Quality Ayurveda centre on site. ₹4500

Keratheeram Beach Resort ☎ 99462 20283 or ☎ 98461 38899, ⓦ keratheeramvarkala.com. Set back a bit from the clifftop strip, this nice budget hotel ("resort" is stretching it) feels secure and private. The downstairs rooms have their own hammocks and the whole place has a chilled-out vibe, particularly on the covered rooftop area where you can do yoga in the morning (donation requested). ₹1000

Oceanic ☎ 0470 260 1413 or ☎ 98460 96912, ⓔ oceanic residence@yahoo.co.in. Very pleasant rooms, with flowering climbers trailing from its balconies, close to the clifftop. Among the better-run, better-value budget options close to the strip. ₹500 extra for a/c. ₹1500

SOUTH CLIFF

KR House ☎ 0470 260 6400 or ☎ 93497 41998, ⓔ ramachandran.krhouse@yahoo.co.in. A gem of a budget place, in a plum spot, with comfy mattresses, spotless bathrooms and balconies overlooking a narrow garden running to the cliff edge, from where a flight of steps drops steeply down to the beach. It's quiet, and run with great efficiency by the kindly Mr Ramachandran. ₹1000

★ **Oceano** ☎ 93493 92022 or ☎ 4703 251546, ⓦ the oceanoresort.com. Set on the highest stretch of secluded South Cliff, rooms in this Dutch-managed guesthouse are light, cool, stylish and good value, with spectacular views from the pricier sea-facing suites (₹6350). You eat meals (including a complimentary breakfast) in little thatched gazebos on the cliff edge, from where steps lead to the beach via a spectacularly sited yoga platform. ₹3200

Villa Jacaranda Temple Rd West ☎ 0470 261 0296, ⓦ villa-jacaranda.biz. Bijou boutique guesthouse nestled amid the leafy lanes near the temple. It's small (just four

rooms) but perfectly formed, with cool wooden furniture, crisp white sheets, fresh jasmine flowers in your room and a fragrant garden. Room 4 – which costs a little extra – has expansive sea views from its private terrace. Prices are not increased at Christmas. ₹6000

ODAYAM

Blue Water ☎ 94468 48534, ⓦ bluewaterstay.com. A nicely set up, welcoming option, comprising fourteen varnished palm-wood chalets with tiled roofs – not all that spacious, but comfortably furnished, with floating flowers in terracotta pots, cane blinds and silk throws on the beds. All have sea views. The open-sided restaurant, overlooking the waves at the bottom of a terraced plot, is also the best place to eat and drink hereabouts. ₹6000

The First Place ☎ 0470 299 2090 or ☎ 97469 83783, ⓦ thefirstplace-odayam.com. Ecofriendly Swedish-run guesthouse on the bluff overlooking the beach, with its own shady garden. The rooms aren't large, but they're nicely done – freshly painted with little wooden shelves, glossy red-oxide floors and mozzie nets – with Scandinavian touches that give them a boutique feel. Home-cooked Indian food and an outdoor space for yoga. High season only. ₹2500

Maadathil Cottages Manthara Temple Rd ☎ 97461 13495 (Muhajir), ⓦ maadathilcottages.com. Row of locally owned and run holiday cottages in traditional Keralan style (gabled, red-tiled roofs, wood railings and split-cane blinds) in a sweet spot under the coconut trees behind Odayam beach. There's a pricier, larger cottage with a lovely rear veranda looking on to a lotus pond filled with egrets and butterflies. ₹4500

Mektoub ☎ 94479 71239, ⓔ mektoubexperience @gmail.com. A perfect place to soak up the unspoiled vibe that still holds sway in Odayam. In an idyllic setting between coconut groves and paddy fields, it comprises a campus of red-laterite buildings with spacious rooms and sea-facing verandas. Bargain rates considering the level of comfort, and owner Rafik is a great cook. It's hard to find; call ahead to be met. ₹3500

★ **Palm Tree Heritage** ☎ 99460 55036, ⓦ palmtree heritage.com. Stylish, part-Swedish-owned boutique place right behind the beach, set in well-watered gardens. The architecture is delightful and the interiors cool and comfortable, blending traditional, handmade Keralan woodwork and modern comforts, including luxurious bathrooms. They also recently took over (and revamped) *Pink Aana*'s simple non-a/c bamboo huts (₹3000). The food's terrific, and Babu and his staff are unfailingly courteous. ₹7000

EATING

Varkala's clifftop **café-restaurants** specialize in locally caught seafood (you'll also find plenty of Italian, Thai and Mexican dishes on offer – but they won't taste much like the real thing). Prices are high, even by Keralan standards, and service painfully slow, but the superb location more than compensates. Although alcohol is available in just about all the clifftop places, due to Varkala's religious importance **beer** tends to be served in discreet teapots. Once the restaurants finish serving, **nightlife** is generally low-key.

★**Café del Mar** North Cliff. The most professionally run place to eat on North Cliff, with an Italian coffee machine and polite, uniformed service. It offers the usual jack-of-all-trades menu, but they can actually cook everything on it. Made with imported cheeses, the Italian dishes are especially good (try the baked aubergine lasagne) and there are plenty of light bites and healthy salads. Most mains ₹250–400. Daily 7.30am–late.

Coffee Temple North Cliff. Hot contender (along with *Café del Mar*) for the crown of "Best Coffee in Varkala" and with a loyal following. The cakes are uninspiring *German Bakery* fare, but the Western menu is a hit with backpackers making use of the free wi-fi. Espresso from ₹80. Free filter water. Daily 8am–11pm.

Juice Shack North Cliff ☎ 99952 14515. Fresh juices churned out by the larger-than-life, resplendently bearded Umesh and his team. They also do a range of healthy snacks (wraps and crunchy salads; ₹150) and host popular buffets (non-veg ₹500) on Wed and Sat (buy your ticket in advance). Daily 7am–11pm.

Little Tibet North Cliff. Decorated with cheerful prayer flags and Buddhist *thangkas*, this large bamboo and palm-thatch place catches the breezes at a prime upstairs cliff-edge location. Mexican and Italian specialities are offered, but most people come for the tasty Tibetan *momo* dumplings (₹150–230) and *thukpa* soup (₹150). Very friendly, professional service. Daily 8am–late.

Sri Padmam Temple Junction. This dingy-looking café on the temple crossroads serves freshly made, cheap and tasty South Indian veg food (including ₹90 "meals" at lunchtime). You can walk through the front dining room to a large rear terrace affording prime views of the tank – particularly atmospheric at breakfast time. Daily 6am–9pm.

Suprabhatam Varkala town. The cheapest and best pure veg joint in Varkala, just off the main roundabout in a dining hall lined with coir mats. Their dosas and other fried snacks aren't great, but the lunchtime "unlimited" rice-plate "meals" (noon–3pm; ₹45), featuring the usual *thoran*, *avial*, dhal, *rasam*, buttermilk, curd, *papad* and red or white rice, pull in streams of locals and foreigners alike. Daily 8am–9pm.

DIRECTORY

Banks There's an ATM on Temple Junction, and several banks up in Varkala town, just off the main roundabout.

Cookery classes Khan's Cookery offers daily classes in a spruce little kitchen behind *Little Tibet* on North Cliff (₹600/₹800 for veg/non-veg; book on ☎ 98956 33896).

Internet There's free wi-fi with a good connection at *Coffee Temple* (see above).

Post office Just north of Temple Junction (Mon–Sat 10am–2pm), near the *Sri Padmam* restaurant.

Kollam (Quilon)

Sandwiched between the sea and Ashtamudi ("eight inlets") Lake, **KOLLAM** (pronounced "Koillam", and previously known as **Quilon**), was for centuries the focal point of the Malabar's spice trade. Phoenicians, Arabs, Greeks, Romans and Chinese all dispatched ships to the city, before the rise of Calicut and Cochin eclipsed the port. These days, it's a workaday market town and busy transport hub for the southern backwater region, with surprisingly few vestiges of its former prominence. Many travellers stay overnight here, however, en route to or from Alappuzha on the excursion boats that leave each morning from its lakeside ferry jetty. If the traffic in the centre gets too much, take a short auto-rickshaw ride south to the main **beach**, or a couple of kilometres west along the coastal road to the **Thangassery Lighthouse** (daily 10am–5pm; ₹25), which is well worth the climb to the top for views of the fishing harbour.

In the evening, a stroll through the town's traditional **bazaar**, with its old wooden houses and narrow backstreets lined by coir warehouses, rice stores and cashew traders, is a pleasant diversion.

Old British Residency and around

Residency Rd, Ashtamudi Lake

Of the few surviving colonial vestiges, the only one worth a detour is the former **British Residency**, a magnificent 250-year-old mansion on the shores of the lake, now only open for official events. Among the last monuments surviving in India from the earliest days of the Raj, it perfectly epitomizes the openness to indigenous influences that characterized the era, with typically Keralan gable roofs surmounting British pillared verandas. There are no set visiting hours – just turn up and ask the manager if you can have a look around.

Just nearby, another colonial-era building has been transformed into the **8 Point Art Gallery & Café**, which is a great place for a break.

6

ARRIVAL AND DEPARTURE
                                                                        KOLLAM (QUILON)

By train Kollam's busy mainline railway station lies east of the clock tower that marks the centre of town, and is easily reached by auto-rickshaw. Note that most Thiruvananthapuram-bound trains do not stop in Varkala. Destinations Alappuzha/Alleppey (9 daily; 1hr 15min–2hr); Ernakulam/Kochi (every 30min; 3–4hr); Thiruvananthapuram (hourly; 1hr 15min–2hr 30min); Varkala (hourly; 20–30min).

By bus The KSRTC bus stand is on the west side of town, near the boat jetty on Ashtamudi Lake. You can book express buses in advance but not local or "limited stop" services. Destinations Alappuzha/Alleppey (hourly; 2hr); Ernakulam/Kochi (every 45min–1hr; 3hr–3hr 20min); Thiruvananthapuram (every 30min; 1hr 45min).

By boat There are some backwater ferry services from Kollam (see box opposite).

INFORMATION

Tourist information The District Tourism Promotion Council (DTPC) has a tourist office (daily 8am–7pm; ☎ 0474 274 5625, ⊕ dtpckollam.com) at the boat jetty on Ashtamudi Lake, where you can book tickets for the daily tourist backwater cruises (see box opposite) and other tours. The local Alappuzha Tourism Development Council office (ATDC; daily 8am–8pm; ☎ 0474 276 7440, ⊕ atdcalleppey.com), across the road, offers comparable services.

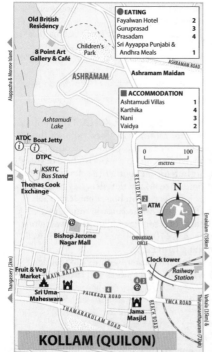

EATING
Fayalwan Hotel	2
Guruprasad	3
Prasadam	4
Sri Ayyappa Punjabi & Andhra Meals	1

ACCOMMODATION
Ashtamudi Villas	1
Karthika	4
Nani	3
Vaidya	2

KOLLAM (QUILON)

ACCOMMODATION

★ **Ashtamudi Villas** 2km north of Kollam, on the far side of Thevally Bridge ☎ 98471 32449, ⊕ ashtamudivillas.com. Buried deep in the backwaters on the outskirts of town, this place is right on the water's edge, with hammocks strung between the palm trees. The rooms, in a row of ecofriendly brick chalets, are spacious, bright and cool (get the detached one if it's available). You can phone ahead to arrange a pick-up. Local tours arranged from here are recommended. ₹1500

Karthika Paikkada Rd, near the Jama Masjid mosque ☎ 0474 275 1831. Large, popular, central budget hotel offering a range of acceptably clean, plain rooms (some a/c) ranged around a courtyard that centres, rather unexpectedly, on three huge nude figures. ₹600

Nani Opposite the clock tower ☎ 0474 275 1141, ⊕ hotelnani.com. A decent hotel, in a quirky, Keralan-gabled redbrick tower block near the railway station. The comfortably furnished, standard rooms are the real bargain, though couples might appreciate the extra space of the "executive" deluxe options (₹3250). ₹2000

Vaidya Residency Rd, Chinnakkada ☎ 0474 274 8432, ⊕ thehotelvaidya.com. This place is fine if you just want somewhere comfortable to crash for a night and aren't fussy about the view. On the north side of town, the business-orientated, characterless rooms have no balconies and zero outlook, but are clean, and huge for the price. The standard ones (referred to as "deluxe") are the best value. ₹1950

BACKWATER CRUISES FROM KOLLAM

DTPC run popular **cruises from Kollam to Alappuzha** (10.30am; 8hr; ₹400) on alternate days, with stops for lunch and tea. Tickets can be bought on the day from their tourist office at the boat jetty on Ashtamudi Lake, and at some of the hotels. They also offer exclusive overnight *kettu vallam* cruises, and half-day canal trips to nearby **Monroe Island** (daily 9am–1pm & 2–6.30pm; ₹600), as well as guided village tours taking in Ayurveda factories, coir-makers, boat-builders and bird-nesting sites.

You may find that you get a far better impression of backwater life by hopping between villages on the very cheap **local ferries**. DTPC have timetables and route information; tickets are sold on the boats themselves.

6

EATING

Fayalwan Hotel Main bazaar. Come here for speedy service, traditional Keralan breakfasts (₹60) and the best mutton biryani in town (lunchtime only; ₹140). Recently renovated, it's run by the third generation of the same family and the walls of the clean, fan-cooled interior still sport pictures of traditional wrestlers – the *fayalwans* after which the restaurant is named. Daily 8am–9pm.

Guruprasad Main bazaar. Cramped and sweaty, but offering wonderfully old-school "meals" (₹50): blue-and-cream walls, framed ancestral photos and Hindu devotional art provide the typical backdrop for great pure-veg rice plates and Udupi-style snacks. Daily 7.30am–10pm.

★**Prasadam** Nani hotel, opposite the clock tower ☎ 0474 275 1141, ⓦ hotelnani.com. Kollam's best food,

served in plush a/c comfort. Traditional South Indian thalis are the most popular lunchtime options from an exhaustive menu, but this is also great for fresh local seafood and backwater cuisine, like the *karimeen pollichathu* (white fish steamed in banana leaf; ₹225) and a blow-out seafood platter. Daily 7.30–10am, noon–3pm & 7–10.30pm.

Sri Ayyappa Punjabi & Andhra Meals Main bazaar, near Dhanya Super Market. Situated down a tiny alleyway off Kollam's main bazaar, this place is a real hidden gem. Look for the sign just east of the Indian Bank, on the north side of the road. Superb Punjabi cuisine (a rarity in these parts) includes a delicious *paneer* butter masala (₹45) and dhal fry (₹35), hot naan breads and heavenly lassis. Mon–Sat noon–9.30pm.

DIRECTORY

ATM ATMs can be found in the smart Bishop Jerome Nagar shopping mall just south of the main road between the jetty and the clock tower. The efficient Axis bank also has a dependable ATM next to the *Vaidya* hotel, and there's a

Thomas Cook Exchange on the crossroads not far from the boat jetty.

Internet Cyber.com, just south of the clock tower on the first floor of Yeskay Towers, charges just ₹35/hr.

Alappuzha (Alleppey)

From the mid-nineteenth century, **ALAPPUZHA** (or "**Alleppey**") served as the main port for the backwater region. Spices, coffee, tea, cashews, coir and other produce were shipped out from the inland waterways to the sea via its grid of canals and rail lines. Tourist literature loves to dub the town as "the Venice of the East", but in truth the comparison does few favours to Venice. Apart from a handful of colonial-era warehouses and mansions, and a derelict pier jutting into the sea from a sun-blasted and dirty **beach**, few monuments survive, while the old canals enclose a typically ramshackle Keralan market of bazaars and noisy traffic.

That said, Alappuzha makes a congenial place to while away an evening en route to or from the **backwaters**. Streams of visitors do just that during the winter season, for the town has become Kerala's pre-eminent **rice boat cruising** hub, with an estimated four hundred *kettu vallam* moored on the fringes of nearby Vembanad and Punnamada lakes. To cash in on the seasonal influx, the local tourist offices lay on excursion boats for day-trips, while in mid-December the sands lining the west end of town host a popular **beach festival**, during which cultural events and a procession of fifty caparisoned elephants are staged with the dilapidated British-built pier as a backdrop. Alappuzha's really big day, however, is the second Saturday of August, in the middle of the monsoon,

6

DAY-CRUISES AND CANOE TRIPS AROUND ALAPPUZHA

The obvious destination for a day-trip from Alappuzha is **Vembanad Lake** on the town's north and eastern fringes: **Punnamada Lake** (also called Punnamada Kayal) is the local section of this vast waterway. Reaching either from town is most straightforward by water. For short cruises, it's possible to charter diesel-powered motorboats (₹400/hr), but a better option would be to dispense with engines altogether and opt for a guided village tour in a hand-paddled canoe. Aside from being more "green", these allow you to penetrate narrow waterways beyond the range of the other tourist boats. DTPC offers its own punted tours, carrying two people for ₹250/hr.

A recommended private operator who's been ferrying tourists around Alappuzha's off-track backwaters for years is **Mr K.D. Prasenan** (☎ 93888 44712), based at the *Palm Grove Lake Resort* on the Punnamada Kayal, 3.5km north of the boat jetty (see below). He offers tours in a slender 10m boat (₹350/hr for two people).

Alternatively, **Paddyland** tours charges ₹1000 per person for an 8hr trip, which includes a transfer to and from town on the ferry, and breakfast and lunch in the boatman's home. Contact Mr Joseph on ☎ 94465 84905, ⊛ paddylandtours.com.

---

when it serves as the venue for one of Kerala's major spectacles – the **Nehru Trophy snake boat race** (see box, p.301).

ARRIVAL AND DEPARTURE

By bus The filthy KSRTC bus stand is at the northeast edge of town, 1min from the boat jetty. For Fort Cochin, catch any of the fast Ernakulam services along the main highway and get down at Thoppumpady (7km south), from where local buses run the rest of the way.

Destinations Ernakulam/Kochi (every 30min; 1hr 30min); Kollam/Quilon (9 daily; 1hr 15min–2hr); Kottayam (every 20min; 1hr 20min); Thiruvananthapuram (every 30min; 3hr 30min); Varkala (1 daily; 3hr 30min).

By boat The main boat jetty is on Vadai Canal, close to the KSRTC bus stand, from where the daily tourist ferries to and from Kollam run, as well as cheaper local (and less direct) ferries to and from Kottayam (dep. 7.30am, 9.35am, 11.30am, 2.30pm & 5.15pm). Regular services also connect Alappuzha with Champakulam, where you pick up less frequent boats to Neerettupuram and Kidangara, and back to Alappuzha. This round route ranks among Kuttanad's

classic trips; the tourist offices can help you make sense of the timetables (also found at ⊛ swtd.gov.in).

By train The station, on the main Thiruvananthapuram–Ernakulam line, lies 3km southwest across town, on the far side of Alappuzha's main waterway, Commercial Canal. As the backwaters prevent trains from continuing directly south beyond Alappuzha, only a few major daily services and a handful of passenger trains depart from here. For points further north along the coast, take the *Jan Shatabdi Express* (#12076) and change at Ernakulam, as the afternoon *Alleppey–Cannanore Express* (#16307), which runs as far as Kozhikode and Kannur, arrives at those destinations rather late at night. It is, however, a good bet if you want to get to Thrissur.

Destinations Ernakulam/Kochi (12 daily; 1hr–1hr 30min); Thiruvananthapuram (10 daily; 3hr–3hr 40min); Varkala (6 daily; 2hr–2hr 40min).

INFORMATION

Tourist information The town has several rival tourist departments, all of them eager to offer advice and book you onto their houseboat tours. The most conveniently situated – at the jetty itself on VCSB (Vadai Canal South Bank) Rd – are the DTPC tourist reception centre (daily 9am–5pm; ☎ 0477 225 1796) and adjacent Kerala Tourism office (Mon–Sat 10am–5pm; ☎ 0477 226 0722, ⊛ kerala tourism.org). The ATDC office (☎ 0477 226 4462, ⊛ atdc alleppey.com) is tucked away on the corner of VCNB Rd and Mullackal Rd, on the second floor of a shopping

complex. Both ATDC and DTPC sell tickets for their ferries, backwater cruises and charter boats, and can help you fathom the intricacies of local ferry timetables. Though many of the houseboat booking agencies dotted around town call themselves "tourist information offices" they're nothing of the kind; their sole purpose is to sell their cruises.

Services You can change money at the efficient UTI bank on Mullackal Rd (Mon–Sat 9.30am–4.30pm). Both this and the State Bank of India opposite have reliable ATMs.

ACCOMMODATION

There are some great **homestay** possibilities if you're willing to travel to the outskirts and pay a little more, along with some good options a taxi ride away in the surrounding **backwaters** and further up the coast. Nearly everywhere, whatever its price bracket, has some kind of tie-in with a houseboat operator: good-natured encouragement tends to be the order of the day rather than hard-sell tactics, but you may be able to negotiate a reduction on your hotel tariff if you do end up booking a backwater trip. Whenever you come, and wherever you choose to stay, brace yourself for clouds of **mosquitoes**.

ALAPPUZHA TOWN

Alasr Commercial Canal, North Bank Rd, west of Kochukada Bridge ⊕99478 20002 or ⊕96050 66611. Bona fide heritage hotels offering rooms for less than ₹1000 are as rare as hen's teeth in Kerala, but *Alasr* is just that – a splendid two-hundred-year-old merchant's mansion overlooking one of Alappuzha's main canals, offering a range of huge, affordable rooms of various sizes. There's none of the style and retro-chic of a boutique place and they can be tricky to get hold of: use ⓦairbnb.com to book. ₹**700**

★**Bella Homestay** Near Nehru Trophy Finishing Point ⊕90617 93196 or ⊕0477 223 0201, ⓦbellakerala.com. Tucked away in a leafy, quiet backstreet, this homestay in a modern house within walking distance of the main houseboat terminal is a great mid-range option. The impeccably clean rooms are spacious and individually furnished with splashes of colour, the welcome from Keralan-Polish hosts Biju and Natasha is warm, and the breakfasts are great. ₹**2500**

Cherukara Nest 9 774 Cherukara Building ⊕0477 225 1509 or ⊕99470 59628. 1940s "heritage" home, on a quiet canal road just a short walk around the corner from the KSRTC bus stand. Breakfast is served in an old courtyard under a huge mango tree. Ecofriendly houseboat cruises are a sideline. A/c ₹600 extra. ₹**900**

Palm Grove Lake Resort Punnamada Kayal, 3.5km north of boat jetty ⊕0477 223 5004 or ⊕98470 10429, ⓦpalmgrovelakeresort.com. Near where the canal meets Punnamada Lake, this relaxed resort overlooks the water – a perfect, tranquil spot from which to watch the snake boat races. Shaded by areca and coconut palms, its pretty cottages have gabled tile roofs, private outdoor showers and sitouts opening onto the garden. A/c ₹1000 extra. ₹**2300**

Palmy Lake Resort Thathampally, 2km north of boat jetty ⊕0477 223 5938 or ⊕94476 67888, ⓦpalmyresort .com. Spacious, neatly painted red-tiled "cottages" (a/c and non-a/c), grouped behind a modern family home on the northeastern limits of town. It isn't actually on the lake, but offers exceptional value; all rooms have private pillared verandas opening onto a restful garden. ₹**1000**

Venice Castle Behind Canara Bank, close to KSRTC bus stand ⊕0477 223 777 or ⊕99470 84414, ⓦvenicecastle .com. Substantial, modern Keralan home a stone's throw from the bus stand and town centre, but sheltered behind a screen of lush greenery. Huge rooms for the price, and well aired, with comfy beds, decent bathrooms and views over mango and palm trees. A/c ₹300 extra. ₹**1200**

ALAPPUZHA (ALLEPPEY)

■ ACCOMMODATION	
Akkarikkulam Memoirs	3
Alasr	2
Angeo Beach House	1
Bella Homestay	8
Cherukara Nest	7
Lake & Paddy	4
Palm Grove Lake Resort	9
Palmy Lake Resort	10
Pooppally's	5
Venice Castle	6

● EATING
Dreamers	1
Halay's	2
Thaff	3

CHETTIKAD

Angeo Beach House Chettikad Beach, Priyadarsini Rd, Thumpoly ☏ 80867 52586. A simple and secluded homestay right on the beach. The charming hosts cook great Keralan food – though only their son Martin, who runs *Dreamers* in Alappuzha (see opposite), speaks English. Each of the three rooms has a veranda and there's a hammock and a little sitout in the shaded garden. They plan to add a couple of bamboo huts, too. ₹2500

ALAPPUZHA BACKWATERS

Akkarikkulam Memoirs Chennamkary ☏ 0477 276 2345 or ☏ 94463 66066, ⊛ akkarakalammemoirs.com. One of the few proper heritage hotels in the backwaters (as opposed to homestays), in a recently converted Syrian-Christian mansion overlooking the Pamba River. Great value, and the rates include a sunset cruise, use of a rowing boat, bicycles, night fishing tours and guided walks around the area. ₹5500

Lake & Paddy Pamba riverside, 2.5km east of town centre at Chungam. Tiny and colourful budget guest-house, run by hospitable brothers, situated right on the Pamba River with rice fields to the rear. Two lovely tile-floored cottages make the most of the green views (₹900); two other cheapie rooms in the main house are bamboo lined and share a bathroom. A fantastic location for watching village and river life roll by, and easily reached by auto-rickshaw or government ferry from Alappuzha. ₹600

KUTTANAD: THE BACKWATERS OF KERALA

One of the most memorable experiences for travellers in India is the opportunity to take a boat journey on the **backwaters of Kerala**. The area known as **Kuttanad** stretches for 75km from Kollam in the south to Kochi in the north, sandwiched between the sea and the hills. This bewildering labyrinth of shimmering waterways, composed of lakes, canals, rivers and rivulets, is lined with dense tropical greenery and preserves rural Keralan lifestyles that are completely hidden from the road.

The region's bucolic way of life has long fascinated visitors. And the ever entrepreneurial Keralans were quick to spot its potential as a visitor destination – particularly after it was discovered that foreigners and wealthy tourists from India's cities were prepared to pay vast sums in local terms to explore the area aboard converted **rice barges**, or *kettu vallam*. Since its inception in the early 1990s, the houseboat tour industry has grown exponentially in both size and sophistication, and has brought with it major environmental drawbacks as well as increased prosperity. You can, however, explore this extraordinary region in lower-impact ways, too.

TOURIST CRUISES

The most popular excursion in the Kuttanad region is the full-day journey between **Kollam** and **Alappuzha**. All sorts of private hustlers offer their services, but the principal boats are run on alternate days by the ATDC and the DTPC (see box, p.319). The double-decker boats leave from both Kollam and Alappuzha daily, departing at 10.30am (10am check-in); tickets (₹400) can be bought in advance or on the day at the ATDC/DTPC counters, other agents and some hotels. Both companies make three stops during the 8hr journey, including one for lunch, and another 3hr north of Kollam at the **Mata Amritanandamayi Math** (see p.52) at Amritapuri (where "Amma" offers devotees her trademark hugs). Although this is by far the main backwater route, many tourists find it too long, with crowded decks and intense sun. There's also something faintly embarrassing about being cooped up with a crowd of fellow tourists, madly photographing any signs of life on the water or canal banks, while gangs of kids scamper alongside the boat screaming "one pen, one pen".

VILLAGE TOURS AND CANOES

Quite apart from their significant environmental impact, most boats are too wide to squeeze into the narrower inlets connecting small villages. To reach these more idyllic, remote areas, therefore, you'll need to charter a punted **canoe**. The slower pace means you cover less distance in an hour, but the experience of being so close to the water, and those who live on it, tends to be correspondingly more rewarding. You'll also find more formal "**village tours**" advertised across the Kuttanad area, tying together trips to watch coir-makers, rice farmers and boat-builders in action, with the opportunity to dine in a traditional Keralan village setting.

KETTU VALLAM (HOUSEBOATS)

Whoever dreamed up the idea of showing tourists around the backwaters in old rice barges, or **kettu vallam**, could never have imagined that, more than two decades on,

Pooppally's Ponga, Pooppally, on the Pamba River ⊕ 0477 276 2034 or ⊕ 93435 75080, ⊕ pooppallys.com. This old ancestral mansion is a typically Syrian-Christian home with double-gabled roof and guest rooms in twin wings opening on to a central courtyard garden next to the river. They're not overly large, but have delightful wood-pillared verandas. If it's free, splash out on the romantic, 200-year-old *nalukettu* (₹5000), which sits on stilts above a pond in the back garden. *Pooppally's* is accessible by ferry or road. ₹4000

EATING

In addition to the **restaurants** listed here, most of Alappuzha's homestays and guesthouses provide meals for guests, usually delicious, home-cooked Keralan cooking that's tailored towards sensitive Western palates.

★**Dreamers** Alappuzha beach ⊕ 80867 52586, ⊕ dreamersrestaurant.com. With its sea view and rustic decor, this place is like a cross between a treehouse and dune shack. The menu includes fresh pasta and pizza with real olive oil (₹250–300) – *Dreamers* is part-owned by an Italian – plus fresh salads and local seafood (the roast crab is a winner). Springsteen, Clapton and Rihanna dominate a rather random soundtrack. Daily noon–11pm.

nine hundred or more of them would be chugging around Kuttanad waterways. These **houseboats**, made of dark, oiled jackwood with canopies of plaited palm thatch and coir, are big business, and almost every accommodation seems to have one. The flashiest are fitted with a/c rooms, jacuzzis and widescreen plasma TVs on their teak sun decks and have bottles of imported wine in their fridges. At the opposite end of the scale are rough-and-ready transport barges with gut-thumping diesel engines, cramped bedrooms and minimal washing facilities.

Rates vary hugely depending on the quality, more than double over Christmas and New Year, and halve off-season during the monsoons. In practice, ₹7500–18,000 is the usual bracket for a trip on a two-bedroom, a/c boat with a proper bathroom, including three meals, in early December or mid-January. The cruise should last a minimum of 22 hours, though don't expect to spend all of that on the move: running times are carefully calculated to spare gas. From sunset onwards you'll be moored at a riverbank.

You'll save quite a lot of cash, and be doing the fragile ecosystem a big favour, by opting for a more environmentally friendly **punted** *kettu vallam*. Rice barges were traditionally propelled by punt, and though it means you travel at a more leisurely pace, the experience is silent (great for wildlife-spotting) and altogether more relaxing.

Houseboat operators work out of **Kollam** and **Kumarakom**, but most are in **Alappuzha**, where you'll find the lowest prices – but also the worst congestion on more scenic routes. Spend a day shopping around for a deal (your guesthouse or hotel-owner will be a good first port of call), or if you're in Alappuzha, head to the main houseboat terminal at 9am to meet returning *kettu vallam* and question travellers as they disembark. Always check the boat over beforehand. It's also a good idea to get the deal fixed on paper before setting off, and to withhold a final payment until the end of the cruise in case you're not satisfied.

Dependable operators include: **Lakes and Lagoons** (⊕ 0477 226 6842, ⊕ lakeslagoons.com); **Angel Queen** (⊕ 98951 89095, ⊕ angelqueencruise.in); Xandari Riverscapes (⊕ 0484 6503 044 or ⊕ 0484 311 5036, ⊕ raxacollective.com); and the upmarket **Spice Routes Luxury Cruises** (⊕ 0484 600 3300 or ⊕ 86060 00430, ⊕ spiceroutes.com).

LOCAL FERRIES

Kettu vallam may offer the most comfortable way of cruising the backwaters, but you'll get a much more vivid experience of what life is actually like in the region by jumping on one of the local ferries that serve its towns and villages. Particularly recommended is the trip from **Alappuzha to Kottayam** (dep. 7.30am, 9.30am, 11.30am, 2.30 & 5.15pm; 2hr 30min; ₹20), which winds across open lagoons and narrow canals, through coconut groves and islands. Arrive early to get a good place with uninterrupted views.

Good places to aim for from Alappuzha include Neerettupuram, Kidangara and Chambakulam; all are served by regular daily ferries, but you may have to change boats once or twice along the way, killing time in local cafés and toddy shops (all of which adds to the fun, of course).

6

THREATS TO THE BACKWATER ECOSYSTEM

The **African moss** that often carpets the surface of the narrower waterways may look attractive, but it is a symptom of the many serious **ecological problems** currently affecting the region, whose population density ranges from between two and four times that of other coastal areas in southwest India. This has put growing pressure on land, and consequently a greater reliance on fertilizers that eventually work their way into the water and cause the build-up of moss.

Illegal land reclamation poses the single greatest threat to this fragile ecosystem. In little more than a century, the total area of water in Kuttanad has been reduced by two-thirds, while mangrove swamps and fish stocks have been decimated by pollution and the spread of towns and villages around the edges of the backwater region. Tourism adds to the problem, as the film of oil from motorized ferries and houseboats spreads through the waters, killing yet more fish, which has in turn led to a reduction of more than fifty percent in the number of bird species found in the region.

Halay's CCSB Rd. Proper Keralan-Muslim restaurant that's been an Alappuzha institution for generations. Much of its old-world character disappeared in a recent face-lift, but the food's as delicious as ever. Nearly everyone comes for their chicken biryanis (₹180) or their blow-out "meals" (₹380), to be enjoyed with the legendary house date pickle. Daily noon–10.30pm.

Thaff YMCA Junction. It looks a bit down on its luck from the outside, but this is the best place in town for inexpensive non-veg Indian food, from local fish to chicken and mutton specialities, and all the standard veggie dishes. Intense Keralan flavours and rock-bottom prices are guaranteed, with filling thalis for ₹60. Daily 8–10am, 11am–3pm & 4–10pm.

Mararikulam

Fourteen kilometres north of Alappuzha a number of high-end eco-resorts have sprung up in the fishing village of **MARARIKULAM**; the attraction here is that there's little to do except lounge on the uninterrupted stretch of white-sand **beach**. One nearby place of interest is sixteenth-century **St Andrew's Basilica** (@arthunkalchurch.org; ₹50 donation requested) 6km north in **Arthungal** – not to be missed in January when Christian pilgrims flock here for the Feast of San Sebastian.

ARRIVAL AND DEPARTURE   MARARIKULAM

By bus Buses from Alappuzha drop passengers at St Augustine's church, a short walk from the beach (frequent; 40min). For services further afield, you'll need to get an auto-rickshaw up to the main highway, NH-47.

By taxi Cars line up outside *Marari Beach Resort*. Laiju is a recommended local driver (☎ 99463 83081).

ACCOMMODATION

Most visitors will have booked into one of the expensive resorts in advance; those listed below are independent, local options. Note that the lane from St Augustine's church (on Beach Rd) towards the beach is lined with budget **homestays** that usually have space.

Arakal Heritage Chethy, 3km north of Marari Beach ☎ 0478 286 5545 or ☎ 98472 68661, @arakal.com. Three-hundred-year-old heritage home tucked away in a shady spot at the far end of Marari Beach. Individual cottages have bags of Keralan character, with traditional gabled roofs and dark-wood antique furniture – one even has a mango tree growing through it. Mini and Abi are wonderful hosts who will arrange cookery classes and lend you a canoe to paddle in the backwaters. Full board. ₹7000

Austin's Beach Villa Marari Beach ☎ 94475 04293, @marariaustinbeachvilla.com. Right on the beachfront, this solid option has four rooms, the slightly pricier two on the first floor with a terrace and a/c. Rooms and bathrooms are spotless and there's solar hot water. Breakfast included. ₹3500

Marari Arapakal Beach Villa Marari Beach ☎ 99474 40334 or ☎ 94001 37713, @marariarapakalbeach.com. These two newish buildings in the grounds of a family home might not have much character, but they're clean and secure and just a few minutes' walk from the beach. Dominic also owns a more basic shack right on the beach with two rooms for the same price. Breakfast included. ₹2500

★**Marari Dreamz** Mararikulam ☎87144 14309 or ☎96564 96556, ⓦmararidreamz.com. Somehow the location on the wrong side of Beach Rd doesn't seem to matter. Behind a standard suburban facade this lovely hideaway has large and very private rooms; each comfortably sleeps three and has its own shady veranda in the garden. There are bicycles and motorbikes to rent and young hosts Allwyn and Jency go out of their way to look after guests. ₹4000

Kottayam and around

6

Some 76km southeast of Kochi and 37km northeast of Alappuzha, **KOTTAYAM** is a compact, busy Keralan town strategically located between the backwaters and the mountains of the Periyar Wildlife Sanctuary. The many **rubber plantations** around town, introduced by British missionaries in the 1820s, have for more than a century formed the bedrock of a booming local economy, most of it controlled by landed **Syrian Christians**. Author Arundhati Roy grew up in nearby **Ayemenem**, the magical setting for her acclaimed novel *The God of Small Things* and partway towards vast **Vembanad Lake**, where the **Kumarakom Bird Sanctuary** spreads across a cluster of islands.

Kottayam's churches

The presence of two thirteenth-century **churches** on a hill 5km northwest of the centre (accessible by auto-rickshaw) attests to the area's deeply rooted Christian heritage. Two eighth-century Nestorian stone crosses with Palavi and Syriac inscriptions, on either side of the elaborately decorated altar of the **Valliapalli** ("big") church, are among the earliest solid traces of Christianity in India. The visitors' book contains entries from as far back as the 1890s, including one each from the Ethiopian king, Haile Selassie, and a British viceroy. The apse of the nearby **Cheriapalli** ("small") church is covered with lively paintings, thought to have been executed by a Portuguese artist in the sixteenth century. If the doors are locked, ask for the key at the church office (9am–1pm & 2–5pm).

Kumarakom

A twenty-minute bus ride west of Kottayam brings you to the shores of **Vembanad Lake**, where the **Kumarakom Bird Sanctuary** forms the focus of a line of ultra-luxurious resorts on the water's edge. A **backwaters cruise** hereabouts is a much better bet for peace and quiet than in Alappuzha or Kollam, although you will have to pay a little more if you want to arrange things from here: your hotel or homestay will be able to help.

Kumarakom Bird Sanctuary
Daily dawn–dusk • ₹150 (₹50); guide ₹300

The small **Kumarakom Bird Sanctuary** in the wetlands is a good place to spot domestic and migratory birds such as egrets, osprey, flycatchers and racket-tail drongos, as well as glimpses of otters and turtles in the water. There's a paved walkway for a lot of the route, but it does get tricky in parts. The best time to visit is between November and May before the sun rises; the one and only official guide can't be booked in advance and is snapped up by 6.30am.

Bay Island Driftwood Museum
Outskirts of Kumarakom village • Tues–Sat 10am–5pm, Sun 11.30am–5.30pm • ₹50 • ⓦbayislandmuseum.com

Birds, or representations of them, feature prominently in the area's most bizarre visitor attraction, the **Bay Island Driftwood Museum**, just off the main road, in which lumps of driftwood sculpted by the sea are displayed in an idiosyncratic gallery.

Ettumanur

12km north of Kottayam • Admission is free for foreigners, but you'll need to buy a camera ticket (₹20, video ₹50) from the counter on the left of the main gateway

Another possible day-trip from Kottayam is the magnificent Mahadeva (Shiva) temple at **ETTUMANUR**, on the road to Ernakulam, whose entrance porch holds some of Kerala's most celebrated medieval **wall paintings**. The most spectacular depicts Nataraja (Shiva) executing a cosmic *tandava* dance, trampling evil in the form of a demon underfoot.

6

ARRIVAL AND INFORMATION

By train Kottayam railway station, 2km north of the centre, sees a constant flow of traffic between Thiruvananthapuram (3hr 30min) and points north, including Ernakulam/Kochi (1hr 30min). There's a prepaid auto-rickshaw stand outside the main entrance.

By bus Kottayam's KSRTC bus stand, 500m south of the centre on TB Rd (not to be confused with the private stand for local buses on MC Rd), is an important stop on routes to and from major towns in South India.

Destinations Ernakulam/Kochi (every 30min; 2hr); Kollam/ Quilon (5 daily; 2hr 30min); Kumily/Periyar (every 30min;

KOTTAYAM AND AROUND

3–4hr); Madurai (4 daily; 7hr); Thiruvananthapuram (every 15–30min; 4hr).

By ferry The public ferry leaves for Alappuzha (2hr 30min) at 7am, 9am, 11am, 1.30pm and 3.30pm.

Tourist information DTPC maintains a tiny tourist office at the jetty (daily 10am–5pm; ☎ 0481 256 0479).

Services The best place to change money is the Canara Bank on KK Rd, which also has one of several ATMs around the main square. Internet facilities are available at Intimacy (₹30/hr), also on KK Rd, just north of the KSRTC bus stand.

ACCOMMODATION

Akkara Mariathuruthu ☎ 0481 251 6951, ⓦ akkara.in. Just a 15min drive out of town, this welcoming homestay occupies an ancestral Syrian-Christian homestead sitting proudly on the riverbank – an idyllic, typically Keralan building, with traditional gabled architecture and interiors. In 2016 they opened an Ayurvedic centre on site and packages are available. Access is by road or dugout canoe. A/c ₹500 extra. ₹2500

Arcadia TB Rd ☎ 0481 256 9999, ⓦ arcadiahotels.net. The town's top hotel, occupying its tallest building – a towering, white, angular monster block just south of the centre. Its rooms look much nicer from the inside, however, and are very good value (especially the "standard doubles"); there's also a fantastic rooftop pool on the fourteenth floor, as well as a restaurant (*Déja Vu*) and bar (*Ice Lounge*). ₹2200

Backwater Breeze Cheepumkal, 5km north of Kumarakom, near the bird sanctuary ☎ 99954 99320, ⓦ backwaterbreeze.com. Ajish and his family live

downstairs, with the four large guest rooms upstairs sharing a veranda overlooking the canal towards Vembanad Lake. Breakfast is included and there's a restaurant next door where you can order dinner. A/c ₹500 extra. ₹1500

★**GK's Riverview** Thekkakarayil, Kottaparambil, near Pulikkuttssery, 4km by water from Kumarakom ☎ 0481 259 7527 or ☎ 94471 97527, ⓦ gkhomestay-kumarakom .com. Award-winning rustic homestay, buried deep in the watery wilds between Kottayam and Kumarakom. The accommodation comprises four comfortable a/c guest rooms in a separate block behind a family home, overlooking paddy fields. Charming hosts George and Dai are mines of information about the area; they'll pick you up from Kottayam if you phone ahead. Half board ₹3000

Homestead KK Rd ☎ 0481 256 0467. This long-standing hotel is the best mid-priced option, though the beds in the economy rooms are rock hard and it's well worth shelling out an additional ₹200 for a "deluxe" with more space, better furniture and thicker mattresses. ₹785

EATING

Anand KK Rd. For a delicious, pure-veg thali or Udupi snack, you won't do better than this place on the ground floor of the *New Anand Lodge*, just off the northeast side of the main square. Of the two rooms the a/c family hall is more relaxing (though both are a little rough around the edges) and meals only cost ₹10 more. A range of rice meals for under ₹100, and scrumptious masala dosas for ₹45. Daily 6.30am–9pm.

Meenachil Homestead Hotel KK Rd. Quality non-veg Keralan food such as *kozhi* (chicken) *varutha* curry (₹140) and Chinese duck (₹120) is served on the a/c floor; the cheaper "Thali" section downstairs opens earlier for breakfast, as well as serving set Keralan "meals" for ₹105 (veg) and ₹140 (fish) at lunchtime. Daily 8am–9.30pm.

Periyar and around

One of the largest national parks in India, the **Periyar Wildlife Sanctuary** (also known as the Periyar Tiger Reserve) occupies 925 square kilometres of the Cardamom Hills region of the Western Ghats. The majority of its visitors come in the hope of seeing **wild elephants** – or even a rare glimpse of a **tiger** – grazing the shores of the reservoir at the heart of the reserve. Daily safari boats ferry day-trippers around this sprawling, labyrinthine lake, where sightings are most likely at the height of the dry season in April. However, for the rest of the year, wildlife is less abundant than you might expect given Periyar's overwhelming popularity.

6

Just a few hours by road from the Keralan coastal cities and Madurai in Tamil Nadu, Periyar ranks among India's busiest reserves, attracting thousands of visitors over holiday periods. The park's ageing infrastructure, however, has struggled to cope with the recent upsurge in numbers. Just how overburdened facilities had become was horribly revealed in September 2009 when an excursion boat capsized on the lake, killing 45 tourists. Since that **Thekkady disaster**, strict restrictions have been imposed, but the lake safari experience hasn't improved; most foreign visitors leave disappointed, not merely with the park, but also its heavily commercialized surroundings and apparent paucity of wildlife.

That said, if you're prepared to **trek** into the forest, Periyar can still be worth a stay. Elephant, sambar, Malabar giant squirrel, gaur, stripe-necked mongoose and wild boar are still commonly spotted in areas deeper into the park, where birdlife is also prolific. Another selling point is Periyar's much vaunted **ecotourism** initiative. Instead of earning their livelihoods through poaching and illegal sandalwood extraction, local Manna people are these days employed by the Forest Department to protect vulnerable parts of the sanctuary. Schemes such as "Border Hiking", "Tiger Trail" and "Jungle Scout" tours, in which visitors accompany tribal wardens on their duties, serve to promote community welfare and generate income for conservation work.

In addition, the area **around Periyar** holds plenty of engaging day-trip destinations, such as **spice plantations** and an **elephant camp**, as well as lots of scope for **trekking** in the surrounding hills and forest. It's also a lot cooler up here than down on the more humid coast, and many foreign visitors are glad of the break from the heat.

Kumily

As beds inside the wildlife sanctuary are in short supply, most visitors to Periyar stay in nearby **KUMILY**, a typical High Range town, centred on a hectic roadside market, 1km or so north of the main park entrance (known as **Thekkady**). Hotels and Kashmiri handicrafts emporia have spread south from the bazaar to within a stone's throw of the park, and tourism now rivals the spice trade as the area's main source of income. That said, you'll still see plenty of little shops selling local herbs, essential oils and cooking spices, while in the busy **cardamom sorting yard** behind the *Spice Village* resort, rows of Manna women sift through heaps of fragrant green pods using heart-shaped baskets.

Periyar Wildlife Sanctuary

Daily 6am–6pm · ₹450 (₹33) · ⑩ periyartigerreserve.org

Centred on a vast artificial **lake** created by the British in 1895 to supply water to the drier parts of neighbouring Tamil Nadu, the **Periyar Wildlife Sanctuary** lies at altitudes of between 900m and 1800m, and is correspondingly cool: temperatures range from 15°C to 30°C. The royal family of Travancore, anxious to preserve favourite hunting grounds from the encroachment of tea plantations, declared it a forest reserve, and built the Edapalayam Lake Palace to accommodate their guests in 1899.

Seventy percent of the protected area, which is divided into core, buffer and tourist zones, is covered with evergreen and semi-evergreen forest. The **tourist zone** – logically

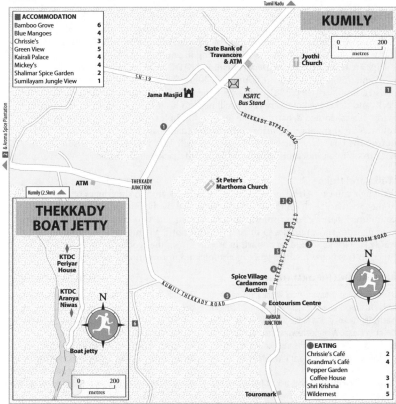

enough, the part accessible to casual visitors – surrounds the lake, and consists mostly of semi-evergreen and deciduous woodland interspersed with grassland, both on hilltops and in the valleys. Although excursions on the lake (either by diesel-powered launch or paddle-powered bamboo raft) are the standard ways to experience the park, you can get much more out of a visit by **walking** with a local guide in a small group away from the crowd. However, avoid the period immediately after the monsoons, when **leeches** make hiking virtually impossible. The **best time to visit** is between December and April, when the dry weather draws animals from the forest to drink at the lakeside.

Bamboo rafting trips

By far the best option for wildlife viewing from the lake is to sign up for one of the Forest Department's excellent **bamboo rafting trips**, which start with a short hike from the boat jetty at 8am, with the half-day trip returning at 2pm and the full-day option at 5pm. The rafts carry four or five people and, because they're paddled rather than motor-driven, can approach the lakeshore in silence, allowing you to get closer to the grazing animals and birds. Tickets cost ₹2000 per person for a full day and may be booked in advance from the ecotourism centre on Ambadi Junction (see p.330). Note that during busy periods places sell out quickly, so reserve as far ahead as possible.

Boat tours

Although **boat tours** are considerably less expensive than the bamboo rafting trips, it's quite a hassle to book yourself on one, and the trips themselves can come as a disappointment. It's unusual to see many animals – engine noise and the presence of dozens of other people make sure of that. To maximize your chances of sighting elephants, wild boar or sambar grazing by the water's edge, take the 7.30am service (for which you'll need to wear warm clothing in winter).

Trips are run by the **Forest Department** and **KTDC** and depart at the same times (7.30am, 9.30am, 11.15am, 1.45pm & 3.30pm; ₹150). Since the 2009 Thekkady disaster, however (see p.328), only twenty people are permitted to travel on the upper decks and tickets sell out very fast; you'll need to be at the lakeside at least two hours before the scheduled departure time (or 1hr 30min for the 7.30am boat). Sales counters are just above the main **visitor centre** (daily 6am–6pm; ☎04869 224571), next to the boat jetty; the Forest Department will issue two seats per person. You'll need to fill in an indemnity form, and wear a life-jacket at all times.

Walks and treks

Although you can – leeches permitting – trek freely around the fringes of Periyar, access to the sanctuary itself on foot is strictly controlled by the Forest Department. Their community-based ecotourism programme offers a variety of structured **walking tours**, ranging from short rambles to three-day expeditions, all guided by local Manna tribal wardens. Tickets should be booked in advance from the ecotourism centre on Ambadi Junction (see below), where you can also pick up information on the trips.

ARRIVAL AND INFORMATION   PERIYAR AND AROUND

By bus Buses from Kottayam (every 30min; 4hr), Ernakulam/ Kochi (10 daily; 5hr) and Madurai in Tamil Nadu (at least hourly; 5hr 30min) pull in to the scruffy bus stand east of the main bazaar. Auto-rickshaws will run you from here to the visitor centre inside the park for around ₹60–70, stopping at the park entrance at Thekkady where you can pay the reserve fee.

Tourist information To book any of Periyar's popular ecotours (see below), you'll have to walk down the

Thekkady Rd to the ecotourism centre on Ambadi Junction (daily 6.30am–8.30pm, last tickets sold at 7.30pm; ☎04869 224571) – or better still, book in advance on ⊕ periyartigerreserve.org.

Services Both the State Bank of Travancore (which has an ATM), near the bus stand, and the Thekkady Bankers in the main bazaar can change currency and travellers' cheques. Internet facilities are available around Thekkady Junction for about ₹40/hr.

TOURS AND TREKS

Tours As well as the attraction of the wildlife sanctuary, tours to tea factories and spice plantations are offered by almost every hotel and tourist agency in Kumily. Unfortunately, many places have become heavily commercialized, so it's worth shopping around; often the best way to organize a tour is to ask at your hotel. There are only a couple of certified organic spice gardens in the area, Aroma at Chelimada, a short walk west of Kumily on the Kottayam Rd (₹250/person; contact the owner Mr Sebastian on ☎ 94953 67837), and Manu Abraham's idyllic plantation out on the Kumily–Attapallum main road (₹300/person; book in advance on ☎ 94464 02276).

Treks The windy, grassy ridgetops and forests around Periyar afford many fine treks, with superb views over the High

Range guaranteed. One especially rewarding half-day trip is the hike up Kurusamalai (3hr), the peak towering to the northwest of Kumily, whose summit is crowned with a Holy Cross. As the summit falls within the national park boundaries, you're only permitted to hike to it under the auspices of the ecotourism centre (see above), who market it as their "Cloud Walk" (₹300). Although hilly, this area is also good cycling territory; you can rent bikes from stalls in the market, and Touromark (☎ 04869 224332, ⊕ touromark .com), midway between Kumily and Thekkady, have imported 21-speed mountain bikes for rent. They also offer guided trips, ranging from 4hr/15km hacks through local spice gardens, coffee plantations and woodlands to a three-night/four-day ride across the Cardamom Hills to Munnar.

ACCOMMODATION

Kumily has **accommodation** to suit all pockets, with a number of small homestay guesthouses on the fringes of the village offering particularly good value; the three KTDC-run hotels actually inside the park are either ludicrously expensive or shabby, or both. The forest department has a decent campsite, 16km away, just beyond Vallakkadavu checkpoint; they also offer camping inside the park on their "Tiger Trail" trek (contact the ecotourism centre).

Bamboo Grove Off Kumily Thekkady Rd; book via the ecotourism centre ☎0486 922 4571, ⓦperiyartiger reserve.org. Though not in the park itself, *Bamboo Grove* is run by the forest department and aims to support local communities. The fifteen individual cottages are a little dark, but they're clean and private and set in lovely gardens. The two-day package (₹4500 for two adults) is great value as it includes food, a jungle trek, tribal visit and boat tour. ₹1500

Blue Mangoes Bypass Rd ☎04869 224603 or ☎97449 95253. Simple rooms (with sitouts and balconies) in an impeccably clean modern block, plus a larger family "cottage". Rock-bottom rates, but good bedding and a quiet location. Owner Bobby speaks excellent English. ₹650

Chrissie's Bypass Rd ☎0486 922 4155 or ☎94476 01304, ⓦchrissies.in. Smart four-storey hotel below the bazaar, run by Adel and his long-standing staff. It's pricier than most homestays in the area, but you get more privacy and better views, and homely interiors decorated with unique artwork. There's also a great yoga *shala* on the rooftop, and a popular little café-restaurant on the ground floor (see p.332). ₹2300

Green View Bypass Rd ☎0486 922 4617 or ☎94474 32008, ⓦsureshgreenview.com. One of Kumily's most popular homestays, in a newish house just off the Thekkady Rd. The seventeen rooms range from basic options with bucket hot water to large rooms with solar-heated showers and balconies looking across the valley to Kurusamalai Mountain (₹1750); the rooftop where you can do yoga shares the same view. A lovely rear garden attracts lots of wild birds. ₹750

Kairali Palace Bypass Rd ☎0854 782 2285 or ☎98951 87789, ✉nitheeshmeera@gmail.com. Outstandingly attractive homestay in a fusion building that blends traditional and modern styles, with gabled roofs and wooden railings wrapped around the airy first-floor terrace. It has just two rooms, both well furnished for the price. ₹950

Mickey's Bypass Rd ☎0486 922 3196 or ☎94472 84160. One of the oldest guesthouses in Kumily, whose smiling owner, Sujata, offers a range of rooms and cottages (₹1250), all with balconies or sitouts littered with comfortable cane furniture. ₹750

Shalimar Spice Garden Murikaddy, 6km from Kumily ☎04869 222132, ⓦshalimarkerala.net. Teak huts in traditional Keralan style with elephant-grass roofs, whitewashed walls, chic interiors and verandas looking straight onto forest, on the edge of an old cardamom and pepper estate. Facilities include a beautiful Ayurveda centre, an outdoor pool set amid the trees and an open-sided restaurant where you can fine dine at rough-hewn

6

THE AYAPPA CULT

Throughout December and January, Kerala is packed with huge crowds of men wearing black *dhotis*; you'll see them milling about railway stations, driving in overcrowded and gaily decorated jeeps and cooking a quick meal on the roadside by their tour bus. They are pilgrims on their way to the Sri Ayappa forest temple (also known as Hariharaputra or Shasta) at **Sabarimala**, in the western section of Periyar, around 200km from both Thiruvananthapuram and Kochi. The **Ayappa devotees** can seem disconcertingly ebullient, chanting "*Swamiyee Sharanam Ayappan*" ("Give us protection, god Ayappa") in a lusty call-and-response style reminiscent of English football fans.

Ayappa – the offspring of a union between Shiva and Mohini, Vishnu's beautiful female form – is primarily a Keralan deity, but his appeal has spread phenomenally in the last thirty years across South India, to the extent that this is said to be **the largest pilgrimage in the world**, with as many as 40 to 50 million devotees each year. Pilgrims are required to remain celibate, abstain from intoxicants, and keep to a strict vegetarian diet for 41 days before setting out on the four-day walk through the forest from the village of **Erumeli** (61km, as the crow flies, northwest) to the shrine at Sabarimala. Less-keen devotees take the bus to the village of Pampa, and join the 5km queue. When they arrive at the modern temple complex, pilgrims who have performed the necessary penances may ascend the famous eighteen **gold steps** to the inner shrine. There they worship the deity, throwing donations down a chute that opens onto a subterranean conveyor belt, where the money is counted and bagged.

The pilgrimage reaches a climax during the festival of Makaravilakku or **Makar Sankranti**, when massive crowds congregate at Sabarimala. On January 14, 1999, 51 devotees were buried alive when part of a hill crumbled under the crush of a stampede. The pilgrims had gathered at dusk to catch a glimpse of the final sunset of **makara jyoti** ("celestial light") on the distant hill of Ponnambalamedu.

Although males of any age and even of any religion can take part in the pilgrimage, **females** between the ages of 9 and 50 are barred.

granite tables. ₹12,500

★**Sumilayam Jungle View** On the eastern edge of town ☎0486 922 3582 or ☎94461 36407, ✉jungle view8@yahoo.com. The best-value budget homestay in Kumily, a 10min plod (or short auto-rickshaw ride) from the bus stand – literally on the Tamil Nadu–Kerala border.

The clean, bright guestrooms are comfortably furnished; those on the upper storey open onto a marble-floored veranda just metres from jungle. Free nocturnal wildlife-spotting walks in the gardens are offered by your welcoming host, Mr Ramachandran. ₹850

6

EATING

You're more likely to take **meals** at your guesthouse or hotel than eat out in Kumily, but for a change of scene the following places are the best options within walking distance of the bazaar.

Chrissie's Café Bypass Rd ☎0486 922 4155, ⊚chrissies .in. This relaxing expat-run café, on the ground floor of *Chrissie's* hotel, pulls in a steady stream of foreigners through-out the day and evening for its delicious pizzas (₹175–250), made with Kodai mozzarella, and Middle Eastern options; check out the specials board. They also do healthy breakfasts, home-made cakes and proper coffee. Count on ₹400–500/head. Daily 8am–9pm.

Grandma's Café Bypass Rd ☎99953 17261. This arty café is adored by backpackers for its laidback vibe and tasty grub; try the *ularthiyathu* with mushrooms (₹160) or prawns (₹330). Service can be a little slow, but for distraction there's a projector for films and most nights a campfire is lit. Daily 7.30am–10.30pm.

Pepper Garden Coffee House Thamarkandam Rd. In a garden filled with cardamom bushes behind a prettily painted blue-and-green house, a former park guide and his wife whip up tempting travellers' breakfasts (date and

raisin pancakes, porridge with jungle honey, fresh coffee and Nilgiri tea), in addition to home-cooked lunches of veg fried rice, curry and dhal, using mostly local organic produce. Mains ₹65–150. Daily 8.30am–9.30pm.

Shri Krishna Bypass Rd. Run by a Bihari family, this pure-veg restaurant serves authentic North Indian dishes, including cheap and filling Gujarati and Marwari thalis (₹70–110), served on the usual tin trays or leaves. Daily 8am–9pm.

Wildernest Thekkady Rd ☎0486 922 4030, ⊚wildernest-kerala.com. Filling Continental buffet breakfasts (fruit, juices, cereals, eggs, toast, peanut butter, home-made jams and freshly ground coffee; ₹250) served in the ground-floor café of a stylish small hotel (rooms ₹5500; those on the first floor with terraces are best). They also serve afternoon tea and cakes (including a delicious, very British, warm plum cake). Daily 8am–7pm.

Munnar and around

MUNNAR, 130km east of Kochi and 110km north (4hr 30min by bus) of the Periyar Wildlife Sanctuary, is the centre of Kerala's principal tea-growing region. A scruffy agglomeration of corrugated-iron-roofed cottages and tea factories, its centre on the valley floor fails to live up to its tourist-office billing as "hill station", but there's plenty to enthuse about in the surrounding mountains, whose lower slopes are carpeted with lush tea gardens and dotted with quaint old colonial bungalows. Above them, the grassy ridges and crags of the High Range offer superlative **trekking** routes, many of which can be tackled in day-trips from the town – though note that peninsular India's highest peak, **Ana Mudi** (2695m), is closed to visitors for the time being.

It's easy to see why the pioneering Scottish planters who developed this hidden valley in the 1870s and 1880s felt so at home here. At an altitude of around 1600m, Munnar enjoys a refreshing **climate**, with crisp mornings and sunny blue skies in the winter – though as with all of Kerala, torrential rains descend during the monsoons. Munnar's greenery and cool air draw streams of well-heeled honeymooners and weekenders from South India's cities. However, increasing numbers of foreign visitors are stopping for a few days too, enticed by the superbly scenic bus ride from Periyar, which takes you across the high ridges and lush tropical forests of the Cardamom Hills, or for the equally spectacular climb across the Ghats from Madurai.

Clustered around the confluence of three mountain streams, Munnar town is a typical hill bazaar of haphazard buildings and congested market streets; the daily vegetable **market** in the main bazaar is a good place for a wander (closed Wed).

HIKING AROUND MUNNAR

Although South India's highest peak, Ana Mudi, is off-limits due to the Nilgiri tahr conservation programme (see p.334), several of the other summits towering above Munnar can be reached on day-treks. The hiking scene is surprisingly undeveloped and it makes sense to use the services of a guide, particularly for **Meesapulimalai Peak** (2640m), which can be accessed from Silent Valley or Kolukkumalai estates and could easily be incorporated into a multiday excursion. Always check whether transport to and from the trailhead is included.

OPERATORS

Greenview Pleasure Holidays ⓦmunnartrekking .com. The owner of the *Green View* guesthouse (see p.335) and his enthusiastic young team lead groups of two or more on nearby routes; rates range from ₹650/ person for soft treks up to ₹1250 for longer, more challenging outings.

Kestrel Adventures ☎0486 5208565 or ☎94470 31040, ⓦkestreladventures.com. This professionally run local adventure company arranges treks (₹4200 for 2–3hr for two people at Chinnar, including transport), sightseeing by jeep (₹2000 for a full day) and mountain biking (₹6100 for two people for a full day off road –

plus tax and jeep rental).

KFDC See p.334. The Kerala Forest Development Corporation arranges 24hr treks (₹7000), including basic overnight accommodation in Silent Valley and transfers in packed jeeps.

Kolukkumalai ⓦkolukkumalai.in. Your best bet for multiday bespoke trips on Meeshapulimalai and the surrounding grasslands. English-speaking guides and delicious food – plus you can opt to stay in a mountain hut nestled in the highest tea estate in the world. Prices start at ₹2500 for a day-trek (plus transport and accommodation).

Kanan Devan Hills Tea Museum

Nallathany Rd · Tues–Sun 10am–4pm · ₹95, camera ₹25 · ⓦ kdhptea.com/TeaMuseum.html

Although it doesn't physically demonstrate how tea is made, the **Kanan Devan Hills Tea Museum**, 2km northwest of the centre, is worth a visit for its collection of antique machinery and exhibition of photos of the area's tea industry, ranging from 1880s pioneers to the modern Tata tea conglomerate. The highlight of the visit is a short audiovisual presentation outlining how tea was introduced to the region and how it is processed today, rounded off with a tasting session; and there's a shop selling various KDH products.

Around Munnar

Buses wind their way up to the aptly named **Top Station**, a hamlet famed for its views and meadows of **Neelakurunji plants**, and to the more distant nature sanctuaries of Eravikulam and Chinnar, where you can spot Nilgiri tahr, elephant and many other wild animals. To reach the most remote attractions, however, you might want to hire a taxi for the day.

Top Station

34km northeast of Munnar · 10 daily buses (from 5.30am; 1hr 30min); jeep taxis do the return trip for ₹1200

One of the most popular **excursions** from Munnar is the long climb through some of the Subcontinent's highest tea estates to **TOP STATION**, a tiny hamlet on the Kerala–Tamil Nadu border which, at 1600m, is the highest point on the interstate road. The settlement takes its name from the old aerial **ropeway** that used to connect it with the valley floor, the ruins of which can still be seen in places.

Eravikulam National Park

13km northeast of Munnar · Daily 8am–4.30pm; closed for calving season Feb to early April, check ahead · ₹370 (₹90), tickets can be purchased in advance (additional ₹50) online to avoid the queues · ⓦ eravikulam.org

Encompassing 100 square kilometres of moist evergreen forest and grassy hilltops in the Western Ghats, **Eravikulam National Park** is the last stronghold of one of the world's

6

THE NEELAKURUNJI PLANT

Apart from the marvellous views over the Tamil plains, the hills around Munnar are renowned for the very rare **Neelakurunji plant** (*Strobilatanthes*), which flowers only once every twelve years. Huge crowds climb up to Top Station and other viewpoints to admire the cascades of violet blossom spilling down the slopes (the next flowering is due in Sept/Oct 2018). Views are best before the mist builds at 9am.

---

rarest mountain goats, the **Nilgiri tahr**. Its innate friendliness made the tahr pathetically easy prey during the hunting frenzy of the colonial era. Today, however, numbers are healthy, and the animals have regained their tameness, largely thanks to the efforts of the American biologist Clifford Rice, who studied them here in the early 1980s. Unable to get close enough to observe the creatures properly, Rice followed the advice of locals and attracted them using salt, and soon entire herds were congregating around his camp. The tahrs' salt addiction also explains why so many hang around the park gates at **Vaguvarai**, where visitors – despite advice from rangers – slip them salty snacks.

You're almost guaranteed sightings of tahr from the minute you enter the park gates, reached by shuttle bus (₹20). From there, you can walk a further 1500m up a winding single-track road before the rangers turn you around, but expect to do so in the company of hundreds of other tourists on weekends – a rather hollow experience.

Chinnar Wildlife Sanctuary

58km north of Munnar • Daily 6am–7pm • ₹100 (₹10) • ⓦ chinnar.org • Any bus running between Munnar and Udumalpet will stop at the sanctuary

Although it borders Eravikulam, the **Chinnar Wildlife Sanctuary** is far less visited, not least because its entrance lies a two-hour drive from Munnar along winding mountain roads. The reserve, in the rain shadow of the High Range and thus much drier than its neighbour, is one of the best spots in the state for birdwatching, with 225 species recorded to date. But the real star attractions are the resident **grizzled giant squirrels**, who scamper in healthy numbers around the thorny scrub here, and the near-mythical "white bison of Manjampatti", thought to be an albino Indian gaur.

Members of local tribal communities (who won't be fluent in English) act as guides for popular day-treks that might take in prehistoric rock art, dolmen sites or a waterfall – all of which can be arranged on spec at a counter next to the Chinnar Forest Check Post. For multiday treks you can camp or book a bed in the thirty-bed dormitory, but this needs to be arranged in advance at the Forest Information Centre in Munnar or with Kestrel Adventures (see box, p.333).

ARRIVAL AND INFORMATION   MUNNAR

By bus State-run and private buses pull into the town bus stand in the modern main bazaar, near the river confluence and Tata headquarters; state buses continue through town, terminating nearly 3km south. For most hotels you should ask to be dropped off at Old Munnar, 2km south of the centre, near the ineffectual DTPC tourist office (daily 8.30am–7pm; ⓣ 04865 231516).

Destinations Ernakulam/Kochi (every 30min; 5hr 30min); Kottayam (5 daily; 5hr); Kumily (3 daily; 5hr).

KFDC office Based in the Rose Gardens, 2km east on Mattupetty Rd (ⓣ 0486 523 0332, ⓦ munnar.kfdceco tourism.com), KFDC can arrange a whistlestop day-tour around Munnar (₹1000/person) as well as multiday treks (see box, p.333).

Forest Information Centre Near Mount Carmel Church in the centre of Munnar town (ⓣ 0486 523 1587). Drop in to organize trips to Chinnar Wildlife Sanctuary.

ACCOMMODATION

Munnar's **accommodation** costs significantly more than elsewhere in the High Range region, reflecting the high demand for beds from middle-class tourists from the big cities. Rooms at the low end of the scale are in particularly short supply; the few that exist are blighted by racket from the bus stand and bazaar. There are some options outside town that would suit travellers with their own transport.

Anaerangal Camp at Suryanelli 25km east of Munnar on the Periyar road ☎ 0484 209 2280 or ☎ 0484 401 2700, ⊕ munnarcamps.com. Half a dozen spacious fixed tents, fitted with beds and bathrooms, facing a magnificent panorama of mountain peaks, lake and forest. Keralan food, prepared at kitchens on site, is included in the rate, along with trekking to the lake and nearby peak, plantation visits and an evening camp fire. An inspiring location, but not the quality outfit it once was. ₹6000

Green Valley Vista Chekuthan Mukku, Chithirapuram, 8km south of Munnar ☎ 0486 5263 261 or ☎ 94474 32008, ⊕ greenvalleyvista.com. On the main road (ask the bus to drop you at the stop 20m away), so it's worth paying a bit extra for the larger quieter rooms at the back, which have the added advantage of gorgeous valley views. Sister to the *Green View* in Kumily, it offers the same good-value, clean rooms but with a bit less character. ₹1500

Green View Sri Parvati Amman Kovil St, near the KSRTC bus stand ☎ 0486 523 0189 or ☎ 94478 25447 (Deepak). Clean and friendly budget guesthouse on the valley floor, down a side road just off the main drag, with rooms of various sizes – the best of them, no. 402, is a tiny double with big windows and hill views. Pitched squarely at foreign backpackers, it's run by an enthusiastic, competent young crew who do a sideline in guided day-treks (see box, p.333). They have some quieter properties outside town; enquire about *River Green Villa* and *Greenwoods Cottage*. ₹600

★ **High Range Club** Kanan Devan Hills Rd ☎ 0486 523 0253, ⊕ highrangeclubmunnar.com. This old Raj-era club, founded by British planters in 1909, must have been a nightmare of suffocating imperialism in its heyday. Now the faded colonial ambience, with lounges filled with 1940s furniture and moth-eaten hunting trophies, feels undeniably quaint (though there *is* still a dress code on Sat evenings). The club's guest wing holds three kinds of rooms and cottages (₹3500–4500), varying in size and comfort. Breakfast, lunch and dinner available for an extra ₹745. ₹3000

JJ Cottage Sri Parvati Amman Kovil St, near the KSRTC bus stand ☎ 0486 523 0104. Next door to *Green View*, and very much in the same mould, though it's been open longer, charges more and tends to get booked up earlier. Like its neighbour, the nicest of its clean, variously sized rooms is the one at the top (frontside), which has wood-panelled walls and fine views. A warm family welcome is guaranteed. ₹650

★ **Rosegardens** Karadipara, near the viewpoint on NH-49, 10km southwest of Munnar ☎ 0486 4278 243 or ☎ 94473 78524, ⊕ munnarhomestays.com. This gem of a homestay has five rooms, all with terraces. It's the two-acre setting that steals the show and hosts Tomy and Rajee are justly proud of their beautiful gardens. There's no TV here – instead you have meals with the family and plenty of peace and quiet. Trekking and cookery courses can be arranged, and there's decent driver accommodation. ₹4500

Zina Cottages Kad ☎ 0486 523 0349 or ☎ 94471 90954. British-era stone bungalow, nestled amid tea gardens high on the hillside above Munnar. The basic rooms can be chilly, but the flower-filled front terrace has magnificent views across the town to Ana Mudi, and the young host will fill you in on local walks over flasks of hot tea in his sitting room. Come here less for creature comforts than for atmosphere, of which it has plenty. ₹750

EATING

The **thattukada** (hot food stall market) just south of the main bazaar, opposite the taxi stand, gets into its stride around 7.30pm and runs through the night, serving delicious, piping-hot Keralan food – dosas, *parathas*, *iddiappam*, green-bean curry, egg masala – ladled onto tin plates and eaten on rough wood tables in the street.

Guru Bhavan Mattupetty Rd ☎ 94478 25941. This place, a 10min uphill walk from the bazaar, is packed out with locals enjoying veg and non-veg (mostly) South Indian dishes; veg "meals" are stupendous value at ₹50. Drop by in the morning for cheap and delicious breakfast staples like *idli* and dosas. Daily 7am–10pm.

Saravan Bhavan Munnar Market. The best pure-veg South Indian restaurant in town, serving the standard range of tasty Udupi dosas (₹30–50) and thali meals (₹70) – in addition to popular mini-*idli* plates and delicious buttermilk. Tucked away down a narrow side street, but there's a large sign on the roadside in the main bazaar, directly behind the Gandhi statue. Daily 8am–9pm.

Kochi (Cochin)

Spreading across islands and promontories between the Arabian Sea and the backwaters, **KOCHI** (long known as **Cochin**) is Kerala's prime tourist destination. Its main sections – modern **Ernakulam** and the old peninsular districts of **Mattancherry** and **Fort Cochin** to the west – are linked by bridges and a complex system of ferries. Although some visitors

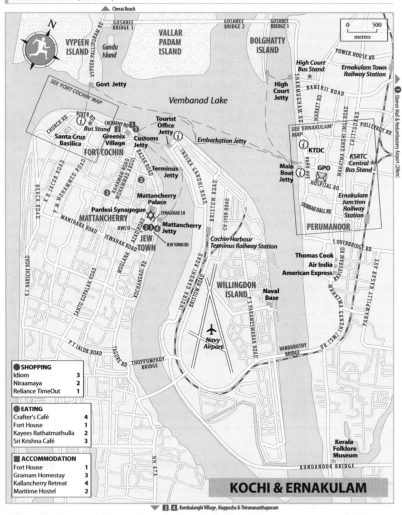

Cherai Beach

GOSHREE BRIDGE 3 **GOSHREE BRIDGE 2** **GOSHREE BRIDGE 1**

VYPEEN ISLAND
Gundu Island

VALLAR PADAM ISLAND

BOLGHATTY ISLAND

POWER HOUSE RD

High Court Bus Stand
Ernakulam Town Railway Station

SEE FORT COCHIN MAP

Govt Jetty

BANERJI ROAD

MARKET RD

High Court Jetty

Vembanad Lake

PULLEPADY RD

SEE ERNAKULAM MAP

RIVER RD

CHURCH RD

CALVATHY RD

Tourist Office Jetty

KTDC

Santa Cruz Basilica
Greenix Village
Customs Jetty

Embarkation Jetty

KSRTC Central Bus Stand

FORT COCHIN

Main Boat Jetty

GPO

HOSPITAL RD

Terminus Jetty

Ernakulam Junction Railway Station

Mattancherry Palace

DURBAR HALL RD

PERUMANOOR

Pardesi Synagogue
MATTANCHERRY

SYNAGOGUE LN

JEWS ST

Mattancherry Jetty

JEW TOWN

JEW TOWN RD

Cochin Harbour Terminus Railway Station

S OVERBRIDGE RD

Thomas Cook
Air India
American Express

WILLINGDON ISLAND

Naval Base

PARAMPILLY NAGAR AVE

Navy Airport

VANDURUTHY BRIDGE

P T JACOB ROAD

THOPPUMPADY BRIDGE

Kerala Folklore Museum

● **SHOPPING**
Idiom	3
Niraamaya	2
Reliance TimeOut	1

KUNDANOOR BRIDGE

● **EATING**
Crafter's Café	4
Fort House	1
Kayees Rathatmathulla	2
Sri Krishna Café	3

KOCHI & ERNAKULAM

■ **ACCOMMODATION**
Fort House	1
Gramam Homestay	3
Kallancherry Retreat	4
Maritime Hostel	2

3, 4, Kumbalanghi Village, Alappuzha & Thiruvananthapuram

opt to stay in the more convenient Ernakulam, the overwhelming majority base themselves in Fort Cochin, where the city's complex history is reflected in an assortment of architectural styles. Spice markets, Chinese fishing nets, a synagogue, a Portuguese palace, India's first European church and seventeenth-century Dutch homes can all be found within an easy walk.

Brief history

Kochi sprang into being in 1341, when a flood created a safe natural port that swiftly replaced Muziris (now Kodungallur, 50km north) as the chief harbour on the Malabar Coast. The royal family moved here in 1405, after which the city grew rapidly, attracting Christian, Arab and Jewish settlers from the Middle East. The history of **European** involvement from the early 1500s onwards is dominated by the aggression of the Portuguese, Dutch and British, who successively competed to control the port and its lucrative spice trade. From 1812 until Independence in 1947 it was administered by a succession of *diwans*, or finance ministers. In the 1920s, the British expanded the port to accommodate modern ocean-going ships, and Willingdon Island, between Ernakulam and Fort Cochin, was created by extensive dredging.

Old Kochi: Fort Cochin and Mattancherry

Old Kochi, the thumb-shaped peninsula whose northern tip presides over the entrance to the city's harbour, formed the focus of European trading activities from the sixteenth century onwards. With high-rise development restricted to Ernakulam across the water, its twin districts of **Fort Cochin**, in the west, and **Mattancherry**, on the headland's eastern side, have preserved an extraordinary wealth of early colonial architecture, spanning the Portuguese, Dutch and British eras – a crop unparalleled in India. As you approach by ferry, the waterfront, with its sloping red-tiled roofs and ranks of peeling, pastel-coloured *godowns* (warehouses), offers a view that can have changed little in centuries.

Closer up, however, Old Kochi's historic patina has started to show some ugly cracks. The spice trade that fuelled the town's original rise is still very much in evidence. But over the past twenty years an extraordinary rise in visitor numbers has had a major impact. Thousands of tourists pour through daily in winter, and with no planning or preservation authority to take control, the resulting rash of new building threatens to destroy the very atmosphere people come here to experience. That said, tourism has also brought some benefits, inspiring renovation work to buildings that would otherwise have been left to rot.

Fort Cochin

Fort Cochin, the grid of old streets at the northwest tip of the peninsula, is where the Portuguese erected their first walled citadel, Fort Immanuel, which the Dutch East India Company later consolidated with a circle of well-fortified ramparts. Only a few fragments of the former battlements remain (the outline of the old walls is traced by the district's giant rain trees, some of which are more than two centuries old), but dozens of other evocative European-era monuments survive.

A good way to get to grips with Fort Cochin's many-layered history is to pick up the free **walking-tour maps** produced by Kerala Tourism and the privately run Tourist Desk (see p.342). They lead you around some of the district's more significant landmarks, including the early eighteenth-century Dutch Cemetery, Vasco da Gama's supposed house and several traders' residences.

Walking around the old quarter you'll come across several small exhibition spaces and **galleries** – evidence of Fort Cochin's newfound status as one of India's contemporary art hubs. The scene takes centre stage between mid-December and March when the **Kochi-Muziris Biennale** (ⓦkochimuzirisbiennale.org) draws artists and collectors from across the country with its mix of film, art, performance art and new media hosted by half a dozen different venues.

Chinese fishing nets
Daily 6.30am–11am & 5–7pm

Probably the single most familiar photographic image of Kerala, the huge, elegant **Chinese fishing nets** lining the northern shore of Fort Cochin add grace to the waterfront view. Traders from the court of Kublai Khan are said to have introduced them to the Malabar region. Known in Malayalam as *cheena vala*, they can also be seen throughout the backwaters further south. The nets, which are suspended from poles and operated by levers and weights, require at least four men to control them. If you linger, the fishermen will beckon you over to help (for a small tip).

6

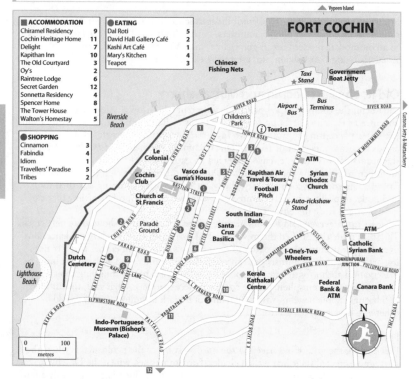

▲ Vypeen Island

FORT COCHIN

■ ACCOMMODATION	
Chiramel Residency	9
Cochin Heritage Home	11
Delight	7
Kapithan Inn	10
The Old Courtyard	3
Oy's	2
Raintree Lodge	6
Secret Garden	12
Sonnetta Residency	4
Spencer Home	8
The Tower House	1
Walton's Homestay	5

● EATING	
Dal Roti	5
David Hall Gallery Café	2
Kashi Art Café	1
Mary's Kitchen	4
Teapot	3

● SHOPPING	
Cinnamon	3
Fabindia	4
Idiom	1
Travellers' Paradise	5
Tribes	2

Church of St Francis and around

Parade Ground • Daily 8.30am–6.30pm • Free

South of the Chinese fishing nets on Church Road (the continuation of River Road) is the large, typically English **Parade Ground**. Overlooking it, the **Church of St Francis** was the first built by Europeans in India. Its exact age is not known, though the stone structure is thought to date back to the early sixteenth century. The facade, meanwhile, became the model for most Christian churches in India. Vasco da Gama was buried here in 1524, but his body was later removed to Portugal. Under the Dutch, the church was renovated and became Protestant in 1663, then Anglican with the advent of the British in 1795. Inside, the earliest of various tombstone inscriptions placed in the walls dates from 1562.

Mattancherry

Mattancherry, the old district of red-tiled riverfront wharves and houses occupying the northeastern tip of the headland, was once the colonial capital's main market area – the epicentre of the Malabar's spice trade, and home to its wealthiest Jewish and Jain merchants. Like Fort Cochin, its once grand buildings have lapsed into advanced states of disrepair, with most of their original owners working overseas. When Mattancherry's Jews emigrated en masse to Israel in the 1940s, their furniture and other unportable heirlooms ended up in the **antique shops** for which the area is now renowned – though these days genuine pieces are few and far between.

Mattancherry Palace

Jew Town Rd • Daily except Fri 9am–5pm • ₹5

The sight at the top of most itineraries is **Mattancherry Palace**, on the roadside a short walk from the Mattancherry Jetty, 1km or so southeast of Fort Cochin. Known locally as the Dutch Palace, the two-storey building was actually erected by the Portuguese, as a gift to the raja of Cochin, Vira Keralavarma (1537–61) – though the Dutch did add to the complex. While its squat exterior is not particularly striking, the interior is captivating, with some of the finest examples of Kerala's underrated school of **mural** painting, along with Dutch maps of old Cochin, coronation robes belonging to past maharajas, royal palanquins, weapons and furniture.

Pardesi Synagogue

Synagogue Lane, Jew Town • Sun–Thurs 10am–1pm & 3–5pm, Fri 10am–1pm • ₹5

The neighbourhood immediately behind and to the south of Mattancherry Palace is known as **Jew Town**, home of a vestigial Jewish community whose place of worship is the **Pardesi (White Jew) Synagogue**. Founded in 1568 and rebuilt in 1664, the building is best known for its interior, an incongruous hotchpotch paved with hand-painted eighteenth-century blue-and-white tiles from Canton. An elaborately carved Ark houses four scrolls of the Torah, on which sit gold crowns presented by the maharajas of Travancore and Cochin, testifying to good relations with the Jewish community. The synagogue's oldest artefact is a fourth-century copperplate inscription from the raja of Cochin.

Ernakulam

With its fast-paced traffic, broad streets and glittering gold emporia, **ERNAKULAM** has more of a big-city feel than Thiruvananthapuram – despite the fact it's marginally smaller. Other than the contemporary art on display at the small

---

KATHAKALI IN KOCHI

Kochi is the only city in Kerala where you are guaranteed the chance to see live **kathakali**, the state's unique form of ritualized theatre (see box, p.304). Whether in its authentic setting, in temple festivals held in winter, or at the shorter tourist-oriented shows that take place year-round, these mesmerizing dance dramas – depicting the struggles of gods and demons – are an unmissable feature of Kochi's cultural life.

Four venues in the city currently hold daily shows, each preceded by an **introductory talk** at around 6.30pm. You can watch the dancers being made up if you arrive an hour or so beforehand; keen photographers should turn up well before the start to ensure a front-row seat. **Tickets** (usually around ₹250) can be bought at the door. Most visitors only attend one performance, but you'll gain a much better sense of what kathakali is all about if you take in at least a couple. The next step is an **all-night recital** at a temple festival.

Greenix Village Opposite Fort House, Fort Cochin ☏ 0484 221 7000, ⊕ greenix.in. You've a choice between a short kathakali recital (₹350) or longer "kaleidoscope" culture show (₹650) combining excerpts from kathakali plays with displays of mohiniyattam dance, kalarippayat martial art and, on Sun, theyyem, set against a combination of live and prerecorded music. Performances aren't of the highest standard, but costumes and acts change in quick succession and the make-up is particularly stunning. Note that it costs ₹50 extra to take photos.

Kerala Folklore Museum Theyvara, near Kundanur Bridge, southeastern edge of Ernakulam ☏ 0484 266 5452, ⊕ keralafolkloremuseum.org. The most atmospheric venue – an a/c theatre decorated with wonderful Keralan murals and traditional wooden architecture – though it's a long trek across town if you're staying in Fort Cochin and sadly you have to book the entire theatre for an exclusive (and eye-wateringly expensive) show. Most visitors tour the museum downstairs (see p.340) and just take a peek at the theatre.

Kerala Kathakali Centre Bernard Master Lane, near Santa Cruz Basilica, just off KB Jacob Rd, Fort Cochin ☏ 0484 221 7552, ⊕ kathakalicentre.com. Popular performances in a dedicated a/c theatre from a company of graduates of the renowned Kalamandalam academy. You usually get to see three characters, and the music is live. Shows (₹300) 6–7.30pm (make-up 5pm), plus classical music recitals at 8pm every night except Sat (₹250) and kalarippayat martial art daily at 4pm (₹250).

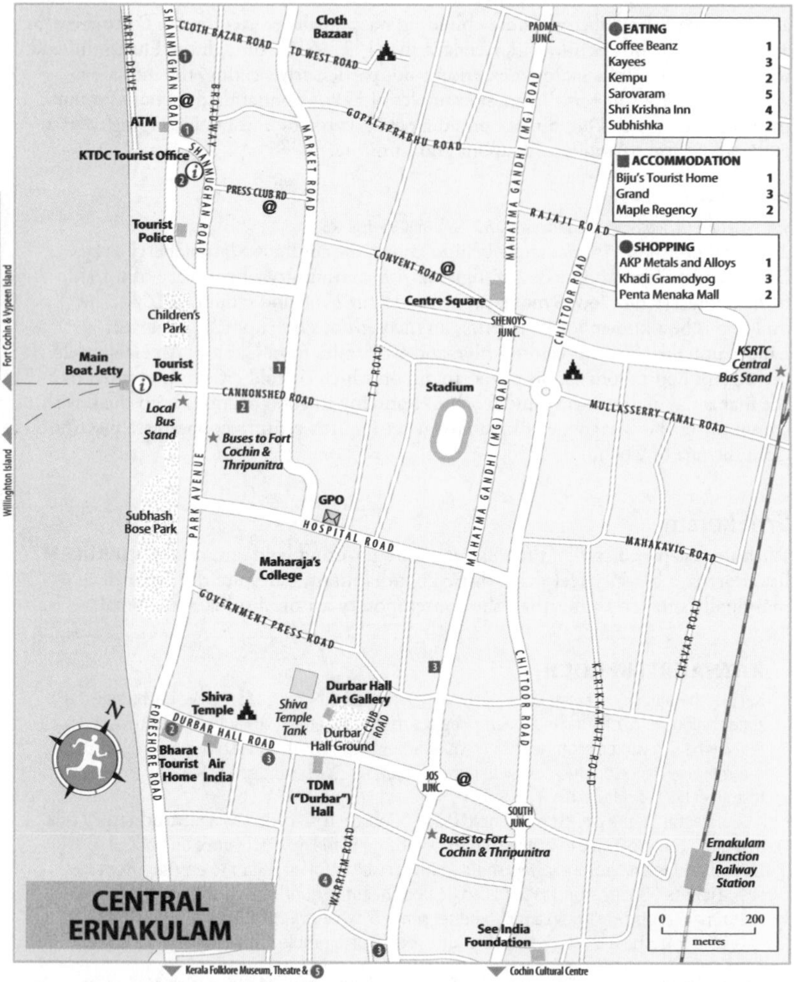

6

EATING
Coffee Beanz	1
Kayees	3
Kempu	2
Sarovaram	5
Shri Krishna Inn	4
Subhishka	2

ACCOMMODATION
Biju's Tourist Home	1
Grand	3
Maple Regency	2

SHOPPING
AKP Metals and Alloys	1
Khadi Gramodyog	3
Penta Menaka Mall	2

CENTRAL ERNAKULAM

Fort Cochin & Vypeen Island

Willingthon Island

Kerala Folklore Museum, Theatre & ⑤   Cochin Cultural Centre

Durbar Hall Art Gallery on Durbar Hall Road (daily 11am–7pm; free), and the remarkable **folklore museum** on the southern outskirts, there's little in the way of sights – if you spend any time here, it'll probably be to eat at one of the area's famous Keralan **restaurants**.

Running parallel to the seafront, roughly 500m inland, **Mahatma Gandhi (MG) Road** is its main thoroughfare, where you'll find some of the largest textile stores, jewellery shops and hotels.

Kerala Folklore Museum

Theyvara, near Kundanur Bridge • Daily 9.30am–6pm • ₹200, camera ₹100 • ☎ 0484 266 5452, ⓦ keralafolkloremuseum.org • Auto-rickshaws charge around ₹200 for the trip out to the museum from the Main Boat Jetty in Ernakulam – ask for Riviera Junction, or Kundanur Bridge

Ernakulam's one outstanding visitor attraction is the **Kerala Folklore Museum**, on the distant southeast fringes of the city. Housed in a multistorey laterite building encrusted with traditional wood- and tile-work, the collection of antiques includes dance-drama masks and costumes, ritual paraphernalia, musical instruments, pieces of temple architecture, 3000-year-old burial urns, cooking utensils, portraits and ancestral photographs – to name but a few of the categories amassed by founder and avid antiques collector, George Thaliyath.

Its crowning glory is an exquisitely decorated **theatre** on the top floor, decorated with swirling Keralan temple murals and dark wooden pillars. It's only open for exclusive, prearranged *kathakali* performances (see p.339).

ARRIVAL AND DEPARTURE   KOCHI (COCHIN) 6

By plane Kochi's international airport (🌐 cochinairport .com) – one of India's most modern and efficient – is at Nedumbassery, near Alwaye (aka Alua), 29km north of Ernakulam. A prepaid taxi into town costs around ₹600 and takes 45min or so, traffic permitting. Modern, comfortable a/c airbuses also cover the route more or less hourly, running to Fort Cochin (9 daily; 45min–1hr 30min; ₹80).

By train There are two main railway stations, Ernakulam Junction, near the centre, and Ernakulam Town, 2km further north. The Cochin Harbour Terminus, on Willingdon Island, serves the island's luxury hotels. Ernakulam Town lies on Kerala's main broad-gauge line and sees frequent services to and from Thiruvananthapuram via Kottayam, Kollam and Varkala. In the opposite direction, trains connect Ernakulam and Thrissur, and Chennai across the Ghats in Tamil Nadu. Since the opening of the Konkan Railway, a few express trains travel along the coast all the way to Goa and Mumbai. Although most long-distance express and mail trains depart from Ernakulam Junction, a couple of key services leave from Ernakulam Town. To confuse matters further, a few also start at Cochin Harbour station, so be sure to check the departure point when you book your ticket. The main reservation office, good for trains leaving all the stations, is at Ernakulam Junction.

Destinations Alappuzha/Alleppey (16 daily; 1hr–1hr 30min); Bengaluru (5 daily; 11hr 20min–13hr); Chennai (7 daily; 12–15hr); Goa (4 daily; 12hr 25min–15hr); Kozhikode/Calicut (15 daily; 3hr 50min–4hr 40min); Mumbai (6 daily; 20hr 45min–27hr); Varkala (hourly; 3–4hr).

By bus The KSRTC Central bus stand (☎ 0484 237 2033), beside the railway line east of MG Rd and north of Ernakulam Junction, is for state-run long-distance services. Reservations for services originating here can be made up to twenty days in advance. There are also two stands for pricier private services: the Kaloor Stand (rural destinations to the south and east) is across the bridge from Ernakulam Town railway station on the Alwaye Rd, while the High Court Stand (buses to Kumily, for Periyar Wildlife Reserve, and north to Thrissur, Guruvayur and Kodungallur) is opposite the High Court ferry jetty. The Fort Cochin bus terminus serves tourist buses, local services to Ernakulam and the airport bus.

Destinations Alappuzha/Alleppey (every 15–30min; 1hr 30min); Coimbatore (8–11 daily; 4–5hr); Kottayam (hourly; 2hr); Kozhikode/Calicut (every 1–2hr; 5hr–5hr 30min); Kumily (9–10 daily; 5hr 30min–6hr); Munnar (every 30–45min; 5hr); Thiruvananthapuram (every 30min; 5hr); Thrissur (every 15min; 1hr 45min).

RECOMMENDED TRAINS FROM KOCHI/ERNAKULAM

The trains listed below are recommended as the fastest and/or most convenient services from Ernakulam. If you're heading to **Alappuzha** for the backwater trip to Kollam, take the bus, as the only trains that can get you there in time invariably arrive late.

Destination	Name	No.	Station	Departs	Arrives
Bengaluru (Bangalore)	*Kanyakumari–Bangalore Express*	#16525	ET	daily 6.05pm	7.20am+
Kozhikode (Calicut)	*Netravati Express*	#16346	EJ	daily 2.05pm	7pm
Madgaon (Margao)	*Netravati Express*	#16346	EJ	daily 2.05pm	4.55am+
Mumbai	*Mangala Ldweep*	#12617	EJ	daily 1.15pm	12.55pm+
Thiruvananthapuram	*Jan Shatabdi*	#12081	ET	Mon, Tues & Thurs–Sat 9.45am	1.50pm
Varkala	*Sabari Express*	#17230	ET	daily 1.15pm	5.04pm

EJ = Ernakulam Junction
ET = Ernakulam Town
* = a/c only, meals included, + = next day

6

GETTING AROUND

By ferry Kochi's dilapidated ferries provide a cheap and relaxing way to reach the various parts of the city. The most popular route for visitors is the one connecting Ernakulam's Main Boat Jetty and Fort Cochin/Mattancherry's Customs Jetty (5.50am–9.30pm; every 20–30min). Also leaving from Ernakulam are ferries to Bolghatty Island (6.30am–9pm; every 30min) and Vypeen Island (7am–9.30pm; every 20–30min). The latter has two routes – one direct, and another slower service via Willingdon Island. From Fort Cochin's Government Jetty (10min walk west of Customs Jetty), you can also hop on a flat-bottomed vehicle ferry across the harbour mouth to Vypeen Island (6.30am–9pm; every 15min). Tickets should be purchased prior to embarkation from the hatch (separate queues for ladies and gents).

By bus KSRTC is in the process of upgrading its ageing fleet with new, state-of-the-art, low-floored Volvo buses, coloured bright green or orange. The new vehicles – used on prime routes such as the run between Fort Cochin and the airport – are cleaner and more comfortable, but there remain plenty of the old rust buckets in circulation and they're invariably crammed to bursting point. Frequent services run throughout the day between Ernakulam and Fort Cochin, though the ferry is a lot more enjoyable. If you miss the last boat back at 9.30pm, don't wait around for a bus (departures are sporadic and horrendously packed at that time of night); jump in an auto-rickshaw instead (₹250–300).

By bike Bicycles can be rented from many hotels and guesthouses in Fort Cochin.

By motorbike I-One's-Two Wheelers, at 1/946-A Njaliparambu (the lane opposite the entrance to the Kerala Kathakali Centre, near the Basilica in Fort Cochin) has Enfields for rent, as well as a few automatic Honda Activas. You'll need to leave your passport as security. Contact Ivan Joseph (☎98471 55306, ⚲rentabikecochin.com).

INFORMATION

Tourist information India Tourism's main office (Mon–Fri 9am–5.30pm, Sat 9am–noon; ☎0484 266 8352, ⚲incredibleindia.org), providing reliable information and qualified guides for visitors, is inconveniently situated on Willingdon Island, between the *Vivanta by Taj Malabar Hotel* and Tourist Office Jetty; they also have a desk at the airport. KTDC's reception centre, on Shanmugham Rd, Ernakulam (daily 8am–7pm; ☎0484 235 3234, ⚲ktdc .com), books rooms in their hotel chain and organizes sightseeing and backwater tours. For general advice the most convenient source is the tiny, independently run Tourist Desk (daily 9am–6pm; ☎0484 237 1761, ⚲tourist desk.in) near the entrance to the Main Boat Jetty in Ernakulam (follow the path branching to the right – north – as you approach the jetty terminal, or to the left if arriving from Fort Cochin). There's a subsidiary office opposite the chidren's park on Tower Rd in Fort Cochin (10am–6.30pm; ☎0484 221 6129). Both hand out maps of the town and backwaters – and walking-tour maps and guides to Fort Cochin – but the former is more helpful when it comes to checking ferry and bus times, and for finding temple festivals in the area and further afield.

TOURS AND BACKWATER TRIPS

The Tourist Desk (see above) at the Main Jetty in Ernakulam and Tower Rd in Fort Cochin runs tours to Wayanad, and can organize beach and backwater stays in its own guesthouses around Kannur.

Backwater trips KTDC offers day-trips into the backwaters south of Kochi (daily 8.15am–5.30pm; ₹1250), but they're not as good as those run by the Tourist Desk (daily 8am–6pm; ₹1250; book at their counters in Fort Cochin and Ernakulam; ⚲touristdesk.in/watervalleytour.htm). The cost includes hotel pick-up, transfer to the departure point 5km north of Alappuzha, a morning cruise (in a motorized boat) on the open backwaters, a village tour, a Keralan lunch buffet and an afternoon trip through narrow waterways in a much smaller punted canoe. In a similar vein are the community-based tours run by the villagers of Kumbalanghi on Kallancherry Island, 14km south of Fort Cochin (☎0484 224 0329 or ☎93889 75508, ⚲kumbalanghivillagetours.com), profits from which go to the farmers, coir producers and fishermen who show you around (see p.347).

Cruises If you are pushed for time, KTDC's half-day Kochi boat cruise (daily 9.30am–1pm & 2.30–6pm; ₹200) is a good way to orient yourself, but it doesn't stop long in either Mattancherry or Fort Cochin. Book at the reception centre on Shanmugham Rd (see above).

ACCOMMODATION

Most foreign visitors opt to stay in **Fort Cochin**, with its uncongested backstreets and charming colonial-era architecture. There are, however, drawbacks: room rates are grossly inflated (especially over Christmas and New Year), with few options at the budget end of the scale. **Ernakulam** may suffer a dearth of historic ambience, but it's far more convenient for travel connections and offers lots of choice and better value in all categories. Wherever you choose to stay, book well in advance.

ERNAKULAM

Biju's Tourist Home Corner of Cannonshed and Market roads ☎0484 238 1881, ⊛bijustouristhome .com; map p.340. A friendly, efficiently run budget hotel just a 5min walk from the boat jetty, with 27 spotless, well-aired and sizeable rooms that cater to a business crowd. It has its own clean water supply and offers a cheap same-day laundry service. Phone reservations accepted. A/c ₹500 extra. **₹980**

Grand MG Rd ☎0484 238 2061, ⊛grandhotelkerala .com; map p.340. The most classically glamorous place to stay in central Ernakulam. Spread over three floors of a 1960s building, its relaxing a/c rooms are done in retro-colonial style, with varnished wood floors and split-cane blinds. The good hotel restaurant warrants a visit in its own right. **₹3900**

Maple Regency XL/1511 Cannonshed Rd ☎0484 235 5156 or ☎0484 237 1711, ⊛hotelmapleregency .com; map p.340. The best of the few rock-bottom options in the streets immediately east of the Main Boat Jetty. Although the thirty cheap, clean, non-a/c rooms in the main block are OK, the couple of old ancestral bungalows in the rear are much nicer (₹940, ₹1625 a/c). They've been converted into pleasant chalet-style "cottages", with red-tiled floors, long pillared verandas and a lot more charm than anything else in this price bracket. *Boat Jetty Bungalow* next door is run by the same outfit and it's worth checking a couple of rooms for comparison. **₹690**

FORT COCHIN

Chiramel Residency 1 296 Lilly St ☎0484 221 7310 or ☎94478 18930, ⊛chiramelhomestay.com; map p.338. A great seventeenth-century heritage homestay, with welcoming owners and five lofty and carefully restored rooms set around a fancily furnished communal sitting room. All have big wooden beds, teak floors and modern bathrooms. There's a cheaper, newer block too, with a similarly nice communal feel. Breakfast included. **₹3000**

Cochin Heritage Home Vadatazha Rd, near Bishop's Palace ☎0484 221 6123 or ☎94474 32636, ⊛cochin heritage.com; map p.338. The property with the most traditional Keralan character in Fort Cochin. With their high beamed ceilings, oxide tiled floors and antique wooden doors, the rooms are simply but attractively furnished, and open onto a polished-pillar veranda where breakfast is served in the shade of split-cane blinds. Just four rooms, so book ahead. Rates include breakfast. **₹3000**

Delight Ridsdale Rd, opposite the parade ground ☎0484 221 7658 or ☎98461 21421, ⊛delightful homestay.com; map p.338. Occupying an annexe tacked onto a gleaming three-hundred-year-old Portuguese mansion, David and Flowery's homestay holds seven spacious, comfortable and well-aired rooms, all equipped with new bathrooms and quiet ceiling fans. Some open onto a lovely courtyard garden; another has a long veranda overlooking the parade ground. Breakfast included. **₹2000**

Fort House 6A Calvathy Rd ☎0484 221 7103, ⊛hotel forthouse.com; map p.336. Stylishly simple rooms flank a sandy courtyard littered with pot plants and votive terracotta statues. Those in the better block (rooms 1–6) have comfy king-sized beds and good showers in their chic wet-room bathrooms – though the a/c units can be noisy. Avoid the older budget block on the west side. Rates include breakfast. **₹6000**

Kapithan Inn 931 KL Bernard Rd ☎0484 221 6560, ⊛kapithaninn.com; map p.338. Scrupulously clean, very nicely furnished rooms in a friendly homestay behind Santa Cruz Basilica, with four smarter, larger a/c cottages (₹2500) to the rear (large enough for families). Various rooms at varying rates, but all are a real bargain, plus there's a lovely rooftop space. A/c ₹500 extra. **₹1000**

Maritime Hostel 2/227 Calvathy St ☎0484 656 7875, ⊛thehostelcrowd.com; map p.336. It's unusual to find a backpacker hostel in Kerala and this one, in a colonial building on the road towards Customs Jetty, is a real gem. There's both a mixed and female-only dorm, plus a couple of private rooms and although the dorms are fairly compact, they are beautifully clean and comfortable (note that the girls' room isn't en-suite). There's a glimpse of water from the shared terrace and a cute nautical theme runs throughout; dosa breakfast included. Dorms **₹500**, doubles **₹1800**

The Old Courtyard 1/371–2 Princess St ☎0484 221 6302 or ☎0484 221 5035, ⊛oldcourtyard.com; map p.338. Another delightful heritage hotel, with eight rooms around a seventeeth-century courtyard, framed by elegant Portuguese arches and bands of original *azulejo* tiles. For once the decor and antique furnishings (including romantic four-posters) are in keeping with the building – though perhaps a bit dark and lacking mod cons. Upper-storey rooms are less disturbed by noise from the courtyard café. **₹3000**

Oy's Burgher St ☎96333 27930, ⊛oys.co.in; map p.338. Pleasant, clean and friendly backpackers' hideaway, with just three cosy rooms, down the lane from *Kashi Arts Café*. Barred windows look onto a little raised terrace and there's a pleasant little travellers' café on the ground floor. **₹800**

Raintree Lodge Peter Celli St ☎0484 325 1489 or ☎98470 29000, ⊛fortcochin.com; map p.338. Five outstandingly smart rooms furnished in modern style (three of them with tiny balconies) in a cosy guesthouse that's within easy walking distance of the sights, but still tucked away. The really nice thing about this place is its plant-filled roof terrace, which has panoramic views. No breakfast, however. **₹2500**

6

6

★**Secret Garden** 745 Bishop Garden Lane, near Pattalam Market ☎0484 221 6658 or ☎98955 81489, ⓦsecretgarden.in; map p.338. Buried in a maze of narrow back lanes, this unique place is run by Icelandic architect Thóra Guðmundsdóttir. Huge rooms with high wooden ceilings, hand-carved beds and brightly painted traditional Indian murals open onto balconies fronting an exotic garden with a sizeable pool. Morning yoga on the rosewood deck can be arranged, and there are books and bicycles to borrow. Family rooms are particularly good value. ₹7000

Sonnetta Residency 387 Princess St ☎0484 221 5744 or ☎98955 43555, ⓦsonnettaresidency.com; map p.338. This small, old-fashioned guesthouse has to be one of the cleanest places to stay in Kerala: the surfaces are gleaming, bed linen boil-washed and bathrooms polished. It lacks character, and has no outside sitting space, but is efficiently run and provides a secure, convenient base, with some of the cheapest a/c rooms (₹550 extra) in the district. ₹900

Spencer Home 298 Parade Rd ☎0484 221 5049, ⓦspencerhome-fortkochi.blogspot.co.uk; map p.338. Warm-toned wood pillars and gleaming ceramic tiled floors line the verandas fronting this Portuguese-era house's eleven immaculate rooms, which open onto a painstakingly kept garden. Peaceful and good value for the area. A/c ₹500 extra. ₹1500

The Tower House 320–321 Tower St ☎0484 221 6960, ⓦneemranahotels.com; map p.338. Graceful period house perfectly situated opposite the Chinese fishing nets. The airy interiors are scrupulously in period, and there's a secluded pool. Don't expect the slick service of other places in this bracket, but note that rates plummet in the off season. ₹7500

★**Walton's Homestay** 39 Princess St ☎0484 221 5309 or ☎92497 21935, ⓦwaltonshomestay.com; map p.338. Among Cochin's most characterful homestays, run by philosopher and local historian Mr Christopher Edward Walton, in a centuries-old Dutch house. The rooms, many of which open onto a delightful rear garden, have been beautifully renovated, with modern bathrooms, ceiling fans, solar-powered hot water and comfy beds (a/c ₹400 extra). Book-swap library available; breakfast on the terrace is included. ₹1500

KUMBALANGHI VILLAGE

Gramam Homestay Neduveli House, North Kumbalanghi ☎0484 2240278 or ☎94471 77312, ⓦgramamhomestay.com; map p.336. Welcoming homestay offering accommodation in a beautifully converted coconut warehouse, slap on the banks of a lagoon. Chill in a hammock under the palms, go for cycle and canoe rides around the village, watch local fishermen and toddy tappers at work and generally soak up the peaceful rural atmosphere. Hosts Jos and Lyma provide breakfast (and dinner on request) and there's a self-catering cottage too. Double ₹3500, cottage ₹6000

★**Kallancherry Retreat** Kumbalanghi village ☎0484 224 0564 or ☎98474 46683, ⓦkallancherryretreat.com; map p.336. Charming little family homestay, a world away from the crowded streets of Fort Cochin, set under palm trees on the banks of a huge lagoon just a 30min ride out of town. The rooms are squeaky clean and have balconies. ₹2000

EATING

Foreign tourists tend to congregate at the pavement joints along **Tower Rd** near the Chinese fishing nets, drinking warm beer disguised in teapots. The food served in these cafés, however, is notoriously unhygienic. Your rupees will stretch further in **Ernakulam**, where you'll find some of the best traditional food in all South India.

ERNAKULAM

Coffee Beanz Shanmugham Rd ⓦcoffeebeanz.in; map p.340. Trendy a/c cappuccino bar, patronized in the main by well-heeled students from the local management college shrieking into their mobiles over a full-on MTV soundtrack. The din notwithstanding, it's a good spot to beat the heat and grab a good coffee or quick meal (burgers, grilled sandwiches, dosas and fish curries, mostly under ₹200). Daily 11am–11pm.

Kayees Durbar Hall Rd; map p.340. This salubrious branch of the city's most famous Muslim restaurant is a modern dining hall in the heart of the downtown area, with an a/c section on the first floor. The menu is comprehensive, but everyone comes for the Malabari biryanis (veg, chicken or mutton; ₹150–190), served with Kayees' mellow palm-date pickle and Arabian tea. Packed at lunchtime, and on Sun. Pay for your meal token in advance. Daily 11.30am–10pm.

Kempu Ground floor, Bharat Tourist Home, Durbar Hall Rd ☎0484 230 5519, ⓦbharathotel.com; map p.340. The decor – terracotta murals, thick stone floors and dark Keralan wood – is soothing, and the South Indian bites dependably good. Try their *bonda* – spicy vegetable and peanut balls (₹35), served with coconut-chilli *chatni* that's so thick you have to spread it with a knife. A good place for a coffee break after a shopping trip on nearby MG Rd. Daily 3.30pm–2am.

★**Sarovaram** Bypass Rd, Kudunnur ☎0484 2305519; map p.340. People travel from across the city for *Sarovaram's* famous lunchtime *sadyas* (noon–2.30pm;

₹170), served on banana leaves in a typical Laurie Baker building, with exposed bricks and stone floors. The pure veg food is unrivalled in the city and the atmosphere is much more Keralan, though it's a long trek across town – you might want to combine it with a trip to the Folklore Museum (see p.340), about 15min away in a rickshaw. Daily 7am–10.30pm.

Shri Krishna Inn Warriam Rd ☏ 0484 236 6664; map p.340. The sumptuous South Indian thalis served in this smart, dimly lit a/c vegetarian restaurant are on a par with nearby *Subhishka's*, but the decor is more appealingly traditional, with lathe-turned wooden pillars and earthy-toned Keralan murals setting the tone. As well as unlimited thalis (₹130–180), they do a huge range of ice creams. Daily 7.30am–11pm.

Subhishka Bharat Tourist Home, Durbar Hall Rd ☏ 0484 230 5519, ⓦ bharathotel.com; map p.340. The same banana leaf *sadyas* as at *Sarovaram* (₹160 unlimited), served in more contemporary surroundings, with incongruous music and a/c. Hidden at the back of the hotel lobby, it's a great place for crowd-watching, especially on Sun when everyone appears in their best saris and shirts for the big family meal. Daily 7am–3.30pm & 7–11pm.

FORT COCHIN

★**Dal Roti** 1 293 Lilly St; map p.338. The first choice among Fort Cochin's hungry travellers, despite the erratic service and shortage of tables. You'll know why as soon as you taste their signature *kati* rolls – deliciously flaky wraps filled with egg, chicken or vegetables – or good-value thalis (₹170 for the delicious veg option). The food is authentic North Indian and full of smoky, spicy flavours you don't get to enjoy that often in Kerala. Wed–Mon noon–3.30pm & 6.30–10.15pm.

David Hall Gallery Café Parade Ground ⓦ davidhall .in; map p.338. Delicious pizzas (₹300–400; noon–3pm & 6–9pm only), made in a proper pizza oven and served alfresco in a lovely green oasis behind the David Hall art space. They also serve freshly ground coffee, quality teas and juices. Don't miss the amazing seventeenth-century Dutch timbers on your way through the exhibition space. Daily 10am–9pm.

Fort House 6A Calvathy Rd ☏ 0484 221 7103, ⓦ hotel forthouse.com; map p.336. Carefully prepared Keralan specialities – including delicious seafood options and not-so-traditional roast chicken – served on a romantic, candlelit jetty. The food is consistently good, and not too pricey (most mains ₹300–400), and the location's perfect for watching the ships chugging in and out of the docks. Daily 7.30am–7.30pm.

Kashi Art Café Burgher St ⓦ kashiartgallery.com; map p.338. Cool, open-air gallery café, with floors made from pebbles and railway sleepers, patronized mainly by well-heeled metropolitan Indian tourists. Freshly ground espresso (₹70) is the big draw, along with their famous house cakes (the old-fashioned chocolate gateau is legendary; ₹110), but they also do light meals and savoury snacks – check the specials board, and expect perfunctory service. Daily 8.30am–7.30pm.

Mary's Kitchen 1/957 KB Jacob Rd ☏ 94460 14385; map p.338. This small rooftop restaurant across from Santa Cruz Basilica is lovingly run by husband-and-wife team Mary and Martin. Everything is home-cooked from scratch and it's the place to come for true Keralan specialities, particularly at breakfast. *Kozhukkotta* (coconut dumplings) and banana *ada* (steamed rice-flour parcels made with coconut and jaggery) are fresh and filling – and remarkably cheap (₹50–75). Ask about cookery classes. Daily 8am–9.30pm.

Teapot Peter Celli St ☏ 0484 221 8035; map p.338. With its massive collection of teapots from around the world, shabby-chic colour-washed wood floors and walls, tea-chest tables and funky little mezzanine floor, this backstreet tearoom gives *Kashi* some much-needed competition. Quality teas (₹90) and coffees (₹60) are the mainstay, but they also do light meals (₹200–300) and delicious home-made cakes. Daily 8.30am–9pm.

MATTANCHERRY

Crafters Café Next to Heritage Arts shop, Jew Town Rd ☏ 0484 222 3346, ⓦ crafters.in; map p.336. Handy pit stop if you're visiting the nearby synagogue. Tables on their wonderful little blue-pillared balcony are great for people-watching as you enjoy a plate of delicious butterfly prawns (₹280), *appam* with coconut-veg stew (₹150) or a freshly cut sandwich (₹100–160). They also do proper espresso and cakes. Daily 9.30am–6.30pm.

★**Kayees Rahatmathulla** Rahatmathulla Hotel, New Rd; map p.336. This Muslim joint in the backstreets of Mattancherry is legendary across the state for its fragrant biryanis, prepared fresh each morning according to a traditional, closely guarded Malabari recipe. There are frequently queues out the door, so get here before 1pm (ideally earlier) to avoid disappointment. You've a choice of chicken (₹110) or mutton (₹140) biryanis, accompanied by the wonderful house date pickle. Daily 5am–11.30am, noon–3pm & 5.30–9pm.

★**Sri Krishna Café** Mattancherry Palace/Cheralai Rd; map p.336. Typical South Indian, pure-veg restaurants are thin on the ground on this side of the water, so it's worth jumping in a rickshaw from Fort Cochin to eat at this famous old Udupi café in the temple district of Mattancherry, where traditional Keralan "meals" cost ₹55. Daily 8am–9.30pm.

SHOPPING

While serious shopping in **Ernakulam** tends to be focused on MG Rd and the **mega malls** to the north of the city (see box below), over in the tourist enclave of Fort Cochin, a combination of lookalike Kashmiri emporia (best avoided) and more individual boutiques, handicraft and curio shops cater for the passing foreign trade; the **Ethnic Passage** next to the synagogue in Jew Town has a number of these under one renovated two-thousand-year-old roof. **Jew Town** is also the hub of an established **antiques** scene, with some of the largest and most spectacular showrooms in India – a legacy of the post-1960s exodus of the district's Jewish population to Israel, when a large amount of family furniture was left behind. Some approach the scale of small museums, with chunks of temple masonry, carved wood pillars, religious sculpture, doors, windows and even, in one instance, a huge Keralan snake boat for sale – though don't expect to find any bargains. **Original art** by local painters also features prominently in the galleries of Jew Town.

AKP Metals and Alloys Broadway, Ernakulam ⓦ akp metallodrome.com; map p.340. The city's largest metalware emporium, showcasing a vast selection of traditional Keralan items in brass, copper, silver and bell metal. Mon–Sat 10.30am–8pm.

Cinnamon Trinity Hotel, 658 Ridsdale Rd, Parade Ground, Fort Cochin ☎0484 221 7124; map p.338. The Fort Cochin branch of the hip Bengaluru lifestyle chain sells clothes, shoes and items for the home from a range of top Indian designers in a light and airy boutique. Women's garments are particularly striking: unusual pieces in gorgeous natural colours. Mon–Sat 10am–7pm.

Fabindia 279(I), Napier St, near Parade Ground, Fort Cochin ☎0484 304 3517, ⓦfabindia.com; map p.338. Specializing in garments made from traditional Indian textiles, the nationwide chain boasts five branches in the city, the most convenient of them in Fort Cochin. Browse a huge range of vibrant *kurtas*, tops, skirts, bedspreads and cushion covers – all at reasonable (fixed) rates. Mon–Sat 10.30am–8.30pm.

Idiom Bastion St near Princess St, Fort Cochin; map p.336. The best place to browse for books on travel, Indian and Keralan culture, flora and fauna, religion and art; they also have an excellent range of fiction. There's a second branch in Mattancherry. Mon–Sat 9am–6pm.

Khadi Gramodyog Bhavan Pallimuku, MG Rd, Ernakulam; map p.340. The usual assortment of climate-friendly, hand-spun cotton and silk, sold by length or as ready-made garments, as well as items for the home, incense, honey, sandalwood and other village handicrafts at fixed prices. Mon–Sat 10.30am–8pm.

Niraamaya Behind the Pardesi Synagogue, Mattancherry ⓦayurvastraonline.com; map p.336. This innovative little boutique in Jew Town sells clothes made from organic cotton infused with healing Ayurvedic herbs. Dyed in subtle colours, they're perfect for the sticky Keralan heat. Also bed linen and yoga mats from natural materials. Another branch on Quiros St in Fort Cochin. Mon–Sat 10am–5pm.

Penta Menaka Mall Marine Drive, Ernakulam; map p.340. The best place in the city for electronic goods, computer/video games and movies – at a fraction of the price you'd pay back home (they're mostly pirated). Daily 10.30am–9.30pm.

Reliance TimeOut Level 02, Oberon Mall, north Ernakulam; map p.336. The widest range of branded CDs and DVDs in the city – both regional and international – along with a huge section of books, toys and writing and art materials. Mon–Fri 10.30am–9.30pm, Sat & Sun 10.30am–10pm.

Travellers' Paradise KL Bernard Master Rd, Fort Cochin ⓦbloominthenaturalway.com; map p.338. French designer Sophie Debiève set up this collective to market original pieces made by local Keralan women – mostly silk and cotton in beautiful Indian colours, and incorporating floral French print motifs. The range includes original household linen, bags and cards. The adjoining *Masters Art Café* is a nice place to have a breather. Mon–Sat 10am–6pm.

Tribes Next to Head Post Office, Fort Cochin ⓦtribesindia .com; map p.338. Jewellery, textiles, paintings, terracotta and stone work, metal crafts and organic food products produced by tribal communities across the country. Standout pieces range from bead necklaces by the Wancho of Arunachal Pradesh to coral bracelets from the Konyak Nagas and vibrant Pithora ritual art by the Bhils of Madhya Pradesh. Profits go towards development projects in the artists' communities. Mon–Sat 10am–6pm.

KOCHI'S SHOPPING MALLS

Kochi's massive **shopping malls** are prime leisure destinations for the city's well-heeled middle classes (daily 10am–10pm). On Ernakulam's MG Road, **Centre Square** (ⓦcentresquarekochi.com) has a food court and the eleven-screen Cinépolis, plus the usual international, air-conditioned stores. Some 7km north of the centre, around Edapally Junction and spread over six storeys, the **Oberon** (ⓦoberonmall.com) used to be the high temple of modern Keralan consumerism until it was usurped by the colossal **LuLu Mall** (ⓦlulumall.in), a sixteen-acre complex 2km further north, with a seven-screen multiplex, eighteen food outlets and parking for three thousand cars.

DIRECTORY

Banks All the major South Indian banks have branches on MG Rd in Ernakulam. In Kochi, head to Kunnumpuram Junction for banks; ATMs are dotted everywhere around town.

Cinemas The largest multiplex in Kochi is Cinépolis, on the sixth floor of Centre Square Mall (see box opposite). It has eleven screens, swanky VIP sofas, and shows all the latest Hollywood and Bollywood offerings.

Hospitals The six-hundred-bed Medical Trust Hospital on MG Rd (☏ 0484 235 8001, ⌨ medicaltrusthospital.com) is one of the state's most advanced private hospitals and has a 24hr casualty unit and ambulance service.

Laundry The municipal laundry in Fort Cochin is the Dhobi Khanna, on the south side of the district, a 3km/₹40 rickshaw ride from the tourist enclave. ₹10–15 for shirts; ₹25 for trousers. Allow 24hr.

Taxis Ashik Taxis (☏ 92881 57145 or ☏ 96567 98481) cover the entire state, and offer day-trips at fair prices. If you'd like to hire a car and driver for a few days or more, get in touch with Baiju (☏ 94468 27117), who is reliable and friendly and speaks great English.

6

Around Kochi

While the majority of visitors use the city as a base for day-trips into the surrounding backwaters and satellite villages, there's nothing to stop you doing the opposite, basing yourself in quiet backwater locations out of town – such as **Vypeen Island** to the north, or **Kumbalanghi** to the south – and travelling in to see the sights by bus, taxi or auto-rickshaw. There is some outstanding homestay accommodation in Kumbalanghi village (see p.344).

Backwater trips

Coir-production, rope-making, toddy-tapping, fishing and crab-farming are the main sources of income in the **backwater villages** south of Kochi. Easily reachable via the national highway, they're scattered over an expanse of huge lagoons and canals, flowing west behind a near continuous beach.

You can dip into the region for a day on one of the popular trips run out of Fort Cochin by KTDC and the Tourist Desk (see p.342), or with a community-based tourism initiative based at Kumbalanghi village (see p.344) – an award-winning project where proceeds are shared among the locals. The cost of the latter tour is ₹1400 (or ₹800 without lunch). You also have to budget for transport to and from the village. The trip is most easily done by auto-rickshaw (₹300–350 each way); if travelling by bus, head for Perumamapadappu, aka "Perumbadapu" on Google maps, and catch an auto from there for the remaining couple of kilometres.

Thripunitra

Some 12km southeast of Ernakulam and a short bus or auto-rickshaw ride from the bus stand just south of Jos Junction on MG Road, the small suburban town of **THRIPUNITRA** is worth a visit for its dilapidated colonial-style **Hill Palace**, now an eclectic museum, as well as its fabulous **temple festival**, held in October or November.

Hill Palace

Tues–Sun 9am–5pm • ₹10

The royal family of Cochin at one time had around forty palaces – the **Hill Palace** was confiscated by the state government after Independence, and has slipped into dusty decline over the past decades. One of the museum's finest exhibits is an early seventeenth-century wooden *mandapa* (hall) featuring carvings of episodes from the Ramayana. Of interest too are the silver filigree jewel boxes, gold and silver ornaments, and ritual objects associated with grand ceremonies. Artefacts in the **bronze gallery** include a *kingini katti* knife, whose decorative bells belie the fact that it was used for beheading, and a body-shaped cage in which condemned prisoners would be hung while birds pecked them to death.

6

LAKSHADWEEP

Visitors to Kerala in search of an exclusive tropical paradise may well find it in **Lakshadweep** (W lakshadweep.nic.in), the islands that lie between 200km and 400km offshore in the deep blue of the Arabian Sea. The smallest Union Territory in India, Lakshadweep's 27 tiny, coconut-palm-covered coral islands are the archetypal tropical hideaway, edged with pristine white sands and surrounded by calm lagoons where average water temperature stays around 26°C all year. Beyond the lagoons lie the **coral reefs**, home to sea turtles, dolphins, eagle rays, lionfish, parrotfish, octopus, barracudas and sharks. Only ten of the islands are inhabited, with a total **population** of just over 65,000, the majority of whom are Malayalam-speaking Sunni Muslims said to be descended from seventh-century Keralan Hindus who converted to Islam.

Theoretically, it's possible to **visit** Lakshadweep year round; the hottest time is April and May, when temperatures can reach 33°C; the monsoon (May–Sept) attracts approximately half the rainfall seen in Kerala, in the form of passing showers rather than deluges, although the seas are rough. Concerted attempts are being made to minimize the ecological impact of tourism in the islands; all visits must be arranged in Kochi through the **Society for Promotion of Recreational Tourism and Sports (SPORTS)** on IG Rd, Willingdon Island (📞 0484 266 8387, W lakshadweep tourism.com). At the time of writing, basic but pricey **accommodation** – run by the Lakshadweep department of tourism – was available on Kadmat, Kavaratti, Bangaram, Thinnakara and Minicoy. Access by plane is to the gateway island of **Agatti** (Mon–Sat; daily 1hr 30min), from where you'll be transferred by speedboat; or you can travel by sea from Kochi (14–18hr). SPORTS also offers a five-day **cruise** package taking in Kavaratti, Kalpeni and Minicoy (₹25,000/person). Meals are included, and permits taken care of, but diving costs extra. Week-long **diving** courses (see p.456) are available in Kadmat, Kavaratti and Minicoy from ₹20,000/person.

Sri Purnathrayisa Temple

Performances of theatre, classical music and dance, including all-night **kathakali**, are held over a period of eight days during the annual **Vrishikolsavam** festival (Oct/Nov) at the **Sri Purnathrayisa Temple** on the way to the palace. Inside the temple compound, both in the morning and at night, massed drum orchestras perform *chenda melam* in procession with fifteen caparisoned elephants.

Cherai Beach

The closest beach to Kochi worth the effort of getting to is **Cherai**, 25km north on **Vypeen Island**. A 3km strip of golden sand and thumping surf, it's sandwiched on a narrow strip of land between the sea and a very pretty backwater area of glassy lagoons. Chunky granite sea defences prevent the waves from engulfing the ribbon of fishing villages that subsist along this strip. Nowhere, however, is the sand more than a few metres wide at high tide, and the undertow can get quite strong. Even so, Cherai is gaining in popularity each year, and a row of small resorts and guesthouses has sprung up to accommodate the trickle of mainly foreign travellers who find there way up here from Fort Cochin.

ARRIVAL AND DEPARTURE   CHERAI BEACH

By ferry and bus To get to Cherai, you can jump on the car ferry (*jangar*) across to Vypeen Island from the jetty next to Brunton Boatyard in Fort Cochin, then transfer onto the hourly bus waiting on the other side, or catch one of the more frequent buses from opposite the High Court Jetty in Ernakulam.

By scooter Alternatively, you can hire a scooter (see p.342) and ride up – in which case, a preferable route to the main road is the more picturesque coastal lane hugging the sea wall; you can pick this up by turning west (left) down a bumpy backroad at Nayarambalam, 1km north of Narakkal, or via any of the lanes peeling left further on.

ACCOMMODATION

Brighton Beach House 3/783 Palli Fort, Convent Beach Rd, 2.5km north of Cherai 📞 99465 65555, 📞 99474 40449, W brightonbeachhouse.org. Fairly basic rooms

(some a/c) opening on to a yard right next to the sea wall, a 5min drive north of the main beachfront. Meals and sundowners are served in a small gazebo-cum-sun-terrace overlooking the sand, which is particularly narrow here. A/c ₹800 extra. ₹2000

La Dame Rouge Kizhakke Veedu, Manapilly ☎0484 2481 062 or ☎92494 10523, ⊚ladamerouge.com. This small, French-owned boutique guesthouse is a true labour of love – beautifully designed and run by host Marco, a former consular official who's been here for decades. The rooms and duplex suites are exquisitely decorated, with colour-washed walls, four-posters and Indian antiques – and the location, near a huge backwater, is superb. Canoe trips to the local market, Ayurvedic massages and fragrant Indo-Gallic fusion cooking are all on offer. Half board ₹5500

Kuzhupilly Beach House Kuzhupilly, 4.5km south of Cherai ☎0484 2531456 or ☎94471 07028, ⊚kuzhupilly

beachhouse.com. Little budget guesthouse just 30min by taxi from the Vypeen–Fort Cochin ferry dock, but overlooking a deserted stretch of beach and backwaters. The best rooms (₹2500) are on the upper floor and have fine sea views. Delicious, authentic Keralan home-cooking is on offer, along with bicycles and canoe tours. You can get most of the way there by bus (much cheaper); phone ahead for instructions. ₹2000

Ocean Breath Cherai ☎98476 35206, ⊚beachand backwater.com. The best-value budget option in Cherai, and the one with most Keralan atmosphere. No sea views (it's set back across the road from the sea wall) but the rooms are pleasant, with high, traditional Keralan ceilings and carved gables, shiny ceramic floors and small sitouts. ₹1500

Thrissur (Trichur)

THRISSUR (Trichur), a busy market hub and temple town roughly midway between Kochi (74km south) and Palakkad (79km northeast) on the NH-47, is a convenient, albeit traffic-clogged, base for central Kerala. Close to the Palghat (Palakkad) Gap – an opening in the natural border made by the Western Ghat mountains – Thrissur presided over the main trade route into the region from Tamil Nadu and Karnataka and for years was the capital of Cochin state.

Today, Thrissur is home to several influential art institutions and prides itself on being the cultural capital of Kerala. One of the state's principal Hindu temples, **Vadukkunnathan**, is here too, at the centre of a huge circular maidan that hosts all kinds of public gatherings, not least Kerala's most extravagant, noisy and sumptuous festival, **Puram**. The town derives most of its income from remittance cheques sent by expatriates in the Gulf – hence the predominance of ostentatious modern houses in the surrounding villages. The hinterland also serves as a storehouse, dotted with communities and pilgrimage sites where both contemporary party politics and ancient art traditions are pursued with great enthusiasm, despite the disruptive impact on local life of mass out-migration.

Vadakka Madham Brahmaswam

Thakkemadham Rd • Daily 7.30am–2.30pm • Donation requested • ☎0487 244 0877

The mighty Vadukkunnathan Temple, in the centre of the Round, may be closed to non-Hindus, but you can gain a sense of how ancient its roots are at the nearby **Vadakka Madham Brahmaswam**, five minutes' walk west of the temple, where young Namboodiri Brahmin boys attend **chanting** classes at a traditional *madham*, or college. Wearing traditional white *mundu*, sacred threads and ash marks on their skin, the students sit cross-legged in traditional Keralan halls while they repeat verses from three-thousand-year-old texts modelled for them by their gurus. If you'd like to visit, telephone ahead to ensure classes will be in progress.

Basilica of Our Lady of Dolours

Church Rd • **Tower** Tues–Fri 9am–1pm & 2–6pm, Sat & Sun 10am–1pm & 2–7.30pm • ₹20 • ⊚doloursbasilicathrissur.com

Not to be outdone by the scale of the Hindu temple across town, the vast Indo-Gothic **Basilica of Our Lady of Dolours** (**Puthan Pally** in Malayalam) dominates the skyline southeast of the Round, thanks to its gigantic 79m-high belfry – the tallest in India. Take the lift to the top, where superb views extend across the palm forest

6

THRISSUR PURAM

Thrissur is best known to outsiders as the venue for Kerala's biggest annual festival, **Puram**, which takes place on one day in the Hindu month of Medam (April–May; ask at a tourist office or check online for the exact date). Inaugurated by Shaktan Tampuran, the raja of Cochin, between 1789 and 1803, the event is the culmination of eight days of festivities spread over nine different temples to mark obeisance to Lord Shiva, at the peak of the summer's heat. Like temple festivals across Kerala, it involves the stock ingredients of caparisoned elephants, massed drum orchestras and firework displays, but on a scale, and performed with an intensity, unmatched by any other.

Puram's grand stage is the long, wide path leading to the southern entrance of **Vadukkunnathan Temple** on the Round. Shortly after dawn, a sea of onlookers gathers here to watch the first phase of the 36-hour marathon – the **kudammottom**, or "Divine Durbar" – in which two majestic **elephant processions**, representing Thrissur's Tiruvambadi and Paramekkavu temples, advance towards each other down the walkway, like armies on a medieval battlefield, preceded by ranks of drummers and musicians. Both sides present thirteen tuskers sumptuously decorated with gold caparisons (*nettipattom*), each ridden by three young Brahmins clutching objects symbolizing royalty: silver-handled whisks of yak hair, circular peacock-feather fans and colourful silk umbrellas fringed with silver pendants. At the centre of the opposing lines, the principal elephant carries an image of the temple's presiding deity. Swaying gently, the elephants stand still much of the time, ears flapping, seemingly oblivious to the crowds and huge orchestra that plays in front of them, competing to create the most noise and greatest spectacle. When the music reaches its peak around sunset, the two groups set off towards different districts of town. This signals the start of a spectacular **firework display** that begins with a series of deafening explosions and lasts through the night, with the teams once again trying to outdo each other to put on the most impressive show.

If you venture to Thrissur for Puram, be prepared for packed buses and trains, and book **accommodation** well in advance. As is usual for temple festivals, many men use the event as an excuse to get hopelessly drunk. Women are thus advised to dress conservatively and only to go to the morning session, or to watch with a group of Indian women – and at all times avoid the area immediately in front of the drummers, where the "rhythm madmen" congregate.

surrounding Thrissur, but coming down choose the stairs so you can view the artwork adorning the walls; an eclectic mix of wood, stained glass and brass depict stories from the Bible.

Archeological Museum

Karunkaram Nambiar Rd • Tues–Sun 9.30am–1pm & 2–4.30pm • ₹20

Of the town's **museums**, grouped to the north of the Round, the only one worth visiting – not least for the splendid Keralan architecture of the former palace it's housed in – is the **Archeological Museum**, opposite the Priya Darshini bus stand, a five-minute walk north of the Round on Karunkaram Nambiar Road. Former residence of the Cochin royal family, the two-hundred-year-old **Shaktan Thampuran Palace** is beautifully decorated with intricate wood- and tile-work. Exhibits include fifteenth- and eighteenth-century hero stones, a fearsome selection of beheading axes and a massive iron-studded treasury box.

ARRIVAL AND INFORMATION   THRISSUR (TRICHUR)

The principal point of orientation in Thrissur is the **Round**, a road (subdivided into North, South, East and West) which circles the Vadukkunnathan Temple complex and maidan in the town centre.

By train On the main line to Chennai and other points in neighbouring Tamil Nadu, and with good connections to Ernakulam/Kochi and Thiruvananthapuram, the railway station is 1km southwest.

THEYYEM RITUAL, KANNUR (P.358) >

Destinations Ernakulam/Kochi (every 30min; 1hr 20min); Kozhikode/Calicut (2hr 15min–3hr 40min); Thiruvananthapuram (hourly; 6hr).

By bus The KSRTC long-distance bus stand is opposite the station. The Shakthan Thampuran bus stand, on TB Rd, around 1km from Round South, serves local destinations south such as Irinjalakuda, Kodungallur and Guruvayur.

Tourist information The primary purpose of the volunteer-run DTPC tourist office (Mon–Sat 10am–5pm; ☎0487 232 0800), on Palace Rd opposite the Town Hall (5min walk off Round East), is to promote the Puram festival, but they also hand out maps of Thrissur.

ACCOMMODATION

Thrissur has plenty of competitively priced mid-range hotels but only a couple of decent budget ones. If you're planning to be here during **Puram**, book well in advance and bear in mind that room rates soar – some of the more upmarket hotels, and those overlooking the Round, charge up to ten times their usual prices.

Ashoka Inn TB Rd ☎0487 244 4333, ⊛ashokainn.co.in. Best value among the business-oriented three-stars in the Shakthan Thampuran bus stand district, in a gleaming, glass-sided tower block with spacious, impeccably clean rooms. Breakfast included. ₹3500

Gurukripa Heritage Chembottil Lane ☎0487 242 1895, ⊛gurukripalodge.com. Run with great efficiency by the venerable Mr Venugopal, the *Gurukripa*, just off Round South, offers a variety of simple rooms, (including several great-value singles) ranged around a long inner courtyard. ₹800

★**Kuruppath** Mannadiara Lane, off Kuruppam Rd ☎94952 60000 or ☎98460 45696, ⊛kuruppathheritage .com. An impeccably restored heritage bungalow, cowering amid the high-rise tower blocks in the heart of town, just a stone's throw from Round South. Filled with dark wood and antique tiles, the interiors are light, cool and astonishingly peaceful, considering the location. ₹3000

EATING AND DRINKING

There are plenty of dependable places to eat in Thrissur, with many hotels and busy "meals" joints lining the Round. In the evening, from 8.30pm, you can also join the auto-rickshaw-wallahs, hospital visitors, itinerant mendicants, Ayappa devotees and students who congregate at the popular *thattukada* **hot food market** on the corner of Round South and Round East, opposite the Medical College Hospital. The rustic Keralan cooking – omelettes, dosas, *parathas, iddiappam,* bean curries and egg masala – is freshly prepared, delicious and unbelievably cheap.

Akshaya Luciya Palace, Marar Rd, just off the southwest corner of the Round ⊛hotelluciyapalace.com. Fairly bland hotel restaurant where waiters in bow ties serve quality Keralan meals at lunchtime (₹195) in a blissfully cold a/c dining hall. From 7.30pm you can order from an exhaustive multicuisine menu, sitting outside in a pleasant garden illuminated by fairy lights. Beer is permitted with meals. Daily noon–3pm & 6–10.30pm.

★**Bharath Hotel** Chembottil Lane, 50m down the road from the Elite Hotel ☎0487 242 1720. Thrissur's top pure-veg place, packed from 7.30am onwards. The food is unfailingly fresh and delicious, and the queues stretch out the door on weekends. Be sure to leave room for the *ada*, a mix of sugar cane, coconut and rice steamed in a banana leaf (which tastes disconcertingly like old-fashioned British treacle pudding and costs just ₹25). Daily 6.30am–10.30pm.

DIRECTORY

Banks There are ATMs all over the centre of town. The best place to change money and travellers' cheques is the UTI Bank in the City Centre Shopping building (Mon–Fri 9.30am–3.30pm, Sat 9.30am–1.30pm) on Round West. The UAE Exchange & Financial Services (Mon–Sat 9.30am–6pm, Sun 9.30am–1.30pm) in the basement of the *Casino Hotel* building also changes currency and travellers' cheques.

Internet Available for ₹30/hr at Hugues Net on the top floor of the City Centre Shopping building and at SS Consultants next to the *Luciya Palace* hotel.

Post office The main post office is on the southern edge of town, just off Round South.

Around Thrissur

Guruvayur, 19km west of Thrissur, is the site of South India's most revered Krishna temple, with hundreds of thousands of Hindu pilgrims pouring in all year to worship at the shrine. As usual, non-Hindus are barred from entering, but there is a cultural institution that has opened its doors to visitors; learn all about *kathakali* in **Cheruthuruthy**'s Kerala Kalamandalam.

Cheruthuruthy

CHERUTHURUTHY, on the banks of the Bharatpuzha (aka "Nila") River 32km north of Thrissur, is internationally famous as the home of **Kerala Kalamandalam** (☎0488 426 2305, ⊚kalamandalam.org), the state's flagship training school for *kathakali* and other indigenous Keralan performing arts. The academy was founded in 1927 by the revered Keralan poet Vallathol (1878–1957), and has since been instrumental in the large-scale revival of interest in unique Keralan art forms. Non-Hindus are welcome to attend *kathakali*, *kudiyattam* and *mohiniyattam* performed in the school's wonderful **theatre**, which replicates the style of the wooden, sloping-roofed traditional *kuttambalam* auditoria found in Keralan temples. You can also sit in on classes, watch demonstrations of mural painting, and visit exhibitions of costumes by signing up for the fascinating "**a day with the masters**" cultural programme (Mon–Sat 9.30am–1pm; ₹1000, including lunch).

6

ARRIVAL AND DEPARTURE   CHERUTHURUTHY

By train Served by express trains to and from Mangalaru, Chennai and Kochi, the nearest mainline railway station is Shoranur Junction, 3km south.

By bus Buses heading to Shoranur from Thrissur's Priya Darshini (aka "Wadakkancheri") stand pass through Cheruthuruthy.

ACCOMMODATION

River Retreat Heritage Ayurvedic Resort 2km from Kalamandalam ☎04884 262244, ⊚riverretreat.in. Accommodation in Cheruthuruthy is limited to the luxurious *River Retreat Heritage Ayurvedic Resort*, former palace of the raja of Cochin. The three-star hotel and Ayurveda spa occupies an idyllic position on the banks of the Nila, where you can swim in a crystalline pool, partly shaded by coconut palms. ₹2900

Kozhikode (Calicut)

Formerly one of Asia's most prosperous trading capitals, the busy coastal city of **KOZHIKODE** (**Calicut**), 225km north of Kochi, occupies an extremely important place in Keralan legend and history. It's also significant in the chronicles of European involvement on the Subcontinent, as Vasco da Gama landed at nearby Kappad beach in 1498. After centuries of decline following the Portuguese destruction of the city, Kozhikode is once again prospering thanks to the flow of remittance cheques from the Gulf – a legacy of its powerful, Moppila-Muslim merchant community, who ran the local ruler's (Zamorin's) navy and trade. The recent building boom has swept aside most monuments dating from the golden age, but a few survive, notably a handful of splendid Moppila **mosques**, distinguished by their typically Keralan, multitiered roofs.

The Moppila mosques

The three most impressive mosques lie off a backroad running through the **Muslim** quarter of **Thekkepuram**, 2km southwest of the maidan (the auto-rickshaw-wallahs will know how to find them). Start at the 1100-year-old **Macchandipalli Masjid**, between Francis Road and the Kuttichira Tank, whose ceilings are covered in beautiful polychrome stucco and intricate Koranic script. A couple of hundred metres further north, the eleventh-century **Jama Masjid**'s main prayer hall, large enough for a congregation of 1200 worshippers, holds another elaborately carved ceiling. The most magnificent of the trio of mosques, however, is the **Mithqalpalli** (aka **Jama'atpalli**) **Masjid**, hidden down a lane behind Kuttichira tank. Resting on 24 wooden pillars, its four-tier roof and turquoise walls were built more than seven hundred years ago.

ARRIVAL AND DEPARTURE   KOZHIKODE (CALICUT)

By plane Kozhikode's international airport (⊚calicutairport .com), at Karippur, 23km south of the city, is primarily a gateway for emigrant workers flying to and from the Gulf, but also has direct flights to many other Indian cities, including

Mumbai, Delhi, Kochi, Chennai and Hyderabad. A taxi from the airport into town costs around ₹550.

Destinations Chennai (1–2 daily; 1hr 20min); Cochin (1 daily; 45min); Coimbatore (1 daily; 35min); Hyderabad (1 daily; 1hr 50min); Mumbai (34 daily; 1hr 40min–2hr).

By train The railway station (☎ 0495 270 1234), near the centre of town, is served by coastal expresses, slower passenger trains and superfast express trains to and from Goa, Mumbai, Kochi and Thiruvananthapuram.

Destinations Bengaluru (1 daily; 12hr); Chennai (4 daily; 12–18hr); Goa (22 daily; 8–11hr 30min); Kannur (every 30min–1hr; 1hr 20min–1hr 45min); Ernakulam/Kochi (every 30min; 4–5hr); Mumbai (20 daily; 19–22hr); Thiruvananthapuram (hourly; 7hr 15min–10hr).

By bus There are three bus stands. Government-run services pull in at the KSRTC bus stand, on Mavoor Rd (aka Indira Gandhi Rd). Private long-distance – mainly overnight – buses stop at the New Moffussil private stand, 500m away on the other side of Mavoor Rd. The Palayam bus stand, off MM Ali Rd, just serves the city.

Destinations Bengaluru (8–10 daily; 10–11hr); Kannur (hourly; 1hr 30min–3hr); Kalpetta/Wayanad (every 30min; 2hr); Kottayam (8–12 daily; 7–8hr); Ooty (3–4 daily; 5hr 30min–6hr); Thrissur (hourly; 3hr 30min).

INFORMATION

Tourist information KTDC's tourist information booth (officially daily 9am–7.30pm; ☎ 0495 270 0097), at the railway station, has information on travel connections and sights, but opening hours are erratic. The main KTDC tourist office (☎ 0495 272 2391), in the *Malabar Mansion* hotel at the corner of SM St, can supply limited information about the town and area.

ACCOMMODATION

Hotels in Kozhikode are plentiful, except at the bottom end of the range, where decent places are few and far between. This is one city where travellers on tighter budgets might be tempted to **upgrade**. The beach is a great place to stay, though you'll need to head into town for the best places to eat.

Alakapuri Guest House Chinthavalappu Junction, MM Ali Rd, near the Palayam bus stand ☎ 0495 272 3451, ⊚ hotelalakapuri.com. Opening on to a large central garden, the rooms in this popular place range from old-fashioned, spartan, a/c doubles to more spacious "cottages" with polished wood chairs, pillared sitouts and sofas (₹1600). All are neatly painted and clean. In the evening, you can eat on the lawn or in their cavernous dining hall under the watchful gaze of a giant plaster elephant. ₹1000

Beach Hotel Beach Rd, 2km west of the centre ☎ 0495 276 2056, ⊚ beachheritage.com. Dating from 1890, the premises of the colonial-era Malabar English Club, with its closely cropped lawns and high-pitched tiled roofs, now house a heritage hotel with loads of lovely character. The six rooms come with balconies or private patios, split-cane blinds, paddle fans and a/c. Those on the upper floor are larger and have the best sea views. Good value. ₹3500

Calicut Tower Markaz Complex, off IG Rd ☎ 0495 272 3202, ⊚ calicutower.com. This ninety-room tower block, tucked away down a quiet side street close to the KSRTC bus station and popular mainly with visiting Gulf Arab medical tourists, offers by far the best value in Kozhikode's lower-mid-range bracket. Impeccably clean, with shiny tiled floors and well-scrubbed bathrooms, its "standard a/c" rooms (just ₹300 pricier than the stuffier non-a/c options) are huge for the price. Strictly no alcohol. ₹1700

★ **Harivihar** 4km north of the centre in the residential suburb of Bilathikulam ☎ 0495 276 5865, ⊚ harivihar .com. Ancestral home of the Kadathanadu royal family, converted into a particularly desirable heritage homestay. Set among lawns, herb beds, lotus ponds and an original laterite-lined bathing tank (which guests are welcome to use), the mansion is a model of traditional Keralan refinement. Distractions include short courses in yoga, astrology, cookery and Indian mythology, but the focus is the top-grade Ayurvedic centre. Generously sized rooms make the Ayurveda yoga 21-day retreats an even nicer prospect. ₹9000

Sea Queen Beach Rd ☎ 0495 236 6604, ⊚ seaqueenhotel .com. This modern four-storey building is a good option if your budget can stretch to one of the pleasant, spacious a/c rooms, the best of which is the sea-facing "a/c-deluxe" (no. 213; ₹3000). The non-a/c rooms are fusty and not nearly as nice. Breakfast, served alfresco on the rooftop, is included in the price (there's an a/c restaurant up there too). ₹2000

EATING

Kozhikode is famous for its **Moppila cuisine**, which has its roots in the culinary traditions of the city's former Arab traders. Fragrant chicken biryanis and seafood curries with distinctive Malabari blends of spices crop up on most non-veg restaurant menus. **Mussels** are also big news here; deep-fried in their shells in crunchy, spicy millet coatings, they're served everywhere during the season (Oct–Dec); at any other time, they'll have been imported and won't be as fresh. Finally, no Kozhikode feast is complete without a serving of the city's legendary **halwa**: a sticky Malabari sweet made from rice flour, coconut, jaggery (unrefined sugar) and ghee, it comes in a dazzling variety of colours and flavours.

★**Paragon** Off the Kannur Rd ☏0495 404 0000, ⓦparagonrestaurant.net. *Paragon* has been a city institution since it opened in 1939. Don't be put off by the gloomy setting beneath a flyover: the Malabari cooking here is as good as you'll find anywhere. Seafood dishes are the speciality – especially fish tamarind, fish-mango curry, *pollichathu* and *mollee* – but there are dozens of alternatives. Whatever you order, make sure it's accompanied by their famously light *appam* and *paratha* combo. Most mains ₹150–225. Daily 6am–10.45pm.

Sagar Mavoor/IG Rd ⓦfacebook.com/calicutsagar. Another old favourite of Calicut's middle classes, now with two branches. Both are housed in distinctive laterite buildings, with non-a/c on the ground floor, and brighter a/c "family" dining halls on the floors above. Ignore the generic North Indian/Chinese/multicuisine menu. Everyone comes for the Malabari dishes such as egg curry, fish korma and, best of all, the flavour-packed chicken *pollichathu*. Most mains under ₹175. Daily 6am–midnight.

Zain's Hotel Convent Cross Rd ☏0495 236 6331. An unassuming, red-painted family house down a dingy lane in the west end of town is hardly what you'd expect the Holy Grail of Moppila cuisine to look like, but people travel from across the city to eat here. You'll find a choice of biryanis (fish, chicken or mutton; ₹140–230), various fiery seafood curries and a range of different *pathiris* – the definitive Malabari rice-flour bread. Most mains ₹125–175. Daily noon–10.30pm.

DIRECTORY

Banks and exchange The UAE Exchange on Bank Rd, next to *Hyson Heritage* (Mon–Sat 9.30am–1.30pm & 2–6pm, Sun 9.30am–1.30pm), changes cash and travellers' cheques, while the Union Bank of India and the State Bank of India, opposite each other on MM Ali Rd, are two of many large branches with ATMs.

Internet Available at the Hub, on the first floor of the block to the right of *Nandhinee Sweets*, MM Ali Rd, and at Internet Zone, near KTDC *Malabar Mansion* (both ₹40/hr).

Wayanad

The seven mountains encircling the hill district of **Wayanad**, 70km inland from Kozhikode, enfold some of the most dramatic scenery in all of South India. With landscapes varying from semitropical savanna to misty tea and coffee plantations, and steep slopes that rise through dense forest to distinctive, angular summits of exposed grassland, the region ranges over altitudes of between 750m and 2100m. Even at the base of the plateau, scattered with typically ramshackle Indian hill bazaars, it's cooler than down on the plains.

The main Mysuru–Kozhikode highway, NH-17, slices through Wayanad. Since the late 1990s, it has been the source of new income in the form of overstressed dot-com executives and their families from Bengaluru and Delhi, with numerous high-end resorts, eco-hideaways and plantation stays springing up to service the screen-weary. Even if you can't afford to stay in one of these bijou retreats, however, there are plenty of reasons to venture up here. Abutting the Tamil Nadu and Karnatakan borders, the twin reserves of **Muthanga** in the southeast and **Tholpetty** in the north collectively comprise the **Wayanad Wildlife Sanctuary** – part of the world-famous Nilgiri Biosphere and one of the best places in India to spot wild **elephant**.

Southern Wayanad

If you're travelling on all but the most flexible of budgets, you'll probably have to stay in the district's capital, **Kalpetta**. A hectic market hub straddling the main road, the town has little to commend it as a place to hang out, but does have budget accommodation, as well as good transport connections to points east. The other centres are **Mananthavady** and **Sulthan Bathery**, which is closest to **Muthanga Wildlife Sanctuary**.

Muthanga Wildlife Sanctuary

40km east of Kalpetta • Daily 7–10am & 3–5pm • ₹300, plus jeep entry ₹75 and hire ₹600

Part of a network of protected reserves with neighbouring states, **Muthanga Wildlife Sanctuary** is noted primarily for its elephants, but also shelters Indian bison (gaur), deer, wild boar, bear and a handful of tigers. There is currently no trekking allowed inside the sanctuary.

Edakkal Caves

28km east of Kalpetta, near Adikavala • Tues–Sun 9am–4pm • ₹20, camera ₹30

The prehistoric rock art site of **Edakkal**, which means "stone in between", was rediscovered in 1894 and is now overrun most days. It's a 1km hike up to the entry gate, after which there are a *lot* of stairs to navigate, but it's worth it to see where people etched human figures and animals – and geometric symbols of the sun – more than six thousand years ago. In nearby Adikavala, the **Wayanad Heritage Museum** (daily 9am–6pm; ₹20) gives a bit of background.

ARRIVAL AND DEPARTURE   SOUTHERN WAYANAD

By bus Some buses will terminate at either Kalpetta or Sulthan Bathery, but it's easy to hop on a local bus between the two (30min). Most services for Kannur depart from Mananthavady, 30km north of Kalpetta.

Destinations Kannur (hourly; 4hr); Kozhikode/Calicut (every 30min; 2hr); Mysuru (Karnataka; hourly; 4hr); Ooty/Udhagamandalam (Tamil Nadu; 3–4 daily; 4hr; daylight hours only).

INFORMATION AND TOURS

DTPC office Close to *Green Gates* hotel in North Kalpetta (Mon–Sat 10am–5pm; ☎0493 620 2134, ⊛dtpcwayanad.com). Staff will help with permits, tours and trekking.

Wayanad Nature Tours By far the best guide is Sabu (☎99612 84874, ⊛wayanad-naturetours.com) who can

take you to tea estates and tribal villages, into forests to spot wildlife or on a challenging trek into the mountains (though you could only ascend halfway up Chembra Peak at the time of writing). His website is a useful resource, updated daily with the latest from Wayanad.

ACCOMMODATION

★Aranyakam Valathur–Rippon, Meppadi ☎04936 280261 or ☎94477 81203, ⊛aranyakam.com. Rooms and suites in a handsome Keralan-style bungalow, with wood floors and verandas on both sides, the rear ones just a few metres from the coffee bushes. Best options, if you can stretch to them, are their two huts (₹6500/₹8000), which look across a spectacular wilderness of pristine forest and mountain. ₹4000

Chandragiri Main Rd, Kalpetta ☎04936 203049, ⊖chandragiri4inn@gmail.com. The best cheapie in Kalpetta, in a modern block at the north end of town, and the only place with beds under ₹750 that you'd want to sleep in. It has three kinds of room, varying in size from tiny to small, but they're well scrubbed and aired. ₹600

Green Gates TB Rd, North Kalpetta ☎04936 202001, ⊛greengateshotel.com. Tucked away in its own lush grounds 300m north of the DTPC office, with rooms in the main multistorey block (ask for a balcony; ₹3000), or more private cottages to its rear (₹5250). There's a pool (the only area with wi-fi), plenty of chillout space in the gardens

and an Ayurveda centre. The most comfortable option in Kalpetta, but not a great location. Breakfast and dinner included. ₹3500

Mint Flower Chungam Sulthan's Battery ☎0494 6222 206 or ☎97452 22206, ⊛hotelmintflower.com. This modern mid-range hotel on the main road through town has 36 spotless rooms; the more expensive ones have huge bathrooms. South Indian breakfast included, but the food highlight is the ridiculously cheap snacks – samosas are ₹12 – at the bakery out front. Wi-fi in reception only, a/c 300 extra. ₹1175

Tranquil Kappamudi Estate, Kolaggappara ☎04936 220244 or ☎99475 88507, ⊛tranquilresort.com. The crème de la crème of Wayanad's homestays, set amid 400 acres of rambling coffee, cardamom and vanilla plantations. The planter's bungalow itself holds eight comfy rooms (from US$335), all opening on to a glorious veranda wrapped in manicured gardens, and there are two palatial treehouses (US$435–470) as well as a large pool. The cooking's terrific, and the Dey family are perfect hosts. Minimum two nights. ₹15,500

North Wayanad

The teak forest takes over completely as you climb towards the northern limits of Wayanad, tracked by the savanna grass summits of the Brahmagiri massif. Some travellers use the pot-holed trunk road cutting north towards Mysuru to reach the Nagarahole National Park or the Kodagu (Coorg) district in neighbouring Karnataka.

But the majority of people who venture up here do so for a glimpse of wild elephants at the **Tholpetty Wildlife Sanctuary**, on the state border.

Tholpetty Wildlife Sanctuary

25km northeast of Mananthavady • Daily 7–10am & 3–5pm • ₹300, plus jeep entry ₹75 and hire ₹600 • Taxis charge ₹850 for the trip (with waiting time) from Mananthavady and the frequent KSRTC buses to Kutta will drop you off at the sanctuary entrance

Forming the northern sector of the Wayanad reserve, **Tholpetty Wildlife Sanctuary** is one of the best parks in South India for sighting elephant, as well as bison, boar, sambar, spotted deer, macaques and Nilgiri langurs. Tigers also inhabit the reserve and their pug marks are commonly encountered along the muddy margins of forest trails; numbers are steadily increasing, although you'd be lucky to see one in the flesh.

The Forest Department runs 24km **jeep safaris** from the park's main gates along a network of rutted tracks, passing through stands of old teak and bamboo groves. There is currently no trekking allowed inside the sanctuary.

Sree Thirunelli

30km northwest of Mananthavady • A dozen buses daily connect Mananthavady to Thirunelli; jeeps will run you out there for around ₹400

One of Wayanad's most celebrated temples, **Sree Thirunelli**, lies in a remote part of the district, reached via a bumpy backroad winding west off the Kogadu road. Set amid an awesome amphitheatre of mountains draped in vegetation, the temple is an unusual mix of Keralan tiled roofs and North Indian-style pillared halls. The forest road is a good one to drive at dusk to spot elephants.

ACCOMMODATION	NORTH WAYANAD

Enteveedu Kayakkunnu, Pananaram ☎ 0493 522 0008, ⊛ enteveedu.co.in. Meaning "my own home", this wonderful out-of-the-way place halfway between Kalpetta and Mananthavady has large comfortable rooms; one has three double beds, others interconnect so you can book as a family or group. Shared sitout areas look over the surrounding paddy fields and coffee plantations. Breakfast included, veg meals ₹250. A/c ₹500 extra. ₹2500

Pachyderm Palace Near the Tholpetty Forest Check Post ☎ 82742 44999, ⊛ pachydermpalace.com. Traditional Keralan bungalow run by the Tourist Desk in Kochi (see p.342), with five simple rooms and garden hut on stilts. Many guests are initially surprised by how basic

rooms are for the price, but are invariably won over by the authentic Keralan cuisine (rates are all-inclusive) and friendly welcome. Jeeps for wildlife drives can be arranged here, along with guides for treks into the nearby Brahmagiri range. ₹2500

Wildlife Resort 500m from the Tholpetty Forest Check Post ☎ 96565 66977 or ☎ 97447 70500, ⊛ wildlife resorts.in. The most comfortable option within easy walking distance of the Tholpetty park gate. Its recently built laterite, red-tiled "cottages", set in steeply sloping gardens just off the main road, are bland, and a tad overpriced, but well furnished with good mattresses and private sitouts. ₹4000

The far north

The beautiful coast **north of Kozhikode** is a seemingly endless stretch of coconut palms, wooded hills and virtually deserted beaches. The small fishing towns ranged along it hold little of interest for visitors, most of whom bypass the area completely – missing out on some exquisite, quiet coves, and the chance to see **theyyem**, the extraordinary masked trance dances that take place in villages throughout the region between November and May (see box, p.358).

The only village in Kannur district where you can be guaranteed a glimpse of *theyyem* is **Parassinikadavu**, a thirty-minute drive north of Kannur, where temple priests don elaborate costumes, dance and make offerings to the god Muthappan each morning and evening. With an early enough start, it's possible to catch the morning session and still have time to continue north to explore the little-visited **Valiyaparamba backwater** region.

6

THEYYEM

Theyyem (or *theyyam*) – the dramatic spirit-possession ceremonies held at village shrines throughout the northern Malabar region in the winter – rank among Kerala's most extraordinary spectacles. More than four hundred different manifestations of this arcane ritual exist in the area around Kannur alone, each with its own distinctive costumes, elaborate jewellery, body paints, face make-up and, above all, gigantic headdresses (*mudi*).

Unlike in *kathakali* and *kudiyattam*, where actors impersonate goddesses or gods, here the performers actually become the deity being invoked, acquiring their magical powers. These allow them to perform superhuman feats, such as rolling in hot ashes or dancing with a crown that rises to the height of a coconut tree. By watching the *theyyem*, members of the audience believe they can partake of the deity's powers – to cure illness, conceive a child or get lucky in a business venture.

Traditionally staged in small clearings (*kaavus*) attached to village shrines, *theyyem* rituals are always performed by members of the lowest castes; Namboodiri and other high-caste people may attend, but they do so to venerate the deity – a unique inversion of the normal social hierarchy. Performances generally have three distinct phases: the *thottam*, where the dancer, wearing a small red headdress, recites a simple devotional song accompanied by the temple musicians; the *vellattam*, in which he runs through a series of more complicated rituals and slower, elegant poses; and the *mukhathezhuttu*, the main event, when he appears in full costume in front of the shrine. From this point on until the end of the performance, which may last all night, the *theyyem* is manifest and empowered, dancing around the arena in graceful, rhythmic steps that grow quicker and more energetic as the night progresses, culminating in a frenzied outburst just before dawn, when it isn't uncommon for the dancer to be struck by a kind of spasm.

Increasing numbers of visitors are making the journey up to Kannur to experience *theyyem*, but **finding rituals** requires time, patience and stamina. The best sources of advice are local guesthouse owners, who can check the Malayalai newspapers for notices; ⓦ keralatourism.org /theyyamcalendar is also useful, as is the leaflet *A Hundred Festivals for You*, published by the Tourist Desk in Kochi (see p.342). Anyone pushed for time might consider a trip out to **Parassinikadavu** (see p.360), where a form of *theyyem* is staged daily.

Pressing on further north into Kasaragod district, it's worth splashing out on a night in one of the boutique retreats that have sprung up recently – the loveliest of them near the roadside town of **Nileshwar**, at the head of the Valiyaparamba backwaters. Larger hotel complexes, pitched at wealthy holiday-makers from Bengaluru, are beginning to appear further north still around **Bekal Fort**, where you can walk along impressive ramparts overlooking kilometres of empty coast.

Kannur (Cannanore)

KANNUR (Cannanore), a large, predominantly Moppila Muslim fishing and market town 92km north of Kozhikode, was for many centuries the capital of the Kolathiri rajas, who prospered from the maritime spice trade through its port. India's first Portuguese Viceroy, Francisco de Almeida, took the stronghold in 1505, leaving in his wake an imposing triangular bastion, **St Angelo's Fort**. This was taken in the seventeenth century by the Dutch, who sold it a hundred or so years later to the Arakkal rajas, Kerala's only ruling Muslim dynasty.

These days, the town is the largest in the northern Malabar region – a typically Keralan market and transport hub jammed with giant gold emporia and silk shops, and seething with traffic. Land prices are booming ahead of the opening of an international airport, which will doubtless see more skyscrapers rise on the outskirts. Kannur's few sights can be slotted into a morning, but increasing numbers of travellers are using the beaches to the south as bases from which to venture into the hinterland in search of **theyyem** rituals.

St Angelo's Fort

Daily 8am–6pm • Free, car park ₹10

Accessed through a gateway on its northern side, **St Angelo's Fort** remains in good condition and is worth visiting to wander the gardens and scale the massive laterite ramparts, littered with British cannons, for views over the town's massive Norwegian-funded fishing anchorage.

Arakkal Heritage Museum

Mon–Sat 10am–5.30pm • ₹50

The somewhat dilapidated whitewashed building facing the beachfront below the fort – once the raja and bibi of Arrakal's palace – now houses the government-run **Arakkal Heritage Museum**. Here documents, weapons, various pieces of four-hundred-year-old rosewood furniture and other heirlooms relating to the family's history are displayed – though they're somewhat upstaged by the old building itself, with its high-beamed ceilings and original floorboards.

Folklore Museum

Chirakkal, 5km north of Kannur town • Mon–Sat 10am–5pm • ₹10 • ☎ 0497 277 8090 • Rickshaws charge ₹150–200 for the trip, and buses run every 30min from the Padanna Paalam bus stand on the north edge of Kannur town

Extravagant costumes worn in *theyyem* and other less-known local art and ritual forms, including the Muslim dance style *oppana*, dominate the collection of the **Folklore Museum**, in the village of **Chirakkal** just off NH-17. Housed in the 130-year-old palace, the engaging collection also features masks and weapons used in *patayani* rituals performed in local Bhadrakali temples, and displays of *todikkalam* murals.

ARRIVAL AND DEPARTURE   KANNUR (CANNANORE)

Straddling the main coastal transport artery between Mangalaru in Karnataka and Kochi/Thiruvananthapuram, Kannur is well connected by bus and train to most major towns and cities in Kerala.

By train The busy railway station, right in the centre of town, is Kannur's principal landmark, and the best place to pick up auto-rickshaws and taxis for trips further afield. Kerala Tourism has an info counter on the main concourse (Mon–Sat 9am–4pm; ☎0497 270 3121) where you can find out about homestays and *theyyem* rituals.

Destinations Goa (22 daily; 6hr 40min–9hr); Ernakulam/Kochi (hourly; 5hr 30min–6hr 30min); Kozhikode/Calicut (every 30min–1hr; 1hr 20min–1hr 45min); Mangalaru (hourly; 2–3hr); Mumbai (20 daily; 16–21hr).

By bus Most local services, including those from other towns in Malabar, work out of the New Bus Stand, a 5min walk southeast of the railway station; the hub for long-distance Kerala state services is the KSRTC stand, a short hop by auto-rickshaw north. Fleets of private buses – the most garishly painted coaches in India – also cover the same routes.

Destinations The following refers only to Kerala and Karnataka State Transport Corporation services: Kalpetta, Wayanad (2 daily; 4hr); Ernakulam/Kochi (4–6 daily; 8hr); Kozhikode/Calicut (hourly; 1hr 30min–3hr); Madurai (1 nightly; 11hr 30min–13hr); Mangalaru (3 daily; 4–5hr); Mysuru (5 daily; 8hr).

KANNUR COOPERATIVES

Local guesthouse owners can point you towards **handloom weaving workshops** dotted around nearby villages – a legacy of the old calico cotton trade. A couple that are used to receiving visitors (Mon–Sat) are the **Kanhirode Co-operative**, 13km northeast of Kannur on the main road to Mattanur (☎0497 285 7865, ☻weaveco.com), which employs around four hundred workers to make upholstery and curtain fabrics, plus material for luxury shirts and saris, and **Lokanath Weavers Co-operative**, 3km east of Kannur on the Edapally–Panvell Hwy (☎0497 272 6330, ☻lokfab.com). The **Kerala Dinesh Beedi Co-operative** in Thottada 7km south of Kannur (☎0497 270 1699, ☻keraladinesh.com) makes an interesting visit to see workers deftly rolling thousands of skinny Indian cigarettes – though you can't actually buy them here.

ACCOMMODATION

Kannur's noisy and congested centre is jammed with **hotels**, but you'll find better options further east in the cantonment district behind **Baby Beach**, and further north at **Palliyamoola Beach** (a ₹75 ride away), where a number of small resorts and homestays stand close to the sea. Southeast of town down the coast, a string of four spectacular beaches hold even more desirable places to stay.

Blue Mermaid Thottada Beach ☎94973 00234, ⓦbluemermaid.in. Gorgeous homestay resort comprising a modern block of spacious, well-furnished a/c rooms, a detached cottage on the headland (₹3800) and a romantic bamboo honeymoon lodge (₹4000) – all in a heavenly setting overlooking one of the area's loveliest beaches. Keralan meals and yoga lessons on site. Half board ₹3400

Chera Rocks 14km south at Chera Kalle, Tayeechery ☎0490 234 3211 or ☎94466 10131, ⓦcherarocks.com. If you're dreaming of a room where you can watch the moonlight on the waves and fall asleep to the sound of surf crashing through the coconut trees, look no further. Here is a pretty three-bedroom cottage (₹5600) huddled in a palm grove behind an idyllic beach, and less pricey "deluxe" rooms occupying a white house set back just behind it. Rates include full board and station pick-up. ₹3300

★**Costa Malabari** 10km south near Thottada village; book through the Tourist Desk, Main Jetty, Kochi ☎0484 237 1761 or ☎94477 75691, ⓦtouristdesk.in /costamalabari.htm. Three traditional Keralan bungalows, surrounded by cashew and coconut groves on the bluff above pretty Thottada Beach. *Costa Malabari II* is the pick of the crop (and costs ₹1000 more than *I* & *III*), perched on a clifftop where a flight of rickety wooden steps descends to a golden-sand cove. The food, which is included and served on a picturesque veranda, gets rave reviews. Pick-up from

Kannur by arrangement. ₹3000

Ezhara Beach House Near Ezhara Moppila School, Ezhara Kadappuram, Kuttikkagam ☎0497 283 5022 or ☎98468 19941, ⓦezharabeachhouse.com. Tucked under the palms, this slightly shabby, blue-painted bungalow is incredibly private and the sort of place travellers pitch up and stay for weeks. It's a stone's throw from an empty beach, but visitors are asked to respect the fact it's in a Muslim village and cover up. Hyacinth is a great host; you get a whole floor to yourself. Half board ₹3500

★**Kannur Beach House** Thottada ☎98471 86330 or ☎98471 84535, ⓦkannurbeachhouse.com. Sandwiched on a sliver of land between a river and the beach, this friendly little guesthouse has a sublime location and the rooms, with their antique wooden doors and windows, luminous interiors and lovely verandas, are perfect havens. Half board ₹3200

Palm Grove Heritage Mill Rd, near Government Guesthouse, Kannur town ☎0497 270 3182, ⓦpalm groveheritageretreat.com. Dating from the 1930s, this former palace once belonged to the last raja of Arikkal but now accommodates an offbeat hotel, with a choice of bargain rooms or threadbare suites in the old portion, and large, modern, good-value doubles in the two adjacent, multistorey blocks that sometimes host conferences. Breakfast not included. Doubles ₹700, suites ₹1800

EATING

Geetha Station Rd. For a real Keralan experience stop at this diminutive, slightly grubby four-table "bakery" opposite the railway station exit. The menu isn't in English so you'll have to point at what you want from the glass case (samosa,

buttery *paratha*, *ela ada*...). The masala curry is spicy, the chai sweet and strong, and you'll have lunch for two for under ₹100. Daily 7am–9pm.

Parassinikadavu

The **Parassini Madammpura** temple in the village of **PARASSINIKADAVU**, 20km north of Kannur beside the River Valapatanam, is visited in large numbers by Hindu pilgrims for its **theyyem** rituals (daily 6.30–8.30am & 5.45–8.30pm). Elaborately dressed and accompanied by a traditional drum group, the resident priest, or *madayan*, becomes possessed by the temple's presiding deity – Lord Muthappan, Shiva, in the form of a *kiratha*, or hunter – and performs a series of complex offerings. The two-hour ceremony culminates when the priest/deity dances forward to bless individual members of the congregation – an extraordinary spectacle, even by Keralan standards.

ARRIVAL AND DEPARTURE
PARASSINIKADAVU

By bus and taxi Regular local buses leave Kannur for Parassinikadavu from around 7am, dropping passengers at the top of the village. If you want to get here in time for

the earliest *theyyem*, however, you'll have to fork out for one of the Ambassador taxis that line up outside Kannur bus stand (around ₹400 return). Cabbies sleep in their cars, so you can arrange the trip on the spot by waking one up; taxis may also be arranged through most hotels. Either way, you'll have to leave around 4.30am – or else spend the night nearer the temple.

ACCOMMODATION

Thai Resort 80m from the temple ☎0497 278 4242, ⓦ thairesort.in. Shaded by coconut trees, seven circular stone cottages are dotted around a well-kept garden with cool, comfortable rooms. They're a bit gloomy, but well aired, and the location's perfect. ₹2200

Thapasya Heritage Temple Rd ☎0497 278 2944 or ☎94470 65108, ⓦ thapasyaheritage.com. Situated on the hillside just south of the village, this is by far the best-value budget option within walking distance of the temple, and is very popular because of it. The building's modern, the beds have crisp linen and comfy mattresses, and the bathrooms are clean. A/c ₹1000–1300. ₹650

Valiyaparamba

If you were overwhelmed by the crowded backwaters in the south and are yearning for quiet white-sand beaches and coconut trees, push on 50km north of Kannur to one of the quietest stretches of coast in the state. The **Valiyaparamba backwaters** centre on a small, 30km delta fed by four rivers and their various bands and tributaries. Though local ferries crisscross this fascinating necklace of lagoons and islets, and a few companies organize houseboat trips from Ayitti Jetty, Valiyaparamba holds comparatively few permanent dwellings and traffic on its waterways largely consists of country fishing boats. It makes a wonderful region for off-track explorations; foreign tourists are few and far between.

ACCOMMMODATION

★**Kanan Beach Resort** Nileswar ☎0467 228 8880 or ☎86062 08880, ⓦ kananbeachresort.com. Of all the swanky resorts in the area, this has the most Keralan character. The self-contained, gable-roofed cottages – the size of small villas – come with a kitchen and sea- and sunset-facing verandas. There's a quiet pool and the location in a coconut grove alongside the beach is unbeatable. ₹13,500

Valiyaparamba Retreat Oriyara village, 15km north of Payyanur; book through the Tourist Desk, Main Jetty, Kochi (☎0484 237 1761, ⓦ touristdesk.in). This three-bedroom house facing the backwater on the northern side of Valiyaparamba has a welcoming host, tasty food and all the basics for a comfy stay. Regular buses run to Oriyara (30min) from the nearest railway station at Payyanur: get directions when booking with the Tourist Desk. Full board ₹3500

Bekal

BEKAL, 24km north of Nileshwar and the Valiyaparamba backwaters, is popular among Keralans as a weekend day-trip destination, with huge **Bekal Fort** (daily 8am–5.30pm; ₹100) standing on a hot and dusty promontory north of palm-fringed **Bekal Beach**. Both spots are great for people-watching in the late afternoon as families in their Sunday best stroll and paddle in the sea.

Tamil Nadu

368 Chennai

381 The northeast

401 Central Tamil Nadu: the Chola heartland

412 Tiruchirapalli (Trichy) and around

415 Madurai

422 Chettinadu

423 Rameshwaram

425 Kanyakumari

427 The Ghats

MEENAKSHI TEMPLE, MADURAI

Tamil Nadu

When Indians refer to "the South", it's usually Tamil Nadu they're talking about. While Karnataka and Andhra Pradesh are essentially cultural transition zones buffering the Hindi-speaking north, and Kerala and Goa maintain their own distinctively idiosyncratic identities, the peninsula's massive Tamil-speaking state is India's Dravidian Hindu heartland. Traditionally protected by distance and the military might of the southern Deccan kingdoms, the region has, over the centuries, been less exposed to northern influences than its neighbours. As a result, the three powerful dynasties dominating the South – the Cholas, the Pallavas and the Pandyans – were able, over a period of more than a thousand years, to develop their own unique religious and political institutions, largely unmolested by marauding Muslims.

The most visible legacy of this protracted cultural flowering is a crop of astounding **temples**, whose gigantic gateway towers, or *gopuras*, still soar above just about every town. It is the image of these colossal wedge-shaped pyramids, high above the canopy of dense palm forests, or against patchworks of vibrant green paddy fields, which Edward Lear described as "stupendous and beyond belief". Indeed, the garishly painted deities and mythological creatures sculpted onto the towers linger long in the memory of most travellers.

The great Tamil temples, however, are merely the largest landmarks in a vast network of **sacred sites** – shrines, bathing places, holy trees, rocks and rivers – interconnected by a web of ancient pilgrims' routes. Tamil Nadu harbours 274 of India's holiest Shiva temples, and 108 are dedicated to Vishnu. In addition, five shrines devoted to the five Vedic elements (Earth, Wind, Fire, Water and Ether) are to be found here, along with eight to the planets, as well as other places revered by Christians and Muslims. Scattered from the pale orange crags and forests of the Western Ghats, across the fertile deltas of the **Vaigai** and **Kaveri** rivers to the Coromandel coast on the Bay of Bengal, these sites were celebrated in the hymns of the Tamil saints, composed between one and two thousand years ago. Today, so little has changed that the same devotional songs are still widely sung and understood in the region and it remains one of the last places in the world where a classical culture has survived well into the present.

The Tamils' living connection with their ancient Dravidian past has given rise to a strong **nationalist movement**. With a few fleeting lapses, one or other of the pro-Dravidian parties has been in power here since the 1950s, spreading their

---

BEST TIME TO VISIT

Tamil Nadu can be visited year-round, although by far the most popular time is between December and March, when the skies are mostly blue and the weather not as hot as it becomes from April to June, especially on the inland plains. Coastal areas, however, only ever vary a few degrees either side of 30°C but humidity levels are consistently high from April through September.

The main summer monsoon largely misses Tamil Nadu but the state does receive plenty of precipitation during the northeast monsoon season from October to early December, when violent cyclones can be a threat, sometimes causing floods and wreaking havoc with transport links.

During the hotter months, the hill stations of the Western Ghats provide welcome respite from the heat but they can be pretty chilly, at least at night, in the winter. The Christmas and New Year period gets busy and prices are higher then and for local festivals, of which the state has many.

Highlights

❶ Mamallapuram Stone-carvers' workshops, a long sandy beach and wonderful Pallava monuments have made this a top tourist attraction. **See p.381**

❷ Puducherry Former French colony that has retained the ambience of a Gallic seaside town: croissants, a promenade and gendarmes wearing *képis*. **See p.394**

❸ Thanjavur Home to some of the world's finest Chola bronzes, this town is dominated by the colossal tower of the Brihadishwara Temple. See p.407

❹ Madurai The love nest of Shiva and his consort Meenakshi, this busy city's major

temple hosts a constant round of festivals. **See p.415**

❺ Kanyakumari At the southern tip of the Subcontinent, Kanyakumari marks the sacred meeting point of the Bay of Bengal, Indian Ocean and Arabian Sea. **See p.425**

❻ The Ghats The spine of southern India, excellent for trekking through lush mountains and tea plantations from its refreshingly cool hill stations. **See p.427**

❼ Mudumalai Wildlife Sanctuary This densely forested park is becoming increasingly popular for its wild elephants and excellent accommodation. **See p.438**

HIGHLIGHTS ARE MARKED ON THE MAP ON P.366

anti-brahmin, anti-Hindi proletarian message to the masses principally through the medium of movies. Indeed, since Independence, the majority of Tamil Nadu's political leaders have been drawn from the state's prolific **cinema** industry.

With its seafront fort, grand mansions and excellence as a centre for the performing arts, the state capital **Chennai** is nonetheless a hot, chaotic, noisy Indian metropolis that still carries faint echoes of the Raj. However, it can be used as a base for visiting **Kanchipuram**, a major pilgrimage and sari-weaving centre, filled with reminders of an illustrious past.

TAMIL NADU

0 — 50 kilometres

ANDHRA PRADESH

KARNATAKA

Pulicat
Tiruttani
Chennai
Bengaluru
Arakkonam
Ranippettai
Dakshina Chitra
Vellore
Chengalpattu
Krishnagiri
Kanchipuram
Maduranthakam
① Mamallapuram
VEDANTHANGAL BIRD SANCTUARY
Mysuru

TAMIL NADU

Tiruvannamalai
Gingee
Tindivanam
Auroville
Villupuram
② Puducherry
Stanley
Yercaud
Cuddalore
MUDUMALAI WILDLIFE SANCTUARY
Theppakkadu
Masinagudi
Salem
Vriddhachalam
Chidambaram
⑦ Dodabetta
BAY OF BENGAL
Gudalur
Udhagamandalam (Ooty)
Gangaikondacholapuram
Coonoor
Kotagiri
Erode
Mayiladuturai
Tharamgambadi
Mettupalayam
Namakkal
Swamimalai
Karaikal
⑥ Coimbatore
Tiruppur
Srirangam
Darasuram
Kumbakonam
Nagur
Karur
Kulittalai
Nagappattinam
Nilgiri Blue Mountain Railway
Tiruchirapalli
Thiruvaiyaru
Thiruvarur
Velankanni
Pollachi
Thanjavur
INDIRA GANDHI WILDLIFE SANCTUARY
Palani
Tiruthuraipondi
Lake Vyapuri
Dindigul
Pudukottai
Kollidam
Vedaranyam
Kodaikanal
Kanadukathan
CHETTINADU
Algarkovil
④ Madurai
Karaikudi
KERALA
Tiruparankundrum
Manamadurai
Jaffna
Alappuzha
Shrivilliputhur
NILGIRIS
Rajapalaiyam
Ramanathapuram
Rameshwaram
Palk Strait
Mandapam
Talaimannar
SRI LANKA
Adam's Bridge
Mannar
Gulf of Mannar
Kollam
Kuttalam
Tenkasi
Tuticorin
Thiruvananthapuram
Tirunelveli
Kovalam
Mundanthurai
Palayankottai
LAKSHADWEEP SEA
Nanguneri
Tiruchendur
Tambraparni
Padmanabhapuram
Marunthu Malai
Suchindram
⑤
Nagercoil
Kanyakumari

HIGHLIGHTS
① Mamallapuram   ⑤ Kanyakumari
② Puducherry   ⑥ The Ghats
③ Thanjavur   ⑦ Mudumalai Wildlife Sanctuary
④ Madurai

FESTIVALS IN TAMIL NADU

Pongal (mid-Jan). One of the most colourful and important Tamil festivals, celebrating the harvest, when thresholds are decorated with beautiful designs.

Thiruvaiyaru Thyagaraja Aradhana (Jan). A five-day celebration of Carnatic classical music at Thiruvaiyaru, near Thanjavur, in honour of the great Carnatic composer-saint. See p.409.

Teppam Floating Festival (Jan/Feb). Worshippers take boats to the shrine in the middle of the great bathing tank in Madurai. See p.419.

Mamallapuram Dance Festival (Jan–Feb). Month-long classical dance performances against the wonderful backdrop of Arjuna's Penance.

Natyanjali Dance Festival (Feb/March). Five-day dance festival at the great temple in Chidambaram, with occasional offshoots in Kumbakonam and Thanjavur.

Chithirai (April/May). Maybe the most important Madurai festival, celebrating the marriage of the principal deities of the great Meenakshi-Sundareshwarar Temple. See p.418.

King Rajaraja's birthday (Oct). Vibrant ten-day affair when Thanjavur's magnificent Brihadishwarar temple is decked out fully to celebrate its creator's birthday. See p.409.

Kartigai Deepam (Nov/Dec). Statewide extension of Diwali, especially lively in Tiruvannamalai, where pilgrims circumambulate Arunachala.

Chennai festival season (Dec–Feb). A series of Indian classical concerts and dance performances takes place at various venues throughout the city.

Much the best place to start a temple tour is in nearby **Mamallapuram**, a seaside village that – quite apart from some exquisite Pallava rock-cut architecture – boasts a long and lovely beach. Further down the coast lies the one-time French colony of **Puducherry**, now home to the famous Sri Aurobindo ashram; nearby, **Auroville** has carved out a role for itself as a popular New Age centre. The road south from Puducherry puts you back on the temple trail, leading to the tenth-century Chola kingdom and the extraordinary architecture of **Chidambaram**, **Gangaikondacholapuram**, **Kumbakonam** and **Darasuram**. For the best Chola bronzes, however, and a glimpse of the magnificent paintings that flourished under Maratha rajas in the eighteenth century, travellers should head for **Thanjavur**. Chola capital for four centuries, the city boasts almost a hundred temples and was the birthplace of Bharatanatyam dance, famous throughout Tamil Nadu.

In the very centre of Tamil Nadu, **Tiruchirapalli**, a commercial town just northwest of Thanjavur, held some interest for the Cholas, but reached its heyday under later dynasties, when the temple complex in neighbouring **Srirangam** became one of South India's largest. Among its patrons were the Nayaks of **Madurai**, whose erstwhile capital further south, bustling with pilgrims, priests, peddlers, tailors and tourists, is an unforgettable destination. The deeply rural area of **Chettinadu** to the northwest hides many delightful villages with splendid mansions, a fine break from the temple trail. **Rameshwaram**, on the long spit of land reaching towards Sri Lanka, and **Kanyakumari** at India's southern tip are both important pilgrimage centres, and have the added attraction of welcome cool breezes and vistas over the sea.

While Tamil Nadu's temples are undeniably its major attraction, the hill stations of **Kodaikanal** and **Udhagamandalam** (**Ooty**) in the west of the state are popular destinations on the well-beaten tourist trail between Kerala and Tamil Nadu. The verdant, cool hills offer mountain views and gentle trails through the forests and tea and coffee plantations. You can also spot wildlife in the teak forests of **Mudumalai Wildlife Sanctuary** and bamboo groves of **Indira Gandhi Wildlife Sanctuary**, situated in the Palani Hills.

Brief history

Since the fourth century BC, Tamil Nadu has been shaped by its majority **Dravidian** population, a people of uncertain origins and physically quite different from north Indians. The influence of the powerful *janapadas*, established in the North by the fourth and third centuries BC, extended as far south as the Deccan, but they made few incursions into **Dravidadesa** (Tamil country). Incorporating what is now Kerala and Tamil Nadu, Dravidadesa was ruled by three dynasties: the **Cheras**, who held sway over much of the Malabar coast (Kerala), the **Pandyas** in the far south and the **Cholas**, whose realm stretched along the eastern Coromandel coast.

In the fourth century, the **Pallava** dynasty established a powerful kingdom centred in **Kanchipuram**. By the seventh century, the successors of the first Pallava king, Simhavishnu, were engaged in battles with the southern Pandyas and the forces of the Chalukyas, based further west in Karnataka. This was also an era of social development. **Brahmins** became the dominant community. The emergence of *bhakti*, devotional worship, placed temples firmly at the centre of religious life, and the inspirational *sangam* literature of saint-poets fostered a tradition of dance and music that has become Tamil Nadu's cultural hallmark.

In the tenth and eleventh centuries, the Cholas experienced a profound revival, ploughing their new wealth into the construction of splendid and imposing temples. Subsequently, the **Vijayanagars**, based in Hampi (Karnataka), resisted Muslim incursions from the North and spread to cover most of South India by the sixteenth century. This prompted a new phase of architectural development, including the introduction of colossal *gopuras*. In Madurai, the Vijayanagar governors, **Nayaks**, set up an independent kingdom whose impact spread as far as Tiruchirapalli.

Simultaneously, the South experienced its first significant wave of **European settlement**. First came the Portuguese, followed by the British, Dutch and French. The Western powers soon found themselves engaged in territorial disputes, most markedly between the French, based in **Pondicherry**, and the British, whose stronghold since 1640 had been Fort St George in **Madras**. It was the British who prevailed, confining the French to Pondicherry.

As well as occasional rebellions against colonial rule, Tamil Nadu also saw anti-brahmin protests, in particular in the 1920s and 1930s. **Independence** in 1947 signalled the need for state boundaries, and by 1956 the borders had been demarcated on a linguistic basis. Thus in 1965 Madras Presidency became **Tamil Nadu**.

Since Independence, Tamil Nadu's industrial sector has mushroomed. The state was a Congress stronghold until 1967, when the **DMK** (Dravida Munnetra Kazhagam), championing the lower castes and reasserting Tamil identity, won a landslide victory on a wave of anti-Hindi and anti-central government sentiment. Power has ping-ponged back and forth between the DMK and the breakaway party AIADMK ever since (see box, p.370).

Chennai

In the northeastern corner of Tamil Nadu on the Bay of Bengal, **CHENNAI** (still commonly referred to by its former British name, **Madras**) is India's fourth largest city, with a population nudging seven and a half million. Hot, congested and noisy, it's the major transport hub of the South and most travellers stay just long enough to book a ticket for somewhere else. The attractions of the city itself are sparse, though it does boast fine specimens of **Raj architecture**, pilgrimage sites connected with the apostle **Doubting Thomas**, superb **Chola bronzes** at its state museum, and plenty of classical music and dance performances.

Geographically Chennai divides into three main sectors. North of the River Cooum stands **Fort St George**, site of the first British outpost in India, and **George Town**, the commercial centre, which developed during British occupation. George Town's principal landmark is **Parry's Corner**, located at the southern end of Rajaji Salai. Sandwiched between the Cooum and Adyar rivers is **central Chennai**, the modern, commercial heart of the metropolis, crossed and served by the city's main thoroughfare,

Anna Salai. East of Anna Salai is the atmospheric old Muslim quarter of **Triplicane** and beyond is the long straight **Marina** with its massive beach, fishing boats and hordes of domestic tourists, saris and trousers hitched up, enjoying a paddle. Further south along the coast is the district of **Mylapore**, inhabited by the Portuguese in the 1500s, with its two important places of pilgrimage and tourist attractions, **Kapalishvara Temple** and **San Thomé Cathedral**.

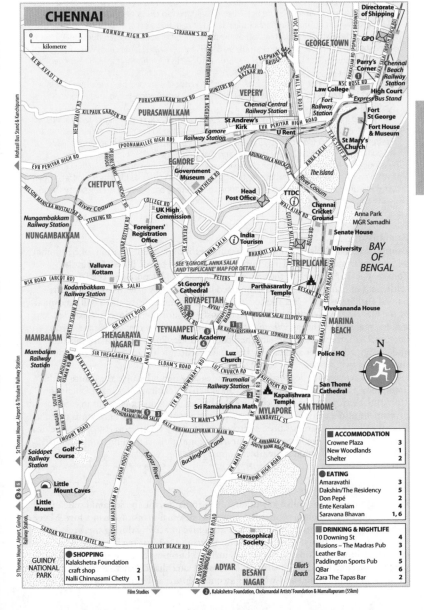

CHENNAI

■ ACCOMMODATION	
Crowne Plaza	3
New Woodlands	1
Shelter	2

● EATING	
Amaravathi	3
Dakshin/The Residency	5
Don Pepé	2
Ente Keralam	4
Saravana Bhavan	1, 6

■ DRINKING & NIGHTLIFE	
10 Downing St	4
Illusions – The Madras Pub	3
Leather Bar	1
Paddington Sports Pub	5
QBar	6
Zara The Tapas Bar	2

● SHOPPING	
Kalakshetra Foundation craft shop	2
Nalli Chinnasami Chetty	1

OF MOVIE STARS AND MINISTERS

One notable difference between the Chennai-based Tamil movie industry and the mainstream Bollywood movies from Mumbai is the influence of **politics** on Tamil films. Traditional folk ballads about low-caste heroes vanquishing high-caste villains were perfect propaganda vehicles for the nascent Tamil nationalist movement, the Dravida Munnetra Kazhagam (**DMK**). It is no coincidence that the party's founding father, **C.N. Annadurai**, was a top script- and screenplay-writer. He and his colleagues used the popular film genres of the time to convey their political ideas to the masses and this politicization of the big screen created the **fan clubs**, or *rasigar manrams*, that play a key role in mobilizing support for the nationalist parties in elections.

Perhaps the most influential fan club of all time was that of superstar Marudur Gopalamenon Ramachandran, known to millions simply as "**MGR**". He generated fanatical grass-roots support in the state and rose to become chief minister in 1977. His eleven-year rule is still regarded by liberals as a dark age of chronic corruption, police brutality, political purges and rising organized crime. When he died in 1987, two million people attended his funeral and even today, MGR's statue, sporting trademark sunglasses and lamb's-wool hat, is revered across Tamil Nadu at roadside shrines.

MGR's political protégée, and eventual successor, was teenage screen starlet **J. Jayalalithaa**, a convent-educated brahmin's daughter whom he recruited to be both his leading lady and mistress. After 25 hit films together, Jayalalithaa followed him into politics, becoming leader of the AIADMK, the party MGR set up after being expelled from the DMK in 1972. Despite allegations of fraud and corruption that even saw her jailed at one point, Jayalalithaa enjoyed five spells as chief minister and was deified by her supporters. Her sudden death in December 2016 (of cardiac arrest following complications from sepsis) prompted wild conspiracy theories in the press and left a political vacuum in Tamil Nadu.

7

Brief history

As capital of Tamil Nadu, Chennai is a comparatively modern creation, like Mumbai and Kolkata. It was founded as a fortified trading post by the **British East India Company** in 1639, north of the ancient Tamil port of **Mylapore** and the Portuguese settlement of San Thomé. It was completed on St George's Day in 1640 and thus named **Fort St George**. Over the course of the following century and a half, as capital of the **Madras Presidency**, which covered most of South India, the city expanded to include many surrounding villages. It was briefly lost to the French but three years later, in 1746, the British re-established control under **Robert Clive** (Clive of India) and continued to use it as their southern base, although it was surpassed in national importance by Calcutta.

The city's renaissance began after Independence, when it became the centre of the Tamil **movie industry**, and a hotbed of **Dravidian nationalism**. Renamed Chennai in 1997, the metropolis has boomed since the Indian economy opened up to foreign investment in the early 1990s. The flip side of this rapid economic growth is that Chennai's infrastructure has been stretched to breaking point: poverty, oppressive heat and pollution are more likely to be your lasting impressions than the conspicuous affluence of the city's modern marble shopping malls.

Fort St George

Fort St George is quite unlike any other fort in India. Facing the sea amid state offices, it looks more like a complex of well-maintained colonial mansions than a fort. Many of its buildings are today used as offices and are a hive of activity during the week.

The fort was the first structure of Madras town and the first territorial possession of the British in India. Construction began in 1640 but most of the original buildings were damaged during French sieges and replaced later that century. The most imposing structure is the slate-grey-and-white eighteenth-century colonnaded **Fort House**.

Fort Museum

York St · Daily except Fri 9am–5pm · ₹100 (₹5), no photography

The modestly proportioned **Exchange Building** houses the excellent **Fort Museum**. The collection within faithfully records the central events of the British occupation of Madras with portraits, regimental flags, weapons, East India Company coins, medals, stamps and thick woollen uniforms that make you wonder how the Raj survived as long as it did. The first floor is now an **art gallery**, where portraits of prim officials and their wives sit side by side with fine sketches of the British embarking at Chennai in aristocratic finery, attended by Indians in loincloths. Also on display are etchings by the famous artist **Thomas Daniell**, whose work largely defined British perceptions of India at the end of the eighteenth century.

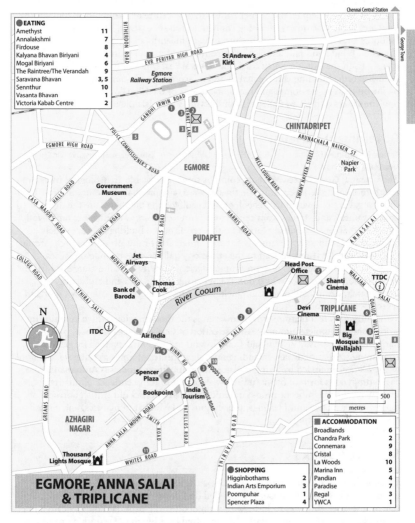

Chennai Central Station

George Town

7

● EATING	
Amethyst	11
Annalakshmi	7
Firdouse	8
Kalyana Bhavan Biriyani	4
Mogal Biriyani	6
The Raintree/The Verandah	9
Saravana Bhavan	3, 5
Sennthur	10
Vasanta Bhavan	1
Victoria Kabab Centre	2

■ SHOPPING	
Higginbothams	2
Indian Arts Emporium	3
Poompuhar	1
Spencer Plaza	4

■ ACCOMMODATION	
Broadlands	6
Chandra Park	2
Connemara	9
Cristal	8
La Woods	10
Marina Inn	5
Pandian	4
Paradise	7
Regal	3
YWCA	1

EGMORE, ANNA SALAI & TRIPLICANE

St Mary's

St Thomas St • Daily 9am–5pm

South of the Fort Museum, past the State Legislature, stands the oldest surviving Anglican church in Asia, **St Mary's**, built in 1678 and partly renovated after the battle of 1759. It's distinctly English in style, crammed with plaques and statues in memory of British soldiers, politicians and their wives. The grandest plaque, made of pure silver, was presented by Elihu Yale, former governor of Fort St George (1687–96) and founder of Yale University. A collection of photographs of visiting dignitaries, including Queen Elizabeth II, is on display in the entrance porch.

George Town

Bus #18 from Anna Salai

North of Fort St George, the former British trading centre of **George Town** remains the focal area for banks, offices, shipping companies and street stalls. This network of streets harbours a fascinating medley of architecture: eighteenth- and nineteenth-century churches, Hindu and Jain temples and a scattering of mosques, interspersed with grand mansions. In the east, on Rajaji Salai, the **General Post Office** occupies a robust earth-red Indo-Saracenic building constructed in 1884. George Town's southern extent is marked by the bulbous white domes and sandstone towers of the **High Court** and the even more opulent towers of the **Law College**, both showing strong Islamic influence.

Government Museum

Pantheon Rd • Daily except Fri 9.30am–5pm • ₹250 (₹15), camera ₹200, video camera ₹500 • ⓦ chennaimuseum.org • Bus #23C from Anna Salai

The Chennai **Government Museum** contains some remarkable archeological finds from South India and the Deccan. Inside the deep-red, circular **main building**, built in 1851, the first gallery is devoted to archeology and geology; the highlights are the dismantled panels, railings and statues from the second-century AD *stupa* complex at **Amaravati** (see p.289). These sensuously carved marble reliefs of the Buddha's life are widely regarded as the finest achievements of early Indian art. To the left of here high, arcaded halls full of stuffed animals lead to the **ethnology gallery**, where models, clothes, weapons and photographs of expressionless faces in orderly lines illustrate local tribal societies, some long since wiped out. A fascinating display of wind and string **instruments**, drums and percussion includes the large predecessor of today's sitar and several very old tablas.

The museum's real treasure-trove, however, is the modern wing, which contains the world's most complete and impressive selection of **Chola bronzes** (see box, p.410). Large statues of Shiva, Vishnu and Parvati stand in the centre, flanked by glass cases containing smaller figurines, including several sculptures of Shiva as **Nataraja**, the Lord of the Dance, encircled by a ring of fire. One of the finest models is **Ardhanarishvara**, the androgynous form of Shiva (united with Shakti in transcendence of duality). Elsewhere, the magnificent Indo-Saracenic **art gallery** houses old British portraits of figures such as Clive and Hastings, plus Rajput and Mughal miniatures, and a small display of ivory carvings.

St Andrew's Kirk

Off Periyar EVR High Rd

Just northeast of Egmore Station, **St Andrew's Kirk**, consecrated in 1821, is a fine example of Georgian architecture. Modelled on London's St Martin-in-the-Fields, it's one of just three churches in India with a circular seating plan, laid out beneath a huge dome painted blue with gold stars and supported by a sweep of Corinthian columns.

Marble plaques around the church give a fascinating insight into the kind of people who left Britain to work for the imperial and Christian cause. A staircase leads onto the flat roof, surrounding the dome, from where you can climb further up into the steeple past the massive bell to a tiny balcony affording excellent views of the city.

The Marina

One of the longest city beaches in the world, the **Marina** (Kamaraj Salai) stretches 5km from the harbour at the southeastern corner of George Town to near San Thomé Cathedral. Going south, you'll pass the Indo-Saracenic **Presidency College** (1865–71), one of a number of stolid Victorian buildings that make up the **University**, as well as adjacent **Vivekananda House** (see below).

Today the **beach** itself is a sociable stretch, peopled by idle paddlers, picnickers and pony-riders; every afternoon crowds gather around the beach market. However, its location, just a little downstream from the port, which belches out waste and smelly fumes, combined with its function as the toilet for the fishing community, detract somewhat from its natural beauty.

Vivekananda House

Mon 10am–12.15pm, Tues–Sun 10am–12.15pm & 3–7.15pm • ₹10 • ⓦ vivekanandahouse.org

Housed in a splendidly rotund and ornate stone building, the nineteenth-century Madras depot of the Tudor Ice Company has been converted into the interesting **Vivekananda House** museum, which gives an excellent account of the life of the nineteenth-century saint, Swami Vivekananda, who stayed here for some time in 1897. Now a branch of the Sri Ramakrishna Math organization (see p.374), the museum contains attractive visual displays of Hindu beliefs, as well as photographic and detailed textual material on Vivekananda's life.

Mylapore

Buses #4, #5 or #21 from the LIC building on Anna Salai

Long before Madras came into existence, **Mylapore**, south of the Marina, was a major settlement; the Greek geographer Ptolemy mentioned it in the second century AD as a thriving port. During the Pallava period (fifth to ninth centuries) it was second only to Mamallapuram. Its two outstanding sights are venerable **San Thomé Cathedral** and the mighty **Kapalishvara Temple**, while the **Sri Ramakrishna Math** also warrants a visit.

San Thomé Cathedral

San Thomé High Rd • Daily 6am–8pm • ⓦ santhomechurch.com

An important stop on the St Thomas pilgrimage trail, **San Thomé Cathedral** marks the eastern boundary of Mylapore, lying close to the sea at the southern end of the Marina on San Thomé High Road. Although the present neo-Gothic structure dates from 1896, it stands on the site of two earlier churches built over the tomb of St Thomas. The saint's **relics** are kept inside the nave, accessed by an underground passage from the small **museum** at the rear of the courtyard, and are the object of great reverence. The museum itself houses stones inscribed in Tamil, Sanskrit (twelfth-century Chola) and early Portuguese, and a map of India, dated 1519.

Kapalishvara Temple

N Mada St • Daily 6am–noon & 4–9.30pm

The huge **Kapalishvara Temple** sits just under 1km west of the San Thomé Cathedral, off RK Mutt Road. Seventh-century Tamil poet-saints sang its praises, but the present structure, dedicated to Shiva, probably dates from the sixteenth century. The huge (40m) *gopura* towering above the main east entrance, plastered in stucco figures, was added in 1906. Surrounding an assortment of busy shrines, where priests offer blessings for devotees and non-Hindus alike, the courtyard features an old tree where a small shrine to Shiva's consort, Parvati, shows her in the form of a peahen (*mayil*) worshipping a lingam.

Sri Ramakrishna Math

31 Ramakrishna Math Rd • Temple daily 5–11.45am & 3–9pm • ⓦ chennaimath.org

A short walk south of the Kapalishvara Temple, lie the peaceful and extensive grounds of the **Sri Ramakrishna Math**, an active place of study for devotees wishing to follow the teachings of the famous nineteenth-century master. The focus of interest for the casual visitor is the **Universal Temple of Sri Ramakrishna**, an elegant construction combining architectural motifs from Hindu, Buddhist and Jain temples, as well as European churches, while the manicured forecourt echoes the Islamic themes of the Mughals. Within the temple itself are a series of prayer halls, approached by steps, and the inner sanctum contains a solid marble statue of Ramakrishna seated on a lotus.

7

Little Mount Caves

Little Mount, off Mount Rd • Bus #18A, #18B, or #52C from Anna Salai

St Thomas is said to have sought refuge from persecution in the **Little Mount Caves**, 8km south of the city centre. Entrance to the caves is beside steps leading to a statue of Our Lady of Good Health. Inside, next to a small natural window in the rock, are impressions of what are believed to be St Thomas' handprints, created when he made his escape through this tiny opening. Behind the new circular church of Our Lady of Good Health is a natural **spring**. Tradition has it that this was created when Thomas struck the rock, so the crowds that came to hear him preach could quench their thirst; samples of its holy water are on sale.

St Thomas Mount

Mount Rd • Take a suburban train to Guindy railway station and walk from there

It's said that St Thomas was speared to death while praying before a stone cross on **St Thomas Mount**, 11km south of the city centre. **Our Lady of Expectation Church** (1523), at the summit of the Mount, can be reached by 134 granite steps marked with the fourteen stations of the Cross, or by a road which curls its way to the top, where a huge old banyan tree provides shade for devotees who come to fast, pray and sing. Inside the church, St Thomas' cross is rumoured to have bled in 1558, while the altar is said to mark the exact spot of the apostle's death; the painting of the Madonna and Child above the altar is attributed to St Luke.

Theosophical Society headquarters

Adyar Bridge Rd, Besant Nagar (south of Mylapore) • **Grounds** Mon–Sat 8.30–10am & 2–4pm **Bookshop** Mon–Sat 9.30am–12.30pm & 2.30–5.30pm **Library** Tues–Sun 9am–5pm • Free • ⓦ ts-adyar.org • Buses #5, #5C or #23C from George Town/Anna Salai

The **Theosophical Society** was established in New York in 1875 by American Civil War veteran Colonel Henry S. Olcott and the eccentric Russian aristocrat Madame Helena Petrovna Blavatsky, who claimed to have occult powers. Based on a fundamental belief in the equality and truth of all religions, the society in fact propagated a modern form of Hinduism, praising all things Indian and shunning Christian missionaries. Needless to say, its two founders were greeted enthusiastically when they transferred their operations to Madras in 1882, establishing their headquarters near Elliot's Beach in Adyar.

The society's buildings still stand today, sheltering several shrines and an excellent **library** of books on religion and philosophy. The collection includes 800-year-old scroll pictures of the Buddha; rare Tibetan xylographs; exquisitely illuminated Korans; a giant copy of Martin Luther's *Biblia* printed in Nuremberg three hundred years ago; and a thumbnail-sized Bible in seven languages. Anybody is welcome to look around, but to gain full use of the library you have to register as a member.

The 270 acres of woodland and gardens surrounding the society's headquarters make a serene place to sit and restore the spirits. In the middle, a vast 400-year-old **banyan tree**, said to be the second largest in the world, can provide shade for up to three thousand people at a time.

Kalakshetra Foundation

Kalakshetra Rd, Thiruvanmiyur, 15km south of the centre • Daily 8.30–11.30am, except 2nd & 4th Sat of month • ₹500 (₹100) • ⓦ kalakshetra.in • Take one of the many city bus routes to Thiruvanmiyur bus stand, 500m away

Set in delightfully landscaped and shady grounds, the **Kalakshetra Foundation** was created in 1936 and has since established itself as the prime cultural organization for the study and performance of traditional Tamil song and dance. Visitors are welcome to quietly witness the morning classes and, of course, are encouraged to attend an evening performance whenever they are scheduled. The small **Rukmini Devi Museum**, named after the dancer whose success inspired the foundation, contains her personal collection of artistic objects, from stone and brass sculptures to delicate fabrics and fine paintings; unfortunately, at the time of writing it was closed for major refurbishment. There is also a great craft centre, complete with shop (see p.380).

7

Cholamandal Artists' Village

Injambakkam, 24km south of the centre • Daily 9am–6.30pm • Grounds free; museum ₹20 • ⓦ cholamandalartistvillage.com • Any ECR bus destined for Mamallapuram and Puducherry passes close to the entrance

Tucked beside the beach in the sprawling southern suburbs of Chennai, the **Cholamandal Artists' Village** was established in the mid-1960s to encourage contemporary Indian art. In a country where visual culture is so comprehensively dominated by convention, fostering innovation and artistic experimentation proved no easy feat. Despite an initially hostile response from the Madrasi establishment (who allegedly regarded the tropical storm that destroyed the artists' first settlement as an act of nemesis), the village has prospered. Today, Cholamandal's thirty-strong community has several studios and a large **museum** filled with paintings, sketches, sculpture and metalwork, as well as a shop selling work produced here.

ARRIVAL AND DEPARTURE — CHENNAI

BY PLANE

Chennai airport The airport, in Tirisulam, 16km southwest of the city centre on NH-45, is comprehensively served by international and domestic flights. The new international and domestic terminals are a short walk from each other, on opposite sides of the old terminal. Facilities at both are much better on the air side than the land side. The Tamil Nadu Tourist Information Centre at the arrivals exit can book accommodation.

Getting into town The quickest and cheapest way to get into town is by suburban train (see p.377) from Tirisulam station, 400m from the airport on the far side of the road, to Park, Egmore and North Beach stations (30–40min). There are prepaid taxi counters at both terminals for the ever-congested ride to the main hotels or railway stations; from the main road, rickshaws charge ₹400, not much less than taxis. Taxis straight down the coast to Mamallapuram

cost around ₹1300. Buses #70 and #70A go to Mofussil Bus Stand (see p.376) in Koyambedu suburb, from where you can connect to other destinations.

Airlines, international Air India ☎044 2345 3303, airport ☎044 2256 6002; American Airlines ☎1800 200 1800; British Airways ☎1800 102 3592; Emirates ☎044 6683 4400; Gulf Air ☎044 2256 1156; Lufthansa ☎1800 102 5838; Qatar Airways ☎044 4289 6000; Singapore Airlines ☎044 3254 7771; Sri Lankan Airlines ☎044 4392 1234; Thai Airways ☎044 4206 3311. Most offices are open Mon–Fri 10am–5pm, Sat 10am–1pm.

BY TRAIN

Chennai has two main long-distance railway stations – Egmore and Central, both on the north side of the city centre and just 1.5km apart. Egmore station is the arrival point for most trains from Tamil Nadu and Kerala; its

RECOMMENDED TRAINS FROM CHENNAI

Destination	Name	No.	From	Departs	Arrives
Bengaluru	Shatabdi Express	#12007	Central	6am*	10.50am
	Bangalore Express	#12609	Central	1.35pm	8.05pm
Coimbatore	Kovai Express	#12675	Central	6.15am	1.45pm
	Cheran Express	#12673	Central	10.10pm	6.15am+
Hyderabad	Charminar Express	#12759	Central	6.10pm	8am+
Kanyakumari	Kanyakumari Express	#12633	Egmore	5.30pm	6.50am+
Kochi/Ernakulam	Alleppey Express	#22639	Central	8.45pm	8.25am+
	Trivandrum Mail	#12623	Central	7.45pm	7.08am+
Kodaikanal Road	Pandian Express	#12637	Egmore	9.20pm	5am+
Madurai	Vaigai Express	#12635	Egmore	1.20pm	9.25pm
	Pandian Express	#12637	Egmore	9.20pm	6.15am+
Mettupalayam (for Ooty)	Nilagiri Express	#12671	Central	9.15pm	6.15am+
Mumbai	Mumbai Express	#11042	Central	11.55am	1.35pm+
	Chennai Express	#12164	Egmore	6.50am	6am+
Mysuru	Shatabdi Express	#12007	Central	6am*	1pm
	Mysore Express	#22682	Central	11.30pm	8.20am+
Rameshwaram	R'waram Express	#16713	Egmore	5pm	4.45am+
Thanjavur	Trichy Express	#16853	Egmore	8.15am	2.43pm
Tiruchirapalli	Guruvayur Express	#16127	Egmore	7.40am	1.10pm
	Vaigai Express	#12635	Egmore	1.20pm	6.30pm
Thiruvananthapuram	Trivandrum Mail	#12623	Central	7.45pm	11.45am+
Tirupati	Sapthagiri Express	#16057	Central	6.25am	9.40am

*Except Wed; a/c only, + next day

booking office, up the stairs left of the main entrance, handles bookings for both stations. There is also an efficient tourist reservation counter (Mon–Sat 8am–8pm, Sun 8am–2pm) on the first floor of the Moore Market Complex (next to the main Central station building), which sells tickets for trains from both stations. Both stations have left-luggage offices. The occasional service for southern Tamil Nadu leaves from the suburban Tambaram station.

BY BUS

Mofussil Bus Stand Buses from all long-distance destinations use the huge Mofussil Bus Stand, inconveniently situated in the suburb of Koyambedu, more than 10km west of the centre. Mofussil is linked to other parts of Chennai by a host of city buses, which depart from the well-organized platforms outside the main terminal: buses #27, #15B, #15F and #17E go to the Egmore/Central area and Parry's Corner; bus #27B also goes on to Triplicane; while buses #70 and #70A link the bus stand with the airport. Note that all express ECR buses from Mamallapuram, Puducherry and other coastal towns to the south of Chennai stop at Guindy suburban railway station; taking a train in from there saves time.

Destinations The six platforms at Mofussil are each divided into thirty-odd bays, with frequent services to destinations throughout Tamil Nadu and neighbouring states, including Bengaluru (every 15–30min; 8–10hr); Chengalpattu (every 5–10min; 1hr 30min–2hr); Chidambaram (20 daily; 6–7hr); Coimbatore (every 30min; 11–12hr); Kanchipuram (every 20min; 1hr 30min–2hr); Kanyakumari (10 daily; 15–17hr); Kodaikanal (1 daily; 14–15hr); Kumbakonam (every 30min; 7–8hr); Madurai (every 20–30min; 10hr); Mamallapuram (every 15–30min; 2hr); Puducherry (every 15–30min; 4–5hr); Rameshwaram (3 daily; 13–14hr); Thanjavur (20 daily; 8–9hr); Thiruvananthapuram (6 daily; 18–20hr); Tiruchirapalli (every 15–30min; 8–10hr); Tirupati (every 30min–1hr; 4–5hr); Tiruvannamalai (every 20–30min; 4–5hr); Udhagamandalam (Ooty) (2 daily; 14–15hr).

BY BOAT

Boats leave Chennai every week/ten days for Port Blair, capital of the Andaman Islands. The first thing you'll need to do is contact the Shipping Corporation of India at 17 Rajaji Salai, Jawahar Building, George Town (☎044 2523 1401, ⊛shipindia.com) to find out when the next sailing is and when tickets go on sale, usually up to a month prior to departure. There are no ticket sales on the day of sailing. Permits for up to thirty days are given on arrival in Port Blair. The Andaman Information Centre (Mon–Fri 10am–5.30pm, Sat 10am–1pm; ☎044 2533 3952) is in the Tamil Nadu Tourism Complex, 2 Wallajah Rd, Triplicane. For more details, see the Andaman Islands chapter (see p.448).

GETTING AROUND

Chennai's sights and facilities are spread over such a wide area that it's impossible to get around without using some form of **public transport**. Most visitors jump in auto-rickshaws, but outside rush hours you can travel around comfortably by **bus** or on the suburban **train** (Mass Rapid Transport System; see below). At the time of writing, the section of the new Chennai metro (⊕ chennaimetrorail.gov.in) between Koyambedu and Alandur was up and running, while the line from Little Mount to the airport was expected to open sometime in 2016.

By train If you want to travel south from central Chennai to Guindy (Deer Park) or the airport, the easiest way to go is by suburban train (aka the MRST). Services run every 15min (on average) between 4.30am and 11pm, prices are minimal, and they only get overcrowded during rush hours (around 7–9am & 4–6pm). Buy a ticket before boarding. City trains travel between Beach (opposite the GPO), Fort, Park (for Central), Egmore, Nungambakkam, Kodambakkam, Mambalam (for T Nagar and silk shops), Saidapet (for Little Mount Church), Guindy, St Thomas Mount and Tirisulam (for the airport).

By bus Local bus routes radiate out from the amalgamated Express and Broadway bus stands, between Central train station and George Town. On Anna Salai and other major thoroughfares buses have dedicated stops, but on smaller streets you have to flag them down, or wait with the obvious crowd. Numbers of services to specific places of interest in the city are listed in the relevant accounts, while those to and from the Mofussil Bus Stand are listed in "Arrival and departure" (see p.375).

By rickshaw Auto-rickshaw drivers in Chennai are notorious for demanding high fares from locals and tourists alike. The diversions and one-way systems in place due to the construction of the metro are having a considerable effect on journey times and hence rickshaw prices. It's worth asking two or three drivers to compare prices and then haggle. If you need to get to the airport or station early in the morning, expect to pay up to ₹500. Arrange in advance.

By taxi Chennai's yellow-top Ambassador taxis have meters but drivers often refuse to use them, so prepare yourself for some hard bargaining. At around ₹200 from Central station to Triplicane, they're practically pricing themselves out of business. For this reason, more reliable and economical radio taxis such as Bharati Call Taxi (☎ 044 2814 2233) are popular.

By car Private cars (with driver) can be booked at any of the city's upmarket hotels, through TTDC or with one of the numerous private tour agents (see p.381).

INFORMATION

Tourist information The Tamil Nadu Tourism Development Office, 2 Wallajah Rd, Triplicane (theoretically open 24hr; ☎ 044 2533 3333, ⊕ tamilnadutourism.org), houses several other state tourist offices including the office of the Andamans. You can pick up Chennai and Tamil Nadu maps here. There is another branch opposite the Central railway station at 4 EVR Salai (Mon–Fri 10am–1.30pm & 2pm–5.45pm; ☎ 044 2538 4356).

The India Tourism Office, 154 Anna Salai (Mon–Fri 9.15am–5.45pm; ☎ 044 2846 0285, ⊕ incredibleindia .org), is far more helpful and provides information, maps and brochures for the whole of India.

Services A useful and centrally located travel agent and exchange facility is Thomas Cook, 45 Montieth Rd (Mon–Sat 10.30am–6pm; ☎ 044 6677 4600).

CHENNAI TOURS

One good way to get around the sights of Chennai is on a TTDC **bus tour**; bookings are taken at its office (see above). They're good value, albeit rushed, and the guides can be very helpful. The TTDC **half-day tour** (daily 8am–1pm or 1.30–6.30pm; ₹300 non-a/c, ₹375 a/c) takes in Fort St George, the Government Museum (Birla Planetarium on Fri), the Snake Park, Kapalishvara Temple, and Marina Beach. TTDC also offers good-value **day-trips**, including visits to Mamallapuram, Kanchipuram (daily 6.30am–7pm; ₹825 non-a/c, ₹1025 a/c), and Puducherry (Sat & Sun 6.30am–7pm; ₹750 non-a/c, ₹925 a/c), with meals included in the tariff; check at the office for other itineraries and further details.

Storytrails (☎ 044 4501 0202, ⊕ storytrails.in) conducts a number of fascinating and expertly led, themed **walking tours**, with enticing titles such as Bazaar Trail, Spice Trail, British Blueprints and Steeple Chase. Prices vary according to the number of people but reckon on around ₹1000 per person for a small group. A perennially popular tour among bikers is the one offered by the **Royal Enfield motorcycle factory** around 18km north of the centre in Tiruvottiyur (every 2nd & 4th Sat of month 10am; ₹600 per person; ☎ 044 4223 0400, ⊕ royalenfield.com).

7

ACCOMMODATION

Finding an inexpensive **place to stay** in Chennai can sometimes be a problem. With the 24hr checkout system it's difficult to predict availability and some of the cheaper places don't take advance bookings. The good news is that standards in the cheapies are better than in other cities. Most of the mid-range and inexpensive hotels are around the railway station in **Egmore** and further east in **Triplicane**. The bulk of the top hotels are in the south of the city and several offer courtesy buses to and from the airport.

EGMORE

Chandra Park 9 Gandhi Irwin Rd, opposite the station ☎044 2819 1177, ⓦhotelchandrapark.com; map p.371. Clean-cut business hotel with central a/c, foreign exchange, 24hr coffee shop, bar and rather disappointing restaurant. The spacious, light and well-furnished standard rooms are a very good deal. ₹1500

Marina Inn 55/31 Gandhi Irwin Rd ☎044 2819 2919, ⓦmarinainn.in; map p.371. Very smart business-style hotel with central a/c around 200m to the right as you exit Egmore station. The double rooms, though not big, are tastefully decorated and very clean, with 32" LCD TVs; there's also a multicuisine restaurant and bar. ₹2100

★**Pandian** 15 Kennet Lane ☎044 2819 1010, ⓦhotelpandian.com; map p.371. Very smart two-star hotel with spotless, brightly coloured rooms, breakfast included and free wi-fi for 1hr/day. There are some singles (from ₹950) while doubles with a/c cost ₹2200. ₹1500

Regal 15 Kennet Lane ☎044 2819 1122; map p.371. Cleanish, modern building close to the station with good-value rooms (a/c ₹990), all with attached bathrooms and TV. No advance booking. The adjoining *Masa* is very similar. No wi-fi in either. ₹500

★**YWCA** 1086 Periyar EVR High Rd ☎044 2532 4234, ⓦywcamadras.org; map p.371. Attractive hotel in quiet gardens behind Egmore station, with spotless, spacious rooms, safe-deposit and a good restaurant. A highly recommended, safe and friendly place; book in advance. Rates include a buffet breakfast. Wi-fi ₹100/day. ₹1265

ANNA SALAI AND TRIPLICANE

Broadlands 18 Vallaba Agraharam St, Triplicane ☎044 2854 5573, ⓔbroadlandshotel@yahoo.com; map p.371. Reception is in an old whitewashed house, from which stretches a maze of corridors, outbuildings and courtyards. This is a budget travellers' enclave with character. There's a wide range of rooms, some with private balconies, with singles starting from ₹400 and one a/c double for ₹1000. No wi-fi. ₹450

Connemara Binny Rd ☎044 6600 0000, ⓦvivanta bytaj.com; map p.371. Dating from the Raj era, this whitewashed Art Deco five-star near Anna Salai, owned by the Taj group, is a Chennai institution. The large heritage

rooms feature Victorian decor, dressing rooms and verandas overlooking the pool; suites go up to ₹45,000. There's also a health club, 24hr coffee shop, two excellent restaurants (see opposite) and a bar. ₹11,000

Cristal 34 CNK Rd, Triplicane ☎044 2851 3011; map p.371. Down a lane off Quaide Milleth Salai (opposite the *Firdouse* hotel) and thus a little quieter, this is as cheap as it gets in Chennai. Rooms are tiled and all have attached showers. The a/c rooms start at ₹800, depending on size and facilities. No wi-fi. ₹400

La Woods 1 Woods Rd ☎044 2846 0677, ⓦlawoods hotel.com; map p.371. Good-value, mid-range hotel with central a/c. The comfortable and nicely decorated rooms have modern plumbing, lighting and media hub, while Italian marble flooring throughout gives a bright and airy feel. Breakfast included; wi-fi in lobby. ₹3000

★**Paradise** 17/1 Vallaba Agraharam St, Triplicane ☎044 2859 4252, ⓦparadiseguesthouse.co.in; map p.371. A friendly and dependable hotel, offering inexpensive rooms with attached bathrooms, TVs and a choice of Western or Indian loos. There are two blocks, old and new, right next to each other; rooms (a/c ₹1100) in the new block are slightly bigger and cleaner. There's also a large roof terrace, travel facilities and exchange. Good value. ₹700

OUTSIDE THE CENTRE

Crowne Plaza 132 TTK Rd ☎044 2499 4101, ⓦcrowne plaza.com; map p.369. The last word in American-style executive luxury, with great online deals. There are several excellent restaurants (see opposite), a 24hr coffee shop, gym and spa. The spacious rooms with plush furnishings make it a first-rate choice. ₹6460

New Woodlands 72–75 Dr Radhakrishnan Salai ☎044 2811 3111, ⓦnewwoodlands.com; map p.369. Sprawling complex of spacious, self-contained apartments called cottages (non-a/c ₹4000, a/c ₹5485) and clean, reasonably sized rooms in the main block. There are also two good restaurants and a swimming pool. ₹2500

Shelter 19–21 Venkatesa Agraharam St, Mylapore ☎044 4924 1919, ⓦhotelshelter.com; map p.369. A stone's throw from the Kapalishvara Temple, this sparklingly clean luxury three-star hotel with good restaurants and a bar is better value than most more upmarket places. ₹4500

EATING

Chennai offers the complete range of dining options you would expect from a major city, ranging from dirt-cheap vegetarian "meals" joints to high-class Westernized hotel restaurants, with some unique independent venues in between.

EGMORE

Kalyana Bhavan Biriyani 139/140 Marshalls Rd ☏ 044 6525 3111; map p.371. As the name suggests, this is a specialist biryani place, serving tasty plain, chicken and mutton versions (₹85–170) on banana leaves, accompanied by aubergine sauce and a semolina sweet. Daily 11am–4pm & 6–9pm.

Saravana Bhavan 21 Kennet Lane ☏ 044 2819 2055, ⓦ saravanabhavan.com; map p.371. This famous South Indian fast-food chain is an institution in Chennai, with more than twenty branches dotted around the city, plus more statewide and international locations. Try one of the many set meals (around ₹100) and finish with freshly made *ladoo* or *barfi* from the sweets counter. Daily 6am–10pm.

★ **Vasanta Bhavan** 20 Gandhi Irwin Rd ☏ 044 2819 2354; map p.371. One of the best-value "meals" joints around the station, with ranks of attentive waiters and delicious pure-veg food – ₹85 for a generous limited thali, plus great dosas and so on. It's busy, spotlessly clean, and its coffee and sweets are delicious too. Daily 6am–10.30pm.

Victoria Kabab Centre 3 Kennet Lane ☏ 044 2819 3638; map p.371. Bright modern canteen-style joint with an open-view kitchen, where the busy chefs turn out a range of delicious barbecue items, such as Irani chops (₹180), plus soups, gravy items and some Chinese. Daily 11am–midnight.

ANNA SALAI AND TRIPLICANE

Amethyst Next to Corporation Bank, White's Rd ☏ 044 4599 1633, ⓦ amethystchennai.com; map p.371. Delightfully lush garden café with tables set among ferns and palms along a veranda and in an a/c hall. There are toasted sandwiches (from ₹225), a range of coffees, fresh veg and fruit juices (from ₹120) and filling main courses such as bangers and mash for around ₹400. Wi-fi ₹50/hr. Daily 10am–10pm.

★ **Annalakshmi** 1st floor, Sigapi Achi Building (behind Air India office), 18/3 Rukmani Lakshmipathy Rd ☏ 044 2852 5109; map p.371. This beautifully decorated restaurant is a charitable venture run voluntarily by Sivananda devotees, whose profits go to the community. You can choose between pricey set menus with different Ayurvedic properties or order à la carte dishes for around ₹250–400. Tues–Sun 11am–3pm & 7–9pm.

Firdouse 307 Quaide Milleth Salai ☏ 044 4215 7174; map p.371. One of Triplicane's best, with an extensive menu of north and South Indian food: *aloo parathas*, a range of chicken dishes, vegetarian options and biryanis, all in the ₹100–200 range; also caramel custard. Clean, with a separate a/c dining area. Daily 11am–midnight.

Mogal Biriyani Triplicane High Rd, near the junction

with Wallajah Rd; map p.371. A tiny *dhaba*, the best of many such places on this road, with few tables but serving up tasty chicken in tandoori, kebab and biryani for under ₹100. Daily 11am–11pm.

The Raintree/The Verandah Connemara hotel, Binny Rd ☏ 044 6600 0000; map p.371. Occupying a classy wooden building at the rear of the compund, *The Raintree* specializes in set Chettinad meals from ₹1450, while *The Verandah* is a high-quality multicuisine restaurant, with meals for around ₹1000. Both daily: The Raintree 12.30–3pm & 7.30pm–midnight; The Verandah 24hr.

Sennthur 154 Anna Salai, opposite Spencer Plaza ☏ 044 6546 8316; map p.371. Large, centrally located "banana-leaf" restaurant very popular with locals. There are two main eating areas, non-a/c at the front and a slightly more expensive a/c hall at the back. "Meals" are served from 11.30am–3.30pm (standard meals ₹70; specials with extra dishes and dessert ₹100); also North Indian dishes. Daily 7am–11pm.

OUTSIDE THE CENTRE

Amaravathi Corner of Cathedral and TTK roads ☏ 044 2811 7000; map p.369. One of four dependable options in this complex of regional speciality restaurants, south of the downtown area. This one does excellent Andhran food, including particularly tasty biryanis (from ₹250). Daily noon–4pm & 7–11pm.

★ **Dakshin/The Residency** Crowne Plaza hotel, 132 TTK Rd ☏ 044 2499 4101; map p.369. The *Dakshin* is one of the country's top South Indian restaurants, serving a range of unusual dishes, including seafood in marinated spices, Karnataka mutton biryani and *appam*. Live Carnatic music in the evenings. Book in advance and expect to pay at least ₹1000 for a meal with starter and drink. *The Residency* serves multicuisine, including Southeast Asian, Chinese and European dishes. Daily 12.15–3pm & 7.15–11pm.

Don Pepé 1st floor, above Hot Breads, 73 Cathedral Rd ☏ 044 2811 0343; map p.369. Swish a/c Tex-Mex joint, serving a predictable menu of fajitas, enchiladas, tortillas and burritos, plus a selection of average pasta dishes (dubbed "Euro-Mex"). Meat dishes cost in the region of ₹300–400. Daily 11am–10pm.

Ente Keralam 1 Kasturi Estate, First St, Poes Garden ☏ 044 3221 6591, ⓦ entekeralam.in; map p.369. Food is served in seven separate rooms at this top-notch Keralan restaurant, giving it a homely feel. Try a backwater speciality, Karimeen fish (₹400–600 depending on size), one of the veggie coconut curries (₹200) or the meat dishes (around ₹350). The lunchtime menu offers sixteen dishes for ₹250. Daily noon–3pm & 7–11pm.

DRINKING AND NIGHTLIFE

Chennai's bar and club scene has been growing along with the disposable income of the local middle class. Triplicane, however, is almost dry and Egmore doesn't offer much, so most of the major nightspots are located in the top-end hotels

7

dotted around the south side of the city. Expect cover charges including a drink of up to ₹1000 per person. Check out ⓦwhatshot.in/chennai for the latest trends.

10 Downing St Kences Inn, 50 North Boag Rd, T Nagar ☏044 4354 6565, ⓦ10ds.in/chennai; map p.369. As you might guess from the name, there's an austere English feel to the decor at this chain pub but there's no holds barred on the fun front, with ladies' nights on Wednesdays and karaoke Thursdays. Daily 11am–1pm.

Illusions – The Madras Pub 105 Dr Radhakrishnan Salai, Mylapore ☏044 4214 4449; map p.369. First-floor bar with snazzy modern design in its artwork and furniture. Popular with clubbers and celebrities for its mix of rock, hip-hop and Bollywood nights. Daily 12.30–3pm & 6.30pm–midnight.

Leather Bar Park hotel Plot 601, Anna Salai ☏90251 78535, ⓦtheparkhotels.com; map p.369. A favourite of Chennai's young moneyed crowd – especially at weekends – this smart hotel bar gains its name from the black leather furniture throughout. The wide range of drinks include plenty of cocktails, which you can sip alfresco on the spill-out terrace area. Daily 11am–midnight.

Paddington Sports Pub 132 Chamiers Rd, Nandanam ☏90251 48252, ⓦgotopaddington.co.in; map p.369. Large sports bar complete with billiards room, smart restaurant area and a goalpost-shaped bar. They also serve Indian and Chinese food. Daily 11am–1pm.

QBar Hilton Chennai, 10th Floor, 124/1 Jawaharlal Nehru Salai, Guindy ☏90251 83174; map p.369. Poolside rooftop club with a chill-out soundtrack provided by the resident DJ. They serve a good selection of beers and wines, cocktails and mocktails. Daily noon–11pm.

Zara The Tapas Bar 71 Cathedral Rd, Gopalapuram ☏044 2811 1462; map p.369. A dizzying mishmash of neon lighting, TV screens flashing images and trendy decor, where you can sample good cocktails and snack on the idiosyncratic take on tapas. Themed club nights such as Retro Thursdays. Daily 11am–11pm.

ENTERTAINMENT

Cinema There is plenty of entertainment on offer in Chennai, including a number of high-quality cinemas showing English, Hindi and, of course, Tamil films, such as the swish Sathyam chain (ⓦspicinemas.in).

Music The annual Carnatic music festival runs from mid-December to mid-February, with the main concerts taking place at the music academy on TTK Rd. You can find details of other classical music and dance performances at ⓦkutcheribuzz.com.

SHOPPING

Higginbothams 116 Anna Salai ☏044 2852 0640; map p.371. One of the largest stores of the nationwide bookseller, packed with hardbacks and paperbacks on every subject imaginable. Very strong history, philosophy and religion sections. Mon–Sat 9am–8pm, Sun 10.30am–7.30pm.

Indian Arts Emporium 152 Anna Salai ☏044 2846 0560; map p.371. This jointly managed row of several crafts shops has a wide range of bronzes, ornaments, silks and carpets. Mon–Sat 10.30am–7.30pm, Sun 10.30am–4pm.

Kalakshetra Foundation craft shop Kalakshetra Rd, Thiruvanmiyur ☏044 2452 5423, ⓦkalakshetra.in; map p.369. The shop here sells a huge array of quality handmade crafts, from silk and silk/cotton saris to larger woven items and accessories such as bags. Mon–Sat 9am–5pm.

Nalli Chinnasami Chetty 9 Nageswaran Rd, T Nagar ☏044 2434 4115, ⓦnallisilks.com; map p.369. Huge branch of this famous silk shop, selling an array of saris and other items, including some of Kanchipuram's best products. Daily 9am–9pm.

Poompuhar 108 Anna Salai ☏044 2852 0624, ⓦtnpoompuhar.org; map p.371. Tamil Nadu's official state handicrafts showroom stocks all sorts of souvenirs, from small trinkets to huge bronze Nataraj replicas. Mon–Sat 10am–8pm.

Spencer Plaza Anna Salai ☏044 2849 1001; map p.371. Chennai's original mall with its glass-roofed atrium is packed with hundreds of shops, from chains such as Bata to small independent clothes outlets. Also boasts forex agents and fast food aplenty. Daily 9.30am–9.30pm.

DIRECTORY

Banks and currency exchange Chennai has plenty of banks, though the major hotels offer exchange facilities to residents only. Thomas Cook (Mon–Sat 9am–6pm) has offices at the Ceebros Centre, 45 Montieth Rd, Egmore, at the G-4 Eldorado Building, 112 Uttar Gandhi Salai. There are forex agents at the airport and in Spencer Plaza (see above). **Consulates** Australia, 9th Floor, Express Chambers, 49–50 Whites Rd, Royapettah ☏044 4592 1300; Canada, YAFA Tower, Khader Kawaz Khan Rd, Nungambakkam ☏044 2833 0888; New Zealand, 132 Cathedral Rd ☏044 2811 2472; South Africa, 234 NSC Bose Rd ☏044 2530 6789; Sri Lanka, 56 Sterling Rd, Nungambakkam ☏044 2824 1896; UK, 20 Anderson Rd, Nungambakkam ☏044 4219 2151; US, Gemini Circle, Anna Salai ☏044 2857 4000.

Hospitals Chennai's best-equipped private hospital is the Apollo, 21 Greams Lane (☎ 044 2829 3333, ⓦ chennai.apollohospitals.com). For an ambulance, try ☎ 102, but it's usually quicker to jump in a taxi.

Post office Chennai's main post office is opposite Shanti theatre on Anna Salai (Mon–Sat 8am–8pm, Sun 10am–5pm). There are smaller branches in both Egmore and Triplicane.

Travel agents Reliable agents include Macro Hawk Flight Travels, Munoth Centre, 343 Triplicane High Rd ☎ 044 2852 8585, ⓔ macrohawk05@yahoo.com; Thomas Cook, Eldorado Building, 112 Nungambakkam High Rd ☎ 044 2827 5052, ⓦ thomascook.in; Trade-wings, 713 Anna Salai ☎ 044 4203 7101, ⓦ tradewingstravels.in; and Welcome Tours & Travels, 150 Anna Salai ☎ 044 2846 0677, ⓦ allindiatours.com.

The northeast

Fazed by the heat and air pollution of Chennai, most visitors escape as fast as they can, heading down the Coromandel coast to India's stone-carving capital, **Mamallapuram**. En route, it's worth stopping at **Dakshina Chitra**, a folk museum around 30km south of Chennai, where traditional buildings from across South India have been beautifully reconstructed. Further inland, **Kanchipuram** is an important pilgrimage and silk-sari-weaving town from where you can loop southwest to the atmospheric temple town of **Tiruvannamalai**, situated at the base of the sacred mountain, Arunachala. Along the coast, you can breakfast on croissants and espresso coffee in the former French colony of **Puducherry**. A short way north, **Auroville**, the Utopian settlement founded by followers of the Sri Aurobindo Ghose's spiritual successor, The Mother, provides a New Age haven for soul-searching Westerners and an economy for the local population.

Mamallapuram and around

Scattered around the base of a colossal mound of boulders 58km south of Chennai is the small seaside town and UNESCO World Heritage Site of **MAMALLAPURAM** (formerly Mahabalipuram). From dawn till dusk, the rhythms of chisels chipping granite resound down its sandy lanes – evidence of a stone-carving tradition that has endured since this was a major port of the Pallava dynasty, between the fifth and ninth centuries. It is only possible to speculate about the purpose of much of the boulder sculpture, but it appears that the friezes and shrines were not made for worship at all, but rather as showcases for the talents of local artists. Due in no small part to the maritime activities of the Pallavas, their style of art and architecture had wide-ranging influence, spreading from South India as far north as Ellora, as well as to Southeast Asia.

Mamallapuram's monuments divide into four categories: open-air **bas-reliefs**, structured **temples**, man-made **caves** and **rathas** ("chariots" carved in situ from single boulders to resemble temples or the chariots used in temple processions). The famous bas-reliefs, **Arjuna's Penance** and the **Krishna Mandapa**, adorn massive rocks near the centre of the village, while the beautiful **Shore Temple**, one of India's most photographed monuments, presides over the beach. Sixteen man-made caves and monolithic structures, in different stages of completion, are scattered through the area, but the most complete of the nine *rathas* are in a group, named after the five Pandava brothers of the Mahabharata.

Given the coexistence of so many stunning archeological remains with a long sandy **beach**, it was inevitable this would become a major destination for Western travellers, with the inevitable presence of Kashmiri emporia, beach hawkers, budget hotels and fish restaurants – and more recently hordes of Chennai-escapees descending at the weekends as well. The sandy hinterland and flat estuarine paddy fields around Mamallapuram also harbour a handful of sights well worth making forays from the coast to see. You can take any coastal bus between Mamallapuram and Chennai, or rent a moped for the day.

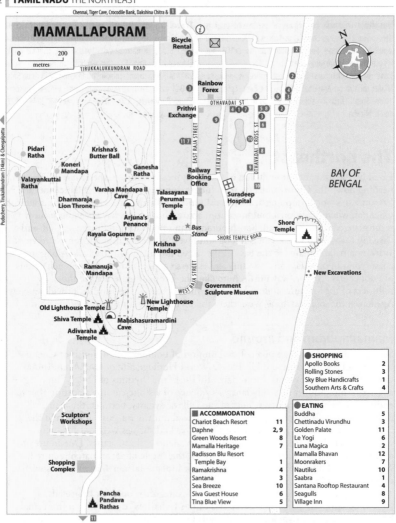

Chennai, Tiger Cave, Crocodile Bank, Dakshina Chitra &

MAMALLAPURAM

0   200
metres

TIRUKKALUKKUNDRAM ROAD

Bicycle Rental

Rainbow Forex

Prithvi Exchange

OTHAVADAI ST

EAST RAJA STREET

THIRUKULA ST

OTHAVADAI CROSS ST

Pidari Ratha

Krishna's Butter Ball

Koneri Mandapa

Ganesha Ratha

Valayankuttai Ratha

Varaha Mandapa II Cave

Dharmaraja Lion Throne

Railway Booking Office

Talasayana Perumal Temple

Suradeep Hospital

BAY OF BENGAL

Arjuna's Penance

Rayala Gopuram

Bus Stand

SHORE TEMPLE ROAD

Shore Temple

Krishna Mandapa

Ramanuja Mandapa

WEST RAJA STREET

New Excavations

Government Sculpture Museum

Old Lighthouse Temple

New Lighthouse Temple

Shiva Temple

Mahishasuramardini Cave

Adivaraha Temple

Sculptors' Workshops

Shopping Complex

Pancha Pandava Rathas

● SHOPPING	
Apollo Books	2
Rolling Stones	3
Sky Blue Handicrafts	1
Southern Arts & Crafts	4

■ ACCOMMODATION		● EATING	
Chariot Beach Resort	11	Buddha	5
Daphne	2, 9	Chettinadu Virundhu	3
Green Woods Resort	8	Golden Palate	11
Mamalla Heritage	7	Le Yogi	6
Radisson Blu Resort		Luna Magica	2
Temple Bay	1	Mamalla Bhavan	12
Ramakrishna	4	Moonrakers	7
Santana	3	Nautilus	10
Sea Breeze	10	Saabra	1
Siva Guest House	6	Santana Rooftop Restaurant	4
Tina Blue View	5	Seagulls	8
		Village Inn	9

Puducherry, Tirukkalikundram (14km) & Chengalpattu

7

The Shore Temple

Daily 6am–6pm (ticket office closes 5.30pm) • ₹250 (₹10), includes Pancha Pandava *rathas* if visited on the same day

With its unforgettable silhouette, visible for kilometres along the beach, Mamallapuram's **Shore Temple** dates from the early eighth century and is considered to be the earliest stone-built temple in South India. Today, due to the combined forces of wind, salt and sand, much of the detailed carving has eroded, giving the whole temple a soft, rounded appearance.

The taller of the towers is raised above a cell that faces out to sea – don't be surprised to see mischievous monkeys crouching inside. Approached from the west through two low-walled enclosures lined with small Nandi (bull) figures, the temple comprises two lingam shrines (one facing east, the other west), and a third shrine between them housing an image of the reclining Vishnu. Recent excavations, revealing a tank containing a structured stone column thought to have been a lantern, and a large

Varaha (boar incarnation of Vishnu) aligned with the Vishnu shrine, suggest that the area was sacred long before the Pallavas chose it as a temple site.

Arjuna's Penance

Mamallapuram's most celebrated bas-relief, **Arjuna's Penance** (also referred to as the "Descent of the Ganges"), lies directly west of the bus stand behind the modern Talasayana Perumal Temple. The surface of this rock erupts with detailed carving, most notably endearing and naturalistic renditions of animals. On the left-hand side, Arjuna, one of the Pandava brothers and a consummate archer, is shown standing on one leg. He is looking at the midday sun through a prism formed by his hands, meditating on Shiva, who is represented by a nearby statue fashioned by Arjuna himself. The Shiva Purana tells that Arjuna made the journey to a forest on the banks of the Ganges to do penance, in the hope that Shiva would part with his favourite weapon, the *pashupatashastra*, a magic staff or arrow. Shiva eventually materialized in the guise of Kirata, a wild forest-dweller, and picked a fight with Arjuna over a boar they both claimed to have shot. Arjuna only realized he was dealing with the deity after his attempts to drub the wild man proved

7

THE TEMPLES OF TAMIL NADU

No Indian state is more dominated by its **temples** than Tamil Nadu, where temple architecture catalogues the tastes of successive dynasties and testifies to the centrality of religion in everyday life. Most temples are built in honour of Shiva, Vishnu and their consorts; all are characterized not only by their design and sculptures, but also by constant activity: devotion, dancing, singing, pujas, festivals and feasts. Each is tended by brahmin priests, recognizable by their *dhotis* (loincloths), a sacred thread draped over the right shoulder, and marks on the forehead. One to three horizontal (usually white) lines distinguish Shaivites; vertical lines (yellow or red), often converging into a near-V shape, are common among Vaishnavites.

DRAVIDA ARCHITECTURE

Dravida, the temple architecture of Tamil Nadu, first took form in the Pallava port of **Mamallapuram**. A step-up from the cave retreats of Hindu and Jain ascetics, the earliest Pallava monuments were **mandapas**, shrines cut into rock faces and fronted by columns. This sculptural skill was transferred to freestanding temples, **rathas**, carved out of single rocks and incorporating the essential elements of Hindu temples: the dim inner sanctuary, the *garbhagriha*, capped with a modest tapering spire featuring repetitive architectural motifs.

CHOLA ARCHITECTURE

Pallava themes were developed in Karnataka by the Chalukyas and Rashtrakutas, but it was the Shaivite **Cholas** who spearheaded Tamil Nadu's next architectural phase, in the tenth century. In **Thanjavur**, Rajaraja I created the Brihadishvara Temple principally as a status symbol; its proportions far exceed any attempted by the Pallavas. Set within a vast walled courtyard, the sanctuary, fronted by a small *mandapa*, stands beneath a sculpted *vimana* that soars more than 60m high. Most sculptures once again feature Shiva, but the *gopuras* each side of the eastern gateway to the courtyard were an innovation, as were the lions carved into the base of the sanctuary walls, and the pavilion erected over Nandi in front of the sanctuary.

VIJAYANAGAR ARCHITECTURE

By the time of the thirteenth-century **Vijayanagar** kings, the temple was central to city life, the focus for civic meetings, education, dance and theatre. The Vijayanagars extended earlier structures, adding enclosing walls around a series of **prakaras**, or courtyards, and erecting freestanding *mandapas* for use as meeting halls, elephant stables, stages for music and dance, and ceremonial marriage halls (*kalyan mandapas*). Raised on superbly decorated columns, these *mandapas* became known as **thousand-pillared halls**. **Tanks** were added, doubling as water stores and washing areas, and used for festivals when deities were set afloat in boats.

Under the Vijayanagars, the *gopuras* were enlarged and set at the cardinal points over the high gateways to each *prakara*, to become the dominant feature. **Madurai** is the place to check out Vijayanagar architecture.

futile; narrowly escaping death at the playful hand of Shiva, he was finally rewarded with the weapon. To the right of Arjuna, a natural cleft represents the **Ganges**, complete with *nagas* – water spirits in the form of cobras. You may well see sudden movements among the carved animals: lazing goats often join the permanent features.

Ganesha Ratha and Krishna's Butter Ball

Just north of Arjuna's Penance a path leads west and uphill to a single monolith, the **Ganesha Ratha**. Its image of Ganesh dates from this century; some say it was installed at the instigation of England's King George V. The sculpture at one end, of a protecting demon with a tricorn headdress, is reminiscent of the Indus Valley Civilization's 4000-year-old horned figure known as the "proto-Shiva". Further north up the hill, precipitously balanced on the top of a ridge, is a massive, natural, almost spherical boulder called **Krishna's Butter Ball**. Picnickers and goats often rest in its perilous-looking shade.

Varaha Mandapa II Cave

On the hill behind Arjuna's Penance, southwest of the Ganesha Ratha, is the **Varaha Mandapa II Cave**, whose entrance hall has two pillars with horned lion-bases and a cell flanked by two *dvarapalas*, or guardians. One of four **panels** shows the boar-incarnation of Vishnu, who stands with one foot resting on the *naga* snake-king as he lifts a diminutive Prithvi – the Earth – from the primordial ocean. Another is of Gajalakshmi, the goddess Lakshmi seated on a lotus being bathed by a pair of elephants. Trivikrama, the dwarf brahmin who becomes huge and bestrides the world in three steps to defeat the demon king Bali, is shown in another panel, and finally a four-armed Durga is depicted in another.

The Krishna Mandapa

Immediately south of Arjuna's Penance, the enormous bas-relief known as the **Krishna Mandapa** shows Krishna raising Mount Govardhana aloft in one hand. The sculptor's original intention must have been for the rock above Krishna to represent the mountain, but the seventeenth-century Vijayanagar addition of a columned *mandapa*, or entrance hall, prevents a clear view of the carving. Krishna is also depicted seated milking a cow, and standing playing the flute. Other figures are *gopas* and *gopis*, the cowboys and -girls of his pastoral youth.

The lighthouses

Around 300m south of Arjuna's Penance, at the highest point in an area of steep paths, unfinished temples, ruins, scampering monkeys and massive rocks, the **New Lighthouse** affords fine views east to the Shore Temple, and west across paddy fields and flat lands littered with rocks. Next to it, the **Olakanesvara** ("flame-eyed" Shiva), or **Old Lighthouse Temple**, used as a lighthouse until the early twentieth century, dates from the Rajasimha period (674–800 AD).

Mahishasuramardini Cave

Nestling between the two lighthouses is the **Mahishasuramardini Cave**, whose central image portrays Shiva and Parvati with the child Murugan seated on Parvati's lap. Shiva's right foot rests on the back of the bull Nandi, and Parvati sits casually, leaning on her left hand. On the left wall, beyond an empty cell, a panel depicts Vishnu reclining on the serpent, his attitude of repose contrasted with the weapon-brandishing demons, Madhu and Kaithaba. Other figures seek Vishnu's permission to chase them. Opposite, an intricately carved panel shows the eight-armed goddess Durga as Mahishasuramardini, the "crusher" of the buffalo demon Mahishasura. The panel shows Durga riding a lion, in the midst of the struggle. Accompanied by dwarf *ganas*, she wields a bow and other weapons; Mahishasura, equipped with a club, can be seen to the right, in flight with fellow demons.

Government Sculpture Museum

West Raja St • Daily 9.30am–5pm • ₹10

The small **Government Sculpture Museum**, located on the main road south of the bus stand, has a rather motley collection of unlabelled Pallava sculpture found in and around Mamallapuram, some of it quite colourful and attractive. Many of the best pieces stand on the front lawn, perfectly visible from the road. The building itself, though modern, is also appealing and resembles a temple more than a museum.

Pancha Pandava Rathas (Five Rathas)

Daily 6am–6pm (ticket office closes 5.30pm) • ₹250 (₹10) including the Shore Temple on the same day

In a sandy compound 1.5km south of the village centre stands the stunning group of monoliths known as the **Pancha Pandava Rathas**, the five chariots of the Pandavas. Dating from the period of Narasimhavarman I (c.630–670 AD), they consist of five separate freestanding sculptures that imitate structured temples, plus some beautifully carved life-sized animals.

The "architecture" of the *rathas* reflects a variety of styles and stands almost as a model for much subsequent development in the southern style. Carving was always executed from top to bottom, enabling the artists to work on the upper parts with no fear of damaging anything below. Intriguingly, it's thought that the *rathas* were never used for worship.

The southernmost and tallest of the *rathas*, named after the eldest of the Pandavas, is the pyramidal **Dharmaraja**. Set on a square base, the upper part comprises a series of diminishing storeys, each with a row of pavilions. Four corner blocks, each with two panels and standing figures, are broken up by two pillars and pilasters supported by squatting lions. Figures on the panels include Ardhanarishvara (Shiva and female consort in one figure), Brahma, the king Narasimhavarman I and Harihara (Shiva and Vishnu combined). The central tier includes sculptures of Shiva Gangadhara and one of the earliest representations in Tamil Nadu of the dancing Shiva, Nataraja, who became all-important in the region. Alongside, the **Bhima** *ratha*, the largest of the group, is the least complete. Devoid of carved figures, the upper storeys, as in the Dharmaraja, feature false windows and repeated pavilion-shaped ornamentation.

The Arjuna and Draupadi *rathas* share a base. Behind the **Arjuna**, the most complete of the entire group and very similar to the Dharmaraja, stands a superb unfinished sculpture of Shiva's bull Nandi. **Draupadi** is unique in terms of rock-cut architecture, with a roof that appears to be based on a straw-thatched hut. There's an image of Durga inside, but the figure of her lion vehicle outside is aligned side-on and not facing the image, suggesting this was not a real temple. To the west, close to a life-sized carving of an elephant, stands the *ratha* named after the twin brothers **Nakula and Sahadeva**.

Tiger Cave

Main highway, 4km north of Mamallapuram • Daily sunrise–sunset • Free

Set amid trees close to the sea, the extraordinary **Tiger Cave** contains a shrine to Durga, approached by a flight of steps that passes two subsidiary cells. Following the line of an irregularly shaped rock, the cave is remarkable for its elaborate exterior, which features multiple lion-heads surrounding the entrance to the main cell. If you sit for long enough, the section on the left with seated figures in niches above two elephants begins to resemble an enormous owl.

Crocodile Bank

14km north of town on the road to Chennai • Tues–Sun 8.30am–5.30pm • ₹35, camera ₹20, video camera ₹100 • **Night Safari** Sat & Sun 7–8.30pm • ₹200 • ☎ 044 2747 2447, ⓦ madrascrocodilebank.org

The **Crocodile Bank** at Vadanemmeli was set up in 1976 by the American zoologist Romulus Whittaker to protect and breed indigenous crocodiles. The Bank has been so successful (from fifteen crocs to five thousand in the first fifteen years) that its remit now extends to saving endangered species, such as turtles and lizards, from around the world.

Low-walled enclosures in its garden compound house hundreds of inscrutable crocodiles, soaking in ponds or sunning themselves on the banks. Breeds include the fish-eating, knobbly-nosed gharial, and the world's largest species, the saltwater *Crocodylus porosus*, which can grow to 8m in length.

There are **feeding demonstrations** at 11.30am, 12.30pm, 4.30pm and 5.30pm on Sundays. The temptation to take photos is tempered by the sight of those hungry saurians clambering over each other to snap up the chopped flesh, within centimetres of the top of the wall. Another attraction is the weekend **Night Safari**, when the crocodiles are far more active, which has to be booked at least 48 hours in advance.

Another important field of work is conducted with the collaboration of local Irula people, whose traditional expertise is with snakes. Cobras are brought to the bank for **venom collection**, to be used in the treatment of snakebites. Elsewhere, snakes are repeatedly "milked" until they die, but here only a limited amount is taken from each snake, enabling them to return to the wild. To visit this section costs an extra ₹5.

7

Dakshina Chitra

Main Coast Rd • Daily except Tues 10am–6pm • ₹200 (₹100), camera ₹20, video camera ₹75 • ☎ 044 2747 2603, ⓦ dakshinachitra.net

Occupying a patch of sand dunes midway between Chennai and Mamallapuram, **Dakshina Chitra**, literally "Vision of the South", is one of India's best-conceived folk museums, devoted to the rich architectural and artistic heritage of Kerala, Karnataka, Andhra Pradesh and Tamil Nadu. Set up by the Chennai Craft Foundation, the museum exposes visitors to many disappearing traditions of the region, which you might otherwise not be aware of, from tribal fertility cults and Ayyannar field deities to pottery and leather shadow-puppets.

A selection of traditional buildings from across peninsular India has been painstakingly reconstructed using original materials. Exhibitions attached to them convey the environmental and cultural diversity of the South, most graphically expressed in a wonderful textile collection featuring antique silk and cotton saris from various castes and regions. Snacks are available on site.

ARRIVAL AND DEPARTURE   MAMALLAPURAM AND AROUND

By train The nearest railway station is in Chengalpattu, 29km to the northeast for mainline trains to Chennai, Tiruchirapalli and beyond. There are frequent bus connections from Chengalpattu to Mamallapuram (see below).

By bus The bus stand is in the centre of the village in front of the Talasayana Perumal Temple. There are services roughly every 30min to Chennai (4.15am–10pm; 2hr), six daily to Kanchipuram (2hr) and regular services to Chengalpattu (for Tiruvannamalai and better connections to Kanchipuram). Mamallapuram lies just off the East Coast Rd between Chennai and Puducherry; buses between the two run every 15–20min but don't come in to Mamallapuram – you need to either walk or take an auto-rickshaw (₹50) the 1.5km northwest to the bus stop on the East Coast Rd.

By taxi Taxis to and from the centre of Chennai cost around ₹1600 or ₹1300 to and from the airport. Puducherry is a ₹1800 ride.

GETTING AROUND AND INFORMATION

By bike and motorbike By far the best way to get to the important sites is by bicycle. You can rent bikes from shops on East Raja St for ₹20/hr or ₹75/day. Scooters and Enfield motorcycles can also be rented for around ₹400/day – check at your guesthouse.

Tourist information The Government of Tamil Nadu Tourist Office (Mon–Fri 10am–5.45pm; ☎ 044 2744 2232) is one of the first buildings you see in the village, on your left as you arrive from Chennai, but is not much use. A better resource is ⓦ mahabalipuram.co.in.

ACCOMMODATION

Mamallapuram village has dozens of guesthouses and small hotels in the budget and mid-range categories but it suffers badly from aggressive touting by a small number of places; ignore the touts and walk to your chosen destination – it's a small place. The more luxurious resorts are dotted along the coast, mostly to the north.

Chariot Beach Resort 69 Five Rathas Rd ☎94449 92726, ⓦchariotbeachresorts.com. A luxurious resort at the southern end of town with massive garden area, unobstructed sea views and a 57m swimming pool. All rooms are spacious and beautifully furnished, and there's also the option of luxurious cottages (₹9500) and sea-view suites (₹13,500). ₹7500

Daphne Fishermens Colony (reception at Daphne's Hotel Othavadai, Cross St) ☎98942 82876, ⓔhotel daphne1@yahoo.com. The very last guesthouse on the beach strip with just nine rooms on three floors, a roof terrace and sea views. The place in the village is fine too. ₹1000

★**Green Woods Resort** 12 Othavadai Cross St ☎044 2744 3318, ⓔgreenwoods_resort@yahoo.com. Very friendly and extremely good value family-run place, set round a leafy courtyard garden, which does attract mosquitoes. There's a wide range of very clean rooms (the best a/c rooms cost just ₹1400), some with swing chairs, private balconies, terraces and TVs, plus excellent Ayurvedic massage on site. ₹700

Mamalla Heritage 104 East Raja St ☎044 2744 2060, ⓦhotelmamallaheritage.com. Efficient and modern hotel on the main road through the village with comfortable and spotless a/c rooms overlooking a courtyard. There's a choice of standard and slightly bigger deluxe (₹3120) rooms, all with fridge and TV, and there are two very good restaurants on site (see below). ₹2400

Radisson Blu Resort Temple Bay 57 Kovalam Rd, 1km north of the village ☎044 2744 3636, ⓦradissonblu .com. A luxurious resort with a swimming pool and excellent restaurant, which backs right on to the beach. There are eight different categories of room, from standard doubles to sea-view villas with jacuzzis and sitout areas. ₹5600

Ramakrishna 8 Othavadai St ☎044 2744 2331, ⓦhotel ramakrishna.com. Bigger than many of the surrounding hotels, its rooms have been completely refurbished with hardwood floors, new bathrooms and flatscreen TVs. There's also a breezy rooftop restaurant. ₹1500

Santana 178 Othavadai St ☎97910 77352, ⓔbabu santana@rediffmail.com. Six sizeable and spotless first-floor rooms (a/c ₹1400); the seafront one is a gem, sandwiched in between its popular ground-floor beachside restaurant and roof terrace. It also offers a travel service. ₹1000

★**Sea Breeze** Othavadai Cross St ☎044 2744 3035, ⓦhotelseabreeze.net. The only bona fide beach resort within the village, featuring a range of a/c rooms whose prices vary according to size and view – the large sea-view rooms with private balcony and king-size beds are the best. The swimming pool is open to non-residents (₹400/day) and there's an Ayurveda centre. Breakfast included. ₹3000

Siva Guest House 2 Othavadai Cross St ☎044 2744 3534, ⓦsivaguesthouse.com. A small but clean and tidy lodge with just fifteen rooms, which are spread over three floors. Mandala-patterned bedsheets add flavour and there is a choice of non-a/c and a/c rooms (₹1000). Good value. ₹400

Tina Blue View 48 Othavadai St ☎044 2744 2319. Established family guesthouse with simple turquoise and whitewashed rooms, some in the main block and others in an annexe in the pleasant garden. All rooms have attached bathrooms and mosquito nets. There are also some single rooms (₹400) and a new a/c cottage (₹1300). ₹600

EATING

Mamallapuram is crammed with small restaurants specializing in **seafood** – tiger prawns, pomfret, tuna, shark and lobster – usually served marinated and grilled with chips and salad; always establish in advance exactly how much it will cost. As this is a travellers' hangout, there are also numerous places offering the usual array of pasta, pancakes and bland Indian dishes. **Beer** is widely available, but it's pricey (₹180–200) and there are no dedicated bars. If you want to enjoy real Indian food, head to the *dhabas* by the bus stand and the banana-leaf places on East Raja St.

Buddha 46 Othavadai St ☎97890 70754. Yellow walls adorned with Buddhas and the leafy outlook create a pleasant ambience. The usual travellers' breakfasts are available (omelette, toast and muesli), plus salads including Thai and pesto, as well as fish and seafood for around ₹300. There's also an unexpected range of cocktails at ₹180. Daily 7am–11pm.

Chettinadu Virundhu 10 East Raja St ☎98403 65621. Smart new canteen-style place with an a/c corner, serving a range of tasty recipes from the Chettinad region for ₹150–200, plus other Indian and Chinese standards. Daily 11.30am–4pm & 6.30–10.30pm.

★**Golden Palate** Mamalla Heritage hotel, 104 East Raja St ☎044 2744 2060. Blissfully cool café with a/c and tinted windows, serving the best veg food in the village:

₹150 "meals" at lunchtime (noon–3pm), North Indian tandoori in the courtyard in the evenings and wonderful ice-cream sundaes. The equally popular rooftop *Waves* restaurant serves chicken and grilled fish for ₹300–400. Golden Palate daily 7am–10.30pm; Waves daily noon–4pm & 7–11pm.

★**Le Yogi** 19 Othavadai St ☎98407 06340. Run by a French/Indian couple, this relaxed place is a good spot to chill, serving French crêpes (around ₹140), a range of salads with brown sesame bread, pasta dishes for up to ₹270, plus good coffee and lassis. Daily 8am–11pm.

Luna Magica Bajanai Kovil St, Fisherman Colony ☎98401 00519. Beach restaurant serving top-notch seafood, kept alive in a tank and sold by weight. They specialize in tiger prawns and lobster in a choice of tasty

7

sauces such as tomato or garlic butter and also offer fish curry, plus grilled fish, shark and tuna steaks for ₹200–350. Red wine and cold beer are available but expensive. Daily 7.30am–10pm.

Mamalla Bhavan Shore Temple Rd, opposite the bus stand. A very popular pure-veg and "meals" joint that's invariably packed. At ₹70–90, the unlimited lunchtime "meals" (11.30am–3.30pm) are a bargain, and they also serve good South Indian breakfasts including *pongal*, masala dosas and coffee. Daily 6.30am–9.30pm.

Moonrakers 34 Othavadai St ☎ 044 2744 2115. Cool jazz and blues sounds, great fresh seafood and slick service ensure this place, with its three floors, is often packed with travellers. The owners are constantly touting passers-by for custom. Good seafood platter (fish, prawns, calamari) for ₹500. Daily 11.30am–11.30pm.

Nautilus Othavadai Cross St. Popular café/restaurant run by a French chef. The menu features soups, a wide range of French salads (₹100–150), ratatouille and non-veg mains such as seafood, beef and the usual travellers' favourites for ₹240–380. Daily 9am–11pm.

Saabra 5/4 Kovalam Rd ☎ 94448 95862. First-floor joint that does great veg, egg and chicken *kaati* rolls for ₹50–80, as well as Indian and Chinese dishes such as tandoori and biryanis for ₹100–200. Daily 11am–10pm.

Santana Rooftop Restaurant Santana hotel, 178 Othavadai St ☎ 94442 90832. The breezy rooftop is much nicer than the ground-floor dining area, especially if you can get a front seat. Lobster per kilo, fish dishes, calamari and seafood platters with rice and salad go for ₹300–600. Daily 7am–11pm.

Seagulls Tina Blue View, 48 Othavadai St ☎ 044 2744 2319. A large and pleasant rooftop restaurant serving a decent, extensive seafood menu including tuna steak with chips and salad, seafood platters, fish and prawn curries, veggie dishes and chicken, all in the ₹250–400 range. Daily 7am–11pm.

Village Inn Thirukulam St, off Othavadai St ☎ 94441 16406. A small, pleasant restaurant with cane furniture and classical Indian music, dishing up grilled seafood for around ₹300, plus cheaper fish curry, biryanis and veggie dishes. One of the cheaper places for beer. Daily 9am–10.30pm.

SHOPPING

Apollo Books 150/1 Fisherman Colony ☎ 044 2744 2992. Excellent and friendly bookshop, owned by knowledgeable Apollo himself, who stocks a fine range of literature and titles on art, history, culture and religion. Daily 10am–8pm.

Rolling Stones 4 Othavadai Cross St ☎ 80561 13998. Tiny stone-carving shop, whose charming owner not only sells his work at fair prices but offers carving lessons so you can make your own piece. Daily 9am–9pm.

Sky Blue Handicrafts 8 Othavadai St ☎ 044 2744

VEDANTHANGAL BIRD SANCTUARY

One of India's most spectacular bird sanctuaries lies roughly 1km east of the village of **Vedanthangal**, 30km from the east coast and 86km southwest of Chennai. The **sanctuary** is busiest with birdlife between December and February, when it's totally flooded. The rains of the northeast monsoon, sweeping through in October or November, bring local and migratory waterbirds, including some that nest and settle here until the dry season (usually April), when they leave for wetter areas. Abundant trees on mounds above water level provide perfect nesting spots, alive by January with fledglings. Visitors can watch the avian action from a path at the water's edge, or from a watchtower (fitted out with strong binoculars). Try to come at sunset, when the birds return from feeding. Common Indian **species** to look out for are openbill storks, spoonbills, pelicans, black cormorants, and herons of several types. You may also see ibises, grey pelicans, migrant cuckoos, sandpipers, egrets (which paddle in the rice fields), and darting bee-eaters.

ARRIVAL AND DEPARTURE

By bus Getting to Vedanthangal can present a few problems. The nearest town is Maduranthakam, 8km east, on NH-45 between Chengalpattu and Tindivanam, from where there are hourly buses to the sanctuary. Alternatively, direct services run every hour or two from Chengalpattu.

By taxi Taxis make the journey from Maduranthakam for ₹500 but cannot be booked from Vedanthangal.

INFORMATION

Opening hours Daily 6am–6pm. The best months to visit are Nov–Feb, although weekends and holidays can be crowded and noisy.

Entry fees Entry to the sanctuary is ₹5 (camera ₹25, video camera ₹150).

Accommodation To arrange accommodation in the *Forest Department Resthouse*, call the Forest Ranger (☎ 94442 66213) or Wildlife Warden in Chennai (☎ 044 2235 1471).

3729. Easily the friendliest and most reputable Kashmiri shop in the village, where you can find lots of authentic fabrics, dresses, bags and silver jewellery. Daily 8am–10pm.

Southern Arts & Crafts 72 East Raja St ☎044 2744 3675, ⓦsouthernarts.in. Smart showroom for stone carving, bronzes, paintings and other local artefacts. Daily 9am–8pm.

DIRECTORY

Banks and exchange Two of the best places to change money are Prithvi Exchange, 23/12 East Raja St (daily 9.30am–7pm; ☎044 2744 3265), and The Rainbow Forex, 14 Othavadai St (daily 9.30am–9pm; ☎91767 04374).

Hospital If you need medical treatment, Suradeep Hospital 15, Thirukulam St (☎044 2744 2335), is highly recommended.

Surfing A relatively new activity in Mamallapuram, available through Mumu Surf School (☎97898 44191, ⓦmumusurfer

.wix.com/indiasurfing), where you can take lessons from ₹750 per person, depending on group size. If you know what you're doing, board rental goes from ₹250/hr.

Travel agents Delhi-based Hi! Tours at 125 East Raja St (☎044 2744 3260, ⓦhi-tours.com) offer car rental, ticketing and other services. Travels Partners (☎98403 77033, ⓔtravelspartners@gmail.com) on Othavadai St provide friendly service.

Kanchipuram

KANCHIPURAM is situated on the Vegavathi River 70km southwest of Chennai. Ask any Tamil what Kanchipuram (aka "Kanchi") is famous for, and they'll probably say silk saris, shrines and saints – in that order. A dynastic capital throughout the medieval era, it remains one of the country's seven holiest cities, sacred to both Shaivites and Vaishnavites, and among the few surviving centres of goddess worship in the South. Year round, pilgrims pour through for a quick puja stop on the Tirupati tour circuit and, if they can afford it, a spot of shopping in the sari emporia. For non-Hindu visitors, however, Kanchipuram holds less appeal. Although the temples are undeniably impressive, the town itself is unremittingly hot, with only basic accommodation and amenities. Some people prefer to visit Kanchipuram as a **day-trip** from Chennai or Mamallapuram, both of which are a two-hour bus ride away.

Established by the **Pallava** kings in the fourth century AD, Kanchipuram served as their **capital** for five hundred years, and continued to flourish throughout the Chola, Pandya and Vijayanagar eras. Under the Pallavas, it was an important scholastic forum, and a meeting point for Jain, Buddhist and Hindu cultures. Its **temples** dramatically reflect this enduring political prominence, spanning the years from the peak of Pallava construction to the seventeenth century, when the ornamentation of the *gopuras* and pillared halls was at its most elaborate. You might need to be a little firm to resist the attentions of pushy puja-wallahs, who try to con foreigners into overpriced ceremonies. If you've come for silk, head for the shops that line Gandhi and Thirukatchininambi roads.

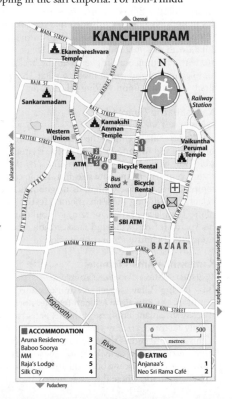

KANCHIPURAM

N MADA STREET
Ekambareshvara Temple
RAJA ST
Sankaramadam
WEST RAJA ST
PUTTERI STREET
Western Union
Kailasanatha Temple
PUTHUPALAYAM STREET
RAJA STREET
Kamakshi Amman Temple
NELLUKKARA ST
ATM
Bus Stand
KAMARAJAR STREET
MADAM STREET
ATM
CAR STREET
MADRAS ROAD
EAST RAJA STREET
Bicycle Rental
Bicycle Rental
SBI ATM
BAZAAR
GANDHI ROAD
Vegavathi River
VILAKKADI KOIL STREET
Chennai
Railway Station
Vaikuntha Perumal Temple
GPO
RAILWAY STATION RD
Varadarajaperumal Temple & Chengalpattu
Puducherry

■ ACCOMMODATION
Aruna Residency	3
Baboo Soorya	1
MM	2
Raja's Lodge	5
Silk City	4

0   500
metres

● EATING
| Anjanaa's | 1 |
| Neo Sri Rama Café | 2 |

7

Ekambareshvara Temple

North Mada St • Daily; closed noon–4pm • Camera ₹20, video camera ₹100

On the north side of town, Kanchipuram's largest temple and most important Shiva shrine, the **Ekambareshvara Temple** – also known as Ekambaranatha – is easily identified by its colossal whitewashed *gopuras*, which rise to almost 60m. The main temple contains some Pallava work, but was mostly constructed in the sixteenth and seventeenth centuries, and stands within a vast walled enclosure beside some smaller shrines and a large fish-filled water tank.

The entrance is through a high-arched passageway beneath an elaborate *gopura* in the south wall which leads to an open courtyard and a majestic "thousand-pillared hall", or *kalyan mandapa*. This faces the tank in the north and the sanctuary in the west that protects the emblem of Shiva (here in his form as **Kameshvara**, Lord of Desire), Prithvi lingam (one of five lingams in Tamil Nadu that represent the elements, in this case *Prithvi*, the Earth). Behind the sanctum, accessible from the covered hallway around it, an eerie, bare hall lies beneath a profusely carved *gopura*, and in the courtyard a venerable **mango tree** represents the tree under which Shiva and Kamakshi were married. This union is celebrated during a festival each April, when many couples are married in the *kalyan mandapa*.

Sankaramadam

Raja St • Daily; closed noon–4pm

Kanchipuram is the seat of a line of holy men bearing the title **acharya**, whose line dates back perhaps as far as 1300 BC to the saint Adi Sankaracharya. The 68th acharya, the highly revered Sri Chandrasekharendra Sarasvati Swami, died in January 1994 at the age of 101. Buried in the sitting position, as is the custom for great Hindu sages, his mortal remains are enshrined in a *samadhi* at the **Sankaramadam**, a *math* (monastery for Hindu renouncers) down the road from the Ekambareshvara Temple. Lined with old photographs from the life of the former swami, with young brahmin students chanting Sanskrit verses in the background, it's a typically Tamil blend of simple sanctity and garish modern glitz. The *math*'s two huge elephants are available to bestow blessings upon visiting pilgrims for a small fee.

Kailasanatha Temple

Western outskirts • Daily; closed noon–4pm

The **Kailasanatha Temple**, the oldest structure in Kanchipuram and the finest example of Pallava architecture in South India, is situated among several low-roofed houses just over 1km west of the town centre. Built by the Pallava king Rajasimha early in the eighth century, its intimate size and simple carving distinguish it from the town's later temples. Usually quieter than its neighbours, the shrine becomes the focus of vigorous celebrations during the **Mahashivratri festival** each March. Like its contemporary, the Shore Temple at Mamallapuram, it is built of soft sandstone, but its sheltered position has spared it from wind and sand erosion, and it remains remarkably intact, despite some rather clumsy renovation work.

Kamakshi Amman Temple

Raja St • Daily; closed noon–4pm • ⓦ kanchikamakshi.com

Built during Pallava supremacy and modified in the fourteenth and seventeenth centuries, the **Kamakshi Amman Temple**, north of the bus stand, combines several styles, with an ancient central shrine, gates from the Vijayanagar period, and high, heavily sculpted, creamy *gopuras* set above the gateways.

This is one of India's three holiest shrines to Shakti, Shiva's cosmic energy depicted in female form, usually as his consort. The goddess Kamakshi, a local form of Parvati, shown with a sugar-cane bow and arrows of flowers, is honoured for having lured Shiva to Kanchipuram, where they were married, and thus having forged the connection between the local community and the god. In February or March, deities are wheeled to the temple in huge wooden "cars", decked with robed statues and swaying plantain leaves.

ARRIVAL AND DEPARTURE   KANCHIPURAM

By train The railway station in the northeast of town sees twelve daily passenger services from Chengalpattu (originating in Chennai, Arakkonam, Tirupati and Puducherry) and two express trains (the weekly *Mumbai–Madurai Express* and biweekly *Mumbai–Nagercoil Express*).
By bus Buses from Chennai, Mamallapuram and Chengalpattu stop at the stand in the town centre just off Kosa St.
Destinations Chennai (every 10–15min; 1hr 30min–2hr); Madurai (4 daily; 8–9hr); Puducherry (hourly; 3–4hr); Tiruchirapalli (12 daily; 7–8hr); Tiruvannamalai (10 daily; 3–4hr).

GETTING AROUND

By bike The best way to get around Kanchi is by bicycle. Most of the main roads are fairly wide and traffic just about manageable. Bikes are available (₹10/hr) from stalls at both the west and northeast entrances to the bus stand.

ACCOMMODATION

Aruna Residency 15 Ulakalanthar Maada St, tucked away 50m down from the main junction ☎ 044 2722 4274, ✉ arunamahal@gmail.com. A large, quiet mid-range place that offers very good deals on single occupancy rooms. The double rooms (a/c ₹1650), complete with TV, are a good size, light and airy. ₹1200
★**Baboo Soorya** 85 East Raja St ☎ 044 2722 2555, ⓦ hotelbaboosoorya.com. The smartest place in town and set back from the noise of the main road in its own grounds. The 38 a/c rooms are well kept and represent good value. There's also a restaurant and a/c bar. It's a good idea to book in advance. ₹1500
MM 65/66 Nellukkara St ☎ 044 2722 7250, ⓦ mm hotels.com. Large, clean, medium-priced hotel, situated right in the heart of the town. The wood-panelled a/c

rooms (₹1800) have armchairs but are a little on the small side; the non-a/c rooms are plainer but slightly bigger. There's a *Saravana Bhavan* restaurant franchise on the ground floor. ₹1200
Raja's Lodge 20-B Nellukkara St ☎ 044 2722 2603. One of the best budget options in town, although little English is spoken. The rooms are on the small side and somewhat dingy. The same rooms can be a/c activated for an extra ₹300. No wi-fi. ₹500
Silk City 1st Floor, 77 Nellukara St ☎ 044 2722 7573, ✉ hotelsilkcity@gmail.com. Brand-new hotel in a central location with immaculate, spacious a/c rooms. A kettle, TV and towels are provided in all rooms, and the large attached bathrooms are spotless. Excellent value. No alcohol or wi-fi. ₹1200

EATING

Anjanaa's Baboo Soorya, 85 East Raja St ☎ 044 2723 3101. An excellent Chettinad restaurant on the ground floor of the hotel, serving lunchtime "meals" and a range of veg, chicken and fish dishes cooked Chettinad style for ₹150–300. Across the reception is its large and busy a/c bar serving cold beers for ₹200. Daily 10.30am–3.30pm

& 6.30–10.30pm.
Neo Sri Rama Café 20 Nellukkara St ☎ 044 2722 2435. Great value if slightly dingy restaurant, churning out filling unlimited "meals" for only ₹55. The sort of place where you are likely to attract the interest of the locals. Daily 7am–10.30pm.

Tiruvannamalai

Synonymous with the fifth Hindu element of Fire, **TIRUVANNAMALAI**, 100km southwest of Kanchipuram, ranks, along with Madurai, Kanchipuram, Chidambaram and Trichy, as one of the five holiest towns in Tamil Nadu. Its name, meaning "Red Mountain", derives from the spectacular extinct volcano, **Arunachala**, which rises behind it, and which glows an unearthly crimson in the dawn light. This awesome natural backdrop, combined with the colossal **Arunachaleshvara Temple** in the centre of town, make Tiruvannamalai one of the region's most memorable destinations. Well off the tourist trail, it's a perfect place to get to grips with life in small-town Tamil Nadu, especially for anyone with an interest in Hinduism.

Mythology identifies Arunachala as the place where Shiva asserted his power over Brahma and Vishnu by manifesting himself as a lingam of fire, or **agni-lingam**. The event is commemorated each year at the rising of the full moon in November/December, when

THE PRADAKSHINA

During the annual Kartigai festival, Hindu pilgrims are supposed to perform an auspicious circumambulation of Arunachala, known as the **pradakshina** (*pra* signifies the removal of all sins, *da* the fulfilment of desires, *kshi* freedom from the cycle of rebirth, and *na* spiritual liberation). Along the way, offerings are made at a string of shrines, tanks, temples, lingams, pillared meditation halls, sacred rocks, springs, trees and caves related to the Tiruvannamalai legends. Although hectic during the festival, the paved path linking them all together is quiet for most of the year, and makes a wonderful day-hike, affording fine views of the town and its environs.

a vast vat of two thousand litres of ghee and a 30m-wide wick is lit by priests on the summit of Arunachala. This symbolizes the fulfilment of Shiva's promise to reappear each year to vanquish the forces of darkness and ignorance with firelight.

The sacred Red Mountain is also associated with the famous twentieth-century saint, **Sri Ramana Maharishi**, who chose it as the site for his 23-year meditation retreat. A crop of small ashrams have sprung up on the edge of town below Sri Ramana's Cave, some of them more authentic than others, and the ranks of white-cotton-clad foreigners floating between them have become a defining feature of Tiruvannamalai.

Arunachaleshvara Temple
Daily; closed noon–4pm

Known to Hindus as the "Temple of the Eternal Sunrise", the enormous **Arunachaleshvara Temple**, built over a period of almost a thousand years, consists of three concentric courtyards whose gateways are topped by tapering *gopuras*, the largest of which cover the east and north gates. The best spot from which to view the precinct, a breathtaking spectacle against the sprawling plains and lumpy, granite Shevaroy Hills, is the path up to Sri Ramana Maharishi's meditation cave, Virupaksha (see below), on the lower slopes of Arunachala. To enter the temple, however, head for the huge eastern gateway, which leads through the thick outer wall carved with images of deities, local saints and teachers. In the basement of a raised hall to the right before entering the next courtyard is the Parthala lingam, where Sri Ramana Maharishi is said to have sat in a state of Supreme Awareness while ants feasted on his flesh.

The caves

Opposite the western entrance of the temple complex, a path leads up a holy hill (15min) to the **Virupaksha Cave**, where the Maharishi stayed between 1899 and 1916. He personally built the bench outside and the hill-shaped lingam and platform inside, where all are welcome to meditate in peace. When this cave became too crowded, Ramana shifted to another, hidden away a few minutes further up the hill. He named this one, and the small house built onto it, **Skandasramam**, and lived there between 1916 and 1922. The inner cave here is also set aside for meditation, and the front patio affords splendid views across the temple, town and surrounding plains.

Sri Ramana ashram
Main Rd · ⓦ sriramanamaharshi.org

The caves can also be reached via the pilgrims' path winding uphill from the **Sri Ramana ashram**, 2km south of the temple along the main road. This simple complex is where the sage lived after returning from his retreat on Arunachala, and where his body is today enshrined. The *samadhi* has become a popular place for Sri Ramana's devotees on pilgrimage, but interested visitors are welcome to stay in the dorms here. There's also an excellent bookshop (daily 8–11am & 2–6pm) stocking a huge range of titles on the life and teachings of the guru, as well as quality postcards, calendars, devotional music and DVDs.

ARRIVAL AND INFORMATION

By train The railway station, 500m east of the temple, is on the main Tirupati–Madurai line, with a daily service in each direction.

By bus Buses arrive at the town bus stand on Chinnakadai St, 1km north of the temple. Coming from the coast, it's easiest to make your way on one of the numerous buses from Tindivanam, which pass through Gingee. There are excellent bus connections to Chennai (every 10min; 4hr), Chengalpattu (every 10min; 2hr 30min; change for Mamallapuram), Puducherry (every 30min; 3hr), Trichy (hourly; 4–5hr) and Kanchipuram (every 2hr; 2hr 30min).

Services There is intermittent internet access at the Image Computer Centre, 52 Car St, and Sri Sai, 14-A Kadambarayam St. There are a few ATMs and a couple of Western Union offices but the best place to change money is the India Boutique/Forex, 138 Raj Chettiyar Complex on Chengam Rd, near the ashram (☎04175 238248).

ACCOMMODATION

Arunachala 5 Vada Sannathi St ☎04175 228300, ⓦhotelarunachala.in. Large, clean and comfortable hotel situated right outside the main temple entrance. There is a choice of non-a/c and a/c rooms (₹1500), all of which are a good size and have TVs. Not the quietest place to stay, but certainly atmospheric. ₹900

Park 26 Kosmadam St ☎04175 222471. Reliable budget option a 5min walk from the junction of North and East Car streets. The rooms are fairly basic but clean, with TVs and buckets but no showers. There's a vegetarian canteen on the ground floor. No wi-fi. ₹500

Ramakrishna 34-F Polur Rd, 5min from the bus station on the main Gingee road (turn right out of the bus station and veer left at the fork) ☎04175 250003, ⓦhotelramakrishnatiruvannamalai.com. One of the best places in town, with sizeable, clean rooms with TV and attached bathrooms and a choice of Indian or Western loos. There are also larger deluxe rooms and a/c rooms from ₹1250. Excellent a/c restaurant next door to the reception (see below). ₹950

SASA Lodge Chinnakadai St, almost opposite the bus stand ☎04175 252293. One of the cheapest lodges in town, painted a bright blue and white. Rooms (some with a/c; ₹750) are basic and clean enough, but most of them are windowless. The front-facing rooms have light but are rather noisy. No wi-fi. ₹450

Trishul 6 Kanagarayar St ☎04175 222219, ⓦhotel trishul.com. Tucked away down a lane off Kosmadam St near the *Park* in a quiet location away from the hustle, this hotel has a rooftop terrace with views of the temple, a good restaurant and a bafflingly dark a/c bar. Choice of decent-sized non-a/c and a/c rooms (₹1850). ₹1500

EATING

Nala Residency 21 Anna Salai ☎04175 222322. A couple of hundred metres beyond the *Park*, this hotel restaurant has an extensive menu (veg and non-veg) and serves quality food. Veggie dishes cost under ₹100 and chicken dishes around ₹150. Try the delicious butter *paneer* masala. Daily 7.30am–midnight.

★**Ramakrishna** 34-F Polur Rd ☎04175 250005. Excellent food served quickly and efficiently in a/c comfort. Good breakfasts, excellent eleven-dish "meals" (11am–3pm; ₹90) and a range of north and South Indian food available in the evenings. Daily 6.30am–10.30pm.

Udipi Brindhavan Car St ☎04175 222693. Located down a small lane opposite the temple's east entrance, this long and narrow *dhaba* is a typical Udupi restaurant, serving very cheap lunchtime "meals" (11am–4pm; ₹60) and excellent *parathas*. Daily 6am–11pm.

Vickys Trishul hotel 6 Kanagarayar St ☎04175 222219. Posh a/c ground-floor restaurant with a vaguely oriental vibe and decor, and a wall-length aquarium. Prices range between ₹80 and ₹150 for veg, chicken, the usual lunchtime "meals" option, and tandoori in the evenings. Daily 7.30am–10.30pm.

Gingee Fort

Daily 9am–5pm · ₹100 (₹5) · ⓦ gingeefort.com · The half-hourly buses between Tiruvannamalai (1hr) and Puducherry (2hr) all stop on demand right by the gate of the fort

An epic landscape of huge boulder hills, interspersed by lush splashes of rice paddy≈and banana plantations, stretches east of Tiruvannamalai towards the coast. The scenery peaks at **GINGEE** (pronounced "*Shinjee*" and also spelt Senji), 37km east of the Red Mountain, where the ruins of Tamil Nadu's most spectacular **fort** sprawl over a vast swathe of sun-scorched granite, left to the mercy of the weeds and tropical weather. Only on weekends, when bus parties pour around the most accessible monuments, does the site receive more than a trickle of visitors.

Bisected by the main Tiruvannamalai–Puducherry road, Gingee Fort comprises three separate citadels, crowning the summits of three dramatic hills: **Krishnagiri** to the north, **Rajagiri** to the west and **Chandrayandurg** to the southeast. Connecting them to form an enormous triangle, 1.5km from north to south, are 20m-thick walls, punctuated by bastions and gateways giving access to the protected zones at the heart of the complex. A network of raised, paved paths links the site's principal landmarks. From the road, head south to the main east gate, where a snaking passage emerges, after no fewer than four changes of direction, inside the **palace** enclave. Of the many structures that were unearthed by archeologists here, the most distinctive is the square seven-storey **Kalyana Mahal tower**, focal point of the former governor's residence; featuring an ingenious hydraulic system that carried water to the uppermost levels, it is crowned by a tapering pyramidal tower.

It's hard to imagine such defences ever being overrun, but they were on numerous occasions following the fort's foundation by the Vijayanagars in the fifteenth century. The Muslim Adil Shahis from Bijapur (now Vijayapura), Shivaji's Maharatas and the Mughals all conquered Gingee, using it to consolidate the vulnerable southern reaches of their respective empires. The French also took it in 1750, but were ousted by the British after a bloody five-week siege eleven years later.

Puducherry

First impressions of **PUDUCHERRY** (**Pondicherry**, also often referred to simply as Pondy), the former capital of French India, can be unpromising. Instead of the leafy boulevards and *pétanque* pitches you might expect, its messy outer suburbs and bus stand are as cluttered and chaotic as any typical Tamil town. Closer to the seafront, however, the atmosphere grows tangibly more Gallic, as the bazaars give way to rows of houses whose shuttered windows and colourwashed facades wouldn't look out of place in Montpellier. For anyone familiar with the British colonial imprint, the town can induce culture shock with its richly ornamented Catholic churches, French road names and policemen in De Gaulle-style *képis*, and *boules* played in the dusty squares. Many of the seafront buildings were damaged by the 2004 tsunami, but Puducherry's tourist infrastructure remained intact.

Brief history

Known to Greek and Roman geographers as "Poduke", Puducherry was an important staging post on the second-century maritime trade route between Rome and the Far East. When the Roman Empire declined, the Pallavas and Cholas took control and were followed by a succession of colonial powers, from the Portuguese in the sixteenth century to the French, Danes and British, who exchanged the enclave several times after the various battles and treaties of the Carnatic Wars in the early eighteenth century. Puducherry's heyday, however, dates from the arrival of the French governor Joseph **Dupleix**, who accepted the governorship in 1742 and immediately set about rebuilding a town decimated by its former British occupants. It was Dupleix who instituted the street plan of a central grid encircled by a broad oblong boulevard, bisected north to south by a canal dividing the "Ville Blanche", to the east, from the "Ville Noire", to the west.

Although relinquished by the French in 1954 – when the town became the headquarters of the **Union Territory of Pondicherry**, administering the three other former colonial enclaves scattered across South India – Puducherry's split personality still prevails. The seaside promenade, **Goubert Salai** (formerly Beach Road), has the forlorn look of an out-of-season French resort, complete with its own white Hôtel de Ville. Many visitors are grave Europeans in white Indian costume, busy about their spiritual quest. It was here that **Sri Aurobindo Ghose** (1872–1950), a leading figure in the freedom struggle in Bengal, was given shelter after it became unwise for him to live close to the British in Calcutta. His ashram attracts thousands of devotees from all around the world, most particularly from Bengal.

Goubert Salai

Puducherry's beachside promenade, **Goubert Salai**, is a favourite place for a stroll, though there's little to do other than watch the world go by. The Hôtel de Ville, today housing the Municipal Offices building, is still an impressive spectacle, and a 4m-tall

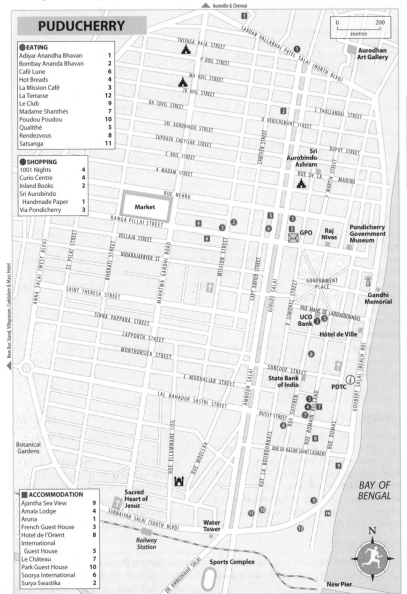

PUDUCHERRY

● EATING	
Adiyar Anandha Bhavan	1
Bombay Ananda Bhavan	2
Café Lune	6
Hot Breads	4
La Mission Café	3
La Terrasse	12
Le Club	9
Madame Shanthés	7
Poudou Poudou	10
Qualithé	5
Rendezvous	8
Satsanga	11

● SHOPPING	
1001 Nights	4
Curio Centre	4
Inland Books	2
Sri Aurobindo Handmade Paper	1
Via Pondicherry	3

■ ACCOMMODATION	
Ajantha Sea View	9
Amala Lodge	4
Aruna	1
French Guest House	3
Hotel de l'Orient	8
International Guest House	5
Le Château	7
Park Guest House	10
Soorya International	6
Surya Swastika	2

Gandhi memorial, surrounded by ancient columns, dominates the northern end. Nearby, a French memorial commemorates French Indians who lost their lives in World War I.

Just north of the Hôtel de Ville, a couple of streets back from the promenade, is the leafy old French-provincial-style square now named **Government Place**. On the north side, the impressive, gleaming white **Raj Nivas**, official home to the present lieutenant-governor of Puducherry Territory, was built late in the eighteenth century for Joseph Francis Dupleix.

Pondicherry Government Museum

Ranga Pillai St • Tues–Sun 10am–1pm & 2–5pm • ₹50 (₹2)

The **Pondicherry Government Museum** is opposite Government Place. The archeological collection includes Neolithic 2000-year-old remains from Arikamedu, a few Pallava (sixth- to eighth-century) and Buddhist (tenth-century) stone sculptures, bronzes, weapons and paintings. Alongside are a bizarre assembly of French salon furniture and bric-à-brac from local houses, including a velvet S-shaped "conversation seat".

Sri Aurobindo Ashram

Rue de la Marine • Daily 8am–noon & 2–6pm • Free, no children under 3, photography with permission • ⓦ sriaurobindoashram.org

The **Sri Aurobindo Ashram** is one of the best-known and wealthiest ashrams in India. Founded in 1926 by the Bengali philosopher-guru, Aurobindo Ghosh, and his chief disciple, personal manager and mouthpiece "The Mother", it serves as the headquarters of the Sri Aurobindo Society, or SAS. Today the SAS owns most of the valuable property and real estate in Puducherry, and wields what many consider to be a disproportionate influence over the town. The **samadhi**, or mausoleum, of Sri Aurobindo and "The Mother" is covered daily with flowers and usually surrounded by supplicating devotees with their hands and heads placed on the tomb. Inside the main building, an incongruous and very bourgeois-looking Western-style room, complete with three-piece suite and Persian carpet, is where "The Mother" and Sri Aurobindo chilled out. The adjacent bookshop sells a range of literature and tracts, while the building opposite hosts frequent cultural programmes.

Botanical Gardens

Subbaiyah Salai • Daily 10am–6pm • Free; aquarium ₹10

Established in 1826, the **Botanical Gardens** offer many quiet paths to wander. The French planted nine hundred species here, experimenting to see how they would do in Indian conditions; one mahogany tree, the *Khaya senegalensis*, has grown to a height of 25m. You can also see an extraordinary fossilized tree, found about 25km away in Tiravakarai. The aquarium inside the gardens is uninspiring.

ARRIVAL AND DEPARTURE   PUDUCHERRY

By train Puducherry's railway station is in the south, a 5min walk from the sea off Subbaiyah Salai. There are daily express and passenger trains to Chennai and Tirupati and weekly fast express trains to Bhubaneswar (Wed), Mangaluru (Tues), New Delhi (Wed) and Howrah, Kolkata (Wed).

By bus All buses pull into New Bus Stand, which lies on the western edge of town. From here, auto-rickshaws charge at least ₹50 into the old town, taxis double that; but you can jump in a *tempo* to central Ambour Salai for ₹10.

Destinations Bengaluru (4 daily; 10–11hr); Chennai (every 15–20min; 2hr 30min–3hr); Chidambaram (every 20min; 2hr); Coimbatore (10 daily; 9hr); Kanchipuram (10 daily; 3–4hr); Kanyakumari (hourly; 12–13hr); Madurai (hourly; 9–10hr); Mamallapuram (every 15–20min; 1hr 30min–2hr); Thanjavur (hourly; 5hr); Tiruchirapalli (every 30min; 5hr 30min–6hr); Tiruvannamalai (every 30min; 3hr).

GETTING AROUND

By auto-rickshaw Puducherry is well served by auto-rickshaws, which can negotiate the narrow and chaotic streets efficiently.

By bicycle/scooter You can rent a bicycle for ₹75/24hr from one of the many stalls dotted about town, such as Sri Durga Pharameshwari Cycle Stores, 106-B Mission St

(T 98941 21133), and JDR, 47 Mission St (T 0413 319 4888), which also rents scooters (₹400/24hr), useful for trips further afield such as Auroville.

INFORMATION AND TOURS

Tourist information The Puducherry Tourism Development Corporation (PTDC) office is at 40 Goubert Salai (daily 8.30am–7.30pm; T 0413 233 9497, W pondytourism.in). The staff are extremely helpful, providing leaflets and a city map, and information about Auroville.

Tours PTDC run city tours to all the main attractions (half-day 1.30–5.30pm, non-a/c ₹150, a/c ₹200; full-day 9.30am–5.30pm, non-a/c ₹250, a/c ₹300), a fine Heritage Walking Tour (daily 8am–12.30pm; free) and can help arrange car rental.

Services Muthu Forex, 161 Mission St (T 0413 222 4239), has a Western Union transfer facility. Thomas Cook is at 2A Rue Labourdonnais (T 0413 222 4008). Other places to change money include the State Bank of India, 15 Suffren St, and UCO Bank on Rue Mahe de Labourdonnais.

ACCOMMODATION

7

Puducherry's **basic lodges** are concentrated around the main market area, Ranga Pillai St and Rue Nehru, while trendy boutique hotels now punctuate the French quarter. Guesthouses belonging to the Sri Aurobindo Ashram offer good value for money but are not overly welcoming, with a lot of regulations, curfews and overpowering "philosophy of life" notices.

Ajantha Sea View 50 Goubert Salai T 0413 234 9032, W ajanthaseaviewhotel.com. Just about the only hotel on the seafront, whose large and comfortable if slightly faded rooms all have balconies with direct or partial sea views. ₹3500

Amala Lodge 92 Ranga Pillai St T 0413 233 8910. This centrally located hotel is one of the best of the budget options. The rooms, some with shared bathrooms, are clean enough but a little bit on the small side. There is also a three-bed room available with a/c for ₹800. No wi-fi. ₹350/₹400

Aruna 3 Zamindar Garden, SV Patel Rd T 0413 233 7756, E hotelarunapondy@gmail.com. Located on a quiet side street, up in the northern sector of town. It has pleasant double rooms (some a/c; ₹1100) with TV and balcony, some of which catch the morning sun. ₹850

French Guest House 38 Ambour Salai T 0413 420 0853. Clean, reasonably sized rooms, including some family suites, in a welcoming centrally located hotel with a comical Eiffel Tower mural. The a/c rooms are slightly cleaner and brighter for only ₹200 more. No wi-fi. ₹600

★**Hotel de l'Orient** 17 Rue Romain Rolland T 0413 234 3067, W neemranahotels.com. A beautiful, UNESCO heritage-accorded French house boasting sixteen individually decorated rooms with French antiques, tiled balconies and long shuttered windows overlooking the leafy courtyard restaurant. Four categories of room with the most expensive, featuring an anteroom and four-poster bed, costing ₹8000. ₹3500

International Guest House 47 NSC Bose Salai T 0413 233 6699, E ingh@aurosociety.org. The largest Aurobindo establishment in town, with dozens of very large, clean rooms, some of which are a/c. It's a good budget option but typically institutional, with a 10.30pm curfew. Often full, so best book in advance. Rooms in the new wing are slightly more expensive. No wi-fi. ₹550

★**Le Château** 11A Rue Romain Rolland T 0413 222 9500, W lechateau.co.in. No detail has been spared in the conversion of this colonial house into a very smart but reasonably priced boutique hotel. The balconied, all a/c rooms are well appointed and there's a fine ground-floor restaurant. Wi-fi in lobby. ₹2800

Park Guest House Goubert Salai T 0413 223 3644, E parkgh@sriaurobindoashram.org.in. Another Sri Aurobindo Society place with the same strict rules (no alcohol and a 10.30pm curfew), for ashram visitors only. Spotless and very comfortable rooms (a/c only ₹900) with mosquito nets and sitouts, overlooking garden and sea. Bike rental and restaurant but no TV or wi-fi. ₹800

Soorya International 55 Ranga Pillai St T 0413 222 7485, W hotelsooryainternational.com. Decent, all a/c hotel, located in the centre of town. Good-sized, comfortable standard rooms and bigger deluxe rooms complete with sofa and balcony. It also has a multicuisine restaurant. No wi-fi. ₹1000

Surya Swastika 11 Eswaran Koil St T 0413 234 3092, E suryaswastika@gmail.com. A traditional Tamil guesthouse in a quiet corner of town, with nine basic rooms dotted around a covered central courtyard. Quintessential budget travellers' place – incredibly cheap, friendly and clean enough. Wi-fi ₹20/hr. ₹300/₹350

EATING

If you've been on the road for a while and are hankering for healthy salads, fresh coffee, crusty bread, cakes and real pastry, you'll be spoilt for choice in Puducherry. **Beer** is available just about everywhere (except the SAS-owned establishments) and is much lower than the regular Tamil Nadu price, starting at around ₹80 a bottle.

Adiyar Anandha Bhavan Rue Nehru ☎0413 222 3333. Very popular pure-veg restaurant with three counters under one brightly lit roof. Samosas, chaat and snacks on the left, a sweet counter in the centre and veggie dishes to the right, all under ₹100. Pay first and show receipt. Daily 7am–11pm.

Bombay Ananda Bhavan 199 Mission St ☎0413 222 8293. Clean and very popular south-Indian pure-veg joint, serving good South Indian breakfasts of *pongal, vada* and excellent masala dosas for ₹45, plus the usual lunchtime "meals" for ₹70. Daily 7am–10pm.

Café Lune Rue Suffren, near the State Bank of India ☎0413 233 8987. This tiny café, which opened in 1961, is popular with the locals, who gather to drink coffee, prepared with great pomp and style. The ultra-cheap lunchtime plate of lemon rice is a snip at only ₹10 and the *vada* is very good. Mon–Fri 7am–1pm & 4–7pm, Sat 7am–1pm.

Hot Breads 42 Ambour Salai ☎0413 222 7886, ⓦhotbreads.in. Squeaky-clean *boulangerie*-café popular with the French expats. Classic fresh croissants, crusty baguettes and delicious savoury pastry snacks are available, their tempting smells wafting out onto the street. Great breakfast combos for ₹55–80, plus pizza, burgers and hot dogs later on. Daily 7.30am–9.30pm.

La Mission Café 180 Mission St ☎0413 420 4210. Small modern a/c basement café with a nice selection of teas, coffees, cakes and snacks. Free wi-fi. Daily 6am–8.30pm.

★**La Terrasse** 5 Subbiah Salai ☎0413 222 0809. Popular French restaurant, especially for European back-packers, who hang out here to sip an alfresco cappuccino. The prawn dishes (₹200–400) and pizzas are excellent, and there's a range of Indian, Chinese and French food. Daily except Wed 8.30am–10pm.

★**Le Club** 38 Rue Dumas ☎0413 233 9745, ⓦleclubraj .com. One of the best-known restaurants in town. The menu is predominantly French and features their famous *coq au vin*,

steak au poivre and seafood dishes (all around ₹500), plus a full wine list and cocktails. Daily 8am–10.30pm.

★**Madame Shanthés** 40A Rue Romain Rolland ☎0413 222 2022. Very friendly rooftop restaurant, with lovely ambience and evening illuminations, that serves tasty French, Indian and Chinese dishes. The speciality is seafood: pasta *marinara* (₹240) and a superb, excellent-value seafood platter but they also do meat like chicken stroganoff for ₹280. Daily 11am–11pm.

Poudou Poudou 31 Rue Labourdonnais ☎0413 421 0535. One of the only purely Indian restaurants in the old part of town, this place also serves some seafood and fish curries. There is a small a/c dining area and two rooftop terraces, the upper one accessed through a dead tree trunk. Most dishes cost less than ₹200. Daily 10am–11.30pm.

Qualithé 3 Rue Mahe de Labourdonnais, opposite Government Place. An airy rooftop restaurant has been created above the hotel, while the dingy old bar on the ground floor is also being refurbished. Tuck into delights such as crispy kalamari (₹240) or pepper steak (₹350). Free wi-fi. Daily 6–10.30pm.

★**Rendezvous** 30 Rue Suffren ☎0413 222 7677, ⓦrendezvouscafe.co.in. This delightful upstairs restaurant has been completely revamped with white leather seating and sleek decor. The quality of the Indo-Gallic cuisine is superb, with seafood costing around ₹500–1000. The fine cocktails are two for one from 6.30–7.30pm. Daily except Tues 11am–3.30pm & 6–10pm.

Satsanga 54 Rue Labourdonnais ☎0413 222 5867. The food here is prepared by the French *patron*: organic salads, tzatziki, garlic bread, sauté potatoes and *tagliatelle alla carbonara* complement the fresh fish and French beef dishes, mostly under ₹400. Also a wide Indian menu. Two dining areas – a courtyard or rooftop. Tues–Sun 12–3pm & 6–11pm.

SHOPPING

1001 Nights 40A Rue Romain Rolland ☎0413 234 0073. Jam-packed with all sorts of carpets, rugs, dresses, accessories, jewellery and souvenirs, this Kashmiri shop is fairly laidback in terms of sales technique. Daily 9am–9pm.

Curio Centre 40 Rue Romain Rolland ☎0413 222 5676. Classy if slightly ramshackle old place with high ceilings. In between the larger items of furniture, you can discover some unusual ornaments. Daily 9.30am–8pm.

Inland Books 1 Rue Suffren ☎95004 30856. Large bookshop belonging to the town's main publisher, with a wide range of subjects in English. Daily 9am–9pm.

Sri Aurobindo Handmade Paper 50 Sardar Vallabhai Patel Salai ☎0413 233 7463, ⓦsriaurobindopaper.com. Something of an institution, this place sells colourful paper gifts and all sorts of stationery from within a leafy compound where you can also witness the traditional manufacturing process. Mon–Sat 9am–5.30pm, Sun 10am–1pm.

Via Pondicherry 20 Rue Romain Rolland ☎0413 222 3319, ⓦviapondicherry.com. Created and run by a vivacious classical dancer and designer, this little shop is a veritable swirl of colour, with all sorts from bags to shawls and bright decorations. Daily 9am–1pm & 3–8pm.

Auroville

The most New Age place anywhere in India must surely be **AUROVILLE**, the planned "City of Dawn", 10km north of Pudicherry, straddling the border of the Union

Territory and Tamil Nadu. Founded in 1968, Auroville was inspired by "The Mother", the spiritual successor of Sri Aurobindo. Around 1700 people live in communes (two thirds of them non-Indians), with such names as Fertile, Certitude, Sincerity, Revelation and Transformation, in what it is hoped will eventually be an ideal city for a population of fifty thousand. Architecturally experimental buildings, combining modern Western and traditional Indian elements, are set in a rural landscape of narrow lanes, deep red earth and lush greenery. Income is derived from agriculture, handicrafts, alternative technology, educational and development projects and Aurolec, a computer software company.

Considering how little there is to see here, Auroville attracts a disproportionately large number of day-trippers – much to the chagrin of its inhabitants, who rightly point out that you can only get a sense of what the settlement is all about if you stay a while. Interested visitors are welcomed as paying guests in most of the communes (see below), where you can work alongside permanent residents.

7

The Visitor Centre

Daily 9am–5.30pm • ☎ 0413 262 2239, ⓦ auroville.org

The **Visitor Centre** is the focal point of any tourist visit to Auroville. You need to get tickets here for an exterior viewing of Matri Mandir (see below), but before they are issued, you're shown a short video presentation about the village. The adjacent bookshop has plenty of literature on Auroville and it's worth checking the notice board, which has details of **activities** in which visitors may participate (including yoga, reiki and Vipassana meditation, costing around ₹200/session). The nearby **Bharat Niwas** houses a permanent exhibition on the history and philosophy of the settlement. There are also three quality handicraft outlets and several pleasant vegetarian cafés serving snacks, meals and cold drinks.

Matri Mandir

Mon–Sat 10am–noon & 2–4pm, Sun 10am–noon • Free • Tickets available from the Visitor Centre • To obtain "concentration entry" for the Matri Mandir to meditate on the crystal, you must book two days ahead

Begun in 1970, the space-age **Matri Mandir** – a gigantic, almost spherical high-tech meditation centre at the heart of the site – was conceived as "a symbol of the Divine's answer to man's inspiration for perfection". Earth from 124 countries was symbolically placed in an urn, and is kept in a concrete cone in the amphitheatre adjacent to Matri Mandir, from where a speaker can address an audience of three thousand without amplification. The focal point of the interior of the Matri Mandir is a 70cm crystal ball symbolizing the neutral but divine qualities of light and space.

ARRIVAL AND INFORMATION   AUROVILLE

Auroville lies 15km north of Puducherry, off the main Chennai road; you can also get here via the coastal highway, turning off at the village of Chinna Mudaliarchavadi.

By bus Buses from Puducherry run every 20–30min but as Auroville is spread over some fifty square kilometres it's best to come with your own transport.

By auto-rickshaw or taxi From Puducherry to Auroville costs around ₹300 for the 30min journey in an auto-rickshaw or around ₹400 in a taxi.

Tours Alternatively, there's the PTDC half-day tour from Puducherry (see p.397).

ACCOMMODATION AND EATING

The information desk at the Visitor Centre is a good place to enquire about **accommodation** or you can contact the Auroville guest accommodation service (☎ 0413 262 2704, ⓦ guesthouses.auroville.org). This should be done months ahead for the peak winter months. Officially there's no lower limit on the time you have to stay, but visitors are encouraged to stick around for at least a week and to help out on communal projects. There are many excellent privately-run **restaurants** dotted around the ashram and a café at the Visitor Centre.

Central Tamil Nadu: the Chola heartland

To be on the banks of the Cauvery listening to the strains of Carnatic music is to have a taste of eternal bliss.

Tamil proverb

Continuing south of Puducherry along the Coromandel coast, you enter the flat landscape of the **Kaveri** (aka Cauvery) **Delta**, a watery world of canals, dams, dykes and rivulets that has been intensively farmed since ancient times. Just 160km in diameter, it forms the verdant rice-bowl core of Tamil Nadu, crossed by more than thirty major rivers and countless streams. The largest of them, the River Kaveri, known in Tamil as Ponni, "The Lady of Gold" (a form of the Mother Goddess), is revered as a conduit of liquid *shakti*, the primordial female energy that nurtures the millions of farmers who live on her banks and tributaries. The landscape here is one endless swathe of green paddy fields, dotted with palm trees and little villages of thatched roofs and market stalls; it comes as a rude shock to land up in the hot and chaotic towns.

This mighty delta formed the very heartland of the **Chola** empire, which reached its apogee between the ninth and thirteenth centuries, an era often compared to classical Greece and Renaissance Italy both for its cultural richness and the sheer scale and profusion of its architectural creations. Much as the Cholas originally intended, every visitor is immediately in awe of their huge temples, not only at cities such as **Chidambaram**, **Kumbakonam** and **Thanjavur**, but also out in the countryside at places like **Gangaikondacholapuram**, where the magnificent temple is all that remains of a once-great city. Exploring the area for a few days will bring you into contact with the more delicate side of Chola artistic expression, such as the magnificent **bronzes** of Thanjavur.

Chidambaram

CHIDAMBARAM, 58km south of Puducherry, is so steeped in myth that its history is hard to unravel. As the site of the *tandav*, the cosmic dance of Shiva as **Nataraja**, King of the Dance, it's one of the holiest sites in South India, and a visit to its **Sabhanayaka Temple** affords a fascinating glimpse into ancient Tamil religious practice and belief. The legendary king **Hiranyavarman** is said to have made a pilgrimage here from Kashmir, seeking to rid himself of leprosy by bathing in the temple's Shivaganga tank. In thanks for a successful cure, he enlarged the temple. He also brought three thousand brahmins, of the Dikshitar caste, whose descendants, distinguishable by top-knots of hair at the front of their heads, are the ritual specialists of the temple to this day.

Few of the fifty *mathas* (monasteries) that once stood here remain, but the temple itself is still a hive of activity and hosts numerous **festivals**. The two most important are ten-day affairs, building up to spectacular finales: on the ninth day of each, temple chariots process through the four Car streets in a **car festival**, while on the tenth there is an **abhishekham**, when the principal deities in the Raja Sabha (thousand-pillared hall) are anointed. For exact dates (one is in May/June, the other in Dec/Jan), contact any TTDC tourist office and plan well ahead, as they are very popular. Other local festivals include fire-walking and *kavadi* folk dance (dancing with decorated wooden frames on the head) at the Thillaiamman Kali (April/May) and Keelatheru Mariamman (July/Aug) temples respectively.

Chidambaram revolves around the Sabhanayaka Temple and the busy market area that surrounds it, along North, East, South and West Car streets. The town also has a large student population, based at Annamalai University to the east, a centre of Tamil studies.

Sabhanayaka Nataraja Temple

Daily 4am–noon & 4–10pm

For South India's Shaivites, the **Sabhanayaka Nataraja Temple**, where Shiva is enthroned as Lord of the Cosmic Dance (Nataraja), is the holiest of holies. Its huge *gopuras*, whose lights are used as landmarks by sailors far out to sea in the Bay of Bengal, soar above a 55-acre complex, divided by four concentric walls. The oldest parts now standing were built under the Cholas, who adopted Nataraja as their chosen deity and crowned several kings here. If you have the time the best way to tackle the complex is to work slowly inwards from the third enclosure in clockwise circles.

Frequent **ceremonies** take place at the innermost sanctum, the most popular being at noon and 6pm, when a fire is lit, great gongs are struck and devotees rush forward to catch a last glimpse of the lingam before the doors are shut. On Friday nights before the temple closes, during a particularly elaborate puja, Nataraja is carried on a palanquin accompanied by music and attendants carrying flaming torches and tridents. At other times, you'll hear ancient devotional hymns from the Tevaram.

The gopuras

The west *gopura* is the most popular entrance, as well as being the most elaborately carved and probably the earliest (c.1150 AD). Turning north (left) from here, you come to the colonnaded **Shivaganga tank**, the site of seven natural springs. From the broken pillar at the tank's edge, all four *gopuras* are visible. In the northeast corner, the largest building in the complex, the **Raja Sabha** (fourteenth- to fifteenth-century) is also known as "the thousand-pillared hall"; tradition holds that there are only 999 actual pillars, the thousandth being Shiva's leg. During festivals the deities Nataraja and Shivakamasundari are brought here and mounted on a dais for the anointing ceremony, *abhishekha*.

The importance of **dance** at Chidambaram is underlined by the reliefs of dancing figures inside the east *gopura*, demonstrating 108 *karanas* (a similar set is to be found in the west *gopura*). A *karana* is a specific point in a phase of movement prescribed by the extraordinarily comprehensive Sanskrit treatise on the performing arts, the *Natya Shastra* (c.200 BC–200 AD) – the basis of all classical dance, music and theatre in India.

The second enclosure

To get into the square **second enclosure** head for its western entrance (just north of the west *gopura* in the third wall), which leads into a circumambulatory passageway. Once beyond this second wall you may become disorientated as the roofed inner enclosure sees little light and is supported by a maze of colonnades.

Govindaraja shrine

The innermost **Govindaraja shrine** is dedicated to Vishnu – no surprise, as most Shiva temples have a Vishnu shrine inside them, though no Vaishnavite temple has a shrine for Shiva. The deity is attended by non-Dikshitar brahmins who, it is said, don't always get along with the Dikshitars. From outside the shrine, non-Hindus can see through to the most sacred part of the temple, the **Kanaka Sabha** and the **Chit Sabha**, adjoining raised structures, roofed with copper and gold plate and linked by a hallway. The latter houses bronze images of Nataraja and his consort Shivakamasundari; behind and to the left of Nataraja, a curtain, sacred to Shiva and strung with rows of leaves from the *bilva* tree, demarcates the most potent area of all. Within it lies the **Akashalingam**, known as the *rahasya*, or "secret", of Chidambaram: made of the most subtle of the elements, Ether (*akasha*) – from which Air, Fire, Water and Earth are born – the lingam is invisible, signifying the invisible presence of God in the human heart.

A crystal lingam, said to have emanated from the light of the crescent moon on Shiva's brow, and a small ruby Nataraja are worshipped in the Kanaka Sabha. They are ritually bathed in the flames of the priests' camphor fire or oil lamps six times a day. This inner area is where you're most likely to hear **oduvars**, hereditary singers from the middle, non-brahmin castes, intoning verses of ancient Tamil poetry. The songs with which they regale the deities at puja time, drawn from compilations such as the Tevaram or earlier Sangam, are believed to be more than a thousand years old.

ARRIVAL AND INFORMATION

By train The railway station is just over 1km southeast of the centre. There are daily trains to Chennai Egmore (5hr 30min–6hr) and Tiruchirapalli (3hr 30min) via Thanjavur (2hr 30min).

By bus Buses from Chennai, Thanjavur, Mamallapuram and Madurai pull in at the bus stand, about 500m from the temple.

Destinations Chengalpattu (every 20–30min; 4hr 30min–5hr); Chennai (every 20–30min; 5–6hr); Coimbatore (8 daily; 7hr); Kanchipuram (hourly; 7–8hr); Kanyakumari (4 daily; 9–10hr); Kumbakonam (every 10min; 2hr 30min);

Madurai (6 daily; 7hr 30min–8hr); Puducherry (every 15–20min; 2hr); Thanjavur (every 15–20min; 3hr); Tiruchirapalli (every 30min; 4hr 30min); Tiruvannamalai (hourly; 3hr 30min).

Tourist information The TTDC tourist office (Mon–Fri 9.45am–5.45pm; ☎04144 238739) is next to *Vandayar Gateway Inn* hotel on Railway Feeder Rd. Friendly, helpful staff but not a lot of leaflets.

Services None of the banks in Chidambaram change money, although the *Saradharam* hotel, near the bus stand, will.

ACCOMMODATION

A1 Ritz 2 VGP St, near the bus stand ☎04144 646675, ✉alritzhotel@gmail.com. One of the better places in town, this comfortable hotel is conveniently located and has good-sized clean rooms (a/c ₹1200), all with TV, and a good restaurant. No wi-fi. **₹1000**

Akshaya 17/18 East Car St ☎04144 220192, ⬡hotel-akshaya.com. Pleasant, clean, mid-range hotel, with a garden backing right onto the temple wall. There's a choice of non-a/c and a/c rooms (₹1800), though the non-a/c are much better value, and a couple of restaurants. Wi-fi in lobby. **₹1200**

Mansoor Lodge 91 East Car St ☎04144 221072, ✉mansoorlodge@rediffmail.com. A cheap, friendly and good-value hotel, right opposite the temple. The rooms (some singles at ₹300) have tiled floors and clean bathrooms and there is a TV in each one. No wi-fi. **₹500**

Raja Rajan 162 West Car St ☎04144 222690. Close to

the west gate of the temple, this tall skinny building is another budget option with clean rooms and tiled bathrooms. There are some cheap singles (₹250) and good-value a/c rooms (₹750). No wi-fi. **₹400**

Sabanayagam 7 East Sannathi St, off East Car St ☎04144 220896. Despite its flashy exterior, this is a run-of-the-mill budget place located 10m down the main temple entrance lane. Rooms (some windowless; a/c ₹1200) are clean, with a choice of Western or Indian toilets, but off dim corridors. No wi-fi. **₹600**

Saradharam 19 Venugopal Pillai St, opposite the bus stand ☎04144 221336, ⬡hotelsaradharam.co.in. Large, clean, well-kept rooms, some with balconies, in a modern building; a/c rooms (₹1800) include breakfast. The hotel also has three decent restaurants (including the multicuisine *Anupallavi*), a garden, cocktail lounge, laundry service and foreign exchange. Wi-fi in lobby. **₹990**

EATING

Palagaram.com West Car St (just north of west gate) ☎04144 224228. Oddly named but smart, new a/c restaurant, where you can enjoy a variety of filling set meals for ₹60–140. Daily 7.30am–10.30pm.

Southern Spice Vandayar hotel, 12 VGP St ☎04144 225374. This comfortable a/c dining hall offers a range of Indian and Chinese food, with non-veg dishes such as shell-less crab in the ₹150–200 bracket. Daily 7am–10pm.

Sri Krishna Vilas 93 East Car St ☎94432 12328. Simple but very good, South Indian food served in a clean

environment with deities adorning the walls and early morning pujas. Small range of breakfast dishes including tasty *pongal*. No menu as such – just ask for what you want – but all items ₹50 or less. Daily 7.15am–2pm & 4–10pm.

Thillai Ganesa Bhavan 137/4 SP Kovil St, opposite the hospital ☎98652 82004. Around the corner from the bus station, this small place, adorned with Lakshmi pictures on the walls, is a popular choice, serving tasty South Indian breakfasts, good coffee and lunchtime "meals" (₹70) from 11am–3.30pm. Daily 6.30am–10pm.

Gangaikondacholapuram

Devised as the centrepiece of a city built by the Chola king Rajendra I (1014–42) to celebrate his conquests, the magnificent **Brihadishwara Temple** (a replica of the Tanjore temple) stands in the tiny village of **GANGAIKONDACHOLAPURAM** in Ariyalur District, 35km north of Kumbakonam. The tongue-twisting name means "the town of the Chola who took the Ganges". Under Rajendra I, the Chola empire did indeed stretch as far as the great river of the North, an unprecedented achievement for a southern dynasty. Aside from the temple and the rubble of Rajendra's palace, 2km east at Tamalikaimedu, nothing of the city remains. Nonetheless, this is among the most extraordinary archeological sites in South India, outshone only by Thanjavur, and the fact that it's devoid of visitors most of the time gives it a memorably forlorn feel. Note there are scarcely any facilities beyond a couple of stalls, so avoid getting stuck here when the temple is closed.

Brihadishwara Temple

Daily 6am–noon & 4–8pm

Dominating the village landscape, the **Brihadishwara Temple** sits in a well-maintained grassy courtyard, flanked by a closed *mandapa* hallway. Over the sanctuary, to the right, a massive pyramidal tower (*vimana*) rises 55m in nine diminishing storeys.

Turning right (north) inside the courtyard, before you reach a small shrine to the goddess **Durga**, containing an image of Mahishasuramardini (the slaying of the buffalo demon), you come across a small well, guarded by a lion statue, known as Simha-kinaru and made from plastered brickwork. King Rajendra is said to have had Ganges water placed in the well to be used for the ritual anointing of the lingam in the main temple. The lion, representing Chola kingly power, bows to the huge Nandi respectfully seated before the eastern entrance of the temple, in line with the *shivalingam* contained within.

Directly in front of the eastern entrance to the temple stands a small altar for offerings. Two parallel flights of stairs ascend to the *mukhamandapa* or porch, which leads to the long pillared *mahamandapa* hallway, the entrance of which is flanked by a pair of large guardian deities. Immediately inside the temple a guide can show you the way to the tower, up steep steps. If you enter alone, a torch is useful because parts of the interior are extremely dark. On either side of the temple doorway, sculptures of Shiva in his various benevolent (*anugraha*) manifestations include him blessing Vishnu, Devi, Ravana and the saint Chandesha. In the northeast corner, an unusual square stone block features carvings of the nine planets (*navagraha*). A number of **Chola bronzes** (see box, p.410) stand on the platform; the figure of Karttikeya, the war god, carrying a club and a shield, is thought to have had particular significance

The base of the main temple sanctuary is decorated with lions and scrollwork. Above this decoration, running from the southern to the northern entrance of the *ardhamandapa*, a series of sculpted figures in plastered niches portray different images of Shiva. The most famous is at the northern entrance, showing Shiva and Parvati garlanding the saint Chandesha, who here is sometimes identified as Rajendra I.

Archeological Museum

Daily except Fri 10am–1pm & 2–5.45pm • Free

Two minutes' walk northeast along the main road (turn right from the car park), the tiny **Archeological Museum** contains Chola odds and ends discovered locally. The finds include terracotta lamps, coins, weapons, tiles, bronze, bangle pieces, palm-leaf manuscripts and an old Chinese pot.

ARRIVAL AND DEPARTURE   **GANGAIKONDACHOLAPURAM**

By bus Although it is marginally closer to Chidambaram, bus connections are better to and from Kumbakonam (every 15–30min; 1hr 30min). Some Trichy-to-Chidambaram services also stop here.

Kumbakonam and around

Sandwiched between the Kaveri (Cauvery) and Arasalar rivers, 74km southwest of Chidambaram and 38km northeast of Thanjavur, is **KUMBAKONAM**. Hindus believe this to be the place where a water pot (*kumba*) of *amrita* – the ambrosial beverage of immortality – was washed up by a great deluge from atop sacred Mount Meru in the Himalayas. Shiva, who just happened to be passing through in the guise of a wild forest-dwelling hunter, for some reason fired an arrow at the pot, causing it to break. From the shards, he made the lingam that is now enshrined in **Kumbeswara Temple**, whose *gopuras* today tower over the town, along with those of some seventeen other

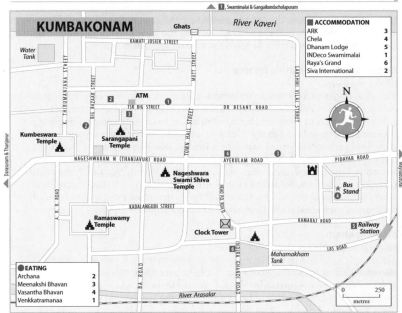

▲ 1 Swamimalai & Gangaikondacholapuram

major shrines. A former capital of the Cholas, who are said to have kept a high-security treasury here, Kumbakonam is the chief commercial centre for the Thanjavur region. The main bazaar, **TSR Big Street**, is especially renowned for its quality costume jewellery.

The main reason to stop in Kumbakonam is to admire the exquisite sculpture of the **Nageshwara Swami Shiva Temple**, which contains the most refined Chola stone carving still in situ. The town also lies within easy reach of the magnificent Darasuram and Gangaikondacholapuram temples, both spectacular ancient monuments that see very few visitors. The village of Swamimalai, just a bike ride away, is the state's principal centre for traditional **bronze casting**.

Kumbeswara Temple

Nageshwaram Rd · Daily 6am–noon & 4–8pm

Surmounted by a multicoloured *gopura*, the east entrance of Kumbakonam's seventeenth-century **Kumbeswara Temple**, home of the famous lingam from which the town derived its name, is approached via a covered market selling a huge assortment of cooking pots, a local speciality, as well as the usual glass bangles and trinkets. At the gateway, you may meet the temple elephant, with a painted forehead and necklace of bells. Beyond the flagstaff, a *mandapa* houses a fine collection of silver *vahanas*, vehicles of the deities, used in festivals, and *pancha loham* (compound of five metals) figures of the 63 Nayanmar poet-saints.

Sarangapani Temple

Off ISR Big St · Daily 6am–noon & 4–8pm · ⓦ srirangapanitemple.org

The principal and largest of the Vishnu temples in Kumbakonam is the thirteenth-century **Sarangapani Temple**, entered through a ten-storey pyramidal *gopura* gate, more than 45m high. The **central shrine** dates from the late Chola period, with many later accretions. Its entrance, within the innermost court, is guarded by huge *dvarapalas*, identical to Vishnu whom they protect. Between them are carved stone *jali* screens, each different, and in front of them stands the sacred, square *homam* fireplace. During the day, rays of light from tiny ceiling windows penetrate the darkness around the sanctum, designed to resemble a chariot with reliefs of horses, elephants and wheels. A painted cupboard contains a mirror for Vishnu to see himself when he leaves the sanctum sanctorum.

Nageshwara Swami Shiva Temple
Daily 6am–noon & 4–8pm

The small **Nageshwara Swami Shiva Temple**, in the centre of town, is Kumbakonam's oldest, founded in 886 and completed a few years into the reign of Parantaka I (c.907–940). First impressions are unpromising, as much of the original building has been hemmed in by later Disney-coloured additions, but beyond the main courtyard, occupied by a large columned *mandapa*, a small *gopura*-topped gateway leads to an inner enclosure where the earliest Chola shrine stands. Framed in the main niches around its sanctum wall are a series of exquisite stone figures, regarded as the finest surviving pieces of **ancient sculpture** in South India. With their languid stance and mesmeric, half-smiling facial expressions, these modest-sized masterpieces far outshine the more monumental art of Thanjavur and Gangaikondacholapuram.

Mahamakham
Indira Gandhi Rd • Daily 6am–noon & 4–8pm

The most famous and revered of many sacred **water tanks** in Kumbakonam, the **Mahamakham** in the southeast of town is said to have filled with ambrosia (*amrit*) collected from the pot broken by Shiva. Every twelve years, when Jupiter passes the constellation of Leo, it is believed that water from the Ganges and eight other holy rivers flows into the tank, thus according it the status of *tirtha*, or sacred river crossing. At this auspicious time, as many as four million pilgrims come here for an absolving bathe; the last occasion was in early 2016.

Airavateshwara Temple
Temple daily 5am–7pm • From central Kumbakonam it is a short bus, auto-rickshaw or an easy 4km bike ride (on the Thanjavur route) southwest; the route is flat enough, but keep your wits about you on the Thanjavur Main Rd

The **Airavateshwara Temple**, built by King Rajaraja II (c.1146–73), stands in the village of **Darasuram**, now more of a suburb of Kumbakonam. This superb, if little-visited, Chola monument ranks alongside those at Thanjavur and Gangaikondacholapuram; but while the others are grandiose, emphasizing heroism and conquest, this is far smaller, exquisite in proportion and detail, and said to have been decorated with *nitya-vinoda*, "perpetual entertainment", in mind. At this temple, Shiva is called Airavateshwara because he was worshipped here by Airavata, the white elephant belonging to Indra, king of the gods.

Darasuram's finest pieces of sculpture are the Chola black-basalt images adorning wall niches in the *mandapa* and inner shrine. These include images of Nagaraja, the snake-king, with a hood of cobras, and Dakshinamurti, the "south-facing" Shiva as teacher, expounding under a banyan tree.

Swamimalai
8km west of Kumbakonam on the NH-22 route to Trichy • Temple daily 5am–noon & 4–10pm • ⦿ swamynathaswamytemple.tnhrce.in • To reach Swamimalai by bicycle from Darasuram, head northwest and ask frequently for directions through the convoluted country lanes

SWAMIMALAI, 8km west of Kumbakonam, is revered as one of the six sacred abodes of Lord Murugan, Shiva's son, whom Hindu mythology records became his father's religious teacher (*swami*) on a hill (*malai*) here. The site of this epic role-reversal now hosts one of the Tamils' holiest shrines, the **Arulmigu Swaminatha Swamy Temple**, crowning the hilltop of the centre of the village, but of more interest to non-Hindus are the **bronze-casters'** workshops dotted around the bazaar and the outlying hamlets.

Known as **sthapathis**, Swamimalai's casters still employ the "lost wax" process perfected by the Cholas to make the most sought-after temple idols in South India.

Their finished products are displayed in numerous showrooms along the main street, from where they are exported worldwide, but it is more memorable to watch the *sthapathis* in action, fashioning the original figures from beeswax and breaking open the moulds to expose the mystical finished metalwork inside.

ARRIVAL AND DEPARTURE

By train Kumbakonam's small railway station, in the southeast of town 2km from the main bazaar, is well served by trains in both directions, and has a 24hr left-luggage office and decent (non-a/c and a/c) retiring rooms.
By bus The hectic bus stand is in the southeast of town, just northwest of the railway station. All the timetables are in Tamil, but there's an enquiry office with English-speaking

KUMBAKONAM AND AROUND

staff. Buses leave for Gangaikondacholapuram (every 15–30min; 1hr 30min), Puducherry (hourly; 4hr) and Thanjavur (every 5–10min; 1hr 30min), many going via Darasuram. Frequent services run to Chennai (every 30min; 7–8hr), Trichy (every 5–10min; 2hr 30min), and there's a daily service to Bengaluru at 6pm (11hr).

ACCOMMODATION

ARK 21 TSR Big St ☎ 0435 242 1942, ✉ info@hotelark .com. Centrally located hotel with five floors and fifty spacious and very clean rooms (a/c from ₹1400) and suites, all with TV and decent-sized bathrooms. There's also an a/c bar serving overpriced beer. ₹1000
Chela 9 Ayekulam Rd ☎ 0435 243 0336, ⓦ hotelchela .com. Large mid-range place located between the bus stand and the centre, with a pale green mock-classical front. The good-sized clean rooms (a/c ₹1100) have pleasant bathrooms and TV, plus there's a multicuisine restaurant and bar. ₹800
Dhanam Lodge 188 Kamaraj Rd ☎ 0435 242 3864. Good, basic but perfectly clean budget lodge, with compact rooms. Equally convenient for the bus stand and train station. No wi-fi. ₹650
INDeco Swamimalai In the hamlet of Thimmakkudy,

6km west of Kumbakonam ☎ 0435 248 0044, ⓦ indeco hotels.com. Set in its own grounds, this heritage resort is in a beautifully restored nineteenth-century brahmin's mansion, modern facilities in teak- and rosewood-furnished rooms. Suites ₹4500. Three restaurants, a small swimming pool and massage. Good online deals. ₹3000
Raya's Grand 23/25 Mahamaham Tank West ☎ 0435 242 6611, ⓦ hotelrayas.com. Spanking-new business-oriented hotel with large, lavishly furnished a/c rooms, all with mini-fridges and large flatscreen TVs. Great views of the tank from the front rooms. ₹1975
Siva International 104/5 TSR Big St ☎ 0435 242 4014. This huge hotel complex is one of the tallest buildings in town. The rooms (a/c ₹800) are a good size and it's clean enough, but there are some grungy corridors. Great views from the rooftop. No wi-fi. ₹500

EATING

Archana Big Bazaar St ☎ 0435 243 2357. Right in the thick of the market, serving good-value South Indian "meals" for only ₹50 and great *uttapams*, this place is popular with the locals. Foreigners aren't often seen here, though will be made very welcome. Beware: it can get hot and stuffy inside. Daily 6am–10.30pm.
Meenakshi Bhavan Ayekulam Rd ☎ 0435 6454251. Excellent, clean south-Indian veg joint, which serves some rarer snacks like *adai*, a form of spicy rice cake, and very good dosas. "Meals" go from ₹70 or a bit more in the a/c room. Daily 7am–11pm.

Vasantha Bhavan Bus stand ☎ 0435 6533996. Good veg restaurant serving full range of South Indian breakfasts to fuel any onward journey. "Meals" are served from 11am (₹80) and there's plenty of chai and coffee. Daily 6am–midnight.
Venkkatramanaa 40 Gandhi Park North ☎ 0435 2400736. Huge and very popular restaurant, adorned with pictures of Sri Ramana. There's no English menu, but the staff are friendly and helpful. A small range of dishes including "meals" and South Indian specials, all ₹75 or less. Daily 5am–9.45pm.

Thanjavur

One of the busiest commercial towns of the Kaveri Delta, **THANJAVUR** (aka Tanjore), 55km east of Tiruchirapalli and 35km southwest of Kumbakonam, is nevertheless well worth a visit. Its history and treasures – among them the breathtaking **Brihadishwara Temple**, Tamil Nadu's most awesome Chola monument – give it a crucial significance to South Indian culture. The home of the world's finest Chola bronze collection, it holds enough of interest to keep you enthralled for at least a couple of days plus it's a good base for short trips to nearby Gangaikondacholapuram, Darasuram and Swamimalai.

7

Thanjavur divides into two sections, separated by the east–west **Grand Anicut Canal**. The **old town**, north of the canal and once entirely enclosed by a fortified wall, was chosen, between the ninth and the end of the thirteenth century, as the capital of their extensive empire by all the Chola kings save one. None of their secular buildings survive, but you can still see as many as ninety temples, of which the Brihadishwara most eloquently epitomizes the power and patronage of Rajaraja I (985–1014), whose military campaigns spread Hinduism to the Maldives, Sri Lanka and Java. Under the Cholas, as well as the later Nayaks and Marathas, literature, painting, sculpture, Carnatic classical music and Bharatanatyam dance all thrived here. Quite apart from its own intrinsic interest, the Nayak **royal palace compound** houses an important library and museums including a famous collection of bronzes.

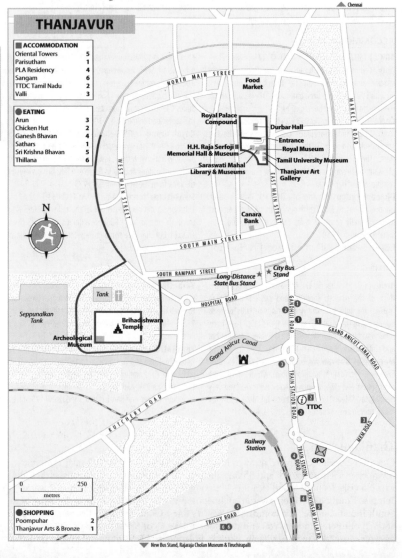

THANJAVUR

ACCOMMODATION

Oriental Towers	5
Parisutham	1
PLA Residency	4
Sangam	6
TTDC Tamil Nadu	2
Valli	3

EATING

Arun	3
Chicken Hut	2
Ganesh Bhavan	4
Sathars	1
Sri Krishna Bhavan	5
Thillana	6

SHOPPING

Poompuhar	2
Thanjavur Arts & Bronze	1

Chennai

NORTH MAIN STREET

Food Market

MARKET ROAD

Royal Palace Compound

Durbar Hall

Entrance

H.H. Raja Serfoji II Memorial Hall & Museum

Royal Museum

Tamil University Museum

Saraswati Mahal Library & Museums

Thanjavur Art Gallery

WEST MAIN STREET

EAST MAIN STREET

N

Canara Bank

SOUTH MAIN STREET

SOUTH RAMPART STREET

Long-Distance State Bus Stand

City Bus Stand

Tank

HOSPITAL ROAD

GANDHI ROAD

Seppunalkan Tank

Brihadishwara Temple

GRAND ANICUT CANAL ROAD

Archeological Museum

Grand Anicut Canal

TRAIN STATION ROAD

KUTCHERY ROAD

TTDC

0   250
metres

Railway Station

TRAIN STATION ROAD

GPO

MKM ROAD

SRINIVASAM PILLAI RD.

TRICHY ROAD

New Bus Stand, Rajaraja Cholan Museum & Tiruchirapalli

Of major local **festivals**, the most lavish celebrations at the Brihadishwara Temple are associated with the birthday of King Rajaraja, in late October. A five-day celebration of **Carnatic classical music** is held each January at the Panchanateshwara Temple at **Thiruvaiyaru**, 13km away, to honour the great Carnatic composer-saint, Thyagaraja.

Brihadishwara Temple
Temple Daily 6am–8pm • **Museum** Daily 9am–6pm • Free • ☎ 04362 274476, ⊕ brihadeeshwarartemple.com

Thanjavur's skyline is dominated by the huge tower of the **Brihadishwara Temple**, which for all its size and UNESCO World Heritage status lacks the grandiose excesses of later periods. The temple was constructed as much to reflect the power of its patron, King Rajaraja I, as to facilitate the worship of Shiva. Profuse **inscriptions** on the base of the main shrine provide incredibly detailed information about the organization of the temple, showing it to have been rich, both in financial terms and in ritual activity. No fewer than four hundred female dancers, **devadasis** (literally "slaves to the gods", married off to the deity), were employed, and each provided with a house. Other staff – another two hundred people – included dance teachers, musicians, tailors, potters, laundrymen, goldsmiths, carpenters, astrologers, accountants and attendants for all manner of rituals and processions.

The temple entrance
Entrance to the complex is on the east, through two **gopura** gateways some way apart. Although the outer one is the larger, both are of the same pattern: massive rectangular bases topped by pyramidal towers with carved figures and vaulted roofs. At the core of each is a monolithic sandstone lintel, said to have been brought from Tiruchirapalli, more than 50km away. The outer facade of the inner *gopura* features mighty, fanged *dvarapala* door guardians, mirror images of each other, and thought to be the largest monolithic sculptures in any Indian temple. "Elephant blessings" are sometimes available just through the arch.

The main temple
Once you are inside, the gigantic **courtyard** gives plenty of space to appreciate the buildings. The **main temple**, constructed of granite, consists of a long pillared *mandapa* hallway, followed by the *ardhamandapa*, or "half-hall", which in turn leads to the inner sanctum, the *garbha griha*. Above the shrine, the pyramidal 61m *vimana* tower rises in thirteen diminishing storeys, the apex being exactly one third of the size of the base. This *vimana* is an example of a "structured monolith", a stage removed from the earlier rock-cut architecture of the Pallavas, in which blocks of stone are assembled and then carved. As the stone that surmounts it is said to weigh eighty tonnes, there is considerable speculation as to how it got up there; the most popular theory is that the rock was hauled up a 6km-long ramp. Others have suggested the use of a method comparable to the Sumer Ziggurat style of building, in which logs were placed in gaps in the masonry and the stone raised by leverage.

The black *shivalingam*, more than 3.5m high, in the **inner sanctum**, is called Adavallan, "the one who can dance well" – a reference to Shiva as Nataraja, the King of the Dance, who resides at Chidambaram and was the *ishtadevata*, chosen deity, of the king. The lingam is only on view during pujas, when a curtain is pulled back to reveal the god to the devotees.

The Archeological Museum
Outside, the walls of the courtyard are lined with **colonnaded passageways** – the one along the northern wall is said to be the longest in India. In the southwest corner of the courtyard, the small **Archeological Museum** houses an interesting collection of sculpture. Here you can also buy the excellent ASI booklet, *Chola Temples*, which gives detailed accounts of Brihadishwara and the temples at Gangaikondacholapuram and Darasuram.

7

CHOLA BRONZES

Originally sacred temple objects, **Chola bronzes** are the only art form from Tamil Nadu to have penetrated the world art market. The most memorable bronze icons are the **Natarajas**, or dancing Shivas. The image of Shiva, standing on one leg, encircled by flames, with wild locks caught in mid-motion, has become almost as recognizably Indian as the Taj Mahal.

The principal icons of a temple are usually stationary and made of stone. Frequently, however, ceremonies require an image of the god to be led in procession outside the inner sanctum, and even through the streets. According to the canonical texts known as *Agamas*, these moving images should be made of metal. Indian bronzes are made by the **cire-perdue** ("**lost wax**") process, known as *madhuchchishtavidhana* in Sanskrit. Three layers of clay mixed with burned grain husks, salt and ground cotton are applied to a figure crafted in beeswax, with a stem left protruding at each end. When that is heated, the wax melts and flows out, creating a hollow mould into which molten metal – a rich five-metal alloy (*panchaloha*) of copper, silver, gold, brass and lead – can be poured through the stems. After the metal has cooled, the clay shell is destroyed, and the stems filed off, leaving a unique completed figure, which the caster-artist, or *sthapathi*, remodels to remove blemishes and add delicate detail.

Those bronzes produced by the few artists practising today invariably follow the Chola model; the chief centre is now **Swamimalai** (see p.406). Original Chola bronzes are kept in many Tamil temples, but as the interiors are often dark it's not always possible to see them properly. Important **public collections** include the Royal Palace Compound at Thanjavur (see below), the Government Museum at Chennai (see p.372) and the National Museum, New Delhi.

Royal Palace Compound

East Main St (a continuation of Gandhiji Rd) • **Palace Compound** Daily 9am–6pm • Free • **Durbar Hall** Daily 10am–5pm • ₹50 (₹10), camera ₹30, video camera ₹100

Members of the erstwhile royal family still reside in the **Royal Palace Compound**, 2km northeast of Brihadishwara Temple. Work on the palace began in the mid-sixteenth century under Sevappa Nayak, the founder of the Nayak kingdom of Thanjavur; additions were made by the Marathas from the end of the seventeenth century onwards. Dotted around the compound are several reminders of Thanjavur's past under these two dynasties, including an exhibition of oriental manuscripts and a superlative museum of **Chola bronzes**. Unfortunately, many of the palace buildings remain in a sorry state, despite various promises of funds for renovation.

Remodelled by Shaji II in 1684, the **Durbar Hall**, or hall of audience, houses a throne canopy decorated with the mirrored glass distinctive of Thanjavur. Although damaged, the ceiling and walls are elaborately painted. Five domes are striped red, green and yellow, and on the walls, friezes of leaf and pineapple designs and trumpeting angels in a night sky show European influence. The **courtyard** outside the Durbar Hall was the setting for one of the more poignant moments in Thanjavur's turbulent history when, in 1683, the last of the Nayak kings gave himself up to the king of Madurai. Its most imposing structure, the Sarja Madi or "seven-storey" bell tower, built by Serfoji II in 1800, is closed to the public due to its unsafe condition.

Saraswati Mahal Library Museum

Daily 10am–1pm & 1.30–5pm • Free

The **Saraswati Mahal Library** holds one of the most important oriental manuscript collections in India, used by scholars from all over the world. The library is closed to the general public, but a small **museum** displays a bizarre array of books and pictures from the collection. Among the palm-leaf manuscripts is a calligrapher's *tour de force* in the form of a visual mantra, where each letter in the inscription "Shiva" comprises the god's name repeated in microscopically small handwriting. Most of the Maratha manuscripts, produced from the end of the seventeenth century, are on paper; they include a superbly illustrated edition of the Mahabharata. Sadists will be delighted to see the library managed to hang on to its copy of the explicitly illustrated **Punishments**

in China, published in 1804. Next to it, full rein is given to the imagination of French artist **Charles Le Brun** (1619–90), in a series of pictures on the subject of physiognomy. Animals such as the horse, bullock, wolf, bear, rabbit and camel are drawn in painstaking care above a series of human faces which bear an uncanny, if unlikely, resemblance to them. You can buy postcards of this scientific study and exhibits from the other palace museums in the **shop** next door.

Thanjavur Art Gallery

East Main St • Daily 9am–1 & 3pm–6pm • ₹60 (₹7), camera or video camera ₹100 (₹30)

A magnificent collection of **Chola bronzes** – the finest of them from the Tiruvengadu hoard, unearthed in the 1950s – fills the **Thanjavur Art Gallery**, a high-ceilinged audience hall with massive pillars, dating from 1600. The elegance of the figures and delicacy of detail are unsurpassed. A tenth-century statue of Kannappa Nayannar (#174), a hunter-devotee, shows minutiae right down to his embroidered clothing, fingernails and the fine lines on his fingers. The oldest bronze, four cases left of the main doorway (#58), shows Vinadhra Dakshinamurti ("south-facing Shiva") who, with a deer on one left hand, would have originally been playing the *vina* – the musical instrument has long since gone. However, the undisputed masterpiece of the collection shows Shiva as Lord of the Animals (#86), sensuously depicted in a skimpy loincloth, with a turban made of snakes. Next to him stands an equally stunning Parvati, his consort (#87), but the cream of the female figures, a seated, half-reclining Parvati (#97), is displayed on the opposite side of the hall.

ARRIVAL AND INFORMATION   **THANJAVUR**

By train Thanjavur's railway station is located south of the old town, canal and Brihadishwara temple complex.
Destinations Chennai Egmore (5 daily; 7–8hr); Kumbakonam (10 daily; 45min–1hr 15min); Madurai (2 daily; 3hr 55min–4hr 40min); Rameshwaram (1 daily; 8hr 5min); Trichy (10 daily; 1hr–1hr 50min).
By bus Most buses, including those from Madurai, Tiruchirapalli and Kumbakonam, terminate at the New Bus Stand, 6km southwest of the centre. Rickshaws into town from here cost ₹150, or you can jump on one of the #57, #74 or #75 buses that shuttle to and from the centre every

few minutes. Buses from northern destinations such as Chennai, Puducherry and Kumbakonam pass through town, so you can get off near the temple.
Destinations Kumbakonam (every 5min; 1hr 30min); Madurai (every 15min; 6hr); Trichy (every 5min; 1hr 30min).
Tourist information The TTDC tourist office (Mon–Fri 10am–5.45pm; ☎04362 230984) is located in the compound of *TTDC Tamil Nadu* hotel on Gandhiji Rd.
Services You can change money at Canara Bank on South Main St.

ACCOMMODATION

Oriental Towers 2889 Srinivasam Pillai Rd ☎04362 230450, ⓦhotelorientaltowers.com. Huge hotel-cum-shopping complex, with small swimming pool, internet access, a multicuisine restaurant and luxurious a/c rooms. Four rooms on each floor have good temple views, while deluxe rooms are larger and cost an extra ₹500. Good value. ₹2700
Parisutham 55 Grand Anicut Canal Rd ☎04362 231801, ⓦhotelparisutham.com. Luxurious hotel with spacious, a/c rooms, a large palm-fringed pool, Ayurvedic treatments, multicuisine restaurant, craft shop, foreign exchange and travel agent. It's popular with tour groups, so book ahead. ₹3600
PLA Residency 2886 Srinivasam Pillai Rd ☎04362 278391, ⓦplaresidency.com. Small but immaculate rooms with large flatscreen TVs and fab attached bathrooms with modern plumbing and serious shower heads. It's worth paying an extra ₹200 for the bigger exec double. Good rooftop restaurant and a new annexe two doors along. ₹1680

Sangam Trichy Rd ☎04362 239451, ⓦsangamhotels .com. Luxury four-star hotel on the road in from the bus stand, with comfortable a/c rooms, an excellent restaurant (see p.412), pool (₹250 for non-residents) and beautiful Tanjore paintings – the one in the lobby is worth a trip here in itself. ₹4500
TTDC Tamil Nadu Gandhiji Rd ☎04362 231325, ⓦttdconline.com. A 10min walk from the railway station, this state-run hotel, once the raja's guesthouse, manages to maintain lots of character. Large, comfortable and very clean a/c rooms with a sofa and armchairs, all of them set around a pleasant enclosed garden. ₹1400
★**Valli** 2948 MKM Rd ☎04362 231580, ☻arasu_tnj @rediffmail.com. At the end of an industrial lane, this friendly hotel has clean rooms, some a/c, with a choice of Indian or Western loos, a rooftop terrace and convenient but rather average restaurant. The best budget option in town. Wi-fi in lobby and restaurant. ₹650

EATING

Arun Court Rd ☎04362 277310. Conveniently located on the corner of Gandhiji and Court roads, this small pure-veg South Indian restaurant has an extensive menu featuring 96 dishes, most of which cost around ₹60–70. Fine masala dosas too. Daily 6.30am–10pm.

Chicken Hut 82 Gandhiji Rd ☎04362 231133. Far superior to the average fast-food joint, serving Chinese, pizza and burgers as well as the tasty fried chicken of the name – four-piece meal only ₹330. Daily 11.30am–3pm & 6.30–10.30pm.

Ganesh Bhavan 2905 Srinivasam Pillai Rd ☎04362 277032. Large, clean, South Indian *dhaba* situated on the first floor. Serves a wide range of veg dishes, a selection of noodle dishes (around ₹100), masala dosas (₹60) and tandoori food after 4pm. Daily 7am–10.30pm.

Sathars 167 Gandhiji Rd ☎04362 277032. The most popular non-veg restaurant in town, serving a variety of chicken and prawn dishes for ₹150–230, and a few cheaper veggie favourites. There are three separate sections, including an a/c hall upstairs. Daily 12.30–4.30pm & 6.30–11.30pm.

★**Sri Krishna Bhavan** 68A VAC Nagar Trichy Rd ☎04362 233344. Very clean and popular pure-veg restaurant, which serves delicious, unlimited thalis for just ₹70 and a good range of curries and breads. Its a/c hall is open from 10am to 10pm. Daily 7am–10pm.

★**Thillana** Sangam hotel, Trichy Rd ☎04362 239451. Swish multicuisine restaurant renowned for its superb lunchtime south-Indian thalis (₹300). In the evening, the extensive à la carte menu, featuring superb *chettinad* specialities (₹280–475), is served up with live Carnatic music. Daily noon–3pm & 7–11pm.

SHOPPING

Poompuhar Gandhiji Rd ☎04362 230060, ⓦtn poompuhar.org. This state government shop near the TTDC hotel is a safe bet for reasonable prices on replica bronzes and an array of other handicrafts and souvenirs. Daily 10am–8pm.

Thanjavur Arts & Bronze 138 Gandhiji Rd ☎04362 232290. One of the best private emporia, with a particularly good selection of bronzes and paintings. Daily 10am–8pm.

Tiruchirapalli (Trichy) and around

TIRUCHIRAPALLI – more commonly referred to as **Trichy** – stands in the plains between the Shevaroy and Palani hills, just under 100km north of Madurai. Dominated by the dramatic Rock Fort, it's a sprawling commercial centre with a modern feel. Most of its business is in the southern **Trichy Junction** district, where the **bazaars**, immediately north of the Junction, heave with locally made cigars, textiles and fake diamonds, made into inexpensive jewellery and sewn into dance costumes. Head north along Big Bazaar Road and you're confronted by the dramatic profile of the **Rock Fort**, topped by the seventeenth-century Vinayaka (Ganesh) Temple. There are several British churches dotted around the town, the most notable of which is **Our Lady of Lourdes**, west of the Rock Fort, which is modelled on the basilica of Lourdes.

North of the fort, the River Kaveri marks a wide boundary between the crowded business districts and the somewhat more serene temples beyond the river. The spectacular **Ranganathaswamy Temple** in **Srirangam**, 6km north of central Trichy, is so large it holds much of the village within its courtyards. Also north of the Kaveri is the elaborate **Sri Jambukeshwara Temple**.

Brief history

The precise date of Trichy's foundation is uncertain, but though little early architecture remains, it is clear that between 200 and 1000 AD control of the city passed between the Pallavas and Pandyas. The Chola kings who gained supremacy in the eleventh century embarked upon ambitious building projects, reaching a zenith with the Ranganathaswamy Temple. In the twelfth century, the Cholas were ousted by the Vijayanagar kings of Hampi, who then stood up against Muslim invasions until 1565, when they succumbed to the might of the sultans of the Deccan. Less than fifty years later the Nayaks of Madurai came to power, constructing the fort and firmly establishing Trichy as a trading city. After almost a century of struggle against the French and British,

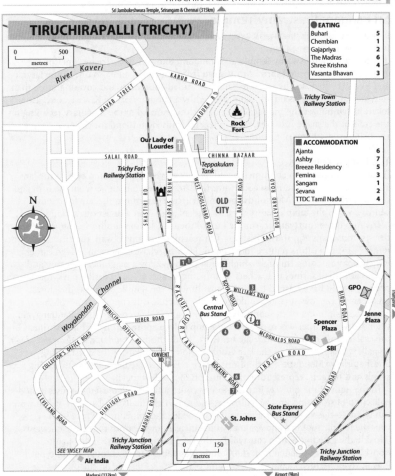

who both sought lands in southeast Tamil Nadu, the town came under British control until it was declared part of Tamil Nadu State in 1947.

The Rock Fort

Daily 6am–8pm • ₹3, camera ₹20, video camera ₹100 • ☎ 0431 270 4621, ⊛ trichyrockfort.tnhrce.in • Bus #1 from outside the railway station or Dindigul Rd

The massive sand-coloured rock on which Trichy's **Rock Fort** rests towers to a height of more than 80m, its irregular sides smoothed by wind and rain. The Pallavas were the first to cut into it, but it was the Nayaks who grasped the site's potential as a fort, adding only a few walls and bastions as fortifications. From the entrance, off China Bazaar, a long flight of red-and-white-painted steps cuts steeply uphill, past a series of Pallava and Pandya rock-cut temples (closed to non-Hindus), to the **Ganesh Temple** crowning the hilltop. The views from its terrace are spectacular, taking in the Ranganathaswamy and Jambukeshwara temples to the north, their *gopuras* rising from a sea of palm trees, and the cubic concrete sprawl of central Trichy to the south.

Sri Ranganathaswamy Temple

Srirangam • Daily 5.30am–9pm • Free, camera ₹50, video camera ₹100; official guides ₹300/2hr • Ⓦ srirangam.org • Frequent buses from Trichy pull in and leave from the southern gate

The **Sri Ranganathaswamy Temple** at **Srirangam**, 8km north of Trichy Junction, is among the most revered shrines to Vishnu in South India, and also one of the largest and liveliest. Enclosed by seven rectangular walled courtyards and covering more than sixty hectares, it stands on an island defined by a tributary of the River Kaveri. This location symbolizes the transcendence of Vishnu, housed in the sanctuary reclining on the coils of the snake Adisesha, who in legend formed an island for the god, resting on the primordial Ocean of Chaos.

The temple complex

A gateway topped with an immense and heavily carved *gopura*, completed in the late 1980s, leads to the outermost courtyard, the latest of seven built between the fifth and seventeenth centuries. Most of the present structure dates from the late fourteenth century, when the temple was renovated and enlarged after a disastrous sacking in 1313.

The first **three courtyards** form the hub of the temple community, housing ascetics, priests, musicians and souvenir shops. On reaching the fourth wall, the entrance to the temple proper, visitors remove footwear and can purchase camera and video camera tickets before passing through a high gateway, topped by a magnificent *gopura* and lined with small shrines to teachers, hymn-singers and sages. In earlier days, this **fourth** *prakara* would have formed the outermost limit of the temple, and was the closest members of the lowest castes could get to the sanctuary. It contains some of the finest and oldest buildings of the complex, including a temple to the goddess **Ranganayaki** in the northwest corner where devotees worship before approaching Vishnu's shrine. On the eastern side of the *prakara*, the heavily carved "thousand pillared" *kalyan mandapa*, or hall, was constructed in the late Chola period. The pillars of the outstanding **Sheshagiriraya Mandapa**, south of the *kalyan mandapa*, are decorated with rearing steeds and hunters, representing the triumph of good over evil.

To the right of the gateway into the fourth courtyard, a small **museum** houses a modest collection of stone and bronze sculptures and some delicate ivory plaques. For ₹10, you can climb to the roof of the fourth wall from beside the museum and take in the view over the temple rooftops and *gopuras*, which increase in size from the centre outwards.

Inside the gate to the **fifth courtyard** – the final section of the temple open to non-Hindus – is a pillared hall, the **Garuda Mandapa**, carved throughout in typical Nayak style. Maidens, courtly donors and Nayak rulers feature on the pillars that surround the central shrine to Garuda, the man-eagle vehicle of Vishnu.

ARRIVAL AND DEPARTURE   TIRUCHIRAPALLI (TRICHY) AND AROUND

By plane Trichy's airport (enquiries and bookings ☏ 0431 248 0233) is 8km south of the centre and has daily flights to and from Chennai, several weekly to Thiruvananthapuram and Kozhikode, and frequent services to Sri Lanka and the Gulf states. The journey into town, by taxi (around ₹350) or bus (#7, #28, #59, #63 or #K1) takes less than 30min.

By train The main railway station, Trichy Junction, which has given its name to the southern district of town, is within easy reach of most hotels and restaurants.

Destinations Bengaluru (1 daily; 9hr 15min); Chengalpattu (6–7 daily; 4hr–5hr 30min); Chennai (16–17 daily; 5hr 40min–7hr 55min); Coimbatore (4 daily; 4hr 50min–5hr 20min); Ernakulam for Kochi (2 daily; 10hr 30min–14hr); Kanyakumari (3 daily; 7hr 30min–9hr); Kodaikanal Rd (3–4 daily; 1hr 50min–2hr 15min); Madurai (11–14 daily; 2hr

20min–3hr 15min); Thanjavur (10 daily; 38min–1hr 40min).

By bus There are two main bus stands in Trichy, State Express and Central, both served by a mixture of state and private buses. The efficient local city service (#1) that leaves from the platform on Rockins Rd, opposite the *Shree Krishna* restaurant, is the most convenient way of getting to the Rock Fort, the temples and Srirangam. Auto-rickshaws are also widely available.

Destinations Chengalpattu (every 15–30min; 7–8hr); Chennai (every 15–30min; 8hr 30min–9hr 30min); Coimbatore (every 30min; 5hr); Kanchipuram (3 daily; 7hr); Kanyakumari (every 30min; 10–11hr); Kodaikanal (8–10 daily; 5–6hr); Madurai (every 20–30min; 4–5hr); Puducherry (every 30min; 5–6hr); Thanjavur (every 10min; 1hr–1hr 30min); Tiruvannamalai (5 daily; 6hr).

INFORMATION

Tourist information The tourist office (Mon–Fri 10am–5.30pm; ☎ 0431 246 0136), which offers travel information but no maps, is just outside the *Tamil Nadu* hotel, opposite the Central Bus Stand.

Services There are many places to change money, such as the Highway forex office (Mon–Sat 10am–6pm) in the Plaza and the State Bank of India on Dindigul Rd.

ACCOMMODATION

Ajanta 6A Rockins Rd ☎ 0431 241 5501. A huge, 85-room complex centred on its own Vijayanagar shrine, and with an opulent Tirupati deity in reception, which is popular with middle-class pilgrims. The rooms (a/c ₹1500; good-value singles ₹540) are fairly spartan but clean. No wi-fi. **₹900**

Ashby 17-A Rockins Rd ☎ 0431 246 0652, ⓦ ashbyhotel .com. This atmospheric Raj-era place is first choice for most foreign tourists, though it's seen better days. The rooms (a/c ₹1610) are large and cleanish, with cable TV and mosquito coils, and there's a decent little courtyard restaurant. No wi-fi. **₹690**

Breeze Residency 3/14 McDonald's Rd ☎ 0431 404 5333, ⓦ breezeresidency.com. This large, centrally located a/c hotel boasts good-sized, comfortably furnished rooms, a nicely decorated foyer, swimming pool and a very good restaurant, *The Madras* (see below). **₹2900**

★**Femina** 109 Williams Rd, near Central Bus Stand ☎ 0431 241 4501, ⓦ feminahotel.net. Well-maintained, sprawling block of a/c rooms, some with balconies offering views of the Rock Fort. The hotel has a flashy marble

lobby and houses two plush restaurants, travel services, shops, a pool, fitness centre and 24hr coffee bar. **₹1850**

Sangam Collector's Office Rd ☎ 0431 241 4700, ⓦ sangamhotels.com. Trichy's top hotel, with all the facilities expected of a four-star: a very nice swimming pool (₹250 for non-residents) and an excellent restaurant, *Chembian* (see below), with live music at weekends. **₹4275**

Sevana 5 Royal Rd ☎ 0431 241 5201, ⓔ hotelsevana @gmail.com. Set in its own grounds 100m back from the main road, this hotel lacks character but offers clean, spacious doubles with king-size beds and towels provided. There's a good-value 33-percent discount for single occupancy and the a/c tariff (₹1450) includes breakfast. No wi-fi. **₹750**

TTDC Tamil Nadu McDonald's Rd ☎ 0431 241 4346, ⓦ ttdconline.com. One of TTDC's better hotels, and just far enough from the bus stand to escape the din. There are two categories of a/c room (standard ₹995; larger deluxe ₹1450), all with cable TV, but the non-a/c rooms are better value. **₹775**

EATING

Buhari Annamalai Complex, McDonald's Rd ☎ 0431 645 9814. Refreshingly cool, a/c, North Indian restaurant with yellow walls, serving chicken, mutton, fish and veg dishes, with or without gravy, plus some Chinese. Daily 11.30am–11pm.

Chembian Sangam hotel, Collector's Office Rd ☎ 0431 424 4555. This excellent restaurant offers a range of delicious Indian dishes as well as unusually good Western and Chinese cuisine, in an atmospheric, beautifully decorated dining hall. Non-veg mains around ₹300–400. Live Carnatic music at weekends. Daily 11.30am–3.30pm & 7–11pm.

Gajapriya Royal Rd, ground floor of the Gajapriya hotel. Non-veg North Indian and noodle dishes are specialities of this small but blissfully cool and clean a/c restaurant, where meat dishes cost ₹100–150. Dingy bar next door. Daily 6.30–11pm.

The Madras Breeze Residency, 3/14 McDonald's Rd ☎ 0431 404 5333. Worth a visit for its excellent-value

weekday lunchtime (₹250) and dinner buffets (₹400), which feature a wide range of Indian and Chinese dishes and a few random Mexican treats thrown into the mix. Prices higher at weekends. Daily 12.30–3.30pm & 7–11pm.

Shree Krishna 1 Rockins Rd, opposite Central Bus Stand ☎ 0431 241 4737. Delicious and very filling American or South Indian set breakfasts (₹100), unlimited banana-leaf thalis at lunchtime (₹70) and a range of veggie curries (all under ₹100) in the evenings – all served with a smile. Daily 6am–11pm.

Vasanta Bhavan Abhirami hotel complex, 10 Rockins Rd, opposite Central Bus Stand ☎ 0431 241 5001. Trichy's best-known South Indian restaurant, serving up unbeatable-value lunchtime "meals" (₹80) and the standard range of snacks the rest of the day. The fast-food counter serves fine dosas and *uttapams* all day. Daily 6am–11pm.

Madurai

One of the oldest cities in South Asia, **MADURAI**, on the banks of the River Vaigai, has been an important centre of worship and commerce for as long as there has been civilization in South India. It was often described as "the Athens of the East"

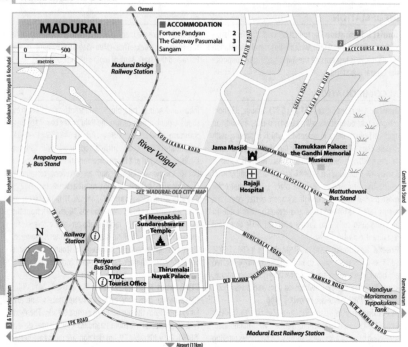

and indeed, when the Greek ambassador Megasthenes visited in 302 BC, he wrote of its splendour and described its queen, Pandai, as "a daughter of Herakles". The Roman geographer Strabo also wrote of Madurai, complaining that the city's silk, pearls and spices were draining the imperial coffers of Rome. It was this lucrative trade that enabled the **Pandyan** dynasty to erect the mighty **Meenakshi-Sundareshwarar temple**. Although now surrounded by a sea of modern concrete cubes, the massive *gopuras* of this vast complex, writhing with multicoloured mythological figures and crowned by golden finials, remain the greatest man-made spectacle of the South. No fewer than 15,000 people pass through its gates every day and on Fridays (sacred to the goddess Meenakshi) numbers swell to more than 25,000, while the temple's ritual life spills out into the streets in an almost ceaseless round of festivals and processions.

Although considerably enlarged and extended through the ages, the overall layout of Madurai's **old city**, south of the River Vaigai, has remained largely unchanged since the first centuries AD, comprising a series of concentric squares centred on the massive **Meenakshi Temple**. Aligned with the cardinal points, the street plan forms a giant mandala, whose sacred properties are activated during the regular mass clockwise circumambulations of the central temple. **North of the river**, Madurai becomes markedly more mundane and irregular. You're only likely to cross the Vaigai to reach the city's more expensive hotels or the Gandhi Museum.

Brief history

Although invariably interwoven with myth, the traceable history and fame of Madurai stretches back well over two thousand years. Numerous natural **caves** in local hills, and boulders often modified by the addition of simple rock-cut beds, were used both in prehistoric times and by ascetics such as the Ajivikas and Jains, who practised withdrawal and penance.

Madurai appears to have been capital of the Pandyan empire without interruption for at least a thousand years. It became a major commercial city, trading with Greece, Rome and China, and *yavanas* (a generic term for foreigners) were frequent visitors to Pandyan seaports. The Tamil epics describe them walking around town with their eyes and mouths wide open with amazement. Under the Pandya dynasty, Madurai also became an established seat of Tamil culture, credited with being the site of three **sangams**, "literary academies", said to date back ten thousand years and which supported some eight thousand poets.

The Pandyas' capital fell in the tenth century, when the **Chola** king Parantaka took the city. In the thirteenth century, the Pandyas briefly regained power until the early 1300s, when the notorious **Malik Kafur**, the Delhi Sultanate's "favourite slave", made an unprovoked attack during a plunder-and-desecration tour of the South, and destroyed much of the city. Forewarned of the raid, the Pandya king, Sundara, fled with his immediate family and treasure, leaving his uncle and rival, Vikrama Pandya, to repel Kafur. Nevertheless, the latter returned to Delhi with booty said to consist of "six hundred and twelve elephants, ninety-six thousand *mans* of gold, several boxes of jewels and pearls and twenty thousand horses".

Shortly after this raid Madurai became an independent Sultanate. In 1364, it joined the Hindu **Vijayanagar** empire, ruled from Hampi and administered by governors, the **Nayaks**. In 1565, the Nayaks asserted their own independence. Under their supervision and patronage, Madurai enjoyed a renaissance, being rebuilt on the pattern of a lotus centring on the Meenakshi Temple. Part of the palace of the most illustrious of the Nayaks, **Thirumalai** (1623–55), survives today. The city remained under Nayak control until the mid-eighteenth century when it was gradually taken over by the British. A hundred years later the British de-fortified Madurai, filling its moat to create the four Veli streets that today mark the boundary of the old city.

7

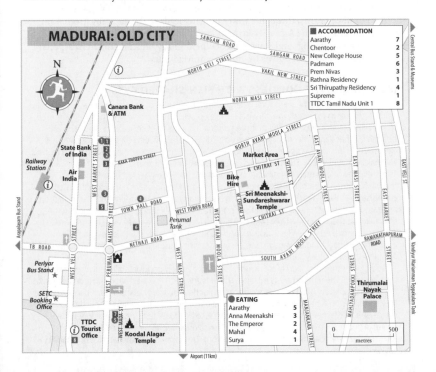

MADURAI: OLD CITY

N

ACCOMMODATION	
Aarathy	7
Chentoor	2
New College House	5
Padmam	6
Prem Nivas	3
Rathna Residency	1
Sri Thirupathy Residency	4
Supreme	1
TTDC Tamil Nadu Unit	8

SANGAM ROAD
SANGAM ROAD
NORTH VELI STREET
VAKIL NEW STREET
NORTH MASI STREET
Canara Bank & ATM
NORTH AVANI MOOLA STREET
State Bank of India
Railway Station
KAKA THOPPU STREET
Air India
Market Area
N CHITRAL ST
Bike Hire
Sri Meenakshi-Sundareshwarar Temple
WEST MARKET STREET
MAISTRY STREET
TOWN HALL ROAD
WEST TOWER ROAD
Perumal Tank
S CHITRAL ST
NETHAJI ROAD
WEST AVANI MOOLA STREET
EAST AVANI MOOLA STREET
CHITRAL ST
EAST MASI STREET
EAST MARKET
EAST VELI ST
SOUTH AVANI MOOLA STREET
RAMANATHAPURAM ROAD
TB ROAD
Periyar Bus Stand
WEST VELI STREET
WEST PERUMAL STREET
WEST MASI STREET
SETC Booking Office
Thirumalai Nayak Palace
MAHLYADAMPOKKI STREET
MANJANKARA STREET
TTDC Tourist Office
WEST MARK ST
Koodal Alagar Temple

EATING	
Aarathy	5
Anna Meenakshi	3
The Emperor	2
Mahal	4
Surya	1

0 — 500
metres

Aappalayam Bus Stand

Central Bus Stand & Museums

Vandiyur Mariamman Teppakulam Tank

Airport (11km)

Sri Meenakshi-Sundareshwarar Temple

Daily 4am–12.30pm & 4–10pm • No shorts or cameras, mobiles ₹50

Enclosed by a roughly rectangular 6m-high wall, in the manner of a fortified palace, and with modern security measures to match, the **Sri Meenakshi-Sundareshwarar Temple** is one of the largest temple complexes in India. Much of it was constructed during the Nayak period between the sixteenth and eighteenth centuries, but certain parts are very much older.

For the first-time visitor, confronted with a confusing maze of shrines, sculptures and colonnades, and unaware of the logic employed in their arrangement, it's very easy to get disorientated. Quite apart from the estimated 33,000 sculptures to arrest your attention, the life of the temple is absolutely absorbing, with the endless round of puja ceremonies, loud *nagaswaram* and *tavil* music, weddings, brahmin boys under religious instruction in the Vedas, the prostrations of countless devotees and the glittering market stalls inside the east entrance. If you're braving the heat of late spring, check when the stunning **Chithirai festival** is taking place to celebrate the marriage of Meenakshi and Sundareshwarar (Shiva), marked by vivid chariot processions. Even if you're not lucky enough to see a festival procession, something is always going on to make this one of the most compelling places in Tamil Nadu. Approximately fifty priests live and work here, recognizable by the white *dhotis* tied between their legs and silk cloth worn around their waists. You can roam freely within the complex but the main shrines can only be entered by Hindus.

The entrance

Madurai takes the **gopura**, prominent in all southern temples, to its ultimate extreme. The entire complex has no fewer than twelve such towers. Built into the outer walls, the four largest reach a height of around 46m and are covered with a profusion of gaily painted stucco gods and demons.

The most popular **entrance**, on the east side, leads directly to the Shiva shrine. Another entrance nearby, through a towerless gate, leads to the adjacent Meenakshi shrine deep inside. In the **Ashta Shakti Mandapa** ("Eight Goddesses Hallway"), a market sells puja offerings and souvenirs. Sculpted pillars illustrate different aspects of the goddess Shakti, and Shiva's 64 miracles at Madurai.

MEENAKSHI: THE GODDESS WITH FISH-SHAPED EYES

The goddess **Meenakshi** of Madurai emerged from the flames of a sacrificial fire as a 3-year-old child, in answer to the Pandyan king Malayadvaja's prayer for a son. The king, not only surprised to see a female, was also horrified that she had three breasts. In every other respect, she was beautiful, as her name, Meenakshi ("fish-eyed"), suggests; fish-shaped eyes are classic images of desirability in Indian love poetry. Dispelling his concern, a mysterious voice told the king that Meenakshi would lose the third breast on meeting her future husband.

In the absence of a male heir, the adult Meenakshi succeeded her father as Pandyan monarch. With the aim of world domination, she embarked on a series of successful battles, culminating in the defeat of Shiva's armies in his Himalayan abode, Mount Kailash. Shiva then appeared on the battlefield and upon seeing him, Meenakshi immediately lost her third breast thus fulfilling the prophecy. They then travelled to Madurai, where they were duly married. They assumed a dual role – firstly as king and queen of the Pandya kingdom, with Shiva assuming the title Sundara Pandya, and secondly as the presiding deities of the Madurai temple, into which they subsequently disappeared.

Today, their shrines in Madurai are the focal point of a hugely popular fertility cult centred on their "coupling". The temple priests maintain that this ensures the preservation and regeneration of the universe, so every night the pair are placed in Sundareshwarar's bedchamber – but not before Meenakshi's nose ring is carefully removed so that in the heat of passion it won't cut her husband. However, fidelity is never taken for granted, and has to be ritually tested each year when the beautiful goddess Cellattamman is brought to Sundareshwarar "to have her powers renewed". After she is spurned, she flies into a fury that can only be placated with the sacrifice of a buffalo.

Golden Lotus Tank

Continuing straight on from the Ashta Shakti Mandapa, you cross East Ati Street and having passed through the seven-storey **Chitrai gopura** you then enter a passageway which leads to the eastern end of the **Pottamarai Kulam** ("Golden Lotus Tank"), where Indra bathed before worshipping the *shivalingam*. From the east side of the tank you can see the glistening gold of the Meenakshi and Sundareshwarar *vimana* towers. Facing Meenakshi, just beyond the first entrance and in front of the sanctum sanctorum, stands Shiva's bull-vehicle, Nandi. At around 9pm, the moveable images of the god and goddess are carried to the **bed chamber**. Here the final puja ceremony of the day, the **lalipuja**, is performed, when for thirty minutes or so the priests sing lullabies (*lali*), before closing the temple for the night.

Every Friday (6–7pm) Sundareshwar and Meenakshi are brought to the sixteenth-century **Oonjal Mandapa**, where they are placed on a swing (*oonjal*) and serenaded by members of a special caste, the Oduvars.

Sundareshwarar shrine

Walking back north, past the Meenakshi shrine and through a towered entrance, you arrive at the Sundareshwarar shrine. Inside is the huge monolithic Ganesh, **Mukkuruni Vinayaka**, thought to have been unearthed during excavation of the Mariamman Teppakulam tank. Chubby Ganesh is well known for his love of sweets and during the annual **Vinayaka Chaturthi festival** (Sept), a special *prasad* (food offering) is concocted using 300 kilos of rice, ten kilos of sugar and 110 coconuts.

North of the flagstaffs are statues of Shiva and Kali in the throes of a dance competition; a nearby stall sells tiny **butter balls** for visitors to throw at the deities "to cool them down".

The Thousand Pillar Hall

Art Museum Daily 6.30am–12.30pm & 4–9pm • ₹5

Leaving through the east gateway of the Sundareshwarar shrine you come to the fifteenth-century **Ayirakkal Mandapa** (thousand-pillared hall) in the northeast corner, which now houses the temple **Art Museum**. Throughout the hall, large sculptures of strange mythical creatures and cosmic deities rear out at you from the broad stone pillars, some of which have startlingly metallic-like musical tones when tapped.

Vandiyur Mariamman Teppakulam

Ramnad Rd • Bus #4 or #4A

At one time, the huge **Vandiyur Mariamman Teppakulam** tank in the southeast of town, with its constant supply of water, flowing via underground channels from the Vaigai, was always full. Nowadays it is only filled during the spectacular Teppam **floating festival** (Jan/Feb), when pilgrims take boats out to the goddess shrine in the centre. Before their marriage ceremony, Shiva and Meenakshi are brought in procession to the tank, where they float on a beautifully illuminated raft pulled by devotees, which encircles the shrine. The boat trip is the overture to a seduction that reaches its passionate conclusion later that night in the temple. This traditionally makes the Teppam the most auspicious time of year for young couples to get married.

Thirumalai Nayak Palace

Mahlyadampokki St • **Palace** Daily 9am–5pm • ₹50 (₹10), camera ₹30, video camera ₹100, includes Palace Museum • **Sound-and-light show** English 6.45–7.35pm, ₹50; Tamil 8–8.50pm, ₹25; tickets issued 15min before the show • ☏ 0452 233 2945 • Bus #4, #14 or #47

Today only a quarter of the seventeenth-century **Thirumalai Nayak Palace**, located 1.5km southeast of the Meenakshi Temple, survives. Much of it was dismantled by Thirumalai's grandson, Chockkanatha Nayak, and used to build a new palace at

Tiruchirapalli. The remains were renovated in 1858 by Lord Napier, then governor of Madras, and once again in 1971 for the Tamil World Conference. The palace originally consisted of two residential sections, a theatre, private temple, harem, royal bandstand, armoury and gardens. The **Palace Museum** in an adjacent hall includes unlabelled Pandyan, Jain and Buddhist sculptures, terracottas and an eighteenth-century print of the palace in a dilapidated state. A nightly **sound-and-light show** (in both English and Tamil) recalls the story of the Tamil epic, Shilipaddikaram, and the history of the Nayaks.

Tamukkam Palace: the Gandhi Memorial Museum

Tamukkan Rd · Daily except Fri 10am–1pm & 2–5.45pm · Free · Bus #1, #2A, #22, #24, #44 & #77 (from Periyar bus stand 20min)

Across the Vaigai, 5km northeast of the centre near the Central Telegraph Office, stands **Tamukkam**, the seventeenth-century multipillared and arched palace of Queen Rani Mangammal. Built to accommodate such regal entertainment as elephant fights, Tamukkam was taken over by the British, used as a courthouse and collector's office, and in 1955 became home to the Gandhi and Government museums. The **Gandhi Memorial Museum** charts the history of India since the landing of the first Europeans, viewed in terms of the freedom struggle. The perspective is national, but where appropriate, reference is made to the role played by Tamils. Wholeheartedly critical of the British, it states its case clearly and simply, quoting the condemnation by Englishman John Sullivan of his fellow countrymen's insulting treatment of Indians. One chilling artefact, kept in a room painted black, is the bloodstained *dhoti* the Mahatma was wearing when he was assassinated. Next door to the museum, the **Gandhi Memorial Museum Library** houses a reference collection, open to all, of fifteen thousand books, periodicals, letters and microfilms.

ARRIVAL AND DEPARTURE   MADURAI

By plane Madurai's small domestic airport (☏ 0452 269 0433), 12km south of the centre, is served by direct domestic flights to and from Chennai (10 daily; 1hr 5min–1hr 20min), Bengaluru (1 daily; 1hr 20min) and Hyderabad (1 daily; 1hr 50min), as well as international connections to Colombo (1–2 daily; 1hr) and Dubai (3hr 5min). To get to the airport, catch a taxi (around ₹300) or take city bus #10A from the Periyar Bus Stand.

By train The reservations office is to the left of the main hall. There's a prepaid auto-rickshaw and taxi booth outside the main entrance. Madurai is well connected with most major towns and cities in South India and some beyond. It's possible to reach the railhead for Kodaikanal by train, but the journey is much faster by express bus.

Destinations Bengaluru (2–3 daily; 9hr 15min–10hr 50min); Chennai (10–13 daily; 7hr 40min–11hr 40min); Delhi (2 weekly; 41hr 45min); Ernakulam for Kochi (1 daily; 11hr); Kanyakumari/Nagercoil (6–8 daily; 4hr 25min–6hr 20min); Mumbai (5 weekly; 34hr 55min–36hr 15min); Rameshwaram (3–4 daily; 3hr 40min–4hr 30min); Trichy (11–15 daily; 1hr 55min–3hr 40min); Trivandrum (3 daily; 6hr 50min–7hr 40min).

By bus The Central Bus Stand is the arrival point for all services except those from Kerala and west Tamil Nadu, which arrive at Arapalayam Bus Stand. The Central Bus Stand is 7km from the centre, east of the river, and is connected to the centre by city buses #700 and #75, while Arapalayam Bus Stand is in the northwest, about 2km from the railway station. Periyar Bus Stand, on West Veli St, is for local city buses. Next to Periyar is the Tamil Nadu State

RECOMMENDED TRAINS FROM MADURAI

Destination	Name	No.	Departs	Arrives
Bengaluru	*Bangalore Express*	#17236	11.50pm	9.05am+
Chennai	*Vaigai Express*	#12636	7am	2.40pm
	Pandian Express	#12638	8.35pm	5.35am+
Nagercoil	*Guruvayur Express*	#16127	4.15pm	9.25pm
Rameshwaram	*Rameshwaram Express*	#16734	4.05pm	7.45pm
Trichy	*Vaigai Express*	#12636	7am	8.55am

+ Next day

Express reservation office (8am–2pm & 4–8pm) for a/c buses to Chennai and other destinations including several Keralan towns and Bengaluru.

Destinations (from the Central Bus Stand unless otherwise stated): Chengalpattu (every 20–30min; 8–9hr); Chennai (every 20–30min; 10–11hr); Chidambaram (6 daily; 7hr 30min–8hr); Coimbatore (Arapalayam stand, every 30min; 5–6hr); Kanchipuram (4 daily; 9–10hr); Kanyakumari (every 30min; 5hr 30min–6hr); Kochi/Ernakulam via Kottayam (Arapalayam stand, 9 daily; 9hr 30min–10hr); Kodaikanal (Arapalayam stand, hourly; 4hr–4hr 30min); Kumbakonam (8 daily; 6hr–6hr 30min); Kumily, for Periyar Wildlife Sanctuary (Arapalayam stand, hourly; 5hr); Mysuru (5 daily; 10–11hr); Puducherry (hourly; 9–10hr); Rameshwaram (every 30min–1hr; 4hr); Thanjavur (every 30min; 4–5hr); Thiruvanantha-puram, Kerala (hourly; 7–8hr); Tiruchirapalli (every 30min; 4–5hr); Tirupati (4 daily; 15hr). There are no direct services from Madurai to Ooty – you need to change in Coimbatore.

GETTING AROUND

By bike Cheap bike rental is available at SV, West Tower St, near the west entrance to the temple, or the stall on West Veli St, opposite the *Tamil Nadu* hotel.

By taxi If you want a taxi to see the outlying sights, head to the rank outside the main railway station, which abides by government set rates; a 5hr city tour will cost around ₹1200.

INFORMATION

Tourist information The TTDC tourist office, on West Veli St (Mon–Fri 10am–5.45pm, plus Sat 10am–1pm during festivals; ☎ 0452 233 4757), is useful for general information and maps, and can provide information on car rental and approved guides. In the main hall of the railway station itself you'll find a very helpful branch of the Tourism Department information centre (daily 6.30am–8.30pm).
Services The State Bank of India at 6 West Veli St can change cash.

7

ACCOMMODATION

Aarathy 9 Perumal Koil, West Mada St ☎ 0452 233 1571; map p.417. Popular hotel in a great location over-looking the Koodal Alagar Temple; it's often booked up. All rooms (a/c from ₹1200) have TV and some have balconies, but there's quite a range so it's worth checking a few. Good a/c restaurant and alfresco eating in the courtyard. ₹750
Chentoor 106 West Perumal Maistry St ☎ 0452 307 7777 ⓦ hotelchentoor.in; map p.417. Good-value tower-block hotel with very nice, clean all-a/c rooms with TV and king-size beds. The Star Suite goes for ₹3500. Also has a good rooftop restaurant. ₹1500
Fortune Pandyan Racecourse Rd, north of the river ☎ 0452 4356789, ⓦ fortunehotels.in; map p.416. Smart, a/c hotel with a range of large, comfortable rooms all with TV and lavishly decorated with period-style furnishings. Quiet and relaxed, but some way from the centre. Good restaurant, a bar, exchange facilities and travel agency. ₹4500
★**The Gateway Pasumalai** 40 TPK Rd, Pasumalai Hills ☎ 0452 663 3000, ⓦ thegatewayhotels.com; map p.416. Madurai's most exclusive hotel, a beautifully refurbished colonial house in 25 acres of manicured gardens in the hills, overlooking the city from 6km away. Superior rooms in the old building are the most atmos-pheric, but the executive rooms have the best views. There is a gourmet restaurant, swimming pool, tennis court and bar. Good early-bird online specials. ₹5525
New College House 2 Town Hall Rd ☎ 0452 234 2971, ⓔ collegehouse_mdu@yahoo.co.in; map p.417. This huge, maze-like place has more than 200 rooms, and one of the town's best "meals" canteens. The cheapest rooms are grubby but the cleaner deluxe rooms cost only ₹200 extra.

No wi-fi but a browsing centre on the ground floor. ₹650
Padmam 1 Perumal Tank West St ☎ 0452 234 0702, ⓔ hotel_padmam@hotmail.com; map p.417. Clean, comfortable, modern hotel in a central location with a rooftop restaurant. All rooms have TV, some have small balconies and a few are a/c (₹1770). The front rooms, which overlook the ruined Perumal tank and have views of the temple *gopuras*, are more expensive. ₹1330
Prem Nivas 102 West Perumal Maistry St ☎ 0452 234 2532; map p.417. The swanky exterior belies a slightly grubby interior, although bed linen is clean and the rooms (a/c ₹1200; good-value singles ₹450) are a reasonable size, with flatscreen TVs. ₹680
Rathna Residency 109 West Perumal Maistry St ☎ 0452 437 4444, ⓦ hotelrathnaresidency.com; map p.417. This is a standard mid-range hotel with central a/c and clean, decent-sized rooms. There's also a money exchange facility and a good restaurant, *The Sangam*. Breakfast included. ₹1800
Sangam Alagar Koil Rd ☎ 0452 424 4555, ⓦ hotel sangam.com; map p.416. Situated in its own grounds, this plush, centrally a/c hotel has very comfortable rooms (deluxe ₹5200 with bath and sofa), a bar and currency exchange. There is a decent swimming pool (₹200 for non-residents), nice gardens and an excellent restaurant. ₹3750
★**Sri Thirupathy Residency** 20 West Avani Moola St ☎ 0452 234 7431; map p.417. This small hotel, right next to the temple, has spotless non-a/c doubles and is a popular choice with travellers. The "deluxe" a/c rooftop room (₹1500) has a great view of the western *gopura*. Book in advance. ₹660

Supreme 110 West Perumal Maistry St ☎ 0452 234 3151, ⓦ hotelsupreme.in; map p.417. A large, central hotel in a seven-storey block with comfortable a/c rooms, some of which have temple views. There are good facilities, including foreign exchange, a travel counter, and two restaurants (see below). Lukewarm reception. ₹2500

TTDC Tamil Nadu Unit I West Veli St ☎ 0452 233 7471, ⓦ ttdconline.com; map p.417. Situated a little out of the way from the atmosphere of the temples and the bazaar, this hotel offers spacious rooms overlooking a leafy courtyard. The non-a/c rooms are very good value; the a/c rooms (from ₹1400) are larger and very comfortable. No wi-fi. ₹900

EATING

When the afternoon heat gets too much, head for one of the **juice bars** dotted around the centre, where you can order freshly squeezed pomegranate, pineapple, carrot or orange juice for around ₹30 a glass. Madurai is hardly a drinking town, but most of the pricier hotels have a bar, perhaps the most eccentric being the *Apollo 96*, a sci-fi-themed extravaganza at the *Supreme* hotel (see above).

Aarathy Aarathy hotel, 9 Perumal Koil, West Mada St ☎ 0452 233 1571; map p.417. This place serves South Indian breakfasts (7–10.30am), very good lunchtime "meals" (11.30am–3.30pm; ₹100) and a good range of veg and non-veg dishes (4.30–10.30pm). There's an a/c dining room and tables in a courtyard, where the temple elephant is led twice a day. Daily 6am–10.30pm.

★**Anna Meenakshi** West Perumal Maistry St; map p.417. One of the best-value places to eat in the centre, this upmarket branch of *New College House*'s more traditional canteen serves good pure-veg food. Delicious coconut and lemon rice "meals" (₹65), banana-leaf "meals" (₹120), plus some North Indian dishes. Daily 6am–11pm.

★**The Emperor** Chentoor hotel, 106 West Perumal Maistry St ☎ 0452 307 7777; map p.417. With a lovely breeze and great city and temple views, this multicuisine rooftop restaurant is a great place to eat. They serve good Indian food, including biryanis, chicken dishes (₹150–250), sizzlers, and Chinese cuisine. Daily 6am–11pm.

Mahal 21 Town Hall Rd ☎ 0452 234 2700; map p.417. Well-established and nicely decorated street-level restaurant serving small but tasty portions of fish and chips, plus half tandoori chicken for ₹190 and cheap South Indian veg snacks. Daily noon–10.30pm.

Surya Supreme hotel, 110 West Perumal Maistry St ☎ 0452 234 3151; map p.417. This is one of Madurai's most popular rooftop restaurants, with great views of the city and temple. The pure-veg food is average and the service a little lax, but it's still worth checking out. A/c hall on ground floor. Main courses ₹150–280. Daily 4pm–midnight.

SHOPPING

Old Madurai is crowded with **textile and tailors' shops**, particularly in West Veli, Avani Moola and Chitrai streets, and Town Hall Rd. At the tailors' shops near the temple, locally produced textiles are generally good value, and tailors pride themselves on turning out faithful copies of favourite clothes in a matter of hours. South Avani Moola Street is packed with **jewellery**, particularly gold shops, while stores on West Veli Street sell crafts, oil lamps, Meenakshi sculptures and *khadi* cloth and shirts.

Chettinadu

The tranquil rural area known as **Chettinadu** occupies a swathe of land about equidistant from Madurai to the southwest and Trichy and Thanjavur to the north. It is the traditional home of the **Chettiars**, also known as the Nagarathas, a merchant community who date back to the Chola empire and came to prominence in the nineteenth century, when they played an important role in the British trade routes to countries on the Subcontinent and Southeast Asia. The great wealth accumulated during this period allowed them to build lavish **mansions** and notable temples in their 96 villages, of which 72 remain, plus the larger towns of **Karaikudi** and **Pudukottai**. These urban areas grew from villages and provide the gateway to the area, especially the former.

It would take days if not weeks to explore the area thoroughly, so it is best to base yourself at one of the most picturesque villages, such as **Kanadukathan**, 15km north of Karaikudi, en route to Pudukottai. Many of the mansions here and in other villages fell into disrepair when their owners emigrated but have recently been beautifully refurbished as heritage hotels, often by returning Chettiars themselves. Chettinadu is also renowned for its **cuisine** (see box opposite), with examples of it often to be found on Indian menus worldwide.

FOOD IN TAMIL NADU

As befits the heartland of the South, Tamil Nadu's **cuisine** is typical of South India's finest, especially the rice-based thali, known throughout the state simply as **"meals"**. This inexpensive lunchtime feast comprises a pile of rice, often served on a section of **banana leaf**, accompanied by a papad and a selection of dishes in tiny metal pots. These can vary but usually include the likes of *sambhar* (a spicy lentil soup) or *rasam* (a peppery tamarind juice soup), *kootu* (vegetable curried with more lentils), spicy potato fry, *kosumari* salad (grated carrot and coconut in lime juice), *medu vadai* (lentil dumpling), mango or lime pickle, and curd. Often there is a pot of a sweet concoction such as *akkaravadisal* (made with rice and lentils) thrown in for good measure. These meals are sometimes "limited"(i.e. a fixed amount) but more often "unlimited", which means they keep coming round dolloping more on your plate (or leaf) until you beg them to stop.

One of the most celebrated types of Tamil cooking is **Chettinad** cuisine, renowned for its skilful use of aromatic spices such as tamarind, star aniseed, a lichen called *kalpasi*, fennel seeds, fenugreek and whole red chillies. Chettinad chicken and Chettinad fish are the dishes most commonly found on menus outside India. Another item seen throughout India that originated here is Chicken 65, so called because the combination of spices was said to preserve the meat for 65 days on long commercial sea voyages.

7

Kanadukathan

Set amid vivid rice paddies and sugar cane fields, just a couple of kilometres off the main highway, **KANADUKATHAN** epitomizes the effortless class that is exuded by most Chettinad villages. It takes barely ten minutes to walk from one side of it to the other, during which time your eye will marvel at the ornate architecture of the houses and mansions on display. Some heritage houses, usually bearing the owner's initials, such as CVRM and VVR, can be entered by paying a small fee to the janitor. The main attraction, just a block the other side of the large temple bathing tank from the central crossroads, is the **Maharaja Palace**. This large two-storey edifice is not open to the public but you can admire the startling white walls and arches, counterpointed by vivid flashes of reds and blues from outside.

ARRIVAL AND DEPARTURE

KANADUKATHAN

By bus Kanadukathan is most easily accessed from Karaikudi (every 15–30min; 30min).
By taxi As the Chettinadu villages are spread over a wide

area, many people choose to hire a vehicle and driver for their visit from Madurai, Trichy or Thanjavur – reckon on around ₹2500/day.

ACCOMMODATION AND EATING

★**Chettinadu Mansion** Three blocks behind the palace ☎04565 273080, ⊛chettinadmansion.com. This splendid 1902 mansion has been converted into a luxury hotel while preserving many of its original features, such as the classy halls, period furniture and family photos. Quality food is available to guests. The gentlemanly owner lives on the premises and his less expensive *Chettinad Court* is nearby. Breakfast included. ₹6650
Chettinadu Narayana Vilas 2 blocks behind the palace ☎04565 283199, ⊛chettinadunarayanavilas

.com. Attractive mansion that has been decorated in warm and vibrant colours but maintains its character. The smart bedrooms have a modern feel and the Chettinad cooking is excellent. Breakfast included. ₹5000
Visalam On the main village street ☎04565 273301, ⊛cghearth.com. The largest local mansion has been taken over by this eco-conscious luxury chain, which has created top-notch rooms, quality dining and drinking areas in the lush grounds, plus a sizeable pool. Breakfast included. ₹16,300

Rameshwaram

The sacred island of **RAMESHWARAM**, 163km southeast of Madurai and less than 20km from Sri Lanka across the Gulf of Mannar, is, along with Madurai, South India's most important pilgrimage site. Rameshwaram is mentioned in the Ramayana as the place where the god Rama, as an incarnation of Vishnu, worshipped Shiva, and consequently attracts followers of both Vishnu and Shiva. The **Ramalingeshwara Temple** complex, with its magnificent pillared walkways, is the most famous on the island, but there are several other small temples of interest, such as the **Gandhamadana Parvatam**, sheltering Rama's footprints, and the **Nambunayagi Amman Kali Temple**, frequented for its curative properties. **Danushkodi** (Rama's Bow) at the eastern end is where Rama is said to have bathed. The boulders peppering the sea between here and Sri Lanka, making "Rama's bridge" (*Rama Sethu*), were strategically placed by Hanuman's monkey army so they could cross to Lanka in their search for Rama's wife Sita, after her abduction by the demon king Ravana. The town offers uncommercialized **beaches** (not India's most stunning) where you can unwind, bathe and do ablutions.

Rameshwaram, whose streets radiate out from the vast block enclosing the Ramalingeshwara, is always crowded with day-trippers and ragged mendicants who camp outside the Ramalingeshwara and the **Ujainimahamariamman**, the small goddess shore temple. An important part of their pilgrimage is to bathe in the main temple's sacred tanks and in the sea; the narrow strip of beach is shared by groups of bathers, relaxing cows and mantra-reciting *swamis* sitting next to sand lingams. As well as fishing – prawns and lobsters for packaging and export to Japan – shells are a big source of income in the coastal villages.

Ramalingeshwara Temple

The core of the **Ramalingeshwara** (or Ramanathaswamy) **Temple** was built by the Cholas in the twelfth century to house two much-venerated **shivalingams** associated with the Ramayana. After rescuing his wife Sita from the clutches of Ravana, Rama was advised to atone for the killing of the demon king – a brahmin – by worshipping Shiva. Rama's monkey lieutenant, Hanuman, was despatched to the Himalayas to fetch a *shivalingam*, but when he failed to return by the appointed day, Sita fashioned a lingam from sand (the *Ramanathalingam*) so the ceremony could proceed. Hanuman eventually made it back bearing a lingam and in order to assuage the monkey's guilt Rama decreed that in future, of the two, Hanuman's should be worshipped first. The lingams are now housed in the inner section of the Ramalingeshwara, but can only by viewed by Hindus. Much of what can be visited dates from the 1600s, when the temple received generous endowments from the Sethupathi rajas of Ramanathapuram.

The temple is enclosed by high walls, which form a rectangle with huge pyramidal *gopura* entrances on each side. Each gateway leads to a spacious closed ambulatory, flanked on either side by continuous platforms with massive pillars set on their edges. These **corridors** are the most famous attribute of the temple, their extreme length – 205m, with 1212 pillars on the north and south sides – giving a remarkable impression of receding perspective. Before entering the inner sections of the temple, pilgrims are expected to bathe at each of the 22 temple **tirthas** (tanks) in the temple – hence the groups of dripping-wet pilgrims, most of them fully clothed, making their way from tank to tank, to be soaked by bucket-wielding temple attendants. Monday is Rama's auspicious day, when the Padilingam puja takes place. **Festivals** of particular importance at the temple include **Mahashivaratri** (ten days during Feb/March), **Brahmotsavam** (ten days during March/April) and **Thirukalyanam** (July/Aug), celebrating the marriage of Shiva to Parvati.

ARRIVAL AND INFORMATION   RAMESHWARAM

By train The railway station is 1km southwest of the centre; trains from Chennai and further afield all terminate here. There are daily services to Chennai Egmore (13hr 30min) via Trichy (5hr 30min) and Thanjavur (6hr 25min).

By bus The NH-49 links Madurai to Mandapam on the coast and the impressive 2km-long Indira Gandhi Bridge links the mainland to the island of Rameshwaram. Frequent services from Madurai (every 30min–1hr; 4hr),

Trichy (hourly; 7–8hr) and beyond arrive at the bus stand 2km west of the centre. Local bus #1 (every 10min) connects the bus stand, temple and railway station.

Tourist information The main TTDC tourist office, a dilapidated two-storey peach-coloured building next to the bus stand (daily 10am–5.45pm; ☎04573 221371) gives out information about guides, accommodation and boat trips, but opens rather erratically.

ACTIVITIES

Kitesurfing Gradually on the rise in India, kitesurfing can be enjoyed at several locations around the island, between Rameshwaram and Danushkodi, from around ₹1400/hr with Quest Asia (☏ 98203 67412, ⊚ thekitesurfingholiday .com), who can also provide accommodation with full board.

ACCOMMODATION

Accommodation in Rameshwaram comprises a mixture of basic old lodges in the streets round the temple and newer hotels, mostly in the direction of the transit points. The temple authorities also provide pilgrim rooms; ask at the Devasthanam Office, East Car St (☏ 04573 221223). During holidays and festivals, rooms are like gold dust and just as pricey.

Daiwik NH-49 near the bus stand ☏ 04573 223222, ⊚ daiwikhotels.com. This is one of several new hotels on the main highway into town. Immaculate, spacious and comfortable rooms with king-size beds and flatscreen TVs. Deluxe rooms ₹1000 more. On-site massage and restaurant. ₹**2600**

Island Star 41A South Car St ☏ 04573 221472. This is a fair-sized hotel with clean and pleasantly appointed rooms, most of which have sea views. The non-a/c rooms are quite good value; a/c doubles are over twice the price. No wi-fi. ₹**400**

Maharaja's 7 Middle St ☏ 04573 221271, ⊜ hotel maharajas@gmail.com. Located near the west gate of the temple, this hotel has clean and comfortable rooms with attached bathrooms and TV. Some rooms have temple views from the balcony. The a/c rooms cost double. No wi-fi. ₹**605**

Sri Kumaram 1/54 West Car St ☏ 90800 50040. Smart modern lodge that backs right onto the temple near the west *gopura*. The rooms are compact but neat and a/c rates are only fifty percent higher. ₹**1000**

★ **TTDC Tamil Nadu** Near the beach, 500m from the corner of North Car and East Car streets ☏ 04573 221277, ⊚ ttdconline.com. The best option in the temple area of Rameshwaram, situated in its own grounds with restaurant and bar. There are some sea-facing rooms and cheaper ones (a/c from ₹1500) in the new block with outdoor seats. Breakfast included. ₹**980**

Vinayaga 5 Railway Feeder Rd ☏ 04573 222361, ⊚ vinayagahotel.com. A pleasant hotel in a three-storey block just 100m from the railway station precinct. Clean and well kept, with 45 light, spacious and airy a/c rooms (deluxe rooms cost an extra ₹400). Removed from the temple area but quieter for it. ₹**2100**

EATING

Abhirami Shore Rd, near the east entrance to the main temple ☏ 04573 221178. Reasonably clean south-Indian veg joint on the way to the seashore, with street views from the tables. Lunchtime "meals" are served from 11.30am–3pm at the pilgrim price of ₹50. Daily 6.30am–11.30pm.

Ananda Bhavan 1/4 West Car St ☏ 97873 44774. Clean and spacious south-Indian-style restaurant serving good South Indian breakfasts. "Meals" available from 11.30am–3.30pm (₹70) plus pure-veg dishes costing under ₹100. Daily 7am–11pm.

Ganesh Mess Middle St, off Car St West ☏ 99940 63984. A small restaurant with just eight tables and pleasant and friendly service. The lunchtime "meals" cost ₹65 and they also serve masala dosas (₹40) and other South Indian snacks throughout the day. Daily 7.15am–10.30pm.

Saravana Bhavan 6 Middle St, off Car St West ☏ 04573 222733. Spotless franchise of the ever-popular and reliable chain, churning out copious quantities of snacks and meals, all under ₹100. This one also has a good bakery. Daily 7am–10.30pm.

TTDC Tamil Nadu Near the beach. Gigantic, noisy, high-ceilinged glass building serving all-you-can-eat pure veg breakfast, lunch and dinner buffets (from ₹80–130). There is also an a/c bar in the grounds opposite reception. Daily 7.30–10am, 12.30pm–2.30pm & 7.30–9.30pm.

Kanyakumari

At the southernmost extremity of India, **KANYAKUMARI** is almost as compelling for Hindus as Rameshwaram. It's significant not only for its association with a virgin goddess, Devi Kanyakumari, but also as the meeting point of the Bay of Bengal, Indian Ocean and Arabian Sea, thus regarded as a holy *sangam*. Watching the sun rise and set from here is the big attraction, especially on full-moon day in April, when it's possible to see both the setting sun and rising moon on the same horizon. Although Kanyakumari is in the state of Tamil Nadu, most foreign visitors arrive on day-trips from Kerala. While the place is of enduring appeal to pilgrims and those who just want to see India's tip, some may find it bereft of atmosphere, its magic obliterated by ugly concrete buildings and hawkers. Kanyakumari was devastated by the 2004 tsunami, although the seafront and jetty have since been rebuilt.

Kumari Amman Temple

Sannathi St • Daily 4.30am–12.15pm & 4–8.15pm

The shoreline **Kumari Amman Temple** is dedicated to the virgin goddess **Devi Kanyakumari**, who may have originally been the local guardian deity of the shoreline but was later absorbed into the figure of Devi, or Parvati, consort of Shiva. The image of Devi Kanyakumari inside the temple wears a diamond nose stud of such brilliance that it's said to be visible from the sea. Male visitors must be shirtless and wear a *dhoti* before entering the temple; non-Hindus are not allowed in the inner sanctum. It is especially auspicious for pilgrims to wash at the bathing *ghat* here.

Gandhi Mandapam

Daily 7am–7pm

Resembling a prewar British cinema, the **Gandhi Mandapam**, 300m northwest of the Kumari Amman Temple, was actually conceived as a modern imitation of an Odishan temple. It was so designed that at noon on October 2, Mahatma Gandhi's birthday, the sun strikes the auspicious spot where his ashes were laid prior to immersion in the sea.

The rocks

Ferry every 20min; daily 7.45am–4pm • ₹34, 150 people/boat

Possibly the original sacred focus of Kanyakumari were the two **rocks**, about 60m apart, jutting out of the sea 500m off the coast. They can be reached by the Poompuhar ferry service leaving from the jetty on the east side of town. Known as the Pitru and Matru *tirthas*, they attracted the attention of the Hindu reformer Vivekananda (1862–1902), who swam out to the rocks in 1892 to meditate on the syncretistic teachings of his recently dead guru, Ramakrishna Paramahamsa. Incorporating elements of architecture from around the country, the 1970 **Vivekananda Memorial** (daily 8am–4pm; ₹20; ⓦvivekanandakendra.org) houses a statue of the saint. The footprints of Devi Kanyakumari can also be seen here, at the spot where she performed her penance. The other rock features an imposing 40m-high statue of the ancient Tamil saint and poet **Thiruvalluvar**, who is revered throughout the state.

Wandering Monk Museum (Vivekananda Puram)

Beach Rd, just round the corner from Rock St • Daily 8am–noon & 4–8pm • ₹10

The small **Wandering Monk Museum** is dedicated to the life and teachings of Vivekananda, one of the first Hindu masters to take the teachings of *advaita* non-dualism to the West. The recently modernized exhibition in English, Tamil and Hindi concentrates on providing a meticulously detailed account of the *swami's* odyssey around the Subcontinent at the end of the nineteenth century, using a series of attractively illustrated panels.

ARRIVAL AND INFORMATION — KANYAKUMARI

By train Trains from all over the Subcontinent (even once a week from Jammu – at 70hr the longest rail journey in India) stop at the railway station in the north of town, 2km from the seafront, although even more services terminate at Nagercoil, only 10km away and connected by frequent buses.

Destinations from Kanyakumari or Nagercoil: Bengaluru (2–3 daily; 14hr–20hr 50min); Chennai (3 daily; 13hr 30min–15hr 50min); Coimbatore (3 daily; 11hr 5min–12hr 20min); Ernakulam for Kochi (5–7 daily; 5hr 10min–7hr 30min); Madurai (6–8 daily; 4hr 10min–7hr 40min); Mumbai (1–4 daily; 29hr 50min–45hr 45min); Thiruvananthapuram (7–9 daily; 1hr 30min–2hr 10min); Tiruchirapalli (3–4 daily; 7hr 10min–8hr 40min).

By bus The Express Bus Stand, near the lighthouse on the west side of town, has frequent services to Thiruvananthapuram and Madurai, plus regular buses to more distant destinations. Changing in Nagercoil sometimes gives you more options too.

Destinations Chennai (8 daily; 15–17hr); Kovalam (10–12 daily; 2hr); Madurai (every 30min; 5hr 30min–6hr); Puducherry (1 daily; 11–12hr); Rameshwaram (3 daily; 10hr); Thiruvananthapuram (every 30min–1hr; 2hr 30min–3hr); Tiruchirapalli (every 30min; 10–11hr).

Tourist information The main Tamil Nadu tourist office on Beach Rd (Mon–Fri 10am–1pm & 2–5.45pm; T 04652 246276) has maps and brochures.

ACCOMMODATION

★Lakshmi Tourist Home East Car St T 04652 246333. This small neat hotel is a popular choice, with comfortable rooms, some of which are sea-facing. Choice of non-a/c and a/c rooms (₹1500). There's also an excellent non-veg restaurant. No wi-fi. ₹650

Maadhini East Car St T 04652 246787, W hotelmaadhini.com. Large hotel right on the seafront above the fishing village. Comfortably furnished rooms (a/c ones a third more expensive), some with fine sea views. It has one of the best restaurants in town (see below), an a/c bar and a rooftop terrace. Wi-fi in lobby. ₹900

Manickam Tourist Home North Car St T 04652 246387, W hotelmanickam.com. Large hotel block and sister hotel to the *Maadhini* (same owners). It has spacious, clean rooms, some with balconies and sea views. Avoid the basement rooms. Also has a rooftop terrace. ₹800

Samudra Sannathi St T 04652 246162, E hotelsamudra@yahoo.com. Smart hotel towards the bottom of Sannathi St, near the temple entrance. It has forty well-furnished deluxe rooms (a/c ₹1600), all facing the sea. All rooms have cable TV and the hotel also has its own generator. ₹800

TTDC Tamil Nadu Near the lighthouse on Seafront T 04652 246257, W ttdconline.com. Up the hill and a little further from the temple and main drag. Choice of rooms (a/c ₹2100) in the main block or separate family cottages. The on-site restaurant (7.30–10pm) serves veg and non-veg. No wi-fi. ₹1500

7

EATING

Archana Maadhini East Car St T 04652 246787. A comfortable a/c basement dining-hall option that has an extensive veg and non-veg multicuisine menu for ₹80–250. In the evening you can also eat in the alfresco courtyard and they boast the town's widest selection of ice creams. Daily 7am–10.30pm.

Hotel Viswa Corner of South Car St and Periyar Main Rd T 04652 246047. Spotlessly clean corner joint with floral designs on the wall, hundreds of hanging bananas and great masala dosas for ₹50. Daily 7am–midnight.

Saravana Bhavan Sannathi St T 04652 246357. Opposite the *Samudra*, to which it belongs, this very large dining hall is arguably the best of Kanyakumari's many "meals" restaurants, although service can be slow. Serves the usual snacks in the morning and evening and ₹80 "meals" at lunchtime. Daily 6.30am–10pm.

Sebaa 2/19 South Car St T 04652 246396. On the corner with East Car St, this pleasant restaurant serves up a range of prawn and fish curries, mutton biryanis (₹240) and some chicken dishes for ₹150–200. Daily 11am–10.30pm.

Sree Devi Tiffin Stall Top of Rock St, at the junction with Beach Rd. Small but very popular local *dhaba*, serving *parathas*, omelettes and various snacks, along with a small selection of chicken curries (₹60). It's also a great place to sit, enjoy a chai and watch the world go by. Daily 6am–11pm.

The Ghats

Around sixty million years ago, what is today called peninsular India was a separate land mass drifting northwest across the ocean towards Central Asia. Geologists believe this mass originally broke off from the African continent along a fault line. This line is still discernible today as the north–south ridge of volcanic mountains, known as the **Western Ghats**, which stretch 1400km down the west coast of India. Rising to a height of around 2500m, it is India's second highest mountain chain after the Himalayas.

Forming a natural barrier between the Tamil plains and coastal Kerala and Karnataka, the Ghats (literally "steps") soak up the bulk of the southwest monsoon, which drains east to the Bay of Bengal via the mighty Kaveri and Krishna river systems. The massive amount of rain that falls here between June and October (around 2.5m) allows for an incredible **biodiversity**. Nearly one third of all India's flowering plants can be found in the dense evergreen and mixed deciduous forests cloaking the Ghats, while the woodland undergrowth supports the Subcontinent's richest array of wildlife.

It was this abundance of game, and the cooler temperatures of the range's high valleys and grasslands, that attracted the British away from the withering summer heat on the southern plains. They also realized the economic potential of the local climate, fertile soil and plentiful rainfall. As the forests were felled to make way for tea plantations, and the region's many tribal groups – among them the Todas – were forced deeper into the mountains, permanent **hill stations** were established. Today, as in the days of the Raj, these continue to provide welcome escapes from the incessant heat, as well as romantic getaways for the emergent Indian middle classes and nostalgia for foreign tourists.

The best known of the hill resorts is **Udhagamandalam** (formerly Ootacamund, and known just as "**Ooty**") nestling in the **Nilgiris** (from *nila-giri*, "blue mountains"). The ride up to Ooty on the **miniature railway** via Coonoor is fun, and the views breathtaking, but the town centre suffers from heavy traffic pollution and actually has little to offer. Further south and reached by a scenic switchback road, the other main hill station is **Kodaikanal**. The lovely walks around town provide views and fresh air in abundance, while the bustle of Indian tourists around the lake makes a pleasant change from life in the city.

The forest areas lining the state border harbour Tamil Nadu's principal **wildlife sanctuaries**, **Indira Gandhi** and **Mudumalai**, which comprise part of the vast **Nilgiri Biosphere Reserve**, the country's most extensive tract of protected forest. Road building, illegal felling, hydroelectric projects and overgrazing have whittled away large parts of this huge wilderness area over the past two decades, but what's left is still home to an array of wildlife. The main route between Mysuru and the cities of the Tamil plains wriggles through the Nilgiris, and you may well find yourself pausing for a night or two along the way. Whichever direction you're travelling in, a stopover in the dull textile city of **Coimbatore** is hard to avoid.

Kodaikanal

Perched on top of the Palani range, around 120km northwest of Madurai, **KODAIKANAL**, also known as **Kodai**, owes its perennial popularity to its hilltop position which, at an altitude of 2133m, affords breathtaking views over the blue-green reaches of the Vaigai plain. Raj-era bungalows and flower-filled gardens add atmosphere, while short walks out of the centre lead to rocky outcrops, waterfalls and dense *shola* forest. With the more northerly wildlife sanctuaries and forest areas of the Ghats closed to visitors, Kodai's outstandingly scenic hinterland also offers South India's best **trekking** terrain.

After a while in the South Indian plains, a retreat to Kodai's cool heights is more than welcome. However, in the height of summer (April–July) when temperatures compete with those in the lowlands, it's not worth the trip – nor is it a good idea to come during the monsoon (Oct–Dec), when the town is shrouded in mist and prone to heavy downpours. From January to early March the nights are chilly so the **peak tourist season** runs from April to June, when prices soar.

The lake

Kodai's focal point is its **lake**, sprawling like a giant amoeba over sixty acres just west of the town centre. This is a popular place for strolls or bike rides along the 5km path that fringes the water's edge; a leisurely circumambulation is a very pleasant way to while away an hour or two and also makes a good excuse for an evening indulging in Kodai's locally made chocolate. Pedal boats (₹70–140) and rowing boats (₹35 per person plus ₹60 for the boatman) can be rented on the eastern shore. Horseriding is also an option here – ₹100 to be led along the lakeside for 1km and ₹500 for an hour's ride. Shops, restaurants and hotels are concentrated in a rather congested area east of and downhill from the lake. The only monuments to Kodai's colonial past are the neat **British bungalows** that overlook the lake, and Law's Ghat Road on the eastern edge of town. The British first moved here in 1845, to be joined later by members of the American Mission, who set up schools for European children.

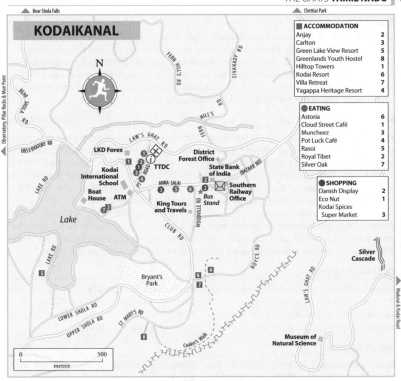

Bear Shola Falls   Chettiar Park

KODAIKANAL

ACCOMMODATION

Anjay	2
Carlton	3
Green Lake View Resort	5
Greenlands Youth Hostel	8
Hilltop Towers	1
Kodai Resort	6
Villa Retreat	7
Yagappa Heritage Resort	4

EATING

Astoria	6
Cloud Street Café	1
Muncheez	3
Pot Luck Café	4
Rasoi	5
Royal Tibet	2
Silver Oak	7

SHOPPING

Danish Display	2
Eco Nut	1
Kodai Spices Super Market	3

Observatory, Pillar Rocks & Moir Point

LKD Forex

Kodai International School

Boat House   ATM

Lake

District Forest Office

TTDC

ANNA SALAI

State Bank of India

King Tours and Travels

Bus Stand

Southern Railway Office

CLUB RD

Bryant's Park

NOYCE RD

Silver Cascade

Museum of Natural Science

Coaker's Walk

LOWER SHOLA RD   UPPER SHOLA RD   ST MARY'S RD

0   500
metres

Madurai & Kodai Road

7

Bryant's Park

Park Daily 9am–6.30pm, last entry 6pm · ₹30, camera ₹50, video camera ₹100 · **Coaker's Walk** Daily 7am–7pm · ₹10

Southeast of the lake is **Bryant's Park**, with tiered flowerbeds, rhododendrons, pine, eucalyptus and wattle. A flower show is held here in May. On the opposite side of the road a path, known as **Coaker's Walk**, skirts the precipitous hillside, winding from the *Villa Retreat* to *Greenlands Youth Hostel* (10min), offering remarkable views that stretch as far as Madurai on a clear day.

Pillar Rocks and Bear Shola Falls

One of Kodai's most popular natural attractions is the **Pillar Rocks**, 7km south of town, where a series of granite cliffs rise more than 100m above the hillside. To get here, follow the westbound Observatory Road from the northernmost point of the lake (a steep climb) until you come to a crossroads; the southbound road passes the gentle **Fairy Falls** on the way to Pillar Rocks. Some 2km west of the lake, the signposted **Bear Shola Falls** is now barely a trickle of water but remains a popular picnic and photo-stop for local tourists.

Museum of Natural Science

3km down Law's Ghat Rd · Daily except Tues 10am–5pm · ₹10, camera ₹10

Downhill and southeast of the town centre, within the premises of Sacred Heart College, the **Museum of Natural Science** has a very uninviting array of stuffed animals. However, the spectacular orchid house contains one of India's best collections, which can be viewed by appointment only; ask at the tourist office (see p.430).

Chettiar Park

On the very northeast edge of town, around 3km from the lake at the end of a winding uphill road, **Chettiar Park** has an abundance of trees and flowers all year round. Every twelve years it is also flushed with a haze of pale-blue **Kurinji blossoms** (the next flowering is due in 2018). These unusual flowers are associated with the god Murugan, the Tamil form of Karttikeya (Shiva's second son), and god of Kurinji, one of five ancient divisions of the Tamil country. A temple in his honour stands just outside the park.

ARRIVAL AND DEPARTURE   KODAIKANAL

By train Tickets for onward rail journeys from Kodai Rd can be booked at the Southern Railway office, at the GPO – follow signs for the Philatelic Counter (Mon–Fri 9.30am–1.30pm & 2.30–3.30pm, Sat 9.30am–noon). Several travel agents in town, such as King Tours and Travels on Woodville Rd (☏ 04542 243357, ⊛ kodaikingtravels.com), can reserve trains, buses and planes within South India.

By bus The buses from Madurai and Dindigul that climb the steep road up to Kodai pull in at the stand in the centre of town. There are two roads to Kodaikanal: the less-used

route from Palani is by far the more spectacular approach, and during the monsoon may be the only one open. Unless you're travelling long distances the bus is more convenient than the train, as the nearest railhead, Kodai Rd, is 3hr away by bus. The TNSTC reservation counter (daily 10am–1pm & 2–4pm) is at the bus station.

Destinations Coimbatore (2 daily; 6hr); Madurai (15 daily; 4hr); Palani (10 daily; 3hr). There are also daily ultra-deluxe SETC departures to Bengaluru (5.30pm; 12hr), Chennai (6.30pm; 12hr) and Kanyakumari (9am; 10hr).

GETTING AROUND

By taxi Taxis line Anna Salai in the centre of town, offering sightseeing at high fixed rates (₹900/half-day).

By bike Bicycles are a popular and convenient way to travel both in and around Kodaikanal. They can be rented

from the bike stall on Anna Salai or from numerous stalls around the lake (₹20/hr or around ₹100/day). While freewheeling downhill is fun, what goes down must come up, so walking is usually the best bet.

INFORMATION

Tourist information The tourist office (Mon–Fri 10am–5.45pm; ☏ 04542 241675) on PT Rd is minimally helpful. *Greenlands Youth Hostel* (see below) can arrange treks of varying lengths, such as the 5hr trek in the hills around Kodaikanal itself or the three-day trek of moderate

difficulty across the mountains to Munnar in Kerala. Rates depend on group numbers.

Services There are several foreign exchange places; the State Bank of India and Canara Bank are both on Anna Salai.

ACCOMMODATION

Kodaikanal's inexpensive **lodges** are grouped at the lower end of Anna Salai. It is worth asking whether blankets and hot water are provided (the latter should be free, but you may be charged in budget places).

Anjay Anna Salai ☏ 04542 241089, ⊛ hotelanjay.com. Simple, clean and pleasant hotel centrally located near the bus stand. Rooms are smarter than you'd expect from the outside, all with balconies and TV; the deluxe rooms (from ₹100 more) have the best views. **₹700**

Carlton Off Lake Rd ☏ 04542 240056, ⊛ kraheja hospitality.com. The most luxurious hotel in Kodaikanal, a spacious, tastefully renovated and well-maintained colonial house overlooking the lake. All rooms have a lake view and exude Raj-era charm. There are also cottages within the grounds, a restaurant, bar and comfortable lounge. All rates include full board. Wi-fi ₹100/hr. **₹9700**

Green Lake View Resort 11/213 Lake Rd ☏ 04542 242384, ⊛ greenlakeviewresort.com. Pleasant resort set in its own extensive grounds on a quiet corner of the lake with lovely gardens and swings. There is a wide range of

different rooms priced, according to size and hot water availability. No wi-fi. **₹2500**

★**Greenlands Youth Hostel** Coaker's Walk, off St Mary's Rd ☏ 04542 241099, ⊛ greenlands kodaikanal.com. An attractive old stone house with unrivalled views and sunsets from its deep verandas. There's a variety of decent-sized rooms with wooden beds, colourful linens and attached bathrooms, plus also a dorm. Very popular with groups, so book ahead. Dorms **₹300**, doubles **₹1200**

Hilltop Towers Club Rd ☏ 04542 240413, ⊛ hilltop group.in. Decent hotel, 5min from the lake, with modern, comfortable rooms featuring arched doors, large beds and TV. There's also a cosy and romantic honeymoon suite with a circular bed, plus three good restaurants and a bakery. **₹2100**

Kodai Resort Noyce Rd, near Coaker's Walk ☎04542 241301, ⓦkodairesorthotel.com. Large complex of fifty incongruous-looking but very pleasant cottages housing comfortable bedrooms with king-sized beds, TVs and huge individual roof terraces with good views. Also a health club, restaurant and resident emu. Wi-fi in lobby. ₹2900

Villa Retreat Coaker's Walk, off Club Rd ☎04542 240940, ⓦvillaretreat.com. Comfortable old stone house, with more character than most, situated in lovely gardens that afford superb views. Though a touch over-priced, rooms (priced according to views) have 24hr hot water; some also have real fires. Wi-fi in lobby. ₹2900

Yagappa Heritage Resort Noyce Rd ☎04542 241235, ⓔyagapparesort@yahoo.com. Good mid-range budget option with very clean rooms in three buildings, set around a lawn-cum-courtyard with views to the rear. There's a choice of standard and deluxe rooms (with balcony) and a small dining area for guests only. ₹2200

EATING

Astoria Anna Salai ☎04542 240524. Large clean dining area that dishes up ample quantities of South Indian "meals" (₹115–155) and all the usual snacks and standard menu items. Daily 7am–10pm.

Cloud Street Café PT Rd ☎04542 246425. Large, pleasant, upstairs café with travellers' vibe and secondhand book swap. Veggie breakfasts with mushrooms, tomatoes and beans are served until 11.30am after which there are wood-oven pizzas (from ₹410), pasta, cakes and chocolate brownies. Occasional live music. Daily 9am–9pm.

★**Muncheez** PT Rd ☎04542 240046. Mostly a take-away joint with a single pavement table, you can choose your own fillings for their excellent Mexican-style wraps (₹60–150); they also do burgers, potato wedges and desserts. Daily 11am–9.30pm.

Pot Luck Café PT Rd ☎04542 240244. Tiny café with just two tables squeezed onto a narrow veranda serving travellers' favourites (mostly ₹100–150), including pancakes, club sandwiches, burgers, spaghetti and tempting drinks such as Mayan hot chocolate. Daily except Tues 9am–5.30pm.

Rasoi Anna Salai, above the Cocoa Bean ☎98651 04664. Tiny first-floor *dhaba* with just eight tables, serving delicious Punjabi and Gujarati food for ₹100–175: excellent *aloo parathas*, a range of North Indian vegetarian dishes, limited Punjabi thalis and unlimited Gujarati thalis. Daily 10am–10pm.

★**Royal Tibet** J's Heritage Complex, PT Rd ☎04542 243804. Small, friendly Tibetan joint, serving thick home-made bread and particularly tasty *momos*, soups and noodles. There's a range of chicken, mutton, beef and vegetarian dishes, including some Indian and Chinese, all for under ₹150. Daily noon–4pm & 5.30–9pm.

Silver Oak Carlton hotel, off Lake Rd ☎04542 240056. Splash out at Kodai's top hotel on its evening buffet spread (veg and non-veg; ₹850), rounded off with a *chhota* peg of Scotch in the bar. Lunchtime buffet also available (₹800), as are à la carte items. Daily 7.30–10am, 12.30–3pm & 7.30–10.30pm.

SHOPPING

Danish Display Anna Salai ☎04542 242455. Lots of handicrafts and trinkets to be found here, from religious items to wood and bronze ornaments, plus colourful clothes and scarves. Mon–Sat 9.30am–9pm, Sun 11.30am–9pm.

Eco Nut J's Heritage Complex, PT Rd ☎04542 243296. One of South India's few bona fide Western-style wholefood shops, and a great place to stock up on trekking supplies: muesli, home-made jams, breads, pickles and muffins, high-calorie "nutri-balls" and delicious cheeses from Auroville. Daily 9am–5.30pm.

Kodai Spices Super Market Anna Salai ☎98421 98894. All sorts of spices, herbs, honey and nuts can be found here, good for travels or the cupboard at home. Daily 9am–9pm.

Indira Gandhi (Anamalai) Wildlife Sanctuary

Indira Gandhi (Anamalai) Wildlife Sanctuary is a 958-square-kilometre tract of forest on the southern reaches of the Cardamom Hills, 37km southwest of the busy junction town of **Pollachi**. Vegetation ranges from *shola*-grassland to dry deciduous to tropical evergreen, and the sanctuary is home to lion-tailed macaques (black-maned monkeys), gaur, sambar, spotted and barking deer, sloth bear, as well as leopards and tigers. Birds such as hornbills and frogmouths are also seen here. It's possible to **trek** through the giant creaking stands of bamboo with a guide and the Forestry Department also runs **safari tours** by minibus and **elephant safaris**. For reservations, contact the park reception office (see p.432).

ARRIVAL AND DEPARTURE   INDIRA GANDHI (ANAMALAI) WILDLIFE SANCTUARY

By bus There are good bus connections between Pollachi and both Coimbatore and Palani. From Pollachi there are three buses a day (6.15am, 11.15am & 3.15pm) up to the park's reception centre (☎ 04253 238360) at Top Slip.
By car/taxi Rented cars/taxis, available at Pollachi, run to

the official entrance at the Sethumadai checkpost from 6.30am–6pm daily. Private vehicles can drive into the park with prior permission from the Field Director, Wildlife Warden Office, 178 Meenkarai Rd, Pollachi (☎ 04253 225356).

ACCOMMODATION AND EATING

The Forestry Department runs six **resthouses**, ranging from the basic *Hornbill* to the luxurious *Pillar Top*. Most are within easy walking distance of the reception centre and should be booked in advance through the Field Director in Pollachi. The canteen next to the reception centre serves basic **meals** and drinks and the local shop has equally basic provisions.

Coimbatore

Visitors tend only to use the busy industrial city of **COIMBATORE** as a stopover on the way to Ooty, 90km northwest. Once you've climbed up to your hotel rooftop to admire the blue, cloud-capped haze of the Nilgiris in the west, there's little to do here other than kill time wandering through the nuts-and-bolts bazaars, lined with lookalike textile showrooms, "General Traders" and shops selling motor parts.

ARRIVAL AND DEPARTURE   COIMBATORE

By train For Ooty, catch the daily #12671 *Nilagiri Express* at 5.15am, which gets into Mettupalayam at 6.15am, in time to connect with the Toy Train (see box, p.436) for Ooty.
By bus Coimbatore has half a dozen bus stands, linked to each other and the railway station by local buses from the busy Central Bus Stand, 2km north of the railway station. The Thiruvalluvar Bus Stand is the main state and interstate station, while most buses to and from Ooty, Coonoor and Mettupalayam use the Mettupalayam New Bus Stand 4km

north of town. The south of town holds a fourth bus stand, Ukkadam, which serves Palani, Pollachi, Madurai, Trichy and towns in northern Kerala.
Destinations Chennai (every 30min–1hr; 7–8hr); Kodaikanal (4 daily; 6hr); Madurai (every 30min; 5–6hr); Udhagamandalam (Ooty) (every 30min; 3hr 30min–4hr); Palani (hourly; 2hr 30min–3hr); Pollachi (every 30min; 1hr); Tiruchirapalli (every 30min; 5hr).

ACCOMMODATION AND EATING

City Tower 56 Sivasamy Rd ☎ 0422 223 6999, ⓦ hotel citytower.com. A smart high-rise hotel, 5min walk south of the Central Bus Stand, with decent rooms featuring leatherette and vinyl. The "executive" rooms are more spacious and have a minibar and balcony; a/c about half as much again. Quality multicuisine restaurant. ₹1450
KK Residency 7 Shastri Rd ☎ 0422 430 0222, ⓦ hotel kkresidency.com. Large, business-style hotel in a tower block behind the Central Bus Stand, with very clean rooms (a/c ₹1300; good deals for single occupancy) and two good restaurants. ₹700
★ **Naalukettu** Nehru St opposite the Blue Star ☎ 0422 223 1402. Stylish, clean and reasonably priced restaurant with nice courtyard garden and interior. It serves a range

of veg and non-veg food including various biryanis (₹150), including prawn, and chicken dishes. Daily noon–10.30pm.
New Vijaya Lodge 8/81 Geetha Hall Rd ☎ 0422 230 1570, ⓔ newvijayalodgemka@yahoo.com. Close to the railway station and one of the best (of many) budget options on this street. Rooms (a/c ₹1000) are clean, simple and compact, with TV, hot water in the mornings and towels provided. ₹550
TTDC Tamil Nadu 2 Dr Nanjappa Rd ☎ 0422 230 2177, ⓦ ttdconline.com. Conveniently located opposite the Central Bus Stand, with clean, pleasant rooms (a/c ₹1400). There's a tourist information service and its own very good restaurant next door. Often fully booked, so phone ahead. ₹975

Coonoor

At an altitude of 1858m, **COONOOR**, a scruffy bazaar and tea-planters' town on the Nilgiri Blue Mountain Railway (see box, p.436) lies at the head of the Hulikal ravine, on the southeastern side of the Dodabetta mountains, 27km north of Mettupalayam and 19km south of Ooty. Thanks to its proximity to its more famous neighbour, Coonoor has avoided Ooty's overcommercialization, and can make a pleasant place for a short stop.

COONOOR'S TEA ESTATES

Visible from far away as tiny orange or red dots amid the green vegetation, **tea-pickers** work the slopes around Coonoor, carrying wicker baskets of fresh leaves and bamboo rods that they use like rulers to ensure that each plant is evenly plucked. Once the leaves reach the factory, they're processed within a day, producing seven grades of tea. **Orange pekoe** is the best and most expensive; the seventh lowest grade, a dry dust of stalks and leaf swept up at the end of the process, will be sold on to make instant tea. To visit a tea or coffee plantation, contact **UPASI** (United Planters' Association of Southern India) at Glenview House, Coonoor (☏0423 223 0270, ⓦupasi.org), just along from *Vivek Tourist Home*. Or you can go directly to one such as **High Field Estate** (Mon–Sat 9am–5pm; free; ☏0423 223 0023), less than 2km past Sim's Park; it also has a fine shop.

Coonoor consists of two "levels", **Lower Coonoor**, with its small but atmospheric hill market, which specializes in leaf tea and fragrant essential oils and **Upper Coonoor**, with its old Raj-era bungalows and narrow lanes with flower-filled hedgerows. At the top lies **Sim's Park**, a lush botanical garden on the slopes of a ravine with hundreds of rose varieties (daily 7am–6.30pm; ₹30, camera ₹50, video camera ₹100).

Around the town, rolling hills and valleys carpeted with spongy green tea bushes and stands of eucalyptus and silver oak offer some of the most beautiful scenery in the Nilgiris, immortalized in many a Hindi-movie dance sequence. Cinema fans from across the South flock here to visit key locations from their favourite blockbusters, among them **Lamb's Nose** (5km) and **Dolphin's Nose** (9km), former British picnicking spots with paved pathways and dramatic views of the Mettupalayam plains. If you take an early morning bus to Dolphin's Nose, it's possible to walk the 9km back into town via Lamb's Nose – a very pleasant scenic amble that takes you through tea estates and dense forest.

ARRIVAL AND DEPARTURE   COONOOR

By train The railway station is in Lower Coonoor across the bazaar from the bus station. There are four trains daily to Ooty (7.45am, 10.40am, 12.35pm & 4.30pm) and one daily service to Mettupalayam at 3.15pm, which arrives at 5.30pm. The ticket office is open daily 7.30am–5.30pm.

By bus Buses to and from Mettupalayam, Coimbatore, Kotagiri and Ooty all use the bus stand, a large blue building at the entrance to Lower Coonoor. Local buses run to Dolphin's Nose every 2hr, starting at 7am.

ACCOMMODATION

There are a few decent places to stay in Coonoor but it's spread over a wide area, so it's best to arrive early to look for a room; you'll need an auto-rickshaw to find most of the hotels. Those around the bus stand are either not worth staying in or won't accept foreigners. Expect to pay around ₹60 from the bus stand to Bedford Circle or jump on a bus bound for Kotagiri.

Gateway (By Taj Group) Church Rd, Upper Coonoor ☏0423 222 5400, ⓦtajhotels.com. Luxurious colonial-era hotel with spectacular views from the gardens. Ayurvedic treatments, excellent lunchtime buffets and a range of sports and activities. The largest "superior" rooms cost up to ₹10,000 but there are usually good online discounts. ₹4750

Highfield Stay High Field, 1.5km beyond Sim's Park ☏0423 222 2299, ⓦhighfieldstay.com. Huge, comfortably furnished rooms in an attractive building amidst a tea plantation. Guests are charged ₹1000 each and there is food on demand. The owners have another property 4km further out. ₹2000

Velan (aka Ritz) Ritz Rd, Bedford Circle ☏0423 223 0784, ⓦvelanhotels.com. Mid-range hotel with character,

set in a great location on the outskirts of town. It has deep balconies, fine views and spacious rooms – the standard rooms have tiled floors, while the deluxe suites (₹3000) have wooden floors. Good restaurant. ₹2000

Vivek Tourist Home 42 Figure of Eight Rd, near Bedford Circle ☏0423 223 0658, ⓦhotelvivek.com. Clean rooms in a slightly institutional atmosphere; some have tiny balconies overlooking the lawn and tea terraces. Standard rooms have hot water by bucket only in the morning; deluxe rooms (₹2000) have 24hr hot showers. ₹1100

★YWCA Guest House Wyoming, near Nankem hospital, 500m down from Bedford Circle ☏0423 223 4426, ⓦywcaagooty.com. There are only fourteen rooms

7

– five doubles, five singles (₹700) and dorms – in this Victorian-era house, full of character on a bluff overlooking town. Superb home-cooked meals are available at very reasonable rates, and there's a flower garden with fine views of the tea terraces. No alcohol or wi-fi. Dorms ₹180, doubles ₹970

EATING

Dragon Bedford Circle ☎0423 223 2158. Chinese restaurant serving up authentic Chinese dishes including spring rolls, a range of chop suey, chow mein and a few Indian dishes, all in the ₹100–200 range. Daily 10am–4pm & 6.30–11pm.

★**Hyderabad Biriyani House** Cash Bazaar, Lower Coonoor ☎0423 223 2223. Spanking new first-floor restaurant and a splendid selection of filling biryanis for around ₹200, as well as other veg, chicken, mutton, fish and prawn dishes. Good service and free wi-fi. Daily 11am–11pm.

Mirchi Bedford Circle ☎90035 57477. Clean restaurant with pleasant decor serving a range of veg and non-veg Indian food (₹120–220), including a selection of spicy Chettinad dishes. Also serves soups (₹70) and lunchtime "meals". Daily 10am–11pm.

Sri Ramachendra Lunch Home Cash Bazaar, Lower Coonoor ☎0423 220 6309. Simple pure-veg place serving traditional South Indian breakfasts and great lunchtime "meals" for only ₹60. Could do with a lick of paint but clean enough. Daily 6.30am–9.30pm.

Kotagiri

Forming the third point of an almost equilateral triangle with Coonoor and Ooty, **KOTAGIRI** is another tea town, which sees far fewer visitors than its more famous neighbours. It is for that very reason that it is worth making the detour here, in order to stroll along the ridges draped with vivid green tea plantations or among the locals busying themselves in the lively little bazaar on the hill above the bus stand. Further downhill to the south, the town's most notable building is the huge yellow 1867 **St Mary's Church**, built by an order of Franciscan nuns.

ARRIVAL AND DEPARTURE KOTAGIRI

By bus Kotagiri is served by buses from Coonoor (every 20–30min; 1hr) and Ooty (every 30min–1hr; 1hr 15min).

ACCOMMODATION AND EATING

Suthy's Resort On the main road into town ☎04266 272444, ⊕suthysresorts.com. Surprisingly palatial two-storey building with unique floral designs in the guest rooms and elsewhere. Smart multicuisine restaurant and superb views across the valley. ₹2000

Top Hill Lodge Uphill from the bazaar ☎04266 271473. Large block perched on a hill, which offers average-sized, cleanish rooms at inexpensive rates, though service is a little lackadaisical. No restaurant or wi-fi. ₹600

Udhagamandalam (Ooty)

In the early nineteenth century, when the British burra sahib John Sullivan first ventured into this region of the Nilgiris through the Hulikal ravine and "discovered" **UDHAGAMANDALAM** (anglicized to **Ootacamund**, abbreviated to Ooty), the territory was the traditional homeland of the pastoralist **Toda** hill tribe. Until this moment, the Todas had lived in almost total isolation from the cities of the surrounding plains and Deccan plateau lands. Sullivan quickly realized the agricultural potential of the area, acquired tracts of land for ₹1 per acre from the Todas, and set about planting flax, barley and hemp, as well as potatoes, soft fruit and, most significantly, **tea**, all of which flourished in the mild climate. Within twenty years, the former East India Company clerk had made a fortune. Needless to say, he was soon joined by other fortune-seekers, and a town was built, complete with artificial lake, churches and stone houses that wouldn't have looked out of place in Surrey or the Scottish Highlands. **Ooty** was the "Queen of Hill Stations" and the most popular hill retreat in India outside the Himalayas.

By a stroke of delicious irony, the Todas outlived the colonists whose cash crops originally displaced them – but only just. Having retreated with their buffalo into the surrounding hills and wooded valleys, they continue to preserve a more-or-less traditional way of life, albeit in greatly diminished numbers. Until the mid-1970s "Snooty Ooty" continued to be "home" to the notoriously snobbish British inhabitants who chose to "stay on" after Independence. Since then, visitors have continued to be attracted by Ooty's cool climate and peaceful green hills, forest and grassland. However, indiscriminate **development** and a deluge of domestic holiday-makers mean that the quaint vestiges of the Raj have been somewhat diluted and are now few and far between.

Situated 2286m above sea level, the town sprawls over a large area with plenty of winding roads and steep climbs. The focal point is **Charing Cross**, a busy junction at the end of **Commercial Road**, the main shopping street running south to the Big Bazaar and municipal vegetable market.

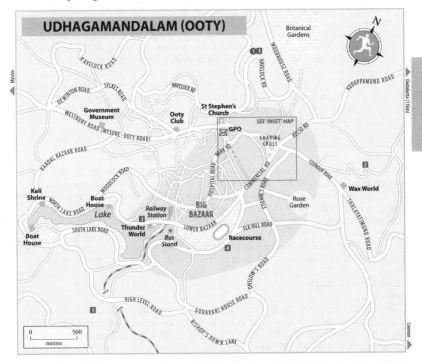

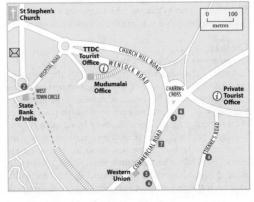

ACCOMMODATION	
Co-operators Guest House	6
Hills Palace	7
King's Cliff	1
Reflections Guest House	3
Regency Royale Villas	5
Sherlock	2
YWCA Anandagiri	4

● EATING	
Chandan	3
Earl's Secret	1
Hyderabad Biriyani House	5
Preethi Palace	4
Shinkows	2
Willy's	6

7

THE NILGIRI BLUE MOUNTAIN RAILWAY

The famous narrow-gauge **Nilgiri Blue Mountain Railway** climbs up from Mettupalayam on the plains, via Hillgrove (17km) and Coonoor (27km) to Udhagamandalam, a journey of 46km that passes through sixteen tunnels, eleven stations and nineteen bridges. It's a slow haul of four and a half hours or more – sometimes the train moves little faster than walking pace, and always takes at least twice as long as the bus – but the **views** are absolutely magnificent, especially along the steepest sections in the Hulikal ravine.

The line was built between 1890 and 1908, paid for by the tea-planters and other British inhabitants of the Nilgiris. It differs from India's two comparable narrow-gauge lines, to Darjeeling and Shimla, for its use of the so-called **Swiss rack system**, by means of which the tiny locomotives are able to climb gradients of up to 1 in 12.5. Special bars were set between the track rails to form a ladder, which cogs of teeth, connected to the train's driving wheels, engage like a zip mechanism. Because of this novel design, only the original locomotives can still run the steepest stretches of line, which is why the section between Mettupalayam and Coonoor has remained one of South Asia's last functioning **steam routes**. The chuffing and whistle screeches of the tiny train, echoing across the valleys as it pushes its blue-and-cream carriages up to Coonoor (where a diesel locomotive takes over) rank among the most romantic sounds of South India, conjuring up the determined gentility of the Raj era. Even if you don't count yourself as a trainspotter, a boneshaking ride on the Blue Mountain Railway should be a priority.

Botanical Gardens

Woodhouse Rd • Daily 7am–6.30pm • ₹30, camera ₹50, video camera ₹100 • ☏ 0423 244 2545

A little way north of Charing Cross, the **Botanical Gardens**, laid out in 1847 by gardeners from London's Kew Gardens, consist of fifty acres of immaculate lawns, lily ponds and beds, with more than a thousand varieties of shrubs, flowers and trees. There's a refreshment stand in the park, and shops in the small Tibetan market sell ice creams and snacks. The **Rose Garden** (same hours and fees), south of Charing Cross along a lane off Etienne's Road, has 2800 varieties of rose and is the largest collection in the whole of India. It's worth a visit for any budding botanists and gardeners, particularly in season, when the flowers proudly flaunt their petals and perfumes.

St Stephen's Church

Mysore–Ooty road

Northwest of Charing Cross, the small Gothic-style **St Stephen's Church** was one of Ooty's first colonial structures, built in the 1820s on the site of a Toda temple; timber for its bowed teak roof was taken from Tipu Sultan's palace at Srirangapatna and hauled up here by elephant. The area around the church gives some idea of what the hill station must have looked like in the days of the Raj. To the right is the rambling and rather dilapidated **Spencer's store**, which opened in 1909 and sold everything a British home in the colonies could ever need; it's now a computer college.

The lake

Boathouse daily 9am–6pm • ₹10, camera ₹20, video camera ₹125

Situated in the southwest corner of Ooty, the long and narrow **lake**, constructed in the early 1800s, is still one of Ooty's main tourist attractions, despite being somewhat polluted by sewage. The circumference of the lake is about 4.5km and makes for a very pleasant walk, conveniently peppered with juice and chai stalls. Renting one of a range of lake-worthy vessels from the busy **boathouse** is a quintessential part of the domestic holiday scene, with a small percentage of foreigners also choosing to brave the waters. Once inside the boathouse, various boats can be rented (pedal boats ₹120–200, rowing boats ₹145–185, charter motor boats seating 8–15 people ₹420–1800). Back outside, you can hire a horse and ride around the lake for ₹400 per hour. Another increasingly popular feature of destinations like Ooty is theme parks and North Lake Road now boasts Thunder World (daily 10am–8.30pm; ₹10, unlimited rides ₹300), India's largest dinosaur park. It's predictably cheesy but kids might enjoy the various rides and seeing the giant model creatures on display.

Wax World

Dodabetta Rd • Daily 9.30am–6.30pm • ₹30, camera ₹10 • ☎ 97903 43296, ⓦ waxworld.in

A kilometre from Charing Cross, **Wax World** is a rather lifeless exhibition of twenty famous and infamous social and political figures, mostly from the twentieth century. Interesting in its own way, and with helpful guides to commentate, you may pick up the odd historical nugget. Watch out for the "disturbing scene". There are no Bollywood divas or sports heroes as yet.

ARRIVAL AND DEPARTURE

UDHAGAMANDALAM (OOTY)

By train Ooty's station for the miniature Nilgiri Blue Mountain Railway (see box opposite) from Coonoor and Mettupalayam is near Big Bazaar and close to the bus station. The station has a booking office (6.30am–7pm), where you can buy tickets for the little train, and a reservation counter (daily 8am–12.30pm & 2.30–4.30pm) for booking onward services to most other destinations in the South. Four trains daily (9.15am, 12.15pm, 2pm & 6pm) pootle down the narrow-gauge track to Coonoor but only the 2pm train continues down to Mettupalayam, on the main broad-gauge network, arriving at 6.30pm. If you are Chennai-bound you can connect with the daily #12672 *Nilagiri Express*, which departs at 7.45pm.

By bus Buses from all destinations arrive at the bus stand, in the southwest of Ooty, near the racecourse and Big Bazaar. Auto-rickshaws and taxis are available just outside the bus stand. There is an enquiry office (daily 7am–8pm) on the left side of the station (as you enter) on the first floor. Both Tamil Nadu and Karnataka State Transport run regular and super-deluxe state buses out of Ooty.

Destinations Bengaluru (9 daily; 7–8hr), Masingudi (4 daily; 2hr–2hr 30min), Mettupalayam (every 10 min; 2hr), Mysuru (every 30min; 4hr 30min–5hr) and other destinations in Tamil Nadu and Kerala. Private buses to Mysuru, Bengaluru and Kodaikanal can be booked at the bigger hotels and agents dotted around the town.

INFORMATION

Tourist information The TTDC tourist office (Mon–Fri 10am–5.45pm; ☎ 0423 244 3977) is next door to the TTDC *Hotel Tamil Nadu* just above Wenlock Rd. You can book tours here, including a mammoth day-trip (daily 9am–8pm; ₹300/head or ₹2500/car) that includes Kamarajasagar Dam, Mudumalai and a jungle ride. There's also a day-trip around Ooty and Coonoor (daily 9am–6pm; ₹250/head, ₹1400/car), which goes to Ooty Lake, Doddabetta Peak, the Botanical Gardens, Sim's Park, Lamb's Nose, Dolphin's Nose and a tea garden. There's an erratically opening private

tourist information centre (Mon–Fri 10am–1pm & 2–6pm) in the clock tower building at Charing Cross that gives out leaflets and hotel information. The Mudumalai Forest Ranger Officer's office (Mon–Fri 10am–1pm & 2–5.45pm; ☎ 0423 244 4098, ⓦ mudumalaitigerfoundation.in) is just up behind the TTDC office.

Services The State Bank of India on West Town Circle changes currency, as does the Western Union Office on Commercial Rd.

ACCOMMODATION

Ooty's **accommodation** is a lot more expensive than in many places in India and during the peak season (April and May), prices can rise by thirty to a hundred percent. It also gets very crowded, so you may have to hunt around.

Co-operators Guest House Commercial Rd, just along from Charing Cross ☎ 0423 244 4046. This centrally located hotel is a good budget option. Set slightly back from the main road, the Raj-era building has clean rooms and yellow-and-turquoise balconies overlooking a courtyard. No wi-fi. **₹750**

Hills Palace Commercial Rd ☎ 0423 244 6483, ⓦ egh planet.com. Centrally located place set back from the main road and insulated from the traffic noise. Friendly, with spotlessly clean rooms (bigger rooms cost an extra ₹400), all with 24hr hot water and TV. Cheaper rates during

weekdays. No wi-fi. **₹1200**

King's Cliff Havelock Rd ☎ 0423 245 2888, ⓦ littlearth .in. Imposing ancestral mansion with nine lavishly furnished rooms, executive, standard and deluxe (₹4975), each with a Shakespearean theme. The place is full of character and has a stylish lounge and dining room. **₹2475**

★ **Reflections Guest House** North Lake Rd ☎ 0423 244 3834, ✉ reflectionsin@yahoo.co.in. Homely, relaxing guesthouse by the lake, just 5min walk from the railway station. Rooms open onto a small terrace and most have lake views. Limited food menu. Easily the best budget option in Ooty, but it's small and fills up quickly, so book in advance. ₹770

Regency Royale Villas Fernhill Post, High Level Rd ☎0423 2443911, ⓦwelcomheritagehotels.in. Luxury heritage hotel in converted Fernhills Palace, the maharaja of Mysore's former summer residence. The original exterior remains, but the ninteeen rooms and cottages were undergoing further renovation at the time of writing, so check the website for reopening and the new rates.

★**Sherlock** Tiger Hill Rd, 3km east of Charing Cross ☎0423 244 4000, ⓦlittlearth.in. Beautifully landscaped Victorian mansion with a Conan Doyle theme and stunning views from the grassy terrace. All nine rooms, standard or deluxe (₹3975), are tastefully furnished and have sitouts. Cheaper during the week. Friendly service and good food, too. ₹2975

YWCA Anandagiri Etienne's Rd ☎0423 244 4262, ⓦywcaagooty.com. Charming 1920s building set in spacious grounds near the racecourse. There are seven different types of room (tariffs vary according to size and hot water availability), bungalows and four dorms. Excellent value and popular, so best book ahead. No wi-fi. Dorms ₹200, doubles ₹800

EATING

Chandan Nahar hotel, Commercial Rd, near Charing Cross. Carefully prepared North Indian specialities, including a selection of tandoori vegetarian dishes, and some Chinese, served inside a posh restaurant. The complex also has a South Indian garden restaurant and a café. Main courses ₹180–290. Daily 12.30–3.30pm & 7.30–10.30pm.

Earl's Secret King's Cliff hotel, Havelock Rd ☎0423 245 2888. Extensive menu of more than two hundred quality dishes, including quail, chicken, seafood and veggie as well as delicious home-baked desserts, served in atmospheric surroundings. Expect to pay ₹350–500 for a main course. The hotel's resident singer/guitarist serenades diners from 8.45pm. Daily noon–3pm & 7–11pm.

Hyderabad Biriyani House Walsham Rd ☎0423 244 5080. Small, brightly lit, modern restaurant in the thick of the market that dishes up excellent filling biryanis and a range of other dishes for around ₹180–250. Free wi-fi. Daily 11am–11pm.

★**Preethi Palace** Etienne's Rd near Charing Cross ☎0423 244 2789. Excellent and very popular restaurant serving great lunchtime "meals" (Bengali ₹120, North Indian and Gujarati ₹180) and a range of delicious pure-veg Jain food throughout the day. Daily 7am–10pm.

Shinkows 42 Commissioners Rd ☎0423 244 2811. Good-value, authentic Chinese restaurant serving decent-sized portions on the spicy and pricey side – main meat and fish courses are around ₹200–300, veggie dishes ₹80–160. Daily noon–4pm & 6.30–10pm.

Willy's KRC Arcade, Walsham Rd ☎0423 244 8646. Second-floor café with a laidback ambience and 70s-style dolphin mural, where you can chill out over a coffee, cake, toasted sandwich or Indian snack (all under ₹100) and browse the impressive lending library. Wi-fi ₹30/hr. Daily 10am–10pm.

Mudumalai Wildlife Sanctuary

Elephant Camp Daily 8.30–9am & 5.30–6pm • ₹15 • **Elephant safari** Daily 7–8am & 4–5pm • ₹865/up to four people • **Vehicle safari tour** Daily 7–9am & 3–5.30pm; 40min • ₹135/person, camera ₹25, video camera ₹150 • ☎0423 252 6235, ⓦmudumalaitigerfoundation.in

Set 1140m up in the Nilgiri Hills, the **Mudumalai Wildlife Sanctuary** covers 322 square kilometres of deciduous forest, split by the main road from Ooty (64km to the southeast) to Mysore (97km to the northwest). Occupying the thickly wooded, lower northern reaches of the hills, it boasts one of the largest populations of elephants in India, along with wild dogs, gaur (Indian bison), common and Nilgiri langurs and bonnet macaques (monkeys), jackals, hyenas, sloth bears and even a few tigers and leopards. The abundant local flora includes the dazzling red flowers of the Flame of the Forest.

The main focus of interest by the park entrance at **Theppakkadu** is the **Elephant Camp** show, where you can watch the sanctuary's tame pachyderms being fed and bathed. This is also the starting point for the government **safari tour**, either on elephant back or by vehicle, which is the only way of accessing the official park limits. However, you may well see more creatures if you take a private **jeep tour** or **guided trek** into some of the parts of Mudumalai that are outside the state-controlled area. These can be arranged through your guesthouse or direct at Nature Safari in Masinagudi (☎0423 252 6340, ⓔsaveelephasmaximus@yahoo.co.in).

ARRIVAL AND DEPARTURE

By bus The main route to Mudumalai from Ooty plied by buses to Mysore and Bengaluru takes 2hr 30min to reach Theppakkadu. The alternative route, a tortuous journey of very steep gradients and hairpin bends, can only be

MUDUMALAI WILDLIFE SANCTUARY

attempted by taxis, 4WD and minibuses. These take around 1hr and end up in Masinagudi, which is closer to most of the area's accommodation.

ACCOMMODATION

Forest Resthouses Theppakkadu & Masinagudi ☎ 0423 244 4098, ⓦ mudumalaitigerfoundation.in. The Forest Department has a selection of rustic resthouses in or just outside the park, including some basic but nonetheless pleasant wood houses. Best budget option. No wi-fi. Dorms ₹165, doubles ₹735

★**Jungle Retreat** Bokkapuram, 6km southwest of Masinagudi ☎ 0423 252 6469, ⓦ jungleretreat.com. The biggest and most luxurious sanctuary resort, with eco-friendly swimming pool and a range of accommodation including dorm beds, various rooms and luxury treehouses (₹12,000). The daily food tariff (₹2000/person) covers three sumptuous buffet meals and unlimited tea and coffee. They can also arrange treks and plantation visits. Dorms ₹1000, doubles ₹5440

Secret Ivory Masinagudi ☎ 0423 252 6844, ⓦ secret

ivory.com. Luxury guesthouse with just eight rooms and a treehouse (₹4800). They serve delicious farm-fresh veg, grown on their own land and also organize treks and safaris. ₹2400

TTDC Tamil Nadu Theppakkadu ☎ 0423 252 6580, ⓦ ttdconline.com. The somewhat dowdy TTDC hotel is one of the park's few budget options. There is a choice of doubles, four-bed family rooms (₹1400) and very cheap dorm accommodation. Dorms ₹125, doubles ₹600

Wild Haven Chadapatti, 6km south of Masinagudi ☎ 0423 252 6490, ⓦ wildhaven.in. This lodge is in open land with great mountain views. There is a choice of simple, spacious double rooms in the stone block or accommodation in cottages. Breakfast included but other meals only available for large groups. ₹3000

7

The Andaman Islands

445 South Andaman

453 Neil

454 Havelock

458 Long Island

458 Middle Andaman

459 Interview Island

460 North Andaman

461 Little Andaman

BEACH, HAVELOCK

The Andaman Islands

India's most remote state, the Andaman Islands are situated more than 1000km off the east coast in the middle of the Bay of Bengal, connected to the mainland by flights and ferries from Kolkata, Chennai and Visakhapatnam. Thickly covered by deep green tropical forest, the archipelago supports a profusion of wildlife, including some extremely rare species of bird, but the principal attraction for tourists lies in the beaches and the pristine reefs that ring most of the islands. Filled with colourful fish and kaleidoscopic corals, the crystal-clear waters of the Andaman Sea feature some of the world's richest and least spoilt marine reserves – perfect for snorkelling and scuba diving. Although parts of the archipelago still see few visitors, the Andamans are now firmly on the tourist circuit.

For administrative purposes, the Andamans are grouped with the **Nicobar Islands**, 200km further south, but these remain strictly off-limits to foreigners, as well as Indians with no direct business there. Approximately two hundred islands make up the Andaman group and nineteen the Nicobar. They are of varying size, the summits of a submarine mountain range stretching 755km from the Arakan Yoma chain in Burma to the fringes of Sumatra in the south. All but the most remote are populated in parts by **indigenous tribes** whose numbers have been slashed dramatically as a result of nineteenth-century European settlement and, more recently, rampant **deforestation**, now banned at least in theory.

With the timber-extraction cash cow now largely tethered, **tourism** has gradually been replacing tree-felling as the main source of revenue on the Andamans. However, the extra visitor numbers are already beginning to overtax an already inadequate infrastructure, aggravating seasonal water shortages and sewage disposal problems. Given India's track record with tourism development, it's hard to be optimistic about how these issues will be managed. Consequently, it's no small mercy that plans to allow flights from Southeast Asia and even further afield to enter India at Port Blair seem to be on permanent hold, as the impact on this culturally and ecologically fragile region could be catastrophic.

The point of arrival for boats and planes is the small but busy capital, **Port Blair** in **South Andaman**, which holds almost half the total population. The only island to have fully developed a tourist infrastructure is **Havelock**, although its smaller neighbour **Neil** is heading in the same direction; these two are the only inhabited islands of **Ritchie's Archipelago**. The other places where foreigners can spend the night are on the large islands of **Middle** and **North Andaman**, connected to South Andaman by the Andaman Trunk Road (ATR), diminutive **Long Island** and remote **Little Andaman**, a long voyage to the south.

The outlying islands are richest in natural beauty, with the beaches of **Smith** and the coral around **Cinque** of particular note. Such spots are not always easy to reach, as connections and transport can be erratic, frequently uncomfortable and severely limited.

BEST TIME TO VISIT

The Andaman Islands enjoy a consistently warm climate, rarely departing from the parameters of 22–32°C all year round, even at night, while humidity never drops below seventy percent. There is a lot of rain from May to September and they also catch the northeast monsoon in the autumn, with occasionally violent cyclones prone to hit during either period, so the ideal months to visit from a climatic perspective are December to April. Increased tourism, however, means that Diwali and the Christmas/New Year periods are busy, with prices at their peak. Not all accommodation in the more remote parts such as Little Andaman opens outside peak season.

SCUBA DIVING

Highlights

❶ Wandoor The white sandy beach and islets of the Mahatma Gandhi National Marine Park are the most popular day-trip destination from capital Port Blair, and a good appetizer for more remote parts. **See p.452**

❷ Havelock For the best diving and partying, head for Havelock, still relaxed and convivial despite being the most developed of the Andamans. **See p.454**

❸ Scuba diving The Andamans' beautiful coral reefs teem with vivid underwater life. **See box, p.456**

❹ Long Island This is the place to head to get an idea of what Havelock was like two decades ago and a chance to unwind in a friendly, laidback village. **See p.458**

❺ North Andaman The long haul by bus or boat from Port Blair is worthwhile for the backdrop of thick rainforest and the dazzling tropical beaches when you arrive. **See p.460**

❻ Little Andaman As very few travellers make it to the archipelago's southernmost island, you may well have the stunning forest-fringed beaches to yourself. **See p.461**

HIGHLIGHTS ARE MARKED ON THE MAP ON P.444

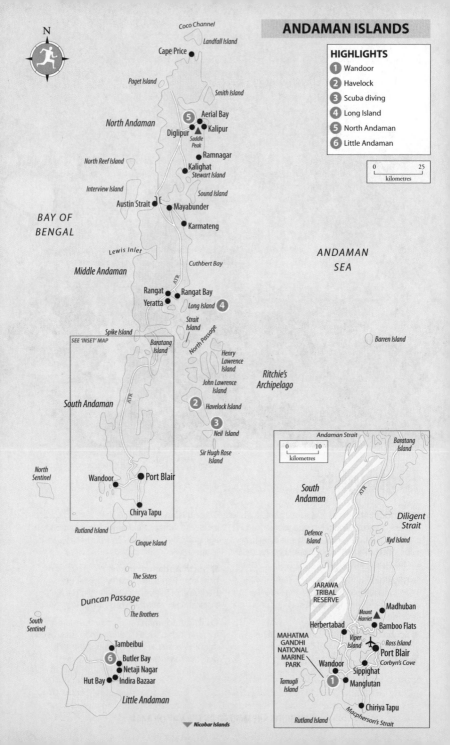

ANDAMAN ISLANDS

HIGHLIGHTS

1. Wandoor
2. Havelock
3. Scuba diving
4. Long Island
5. North Andaman
6. Little Andaman

0   25
kilometres

Coco Channel

Landfall Island

Cape Price

Paget Island

Smith Island

North Andaman

5 Aerial Bay
Kalipur
Diglipur
Saddle Peak

Ramnagar

Kalighat
Stewart Island

North Reef Island

Interview Island

Sound Island

Austin Strait   Mayabunder

**BAY OF
BENGAL**

Karmateng

Lewis Inlet

Cuthbert Bay

**ANDAMAN
SEA**

Middle Andaman

Rangat   Rangat Bay
Yeratta
Long Island 4

Spike Island

*Strait
Island*

North Passage

SEE 'INSET' MAP

*Baratang
Island*

*Henry
Lawrence
Island*

*John Lawrence
Island*

*Ritchie's
Archipelago*

Barren Island

South Andaman

2 *Havelock Island*

3
Neil Island

*Sir Hugh Rose
Island*

*North
Sentinel*

Wandoor   ● Port Blair

Chirya Tapu

Rutland Island

Cinque Island

The Sisters

Duncan Passage

The Brothers

*South
Sentinel*

Tambeibui
6 Butler Bay
Netaji Nagar
Hut Bay Indira Bazaar

Little Andaman

▼ *Nicobar Islands*

Andaman Strait

0   10
kilometres

*Baratang
Island*

**South
Andaman**

*Diligent
Strait*

*Defence
Island*

Kyd Island

**JARAWA
TRIBAL
RESERVE**

Madhuban
*Mount
Harriet*
Herbertabad   Bamboo Flats

**MAHATMA
GANDHI
NATIONAL
MARINE
PARK**

*Viper
Island*
Wandoor
1   Sippighat
Manglutan

Ross Island
Port Blair
Corbyn's Cove

*Tamugli
Island*

Chiriya Tapu

Rutland Island   *Macpherson's Strait*

N

Brief history

The earliest mention of the Andaman and Nicobar islands is found in **Ptolemy**'s geographical treatises of the second century AD. Other records from the Chinese Buddhist monk I'Tsing some five hundred years later and Arabian travellers who passed by in the ninth century depict the inhabitants as fierce and cannibalistic. It is unlikely, however, that the Andamanese were cannibals, as the most vivid reports of their ferocity were propagated by Malay pirates who held sway over the surrounding seas, and needed to keep looters well away from trade ships that passed between India, China and the Far East.

During the eighteenth and nineteenth centuries, **European missionaries** and trading companies turned their attention to the islands with a view to colonization. A string of unsuccessful attempts to convert the Nicobaris to Christianity was made by the French, Dutch and Danish, all of whom were forced to abandon their plans in the face of hideous diseases and a severe lack of food and water. Though the missionaries themselves seldom met with any hostility, several fleets of trading ships that tried to dock on the islands were captured, and their crews murdered, by Nicobari people.

In 1777, the British Lieutenant Archibald Blair chose the South Andaman harbour now known as **Port Blair** as the site for a **penal colony**, although it was not successfully established until 1858, when political activists who had fuelled the Mutiny in 1857 were made to clear land and build their own prison. Out of 773 prisoners, 292 died, escaped or were hanged in the first two months. Many also lost their lives in attacks by Andamanese tribes who objected to forest clearance, but by 1864 the number of convicts had grown to three thousand. The prison continued to confine political prisoners until 1945 and still stands as Port Blair's prime "tourist attraction" (see p.446).

During World War II the islands were occupied by the **Japanese**, who tortured and murdered hundreds of indigenous islanders suspected of collaborating with the British, and bombed the homes of the Jarawa tribe. British forces moved back in 1945, and at last abolished the penal settlement. After **Partition**, refugees – mostly low-caste Hindus from Bengal – were given land in Port Blair and North Andaman, where the forest was clear-felled to make room for rice paddy, cocoa plantations and new industries. Since 1951, the population has increased more than tenfold, further swollen by repatriated Tamils from Sri Lanka, ex-servicemen given land grants, economic migrants from poorer Indian states including thousands of Bihari labourers, and the legions of government employees packed off here on two-year "punishment postings". This replanted population greatly outnumbers the Andamans' indigenous people (see box, p.448), who currently comprise around 0.5 percent of the total.

8

INFORMATION   THE ANDAMAN ISLANDS

Health It's worth pointing out that a minority of travellers fall sick in the Andamans. The dense tree cover, marshy swamps and high rainfall combine to provide the perfect breeding ground for mosquitoes, and malaria is endemic in even the most remote settlements. Sandflies are also ferocious in certain places and tropical ulcer infections from scratching the bites are a frequent hazard.

Permits Foreign tourists are only permitted to visit certain parts of the Andaman group and some of those only as day-trips. Free thirty-day permits are granted on arrival by both sea and air and can be extended at Port Blair, Havelock and Neil for fifteen days on production of an outbound ticket.

Time Despite being so far east, the islands run on Indian time, so the sun rises as early as 4.30am in summer and darkness falls soon after 5pm.

South Andaman

South Andaman is the most heavily populated of the Andaman Islands – particularly around the capital, **Port Blair** – thanks in part to the drastic thinning of tree cover to make way for settlement. Foreign tourists can only visit its southern and east-central reaches – including the beaches at **Corbyn's Cove** and **Chiriya Tapu**, the fine reefs on the western shores at **Wandoor**, 35km southwest of Port Blair, and the environs of **Madhuban** and **Mount Harriet**, on the east coast across the bay from the capital. With your own transport it's easy to find your way along the narrow bumpy roads that connect small villages, weaving through forests and coconut fields, and skirting the swamps and rocky outcrops that form the coastline.

Port Blair

An odd combination of refreshingly scenic hills and characterless tin-roofed buildings tumbling towards the sea in the north, east and west, and petering out into fields and forests in the south, **PORT BLAIR** merits only a short stay. There's little to see here – just the **Cellular Jail** and a few small **museums** – but as it's the point of arrival for the islands and the place with the most facilities, you may well find yourself staying longer than you'd ideally want to. The hub of the town's activities and facilities is the cluster of streets known as Aberdeen Bazaar. Generally, street names are in short supply all over town, and are rarely used.

Cellular Jail

GB Pant Rd · **Jail and museum** Tues–Sun 9am–noon & 2–5pm · ₹10, camera ₹20 · **Sound-and-light show** Mon, Wed & Fri 6.45pm · ₹50

Port Blair's only firm reminder of its gloomy past, the sturdy brick **Cellular Jail**, overlooks the sea from a small rise in the northeast of town. Built between 1896 and 1905, its tiny solitary cells were quite different and far worse than the dormitories in other prison blocks erected earlier. Only three of the seven wings that originally

8

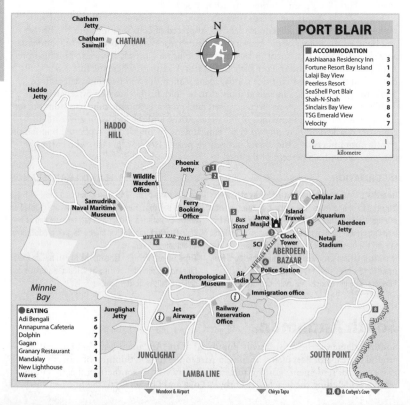

PORT BLAIR

■ ACCOMMODATION
Aashiaanaa Residency Inn	3
Fortune Resort Bay Island	1
Lalaji Bay View	4
Peerless Resort	9
SeaShell Port Blair	2
Shah-N-Shah	5
Sinclairs Bay View	8
TSG Emerald View	6
Velocity	7

0 — 1 kilometre

● EATING
Adi Bengali	5
Annapurna Cafeteria	6
Dolphin	7
Gagan	3
Granary Restaurant	4
Mandalay	1
New Lighthouse	2
Waves	8

Chatham Jetty
Chatham Sawmill · CHATHAM
Haddo Jetty
HADDO HILL
Phoenix Jetty
Wildlife Warden's Office
Samudrika Naval Maritime Museum
Ferry Booking Office
Bus Stand · Jama Masjid
Island Travels
Cellular Jail
Aquarium
Aberdeen Jetty
MOULANA AZAD ROAD
Clock Tower
Netaji Stadium
SCI · ABERDEEN BAZAAR
Police Station
Air India
Anthropological Museum
Immigration office
Minnie Bay
Junglighat Jetty
Jet Airways
Railway Reservation Office
JUNGLIGHAT
SOUTH POINT
LAMBA LINE

▼ Wandoor & Airport ▼ Chirya Tapu 9, 8 & Corbyn's Cove ▼

radiated from the central tower now remain. Visitors can peer into the 3m by 3.5m cells and imagine the grim conditions in which the prisoners lived. Cells were dirty and poorly ventilated, drinking water was limited to two glasses per day, and the convicts were expected to wash in the rain as they worked clearing forests and building prison quarters. Food, brought from the mainland, was stored in vats where the rice and pulses became infested with worms; more than half the prison population died long before their twenty years' detention was up. Protests against conditions led to several hunger strikes, and frequent executions took place at the gallows that still stand in squat wooden shelters in the courtyards, in full view of the cells. The **sound-and-light show** outlines the history of the prison, and a small **museum** by the entrance gate exhibits lists of convicts, photographs and grim torture devices.

Anthropological Museum

MG Rd • Tues–Sun 9am–1pm & 1.30–4.30pm • ₹20, camera ₹20

On the south side of the centre, close to the Directorate of Tourism, the diverting **Anthropological Museum** has exhibits on the Andaman and Nicobar tribes, including weapons, tools and rare photographs of the region's indigenous people taken in the 1960s. Among the most striking of these is a sequence featuring the Sentinelese, taken on April 26, 1967, when a party of Indian officials made the first contact with the tribe. After scaring the aborigines, the visitors marched into one of their hunting camps and made off with the bows, arrows and other artefacts now displayed in the museum.

Samudrika Naval Maritime Museum

Haddo Rd, Delanipur • Tues–Sun 9am–5.30pm • ₹50

To the northwest of town in the area known as Delanipur, the **Samudrika Naval Maritime Museum** is an excellent primer if you're heading off to more remote islands, with a superlative shell collection and informative displays on various aspects of local marine biology. One of the exhibits features a cross-section of the different corals you can expect to see on the Andamans' reefs, followed by a rundown of the various threats these fragile organisms face, from mangrove depletion and parasitic starfish to clumsy snorkellers.

8

ARRIVAL AND DEPARTURE

PORT BLAIR

Port Blair is the departure point for all flights and ferry crossings to the **Indian mainland**; it is also the hub of the Andamans' inter-island bus and ferry network. **Booking tickets** for boats (especially back to Chennai, Kolkata or Visakhapatnam) can be time-consuming, and many travellers are obliged to come back here well before their permit expires to make reservations before heading off to more pleasant parts of the islands again. Port Blair has an efficient computerized Southern Railways reservation office near the Secretariat (Mon–Sat 8.30am–1pm & 2–4pm) – useful for travellers intending to catch onward **trains** from their port of arrival on the mainland.

BY PLANE

Veer Savarkar airport The smart airport terminal is less than 4km south of town at Lamba Line. Taxis and auto-rickshaws are on hand for short trips into town (₹60–100), while mid- or upper-range hotels usually have shuttle buses to collect guests. Local buses also frequently ply the route to town from outside the shop on the far side of the main road, barely 100m from the terminal building.

To and from the mainland Port Blair is currently served by flights from Chennai (5–6 daily; 2hr) and Kolkata (4 daily; 2hr), operated by Air India, Jet Airways, Spicejet and Go Air; Air India and its subsidiary Alliance Air fly nonstop from Bhubaneswar (6 weekly; 2hr); and Air India has a daily flight from Visakhapatnam (2hr). Flights at peak times like Diwali, Christmas and New Year through to

February can be heavily subscribed, so book early. These periods also see prices soar as high as ₹20,000 one way; at other times they can be as low as ₹5000. The Air India office (☎03192 233108) is diagonally opposite the tourist office, while Jet Airways (☎03192 236922) is on the first floor at 189 Main Rd, Junglighat, next to the Incredible India office. Spicejet and Go Air can only be booked online or through travel agents such as the efficient Island Travels (Mon–Sat 9am–6pm; ☎03192 233034), between the clock tower and marina.

Inter-island services In 2012 a new private seaplane service started to Havelock and Diglipur but it was not operating at the time of writing. There is an inexpensive (₹2500–4000) helicopter service connecting Port Blair with Havelock, Diglipur and Little Andaman but tourists

NATIVE PEOPLE OF THE ANDAMAN AND NICOBAR ISLANDS

Quite where the **indigenous population** of the Andaman and Nicobar islands originally came from is a puzzle that has preoccupied anthropologists since Alfred Radcliffe-Brown conducted his famous fieldwork among the Andamanese at the beginning of the twentieth century. Asian-looking groups such as the Shompen may have migrated here from the east and north when the islands were connected to Burma, or the sea was sufficiently shallow to allow transport by canoe, but this doesn't explain the origins of the black populations, whose appearance suggests African roots.

The survival of the islands' first inhabitants has long been threatened by traders and colonizers, who introduced disease and destroyed their territories through widespread tree-felling. Thousands also died from addiction to the alcohol and opium that the Chinese, Japanese and British exchanged for valuable shells. Many have had their populations decimated, while others like the Nicobarese have assimilated to modern culture, often adopting Christianity. The indigenous inhabitants of the Andamans, divided into *eramtaga* (those living in the jungle) and *ar-yuato* (those living on the coast), traditionally subsisted as hunter-gatherers, living on fish, turtles, turtle eggs, pigs, fruit, honey and roots. For more information on the islands' original inhabitants, visit Survival International's website, ⓦ survival-international.org.

THE GREAT ANDAMANESE

Although they comprised the largest group when the islands were first colonized, only around fifty **Great Andamanese** now survive. In the 1860s, the Rev Henry Corbyn set up a "home" for the tribe to learn English on Ross Island, insisting that they wear clothes and attend reading and writing classes. Five children and three adults from Corbyn's school were taken to Calcutta in 1864, where they were shown around the sights but treated more as curiosities themselves. Within three years, almost the entire population had died, victims of either introduced diseases or addiction. In recent years the surviving Great Andamanese were forcibly settled on Strait Island, north of South Andaman, as a "breeding centre", where they were forced to rely on the Indian authorities for food and shelter. Sadly, the last speaker of Bo, one of the oldest Andamanese languages, died in 2010.

THE JARAWAS

The **Jarawas**, who were shifted from their original homes when land was cleared to build Port Blair, currently number around three hundred and live on the remote western coasts of Middle and South Andaman. They are hemmed in by the Andaman Trunk Road (ATR), which since the 1970s has cut them off from hunting grounds and freshwater supplies. During the 1980s and 1990s, encroachments on their land by loggers, road builders and settlers met with fierce resistance, and dozens, possibly hundreds, of people died in **skirmishes**, mostly on or near the

can only book tickets one day in advance and seats are often taken up by officials. Flights are also prone to cancellation due to bad weather and there is a 6kg baggage limit. Contact the Secretariat in Port Blair to check (ⓣ 03192 230093).

BY BOAT

Jetties Port Blair has two main jetties: boats from the mainland moor at Haddo Jetty, nearly 2km northwest of Phoenix Jetty, arrival point for inter-island ferries. The Director of Shipping Services (DSS; ⓣ 03192 245555) at Phoenix Jetty has the latest information on boats and ferries, but you can also check details of forthcoming departures in the shipping news column of the local newspaper, the *Daily Telegrams*. Boats can get cramped and uncomfortable, sometimes lacking shade outside and space inside; take adequate supplies of food and water, as minimal sustenance is sold on board.

To and from the mainland Services to and from Chennai (see p.376) can be relied upon to leave in each direction once every week to ten days, while those to and from Kolkata sail roughly every two weeks; boats to and from Visakhapatnam are altogether more erratic, averaging once a month in each direction – call the Shipping Office there on ⓣ 0891 256 5597 for more information. Although much cheaper than flying (from ₹1600), sea crossings are long (3–5 days), uncomfortable and often delayed by bad conditions. Tickets for all three mainland ports (Chennai, Kolkata and Visakhapatnam) are handled by the DSS and go on sale a week in advance of departure at the allotted booths within the Computerized Reservation Centre (Mon–Fri 9am–1pm & 2–4pm, Sat 9am–noon) at Phoenix Jetty. When they do go on sale, it's wise to be there to join the fray ahead of time. Make sure you get a ticket before your permit expires, as you will need to show it to get the fifteen-day extension (see p.445).

ATR. Some more amicable **contact** between settlers and tribals was subsequently made through gift exchanges at each full moon, although the initiative was later cancelled. These meetings nevertheless led to some Jarawas becoming curious about what "civilization" had to offer, and they started to hold their hands out to passing vehicles and even visiting Indian settlements near their territory. Despite the authorities trying to minimize contact, it is still common for Jarawas to approach buses, and some private vehicles ignore the rules and stop for photo shoots. The government has increased Jarawa land by 180 square kilometres, but lodged an ongoing appeal over a 2002 Indian Supreme Court order to close the ATR – a ruling made following protests by international pressure groups such as Survival International. A disturbing legal reversal made early in 2013 has also once again allowed "human safaris" to take place.

THE ONGE

Relations with the **Onge**, who call themselves the **Gaubolambe**, have been relatively peaceful. Distinguished by their white-clay and ochre body paint, they continue to live in communal shelters and construct temporary thatched huts on Little Andaman. The remaining population of just under one hundred retain their traditional way of life on two small reserves. Contact with outsiders is limited to an occasional trip into town to purchase liquor, and visits from rare parties of anthropologists. The reserves are strictly off-limits to foreigners, but you can learn about the Onge's traditional hunting practices, beliefs and rituals in Vishvajit Pandya's wonderful ethnographic study, *Above the Forest*.

THE NICOBARESE AND OTHER TRIBES

On the Nicobars, the most assimilated and numerous tribe, the **Nicobarese**, are of Mongoloid descent and number well over twenty thousand. They live in villages, ruled by a headman, and have largely cordial relations with the Indian settlers. By contrast, only very limited contact is ever had with the isolated **Shompen** tribe of Great Nicobar, whose population of around four hundred manage to lead a traditional hunting-and-gathering existence. The most elusive tribe of all, the **Sentinelese**, live on North Sentinel Island west of South Andaman. Following the first encounter with Indian settlers in 1967, some contact was made with them in 1990, after a team put together by the local administration left gifts on the beaches every month for two years, but subsequent visits have invariably ended in a hail of arrows and two Indian fishermen who ventured too close to the island were killed in 2006. Since the early 1990s, the authorities have effectively given up trying to contact the Sentinelese, who are estimated to number anywhere between forty and two hundred. Flying in or out of Port Blair, you pass above their island, ringed by a spectacular coral reef. It's reassuring to think that the people sitting at the bottom of the plumes of smoke drifting up from the forest canopy still manage to resist contact with the outside world.

Inter-island services Most of the islands open to foreign tourists are accessible by government-run boats from Phoenix Jetty. Details of sailings to and from Port Blair for the following two to five days are posted in the *Daily Telegrams* newspaper. More details of boat services between destinations outside the capital appear in the relevant accounts of this guide. The only way to guarantee a passage is to book tickets in advance at the Inter-Island booths in the Computerized Reservation Centre at Phoenix Jetty, though any unsold tickets are issued prior to departure on the quay. You can avoid these scrums by paying an agent such as Island Travels to get a ticket for you. Fares are very reasonable, even allowing for the two-tier pricing system for islanders and non-islanders: Havelock, for example, costs ₹300–400, Little Andaman just ₹220. Havelock and Neil also have a smart private catamaran service, the *Makruzz* (1–2 daily; 2hr; from ₹990; ⓦmakruzz.com), while the upmarket private *Green Ocean* ferry serves just Havelock

(1 daily; 2hr 30min; ₹900; ⓦgreenoceancruise.com). Destinations Aerial Bay on North Andaman (3 weekly; 8–9hr); Havelock (3–4 daily; 2hr–3hr 30min); Hut Bay on Little Andaman (5–6 weekly; 6–9hr); Long Island (4 weekly; 5–6hr); Neil (2–3 daily; 2hr); Rangat on Middle Andaman (4 weekly; 6–7hr).

BY BUS

Buses connect Port Blair with most of the major settlements on Middle and North Andaman via the Andaman Trunk Road. From the bus stand in the centre of town, there are government services to Rangat (3 daily; 6hr), Mayabunder (2 daily; 9hr) and Diglipur (2 daily; 11hr). Several private companies, including Ananda (☎03192 233252), who have an office near the bus stand, run deluxe or video coach services to the same destinations; these leave from outside the bus stand between 5am and 10am. Tickets for both categories of service are cheap at ₹200–400.

GETTING AROUND

By taxi and auto-rickshaw Taxis gather opposite the bus stand in central Port Blair. They all have meters and there's a prepaid booth, but negotiating the price before leaving is the usual practice. Expect to pay at least ₹120 for a trip from the centre of town to Corbyn's Cove; auto-rickshaws try to charge just as much as taxis but a ride within town shouldn't cost more than ₹50.

By bus Local buses run from the bus stand frequently to Wandoor (hourly) and less so to Chiriya Tapu (every 2hr), so they can be used for day-trips.

By motorbike It's pleasant to rent a motorbike or scooter but there are few outlets – try Green Island Tours & Travels (☎03192 230226), near the clock tower in Aberdeen Bazaar. The only petrol pumps are on the crossroads west of the bus stand and on the airport road.

INFORMATION AND TOURS

Tourist information The counter at the airport (☎03192 232414) hands out a useful general brochure, but trying to get more than basic tour and hotel information from the main A&N Directorate of Tourism office (Mon–Sat 8am–8pm; ☎03192 232747, ⊛and.nic.in), situated on a hill south of Aberdeen Bazaar, can be frustrating. Further southwest on Junglighat Main Rd, the Incredible India office (Mon–Fri 8.30am–5pm; ☎03192 233006, ⊛incredibleindia.org) is not much better.

Permits The Immigration Office (Mon–Fri 8.30am–1pm & 2–5.30pm, Sat 8.30am–1pm; ☎03192 239247) in Aberdeen Bazaar, is the place to go for the free fifteen-day permit extension (see p.445). If you intend to visit Interview Island (see p.459), you must first obtain a free permit from the Chief Wildlife Warden, whose office (☎03192 233270) is next to the zoo in Haddo.

Hospital The main hospital for the whole archipelago is GB Pant Hospital on GB Pant Rd (☎03192 232102).

Services It's wise to stock up on rupees in Port Blair as the banks and agencies here are the only places on the islands officially allowed to exchange cash. There are several ATMs dotted around the town (and now a couple on Havelock too).

Tours A couple of smart private tourist boats such as the MV *Mark Marina* (☎96795 38188) conduct various harbour cruises (2–7hr; ₹250–1100) from Phoenix Jetty around the harbour, taking in North Bay, Viper and Ross islands (see opposite).

ACCOMMODATION

Port Blair boasts numerous places to stay in most budget ranges. The abundance of options means availability is only an issue around Christmas and New Year, when prices are also hiked; they drop during the monsoon season.

Aashiaanaa Residency Inn Marine Hill ☎94742 17008, ✉shads_maria@hotmail.com. An attractive ochre-coloured building, very conveniently located for Phoenix Jetty. There is a selection of decent-sized, mostly attached rooms, some with balconies. Wi-fi in lobby ₹60/hr. **₹500/₹650**

Fortune Resort Bay Island Marine Hill ☎03192 234101, ⊛fortunehotels.in. Port Blair's swishest hotel is elegant and airy with polished dark wood. All rooms have carpets and balconies overlooking Phoenix Jetty. There's a good restaurant, gardens and an open-air seawater swimming pool. Check for online deals. **₹7650**

Lalaji Bay View RP Rd ☎03192 230551, ⊛lalajibayview.com. Popular budget guesthouse on a bayside hill above Aberdeen Bazaar, which offers good-value attached rooms, the cheapest ones windowless. It also has a good sociable rooftop restaurant that serves beer, but service is slow. Wi-fi in restaurant ₹60/hr. **₹600**

Peerless Resort Corbyn's Cove ☎03192 229263, ⊛peerlesshotels.com. The setting is lovely, with a white-sand beach opposite, and gardens of palms, jasmine and bougainvillea, but the balconied a/c rooms and cottages are a bit tatty for the prices they charge. There's a bar and mid-priced restaurant with an average evening buffet. **₹6600**

★**SeaShell Port Blair** Marine Hill ☎03192 242773, ⊛seashellhotels.net. Excellent modern hotel suitable for business travellers and tourists alike. Spacious, beautifully furnished and decorated rooms with great showers and flatscreen TVs. The more expensive rooms have balconies overlooking the sea. **₹7500**

Shah-N-Shah Mohanpura ☎03192 233696, ✉apsara tours786@yahoo.com. Conveniently located between the bus stand and Phoenix Jetty, this is very basic but friendly, with mostly attached rooms and a travel agent. Cheap single occupancy. No wi-fi. **₹400/₹600**

Sinclairs Bay View On the coast road to Corbyn's Cove ☎03192 227824, ⊛sinclairshotels.com. Clifftop hotel offering spotless carpeted rooms with balconies, large bathrooms and dramatic views, as well as a much-improved restaurant. **₹8000**

★**TSG Emerald View** 25 Moulana Azad Rd ☎03192 246488, ⊛tsgemerald.com. Smart mid-range place with a sparkling new lobby and spacious, colourfully furnished a/c rooms, boasting all mod cons. Also has a decent restaurant. **₹2500**

Velocity Moulana Azad Rd ☎03192 238238, ⊛hotel velocity.in. Sleek modern block with some jazzy design features and well-furnished, fair-sized rooms. Breakfast included. **₹1800**

EATING

★ **Adi Bengali** Moulana Azad Rd ☎ 99332 50583. Simple but sparkling clean place serving tasty Bengali dishes such as fish masala, a snip at ₹90. Also offers chicken and a range of veg dishes. Daily 7am–10pm.

Annapurna Cafeteria Aberdeen Bazaar, towards the post office ☎ 03192 234199. Port Blair's best south-Indian joint, serving a range of huge crispy dosas, plus North Indian and Chinese meals, delicious coffee and wonderful *pongal* at breakfast. The lunchtime thalis are also good. Mains ₹80–150. Mon–Sat 6.30–10.30am & 3.30–10.30pm.

Dolphin Marthoma Church Complex, Golgha ☎ 03192 243933. Pleasantly decorated with cane chairs and blinds, serving carefully prepared Indian and Chinese dishes, as well as some Continental options and a few house specialities involving chicken and seafood (around ₹100–200). Daily noon–10pm.

Gagan Aberdeen Bazaar, opposite the clock tower ☎ 03192 212140. Simple canteen with a decent range of north and South Indian veg and non-veg dishes for around ₹70–180, including tasty fried fish. Daily 7am–10pm.

Granary Restaurant Islanderr Inn, Moulana Azad Rd ☎ 03192 234234. Colourful ground-floor restaurant in a modern hotel, serving a standard range of Indian and Chinese food for ₹100–200 and a ₹400 evening buffet. Daily 8am–3pm & 6–10pm.

Mandalay Fortune Resort, Marine Hill ☎ 03192 234101. À la carte main courses (₹250–400) or, when demand allows, a reasonable dinner buffet for around ₹600, can be enjoyed in the airy open restaurant with great bay views. Service can be a bit lax for its class. The adjacent *Nico Bar* is a decent bet for a drink. Daily noon–10.30pm.

★ **New Lighthouse** Near Aberdeen Jetty ☎ 03192 237356. Popular place with outdoor seating and an airy rooftop, where you can catch the sea breeze while feasting on some of the cheapest lobster and other seafood (₹150–300) in the Andamans. Daily 11am–10.30pm.

Waves Peerless Resort, Corbyn's Cove ☎ 03192 229263. Slightly pricey but very congenial alfresco hotel restaurant under a shady palm grove, and one of the few places in town you can order a beer with your meal. Most dishes ₹250–500. Daily 11am–11pm.

Around Port Blair

At some point, you're almost certain to find yourself killing time in Port Blair, waiting for boats to show up or tickets to go on sale. Rather than wasting days in town, it's worth exploring the **coast** of South Andaman which, although far more densely populated than other islands in the archipelago, holds a handful of easily accessible beauty spots and historic sites. Among the latter, the ruined colonial monuments on **Viper** and **Ross islands** can be reached on daily harbour cruises or regular ferries from the capital (see opposite). For **beaches**, head to nearby **Corbyn's Cove**, or cross South Andaman to reach the more pleasingly secluded **Chiriya Tapu**, which is easily accessible on a day-trip if you rent a motorbike or scooter, and is the jumping-off point for Cinque. By far the most rewarding way to spend a day out of town, however, is to catch the tourist boat from **Wandoor** to **Jolly Buoy** or **Red Skin islands** in the **Mahatma Gandhi National Marine Park** opposite, which boasts some of the Andamans' best snorkelling. The other area worth visiting is **Mount Harriet** and **Madhuban** on the central part of South Andaman, north across the bay from Port Blair.

Viper Island

First stop on the harbour cruises from Port Blair is generally **Viper Island**, named not after the many snakes that doubtless inhabit its tangled tropical undergrowth, but a nineteenth-century merchant vessel that ran aground on it during the early years of the colony. Lying a short way off Haddo Jetty, it served as an isolation zone for the main prison, where escapees and other convicts were sent to be punished. Whipping posts and

---

A WALK ON THE WET SIDE

One new activity that has started up in recent years is **sea walking** at North Bay. In this rather peculiar piece of fun, people are fitted into a large and rather unwieldy space-type helmet, which is connected to a non-pressurized oxygen source on the surface, and lowered down for a stroll around the seabed at a depth of five to eight metres. A sea walk of up to twenty minutes costs from ₹3200 and can be organized through Sea Link Adventures at 43 MA Rd, Phoenix Bay (☎ 96795 78661, ⊛ sealinkadventures.com).

crumbling walls, reached from the jetty via a winding brick path, remain as relics of a torture area, while occupying the site's most prominent position are the original gallows.

Ross Island

₹20 • Several daily boats from Phoenix Jetty (see p.449) • **Sound-and-light show**, including government boat 4.15pm, returns 7.15pm; ₹250

Eerie decaying colonial remains are to be found on **Ross Island**, at the entrance to Port Blair harbour, where the British sited their first penal settlement in the Andamans. Originally cleared by convicts wearing iron fetters, Ross witnessed some of the most brutal excesses of British colonial history, and was the source of the prison's infamy as **Kalapani**, or Black Water. Of the many convicts transported here, distinguished by their branded foreheads, the majority perished from disease or torture before the clearance of the island was completed in 1860. Thereafter, it served briefly as the site of Rev Henry Corbyn's **Andaman Home** – a prison camp created with the intention of "civilizing" the local tribespeople – and then the headquarters of the revamped penal colony before the British were forced to evacuate by the Japanese entry into World War II. Little more than the hilltop **Anglican church**, with its weed-infested graveyard, has survived the onslaught of tropical creepers and vines. There is a sound-and-light show every evening, but only in Hindi.

Corbyn's Cove

The best beach within easy reach of the capital lies 6km southeast, at **Corbyn's Cove**, a small arc of smooth white sand backed by a swaying curtain of palms. There's a large hotel here, *Peerless Resort* (see p.450), but the water isn't particularly clear, and bear in mind that lying around scantily clothed may bring you considerable attention from crowds of local workers.

Chiriya Tapu

For a little isolation, take a bus 30km south of Port Blair to **Chiriya Tapu** ("Bird Island"), at the tip of South Andaman. The walkable track running beyond this small fishing village leads through thick jungle overhung with twisting creepers to a large bay, where swamps give way to shell-strewn beaches. Other than at lunchtime, when it often receives a deluge of bus parties, the beach offers plenty of peace and quiet, forest walks on the woodcutters' trails winding inland and easy access to an inshore reef. However, the water here is nowhere near as clear as at outlying spots in the archipelago.

Cinque Island

Cinque, two hours south of Chiriya Tapu, actually comprises two islets, joined by a spectacular sand isthmus with shallow water either side that covers it completely at high tide. The main incentive to come here is the superb diving and snorkelling around the reefs. However, heaps of dead coral on the beach attest to damage wreaked by the Indian navy during the construction of the swish "cottages" overlooking the beach. Rumour has it that these were built for the visit of a Thai VIP in 1996, but local government officials now use them as bolt holes from Port Blair.

Although there are no **ferries** to Cinque, it is possible to charter a dinghy and boatman for around ₹2500 per day from Chiriya Tapu. Foreigners are not allowed to stay the night.

Wandoor

Much the most popular excursion from Port Blair is to **WANDOOR**, 30km southwest. The long white **beach** here is littered with the dry, twisted trunks of trees torn up and flung down by annual cyclones. It's fringed not with palms but with dense forest teeming with birdlife. You should only snorkel here at high tide, as the coral is easily damaged when the waters are shallow.

ACCOMMODATION   WANDOOR

Sea Princess Beach Resort 500m back from the car park ☎03192 280002, ⊛seaprincessandaman.com.

This smart resort, set in nicely landscaped grounds, offers luxury cottages, rooms and suites. The restaurant is also very pleasant. ₹6000

Wandoor Paradise Resort On the beach ☏94342 72135. The only budget option in Wandoor are the two ramshackle huts here, though the seaside location is made less idyllic because the restaurant is mainly a drinking den. No wi-fi. ₹500

The Mahatma Gandhi National Marine Park

Park entry ₹500 (₹50) • Boats from Wandoor Tues–Sun 10am; ₹500

Most people take a cruise around the fifteen islets comprising the **Mahatma Gandhi National Marine Park**, which boasts one of the richest coral reefs in the region. From the jetty at Wandoor, the boats chug through broad creeks lined with dense mangrove swamps and pristine forest to either **Red Skin Island** or, more commonly, **Jolly Buoy**. The latter, an idyllic deserted island, boasts an immaculate shell-sand beach ringed by a bank of superb coral. The catch is that the boat only stops for around an hour, which isn't nearly enough time to explore the shore and reef. While snorkelling off the edges of the reef, beware of **strong currents**.

Mount Harriet and Madhuban

Park entry ₹250 (₹25) • Passenger ferries from Chatham Jetty every 30min, vehicle ferries from Phoenix Jetty 8 daily

The richly forested slopes of **Mount Harriet** make for some decent exercise and can easily be visited on a day-trip from Port Blair. From the ferry landing at **Bamboo Flats**, it's a pleasant 7km stroll east along the coast and north up a path through trees hung with thick vines and creepers to the 365m summit, which affords fine views back across the bay. An intermittent bus service runs between Bamboo Flats and Hope Town, where the uphill path starts, and saves you the 3km coastal stretch. Alternatively, jeeps and taxis are available to take you all the way to the top, but they charge at least ₹500. The Mount Harriet National Park checkpost is on the road so you probably won't be asked if you take the path. It's 2.5km from the checkpost up to the resthouse and viewing tower at the summit. If you have strong legs, you can reach the small settlement of **Madhuban** on the coast northeast of the mountain by the 16km round route via Kala Patthar (Black Rock) and back via the coast. There is a decent beach at Madhuban but not much else.

8

Neil

Tiny, triangular-shaped **Neil** is the most southerly inhabited island of **Ritchie's Archipelago**, barely two hours northeast of Port Blair on a fast ferry. The source of much of the capital's fresh fruit and vegetables, its fertile centre, ringed by a curtain of stately tropical trees, comprises vivid patches of green paddy dotted with small farmsteads and banana plantations. The beaches are mediocre by the Andamans' standards but worth a day or two en route to or from Havelock and, as it is far less developed with little more than ten accommodation options, some visitors prefer it to its busier neighbour for more extended stays.

Neil boasts five **beaches**, all of them within easy cycling distance of the small bazaar just up the lane from the jetty. The best place to swim is **Neil Kendra**, a gently curving bay of white sand on the north coast which straddles the jetty and is scattered with picturesque wooden fishing boats. This blends into **Bharatpur** to the east and **Lakshmanpur**, which continues for nearly 3km west: to get to Lakshmanpur by road, head right when the road from the jetty meets the bazaar and follow it for around twenty minutes until it dwindles into a surfaced track, then take a right. Wrapped around the headland, the beach is a broad spur of white-shell sand, with shallow water offering good snorkelling, although footing is difficult when entering the water at any time other than high tide.

Exposed to the open sea and thus prone to higher tides, **Sitapur** beach, 6km southeast of Neil Kendra, is also appealing and has the advantage of a sandy bottom extending into the sea. The ride there across Neil's central paddy land is pleasant, but there are no facilities beyond the two new guesthouses on intermediate **Ram Nagar** beach.

ARRIVAL AND DEPARTURE

By boat Neil is well connected with Havelock (2–3 daily; 1hr 30min) and Port Blair (2–3 daily; 2hr), plus there are four weekly ferries to Long Island (4hr 30min) and Rangat (5hr 30min–6hr).

GETTING AROUND

By bus An hourly bus runs between the bazaar and Sitapur. You can also rent bicycles (₹60/day) or mopeds (₹300/day) at guesthouses or stalls in the market.

ACCOMMODATION

A-N-D Beach Resort 250m east of the jetty, Neil Kendra ☎ 96795 25789. Tucked along the path behind the beach, this welcoming place has some very cheap huts with common bathrooms and a few attached ones, as well as a decent restaurant. No wi-fi. ₹300/₹500

Breakwater Ram Nagar ☎ 95318 52332. Ever-expanding group of mostly attached bamboo huts, plus some larger concrete rooms, arranged around a patch of open land behind the beach. The restaurant does good food and is a sociable gathering place. No wi-fi. ₹300/₹500

★**Emerald Gecko** Sitapur ☎ 94742 50821, ⓦ emerald -gecko.com. Great new offshoot of the Havelock favourite, with large and sturdy bungalow-style and two-storey bamboo huts, plus a sociable and fine-quality restaurant. No wi-fi. ₹2500

Kalapani Ram Nagar ☎ 94742 74991. Though not quite as appealing as those at nearby *Breakwater*, the huts here are perfectly habitable and some of them have shared facilities. Free cooking lessons. No wi-fi. ₹200/₹600

SeaShell Lakshmanpur ☎ 03192 242773, ⓦ seashell hotels.net. The latest venture from the *SeaShell* group is by far Neil's most upmarket resort, with superbly furnished thatched cottages set in lush landscaped gardens. Look for online deals in advance. ₹9000

★**Tango Beach Resort** Lakshmanpur ☎ 03192 282634, ⓦ tangobeachandaman.com. This friendly place right on the beach offers a range of accommodation from small non-attached bamboo huts to larger ones with verandas and the pricey Lagoon suites. It also has a new rooftop restaurant. No wi-fi. ₹500/₹950

EATING

Blue Sea Ram Nagar beach ☎ 94760 13330. This joint just back from the beach offers keenly priced seafood, plus pasta, Indian dishes and filling sizzlers for around ₹100–300. Daily 8.30am–11pm.

Chand Restaurant In the bazaar ☎ 94742 22395. Small *dhaba*-style establishment, which serves up tasty, albeit somewhat oily, food. It's mostly Indian, with a range of thalis, including fish, for ₹100–180, plus some Western dishes. Daily 6am–10.30pm.

Garden View Near Sitapur ☎ 99332 21552. Friendly family restaurant in a field just beside the main road, which does fresh fish curry for ₹150, as well as a lot of veggie and some chicken dishes. Daily 7am–10pm.

★**Gyan Garden** 400m west of the bazaar ☎ 99332 93078. Far and away the best place to eat, this delightful and welcoming garden restaurant cooks fresh fish (₹150–200) and home-grown veg dishes are also a speciality. Daily 8am–10pm.

Havelock

Havelock is the largest island in Ritchie's Archipelago, and the most intensively cultivated, settled – like many in the region – by Bengali refugees after Partition. Thanks to its regular ferry connections with the capital, it is also visited in far greater numbers than anywhere else in the Andamans. In peak season, several thousand tourists can be holed up here at one time, including an increasing number of well-heeled Indians, which has led to an explosion in accommodation and tourist shops, many (as in the rest of the country) owned by Kashmiris.

The east coast

Havelock's hub of activity is not the **jetty village**, which just has a few stalls, a couple of dowdy lodges, the odd restaurant and the police station, but the **Main Bazaar**, which you come to if you follow the road straight ahead from the jetty for 2km, passing Beach #2 on the way. Here you'll find a greater variety of shops and places to eat, the only bank and the island's main junction.

If you take the left turn through the busier strip of Main Bazaar, the road leads on past **beaches #3 and #5**, where most of the beach huts and resorts are located. As on Neil's north coast, these east-facing beaches, though exquisitely scenic, have fairly thin strips of golden-white sand, and when the sea recedes across the lumps of broken coral and rock lying offshore, swimming becomes all but impossible. After Beach #5 the road continues south for several kilometres before turning slightly inland and eventually petering out at **Kalapathar** beach. The entire southern half of Havelock consists of impenetrable forest.

The west coast

The right turn from the island's main junction leads 9km through paddy fields and other crops before dropping through some spectacular woodland to **Radhnagar** (Beach #7), a 2km arc of perfect white sand, backed by stands of giant *mowhar* trees and often touted as the most beautiful in India. The water is a sublime turquoise colour and, although the coral is sparse, marine life here is diverse and plentiful, especially among the rocks around the corner from the main beach (accessible at low tide). The main drawback, which can make sunbathing uncomfortable, is a preponderance of pesky sandflies. Another hazard, around the lagoon at the far northern end, is saltwater **crocodiles**.

As the nesting site for a colony of olive ridley **turtles**, Radhnagar is strictly protected by the Forest Department, whose wardens ensure tourists don't light fires or sleep on the beach. There's not much accommodation here, but a clutch of *dhabas* provides ample sustenance for day-trippers.

A couple of kilometres before the road descends to Radhnagar, a path on the right leads over a hill and down through some scattered settlements to far wilder **Elephant Beach**, although the only trunks you are likely to spot are those of huge fallen trees. Snorkelling here is good, and coral reefs are accessible from the shore, but it can be tough to find the way; look out for the start of the path at a sharp bend in the road with a Forest Department noticeboard and then keep asking the way whenever you see a local.

HAVELOCK

■ ACCOMMODATION		● EATING	
Barefoot at Havelock	5	Anju-coco	4
Barefoot Scuba Resort	3	Barefoot Bar & Brasserie	1
Dreamland Resort	7	Blackbeard's Bistro	7
Emerald Gecko	8	Café del Mar	2
The Flying Elephant	9	Fat Martin	5
Green Valley	4	Full Moon Café	3
SeaShell Havelock	1	Nala's Kingdom	1, 8
Sea View	2	Red Snapper	6
Wild Orchid	6	■ DRINKING & NIGHTLIFE	
		Cicada	1

8

ARRIVAL AND INFORMATION

HAVELOCK

By boat Havelock's main jetty is on the north side of the island, at the village known as Beach #1. If you've booked accommodation in advance, most places arrange a pick-up.
Destinations Ferries: Long Island (4 weekly; 4hr–4hr 30min); Neil (2–3 daily; 1hr 30min); Port Blair (3–4 daily; 2hr–3hr 30min); Rangat (4 weekly; 5hr–5hr 30min). There are also one or two daily *Makruzz* catamaran sailings for Port Blair.

Tourist information When staffed, the small tourist office just outside the jetty gates is moderately helpful (daily 8am–5pm; ☏ 94742 22245).
Services The only place to change money is the State Co-operative Bank (Mon–Fri 9am–1pm, Sat 9–11am), at the Main Bazaar, 2km inland of the main jetty, although there are now two ATMs en route. Numerous places now offer satellite internet connections, but charge as much as ₹300/hr.

SCUBA DIVING IN THE ANDAMAN ISLANDS

The seas around the Andaman Islands are some of the world's most unspoiled. Marine life is abundant, with an estimated 750 species of fish existing on one reef alone, and parrot, trigger and angel fish living alongside manta rays, reef sharks and loggerhead turtles. Many species of fish and coral are unique to the area, and fascinating ecosystems exist in ash beds and cooled lava based around the volcanic Barren Island. For a quick taste of marine life, you could start by **snorkelling**; most hotels can supply masks and snorkels, though some equipment is in dire need of replacement. The only way to get really close, and venture out into deeper waters, is to **scuba dive**. The undisputed home of **diving** is Havelock, with eight centres up and running at the last count, and there are also operators on Neil, Long and South Andaman. Since 2013 the **decompression chamber** at the naval base in Port Blair has been open to any divers with suspected bends, boosting safety.

PRICES AND COURSES

Prices are very similar at all the centres, with certified divers paying around ₹4500–5000 for two tanks; more economical packages, often including accommodation and food, are available for multiple dives, while Discover Scuba introductory days go for ₹4000–5000. **Courses** cost about ₹18,000 for a basic four-day PADI open-water qualification, ₹15,500 for advanced or ₹50,000 to go all the way up to Divemaster, including all the tanks.

DIVING ADVICE

Underwater, it's not uncommon to come across schools of reef shark, which rarely turn hostile, but one thing to watch out for and avoid is the **black-and-white sea snake**. Though these seldom attack – and, since their fangs are at the back of their mouths, would find it difficult to get a grip on any human – their bite is twenty times deadlier than that of the cobra.

Increased tourism inevitably puts pressure on the delicate marine ecosystem, and poorly funded wildlife organizations can do little to prevent damage from insensitive visitors. Ensure your presence in the sea around the reefs does not harm the coral by observing the following **Green Coral Code** while diving or snorkelling:

• Never touch or walk on living coral, or it will die.
• Try to keep your feet away from reefs while wearing fins; the sudden sweep of water caused by a flipper kick can be enough to destroy coral.
• Always control the speed of your descent while diving; enormous damage can be caused by divers landing hard on a coral bed.
• Never break off pieces of coral from a reef, and remember that it is illegal to export dead coral from the islands, even fragments you may have found on a beach.

DIVE CENTRES

Andaman Bubbles Beach #5, Havelock ☎95318 35655, ⌨andamanbubbles.com. Top-quality centre with excellent equipment and nitrox diving.

Barefoot Scuba Beach #3, Havelock ☎03192 282181, ⌨diveandamans.com. A PADI 5-star-rated operator with expert divemasters. Offers cheap accommodation with multiple dive packages.

Dive India Beach #5, Havelock ☎03192 214247, ⌨diveindia.com. One of the more established operations on Havelock. It has another branch on Neil, too.

India Scuba Explorers Neil Kendra, Neil ☎99332 71450, ⌨indiascubaexplorers.com. Small but professional German-run dive centre.

Infiniti Live-Aboard Chiriya Tapu, South Andaman ☎99200 88435, ⌨infinitiliveaboard.com. Reliable company run by a team of enthusiastic mainlanders with a smart boat with sleeping facilities, good for getting to Cinque and other more distant sites.

Lacadives Chiriya Tapu, South Andaman ☎98209 28271, ⌨lacadives.com. After nearly twenty years of experience in the Lakshadweeps, Lacadives now explore the reefs around South Andaman.

GETTING AROUND

By bus From the jetty buses run hourly from 6.30am to Radhnagar (aka Beach #7), the last returning at 6pm. Another service runs several times daily to Kalapathar, passing down the east coast, where the bulk of the accommodation is located.

By bike You can rent a scooter, motorbike (around ₹350/day) or cycle (₹60/day) at the guesthouses.

ACCOMMODATION

With the only fully developed tourist scene in the Andamans, Havelock now has nearly a hundred accommodation establishments to choose from, offering everything from the most basic huts to luxuriously furnished cottages. Prices can rise by fifty percent from mid-December to mid-January, and drop considerably between May and October.

Barefoot at Havelock Radhnagar ☎03192 220191, ⓦbarefoot-andaman.com. Havelock's most luxurious resort, with fan-cooled duplexes, "Nicobari" cottages, a/c "Andaman" villas and top-quality a/c Rajasthani tents. The fine restaurant and bar area are also attractive timber-and-thatch structures. ₹9500

★**Barefoot Scuba Resort** Beach #3 ☎03192 282343, ⓦdiveandamans.com. The home of Barefoot's dive centre offers luxury Rajasthani tents and smart bamboo duplexes with attached bathrooms, as well as humble huts for people on dive packages. ₹4000

Dreamland Resort Radhnagar ☎94742 24166. Just 200m back along the main road from the beach, offering ten basic, blue raffia huts with shared bathrooms, plus some smart new attached rooms. The only cheapie at Havelock's best beach. No wi-fi. ₹700/₹1200

★**Emerald Gecko** Beach #5 ☎94742 50821, ⓦemerald-gecko.com. The nicest mid-range resort, with ten modest huts (with or without private bathroom) and half a dozen superbly designed two-tier cottages. Breakfast included. No wi-fi. ₹1400/₹2300

The Flying Elephant Kalapathar ☎94760 13943, ⓦflying-elephant.in. The most remote place to stay on the island, with five spacious duplexes and four huge bungalows, connected by an elevated boardwalk, plus a yoga room. There's a restaurant on the opposite side of the road. No wi-fi. ₹4000

Green Valley Beach #5 ☎94760 02984, ⓦgreenvalleyhavelock.com. This mixture of compact bamboo huts and sturdier plywood ones is one of the few remaining cheapies anywhere, although the a/c options are much costlier. Wi-fi ₹200/hr. ₹600

SeaShell Havelock Beach #2 ☎03192 211830, ⓦseashellhotels.net. Arranged around a manicured lawn barely 1km from the jetty, there are five types of a/c lodgings from traditional villas to chalets, which offer all mod cons including flatscreen TVs. ₹8000

Sea View Beach #3 ☎94342 98979. Very simple but spacious ecofriendly bamboo huts, all with attached bathrooms and mosquito nets. The restaurant does decent, mostly Indian food. No wi-fi. ₹600

★**Wild Orchid** Beach #5 ☎95318 35655, ⓦwildorchidandaman.com. Easily the best value higher-end resort, for its classy cottages (some with a/c), splendidly constructed timber restaurant and lounge, and all-round laidback atmosphere. Breakfast included. No wi-fi. ₹6000

8

EATING

★**Anju-coco** Beach #5 ☎94760 76405. Havelock's best independent roadside restaurant, in expanded new premises. Filling ₹50 breakfasts, cheap fish and chips, Tibetan *momos* and more adventurous dishes for ₹180–250. Try the dramatic Fire Waterfall cocktail. Daily 8am–10.30pm.

Barefoot Bar & Brasserie Main jetty ☎94742 24212. Smart upper-storey wooden deck with film posters and expensive food. Most mains around ₹300 and seafood sizzlers up to ₹800. Inexpensive lunchtime thalis served downstairs. Daily 11am–4.30pm & 6–10pm.

Blackbeard's Bistro Emerald Gecko, Beach #5 ☎03192 206084. The lovely open dining area has a bar and furniture created from recycled timber, and often offers rare dishes such as ceviche as well as fresh fish cooked in delicious and imaginative sauces for ₹300–350. Daily 7–10.30am, noon–2pm & 6–9.30pm.

Café del Mar Barefoot Scuba Resort, Beach #3 ☎03192 282343. Convivial joint serving Indian, Chinese and Western dishes. Excellent meat and seafood specials for ₹200–250. Daily 6.30am–9pm.

Fat Martin At Andaman Bubbles Beach #5 ☎94760 71965. Gradually expanding around the dive shop, this place rustles up superb masala dosas for ₹80, as well as main courses ranging from ₹150–400. Daily 7am–8pm.

★**Full Moon Café** Island Vinnie's, Beach #3 ☎01392 282222. Wide menu, including some genuinely spicy Indian cuisine, plus many Western favourites and fresh seafood, mostly ₹150–400. Try the succulent fish tikka. Daily 7am–11pm.

Nala's Kingdom Main jetty ☎01392 282233. The most salubrious place in the jetty area, serving Bengali, South Indian, Chinese and various fish dishes for under ₹200. Great thalis too. New branch at Beach #5. Daily 7am–4pm & 7–9.30pm.

★**Red Snapper** Wild Orchid, Beach #5 ☎03192 282472. Excellent upmarket seafood, meat and veg menu, served in classy surroundings. Most dinners are in the ₹400–500 range. Occasional recitals of traditional Bengali music. Daily 7–10.30am, noon–2.30pm & 6.30–9pm.

DRINKING AND NIGHTLIFE

Cicada Beach #5 ☎94742 67689. The island's only dedicated nightspot, set amid the palm groves inland from the road, has recorded and occasional live music, as well as great cocktails. Only operates in the dry months. Daily 9pm–midnight.

Long Island

Just off the southeast coast of Middle Andaman, **Long Island** is attracting a growing number of travellers, with a couple of excellent beaches in **Marg Bay** and **Lalaji Bay**. Both of these are most easily approached by chartering a fisherman's dinghy from the jetty (around ₹500 each way), if you can find one, although Lalaji can be reached on foot by following the red arrows across the island and then turning left along the coast. You should not attempt this at high tide, and even when the sea is out it's quite an obstacle course of rocks and fallen trees.

The main settlement by the jetty has the island's only facilities, which amount to a handful of shops, a couple of basic *dhabas*, and the only two places to stay.

ARRIVAL AND DEPARTURE

LONG ISLAND

By boat Long Island has four weekly ferries to and from Havelock (4hr–4hr 30 min), Neil (5hr–5hr 30min), Port Blair (6–7hr) and Rangat (1hr), as well as a small local ferry connection with Yeratta (2 daily; 1hr 15min), 9km from Rangat.

ACCOMMODATION AND EATING

Blue Planet Signposted with blue arrows from the jetty ☎03192 215923, ⊕ blueplanetandamans.com. Around a dozen adjoining rooms of varying sizes, some attached, arranged compactly around the courtyard restaurant whose centrepiece is a giant *mowhar* tree. Also a couple of large cottages and campsite nearby. ₹600/₹1200

Forest Office Guesthouse Near the jetty ☎03192 278532. Some people see if there is any availability at the Forest Office's guesthouse, which has a couple of spartan attached rooms usually occupied by officials. ₹500

Hotel GKR Opposite the village football pitch ☎94742 08368. A very basic restaurant that serves South Indian snacks, fish fry and fairly skimpy thalis for ₹100. Daily 6am–9pm.

Middle Andaman

For most travellers, **Middle Andaman** is a gruelling rite of passage to be endured en route to or from the north. The sinuous Andaman Trunk Road, hemmed in by walls of towering forest, winds through kilometres of jungle, and crosses the strait that separates the island from its neighbour, **Baratang**, by means of a rusting flat-bottomed ferry. The island's frontier feeling is heightened by the knowledge that the impenetrable forests west of the ATR comprise the **Jarawa Tribal Reserve** (see box, p.448). Of its two main settlements, the more northerly **Mayabunder**, the port for alluring **Interview Island** (see opposite), is slightly more appealing than characterless inland **Rangat** because of its pleasant setting by the sea, but neither town gives any reason to dally. Baratang, meanwhile, has some interesting mud volcanoes and limestone caves, which can be accessed on the boat trips that run daily except Sunday according to demand (₹350).

Rangat

At the southeast corner of Middle Andaman, **RANGAT** consists of a ramshackle sprawl around two rows of chai shops and general stores divided by the ATR, which is now at least paved. However, as a major staging post on the journey north, it's impossible to avoid – just don't get stranded here if you can help it.

ARRIVAL AND DEPARTURE

RANGAT

By boat The four weekly ferries from Port Blair via Havelock, Long Island and Neil dock at Rangat Bay, 8km east, from where you can take a bus or auto-rickshaw into town; there are also small daily ferries to Long Island from nearby Yeratta.

By bus Rangat is served by two daily government buses to Port Blair (6–7hr) as well as some private services, which pass through in the morning from further north. There are several daily buses to Mayabunder (2hr 30min–3hr) and Diglipur (4hr 30min–5hr).

ACCOMMODATION AND EATING

APWD Rest House ⊙ 03192 274237. The Andaman Public Works Department (APWD)'s *Rest House*, pleasantly situated up a winding hill from the bazaar with views across the valley, is the best place to stay and eat, providing good, filling fish thalis (₹100). No wi-fi. ₹600

Aroma Restaurant Main Rd ⊙ 94742 73527. Other than a couple of *dhabas*, this first-floor place, offering north and South Indian and Chinese staples, is the only place to eat in town. Daily 11am–10pm.

Hawksbill Nest 15km north at Cuthbert Bay (aka RRO)

⊙ 03192 279159. The rooms (some a/c) are characterless but comfortable at this A&N Tourism hotel, which is invariably empty. Buses between Rangat and Mayabunder stop here on request and there is a fine beach nearby. No wi-fi. Dorms ₹150, doubles ₹600

Sea Shore Lodge ⊙ 03192 274464. If you have an early ferry out of Rangat Bay, it's better to stay down near the jetty at the friendly *Sea Shore Lodge*. Basic meals can be had from the motley conglomeration of stalls between the lodge and the jetty. No wi-fi. ₹600

Mayabunder

Only 70km north of Rangat by road, **MAYABUNDER** is perched on a long promontory right at the top of the island and surrounded by mangrove swamps. Unfortunately, the bus journey from Rangat can exceed three hours due to continual stops on the surprisingly populated route. Home to a large minority of former Burmese **Karen** tribal people who were originally brought here as cheap logging labour by the British, the village is more spread out and more appealing than Rangat. At the brow of the hill, before it descends to the jetty, a small hexagonal wooden structure houses the **Forest Museum** (Mon–Sat 8am–noon & 1–4pm; free), which holds a motley collection of turtle shells, snakes in formaldehyde, dead coral and a crocodile skull.

8

ARRIVAL AND DEPARTURE — MAYABUNDER

By bus Some of the buses from Port Blair (9–10hr) and Rangat (2hr 30min–3hr) now continue over the new bridge to Diglipur on North Andaman (2hr from Mayabunder).

ACCOMMODATION AND EATING

Anmol Lodge Middle of the bazaar in the village centre ⊙ 03192 262695. This once humble lodge has been fully renovated so all rooms are now attached, with cable TV and some a/c. Food must be pre-ordered. No wi-fi. ₹700

APWD Rest House Next door to the Forest Museum ⊙ 03192 273211. The rooms (some a/c) are large and very comfortable, plus there's a pleasant garden and gazebo overlooking the sea, and a dining room serving good

set meals (around ₹100). Often booked up by officials. No wi-fi. ₹600

Sea'N'Sand 1km south of the centre ⊙ 03192 273454, ⊙ thanzin_the_great@yahoo.co.in. Nicely located by the sea, this very welcoming Karen-run lodge has a range of simple rooms, mostly attached, and a reasonable restaurant. ₹300/₹600

Interview Island

Mayabunder is the jumping-off place for **Interview Island**, a windswept nature sanctuary off the remote northwest coast of Middle Andaman – if you've come to the Andamans to watch **wildlife**, it should be top of your list. Large and mainly flat, it is completely uninhabited save for a handful of unfortunate forest wardens, coastguards and policemen, posted here to ward off poachers. Foreigners aren't permitted to spend the night on the island, and to do a day-trip you must first obtain a ₹500 **permit** from the Forest Museum in Mayabunder (see above). The only way to reach Interview is to charter a private fishing dinghy from Mayabunder jetty for around ₹4000 to ₹5000. Arrange one the day before and leave at first light. Ask your boatman to moor by the **beach** at the southern tip of the island, which has a perennial freshwater pool inside a low cave; legend has it that the well, a nesting site for white-bellied **swifts**, has no bottom. At the forest post, where you have to sign an entry ledger, ask the wardens about the movements of Interview's feral **elephants**, descendants of trained elephants deserted here by a Kolkata-based logging company after its timber operation failed in the 1950s. **Saltwater crocodiles** are found on the island's eastern coastline.

North Andaman

Shrouded in dense jungle, **North Andaman** is the least populated of the region's large islands, crossed by a single road linking its scattered Bengali settlements. Although parts have been seriously logged, the total absence of driveable roads into northern and western areas has ensured blanket protection for a vast stretch of convoluted coastline, running from Austin Strait in the southwest to the northern tip, Cape Price; it's reassuring to know at least one extensive wilderness survives in the Andamans.

Despite the completion of the ATR's final section and the bridge from Middle Andaman, the main settlement of **DIGLIPUR** continues to exist in relative seclusion, though this may well change if the projected airport towards Kalipur opens. Known in the British era as Port Cornwallis, North Andaman's largest settlement is another disappointing market town where you're only likely to pause long enough to pick up a local bus further north to the coast. Unless you are catching a boat (to Smith or Ross islands or back to Port Blair) straightaway from the port of **Aerial Bay**, 9km northeast, it's better to continue another 9km to **Kalipur**, where there's an excellent deserted beach, backed by lush forest and covered in photogenic driftwood. Swimming is best at high tide because the water recedes across rocky mud pools. Offshore snorkelling is also excellent, especially along the reef that runs towards the islet barely 500m away.

It's possible to walk from Kalipur to **Saddle Peak**, the highest mountain in the Andamans at 737m, which rises dramatically to the south, swathed in lush jungle. A permit (₹250/25) to make the three- to four-hour climb must be obtained from the Range Officer at the forest checkpost near the start of the ascent, but don't attempt it without a guide and plenty of drinking water. Another enjoyable day-trip is to the **limestone caverns**, 12km south near Ramnagar beach, best accessed by dinghy from Kalipur. You can arrange a dinghy, or guide for the Saddle Peak climb, at *Pristine Beach Resort* (see below).

Smith and Ross islands

Many tourists find their way up here in order to explore the various **islands** dotted around the gulf north of Aerial Bay, particularly **Smith** and **Ross** (not to be confused with its namesake near Port Blair), whose white sandbars, coral reefs and flora are splendid. At low tide it is possible to walk between the two islands. You can organize the requisite ₹500 permit from the Wildlife Information booth at Aerial Bay and rent a boat (₹2500) for the return trip yourself, or through one of the area guesthouses – try *Pristine Beach Resort* (see below).

ARRIVAL AND DEPARTURE   NORTH ANDAMAN

By boat There are three boats a week in each direction from Aerial Bay to Port Blair (7–9hr).

By bus Several buses a day leave in the early morning for Port Blair (11–12hr) via Mayabunder (2hr) and Rangat (4hr 30min–5hr). There are 10–12 daily buses from Diglipur to Aerial Bay (20min) and Kalipur (45min).

ACCOMMODATION AND EATING

DIGLIPUR
APWD Rest House ☎ 03192 272203. On the hill above the main road, the *APWD Rest House* offers the village's nicest accommodation. ₹600

Maa Yashoda On the main road ☎ 99332 55086. This selection of ultra-basic rooms above a shop have bathrooms but not a lot else. ₹400

KALIPUR
★**Pristine Beach Resort** ☎ 03192 271793. Easily the most congenial place to stay on North Andaman, with a huge range of options from small but tidy huts through sturdy duplexes to luxury cottages, all set in lovely grounds near the beach. Very good restaurant too (most dishes ₹150–300). Free wi-fi 7–9am. ₹900

Turtle Resort ☎ 03192 272553. Typically institutional A&N Tourism hotel, which enjoys a prime location on a hilltop above the bay. The rooms are plain but large. Dorms ₹150, doubles ₹600

Little Andaman

Little Andaman is the furthest point south in the archipelago that foreigners can travel to on their tourist permit. Most of the island has been set aside as a tribal reserve for the **Onge** and is thus off-limits. It was also the only island open to foreigners to sustain extensive damage in the 2004 **tsunami**, but although a number of buildings were destroyed, and 64 people died, Little Andaman has recovered well. Relatively few visitors make it down here, although a slight improvement in tourist infrastructure renders it increasingly worthwhile for those who do. Still, it is worth noting that boats can be infrequent outside peak months and not all accommodations operate outside high season.

The main settlement, **INDIRA BAZAAR**, is 2km north of the jetty at **Hut Bay**, which curves gradually round in a majestic 8km sweep, the quality of the sand and beauty of the adjacent jungle increasing the further north you go. The top stretch is named **Netaji Nagar** after the village on the island's only road, which runs behind it. En route, you can detour 1km inland at the huge signpost about 2.5km north of Indira Bazaar to see the **White Surf Waterfalls** (daily dawn–dusk; ₹20). Made up of three 10- to 15m-high cascades, it's a relaxing spot; you can clamber into the right-hand fall for a soothing shower – yet crocodiles are said to inhabit the surrounding streams. Over the headland at the top of Hut Bay, 12km or so from the jetty, lies the smaller but equally picturesque crescent of **Butler Bay**. There's not much to do here but swim, sunbathe or look around the slightly eerie remains of the government beach resort, which was swept away by the tsunami – that is unless you've brought your surfboard with you: Little Andaman has a cult reputation among surfers for having some of the best conditions anywhere in South Asia.

8

ARRIVAL AND DEPARTURE   LITTLE ANDAMAN

By boat Daily ferries from Port Blair arrive at Hut Bay, the faster ones making the voyage in less than 6hr.

GETTING AROUND

Bicycles (₹50/day) and **mopeds** (₹300/day) can be rented through the guesthouses, but are in very short supply.

ACCOMMODATION AND EATING

Blue View Netaji Nagar ☎ 97344 80842. A motley mixture of huts and rooms, all with shared facilities, spaced around open ground, plus a good seafood restaurant (dishes ₹150–200). Only opens from late Nov to May. No wi-fi. ₹350

★**Jina Resort** Netaji Nagar ☎ 94760 38057. Pleasant and welcoming place with a sociable eating area and great banana leaf fish (₹200) on the menu. There are huts and rooms of varying sizes but all are non-attached. Only opens from late Nov to May. No wi-fi. ₹250

Palm Grove Indira Bazaar ☎ 94342 99212. Decent government-run restaurant which offers a limited menu of fish, chicken and veg dishes, mostly Indian. Filling thalis go for ₹130. Daily 7am–9pm.

Sealand Tourist Home Indira Bazaar ☎ 03192 284306. The best place to stay in the main settlement is this two-storey lodge, whose splendid bay-front location is marred by the architect's inexplicable decision to have all windows facing the interior. Some rooms a/c, all attached. No wi-fi. ₹500

Vvet Guest House Indira Bazaar ☎ 03192 284155. Functional government-run guesthouse whose staff can take some persuading to let you stay, but the small, pleasant garden makes the wrangling just about worthwhile. No wi-fi. ₹350

MURALS, KERALA

Contexts

463 History

481 Religion

488 Music and dance

490 Wildlife

496 Books

499 Language

507 Glossary

History

For many centuries, the geographical isolation of South India – separated from the North by the Vindhya range of sheer-sided table mountains – left the region insulated from the waves of invasion and assimilation that took place in the North. The influences of these invaders – among them the Aryans, Mauryans, and Mughals – did traverse the Vindhyas and the fertile Deccan Plateau, but they invariably did so slowly, by a process of gradual assimilation rather than conquest, enabling the societies of the peninsula to develop in their own way. Moreover, some of India's most defining cultural traits and traditions originated in the deep Dravidian south, from where they spread northwards.

Prehistory

Compared to the extraordinary wealth of archeological finds in northwestern India, evidence of **prehistoric settlement** in the South is scant – although one of the oldest human artefacts ever unearthed in Asia was discovered at Pallavaram, near Chennai (Madras), in 1863, by British archeologist Bruce Foote, who found an oval-shaped hand-axe which he surmised must have originated in the Lower Paleolithic era.

While hunter-gatherers roamed across the region, the development of rice cultivation and metalwork, were probably imported from the Northwest, primarily the Indus Valley region on the present-day border with Pakistan. Roughly contemporaneous with those of Sumer and ancient Egypt, the sophisticated **Indus Valley civilization** (or Harappan civilization), displayed remarkable longevity, surviving for a thousand years until its sudden demise around 1700 BC, probably caused by a catastrophic series of droughts, when its peoples began to move southwards.

Some historians have advanced this migration theory to account for the origins of the **Dravidians**, who are believed to have colonized the southwest of India around 1800 BC – the same time that the Indus Valley civilization went into decline. This is supported by research revealing that the main languages of the South have more in common with Brahui, an obscure Asiatic tongue spoken by nomads on the Iran–Pakistan border, than they do with the Indo-Aryan-based languages of the North.

By the dawn of the **Iron Age** early in the first millennium BC, much of northwest India had been colonized by the Aryans, a fairer-skinned nomadic people, thought to have originated in a region around the Caucasus Mountains (their language, an antiquated form of Sanskrit, has astonishingly close affinities with Latin, Greek and Celtic).

Dravidadesa: the early kingdoms

As North India came under the sway of the Aryans and Persians as well as seeing the arrival of two new religions, Buddhism and Jainism, the South remained something of a backwater. The rise of the **Mauryan Empire** under Chandragupta Maurya (340–298BC) and his son, **Ashoka** (c.268–232BC) the most famous of India's early rulers, extended only as far south as Mysore. Beyond here lay the three independent kingdoms of the **Cholas**, of the Coromandel region and Cauvery basin; the **Pandyas**, whose

1500–1000 BC	c. 1000 BC	c. 566–483 BC
The world's oldest surviving sacred texts, the Vedas, are composed in northern India	Rise of the caste system	Lifetime of Gautama Buddha, founder of the Buddhist faith

capital was at Madurai; and the **Cheras**, from southwest Kerala. Collectively, the kingdoms of these three undefeated dynasties comprised a domain known to northerners as **Dravidadesa**, "Land of the Tamils".

A wealth of historical detail relating to the early kingdoms of the South has survived, most of it in a remarkable body of classical Tamil poetry known as the **Sangam**, composed between the first and third centuries AD in Madurai. The texts, which were only rediscovered in the nineteenth century, refer to an era when the indigenous Dravidian culture of the deep south was being transformed by Sanskritic influences from the North. Nevertheless, they vividly demonstrate that some of the most distinctive characteristics of Indian civilization – including yoga, *tantra*, the cult of the god Murugan and goddess worship – were almost certainly indigenous to the South, and widespread well before the Aryans came to dominate the region completely.

The Sangam also records the stormy political relations between the three dynasties, who were frequently at war with each other, or with the rulers of neighbouring Sri Lanka. Ultimately, however, all three seem to have succumbed to an enigmatic fourth dynasty, the **Kalabhras**, about whom the Sangam poems say very little other than that they were "bad kings" (*kaliarasar*). Buddhist texts from a later period suggest the Kalabhras were originally hill tribes who swept down from the Deccan Plateau to harass the inhabitants of the river valleys and coastal areas, and later took up Jainism and Buddhism, deposing the Dravidian kings and persecuting the brahmins.

Sea trade and the rise of the Satavahnas

The cultural flowering of the Sangam era in the south, during the first two centuries AD, was stimulated by a rapid growth in **maritime trade** throughout the region. As well as Arab merchants, the ports of the Malabar and Coromandel coasts now began to welcome **Roman** ships and became an entrepôt for valuable foreign goods – notably Chinese silk and perfume from the Gangetic basin.

The vast trade wealth pouring into South India around the turn of the millennium enabled the region's rulers to create larger and more organized kingdoms, backed by well-equipped armies. Conditions were ripe for the rise of a major power, and this came in the first century BC with the advent of the **Satavahanas**, an obscure tribal dynasty from the Deccan who, in the space of a hundred years, assumed the imperial mantle of the Mauryans. By the time Ptolemy was writing his *Geography*, midway through the second century AD, the empire, based in **Pratisthana** (near modern Paithan in Maharashtra), comprised thirty fortified cities and stretched from coast to coast.

The **Satavahanas** (or Andhras, as they are referred to in some ancient texts) were also prolific patrons of the arts, responsible for the greatest monuments in India at that time and many of the most accomplished rock-cut caves of the northwest Deccan. However, the crowning glory of Andhran art was to be the Great Stupa complex at **Amaravati**, in Andhra Pradesh (see p.289), whose exquisite bas-reliefs (some of which are now housed in the Government Museum in Chennai; see p.372) are considered by many scholars to be the finest ancient Indian sculpture.

The Early Middle Ages: 600–1200 AD

The history of the early middle ages in South India, from the time of the Satavahanas' demise to the arrival of the Muslims, revolves around the rise and fall of a mosaic of

265–232 BC	261 BC	375–415 AD	460–477 AD
Reign of the Mauryan emperor Ashoka	Cave monasteries appear in the Deccan region	The Golden Age of Classical India during the reign of Chandra Gupta II	Ajanta's finest cave paintings are commissioned by Emperor Harishena

regional dynasties. These invariably fought each other to gain supremacy for short periods, and then found their rule usurped by one or other of their adversarial neighbours.

Foremost among the states of the southern Deccan were the **Chalukyas**, who founded a capital at Vatapi (**Badami**) and a series of magnificent stone temples. The Chalukyas' conspicuous wealth inevitably attracted the attentions of their neighbours. After fending off two invasions, they eventually succumbed in 753 AD to the **Rashtrakutas**, whose domain extended most of the way across the Deccan.

The Chalukyas' southern enemies, the **Pallavas**, emerged after defeating the Kalabhras, the "bad kings" who originally routed the region's three early dynasties. From the outset, the Pallavas seem to have been keen seafarers, trading with Greeks, Satavahanas and Romans, whose coins have all been found amid the ruins of ancient **Mamallapuram**, just south of Chennai. The extraordinary crop of stone temples (foremost among them the Shore Temple, see p.382), open-air bas-reliefs and finely carved caves dotted around this fishing and stone-carving village recall the era when it ranked among the busiest ports in Asia.

The temples of Mamallapuram provided the main architectural inspiration for the **Cholas**, an offshoot of the ancient dynasty of the same name who asserted their independence from the Pallavas in 897 AD. During their 250-year rule, the Cholas expanded out of their royal capital, **Thanjavur**, in the Cauvery basin, defeating both the Pandyas and Cheras, and later conquering Sri Lanka, the Maldives and the Andamans, in addition to enclaves in Java and Sumatra. Combined with the huge sums in plunder yielded by their military campaigns, the Cholas' trade monopoly financed an awesome building spree including the colossal Brihadishwara temple, in its day the largest in India.

Muslim incursions

At the start of the eleventh century, a new player appeared on the political map of northern India. **Mahmud**, a Turkish chieftain who had established a powerful kingdom at Ghazni, near Kabul in Afghanistan, made seventeen plundering raids into the plains of northern India between 1000 and 1027 AD. His was the first of many Muslim incursions

---

BHAKTI AND THE TAMIL POETS

From the eighth century onwards, the devotional form of Hinduism known as **bhakti**, which first blossomed in Tamil Nadu, spread north into the rest of India to become, as it still is, the dominant strain of Hinduism throughout the country. This was essentially a popular movement which encouraged individual devotees to form a highly personal relationship with a chosen god (*ishtadevata*), an approach which revolutionized Hindu practice by offering a religious path and goal open to all castes.

The great champions of *bhakti* were the **poet-saints** of Tamil Nadu, often said to have "sung" the religions of Jainism and Buddhism out of South India. Although in practice a variety of deities was worshipped, the movement had two strands: the **Nayanmars**, devoted to Shiva, and the **Alvars**, faithful to Vishnu. Collections of their poetry, the greatest literary legacy of South India, remain popular today, and the poets themselves are almost deified, featuring in carvings in many temples.

---

543 AD	700–728 AD	757–790 AD	Early 11th century
Chalukya dynasty found their capital at Badami, erecting India's first freestanding stone temples	Pallava dynasty build the famous Shore Temple at Mamallapuram	Kailash temple carved at Ellora in Maharashtra	The Cholas establish an empire stretching from the far south of India to Sumatra

from the northwest that would, after two hundred years of constant infighting and wars with local rulers, lead to the creation of an Islamic empire based in Delhi.

Founded in 1206 AD, the **Delhi Sultanate** made little impact on the South during its formative years. In 1309, however, the redoubtable Sultan **Allauddin Khilji** set his sights southwards. Having heard rumours of the treasures stored in the great Tamil temples, he took advantage of the Cholas' decline to mount a raid. It is recorded that his general, the ruthless military genius and former Hindu slave **Malik Kafur**, returned with a thousand camels bearing booty, including the famous Koh-i-noor diamond. This, however, was merely a prelude to the sultanate's second expedition of 1310–11, in the course of which Allauddin's army pressed into the deep south itself. Raiding towns and desecrating the splendid Chola temples of the Cauvery Delta, it reached Madurai on April 10, 1311, and mercilessly sacked the Pandyas' capital, massacring the few of its inhabitants who had not fled.

Vijayanagar: 1346–1565

The main bulwark against Muslim incursion, not just from the Delhi Sultanate but also from the emerging **Deccan** and **Bahmani sultanates**, was the southern Hindu kingdom of **Vijayanagar**. Founded on the banks of the River Tungabhadra (at modern-day Hampi), it came to dominate the entire region south of the River Krishna. The dynastic capital, Vijayanagar ("City of Victory") became, for an all too brief period, among the most splendid in the world. Travellers such as Domingo Paes, who stayed there between 1522 and 1524, marvelled at the opulence of its royal court, the richness of its bazaars and the sumptuousness of its festivals. Under the rule of Krishna Deva Raya (1509–29) the South acquired some of its most impressive **temple towers** (*gopuras*), erected by the king to foster loyalty among brahmins and inhabitants of distant regions over which Vijayanagar's hold was precarious.

After Krishna Deva Raya's death in 1529, internal struggles and conflicts with the Portuguese weakened the empire. However, it was the Vijayanagars' old foes, the Bijapuris, who eventually brought their glorious rule to an abrupt and bloody end. Having benefited from the Deccan sultanates' constant feuding for more than a century, the Vijayanagars made a fatal mistake when they desecrated mosques during campaigns in the 1550s. This finally galvanized the sultans to set aside their differences and march on Vijayanagar. The armies met at Talikota in 1565. At first, the battle seemed to be going the Hindus' way, but suddenly turned against them when two of their Muslim generals defected. The Vijayanagar regent, Rama Raya, was captured and beheaded, while his brother, Tirumala, fled with what was left of the army, leaving the capital defenceless.

The ensuing sack lasted six months and reduced Asia's most illustrious city to rubble. Predictably, the Deccan sultans squabbled over the spoils and spent the next century fighting each other, leaving the region vulnerable to invasion by the Mughals.

The Portuguese

Around the same time as Vijayanagar was enjoying its period of greatest prosperity, the harbinger of a new regional power appeared on the horizon of the Arabian Sea. Driven

1000–27	1192	1198
The Muslim warlord Mahmud of Ghazni mounts seventeen bloody incursions into Hindu India from Afghanistan	Muhammad of Ghor defeats Prithviraj III at the Battle of Tarain, laying the foundations of the Delhi Sultanate	Qutbu'd-din Aibak erects the Qutub Minar victory tower in Delhi, marking the start of Muslim rule in India

by the lust for "Christians and spices", **Vasco da Gama**'s arrival on the Malabar Coast in 1498 blazed a trail that would, after only fifteen years, result in the creation of Europe's first bona fide colony in the East.

Formerly a Vijayanagar port, **Goa** had been taken by the Bahmanis, whom the Portuguese, under **Admiral Alfonso de Albuquerque**, expelled in 1510. Thereafter, despite repeated attempts by the Muslims to regain their possession, the colony expanded at a breathless pace. At the height of its power, the city was the lynchpin of a trade network extending from the Philippines to the north Atlantic, with cathedrals to rival Rome's and a population that at one time was greater even than Lisbon's.

Yet, despite enjoying an early monopoly on maritime trade in Asia, ruthlessly enforced by their insurmountable naval supremacy, the Portuguese were unable to sustain an early lead over their European rivals. Repeated outbreaks of disease depleted the population of Goa, while the defeat in 1565 of Vijayanagar, which by that time accounted for a significant portion of the city's trade, had a disastrous effect on the whole Portuguese economy. Unable to maintain control of the sea lanes, Portugal

VASCO DA GAMA'S REVENGE

The essential facts of **Vasco da Gama**'s three expeditions to India have survived thanks to the diaries of Alvaro Velho, one of his soldiers. These describe in detail how the small fleet of five ships set sail from Lisbon in July 1497, the sacred symbol of Christ billowing in their sails. Their route took them around the islands of Cabo Verde (Cape Verde) and four thousand miles southeast to round the Cape of Good Hope at the beginning of November.

At Malindi, da Gama was granted the services of an expert navigator, an Arab sea captain called **Ibn' Masjid**, who piloted the three remaining *caravelas* across the Indian Ocean to Calicut. However, news of atrocities committed by the Portuguese en route had preceded their arrival, and the local *zamorin*, Mana Vikrama, briefly imprisoned da Gama before he was allowed to fill his holds with pepper and leave – an insult the proud Portuguese admiral would never forget.

Four years later he returned to **Calicut**, this time bent on revenge. In addition to his incarceration by the Hindu ruler, he intended to avenge the murder of 53 Portuguese killed during a previous expedition in 1500. As a prelude to the onslaught, da Gama waylaid a Muslim ship en route from Mecca and burned alive all 700 of its passengers and crew. Then he set about bombarding the city. While the cannonade decimated Calicut's temples and houses, da Gama ordered the crews of a dozen or so trade ships anchored in the harbour to be rounded up. Before killing them, he had the prisoners' hands, ears and noses hacked off and the pieces sent ashore.

Leaving Calicut in flames, Da Gama sailed south to **Cochin**, where a mixture of gifts and threats was enough to make the local raja fill the Portuguese ships holds with pepper and cardamom at favourable prices before the admiral began his return voyage, slipping past the waiting navy of the angry *zamorin*.

Da Gama's tactics unleashed turmoil on the Malabar. Within months a major offensive was launched by the *zamorin* to punish the raja of Cochin for his collusion. After some initial success, the invasion was forestalled by the monsoons. It then foundered completely after a Portuguese naval squadron sailed to Cochin's aid in September 1503. The grateful raja responded by granting the Portuguese permission to build a fort at the mouth of his capital's harbour: erected in 1504, **Fort Manuel** – the nucleus of Fort Cochin – would be the first ever colonial stronghold on the Indian coast.

1498	1510	1526
Vasco da Gama completes the sea route across the Arabian Sea to land in Calicut on the Malabar Coast (Kerala)	The Portuguese admiral Alfonso Albuquerque takes the strategically vital port of Goa	Babur defeats Ibrahim Lodi's forces at the Battle of Panipat to found the Mughal dynasty

gradually saw its trade empire whittled away, first by the Dutch, and later by the French and British. Goa actually survived as a Portuguese colony until 1961, but was effectively a spent force by the end of the seventeenth century.

The Mughal Empire

Descendants of Timur and Genghis Khan's Mongols from Samarkand in Central Asia, the **Mughals** staked their claim to North India with Babur's defeat of the Delhi sultan, Ibrahim Lodi, in 1526. Through the revolutionary deployment of small arms and mobile artillery, the invaders routed an army ten times their size. The victory inaugurated an empire that would, by the time of its demise two hundred years later, become the largest and most powerful since Ashoka's, eighteen centuries earlier. Keen patrons of the arts as well as fearsome military strategists, successive emperors blended Persian and Indian culture to create some of the Subcontinent's greatest treasures, including the Red Fort in Delhi and the Taj Mahal in Agra.

Aurangzeb and the Marathas

The Mughals' influence, however, had little impact on the South until the reign of **Shah Jahan** (1627–58), when the northernmost of the Deccan sultanates, Ahmadnagar, was annexed. A hundred years after their sack of Vijayanagar, Bijapur and Golconda also succumbed, this time to the last of the Great Mughals, **Aurangzeb** (1658–1707).

The most expansionist ruler of the dynasty, Aurangzeb was also a devout Sunni, notorious for his rough treatment of Hindus, and for reinstating the much-hated *jizya* tax on non-Muslims that his great-grandfather, Akbar, had repealed. Aurangzeb's arch-adversaries in the Deccan region were a confederacy of low-caste Hindu warriors called the **Marathas**. Unlike the Mughals, they attacked not with large, formal armies, but by mounting guerrilla-style raids, retreating to the safety of impregnable fortresses perched on the top of table mountains.

Under their most audacious and gifted leader, **Shivaji**, whom Aurangzeb named "The Mountain Rat", the Marathas managed on numerous occasions to outwit the Mughal's superior forces, and over time came to dominate a large chunk of western India. Aurangzeb moved his court from Delhi to Aurangabad in order to personally supervise the subjugation of the Marathas. It was from there, too, that he mounted the victorious campaigns against Bijapur and Golconda that extended Mughal rule to its eventual high-water mark.

Aurangzeb may have pushed the empire's boundaries further south than any of his predecessors, but his policies ultimately brought about the dynasty's downfall. To win over the nobles of his new acquisitions in the Deccan, the emperor demanded lower taxes from them, which left an administrative shortfall that he subsequently made up for by over-taxing his farmers. This duly provoked **peasant uprisings**, made more deadly by the proliferation of small arms at that time, which Aurangzeb's cumbersome, elephant-based army was ill suited to quell. In addition, the burden on the shattered Deccan states of reprovisioning an army whose annual losses were calculated at 100,000 men and around 300,000 animals was enormous. In 1702–03, famine and pestilence wiped out an estimated two million people in the region.

1600	1615	1658
The British East India Company is formed	Sir Thomas Roe, British ambassador to the Mughal court, negotiates trade rights with Jahangir	Aurangzeb, last, most devout and austere of the great Mughal emperors, ascends to the throne after murdering his brothers

After the last Great Mughal's death in 1707, half a century of gradual decay was presided over by a succession of eight incompetent emperors. The final blow to the Mughal dynasty came in 1779, when the Persian Nadir Shah raided Delhi and made off with a vast loot that included the Peacock Throne itself. "The streets", wrote one eyewitness, "were strewn with corpses like a garden with weeds. The city was reduced to ashes and looked like a burnt plain."

The Dutch, British and French

The Portuguese domination of the Indian Ocean was complete by the time Babur descended on Delhi, and neither he nor his Mughal successors felt in the least threatened by the presence of foreign powers on their coastal borders. In fact, they welcomed the traders as providers of silver and gold which they could use to mint money. In the course of the seventeenth and eighteenth centuries, however, the European powers would become a force to be reckoned with, eventually replacing the Mughals as India's rulers.

The first challengers of the Portuguese trade supremacy were the **Dutch**, whose cheaper and more manoeuvrable *fluyt* ships easily outsailed the more old-fashioned, ungainly *caravelas* from Lisbon. Determined not to allow Asia to be carved up by the proselytizing Roman Catholics, the Protestant Dutch East India Company – founded in 1602, only a couple of decades after Holland's victorious war of independence over Spain – systematically took control of the international spice trade, relieving the Portuguese of the strategically essential Moluccas in 1641, Ceylon in 1663 and their chief ports on the Malabar Coast soon after.

Although established two years before its Dutch counterpart, the British East India Company lagged behind initially, operating on a more modest scale with a string of trading posts, or **factories**, around the coast, where goods – mostly **textiles** – could be stored awaiting annual shipment. Its first headquarters (from 1612), in Surat, Gujarat, was relocated to Bombay (Mumbai) in 1674, and by the mid-seventeenth century the British possessed 27 such outposts, the largest being **Fort St George** on the Coromandel coast – the forerunner of Madras (modern Chennai).

The greatest threat to Britain's early Indian colonies was not local rulers, but rival Europeans. In the case of Fort St George, the **French** – whose own East India Company, started in 1664, was based further south on the Coromandel coast at **Pondicherry** (now Puducherry) – were to prove the most troublesome, prompted by the War of the Austrian Succession breaking out in Europe.

The Carnatic Wars

The first clash between France and Britain in India (which became known as the **Carnatic Wars**) came in 1746 when the French governor of Pondicherry, the wily diplomat **Joseph François Dupleix**, captured Fort St George with the help of a French fleet commanded by **Admiral La Bourdonnais**. Among those imprisoned during the short French occupation (the fort was handed back two years later) was a young **Robert Clive**, considered one of the founders of the British Raj.

Dupleix had long since learnt that the best way to extend French influence, and trade, was to forge alliances with whichever local ruler looked likely to emerge victorious

1659	1666	1668
The Maratha warlord, Shivaji, defeats the sultan of Bijapur to become the most powerful chief in peninsular India	Shivaji and his son, Sambhaji, escape from Aurangzeb's court by hiding in a box of sweets	Bombay is leased from the British Crown to the East India Company who begin fortifying the city

from the furious in-fighting that wracked the South during the break-up of the Mughal empire. In this way, the British and the French were drawn into the conflicts of regional rulers, often facing each other from opposite ends of a battlefield.

In one such encounter, where the European powers pitched in to support rival sons of the nawab of **Arcot** in 1751, Clive, then only 26 years old, distinguished himself by holding a fortress for fifty days with only two hundred men against a vastly superior force of fifteen thousand French and their Indian allies. The first great triumph of British arms in the history of India, this feat made Clive a hero, a reputation he consolidated soon afterwards by marching through the monsoons to intervene decisively at the siege of **Trichinopoly**. The French lost half their army in this second battle, and saw their protégé, Chandra Sahib, captured and killed. Dupleix's reputation never recovered; he was recalled two years later and died destitute.

The British went on to defeat the French again at Wandiwash in 1760, and finally took Pondicherry after an eight-month siege, effectively bringing to an end the French bid for power in India.

Haider Ali and Tipu Sultan of Mysore

The French were certainly down, but they were not yet quite out, thanks to the one remaining thorn in the side of British territorial ambitions: **Haider Ali**. A former general of the maharaja of Mysore, Haider Ali had usurped his master's throne in 1761 and within a short time ruled over virtually the entire South. The secret of his dramatic success lay in his readiness to learn from the Europeans, in particular the French, whose military tactics he emulated, and who provided him with officers to train his infantry. Between 1767 and 1769, he fought a series of battles with the British, whom he had always, unlike other Indian rulers, regarded as a threat to India as a whole, and whom he eventually coerced into a highly favourable treaty after threatening to attack Madras.

Held back by corrupt officials in both Madras and Calcutta, the British failed to provide a robust response, but rallied during the governorship of **Warren Hastings**. In

---

TEA AND HIGH SOCIETY

The most pervasive of all the British Raj's bequests to its former colony is without doubt **tea**. India is responsible for just over one third of global production, and around a quarter of that comes from plantations in the Nilgiri Hills in the south, which churn out between 180 and 200 million kilograms per year. The bulk of it goes to domestic consumption in the form of CTC ("crush, tear and curled") – a lumpy black powder yielding a dark, flavoursome chai. South Indians like it brewed milky and sweet. Filling glasses from kettles raised to arm's height, chai-wallahs pop up wherever, and whenever, anyone might conceivably need a pick-me-up.

In the broiling South, tea could only be grown in the cool fresh air of the Western Ghat mountains. This was also where homesick Brits could ride, hunt, ramble and sketch without fear of collapsing from the heat. Bungalows were built as hot-season boltholes, and swathed in rose bushes and ivy. Railway lines, racecourses and that most British of institutions, the Members' Club, followed in their wake, eventually coalescing into the hotbed of snobbery and sexual intrigue that would become the "**Hill Station**". Today you can find vestigeas of the empire's prewar twilight in Munnar's tea estates (see p.332), leafy Matheran (p.141) and Ootacamund (see p.434), once known as "Snooty Ooty" and worth visiting for its steam railway.

1674	1757	1779
The French East India Company establish their headquarters in Pondicherry	Robert Clive's military victory in Bengal lays the foundation for two centuries of British rule in India	With the Mughal dynasty in decline, the Persian king Nadir Shah sacks Delhi, slaughtering tens of thousands

1778, they were once again at war with the French, and fending off Marathas in the west, which Haider Ali took as his cue to launch a major offensive. Assisted by the French, who landed troops by sea to join the battle, Haider again forced the British to sue for peace.

This was far from the most honourable period in the imperial history of France and Britain. During their various marches and skirmishes across South India and Kerala, known as the Carnatic Wars temples were regularly desecrated and massacres were commonplace; in all, a million Tamils were killed in the crossfire.

After Haider's death in 1782, his son **Tipu Sultan**, aka "the Tiger of Mysore", carried on his father's campaigns, but did so with diminished support from the French, who had by this time begun to wind down their Indian operations. In the end, Tipu Sultan was let down badly by his father's former allies. In 1799, they failed to dispatch troops to reinforce him when an army, led by Lord Wellesley and his brother Arthur (later the Duke of Wellington, of Waterloo fame) marched on **Srirangapatnam**. Tipu Sultan died defending a breach in his capital's walls (a story that later inspired Wilkie Collins's novel, *The Moonstone*), and Mysore was returned to the old Hindu dynasty Haider Ali had deposed. After more than a century of continual conflict between the European powers and their various allies, the struggle for control of India was finally won by the British.

British rule in the South

Following their victory at Srirangapatnam, the British, under Hastings' successor, **Lord Cornwallis**, annexed the coastal areas and interior plains that had been under Tipu Sultan's sway, settling down to a period of relatively trouble-free rule. Stretching from the Telegu-speaking region of present-day Andhra Pradesh to the Malabar Coast, the **Madras Presidency** was a notoriously "hands-off" regime, with vast administrative districts on which colonial officers could make very little impact. Life basically continued as it had before the advent of the British Raj. Unlike in the North, where the economic changes brought about by the Industrial Revolution in Britain had a huge impact, the South's output was geared towards domestic consumption; when the Lancashire mills forced the bottom out of the cotton industry in Bengal, the weavers of Madras were largely unaffected.

Nevertheless, resentment at British rule was not confined to the northern plains, where the so-called **Indian Mutiny** (re-dubbed "the First War of Independence" by nationalist politicians, and referred to in the Guide as the 1857 uprising) broke out in Lucknow. **Uprisings** also occurred in forest regions of Andhra Pradesh, and the Moppila Muslims of the Malabar who took arms against the oppressive rule of both Hindu landowners and the British. Generally, however, opposition to the British came not from low-caste or tribal populations, but ironically from members of the English-speaking, university-educated elite in Madras, where the end of the nineteenth century saw the emergence of a nascent **nationalist movement**.

As this nationalist movement continued to grow, it found expression in the strategy of *swadeshi* ("self-sufficiency"), which involved a boycott of imported goods, in particular British textiles, and the revival of India's own production techniques. *Swadeshi* soon spread across South India, creating economic chaos, and the arrest and imprisonment of one extremist, **Bal Tilak**, caused an uprising that brought Bombay's

1799	1857	1858
Tipu Sultan is killed at the battle of Srirangapatnam, securing British control of the far south	A rebellion by sepoy troops triggers a full-scale uprising against British rule in northern India, suppressed with much brutality	British rule or "Raj" is established with power transferred from the East India Company to the Crown

industry to a standstill; troops were sent onto the streets to quell it and several deaths resulted. In 1916, Tilak joined up with Annie Besant, who strongly believed in India's right to self-government, to form the Home Rule League, based at the Theosophical Society's headquarters in Adyar, Madras. The organization openly objected to the

MAHATMA GANDHI – INDIA'S GREAT SOUL

India's most famous son, **Mohandas Karamchand Gandhi**, was born on October 2, 1869, in Porbandar, Gujarat. Although merchants by caste – Gandhi means grocer – both his grandfather and father rose to positions of political influence. Young Mohandas was shy and sickly, just an average scholar, but from early on he questioned the codes of power around him, even flouting accepted Hindu practice: he once ate meat for a year believing it would give him the physical edge the British appeared to possess. As a teenager, he began to develop an interest in spirituality, particularly the Jain principle of **ahimsa** (non-violence).

At 19, he moved to London to study law, outwardly adopting the appearance and manners of an Englishman while obeying his mother's wish that he resist meat, alcohol and women. Studying the Bible alongside the Bhagavad Gita, he came to view different religions as a collective source of truth from which all could draw spiritual inheritance.

After a brief spell back in India, Gandhi left again to practise law in South Africa. The plight of his fellow Indians there, coupled with his own indignation at being ejected from a first-class train carriage, fuelled his campaigns for racial equality. Gaining crucial victories for minorities against the practices of indentured labour, his public profile grew. At this time he opted to transcend material possessions, donning the peasant's handspun *dhoti* and shawl and taking a vow of celibacy. This turn to ascetic purity he characterized as *satyagraha*, derived from Sanskrit ideas of "truth" and "firmness"; it would become the touchstone of **passive resistance**.

Returning to India with his messianic reputation well established – the poet Tagore named him **"Mahatma"** (Great Soul) – Gandhi travelled the country campaigning for **swaraj** (home rule). He also worked tirelessly for the rights of women and untouchables, whom he called **Harijans** (children of God). Gandhi stepped up his activities in the wake of the brutal massacre of protesters at Amritsar, leading a series of self-sufficiency drives during the 1920s, which culminated in the great **salt march** from Ahmedabad to Dandi in 1930. This month-long 386km journey led a swelling band of followers to the coast, where salt was made in defiance of the British monopoly on production. It drew worldwide attention: although Gandhi was promptly imprisoned, British resolve was seen to have weakened. On his release, he was invited to a round-table meeting in London to discuss home rule. The struggle continued for several years during which Gandhi spent time in the South, founding a model village and ashram at Sevagram (see p.136) in Maharashtra and living under house arrest at Pune's Aga Khan Palace (see p.146) where his wife, Kasturba, died in 1944.

As the nationalist movement gained strength, Gandhi grew more concerned about the state of Hindu-Muslim relations. He responded to outbreaks of communal violence by subjecting his own body to self-purification and suffering through fasting. After Independence, Partition left him with a deep sense of failure. In a bid to stem the ensuing violence, he again fasted in Calcutta as large numbers of Hindus and Muslims flowed between the new countries. Gandhi's commitment to the fair treatment of Muslim Indians and his intention to visit and endorse Pakistan as a neighbour enraged many Hindu fundamentalists. He survived an attempt on his life on January 20, 1948, only to be shot dead from close range by a lone Hindu gunman in Delhi ten days later. Prime minister Nehru announced the loss of a national radio: "Friends and comrades, the light has gone out of our lives and there is darkness everywhere."

1911	1915	1919	1930
Delhi succeeds Calcutta as the British capital	Gandhi returns to India from South Africa	British troops open fire on unarmed civilians during a demonstration in Amritsar, killing 379 people	Gandhi leads mass protests against British rule. Sixty thousand are imprisoned in its wake

colonial regime, spreading its nationalistic message through publications such as *The Hindu* among the literate classes. Tilak's vision for distinct language-based states in the South was later borne out with the State Reorganization Act (see below). He died in 1920, and **Mahatma Gandhi** emerged from his shadow to dominate the Indian National Congress party. Gandhi spent much of the 1920s and 1930s in Bombay, and launched his Quit India campaign in 1942 from his Mani Bhavan home.

Indian Independence was eventually attained on **August 15, 1947**, when a parliamentary system (the Lok Sabha) was established in New Delhi, with **Jawaharlal Nehru** sworn in as Prime Minister.

The South since Independence

Independence passed off relatively peacefully in South India in 1947, as the North succumbed to the horrors of Partition. With the exception of the nizam of Hyderabad, who tried to retain his dominions and had to be ousted by the new Indian army, the Princely States – namely Cochin, Travancore and Mysore – acceded gracefully to the Indian Union. Although deprived of their privy purses and most of their land, many of the former rulers used their privileged backgrounds to secure powerful roles in their new states, becoming members of parliament or industrialists.

The dissolution of British rule also generated an upsurge in regional sentiments. In the South, calls to restructure state boundaries along linguistic lines gained pace, culminating in the 1956 **State Reorganization Act**, when the region was divided into four main states: the Kannada-speaking area became Mysore (later changed to Karnataka); the Telegu zone made up Andhra Pradesh; the former Tamil region of the Madras Presidency became Madras (subsequently renamed Tamil Nadu); and Kerala was created from the Malayalam-speaking Malabar coastal zone. Goa, meanwhile, remained under Portuguese control until 1961, when India's first prime minister, **Jawaharlal Nehru**, lost his patience with the Portuguese dictator Salazar and sent in the troops.

From the start, Nehru vociferously opposed the creation of language-based states, predicting such a move would lead to fragmentation, schisms and regionalism. The political upheavals of the past fifty years have proved him right. With the rise in popularity of the pro-Dravidian **DMK** in Tamil Nadu and the **Telegu Desam** in Andhra Pradesh, the South's political scene has been completely dominated by **regional parties** in one guise or another, reflecting widespread mistrust of central government rule from Delhi. This has been most vehemently expressed in resistance to the imposition of Hindi – the most widely spoken language in northern India – as the medium of education and law. As these parties gained larger shares of the vote, state-specific issues and calls for greater regional autonomy have increasingly dominated the political agendas of all four states.

Caste conflict

Caste (see p.482) has always been more firmly rooted in South Indian society than the more Muslim-influenced North, but political legislation has done little to erase these age-old social divisions. Adopted in 1950, the Constitution of India paved the way for laws to combat caste discrimination, with clauses obliging the states to implement

1931	Aug 15, 1947	Jan 30, 1948
The Gandhi–Irwin Pact secures the release of all political prisoners	India is partitioned as Nehru is sworn in as the country's first prime minister – millions are displaced	Mahatma Gandhi is shot at point-blank range by a Hindu fanatic while attending a prayer meeting in Delhi

THE WAR IN SRI LANKA

The **ethnic conflict** between the majority (Buddhist) Sinhalese and minority Tamil populations of Sri Lanka erupted into full-scale war in 1987. Following several years of escalating clashes between Sri Lankan government forces and the Liberation Tigers of Tamil Eelam (LTTE – popularly known as the **Tamil Tigers**), Sri Lankan president J. R. Jayawardene sent the Sri Lankan Army in against the LTTE stronghold on the Jaffna peninsula in the north of the island. Prime Minister Rajiv Gandhi, under pressure from Indian Tamils concerned at the treatment of their fellow Tamils in Sri Lanka, began talks with the Jayawardene government, and in July 1987 the two countries signed a peace accord, part of which permitted the Indian army to intervene and disarm the LTTE. In the event, however, India became bogged down in a messy war with the LTTE, with high casualties on both sides – it was this debacle, with Indian troops fighting Tamil guerrillas, which led to Rajiv Gandhi's assassination in 1991.

India was only able to extricate itself after the defeat of Rajiv Gandhi in the 1989 elections, following which, in March 1990, the new government withdrew all troops from the island. Ripples from the war in Sri Lanka continued to have a marked influence on political life in the South, until the eventual defeat of the LTTE in 2009.

policies of positive discrimination. "Untouchables" and "Other Backward Castes" (OBCs) were given **quotas** in educational institutions, parliament, regional assemblies and state-sector jobs.

"Affirmative action" policies initiated under Prime Minister **V.P. Singh** in the early 1990s certainly increased the level of lower caste participation in government, but they have had some negative effects too. Inevitably, sought-after university places and public-sector jobs are often granted to unqualified people instead of better-qualified members of higher castes, creating sectarian resentment that has increasingly spilled into violence. Clashes between brahmins and low-caste farmers have led to whole districts of Tamil Nadu being placed under martial law on several occasions.

The other harmful repercussion of positive discrimination has been the **politicization** of caste. In order to be elected or to form power-wielding coalitions, Indian politicians these days have to galvanize **vote banks** – blocks of support from specific caste or ethnic groups. In return, these vote banks look to their leaders to advance their agendas in government, a process that all too often results in national or state interests being subordinated to the demands of minority groups.

Communal violence and Tamil nationalism

Though less pronounced in the South than the North, communal conflict continued to rock India throughout the 1980s and 1990s. In 1984 Prime Minister Indira Gandhi of the ruling Congress party was killed by her Sikh bodyguard after she sanctioned a bloody attack on the Golden Temple in Amritsar. Her son Rajiv Gandhi was elected on a landslide soon afterwards, but he soon became embroiled in the conflict in Sri Lanka (see box above). In 1991 he was assassinated by an LTTE suicide bomber while on the campaign trail in Tamil Nadu.

Violence came to a head on February 14, 1998, when fifteen bombs exploded in crowded districts of Coimbatore, Tamil Nadu killing sixty people. The Home Affairs Minister and BJP leader at that time, L.K. Advani, was due to address a rally in the

1948	**1961**	**1966**
Indian troops and Pakistani insurgents clash for the first time in Kashmir, leading to the fateful partition of the region	451 years of Portuguese rule in Goa come to an end as Nehru orders in the Indian army	Nehru's niece, Indira Gandhi, becomes leader of the Congress Party and India's third prime minister

city, which the Islamic extremist organization Al-Umma decided to use as use as a pretext to settle communal scores for earlier attacks on Muslims in the region.

Following its resounding defeat in the wake of Rajiv's assassination, when it was accused of harbouring and training **separatist guerrillas**, the **DMK**, the then dominant (Tamil nationalist) party had to publically distance itself from the LTTE, despite being aware of the electoral cost of doing so. The other main party to have ruled the state, the **AIADMK**, led by the maverick ex-film starlet **Jayalalithaa** (see box, p.370), consistently exploited this fact to kindle support, forming coalitions with more openly pro-Tiger nationalist parties and leaders.

The rise of the BJP

With the decline of the Congress Party (and corresponding rise of the pro-Hindu, nationalist **BJP**) throughout the 1990s, politics at national level became increasingly fragmented. No longer dominated by a single party, the succession of short-lived governments in New Delhi tended to be formed by shaky coalitions brought together by political expediency. Thus regionalist parties such as the pro-Tamil DMK and AIADMK, who had for decades enjoyed massive support in their home state but wielded disproportionately little influence at national level, emerged as a potent new force.

The political turmoil came to a head during a period of brinkmanship between India and Pakistan over Kashmir. While the world was preoccupied with NATO's bombing of Belgrade, at least eight hundred Pakistani fighters crept across the so-called Line of Control (the de facto border) overlooking the Srinagar-Leh road near **Kargil**. India's response was to move thousands of troops and heavy artillery into the area, swiftly followed up with an aerial bombardment. Within days the two countries were poised on the brink of all-out war, only months after both had successfully tested long-range nuclear missiles. In the event the conflict was contained, but Pakistan took a bloody nose from the encounter, and by July 1999 the Indian army had retaken all the ground previously lost to the militants.

Riding high a wave of patriotism the BJP under Atal Bihari Vajpayee inflicted the biggest defeat Congress had sustained since it first came to power in 1947. Vajpayee's majority was far from as large as he might have hoped, and the BJP-led **National Democratic Alliance** (**NDA**) coalition was fractured and tenuous. But those who gleefully interpreted **Sonia Gandhi**'s second election defeat as the end of dynastic politics in India were to be proved wrong in the most dramatic fashion only five years later.

Back down south meanwhile, Jayalalithaa was thrust into something of a political wilderness, with her party soundly beaten by a BJP-led coalition that included the DMK, led by her arch-rival, the then chief minister of Tamil Nadu, **M. Karunanidhi**. In October 2000, the High Court in Chennai (Madras) found her guilty of corruption, and issued a three-year suspended prison sentence, prompting riots from her supporters.

The turn of the millennium

Despite the charges Jayalalithaa announced she would run in the state elections of 2001, expecting that the corruption charges could be overturned at a later date. Her AIADMK-led coalition including the pro Tamil Tiger PMK and two communist

1975–1977	1984	1987
In response to widespread civil unrest, Indira Gandhi declares a "State of Emergency", suspending elections and civil liberties	Militant Sikhs occupy the Golden Temple in Amritsar. Indira Gandhi orders in the troops. A massacre ensues	India sends peace-keeping forces to war-torn Sri Lanka. Thousands of refugees arrive in Tamil Nadu

parties defeated Kurunanidhi's sixteen party coalition dominated by the DMK and BJP. The new chief minister wasted no time in settling scores with her opponents, ordering Karunanidhi's arrest on corruption charges, along with that of around one thousand of his supporters.

Karunanidhi's release (on "humanitarian grounds") came a few days later, but the ageing former premier had to face his own set of corruption charges. Violent protests accompanied the dispute. A high-ranking BJP government official, dispatched by prime minister Vajpayee from New Delhi to investigate the situation, reported that "no law of the land prevails in Tamil Nadu".

Domestic politics, however, took a back seat in late 2001 when **Indo-Pak relations** and the Kashmiri question returned to the fore as India entered one of the most volatile periods in its history. In October, the **State Assembly building in Srinagar** was destroyed by Islamist suicide car-bombers, and then in December, three Muslim gunmen stormed the **Parliament Building** in New Delhi, killing several police guards before they were picked off by army marksmen. Pakistani involvement was inevitably suspected. Then, in early 2002, a Muslim mob in **Godhra**, Gujarat, attacked a trainload of Hindu pilgrims returning from Ayodhya, killing 59. In the reprisal riots that followed, around two thousand people (mostly Muslims) were slaughtered.

Anti-Muslim sentiment was further fuelled only a month later when an Islamist suicide squad commandeered a tourist bus and used it to attack the **Kaluchak** army camp near Jammu. Coming hot on the heels of yet another promise by Pakistan to clamp down on cross-border militancy, the atrocity provoked outrage in Delhi. Vajpayee, bowing to the hawks on the right of his party, called for a "decisive battle", initiating a massive build-up of troops on the border. An estimated million men in arms were involved in the ensuing standoff as India and Pakistan edged to the brink of war, until US diplomacy diffused the crisis.

FLOODS, TSUNAMIS AND DROUGHT

While South India's cities have seen rapid development, the rural interior has been slow to reap the rewards. During the early 2000s two **natural disasters** battered the region. In 2000, record rainfalls wrought havoc in the southern state of Andhra Pradesh. An estimated twelve million were left marooned or homeless as river levels rose by as much as four metres in places. Four years later the "Boxing Day" tsunami of December 26, 2004 caused catastrophic damage and the loss of around seven thousand lives on the Tamil Nadu coast, southern Kerala and the Andaman and Nicobar Islands. Relief poured in from abroad but, amidst the usual accusations of corruption and incompetence, it took years for the clear-up to be completed and the affected areas to recover.

If this wasn't challenging enough, the South had just borne the brunt of a series of **crop failures** caused by drought, controversial experiments with GM species and pesticide resistance, which hit Andhra Pradesh particularly hard and led to a spate of farmer suicides. Drought continues to be an issue in Tamil Nadu which has seen the normally reliable southwest monsoon fail to replenish groundwater levels since 2015. Emotive protests by farmers in Delhi, some publicly slashing their wrists in desperation, have drawn the attention of the Indian media – if not long-term government assistance.

Oct 31, 1984	May 21, 1991	1992
Indira Gandhi's Sikh bodyguards take revenge by shooting the prime minister in her garden, unleashing a communal bloodbath	Rajiv Gandhi assassinated by Tamil Tiger suicide bomber while campaigning near Chennai	A mob of Hindu extremists destroy the Babri Masjid mosque in Ayodhya, sparking riots and killings across India

Peace talks and the Mumbai bombings

On-off negotiations over Kashmir lasted until early 2004, when, watched by the world's press, President Pervez Musharraf of Pakistan and Atal Bihari Vajpayee of India posed for a historic handshake and committed to a non-violent "Road Map". Not since the start of the troubles had a rapprochement between the Subcontinent's old foes looked so likely to result in a definitive end to hostilities.

Nevertheless, relations between Hindus and Muslims in some parts of India remained at crisis point. On August 25, 2003, two bombs ripped through the centre of downtown **Mumbai**, one next to the Gateway of India, Mumbai's main tourist hub, killing 107 people. No one claimed responsibility, but four suspects believed to have links with Islamic militant groups were arrested soon after. On **July 11, 2006**, seven synchronized explosions within eleven minutes killed more than two hundred people and injured over seven hundred. Two Kashmiri groups, Lashkar-e-Tayyiba and Jaish-e-Mohammed, were immediately suspected of the attack. Initial concerns in the city centred on a potential backlash and communal violence against the Muslim population, while in Delhi there were fears that talks with Pakistan might also be derailed. Talks were temporarily halted, but in September 2006, Prime Minister Manmohan Singh and President Musharraf made a joint statement that peace negotiations would resume.

The 2004 elections

With India booming as never before and peace on the horizon in Kashmir, Prime Minister Vajpayee and his BJP-led coalition decided to cash in on the perceived "feel good" factor and call a snap **election** in May 2004. "India Shining" was their slogan, but the campaign strategy boomeranged badly. True, India was experiencing a period of unparalleled economic growth, but the boom was based largely on information technology (see box, p.478), benefiting the urban professional classes, and had had little impact on the vast majority of the population. Congress leader **Sonia Gandhi** was quick to seize the initiative and appealed directly to poor rural voters to show the government what they thought of Vajpayee's vision of the country. She also played the dynastic card, introducing her son Rahul and daughter Priyanka to the campaign, which caught the imagination of younger voters (half of the Indian electorate is aged under 35).

Far from increasing his majority, as he had expected, Vajpayee and his government were thrown out in the most dramatic political turnaround of recent times. Congress gained the largest share of the vote and Sonia Gandhi was duly invited to form a government. However, she stunned supporters by "humbly declining" the invitation and stepped down. The announcement caused clamorous scenes in parliament, provoking the worst losses ever seen in the 129-year history of India's stock market. Eventually, former finance minister, 71-year-old **Manmohan Singh**, stepped into the breach and was named as prime minister, the first Sikh to lead the country.

One of the casualties of the national elections in the South was Andhran chief minister **Chandrababu Naidu**. The darling of the World Bank, Naidu had come to power vowing to stamp out corruption, make state government more transparent and efficient and transform the region's economy into a high-tech hub. While Hyderabad's professional classes surged ahead, Andhra's rural poor were suffering the worst

Dec 1992–Jan 1993	May 1996	May 11, 1998
Scores die in a spate of communal disturbances in Mumbai. Terrible reprisal bombings take place two months later	A far-right Hindu nationalist party, BJP, wins the general election	India detonates its first atomic bomb. Pakistan follows suit soon after

INDIA'S SILICON VALLEY

If you've ever called up your bank or broadband provider and been put through to a call centre, the chances are it will be in one of South India's **"tech cities"** of Bengaluru, Hyderabad or Chennai. The phenomenon stems from the 1980s when as the *Economist* put it "middle-class engineers from a dirt-poor socialist India somehow persuaded Western firms to outsource their back-office functions to the Subcontinent." Spurred on by tax breaks, an educated English-speaking population and other incentives, this spawned a three-decade boom that saw the likes of Microsoft, Dell and Samsung moving operations to the "**Indian Silicon Valley**". Today Indian software developers outnumber call-centre workers and local firms such as Infosys, TCS and Wipro have begun exporting ideas and workers back to the West. The number of Indian "tech geeks" working in the real Silicon Valley even prompted President Donald Trump to review the US visa system in 2017.

The impact on South India has been marked, with an **emergent middle class** shopping at IKEA and Tesco as much as at traditional street markets. Local tech firms have also begun to target the needs of millions of Indians; for example, bus and train tickets can be bought with the tap of a smartphone rather than queuing at a window in a Victorian train station. With Chennai and Hyderabad set to hit "megacity" status with ten million inhabitants in the 2020s, it's a market that's set to grow ever larger, the challenge being whether India's new generation of start-up entrepreneurs can keep up.

agricultural crisis in decades (see box, p.476). The 2004 elections finally gave the rural population the opportunity to express their opinion of Naidu's experiment: the party suffered a resounding defeat and its reforms were halted. Having pinned its colours to the BJP-led coalition in Delhi, Jayalalithaa's AIADMK also crashed at the polls in Tamil Nadu in 2006 after her government had cut free electricity to farmers and introduced other measures penalizing rural populations.

Continuing growth and the threat of terrorism

Internationally, **relations with the US** had warmed significantly. During the Cold War, India's socialist government was more in tune with Moscow than Washington and the US tended to favour Pakistan, which by the mid 2000s was becoming mired in Islamist violence and accusations of sponsoring terrorism. In 2006 a deal was signed ending a 34-year ban on nuclear trade with India. It meant that India – a state known to possess nuclear weapons – was allowed to buy and sell nuclear fuel and technology with the rest of the world for civilian purposes, without having to join the Nuclear Non-Proliferation Treaty (NPT). The deal significantly changed the political jigsaw of Asia, with India shifting from from "nuclear pariah" to a power at the forefront of the international scene.

Despite the global economic crash of 2008, India's **technological development** continued to rise at a phenomenal rate, with Tamil Nadu and other southern states leading the way (see box above). The rosy economic picture, combined with certain measures to alleviate rural poverty helped the Congress-led United Progressive Alliance to victory in the **2009 elections**, when Manmohan Singh was elected to a second term in power, the first time this had happened in successive elections since Nehru in 1952. Among southern members of the UPA were the DMK in Tamil Nadu and several small leftist parties in Kerala, which has always had a strong communist element.

1999	2000	Dec 2001
India and Pakistan on the brink of war after insurgents occupy Kargil, in Ladakh	Floods and crop failures devastate rural Andhra Pradesh	Islamist gunmen attack the Indian parliament building in protest at the government's Kashmir policy

At the same time as this rapid economic boom, ongoing fears about **terrorism** increased sharply as a result of the horrific "**26/11**" Mumbai attacks in late November 2008. Televised globally, a group of Pakistani gunmen went on a deadly spree through iconic parts of the city centre, killing 164 people. During the rampage they took over and burnt several floors of the landmark *Taj Palace* hotel, fired on bars frequented by tourists, and left the concourse of CST station splattered in blood. The lasting legacy has been strict **security measures** in many public places, with metal detectors a common feature at the entrance to public parks, museums and temples.

A new southern state and a national right turn

The most significant development in South India for decades took place on June 2, 2014, when the new state of **Telangana** was split off from Andhra Pradesh, following years of protests and agitation by the Telangana independence movement. The main administrative headache to be overcome was that Hyderabad itself fell within Telangana and was the obvious choice as capital of the new state, while none of the existing cities in what was left of Andhra Pradesh was regarded as suitable capital material. Eventually a novel solution was reached whereby Hyderabad would continue to act as capital of both states until a brand new one is built for AP at the culturally significant but extremely small town of Amaravati (see p.289), a process likely to take at least a decade.

Meanwhile, the political ground had been shifting nationally. A series of **corruption scandals** emerged in 2010–11 (notably around India's hosting of the Commonwealth Games), and undermined confidence in the Congress-led administration. Protests at the abysmal standards in public life – at local, state and national levels – coalesced around a social activist from Maharashtra named **Anna Hazare**, who staged a series of high-profile, Gandhian-style hunger strikes. A watered-down anti-corruption law in 2011 took the sting out of the movement but the plight of India's poor, the big losers in every government corruption case, remained centre-stage in 2012, as more than a hundred thousand peasant farmers marched to Delhi from all over the country to lobby for greater land rights. **Women's rights** also came to the fore in the wake of the horrific **Delhi rape case** in December 2012, when a young student died after being brutally gang raped on a bus in the capital. Galvanized by the atrocity, people poured on to the streets protesting at perceived police indifference to sexual violence and poor treatment generally of women in India.

Fears over India's **faltering economy** also dominated the news in late 2012, as growth rates remained comparatively sluggish at just over 6 percent. Those who identified corruption and government inefficiency as the culprits felt vindicated after a massive electricity blackout in July paralyzed the country, leaving 700 million people without power. The **general election of 2014** resulted in a landslide victory for the BJP, led by former – and controversial – Gujarat chief minister **Narendra Modi**, who now became prime minister with an outright majority. Seen as more business-friendly than Congress, the BJP launched initiatives such as the Digital India programme, designed to roll out internet access across the country and increase the number of jobs in the IT industry. Falling oil prices also helped the Indian economy, and an economic slowdown in China at the end of 2015 allowed India to outstrip its neighbour in economic

Dec 26, 2004	**2008**	**2010**
The "Boxing Day Tsunami" causes devastation across the Andamans, Andhra Pradesh, Kerala and Tamil Nadu	Terrorists launch a bloody attack on Mumbai; 164 die	Growth rates exceed ten percent as the Indian economy goes into overdrive despite recession elsewhere in the world

growth, keeping it on course to become the world's third largest economy (after the US and China) by around 2035.

In the South, the political world was rocked by the **death of Jayalalithaa** in December 2016, shortly after winning her fifth term as Chief Minister of Tamil Nadu. This left something of a power vacuum in the ruling AIADMK, especially when her lifelong friend and chosen political heir, Sasikala Natarajan, had to be abandoned by the party as she was jailed on various corruption charges in April 2017, leaving the less charismatic figure of **K. Palaniswami** as the state's chief minister.

Overall, despite its economic growth and its burgeoning middle class, grinding **poverty** continues to blight the lives of millions in rural and urban India, as starkly evident in the South as elsewhere. As Goldman Sachs commented, India is home to "nearly a third of the world's software engineers and a quarter of the world's undernourished". Nor is this the only challenge the country faces. The rise of the BJP has been accompanied by increasing **sectarian sentiment** directed largely against Muslims, but also against other religious minorities, most notably Christians, with ugly scenes even occurring in normally tranquil Kerala.

Whether or not the country can continue to evolve at its present pace and achieve its longed-for position on the global stage will be determined not merely by the power of its economy, but also by the extent to which it is able to balance the needs of rich and poor and to curb the corruption endemic in public life. But it is nonetheless apparent that in the long term South India remains an integral part of a country on the up.

Dec 2012–Feb 2013	**May 2014**	**Dec 2016**
Crowds take to the streets across the country to express outrage at the rape and murder of a young student on a moving bus in Delhi	BJP wins overall majority in the general election	Jayalalithaa, the "goddess" of Tamil Nadu politics dies, aged 68

Religion

Long regarded as the bastion of Hindu values, South India boasts many of the finest, oldest and most extravagant temples in the country and the vast pantheon of Hindu deities is manifest everywhere. The South is also home to a substantial Muslim community, mostly concentrated in Hyderabad. Christians, believed to have been living in South India since the first century AD, have developed distinct denominations, and worship in buildings that range from simple thatched huts to the grand basilicas and churches erected by the Portuguese, French and British. Although Jains and Buddhists are now a minute fraction of the southern population, several magnificent temples stand testament to an impressive presence in the past. The once influential Keralan Jews are now a pitifully small group, but their influence can still be strongly felt in Fort Cochin (Kochi).

Hinduism

Hinduism is the product of several thousand years of evolution and assimilation. It has no founder or prophet, no single creed and no single prescribed practice or doctrine; it takes in hundreds of gods, goddesses, beliefs and practices, and widely variant cults and philosophies. Some are recognized by only two or three villages, others are popular right across the Subcontinent. Hindus call their beliefs and practices **dharma**, which defines a way of living in harmony with natural and moral law while fulfilling personal goals and meeting the requirements of society.

The Vedic age

The origins of Hinduism date back to the arrival of the **Aryans** (see p.463). The Aryans believed in a number of gods associated with the elements, including **Agni**, the god of fire, **Surya**, the sun god, and **Indra**, the chief god. Most of these deities faded in importance in later times, but Indra is still regarded as the father of the gods, and Surya was widely worshipped until the medieval period.

Aryan religious beliefs were first set down in a series of four books, the **Vedas** (from the Sanskrit word *veda*, meaning "knowledge"). Transmitted orally for centuries, the Vedas were finally written down, in Sanskrit, between 1000 BC and 500 AD. The earliest and most important of the four Vedas, the **Rig Veda**, contains more than a thousand hymns to various deities, while the other three (the Yajur Veda, Sama Veda and Atharva Veda) contain further prayers, chants and instructions for performing the complex sacrificial rituals associated with this early Vedic religion.

The Vedas were followed by further religious texts, including the **Brahmanas**, a series of commentaries on the Vedas for the use of priests (brahmins) and, more importantly, the **Upanishads**, which describe in beautiful and emotive verse the mystic experience of unity of the soul (*atman*) with Brahma, the absolute creator of the universe, ideally attained through asceticism, renunciation of worldly values and meditation. In the Upanishads the concepts of **samsara**, a cyclic round of death and rebirth characterized by suffering and perpetuated by desire, and **moksha**, liberation from *samsara*, became firmly rooted. As fundamental aspects of the Hindu world-view, both are accepted by all but a handful of Hindus today, along with the belief in **karma**, the certainty that one's present position in society is determined by the effect of one's previous actions in this and past lives.

THE MAHABHARATA AND THE RAMAYANA

Eight times as long as the *Iliad* and *Odyssey* combined, the **Mahabharata** was written around 400 AD and tells of a feuding kshatriya family in northern India during the fourth millennium BC. The chief character is **Arjuna**, who, with his four brothers, represents the **Pandava** clan, supreme fighters and upholders of righteousness. The Pandava clan are resented by their cousins, the evil **Kauravas**, led by Duryodhana, the eldest son of Dhrtarashtra, ruler of the Kuru kingdom.

When Dhrtarashtra hands his kingdom over to the Pandavas, the Kauravas are understandably less than overjoyed. The subsequent battle between the Pandavas and Kauravas is described in the sixth book, the famous **Bhagavad Gita**. Krishna steps into battle as Arjuna's charioteer. Arjuna is in a dilemma, unable to justify the killing of his own kin in pursuit of a rightful kingdom. Krishna consoles him, reminding him that his principal duty is as a warrior, and convincing him that by fulfilling his dharma he not only upholds law and order by saving the kingdom from the grasp of unrighteous rulers, he also serves the gods in the spirit of devotion and thus guarantees himself eternal union with the divine in the blissful state of *moksha*.

The Pandavas finally win the battle and Yudhishtra, one of the five Pandava brothers, is crowned king. Eventually Arjuna's grandson, Pariksit, inherits the throne, and the Pandavas trek to Mount Meru, the mythical centre of the universe and the abode of the gods, where Arjuna finds Krishna's promised *moksha*.

THE RAMAYANA

The Ramayana tells the story of **Rama**, the seventh of Vishnu's eight incarnations. Rama is the oldest of four sons born to Dasaratha, the king of Ayodhya, and heir to the throne. When the time comes for Rama's coronation, Dasaratha's scheming third wife Kaikeyi has her own son Bharata crowned instead, and has Rama banished to the forest for fourteen years. In an exemplary show of filial piety, Rama accepts the loss of his throne and leaves the city with his wife Sita and brother Laksmana.

One day, Suparnakhi, the sister of the demon **Ravana**, spots Rama in the woods and instantly falls in love with him. Being a virtuous husband, Rama rebuffs her advances, while Laksmana cuts off her nose and ears in retaliation. In revenge, Ravana kidnaps Sita, who is borne away to one of Ravana's palaces on the island of **Lanka**.

Determined to find Sita, Rama enlists the help of the monkey god **Hanuman**, and the two of them gather an army and prepare to attack. After much fighting, Sita is rescued and reunited with her husband. On the long journey back to Ayodhya, Sita's honour is brought into question. To prove her innocence, she asks Laksmana to build a funeral pyre and steps into the flames, praying to Agni, the fire god. Agni walks her through the fire into the arms of a delighted Rama. They march into Ayodhya guided by a trail of lights laid out by the local people. Today, this illuminated homecoming is commemorated by Hindus all over the world during **Diwali**, the festival of lights. At the end of the epic, Rama's younger brother gladly steps down, allowing Rama to be crowned as the rightful king.

Hindu society

The stratification of Hindu society is rooted in the **Dharma Sutras**, a further collection of scriptures written at roughly the same time as the later Vedas. These defined four hierarchical classes, or **varnas** (from *varna*, meaning "colour", perhaps a reference to difference in appearance between the lighter-skinned Aryans and the darker indigenous Dravidian population). Each *varna* was assigned specific religious and social duties, with Aryans established as the highest social class. In descending order the *varnas* are: **brahmins** (priests and teachers), **kshatriyas** (rulers and warriors), **vaishyas** (merchants and cultivators) and **shudras** (menials). The first three classes, known as "twice-born", are distinguished by a sacred thread worn from the time of initiation, and are granted full access to religious texts and rituals. Below all four categories, groups whose jobs involve contact with dirt or death (such as undertakers, leather-workers and cleaners) were classified as **untouchables** or **dalits** (*dalit* meaning "oppressed"). Though discrimination against *dalits* is now a criminal offence, in part thanks to the campaigns of Mahatma Gandhi, the lowest stratum of society has by no means disappeared.

Within the four *varna*s, social status is further defined by *jati*, classifying each individual in terms of their family and job (for example, a *vaishya* may be a jewellery seller, cloth merchant, cowherd or farmer). A person's *jati* determines his **caste**, and lays restrictions on all aspects of life from what sort of food he can eat, religious obligations and contact with other castes, to the choice of marriage partners. There are almost three thousand *jatis*; the divisions and restrictions they have enforced have repeatedly been the target of reform movements and critics.

A Hindu has three **aims in life**: to fulfil his social and religious duties (*dharma*); to follow the correct path in his work and actions (*karma*); and to gain material wealth (*artha*). These goals are linked with the four traditional stages in life. The first is as a child and student, devoted to learning from parents and guru. Next comes the stage of householder, expected to provide for a family and raise children. That accomplished, he may then take up a life of celibacy and retreat into the forest to meditate alone, and finally renounce all possessions to become a homeless ascetic, hoping to achieve the ultimate goal of *moksha*. The small number of Hindus who follow this ideal life assume the final stage as saffron-clad **sadhus** who wander throughout India, begging for food and retreating to isolated caves, forests and hills to meditate. They're a common feature in most Indian towns and many stay for long periods in particular temples. Not all have raised families: some assume the life of a sadhu at an early age as *chellas*, pupils of an older sadhu.

The main deities

Alongside the Vedas and Upanishads, the most important Hindu religious texts are the **Puranas** – long mythological stories about the Vedic gods – and the two great epics, the **Mahabharata** and **Ramayana** (see box opposite), thought to have been completed by the first century AD, though subsequently retold, modified and embellished on numerous occasions and in various different regional languages. The Puranas and the two great epics helped crystallize the basic framework of Hindu religious belief, which survives to this day, based on a supreme triumvirate of deities. **Brahma**, the original Aryan godhead, or "creator", was joined by two gods who had begun to achieve increasing significance in the evolving Hindu world-view. The first, **Vishnu**, "the preserver", was seen as the force responsible for maintaining the balance of the cosmos whenever it was threatened by disruptive forces, incarnating himself on earth nine times in various animal and human forms, or avatars, to fight the forces of evil and chaos, most famously as Rama (the god-hero whose exploits are described in the Ramayana) and as Krishna (who appears at the most significant juncture of the Mahabharata). The second, **Shiva**, "the destroyer" (a development of the Aryan god Rudra, who had played a minor role in the Vedas), was charged with destroying and renewing the universe at periodic intervals, though his powers are not merely destructive, and he is worshipped in myriad forms with various attributes (see box, p.484). The three supreme gods are often depicted in a trinity, or *trimurti*, though in time Brahma's importance declined, and Shiva and Vishnu became the most popular deities – the famous Brahma temple at Pushkar is now one of the few in India dedicated to this venerable but rather esoteric god.

Depicted in human or semihuman form and accompanied by an animal "vehicle", other gods and goddesses who came alive in the mythology of the Puranas are still venerated across India. River goddesses, ancestors, guardians of particular places and protectors against disease and natural disaster are as central to village life as the major deities.

Practice and pilgrimage

In most Hindu homes, a chosen deity is worshipped daily in a shrine room. Outside the home, worship takes place in temples and consists of **puja** – sometimes a simple act of prayer, but more commonly a complex process when the god's image is circumambulated, offered flowers, rice, sugar and incense, and anointed with water,

HINDU GODS AND GODDESSES

VISHNU

With four arms holding a conch, discus, lotus and mace, **Vishnu** is blue-skinned, and often shaded by a serpent, or resting on its coils, afloat on an ocean. He is usually seen alongside his half-man-half-eagle vehicle, Garuda. **Vaishnavites**, often distinguishable by two vertical lines of paste on their foreheads, recognize Vishnu as supreme lord, and hold that he has manifested himself on earth nine times. The most popular of Vishnu's manifestations is as **Krishna**, who is represented in various ways: most popularly he is shown as the playful cowherd who seduces and dances with cowgirls (*gopis*), giving each the illusion that she is his only lover. He is also pictured as a small, chubby, mischievous baby, known for his butter-stealing exploits. Like Vishnu, Krishna is blue, and often shown dancing and playing the flute.

SHIVA

Shaivism, the cult of **Shiva**, was also inspired by *bhakti*, requiring selfless love from devotees in a quest for divine communion, but Shiva has never been incarnate on earth. He is presented in many different aspects, such as **Nataraja**, Lord of the Dance, **Mahadev**, Great God, and **Maheshvar**, Divine Lord, source of all knowledge. Though he does have several terrible forms, his role extends beyond that of destroyer, and he is revered as the source of the whole universe.

Shiva is often depicted with four or more faces, holding a trident, draped with serpents, and bearing a third eye in his forehead. In temples, he is identified with the lingam, or phallic symbol, resting in the yoni, a representation of female sexuality. Whether as statue or lingam, Shiva is accompanied by his bull-mount, Nandi, and often by a consort, who also assumes various forms, and is looked upon as the vital energy, **shakti**, that empowers him.

While Shiva is the object of popular devotion all over India, as the terrible **Bhairav** he is also the god of the Shaivite **ascetics**, who renounce family and caste ties and perform extreme meditative and yogic practices.

OTHER GODS AND GODDESSES

Chubby and smiling, elephant-headed **Ganesh**, the first son of Shiva and Parvati, is invoked before every undertaking (except funerals). Seated on a throne or lotus, his image is often placed above temple gateways, in shops and houses; in his four arms he holds a conch, discus, bowl of sweets (or club) and a water lily, and he's always attended by his vehicle, a rat. Ganesh is regarded by many as the god of learning, the lord of success, prosperity and peace.

Durga, the fiercest of the female deities, is an aspect of Shiva's more conservative consort, Parvati (also known as Uma), who is remarkable only for her beauty and fidelity. Among Durga's many aspects, each a terrifying goddess eager to slay demons, are Chamunda, Kali and Muktakeshi, but in all her forms she is Mahadevi (Great Goddess). Statues show her with ten arms, holding the head of a demon, a spear and other weapons; she tramples demons underfoot, or dances upon Shiva's body.

The comely goddess **Lakshmi**, Vishnu's consort, is usually shown sitting or standing on a lotus flower, and sometimes called Padma (lotus). Lakshmi is the embodiment of loveliness and grace, and the goddess of prosperity and wealth. She appears in different aspects alongside each of Vishnu's avatars, including Sita, wife of Rama, and Radha, Krishna's favourite *gopi*. In many temples she is shown as one with Vishnu, in the form of Lakshmi Narayan.

India's great monkey god, **Hanuman**, features in the Ramayana as Rama's chief aide in the fight against the demon-king of Lanka. Depicted as a giant monkey clasping a mace, Hanuman is seen as Rama and Sita's greatest devotee – as his representatives, monkeys find sanctuary in temples all over India.

The most beautiful Hindu goddess, **Saraswati**, the wife of Brahma, with her flawless milk-white complexion, sits or stands on a water lily or peacock, playing a lute, sitar or *vina*. She is revered as the goddess of music, creativity and learning.

Closely linked with the planet Saturn, **Shani** is feared for his destructive powers. His image, a black statue with protruding blood-red tongue, is often found on street corners; strings of green chillies and lemon are hung in shops and houses each Saturday (*Saniwar*) to ward off his evil influences.

milk or sandalwood paste (which is usually done on behalf of the devotee by the temple priest). The aim in puja is to take **darshan** – glimpse the god – and thus receive his or her blessing. Worshippers leave the temple with *prasad*, an offering of food or flowers taken from the holy sanctuary. **Temple ceremonies** are conducted by priests who tend the image in daily rituals in which the god is symbolically woken, bathed, fed, dressed and, at the end of each day, put back to bed. In many villages, shrines to *devatas*, village deities who function as protectors, are more important than temples.

Strict rules address **purity and pollution**, the most obvious of them requiring high-caste Hindus to limit their contact with potentially polluting lower castes. Above all else, **water** is the agent of purification, used in ablutions before prayer and revered in all rivers, especially Ganga (the Ganges). *Ghat*s, steps leading to the water's edge, are common in all river- or lakeside towns, used for bathing, washing clothes and performing religious rituals.

South India has a wealth of **pilgrimage sites** visited by devotees eager to receive *darshan* and attain merit. The Venkateshvara temple atop Tirumala Hill in Andhra Pradesh claims to draw more pilgrims than any other holy place in the world. Every year, another two million or so devotees head up to the Ayappa Forest Temple at Sabarimala in Kerala. At Kanyakumari, the southern tip of India, the waters of the Indian Ocean, the Bay of Bengal and the Arabian Sea are thought to merge at an auspicious point. Pilgrimages here are often combined with visits to the great temples of Tamil Nadu (see p.383), where Shaivite and Vaishnavite saints established cults and India's largest temples were constructed. Madurai, Thanjavur, Chidambaram and Srirangam are major pilgrimage centres, representing the pinnacle of the architectural development that began at Mamallapuram. Their festivals often involve the pulling of deities on vast wooden chariots through the streets, lively and noisy affairs that make for an unforgettable experience. As well as specific temples sacred to particular gods, historical sites, such as the former Vijayanagar capital at Hampi, remain magnets for pilgrims.

Islam

Muslims – some ten percent of the population of South India – form a significant presence in almost every town, city and village, though the only major southern city with a distinctly Islamic flavour is Hyderabad in Andhra Pradesh. Mumbai and Chennai also boast well-established Muslim quarters.

The belief in only one god, Allah, the condemnation of idol worship and the observance of their own strict dietary laws and specific festivals all set Muslims apart from their Hindu neighbours, with whom they have coexisted, not always peacefully, for centuries.

The first Muslims to settle in India were traders who arrived on the southwest coast in the seventh century. Much more significant was the invasion of North India under **Mahmud of Ghazni**. More raids from Central Asia followed in the twelfth century, resulting in the partial colonization of India, while the invading Muslims set themselves up in Delhi as sultans.

Many Muslims who settled in South India intermarried with Hindus, Buddhists and Jains, and the community spread. A further factor in its growth was missionary activity by **Sufis**, who stressed the attainment of inner knowledge of God through meditation and mystical experience. Their use of music, particularly *qawwali* singing, and dance, shunned by orthodox Muslims, appealed to Hindus, for whom singing played an important role in religious practice. Muslims are enjoined to pray five times daily. They may do this at home or in a **mosque** – always full at noon on Friday, for communal prayer (the only exception being the Druze of Mumbai, who hold communal prayers on Thursday).

The position of **women** in Islam is a subject of great debate. It's customary for women to be veiled – though in larger cities many women don't cover their heads – and in strictly orthodox communities most wear a *burqa*, usually black, that covers them from head to toe. Like other Indian women, Muslim women take second place to men in public, but in the home they wield great influence. Contrary to popular belief, polygamy is not widespread; while it does occur (Mohammed himself had several wives), many Muslims prefer monogamy, and several sects actually stress it as a duty. In marriage, women receive a dowry as financial security.

Buddhism

Buddhism was born on the Indian Subcontinent, developing as an offshoot of – and a reaction to – Hinduism, with which it shares many assumptions about the nature of existence. For a time it became the dominant religion in the country, though from around the fourth century AD onwards it was gradually eclipsed by a resurgent Hinduism (which cleverly reappropriated the Buddha, claiming him to be an incarnation of Vishnu), and the subsequent arrival of Islam more or less finished it off. Today Buddhists make up only a tiny fraction of the population in South India, but a collection of superb monuments offer firm reminders of the previous importance of the faith and its central role in southern India's cultural legacy.

The founder of Buddhism, **Siddhartha Gautama**, known as the **Buddha** ("awakened one"), was born into a wealthy kshatriya family in Lumbini, north of the Gangetic plain in present-day Nepal, around 566 BC. Brought up in luxury as a prince, he married at an early age, but renounced family life when he was 30. Unsatisfied with the explanations of worldly suffering proposed by religious gurus, and convinced that asceticism did not lead to spiritual realization, Siddhartha spent years wandering the countryside and meditating. His enlightenment is said to have taken place under a *bodhi* tree in **Bodhgaya** (Bihar). Soon afterwards he gave his first sermon in **Sarnath**, near Varanasi. For the rest of his life he taught, expounding **dharma**, the true nature of the world, human life and spiritual attainment. Before his death (c.483 BC) in Kushinagara (UP), he had established the **Sangha**, a community of monks and nuns who continued his teachings.

The Buddha's world-view incorporated the Hindu concept of *samsara*, and *karma* and *moksha*, which Buddhists call **nirvana** (literally "no wind"). The most important concept outlined by the Buddha was that all things are subject to the inevitability of **impermanence**. There is no independent inherent self due to the interconnectedness of all things, and our egos are the biggest obstacles on the road to enlightenment.

Jainism

The **Jain** tradition has been tremendously influential for at least 2500 years, though there is now only a tiny Jain population in South India, with most families involved in commerce and trade. Similarities to Hindu worship and a shared respect for nature and non-violence have contributed to the decline of the Jain society through conversion to Hinduism, but there is no antagonism between the two faiths.

The Jain doctrine is based upon the teachings of **Mahavira**, or "Great Hero", the last in a succession of 24 **tirthankaras** ("crossing-makers") said to appear on earth every 300 million years. Mahavira (c.599–527 BC) was born as Vardhamana Jnatrputra into a kshatriya family near modern Patna. Like his near-contemporary the Buddha, Mahavira rejected family life at the age of 30 and spent years wandering as an ascetic in an attempt to conquer attachment to worldly values.

Focused on the practice of **ahimsa** (non-violence), Jains follow a rigorous discipline to avoid harm to all **jivas**, or "souls", which exist in humans, animals, plants, water, fire, earth and air. They assert that every *jiva* is pure and capable of achieving liberation from existence in this universe. However, *jivas* are obscured by **karma**, a form of subtle matter that clings to the soul, which is born of action and binds the *jiva* to physical existence. For the most orthodox Jain, the only way to dissociate *karma* from the *jiva* is to follow the path of asceticism and meditation, rejecting passion, attachment and impure action.

Christianity

The **Apostle Thomas** is said to have arrived in Kerala in 54 AD, and according to popular tradition the Church of San Thome is the oldest Christian denomination in the world, with many tales of miracles by "Mar Thoma", as Thomas is known in Malayalam. According to tradition, Thomas was martyred in 72 AD at Mylapore in **Madras**. The tomb has since become a major place of pilgrimage, while the Portuguese added the Gothic **San Thome Cathedral** to the site in the late nineteenth century.

From the sixteenth century onwards, the history of the Church in India is linked to the spread of foreign Christians across the Subcontinent. In 1552, St Francis Xavier arrived in the Portuguese trading colony of **Goa** to establish missions to reach out to the Hindu "untouchables". In 1559, at the behest of the Portuguese king, the Inquisition arrived in Goa. Jesuit missionaries carried out a bloody and brutal campaign to "cleanse" the small colony of Hindu and Muslim religious practice. Early British incomers took the attitude that the Subcontinent was a heathen and polytheistic civilization waiting to be proselytized and made significant numbers of converts. As Christianity is intended to be free of caste stigma, it can be attractive to those seeking social advancement, and of the two million Christians in present-day India, most are *adivasi* (tribal) and *dalit* (untouchable) people.

Today, Christians in Goa and Kerala number nearly a third and a fifth of the population respectively. While most in Goa follow the **Catholicism** of their former Portuguese rulers, Kerala is home to an array of denominations, ranging from Catholic through Syrian and Malankara **Orthodox** to the Church of South India, modelled on **Anglicanism**.

The **Hindu influence** on Christianity remains marked, in any case, and in many churches you can see devotees offering the Hindu *aarti* (a plate of coconut, sweets and rice), and women wearing *tilak* dots on their foreheads. In the same way that Hindus and Muslims consider pilgrimage to be an integral part of life's journey, Indian Christians have numerous devotional sites, including St Jude's Shrine in **Jhansi** and the Temple of Mother Mary in **Mathura**. This sharing of traditions works both ways. At Christmas, for instance, you can't fail to notice the brightly coloured paper stars and small Nativity scenes glowing and flashing outside schools, houses, shops and churches throughout India.

Zoroastrianism

Of all South India's religious communities, Western visitors are least likely to come across – or recognize – **Zoroastrians**, who have no distinctive dress and few houses of worship. Most live in Mumbai, where they are known as **Parsis** (Persians) and are active in business, education and politics. Zoroastrian numbers – roughly ninety thousand – are rapidly dwindling due to a falling birth rate and absorption into wider communities.

The religion's founder, **Zarathustra** (Zoroaster), lived in Iran around the sixth or seventh century BC, and was the first religious prophet to expound a dualistic philosophy, based on the opposing powers of good and evil. For him, the absolute, wholly good and wise God, **Ahura Mazda**, together with his holy spirit and six emanations present in earth, water, the sky, animals, plants and fire, is constantly at odds with an evil power, **Angra Mainyu**, who is aided by **daevas**, or evil spirits. Five daily prayers, usually hymns, uttered by Zarathustra and standardized in the **Avesta**, the main Zoroastrian text, are said in the home or in a temple, before a fire, which symbolizes truth, righteousness and order. For this reason, Zoroastrians are often, incorrectly, called "fire-worshippers".

Music and dance

Religious rituals in South Indian temples invariably feature some kind of musical accompaniment or dance and the region's classical music is one of the highlights of a visit. Styles of music – whether secular or religious – vary greatly from state to state, but among the most singular South Indian idioms are Keralan percussion used in Kathakali performances, and the vibrant folk music of Goa, both of which convey the cultural distinctiveness of these two regions more vividly than anything else. Dance recitals take place throughout the winter, building up to fever pitch during April and May before pausing for the monsoon (June, July & Aug).

Carnatic music

Hindustani music from North India may be better known internationally, but the classical music of the South – called **Carnatic** – is by far the more ancient. Its tenets, once passed on only orally, were codified in Vedic literature between 4000 and 1000 BC, long before Western classical music was even in its infancy. Rather than being the province of an urbane elite, it's an explosion of colour, sound and Hindu worship. While Hindustani music developed close associations with court and palace, Carnatic music remained part of the warp and weft of South Indian culture, both religious and secular. The other major difference is that Carnatic music, lacking written notation, is taught by demonstration and learnt by ear or – in the case of its highly sophisticated rhythmic system – taught by a marvellous, mathematical structure of "finger computing" which enables a percussionist to break down a complex *thaalam* (rhythmic cycle) into manageable units.

The music and the faith which inspired Carnatic music have remained inseparable. Visitors to the vast temples of South India are much more likely to encounter music than in the North. It's usually the piercing sound of the *nagaswaram* (shawm) and the *tavil* (barrel drum). More than likely it accompanies flaming torches and a ceremonial procession of the temple deity.

Goan music

With reggae and techno blaring out of so many beach bars, you'd be forgiven for thinking **Goa's music and dance scene** started with the invention of the synthesizer. However, the state boasts a vibrant musical tradition of its own: a typically syncretic blend of east and west that is as spicy and distinctive as the region's cuisine.

The most famous Goan folk song and dance form is the **mando**. Originally, this slow and expressive dance (whose name derives from the Sanskrit mandala, meaning circular pattern) was traditionally performed in circles, but these days tends to be danced by men and women standing opposite each other in parallel lines, waving fans and coloured handkerchiefs. *Mandos* gather pace as they progress and are usually followed by a series of **dulpods**, quick-time tunes whose lyrics are traditionally satirical, exposing village gossip about errant housewives, lapsed priests and so on. *Dulpods*, in turn, merge into the even jauntier rhythms of **deknis**, bringing the set dances to a tumultuous conclusion. The basic rhythmic cycles, or *ovis*, of Goan folk songs were exploited by early Christian missionaries in their work. Overlaid with lyrics inspired by Bible stories, many were eventually assimilated into the local Catholic tradition.

Aside from the occasional strain of Portuguese fado, most of the sounds you hear around Goa these days are either *filmi* hits from the latest blockbuster Hindi movies, or a mishmash of folk tunes and calypso rhythms known as **Konkani pop**. Backed by groups of women singers and fanfaring mariachi-style brass sections, Konkani lead vocalists croon away with the reverb cranked up against a cacophony of electric guitar and keyboard accompaniment.

Keralan ritual percussion

The noisiest, rowdiest and most intense phase of any Keralan temple festival (see p.358) is the one presided over by the local drum orchestra, or **chenda melam**, whose ear-shattering performances accompany the procession of the deity around the sacred precinct and into the shrine. As impressive for their mental arithmetic as percussion technique, and showing enormous stamina in the intense heat, the musicians play an assortment of upright barrel drums (**chenda**) supported over the shoulder, bronze cymbals and wind instruments – the oboe-like **kuzhal** and the spectacular C-shaped brass trumpets (**kombu**), which emphasize and prolong the drum beating.

It starts slowly with long-lasting musical cycles and works up to a short, fast, powerful climax. During the performance, an elephant, musicians and the crowd process round the temple precinct – after more than two hours, the excited crowd and sweating musicians celebrate the conclusion and follow the elephant and deity into the inner temple.

Dance

The association of music and dance with Hindu thought has a long heritage, beginning with Shiva himself as Nataraja, the Cosmic Dancer, whose potent image is ever present in Hindu iconography. His temple at Chidambaram, for example, is rich with sculptures of dance poses, music-making and musical instruments.

The best-known Indian classical dance style is *bharatanatyam*, a composite term made up of **bharata**, an acronym of "*bhava*" (expression), "*raga*" (melody) and "*tala*" (rhythm) and **natyam,** the Tamil word for 'dance'. It is a graceful form, rich in gesture, and traditionally performed only by women. A popular subject for temple sculptures throughout South India (especially Tamil Nadu), it originated in the dances of the **devadasis**, temple dancing girls who originally performed as part of their devotional duties in the great Tamil shrines. As with other classical dance forms, training is rigorous. Performers are encouraged to dissolve their identity in the dance and become instruments for the expression of divine presence.

The most iconic South Indian dance performances to catch are Keralan **Kathakali** (see box, p.304) and **theyyems** (see box, p.358). Other styles worth seeking out include **Kuchipudi**, originating in Andhra Pradesh and distinguished by the important role given to dialogue and song, and **Kudiyattam**, the oldest continually performed theatre form in the world. Until recently, it was only performed inside temples, and then only in front of the uppermost castes. Visually, it is very similar to its offspring, Kathakali, but its atmosphere is infinitely more archaic. The actors, eloquent in sign language and symbolic movement, speak in the bizarre, compelling intonation of the local brahmins' Vedic chant, unchanged since 1500 BC.

Wildlife

A fast-growing population and the rapid spread of industries have inflicted pressures on the rural landscape of South India, but the region still supports a wealth of distinct flora and fauna. Walking on less frequented beaches or through the rice fields of the coastal plain, you'll encounter dozens of exotic birds, while the hill country of the interior supports an amazing variety of plants and trees. The majority of the peninsula's larger mammals keep to the dense woodland of the Western Ghat mountains, where a string of contiguous reserves affords them some protection from the hunters and loggers who have wrought such havoc on India's fragile forest regions over the past few decades.

Flora

Something like 3500 species of flowering plants have been identified in South India, as well as countless lower orders of grasses, ferns and brackens. Many species were introduced by the Portuguese from Europe, South America, Southeast Asia and Australia, but there are also a vast number of indigenous varieties which thrive in the humid climate.

Along the coast, the rice **paddy** and **coconut** plantations predominate, forming a near-continuous band of lush foliage. Spiky **spinifex** helps bind the shifting sand dunes behind the miles of sandy beaches lining both the Malabar and Coromandel coasts, while **casuarina** bushes form striking splashes of pink and crimson during the winter months.

In towns and villages, you'll encounter dozens of beautiful **flowering trees**. The Indian **laburnum**, or cassia, throws out masses of yellow flowers and long seed pods in late February before the monsoons. This is also the period when mango and Indian **coral trees** are in full bloom; both produce bundles of stunning red flowers.

TOP 5 PLACES TO WATCH WILDLIFE

Cotigao Wildlife Sanctuary (Goa). Tucked away in the extreme south of Goa, near Palolem beach, its extensive mixed deciduous forest and hilly backdrop make up for a relative paucity of wildlife. Best time: November to March. See p.205.

Indira Gandhi (Anamalai) Wildlife Sanctuary (Tamil Nadu). On the southernmost reaches of the Cardamom Hills, this park is more remote than Mudumalai, and consequently less visited, but encompasses some beautiful mountain scenery as well as abundant fauna. Best time: January to March. See p.431.

Mahatma Gandhi National Marine Park (Andaman Islands). The islets in this reserve, encircled by vivid coral reefs, rise out of crystal-clear water that teems with tropical fish, turtles and other marine life. Can be reached by daily excursion boats, via bus links, from the capital, Port Blair. Best time: January to March. See p.453.

Mudumalai Wildlife Sanctuary (Tamil Nadu). Set 1140m up in the Nilgiri Hills, Mudumalai is one of the most easily reached reserves in the South. It offers a full range of accommodation and trails and gives access to huge areas of protected forest. Best time: January to March. See p.438.

Periyar Wildlife Sanctuary (Kerala). A former maharaja's hunting reserve, centred on an artificial lake high in the Cardamom Hills. Occasional tiger sightings, but you're much more likely to spot an elephant. Well placed for trips into the mountains and tea plantations, with good accommodation, including remote observation towers to which you have to trek. Best time: October to March. See p.328

THE INDIAN TIGER: SURVIVAL OR EXTINCTION?

Few animals command such universal fascination as the **Indian tiger** (also known as the Bengal Tiger), and South India is one of the very few places where this rare and enigmatic big cat can still be glimpsed in the wild, stalking through the teak forests and terai grass – a solitary predator, with no natural enemies save one.

As recently as the beginning of the twentieth century, up to 100,000 tigers still roamed the Subcontinent, even though tiger hunting had long been the "sport of kings". It was the trigger-happy British who brought tiger hunting to its most gratuitous excesses, however. Photographs of pith-helmeted, bare-kneed -burra sahibs posing behind mountains of striped carcasses became a hackneyed image of the Raj.

In the years following Independence, **demographic pressures** nudged the Indian tiger perilously close to extinction. As the human population increased in rural districts, more and more forest was cleared for farming, depriving large carnivores of their main source of game and of the cover they needed to hunt. Forced to turn on farm cattle as an alternative, tigers were drawn into direct conflict with humans; some animals, out of sheer desperation, even turned man-eater and attacked human settlements. **Poaching** has taken an even greater toll. The black market has always paid high prices for dead animals – a tiger pelt alone can fetch US$125,000 in China – and for the various body parts believed to hold magical or medicinal properties.

Today there are 48 Tiger Reserves across India with 17 in the South, all part of the government-run Project Tiger Initiative (projecttiger.nic.in). A 2014 survey estimated there were 2226 tigers in India, an apparent **rise of 30 percent** in four years. The increase was hailed by politicians as a huge success, but taken with a pinch of salt by scientists, who suggest that it may at least partly be explained by improved survey methods. They further point out that the number of tigers killed by poachers also went up in that time. The upshot is that, while conservation efforts do appear to be bearing some fruit, the tiger is still endangered as a species, both in India and worldwide.

One of the region's most distinctive trees, found in both coastal and hill areas, is the stately **banyan**, which propagates by sending out roots from its lower branches. The largest specimens spread out over an area of two hundred square metres. The banyan is revered by Hindus, and you'll often find small shrines at the foot of mature trees. The same is true of the **peepal**, which has distinctive spatula-shaped leaves. Temple courtyards often enclose large peepals, which usually have strips of auspicious red cloth hanging from their lower branches.

The Western Ghats harbour a bewildering wealth of flora, from flowering trees and plants to ferns and fungi. **Shola** forests, lush patches of moist evergreen woodland which carpet the deeper mountain valleys, exhibit some of the greatest biodiversity. Sheltered by a leafy canopy, which may rise to a height of twenty metres or more, buttressed roots and giant trunks tower above a luxuriant undergrowth of brambles, creepers and bracken, interspersed by brakes of bamboo. Common tree species include the kadam, sisso or martel, kharanj and teak, while rarer sandalwood thrives on the higher, drier plateaus south of Mysore. There are dozens of representatives of the fig family, too, as well as innumerable (and ecologically destructive) eucalyptus and rubber trees, planted as cash crops by the Forest Department.

Mammals

The largest Indian land mammal is, of course, the Asian **elephant**, stockier and with much smaller ears than its African cousin, though no less venerable. Travelling around Kerala and Tamil Nadu, you'll regularly see elephants in temples and festivals, but for a glimpse of one in the wild, you'll have to venture into the mountains where, in spite of the huge reduction of their natural habitat, around six and a half thousand still survive. Among the best places for sightings are Periyar in Kerala (see p.328) and Nagarhole in Karnataka (see p.239). Today, wild elephants, which are included under the Endangered Species Protection Act, are under increasing threat from villagers: each adult animal eats roughly two hundred kilos of vegetation and drinks one hundred litres of water a day, and their search for sustenance inevitably brings them into conflict with rural communities.

Across India, local villagers displaced by wildlife reserves have often been responsible for the poaching that has reduced **tiger** populations to such fragile levels (see box, p.491). These days, sightings in South India are very rare indeed, though several kinds of big cat survive. Among the most beautiful is the **leopard**, or panther (*Panthera panthus*). Prowling the thick forests of the Ghats, these elusive cats prey on monkeys and deer, and occasionally take domestic cattle and dogs from the fringes of villages. Their distinctive black spots make them notoriously difficult to see amongst the tropical foliage, although their mating call (reminiscent of a saw on wood) regularly pierces the night air in remote areas. The **leopard cat** is a miniature version of its namesake, and more common. Sporting a bushy tail and round spots on soft buff or grey fur, it is about the same size as a domestic cat and lives around villages, picking off chickens, birds and small mammals. Another cat with a penchant for poultry, and one which villagers occasionally keep as a pet if they can capture one, is the docile Indian **civet**, recognizable by its lithe body, striped tail, short legs and long pointed muzzle.

Wild cats share their territory with a range of other mammals unique to the Subcontinent. One you've a reasonable chance of seeing is the **gaur**, or Indian bison. These primeval-looking beasts, with their distinctive sleek black skin and knee-length white "socks", forage around bamboo thickets and shady woods. The bulls are particularly impressive, growing to an awesome height of two metres, with heavy curved horns and prominent humps.

With its long fur and white V-shaped bib, the scruffy **sloth bear** – whose Tamil name (*bhalu*) inspired that of Rudyard Kipling's character in *The Jungle Book* – ranks among the weirder-looking inhabitants of the region's forests. It can occasionally be seen shuffling along woodland trails, but you're more likely to come across evidence of their foraging activities: trashed termite mounds and chewed-up ants' nests. The same is true of both the portly Indian **porcupine**, or *sal*, which you see a lot less often than the mounds of earth it digs up to get at insects and cashew or teak seedlings; and the **pangolin**, or *tiryo*, a kind of armour-plated anteater whose hard, grey overlapping scales protect it from predators.

Full-moon nights and the twilight hours of dusk and dawn are the times to look out for nocturnal animals such as the **slender loris**. This shy creature – a distant cousin of the lemur, with bulging round eyes, furry body and pencil-thin limbs – grows to around twenty centimetres in length. It moves as if in slow motion, except when an insect flits to within striking distance, and is a favourite pet of forest people. The **mongoose** is another animal sometimes kept as a pet to keep dwellings free of scorpions, mice, rats and other vermin. It will also readily take on snakes – you might see one writhing in a cloud of dust when king cobras during performances by snake charmers.

South India boasts four species of **bat**, including the fulvous fruit bat, or *vagul* – so-called because it gives off a scent resembling fermenting fruit juice; Dormer's bat; the very rare rufous horseshoe bat; and the Malay fox vampire, which feeds off the blood of live cattle. **Flying foxes**, the largest of India's bats, are also present in healthy numbers.

Other species to look out for in forest areas are the Indian **giant squirrel**, or *shenkaro*, which has a coat of black fur and red-orange lower parts. Two and a half times larger than its European cousins, it lives in the canopy, leaping up to twenty metres between branches.

Forest clearings and areas of open grassland are grazed by four species of deer. Widely regarded as the most beautiful is the **chital**, or spotted axis deer, which congregates in large groups around water holes and salt licks, occasionally wandering into villages to seek shelter from its predators. The plainer, buff-coloured **sambar** is also common, despite being affected by diseases spread by domestic cattle during the 1970s and 1980s. Two types of deer you're less likely to come across, but which also inhabit the border forests, are the **barking deer**, whose call closely resembles that of a domestic dog, and the aptly named **mouse deer** that grows to a mere thirty centimetres in height. Both of these are highly secretive and nocturnal; they are also the preferred snack of Goa's smaller predators: the **striped hyena**, **jackal** or *colo*, and **wild dog**, which hunt in packs.

Long-beaked **dolphins** are regular visitors to the shallow waters of South India's more secluded bays and beaches. They are traditionally regarded as a pest by local villagers, who believe they eat scarce stocks of fish. However, this long-standing antipathy is gradually being eroded as local people realize the tourist-pulling potential of the dolphins: Palolem beach, in Goa (see p.200), is a dependable dolphin-spotting location.

Finally, no rundown of South Indian mammals would be complete without some mention of **monkeys**. The most common species is the mangy pink-bottomed **macaque**, or *makad*, which hangs out anywhere scraps may be scavenged or snatched from unwary humans: temples and picnic spots are good places to watch them in action. The black-faced Hanuman **langur**, by contrast, is less audacious, retreating to the trees if threatened. It is much larger than the macaque, with pale grey fur and long limbs and tail. In forest areas, the langur's distinctive call is an effective early-warning system against big cats and other predators, which is why you often come across herds of cheetal grazing under trees inhabited by large colonies of them.

Reptiles

Reptiles are well represented in the region, with more than forty species of snakes, lizards, turtles and crocodiles recorded. The best places to spot them are not the interior forests, where dense foliage makes observation difficult, but open, cultivated areas: paddy fields and village ponds provide abundant fresh water, nesting sites and prey (frogs, insects and small birds).

Your hotel room, however, is where you are most likely to come across tropical India's most common reptile, the **gecko** (*Hemidactylus*), which clings to walls and ceilings with its widely splayed toes. The much rarer chameleon is even more elusive, mainly because its constantly changing camouflage makes it virtually impossible to spot. They'll have no problem seeing you, though: independently moving eyes allow them to pinpoint approaching predators, while prey is slurped up with their fast-moving forty-centimetre-long tongues. The other main lizard to look out for is the **Bengal monitor**. Among the few places you can be sure of sighting one is South Andaman, in the Andaman archipelago.

Olive Ridley **turtles** nest at a number of beaches in the region, notably Morgim in north Goa and Havelock Island in the Andamans. Local coastguards and scientists from the Institute of Oceanography in Goa monitor the migration, patrolling the beaches to deter poachers, but the annual egg binge remains a highlight of the local gastronomic calendar, eagerly awaited by fisher families, who sell the illegal harvest in local markets.

An equally rare sight nowadays is the **crocodile**. Populations have dropped almost to the point of extinction, although the Cambarjua Canal near Old Goa, and more remote stretches of the Mandovi and Zuari estuaries, support vestigial colonies of saltwater crocs, which bask on mudflats and river rocks. Dubbed "salties", they occasionally take calves and goats, and will snap at the odd human if given half a chance. The more ominously named mugger crocodile, however, is harmless, inhabiting unfrequented freshwater streams and riversides. You can see all of India's indigenous crocodiles at the wonderful Crocodile Bank near Mamallapuram (see p.385).

Snakes

Twenty-three species of snake are found in South India, ranging from the gigantic **Indian python** – a forest-dwelling constrictor that grows up to four metres in length – to the innocuous worm snake (*Typhlops braminus*), or *sulva*, which is tiny, completely blind and often mistaken for an earthworm.

The eight **poisonous snakes** present in the region include India's four most deadly species: the cobra, the krait, Russel's viper and the saw-scaled viper. Though these are relatively common in coastal and cultivated areas, even the most aggressive snake will slither off at the first sign of an approaching human. Nevertheless, ten thousand Indians die from snake bites each year, and if you regularly cut across paddy fields or plan to do any hiking, it makes sense to familiarize yourself with the following four or five species, just in case; their bites nearly always prove fatal if not treated immediately with anti-venom serum – available at most clinics and hospitals.

Sea snakes (*Enhydrina schistosa*) are common in coastal areas and potentially lethal (with a bite said to be twenty times more venomous than a cobra's), although rarely encountered by swimmers, as they lurk only in deep water off the shore.

Harmless snakes are far more numerous than their killer cousins and frequently more attractive. The beautiful **golden tree snake** (*Chrysopelea ornata*), for example, sports an exquisitely intricate geometric pattern of red, yellow and black markings, while the **green whip snake** (*Dryophis nasutus*), or *sarpatol*, is a stunning parakeet-green. The ubiquitous **Indian rat snake**, often mistaken for a cobra, also has beautiful markings, although it leaves behind a foul stench of decomposing flesh.

Birds

You don't have to be an aficionado to enjoy South India's abundant **birdlife**. Breathtakingly beautiful birds regularly flash between the branches of trees or appear on overhead wires at the roadside. For more information than we have space for here, see ⓦwww.binding.in.

Thanks to the internationally popular brand of Goan beer, the **kingfisher** has become that state's unofficial mascot: it's not hard to see why the brewers chose it as their logo. Three common species of kingfisher frequently crop up amid the paddy fields and wetlands of the coastal plains, where they feed on small fish and tadpoles. With its enormous bill and pale green-blue wing feathers, the stork-billed kingfisher (*Perargopis capensis*) is the largest and most distinctive member of the family, although the white-throated kingfisher (*Halcyon smyrnensis*) – which has iridescent turquoise plumage and a coral-red bill – and the common kingfisher (*Alcedo atthis*), identical to the one frequently spotted in northern Europe, are more alluring.

Other common and brightly coloured species include the green, blue and yellow **bee-eaters** (*Merops*), the stunning **golden oriole** (*Oriolus oriolus*), and the **Indian roller** (*Coracias bengalensis*), famous for its brilliant blue flight feathers and exuberant aerobatic mating displays. **Hoopoes** (*Upupa epops*), recognizable by their elegant black-and-white tipped crests, fawn plumage and distinctive "*hoo...po...po*" call, also flit around fields and villages, as do **purple sunbirds** (*Nectarina asiatica*) and several kinds of **bulbuls**, **babblers** and **drongos** (*Dicrurus*), including the fork-tailed **black drongo** (*Dicrurus macrocercus*) – which can often be seen perched on telegraph wires. If you're lucky, you may also catch a glimpse of the **Asian paradise flycatcher** (*Terpsiphone paradisi*), which is widespread and among the region's most exquisite birds: males of more than four years of age sport a thick black crest and long silver white streamers, while the more often seen females and young males are reddish-brown.

Paddy fields, ponds and saline mudflats usually teem with water birds. The most ubiquitous is the snowy white **cattle egret**, which can usually be seen wherever there are cows and buffalo, feeding off the grubs, insects and other parasites that live on them. The **great egret** is also pure white, although lankier and with a long yellow bill, while the **little egret**, sports a short black bill. Look out too for the mud-brown Indian pond heron, or "**paddy bird**", India's most common heron. Distinguished by its pale green legs, speckled breast and hunched posture, it stands motionless for hours in water, waiting for fish or frogs.

The hunting technique of the beautiful **white-bellied sea eagle** (*Haliaetus leucogaster*), by contrast, is truly spectacular. Cruising twenty to thirty metres above the surface of the water, this black and white osprey stoops at high speed to snatch its prey – usually sea snakes and mackerel – from the waves with its fierce yellow talons. More common birds of prey such as the **brahminy kite** (*Haliastur indus*) – recognizable by its white breast and chestnut head markings – and the **black kite** (*Milvus migrans*) – a dark-brown bird with a fork tail – are widespread around towns and fishing villages, where they vie with raucous gangs of house **crows** (*Corvus splendens*) for scraps.

Other birds of prey to keep an eye open for, especially around open farmland, are the **white-eyed buzzard** (*Butastur teesa*), the **oriental honey buzzard** (*Pernis ptilorhynchus*), the **black-shouldered kite** (*Elanus caeruleus*) – famous for its blood-red eyes – and the **shikra** (*Accipiter badius*), which closely resembles the European sparrowhawk.

Forest birds

The region's forests may have lost many of their larger animals, but they still offer exciting possibilities for bird-watchers. One species every enthusiast hopes to glimpse while in the woods is the magnificent **hornbill**. The Malabar grey hornbill (*Ocyceros griseus*), with its blue-brown plumage and long curved beak, is the most common, although the Indian pied hornbill (*Anthracoceros malabaricus*), distinguished by its white wing and tail tips and the pale patch on its face, often flies into villages in search of fruit and lizards. The magnificent great hornbill (*Buceros bicornis*), however, is more elusive, limited to the most dense forest areas, where it may occasionally be spotted flitting through the canopy. Growing to 130cm in length, it has a black-and-white striped body and wings, and a huge yellow beak with a long curved casque on top.

Several species of **woodpecker** also inhabit the interior forests, among them three types of flameback woodpecker: the common black-rumped flameback (*Dinopium bengalense*) has a wide range and also ventures into gardens and hotel grounds. The Cotigao sanctuary in south Goa is one of the last remaining strongholds of the white-bellied woodpecker (*Dryocopus javensis*); in spite of its bright red head and white rump, this shy bird is more often heard than seen, making loud drumming noises on tree trunks between December and March.

A bird whose call is a regular feature of the Western Ghat forests, though you'll be lucky to catch a glimpse of one, is the wild ancestor of the domestic chicken – the **jungle fowl**. The grey or Sonnerat's jungle fowl (*Gallus sonneratii*), has dark plumage scattered with yellow spots and streaks.

Books

India, and by extension its southern states, is one of the most written-about places on earth, and there are a bewildering number of titles available covering virtually every aspect of the country, ranging from scholarly historical dissertations to racy travelogues. Books marked ★ are particularly recommended.

HISTORY, SOCIETY AND REPORTAGE

A.L. Basham *The Wonder That Was India*. This veritable encyclopedia by one of India's foremost historical authorities positively bristles with erudition.

Oliver Blach *India Rising: Tales From a Changing Nation*. Part reportage, part travel writing, *India Rising* is a personalized account of the modern nation state drawn from a broad cast of everyday lives, ranging from millionaire entrepreneurs to slum dwellers. A vivid account of the contradictions and challenges at the heart of India's rise, and its extraordinary potential.

Katherine Boo *Behind the Beautiful Forevers*. Award-winning investigative journalist Katherine Boo spent three years exploring the Annawadi slum near Mumbai airport, and her account, tracing the impact of a violent crime on the community, races along with an almost cinematic intensity.

Elizabeth Bumiller *May You Be the Mother of a Hundred Sons*. Lucid exploration of the Indian woman's lot, drawn from dozens of first-hand encounters in the 1990s – since when surprisingly little has changed.

David Burton *The Raj at Table*. Vividly evokes the quirky world of British India – commendable both for its extraordinary recipes and as a marvellous piece of social history.

Liz Collingham *Curry*. Original and entertaining account of Indian history seen through its food, from Mughlai biriyanis to mulligatawny soup.

Larry Collins and Dominique Lapierre *Freedom at Midnight*. Readable, if shallow, account of Independence, highly sympathetic to the British and, particularly, to Mountbatten, who was the authors' main source of information.

Anne de Courcy *The Fishing Fleet*. The hitherto untold story of the many British women who, in response to a dearth of eligible bachelors at home, travelled to India in the late nineteenth century in search of husbands. Drawing on mainly unpublished memoirs, diaries and letters, the narrative yields a vivid picture of the Raj at its height from the female perspective.

★**William Dalrymple** *Nine Lives: In Search of the Sacred in Modern India*. The stories of nine different people who follow contrasting religious paths through the vortex of rapid social and cultural change. Each of Dalrymple's subjects is beautifully defined, revealing a wealth of insight into both India's past and present.

★**William Dalrymple** *White Mughals*. Compelling account of the previously forgotten story of British political officer James Achilles Kirkpatrick's marriage to the great-niece of the nizam of Hyderabad's prime minister.

Siddartha Deb *The Beautiful and the Damned: Life in the New India*. Another brilliant portrait of the country, this time focusing on a handful of individuals whose tragicomic lives epitomize some of the tensions underlying India's modern metamorphosis.

Louis Fischer *The Life of Mahatma Gandhi*. Veteran American journalist Louis Fischer knew his subject personally, and his book provides an engaging account of Gandhi as a man, politician and propagandist.

Patrick French *India*. A snapshot of the modern nation divided into themes (politics, economy and religion). Drawing on encounters with Indians from contrasting backgrounds, it manages to be scholarly yet wide-ranging at the same time – and a highly enjoyable read.

Patrick French *Liberty or Death*. The definitive account (and a damning indictment) of the last years of the British Raj.

M.K. Gandhi *The Story of My Experiments with Truth*. Gandhi's fascinating record of his life, including his spiritual and moral quests and gradual emergence to the fore of national politics.

Anand Giridharadas *India Calling*. An intimate portrait of the country written from the perspective of a young American born of Indian parents who emigrated to the US in the 1970s. It's particularly revealing of the impact of new technology and economic change on families.

Noburu Karashima (ed) *A Concise History of South India*. An interesting collection of articles on South Indian history, spanning prehistoric to modern times, written by a group of respected Indian and Japanese scholars.

John Keay *The Honourable Company: A History of the English East India Company*. Readable and balanced account of the East India Company and its strange role in Subcontinental history.

★**John Keay** *India: A History*. The best single-volume history currently in print. Keay manages to coax clear, impartial and highly readable narrative from five thousand years of fragmented events, enlivened with plenty of quirky asides.

John Keay *Into India*. As an all-round introduction to India, this book – originally written in 1973 but reissued in

1999 – is the one most often recommended by old hands, presenting a wide spread of history and cultural background, interspersed with lucid personal observations.

Edward Luce *In Spite of the Gods*. The most authoritative account of the state of the nation currently in print, packed full of sobering statistics and myth-busting facts that challenge common misconceptions about the country.

★ **Suketu Mehta** *Maximum City: Bombay Lost and Found*. Acclaimed portrait of India's largest city, mixing memoir and travelogue, along with penetrating insights into the history, society and people of Mumbai.

Palagummi Sainath *Everybody Loves a Good Drought*. A classic report on India's poorest districts, telling the stories of individual villages that are usually lost in a maze of development statistics.

Amartya Sen *The Argumentative Indian*. A provocative and sharply written collection of essays on identity, religion, history, philosophy and – above all – what it means to be Indian.

Mark Tully *India: the Road Ahead*. Few commentators understand India as well as Mark Tully, the veteran BBC correspondent, who has written a string of books since the early 1990s cataloguing the country's rapid change. This is his most recent, but they're all worth hunting out, from *No Full Stops* (1992) to *India In Slow Motion* (2003) and *India's Unending Journey* (2008).

TRAVEL

James Cameron *An Indian Summer*. Affectionate and humorous description of the veteran British journalist's visit to India in 1972, and his marriage to an Indian woman.

★ **William Dalrymple** *City of Djinns*. Dalrymple's account of a year in Delhi sifts through successive layers of the city's past using a blend of inspired historical sleuth-work and interviews with a cast of characters ranging from Urdu calligraphers to local pigeon fanciers. The *Age of Kali* (published in India as *In the Court of the Fish-Eyed Goddess*) is a collection of essays drawn from ten years' travel in India.

Alexander Frater *Chasing the Monsoon*. Frater's wet-season jaunt up the west coast and across to Shillong took him through an India of muddy puddles and grey skies: an evocative account of the country as few visitors see it, now something of a classic.

Tim Mackintosh-Smith *The Hall of a Thousand Columns*. Quirky, learned and entertaining travelogue following the footsteps of Ibn Battuta through the Delhi of the Tughluq sultan Muhammad Shah and thence south to Kerala, with lashings of offbeat Subcontinental Islamic history en route.

V.S. Naipaul *An Area of Darkness*. One of the finest (and bleakest) books ever written about India: a darkly comic portrait of the country based on a year of travel around the Subcontinent in the early 1960s – dated, but still essential reading. Naipaul followed this up with *India: A Wounded Civilisation*, a damning analysis of Indian society written during the Emergency of 1975–77, and the altogether sunnier *India: A Million Mutinies Now*, published in 1990.

★ **Jerry Pinto (ed.)** *Reflected in Water: Writings on Goa*. A wide-ranging compilation of pieces from travel essays by the likes of William Dalrymple, Graham Greene and David Tomory, to more impressionistic, literary and historical articles on local life – a must for any interested visitor to the region.

Tahir Shah *Sorcerer's Apprentice*. A journey through the weird underworld of occult India. Travelling as an apprentice to a master conjurer and illusionist, Shah encounters hangmen, baby renters, skeleton dealers, sadhus and charlatans.

FICTION

Aravind Adiga *The White Tiger*. Brilliantly dark satire on the "New" India, set largely in Delhi and featuring the relationship between a wealthy employer and his impecunious but murderously ambitious servant.

Mulk Raj Anand *Untouchable* and *Coolie*. First published in 1935, *Untouchable* gives a memorable worm's-eye view of the brutal life of an untouchable sweeper, while the subsequent *Coolie* (1936) describes the death of a 15-year-old child labourer.

Chetan Bhagat *One Night at the Call Centre*. A heart-warming tale by India's most popular novelist about six employees in a Gurgaon call centre. Like most of Bhagat's novels – including *2 States*, about a Punjabi man who wants to marry a Tamil woman, and *Revolution 2020*, about private tuition colleges and corruption – it's never too heavy, but makes some serious points about the problems faced by young urban Indians.

★ **Vikram Chandra** *Sacred Games*. More than a decade elapsed between the publication of Chandra's award-winning debut novel, *Red Earth and Pouring Rain*, inspired by the life of Anglo-Indian soldier James Skinner, and this, his second offering – an epic, page-turning tale of friendship and betrayals, love and violence set in modern Mumbai.

Anita Desai *Fasting, Feasting*. One of India's leading female authors' eloquent portrayal of the frustration of a sensitive young woman stuck in the stifling atmosphere of home while her spoilt brother is packed off to study in America.

Kiran Desai *The Inheritance of Loss*. This Booker Prize-winning novel, partly set in the Himalayan town of Kalimpong, with the Gorkhaland movement as a backdrop, tells the haunting stories of a judge, an orphaned girl and a cook, each one trapped by their dreams.

E.M. Forster *A Passage to India*. Set in the 1920s, this withering critique of colonialism is memorable as much for its sympathetic portrayal of middle-class Indian life as for its insights into cultural misunderstandings.

Amitav Ghosh *The Hungry Tide*. The history and myths of the Sundarbans are brought dramatically to life in this beautifully written novel, which centres on the relationship between a marine biologist – an American of Indian descent – and a Bengali businessman.

Amitav Ghosh *Sea of Poppies*. This first instalment in Ghosh's *Ibis* trilogy centres around the opium trade in the early nineteenth century. Full of fascinating historical detail, with engaging characters who speak an array of local English vernaculars, it's an excellent depiction of Bengal under Company rule.

Rudyard Kipling *Kim*. Cringingly colonialist at times, of course, but the atmosphere of India and Kipling's love of it shine through in this subtle story of an orphaned white boy. Kipling's other key works on India are two books of short stories: *Soldiers Three* and *In Black and White*.

★**Rohinton Mistry** *A Fine Balance*. Magnificent, gut-wrenching novel focusing on two friends who leave their lower-caste rural lives for the urban opportunities of the big smoke (in this case a fictionalized Mumbai). Mistry's *Such a Long Journey* is an acclaimed account of a Mumbai Parsi's struggle to maintain personal integrity in the face of betrayals and disappointment.

R.K. Narayan *Gods, Demons and Others*. Classic Indian folk tales and popular myths told through the voice of a village storyteller. Many of Narayan's beautifully crafted books, full of touching characters and subtle humour, are set in the fictional South Indian territory of Malgudi.

Gregory David Roberts *Shantaram*. Entertaining, albeit rather overlong, semiautobiographical account of an escaped Australian convict taking refuge in India (mainly Mumbai), with memorable, if occasionally clichéd, depictions of the country and its people.

★**Arundhati Roy** *The God of Small Things*. Haunting Booker Prize-winner about a well-to-do South Indian family caught between the snobberies of high-caste tradition, a colonial past and the diverse personal histories of its members.

★**Salman Rushdie** *Midnight's Children*. This story of a man born at the very moment of Independence, whose life mirrors that of modern India itself, won Rushdie the Booker Prize and the enmity of Indira Gandhi, who had it banned in India. Set in Kerala and Mumbai, *The Moor's Last Sigh* was the subject of a defamation case brought by Shiv Sena leader Bal Thackeray.

William Sutcliffe *Are You Experienced?* Hilarious novel sending up the backpacker scene in India. Wickedly perceptive and very readable.

Vikas Swarup *Q&A*. Filmed by Danny Boyle as *Slumdog Millionaire*, this is the story – in turn funny, shocking and heartwarming – of how an illiterate slum dweller's life experiences enable him to answer a series of difficult questions on a high-prize TV quiz show.

Tarun J. Tejpal *The Alchemy of Desire*. Set mainly in the Himalayas, this sensuous contemporary tale focuses on two lovers, mixing its exploration of human relationships with wider reflections on India in the twentieth century.

ART, ARCHITECTURE AND RELIGION

Roy Craven *Indian Art*. Concise general introduction to Indian art, from Harappan seals to Mughal miniatures.

Dorf Hartsuiker *Sadhus: Holy Men of India*. The weird world of India's itinerant ascetics exposed in glossy colour photographs and erudite but accessible text.

Stephen P. Huyler *Meeting God*. Unrivalled overview of the beliefs and practices of contemporary Hinduism, accompanied by fine photographs.

George Michell *The Hindu Temple*. A reasonable primer, introducing Hindu temples, their significance and architectural development.

Grimmet & Inskipp *Birds of Southern India*. The birders' bible, a beautifully organized, written and illustrated 240-page field guide listing every species known in South India.

Wendy O'Flaherty (translator) *Hindu Myths*. Translations of key myths from the original Sanskrit texts, providing an insight into the foundations of Hinduism.

Paramahansa Yogananda *Autobiography of a Yogi*. Uplifting account of religious awakening and spiritual development by one of the most internationally influential Hindu masters.

Language

No fewer than 22 major languages are officially recognized by the Indian constitution, while numerous minor ones and more than a thousand dialects are also spoken across the country. When independent India was organized, the present-day states were largely created along linguistic lines, which helps the traveller make some sense of the complex situation. Considering the continuing prevalence of English, there is rarely any necessity to speak a local language, but some theoretical knowledge of the background and learning at least a few words of one or two can only enhance your visit.

While the main languages of northern India including Hindi and Urdu are all Indo-Aryan, in South India the picture changes completely: the four most widely spoken languages, Tamil (Tamil Nadu), Telugu (Andhra Pradesh and Telangana), Kannada (Karnataka) and Malayalam (Kerala), all belong to the **Dravidian** family, the world's fourth largest group. These and related minor languages grew up quite separately among the non-Aryan peoples of southern India over thousands of years. The exact origins of the Dravidian group have not been established but it's possible that proto-Dravidian was spoken further north in prehistoric times (see p.463).

With **Independence** it was decided by the government in Delhi that Hindi should become the **official language** of the newly created country. A drive to teach Hindi in all schools followed and more than half the country's population are now reckoned to have a decent working knowledge of the language. However, there has always been strong resistance to the imposition of Hindi in certain areas, especially the **Tamil-led** Dravidian south, and the vast majority of people living below the Deccan plateau have little or no knowledge of it.

This is where **English**, the language of the ex-colonists, becomes an important means of communication. Not surprisingly, given India's rich linguistic diversity, **English** remains a **lingua franca** for many people. It is still the preferred language of law, higher education, much of commerce and the media, and to some degree political dialogue; and for many educated Indians, not just those living abroad, it is actually their first language. All this explains why Anglophone visitors can often soon feel surprisingly at

---

INDIAN ENGLISH

During the British Raj, **Indian English** developed its own characteristics, many of which have survived to the present day. It was during this period that Indian words also entered the vocabulary of everyday English, among them veranda, bungalow, sandal, pyjamas, shampoo, jungle, turban, caste, chariot, chilli, cardamom, pundit and yoga. The traveller to India soon becomes familiar with other terms in common usage that have not spread so widely outside the Subcontinent: *dacoit, dhoti, panchayat, lakh* and *crore* are but a few. A full list of Anglo-Indianisms can be found in the famous Hobson-Jobson Anglo-Indian dictionary.

Perhaps the most endearing aspect of Indian English is the way it has preserved forms now regarded as highly old-fashioned in Britain. Addresses such as "Good sir" and questions like "May I know your good name?" are commonplace, as are terms like "tiffin" and "cantonment". This type of usage reaches its apogee in the more flowery expressions of the media, which regularly feature in the vast array of daily newspapers published in English. Thus headlines such as "37 perish in mishap" (referring to a train crash) often appear or passages like this splendid report of a bank robbery: "The miscreants absconded with the loot in great haste. They repaired immediately to their hideaway, whereupon they divided the iniquitous spoils before vanishing into thin air."

home despite the huge cultural differences. It is not unusual to overhear everyday contact between Indians from different parts of the country being conducted in English, and stimulating conversations can often be had, not only with students or businesspeople, but also with chaiwalas and shoeshine boys.

Useful words and phrases

TAMIL

BASIC WORDS

Yes	Aamaam
No	Illai
Goodbye (will return again)	Varavaanga
Please	Koncham dhayavuseydhu
Thanks	Nanri
Thank you very much	Romba nanringa
Excuse me	Enga
Pardon	Mannikkavum
Come (inviting someone in)	Vaanaga
Stop	Neruthu
This	Idhu
That	Adhu
These	Evaikal
What is this/that?	Idhu/adhu ennaanga?
Very good	Romba nallayirukkudhu
Not bad	Paravaayillai
Big	Pareya
Small	Sarreya
Much	Athekam
Little	Kuraivu

TIME

Today	Enrru
Tomorrow	Naalai
Yesterday	Neerru
Day	Pakal/kezhamai
Night	Eravu
Early morning	Athekaalai
Morning	Kaalai
Afternoon	Matïyam
Evening	Maalai
Monday	Thengal
Tuesday	Chavvaay
Wednesday	Buthan
Thursday	Vyaazha
Friday	Valle
Saturday	Chane
Sunday	Gnaayetrru

COMMUNICATING

I don't understand	Enakku puriya-villaiye
I understand	Enakku puriyudhu
I don't know Tamil	Enakku thamizh theriyaathunga
Do you know someone who knows English?	Inge aangilam Therinchavanga yaaraavadhu irukkiraangalaa?
Could you speak slowly?	Koncham methuvaa pesuveengalaa?
Could you speak loudly?	Koncham balamaa pesunga?
What does he say?	Avar enna sollugiraar?

FOOD AND SHOPPING

I am hungry	Enakku pasikkudhu
I am thirsty	Enakku dhaga maayirukkudhu
How much is it?	Athanudaiya vilaienna?
I only want coffee	Enakku kapi maththi-ram than vendum
Please show me	Koncham kan-pikkireengalaa
Coffee	Kapi
Tea	Teyneer
Milk	Paal
Sugar	Sakkaray
Water	Neer
Rice	Arese
Cooked rice	Satham
Vegetables	Kaaykarikal
Cooked vegetables	Kane
Curd/yoghurt	Thayer
Coconut	Thaenkaay

DIRECTIONS

Where is... ?	Enge iruk kuthunga…?
Far	Turam
Near	Arukkil
Is it near here?	Athu ingeyirundhu pakkam thaane?
How far is it from here?	Athu ingeyirundhu evvalavu dhoora mayirukkunga?
Where can I get an auto-rickshaw?	Enga auto enga kidaikunga?

What is the charge to get there?	Anga povad hukku evvalavu?	9	nbathu
Where is the bank?	Vangi enge irukkuthunga?	10	patthu
		11	pathenonrru
		12	panereynndu
Where is the bus stand?	Bas staandu enge irukki radhu?	13	pathemoonrru
		14	pathenaangu
Where is the train station?	Tireyn staashan enge iruk- kuthunga?	15	pathenainthu
		16	pathenaaru
Where is the lavatory?	Kakkoos enge irukkudhu?	17	pathnaezshu
Where is the information office?	Visaranai enge irukki radhu?	18	pathenayttu
		19	pathenthonbathu
Where is… road?	… theru enge irukkiradhu?	20	erapathu
Post office	Anja lagam	30	muppathu
		40	naarpathu
NUMBERS		50	iymbathu
1	onru	60	arupathu
2	eranndu	70	azhupathu
3	mundru	80	aennapathu
4	naangu	90	thonnoorru
5	iyendhu	100	noorru
6	aaru	1000	aayeram
7	aezshu	100,000	latcham
8	ayttu		

MALAYALAM

BASIC WORDS

		2	randu
Yes	Aanaate	3	muunu
No	Alla	4	naalu
Hello	Namaskaram	5	anchu
Please	Dayavuchetu	6	aaru
Thank you	Nanni	7	eylu
Excuse me	Ksamikkuu	8	ettu
How much is it?	Etra?	9	ombatu
I don't understand	Enikka arriyilla	10	pattu
Do you speak English?	Ninal englisha samsaarik-kumo?	11	pationnu
		12	pantrantu
My name is…	Ente pero…	13	pati-muunu
Where is…?	Eviteyaannaa…?	14–18	pati-…
Coffee	Kaappi	19	pattonpattu
Tea	Chaaya	20	irupatu
Milk	Paalu	21	irupattonnu
Sugar	Panchasara	22	irupatti-randu
Medicine	Marunnu	30	muppatu
Water	Vellam	31	muppati-yonnu
Vegetables	Pachakkari	40	nalpatu
Fish	Meen	50	anpatu
Curd	Tairu	60	arupatu
Rice	Ari	70	elapatu
Cooked rice	Choru	80	enpatu
Banana	Pazham	90	tonnuru
Coconut	Teynna	100	nuura
		1000	aayiram
NUMBERS		100,000	laksham
1	onnu		

TELUGU

BASIC WORDS

Yes	Awunu
No	Kaadu
Goodbye	Namaskaram
Please	Dayatesi
Thank you	Dhanyawadalu
Excuse me	Ksamiynchannddi
How much is it?	Enta?
What is your name?	Ni peru eymitti?
My name is…	Naa peru…
I don't understand	Naadu artham kaawattamleydu
Do you speak English?	Miku angalam vaacha?
Where is… ?	Ekkada undi… ?
How far is… ?	… Enta duram?
Big	Pedda
Small	Tsinna
Today	Iroju
Day	Pagalu
Night	Raatri
Coffee	Kaafii
Tea	Tti
Milk	Palu
Sugar	Chakkera
Salt	Uppu
Water	Nillu
Rice	Biyyamu
Fish	Chepa
Vegetables	Kuragayalu

NUMBERS

1	okatti
2	renddu
3	muddu
4	naalugu
5	aaydu
6	aaru
7	eyddu
8	enimidi
9	tommidi
10	padi
11	pada-kondu
12	pad-rendu
13–19	pad-…
20	iruvay
21	iruvay-okatti
30	muppay
31	muppay-okati
40	nalapay
50	yaabay
60	aruvay
70	debbay
80	enabay
90	tombay
100	nuru/wanda
200	renddu-wanda
1000	veyi
100,000	laksha

KANNADA

BASIC WORDS

Yes	Havdu
No	Illa
Hello	Namaskara
Please	Dayavittu
Thank you	Vandanegallu
Excuse me	Kshamisi
Stop	Nillisu
How much is it?	Eshttu?
What is your name?	Nimma hesaru eynu?
My name is…	Nanna hesaru…
Where is… ?	Ellide… ?
I don't understand	Nanage artha aagalla
Do you speak English?	Neevu english mataaddtiiraa?
Day	Hagalu
Night	Raatri
Today	Ivattu
Coffee	Kaafi
Tea	Tea
Milk	Haalu
Sugar	Sakkare
Water	Neeru
Rice	Akki
Vegetables	Tarakari
Fish	Massali
Coconut water	Yella-neeru

NUMBERS

1	ondu	7	eylu
2	eradu	8	entu
3	mooru	9	ombhattu
4	naalku	10	hattu
5	aydu	11	hannondu
6	aaru	12	hanneradu

13	hadi-mooru	60	aravattu
14–18	hadi-...	70	eppattu
19	hattombhattu	80	embattu
20	ippattu	90	tombattu
21	ippattondu	99	tombattombattu
30	muvattu	100	nooru
31	muvattondu	1000	ondu saavira
40	naalvattu	100,000	laksha
50	aivattu		

KONKANI

BASIC WORDS

		Coconut	Nal
Yes	Hoee	Tender coconut	Adzar
No	Na		
Hello	Paypadta	**NUMBERS**	
Goodbye	Miochay	1	ek
Please	Upkar kor	2	dohn
Thank you	Dio borem korunc	3	teen
Excuse me	Upkar korkhi	4	char
How much?	Kitlay?	5	paanch
How much does it cost?	Kitlay poisha lakthele?	6	soh
I don't want it	Mhaka naka tem	7	saht
I don't understand	Mhaka kay samzona na	8	ahrt
Where is...?	Khoy aasa...?	9	nou
Beach	Prayia	10	dha
Road	Rosto	20	vees
Coffee	Kaafi	30	tees
Tea	Chai	40	cha-ees
Milk	Dudh	50	po-nas
Sugar	Shakhar	100	chem-bor
No sugar	Shakhar naka	1000	ek-azaar
Rice	Tandul	100,000	laakh
Water	Oodak		

HINDI AND URDU

Spoken mainly in Maharashtra (including Mumbai), northeast Karnataka and northern Andhra Pradesh

BASIC WORDS AND PHRASES

		Sister	Didi
Hello (said with palms together at chest height as in prayer – not used for Muslims)	Namaste	Sir (Sahib)	Saaheb
		Yes	Haan
		OK/good	Achhaa
		No	Nahiin
Hello (to a Muslim)	Aslaam alequm	How much?	Kitna?
Greetings (in reply to a Muslim)	Ale qum aslaam	Bad	Kharaab
		My name is...	Mera nam... hai
We will meet again (goodbye)	Phir milenge	What is your name? (formal)	Aapka naam kya hai?
Goodbye (may God bless you) (to a Muslim)	Khudaa Haafiz	What is your name? (familiar)	Tumhara naam kya hai
		I don't understand	Samaj nahin aayaa
How are you? (formal)	Aap kaise hain?	It is OK	Thiik hai
How are you? (familiar)	Kya hal hai?	How much?	Kitna?
Brother (a common address to a stranger)	Bhaaii/bhaayaa	Where is the...?	... Kahaan hai?
		How far?	Kitnaa duur?

Stop	Ruko	11	giara
Wait	Thero	12	bara
Medicine	Dawaaii	13	tera
Pain	Dard	14	chawda
Stomach	Pet	15	pandra
Eye	Aankh	16	sola
Nose	Naakh	17	satra
Ear	Kaan	18	atthara
Back	Piit	19	unnis
Foot	Paao	20	bis
		30	tis
NUMBERS		40	chaalis
1	ek	50	pachaas
2	do	60	saath
3	tin	70	sathar
4	char	80	assii
5	paanch	90	nabbe
6	chey	100	saw
7	saat	200	do saw
8	aatth	1000	hazaar
9	now	100,000	laakh
10	das		

FOOD AND DRINK GLOSSARY

Owing to the very distinct languages of South India, an effective glossary of food terms is almost impossible, but the following list highlights the food and the terms you are likely to come across as a visitor. For more detail, see Basics, p.34.

apa de camarão   spicy prawn pie with a rice and semolina crust (Goa)

appam   wok-cooked rice pancake speckled with holes, soft in the middle; a speciality of the Malabar Coast (Kerala)

assado   a spicy pan-cooked beef preparation (Goa)

bagheri   small aubergine

baingan   cooked with peanut paste and spices (Hyderabad)

bebinca   custard made with (chickpea) flour, eggs and coconut juice (Goa)

biriyani   rice baked with saffron or turmeric, whole spices and meat (sometimes vegetables), and often hard-boiled egg (North India and Hyderabad)

Bombay duck   dried bummalo fish (Mumbai)

caldeen   fish marinated in vinegar and cooked in a spicy sauce of coconut and chillies (Goa)

chai   Indian tea; usually boiled with lots of milk and sugar

chapatti   unleavened bread made of wholewheat flour and baked on a round griddle-dish called a *tawa* (universal)

chop   minced meat or vegetable surrounded by breaded mashed potato

cutlet   minced meat or vegetable fried in the form of a flat cake (universal)

dahi rice   a pleasant and light preparation – sometimes lightly spiced – of boiled rice with yoghurt (*dahi*)

dhal   lentils, pronounced "da'al" and found in one form or another throughout India; in the South often replaced by *sambar* (universal)

dhansak   meat and lentil curry, a Parsi speciality; medium-hot (Mumbai)

dosa   rice pancake – should be crispy; when served with a filling it is called a masala dosa and when plain, a *sada dosa* (Andhra Pradesh, Karnataka, Tamil Nadu, universal)

eshtew   a stew, usually made with chicken, cooked with potatoes in a creamy white sauce of coconut milk (Kerala)

ghee   clarified butter sometimes used for festive cooking, and often sprinkled onto food before eating (universal)

idli   steamed rice cake, usually served with *sambar*; *malligi* (jasmine) *idlis* around Mysore are exceptionally fluffy and so-named because of their lightness – the scent of jasmine is said to waft on the breeze (Andhra Pradesh, Karnataka, Kerala, Tamil Nadu, universal)

jaggery   unrefined sugar made from palm sap (universal)

jeera rice   rice cooked with cumin seeds (*jeera*) (universal)

karhi leaf   a type of laurel from which the leaf and the seeds are widely used as a spice throughout South India (universal)

keema   minced meat (Hyderabad)

khichari   rice cooked with lentils in various ways, from plain to aromatic and spicy (Hyderabad, universal)

kofta   balls of minced vegetables or meat in a curry sauce (Hyderabad)

kokum   purple berry with a sweet-sour taste, used as a digestive (Maharashtra)

korma   meat braised in yoghurt sauce; mild (Hyderabad)

kulcha   fried flat bread to accompany curries (Hyderabad)

lassi   yoghurt drink, served either plain or flavoured with salt or fruit (or cannabis in the case of a "bang lassi")

molee   curry with coconut, usually fish; originally Malay (hence the name); hot (Kerala)

mulligatawny   curried vegetable soup, a classic Anglo-Indian dish rumoured to have come from "Mulligan Aunty" but probably South Indian; medium-strength (universal)

naan   white, leavened bread kneaded with yoghurt and baked in a *tandoor* (universal)

pao   round Portuguese-style bread roll (Goa)

papad   crisp, thin, chickpea-flour cracker (universal)

paratha   wholewheat bread made with butter, rolled thin and griddle-fried; a little bit like a chewy pancake, sometimes stuffed with meat or vegetables (universal)

parota   South India's answer to the North Indian *paratha* – a wheat-flour pancake, for which the dough is oiled and coiled into a spiral before being griddle-fried (universal)

pilau   also known as *pilaf*, *pulau* or *pullao*, rice, gently spiced and pre-fried (universal)

pomfret   a flatfish especially popular in Mumbai (universal)

puri	crispy, puffed-up, deep-fried wholewheat bread (universal)	
rasam	spicy pepper water often drunk to accompany "meals" in the South	
roti	loosely used term; often just another name for chapatti, though it should be thicker, chewier and baked in a *tandoor* (universal)	
sambar	soupy lentil and vegetable curry with asafoetida and tamarind; used as an accompaniment to *dosas*, *idlis* and *vadas* (universal)	
sarpotel	pork dish with liver and heart, cooked in plenty of vinegar and spices	

(Goa)

uppma	popular breakfast cereal made from semolina, spices and nuts, and served with *sambar* (Kerala, Tamil Nadu)
uttapam	thick rice pancake often cooked with onions (Karnataka, Tamil Nadu, Kerala, universal)
vadai	also known as *vada*, a doughnut-shaped deep-fried lentil cake, which usually has a hole in its centre
vindaloo	Goan meat – seasoned with vinegar – (sometimes fish) curry, originally pork; very hot (but not as hot as the kamikaze UK version) (Goa, universal)